COLLINS

CANADIAN
ENGLISH DICTIONARY

COLLINS

CANADIAN
ENGLISH DICTIONARY

HarperCollins*PublishersLtd*

This book is based on the
Collins Pocket Reference English Dictionary,

Entered words that we have reason to believe constitute trademarks have been designated as such. However, neither the presence nor absence of such designation should be regarded as affecting the legal status of any trademark.

Printed and bound in the United States

CONTENTS

Preface vii
Arrangement of Entries viii
Pronunciation ix
Abbreviations Used in the Dictionary xii

Dictionary of the English Language 1

Punctuation Marks and Other Symbols 471
Guide to Punctuation and Use of Capitals 472
Guide to Letter-writing and Forms of Address 474
Signs of the Zodiac 476
Roman Numerals 476
Plurals of Nouns 477
Group Names and Collective Nouns 478
Names and Symbols of Metric Units 480
Metric/Imperial Conversion Factors 482
Temperature Conversion Table 483
Mathematical Symbols 484
Chemical Symbols 486
Canada – Provincial Facts 487
Distances by Air 488
World Standard Times 490
Selected Mountain Heights 491
River Lengths 492
Populations of Selected Urban Areas 493
Countries, their Related Nouns and Adjectives and Currencies 494
Geological Time Chart 498

EDITORIAL STAFF

Canadian Editor
Patrick Drysdale
Editor, *A Dictionary of Canadianisms on Historical Principles*

Chief Editor
Patrick Hanks

Managing Editor
Marian Makins

Editors
Danielle McGinley
Diana Adams

PREFACE

Collins Pocket Reference English Dictionary, Canadian Edition, presents a comprehensive survey of today's language, with special coverage of Canadian English.

The entries in the dictionary have been carefully selected to reflect the needs of today's user, with emphasis on the living language – the words most likely to be encountered in daily life. The coverage is generous, with over 39,000 vocabulary references and 45,000 definitions. In addition to its full treatment of general English, the dictionary draws on the *Collins English Dictionaries* language-monitoring research, ensuring that many new words and meanings are included, and that a truly up-to-date account of our language is presented.

The *Pocket Reference English Dictionary* recognizes that Canadian English, while sharing characteristics of both British and American English, is a distinct variety of the language with its own particular features. Thus many purely Canadian words and meanings are included in the dictionary as well as others that are used throughout North America, while numerous definitions have been edited to reflect a Canadian point of view. Canadian preferences in spelling and pronunciation are given wherever possible.

The dictionary contains many features designed to provide practical help to the user. All irregular spelling forms are shown. The pronunciations of all entries are indicated by stress marks, and, in cases where difficulty might arise, by a simple phonetic respelling. Italic labels draw attention to words or meanings the usage of which is generally restricted to a special context, such as informal English, or which are peculiar to one country, or found within a specialist subject area. In addition, the large clear type and layout of the dictionary makes it easy to find the information required.

Collins Pocket Reference English Dictionary thus provides a practical, easy-to-use, and authoritative guide to today's English.

ARRANGEMENT OF ENTRIES

All main entries are arranged in a single alphabetical listing, including abbreviations, foreign words, and combining forms or prefixes. Each such entry consists of a paragraph, with a main, or core, word at the head of it in large bold type. Derived or related words, in smaller bold type, appear later in the paragraph in alphabetical order, with phrases included at the end. Thus, **'labourer'** and **'laborious'** will be found under **'labour'**, **'lends itself to'** under **'lend'**, and so on. Alternative spellings are shown by bracketing optional letters, eg **'judg(e)'ment'** or by placing the variants side by side (**accurs'ed, accurst'**); but if the divergence in spelling is very great there is a separate entry.

The part of speech is shown by an abbreviation placed after the word (or its pronunciation) eg '**dog** *n.*,' for noun. Words which are used as more than one part of speech are only written out once, the change being indicated by a new part of speech label, eg '**ravage** *vt.* lay waste, plunder —*n.* destruction.' In the case of very short, simple entries, parts of speech may be combined, eg '**jest** *n./vi.* joke.' Spelling of verb parts is indicated in brackets after the verbal definitions, eg '**jab** . . . stab abruptly (**-bb-**)'.

When a derived word is included within an entry, its meaning may be understood from the meaning of the headword or another derived word from within the paragraph.

Field labels and usage notes are added in italic type and abbreviated where there will be no confusion.

Although only '-ize' and '-ization' spellings are shown, the reader should understand that spellings in '-ise' and '-isation' are equally acceptable.

PRONUNCIATION

The pronunciation of many words is adequately shown simply by placing an accent (') immediately after the syllable that carries the main stress. All headwords are stressed except those that have only one syllable.

Where the stress mark alone is insufficient to clarify some peculiarity of pronunciation or misleading spelling, a simple phonetic respelling of the whole or part of the word is given in square brackets immediately after the headword. Typical examples are:

cache [kash]; **cach'et** [kash'ā]; **caecum** [sē'kəm]; **caisson'** [kə-soon']; **capercai'lzie** [kap-ər-kā'lyi]; **cappucci'no** [-chē'-].

The special letters used in the phonetic respelling are listed below. All letters *not* listed have their normal pronunciation.

ā	mate	o͞o	food	ch	church
ah	calm	yoo	sinuous	ng	ring
aw	law	yo͞o	few	th	thin
ē	freeze	oi	boil	TH	this
ī	bite	ow	how	y	yes
ō	rope	ə	ago	H	loch
oo	book				

NOTES

1. The position of the stress mark in a headword generally indicates the length of the stressed vowel: if it comes immediately after the vowel, the vowel is usually long (**sa'vour**); if it comes after a consonant, the vowel is usually short (**sav'age**). But there are some exceptions (like **recite', voli'tion, colli'sion**).

2. Though words like *castle, path, fast* are shown as pronounced with an [ah] sound, many speakers use an [a]. Such variations are entirely acceptable and to be assumed by the reader.

3. Though words like *law, laudable, ball* are shown as pronounced with an [aw] sound, for most Canadian speakers this is indistinguishable from [o], so that *cot* and *caught*, for example, are pronounced the same. Some speakers, however, do distinguish between the two sounds, and so this variation is to be assumed.

4. Though the letter 'r' in some positions (as in *fern, fear, arm, car,* etc.) is pronounced by most Canadians, it is not sounded by certain speakers, especially those from Southern England and a few parts of the eastern and southern United States, and some people sound it much more distinctly than others. Again such variations are to be assumed.

5. Though the widely received pronunciation of words like *which, why* is with a simple [w] sound and is so shown in the dictionary, many speakers, in Scotland and elsewhere, preserve an aspirated sound: [hw]. Once again this variation is to be assumed.

6. The symbol ə, the schwa, represents the neutral vowel heard in a wide range of unstressed syllables. In some words, however, among some speakers an [i] sound is heard, as in **listless** [list'ləs *or* list'lis].

7. Where a headword is stressed only and not pronounced by respelling, the following values are assumed for certain letters and letter combinations:

rai'sin	[-ā-]	**cord'ial**	[-awr-]
carp'et	[-ah-]	**board**	[-awr-]
laud'able	[-aw-]	**aloud'**	[-ow-]
fea'ture	[-ē-]	**tu'na**	[-yōō-]
foam	[-ō-]		

Pronunciation

Whenever these letters are pronounced differently, this pronunciation is shown, as:

car'avan [ka'rə-], **caul'iflower** [kol'-], **deaf** [def], **rea'gent** [rē-ā'jənt], **cor'oner** [ko'rə-], **cou'gar** [ko͞o'-], **doub'le** [dub'l], **rou'ble** [ro͞o'-], **ru'by** [ro͞o'-].

ABBREVIATIONS USED IN THE DICTIONARY

a.	adjective	m	metre(s)
abbrev.	abbreviation	*masc.*	masculine
adv.	adverb	mm	millimetre(s)
Afr.	Africa(n)	N	North
Amer.	America(n)	*n.*	noun
Aust.	Australia(n)	N.Z.	New Zealand
Brit.	Britain, British	*obs.*	obsolete, obsolescent
Canad.	Canada, Canadian	*offens.*	offensive
cent.	century	oft.	often
cm	centimetre(s)	orig.	originally
comb.	combining	*pers.*	person
comp.	comparative	pert.	pertaining
conj.	conjunction	*pl.*	plural
cu.	cubic	*pl.n.*	plural noun
dial.	dialect	*poss.*	possessive
dim.	diminutive	*pp.*	past participle
eg	for example	*prep.*	preposition
esp.	especially	*pres.t.*	present tense
fem.	feminine	*pron.*	pronoun
fig.	figuratively	*pr.p.*	present participle
Fr.	French	*pt.*	past tense
g	gram(s)	R.C.	Roman Catholic
Ger.	German	*refl.*	reflexive
Gr.	Greek	S	South
ie	that is	*sing.*	singular
impers.	impersonal	*sl.*	slang
ind.	indicative	Sp.	Spanish
inf.	informal	sq.	square
interj.	interjection	*sup.*	superlative
intr.	intransitive	*tr.*	transitive
It.	Italian	usu.	usually
k	kilogram(s)	*v.*	verb
km	kilometre(s)	*v.aux.*	auxiliary verb
l	litre(s)	*vi.*	intransitive verb
Lat.	Latin	*vt.*	transitive verb
lit.	literally		

R	Registered Trade Mark
A	Australian
UK	United Kingdom
US	United States
C	Canadian
SA	South African

A (of temperature) absolute; alto; ampere
Å angstrom unit
a are (unit of measure)
a. acre; adjective; answer
a, an *a.* the indefinite article meaning one; *an* is used before vowels, and sometimes before unaccented syllables beginning with *h* aspirate
AA Alcoholics Anonymous; anti-aircraft
aard'vark *n.* S African ant bear
A'asia Australasia
AB able-bodied seaman
aback' *adv.* —**taken aback** startled
ab'acus *n.* counting device of beads on wire frame; flat tablet at top of column
abalo'ne [-ō'ni] *n.* edible shellfish, yielding mother-of-pearl
aban'don *vt.* desert; give up altogether —*n.* freedom from inhibitions *etc.* —**aban'doned** *a.* deserted, forsaken; uninhibited; wicked —**aban'donment** *n.*
abase' *vt.* humiliate, degrade —**abase'ment** *n.*
abash' *vt.* (*usu. passive*) confuse, make ashamed —**abash'ment** *n.*
abate' *v.* make or become less, diminish —**abate'ment** *n.*
ab'attoir *n.* slaughterhouse
abb'ey *n.* dwelling place of community of monks or nuns; church of an abbey
abb'ot *n.* head of abbey or monastery (**abb'ess** *fem.*) —**abb'acy** *n.* office, rights of abbot
abbr., abbrev. abbreviation
abbre'viate *vt.* shorten, abridge —**abbrevia'tion** *n.* shortened form of word or phrase
ab'dicate *v.* formally to give up (throne *etc.*) —**abdica'tion** *n.*
ab'domen *n.* belly —**abdom'inal** *a.*
abduct' *vt.* carry off, kidnap —**abduc'tion** *n.*
abeam' *adv.* abreast, in line
abele' *n.* white poplar
Ab'erdeen An'gus breed of cattle, *orig.* Scottish
aberra'tion *n.* deviation from what is normal; flaw; lapse —**aber'rant** *a.*
abet' *vt.* assist, encourage, *esp.* in doing wrong —**abett'er, -or** *n.*
abey'ance *n.* condition of not being in use or action
abhor' *vt.* dislike strongly, loathe —**abhor'rence** *n.* —**abhorr'ent** *a.* hateful
abide' *vt.* endure, put up with —*vi. obs.* stay, reside (**abode', abi'ded, abi'ding**) —**abide by** obey
abil'ity *n.* competence, power; talent
ab ini'tio [-i-nish'i-ō] *Lat.* from the start
ab'ject *a.* humiliated, wretched; despicable —**abjec'tion, ab'jectness** *n.*
abjure' *vt.* to give up by oath, renounce —**abjura'tion** *n.*
ab'lative *n.* case in (*esp.* Latin) nouns indicating source, agent, instrument of action
ab'laut [-lowt] *n.* vowel change within word, indicating modification of use, *eg sink, sank, sunk*
ablaze' *a.* burning
a'ble *a.* capable, competent —**a'bly** *adv.* —**able-bodied** *a.*
ablu'tion *n.* (*usu. pl.*) act of washing (oneself)
ab'negate *vt.* give up, renounce —**abnega'tion** *n.*
abnor'mal *a.* irregular; not usual or typical; freakish, odd —**abnormal'ity** *n.* —**abnor'mally** *adv.*
aboard' *adv.* on board, on ship, train, or aircraft
abode' *n.* home; dwelling —*pt./pp. of* ABIDE
abol'ish *vt.* do away with —**aboli'tion** *n.* —**aboli'tionist** *n.* one who wishes to do away with something, *esp.* slavery
A-bomb *n.* atomic bomb
abom'inate *vt.* detest —**abom'inable** *a.* —**abom'inably** *adv.* —**abomina'tion** *n.* loathing; the object loathed —**abominable snowman** large legend-

ary apelike creature said to inhabit the Himalayas

Aborig'inal *a.* of, relating to the Aborigines of Aust.; (**a-**) indigenous, earliest —*n.* Aborigine

Aborig'ine [-in-ē] *n.* one of race of people inhabiting Aust. when European settlers arrived; (**a-**) original inhabitant of country *etc.*

abort' *v.* (cause to) end prematurely (*esp.* pregnancy) —*vi.* give birth to dead fetus; fail —**abor'tion** *n.* operation to terminate pregnancy; something deformed —**abor'tionist** *n.* one who performs abortion, *esp.* illegally —**abor'tive** *a.* unsuccessful —**abor'tively** *adv.*

abound' *vi.* be plentiful; overflow —**abound'ing** *a.*

about' *adv.* on all sides; nearly; up and down; out, astir —*prep.* round; near; concerning; ready to —**about turn** reversal, complete change

above' *adv.* higher up —*prep.* over; higher than, more than; beyond

ab'racadab'ra *n.* supposedly magic word

abrade' *vt.* rub off, scrape away

abra'sion *n.* place scraped or worn by rubbing (*eg* on skin); scraping, rubbing —**abra'sive** *n.* substance for grinding, polishing *etc.* —*a.* causing abrasion; grating

abreast' *adv.* side by side; keeping up with

abridge' *vt.* cut short, abbreviate —**abridg(e)'ment** *n.*

abroad' *adv.* to or in a foreign country; at large

ab'rogate *vt.* cancel, repeal —**abroga'tion** *n.*

abrupt' *a.* sudden; blunt; hasty; steep —**abrupt'ly** *adv.* —**abrupt'ness** *n.*

ab'scess [-ses] *n.* gathering of pus in any part of the body

abscis'sa [-sis'-] *n. Math.* distance of point from the axis of coordinates (*pl.* **-sas, -sae** [-sē])

abscond' [-sk-] *vi.* leave secretly, *esp.* having stolen something

ab'seil [-āl] *vi.* descend vertical slope by means of rope

ab'sent *a.* away; not attentive —*vt.* [-sent'] keep away —**ab'sence** *n.* —**absentee'** *n.* one who stays away *esp.* habitually —**absentee'ism** *n.* persistent absence from work *etc.* —**ab'sently** *adv.* —**absent-minded** *a.*

ab'sinth(e) *n.* potent aniseed flavoured liqueur

ab'solute *a.* complete; not limited, unconditional; pure (as **absolute alcohol**) —*n.* —**ab'solutely** *adv.* completely —*interj.* [-loot'-] certainly —**ab'soluteness** *n.*

absolve' *vt.* free from, pardon, acquit —**absolu'tion** *n.*

absorb' *vt.* suck up, drink in; engage, occupy (attention *etc.*); receive impact —**absorb'ent** *a.* —**absorp'tion** *n.* —**absorp'tive** *a.*

abstain' *vi.* keep from, refrain from drinking alcohol, voting *etc.* —**abstain'er** *n.* —**absten'tion** *n.* —**ab'stinence** *n.* —**ab'stinent** *a.*

abste'mious *a.* sparing in food or *esp.* drink, temperate —**abste'miously** *adv.* —**abste'miousness** *n.*

ab'stract *a.* existing only in the mind; not concrete; not representational —*n.* summary, abridgment —*vt.* [əb-strakt'] draw from, remove; deduct —**abstract'ed** *a.* preoccupied —**abstrac'tion** *n.* —**ab'stractly** *adv.*

abstruse' *a.* obscure, difficult to understand, profound —**abstruse'ly** *adv.*

absurd' *a.* contrary to reason —**absurd'ity** *n.* —**absurd'ly** *adv.*

abun'dance *n.* great amount —**abun'dant** *a.* plentiful —**abun'dantly** *adv.*

abuse' [-byōōz'] *vt.* misuse; address rudely —*n.* [-byōōs'] —**abu'sive** *a.* —**abu'sively** *adv.* —**abu'siveness** *n.*

abut' *vi.* adjoin, border on (**-tt-**) —**abut'ment** *n.* support, *esp.* of bridge or arch

abuzz' *a.* noisy, busy with activity *etc.*

abys'mal [-z'-] *a.* immeasurable, very great; *inf.* extremely bad —**abys'mally** *adv.*

abyss' *n.* very deep gulf or pit

AC aircraftman; alternating current

A/C account

aca'cia [-kā'shə] *n.* gum-yielding tree or shrub

acad'emy *n.* society to advance arts or sciences; institution for specialized training; secondary school —**academ'ic** *a.* of academy; belonging to University *etc.*; theoretical —**academ'ically** *adv.* —**academi'cian** *n.*

acan'thus *n.* prickly plant; architectural ornament like its leaf (*pl.* **-thuses, -thi** [-thī])

acc. accompanied; account; accusative

accede' [aks-] *vi.* agree, consent; attain (office, right *etc.*)

accel'erate [aks-] *v.* (cause to) increase speed, hasten —**accelera'tion** *n.* —**accel'erative** *a.* —**accel'erator** *n.* mechanism to increase speed, *esp.* in automobile

ac'cent [ak's-] *n.* stress or pitch in speaking; mark to show such stress; local or national style of pronunciation; particular attention or emphasis —*vt.* [-sent']

accent'uate [aks-] *vt.* stress, emphasize —**accent'ual** *a.* —**accentua'tion** *n.*

accept' [ɔks-] *vt.* take, receive; admit, believe; agree to —**acceptabil'ity** *n.* —**accept'able** *a.* —**accept'ably** *adv.* —**accept'ance** *n.* —**accepta'tion** *n.* common or accepted meaning of word *etc.* —**accept'er** *n.*

ac'cess [ak's-] *n.* act, right, or means of entry —**accessibil'ity** *n.* —**acces'sible** *a.* easy to approach —**access'ibly** *adv.*

access'ary *n. see* ACCESSORY

access'ion *n.* attaining of office, right *etc.*; increase, addition

access'ory *n.* additional or supplementary part of automobile, woman's dress *etc.*; person inciting or assisting in crime —*a.* contributory, assisting

ac'cidence [ak's-] *n.* the part of grammar dealing with changes in the form of words

ac'cident [ak's-] *n.* event happening by chance; misfortune or mishap, *esp.* causing injury; nonessential quality —**acciden'tal** *a.* —**accident'ally** *adv.*

acclaim' *vt.* applaud, praise —*n.* applause —**acclama'tion** *n.* acclaim; election without opposition —**acclam'atory** *a.*

accli'matize *vt.* accustom to new climate or environment —**acclimatiza'tion** *n.*

acc'olade *n.* praise, public approval; award, honour; token of award of knighthood

accomm'odate *vt.* supply, *esp.* with board and lodging; oblige; harmonize, adapt —**accomm'odating** *a.* obliging —**accommoda'tion** *n.* lodgings

accom'pany *vt.* go with; supplement; occur with; provide a musical accompaniment (**-panied, -panying**) —**accom'paniment** *n.* that which accompanies, *esp.* in music, part which goes with solos *etc.* —**accom'panist** *n.*

accom'plice [-plis] *n.* one assisting another in criminal deed

accom'plish *vt.* carry out; finish —**accom'plished** *a.* complete, perfect; proficient —**accom'plishment** *n.* completion; personal ability

accord' *n.* (*esp.* **in accord with**) agreement, harmony —*v.* (cause to) be in accord with —*vt.* grant —**accord'ance** *n.* —**accord'ant** *a.* —**accord'ing** *adv.* —**accord'ingly** *adv.* as the circumstances suggest; therefore

accor'dion *n.* portable musical instrument with keys, metal reeds and a bellows —**accor'dionist** *n.* —**piano accordion**

accost' *vi.* approach and speak to, ask question *etc.*

account' *n.* report, description; importance, value; statement of moneys received, paid, or owed; person's money held in bank; credit available to person at store *etc.* —*vt.* reckon; judge —*vi.* give reason, answer (for) —**accountabil'ity** *n.* —**account'able** *a.* responsible —**account'ancy** *n.* keeping, preparation of business accounts, financial records *etc.* —**account'ant** *n.* one practising accountancy —**account'ing** *n.* skill or practice of keeping and preparing business accounts —*a.*

accou'tre [-ōō'-] *vt.* equip —**accou'trements** [-trɔ-] *pl.n.* equipment, *esp.* military; trappings

accred'ited *a.* authorized, officially recognized

accre'tion *n.* growth; something added on

accrue' *vi.* be added; result

acct. account

accu'mulate *v.* gather, become gathered in increasing quantity; collect —**accumula'tion** *n.* —**accu'mulator** *n.* device that collects and stores energy

acc'urate *a.* exact, correct, without errors —**acc'uracy** *n.* —**acc'urately** *adv.*

accurs'ed, accurst' *a.* under a curse; hateful, detestable

accuse' *vt.* charge with wrong doing; blame —**accusa'tion** *n.* —**accu'sative** *n.* grammatical case indicating the direct object —**accu'satory** *a.* —**accu'ser** *n.*

accus'tom *vt.* make used to, familiarize —**accus'tomed** *a.* usual; used (to); in the habit (of)

ace *n.* the one at dice, cards, dominoes; *Tennis* winning serve *esp.* one untouched by opponent; very successful fighter pilot; *inf.* person expert at anything —*a. inf.* excellent

ac'erbate [as'-] *vt.* make worse; make sour, bitter —**acerb'ity** *n.* severity, sharpness; sour bitterness

ac'etate *n.* salt of acetic acid —**acetate rayon** synthetic textile fibre

ace'tic *a.* derived from or having the nature of vinegar

ac'etone [as'-] *n.* colourless liquid used as a solvent

acet'ylene [-set'-] *n.* colourless, flammable gas used *esp.* in welding metals

ache [āk] *n.* continuous pain —*vi.* to be in pain —**a'ching** *a.*

achieve' *vt.* accomplish, perform successfully; gain —**achieve'ment** *n.* something accomplished

achromat'ic [ak-] *a.* free from or not showing colour, as of a lens, colourless

ac'id [as'-] *a.* sharp, sour —*n.* sour substance; *Chem.* one of a class of compounds which combines with bases (alkalis, oxides *etc.*) to form salts —**acid'ic** *a.* —**acid'ify** *vt.* (**-fied, -fying**) —**acid'ity** *n.* —**acid'ulate** *vt.* to make slightly acid —**acid'ulous** *a.* —**acid rain** rain acidified by atmospheric pollution —**acid test** conclusive test of value

ack-ack *n.* anti-aircraft guns or gunfire

acknowl'edge [ək-nol'ij] *vt.* admit, own, recognize; say one has received —**acknowl'edg(e)ment** *n.*

aclin'ic *a.* without inclination, said of the magnetic equator, on which the magnetic needle has no dip

ac'me *n.* highest point

ac'ne *n.* pimply skin disease

ac'olyte *n.* follower or attendant, *esp.* of priest

ac'onite *n.* genus of plants related to the buttercup, including monkshood; drug, poison obtained from such

a'corn [ā'-] *n.* nut or fruit of the oak tree

acou'stic *a.* pert. to sound and to hearing —**acou'stics** *pl.n.* science of sounds; features of room or building as regards sounds heard within it

acquaint' *vt.* make familiar, inform —**acquaint'ance** *n.* person known; personal knowledge —**acquaint'anceship** *n.*

acquiesce' [a-kwi-es'] *vi.* agree, consent without complaint —**acquies'cence** *n.* —**acquies'cent** *a.*

acquire' *vt.* gain, get —**acquire'ment** *n.* —**acquisi'tion** *n.* act of getting; material gain —**acquis'itive** *a.* desirous of gaining —**acquis'itiveness** *n.*

acquit' *vt.* declare innocent; settle, discharge, as a debt; behave (oneself) (**-tt-**) —**acquitt'al** *n.* declaration of innocence in court —**acquitt'ance** *n.* discharge of debts

a'cre [-kər] *n.* measure of land, 4840 square yards —*pl.* lands, estates; *inf.* large area or plenty of —**a'creage** *n.* the extent of land in acres

ac'rid *a.* pungent, sharp; irritating —**acrid'ity** *n.*

ac'rimony *n.* bitterness of feeling or language —**acrimo'nious** *a.*

ac'robat *n.* one skilled in gymnastic feats, *esp.* as entertainer in circus *etc.* —**acrobat'ic** *a.* —**acrobat'ics** *pl.n.* any activity requiring agility

ac'ronym *n.* word formed from initial letters of other words *eg* UNESCO, ANZAC, NATO

acrop'olis *n.* citadel, *esp.* in ancient Greece

across' *adv./prep.* crosswise; from side to side; on or to the other side —**get (*or* put) it across** explain, make (something) understood

acros'tic *n.* word puzzle in which the first, middle, or last letters of each line spell a word or words

acryl'ic [-kril'-] *n.* variety of synthetic materials, *esp.* textiles derived from an organic acid

act *n.* thing done, deed; doing; law or decree; section of a play —*v.* perform, as in a play —*vi.* exert force, work, as mechanism; behave —**ac'ting** *n.* performance of a part —*a.* temporarily performing the duties of —**ac'tion** *n.* operation; deed; gesture; expenditure of energy; battle; lawsuit —**ac'tionable** *a.* subject to lawsuit —**ac'tivate** *vt.* to make active; make radioactive; make chemically active —**activa'tion** *n.* —**ac'tivator** *n.* —**ac'tive** *a.* moving, working; brisk, energetic —*n.* active member —**ac'tively** *adv.* —**ac'tivism** *n.* —**ac'tivist** *n.* one who takes (direct) action to achieve political or social ends —**activ'ity** *n.* —**ac'tor** *n.* one who acts in a play, motion picture *etc.* (*fem.* **-tress**)

ac'tinism *n.* chemical action of sun's rays —**actin'ic** *a.*

actin'ium *n.* radioactive element occurring as decay product of uranium

ac'tual *a.* existing in the present; real —**actual'ity** *n.* —**ac'tually** *adv.* really, indeed

ac'tuary *n.* statistician who calculates insurance risks, premiums *etc.* —**actua'rial** *a.*

ac'tuate *vt.* activate; motivate —**actua'tion** *n.*

acu'ity *n.* keenness, *esp.* in vision or thought

ac'umen *n.* sharpness of wit, perception, penetration

ac'upuncture *n. orig.* Chinese medical treatment involving insertion of needles at various points on the body —**ac'upuncturist** *n.*

acute' *a.* keen, shrewd; sharp; severe; less than 90° —*n.* accent (´) over a letter to indicate the quality or length of its sound *eg* abbé —**acute'ly** *adv.* —**acute'ness** *n.*

AD anno Domini

ad *n. abbrev. of* ADVERTISEMENT

ad'age *n.* much used wise saying, proverb

adag'io [-dahzh'-] *adv./n. Mus.* leisurely, slow (passage)

ad'amant *a.* very hard, unyielding —**adaman'tine** *a.*

Adam's apple projecting part at front of the throat, the thyroid cartilage

adapt' *vt.* alter for new use; fit, modify; change —**adaptabil'ity** *n.* —**adapt'able** *a.* —**adapta'tion** *n.* —**adapt'er, -or** *n. esp.* appliance for connecting two parts (*eg* electrical)

add *v.* join; increase by; say further —**addi'tion** *n.* adding; supplementary building —**addi'tional** *a.* —**add'itive** *n.* something added, *esp.* to foodstuffs

adden'dum *n.* thing to be added (*pl.* **-da**)

add'er *n.* any of various harmless Amer. snakes; UK small poisonous snake

add'ict *n.* one who has become dependent on something, *eg* drugs (a *drug addict*) —*vt.* [ə-dikt'] (*usu. passive*) —**addict'ed** *a.* —**addic'tion** *n.* —**addic'tive** *a.* causing addiction

ad'dle *v.* make or become rotten, muddled

address' *n.* direction on letter; place where one lives; speech —*pl.* courtship —*vt.* mark destination, as on envelope; speak to; direct; dispatch —**addressee'** *n.* person addressed

adduce' *vt.* offer as proof; cite —**addu'cible** *a.* —**adduc'tion** *n.*

ad'enoids *pl.n.* tissue at back of nose —**adenoid'al** *a.*

adept' *a.* skilled —*n.* [ad'-] expert

ad'equate [-kwət] *a.* sufficient, enough, suitable; not outstanding —**ad'equacy** *n.* —**ad'equately** *adv.*

adhere' *vi.* stick to; be firm in opinion *etc.* —**adhe'rent** *n./a.* —**adhe'sion** *n.* —**adhe'sive** *a./n.*

ad hoc' [-hok'] *a./adv.* for a particular occasion only; improvised

adieu' [-dyōō'] *interj.* farewell —*n.* act of taking leave (*pl.* **adieus', adieux'**)

ad infini'tum *Lat.* endlessly

ad in'terim *Lat.* for the meantime

ad'ipose *a.* of fat, fatty

ad'it *n.* almost horizontal entrance into a mine

adj. adjective; adjourned; adjutant

adja'cent *a.* lying near, next (to) —**adja'cency** *n.*

ad'jective *n.* word which qualifies or limits a noun —**adjecti'val** *a.* of adjective

adjoin' *v.* be next to; join —**adjoin'ing** *a.* next to, near

adjourn' [ə-jurn'] *v.* postpone temporarily, as meeting; *inf.* move elsewhere —**adjourn'ment** *n.*

adjudge' *vt.* declare; decide; award —**adjudg(e)'ment** *n.*

adju'dicate *v.* try, judge; sit in judgment —**adjudica'tion** *n.* —**adju'dicator** *n.*

ad'junct *a.* joined, added —*n.* person or thing added or subordinate —**adjunc'tive** *a.*

adjure' *vt.* beg, earnestly entreat —**adjura'tion** *n.*
adjust' *vt.* make suitable, adapt; alter slightly, regulate —**adjust'able** *a.* —**adjust'er** *n.* —**adjust'ment** *n.*
ad'jutant *n.* military officer who assists superiors —**ad'jutancy** *n.* his office, rank
ad' lib *v.* improvise and speak spontaneously —*n.* such speech *etc.* —*a./adv.*
Adm. Admiral; Admiralty
admin'ister *vt.* manage, look after; dispense, as justice *etc.*; apply —**admin'istrate** *vt.* manage business, institution, government department *etc.* —**administra'tion** *n.* —**admin'istrative** *a.* —**admin'istrator** *n.* (*fem.* **-atrix**)
ad'miral *n.* naval officer of highest sea rank —**ad'miralty** *n.* court having jurisdiction over naval affairs —**Admiralty (Board) UK** department in charge of Royal Navy
admire' *vt.* look on with wonder and pleasure; respect highly —**ad'mirable** *a.* —**ad'mirably** *adv.* —**admira'tion** *n.* —**admi'rer** *n.* —**admi'ringly** *adv.*
admit' *vt.* confess; accept as true; allow; let in (**-tt-**) —**admiss'ible** *a.* —**admis'sibly** *adv.* —**admiss'ion** *n.* permission to enter; entrance fee; confession —**admit'tance** *n.* permission to enter —**admit'tedly** *adv.*
admix'ture *n.* mixture; ingredient —**admix'** *vt.*
admon'ish *vt.* reprove; advise; warn; exhort —**admoni'tion** *n.* —**admon'itory** *a.*
ad naus'eam [nawz'-] *Lat.* to a boring or disgusting extent
ado' [a-dōō'] *n.* fuss
ado'be [-bi] *n.* sun-dried brick
adoles'cence *n.* period of life just before maturity —**adoles'cent** *n.* a youth —*a.*
Ado'nis *n.* a beautiful youth beloved of Venus
adopt' *vt.* take into relationship, *esp.* as one's child; take up, as principle, resolution —**adop'tion** *n.* —**adopt'ive** *a.* that which adopts or is adopted
adore' *v.* love intensely; worship —**ador'able** *a.* —**adora'tion** *n.* —**ador'er** *n.* lover
adorn' *vt.* beautify, embellish, deck —**adorn'ment** *n.* ornament, decoration
ADP automatic data processing
ad rem *Lat.* to the point
adre'nal *a.* near the kidney —**adrenal gland** —**adren'alin(e)** *n.* hormone secreted by adrenal glands; this substance used as drug
adrift' *a./adv.* drifting free; *inf.* detached; *inf.* off course
adroit' *a.* skilful, expert; clever —**adroit'ly** *adv.* —**adroit'ness** *n.* dexterity
adsorb' *v.* (of gas, vapour) condense and form thin film on surface —**adsor'bent** *a./n.* —**adsorp'tion** *n.*
ADT Atlantic Daylight Time
adula'tion [-dyoo-] *n.* flattery —**ad'ulate** *vt.* flatter —**ad'ulator** *n.* —**ad'ulatory** *a.*
adult' *a.* grown-up, mature —*n.* grown-up person; full-grown animal or plant
adul'terate *vt.* make impure by addition —**adul'terant** *n.* —**adul'terated** *a.* —**adultera'tion** *n.* —**adul'terator** *n.*
adul'tery *n.* sexual unfaithfulness of a husband or wife —**adul'terer** *n.masc.* (**-ess** *fem.*) —**adul'terous** *a.*
ad'umbrate *vt.* outline; give indication of —**adum'brant, -rative** *a.* —**adumbra'tion** *n.*
adv. adverb(ial); advertisement
ad valor'em *Lat.* according to the value
advance' [-vah-] *vt.* bring forward; suggest; encourage; pay beforehand; *Motoring* to time spark earlier in engine cycle —*vi.* go forward; improve in position or value —*n.* movement forward; improvement; a loan —*pl.* personal approach(es) to gain favour *etc.* —*a.* ahead in time or position —**advanced'** *a.* at a late stage; not elementary; ahead of the times —**advance'ment** *n.* promotion
advan'tage *n.* superiority; more favourable position or state; benefit —**advanta'geous** *a.* —**advanta'geously** *adv.*
ad'vent *n.* a coming, arrival; (**A-**) the four weeks before Christmas —**the Advent** the coming of Christ —**Ad'ventist** *n.* one of number of Christian sects believing in imminent return of Christ
adventi'tious *a.* added; accidental, casual
adven'ture *n.* risk; bold exploit; remarkable happening; enterprise; com-

mercial speculation —*v.* (take) risk —**adven'turer** *n.* one who seeks adventures; one who lives on his wits (**-ess** *fem.*) —**adven'turous** *a.* —**adven'turously** *adv.* —**adven'turousness** *n.*

ad'verb *n.* word added to verb, adjective, or other adverb to modify meaning —**adverb'ial** *a.* —**adverb'ially** *adv.*

ad'verse *a.* opposed to; hostile; unfavourable, bringing harm —**ad'versary** *n.* enemy —**advers'ative** *a.* —**ad'versely** *adv.* —**advers'ity** *n.* distress, misfortune

advert'[1] *vi.* turn the mind or attention to; refer —**advert'ence** *n.* —**advert'ently** *adv.*

ad'vert[2] *n.* **UK** *inf.* advertisement

ad'vertise *vt.* publicize; make known; give notice of, *esp.* in newspapers *etc.* —*vi.* make public request (for) —**adver'tisement** [-iz-] *n.* —**ad'vertiser** *n.* —**ad'vertising** *a./n.*

advice' *n.* opinion given; counsel; information; (formal) notification

advise' *vt.* offer advice; recommend a line of conduct; give notice (of) —**advi's-able** *a.* expedient —**advised'** *a.* considered, deliberate, as in **well-advised** —**advi'sedly** [-id-li] *adv.* —**advi'ser, -or** *n.* —**advi'sory** *a.*

ad'vocaat [-kah, -kaht] *n.* liqueur with raw egg base

ad'vocate *n.* one who pleads the cause of another, *esp.* in court of law; barrister —*vt.* uphold, recommend —**ad'vocacy** *n.* —**advoca'tion** *n.*

advt. advertisement

adze [adz] *n.* carpenter's tool, like axe, but with arched blade set at right angles to handle

ae'gis [ē'jis] *n.* sponsorship, protection (*orig.* shield of Zeus)

Aeo'lian [ē-o'-] *a.* acted on by the wind, as **Aeolian harp**

ae'on [ē'-] *n.* *see* EON

a'erate *vt.* charge liquid with gas, as effervescent drink; expose to air —**aera'tion** *n.* —**a'erator** *n.* apparatus for charging liquid with gas

a'erial *a.* of the air; operating in the air; pertaining to aircraft —*n.* part of radio *etc.* receiving or sending radio waves

ae'rie, ae'ry [ā'-, ī'-] *n.* *see* EYRIE

a'ero- (*comb. form*) air or aircraft as in **aeroengine**

aerobat'ics *pl.n.* stunt flying

aero'bics *pl.n.* exercise system designed to increase the amount of oxygen in the blood

a'erodrome *n.* **UK** airfield

aerodynam'ics *pl.n.* (*with sing. v.*) study of air flow, *esp.* round moving solid bodies

a'erogram *n.* air letter

a'erolite *n.* meteoric stone —**aerolit'ic** *a.*

aerom'etry *n.* measurement of weight or density of gases

a'eronaut *n.* pilot or navigator of lighter-than-air craft —**aeronau'tics** *pl.n.* (*with sing. v.*) science of air navigation and flying in general —**aeronau'tical** *a.*

a'eroplane *n.* **UK** airplane

a'erosol *n.* (substance dispensed as fine spray from) pressurized can

a'erospace *n.* earth's atmosphere and space beyond —*a.*

aesthet'ic [ēs-] *a.* relating to principles of beauty, taste and art (*also* **esthet'ic**) —**aesthet'ics** *pl.n.* study of art, taste *etc.* —**aes'thete** *n.* one who affects extravagant love of art —**aesthet'ically** *adv.* —**aesthet'icism** *n.*

aes'tivate [ēs'-] *vi.* *see* ESTIVATE

ae'ther *see* ETHER

aetiol'ogy [ē-ti-] *n.* *see* ETIOLOGY

AF audio frequency

afar' *adv.* from, at, or to, a great distance

AFC automatic frequency control

aff'able *a.* easy to speak to, polite and friendly —**affabil'ity** *n.* —**aff'ably** *adv.*

affair' *n.* thing done or attended to; business; happening; sexual liaison —*pl.* personal or business interests; matters of public interest

affect' *vt.* act on, influence; move feelings; make show of, make pretence; assume; have liking for —**affecta'tion** *n.* show, pretence —**affect'ed** *a.* making a pretence; moved; acted upon —**affect'edly** *adv.* —**affect'ing** *a.* moving the feelings —**affect'ingly** *adv.* —**affec'tion** *n.* fondness, love —**affec'tionate** *a.* —**affec'tionately** *adv.*

aff'erent *a.* bringing to, *esp.* describing nerves which carry sensation to the brain

affi'ance *vt.* betroth —**affi'anced** *a./n.* (one) promised in marriage
affida'vit *n.* written statement on oath
affil'iate *vt.* connect, attach, as society to federation *etc.*; adopt —**affilia'tion** *n.*
affin'ity *n.* natural liking; resemblance; relationship by marriage; chemical attraction —**affin'itive** *a.*
affirm' *v.* assert positively, declare; maintain statement; make solemn declaration —**affirma'tion** *n.* —**affirm'ative** *a.* asserting —*n.* word of assent —**affirm'atively** *adv.*
affix' *vt.* fasten (to); attach, append —*n.* [af'-] addition, esp. to word, as suffix, prefix
afflict' *vt.* give pain or grief to, distress; trouble, vex —**afflic'tion** *n.* —**afflic'tive** *a.*
aff'luent *a.* wealthy; abundant —*n.* tributary stream —**aff'luence** *n.* wealth, abundance
afford' *vt.* to be able to buy; be able to spare the time *etc.*; produce, yield, furnish
affor'est *vt.* turn land into forest, plant trees —**afforesta'tion** *n.*
affray' *n.* fight, brawl
affront' *vt.* insult openly —*n.* insult; offence
afield' *adv.* away from home; in or on the field
afire' *adv.* on fire
aflame' *adv.* burning
afloat' *adv.* floating; at sea; in circulation
afoot' *adv.* astir; on foot
afore' *prep./adv.* before, usually in compounds as **afore'said, afore'thought, afore'time**
afoul' [-fowl'] *a./adv.* into difficulty (with)
Afr. Africa(n)
afraid' *a.* frightened; regretful
afresh' *adv.* again, anew
Af'rican *a.* belonging to Africa —*n.* native of Africa —**African violet** house plant with pink or purple flowers and hairy leaves
Africand'er *n.* breed of hump-backed S Afr. cattle
Afrikaans' [-kahns'] *n.* language used in S Africa, derived from 17th cent. Dutch —**Afrikan'er** *n.* white native of S Afr. with Afrikaans as mother tongue
Af'ro *n.* fuzzy, bushy hair style
aft *adv.* towards stern of ship
af'ter [ahf'-] *adv.* later; behind —*prep.* behind; later than; on the model of; pursuing —*conj.* at a later time than —*a.* behind; later; nearer ship's stern
af'terbirth *n.* membrane expelled after a birth
af'tercare *n.* care, *esp.* medical, bestowed on person after period of treatment, and *esp.* after childbirth
af'tereffect *n.* subsequent effect of deed, event *etc.*
af'terglow *n.* light after sunset
af'termath *n.* result, consequence
afternoon' *n.* time from noon to evening
af'tershave *n.* lotion applied to face after shaving
af'terthought *n.* idea occurring later
af'terward(s) *adv.* later
Ag *Chem.* silver
again' *adv.* once more; in addition; back, in return; besides
against' *prep.* in opposition to; in contact with; opposite; in readiness for
agape' *a./adv.* open-mouthed as in wonder *etc.*
ag'aric *n.* various fungi, *eg* mushroom —*a.* fungoid
ag'ate *n.* coloured, semiprecious, decorative form of quartz
age [āj] *n.* length of time person or thing has existed; time of life; period of history; maturity; long time —*v.* make or grow old —**a'ged** [ājd *or* ā'jid] *a.* old —*pl.n.* [ā'jid] old people —**a'g(e)ing** *n./a.* —**age'less** *a.* —**age-old** *a.*
agen'da [-jen'-] *pl.n.* (*with sing. v.*) things to be done; programme of business meeting
a'gent [-j-] *n.* one authorized to carry on business or affairs for another; person or thing producing effect; cause; natural force —**a'gency** *n.* instrumentality; business, place of business, of agent
agent provocateur' [a-zhong-] *Fr.* police or secret service spy
agglom'erate *v.* gather into a mass —*n.* confused mass; rock consisting of volcanic fragments —*a.* —**agglomera'tion** *n.* —**agglom'erative** *a.*
agglu'tinate [-gloo͞'-] *vt.* unite with glue *etc.*; form words into compounds —*a.* united, as by glue —**agglutina'tion**

n. —**agglu'tinative** *a.*

agg'randize *vt.* make greater in size, power, or rank —**aggran'dizement** *n.*

agg'ravate *vt.* make worse or more severe; *inf.* annoy —**agg'ravating** *a.* —**aggrava'tion** *n.*

agg'regate *vt.* gather into mass —*a.* gathered thus —*n.* mass, sum total; rock consisting of mixture of minerals; mixture of gravel *etc.* for concrete —**aggrega'tion** *n.*

aggress'ion *n.* unprovoked attack; hostile activity —**aggress'** *vi.* —**aggres'sive** *a.* —**aggress'iveness** *n.* —**aggres'sor** *n.*

aggrieve' *vt.* pain, injure —**aggrieved'** *a.*

aghast' [-gahst'] *a.* struck, stupefied with horror or terror

ag'ile [-jīl] *a.* nimble; active; quick —**ag'ilely** *adv.* —**agil'ity** *n.*

ag'itate [-j-] *vt.* disturb, excite; to keep in motion, stir, shake up; trouble —*vi.* stir up public opinion (for or against) —**agita'tion** *n.* —**ag'itator** *n.*

aglow' *a.* glowing

ag'lu, ag'loo *n.* breathing hole made in ice by seal

AGM Annual General Meeting

agnos'tic *n.* one who holds that we know nothing of things outside the material world —*a.* of this theory —**agnos'ticism** *n.*

ag'nus de'i [dā'i] figure of a lamb emblematic of Christ; part of Mass beginning with these words; the music for it

ago' *adv.* in the past

agog' *a./adv.* eager, astir

ag'ony *n.* extreme suffering of mind or body, violent struggle —**ag'onize** *vi.* suffer agony; worry greatly —**ag'onizing** *a.*

agorapho'bia *n.* fear of open spaces

agra'rian *a.* of agriculture, land or its management —**agra'rianism** *n.*

agree' *v.* be of same opinion; consent; harmonize; determine, settle; suit (**agreed', agree'ing**) —**agreeabil'ity** *n.* —**agree'able** *a.* willing; pleasant —**agree'ableness** *n.* —**agree'ably** *adv.* —**agree'ment** *n.* concord; contract

ag'riculture *n.* art, practice of cultivating land —**agricul'tural** *a.* —**agricul'turist** *n.*

ag'rimony *n.* yellow-flowered plant with bitter taste

agron'omy *n.* the study of the management of the land and the scientific cultivation of crops —**agron'omist** *n.*

aground' *adv.* (of boat) touching bottom

agt. agent

a'gue [-gyōō] *n. obs.* periodic fever with shivering

ahead' *adv.* in front; onwards

ahoy' *interj.* shout used at sea for hailing

AI artificial insemination; artificial intelligence

AID artificial insemination by donor

aid *vt.* to help —*n.* help, support, assistance

aide, aide'-de-camp' [ād'-də-kong'] *n.* military officer personally assisting superior (*pl.* **aides-de-camp**)

AIDS acquired immune (*or* immuno-) deficiency syndrome

aiguille' [ā-gwēl'] *n.* sharp, slender peak; blasting drill

AIH artificial insemination by husband

ail *vt.* trouble, afflict, disturb —*vi.* be ill —**ail'ing** *a.* sickly —**ail'ment** *n.* illness

ai'leron [ā'-] *n.* movable section of wing of aircraft which gives lateral control

aim *v.* give direction to weapon *etc.*; direct effort towards, try to —*n.* direction; object, purpose —**aim'less** *a.* without purpose

ain't *nonstandard* am not; is not; are not; has not; have not

air *n.* mixture of gases we breathe, the atmosphere; breeze; tune; manner —*pl.* affected manners —*vt.* expose to air to dry or ventilate —**air'ily** *adv.* —**air'iness** *n.* —**air'ing** *v.* time spent in the open air —**air'less** *a.* stuffy —**air'y** *a.* —**air base** —**air bed** —**air'borne** *a.* flying, in the air —**air brake** brake worked by compressed air; method of slowing down an aircraft —**air'brush** *n.* atomizer spraying paint by compressed air —**air commodore** —**air-condition** *vt.* maintain constant stream of clean fresh air in building at correct temperature —**air conditioner** —**air conditioning** —**air'craft** *n.* collective name for flying machines; airplane —**aircraft carrier** —**air cushion** pillow which can be inflated; pocket of air supporting hovercraft —**air'field** *n.* landing and taking-off area for aircraft —**air'foil** *n.* cross section of aileron, wing *etc.* —**air force** strength of country in aircraft —**air gun** gun discharged by force of compressed air —**air hostess** stewardess on aircraft —**air letter** air-mail letter form —**air'lift** *n.* transport of goods *etc.* by aircraft —**air'line** *n.* company operating aircraft —**air'lock** *n.* air bubble obstructing flow of liquid in pipe; airtight chamber —**air mail** —**air'man** *n.* —**air'plane** *n.* heavier-than-air flying machine —**air'play** *n.* radio exposure of disc —**air pocket** less dense air where airplane drops suddenly —**air'port** *n.* station for civilian aircraft —**air pump** machine to extract or supply air —**air raid** attack by aircraft —**air'screw** *n.* propeller of any aircraft —**air shaft** passage for air into a mine *etc.* —**air'ship** *n.* lighter-than-air flying machine with means of propulsion —**air'sickness** *n.* nausea caused by motion of aircraft in flight —**air'speed** *n.* speed of aircraft relative to air —**air'strip** *n.* small airfield with only one runway —**air'tight** *a.* not allowing passage of air —**air trap** device to prevent escape of foul gases —**air valve** —**air'way** *n.* regular aircraft route —**air'worthy** *a.* fit for service in the air —**air'worthiness** *n.*

Aire'dale *n.* large rough-coated terrier dog

aisle [īl] *n.* passageway separating seating areas in church, theatre *etc.*

ajar' *adv.* partly open

akim'bo *adv.* with hands on hips and elbows outwards

akin' *a.* related by blood; alike, having like qualities

Al *Chem.* aluminum

al'abaster *n.* soft, white, semitransparent stone —**alabast'rine** *a.* of, like this

à la carte *Fr.* selected freely from the menu

alack' *interj.* cry of sorrow —**alack-a-day** *interj.*

alac'rity *n.* quickness, briskness, readiness

à la mode *Fr.* in fashion

alarm' *n.* sudden fright; apprehension; notice of danger; bell, buzzer; call to arms —*vt.* frighten; warn of danger —**alarm'ing** *a.* —**alarm'ist** *n.* one given to prophesying danger or exciting alarm *esp.* needlessly —**alarm clock** clock which sounds a buzzer or bell at a set time, as to wake someone up

alas' *interj.* cry of grief

alb *n.* long white priestly vestment, worn at Mass

al'batross *n.* large oceanic bird, of petrel family

albe'it [awl-bē'-] *conj.* although

albi'no [-ē'-] *n.* person or animal with white skin and hair, and pink eyes, due to lack of colouring matter (*pl.* **-nos**) —**al'binism** *n.*

al'bum *n.* book of blank leaves, for photographs, stamps, autographs *etc.*; one or more longplaying gramophone records

al'bumen [-byoo-] *n.* egg white

al'bumin, -en [-byoo-] *n.* constituent of animal and vegetable matter, found nearly pure in white of egg —**albu'minous** *a.*

al'chemy [-k-] *n.* medieval chemistry, *esp.* attempts to turn base metals into gold and find elixir of life —**al'chemist** *n.*

al'cohol *n.* intoxicating fermented liquor; class of organic chemical substances —**alcohol'ic** *a.* —*n.* one addicted to alcoholic drink —**al'coholism** *n.* disease, alcohol poisoning

al'cove *n.* recess

al'dehyde *n.* one of a group of organic chemical compounds

al'der [awl'-] *n.* tree related to the birch

al'derman [awl'-] *n.* formerly, member of governing body of a municipality —**alderman'ic** *a.*

ale *n.* drink made from hops fermented rapidly at high temperature; **UK** fermented malt liquor, type of beer, *orig.* without hops —**ale'house** *n. obs.* public house

alert' *a.* watchful; brisk, active —*n.* warning of sudden attack or surprise —*vt.* warn, *esp.* of danger; draw attention to —**alert'ness** *n.* —**on the alert** watchful

Alexan'drine *n.* verse of six iambic feet

alfal'fa *n.* plant used as fodder; a kind of lucerne

alfres'co *adv./a.* in the open air

alg. algebra

al'gae [-jē] *pl.n.* (*sing.* **al'ga** [-gə]) various water plants, including seaweed

al'gebra *n.* method of calculating, using symbols to represent quantities and to show relations between them, making a kind of abstract arithmetic —**algebra'ic(al)** *a.* —**algebra'ist** *n.*

ALGOL *Computers algorithmic oriented language*

al'gorithm *n.* procedural model for complicated calculations

a'lias *adv.* otherwise —*n.* assumed name (*pl.* **a'liases**)

al'ibi [-bī] *n.* plea of being somewhere else when crime was committed; *inf.* excuse

a'lien *a.* foreign; different in nature; repugnant (to) —*n.* foreigner —**alienabil'ity** *n.* —**a'lienable** *a.* able to be transferred to another owner —**a'lienate** *vt.* estrange; transfer —**aliena'tion** *n.*

alight'[1] *vi.* get down; land, settle

alight'[2] *a.* burning; lit up

align' [-līn'] *vt.* bring into line or agreement —**align'ment** *n.*

alike' *a.* like, similar —*adv.* in the same way

aliment'ary *a.* of food —**alimentary canal** food passage in body

al'imony *n.* allowance paid under court order to separated or divorced spouse

al'iped *a.* wing-footed —*n.* animal, like the bat, whose toes are joined by membrane that serves as wing

al'iquot *a.* such part of a number as will divide it without remainder

alive' *a.* living; active; aware; swarming

aliz'arin *n.* brown to red crystalline solid used as dye

al'kali [-lī] *n.* substance which combines with acid and neutralizes it, forming a salt; potash, soda *etc.* are alkalis (*pl.* **-li(e)s**) —**al'kaline** *a.* —**alkalin'ity** *n.* —**al'kalize** *vt.* —**al'kaloid** *n./a.*

all [awl] *a.* the whole of, every one of —*adv.* wholly, entirely —*n.* the whole; everything, everyone —**all fours** hands and feet —**all in** exhausted —**all-in** *a.* *Wrestling* no style debarred —**all-rounder** *n.* person with ability in many fields

Al'lah [-lə] *n.* Moslem name for the Supreme Deity

allay' *vt.* lighten, relieve, calm, soothe

allege' *vt.* state without or before proof; produce as argument —**allega'tion** *n.* —**alleged'** *a.* —**alleg'edly** [-lej'id-] *adv.*

alle'giance *n.* duty of a subject to his sovereign or state, loyalty

all'egory *n.* story with a meaning other than literal one; description of one thing under image of another —**allegor'ic(al)** *a.* —**allegor'ically** *adv.* —**all'egorist** *n.* —**all'egorize** *vt.*

allegrett'o *adv./a./n. Mus.* lively (passage) but not so quick as allegro

alle'gro [-lā'-] *adv./a./n. Mus.* fast (passage)

all'ergy *n.* abnormal sensitivity to some food or substance innocuous to most people —**all'ergen** *n.* substance capable of inducing an allergy —**aller'gic** *a.* having or caused by an allergy; *inf.* having an aversion (to)

alle'viate *vt.* ease, lessen, mitigate; make light —**allevia'tion** *n.* —**alle'viator** *n.*

all'ey *n.* narrow street; walk, path; enclosure for skittles; fine marble (*pl.* **-eys**)

alli'ance *n.* state of being allied; union between families by marriage, and states by treaty; confederation

all'igator *n.* animal of crocodile family found in America

allitera'tion *n.* beginning of two or more words in close succession with same sound, *eg* Sing a Song of Sixpence —**allit'erate** *vi.* —**allit'erative** *a.*

all'ocate *vt.* assign as a share; place —**alloca'tion** *n.*

allocu'tion *n.* formal address —**al'locute** *vi.*

allog'amy *n.* cross-fertilization

allomor'phism *n.* variation of form without change in essential nature; variation of crystalline form of chemical compound

allop'athy *n.* orthodox practice of medicine; opposite of homeopathy

allot' *vt.* distribute as shares; give out (**-tt-**) —**allot'ment** *n.* distribution; portion of land rented for cultivation; portion allotted

allot'ropy *n.* property of some elements of existing in more than one form, *eg* carbon in the form of diamond and charcoal —**all'otrope** *n.* —**allotrop'ic** *a.* —**allot'ropism** *n.*

allow' *vt.* permit; acknowledge; set aside

—*vi.* (*usu. with* for) take into account —**allow'able** *a.* —**allow'ably** *adv.* —**allow'ance** *n.*

all'oy *n.* mixture of two or more metals —*vt.* [ə-loi'] mix metals, debase

all'spice [awl'-] *n.* pimento or Jamaica pepper

allude' [-lood'] *vi.* mention lightly, hint at, make indirect reference to; refer to —**allu'sion** *n.* —**allu'sive** *a.* —**allu'sively** *adv.*

allure' [-loor'] *vt.* entice, win over, fascinate —*n.* attractiveness —**allure'ment** *n.* —**allu'ring** *a.* charming, seductive —**allu'ringly** *adv.*

allu'vial [-oov'-] *a.* deposited by rivers —**allu'vion** *n.* land formed by washed-up deposit —**allu'vium** *n.* water-borne matter deposited by rivers, floods *etc.* (*pl.* **-viums, -via**)

ally' *vt.* join in relationship by treaty, marriage, or friendship *etc.* (**allied'** [-līd'], **ally'ing**) —**allied'** [*or* al'īd] *a.* —**all'y** *n.* state or sovereign bound to another by treaty; confederate (*pl.* **al'lies**)

al'ma mat'er [-maht'-, -mā'-] *Lat.* one's school, university, or college

al'manac [awl'-] *n.* yearly calendar with detailed information on year's tides, events *etc.*

almi'ghty *a.* having all power, omnipotent; *inf.* very great —**The Almighty** God

alm'ond [ahm'-] *n.* kernel of the fruit of a tree related to the peach; tree that bears it

alm'oner [ahm'-] *n.* person who distributes alms

al'most [awl'-] *adv.* very nearly, all but

alms [ahmz] *pl.n.* gifts to the poor

al'oe *n.* genus of plants of medicinal value —*pl.* bitter drug made from plant

aloft' *adv.* on high; overhead; in ship's rigging

alone' *a.* single, solitary —*adv.* separately, only

along' *adv.* lengthwise; together (with); forward —*prep.* over the length of —**along'side** *adv./prep.* beside

aloof' *adv.* withdrawn; at a distance; apart —*a.* uninvolved —**aloof'ness** *n.*

alope'cia *n.* baldness

aloud' *adv.* loudly; audibly

alp *n.* high mountain —**Alps** *pl. esp.* mountains of Switzerland —**al'pine** *a.* —*n.* mountain plant —**al'pinist** *n.* mountain climber —**alp'enstock** *n.* iron-shod staff used by climbers

alpac'a *n.* Peruvian llama; its wool; cloth made from this

al'phabet *n.* the set of letters used in writing a language —**alphabet'ic(al)** *a.* in the standard order of the letters —**alphabet'ically** *adv.*

alread'y [awl-red'i] *adv.* before, previously; sooner than expected

Alsa'tian [al-sā'shən] *n.* **UK** German shepherd dog

al'so [awl'-] *adv.* as well, too; besides, moreover

alt. alternate; altitude; alto

Alta. Alberta

al'tar [awl'-] *n.* raised place, stone *etc.*, on which sacrifices are offered; in Christian church, table on which priest consecrates the Eucharist Forms compounds, as **al'tarcloth** *n.*, **al'tarpiece** *n.*, **altar rails**

al'ter [awl'-] *v.* change, make or become different —**alterabil'ity** *n.* —**al'terable** *a.* —**al'terably** *adv.* —**altera'tion** *n.* —**al'terative** *a.*

alterca'tion [awl-] *n.* dispute, wrangling, controversy —**al'tercate** *vi.* —**al'tercative** *a.*

alt'er e'go *Lat.* second self; close friend

al'ternate [awl'tərnāt] *v.* occur or cause to occur by turns —**alter'nate** [-it] *a.* one after the other, by turns —*n.* [-it] stand-in —**alter'nately** *adv.* —**alterna'tion** *n.* —**alter'native** *n.* one of two choices —*a.* replacing —**alter'natively** *adv.* —**al'ternator** *n.* electric generator for producing alternating current

alt'horn *n.* a tenor saxhorn

although' [awl-THō'] *conj.* despite the fact that

altim'eter *n.* instrument for measuring height

al'titude *n.* height, eminence, elevation, loftiness

al'to *n. Mus.* male singing voice or instrument above tenor; contralto (*pl.* **-tos**)

altogeth'er [awl-] *adv.* entirely; on the whole; in total

al'truism *n.* principle of living and acting for good of others —**altruis'tic** *a.* —**altruis'tically** *adv.*

al'um *n.* mineral salt, double sulphate of

aluminum and potassium —**alu'minous** [-lōō'-] *a.*
alu'minum [-lōō'-] *n.* light nonrusting metal resembling silver —**alu'mina** *n.* oxide of aluminum —**alu'minous** *a.*
alum'nus *n.* graduate of college (*pl.* **-ni** [-nī])
al'ways [awl'-] *adv.* at all times; for ever
al'yssum *n.* garden plant with small yellow or white flowers
AM, am amplitude modulation; ante meridiem
Am. America(n)
am *first person sing. pres. ind. of* BE
amal'gam *n.* compound of mercury and another metal; soft, plastic mixture; combination of elements
amal'gamate *v.* mix, combine or cause to combine —**amalgama'tion** *n.*
amanuen'sis *n.* one who writes to dictation; copyist, secretary (*pl.* **-ses** [-sēz])
am'aranth *n.* imaginary purple everlasting flower; genus of flowered plants —**amaran'thine** *a.* never fading
amaryll'is [-ril'-] *n.* lilylike plant
amass' *v.* collect in quantity —**amass'able** *a.*
am'ateur [-tər] *n.* one who carries on an art, study, game *etc.* for the love of it, not for money; unskilled practitioner —**am'ateurish** *a.* imperfect, untrained —**am'ateurishly** *adv.* —**am'ateurism** *n.*
am'atol *n.* high explosive consisting of ammonium nitrate and trinitrotoluene (TNT)
am'atory *a.* relating to love
amaze' *vt.* surprise greatly, astound —**amaze'ment** *n.* —**ama'zing** *a.* —**ama'zingly** *adv.*
Am'azon *n.* female warrior of legend; tall, strong woman —**Amazo'nian** *a.*
ambass'ador *n.* senior diplomatic representative sent by one state to another (**ambass'adress** *fem.*) —**ambassador'ial** *a.* —**ambass'adorship** *n.*
am'ber *n.* yellowish, translucent fossil resin —*a.* made of, coloured like amber
am'bergris [-grēs] *n.* waxy substance secreted by the sperm whale, used in making perfumes
ambidex'trous *a.* able to use both hands with equal ease —**ambidexter'ity** *n.*
am'bience *n.* atmosphere of a place
am'bient *a.* surrounding
ambig'uous *a.* having more than one meaning; obscure —**ambigu'ity** *n.* —**ambig'uously** *adv.*
am'bit *n.* circuit; compass
ambi'tion [-bish'-] *n.* desire for power, fame, honour; the object of that desire —**ambi'tious** *a.* —**ambi'tiously** *adv.* —**ambi'tiousness** *n.*
ambiv'alence, ambiv'alency *n.* simultaneous existence of two conflicting desires, opinions *etc.* —**ambiv'alent** *a.*
am'ble *vi.* move along easily and gently; move at an easy pace —*n.* this movement or pace —**am'bler** *n.*
ambro'sia *n. Myth.* food of the gods; anything smelling, tasting particularly good
am'bulance [-byoo-] *n.* conveyance for sick or injured
ambuscade' *n.* a hiding to attack by surprise; ambush
am'bush *n.* a lying in wait (for) —*vt.* waylay, attack from hiding, lie in wait for
ame'liorate *v.* make better, improve —**ameliora'tion** *n.* —**ame'liorative** *a.*
amen' [ā-, ah-] *interj.* surely; so let it be
ame'nable *a.* easy to be led or controlled; subject to, liable —**amenabil'ity, ame'nableness** *n.* —**ame'nably** *adv.*
amend' *vi.* grow better —*vt.* correct; improve; alter in detail, as bill in parliament *etc.* —**amend'ment** *n.* —**amends'** *pl.n.* reparation
ame'nity *n.* (*oft. pl.*) useful or pleasant facility or service
Amer'ican *a.* of, relating to, the American continent or the United States of America
am'ethyst *n.* bluish-violet precious stone
a'miable *a.* friendly, kindly —**amiabil'ity, a'miableness** *n.* —**a'miably** *adv.*
am'icable *a.* friendly —**amicabil'ity** *n.* —**am'icably** *adv.*
amid', amidst' *prep.* in the middle of, among
amid'ship(s) *adv.* near, towards, middle of ship
ami'no acid [*or* -mē'-] organic compound found in protein
amiss' *a.* wrong —*adv.* faultily, badly

—**take amiss** be offended (by)

am'ity *n.* friendship

am'meter *n.* instrument for measuring electric current

ammo'nia *n.* pungent alkaline gas containing hydrogen and nitrogen —**ammo'niac, ammoni'acal** *a.* —**ammo'niated** *a.* —**ammo'nium** *n.*

amm'onite *n.* whorled fossil shell like ram's horn

ammuni'tion [-nish'-] *n.* any projectiles (bullets, rockets *etc.*) that can be discharged from a weapon: also *fig.*

amne'sia *n.* loss of memory

am'nesty *n.* general pardon —*vt.* grant this

amniot'ic fluid fluid surrounding baby in womb

amoe'ba [-mē'-] *n.* microscopic single-celled animal found in ponds *etc.* and able to change its shape (*pl.* **-bas, -bae** [-bē])

amok' *see* AMUCK

among' [-mu-], **amongst'** *prep.* mixed with, in the midst of, of the number of, between

amor'al [a-mor'əl] *a.* nonmoral, having no moral qualities —**amor'alism** *n.* —**amor'alist** *n.* —**amoral'ity** *n.*

am'orous *a.* inclined to love; in love —**am'orously** *adv.* —**am'orousness** *n.*

amorph'ous *a.* without distinct shape —**amorph'ism** *n.*

amort'ize *vt.* pay off a debt by a sinking fund

amount' *vi.* come, be equal (to) —*n.* quantity; sum total

amour' [-moor'] *n.* (illicit) love affair

amour-propre [-prop'r] *Fr.* self-respect

amp. amperage; ampere(s)

am'pere *n.* unit of electric current

am'persand *n.* the sign & (and)

amphet'amine [-mēn] *n.* synthetic liquid used medicinally as stimulant, a dangerous drug if misused

amphib'ious *a.* living or operating both on land and in water —**amphib'ian** *n.* animal that lives first in water then on land; vehicle able to travel on land or water; aircraft that can alight on land or water

am'phitheatre *n.* building with tiers of seats rising round an arena

am'phora *n.* two-handled vessel of ancient Greece and Rome

am'ple *a.* big enough; large, spacious —**am'ply** *adv.*

am'plify *vt.* increase; make bigger, louder *etc.* (**-fied, -fying**) —**amplifica'tion** *n.* —**am'plificatory** *a.* —**am'plifier** *n.*

am'plitude *n.* spaciousness, width

am'poule [-pōōl] *n.* container for hypodermic dose

am'putate [-pyoo-] *vi.* cut off (limb *etc.*) —**amputa'tion** *n.*

amuck', amok' *adv.* —**run amuck** rush about in murderous frenzy

am'ulet [-yoo-] *n.* something carried or worn as a charm

amuse' [-myōōz'] *vt.* divert; occupy pleasantly; cause to laugh or smile —**amuse'ment** *n.* entertainment, pastime —**amu'sing** *a.* —**amu'singly** *adv.*

an *see* A

anabap'tist *n.* advocate of adult baptism only, hence the rebaptizing of those baptized as infants

anabol'ic ster'oid any of various hormones used by athletes to encourage muscle growth

an'abranch *n.* stream that leaves a river and enters it further downstream

anach'ronism [-k'-] *n.* mistake of time, by which something is put in wrong historical period; something out-of-date —**anachronis'tic** *a.*

anacolu'thon [-lōō'-] *n.* a sentence or words faulty in grammatical sequence

anacon'da *n.* large snake which kills by constriction

anae'mia [-nē'-] *n. see* ANEMIA

anaesthet'ic [-nis-] *n./a. see* ANESTHETIC

an'agram *n.* word or sentence made by arranging in different order the letters of another word or sentence, *eg ant* from *tan* —**anagrammat'ical** *a.* —**anagram'matist** *n.*

anal *see* ANUS

analge'sia *n.* absence of pain —**analge'sic** *a./n.* (drug) relieving pain

anal'ogy [-ji] *n.* agreement or likeness in certain respects; correspondence —**analog'ical** *a.* —**analog'ically** *adv.* —**anal'ogist** *n.* —**anal'ogize** *v.* explain by analogy —**anal'ogous** [-gəs] *a.* similar; parallel —**anal'ogously** *adv.*

anal'ysis *n.* separation into its elements or components (*pl.* **-yses** [-sēz]) —**an'alyse** *vt.* examine critically; determine the constituent parts —**an'alyst** *n.* one skilled in analysis, *esp.* chemical analysis —**analyt'ic(al)** *a.* —**analyt'ically** *adv.*

an'ap(a)est *n.* metrical foot of two short syllables and one long

an'archy [-k-] *n.* lawlessness; lack of government in a state; confusion —**anar'chic(al)** *a.* —**anarch'ically** *adv.* —**an'archism** *n.* —**an'archist** *n.* one who opposes all government

anas'tigmat *n.* lens corrected for astigmatism

anastomo'sis *n.* interconnection of veins, arteries *etc.*

anat. anatomical; anatomy

anath'ema *n.* anything detested, hateful; ban of the church; curse (*pl.* **-s**) —**anath'ematize** *vt.*

anat'omy *n.* science of structure of the body; detailed analysis; the body —**anatom'ical** *a.* —**anatom'ically** *adv.* —**anat'omist** *n.* —**anat'omize** *vt.*

an'cestor *n.* person from whom another is descended; early type of later form or product —**ances'tral** *a.* —**an'cestry** *n.*

an'chor [-ng'k-] *n.* heavy (*usu.* hooked) implement dropped on cable, chain *etc.* to bottom of sea to secure vessel —*vt.* fasten by or as with anchor —**an'chorage** *n.* act of, place of anchoring

an'chorite [-ng'k-] *n.* hermit, recluse (*fem.* **-choress**)

an'chovy [-ch-] *n.* small savoury fish of herring family

anchu'sa [-kyōō'-] *n.* plant with hairy leaves and blue flowers

an'cient [ān'shənt] *a.* belonging to former age; old; timeworn —*n.* one who lived in an earlier age (*esp. in pl.*) —**an'ciently** *adv.* —**ancient monument** **UK** notable building or site preserved as public property

ancill'ary *a.* subordinate, subservient, auxiliary

and *conj.* is a connecting word, used to join words and sentences, to introduce a consequence *etc.*

andan'te *adv./n. Mus.* moderately slow (passage)

and'iron *n.* iron bar or bracket for supporting logs in a fireplace

an'ecdote *n.* very short story dealing with single incident —**an'ecdotal** *a.*

ane'mia *n.* deficiency in number of red blood cells —**ane'mic** *a.* suffering from anemia; pale, sickly

anem'ograph *n.* instrument recording force and direction of wind

anemom'eter *n.* wind gauge —**anemomet'ric** *a.* —**anemom'etry** *n.*

anem'one [-ni] *n.* flower related to buttercup —**sea anemone** plantlike sea animal

anent' *prep. obs.* concerning

an'eroid *a.* denoting a barometer which measures atmospheric pressure without the use of mercury or other liquid

anesthet'ic [-nis-] *n./a.* (drug) causing loss of sensation —**anesthe'sia** *n.* loss of sensation —**anesthet'ically** *adv.* —**anes'thetist** [-nēs'-] *n.* expert in use of anesthetics —**anes'thetize** *vt.*

an'eurism [an'yə-] *n.* swelling out of a part of an artery

anew' *adv.* afresh, again

an'gel [ān'j-] *n.* divine messenger; ministering or attendant spirit; person with the qualities of such a spirit, as gentleness, purity *etc.* —**angel'ic** [an-] *a.* —**angel'ically** *adv.*

angel'ica [-j-] *n.* aromatic plant; its candied stalks used in cookery

An'gelus [-j-] *n.* devotional service in R.C. Church in memory of the Incarnation, said at morning, noon and sunset

an'ger [-ng'g-] *n.* strong emotion excited by a real or supposed injury; wrath; rage —*vt.* excite to wrath; enrage —**an'grily** *adv.* —**an'gry** *a.* full of anger; inflamed

angi'na (pec'toris) *n.* severe pain accompanying heart disease

an'giosperm [-j-] *n.* plant having a seed vessel

an'gle[1] [ang'gl] *vi.* fish with hook and line —**an'gler** *n.* —**an'gling** *n.*

an'gle[2] [ang'gl] *n.* meeting of two lines or surfaces; corner; point of view; *inf.* devious motive —*vt.* bend at an angle

an'gler (fish) *n.* sea fish with spiny dorsal fin

An'glican [ang'gli-] *a./n.* (member) of the Church of England —**An'glicanism** *n.*

An'glicize [ang'gli-] *vt.* express in English, turn into English form —**An'glicism** *n.* English idiom or peculiarity

An'glo- [ang'glō] (*comb. form*) English, as **Anglo-American** —**An'glo** *n.* Anglophone

Anglopho'bia *n.* dislike of England *etc.*

Anglophone' *n.* native speaker of English

angor'a *n.* goat with long white silky hair which is used in the making of mohair; cloth or wool made from this hair —**angora cat, rabbit** varieties of cat and rabbit with long, silky fur

angostu'ra [-toor'-] *n.* bitter tonic, used as flavouring in alcoholic drinks

ang'strom *n.* unit of length for measuring wavelengths of electromagnetic radiation

an'guish [ang'gw-] *n.* great mental or bodily pain

an'gular *a.* (of people) bony, awkward; having angles; measured by an angle —**angular'ity** *n.*

anhy'drous *a.* (of chemical substances) free from water

an'iline [-lin, -lēn] *n.* product of coal tar or indigo, which yields dyes

animadvert' *vi.* (*with* (up)on) criticize, pass censure —**animadver'sion** *n.* criticism, censure

an'imal *n.* living creature, having sensation and power of voluntary motion; beast —*a.* of, pert. to animals; sensual —**animal'cule** *n.* very small animal, *esp.* one which cannot be seen by naked eye —**animal'cular** *a.* —**an'imalism** *n.* —**an'imally** *adv.*

an'imate *vt.* give life to; enliven; inspire; actuate; make cartoon film of —**an'imated** *a.* lively; in form of cartoons —**anima'tion** *n.* life, vigour; cartoon film —**an'imator** *n.*

an'imism *n.* primitive religion, belief that natural effects are due to spirits, that inanimate things have spirits —**an'imist** *n.* —**animis'tic** *a.*

animos'ity *n.* hostility, enmity

an'imus *n.* hatred; animosity

an'ion [-ī-ən] *n.* ion with negative charge

an'ise [-is] *n.* plant with aromatic seeds, which are used for flavouring

an'iseed *n.* the liquorice-flavoured seed of anise

an'kle [ang'kl] *n.* joint between foot and leg —**an'klet** *n.* ankle-ornament

ann'als *pl.n.* historical records of events —**ann'alist** *n.*

anneal' *vt.* toughen (metal or glass) by heating and slow cooling; temper —**anneal'ing** *n.*

ann'elid, annel'idan *n.* one of class of invertebrate animals, including the earthworm *etc.*

annex' *vt.* add, append, attach; take possession of (*esp.* territory) —**annexa'tion** *n.*

ann'exe *n.* UK addition (building); something added

anni'hilate [-nī'əl-] *vt.* reduce to nothing, destroy utterly —**annihila'tion** *n.* —**anni'hilative** *a.* —**anni'hilator** *n.*

anniver'sary *n.* yearly return of a date; celebration of this

ann'o Dom'ini *Lat.* in the year of our Lord

ann'otate *vt.* make notes upon, comment —**annota'tion** *n.* —**ann'otator** *n.*

announce' *vt.* make known, proclaim —**announce'ment** *n.* —**announ'cer** *n.* broadcaster who announces items in programme, introduces speakers *etc.*

annoy' *vt.* vex; make slightly angry; tease —**annoy'ance** *n.*

ann'ual *a.* yearly; of, for a year —*n.* plant which completes its life-cycle in a year; book published each year —**an'nually** *adv.*

annu'ity *n.* sum or grant paid every year —**annu'itant** *n.* holder of annuity

annul' *vt.* make void, cancel, abolish (**-ll-**) —**annul'ment** *n.*

ann'ular *a.* ring-shaped —**ann'ulated** *a.* formed in rings —**annula'tion** *n.* —**ann'ulet** *n.* small ring or fillet

Annuncia'tion *n.* angel's announcement to the Virgin Mary; (**a-**) announcing —**annun'ciate** *vt.* proclaim, announce

an'ode *n.* *Electricity* the positive pole, or point of entry of current —**an'odize** *vt.* cover a metal object with protective film by using it for an anode in electrolysis

an'odyne *a.* relieving pain, soothing —*n.* pain-relieving drug

anoint' *vt.* smear with oil or ointment; consecrate with oil —**anoint'ment** *n.* —**the Anointed** the Messiah

anom'alous *a.* irregular, abnormal —**anom'aly** *n.* irregularity; deviation from rule

anon' *obs. adv.* in a short time, soon; now and then

anon. anonymous

anon'ymous *a.* nameless, *esp.* without an author's name —**anonym'ity** *n.* —**anon'ymously** *adv.*

anoph'eles [-lēz] *n.* genus of the malarial mosquito

an'orak *n.* lightweight, warm, waterproof, *usu.* hooded jacket

anorex'ia *n.* loss of appetite —**anorexia nervosa** psychological condition characterized by refusal to eat

anoth'er [-uTH'-] *pron./a.* one other; a different one; one more

ans. answer

an'serine *a.* of or like a goose; silly

an'swer [ahn'sər] *v.* reply (to); solve; reply correctly; pay; meet; be accountable (for, to); match; satisfy, suit —*n.* reply; solution —**an'swerable** *a.* accountable —**answering machine** apparatus for answering a telephone automatically and recording messages

ant *n.* small social insect, proverbial for industry —**ant'eater** *n.* animal which feeds on ants by means of a long, sticky tongue —**ant hill** the mound raised by ants

antag'onist *n.* opponent, adversary —**antag'onism** *n.* —**antagonis'tic** *a.* —**antagonis'tically** *adv.* —**antag'onize** *vt.* arouse hostility in

Antarc'tic *a.* south polar —*n.* these regions

an'te *n.* player's stake in poker —*vt.* stake

ante- (*comb. form*) before, as in **an'techamber** *n.* Such words are not given here where the meaning may easily be inferred from the simple word

antece'dent *a./n.* (thing) going before

antedilu'vian [-lōō'-] *a.* before the Flood; ancient

an'telope *n.* deer-like ruminant animal, remarkable for grace and speed

an'te merid'iem *Lat.* before noon

antena'tal *a.* of care *etc.* during pregnancy

antenn'a *n.* insect's feeler; aerial (*pl.* **-ae** [-ē])

ante'rior *a.* to the front; before

an'them *n.* song of loyalty, *esp.* to a country; Scripture passage set to music; piece of sacred music, originally sung in alternate parts by two choirs

an'ther *n.* sac in flower, containing pollen, at top of stamen —**an'theral** *a.*

anthol'ogy *n.* collection of poems, literary extracts *etc.* —**anthol'ogist** *n.* maker of such —**anthol'ogize** *vt.* include poem *etc.* in anthology

an'thracite *n.* hard coal burning slowly almost without flame or smoke

an'thrax *n.* malignant disease in cattle, communicable to man; sore caused by this

an'thropoid *a.* like man —*n.* ape resembling man

anthropol'ogy *n.* scientific study of origins, development of human race —**anthropolog'ical** *a.* —**anthropol'ogist** *n.*

anthropomorph'ize *vt.* ascribe human attributes to God or an animal —**anthropomorph'ic** *a.* —**anthropomor'phism** *n.*

anti-, ant- (*comb. form*) against Makes compounds as **anti-aircraft** *a.* —**antispasmod'ic** *a./n. etc.* Such words are not given here where meaning may easily be inferred from simple word

antibiot'ic *n.* any of various chemical, fungal or synthetic substances, *esp.* penicillin, used against bacterial infection —*a.*

an'tibody *n.* substance in, or introduced into, blood serum which counteracts the growth and harmful action of bacteria

antic'ipate [-tis'-] *vt.* expect; take or consider beforehand; foresee; enjoy in advance —**anticipa'tion** *n.* —**antic'ipative, antic'ipatory** *a.*

anticli'max *n.* sudden descent to the trivial or ludicrous

an'tics *pl.n.* absurd or grotesque movements or acts

anticy'clone *n.* system of winds moving round centre of high barometric pressure

an'tidote *n.* counteracting remedy

an'tifreeze *n.* liquid added to water to lower its freezing point, as in automobile radiators

an'tigen [-j-] *n.* substance stimulating production of antibodies in the blood

antihis'tamine *n.* drug used *esp.* to

treat allergies

antimacass'ar *n.* cover to protect chairs from macassar oil

an'timony *n.* brittle, bluish-white metal

antip'athy *n.* dislike, aversion —**antipathet'ic** *a.*

antiper'spirant *n.* substance used to reduce sweating

an'tiphon *n.* composition in which verses, lines are sung alternately by two choirs; anthem —**antiph'onal** *a.*

antip'odes [-dēz] *pl.n.* countries, peoples on opposite side of the globe (often refers to Aust. and N Zealand) —**antip'odal, antipode'an** *a.*

an'tipope *n.* pope elected in opposition to the one regularly chosen

antipyret'ic *n./a.* (remedy) effective against fever

antique' [-ēk'] *n.* relic of former times, usu. a piece of furniture *etc.* that is collected —*a.* ancient; old-fashioned —**an'tiquary, antiqua'rian** *n.* student or collector of old things —**an'tiquated** *a.* out-of-date —**antiq'uity** *n.* great age; former times

antirrhi'num [-rī'-] *n.* genus of plants including snapdragon

anti-Semit'ic *a.* discriminating against Jews —**anti-Sem'itism** *n.*

antisep'tic *n./a.* (substance) preventing infection —*a.* free from infection

antith'esis *n.* direct opposite; contrast; opposition of ideas (*pl.* **-eses**) —**antithet'ical** *a.* —**antithet'ically** *adv.*

antitox'in *n.* serum used to neutralize disease poisons

antiven'ene, antiven'in *n.* antitoxin to counteract specific venom, *eg* of snake or spider

ant'ler *n.* branching horn of certain deer —**ant'lered** *a.*

an'tonym *n.* word of opposite meaning to another *eg cold* is an antonym of *hot*

a'nus *n.* the lower opening of the bowels —**a'nal** *a.*

an'vil *n.* heavy iron block on which a smith hammers metal into shape

anx'ious [angk'shəs] *a.* troubled, uneasy; concerned —**anxi'ety** [ang-zī'-] *n.* —**anx'iously** *adv.*

an'y [en'i] *a./pron.* one indefinitely; some; every —**an'ybody** *n.* —**an'yhow** *adv.* —**an'yone** *n.* —**an'yplace** *adv. inf.* —**an'ything** *n.* —**an'yway** *adv.* —**an'ywhere** *adv.*

An'zac *a.* of Australian-New Zealand Army Corps in WWI (1914-18) —*n.* soldier of that corps, Gallipoli veteran

AOB any other business

aor'ta [ā-aw'-] *n.* great artery rising from left ventricle of heart —**aor'tal** *a.*

apace' *adv.* swiftly

apart' *adv.* separately, aside; in pieces

apart'heid [-hīt, -hāt] *n.* (*esp.* in S Africa) official government policy of racial segregation

apart'ment *n.* suite of rooms in larger building; **UK** room

ap'athy *n.* indifference; lack of emotion —**apathet'ic** *a.* —**apathet'ically** *adv.*

ape *n.* tailless monkey (*eg* chimpanzee, gorilla); coarse, clumsy person; imitator —*vt.* imitate —**a'pish** *a.* —**a'pishly** *adv.*

ape'rient, aper'itive *a.* mildly laxative —*n.* any such medicine

aperiod'ic [ā-] *a. Electricity* having no natural period or frequency

aper'itif *n.* alcoholic appetizer

ap'erture *n.* opening, hole

a'pex *n.* top, peak; vertex (*pl.* **a'pexes, a'pices**)

apha'sia *n.* dumbness, or loss of speech control, due to disease of the brain

aphe'lion *n.* point of planet's orbit farthest from the sun

a'phis *n.* various sap-sucking insects (*pl.* **a'phides** [-dēz]) —**a'phid** *n.* an aphis

aph'orism *n.* maxim, pithy saying —**aph'orist** *n.* —**aphoris'tic** *a.*

aphrodis'iac *a.* exciting sexual desire —*n.* substance which so excites

a'piary *n.* place where bees are kept —**apia'rian, a'pian** *a.* —**a'piarist** *n.* beekeeper —**a'piculture** *n.*

apiece' *adv.* for each

aplomb' [-plom'] *n.* self-possession, coolness, assurance

apoc'alypse *n.* prophetic revelation, *esp.* of St. John, last book of the New Testament —**apocalyp'tic** *a.* —**apocalyp'tically** *adv.*

apoc'rypha *n.* religious writing of doubtful authenticity —**Apoc'rypha** *pl.n.* collective name for 14 books originally in the Old Testament —**apoc'ryphal** *a.* spurious

apod'osis *n.* consequent clause in conditional sentence, as distinct from protasis or *if* clause (*pl.* **-oses** [-sēz])

ap'ogee [-jē] *n.* point of moon's or satellite's orbit farthest from the earth; climax

apol'ogy *n.* acknowledgment of offence and expression of regret; written or spoken defence; poor substitute (*with* for) —**apologet'ic** *a.* —**apologet'ically** *adv.* —**apologet'ics** *n.* branch of theology charged with defence of Christianity —**apol'ogist** *n.* —**apol'ogize** *vi.*

ap'ophthegm, ap'othegm [-ə-them] *n.* terse saying, maxim —**apothegmat'ic** *a.*

ap'oplexy *n.* loss of sense and often paralysis caused by broken or blocked blood vessel in the brain; a stroke —**apoplec'tic** *a.*

apos'tasy *n.* abandonment of one's religious or other faith —**apos'tate** *n./a.*

a posterio'ri [ā pos-te-ri-aw'ri] *a.* denoting form of inductive reasoning which arrives at causes from effects; empirical

Apos'tle [-sl] *n.* one sent to preach the Gospel, *esp.* one of the first disciples of Jesus; founder of Christian church in a country; (**a-**) leader of reform —**apos'tleship** *n.* —**apostol'ic(al)** *a.*

apos'trophe [-trə-fi] *n.* a mark (') showing the omission of a letter or letters in a word; digression to appeal to someone dead or absent —**apos'trophize** *vt.*

apoth'ecary *n. old name for* one who prepares and sells drugs, *now* pharmacist

ap'othegm *see* APOPHTHEGM

apotheo'sis *n.* deification, act of raising any person or thing into a god (*pl.* **-ses**)

appal' [-awl'] *vt.* dismay, terrify (**-ll-**) —**appall'ing** *a. inf.* dreadful, terrible

appara'tus *n.* equipment, tools, instruments, for performing any experiment, operation *etc.*; means by which something operates

appar'el [-pa'-] *n.* clothing —*vt.* clothe (**-ll-**)

appar'ent [-pa'-] *a.* seeming; obvious; acknowledged, as in *heir apparent* —**appar'ently** *adv.*

appari'tion [-rish'-] *n.* appearance, *esp.* of ghost

appeal' *vi.* (*with* to) call upon, make earnest request; be attractive; refer to, have recourse to; apply to higher court —*n.* request, reference, supplication —**appeal'able** *a.* —**appeal'ing** *a.* making appeal; pleasant, attractive —**appeal'ingly** *adv.* —**appell'ant** *n.* one who appeals to higher court —**appel'late** *a.* of appeals

appear' *vi.* become visible or present; seem, be plain; be seen in public —**appear'ance** *n.* an appearing; aspect; pretence

appease' *vt.* pacify, quiet, allay, satisfy —**appeas'able** *a.* —**appease'ment** *n.*

appell'ant *see* APPEAL

appella'tion *n.* name —**appell'ative** *a./n.*

append' *vt.* join on, add —**append'age** *n.*

appendici'tis *n.* inflammation of vermiform appendix

appen'dix *n.* subsidiary addition to book *etc.*; *Anatomy* projection, *esp.* the small worm-shaped part of the intestine (*pl.* **-dices** [-di-sēz], **-dixes**)

appercep'tion *n.* perception; apprehension; the mind's perception of itself as a conscious agent —**apperceive'** *vt.*

appertain' *vi.* belong, relate to, be appropriate

app'etence, app'etency *n.* desire, craving; sexual appetite —**app'etent** *a.*

app'etite *n.* desire, inclination, *esp.* desire for food —**appet'itive** *a.* —**ap'petize** *vt.* —**app'etizer** *n.* something stimulating to appetite —**app'etizing** *a.* —**app'etizingly** *adv.*

applaud' *vt.* praise by handclapping; praise loudly —**applaud'er** *n.* —**applaud'ing** *a.* —**applaud'ingly** *adv.* —**applause'** *n.* loud approval

ap'ple *n.* round, firm, fleshy fruit; tree bearing it

appli'ance *n.* piece of equipment *esp.* electrical

appli'qué [-plē'kā] *n.* ornaments, embroidery *etc.*, secured to surface of material —*vt.* ornament thus

apply' *vt.* utilize, employ; lay or place on; administer, devote —*vi.* have reference (to); make request (to) (**-lied'**, **-ly'ing**) —**applicabil'ity** *n.* —**app'licable** *a.* relevant —**app'licably** *adv.* —**ap'plicant** *n.* —**applica'tion** *n.* applying something for a particular use; relevance; request for a job *etc.*; concentration, diligence —**applied'** *a.* (of skill, science *etc.*) put to practical use

appoint' *vt.* name, assign to a job or position; fix, settle; equip —**appoint'ment** *n.* engagement to meet; (selection for a) job —*pl.* fittings

appor'tion *vt.* divide out in shares —**appor'tionment** *n.*

app'osite [-zit] *a.* suitable, apt —**ap'positely** *adv.* —**app'ositeness** *n.* —**apposi'tion** *n.* proximity; the placing of one word beside another

appraise' *vt.* set price on, estimate value of —**apprais'able** *a.* —**apprais'al** *n.* —**appraise'ment** *n.* —**apprais'er** *n.*

appre'ciate [-shi-] *vt.* value at true worth; be grateful for; understand; enjoy —*vi.* rise in value —**appre'ciable** *a.* estimable; substantial —**appre'ciably** *adv.* —**apprecia'tion** *n.* —**appre'ciative, appre'ciatory** *a.* capable of expressing pleasurable recognition —**appre'ciator** *n.*

apprehend' *vt.* seize by authority; take hold of; recognize, understand; dread —**apprehensibil'ity** *n.* —**apprehen'sible** *a.* —**apprehen'sion** *n.* dread, anxiety; arrest; conception; ability to understand —**apprehen'sive** *a.*

appren'tice *n.* person learning a trade under specified conditions; novice —*vt.* bind as apprentice —**appren'ticeship** *n.*

apprise' *vt.* inform

approach' *v.* draw near (to); set about; address request to; approximate to —*n.* a drawing near; means of reaching or doing; approximation; (*oft. pl.*) friendly overture(s) —**approachabil'ity** *n.* —**approach'able** *a.*

approba'tion *n.* approval —**ap'probate** *vt.*

appro'priate *vt.* take for oneself; put aside for particular purpose —*a.* suitable, fitting —**appro'priately** *adv.* —**appro'priateness** *n.* —**appropria'tion** *n.* act of setting apart for purpose; parliamentary vote of money —**appro'priative** *a.* —**appro'priator** *n.*

approve' *vt.* think well of, commend; authorize, agree to —**appro'val** *n.* —**appro'ver** *n.* —**appro'vingly** *adv.*

approx. approximate(ly)

approx'imate *a.* very near, nearly correct; inexact, imprecise —*vt.* bring close —*vi.* come near; be almost the same as —**approx'imately** *adv.* —**approxima'tion** *n.* —**approx'imative** *a.*

appur'tenance *n.* thing which appertains to; accessory

Apr. April

après-ski [ap-rā-] *n.* social activities after day's skiing

a'pricot *n.* orange-coloured stone-fruit related to the plum —*a.* of the colour of the fruit

A'pril *n.* the fourth month of the year

a prior'i [ā prī-ōrī] *a.* denoting deductive reasoning from general principle to expected facts or effects; denoting knowledge gained independently of experience

a'pron *n.* cloth, piece of leather *etc.*, worn in front to protect clothes, or as part of official dress; in theatre, strip of stage before curtain; on airfield, tarmac area where aircraft stand, are loaded *etc.*; *fig.* any of a variety of things resembling these

apropos' [-pō'] *adv.* to the purpose; with reference to —*a.* apt, appropriate —**apropos of** concerning

apse *n.* arched recess, *esp.* in a church —**aps'idal** *a.*

apt *a.* suitable; likely; prompt, quick-witted; dexterous —**apt'itude** *n.* capacity, fitness —**apt'ly** *adv.* —**apt'ness** *n.*

aq'ualung *n.* breathing apparatus used in underwater swimming

aquamarine' *n.* precious stone, the beryl —*a.* greenish-blue, sea-coloured

aq'uaplane *n.* plank or boat towed by fast motor-boat —*vi.* ride on aquaplane; (of automobile) be in contact with water on road, not with road surface —**aq'uaplaning** *n.*

aqua'rium *n.* tank or pond for keeping water animals or plants (*pl.* **-riums, -ria**)

Aqua'rius *n.* (the water-bearer) 11th sign of zodiac, operative c. Jan 20-Feb 18

aquat'ic *a.* living, growing, done in or on water —**aquat'ics** *pl.n.* water-sport

aq'uatint *n.* etching, engraving imitating drawings *etc.*

aq'ua vi'tae [vē'tī] *Lat. obs.* brandy

aq'ueduct *n.* artificial channel for water, *esp.* one like a bridge; conduit

a'queous *a.* of, like, containing water

aquile'gia *n.* columbine

aq'uiline *a.* relating to eagle; hooked like an eagle's beak

Ar *Chem.* argon

Ar. Arabic; Aramaic

ar. arrival; arrives

Ar'ab [a-] *n.* native of Arabia; general term for inhabitants of Middle Eastern countries; Arabian horse **—Ar'abic** *n.* language of Arabs *—a.*

arabesque' *n.* classical ballet position; fanciful painted or carved ornament of Arabian origin *—a.*

ar'able [a-] *a.* suitable for ploughing or planting crops

arach'nid [-k'-] *n.* one of the Arachnida (spiders, scorpions, and mites) **—arach'-noid** *a.* **—arachnol'ogy** *n.*

Ar'an [a-] *a.* (of sweaters *etc.*) made with naturally oily, unbleached wool, often with a complicated pattern

ar'biter *n.* judge, umpire (**-tress** *fem.*) **—arbit'rament** *n.* **—ar'bitrarily** *adv.* **—ar'bitrary** *a.* not bound by rules, despotic; random **—ar'bitrate** *v.* decide dispute; submit to, settle by arbitration; act as an umpire **—arbitra'tion** *n.* hearing, settling of disputes, *esp.* industrial and legal, by impartial referee(s) **—ar'-bitrator** *n.*

arb'o(u)r *n.* leafy glade *etc.*, sheltered by trees

arbor'eal, arbor'eous *a.* relating to trees **—arbore'tum** *n.* place for cultivating specimens of trees (*pl.* **-tums, -ta**) **—arb'oriculture** *n.* forestry, cultivation of trees

arc *n.* part of circumference of circle or similar curve; luminous electric discharge between two conductors **—arc lamp —arc light**

arcade' *n.* row of arches on pillars; covered walk or avenue, *esp.* lined by shops

arcane' *a.* mysterious; esoteric

arch[1] *n.* curved structure in building, supporting itself over open space by pressure of stones one against the other; any similar structure; a curved shape; curved part of sole of the foot *—v.* form, make into, an arch **—arched** *a.* **—arch'way** *n.*

arch[2] *a.* chief; experienced, expert; superior, knowing, coyly playful **—arch'ly** *adv.* **—arch'ness** *n.*

arch. archaic; architecture

arch- (*comb. form*) chief, as in **arch-an'gel** [-k-] *n.*, **archen'emy** *n. etc.* Such words are not given here where the meaning may easily be inferred from the simple word

archaeol'ogy [-k-] *n.* study of ancient times from remains of art, implements *etc.* **—archaeolog'ical** *a.* **—ar-chaeol'ogist** *n.*

archa'ic [-k-] *a.* old, primitive **—ar-cha'ically** *adv.* **—arch'aism** *n.* obsolete word or phrase

archbish'op *n.* chief bishop **—arch-bish'opric** *n.*

archdea'con *n.* chief deacon, clergyman next to bishop **—archdea'conate** *n.* **—archdea'conry** *n.* **—archidiac'o-nal** *a.*

archduke' *n.* duke of specially high rank (**archduch'ess** *fem.*) **—arch-du'cal** *a.* **—archduch'y** *n.*

arch'ery *n.* skill, sport of shooting with bow and arrow **—arch'er** *n.*

arch'etype [-k'-] *n.* prototype; perfect specimen **—arch'etypal** *a.*

archiepis'copal [-k-] *a.* of archbishop **—archiepis'copacy** *n.* **—archiepis'-copate** *n.*

archipel'ago [-k-] *n.* group of islands; sea full of small islands, *esp.* Aegean (*pl.* **-agoes**) **—archipel'agic** *a.*

arch'itect [-k'-] *n.* one qualified to design and supervise construction of buildings; contriver **—architecton'ic** *a.* **—architec'tural** *a.* **—arch'itec-ture** *n.*

arch'itrave [-k'-] *Architecture n.* lowest division of the entablature; ornamental band round door or window opening

ar'chives [-kīvz] *pl.n.* collection of records, documents *etc.* about an institution, family *etc.*; place where these are kept **—archi'val** *a.* **—ar'chivist** *n.*

Arc'tic *a.* of northern polar regions; (**a-**) very cold *—n.* region round north pole **—arctic hare** large hare with white fur in winter **—arctic willow** low-growing shrub of Canad. tundra

ard'ent *a.* fiery; passionate **—ard'ency** *n.* **—ard'ently** *adv.* **—ard'o(u)r** *n.* enthusiasm; zeal

ard'uous *a.* laborious, hard to accomplish, difficult, strenuous **—ard'uously** *adv.* **—ard'uousness** *n.*

are[1] *pres. ind. pl. of* BE

are[2] *n.* unit of measure, 100 square metres

a'rea *n.* extent, expanse of any surface; two-dimensional expanse enclosed by boundary (area of square, circle *etc.*); region; part, section; subject, field of activity; small sunken yard

ar'eca [a'ri-kə] *n.* genus of palms, including betel palm

are'na *n.* enclosure for sports events *etc.*; space in middle of amphitheatre or stadium; sphere, scene of conflict

ar'gent [-j-] *n.* silver —*a.* silver, silvery-white, *esp.* in heraldry

ar'gon *n.* a gas, inert constituent of air

arg'osy *n. Poet.* large richly-laden merchant ship

arg'ot [-ō] *n.* slang

ar'gue *vi.* quarrel, dispute; prove; offer reasons —*vt.* prove by reasoning; discuss —**arg'uable** *a.* —**arg'uer** *n.* —**ar'gument** *n.* quarrel; reasoning; discussion; theme —**argumenta'tion** *n.* —**argumen'tative** *a.*

Arg'us *n.* fabulous being with a hundred eyes —**Argus-eyed** *a.* watchful

ar'ia *n.* air or rhythmical song in cantata, opera *etc.*

ar'id [a-] *a.* parched with heat, dry; dull —**arid'ity** *n.*

A'ries [-rēz] *n.* (the ram) 1st sign of zodiac, operative c. Mar 21-Apr 21

aright' *adv.* rightly

arise' *vi.* come about; get up; rise (up), ascend (**arose', aris'en, ari'sing**)

aristoc'racy *n.* government by the best in birth or fortune; nobility; upper classes —**ar'istocrat** *n.* —**aristocrat'ic** *a.* noble; elegant —**aristocrat'ically** *adv.*

arith'metic *n.* science of numbers; art of reckoning by figures —**arithmet'ic(al)** *a.* —**arithmet'ically** *adv.* —**arithmeti'cian** *n.*

ark *n.* Noah's vessel; (**A-**) coffer containing Jewish Tables of Law

arm[1] *n.* limb extending from shoulder to wrist; anything projecting from main body, as branch of sea, supporting rail of chair *etc.*; sleeve Compounds as **arm'chair** *n.* —**arm'ful** *n.* —**arm'hole** *n.* —**arm'let** *n.* band worn round arm —**arm'pit** *n.* hollow under arm at shoulder

arm[2] *vt.* supply with weapons, furnish; prepare bomb *etc.* for use —*vi.* take up arms —*n.* weapon; branch of army —*pl.* weapons; war, military exploits; official heraldic symbols —**arm'ament** *n.*

armad'a [-mahd'-] *n.* large number of ships or aircraft

armadill'o *n.* small Amer. animal protected by bands of bony plates (*pl.* **-os**)

arm'ature *n.* part of electric machine, *esp.* revolving structure in electric motor, generator

arm'istice *n.* truce, suspension of fighting

arm'o(u)r *n.* defensive covering or dress; plating of tanks, warships *etc.*; armoured fighting vehicles, as tanks —**armo'rial** *a.* relating to heraldic arms —**arm'o(u)rer** *n.* —**arm'o(u)ry** *n.*

ar'my *n.* large body of men armed for warfare and under military command; host; great number

arn'ica *n. Bot.* genus of hardy perennials A tincture of *Arnica montana* is used for sprains and bruises

aro'ma *n.* sweet smell; fragrance; peculiar charm —**aromat'ic** *a.* —**aro'matize** *vt.*

arose' *pt. of* ARISE

around' *prep.* on all sides of; somewhere in or near; approximately (of time) —*adv.* on every side; in a circle; here and there, nowhere in particular; *inf.* present in or at some place

arouse' *vt.* awaken, stimulate

arpegg'io [-j'-] *n. Mus.* notes sounded in quick succession, not together; chord so played (*pl.* **-ios**)

arr. arranged; arrival; arrive

arr'ack *n.* coarse spirit distilled from rice *etc.*

arraign' [-ān'] *vt.* accuse, indict, put on trial —**arraign'er** *n.* —**arraign'ment** *n.*

arrange' *v.* set in order; make agreement; adjust; plan; adapt, as music; settle, as dispute —**arrange'ment** *n.*

arr'ant *a.* downright, notorious —**ar'rantly** *adv.*

arr'as *n.* tapestry

array' *n.* order, *esp.* military order; dress; imposing show, splendour —*vt.* set in order; dress, equip, adorn

arrears' *pl.n.* amount unpaid or undone

arrest' *vt.* detain by legal authority; stop; catch attention —*n.* seizure by warrant; making prisoner —**arrest'ing** *a.* attracting attention, striking —**arrest'or** *n.* person who arrests; mechanism to stop or slow moving object

arr'is *n.* sharp ridge or edge

arrive' *vi.* reach destination; (*with* at) reach, attain; *inf.* succeed —**arri'val** *n.*

arr'ogance *n.* aggressive conceit —**ar'rogant** *a.* proud; overbearing —**ar'rogantly** *adv.*

arr'ow *n.* pointed shaft shot from bow —**arr'owhead** *n.* head of arrow; any triangular shape

arr'owroot *n.* nutritious starch from W Indian plant, used as a food

ars'enal *n.* magazine of stores for warfare, guns , ammunition

ars'enic *n.* soft, grey, metallic element; its oxide, a powerful poison —**ars'enate** *n.* —**arsen'ical** *a.* —**arse'nious** *a.*

ars'on *n.* crime of intentionally setting property on fire

art *n.* skill; human skill as opposed to nature; creative skill in painting, poetry, music *etc.*; any of the works produced thus; profession, craft; knack; contrivance, cunning, trick; system of rules —*pl.* certain branches of learning, languages, history *etc.*, as distinct from natural science; wiles —**art'ful** *a.* wily —**art'fully** *adv.* —**art'fulness** *n.* —**art'ist** *n.* one who practises fine art, *esp.* painting; one who makes his craft a fine art —**artiste'** [-tēst'] *n.* professional entertainer, singer, dancer *etc.* —**artis'tic** *a.* —**artis'tically** *adv.* —**art'istry** *n.* —**art'less** *a.* natural, frank —**art'lessly** *adv.* —**art'lessness** *n.* —**art'y** *a.* ostentatiously artistic

art. article; artificial

ar'tefact *n.* something made by man, *esp.* by hand

arterioscleros'sis *n.* hardening of the arteries

ar'tery *n.* one of tubes carrying blood from heart; any main channel of communications —**arte'rial** *a.* pert. to an artery; main, important as **arterial road**

arte'sian *a.* describes deep well in which water rises by internal pressure

arthri'tis *n.* painful inflammation of joint(s) —**arthrit'ic** *a./n.*

ar'thropod *n.* animal with jointed limbs and segmented body *eg* insect, spider

ar'tichoke *n.* thistle-like perennial, edible flower —**Jerusalem artichoke** sunflower with edible tubers like potato

art'icle *n.* item, object; short written piece; paragraph, section; *Grammar* words *the*, *a*, *an*; clause in a contract; rule, condition —*vt.* bind as apprentice

artic'ulate *a.* able to express oneself fluently; jointed; of speech, clear, distinct —*vt.* joint; utter distinctly —*vi.* speak —**artic'ulated** *a.* jointed —**artic'ulately** *adv.* —**artic'ulateness** *n.* —**articula'tion** *n.*

art'ifice *n.* contrivance, trick, cunning, skill —**artif'icer** *n.* craftsman —**artifi'cial** *a.* manufactured, synthetic; insincere —**artificial'ity** *n.* —**artifi'cially** *adv.* —**artificial intelligence** ability of machines, *esp.* computers, to imitate intelligent human behaviour —**artificial respiration** method of restarting person's breathing after it has stopped

artill'ery *n.* large guns on wheels; the troops who use them

art'isan [-z-] *n.* craftsman, skilled mechanic, manual worker

artiste' *see* ART

a'rum lily plant with large white flower

A'ryan [ā'ri-ən] *a.* relating to Indo-European family of nations and languages

As *Chem.* arsenic

as *adv./conj.* denoting: comparison; similarity; equality; identity; concurrence; reason

asap as soon as possible

asbes'tos *n.* fibrous mineral which does not burn —**asbesto'sis** *n.* lung disease caused by inhalation of asbestos fibre

ascend' [ə-send'] *vi.* climb, rise —*vt.* walk up, climb, mount —**ascend'ancy** *n.* control, dominance —**ascend'ant** *a.* rising —**ascen'sion** *n.* —**ascent'** *n.* rise

ascertain' [as-ər-] *v.* get to know, find out, determine —**ascertain'able** *a.* —**ascertain'ment** *n.*

ascet'ic [-set'-] *n.* one who practises severe self-denial —*a.* rigidly abstinent, austere —**ascet'ically** *adv.* —**ascet'icism** *n.*

ascor'bic acid vitamin C, present in green vegetables, citrus fruits *etc.*

ascribe' *vt.* attribute, impute, assign —**ascri'bable** *a.* —**ascrip'tion** *n.*

asep'tic *a.* germ-free —**asep'sis** *n.*
asex'ual [ā-] *a.* without sex
ash[1] *n.* dust or remains of anything burnt —*pl.* ruins; remains, *eg* of cremated body —**ash'en** *a.* like ashes; pale —**ash'y** *a.*
ash[2] *n.* deciduous timber tree; its wood —**ash'en** *a.*
ashamed' [-āmd'] *a.* affected with shame, abashed
ash'lar *n.* hewn or squared building stone
ashore' *adv.* on shore
Ash Wednesday first day of Lent
A'sian *a.* pert. to continent of Asia —*n.* native of Asia or descendant of one —**Asiat'ic** *a.*
aside' *adv.* to or on one side; privately —*n.* words spoken in an undertone not to be heard by some person present
A-side *n.* more important side of disc
as'inine *a.* of or like an ass, silly —**asinin'ity** *n.*
ask [ah-] *vt.* request, require, question, invite —*vi.* make inquiry or request
askance' *adv.* sideways, awry; with a side look or meaning —**look askance** view with suspicion
askew' *adv.* aside, awry
aslant' [-ahnt'] *adv.* on the slant, obliquely, athwart
asleep' *a./adv.* sleeping, at rest
asp *n.* small venomous snake
aspar'agus [-pa'rə-] *n.* plant whose young shoots are a table delicacy
as'pect *n.* look, view, appearance, expression
as'pen *n.* type of poplar tree
asper'ity *n.* roughness; harshness; coldness
asper'sion *n.* (*usu. in pl.*) malicious remarks; slanderous attack
as'phalt *n.* black, hard bituminous substance used for road surfaces *etc.* —**as'phaltic** *a.*
as'phodel *n.* plant with clusters of yellow or white flowers
asphyx'ia *n.* suffocation —**asphyx'iate** *v.* —**asphyx'iated** *a.* —**asphyxia'tion** *n.*
as'pic *n.* jelly used to coat meat, eggs, fish *etc.*; *Bot.* species of lavender
aspidis'tra *n.* plant with broad tapered leaves
aspire' *vi.* desire eagerly; aim at high things; rise to great height —**as'pirant** *n.* one who aspires; candidate —**as'pirate** *vt.* pronounce with full breathing, as "h" —**aspira'tion** *n.* —**aspi'ring** *a.* —**aspi'ringly** *adv.*
as'pirin *n.* (a tablet of) drug used to allay pain and fever
ass *n.* quadruped of horse family; stupid person
ass'agai, ass'egai [-ī] *n.* slender spear of S Afr. tribes
assail' *vt.* attack, assault —**assail'able** *a.* —**assail'ant** *n.*
assass'in *n.* one who kills, *esp.* prominent person, by treacherous violence; murderer —**assass'inate** *vt.* —**assassina'tion** *n.*
assault' *n.* attack, *esp.* sudden —*vt.* attack
assay' *vt.* test, *esp.* proportions of metals in alloy or ore —*n.* analysis, *esp.* of metals; trial, test —**assay'er** *n.*
ass'egai *see* ASSAGAI
assem'ble *v.* meet, bring together; collect; put together (of machinery *etc.*) —**assem'blage** *n.* —**assem'bly** *n.* gathering, meeting; assembling —**assembly line** sequence of machines, workers in factory assembling product
assent' *vi.* concur, agree —*n.* acquiescence, agreement, compliance
assert' *vt.* declare strongly, insist upon —**asser'tion** *n.* —**assert'ive** *a.* —**asser'tively** *adv.*
assess' *vt.* fix value; evaluate, estimate, *esp.* for taxation; fix amount (of tax or fine); tax or fine —**assess'able** *a.* —**assess'ment** *n.* —**assess'or** *n.*
ass'et *n.* valuable or useful person, thing —*pl.* property available to pay debts, *esp.* of insolvent debtor
assev'erate *v.* assert solemnly —**assevera'tion** *n.*
assid'uous *a.* persevering, attentive, diligent —**assidu'ity** *n.* —**assid'uously** *adv.*
assign' [-īn'] *vt.* appoint to job *etc.*; allot, apportion, fix; ascribe; transfer —**assign'able** *a.* —**assigna'tion** [-ig-nā'-] *n.* secret meeting; appointment to meet —**assign'ment** *n.* act of assigning; allotted duty —**assign'or** *n.*
assim'ilate *vt.* learn and understand; make similar; absorb into the system

—**assim'ilable** *a.* —**assimila'tion** *n.* —**assim'ilative** *a.*

assist' *v.* give help; aid —*n.* act of helping —**assist'ance** *n.* —**assist'ant** *n.* helper

assi'zes *pl.n.* formerly, law court held in each area or county of England and Wales

assn. association

assoc. associated; association

asso'ciate *vt.* link, connect, *esp.* as ideas in mind; join —*vi.* keep company with; combine, unite —*n.* companion, partner; friend, ally; subordinate member of association —*a.* affiliated —**associa'tion** *n.* society, club

ass'onance *n.* likeness in sound; rhyming of vowels only —**ass'onant** *a.*

assort' *vt.* classify, arrange —*vi.* match, agree with, harmonize —**assort'ed** *a.* mixed —**assort'ment** *n.*

ASSR Autonomous Soviet Socialist Republic

asst. assistant

assuage' [-sw-] *vt.* soften, pacify; soothe —**assuage'ment** *n.*

assume' *vt.* take for granted; pretend; take upon oneself; claim —**assump'tion** *n.* —**assump'tive** *a.*

assure' *vt.* tell positively, promise; make sure; insure against loss, *esp.* of life; affirm —**assur'ance** *n.* —**assured'** *a.* sure —**assur'edly** [-id-li] *adv.*

AST Atlantic Standard Time

astat'ic *a. Physics* having no tendency to take fixed position

as'ter *n.* plant with star-like flowers; Michaelmas daisy

as'terisk *n.* star (*) used in printing —*vt.* mark thus —**as'terism** *n.*

astern' *adv.* in, behind the stern; backwards

as'teroid *n.* small planet —*a.* star-shaped

asth'ma [as'mə] *n.* illness in which one has difficulty in breathing —**asthmat'ic** *a./n.* —**asthmat'ically** *adv.*

astig'matism *n.* inability of lens (*esp.* of eye) to focus properly —**astigmat'ic** *a.*

astil'be [-bi] *n.* plant with ornamental pink or white flowers

astir' *adv.* on the move; out; in excitement

aston'ish *vt.* amaze, surprise —**aston'ishing** *a.* —**aston'ishment** *n.*

astound' *vt.* astonish greatly; stun with amazement —**astound'ing** *a.* startling

astrakhan' [-kan'] *n.* lambskin with curled wool

as'tral *a.* of the stars or spirit world —**astral body**

astray' *adv.* off the right path, wanderingly

astride' *adv.* with the legs apart, straddling

astrin'gent [-j-] *a.* severe, harsh; sharp; constricting (body tissues, blood vessels *etc.*) —*n.* astringent substance —**astrin'gency** *n.*

astrol. astrology

astrol'ogy *n.* foretelling of events by stars; medieval astronomy —**astrol'oger** *n.* —**astrolog'ical** *a.*

astrom'etry *n.* determination of apparent magnitudes of fixed stars

astron. astronomy

as'tronaut *n.* one trained for travel in space

astron'omy *n.* scientific study of heavenly bodies —**astron'omer** *n.* —**astronom'ical** *a.* very large; of astronomy —**astronomical unit** unit of distance used in astronomy equal to the mean distance between the earth and the sun

astrophys'ics *n.* the science of the chemical and physical characteristics of heavenly bodies —**astrophys'ical** *a.* —**astrophys'icist** *n.*

astute' *a.* perceptive, shrewd —**astute'ly** *adv.* —**astute'ness** *n.*

asun'der *adv.* apart; in pieces

asy'lum *n.* refuge, sanctuary, place of safety; *old name for* home for care of the unfortunate, *esp.* of mentally ill

asymm'etry *n.* lack of symmetry —**asymmet'rical** *a.*

as'ymptote *n.* straight line that continually approaches a curve, but never meets it

asyn'deton *n.* omission of conjunctions between parts of sentence —**asyndet'ic** *a.* without conjunctions or cross references

at *prep./adv.* denoting: location in space or time; rate; condition or state; amount; direction; cause

at. atmosphere; atomic

atarax'ia *n.* calmness, emotional tranquillity

at'avism *n.* appearance of ancestral, not parental, characteristics in human beings, animals or plants —**atavis'tic** *a.*

atax'ia, atax'y *n.* lack of muscular coordination

ate [āt *or* et] *pt. of* EAT

at'elier [-yā] *n.* workshop, artist's studio

a'theism [ā'-] *n.* belief that there is no God —**a'theist** *n.* —**atheis'tic(al)** *a.*

ath'lete *n.* one trained for physical exercises, feats or contests of strength; one good at sports —**athlet'ic** *a.* —**athlet'ics** *pl.n.* sports such as running, jumping, throwing *etc.* —**athlet'ically** *adv.* —**athlet'icism** *n.*

athwart' *prep.* across —*adv.* across, *esp.* obliquely

at'las *n.* volume of maps

atm. atmosphere; atmospheric

at'mosphere *n.* mass of gas surrounding heavenly body, *esp.* the earth; prevailing tone or mood (of place *etc.*); unit of pressure in cgs system —**atmospher'ic** *a.* —**atmospher'ics** *pl.n.* noises in radio reception due to electrical disturbance in the atmosphere

at. no. atomic number

at'oll *n.* ring-shaped coral island enclosing lagoon

at'om *n.* smallest unit of matter which can enter into chemical combination; any very small particle —**atom'ic** *a.* of, arising from atoms —**atomic'ity** [-mis'-] *n.* number of atoms in molecule of an element —**at'omize** *vt.* reduce to atoms or small particles —**at'omizer** *n.* instrument for discharging liquids in a fine spray —**atom(ic) bomb** one whose immense power derives from nuclear fission or fusion, nuclear bomb —**atomic energy** nuclear energy —**atomic number** the number of protons in the nucleus of an atom —**atomic reactor** *see* REACTOR —**atomic weight** the weight of an atom of an element relative to that of carbon 12

atone' *vi.* make reparation, amends (for); expiate; give satisfaction —**atone'ment** *n.*

aton'ic *a.* unaccented

atop' *adv.* at or on the top; above

atro'cious [-shəs] *a.* extremely cruel or wicked; horrifying; *inf.* very bad —**atro'ciously** *adv.* —**atroc'ity** [-tros'-] *n.* wickedness

at'rophy *n.* wasting away, emaciation —*vi.* waste away, become useless (**-phied, -phying**) —**at'rophied** *a.*

att. attention; attorney

attach' *v.* (*mainly tr.*) join, fasten; unite; be connected with; attribute; appoint; seize by law —**attached'** *a.* (*with* to) fond of —**attach'ment** *n.*

attach'é [a-tash'ā] *n.* specialist attached to diplomatic mission (*pl.* **-s**) —**attaché case** small leather hand-case for papers

attack' *vt.* take action against (in war, sport *etc.*); criticize; set about with vigour; affect adversely —*n.* attacking action; bout

attain' *vt.* arrive at; reach, gain by effort, accomplish —**attainabil'ity** *n.* —**attain'able** *a.* —**attain'ment** *n. esp.* personal accomplishment

attain'der *n. Hist.* loss of rights through conviction of high treason

att'ar *n.* a fragrant oil made *esp.* from rose petals

attempt' *vt.* try, endeavour —*n.* trial, effort

attend' *vt.* be present at; accompany —*vi.* (*with* to) take care of; give the mind (to), pay attention to —**attend'ance** *n.* an attending; presence; persons attending —**attend'ant** *n./a.* —**atten'tion** *n.* notice; heed; act of attending; care; courtesy; alert position in military drill —**atten'tive** *a.* —**atten'tively** *adv.* —**atten'tiveness** *n.*

atten'uate *v.* weaken or become weak; make or become thin —**atten'uated** *a.* —**attenua'tion** *n.* reduction of intensity

attest' *vt.* bear witness to, certify —**attesta'tion** *n.* formal confirmation by oath *etc.*

att'ic *n.* space within roof where ceiling follows line of roof —*a.* of Attica, Athens

attire' *vt.* dress, array —*n.* dress, clothing

att'itude *n.* mental view, opinion; posture, pose; disposition, behaviour —**attitu'dinize** *vi.* assume affected attitudes

attor'ney [-tur'-] *n.* one legally appointed to act for another, *esp.* a lawyer (*pl.* **-neys**)

attract' *v.* draw (attention *etc.*); arouse interest of; cause to come closer (as magnet *etc.*) —**attrac'tion** *n.* power to attract; something offered so as to interest, please —**attrac'tive** *a.* —**attrac'tively** *adv.* —**attrac'tiveness** *n.*

attrib'ute *vt.* regard as belonging to or produced by —*n.* [at'-] quality, property or characteristic of anything —**attrib'utable** *a.* —**attribu'tion** *n.* —**attrib'utive** *a.* —**attrib'utively** *adv.*

attri'tion [-trish'-] *n.* wearing away of strength *etc.*; rubbing away, friction

attune' *vt.* tune , harmonize; make accordant

at. wt. atomic weight

Au *Chem.* gold

au'bergine [ō'bər-zhēn] *n.* **UK** eggplant

aubr(i)e'tia *n.* trailing plant with purple flowers

au'burn *a.* reddish brown —*n.* this colour

au courant' [ō-koo-rong'] *Fr.* up-to-date; acquainted with

auc'tion *n.* public sale in which bidder offers increase of price over another and what is sold goes to one who bids highest —*v.* —**auctioneer'** *n.* —**auction bridge** card game —**Dutch auction** one in which price starts high and is reduced until purchaser is found

auda'cious *a.* bold; daring, impudent —**audac'ity** *n.*

au'dible *a.* able to be heard —**audibil'ity** *n.* —**au'dibly** *adv.*

au'dience *n.* assembly of hearers; act of hearing; judicial hearing; formal interview

au'dio- (*comb. form*) relating to sound or hearing

audiovis'ual *a.* (*esp.* of teaching aids) involving, directed at, both sight and hearing, as film *etc.*

au'dit *n.* formal examination or settlement of accounts —*vt.* examine accounts; attend classes outside official course of study —**au'ditor** *n.*

audi'tion *n.* screen or other test of prospective performer; hearing —*vt.* conduct such a test —**auditor'ium** *n.* building for public gatherings or meetings (*pl.* **-s, -ia**) —**au'ditory** *a.* pert. to sense of hearing

au fait' [ō-fā'] *Fr.* fully informed; expert

auf Wie'dersehen [owf-vē'dər-zā-ən] *Ger.* goodbye

Aug. August

au'ger *n.* carpenter's tool for boring holes, large gimlet

aught *n.* anything —*adv.* to any extent

augment' *v.* increase, enlarge —*n.* [awg'ment] increase —**augmenta'tion** *n.* —**augment'ative** *a.* increasing in force

au'gur *n.* among the Romans, soothsayer —*v.* be a sign of future events, foretell —**au'gural** *a.* —**au'gury** *n.*

august' *a.* majestic, dignified

Au'gust *n.* the eighth month

Augus'tan *a.* of Augustus, the Roman Emperor; hence classic, distinguished, as applied to a period of literature

auk *n.* northern web-footed seabird with short wings used only as paddles

aunt [ahnt] *n.* father's or mother's sister, uncle's wife

au pair' [ō-] *n.* young foreigner who receives free board and lodging in return for housework *etc.* —*a.*

au'ra *n.* quality, air, atmosphere considered distinctive of person or thing; medical symptom warning of impending epileptic fit *etc.*

au'ral *a.* of, by ear —**au'rally** *adv.*

aure'ola, aur'eole *n.* gold discs round heads in sacred pictures; halo

au revoir' [ō-rə-vwahr'] *Fr.* goodbye

au'ricle *n.* outside ear; an upper cavity of heart —**auric'ular** *a.* of the auricle; aural

aurif'erous *a.* gold-bearing

au'rochs [-roks] *n.* species of wild ox, now extinct

auror'a *n.* lights in the atmosphere seen radiating from regions of the poles The northern is called **aurora borealis** and the southern, **aurora australis**; dawn (*pl.* **-ras**)

ausculta'tion *n.* listening to movement of heart and lungs with stethoscope —**aus'cultator** *n.* —**auscul'tatory** *a.*

aus'pice [-pis] *n.* omen, augury —*pl.* patronage —**auspi'cious** *a.* of good omen, favourable —**auspi'ciously** *adv.*

austere' [os-] *a.* harsh, strict, severe; without luxury —**austere'ly** *adv.* —**auster'ity** *n.*

aus'tral *a.* southern

Australa'sian [os-] *a./n.* (native or inhabitant) of Australasia (Australia, N Zealand and adjacent islands)

Austra'lian [os-] *n./a.* (native or inhabitant) of Australia
au'tarchy [-ki] *n.* despotism, absolute power, dictatorship
auth. author; authority; authorized
authen'tic *a.* real, genuine, true; trustworthy —**authen'tically** *adv.* —**authen'ticate** *vt.* make valid, confirm; establish truth, authorship *etc.* of —**authentica'tion, authentic'ity** [-tis'-] *n.*
au'thor *n.* writer of book; originator, constructor (**-ess** *fem.*) —**au'thorship** *n.*
author'ity [-tho'ri-] *n.* legal power or right; delegated power; influence; permission; expert; body or board in control, *esp.* in *pl.* —**author'itative** *a.* —**author'itatively** *adv.* —**authoriza'tion** *n.* —**auth'orize** *vt.* empower; permit, sanction
autis'tic *a.* withdrawn and divorced from reality
au'to *n. inf. short for* AUTOMOBILE
au'to- (*comb. form*) self, as in *autograph, autosuggestion etc.* Such words are not given here where the meaning may easily be inferred from the simple word
autobiog'raphy *n.* life of person written by himself —**autobiog'rapher** *n.* —**autobiograph'ical** *a.* —**autobiograph'ically** *adv.*
autoch'thon [-ok'-] *n.* primitive or original inhabitant —**autoch'thonous** *a.*
au'tocrat *n.* absolute ruler; despotic person —**autoc'racy** *n.* —**autocrat'ic** *a.* —**autocrat'ically** *adv.*
au'tocross *n.* motor racing sport over rough course
autoer'otism *n.* self-produced sexual arousal
autog'amy *n.* self-fertilization
autog'enous [-toj'-] *a.* self-generated
au'tograph *n.* a signature; one's own handwriting —*vt.* sign —**autograph'ic** *a.*
autogy'ro [-jī'-] *n.* aircraft like helicopter using horizontal airscrew for vertical ascent and descent
autointoxica'tion *n.* poisoning of tissues of the body as a result of the absorption of bodily waste
au'tomat *n.* vending machine
au'tomate *vt.* make manufacturing process *etc.* automatic
automat'ic *a.* operated or controlled mechanically; done without conscious thought —*a./n.* self-loading (weapon) —**automat'ically** *adv.* —**automa'tion** *n.* use of automatic devices in industrial production —**autom'atism** *n.* involuntary action —**autom'aton** *n.* self-acting machine, *esp.* simulating a human being (*pl.* **-ata**)
au'tomobile *n.* self-propelled road vehicle
auton'omy *n.* self-government —**auton'omous** *a.*
au'topsy *n.* postmortem examination to determine cause of death; critical analysis
autosugges'tion *n.* process of influencing the mind (towards health *etc.*), conducted by the subject himself
au'tumn *n./a.* **UK** fall (season)
aux. auxiliary
auxil'iary *a.* helping, subsidiary —*n.* helper; something subsidiary, as troops; verb used to form tenses of others
AV Authorized Version (of the Bible)
av. average
avail' *v.* be of use, advantage, value (to) —*n.* benefit, as **to be of little avail** *etc.* —**availabil'ity** *n.* —**avail'able** *a.* obtainable; accessible —**avail oneself of** make use of
av'alanche *n.* mass of snow, ice, sliding down mountain; a sudden overwhelming quantity of anything
avant-garde' [av-ong-] *a.* markedly experimental or in advance
av'arice [-ris] *n.* greed for wealth —**avari'cious** *a.* —**avari'ciously** *adv.*
avast' [-vah-] *interj.* stop
avdp. avoirdupois
Ave. Avenue
avenge' *vt.* take vengeance on behalf of (person) or on account of (thing) —**aven'ger** [-j-] *n.*
av'enue *n.* wide, handsome street; an approach; double row of trees
aver' *vt.* affirm, assert (**-rr-**) —**aver'ment** *n.*
av'erage *n.* the mean value or quantity of a number of values or quantities —*a.* calculated as an average; medium, ordinary —*vt.* fix or calculate a mean —*vi.* exist in or form a mean

averse' *a.* disinclined, unwilling —**aver'sion** *n.* dislike, person or thing disliked

avert' *vt.* turn away; ward off

a'viary [ā'vyə-ri] *n.* enclosure for birds —**a'viarist** *n.*

avia'tion [ā-] *n.* art of flying aircraft; transport by aircraft —**a'viator** *n.*

av'id *a.* keen, enthusiastic; greedy (for) —**avid'ity** *n.*

avocad'o [-kahd'-] *n.* tropical tree; its green-skinned edible fruit

avoca'tion *n.* vocation; employment, business

av'ocet *n.* wading bird of snipe family with upward-curving bill

avoid' *vt.* keep away from; refrain from; not allow to happen —**avoid'able** *a.* —**avoid'ance** *n.*

avoirdupois' [av-ər-də-poiz'] *n./a.* system of weights used in many English-speaking countries based on pounds and ounces

avouch' *vt. obs.* affirm, maintain, attest, own —**avouch'ment** *n.*

avow' *vt.* declare; admit —**avow'able** *a.* —**avow'al** *n.* —**avowed'** *a.* —**avow'edly** *adv.*

await' *vt.* wait or stay for; be in store for

awake', awa'ken *v.* emerge or rouse from sleep; become or cause to become alert (**awoke'** *or* **awaked'** [-wākt'], **awa'king**) —*a.* not sleeping; alert —**awa'kening** *n.*

award' *vt.* to give formally (*esp.* a prize or punishment) —*n.* prize; judicial decision

aware' *a.* informed, conscious —**aware'ness** *n.*

awash' *adv.* level with the surface of water; filled or overflowing with water

away' *adv.* absent, apart, at a distance, out of the way —*n. Sport* game played on opponent's ground

awe *n.* dread mingled with reverence —**awe'some** *a.*

aw'ful *a.* very bad, unpleasant; *obs.* impressive; *inf.* very great —**aw'fully** *adv.* in an unpleasant way; *inf.* very much

awhile' *adv.* for a time

awk'ward *a.* clumsy, ungainly; difficult; inconvenient; embarrassed —**awk'wardly** *adv.* —**awk'wardness** *n.*

awl *n.* pointed tool for boring wood, leather *etc.*

awn'ing *n.* (canvas) roof or shelter, to protect from weather

awoke' *pt./pp. of* AWAKE

AWOL absent without leave

awry' [-rī'] *adv.* crookedly; amiss; at a slant —*a.* crooked, distorted; wrong

axe *n.* tool with a sharp blade for chopping; *inf.* dismissal from employment *etc.* —*vt. inf.* dismiss, dispense with

ax'iom *n.* received or accepted principle; self-evident truth —**axiomat'ic** *a.*

ax'is *n.* (imaginary) line round which body spins; line or column about which parts are arranged (*pl.* **ax'es** [-sēz]) —**ax'ial** *a.* —**ax'ially** *adv.*

Ax'is *n.* coalition of Germany, Italy and Japan, 1936-45

ax'le (tree) [ak'sl] *n.* rod on which wheel turns

ayatoll'ah *n.* one of a class of Islamic religious leaders

aye *adv.* yes —*n.* affirmative answer or vote —*pl.* those voting for motion

aza'lea *n.* genus of shrubby flowering plants, allied to the rhododendron

az'imuth *n.* vertical arc from zenith to horizon; angular distance of this from meridian

Az'tec *a./n.* (member) of race ruling Mexico before Spanish conquest

az'ure [azh'-] *n.* sky-blue colour; sky —*a.* sky-blue

B

B bass; *Chess* bishop; *Chem.* boron; British

BA Bachelor of Arts

Ba *Chem.* barium

bab'ble *v.* speak foolishly, incoherently, or childishly —*n.* foolish, confused talk —**bab'bler** *n.* —**bab'bling** *n.*

babe *n.* baby; guileless person

ba'bel *n.* confused noise or scene, uproar

baboon' *n.* large monkey of Africa and Asia —**baboon'ish** *a.*

ba'by *n.* very young child, infant —**ba'byhood** *n.* —**ba'byish** *a.* —**baby carriage** small four-wheeled carriage for baby (*also* **baby buggy** *inf.*) —**baby-sit** *vi.* —**baby-sitter** *n.* one who cares for children when parents are out

bacc'arat [-rah] *n.* gambling card game

bacc'hanal [-k'ən-] *n.* follower of Bacchus; (participant in) drunken, riotous celebration

bach'elor *n.* unmarried man; holder of lowest university degree; *Hist.* young knight —**bach'elorhood, bach'elorship** *n.*

bacill'us [-sil'-] *n.* minute organism sometimes causing disease (*pl.* **bacill'i**) —**bacill'iform** *a.*

back *n.* hinder part of anything, *eg* human body; part opposite front; part or side of something further away or less used; (position of) player in ball games behind other (forward) players —*a.* situated behind; earlier; remote —*adv.* at, to the back; in, into the past; in return —*vi.* move backwards —*vt.* support; put wager on; provide with back or backing —**back'er** *n.* one supporting another, *esp.* in contest; one betting on horse, *etc.* in race —**back'ing** *n.* support; material to protect the back of something; musical accompaniment, *esp.* for pop singer —**back'ward(s)** *adv.* to the rear; to the past; to worse state —**back'ward** *a.* directed towards the rear; behind in education; reluctant, bashful —**back'wardness** *n.* —**backbench'er** *n.* Brit., Aust. and Canad. member of Parliament not holding office in government or opposition —**back'bite** *vt.* slander absent person —**back'biter** *n.* —**back'biting** *n.* —**back'bone** *n.* spinal column —**back'chat** *n.* impudent answer —**back'cloth, back'drop** *n.* painted cloth at back of stage —**backdate'** *vt.* make effective from earlier date —**backfire'** *vi.* ignite at wrong time, as fuel in cylinder of internal-combustion engine; (of plan, scheme, *etc.*) fail to work, *esp.* to the cost of the instigator; ignite wrongly, as gas burner *etc.* —**back'gammon** *n.* game played with checkers and dice —**back'ground** *n.* space behind chief figures of picture *etc.*; past history of person —**back'hand** *n.* stroke with hand turned backwards —**backhand'ed** *a.* (of compliment *etc.*) with second, uncomplimentary meaning —**back'hander** *n.* blow with back of hand; *inf.* a bribe —**back'lash** *n.* sudden and adverse reaction —**back'log** *n.* accumulation of work *etc.* to be dealt with —**back'pack** *n.* type of knapsack —*vi.* —**backside'** *n.* rump —**back'slide** *vi.* fall back in faith or morals —**back'stroke** *n.* swimming stroke performed on the back —**back'up** *n.* support, reinforcement —**back-up light** light on rear of automobile to show it is reversing —**back'wash** *n.* water thrown back by ship's propellers *etc.*; a backward current; a reaction —**back'water** *n.* still water fed by back flow of stream —**back'woods** *pl.n.* sparsely populated forests

ba'con *n.* cured pig's flesh

bacte'ria *pl.n.* (*sing.* **bacte'rium**) microscopic organisms, some causing disease —**bacte'rial** *a.* —**bacte'ricide** *n.* substance that destroys bacteria —**bacteriol'ogist** *n.* —**bacteriol'ogy** *n.* study of bacteria

bad *a.* of poor quality; faulty; evil; immoral; offensive; severe; rotten, decayed (**worse** *comp.*, **worst** *sup.*) —**bad'ly** *adv.* —**bad'ness** *n.*

bade *pt. of* BID

badge *n.* distinguishing emblem or sign

badg'er *n.* burrowing night animal, about the size of fox —*vt.* pester, worry

bad'inage [-ahzh] *n.* playful talk, banter

bad'minton *n.* game like tennis, played with shuttlecocks over high net

baf'fle *vt.* check, frustrate, bewilder —**baf'fler** *n.* —**baf'fling** *a.* —**baf'fle (plate)** *n.* device to regulate or divert flow of liquid, gas, soundwaves *etc.*

bag *n.* sack, pouch; measure of quantity; woman's purse; *offens.* unattractive woman —*pl. inf.* lots (of) —*vi.* swell out; bulge; sag —*vt.* put in bag; kill as game, *etc.* (**-gg-**) —**bagg'ing** *n.* cloth —**bagg'y** *a.* loose, drooping —**bag lady** homeless woman who carries her possessions in shopping bags —**bag'man** *n. inf.* person who solicits money for political party

bagatelle' *n.* trifle; game like pinball played with nine balls and cue on a board

bagg'age *n.* suitcases *etc.*, packed for journey; *offens.* woman

bag'pipes *pl.n.* musical wind instrument, of windbag and pipes —**bag'piper** *n.*

bail[1] *n. Law* security given for person's reappearance in court; one giving such security —*vt.* release, or obtain release of, on security; *inf.* help a person, firm *etc.* out of trouble

bail[2] *n. Cricket* crosspiece on wicket; bar separating horses in stable

bail[3], **bale** *vt.* empty out water from boat —**bail out** leave aircraft by parachute

bai'ley *n.* outermost wall of a castle

Bai'ley bridge bridge composed of prefabricated sections

bai'liff *n.* land steward, agent; sheriff's officer

bai'liwick *n.* jurisdiction of bailiff

bairn *n. Scot.* infant, child

bait *n.* food to entice fish; any lure or enticement —*vt.* set a lure; annoy, persecute

baize *n.* smooth woollen cloth

bake *vt.* cook or harden by dry heat —*vi.* make bread, cakes *etc.*; be scorched or tanned —**ba'ker** *n.* —**ba'kery, bake'-house** *n.* —**ba'king** *n.* —**baking powder** raising agent containing sodium bicarbonate *etc.* used in cooking

Ba'kelite R hard nonflammable synthetic resin, used for dishes, trays, electrical insulators *etc.*

Balaclav'a [-ahv'ə] *n.* close-fitting woollen helmet, covering head and neck

balalai'ka [-lī'-] *n.* Russian musical instrument, like guitar

bal'ance *n.* pair of scales; equilibrium; surplus; sum due on an account; difference between two sums —*vt.* weigh; bring to equilibrium —**balance sheet** tabular statement of assets and liabilities —**balance wheel** regulating wheel of watch

bal'cony *n.* railed platform outside window; upper seats in theatre

bald [bawld] *a.* hairless; plain; bare —**bald'ing** *a.* becoming bald —**bald'ly** *adv.* —**bald'ness** *n.*

bal'derdash [bawl'-] *n.* idle, senseless talk

bal'dric [bawl'-] *n.* shoulder-belt for sword *etc.*

bale[1] *n.* bundle or package —*vt.* make into bundles or pack into cartons —**ba'ler** *n.* machine which does this

bale[2] *vt. see* BAIL[3]

baleen' *n.* whalebone

bale'ful *a.* menacing —**bale'fully** *adv.*

balk [bawk, bawlk] *vi.* swerve, pull up —*vt.* thwart, hinder; shirk —*n.* hindrance; square timber, beam —**balk at** recoil; stop short

ball[1] [bawl] *n.* anything round; globe, sphere, *esp.* as used in games; a ball as delivered; bullet —*vi.* clog, gather into a mass —**ball bearings** steel balls used to lessen friction on bearings —**ball game** game of baseball —**ball'park** *n.* baseball field or stadium —**ball'point (pen)** pen with tiny ball bearing as nib

ball[2] [bawl] *n.* assembly for dancing —**ball'room** *n.*

ball'ad *n.* narrative poem; simple song

ballade' [-ahd'] *n.* short poem with refrain and envoy; piece of music

ball'ast *n.* heavy material put in ship to give steadiness; that which renders anything steady —*vt.* load with ballast, steady

ball'et [-ā] *n.* theatrical presentation of dancing and miming —**balleri'na** [-ē'-] *n.*

ballis'tic *a.* moving as, or pertaining to motion of, a projectile —**ballis'tics** *pl.n.* (*with sing. v.*) scientific study of ballistic motion

balloon' *n.* large bag filled with air or gas to make it rise in the air —*vi.* puff out —**balloon'ing** *n.* —**balloon'ist** *n.*

ball'ot *n.* method of voting secretly, usually by marking ballot paper and putting it into box —*v.* vote or elicit a vote from

ball'yhoo *n.* noisy confusion or uproar; vulgar, exaggerated publicity or advertisement

balm [bahm] *n.* aromatic substance, healing or soothing ointment; anything soothing —**balm'iness** *n.* —**balm'y** *a.*

bal'sa [bawl'-] *n.* Amer. tree with light but strong wood

bal'sam [bawl'-] *n.* resinous aromatic substance obtained from various trees and shrubs; soothing ointment —**balsam'ic** *a.*

bal'uster *n.* short pillar used as support to rail of staircase *etc.* —**bal'ustrade** *n.* row of short pillars surmounted by rail

bamboo' *n.* large tropical treelike reed (*pl.* **bamboos'**)

bamboo'zle *vt.* mystify, hoax

ban *vt.* prohibit, forbid, outlaw (**-nn-**) —*n.* prohibition; proclamation —**ban(n)s** *pl.n.* proclamation of marriage

banal' [-nahl'] *a.* commonplace, trivial, trite —**banal'ity** *n.*

banan'a [-nahn'-] *n.* tropical treelike plant; its fruit

band[1] *n.* strip used to bind; range of values, frequencies *etc.*, between two limits —**ban'dage** *n.* strip of cloth for binding wound

band[2] *n.* company, group; company of musicians —*v.* bind together —**band'master** *n.* —**bands'man** *n.* —**band'stand** *n.*

bandann'a *n.* coloured silk or cotton handkerchief

B & B UK bed and breakfast

band'box *n.* light box of cardboard for hats *etc.*

ban'deau [-ō] *n.* band, ribbon for the hair

ban'dicoot *n.* ratlike Aust. marsupial

ban'dit *n.* outlaw; robber, brigand (*pl.* **ban'dits, bandit'i**)

bandolier', -leer' *n.* shoulder belt for cartridges

band'wagon *n.* —**climb, jump, get on the bandwagon** join something that seems assured of success

ban'dy *vt.* beat to and fro, toss from one to another (**ban'died, ban'dying**) —**ban'dy, bandy-legged** *a.* having legs curving outwards

bane *n.* person or thing causing misery or distress —**bane'ful** *a.* —**bane'fully** *adv.*

bang[1] *n.* sudden loud noise, explosion; heavy blow —*vt.* make loud noise; beat; strike violently, slam

bang[2] *n.* fringe of hair cut straight across forehead

ban'gle [bang'gəl] *n.* ring worn on arm or leg

ban'ish *vt.* condemn to exile; drive away; dismiss —**ban'ishment** *n.* exile

ban'isters *pl.n.* railing and supporting balusters on staircase

ban'jo *n.* musical instrument like guitar, with circular body (*pl.* **-jo(e)s**) —**ban'joist** *n.*

bank[1] *n.* mound or ridge of earth; edge of river, lake *etc.*; rising ground in sea —*v.* enclose with ridge; pile up; (of aircraft) tilt inwards in turning

bank[2] *n.* establishment for keeping, lending, exchanging *etc.* money; any supply or store for future use, as a **blood bank** —*vt.* put in bank —*vi.* keep with bank —**bank'er** *n.* —**bank'ing** *n.* —**bank(er's) card** card guaranteeing payment of cheques by bank up to an agreed amount —**bank'note** *n.* written promise of payment —**bank'roll** *n.* roll of currency notes —**bank on** rely on

bank[3] *n.* tier; row of oars

bank'rupt *n.* one who fails in business, insolvent debtor —*a.* financially ruined —*vt.* make, cause to be, bankrupt —**bank'ruptcy** *n.*

bann'er *n.* long strip with slogan *etc.*; placard; flag used as ensign

banns *pl. n. see* BAN

ban'quet [bang'kwit] *n.* feast —*vi.* feast —*vt.* treat with feast —**ban'queter** *n.*

banquette' [-ket'] *n.* raised firing step behind parapet; upholstered bench

ban'shee [*or* -shē'] *n.* Irish fairy with a wail portending death

ban'tam *n.* dwarf variety of domestic fowl; very light boxing weight

ban'ter *vt.* make fun of —*n.* light, teasing language

Ban'tu *n.* collective name for large group of related native tribes in Africa; family of languages spoken by Bantu peoples

ban'yan, ban'ian *n.* Indian fig tree with spreading branches which take root

ba'obab *n.* Afr. tree with thick trunk and angular branches

Bap'tist *n.* member of Protestant Christian denomination believing in necessity of baptism by immersion, *esp.* of adults

baptize' [-īz'] *vt.* immerse in, sprinkle with water ceremoniously; christen —**bap'tism** *n.* —**baptis'mal** [-z'-] *a.* —**baptis'mally** *adv.* —**bap'tistry** *n.* place where baptism is performed

bar[1] *n.* rod or block of any substance; obstacle; bank of sand at mouth of river; rail in law court; body of lawyers; counter where drinks are served, *esp.* in hotel *etc.*; unit of music —*vt.* fasten; obstruct; exclude (**-rr-**) —*prep.* except —**bar'ring** *prep.* excepting —**bar code** arrangement of numbers and parallel lines on package, electronically scanned at checkout to give price —**bar'maid** *n.* —**bar'man** *n.* —**bar'tender** *n.*

bar[2] *n.* unit of pressure

bar. barometer; barrel; barrister

barb *n.* sharp point curving backwards behind main point of spear, fish hook *etc.*; cutting remark —**barbed** *a.* —**barbed wire** fencing wire with barbs at close intervals

bar'barous *a.* savage, brutal, uncivilized —**barba'rian** *n.* —**barbar'ic** *a.* —**bar'barism** *n.* —**barbar'ity** *n.* —**bar'barously** *adv.*

bar'becue *n.* meal cooked outdoors over open fire; fireplace, grill used for this —*vt.* cook meat *etc.* in this manner

bar'ber *n.* one who shaves beards and cuts hair

barbit'urate *n.* derivative of barbituric acid used as drug —**bar'bitone, bar'bital** *n.*

bard *n.* Celtic poet; wandering minstrel —**bard'ic** *a.* —**the Bard** Shakespeare

bare *a.* uncovered; naked; plain; scanty —*vt.* make bare —**bare'ly** *adv.* only just, scarcely —**bare'ness** *n.* —**bare'backed** *a.* on unsaddled horse —**bare'faced** *a.* shameless

bar'gain [-gin] *n.* something bought at price favourable to purchaser; contract, agreement —*vi.* haggle, negotiate; make bargain

barge *n.* flat-bottomed freight boat; state or pleasure boat —*vi. inf.* interrupt; *inf.* bump (into), push —**barge'man** *n.*

bar'ite [bār'-] *n.* barium sulphate

bar'itone [ba'ri-] *n.* (singer with) second lowest adult male voice —*a.* written for or possessing this vocal range

ba'rium *n.* white metallic element

bark[1] *n.* sharp loud cry of dog *etc.* —*v.* make, utter with such sound —**bark'er** *n.* crier outside fair booth *etc.*

bark[2] *n.* outer layer of trunk, branches of tree —*vt.* strip bark from; rub off (skin), graze (shins *etc.*)

bark[3] *n.* sailing ship, *esp.* large, three-masted one —**bar'kentine** *n.* small bark

bar'ley *n.* grain used for food and making malt —**barley sugar** sweet originally made with barley

barm *n. obs.* yeast; froth —**barm'y** *a. inf.* silly, insane

barn *n.* building to store grain, hay *etc.* —**barn dance** (party with) square dancing —**barn'yard** *n.* farmyard

bar'nacle *n.* shellfish which adheres to rocks and ships' bottoms

bar'ney *inf. n.* noisy argument; fight —*vi.* argue or fight

barom'eter *n.* instrument to measure pressure of atmosphere —**baromet'ric** *a.* —**barom'etry** *n.* —**bar'ograph** *n.* recording barometer

bar'on [ba'rən] *n.* member of lowest rank of peerage; powerful businessman (*fem.* **-ess**) —**bar'onage** *n.* —**baro'nial** *a.* —**bar'ony** *n.*

bar'onet [ba'rə-] *n.* lowest British hereditary title, below baron but above knight —**bar'onetage** *n.* —**bar'onetcy** *n.*

baroque' [-ok', -ōk'] *a.* extravagantly ornamented, *esp.* in architecture and art

barouche' [-o͞osh'] *n.* four-wheeled carriage with folding top over rear seat

barque [bahrk] *n. see* BARK[3]

barr'ack[1] *n.* (*usu. in pl.*) building for lodging soldiers; huge bare building

barr'ack[2] *v. inf.* (*usu. with* for) encourage by cheering, *esp.* at sporting events;

inf. criticize loudly; jeer —**barr'acking** *n.*

barracou'ta, barracu'da *n.* type of large, elongated, predatory fish, mostly tropical

barr'age [-ahzh] *n.* heavy artillery fire; continuous and heavy delivery, *esp.* of questions *etc.*; dam across river

barr'atry *n.* fraudulent breach of duty by master of ship; stirring up of law suits —**barr'ator** *n.* —**barr'atrous** *a.*

barr'el *n.* round wooden vessel, made of curved staves bound with hoops; its capacity; anything long and hollow, as tube of gun *etc.* —*vt.* put in barrel (**-ll-**) —**barr'elled** *a.*

barr'en *a.* unfruitful, sterile; unprofitable; dull —**barr'enness** *n.* —**Barren Lands** *or* **Grounds** sparsely inhabited tundra region in Canada

barricade' *n.* improvised fortification, barrier —*vt.* to protect by building barrier; block

barr'ier *n.* fence, obstruction, obstacle, boundary —**barrier reef** coral reef lying parallel to shore

barr'ister *n.* lawyer who pleads in court

barr'ow[1] *n.* small wheeled handcart; wheelbarrow

barr'ow[2] *n.* burial mound; tumulus

bart'er *v.* trade by exchange of goods —*n.*

bar'yon [ba'ri-] *n. Physics* elementary particle of matter

bary'tes [-ī'tēz] *n. see* BARITE

bas'alt [-awlt] *n.* dark-coloured, hard, compact, igneous rock —**basalt'ic** *a.*

bas'cule *n.* lever apparatus; drawbridge on counterpoise principle

base[1] *n.* bottom, foundation; starting point; centre of operations; fixed point; *Chem.* compound that combines with an acid to form a salt; medium into which other substances are mixed; *Baseball* one of four points round which batters run —*vt.* found, establish —**base'board** *n.* vertical board around margin of floor —**base'less** *a.* —**base'ment** *n.* lowest storey of building

base[2] *a.* low, mean; despicable —**base'ly** *adv.* —**base'ness** *n.* —**base'born** *a.* illegitimate

base'ball *n.* game, orig. Amer., played with bat and ball

bash *inf. v.* strike violently —*n.* blow; attempt

bash'ful *a.* shy, modest —**bash'fully** *adv.* —**bash'fulness** *n.*

BASIC *Computers* Beginners' All-purpose Symbolic Instruction Code

ba'sic *a.* relating to, serving as base; fundamental; necessary

bas'il [baz'-] *n.* aromatic herb

basil'ica [-zil'-] *n.* type of church with long hall and pillars —**basil'ican** *a.*

bas'ilisk [baz'-] *n.* legendary small fire-breathing dragon

ba'sin *n.* deep circular dish; harbour; land drained by river

ba'sis *n.* foundation; principal constituent (*pl.* **-ses** [-sēz])

bask [-ah-] *vi.* lie in warmth and sunshine (*often fig.*)

bask'et [-ah-] *n.* vessel made of woven cane, straw *etc.* —**bask'etry, bask'etwork** *n.* —**bask'etball** *n.* ball game played by two teams

Basque [bask] *n.* one of race from W Pyrenees; their language

bas-relief' *n.* sculpture with figures standing out slightly from background

bass[1] [bās] *n.* lowest part in music; bass singer or voice —*a.*

bass[2] [bas] *n.* any of large variety of fish, *esp.* sea perch

bass'et *n.* type of smooth-haired dog

bassoon' *n.* woodwind instrument of low tone —**bassoon'ist** *n.*

bas'tard *n.* child born of unmarried parents; *inf.* person, as in **lucky bastard** —*a.* illegitimate; spurious —**bas'tardy** *n.*

baste[1] *vt.* moisten (meat) during cooking with hot fat; beat with stick —**ba'sting** *n.*

baste[2] *vt.* sew loosely, tack

bastina'do *n.* beating with stick, *esp.* on soles of feet —*vt.* (**-does, -doing, -doed**)

bas'tion *n.* projecting part of fortification, tower; strong defence or bulwark

bat[1] *n.* any of various types of club used to hit ball in certain sports, *eg* cricket, baseball —*v.* strike with bat or use bat in sport —**batt'er** *n.* —**batt'ing** *n.* performance with bat —**bats'man** *n.*

bat[2] *n.* nocturnal mouselike flying animal

bat[3] *vt.* flutter (one's eyelids)

batch *n.* group or set of similar objects, *esp.* cakes *etc.* baked together

ba'ted *a.* —**with bated breath** anxiously

bath [-ah-] *n.* vessel or place to bathe in; water for bathing; act of bathing —*pl.* place for swimming —*vt.* wash —**bath'robe** *n.* loose gown worn before dressing —**bath'tub** *n.* tub for bathing in

Bath chair invalid chair

bathe [-āTH] *v.* swim; apply liquid; wash; immerse in water (**bathed, ba'thing**) —*n.* —**ba'ther** *n.*

ba'thos *n.* ludicrous descent from the elevated to the ordinary in writing or speech

bath'yscaph, -scaphe [-āf], **-scape** *n.* vessel for deep-sea observation

bat'ik *n.* dyeing process using wax

bat'man *n.* military officer's servant

bat'on *n.* stick, *esp.* of policeman, conductor, marshal

batra'chian [-trā'ki-] *n.* any amphibian, *esp.* frog or toad

battal'ion *n.* military unit consisting of three or more companies

batt'en[1] *n.* narrow piece of board, strip of wood —*vt.* (*esp. with* down) fasten, make secure

batt'en[2] *vi.* (*usu. with* on) thrive, *esp.* at someone else's expense

batt'er *vt.* strike continuously —*n.* mixture of flour, eggs, milk, used in cooking

batt'ery *n.* connected group of electrical cells; any electrical cell or accumulator; number of similar things occurring together; *Law* assault by beating; number of guns; place where they are mounted; unit of artillery; large number of cages for rearing poultry *etc.*

batt'ing *n.* cotton fibre as stuffing

bat'tle *n.* fight between armies, combat —*vi.* fight, struggle —**bat'tleaxe** *n. inf.* domineering woman

bat'tlement *n.* wall, parapet on fortification with openings or embrasures

bat'tleship *n.* heavily armed and armoured fighting ship

batt'y *a. inf.* crazy, silly

bau'ble *n.* showy trinket

baulk [bawk] *n. see* BALK —**baulk'line** *n. Billiards* straight line across table behind which cue balls start the game

baux'ite *n.* clay yielding aluminum

bawd *n.* prostitute; brothel keeper —**bawd'y** *a.* obscene, lewd

bawl *vi.* cry; shout —*n.*

bay[1] *n.* wide inlet of sea; space between two columns; recess —**bay window**

bay[2] *n.* bark; cry of hounds in pursuit —*v.* bark (at) —**at bay** cornered; at a distance

bay[3] *n.* laurel tree —*pl.* honorary crown of victory

bay[4] *a.* reddish-brown

bay'onet *n.* stabbing weapon fixed to rifle —*vt.* stab with this (**bay'oneted, bay'oneting**)

bazaar' [-zahr'] *n.* market (*esp.* in Orient); sale of goods for charity

bazoo'ka *n.* antitank rocket launcher

BBC British Broadcasting Corporation

BC before Christ; British Columbia

BCG Bacille Calmette-Guérin (antituberculosis vaccine)

B.Com., B.Comm. Bachelor of Commerce

BD Bachelor of Divinity

B/D bank draft

BDS Bachelor of Dental Surgery

BE Bachelor of Engineering

B/E bill of exchange

be *vi.* live; exist; have a state or quality (I **am**, he **is**; we, you, they **are**, *pr. ind.* —**was**, *pl.* **were**, *pt.* —**been** *pp.* —**be'ing** *pr.p.*)

beach *n.* shore of sea —*vt.* run boat on shore —**beach'comber** *n.* one who habitually searches shore debris for items of value —**beach'head** *n.* area on beach captured from enemy; base for operations

beac'on *n.* signal fire; lighthouse, buoy; (radio) signal used for navigation

bead *n.* little ball pierced for threading on string of necklace, rosary *etc.*; drop of liquid; narrow moulding —**bead'ed** *a.* —**bead'ing** *n.* —**bead'y** *a.* small and bright

bead'le *n. Hist.* church or parish officer

bea'gle *n.* small hound

beak *n.* projecting horny jaws of bird; anything pointed or projecting; UK *sl.* magistrate

beak'er *n.* large drinking cup; glass vessel used by chemists

beam *n.* long squared piece of wood; ship's cross timber, side, or width; ray of light *etc.*; broad smile; bar of a balance —*vt.* aim light, radio waves *etc.* (to) —*vi.* shine; smile benignly

bean *n.* any of various leguminous plants or their seeds —**full of beans** *inf.* lively —**bean sprout** edible sprout of newly germinated bean, *esp.* mung bean

bear[1] [bār] *vt.* carry; support; produce; endure; press (upon) (**bore** *pt.*, **born** *or* **borne** *pp.*, **bear'ing** *pr.p.*) —**bear'er** *n.*

bear[2] [bār] *n.* heavy carnivorous quadruped —**bear'skin** *n.* Guards' tall fur helmet

beard *n.* hair on chin —*vt.* oppose boldly

bear'ing *n.* support or guide for mechanical part, *esp.* one reducing friction; relevance; behaviour; direction; relative position; device on shield

beast *n.* animal; four-footed animal; brutal man —**beast'liness** *n.* —**beast'ly** *a.*

beat *vt.* strike repeatedly; overcome; surpass; stir vigorously with striking action; flap (wings); make, wear (path) —*vi.* throb; sail against wind (**beat** *pt.*, **beat'en** *pp.*) —*n.* stroke; pulsation; appointed course; basic rhythmic unit in piece of music —*a. sl.* exhausted —**beat'er** *n.* instrument for beating; one who rouses game for shooters

beat'ify [bē-at'-] *vt.* make happy; *R.C. Church* pronounce in eternal happiness (first step in canonization) (**beat'ified, beat'ifying**) —**beatif'ic** *a.* —**beatifica'tion** *n.* —**beat'itude** *n.* blessedness

beau [bō] *n.* suitor (*pl.* **beaux** [bō(z)])

Beau'fort scale system of indicating wind strength (from 0, calm, to 17, hurricane)

beau'ty [byōō'-] *n.* loveliness, grace; beautiful person or thing —**beautic'ian** *n.* one who works in beauty parlour —**beau'teous** *a.* —**beau'tiful** *a.* —**beau'tifully** *adv.* —**beau'tify** *vt.* (**-fied, -fying**) —**beauty parlo(u)r** establishment offering hairdressing, manicure *etc.*

bea'ver *n.* amphibious rodent; its fur —**beaver away** work hard

B.Ec. Bachelor of Economics

becalmed' [-kahmd'] *a.* (of ship) motionless through lack of wind

became' *pt. of* BECOME

because' *adv./conj.* by reason of, since

bêche-de-mer' [besh də mer'] *n.* edible sea slug

beck *n.* —**at someone's beck and call** subject to someone's slightest whim

beck'on *v.* summon or lure by silent signal

become' [-kum'] *vi.* come to be —*vt.* suit (**became'** *pt.*, **become'** *pp.*, **becom'ing** *pr.p.*) —**becom'ing** *a.* suitable to; proper

bed *n.* piece of furniture for sleeping on; garden plot; *Architecture etc.* place in which anything rests; bottom of river; layer, stratum —*vt.* lay in a bed; plant (**-dd-**) —**bedd'ing** *n.* —**bed'pan** *n.* container used as lavatory by bedridden people —**bed'ridden** *a.* confined to bed by age or sickness —**bed'rock** *n.* —**bed'room** *n.* —**bed'sitter** *n.* oneroomed flat —**bed'stead** *n.*

bedev'il *vt.* confuse; torment —**bedev'ilment** *n.*

bed'lam *n.* noisy confused scene

Bed'ouin [-oo-in] *n.* member of nomadic Arab race —*a.* nomadic

bedrag'gle *vt.* dirty by trailing in wet or mud —**bedrag'gled** *a.*

bee *n.* insect that makes honey —**bee-eater** *n.* insect-eating bird —**bee'hive** *n.* —**bee'line** *n.* shortest route —**bees'wax** *n.* wax secreted by bees

beech *n.* European tree with smooth greyish bark and small nuts; its wood —**beech'en** *a.*

beef *n.* flesh of cattle raised and killed for eating; *inf.* complaint —*vi. inf.* complain —**beeves** *pl.n.* cattle —**beef'y** *a.* fleshy, stolid —**beef'burger** *n. see* HAMBURGER —**beef'eater** *n.* **UK** yeoman of the guard; warder of Tower of London —**beef up** *inf.* strengthen, reinforce

been *pp. of* BE

beep *n.* short, loud sound of car horn *etc.* —*v.* make this sound

beer *n.* fermented alcoholic drink made from hops and malt —**beer'y** *a.* —**beer parlo(u)r** licensed place where beer is sold to the public

beet *n.* any of various plants with root used for food or extraction of sugar

bee'tle *n.* class of insect with hard upper-wing cases closed over the back for protection —**beetle-browed** *a.* with prominent brows

befall' [-awl'] *v.* happen (to) (**befell', befall'en**)

befit' *vt.* be suitable to (-**tt**-) —**befit'tingly** *adv.*

befog' *vt.* perplex, confuse (-**gg**-)

before' *prep.* in front of; in presence of; in preference to; earlier than —*adv.* earlier; in front —*conj.* sooner than —**before'hand** *adv.* previously

befoul' *vt.* make filthy

befriend' *vt.* make friend of

beg *vt.* ask earnestly, beseech —*vi.* ask for or live on alms (-**gg**-) —**begg'ar** *n.* —**begg'arly** *a.*

began' *pt. of* BEGIN

beget' *vt.* produce, generate (**begot'**, **begat'** *pt.*, **begott'en, begot'** *pp.*, **beget'ting** *pr.p.*) —**begett'er** *n.*

begin' *v.* (cause to) start; initiate; originate (**began'**, **begun'**, **beginn'ing**) —**begin'ner** *n.* novice —**beginn'ing** *n.*

bego'nia *n.* genus of tropical plant

begot' *pt./pp. of* BEGET

begrudge' *vt.* grudge, envy anyone the possession of

beguile' [-gīl'] *vt.* charm, fascinate; amuse; deceive —**beguil'er** *n.*

begun' *pp. of* BEGIN

behalf' [-hahf'] *n.* favour, benefit, interest, *esp.* in **in behalf of**

behave' *vi.* act, function in particular way —**beha'vio(u)r** *n.* conduct —**behave oneself** conduct oneself well

behead' *vt.* cut off head

beheld' *pt./pp. of* BEHOLD

behest' *n.* charge, command

behind' *prep.* further back or earlier than; in support of —*adv.* in the rear —**behind'hand** *a./adv.* in arrears; tardy

behold' [-hō-] *vt.* watch, see (**beheld'** *pt.*, **beheld'**, **behold'en** *pp.*) —**behold'er** *n.*

behold'en *a.* bound in gratitude

behove' *vi.* be fit, necessary (*only impersonal*)

beige [bāzh] *n.* undyed woollen cloth; its colour

be'ing *n.* existence; that which exists; creature —*pr.p. of* BE

bel *n.* unit for comparing two power levels

bela'bo(u)r *vt.* beat soundly

bela'ted *a.* late; too late

belay' *vt.* fasten rope to peg, pin *etc.*

belch *vi.* void wind by mouth —*vt.* eject violently; cast up —*n.* emission of wind *etc.*

beleag'uer [-ēg'-] *vt.* besiege

bel'fry *n.* bell tower

belie' [-lī'] *vt.* contradict; misrepresent (**belied'** *pt./pp.*, **bely'ing** *pr.p.*)

believe' *vt.* regard as true or real —*vi.* have faith —**belief'** *n.* —**believ'able** *a.* credible —**believ'er** *n. esp.* one of same religious faith

Belish'a bea'con [-lēsh'-] flashing light in orange globe marking a pedestrian crossing

belit'tle *vt.* regard, speak of, as having little worth or value —**belit'tlement** *n.*

bell *n.* hollow metal instrument giving ringing sound when struck; electrical device emitting ring or buzz as signal —**bell'boy, bell'hop** *n.* page in hotel

belladon'na *n.* deadly nightshade

belle *n.* beautiful woman, reigning beauty

bell'icose *a.* warlike

bellig'erent [-ij'-] *a.* hostile, aggressive; making war —*n.* warring person or nation

bell'ow *vi.* roar like bull; shout —*n.* roar of bull; any deep cry or shout

bell'ows *pl.n.* instrument for creating stream of air

bell'y *n.* part of body which contains intestines; stomach —*v.* swell out (**bel'lied, bell'ying**)

belong' *vi.* be the property or attribute of; be a member or inhabitant of; have an allotted place; pertain to —**belong'ings** *pl.n.* personal possessions

belov'ed [-luv'id *or* -luvd'] *a.* much loved —*n.* dear one

below' [-ō'] *adv.* beneath —*prep.* lower than

belt *n.* band; girdle; zone or district —*vt.* surround, fasten with belt; mark with band; *inf.* thrash

belu'ga [-lōō'-] *n.* large white sturgeon

BEM British Empire Medal

bemoan' *vt.* grieve over (loss *etc.*)

bemuse' *v.* confuse, bewilder

bench *n.* long seat; seat or body of judges *etc.* —*vt.* provide with benches —**bench mark** fixed point, criterion

bend *v.* (cause to) form a curve (**bent** *pt./pp.*) —*n.* curve —*pl.* decompression sickness

beneath' *prep.* under, lower than *—adv.* below

benedic'tion *n.* invocation of divine blessing

ben'efit *n.* advantage, favour, profit, good; money paid by a government *etc.* to unemployed *etc.* *—vt.* do good to *—vi.* receive good (**ben'efited, ben'efiting**) —**benefac'tion** *n.* —**ben'efactor** *n.* one who helps or does good to others; patron (**ben'efactress** *fem.*) —**ben'efice** *n.* an ecclesiastical living —**benef'icence** *n.* —**benef'icent** *a.* doing good; kind —**benef'icently** *adv.* —**benefi'cial** *a.* advantageous, helpful —**benefi'cially** *adv.* —**benefi'ciary** *n.*

benev'olent *a.* kindly, charitable —**benev'olence** *n.* —**benev'olently** *adv.*

benight'ed [-nīt'-] *a.* ignorant, uncultured

benign' [-īn'] *a.* kindly, mild, favourable —**benig'nancy** *n.* —**benig'nant** *a.* —**benig'nantly** *adv.* —**benig'nity** *n.* —**benign'ly** *adv.*

bent *pt./pp. of* BEND *—a.* curved; resolved (on); *inf.* corrupt; *inf.* deviant; *inf.* crazy *—n.* inclination, personal propensity

benumb' [-m] *vt.* make numb, deaden

Ben'zedrine R amphetamine

ben'zene *n.* one of group of related flammable liquids used in chemistry and as solvents, cleaning agents *etc.*

bequeath' [-ēTH'] *vt.* leave property *etc.* by will —**bequest'** *n.* bequeathing; legacy

berate' *vt.* scold harshly

ber'beris *n.* shrub with red berries

bereave' *vt.* deprive of, *esp.* by death (**-reaved', -reft'** *pt./pp.*) —**bereave'ment** *n.* loss, *esp.* by death

ber'et [-rā] *n.* round, closefitting hat

berg *n.* large mass of ice

ber'gamot *n.* type of pear with strong flavour; type of orange; perfume, oil produced from this

beriber'i *n.* tropical disease caused by vitamin B deficiency

ber'ry *n.* small juicy stoneless fruit *—vi.* look for, pick, berries

berserk' *a.* frenzied

berth *n.* ship's mooring place; place to sleep in ship or train *—vt.* to moor

ber'yl *n.* variety of crystalline mineral including aquamarine and emerald

beseech' *vt.* entreat, implore (**besought'** *pt./pp.*)

beset' *vt.* assail, surround with danger, problems (**beset', besett'ing**)

beside' *prep.* by the side of, near; distinct from —**besides'** *adv./prep.* in addition (to)

besiege' *vt.* surround (with armed forces *etc.*)

besott'ed *a.* drunk; foolish; infatuated

besought' *pt./pp. of* BESEECH

bespeak' *vt.* engage beforehand (**bespoke'** *pt.*, **bespoke', bespo'ken** *pp.*) —**bespoke'** *a.* (of garments) made to order; selling such garments

best *a./adv. sup. of* GOOD *or* WELL *—vt.* defeat —**best seller** book or other product sold in great numbers; author of one or more of these

bes'tial *a.* like a beast, brutish —**bestial'ity** *n.*

bestir' *vt.* rouse (oneself) to activity

bestow' [-stō'] *vt.* give, confer —**bestow'al** *n.*

bestride' *vt.* sit or stand over with legs apart, mount horse (**bestrode', bestrid'den, bestri'ding**)

bet *v.* agree to pay money *etc.* if wrong (or win if right) in guessing result of contest *etc.* (**bet** *or* **bett'ed** *pt./pp.*, **bet'ting** *pr.p.*) *—n.* money risked in this way

be'tel [bē'tl] *n.* species of pepper —**betel nut** the nut of the areca palm

bête noire' [bet-nwahr'] *Fr.* pet aversion

betide' *v.* happen (to)

beto'ken *vt.* be a sign of

bet'ony *n.* plant with reddish-purple flower spike

betray' *vt.* be disloyal to, *esp.* by assisting an enemy; reveal, divulge; show signs of —**betray'al** *n.* —**betray'er** *n.*

betroth' [-ōTH'] *vt.* promise to marry —**betroth'al** *n.* —**betrothed'** *n./a.*

bett'er *a./adv. comp. of* GOOD *and* WELL *—v.* improve —**bett'erment** *n.*

between' *prep./adv.* in the intermediate part, in space or time; indicating reciprocal relation or comparison

betwixt' *prep./adv. obs.* between

bev'el *n.* surface not at right angle to another; slant *—vi.* slope, slant *—vt.* cut on slant (**-ll-**) *—a.* slanted

bev'erage *n.* drink

bev'y *n.* flock or group

bewail' *vt.* lament

beware' *vi.* be on one's guard, take care

bewil'der *vt.* puzzle, confuse —**bewil'dering** *a.* —**bewil'deringly** *adv.* —**bewil'derment** *n.*

bewitch' *vt.* cast spell over; charm, fascinate —**bewitch'ing** *a.* —**bewitch'ingly** *adv.*

beyond' *adv.* farther away; besides —*prep.* on the farther side of; later than; surpassing, out of reach of

B/F brought forward

bhp brake horsepower

Bi *Chem.* bismuth

bi'as *n.* slant; personal inclination or preference; onesided inclination (*pl.* **bi'ases**) —*vt.* influence, affect (**-s-** *or* **-ss-**) —**bi'ased** *a.* prejudiced

bib *n.* cloth put under child's chin to protect clothes when eating; top of apron or overalls

Bi'ble *n.* the sacred writings of the Christian religion —**bib'lical** *a.* —**bib'licist** *n.*

bibliog'raphy *n.* list of books on a subject; history and description of books —**bibliog'rapher** *n.* —**bibliograph'ical** *a.*

bib'liophil(e) *n.* lover, collector of books —**biblioph'ily** *n.*

bib'ulous *a.* given to drinking

bicar'bonate [-bə-nit] *n.* chemical compound releasing carbon dioxide when mixed with acid

bicente'nary *n.* two hundredth anniversary; its celebration (*also* **bicentennial**)

bi'ceps *n.* two-headed muscle, *esp.* muscle of upper arm

bick'er *vi./n.* quarrel over petty things —**bick'ering** *n.*

bi'cycle *n.* vehicle with two wheels, one in front of other, pedalled by rider —**bi'cyclist** *n.*

bid *vt.* offer; say; command; invite (**bade, bid, bidd'en**) —*n.* offer, *esp.* of price; try; *Card Games* call —**bidd'er** *n.* —**bidd'ing** *n.*

bide *vi.* remain; dwell —*vt.* await —**bi'ding** *n.*

bi'det [bē'dā] *n.* low basin for washing genital area

bienn'ial [bī-en'-] *a.* happening every two years; lasting two years —*n.* plant living two years —**bienn'ially** *adv.*

bier [bēr] *n.* frame for bearing dead to grave

bifo'cal [bī-] *a.* having two different focal lengths —**bifo'cals** *pl.n.* spectacles having bifocal lenses for near and distant vision

big *a.* of great or considerable size, height, number, power *etc.* (**bigg'er** *comp.*, **bigg'est** *sup.*) —**big'ness** *n.* —**big'head** *n. inf.* conceited person —**bighead'ed** *a.* —**big shot** *inf.* important or influential person

big'amy *n.* crime of marrying a person while one is still legally married to someone else —**big'amist** *n.* —**big'amous** *a.*

bight [bīt] *n.* curve or loop in rope; long curved shoreline or water bounded by it

big'ot *n.* person intolerant or not receptive to ideas of others (*esp.* on religion, race *etc.*) —**big'oted** *a.* —**big'otry** *n.*

bike *n. short for* BICYCLE *or* MOTORBIKE

biki'ni [-kē'-] *n.* woman's brief two-piece swimming costume

bilat'eral [bī-] *a.* two-sided

bil'berry *n.* small European moorland plant with edible blue berries

bile *n.* fluid secreted by the liver; anger, ill-temper —**bil'ious** *a.* nauseous, nauseating —**bil'iousness** *n.*

bilge [-j] *n.* bottom of ship's hull; dirty water collecting there; *inf.* nonsense —*vi.* spring a leak —**bilge water**

biling'ual [bī-ling'gwəl] *a.* speaking, or written in, two languages —**bilin'gualism** *n.*

bill[1] *n.* written account of charges; draft of Act of Parliament; poster; commercial document; piece of paper money, note —*vt.* present account of charges; announce by advertisement —**bill'board** *n.* large board for displaying advertisements —**bill'fold** *n.* small folding case, *esp.* for paper money, documents *etc.* —**bill'ing** *n.* degree of importance (*esp.* in theatre *etc.*)

bill[2] *n.* bird's beak —*vi.* touch bills, as doves; caress

bill[3] *n.* tool for pruning; hooked weapon —**bill'hook** *n.* hatchet with hook at end of cutting edge

bill'abong *n.* A pool in intermittent stream

bill'et *n.* civilian quarters for troops; resting-place —*vt.* quarter, as troops

billet-doux' [bil-i-dōō'] *Fr.* love letter

bill'iards *n.* game played on table with balls and cues

bill'ion *n.* US, C thousand millions (UK orig. million millions)

bill'ow *n.* great swelling wave —*pl.* the sea —*vi.* surge; swell out

bill'y[1] *n.* policeman's truncheon

bill'y[2], **bill'ycan** *n.* can with wire handle used for boiling water on open fire

bimonth'ly *adv./a.* every two months; twice a month

bin *n.* receptacle for corn, refuse *etc.*; one particular bottling of wine

bi'nary *a.* composed of, characterized by, two; dual

bind [-ī-] *vt.* tie fast; tie round, gird; tie together; oblige; seal; constrain; bandage; cohere; unite; put (book) into cover (**bound** *pt./pp.*) —**bind'er** *n.* one who, or that which binds —**bind'ery** *n.* —**bind'ing** *n.* cover of book; tape for hem *etc.* —**bind'weed** *n.* convolvulus

binge [-nj] *n. inf.* excessive indulgence in eating or drinking; spree

bing'o [-ng'gō] *n.* game of chance in which numbers drawn are matched with those on a card

binn'acle *n.* box holding ship's compass

binoc'ular *a.* seeing with, made for both eyes —**binoc'ulars** *pl.n.* telescope made for both eyes

bino'mial [bī-] *a./n.* (denoting) algebraic expression consisting of two terms

bio- [bī-ō-] (*comb. form*) life, living, as in **biochem'istry** *n.* Such words are not given here where the meaning may easily be inferred from the simple word

biodegra'dable *a.* capable of decomposition by natural means

biog. biographical; biography

biog'raphy [bī-] *n.* story of one person's life —**biog'rapher** *n.* —**biograph'ical** *a.* —**biograph'ically** *adv.*

biol. biological; biology

biol'ogy [bī-] *n.* study of living organisms —**biolog'ical** *a.* —**biolog'ically** *adv.* —**biol'ogist** *n.*

bion'ics [bī-] *pl.n.* (*with sing. v.*) study of relation of biological and electronic processes —**bion'ic** *a.* having physical functions controlled, augmented by electronic equipment

bi'opsy *n.* examination of tissue removed surgically from a living body

bi'orhythm *n.* cyclically recurring pattern of physiological states

bipartisan' [bī-pahrt-i-zan' *or* -pahrt'-] *a.* consisting of or supported by two political parties

bipart'ite [bī-] *a.* consisting of two parts, parties

bi'ped *n.* two-footed animal —**bipe'dal** *a.*

bi'plane *n.* airplane with two pairs of wings

birch *n.* tree with silvery bark; rod for punishment, made of birch twigs —*vt.* flog

bird *n.* feathered animal; *sl.* young woman or girl

birett'a *n.* square cap worn by Catholic clergy

birl *v.* cause a floating log to spin using the feet

Bi'ro R ballpoint pen

birth *n.* bearing, or the being born, of offspring; parentage, origin; noble descent —**birth control** limitation of childbearing usu. by artificial means —**birth'day** *n.* —**birth'mark** *n.* blemish, *usu.* dark, formed on skin before birth

bis'cuit [-kit] *n.* small cake of bread leavened with soda or baking powder

bisect' [bī-] *vt.* divide into two equal parts —**bisect'or** *n.*

bisex'ual [bī-] *a.* sexually attracted to both men and women; of both sexes

bish'op *n.* clergyman governing diocese; chess piece —**bish'opric** *n.* diocese or office of a bishop

bis'muth [-z-] *n.* reddish-white metal used in medicine *etc.*

bi'son *n.* large wild ox; Amer. buffalo

bi'stro [bē'-] *n.* small restaurant

bit[1] *n.* fragment, piece; *inf.* value of eighth of dollar; biting, cutting part of tool; mouthpiece of horse's bridle

bit[2] *pt./pp. of* BITE

bit[3] *n. Computers* smallest unit of information

bitch *n.* female dog, fox or wolf; *offens. sl.* spiteful woman; *inf.* complaint —*vi. inf.* complain —**bitch'y** *a.*

bite *vt.* cut into *esp.* with teeth; grip; rise

to bait; corrode (**bit** *pt.*, **bit, bitt'en** *pp.*, **bi'ting** *pr.p.*) —*n.* act of biting; wound so made; mouthful —**bi'ter** *n.*

bitt'er *a.* sharp, sour tasting; unpleasant; (of person) angry, resentful; sarcastic —**bitt'erly** *adv.* —**bitt'erness** *n.* —**bit'ters** *pl.n.* essence of bitter herbs —**bitter end** final extremity

bitt'ern *n.* wading bird like heron

bit'umen *n.* viscous substance occurring in asphalt, tar *etc.*

bi'valve *a.* having a double shell —*n.* mollusc with such shell

biv'ouac *n.* temporary encampment of soldiers, hikers *etc.* —*vi.* pass the night in temporary camp (**biv'ouacked, biv'ouacking**)

bizarre' *a.* unusual, weird

blab *v.* reveal secrets; chatter idly (**-bb-**) —*n.* telltale; gossip

black *a.* of the darkest colour; without light; dark; evil; sombre; dishonourable —*n.* darkest colour; black dye, clothing *etc.*; (**B-**) person of dark-skinned race —*vt.* boycott (specified goods *etc.*) in industrial dispute —**black'en** *v.* —**black'ing** *n.* substance used for blacking and cleaning leather *etc.* —**black'ball** *vt.* vote against, exclude —**black'berry** *n.* plant with thorny stems and dark juicy berries, bramble —**black'bird** *n.* common European songbird —**black'board** *n.* UK chalkboard —**black box** *inf. name for* FLIGHT RECORDER —**black'cap** *n.* type of warbler —**black'cock** *n.* male of the black grouse —**black'head** *n.* dark, fatty plug blocking pore in skin —**black'leg** *n.* UK scab; disease of cattle —**black'list** *n.* list of people, organizations considered suspicious, untrustworthy *etc.* —*vt.* put on blacklist —**Black Mari'a** UK patrol wagon —**black market** illegal buying and selling of goods —**black'thorn** *n.* shrub with black twigs —**black'top** *n.* bitumen for paving; road paved with this —**black widow** highly poisonous Amer. spider

black'guard [blag'ahrd] *n.* scoundrel —*a.* unprincipled, wicked —*vt.* revile —**black'guardism** *n.* —**black'guardly** *a.*

black'mail *vt.* extort money from (a person) by threats —*n.* act of blackmailing; money extorted thus —**black'mailer** *n.*

black'out *n.* complete failure of electricity supply; sudden cutting off of all stagelights; state of temporary unconsciousness; obscuring of all lights as precaution against night air attack —*v.*

black'smith *n.* smith who works in iron

bladd'er *n.* membranous bag to contain liquid, *esp.* urinary bladder

blade *n.* edge, cutting part of knife or tool; leaf of grass *etc.*; sword; *obs.* dashing fellow; flat of oar

blain *n.* inflamed swelling; pimple, blister

blame *n.* censure; culpability —*vt.* find fault with; censure —**blam(e)'able** *a.* —**blame'less** *a.* —**blame'worthy** *a.*

blanch [-ah-] *v.* whiten, bleach, take colour out of; (of foodstuffs) briefly boil or fry; turn pale

blancmange' [blə-monzh'] *n.* jellylike dessert made with milk

bland *a.* devoid of distinctive characteristics; smooth in manner

bland'ish *vt.* coax; flatter —**blan'dishment** *n.*

blank *a.* without marks or writing; empty; vacant, confused; (of verse) without rhyme —*n.* empty space; void; cartridge containing no bullet —**blank'ly** *adv.*

blank'et *n.* thick (woollen) covering for bed; concealing cover —*vt.* cover with blanket; cover, stifle

blare *v.* sound loudly and harshly —*n.* such sound

blar'ney *n.* flattering talk

blas'é [blah'zā] *a.* indifferent through familiarity; bored

blaspheme' *v.* show contempt for God or sacred things, *esp.* in speech —**blasphe'mer** *n.* —**blas'phemous** *a.* —**blas'phemously** *adv.* —**blas'phemy** *n.*

blast [-ahst] *n.* explosion; high-pressure wave of air coming from an explosion; current of air; gust of wind or air; loud sound; *sl.* reprimand —*vt.* blow up; remove, open *etc.* by explosion; blight; ruin —**blast furnace** furnace for smelting ore, using preheated blast of air

bla'tant *a.* obvious —**bla'tancy** *n.*

blaze[1] *n.* strong fire or flame; brightness;

outburst *—vi.* burn strongly; be very angry

blaze² *v.* (mark trees to) establish trail *—n.* mark on tree; white mark on horse's face

blaze³ *vt.* proclaim, publish (as with trumpet) *—n.* wide publicity

bla'zer *n.* type of jacket worn *esp.* for sports

bla'zon *vt.* make public, proclaim; describe, depict (arms) *—n.* coat of arms

bleach *v.* make or become white *—n.* bleaching substance

bleak¹ *a.* cold and cheerless; exposed —**bleak'ly** *adv.*

bleak² *n.* small, silvery fish

blear'y(-eyed) *a.* with eyes dimmed, as with tears, sleep

bleat *v.* cry, as sheep; say, speak, plaintively *—n.* sheep's cry

bleed *vi.* lose blood *—vt.* draw blood or liquid from; extort money from (**bled** *pt./pp.*)

bleep *n.* short high-pitched sound —**bleep'er** *n.* small portable electronic signalling device

blem'ish *n.* defect; stain *—vt.* make (something) defective, dirty *etc.* —**blem'ished** *a.*

blench *vi.* start back, flinch

blend *vt.* mix *—n.* mixture —**blend'er** *n.* one who, that which blends, *esp.* electrical kitchen appliance for mixing food

bles'bok *n.* S Afr. antelope

bless *vt.* consecrate; give thanks to; ask God's favour for; (*usu. passive*) endow (with); glorify; make happy (**blessed, blest** *pp.*) —**bless'ed** *a.* —**bless'edness** *n.* —**bless'ing** *n.* (ceremony asking for) God's protection, aid; short prayer; approval; welcome event, benefit

bleth'er [-TH-] *n.* nonsense, gossip *—vi. also* **blath'er**

blew *pt. of* BLOW

blight [blīt] *n.* plant disease; harmful influence *—vt.* injure as with blight

blight'er [blīt'-] *n. inf.* fellow, person

blimp *n.* small, nonrigid airship used for observing

blind [-ī-] *a.* unable to see; heedless, random; dim; closed at one end; *sl.* very drunk *—vt.* deprive of sight *—n.* something cutting off light; window screen; pretext; place of concealment *eg* for hunter —**blind'ly** *adv.* —**blind'ness** *n.* —**blind'ers** *pl.n.* leather flaps to prevent horse from seeing to the side —**blind flying** navigation of aircraft by use of instruments alone —**blind'fold** *vt.* cover the eyes of so as to prevent vision *—n./a.* —**blind man's buff** game in which one player is blindfolded

blink *vi.* wink; twinkle; shine intermittently *—n.* gleam —**blink'ers** *pl.n.* **UK** blinders —**blink at** see, know about, but ignore —**on the blink** *inf.* not working (properly)

blip *n.* repetitive sound or visible pulse, *eg* on radar screen

bliss *n.* perfect happiness —**bliss'ful** *a.* —**bliss'fully** *adv.* —**bliss'fulness** *n.*

blis'ter *n.* bubble on skin; surface swelling, *eg* on paint *—v.* form blisters (on) —**blis'tering** *a.* (of verbal attack) bitter —**blister pack** package for goods with hard, raised, transparent cover

blithe [blīTH] *a.* happy, gay —**blithe'ly** *adv.* —**blithe'ness** *n.*

BLitt Bachelor of Letters

blitz *n.* sudden, concentrated attack

blizz'ard *n.* blinding storm of wind and snow

bloat *v.* puff or swell out *—n.* distension of stomach of cow *etc.* by gas —**bloat'ed** *a.* swollen —**bloat'er** *n.* smoked herring

blob *n.* soft mass, *esp.* drop of liquid; shapeless form

bloc *n.* (political) grouping of people or countries

block *n.* solid (rectangular) piece of wood, stone *etc.* , *esp. Hist.* that on which people were beheaded ; obstacle; stoppage; pulley with frame; large building of offices, flats *etc.*; group of buildings; area enclosed by intersecting streets *—vt.* obstruct, stop up; shape on block; sketch (in) —**block'age** *n.* obstruction —**block'head** *n.* fool, simpleton —**block letters** written capital letters

blockade' *n.* physical prevention of access, *esp.* to port *etc. —vt.*

bloke *n. inf.* fellow, chap

blond *a.* (of hair) light-coloured *—n.* someone with blond hair (**blonde** *fem.*)

blood [blud] *n.* red fluid in veins; race; kindred; good parentage; temperament; passion *—vt.* initiate (into hunting, war *etc.*) —**blood'ily** *adv.* —**blood'less** *a.* —**blood'y** *a.* covered in blood; slaughterous *—a./adv. sl.* a common intensifier

—*v.* make bloody —**blood bank** (institution managing) store of human blood preserved for transfusion —**blood'hound** *n.* breed of large hound noted for keen powers of scent —**blood'shed** *n.* slaughter, killing —**blood'shot** *a.* inflamed (said of eyes) —**blood sport** sport in which animals are killed, *eg* fox-hunting —**blood'sucker** *n.* parasite (*eg* mosquito) living on host's blood; parasitic person —**blood test** examination of sample of blood —**blood'thirsty** *a.* murderous, cruel —**blood transfusion** transfer of blood from one person to another

bloom *n.* flower of plant; blossoming; prime, perfection; glow; powdery deposit on fruit —*vi.* be in flower; flourish —**bloom'ing** *a.*

bloom'ers *pl.n.* wide, baggy knickers

bloop'er *n. inf.* ludicrous mistake

bloss'om *n.* flower; flower bud —*vi.* flower; develop

blot *n.* spot, stain; disgrace —*vt.* spot, stain; obliterate; detract from; soak up ink *etc.* from (**-tt-**) —**blott'er, blotting pad** —**blotting paper**

blotch *n.* dark spot on skin —*vt.* make spotted —**blotch'y** *a.*

blouse [-owz] *n.* light, loose upper garment

blow[1] [blō] *vi.* make a current of air; pant; emit sound —*vt.* drive air upon or into; drive by current of air; sound; spout (of whales); fan; *sl.* squander (**blew, blown**) —*n.* blast; gale —**blow'er** *n.* —**blow-dry** *vt.* style hair after washing using blast of hot air —*n.* —**blow'fly** *n.* fly which infects food *etc.* —**blow'pipe** *n.* dart tube —**blow-out** *n.* sudden puncture in tyre; uncontrolled escape of oil, gas, from well; *sl.* large meal —**blow out** extinguish; (of tyre) puncture suddenly; (of fuse) melt —**blow'torch** *n.* small burner with very hot flame, for removing paint *etc.* —**blow up** explode; inflate; enlarge (photograph); *inf.* lose one's temper

blow[2] [blō] *n.* stroke, knock; sudden misfortune, loss

blown *pp. of* BLOW[1]

blowz'y *a.* slovenly, sluttish; red-faced

blubb'er *vi.* weep —*n.* fat of whales; weeping

bludg'eon [bluj'ən] *n.* short thick club —*vt.* strike with one; coerce (someone into)

blue *a.* of the colour of sky or shades of that colour; livid; depressed; indecent —*n.* the colour; dye or pigment; indigo powder used in laundering —*vt.* make blue; dip in blue liquid (**blued** *pt./pp.*) —**blues** *pl.n. inf.* (*oft. with sing. v.*) depression; form of Amer. Negro folk song in slow tempo, employed in jazz music —**blu'ish** *a.* —**blue baby** baby born with bluish skin caused by heart defect —**blue'bell** *n.* wild spring flower —**blue'berry** *n.* N Amer. shrub with blue-black edible berries —**blue blood** royal or aristocratic descent —**blue'book** *n.* annual statement of government accounts —**blue'bottle** *n.* blowfly —**blue-collar** *a.* denoting manual industrial workers —**blue goose** bluish-grey variety of snow goose —**blue-pencil** *vt.* alter, delete parts of, *esp.* to censor —**blue'print** *n.* copy of drawing; original plan —**blue'stocking** *n.* scholarly, intellectual woman

bluff[1] *n.* cliff, steep bank; clump of trees —*a.* hearty; blunt; steep; abrupt

bluff[2] *vt.* deceive by pretence of strength —*n.* pretence

blun'der *n.* clumsy mistake —*vi.* make stupid mistake; act clumsily

blun'derbuss *n.* obsolete short gun with wide bore

blunt *a.* not sharp; (of speech) abrupt —*vt.* make blunt —**blunt'ly** *adv.* —**blunt'ness** *n.*

blur *v.* make, become less distinct (**-rr-**) —*n.* something vague, indistinct —**blur'ry** *a.*

blurb *n.* statement advertising, recommending book *etc.*

blurt *vt.* utter suddenly or unadvisedly (*usually with* out)

blush *vi.* become red in face; be ashamed; redden —*n.* this effect —**blush'er** *n.* cosmetic to give rosy colour to face

blus'ter *vi./n.* (indulge in) noisy, aggressive behaviour —**blus'tering, blus'tery** *a.* (of wind *etc.*) noisy and gusty

BMX bicycle motocross; bicycle for such riding

BO *inf.* body odour; box office

bo'a *n.* large, nonvenomous snake; long scarf of fur or feathers
boar *n.* male pig; wild pig
board *n.* broad, flat piece of wood ; sheet of rigid material for specific purpose; table; meals; group of people who administer company; governing body; thick, stiff paper *—pl.* theatre, stage; wooden enclosure where ice hockey, box lacrosse is played *—vt.* cover with planks; supply food daily; enter ship *etc.* *—vi.* take daily meals **—board'er** *n.* **—boarding house** lodging house where meals may be had **—boarding school** school providing living accommodation for pupils **—board'room** *n.* room where board of company meets **—board'walk** *n.* promenade, *esp.* along beach, *usu.* made of planks **—above board** beyond suspicion **—on board** in or into ship
boast *vi.* speak too much in praise of oneself, one's possessions *—vt.* brag of; have to show *—n.* something boasted (of) **—boast'er** *n.* **—boast'ful** *a.* **—boast'fully** *adv.* **—boast'fulness** *n.*
boat *n.* small open vessel; ship *—vi.* sail about in boat **—boat'er** *n.* flat straw hat **—boat'ing** *n.* **—boat'hook** *n.* **—boat'house** *n.* **—boat'man** *n.* **—boat'swain** [bō'sən] *n.* ship's officer in charge of boats, sails *etc.*
bob *vi.* move up and down *—vt.* move jerkily; cut (women's) hair short (**-bb-**) *—n.* short, jerking motion; short hairstyle; weight on pendulum *etc.*; *inf.* formerly, shilling **—bobbed** *a.*
bobb'in *n.* cylinder on which thread is wound
bob'ble *n.* small, tufted ball for decoration
bobb'y *n.* **UK** *inf.* policeman
bobby pin *n.* metal hairpin bent to hold hair in place
bob'cat *n.* Amer. wild cat, bay lynx
bob'olink *n.* Amer. songbird
bob'sled *n.* racing sled with steering mechanism
bode *vt.* be an omen of
bod'ice [-is] *n.* upper part of woman's dress
bod'kin *n.* large blunt needle; tool for piercing holes
bod'y *n.* whole frame of man or animal; main part of such frame; corpse; main part of anything; substance; mass; person; number of persons united or organized; matter, opposed to spirit **—bod'iless** *a.* **—bod'ily** *a./adv.* **—bod'yguard** *n.* escort to protect important person **—body popping** 1980s dance with schematic, mechanical movements (*also* **robotics, robot dancing**) **—bod'ywork** *n.* shell of motor vehicle
Boer [boor] *n.* a S Afr. of Dutch or Huguenot descent *—a.*
boff'in *n.* *inf.* scientist, technical research worker
bog *n.* wet, soft ground; **UK** *sl.* lavatory **—bogg'y** *a.* marshy **—bog down** stick as in a bog
bo'gan *n.* sluggish side stream
bo'gey *n.* evil or mischievous spirit; standard golf score for a good player **—bo'geyman** *n.*
bog'gle *vi.* stare, be surprised
bo'gie *n.* low truck on four wheels; pivoted undercarriage, as on railway rolling stock
bo'gus *a.* sham, false
bohe'mian (*also* **B-**) *a.* unconventional *—n.* one who leads an unsettled life **—bohe'mianism** *n.*
boil[1] *vi.* change from liquid to gas, *esp.* by heating; become cooked by boiling; bubble; be agitated; seethe; *inf.* be hot; *inf.* be angry *—vt.* cause to boil; cook by boiling *—n.* boiling state **—boil'er** *n.* vessel for boiling **—boiler suit** garment covering whole body **—boiling point** temperature at which boiling occurs (100°C for water)
boil[2] *n.* inflamed suppurating swelling on skin
boi'sterous *a.* wild; noisy; turbulent **—boi'sterously** *adv.* **—boi'sterousness** *n.*
bold *a.* daring, fearless; presumptuous; striking, prominent **—bold'ly** *adv.* **—bold'ness** *n.*
bole *n.* trunk of a tree
bole'ro [-ā'-] *n.* Spanish dance; [bol'ə-rō] short loose jacket
boll [-ō-] *n.* seed capsule of cotton, flax *etc.*
boll'ard *n.* post on quay or ship to secure mooring lines; short post in road, footpath as barrier or marker
Bol'shevik *n.* violent revolutionary **—bol'shy, bol'shie** *a.* *inf.* rebellious, uncooperative; left-wing

bo'lster *vt.* support, uphold —*n.* long pillow; pad, support

bolt [bō-] *n.* bar or pin (*esp.* with thread for nut); rush; discharge of lightning; roll of cloth —*vt.* fasten with bolt; swallow hastily —*vi.* rush away; break from control

bomb [bom] *n.* explosive projectile; any explosive device; *sl.* large amount of money; *sl.* disastrous failure —*vt.* attack with bombs; *sl.* fail disastrously, flop —**bombard'** *vt.* shell; attack (verbally) —**bombardier'** *n.* artillery noncommissioned officer; snow tractor with caterpillar tracks at rear and skis at front —**bombard'ment** *n.* —**bomb'er** *n.* aircraft capable of carrying bombs —**bomb'shell** *n.* shell of bomb; surprise; *inf.* very attractive girl —**the bomb** nuclear bomb

bom'bast *n.* pompous language; pomposity —**bombas'tic** *a.*

bo'na fi'de [-di] *Lat.* genuine(ly); sincere(ly) —**bona fides** good faith, sincerity

bonan'za *n.* sudden good luck or wealth; mine or vein rich in ore

bond *n.* that which binds; link, union; written promise to pay money or carry out contract —*vt.* bind; store goods until duty is paid on them —**bond'ed** *a.* placed in bond; mortgaged

bond'age *n.* slavery

bone *n.* hard substance forming animal's skeleton; piece of this —*pl.* essentials —*vt.* take out bone —*vi. inf.* (*with* up) study hard —**bone'less** *a.* —**bo'ny** *a.* —**bone'head** *n. inf.* stupid person

bon'fire *n.* large outdoor fire

bon'go *n.* small drum, usu. one of a pair, played with the fingers (*pl.* **-go(e)s**)

bon'homie [bon'ə-mi] *n. Fr.* good humour, geniality

bonk'ers *a. sl.* crazy

bonn'et *n.* hat with strings; cap; **UK** hood of automobile

bonn'y *a.* beautiful, handsome —**bon'nily** *adv.*

bon'sai [-sī] *n.* (art of growing) dwarf trees, shrubs

bon'tebok [-buk] *n.* S Afr. antelope

bo'nus *n.* extra (unexpected) payment or gift (*pl.* **bo'nuses**)

boo *interj.* expression of disapproval or contempt; exclamation to surprise *esp.* child —*v.*

boob *n. sl.* foolish mistake; female breast

boob'y *n.* fool; tropical marine bird —**booby prize** mock prize for poor performance —**booby trap** harmless-looking object which explodes when disturbed; form of practical joke

boo'dle *n. sl.* money

boog'ie-woog'ie *n.* kind of jazz piano playing, emphasizing a rolling bass in syncopated eighth notes

book *n.* collection of sheets of paper bound together; literary work; main division of this —*vt.* reserve room, ticket *etc.*; charge with legal offence; enter name in book —**book'ing** *n.* reservation —**book'ish** *a.* studious, fond of reading —**book'binder** *n.* —**book'case** *n.* —**book-keeping** *n.* systematic recording of business transactions —**book'let** *n.* —**book'maker** *n.* one whose work is taking bets (*also inf.* **book'ie**) —**book'worm** *n.* great reader

boom[1] *n.* sudden commercial activity; prosperity —*vi.* become active, prosperous

boom[2] *vi./n.* (make) loud, deep sound

boom[3] *n.* long spar, as for stretching the bottom of a sail; barrier across harbour; pole carrying overhead microphone *etc.*

boo'merang *n.* curved wooden missile of Aust. Aborigines, which returns to the thrower —*vi.* recoil; return unexpectedly; backfire

boon *n.* something helpful, favour

boor *n.* rude person —**boor'ish** *a.*

boost *n.* encouragement, help; upward push; increase —*vt.* —**boost'er** *n.* person or thing that supports, increases power *etc.*

boot[1] *n.* covering for the foot and ankle; **UK** trunk of automobile; *inf.* kick —*vt. inf.* kick —**boot'ed** *a.* —**boot'ee** *n.* baby's soft shoe

boot[2] *n.* profit, use —**boot'less** *a.* fruitless, vain —**to boot** in addition

booth [-TH] *n.* stall; cubicle

boot'leg *v.* make, carry, sell illicit goods, *esp.* alcohol —*a.* —**boot'legger** *n.*

boo'ty *n.* plunder, spoil

booze *n./vi. inf.* (consume) alcoholic drink —**booz'er** *n. inf.* person fond of drinking; **UK** bar or pub —**booz'y** *a. inf.* —**booze-up** *n. inf.* drinking spree

bor'ax *n.* white soluble substance, compound of boron —**borac'ic** *a.*

bord'er *n.* margin; frontier; limit; strip of garden —*v.* provide with border; adjoin

bore[1] *vt.* pierce, making a hole —*n.* hole; calibre of gun —**bor'er** *n.* instrument for making holes; insect which bores holes

bore[2] *vt.* make weary by repetition *etc.* —*n.* tiresome person or thing —**bore'dom** *n.* —**bor'ing** *a.*

bore[3] *n.* tidal wave which rushes up river estuary

bore[4] *pt. of* BEAR[1]

born *pp. of* BEAR[1]

bor'on *n.* chemical element used in hardening steel, *etc.*

bor'ough [bu'rə] *n.* town

borr'ow *vt.* obtain on loan or trust; appropriate —**borr'ower** *n.*

bor'zoi *n.* breed of tall hound with long, silky coat

bosh *n. inf.* nonsense

bos'om [booz'-] *n.* human breast; seat of passions and feelings

boss[1] *n.* person in charge of or employing others —*vt.* be in charge of; be domineering over —**boss'y** *a.* overbearing

boss[2] *n.* knob or stud; raised ornament —*vt.* emboss

bot. botanical; botany; bottle

bot'any *n.* study of plants —**botan'ic(al)** *a.* —**bot'anist** *n.*

botch *vt.* spoil by clumsiness —**botch-up** *n.* mess

both [bō-] *a./pron.* the two —*adv./conj.* as well

both'er [-TH'-] *vt.* pester; perplex —*vi./n.* fuss, trouble

bot'tle *n.* vessel for holding liquid; its contents —*vt.* put into bottle; restrain —**bot'tler** *n.* —**bot'tlebrush** *n.* cylindrical brush for cleaning bottle —**bot'tleneck** *n.* narrow outlet which impedes smooth flow of traffic or production of goods

bott'om *n.* lowest part of anything; bed of sea, river *etc.*; buttocks —*vt.* put bottom to; base (upon); get to bottom of —**bott'omless** *a.*

bot'ulism *n.* kind of food poisoning

bou'clé [boo'klā] *n.* looped yarn giving knobbly effect

bou'doir [boo'dwahr] *n.* lady's private sitting-room; bedroom

bougainvill'(a)ea [boo-gən-vil'i-ə] *n.* (sub)tropical climbing plant with red or purple bracts

bough [bow] *n.* branch of tree

bought *pt./pp. of* BUY

boul'der [bōl'-] *n.* large weatherworn rounded stone

boule'vard [bool'vahr, -vahrd] *n.* broad street or promenade

bounce *v.* (cause to) rebound (repeatedly) on impact, as a ball —*n.* rebounding; quality in object causing this; *inf.* vitality, vigour —**bounc'er** *n. esp.* one employed to evict undesirables (forcibly) —**bounc'ing** *a.* vigorous, robust —**bounc'y** *a.* lively

bound[1] *n./vt.* limit —**bound'ary** *n.* —**bound'ed** *a.* —**bound'less** *a.*

bound[2] *vi./n.* spring, leap

bound[3] *a.* on a specified course, as **outward bound**

bound[4] *pt./pp. of* BIND —*a.* committed; certain; tied

boun'ty *n.* liberality; gift; premium —**boun'teous, boun'tiful** *a.* liberal, generous

bouquet' [boo-kā'] *n.* bunch of flowers; perfume of wine ; compliment

bour'bon [bur'-] *n.* whiskey made from corn

bour'geois [boor'zhwah] *n./a.* (*oft. disparaging*) middle class; smugly conventional (person)

bout *n.* period of time spent doing something; contest, fight

boutique' [boo-tēk'] *n.* small shop, *esp.* one selling clothes

bo'vine *a.* of the ox or cow; oxlike; stolid, dull

bow[1] [bō] *n.* weapon for shooting arrows; implement for playing violin *etc.*; ornamental knot of ribbon *etc.*; bend, bent line; rainbow —*v.* bend —**bow-legged** *a.* bandy —**bow window** one with outward curve

bow[2] [bow] *vi.* bend body in respect, assent *etc.*; submit —*vt.* bend downwards; cause to stoop; crush —*n.*

bow[3] [bow] *n.* fore end of ship; prow; rower nearest bow

bowd'lerize *vt.* expurgate

bow'el *n.* (*oft. pl.*) part of intestine (*esp.*

with reference to defecation); inside of anything

bow'er *n.* shady retreat; inner room

bowl[1] [-ō-] *n.* round vessel, deep basin; drinking cup; hollow

bowl[2] [-ō-] *n.* wooden ball —*pl.* game played with such balls —*v.* roll or throw ball in various ways —**bowl'er** *n.* —**bowling alley** —**bowling green**

bowl'er [-ō-] *n.* **UK** derby

bow'ser *n.* fuel tanker

bow'sprit [bō'-] *n.* spar projecting from ship's bow

box[1] *n.* (wooden) container, usu. rectangular with lid; its contents; small enclosure; any boxlike cubicle, shelter or receptacle (*eg* letter box) —*vt.* put in box; confine —**box lacrosse** indoor lacrosse —**box the compass** make complete turn

box[2] *v.* fight with fists, *esp.* with padded gloves on —*vt.* strike —*n.* blow —**box'er** *n.* one who boxes; breed of large dog resembling bulldog

box[3] *n.* evergreen shrub used for hedges

boy *n.* male child; young man —*interj.* exclamation of surprise —**boy'hood** *n.*

boy'cott *vt.* refuse to deal with or participate in —*n.*

Br *Chem.* bromine

Br. Breton; Britain; British

br. branch; bronze; brother

bra [brah] *n. abbrev. of* BRASSIERE

brace *n.* tool for boring; clasp, clamp; pair, couple; strut, support —*pl.* **UK** suspenders —*vt.* steady (oneself) as before a blow; support, make firm —**bra'cing** *a.* invigorating —**brace'let** *n.* ornament for the arm —*pl. sl.* handcuffs

brack'en *n.* large fern

brack'et *n.* support for shelf *etc.*; group —*pl.* marks [ ], () used to enclose words *etc.* —*vt.* enclose in brackets; connect

brack'ish *a.* (of water) slightly salty

bract *n.* small scalelike leaf

brad *n.* small nail —**brad'awl** *n.* small boring tool

brag *vi.* boast (**-gg-**) —*n.* boastful talk —**bragg'art** *n.*

Brah'man, Brah'min *n.* member of priestly Hindu caste; breed of beef cattle

braid *vt.* interweave; trim with braid —*n.* length of anything interwoven or plaited; ornamental tape

braille [brāl] *n.* system of printing for blind, with arrangements of raised dots instead of letters

brain *n.* mass of nerve tissue in head; intellect —*vt.* kill by hitting on head —**brain'less** *a.* —**brain'y** *a.* —**brain'-child** *n.* invention —**brain'storm** *n.* sudden mental aberration; (*also* **brain wave**) sudden, clever idea —**brains trust** group of knowledgeable people who answer questions in panel games, quizzes *etc.* —**brain'wash** *vt.* change, distort a person's ideas or beliefs

braise [-āz] *vt.* stew in covered pan

brake[1] *n.* instrument for retarding motion of wheel on vehicle —*vt.* apply brake to

brake[2] *n.* fern; bracken; thicket; brushwood

bram'ble *n.* prickly shrub; blackberry —**bram'bly** *a.*

bram'bling *n.* type of finch

bran *n.* sifted husks of corn

branch [-ah-] *n.* limb of tree; offshoot or subsidiary part of something larger or primary —*vi.* bear branches; diverge; spread —**branched** *a.*

brand *n.* trademark; class of goods; particular kind, sort; mark made by hot iron; burning piece of wood; sword; mark of infamy —*vt.* burn with iron; mark; stigmatize —**brand-new** *a.* absolutely new

bran'dish *vt.* flourish, wave (weapon *etc.*)

bran'dy *n.* spirit distilled from wine

brash *a.* bold, impudent

brass [-ah-] *n.* alloy of copper and zinc; group of brass wind instruments forming part of orchestra or band; *inf.* money; *inf.* (army) officers —*a.* —**brass'y** *a.* showy; harsh

brass'iere *n.* woman's undergarment, supporting breasts

brat *n. contemptuous name for* a child

bravad'o [-vahd'-] *n.* showy display of boldness

brave *a.* bold, courageous; splendid, fine —*n.* warrior —*vt.* defy, meet boldly —**brave'ly** *adv.* —**bra'very** *n.*

bravo' [brah-] *interj.* well done!

brawl *vi.* fight noisily —*n.* —**brawl'-er** *n.*

brawn *n.* muscle; strength; **UK** pickled pork —**brawn'y** *a.* muscular

bray *n.* donkey's cry —*vi.* utter this; give

out harsh, or loud, sounds

braze *vt.* solder with alloy of brass or zinc

bra'zen *a.* of, like brass; impudent, shameless —*vt.* (*usu. with* out) face, carry through with impudence —**bra'zenness** *n.* effrontery —**bra'zier** *n.* brassworker

bra'zier *n.* pan for burning charcoal or coals

breach *n.* break, opening; breaking of rule, duty *etc.*; quarrel —*vt.* make a gap in

bread [-ed] *n.* food made of flour or meal baked; food; *sl.* money —**bread'fruit** *n.* breadlike fruit found in Pacific Islands —**bread'winner** *n.* person supporting dependants by his earnings

breadth [-edth] *n.* extent across, width; largeness of view, mind

break [brāk] *vt.* part by force; shatter; burst, destroy; fail to observe; disclose; interrupt; surpass; make bankrupt; relax; mitigate; accustom (horse) to being ridden; decipher (code) —*vi.* become broken, shattered, divided; open, appear; come suddenly; crack, give way; part, fall out; (of voice) change in tone, pitch (**broke, bro'ken**) —*n.* fracture; gap; opening; separation; interruption; respite; interval; *inf.* opportunity; dawn; *Billiards* consecutive series of successful strokes; *Boxing* separation after a clinch —**break'able** *a.* —**break'age** *n.* —**break'er** *n.* one that breaks, *eg* electrical circuit breaker; wave beating on rocks or shore —**break dance** acrobatic dance style of 1980s —**break'down** *n.* collapse, as nervous breakdown; failure to function effectively; analysis —**break'fast** [brek'-] *n.* first meal of the day —**break-in** *n.* illegal entering of building, *esp.* by thieves —**break'neck** *a.* dangerous —**break'through** *n.* important advance —**break-up** *n.* thawing of ice in lakes and rivers in springtime —**break'water** *n.* barrier to break force of waves

bream *n.* broad, thin fish

breast [brest] *n.* human chest; milk-secreting gland on chest of human female; seat of the affections; any protuberance —*vt.* face, oppose; reach summit of —**breast'stroke** *n.* stroke in swimming

breath [breth] *n.* air used by lungs; life; respiration; slight breeze —**breathe** [brēTH] *vi.* inhale and exhale air from lungs; live; pause, rest —*vt.* inhale and exhale; utter softly, whisper —**brea'ther** [-TH-] *n.* short rest —**brea'thing** [-TH-] *n.* —**breath'less** *a.* —**breath'taking** *a.* causing awe or excitement

Breath'alyser R device that estimates amount of alcohol in breath —**breath'alyse** *vt.*

bred *pt./pp. of* BREED

breech *n.* buttocks; hinder part of anything, *esp.* gun —**breech'es** [brich'iz] *pl.n.* trousers —**breech'loader** *n.*

breed *vt.* generate, bring forth, give rise to; rear —*vi.* be produced; be with young (**bred** *pt./pp.*) —*n.* offspring produced; race, kind —**breed'er** *n.* —**breed'ing** *n.* producing; manners; ancestry —**breeder reactor** nuclear reactor producing more fissionable material than it consumes

breeze *n.* gentle wind —**breez'ily** *adv.* —**breez'y** *a.* windy; jovial, lively; casual

breeze block light building brick made of ashes bonded by cement

breth'ren [-TH-] *n. pl. of* BROTHER, *obs.* except in religious contexts

breve *n.* long musical note

brev'iary [*or* brē'-] *n.* book of daily prayers of R.C. Church

brev'ity *n.* conciseness of expression; short duration

brew [-ōō] *vt.* prepare liquor, as beer from malt *etc.*; make drink, as tea, by infusion; plot, contrive —*vi.* be in preparation —*n.* beverage produced by brewing —**brew'er** *n.* —**brew'ery** *n.* —**brew'ing** *n.*

bri'ar[1], **bri'er**[1] *n.* prickly shrub, *esp.* the wild rose

bri'ar[2], **bri'er**[2] *n.* European shrub —**briar pipe** made from its root

bribe *n.* anything offered or given to someone to gain favour, influence —*vt.* influence by bribe —**bri'ber** *n.* —**bri'bery** *n.*

bric'-a-brac *n.* miscellaneous small objects, used for ornament

brick *n.* oblong mass of hardened clay used in building —*vt.* build, block *etc.* with bricks —**brick'layer** *n.*

bride *n.* woman about to be, or just, married —**bri'dal** *a.* of, relating to, a bride or wedding —**bride'groom** *n.*

man about to be, or just, married —**brides'maid** *n.*

bridge[1] *n.* structure for crossing river *etc.*; something joining or supporting other parts; raised narrow platform on ship; upper part of nose; part of violin supporting strings —*vt.* make bridge over, span —**bridge'head** *n.* advanced position established on enemy territory

bridge[2] *n.* card game

bri'dle *n.* headgear of horse harness; curb —*vt.* put on bridle; restrain —*vi.* show resentment —**bridle path** path suitable for riding horses

brief *a.* short in duration; concise; scanty —*n.* summary of case for counsel's use; papal letter; instructions —*pl.* underpants; panties —*vt.* give instructions —**brief'ly** *adv.* —**brief'ness** *n.* —**brief'case** *n.* hand case for carrying papers

bri'er *see* BRIAR

brig *n.* two-masted, square-rigged ship

Brig. Brigade; Brigadier

brigade' *n.* subdivision of army; organized band —**brigadier'** *n.* high-ranking army officer, usu. in charge of a brigade —**brigadier-general** *n.* army officer next above a colonel

brig'antine *n.* two-masted vessel, with square-rigged foremast and fore-and-aft mainmast

bright [brīt] *a.* shining; full of light; cheerful; clever —**bright'en** *v.* —**bright'ly** *adv.* —**bright'ness** *n.*

brill *n.* European food fish

brill'iant *a.* shining; sparkling; splendid; very clever; distinguished —**brill'iance, brill'iancy** *n.* —**brill'iantly** *adv.*

brim *n.* margin, edge, *esp.* of river, cup, hat —**brimful'** *a.* —**brim'less** *a.* —**brim'ming** *a.*

brim'stone *n.* sulphur

brin'dle(d) *a.* spotted and streaked

brine *n.* salt water; pickle —**bri'ny** *a.* very salty —*n. inf.* the sea

bring *vt.* fetch; carry with one; cause to come (**brought** *pt./pp.*)

brink *n.* edge of steep place; verge, margin

briquette' [-ket'] *n.* block of compressed coal dust

brisk *a.* active, vigorous —**brisk'ly** *adv.* —**brisk'ness** *n.*

brisk'et *n.* joint of meat from breast of animal

bris'tle [-is'l] *n.* short stiff hair —*vi.* stand erect; show temper —**bris'tliness** *n.* —**bris'tly** *a.*

Brit. Britain; Britannia; British

British thermal unit unit of heat equal to 1055 joules

brit'tle *a.* easily broken, fragile; curt, irritable —**brit'tleness** *n.*

broach *vt.* pierce (cask); open, begin

broad [-aw-] *a.* wide, spacious, open; plain, obvious; coarse; general; tolerant; (of pronunciation) dialectal —**broad'en** *vt.* —**broad'ly** *adv.* —**broad'ness** *n.* —**broad'cast** *vt.* transmit by radio or television; make widely known; scatter, as seed —*n.* radio or television programme —**broad'caster** *n.* —**broad-minded** *a.* tolerant; generous —**broad'side** *n.* discharge of all guns on one side; strong (verbal) attack

brocade' *n.* rich woven fabric with raised design

brocc'oli *n.* type of cabbage

bro'chure [-shə] *n.* pamphlet, booklet

brogue [-ōg] *n.* stout shoe; dialect, *esp.* Irish accent

broil[1] *n.* noisy quarrel

broil[2] *vt.* cook over hot coals; grill —*vi.* be heated

broke *pt.* —**bro'ken** *pp. of* BREAK —*a. inf.* penniless

bro'ker *n.* one employed to buy and sell for others; dealer —**bro'kerage** *n.* payment to broker

broll'y *n. inf.* umbrella

bro'mide *n.* chemical compound used in medicine and photography —**bromide paper** photographic printing paper, treated with silver bromide

bro'mine [-mēn] *n.* liquid element used in production of chemicals —**bro'mic** *a.*

bron'chi, -ia [-ng'k-] *pl.n.* branches of windpipe —**bronch'ial** *a.* —**bronchi'tis** *n.* inflammation of bronchi

bronc'o *n.* Amer. half-tamed horse (*pl.* **-cos**)

brontosau'rus *n.* very large herbivorous dinosaur

bronze *n.* alloy of copper and tin —*a.* made of, or coloured like, bronze —*vt.* give appearance of bronze to —**bronzed** *a.* coated with bronze; sunburnt

brooch [-ō-] *n.* ornamental pin or fastening

brood [-ōō-] *n.* family of young, *esp.* of birds; tribe, race —*v.* sit, as hen on eggs; meditate, fret over —**brood'y** *a.* moody, sullen

brook[1] [-ōō-] *n.* small stream —**brook'let** *n.* —**brook trout** Amer. freshwater trout

brook[2] [-ōō-] *vt.* put up with, endure, tolerate

broom [-ōō-] *n.* brush for sweeping; yellow-flowered shrub —**broom'stick** *n.* handle of broom

bros. brothers

broth *n.* thin soup

broth'el *n.* house of prostitution

broth'er [-uTH'-] *n.* son of same parents; one closely united with another —**broth'erhood** *n.* relationship; fraternity, company —**broth'erliness** *n.* —**broth'erly** *a.* —**brother-in-law** *n.* brother of husband or wife; husband of sister

brought *pt./pp. of* BRING

brow *n.* ridge over eyes; forehead; eyebrow; edge of hill —**brow'beat** *vt.* bully (**brow'beat, brow'beaten**)

brown *a.* of dark colour inclining to red or yellow —*n.* the colour —*v.* make, become brown —**browned off** *inf.* bored, depressed

Brown'ie *n.* junior Girl Guide —**Brownie point** notional mark to one's credit for being seen to do the right thing

browse *vi.* look through (book, articles for sale *etc.*) in a casual manner; feed on shoots and leaves

bruise [-ōōz] *vt.* injure without breaking skin —*n.* contusion, discoloration caused by blow —**bruis'er** *n.* strong, tough person

brum'by *n.* Aust. wild horse

brunch *n. inf.* breakfast and lunch combined

brunette' *n.* woman of dark complexion and hair —*a.* dark brown

brunt *n.* shock of attack, chief stress; first blow

brush *n.* device with bristles, hairs, wires *etc.* used for cleaning, painting *etc.*; act, instance of brushing; brief contact; skirmish, fight; bushy tail; brushwood; (carbon) device taking electric current from moving to stationary parts of generator *etc.* —*v.* apply, remove, clean, with brush; touch lightly —**brush'off** *n. inf.* dismissal; refusal; snub; rebuff —**brush'wood** *n.* broken-off branches; land covered with scrub

brusque [-oosk] *a.* rough in manner, curt, blunt

brute *n.* any animal except man; crude, vicious person —*a.* animal; sensual, stupid; physical —**bru'tal** *a.* —**brutal'ity** *n.* —**bru'talize** *vt.* —**bru'tally** *adv.* —**bru'tish** *a.* bestial, gross

bry'ony, bri'ony *n.* wild climbing hedge plant

BS balance sheet ; British Standard

BSc Bachelor of Science

B-side *n.* less important side of disc

Bt. Baronet

Btu British Thermal Unit

bub'ble *n.* hollow globe of liquid, blown out with air; something insubstantial, not serious; transparent dome —*vi.* rise in bubbles; make gurgling sound —**bub'bly** *a.*

bubon'ic plague [byōō-] *n.* acute infectious disease characterized by swellings and fever

buccaneer' *n.* pirate, sea-rover —**buccaneer'ing** *n.*

buck *n.* male deer, or other male animal; act of bucking; *sl.* dollar —*v.* of horse, attempt to throw rider by jumping upwards *etc.*; resist, oppose (something) —**buck'shot** *n.* lead shot in shotgun shell —**buck'teeth** *pl.n.* projecting upper teeth

buck'et *n.* vessel, round with arched handle, for water *etc.*; anything resembling this —*vt.* put, carry, in bucket —**buck'etful** *n.* —**bucket seat** seat with back shaped to occupier's figure

buck'le *n.* metal clasp for fastening belt, strap *etc.* —*vt.* fasten with buckle —*vi.* warp, bend —**buck'ler** *n.* shield —**buckle down** start work

buck'ram *n.* coarse cloth stiffened with size

Bucks. Buckinghamshire

buckshee' *a. sl.* free

bucol'ic [byōō-] *a.* rustic

bud *n.* shoot or sprout on plant containing unopened leaf, flower *etc.* —*vi.* begin to grow —*vt.* graft (**-dd-**)

Budd'hism [-d'izm] *n.* religion founded in India by Buddha —**Budd'hist** *a./n.*

bud'dleia *n.* shrub with mauve flower spikes

budd'y *n. inf.* mate, chum

budge *vi.* move, stir

budg'erigar *n.* small Aust. parakeet (*also* **budg'ie**)

budg'et *n.* annual financial statement; plan of systematic spending —*vi.* prepare financial statement; plan financially

buff[1] *n.* leather made from buffalo or ox hide; light yellow colour; bare skin; polishing pad —*vt.* polish

buff[2] *n. inf.* expert on some subject

buff'alo *n.* any of several species of large oxen; bison (*pl.* **-lo(e)s**)

buff'er *n.* contrivance to lessen shock of concussion

buff'et[1] *n.* blow, slap; misfortune —*vt.* strike with blows; contend against —**buf'feting** *n.*

buff'et[2] [boof'ā] *n.* refreshment bar; meal at which guests serve themselves; sideboard

buffoon' *n.* clown; fool —**buffoon'ery** *n.* clowning

bug *n.* any small insect; *inf.* disease, infection; concealed listening device —*vt.* install secret microphone *etc.*

bug'bear *n.* object of needless terror; nuisance

bugg'er *n.* sodomite; *vulg. sl.* unpleasant person or thing —*sl. vt.* tire; (*with* up) ruin, complicate

bu'gle *n.* instrument like trumpet —**bu'gler** *n.*

bu'gloss *n.* shrub with blue flower clusters

build [bild] *v.* make, construct, by putting together parts or materials (**built** *pt./pp.*) —*n.* make, form —**build'er** *n.* —**build'ing** *n.* —**built-up** *a.* having many buildings

bulb *n.* modified leaf bud emitting roots from base, *eg* onion; anything resembling this; globe surrounding filament of electric light —*vi.* form bulbs —**bulb'ous** *a.*

bul'bul *n.* tropical songbird

bulge *n.* swelling, protuberance; temporary increase —*vi.* swell out —**bulg'iness** *n.* —**bulg'y** *a.*

bulk *n.* size; volume; greater part; cargo —*vi.* be of weight or importance —**bulk'iness** *n.* —**bulk'y** *a.*

bulk'head *n.* partition in interior of ship

bull[1] *n.* male of cattle; male of various other animals —**bull'dog** *n.* thickset breed of dog —**bull'doze** *v.* —**bull'dozer** *n.* powerful tractor with blade for excavating *etc.* —**bu'llock** *n.* castrated bull —**bull'pen** *n.* part of baseball field where relief pitchers warm up —**bull's-eye** *n.* middle part of target

bull[2] *n.* papal edict

bull[3] *sl. n.* nonsense —*v.* talk nonsense (to)

bull'et *n.* projectile discharged from rifle, pistol *etc.*

bull'etin *n.* official report

bull'ion *n.* gold or silver in mass

bull'y *n.* one who hurts, persecutes, or intimidates weaker people —*vt.* intimidate, overawe; illtreat (**bull'ied, bul'lying**) —**bully beef** corned beef

bul'rush *n.* tall reedlike marsh plant with brown velvety spike

bul'wark *n.* rampart; any defence or means of security; raised side of ship; breakwater

bum *sl. n.* buttocks, anus; loafer, scrounger —*vt.* get by scrounging —*a.* useless

bum'ble *v.* perform clumsily —**bum'bler** *n.*

bum'blebee *n.* large bee

bump *n.* heavy blow, dull in sound; swelling caused by blow; protuberance; sudden movement —*vt.* strike or push against —**bump'er** *n.* horizontal bar at front and rear of motor vehicle to protect against damage; full glass —*a.* full, abundant —**bump off** *sl.* murder

bumph, bumf *n. inf.* useless documents, information *etc.*

bump'kin *n.* rustic

bump'tious *a.* offensively self-assertive

bun *n.* small, round cake; round knot of hair

bunch *n.* number of things tied or growing together; cluster; tuft, knot; group, party —*vt.* put together in bunch —*vi.* gather together —**bunch'y** *a.*

bun'dle *n.* package; number of things tied together; *sl.* lot of money —*vt.* tie in bundle; send (off) without ceremony

bung *n.* stopper for cask; large cork —*vt.* stop up, seal, close; *inf.* throw, sling

bun'galow [bung'gə-lō] *n.* one-storeyed house

bun'gle [bung'gl] *vt.* do badly from lack of skill, botch *—vi.* act clumsily, awkwardly *—n.* blunder, muddle **—bun'gled** *a.* **—bun'gler** *n.* **—bun'gling** *a.*

bun'ion *n.* inflamed swelling on foot or toe

bunk[1] *n.* narrow, shelflike bed **—bunk bed** one of pair of beds constructed one above the other **—bunk'house** *n.* building containing sleeping quarters of workers on ranch

bunk[2] *n. see* BUNKUM

bunk'er *n.* large storage container for oil, coal *etc.*; *Golf* sand trap; (military) underground defensive position

bunk'um *n.* nonsense

bunn'y *n. inf.* rabbit

Bun'sen burn'er gas burner, producing great heat, used for chemical experiments

bun'ting[1] *n.* material for flags

bun'ting[2] *n.* bird with short, stout bill

buoy [boi] *n.* floating marker anchored in sea; lifebuoy *—vt.* mark with buoy; keep from sinking; support **—buoy'ancy** *n.* **—buoy'ant** *a.*

bur(r) *n.* head of plant with prickles or hooks

bur'ble *vi.* gurgle, as stream or baby; talk idly

burd'en[1] *n.* load; weight, cargo; anything difficult to bear *—vt.* load, encumber **—burd'ensome** *a.*

burd'en[2] *n.* chorus of a song; chief theme

bur'dock *n.* plant with prickly burs

bu'reau [-rō] *n.* writing desk; office; government department (*pl.* **-reaus, -reaux**) **—bureauc'racy** [-ok'-] *n.* government by officials; body of officials **—bu'reaucrat** *n.* **—bureaucrat'ic** *a.* **—bureaucrat'ically** *adv.*

bur'gee [-jē] *n.* small nautical flag

bur'geon [-jən] *vi.* bud; develop rapidly

bur'gess [-jis] *n.* inhabitant of borough, *esp.* citizen with full municipal rights

burgh [bur'ə] *n.* Scottish borough **—burgh'er** [ber'gər] *n.* citizen

burg'lar *n.* one who enters building to commit crime, *esp.* theft **—burg'lary** *n.* **—burg'larize** *vt.*

bur'gundy *n.* name of various wines, white and red

bur'lap *n.* coarse canvas

burlesque' [-esk'] *n.* (artistic) caricature; ludicrous imitation; (*also* **burlesk**) bawdy comedy show, *esp.* with striptease *—vt.* caricature

bur'ly *a.* sturdy, stout, robust **—bur'liness** *n.*

burn[1] *vt.* destroy or injure by fire *—vi.* be on fire, *lit.* or *fig.*; be consumed by fire (**burned** *or* **burnt** *pt./pp.*) *—n.* injury, mark caused by fire **—burn'ing** *a.*

burn[2] *n. Scot.* small stream

burn'ish *vt.* make bright by rubbing; polish *—n.* gloss, lustre **—burn'isher** *n.*

burp *v. inf.* belch (*esp.* of baby) *—n.*

burr[1] *n.* soft trilling sound given to letter *r* in some dialects

burr[2] *n.* rough edge left after cutting, drilling *etc.*

burr'o *n.* donkey (*pl.* **-os**)

burr'ow [-rō] *n.* hole dug by rabbit *etc.* *—vt.* make holes in ground; bore; conceal oneself

burs'ar *n.* official managing finances of college, school *etc.* **—burs'ary** *n.* scholarship

burst *vi.* fly asunder; break into pieces; rend; break suddenly into some expression of feeling *—vt.* shatter, break violently *—n.* bursting; explosion; outbreak; spurt

bur'y [ber'i] *vt.* put underground; inter; conceal (**bur'ied, bur'ying**) **—bur'ial** *n./a.*

bus *n.* (*orig.* omnibus) large motor vehicle for passengers *—v.* travel or transport by bus

bus. business

bus'by [-z'-] *n.* tall fur hat worn by certain soldiers

bush [-oo-] *n.* shrub; woodland, thicket; (*Aust., S Afr., Canad. etc.*) uncleared country, backwoods, interior; (*also* **bush lot, woodlot**) land on farm where timber is grown and cut **—bushed** *a. inf.* tired out; mentally disturbed from living in isolation **—bush'y** *a.* shaggy **—bush'-baby** *n.* tree-living, nocturnal Afr. animal **—bush fire** widespread destructive fire in the bush **—bush jacket** shirtlike jacket with patch pockets **—bush line** airline operating in bush country **—bush pilot —bush'whack** *v.* travel around in the bush **—bush'whacker** *n.*

bush'el [-oo-] *n.* dry measure of eight gallons

bus'iness [biz'nis] *n.* profession, occupation; commercial or industrial establishment; commerce, trade; responsibility, affair, matter; work —**bus'inesslike** *a.*

busk'er *n.* one who makes money by singing, dancing *etc.* in the street —**busk** *vi.*

bust[1] *n.* sculpture of head and shoulders of human body; woman's breasts

bust[2] *inf.* *v.* burst; make, become bankrupt —*vt.* raid; arrest —*a.* broken; bankrupt —*n.* police raid or arrest; failure, bankruptcy

bus'tard *n.* large swift-running bird

bus'tle[1] [-səl] *vi.* be noisily busy, active —*n.* fuss, commotion

bus'tle[2] [-səl] *n. Hist.* pad worn by ladies to support back of the skirt

bus'y [biz'i] *a.* actively employed; full of activity; engaged —*vt.* occupy (**bus'ied, bus'ying**) —**bus'ily** *adv.* —**bus'ybody** *n.* meddler —**busy lizzie** house plant

but *prep./conj.* without; except; only; yet; still; besides

bu'tane [byōō'-] *n.* gas used for fuel

butch *a./n. sl.* markedly or aggressively masculine (person)

butch'er [-oo-] *n.* one who kills animals for food, or sells meat; bloody, savage man —*vt.* slaughter, murder; spoil work —**butch'ery** *n.*

but'ler *n.* chief male servant

butt[1] *n.* the thick end; target; object of ridicule; bottom or unused end of anything; *inf.* buttocks —*v.* lie, be placed end on to

butt[2] *v.* strike with head; push —*n.* blow with head, as of sheep —**butt in** interfere, meddle

butt[3] *n.* large cask

butt'er *n.* fatty substance got from cream by churning —*vt.* spread with butter; flatter

butt'ercup *n.* plant of genus *Ranunculus* with glossy, yellow flowers

butt'erfly *n.* insect with large wings; inconstant person; stroke in swimming

butt'ermilk *n.* milk that remains after churning

butt'erscotch *n.* kind of hard, brittle toffee

butt'ery *n.* storeroom for food or wine

butt'ock *n.* rump, protruding hinder part (*usu. pl.*)

butt'on *n.* knob, stud for fastening dress; knob that operates doorbell, machine *etc.* —*vt.* fasten with buttons —**butt'onhole** *n.* slit in garment to pass button through as fastening; flower, spray worn on lapel *etc.* —*vt.* detain (unwilling) person in conversation —**butt'onwood, butt'onball** *n.* N Amer. plane tree

butt'ress *n.* structure to support wall; prop —*vt.*

bux'om *a.* full of health, plump, gay; large-breasted

buy [bī] *vt.* get by payment, purchase; bribe (**bought** *pt./pp.*) —**buy'er** *n.*

buzz *vi.* make humming sound —*n.* humming sound of bees; *inf.* telephone call —**buzz'er** *n.* any apparatus that makes buzzing sound —**buzz saw** power-operated circular saw —**buzz word** *inf.* word, oft. orig. jargon, that becomes fashionable

buzz'ard *n.* bird of prey of hawk family

by *prep.* near; along; across; past; during; not later than; through use or agency of; in units of —*adv.* near; away, aside; past —**by and by** soon, in the future —**by and large** on the whole; speaking generally —**come by** obtain

by- (*comb. form*) subsidiary, incidental, out-of-the-way, near, as in **by'path, by'-product, by'stander**

bye *n. Sport* situation where player, team, wins by default of opponent; *Cricket* run scored off ball not touched by batsman

by(e)-election parliamentary election caused by death or resignation of member

by(e)'law *n.* law, regulation made by local subordinate authority

by'gone *a.* past, former —*n.* (*oft. pl.*) past occurrence; small antique

by'pass *n.* road for diversion of traffic from crowded centres

by'play *n.* diversion, action apart from main action of play

byre [bīr] *n.* cowshed

byte *n. Computers* sequence of bits processed as single unit of information

by'word *n.* a well-known name, saying

C

C *Chem.* carbon; Celsius; Centigrade; Conservative

c. carat; cent; century; circa; copyright

CA chartered accountant

Ca *Chem.* calcium

CAA Canadian Automobile Association

cab *n.* taxi; driver's enclosed compartment on locomotive, truck *etc.* —**cab'man, cabb'y** *n.*

cabal' *n.* small group of intriguers; secret plot

cab'aret [-rā] *n.* floor show at a nightclub or restaurant

cabb'age *n.* green vegetable with usu. round head of leaves —**cabb'agetown** *n.* city slum

ca'ber [kā'-] *n.* pole tossed as trial of strength at Highland games

cab'in *n.* hut, shed; small room *esp.* in ship —*vt.* cramp, confine —**cabin boy** —**cabin cruiser** power boat with cabin, bunks *etc.* —**cabin fever** acute depression resulting from being isolated in wilderness

cab'inet *n.* piece of furniture with drawers or shelves; outer case of television, radio *etc.*; committee of politicians governing country; *obs.* small room —**cabinet-maker** *n.* craftsman who makes fine furniture

ca'ble *n.* strong rope; wire or bundle of wires conveying electric power, telegraph signals *etc.*; message sent by this; nautical unit of measurement (100-120 fathoms) —*v.* telegraph by cable —**ca'blegram** *n.* cabled message —**cable television** television service conveyed by cable to subscribers

caboo'dle *n. inf.* —**the whole caboodle** the whole lot

caboose' *n.* ship's galley; small railway car for use by crew of freight train; mobile bunkhouse used by lumberjacks *etc.*

cab'riolet [-lā] *n.* early type of hansom cab

caca'o [-kah'-] *n.* tropical tree from the seeds of which chocolate and cocoa are made

cach'alot [kash'-] *n.* the sperm whale

cache [kash] *n.* secret hiding place; store of food *etc.*

cach'et [kash'ā] *n.* mark, stamp; mark of authenticity; prestige, distinction

cack'le *vi.* make chattering noise, as hen —*n.* cackling noise or laughter; empty chatter

cacoph'ony *n.* disagreeable sound; discord of sounds —**cacoph'onous** *a.*

cac'tus *n.* spiny succulent plant (*pl.* **cac'tuses, cac'ti** [-tī])

cad *n.* dishonourable, unchivalrous person

cadav'er *n.* corpse —**cadav'erous** *a.* corpselike; sickly-looking; gaunt

cadd'ie, -y *n.* golfer's attendant

cadd'y *n.* small box for tea

ca'dence *n.* fall or modulation of voice in music or verse

caden'za *n. Mus.* elaborate passage for solo instrument or singer

cadet' *n.* youth in training, *esp.* for officer status in armed forces

cadge [kaj] *v.* get (food, money *etc.*) by begging —**cadg'er** *n.*

cad'mium *n.* metallic element

cad're [kahd'ər] *n.* nucleus or framework, *esp.* skeleton of regiment

cae'cum [sē'kəm] *n. Anat.* pouch *esp.* at beginning of large intestine (*pl.* **-ca**)

Caesa'rean section surgical incision through abdominal wall to deliver a baby

caf'é [-ā] *n.* small or inexpensive restaurant serving light refreshments —**cafete'ria** *n.* restaurant designed for self-service

caff'eine [-ēn] *n.* stimulating alkaloid found in tea and coffee

caf'tan *n. see* KAFTAN

cage *n.* enclosure, box with bars or wires, *esp.* for keeping animals or birds; place of confinement; enclosed platform of lift, *esp.* in mine —*vt.* put in cage, confine —**ca'gey** *a.* wary, not communicative

cagoule' [kə-gōōl'] *n.* lightweight, *usu.* knee-length, anorak

cahoots' *pl.n. sl.* partnership, as **in cahoots with**

cairn *n.* heap of stones, *esp.* as monument or landmark

cairn'gorm *n.* yellow or brownish coloured gem

caisson' [kə-sōōn'] *n.* chamber for working under water; apparatus for lifting vessel out of the water; ammunition wagon

cai'tiff [kā'-] *n. obs.* mean, despicable fellow —*a.* base, mean

cajole' *vt.* persuade by flattery, wheedle —**cajole'ment** *n.* —**cajo'ler** *n.* —**cajo'lery** *n.*

cake *n.* baked, sweetened, bread-like food; compact mass —*v.* make into a cake; harden (as of mud)

cal'abash *n.* tree with large hard-shelled fruit; this fruit; drinking, cooking vessel made from gourd

cal'aboose *n. inf.* prison

cal'amine *n.* pink powder used medicinally in soothing ointment

calam'ity *n.* great misfortune; deep distress, disaster —**calam'itous** *a.*

calceola'ria *n.* Amer. plant with speckled, slipper-shaped flowers

cal'cium *n.* metallic element, the basis of lime —**calca'reous, -ious** *a.* containing lime —**cal'cify** *v.* convert, be converted, to lime —**cal'cine** [-sīn] *vt.* reduce to quicklime; burn to ashes

cal'culate *vt.* estimate; compute —*vi.* make reckonings —**cal'culable** *a.* —**cal'culating** *a.* able to perform calculations; shrewd, designing, scheming —**calcula'tion** *n.* —**cal'culator** *n.* electronic device for making calculations —**cal'culus** *n.* branch of mathematics; stone in body (*pl.* **cal'culi** [-ī])

cal'dron [kawl'-] *see* CAULDRON

caléche' [-lesh'] *n.* horse-drawn carriage for taking tourists around

cal'endar *n.* table of months and days in the year; list of events, documents, register; list of courses offered by university *etc.* —*vt.* enter in a list; index

calen'dula *n.* marigold

calf[1] [kahf] *n.* young of cow and of other animals; leather made of calf's skin (*pl.* **calves** [kahvz]) —**calve** *vi.* give birth to calf

calf[2] [kahf] *n.* fleshy back part of leg below knee (*pl.* **calves** [kahvz])

cal'ibre [-bər] *n.* size of bore of gun; capacity, character —**cal'ibrate** *vt.* mark scale of measuring instrument *etc.* —**calibra'tion** *n.*

cal'ico *n.* cotton cloth

calk[1] *see* CAULK

calk[2] *n.* set of spikes attached to sole of boot to prevent slipping

call [kawl] *vt.* speak loudly to attract attention; summon; (*oft. with* up) telephone; name —*vi.* shout; pay visit —*n.* shout; animal's cry; visit; inner urge, summons, as to be priest *etc.*; need, demand —**call'er** *n.* —**call'ing** *n.* vocation, profession —**call box UK** telephone booth —**call up** summon to serve in army; imagine

callig'raphy *n.* handwriting, penmanship —**calligraph'ic** *a.*

cal'liper *n.* metal splint for leg —*pl.* instrument for measuring diameters

callisthen'ics [-is-then'-] *pl.n.* light gymnastic exercises —**callisthen'ic** *a.*

cal'lous *a.* hardened, unfeeling —**cal'lously** *adv.* —**cal'lousness** *n.*

cal'low *a.* inexperienced; immature

cal'lus *n.* area of thick, hardened skin

calm [kahm] *a.* still, quiet, tranquil —*n.* stillness; tranquillity; absence of wind —*v.* become, make, still or quiet —**calm'ly** *adv.* —**calm'ness** *n.*

cal'orie, -ory *n.* unit of heat; unit of energy obtained from foods —**calorif'ic** *a.* heat-making —**calorim'eter** *n.*

cal'umet [-yoo-] *n.* tobacco pipe of N Amer. Indians; pipe of peace

cal'umny *n.* slander, false accusation —**calum'niate** *vt.* —**calumnia'tion** *n.* —**calum'niator** *n.* —**calum'nious** *a.*

calyp'so *n.* (West Indies) improvised song on topical subject

ca'lyx *n.* covering of bud (*pl.* **ca'lyxes, ca'lyces** [-sēz])

cam *n.* device to change rotary to reciprocating motion —**cam'shaft** *n.* in motoring, rotating shaft to which cams are fixed to lift valves

camarad'erie [-rahd'-] *n.* spirit of comradeship, trust

cam'ber *n.* convexity on upper surface

of road, bridge *etc.*; curvature of aircraft wing

camboose' [-bōōs'] *n.* cabin where gang of lumberjacks live; open fireplace in such cabin

ca'mbric *n.* fine white linen or cotton cloth

cam'corder *n.* combined portable video camera and recorder

came *pt. of* COME

cam'el *n.* animal of Asia and Africa, with humped back, used as beast of burden

came'llia *n.* ornamental shrub

cam'eo *n.* medallion, brooch *etc.* with profile head or design carved in relief; single brief scene or appearance in motion picture *etc.* by (well-known) actor

cam'era *n.* apparatus used to make photographs —**cam'eraman** *n.* photographer, *esp.* for television or cinema —**camera obscura** darkened chamber in which views of surrounding country are shown on sheet by means of lenses —**in camera** (of legal proceedings *etc.*) conducted in private

cam'isole *n.* underbodice

c(h)am'omile *n.* aromatic creeping plant, used medicinally

cam'ouflage [-ahzh] *n.* disguise, means of deceiving enemy observation, *eg* by paint, screen —*vt.* disguise

camp *n.* (place for) tents of hikers, army *etc.*; cabins *etc.* for temporary accommodation; group supporting political party *etc.* —*a. inf.* homosexual; consciously artificial —*vi.* form or lodge in a camp —**camp'er** *n.* one who camps; vehicle equipped for camping —**camp'ing** *n.*

campaign' [-pān'] *n.* series of coordinated activities for some purpose, *eg* political or military campaign —*vi.* serve in campaign —**campaign'er** *n.*

campanol'ogy *n.* art of ringing bells musically

campan'ula *n.* plant with blue or white bell-shaped flowers

cam'phor *n.* solid essential oil with aromatic taste and smell —**cam'phorated** *a.*

cam'pion *n.* white or pink wild flower

camp'us *n.* grounds of college or university

can[1] *vi.* be able; have the power; be allowed (**could** *pt.*)

can[2] *n.* container, usu. metal, for liquids, foods; *sl.* toilet; *sl.* buttocks —*v.* put in can (**-nn-**) —**canned** *a.* preserved in can; (of music, programmes *etc.*) previously recorded —**cann'ery** *n.* factory where food is canned

Canada Day July 1st, anniversary of establishment of Confederation in 1867

Canada goose large greyish-brown N Amer. goose

Cana'dian *n./a.* (native) of Canada —**Cana'dianize** *v.* make, become Canadian

canal' *n.* artificial watercourse; duct in body —**canaliza'tion** *n.* —**can'alize** *vt.* convert into canal; direct (thoughts, energies *etc.*) into one channel

can'apé [-pē] *n.* small piece of toast *etc.* with savoury topping

cana'ry *n.* yellow singing bird

canas'ta *n.* card game played with two packs

can'can *n.* high-kicking (orig. French music-hall) dance

can'cel *vt.* cross out; annul; call off (**-ll-**) —**cancella'tion** *n.*

can'cer *n.* malignant growth or tumour —**can'cerous** *a.*

Can'cer *n.* crab, 4th sign of zodiac, operative c. June 21-July 21; constellation —**tropic of Cancer** parallel of latitude 23° 27′ N of the equator

cande'la *n.* basic SI unit of luminous intensity

can'did *a.* frank, open, impartial —**can'didly** *adv.* —**can'didness, can'do(u)r** *n.* frankness

can'didate *n.* one who seeks office, appointment *etc.*; person taking examination or test —**can'didature** *n.*

can'dle *n.* stick of wax with wick; light —**candela'brum** [-lahb'-] *n.* large, branched candle holder (*pl.* **-bra**) —**can'dlepower** *n.* unit for measuring light —**can'dlestick** *n.* —**can'dlewick** *n.* cotton fabric with tufted surface

can'dy *n.* crystallized sugar; confectionery in general —*vt.* preserve with sugar —*vi.* become encrusted with sugar (**can'died, can'dying**) —**can'died** *a.*

can'dytuft *n.* garden plant with clusters of white, pink or purple flowers

cane *n.* stem of small palm or large grass; walking stick —*vt.* beat with cane

ca'nine *a.* like, pert. to, dog —**canine**

tooth one of four sharp, pointed teeth, two in each jaw

can'ister *n.* container, *usu.* of metal, *esp.* for storing dry food

cank'er *n.* eating sore; thing that eats away, destroys, corrupts —*vt.* infect, corrupt —*vi.* decay —**cank'ered, can'kerous** *a.* —**cank'erworm** *n.*

cann'a *n.* tropical flowering plant

cann'abis *n.* hemp plant; drug derived from this

cannello'ni *pl. n.* tubular pieces of pasta filled with meat *etc.*

cann'ibal *n.* one who eats human flesh —*a.* relating to this practice —**can'nibalism** *n.* —**cannibalis'tic** *a.* —**can'nibalize** *vt.* use parts from one machine *etc.* to repair another

cann'on[1] *n.* large gun (*pl.* **-ons** *or* **-on**) —**cannonade'** *n./vt.* attack with cannon —**cann'onball** *n.* —**cannon bone** horse's leg bone

cann'on[2] *n.* **UK** carom —*vi.* rebound, collide

cann'ot *negative form of* CAN[1]

cann'y *a.* shrewd; cautious; crafty —**can'nily** *adv.*

canoe' [-noo'] *n.* very light boat propelled with paddle or paddles (*pl.* **-oes'**) —**canoe'ist** *n.*

can'on[1] *n.* law or rule, *esp.* of church; standard; body of books accepted as genuine; list of saints —**canoniza'tion** *n.* —**can'onize** *vt.* enrol in list of saints

can'on[2] *n.* church dignitary, member of cathedral chapter —**canon'ical** *a.* —**canonis'tic** *a.*

can'opy *n.* covering over throne, bed *etc.*; any overhanging shelter —*vt.* cover with canopy (**-opied, -opying**)

cant[1] *n.* hypocritical speech; whining; language of a sect; technical jargon; slang, *esp.* of thieves —*vi.* use cant

cant[2] *v.* tilt, slope; bevel

can'taloupe, -loup, -lope *n.* variety of musk melon

cantank'erous *a.* ill-natured, quarrelsome

cantat'a [-taht'-] *n.* choral work like, but shorter than, oratorio

canteen' *n.* place in factory, school *etc.* where meals are provided; small shop in military camp; case of cutlery; mess tin

can'ter *n.* easy gallop —*v.* move at, make to canter

Can'terbury bell cultivated campanula

can'ticle *n.* short hymn

can'tilever *n.* beam, girder *etc.* fixed at one end only

can'to [-tō] *n.* division of a poem (*pl.* **-tos**)

can'ton *n.* division of country, *esp.* Swiss federal state

canton'ment [-toon'-] *n.* quarters for troops

Canuck' *n./a. inf.* Canadian

can'vas *n.* coarse cloth used for sails, painting on *etc.*; sails of ship; picture

can'vass *vt.* solicit votes, contributions etc.; discuss, examine —*n.* solicitation

can'yon *n.* deep gorge

cap *n.* covering for head; lid, top, or other covering —*vt.* put a cap on; outdo; select for a team (**-pp-**)

ca'pable *a.* able, gifted; competent; having the capacity, power —**capabil'ity** *n.*

capac'ity [-pas'-] *n.* power of holding or grasping; room; volume; character; ability, power of mind —**capa'cious** *a.* roomy —**capac'itance** *n.* (measure of) ability of system to store electric charge —**capac'itor** *n.*

capar'ison [-pa'ri-] *n.* ornamental covering, equipment for horse —*vt.* adorn thus

cape[1] *n.* covering for shoulders

cape[2] *n.* point of land running into sea, headland

ca'per[1] *n.* skip; frolic; escapade; *sl.* crime —*vi.* skip, dance

ca'per[2] *n.* pickled flower bud of Sicilian shrub

capercai'lzie [kap-ər-kā'lyi] *n.* large black grouse

capill'ary *a.* hairlike —*n.* tube with very small bore, *esp.* small blood vessel

cap'ital *n.* chief town; money, stock, funds; large-sized letter; headpiece of column —*a.* involving or punishable by death; serious; chief; leading; excellent —**cap'italism** *n.* economic system which is based on private ownership of industry —**cap'italist** *n.* owner of capital; supporter of capitalism —*a.* run by, possessing, capital, as capitalist state —**cap'italize** *v.* convert into capital; (*with* on) turn to advantage —**cap'itally** *adv.*

capita'tion *n.* tax or grant per head

Cap'itol *n.* U.S. Congress House; a U.S. state legislature building; temple of Jupiter in Rome

capit'ulate *vi.* surrender on terms, give in —**capitula'tion** *n.* —**capit'ulatory** *adj.*

ca'pon *n.* castrated cock fowl fattened for eating —**ca'ponize** *vt.*

cappucci'no [-chē'-] *n.* coffee with steamed milk

caprice' [-ēs'] *n.* whim, freak —**capri'cious** *a.* —**capri'ciousness** *n.*

Cap'ricorn *n.* sea-goat, 10th sign of zodiac, operative c. Dec. 21-Jan. 19; constellation —**tropic of Capricorn** parallel of latitude 23° 27′ S of the equator

cap'sicum *n.* tropical vegetable with mild peppery flavour, sweet pepper

capsize' *vt.* (of boat) upset —*vi.* be overturned —**capsi'zal** *n.*

cap'stan *n.* machine to wind cable, *esp.* to hoist anchor

cap'sule [-syool] *n.* gelatin case for dose of medicine or drug; any small enclosed area or container; seed vessel of plant

Capt. Captain

cap'tain [-tin] *n.* *Army* officer ranking next above a lieutenant and below a major; *Navy* rank equivalent to colonel; commander of vessel or company of soldiers; leader, chief —*vt.* be captain of

cap'tion *n.* heading, title of article, picture *etc.*

cap'tious [-shəs] *a.* ready to find fault; critical; peevish —**cap'tiously** *adv.* —**cap'tiousness** *n.*

cap'tive *n.* prisoner —*a.* taken, imprisoned —**cap'tivate** *vt.* fascinate —**cap'tivating** *a.* delightful —**captiv'ity** *n.*

cap'ture *vt.* seize, make prisoner —*n.* seizure, taking —**cap'tor** *n.*

capybar'a [-bahr'-] *n.* the largest rodent, found in S Amer.

car *n.* automobile; railway vehicle for passengers or freight; streetcar; passenger compartment, as in balloon —**car'fare** *n.* fare that passenger is charged for ride on bus or streetcar

carafe' [-raf'] *n.* glass water-bottle for the table, decanter

car'amel [ka'rə-] *n.* burnt sugar for cooking; type of confectionery —**car'amelize** *v.*

car'at [ka'rət] *n.* small weight used for gold, diamonds *etc.*

car'avan [ka'rə-] *n.* **UK** trailer for living in; company of merchants travelling together for safety in the East

car'away [ka'rə-] *n.* plant of which the seeds are used as a spice in cakes *etc.*

carb'ide *n.* compound of carbon with an element, *esp.* calcium carbide

carb'ine *n.* short rifle —**carbineer'** *n.*

carbohy'drate *n.* any of large group of compounds containing carbon, hydrogen and oxygen, *esp.* sugars and starches as components of food

carbol'ic (acid) disinfectant derived from coal tar

carb'on *n.* nonmetallic element, substance of pure charcoal, found in all organic matter —**carb'onate** *n.* salt of carbonic acid —**carbon'ic** *a.* —**carbonif'erous** *a.* —**carb'onize** *vt.* —**carbonic acid** carbon dioxide; compound formed by carbon dioxide and water —**carbon dioxide** colourless gas exhaled in respiration of animals —**carbon paper** paper coated with a dark, waxy pigment, used for duplicating written or typed matter, producing **carbon copy**

Carborun'dum R artificial silicate of carbon

car'boy *n.* large glass jar protected by wicker casing

car'buncle *n.* inflamed ulcer, boil or tumour; fiery-red precious stone

carburett'or, carburet'or [-byoo-] *n.* device for vaporizing and mixing gasoline with air in internal-combustion engine

carc'ass, carc'ase *n.* dead animal body; orig. skeleton

carcin'ogen [-sin'-] *n.* substance producing cancer

carcino'ma [-sin-] *n.* a cancer

card[1] *n.* thick, stiff paper; piece of this giving identification *etc.*; illustrated card sending greetings *etc.*; one of the 52 playing cards making up a pack; *inf.* a character, eccentric —*pl.* any card game —**card'board** *n.* thin, stiff board made of paper pulp —**card index** index in which each entry is made on separate card

card[2] *n.* instrument for combing wool *etc.* —*vt.* comb —**card'er** *n.*

car'diac *a.* pert. to the heart —*n.* heart stimulant —**car'dioid** *a.* heart-shaped —**car'diograph** *n.* instrument which records movements of the heart —**car'diogram** *n.* graph of such

card'igan *n.* knitted woollen jacket

card'inal *a.* chief, principal —*n.* highest rank, next to the Pope in R.C. church —**card'inalate** *n.* —**cardinal numbers** 1, 2, 3, *etc.* —**cardinal points** N, S, E, W

care *vi.* be anxious; have regard or liking (for); look after; be disposed to —*n.* attention; pains, heed; charge, protection; anxiety; caution —**care'free** *a.* —**care'ful** *a.* —**care'fully** *adv.* —**care'fulness** *n.* —**care'less** *a.* —**care'lessness** *n.* —**care'taker** *n.* person in charge of premises —*a.* temporary, interim

careen' *vt.* lay ship over on her side for cleaning and repair —*vi.* keel over; sway dangerously

career' *n.* course through life; profession; rapid motion —*vi.* run or move at full speed

caress' *vt.* fondle, embrace, treat with affection —*n.* act or expression of affection

car'et [ka'rit] *n.* mark (‸) showing where to insert something omitted

car'go *n.* load, freight, carried by ship, plane *etc.* (*pl.* **-goes**)

car'ibou [ka'ri-bo͞o] *n.* N Amer. reindeer

car'icature [ka'ri-] *n.* likeness exaggerated or distorted to appear ridiculous —*vt.* portray in this way

ca'ries [kā'ri-ēz] *n.* decay of tooth or bone

carill'on [-yən *or* ka'-] *n.* set of bells *usu.* hung in tower and played by set of keys, pedals *etc.*; tune so played

car'minative *n.* medicine to remedy flatulence —*a.* acting as this

car'mine *n.* brilliant red colour (prepared from cochineal) —*a.* of this colour

carn'age *n.* slaughter

carn'al *a.* fleshly, sensual; worldly —**car'nalism** *n.* —**carnal'ity** *n.* —**car'nally** *adv.*

carna'tion *n.* cultivated flower; flesh colour

carn'ival *n.* festive occasion; travelling fair; show or display for amusement

carniv'orous *a.* flesh-eating —**car'nivore** *n.*

car'ob [ka'rəb] *n.* Mediterranean tree with edible pods

car'ol [ka'rəl] *n.* song or hymn of joy or praise (*esp.* Christmas carol) —*vi.* sing (carols) (**-ll-**)

car'om [ka'rəm] *n.* billiard stroke, hitting both object balls with one's own —*vi.* make this stroke

carouse' [-owz'] *vi.* have merry drinking spree —*n.* —**carous'al** *n.* —**carous'er** *n.*

carousel' [-rə-sel'] *n.* merry-go-round

carp[1] *n.* freshwater fish

carp[2] *vi.* complain about small faults or errors; nag —**carp'er** *n.* —**carp'ing** *a.* —**carp'ingly** *adv.*

carp'enter *n.* worker in timber as in building *etc.* —**carp'entry** *n.* this art

carp'et *n.* heavy fabric for covering floor —*vt.* cover floor; call up for censure —**carp'etbag** *n.* travelling bag —**carp'etbagger** *n.* political adventurer

carr'iage [-ij] *n.* **UK** railway passenger car; bearing, conduct; horse-drawn vehicle; act, cost, of carrying —**carr'iageway** *n.* **UK** part of a road along which traffic passes in a single line

carr'iole *n.* small open carriage for one

carr'ion *n.* rotting dead flesh —**carrion crow**

carr'ot *n.* plant with orange-red edible root; inducement —**carr'oty** *a.* red, reddish

carr'y *vt.* convey, transport; capture, win; effect; behave —*vi.* (of projectile, sound) reach (**carr'ied, carr'ying**) —*n.* range —**carr'ier** *n.* one that carries goods; one who, himself immune, communicates a disease to others; aircraft carrier; kind of pigeon —**carr'yall** *n.* valise or case for carrying clothes *etc.* —**carry on** continue; *inf.* fuss unnecessarily

cart *n.* open (two-wheeled) vehicle, *esp.* pulled by horse —*vt.* convey in cart; carry with effort —**cart'age** *n.* —**cart'er** *n.* —**cart'horse** *n.* —**cart'wheel** *n.* large, spoked wheel; sideways somersault —**cart'wright** *n.* maker of carts

carte blanche' [blahnch'] *Fr.* complete discretion or authority

cartel' *n.* industrial combination for the purpose of fixing prices, output *etc.*; alliance of political parties *etc.* to further common aims

Carte'sian *a.* pert. to the French philosopher René Descartes (1596-1650) or his system of coordinates —*n.* an adherent of his philosophy

cart'ilage *n.* firm elastic tissue in the body; gristle —**cartilag'inous** [-aj'-] *a.*

cartog'raphy *n.* map making —**cartog'rapher** *n.*

cart'on *n.* cardboard or plastic container

cartoon' *n.* drawing, *esp.* humorous or satirical; sequence of drawings telling story; preliminary design for painting —**cartoon'ist** *n.*

cart'ridge *n.* case containing charge for gun; container for film, magnetic tape *etc.*; unit in head of phonograph pick-up —**cartridge paper** strong, thick paper

carve *vt.* cut; hew; sculpture; engrave; cut in pieces or slices (meat) —**carv'er** *n.* —**carv'ing** *n.*

caryat'id [karē-] *n.* supporting column in shape of female figure

cascade' *n.* waterfall; anything resembling this —*vi.* fall in cascades

case[1] *n.* instance; event, circumstance; question at issue; state of affairs, condition; arguments supporting particular action *etc.*; *Med.* patient under treatment; law suit; grounds for suit; grammatical relation of words in sentence

case[2] *n.* box, sheath, covering; receptacle; box and contents —*vt.* put in a case —**case-harden** *vt.* harden by carbonizing the surface of (*esp.* iron) by converting into steel; make hard, callous

ca'sein [kā'sē-in] *n.* protein in milk and its products

case'ment [kās'-] *n.* window opening on hinges

cash *n.* money, banknotes and coin —*vt.* turn into or exchange for money —**cashier'** *n.* one in charge of receiving and paying of money —**cash'book** *n.* —**cash dispenser** computerized device outside a bank for supplying cash —**cash'book** *n.* —**cash register** till that records amount of money put in

cashier' *vt.* dismiss from office or service

cash'mere *n.* fine soft fabric; shawl made from goat's wool

casi'no [-sē'-] *n.* building, institution for gambling (*pl.* **-os**)

cask [-ah-] *n.* barrel; container for wine

cask'et [-ah-] *n.* small case for jewels *etc.*; box for corpse

cassat'a [-saht'-] *n.* ice cream, *esp.* containing fruit and nuts

cass'erole *n.* fireproof cooking and serving dish; kind of stew cooked in this dish

cassette' *n.* plastic container for film, magnetic tape *etc.*

cass'ock *n.* long tunic worn by clergymen

cast [kah-] *v.* throw or fling; shed; throw down; deposit (a vote); allot, as parts in play; mould, as metal —*n.* throw; distance thrown; squint; mould; that which is shed or ejected; set of actors; type or quality —**cast'ing** *n.* —**cast'away** *n.* shipwrecked person —**casting vote** decisive vote

castanets' *pl.n.* (in Spanish dancing) two small curved pieces of wood *etc.* clicked together in hand

caste [kah-] *n.* section of society in India; social rank

cast'er sugar [kah-] finely powdered sugar (also **castor sugar**)

cas'tigate *vt.* punish, rebuke severely, correct; chastise —**castiga'tion** *n.* —**cas'tigator** *n.*

cas'tle [kahs'l] *n.* fortress; country mansion; chess piece

cast'or [kah-] *n.* bottle with perforated top; small swivelled wheel on table leg *etc.*

castor oil vegetable medicinal oil

castrate' *vt.* remove testicles, deprive of power of generation —**castra'tion** *n.*

cas'ual [-z'-] *a.* accidental; unforeseen; occasional; unconcerned; informal —**cas'ually** *adv.* —**cas'ualty** *n.* person killed or injured in accident, war *etc.*; thing lost, destroyed, in accident *etc.* (*pl.* **-ties**)

cas'uist [-z'-] *n.* one who studies and solves moral problems; quibbler —**casuis'tical** *a.* —**cas'uistry** *n.*

cat *n.* any of various feline animals, including, *eg* small domesticated furred animal, and lions, tigers *etc.* —**catt'y** *a.* spiteful —**cat'call** *n.* derisive cry —**cat'fish** *n.* mainly freshwater fish with catlike whiskers —**cat'kin** *n.* drooping flower spike —**cat'nap** *vi./n.* doze —**cat'nip** *n.* scented plant —**Cat's'eye** R glass reflector set in road to indicate traffic lanes —**cat'walk** *n.* narrow, raised path or plank

catab'olism *n.* breaking down of complex molecules, destructive metabolism

cat'aclysm [-kli-zəm] *n.* (disastrous) upheaval; deluge —**cataclys'mal** *a.*

cat'acomb [-ko͞om, -kōm] *n.* underground gallery for burial —*pl.* series of underground tunnels and caves

cat'alepsy *n.* condition of unconsciousness with rigidity of muscles —**catalep'tic** *a.*

cat'alogue [-log] *n.* descriptive list; list of courses offered by university *etc.* —*vt.* make such list of; enter in catalogue

cat'alyst *n.* substance causing or assisting a chemical reaction without taking part in it —**cat'alyse** *vt.* —**catal'ysis** *n.*

catamaran' *n.* type of sailing boat with twin hulls; raft of logs

cat'apult *n.* UK slingshot; *Hist.* engine of war for hurling arrows, stones *etc.*; launching device —*vt.*

cat'aract *n.* waterfall; downpour; disease of eye

catarrh' *n.* inflammation of a mucous membrane —**catarrh'al** *a.*

catas'trophe [-fi] *n.* great disaster, calamity; culmination of a tragedy —**catastroph'ic** *a.*

catch *vt.* take hold of, seize, understand; hear; contract disease; be in time for; surprise, detect —*vi.* be contagious; get entangled; begin to burn (**caught** *pt./pp.*) —*n.* seizure; thing that holds, stops *etc.*; what is caught; *inf.* snag, disadvantage; form of musical composition; thing, person worth catching —**catch'er** *n.* —**catch'ing** *a.* —**catch'y** *a.* pleasant, memorable; tricky —**catch'penny** *a.* worthless; made to sell quickly —**catch'word** *n.* popular phrase or idea —**catch 22** inescapable dilemma —**catchment area** area in which rainfall collects to form the supply of river *etc.*; area from which people are allocated to a particular school, hospital *etc.*

cat'echize [-kīz] *vt.* instruct by question and answer; question —**catechet'ical** *a.* —**cat'echism** *n.* —**cat'echist** *n.* —**catechu'men** *n.* one under instruction in Christianity

cat'egory *n.* class, order, division —**categor'ical** [-go'ri-] *a.* positive; of category —**categor'ically** *adv.* —**cat'egorize** *vt.*

ca'ter *vi.* provide what is required or desired, *esp.* food *etc.* —**ca'terer** *n.*

cat'erpillar *n.* hairy grub of moth or butterfly; type of tractor fitted with caterpillar wheels —**caterpillar wheel** articulated belt revolving round two or more wheels to propel heavy vehicle over difficult ground

cat'erwaul *vi.* wail, howl

cathe'dral *n.* principal church of diocese —*a.* pert. to, containing cathedral

cath'ode *n.* negative electrode —**cathode rays** stream of electrons

cath'olic *a.* universal; including whole body of Christians; (**C-**) relating to R.C. Church —*n.* (**C-**) adherent of R.C. Church —**Cathol'icism** *n.* —**catholic'ity** [-lis'-] *n.* —**cathol'icize** *vt.*

cat'tle *pl.n.* beasts of pasture, *esp.* oxen, cows —**cat'tleman** *n.* —**cattle-grid** *n.* heavy grid over ditch in road to prevent passage of livestock

Cau'casoid *a.* of, pert. to, light-complexioned racial group of mankind

cau'cus *n.* group, meeting, *esp.* of members of political party, with power to decide policy *etc.*

caught *pt./pp. of* CATCH

caul'dron *n.* large pot used for boiling

caul'iflower [kol'-] *n.* variety of cabbage with edible white flowering head

caulk [kawk] *vt.* stop up cracks (*orig.* of ship) with waterproof filler —**caulk'er** *n.* —**caulk'ing** *n.*

cause [-z] *n.* that which produces an effect; reason, origin; motive, purpose; charity, movement; lawsuit —*vt.* bring about, make happen —**caus'al** *a.* —**causal'ity** *n.* —**causa'tion** *n.* —**cause'less** *a.* groundless

cause célèb're [-sə-leb'rə] *Fr.* famous case

cause'way [-z-] *n.* raised way over marsh *etc.*; paved street

cau'stic *a.* burning; bitter, severe —*n.* corrosive substance —**cau'stically** *adv.*

cau'terize *vt.* burn with caustic or hot iron —**cauteriza'tion** *n.*

cau'tion *n.* heedfulness, care; warning —*vt.* warn —**cau'tionary** *a.* containing warning or precept —**cau'tious** *a.* —**cau'tiously** *adv.* —**cau'tiousness** *n.*

cavalcade' *n.* column or procession of riders

cavalier' *a.* careless, disdainful —*n.* courtly gentleman; *obs.* horseman; (**C-**) adherent of Charles I in English Civil War —**cavalier'ly** *adv.*

cav'alry *n.* mounted troops

cave *n.* hollow place in the earth; den —**cav'ern** *n.* deep cave —**cav'ernous** *a.* —**cav'ernously** *adv.* —**ca'ving** *n.* sport of exploring caves —**cav'ity** *n.* hollow —**cave'man** *n.* prehistoric cave dweller —**cave in** fall in; submit; give in

caviar(e)' *n.* salted sturgeon roe

cav'il *vi.* find fault without sufficient reason, make trifling objections (**-ll-**) —**cav'iller** *n.*

cavort' *vi.* prance, frisk

ca'vy *n.* small S Amer. rodent

caw *n.* crow's cry —*vi.* cry so

cayenne' (pepper) [kā-] *n.* pungent red pepper

CB Citizens' Band

CBC Canadian Broadcasting Corporation

cc cubic centimetre(s)

Cd *Chem.* cadmium

CD compact disc —**CD-ROM** compact disc storing written information to be displayed on VDU

CDT Central Daylight Time

cease *v.* bring or come to an end —**cease'less** *a.* —**cease'lessly** *adv.*

ce'dar *n.* large evergreen tree; its wood

cede *vt.* yield, give up, transfer, *esp.* of territory

cedill'a *n.* hooklike mark placed under a letter *c* to show the sound of *s*

cei'lidh [kā'li] *n.* informal social gathering for singing and dancing *esp.* in Scotland

cei'ling [sē'-] *n.* inner, upper surface of a room; maximum price, wage *etc.*; *Aviation* lower level of clouds; limit of height to which aircraft can climb —**ceil** *vt.* line (room), *esp.* with plaster

celan'dine *n.* yellow wild flower

cel'ebrate *v.* rejoice or have festivities to mark (happy day, event *etc.*) —*vt.* observe (birthday *etc.*); perform (religious ceremony *etc.*); praise publicly —**cel'ebrant** *n.* —**cel'ebrated** *a.* famous —**celebra'tion** *n.* —**celeb'rity** *n.* famous person; fame

celer'ity *n.* swiftness

cel'ery *n.* vegetable with long juicy edible stalks

celes'tial *a.* heavenly, divine; of the sky

cel'ibacy *n.* single life, unmarried state —**cel'ibate** *n./a.*

cell *n.* small room, *esp.* in prison; small cavity; minute, basic unit of living matter; device converting chemical energy into electrical energy; small local group operating as nucleus of larger political or religious organization —**cell'ular** *a.* —**cel'lule** *n.* small cell

cell'ar *n.* underground room for storage; stock of wine —**cell'arage** *n.* —**cel'larer** *n.*

cell'o [ch-] *n.* stringed instrument of violin family

cell'ophane *n.* transparent wrapping

cell'uloid [-yoo-] *n.* synthetic plastic substance with wide range of uses; coating of photographic film; cinema film

cell'ulose [-yoo-] *n.* substance of vegetable cell wall; group of carbohydrates; varnish

Cel'sius *a./n.* (of) scale of temperature from 0° (melting point of ice) to 100° (boiling point of water)

Cel'tic [kel'tik *or* sel'-] *n.* branch of language including Gaelic and Welsh —*a.* of, or relating to the Celtic peoples or languages

cement' *n.* fine mortar; adhesive, glue —*vt.* unite with cement; join firmly

cem'etery *n.* burial ground, *esp.* other than churchyard

cen'otaph *n.* monument to one buried elsewhere

cen'ser *n.* pan in which incense is burned —**cense** *vt.*

cen'sor *n.* one authorized to examine motion pictures, books *etc.* and suppress all or part if considered morally or otherwise unacceptable —*vt.* —**censor'ial** *a.* of censor —**censor'ious** *a.* fault-finding —**censor'iousness** *n.* —**cen'sorship** *n.*

cen'sure *n.* blame; harsh criticism —*vt.* blame; criticize harshly

cen'sus *n.* official counting of people, things *etc.*

cent *n.* hundredth part of dollar *etc.*

cen'taur *n.* mythical creature, half man, half horse

cente'nary *n.* 100 years; celebration of

hundredth anniversary —*a.* pert. to a hundred —**centena'rian** *n.* one a hundred years old —**centenn'ial** *a.* lasting, happening every hundred years —*n.* 100th anniversary; celebration of this

cent'igrade *a.* another name for Celsius; having one hundred degrees

cent'imetre *n.* hundredth part of metre

cent'ipede *n.* small segmented animal with many legs

cen'tre *n.* midpoint; pivot, axis; point to or from which things move or are drawn; place for specific organization or activity —**cen'tral** *a.* —**central'ity** *n.* —**centraliza'tion** *n.* —**cen'tralize** *vt.* bring to a centre; concentrate under one control —**cen'trally** *adv.* —**cen'tric** *a.* —**centrif'ugal** *a.* tending from centre —**centrip'etal** *a.* tending towards centre —**central heating** method of heating building from one central source —**central processing unit** *Computers* part of a computer that performs logical and arithmetical operations

centu'rion *n.* Roman commander of 100 men

cen'tury *n.* 100 years; any set of 100

ceram'ic *n.* hard brittle material of baked clay; object made of this —*pl.* (*with sing. v.*) art, techniques of making ceramic objects; such objects —*a.*

ce'real *n.* any edible grain, *eg* wheat, rice *etc.*; (breakfast) food made from grain —*a.*

cer'ebral *a.* pert. to brain

cer'emony *n.* formal observance; sacred rite; courteous act —**ceremo'nial** *a./n.* —**ceremo'nially** *adv.* —**ceremo'nious** *a.* —**ceremo'niously** *adv.* —**ceremo'niousness** *n.*

cerise' [sə-rēz'] *n./a.* clear, pinkish red

cert'ain *a.* sure; settled, inevitable; some, one; of moderate (quantity, degree *etc.*) —**cert'ainly** *adv.* —**cert'ainty** *n.* —**cert'itude** *n.* confidence

cert'ify *vt.* declare formally; endorse, guarantee; declare legally insane (**-fied, -fying**) —**certif'icate** *n.* written declaration —*vt.* give written declaration —**certifica'tion** *n.* —**cert'ifier** *n.*

ceru'lean [-rōō'-] *a.* sky-blue

cer'vix *n.* neck, *esp.* of womb —**cer'vical** *a.*

c(a)e'sium [sē'-] *n.* ductile silvery-white element of alkali metal group

cessa'tion *n.* ceasing or stopping, pause

cess'ion *n.* yielding up

cess'pool *n.* pit in which filthy water collects, receptacle for sewage

cf. confer (*Lat.*, compare)

c/f carried forward

CFL Canadian Football League

cg centigram

cgs units metric system of units based on *centimetre, gram, second*

ch. chapter; church

chafe *vt.* make sore or worn by rubbing; make warm by rubbing; vex, irritate

chaff [-ah-] *n.* husks of corn; worthless matter; banter —*v.* tease good-naturedly

chaff'er *vi.* haggle, bargain —*n.* bargaining

chaff'inch *n.* small songbird

chag'rin [sh-] *n.* vexation, disappointment —*vt.* embarrass; annoy; disappoint

chain *n.* series of connected links or rings; thing that binds; connected series of things or events; surveyor's measure Makes compound nouns as **chain armour, chain mail, chain reaction, chain smoker, chain stitch, chain store** *etc.* —*vt.* fasten with a chain; confine; restrain

chair *n.* movable seat, with back, for one person; seat of authority; professorship; iron support for rail on railway —*vt.* preside over; carry in triumph —**chair'lift** *n.* series of chairs fixed to cable for conveying people (*esp.* skiers) up mountain —**chair'man** *n.* one who presides over meeting —**chair'manship** *n*

chaise [shāz] *n.* light horse-drawn carriage —**chaise longue** [-long] sofa

chalced'ony [kal-sed'-] *n.* whitish, bluish-white variety of quartz

chal'et [shal'ā] *n.* Swiss wooden house

chal'ice *n. Poet.* cup or bowl; communion cup

chalk [chawk] *n.* white substance, carbonate of lime; crayon —*v.* rub, draw, mark with chalk —**chalk'iness** *n.* —**chalk'y** *a.* —**chalk'board** *n.* dark-coloured surface for writing on with chalk

chall'enge *vt.* call to fight or account; dispute; stimulate; object to; claim —*n.*

—**chall'enger** *n.* —**chall'enging** *a.* difficult but stimulating

cha'mber *n.* room for assembly; assembly, body of men; compartment; cavity; *obs.* room —*pl.* office or apartments of barrister; lodgings —**cha'mberlain** *n.* official at court of a monarch having charge of domestic and ceremonial affairs —**cha'mbermaid** *n.* servant with care of bedrooms —**chamber music** music for performance by a few instruments —**chamber (pot)** vessel for urine

chame'leon [kə-] *n.* small lizard famous for its power of changing colour

cham'fer *vt.* groove; bevel; flute —*n.* groove

cham'ois [sham'wah] *n.* goatlike mountain antelope; [sham'i] a soft pliable leather

champ[1] *v.* munch (food) noisily, as horse; be nervous, impatient

champ[2] *n. short for* CHAMPION

champagne' [sham-pān'] *n.* light, sparkling white wine of several varieties

cham'pion *n.* one that excels all others; defender of a cause; one who fights for another; hero —*vt.* fight for, maintain —**cham'pionship** *n.*

chance [-ah-] *n.* unpredictable course of events; fortune, luck; opportunity; possibility; risk; probability —*vt.* risk —*vi.* happen —*a.* casual, unexpected —**chan'cy** *a.* risky

chan'cel [-ah-] *n.* part of a church where altar is

chan'cellor [-ah-] *n.* high officer of state; head of university —**chan'cellorship** *n.* —**chan'cellery, -ory** *n.*

Chan'cery [-ah-] *n.* division of British High Court of Justice

chandelier' [sh-] *n.* hanging frame with branches for holding lights

chand'ler [-ah-] *n.* dealer in ropes, ships' supplies *etc.*

change *v.* alter, make or become different; put on (different clothes, fresh coverings) —*vt.* put or give for another; exchange, interchange —*n.* alteration, variation; variety; conversion of money; small money, coins; balance received on payment —**changeabil'ity** *n.* —**change'able** *a.* —**change'ably** *adv.* —**change'ful** *a.* —**change'less** *a.* —**change'ling** *n.* child believed substituted for another by fairies

chann'el *n.* bed of stream; strait; deeper part of strait, bay, harbour; groove; means of passing or conveying; band of radio frequencies; television broadcasting station —*vt.* groove, furrow; guide, convey

chant [-ah-] *n.* simple song or melody; rhythmic or repetitious slogan —*v.* sing or utter chant; speak monotonously or repetitiously

chanticleer' *n.* cock

chant'y [ch-, sh-] *n. see* SHANTY[2]

cha'os [kā'-] *n.* disorder, confusion; state of universe before Creation —**chaot'ic** *a.*

chap[1] *v.* of skin, become dry, raw and cracked, *esp.* by exposure to cold and wind (**-pp-**) —**chapped** *a.*

chap[2] *n. inf.* fellow, man

chap'el *n.* private church; subordinate place of worship; division of church with its own altar; Nonconformist place of worship ; association of printers

chap'eron(e) [sh-] *n.* one who attends young unmarried lady in public as protector —*vt.* attend in this way

chap'lain [-lin] *n.* clergyman attached to chapel, regiment, warship, institution *etc.* —**chap'laincy** *n.* his office

chaps *pl.n.* cowboy's leggings of thick leather

chap'ter *n.* division of book; section, heading; assembly of clergy, bishop's council *etc.*; organized branch of society, fraternity —**chap'terhouse** *n.*

char[1] *vt.* scorch, burn to charcoal (**-rr-**) —**charred** *a.*

char[2] **UK** *inf. n.* charwoman —*v.* act as charwoman (**-rr-**)

char[3] *n.* troutlike small fish

char'acter [ka-] *n.* nature; total of qualities making up individuality; moral qualities; reputation of possessing them; statement of qualities of person; an eccentric; personality in play or novel; letter, sign, or any distinctive mark; essential feature —**characteris'tic** *a.* —**characteris'tically** *adv.* —**characteriza'tion** *n.* —**char'acterize** *vt.* mark out, distinguish; describe by peculiar qualities —**char'acterless** *a.*

charade' [shə-rahd'] *n.* absurd act; travesty —*pl.* word-guessing parlour game with syllables of word acted

char'coal *n.* black residue of wood,

bones *etc.*, produced by smothered burning; charred wood **—charcoal-burner** *n.*

charge *vt.* ask as price; bring accusation against; lay task on; command; attack; deliver injunction; fill with electricity; fill, load *—vi.* make onrush, attack *—n.* cost, price; accusation; attack, onrush; command, exhortation; accumulation of electricity *—pl.* expenses **—charge'able** *a.* **—char'ger** *n.* strong, fast battle horse; that which charges, *esp.* electrically

char'iot [cha-] *n.* two-wheeled vehicle used in ancient fighting; state carriage **—charioteer'** *n.*

charis'ma [kə-riz'-] *n.* special power of individual to inspire fascination, loyalty *etc.* **—charismat'ic** *a.*

char'ity [cha-] *n.* the giving of help, money *etc.* to those in need; organization for doing this; the money *etc.* given; love, kindness; disposition to think kindly of others **—char'itable** *a.* **—char'itably** *adv.*

charl'atan [sh-] *n.* quack, impostor **—char'latanry** *n.*

charles'ton *n.* fast, rhythmic dance of 1920s

charm *n.* attractiveness; anything that fascinates; amulet; magic spell *—vt.* bewitch; delight, attract **—charmed** *a.* **—charm'er** *n.* **—charm'ing** *a.*

charn'el house vault for bones of the dead

chart *n.* map of sea; diagram or tabulated statement *—vt.* map; represent on chart

chart'er *n.* document granting privileges *etc.*; patent *—vt.* let or hire; establish by charter

char'woman, -lady *n.* woman paid to clean office, house *etc.*

cha'ry *a.* cautious, sparing **—cha'rily** *adv.* **—cha'riness** *n.* caution

chase[1] *vt.* hunt, pursue; drive from, away, into *etc.* *—n.* pursuit, hunting; the hunted; hunting ground **—cha'ser** *n.* drink of beer, soda *etc.*, taken after neat spirit

chase[2] *vt.* engrave **—cha'ser** *n.* **—cha'sing** *n.*

chasm [kazm] *n.* deep cleft, fissure; abyss

chass'is [shas'i] *n.* framework, wheels and machinery of motor vehicle excluding body and coachwork; underframe of aircraft

chaste *a.* virginal; pure; modest; virtuous **—chaste'ly** *adv.* **—chas'tity** *n.*

cha'sten [-sən] *vt.* correct by punishment; restrain, subdue **—cha'stened** *a.* **—chastise'** [chas-tīz'] *vt.* inflict punishment on **—chas'tisement** [-tiz-] *n.*

chas'uble [-z'-] *n.* priest's long sleeveless outer vestment

chat[1] *vi.* talk idly, or familiarly (**-tt-**) *—n.* familiar idle talk **—chatt'ily** *adv.* **—chat'ty** *a.* **—chat show** television or radio programme in which guests are interviewed informally

chat[2] *n.* any of various Amer. warblers

chat'eau [shat'ō] *n.* (*esp.* in France) castle, country house (*pl.* **-teaux** [-tō] *or* **-teaus**)

chatt'el *n.* any movable property (*usu. in pl.*)

chatt'er *vi.* talk idly or rapidly; rattle teeth *—n.* idle talk **—chatt'erer** *n.* **—chat'tering** *n.* **—chatt'erbox** *n.* one who chatters incessantly

chau'ffeur [shō'fər] *n.* paid driver of automobile (**chauffeuse'** *fem.*)

chau'vinism [shō'-] *n.* aggressive patriotism; smug sense of superiority

cheap *a.* low in price; inexpensive; easily obtained; of little value or estimation; mean, inferior **—cheap'en** *vt.* **—cheap'ly** *adv.* **—cheap'ness** *n.*

cheat *vt.* deceive, defraud, swindle, impose upon *—vi.* practise deceit to gain advantage *—n.* fraud

check *vt.* stop; restrain; hinder; repress; control; examine for accuracy, quality *etc.;* mark off to indicate correctness *etc.;* (*oft. with* with) correspond or agree; leave in temporary custody; *Hockey* impede (opponent) *—n.* repulse; stoppage; restraint; brief examination for correctness or accuracy; ticket or tag to identify property deposited for custody; pattern of squares on fabric; threat to king at chess **—check'mate** *n.* *Chess* final winning move; any overthrow, defeat *—vt.* *Chess* make the movement ending game; defeat **—check'out** *n.* counter in supermarket where customers pay **—check'room** *n.* place where baggage, coats *etc.* may be left in temporary custody

—**check'up** *n.* examination (*esp.* medical) to see if all is in order

checked *a.* having pattern of small squares

check'er[1] *n.* cashier, *esp.* in supermarket; attendant in checkroom *etc.*

check'er[2] *n.* marking as on chessboard; marble, peg used in games, *eg* Chinese checkers —*pl.* squares like those of chessboard; game played on chessboard with flat round pieces —*vt.* mark in squares; variegate —**check'ered** *a.* marked in squares; uneven, varied

Ched'dar *n.* smooth hard cheese

cheek *n.* side of face below eye; *inf.* impudence —*vt. inf.* address impudently —**cheek'y** *a.*

cheep *vi./n.* (utter) high-pitched cry, as of young bird

cheer *vt.* comfort; gladden; encourage by shouts —*vi.* shout applause —*n.* shout of approval; happiness, good spirits; mood; *obs.* rich food —**cheer'ful** *a.* —**cheer'fully** *adv.* —**cheer'fulness** *n.* —**cheer'ily** *adv.* —**cheer'less** *a.* —**cheer'lessness** *n.* —**cheer'y** *a.*

cheese *n.* curd of milk coagulated, separated from the whey and pressed —**chees'iness** *n.* —**chees'y** *a.* —**cheese'cloth** *n.* loosely woven cotton cloth —**cheese'paring** *a.* mean

chee'tah *n.* large, swift, spotted feline animal

chef [sh-] *n.* head cook, *esp.* in restaurant

chef-d'oeu'vre [shā-dur'vr] *Fr.* masterpiece

chem. chemical; chemistry

chem'istry [k-] *n.* science concerned with properties of substances and their combinations and reactions —**chem'ical** *n./a.* —**chem'ically** *adv.* —**chem'ist** *n.* **UK** pharmacist; one trained in chemistry

chemother'apy [k-] *n.* treatment of disease by chemical means

chem'urgy [k-] *n.* branch of applied chemistry devoted to the development of agricultural products —**chemur'gic(al)** *a.*

chenille' [shə-nēl'] *n.* soft cord, fabric of silk or worsted

cheque [-ek] *n.* written order to banker to pay money from one's account; printed slip of paper used for this —**cheque'book** *n.* book of cheques —**cheque card** banker's card

cheq'uer [-ər] *n./vt. see* CHECKER[2]

cher'ish *vt.* treat with affection; protect; foster

cheroot' [sh-] *n.* cigar with both ends open

cherr'y *n.* small red fruit with stone; tree bearing it —*a.* ruddy, bright red

cher'ub *n.* winged creature with human face; angel (*pl.* **cher'ubim, cher'ubs**) —**cheru'bic** *a.*

cher'vil *n.* a herb

chess *n.* game of skill played by two with 32 pieces on checkered board of 64 squares —**chess'board** *n.* —**chess'men** *pl.n.* pieces used in chess

chest *n.* upper part of trunk of body; large, strong box —**chest of drawers** piece of furniture containing drawers

chest'erfield *n.* padded sofa

chest'nut [-s'n-] *n.* large reddish-brown nut growing in prickly husk; tree bearing it; *inf.* old joke —*a.* reddish-brown

chev'ron [sh-] *n. Mil.* V-shaped band of braid worn on sleeve to designate rank

chew [-o͞o] *v.* grind with teeth —*n.* —**chew'y** *a.* firm, sticky when chewed —**chewing gum**

chian'ti [ki-] *n.* It. wine

chic [shēk] *a.* stylish, elegant —*n.*

chica'nery [shi-] *n.* quibbling; trick, artifice

chick, chick'en *n.* young of birds, *esp.* of hen; *sl.* girl, young woman —**chicken feed** trifling amount (of money) —**chicken-hearted** *a.* cowardly —**chick'enpox** *n.* infectious disease, *esp.* of children —**chick'pea** *n.* dwarf pea —**chick'weed** *n.* weed with small white flowers

chic'ory *n.* salad plant of which the root is ground and used with, or instead of, coffee

chide *vt.* scold, reprove, censure (**chid** *pt.*, **chidd'en, chid** *pp.*, **chi'ding** *pr.p.*)

chief *n.* head or principal person —*a.* principal, foremost, leading —**chief'ly** *adv.* —**chief'tain** *n.* leader, chief of clan or tribe

chiff'on [sh-] *n.* thin gauzy material —**chiffonier'** *n.* ornamental cupboard

chi'gnon [shē'nyon] *n.* roll, knot, of hair worn at back of head

chihua'hua [chi-wah'wah] *n.* breed of tiny dog, *orig.* from Mexico

chil'blain *n.* inflamed sore on hands, legs *etc.*, due to cold

child [-ī-] *n.* young human being; offspring (*pl.* **child'ren** [-i-]) —**child'ish** [-ī-] *a.* of or like a child; silly; trifling —**child'ishly** *adv.* —**child'less** *a.* —**child'like** *a.* of or like a child; innocent; frank; docile —**child'bed** *n.* state of giving birth to child —**child'birth** *n.* —**child'hood** *n.* period between birth and puberty —**child's play** very easy task

chill *n.* coldness; cold with shivering; anything that damps, discourages —*v.* make, become cold (*esp.* food, drink) —**chilled** *a.* —**chill'iness** *n.* —**chill'y** *a.*

chill'i *n.* small red hot-tasting seed pod; plant producing it

chime *n.* sound of bell; harmonious, ringing sound —*vi.* ring harmoniously; agree —*vt.* strike (bells) —**chime in** come into conversation with agreement

chim(a)e'ra [kī-mē'-] *n.* fabled monster, made up of parts of various animals; wild fancy —**chimer'ic(al)** *a.* fanciful

chim'ney *n.* a passage for smoke; narrow vertical cleft in rock (*pl.* **-neys**)

chimpanzee' *n.* gregarious, intelligent ape of Africa

chin *n.* part of face below mouth

chi'na *n.* fine earthenware, porcelain; cups, saucers *etc.* collectively

chinchill'a *n.* S Amer. rodent with soft, grey fur

chine *n.* backbone; joint of meat; ridge or crest of land

Chinese lantern Asian plant cultivated for its orange-red inflated calyx

chink[1] *n.* cleft, crack —*vt.* fill up or make cracks in

chink[2] *n.* light metallic sound —*v.* (cause to) make this sound

chintz *n.* cotton cloth printed in coloured designs

chip *n.* splinter; place where piece has been broken off; very thin, fried slice of potato eaten cold; UK French fried potato; tiny wafer of silicon forming integrated circuit in computer *etc.* —*vt.* chop into small pieces; break small pieces from; shape by cutting off pieces —*vi.* break off (**-pp-**) —**chip in** interrupt; contribute

chip'munk *n.* small, striped N Amer. squirrel

chipolat'a [-lah'-] *n.* small sausage

chirog'raphy [kī-] *n.* calligraphy

chirop'odist [ki-] *n.* one who treats disorders of feet —**chirop'ody** *n.*

chi'ropractor [kī'-] *n.* one skilled in treating bodily disorders by manipulation, massage *etc.* —**chiroprac'tic** *n.*

chirp, chirr'up *n.* short, sharp cry of bird —*vi.* make this sound —**chir'py** *a.* *inf.* happy

chis'el [-z'-] *n.* cutting tool, usu. bar of steel with edge across main axis —*vt.* cut, carve with chisel; *sl.* cheat (**-ll-**)

chit[1] *n.* informal note, memorandum

chit[2] *n.* child, young girl

chiv'alry [sh-] *n.* bravery and courtesy; medieval system of knighthood —**chiv'alrous** *a.* —**chiv'alrously** *adv.*

chive *n.* herb with mild onion flavour

chlor'ine [kl-] *n.* nonmetallic element, yellowish-green poison gas —**chlor'ate** *n.* salt of chloric acid —**chlor'ic** *a.* —**chlo'ride** *n.* compound of chlorine; bleaching agent —**chlor'inate** *vt.* disinfect; purify with chlorine

chlor'oform [kl-] *n.* volatile liquid formerly used as anaesthetic —*vt.* render insensible with it

chlor'ophyll [kl-] *n.* green colouring matter in plants

chock *n.* block or wedge to prevent heavy object rolling or sliding —**chock-full, chock-a-block** *a.* packed full

choc'olate *n.* paste from ground cacao seeds; confectionery, drink made from this —*a.* dark brown

choice *n.* act or power of choosing; alternative; thing or person chosen —*a.* select, fine, worthy of being chosen —**choice'ly** *adv.*

choir [kwīr] *n.* band of singers, *esp.* in church; part of church set aside for them

choke *vt.* hinder, stop the breathing of; smother, stifle; obstruct —*vi.* suffer choking —*n.* act, noise of choking; device in carburettor to increase richness of gasoline-air mixture —**choked** *a.* —**choke'bore** *n.* gun with bore narrowed towards muzzle —**choke'damp** *n.* carbon dioxide gas in coal mines

chol'er [k-] *n.* bile, anger —**chol'eric** *a.* bad-tempered

chol'era [k-] *n.* deadly infectious disease marked by vomiting and diarrhoea

choles'terol [kol-] *n.* substance found in animal tissue and fat

chomp *v.* chew noisily

choose *vt.* pick out, select; take by preference —*vi.* decide, think fit (**chose, cho'sen, choo'sing**) —**choo'ser** *n.* —**choo'sy** *a.* fussy

chop[1] *vt.* cut with blow; hack (**-pp-**) —*n.* hewing blow; slice of meat containing rib or other bone —**chopp'er** *n.* short axe; *inf.* helicopter; *inf.* large motorbike —**chop'py** *a.* (of sea) having short, broken waves

chop[2] *vt.* exchange, bandy, *eg* **chop logic, chop and change** (**-pp-**)

chops *pl.n. inf.* jaws, cheeks

chop'sticks *pl.n.* implements used by Chinese for eating food

chop su'ey [-sōō'-] a kind of rich Chinese stew with rice

chor'al [k-] *a.* of, for, sung by, a choir

chorale' [-rahl'] *n.* slow, stately hymn tune

chord [k-] *n.* emotional response, *esp.* of sympathy; simultaneous sounding of musical notes; straight line joining ends of arc

chore *n.* (unpleasant) task; odd job

choreog'raphy [ko-ri-] *n.* art of arranging dances, *esp.* ballet; art, notation of ballet dancing —**choreog'rapher** *n.* —**choreograph'ic** *a.*

chor'tle *vi.* chuckle happily —*n.*

chor'us [k-] *n.* band of singers; combination of voices singing together; refrain —*vt.* sing or say together —**chor'ic** [kor'-] *a.* —**chor'ister** [kor'i-] *n.*

chose *pt.* —**cho'sen** *pp. of* CHOOSE

chough [chuf] *n.* large black bird of crow family

chow[1] *n. inf.* food

chow[2] *n.* thick-coated dog with curled tail, *orig.* from China

Christ [krīst] *n.* Jesus of Nazareth, regarded by Christians as the Messiah

Chris'tian [kris'chən] *n.* follower of Christ —*a.* following Christ; relating to Christ or his religion —**christ'en** [kris'n] *vt.* baptize, give name to —**Chris'tendom** [-s'n-] *n.* all the Christian world —**Christian'ity** *n.* religion of Christ —**chris'tianize** *vt.* —**Christian name** name given at baptism —**Christian Science** religious system founded by Mrs. Eddy in U.S.A.

Christ'mas [kris'-] *n.* festival of birth of Christ —**Christmas box** tip, present given at Christmas —**Christmas card** —**Christmas tree**

chromat'ic [krə-] *a.* of colour; *Mus.* of scale proceeding by semitones

chro'matin [krō'-] *n.* part of protoplasmic substance in nucleus of cells which takes colour in staining tests

chrome, chro'mium [krō'-] *n.* metal used in alloys and for plating

chro'mosome [krō'-] *n.* microscopic gene-carrying body in the tissue of a cell

chro'mosphere [krō'-] *n.* layer of incandescent gas surrounding the sun

Chron. Chronicles

chron'ic [kr-] *a.* lasting a long time; habitual

chron'icle [kr-] *n.* record of events in order of time; account —*vt.* record —**chron'icler** *n.*

chronol'ogy [kr-] *n.* determination of sequence of past events; arrangement in order of occurrence —**chronolog'ical** *a.* arranged in order of time —**chronolog'ically** *adv.* —**chronol'ogist** *n.*

chronom'eter [kr-] *n.* instrument for measuring time exactly; watch —**chronomet'rical** *a.* —**chronom'etry** *n.*

chrys'alis [kris'-] *n.* resting state of insect between grub and butterfly *etc.*; case enclosing it (*pl.* **chrys'alises, chrysal'ides** [-idēz])

chrysan'themum [kri-] *n.* garden flower of various colours

chubb'y *a.* plump

chuck[1] *inf. vt.* throw; pat affectionately (under chin); give up, reject

chuck[2] *n.* cut of beef; device for gripping, adjusting bit in power drill *etc.*

chuck'le *vi.* laugh softly —*n.* such laugh

chukk'er *n.* period of play in game of polo

chum *n. inf.* close friend —**chumm'y** *a.*

chunk *n.* thick, solid piece —**chunk'y** *a.*

church *n.* building for Christian worship; (**C-**) whole body or sect of Christians; clergy —**church'man** *n.* —**churchward'en** *n.* officer who represents interests of parish; long clay pipe —**church'yard** *n.*

churl *n.* rustic; ill-bred fellow —**churl'ish** *a.* —**churl'ishly** *adv.* —**churl'ishness** *n.*

churn *n.* large container for milk; vessel for making butter —*v.* shake up, stir (liquid) violently

chute [shoot] *n.* slide for sending down parcels, coal *etc.*; channel; narrow passageway, *eg* for spraying, counting cattle, sheep *etc.*; *inf. short for* PARACHUTE

chut'ney *n.* pickle of fruit, spices *etc.*

CIA US Central Intelligence Agency

cica'da [si-kah'-] *n.* cricketlike insect

cic'atrix [sik'-] *n.* scar of healed wound —**cic'atrize** *v.* heal —**cicatriza'tion** *n.*

CID UK Criminal Investigation Department

ci'der *n.* drink made from apples

cigar' *n.* roll of tobacco leaves for smoking —**cigarette'** *n.* finely-cut tobacco rolled in paper for smoking

C-in-C Commander-in-Chief

cinch *n.* leather or cloth band put round horse to hold saddle *etc.* —*vt.* surround, secure with cinch

cin'der *n.* remains of burned coal

cine camera [sin'i] **UK** movie camera

cin'ema *n.* motion picture; motion-picture theatre; motion pictures generally or collectively —**cinematog'raphy** *n.*

cin'erary *a.* pert. to ashes

cinn'amon *n.* spice got from bark of Asian tree; the tree —*a.* of a light-brown colour

cinque'foil [singk'-] *n.* plant with five-lobed leaves

ci'pher, cy'pher *n.* secret writing; arithmetical symbol; person of no importance; monogram —*vt.* write in cipher

cir'ca *Lat.* about, approximately

cir'cle *n.* perfectly round figure; ring; *Theatre* section of seats in balcony; group, society with common interest; spiritualist seance; class of society —*vt.* surround —*vi.* move round —**circ'ular** *a.* round; moving round —*n.* letter sent to several persons —**circ'ulate** *vi.* move round; pass from hand to hand or place to place —*vt.* send round —**circula'tion** *n.* flow of blood from, and back to, heart; act of moving round; extent of sale of newspaper *etc.* —**cir'culatory** *a.*

circ'uit [-k'it] *n.* complete round or course; area; path of electric current; round of visitation, *esp.* of judges; series of sporting events; district —**circu'itous** *a.* roundabout, indirect —**circu'itously** *adv.* —**circ'uitry** *n.* electrical circuit(s)

circ'umcise [-z] *vt.* cut off foreskin of —**circumcis'ion** *n.*

circum'ference *n.* boundary line, *esp.* of circle

circ'umflex *n.* accent (ˆ) over vowel to indicate length of its sound

circumlocu'tion *n.* roundabout speech

circumnav'igate *vt.* sail or fly right round —**circumnaviga'tion** *n.* —**circumnav'igator** *n.*

circ'umscribe [*or* -skrīb'] *vt.* confine, bound, limit, hamper

circ'umspect *a.* watchful, cautious, prudent —**circ'umspectly** *adv.* —**circumspec'tion** *n.*

circ'umstance *n.* detail; event; matter of fact —*pl.* state of affairs; condition in life, *esp.* financial; surroundings or things accompanying an action —**circumstan'tial** *a.* depending on detail or circumstances; detailed, minute; incidental —**circumstantial'ity** *n.* —**circumstan'tially** *adv.* —**circumstan'tiate** *vt.* prove by details; describe exactly

circumvent' *vt.* outwit, evade, get round —**circumven'tion** *n.*

circ'us *n.* (performance of) travelling group of acrobats, clowns, performing animals *etc.*; circular structure for public shows (*pl.* **-es**)

cirrho'sis [si-rō'-] *n.* any of various chronic progressive diseases of liver —**cirrhot'ic** *a.*

cirr'us *n.* high wispy cloud (*pl.* **cirr'i** [-ī])

cis'co [sis'ko] *n.* N Amer. whitefish (*pl.* **-o(e)s**)

cis'tern *n.* water tank

cit'adel *n.* fortress in, near, or commanding a city

cite *vt.* quote; bring forward as proof —**cita'tion** *n.* quoting; commendation for bravery *etc.*

cit'izen *n.* native, naturalized member of state, nation *etc.*; inhabitant of city —**cit'izenship** *n.*

cit'ron *n.* fruit like a lemon; the tree —**cit'ric** *a.* of the acid of lemon or citron

—**citrus fruit** citrons, lemons, limes, oranges *etc.*

cit'y *n.* a large town

civ'et *n.* strong, musky perfume —**civet-cat** *n.* catlike animal producing it

civ'ic *a.* pert. to city or citizen —**civ'ics** *pl.n.* (*with sing. v.*) study of government and its workings; study of the rights and responsibilities of citizenship

civ'il *a.* relating to citizens of state; not military; refined, polite; *Law* not criminal —**civil'ian** *n.* nonmilitary person —**civil'ity** *n.* —**civ'illy** *adv.* —**civil service** service responsible for the public administration of the government of a country

civ'ilize *vt.* bring out of barbarism; refine —**civiliza'tion** *n.* —**civ'ilized** *a.*

civv'y *sl. n.* civilian —*pl.* civilian clothing

Cl *Chem.* chlorine

cl centilitre

clack *n.* sound, as of two pieces of wood striking together —*v.*

clad *pt./pp. of* CLOTHE

cladd'ing *n.* material used for outside facing of building *etc.*

claim *vt.* demand as right; assert; call for —*n.* demand for thing supposed due; right; thing claimed; plot of mining land marked out by stakes as required by law —**claim'ant** *n.*

clairvoy'ance [-voi'-] *n.* power of seeing things not present to senses, second sight —**clairvoy'ant** *n./a.*

clam *n.* edible mollusc

clam'ber *vi.* to climb with difficulty or awkwardly

clamm'y *a.* moist and sticky —**clam'miness** *n.*

clam'o(u)r *n.* loud shouting, outcry, noise —*vi.* shout, call noisily (for) —**clam'orous** *a.* —**clam'orously** *adv.*

clamp' *n.* tool for holding or compressing —*vt.* fasten, strengthen with or as with clamp

clan *n.* tribe or collection of families under chief and of common ancestry; faction, group —**clann'ish** *a.* —**clan'nishly** *adv.* —**clann'ishness** *n.*

clandes'tine *a.* secret; sly

clang *v.* (cause to) make loud ringing sound —*n.* loud ringing sound —**clang'er** *n. inf.* conspicuous mistake; that which clangs

clank *n.* short sound as of pieces of metal struck together —*v.* cause, move with, such sound

clap[1] *v.* (cause to) strike with noise; strike (hands) together; applaud —*vt.* pat; place or put quickly (**-pp-**) —*n.* hard, explosive sound; slap —**clapp'er** *n.* —**clap'ping** *n.* —**clap'trap** *n.* empty words

clap[2] *n. sl.* gonorrhoea

clap'board *n.* thin board with one edge thicker than the other used in wood-frame construction

clar'et [kla'rət] *n.* a dry dark red wine of Bordeaux

clar'ify [kla'ri-] *v.* make or become clear, pure, or more easily understood (**-fied, -fying**) —**clarifica'tion** *n.* —**clar'ity** *n.* clearness

clarinet' *n.* woodwind musical instrument

clar'ion [kla'ri-] *n.* clear-sounding trumpet; rousing sound

clash *n.* loud noise, as of weapons striking; conflict, collision —*vi.* make clash; come into conflict; (of events) coincide; (of colours) look ugly together —*vt.* strike together to make clash

clasp [-ah-] *n.* hook or other means of fastening; embrace —*vt.* fasten; embrace, grasp —**clasp knife**

class [-ah-] *n.* any division, order, kind, sort; rank; group of school pupils *etc.* taught together; division by merit; quality; *inf.* excellence or elegance —*vt.* assign to proper division —**class'ify** [klas'-] *vt.* arrange methodically in classes (**-fied, -fying**) —**classifica'tion** *n.* —**class'ified** *a.* arranged in classes; secret; (of advertisements) arranged under headings in newspapers —**class'y** [-ah-] *a. inf.* stylish, elegant

class'ic *a.* of first rank; of highest rank generally, but *esp.* of art; refined; typical; famous —*n.* (literary) work of recognized excellence —*pl.n.* ancient Latin and Greek literature —**class'ical** *a.* of Greek and Roman literature, art, culture; of classic quality; *Mus.* of established standards of form, complexity *etc.* —**clas'sically** *adv.* —**class'icism** *n.* —**class'icist** *n.*

clatt'er *n.* rattling noise; noisy conversation —*v.* (cause to) make clatter

clause [-z] *n.* part of sentence, containing verb; article in formal document as treaty, contract *etc.*

claustropho'bia *n.* abnormal fear of confined spaces

clav'ichord [-k-] *n.* musical instrument with keyboard, forerunner of piano

clav'icle *n.* collarbone —**clavic'ular** *a.* pert. to this

claw *n.* sharp hooked nail of bird or beast; foot of bird of prey; clawlike article —*vt.* tear with claws; grip

clay *n.* fine-grained earth, plastic when wet, hardening when baked; earth —**clay'ey** *a.*

clay'more *n.* ancient Highland two-edged sword

CLC Canadian Labour Congress

clean *a.* free from dirt, stain, or defilement; pure; guiltless; trim, shapely —*adv.* so as to leave no dirt; entirely —*vt.* free from dirt —**clean'er** *n.* —**clean'liness** [klen'-] *n.* —**clean'ly** [klēn'-] *adv.* —*a.* [klen'-] clean —**clean'ness** [klēn'-] *n.* —**cleanse** [klenz] *vt.* make clean —**come clean** *inf.* confess

clear *a.* pure, undimmed, bright; free from cloud; transparent; plain, distinct; without defect or drawback; unimpeded —*adv.* brightly; wholly, quite —*vt.* make clear; acquit; pass over or through; make as profit; free from obstruction, difficulty; free by payment of dues —*vi.* become clear, bright, free, transparent —**clear'ance** *n.* making clear; removal of obstructions, surplus stock *etc.*; certificate that ship has been cleared at custom house; space for moving part, vehicle, to pass within, through or past something —**clear'ing** *n.* land cleared of trees —**clear'ly** *adv.* —**clear'ness** *n.* —**clear-sighted** *a.* discerning

cleat *n.* wedge; piece of wood or iron with two projecting ends round which ropes are made fast

cleave[1] *vt.* split asunder —*vi.* crack, part asunder (**clove, cleft** *pt.* **clo'ven, cleft** *pp.* **cleav'ing** *pr.p.*) —**cleav'age** *n.* —**cleav'er** *n.* short chopper

cleave[2] *vi.* stick, adhere; be loyal (**cleaved, cleav'ing**)

clef *n. Mus.* mark to show pitch of stave

cleft *n.* crack, fissure, chasm; opening made by cleaving —*pt./pp. of* CLEAVE[1]

clem'atis [*or* -ā'tis] *n.* flowering climbing perennial plant

clem'ent *a.* merciful; gentle; mild —**clem'ency** *n.* —**clem'ently** *adv.*

clench [-ch, -sh] *vt.* set firmly together; grasp, close (fist)

cler'gy *n.* body of appointed ministers of Christian church —**cler'gyman** *n.*

cler'ic [kler'ik] *n.* clergyman —**cler'icalism** *n.*

cler'ical [kler'ik-] *a.* of clergy; of, connected with, office work

clerk *n.* shop assistant; subordinate who keeps files *etc.* in an office; officer in charge of records, correspondence *etc.*, of department or corporation —**clerk'ly** *a.* —**clerk'ship** *n.*

clev'er *a.* intelligent; able, skilful, adroit —**clev'erly** *adv.* —**clev'erness** *n.*

cli'ché [klē'shā] *n.* stereotyped hackneyed phrase (*pl.* **-s**)

click[1] *n.* short, sharp sound, as of latch in door; catch —*vi.* make this sound

click[2] *vi. sl.* be a success; *inf.* become clear; *inf.* strike up friendship

cli'ent [klī'-] *n.* customer; one who employs professional person —**clientele'** [klē-on-tel'] *n.* body of clients

cliff *n.* steep rock face —**cliff'hanger** *n.* tense situation, *esp.* in movie *etc.*

cli'mate *n.* condition of country with regard to weather; prevailing feeling, atmosphere —**climat'ic** *a.* of climate

cli'max *n.* highest point, culmination; point of greatest excitement, tension in story *etc.* —**climac'tic** *a.*

climb [klīm] *v.* go up or ascend; progress with difficulty; creep up, mount; slope upwards —**climb'er** *n.* —**climb'ing** *n.*

clime *n.* region, country; climate

clinch *vt. see* CLENCH; settle, conclude (an agreement) —**clinch'er** *n. inf.* something decisive

cling *vi.* adhere; be firmly attached to; be dependent (**clung** *pt./pp.*)

clin'ic *n.* place for medical examination, advice, or treatment; group or centre that offers advice or instruction —**clin'ical** *a.* relating to clinic, care of sick *etc.*; objective, unemotional; bare, plain —**clin'ically** *adv.* —**clinical thermometer** used for taking body temperature

clink[1] *n.* sharp metallic sound —*v.* (cause to) make this sound

clink[2] *n. sl.* prison

clink'er *n.* fused coal residues from fire or furnace; hard brick

clinker-built *a.* (of boat) with outer boards or plates overlapping

clip[1] *vt.* cut with scissors; cut short (**-pp-**) —*n. inf.* sharp blow —**clipp'er** *n.*

clip[2] *n.* device for gripping or holding together, *esp.* hair, clothing *etc.*

clipp'er *n.* fast sailing ship

clique [-ēk] *n.* small exclusive set; faction, group of people —**clique'ish** *a.*

clit'oris *n.* small erectile part of female genitals

cloak *n.* loose outer garment; disguise, pretext —*vt.* cover with cloak; disguise, conceal —**cloak'room** *n.* place for keeping coats, hats, luggage

clobb'er *inf. vt.* beat, batter; defeat utterly —*n.* **UK** belongings

cloche [klosh] *n.* cover to protect young plants; woman's close-fitting hat

clock *n.* instrument for measuring time; device with dial for recording or measuring —**clock'wise** *adv./a.* in the direction that the hands of a clock rotate —**clock'work** *n.* mechanism similar to that of a clock, as in a wind-up toy —**clock in** *or* **on, out** *or* **off** record arrival or departure on automatic time recorder

clod *n.* lump of earth; blockhead —**clod'dish** *a.*

clog *vt.* hamper, impede, choke up (**-gg-**) —*n.* obstruction, impediment; wooden-soled shoe —**clog dance**

cloisonn'é [klwah-zon'ā] *n.* enamel decoration in compartments formed by small fillets of metal —*a.*

cloi'ster *n.* covered pillared arcade; monastery or convent —**cloi'stered** *a.* confined, secluded, sheltered

clone *n.* group of organisms, cells of same genetic constitution as another, derived by asexual reproduction, as graft of plant *etc.* —*v.*

clop *vi.* move, sound, as horse's hooves

close[1] [-s] *a.* adjacent, near; compact; crowded; affectionate, intimate; almost equal; careful, searching; confined; secret; unventilated, stifling; reticent; niggardly; strict, restricted —*adv.* nearly; tightly —*n.* shut-in place; precinct of cathedral —**close'ly** *adv.* —**close'ness** *n.* —**close-fisted** *a.* mean; avaricious —**close season** when it is illegal to kill certain kinds of game and fish —**close'-up** *n.* close view, *esp.* portion of motion picture

close[2] [-z] *vt.* shut; stop up; prevent access to; finish —*vi.* come together; grapple —*n.* end

closed shop place of work in which all workers must belong to a trade union

clos'et [-oz'-] *n.* cupboard; small private room; water closet, lavatory —*vt.* shut up in private room, *esp.* for conference

clo'sure [-zh-] *n.* act of closing; ending of debate by majority vote or other authority

clot *n.* mass or lump; *Med.* coagulated mass of blood —*vt.* form into lumps —*vi.* coagulate (**-tt-**)

cloth [-th] *n.* woven fabric —**clothes** [-TH-] *pl.n.* dress; bed coverings —**clothe** *vt.* put clothes on (**clothed** [klōTHd] *or* **clad** *pt./pp.*) —**clo'thier** *n.* —**clo'thing** *n.*

cloud *n.* condensed water vapour floating in air; state of gloom; multitude —*vt.* overshadow, dim, darken —*vi.* become cloudy —**cloud'less** *a.* —**cloud'y** *a.*

clout *n. inf.* blow; short, flat-headed nail; influence, power —*vt.* strike

clove[1] *n.* dried flower bud of tropical tree, used as spice; one of small bulbs making up compound bulb

clove[2] *pt.* —**clo'ven** *pp. of* CLEAVE[1]

clo'ver *n.* low-growing forage plant, trefoil —**be in clover** be in luxury

clown *n.* comic entertainer in circus; jester, fool —**clown'ish** *a.*

cloy *vt.* weary by sweetness, sameness *etc.*

club *n.* thick stick; bat, stick used in some games; association for pursuance of common interest; building used by such association; one of the suits at cards —*vt.* strike with club —*vi.* join for a common object (**-bb-**) —**club car** first-class railway car for day use

club foot deformed foot

cluck *vi./n.* (make) noise of hen

clue *n.* indication, *esp.* of solution of mystery or puzzle —**not have a clue** be ignorant or incompetent

clump[1] *n.* cluster of trees or plants; compact mass

clump[2] *vi.* walk, tread heavily *—n.*
clum'sy [-z-] *a.* awkward, unwieldy, ungainly; badly made or arranged **—clum'sily** *adv.* **—clums'iness** *n.*
clung *pt./pp. of* CLING
clunk *n.* (sound of) blow or something falling
clus'ter *n.* group, bunch *—v.* gather, grow in cluster
clutch[1] *v.* grasp eagerly; snatch (at) *—n.* grasp, tight grip; device enabling two revolving shafts to be connected and disconnected at will
clutch[2] *n.* set of eggs hatched at one time; brood of chickens
clutt'er *v.* strew; crowd together in disorder *—n.* disordered, obstructive mass of objects
cm centimetre(s)
CO Commanding Officer
Co *Chem.* cobalt
Co. Company; County
c/o care of; carried over
coach *n.* long-distance or touring bus; large four-wheeled carriage; railway passenger car with cheapest seats; tutor, instructor *—vt.* instruct **—coach'man** *n.*
coag'ulate *v.* curdle, clot, form into a mass; congeal, solidify **—coagula'tion** *n.*
coal *n.* mineral consisting of carbonized vegetable matter, used as fuel; glowing ember *—v.* supply with or take in coal **—coal'field** *n.* district in which coal is found
coalesce' [-les'] *vi.* unite, merge **—coales'cence** *n.*
coal'fish *n.* food fish with dark-coloured skin
coali'tion *n.* alliance, *esp.* of political parties
coarse *a.* rough, harsh; unrefined; indecent **—coarse'ly** *adv.* **—coarse'ness** *n.*
coast *n.* sea shore *—v.* move under momentum; proceed without making much effort; sail by the coast **—coast'er** *n.* small ship; that which, one who, coasts; small table mat for glasses *etc.*
coat *n.* sleeved outer garment; animal's fur or feathers; covering layer *—vt.* cover with layer; clothe **—coat of arms** armorial bearings
coax [kōks] *vt.* wheedle, cajole, persuade, force gently
coax'ial [kō-aks'-] *a.* having the same axis **—coax'ially** *adv.*
cob *n.* short-legged stout horse; male swan; head of corn; round loaf of bread
co'balt *n.* metallic element; blue pigment from it
cob'ble *vt.* patch roughly; mend shoes *—n.* round stone **—cobb'ler** *n.* shoe mender
co'bra *n.* venomous, hooded snake of Asia and Africa
cob'web *n.* spider's web
Coca-Cola ® carbonated soft drink
cocaine' [-kān'] *n.* addictive narcotic drug used medicinally as anaesthetic
cochineal' *n.* scarlet dye from Mexican insect
cock *n.* male bird, *esp.* of domestic fowl; tap for liquids; hammer of gun; its position drawn back *—vt.* draw back (gun hammer) to firing position; raise, turn in alert or jaunty manner **—cock'erel** *n.* young cock **—cock'eye(d)** *a.* crosseyed; with a squint; askew **—cock'fight** *n.* staged fight between roosters
cockade' *n.* rosette, badge for hat
cockatoo' *n.* Aust., New Guinea, crested parrot
cock'atrice *n.* fabulous animal similar to basilisk
cock'chafer *n.* large, flying beetle
coc'kle[1] *n.* shellfish
coc'kle[2] *v.* wrinkle; pucker
Cock'ney [-ni] *n.* native of London (*pl.* **-neys**)
cock'pit *n.* pilot's seat, compartment in small aircraft; driver's seat in racing car; *orig.* enclosure for cockfighting
cock'roach *n.* kind of insect, household pest
cock'tail *n.* short drink of spirits with flavourings *etc.*; appetizer
cock'y *a.* conceited, pert
co'coa [-kō] *n.* powder made from seed of cacao (tropical) tree; drink made from the powder
co'conut *n.* tropical palm; very large, hard nut from this palm
cocoon' *n.* sheath of insect in chrysalis stage; any protective covering
COD cash on delivery
cod *n.* large sea fish of northern hemisphere

co'da *n. Mus.* final part of musical composition

cod'dle *vt.* overprotect, pamper

code *n.* system of letters, symbols and rules for their association to transmit messages secretly or briefly; scheme of conduct; collection of laws —**co'dify** *vt.* (**-fied, -fying**) —**codifica'tion** *n.*

co'deine [-dēn] *n.* alkaline sedative, analgesic drug

co'dex *n.* ancient manuscript volume, *esp.* of Bible *etc.* (*pl.* **co'dices** [-sēz])

codg'er *n. inf.* man, *esp.* old

cod'icil *n.* addition to will —**codicil'lary** *a.*

coeduca'tional *a.* of education of boys and girls together in mixed classes —**coed** *n.* coeducational school *etc.* —*a.*

coeffi'cient [-fish'-] *n. Maths.* numerical or constant factor

coe'liac [sē'-] *a.* pert. to the belly

coerce' [kō-ers'] *vt.* compel, force —**coer'cive, coer'cible** *a.* —**coer'cion** *n.* forcible compulsion or restraint

coe'val [kō-ē'-] *a.* of same age or generation

coexist' *vi.* exist together —**coexis'tence** *n.* —**coexis'tent** *a.*

C of E Church of England

coff'ee *n.* seeds of tropical shrub; drink made from roasting and grinding these

coff'er *n.* chest for valuables; treasury, funds

coff'er(dam) *n.* watertight structure enabling construction work to be done under water

coff'in *n.* **UK** casket

cog *n.* one of series of teeth on rim of wheel; person, thing forming small part of big process, organization *etc.* —**cog'wheel** *n.*

co'gent *a.* convincing, compelling, persuasive —**co'gency** *n.* —**co'gently** *adv.*

cog'itate [koj'-] *vi.* think, reflect, ponder —**cogita'tion** *n.* —**cog'itative** *a.*

cogn'ac [kon'yak] *n.* French brandy

cog'nate *a.* of same stock, related, kindred —**cogna'tion** *n.*

cogni'tion [-nish'-] *n.* act or faculty of knowing

cog'nizance [*or* kon'-] *n.* knowledge, perception —**cog'nizable** *a.* —**cog'nizant** *a.*

cogno'men *n.* surname, nickname (*pl.* **cogno'mens**)

cognoscen'ti [kon-yō-shen'ti] *pl.n.* people with knowledge in particular field, *esp.* arts

cohab'it *vi.* live together as husband and wife

coheir' [kō-ār'] *n.* a joint heir (**coheir'ess** *fem.*)

cohere' *vi.* stick together, be consistent —**cohe'rence** *n.* —**cohe'rent** *a.* capable of logical speech, thought; connected, making sense; sticking together —**cohe'rently** *adv.* —**cohe'sion** *n.* cohering —**cohe'sive** *a.*

co'hort *n.* troop; associate

coiffeur' [kwah-fer'] *n.* hairdresser

coiffure' [kwah-fyoor'] *n.* hairstyle

coil *vt.* lay in rings; twist into winding shape —*vi.* twist, take up a winding shape or spiral —*n.* series of rings; device in vehicle *etc.* to transform low tension current to higher voltage for ignition purposes; **UK** contraceptive device inserted in womb

coin *n.* piece of money; money —*vt.* make into money, stamp; invent —**coin'age** *n.* coining; coins collectively —**coin'er** *n.* maker of counterfeit money

coincide' [kō-in-] *vi.* happen together; agree exactly —**coin'cidence** *n.* —**coin'cident** *a.* coinciding —**coinciden'tal** *a.*

coir *n.* fibre of coconut husk

coit'ion [kō-ish'-] *n.* sexual intercourse (*also* **co'itus** [kō'it-])

coke[1] *n.* residue left from distillation of coal, used as fuel

coke[2] *sl. n.* Coca-Cola; cocaine

col *n.* high mountain pass

Col. Colonel; Colossians

co'la *n.* tropical tree; its nut, used to flavour drink; a drink so flavoured

col'ander, cull'ender *n.* culinary strainer perforated with small holes

cold *a.* lacking heat; indifferent, unmoved, apathetic; dispiriting; reserved or unfriendly; (of colours) giving an impression of coldness —*n.* lack of heat; illness, marked by runny nose *etc.* —**cold'ly** *adv.* —**cold'ness** *n.* —**cold-blooded** *a.* lacking pity, mercy; having body temperature that varies with that of the surroundings —**cold chisel** toughened steel chisel —**cold feet** *sl.* fear —**cold**

storage method of preserving perishable foods *etc.* by keeping them at artificially reduced temperature —**cold war** economic, diplomatic but nonmilitary hostility

cole'slaw *n.* salad dish based on shredded cabbage

co'leus [kō'li-əs] *n.* plant cultivated for its variegated leaves (*pl.* **-es**)

col'ic *n.* severe pains in the intestines —**coli'tis** *n.* inflammation of the colon

collab'orate *vi.* work with another on a project —**collabora'tion** *n.* —**collab'orator** *n.* one who works with another, *esp.* one who aids an enemy in occupation of his own country

collage' [-ahzh'] *n.* (artistic) composition of bits and pieces stuck together on background

collapse' *vi.* fall; give way; lose strength, fail —*n.* act of collapsing; breakdown —**collaps'ible, -able** *a.*

coll'ar *n.* band, part of garment, worn round neck —*vt.* seize by collar; *inf.* capture, seize —**coll'arbone** *n.* bone from shoulder to breastbone

collate' *vt.* compare carefully; place in order (as printed sheets for binding) —**colla'tion** *n.* collating; light meal

collat'eral *n.* security pledged for repayment of loan —*a.* accompanying; side by side; of same stock but different line; subordinate

coll'eague [-ēg] *n.* associate, companion in office or employment, fellow worker

collect'[1] *vt.* gather, bring together —*vi.* come together; *inf.* receive money —**collect'ed** *a.* calm; gathered —**collec'tion** *n.* —**collect'ive** *n.* factory, farm *etc.*, run on principles of collectivism —*a.* —**collect'ively** *adv.* —**collect'ivism** *n.* theory that the State should own all means of production —**collect'or** *n.*

coll'ect[2] *n.* short prayer

coll'ege [-lij] *n.* place of higher education; society of scholars; association —**colle'giate** *a.* —**collegiate institute** in some provinces, secondary school providing specified facilities and specialist staff

collide' *vi.* strike or dash together; come into conflict —**colli'sion** [-lizh'ən] *n.* colliding

coll'ie *n.* silky-coated breed of sheepdog

coll'ier *n.* coal miner; coal ship —**coll'iery** *n.* coal mine

coll'ocate *vt.* group, place together —**colloca'tion** *n.*

collo'dion *n.* chemical solution used in photography and medicine

coll'oid *n.* suspension of particles in a solution

collo'quial *a.* pert. to, or used in, informal conversation —**collo'quialism** *n.* —**coll'oquy** [-kwi] *n.* conversation; dialogue

collu'sion [-lōō'-] *n.* secret agreement for a fraudulent purpose, *esp.* in legal proceedings —**collu'sive** *a.*

cologne' [kə-lōn'] *n.* perfumed liquid

co'lon[1] *n.* mark (:) indicating break in a sentence

co'lon[2] *n.* part of large intestine from caecum to rectum

colonel [kur'nəl] *n.* army officer ranking next below a brigadier-general —**colonelcy** [kur'-] *n.*

colonnade' *n.* row of columns

col'ony *n.* body of people who settle in new country but remain subject to parent state; country so settled; distinctive group living together —**colo'nial** *a.* of colony —**col'onist** *n.* —**coloniza'tion** *n.* —**col'onize** *vt.*

col'ophon *n.* publisher's imprint or device

col'o(u)r [kul'ər] *n.* hue, tint; complexion; paint; pigment; *fig.* semblance, pretext; timbre, quality; mood —*pl.* flag —*vt.* stain, dye, paint, give colour to; disguise; influence or distort —*vi.* become coloured; blush —**colora'tion** *n.* —**col'o(u)red** *a.* non-White; in S Africa, of mixed descent —**col'o(u)rful** *a.* with bright or varied colours; distinctive

coloss'us *n.* huge statue; something, somebody very large (*pl.* **coloss'i** [-ī], **-suses**) —**coloss'al** *a.* huge, gigantic

colt [-ō-] *n.* young male horse

colts'foot *n.* wild plant with heart-shaped leaves and yellow flowers

col'umbine *n.* flower with five spurred petals

col'umn [-m] *n.* long vertical cylinder, pillar; support; division of page; body of troops —**colum'nar** *a.* —**col'umnist** *n.* journalist writing regular feature for newspaper

co'ma *n.* state of unconsciousness —**co'matose** *a.*

comb [kōm] *n.* toothed instrument for tidying, arranging, ornamenting hair; cock's crest; mass of honey cells —*vt.* use comb on; search with great care

com'bat *vt./n.* fight, contest —**com'batant** *n.* —**com'bative** *a.*

combine' *v.* join together; ally —*n.* [kom'-] trust, syndicate, *esp.* of businesses, trade organizations *etc.* —**combina'tion** *n.* —**com'binative** *a.* —**combine harvester** machine to harvest and thresh grain in one operation

combus'tion *n.* process of burning —**combustibil'ity** *n.* —**combus'tible** *a.*

come [kum] *vi.* approach, arrive, move towards; reach; happen to; occur; be available; originate (from); become; turn out to be (**came, come, com'ing**) —**come'back** *n. inf.* return to active life after retirement; *inf.* retort —**come'down** *n.* setback; descent in social status

com'edy *n.* dramatic or other work of light, amusing character; humour —**come'dian** *n.* entertainer who tells jokes *etc.*; actor in comedy (**comedienne'** *fem.*)

come'ly [kum'-] *a.* fair, pretty, good-looking —**come'liness** *n.*

comest'ible *n.* (*usu. pl.*) food

com'et *n.* luminous heavenly body consisting of diffuse head, nucleus and long tail —**com'etary** *a.*

com'fit [kum'-] *n.* sweet

com'fort [kum'-] *n.* wellbeing; ease; consolation; means of consolation or satisfaction —*vt.* soothe; cheer, gladden, console —**com'fortable** *a.* free from pain *etc.*; *inf.* well-off financially —**com'fortably** *adv.* —**com'forter** *n.* one who comforts; quilted bed covering; **UK** woollen scarf

com'ic *a.* relating to comedy; funny, laughable —*n.* comedian —*pl.* drawings in newspapers *etc.* relating to humorous story —**com'ical** *a.* —**com'ically** *adv.*

Comm. Commonwealth; Communist

comm'a *n.* punctuation mark (,) separating short parts of sentence

command' [-mahnd'] *vt.* order; rule; compel; have in one's power; overlook, dominate —*vi.* exercise rule —*n.* order; power of controlling, ruling, dominating, overlooking; knowledge, mastery; post of one commanding; district commanded, jurisdiction —**comm'andant** *n.* —**commandeer'** *vt.* seize for military use, appropriate —**command'er** *n.* —**command'ing** *a.* in command; with air of authority —**command'ment** *n.*

comman'do [-mahn'dō] *n.* (member of) special military unit trained for airborne, amphibious attack (*pl.* **-dos**)

commem'orate *vt.* celebrate, keep in memory by ceremony; be a memorial of —**commemora'tion** *n.* —**commem'orative** *a.*

commence' *v.* begin —**commence'ment** *n.* start, beginning; ceremony for presentation of awards at secondary school or college

commend' *vt.* praise; commit, entrust —**commend'able** *a.* —**commend'ably** *adv.* —**commenda'tion** *n.* —**commend'atory** *a.*

commen'surate *a.* equal in size or length of time; in proportion, adequate

comm'ent *n.* remark, criticism; gossip; note, explanation —*vi.* remark, note; annotate, criticize —**comm'entary** *n.* explanatory notes or comments; spoken accompaniment to motion picture *etc.* —**comm'entate** *vi.* —**comm'entator** *n.* author, speaker of commentary

comm'erce *n.* buying and selling; dealings; trade —**commer'cial** *a.* of, concerning, business, trade, profit *etc.* —*n.* advertisement, *esp.* on radio or television

commis'erate [-miz'-] *vt.* pity, condole, sympathize with —**commisera'tion** *n.*

comm'issar *n.* official of Communist Party responsible for political education

commissa'riat *n.* military department of food supplies and transport

commiss'ion [-sh'-] *n.* something entrusted to be done; delegated authority; body entrusted with some special duty; payment by percentage for doing something; warrant, *esp.* royal warrant, giving authority; document appointing soldier, sailor or airman to officer's rank; doing, committing —*vt.* charge with duty or task; *Mil.* confer a rank; give order for —**commiss'ioner** *n.* one empowered to act by commission or warrant; member of commission

commissionaire' *n.* messenger, porter, doorkeeper (*usu.* uniformed)

commit' *vt.* entrust, give in charge; perpetrate, be guilty of; pledge, promise; compromise, entangle; send for trial (-tt-) —**commit'ment** *n.* —**commit'tal** *n.*

committ'ee *n.* body appointed, elected for special business usu. from larger body

commode' *n.* chest of drawers; stool containing chamber pot

commo'dious *a.* roomy

commod'ity *n.* article of trade; anything useful

comm'odore *n.* naval officer, senior to captain; president of yacht club; senior captain in convoy of merchant ships

comm'on *a.* shared by or belonging to all, or to several; public, general; ordinary, usual, frequent; inferior; vulgar —*n.* land belonging to community —*pl.* ordinary people; (**C**-) lower House of British Parliament, House of Commons —**com'monalty** *n.* general body of people —**com'moner** *n.* one of the common people, *ie* not of the nobility —**com'monly** *adv.* —**comm'onplace** *a.* ordinary, everyday —*n.* trite remark; anything occurring frequently —**common sense** sound, practical understanding —**comm'onwealth** *n.* republic; (**C**-) federation of self-governing states

commo'tion *n.* stir, disturbance, tumult

commune'[1] [-myōō-] *vi.* converse together intimately —**commu'nion** *n.* sharing of thoughts, feelings *etc.*; fellowship; body with common faith; (**C**-) participation in sacrament of the Lord's Supper; (**C**-) that sacrament, Eucharist

comm'une[2] *n.* group of families, individuals living together and sharing property, responsibility *etc.* —**comm'unal** *a.* for common use

commu'nicate *vt.* impart, convey; reveal —*vi.* give or exchange information; have connecting passage, door; receive Communion —**commu'nicable** *a.* —**commu'nicant** *n.* one who receives Communion —**communica'tion** *n.* act of giving, *esp.* information; information, message; (*usu. pl.*) passage (road, railway *etc.*), or means of exchanging messages (radio, post *etc.*) between places —*pl.* connections between military base and front —**commu'nicative** *a.* free with information

commu'niqué [-ni-kā] *n.* official announcement

comm'unism *n.* doctrine that all goods, means of production *etc.*, should be property of community —**com'munist** *n./a.* —**communis'tic** *a.*

commu'nity *n.* body of people with something in common, *eg* district of residence, religion *etc.*; society, the public; joint ownership; similarity, agreement —**community centre** building for communal activities —**community college** nonresidential college offering two-year courses of study

commute' [-myōō-] *vi.* travel daily some distance to work —*vt.* exchange; change (punishment *etc.*) into something less severe; change (duty *etc.*) for money payment —**commuta'tion** *n.* —**com'mutator** *n.* device to change alternating electric current into direct current —**commu'ter** *n.* one who travels some distance daily to work

compact'[1] *a.* neatly arranged or packed; solid, concentrated; terse —*v.* make, become compact; compress —**compact'ly** *adv.* —**compact'ness** *n.* —**com'pact disc** small disc on which sound is recorded as series of metallic pits enclosed in PVC and played back by optical scanning by laser

com'pact[2] *n.* small case to hold face powder , powder puff and mirror

com'pact[3] *n.* agreement, covenant, treaty, contract

compan'ion[1] *n.* mate, fellow, comrade, associate; person employed to live with another —**compan'ionable** *a.* —**compan'ionship** *n.*

compan'ion[2] *n.* raised cover over staircase from deck to cabin of ship; deck skylight —**compan'ionway** *n.* staircase from deck to cabin

com'pany [kum'-] *n.* gathering of persons; companionship, fellowship; guests; business firm; division of regiment under captain; crew of ship; actors in play

compare' *vt.* notice or point out likenesses and differences of things; liken; make comparative and superlative of adjective or adverb —*vi.* be like; compete with —**comparabil'ity** *n.* —**com'parable** *a.* —**compar'ative** [-pa'rə-] *a.*

that may be compared; not absolute; relative, partial; *Grammar* denoting form of adjective, adverb, indicating 'more' —*n.* —**compar'atively** *adv.* —**compar'ison** [-pa'ri-] *n.* act of comparing

compart'ment *n.* division or part divided off, *eg* in railway carriage; section

com'pass [kum'-] *n.* instrument for showing the north; (*usu. pl.*) instrument for drawing circles; circumference, measurement round; space, area; scope, reach —*vt.* surround; comprehend; attain, accomplish

compass'ion [-sh'-] *n.* pity, sympathy —**compass'ionate** *a.* —**compas'sionately** *adv.*

compat'ible *a.* capable of harmonious existence; consistent, agreeing with —**compatibil'ity** *n.* —**compat'ibly** *adv.*

compat'riot *n.* fellow countryman —*a.*

com'peer *n.* equal, associate, companion

compel' *vt.* force, oblige; bring about by force (**-ll-**)

compend'ium *n.* collection of different games; abridgment, summary (*pl.* **-s, -ia**) —**compend'ious** *a.* brief but inclusive —**compend'iously** *adv.*

com'pensate *vt.* make up for; recompense suitably; reward —**compensa'tion** *n.*

com'père [kom'per] *n.* one who presents artists in cabaret, television shows *etc.* —*vt.*

compete' *vi.* (*oft. with* with) strive in rivalry, contend for, vie with —**competi'tion** *n.* —**compet'itive** *a.* —**compet'itor** *n.*

com'petent *a.* able, skilful; properly qualified; proper, due, legitimate; suitable, sufficient —**com'petence** *n.* efficiency —**com'petently** *adv.*

compile' *vt.* make up (*eg* book) from various sources or materials; gather, put together —**compila'tion** *n.* —**compi'ler** *n.*

compla'cent *a.* self-satisfied; pleased or gratified —**compla'cence, -cency** *n.* —**compla'cently** *adv.*

complain' *vi.* grumble; bring charge, make known a grievance; (*with* of) make known that one is suffering from —**complaint'** *n.* statement of a wrong, grievance; ailment, illness —**complain'ant** *n.*

complai'sant [-lā'z-] *a.* obliging, willing to please, compliant —**complai'sance** *n.* act of pleasing; affability

com'plement *n.* something making up a whole; full allowance, equipment *etc.* —*vt.* add to, make complete —**complemen'tary** *a.*

complete' *a.* full, perfect; finished, ended; entire; thorough —*vt.* make whole, perfect; finish —**complete'ly** *adv.* —**complete'ness** *n.* —**comple'tion** *n.*

com'plex *a.* intricate, compound, involved —*n.* complicated whole; group of related buildings; psychological abnormality, obsession —**complex'ity** *n.*

complex'ion [-ek'shən] *n.* look, colour, of skin, *esp.* of face, appearance; aspect, character; disposition

compli'ant *see* COMPLY

com'plicate *vt.* make intricate, involved, difficult, mix up —**complica'tion** *n.*

complic'ity [-plis'-] *n.* partnership in wrongdoing

com'pliment *n.* expression of regard, praise; flattering speech —*pl.* expression of courtesy, formal greetings —*vt.* praise, congratulate —**complimen'tary** *a.* expressing praise; free of charge

com'plin(e) *n.* last service of day in R.C. Church

comply' *vi.* consent, yield, do as asked (**complied', comply'ing**) —**compli'ance** *n.* —**compli'ant** *a.*

compo'nent *n.* part, element, constituent of whole —*a.* composing, making up

comport' *v.* agree; behave

compose' *vt.* arrange, put in order; write, invent; make up; calm; settle, adjust —**composed'** *a.* calm —**compo'ser** *n.* one who composes, *esp.* music —**com'posite** *a.* made up of distinct parts —**composite school** one offering both academic and nonacademic courses —**composi'tion** *n.* —**compos'itor** *n.* typesetter, one who arranges type for printing —**compo'sure** *n.* calmness

com'pos men'tis *Lat.* of sound mind

com'post *n.* fertilizing mixture of decayed vegetable matter for soil

com'pote [-pōt] *n.* fruit stewed or preserved in syrup

com'pound[1] *n.* mixture, joining; substance, word, made up of parts —*a.* not simple; composite, mixed —*vt.* [kəm-pownd'] mix, make up, put together; intensify, make worse; compromise, settle debt by partial payment; *Law* agree not to prosecute in return for a consideration

com'pound[2] *n.* (fenced or walled) enclosure containing houses *etc.*

comprehend' *vt.* understand, take in; include, comprise —**comprehen'sible** *a.* —**comprehen'sion** *n.* —**comprehen'sive** *a.* wide, full; taking in much —**comprehen'sively** *adv.* —**comprehen'siveness** *n.* —**comprehensive school UK** secondary school for children of all abilities

compress' *vt.* squeeze together; make smaller in size, bulk —*n.* [kom'-] pad of lint applied to wound, inflamed part *etc.* —**compress'ible** *a.* —**compress'ion** [-sh'-] *n.* in internal-combustion engine, squeezing of explosive charge before ignition, to give additional force —**compres'sor** *n. esp.* machine to compress air, gas

comprise' *vt.* include, contain —**compri'sable** *a.*

com'promise [-īz] *n.* meeting halfway, coming to terms by giving up part of claim; middle course —*v.* settle (dispute) by making concessions —*vt.* expose to risk or suspicion

Comptom'eter **R** a calculating machine

comptro'ller [kən-trō'-] *n.* controller (in some titles)

compul'sion *n.* act of compelling; irresistible impulse —**compul'sive** *a.* —**compul'sorily** *adv.* —**compuls'ory** *a.* not optional

compunc'tion *n.* regret for wrongdoing

compute' [-pyōō-] *vt.* reckon, calculate, *esp.* using computer —**computa'tion** *n.* reckoning, estimate —**compu'ter** *n.* electronic machine for storing, retrieving information and performing calculations —**compu'terize** *v.* equip with, perform by computer

com'rade *n.* mate, companion, friend —**com'radeship** *n.*

con[1] *v. inf.* (*short for* confidence game) swindle, defraud

con[2] *n. abbrev. of* contra, against —**pros and cons** (arguments) for and against

con[3] *vt.* direct steering of ship (**-nn-**) —**conn'er** *n.*

concat'enate *vt.* link together —**concatena'tion** *n.* connected chain (as of circumstances)

con'cave [*or* -kāv'] *a.* hollow, rounded inwards —**concav'ity** *n.*

conceal' [-sēl'] *vt.* hide, keep secret —**conceal'ment** *n.*

concede' [-sēd'] *vt.* admit, admit truth of; grant, allow, yield

conceit' [-sēt'] *n.* vanity, overweening opinion of oneself; far-fetched comparison —**conceit'ed** *a.*

conceive' [-sēv'] *v.* think of, imagine; believe; form in the mind; become pregnant —**conceiv'able** *a.* —**conceiv'ably** *adv.*

con'centrate *vt.* focus (one's efforts *etc.*); increase in strength; reduce to small space —*vi.* devote all attention; come together —*n.* concentrated material or solution —**concentra'tion** *n.* —**concentration camp** prison camp, *esp.* one in Nazi Germany

concen'tric *a.* having the same centre

con'cept *n.* abstract idea; mental expression —**concep'tual** *a.* —**concep'tualize** *v.*

concep'tion *n.* idea, notion; act of conceiving

concern' *vt.* relate, apply to; interest, affect, trouble; (*with* in *or* with) involve (oneself) —*n.* affair; regard, worry; importance; business, enterprise —**concerned'** *a.* connected with; interested; worried; involved —**concern'ing** *prep.* respecting, about

con'cert *n.* musical entertainment; harmony, agreement —*vt.* [kən-sert'] arrange, plan together —**concert'ed** *a.* mutually arranged, planned; determined —**concerti'na** [-sər-tē'-] *n.* musical instrument with bellows and keys —*vi.* fold, collapse, as bellows —**concert'o** [-cher'-] *n.* musical composition for solo instrument and orchestra (*pl.* **-tos**)

concess'ion [-sh'-] *n.* act of conceding; thing conceded; grant; special privilege; land division in township survey —**conces'sive** *a.* —**concession road** one of series of roads separating concessions in township

conch [kongk *or* konch] *n.* seashell —**con'choid** [-k-] *n.* shell-like curve —**conchol'ogy** [kong-kol'-] *n.* study, collection of shells and shellfish

concierge' [kon-si-erzh'] *n.* in France, caretaker, doorkeeper

concil'iate *vt.* pacify, win over from hostility —**concilia'tion** *n.* —**concil'iator** *n.* —**concil'iatory** *a.*

concise' [-sīs'] *a.* brief, terse —**concise'ly** *adv.* —**concise'ness** *n.* —**conci'sion** [-si'zh-] *n.*

con'clave *n.* private meeting; assembly for election of Pope

conclude' [-o͞od'] *vt.* end, finish; deduce; settle —*vi.* come to end; decide —**conclu'sion** *n.* —**conclu'sive** *a.* decisive, convincing —**conclu'sively** *adv.*

concoct' *vt.* make mixture, prepare with various ingredients; make up; contrive, plan —**concoc'tion** *n.*

concom'itant *a.* accompanying —**concom'itance** *n.* existence

con'cord *n.* agreement; harmony —*vi.* [-kord'] agree —**concord'ance** *n.* agreement; index to words of book (*esp.* Bible) —**concord'ant** *a.*

con'course *n.* crowd; large, open place in public area

con'crete *n.* mixture of sand, cement *etc.*, used in building —*a.* made of concrete; particular, specific; perceptible, actual; solid —**con'cretely** *adv.* —**concre'tion** *n.* mass of compressed particles; stonelike growth in body

conc'ubine [-ngk'yoo-] *n.* woman living with man as his wife, but not married to him; 'secondary' wife of inferior legal status

concu'piscence *n.* lust

concur' *vi.* agree, express agreement; happen together; coincide (**-rr-**) —**concur'rence** *n.* —**concurr'ent** *a.* —**concur'rently** *adv.* at the same time

concuss' *vt.* injure brain by blow, fall *etc.* —**concuss'ion** *n.* brain injury; physical shock

condemn' *vt.* blame; find guilty; doom; find, declare unfit for use —**condemna'tion** *n.* —**condem'natory** *a.*

condense' *vt.* concentrate, make more solid; turn from gas into liquid; pack into few words —*vi.* turn from gas to liquid —**condensa'tion** *n.* —**conden'ser** *n.* *Electricity* apparatus for storing electrical energy, a capacitor; apparatus for reducing vapours to liquid form; a lens or mirror for focusing light

condescend' *vi.* treat graciously one regarded as inferior; do something below one's dignity —**condescend'ing** *a.* —**condescen'sion** *n.*

con'diment *n.* relish, seasoning for food

condi'tion [-dish'-] *n.* state or circumstances of anything; thing on which statement or happening or existing depends; stipulation, prerequisite; health, physical fitness; rank —*vt.* accustom; regulate; make fit, healthy; be essential to happening or existence of; stipulate —**condi'tional** *a.* dependent on circumstances or events —*n.* *Grammar* form of verbs —**conditioned reflex** in psychology and physiology, automatic response induced by stimulus repeatedly applied

condole' *vi.* grieve with, offer sympathy; commiserate with —**condo'lence** *n.*

con'dom *n.* sheathlike rubber contraceptive device worn by man

condomin'ium *n.* building in which apartments are individually owned and common areas jointly owned; joint rule by two or more states

condone' *vt.* overlook, forgive, treat as not existing

con'dor *n.* large vulture found in the Andes

conduce' [-dyo͞os'] *vi.* help, promote; tend towards —**condu'cive** *a.*

con'duct *n.* behaviour; management —*vt.* [kən-dukt'] escort, guide; lead, direct; manage; transmit (heat , electricity) —**conduc'tion** *n.* —**conduc'tive** *a.* —**conductiv'ity** *n.* —**conduct'or** *n.* person in charge of bus *etc.*, who collects fares; director of orchestra; one who leads, guides; substance capable of transmitting heat, electricity *etc.*; official in charge of passenger train

con'duit [-dit] *n.* channel or pipe for conveying water, electric cables *etc.*

cone *n.* solid figure with circular base, tapering to a point; cone-shaped ice cream wafer; fruit of pine, fir *etc.* —**con'ic(al)** *a.*

confab'ulate *vi.* chat —**con'fab** *n. inf.* shortened form of **confabula'tion** *n.* confidential conversation

confec'tion *n.* prepared delicacy, *esp.* something sweet —**confec'tioner** *n.* dealer in fancy cakes, pastries, candies *etc.* —**confec'tionery** *n.* candies, cakes *etc.*

confed'erate [-rit] *n.* ally; accomplice —*v.* [-rāt] unite —**confed'eracy** *n.* —**confedera'tion** *n.* alliance of political units; (**C-**) federation of Canada inaugurated in 1867

confer' *vt.* grant, give; bestow; award —*vi.* talk with, take advice (**-rr-**) —**con'ference** *n.* meeting for consultation or deliberation; *Sport* league of clubs or teams —**confer'ment** *n.*

confess' *vt.* admit, own; (of priest) hear sins of —*vi.* acknowledge; declare one's sins orally to priest —**confess'ion** *n.* —**confess'ional** *n.* confessor's stall or box —**confess'or** *n.* priest who hears confessions

confett'i *pl.n.* small bits of coloured paper for throwing at weddings

confide' *vi.* (*with* in) tell secrets, trust —*vt.* entrust —**confidant'** *n.* one entrusted with secrets (**-e** *fem.*) —**con'fidence** *n.* trust; boldness, assurance; intimacy; something confided, secret —**con'fident** *a.* —**confiden'tial** *a.* private; secret; entrusted with another's confidences —**confiden'tially** *adv.* —**con'fidently** *adv.* —**confidence game** swindle in which victim entrusts money *etc.*, to thief, believing him honest

configura'tion *n.* shape, aspect, conformation, arrangement

confine' *vt.* keep within bounds; keep in house, bed *etc.*; shut up, imprison —**con'fines** *pl.n.* boundaries, limits —**confine'ment** *n. esp.* childbirth

confirm' *vt.* make sure, verify; strengthen, settle; make valid, ratify; administer confirmation to —**confirma'tion** *n.* making strong, certain; rite administered by bishop to confirm vows made at baptism —**confirm'ative, confirm'atory** *a.* tending to confirm or establish; corroborative —**confirmed'** *a.* (of habit *etc.*) long-established

con'fiscate *vt.* seize by authority —**confisca'tion** *n.*

conflagra'tion *n.* great destructive fire

conflate' *vt.* combine, blend to form whole

con'flict *n.* struggle, trial of strength; disagreement —*vi.* [-flikt'] be at odds with, be inconsistent with; clash

con'fluence, con'flux *n.* union of streams; meeting place —**con'fluent** *a.*

conform' *v.* comply with accepted standards, conventions *etc.*; adapt to rule, pattern, custom *etc.* —**conform'able** *a.* —**conform'ably** *adv.* —**conforma'tion** *n.* structure, adaptation —**conform'ist** *n.* one who conforms, *esp.* excessively —**conform'ity** *n.* compliance

confound' *vt.* baffle, perplex; confuse; defeat —**confound'ed** *a. esp. inf.* damned

confront' [-unt'] *vt.* face; bring face to face with —**confronta'tion** *n.*

confuse' [-fyo͞o-] *vt.* bewilder; jumble; make unclear; mistake (one thing) for another; disconcert —**confu'sion** *n.*

confute' [-fyo͞o-] *vt.* prove wrong; disprove —**confuta'tion** *n.*

con'ga [-ng'g-] *n.* Latin American dance performed by number of people in single file

congeal' [-j-] *v.* solidify by cooling or freezing —**congela'tion** *n.*

conge'nial [-jē'-] *a.* pleasant, to one's liking; of similar disposition, tastes *etc.* —**congenial'ity** *n.* —**conge'nially** *adv.*

congen'ital [-jen'-] *a.* existing at birth; dating from birth

con'ger [-ng'g-] *n.* variety of large, voracious, sea eel

conge'ries [-jē'-] *n. sing. and pl.* collection or mass of small bodies, conglomeration

congest' [-jest'] *v.* overcrowd or clog —**conges'tion** *n.* abnormal accumulation, overcrowding —**congest'ed** *a.*

conglom'erate *n.* thing, substance (*esp.* rock) composed of mixture of other, smaller elements or pieces; business organization comprising many companies —*v.* gather together —*a.* —**conglomera'tion** *n.*

congrat'ulate *vt.* express pleasure at good fortune, success *etc.* —**congratula'tion** *n.* —**congrat'ulatory** *a.*

con'gregate [-ng'gr-] *v.* assemble; collect, flock together —**congrega'tion** *n.* assembly, *esp.* for worship —**congrega'tional** *a.* —**Congrega'tionalism** *n.*

system in which each separate church is self-governing —**Congrega'tionalist** *n.*

con'gress [-ng'gr-] *n.* meeting; formal assembly for discussion; legislative body —**congress'ional** *a.* —**con'gressman** *n.* member of the U.S. Congress

con'gruent [-ng'gr-] *a.* suitable, accordant; fitting together, *esp.* triangles —**con'gruence** *n.* —**congru'ity** *n.* —**con'gruous** *a.*

con'ic *see* CONE

co'nifer [*or* kon'-] *n.* cone-bearing tree, as fir, pine *etc.* —**conif'erous** *a.*

conjec'ture *n.* guess, guesswork —*v.* guess, surmise —**conjec'tural** *a.*

conjoin' *vt.* combine —*vi.* come, or act, together —**conjoint'** *a.* concerted, united —**conjoint'ly** *adv.*

con'jugal *a.* relating to marriage; between married persons —**conjugal'ity** *n.*

con'jugate *v.* inflect verb in its various forms (past, present *etc.*) —**conjuga'tion** *n.*

conjunc'tion *n.* union; simultaneous happening; part of speech joining words, phrases *etc.* —**conjunc'tive** *a.*

conjuncti'va *n.* mucous membrane lining eyelid —**conjunctivi'tis** *n.* inflammation of this

con'jure [kun'jər] *v.* produce magic effects; perform tricks by jugglery *etc.*; invoke devils; [kən-joor'] implore earnestly —**conjura'tion** *n.* —**con'jurer, -or** *n.*

conk *inf. vt.* strike (*esp.* on head) —*vi.* (*oft. with* out) break down

connect' *v.* join together, unite; associate in the mind —**connec'tion, connex'ion** *n.* association; train, *etc.* timed to enable passengers to transfer from another; family relation —**connect'ive** *a.* —**connecting rod** that part of engine which transfers motion from piston to crankshaft

conning tower armoured control position in submarine, battleship, *etc.*; *see* CON[3]

connive' *vi.* plot, conspire; assent, refrain from preventing or forbidding —**conni'vance** *n.*

connoisseur' [kon-i-sur'] *n.* critical expert in matters of taste, *esp.* fine arts; competent judge

connote' *vt.* imply, mean in addition to primary meaning —**connota'tion** *n.*

connu'bial *a.* of marriage

con'quer [kong'kər] *vt.* win by force of arms, overcome; defeat —*vi.* be victorious —**con'queror** *n.* —**con'quest** [kon'kwest] *n.*

consanguin'ity *n.* kinship —**consanguin'eous** *a.*

con'science [-shəns] *n.* sense of right or wrong governing person's words and actions —**conscien'tious** *a.* scrupulous; obedient to the dictates of conscience —**conscien'tiously** *adv.* —**conscientious objector** one who refuses military service on moral or religious grounds

con'scious [-shəs] *a.* aware; awake to one's surroundings and identity; deliberate, intentional —**con'sciously** *adv.* —**con'sciousness** *n.* being conscious

con'script *n.* one compulsorily enlisted for military service —**conscript'** *vt.* —**conscrip'tion** *n.*

con'secrate *vt.* make sacred —**consecra'tion** *n.*

consec'utive *a.* in unbroken succession —**consec'utively** *adv.*

consen'sus *n.* widespread agreement, unanimity

consent' *vi.* agree to, comply —*n.* acquiescence; permission; agreement —**consen'tient** *a.*

con'sequence *n.* result, effect, outcome; that which naturally follows; significance, importance —**con'sequent** *a.* —**consequen'tial** *a.* important —**con'sequently** *adv.* therefore, as a result

conservatoire' [-twahr'] *n.* school for teaching music

conserve' *vt.* keep from change or decay; preserve; maintain —*n.* [*also* kon'-] jam, preserved fruit *etc.* —**conserva'tion** *n.* protection, careful management of natural resources and environment —**conserva'tionist** *n./a.* —**conserv'ative** *a.* tending, or wishing to conserve; moderate —*n. Politics* one who desires to preserve institutions of his country against change and innovation; one opposed to hasty changes or innovations —**conserv'atism** *n.* —**conserv'atory** *n.* greenhouse

consid'er *vt.* think over; examine; make allowance for; be of opinion that; discuss —**consid'erable** *a.* important;

somewhat large —**consid'erably** *adv.* —**consid'erate** *a.* thoughtful for others' feelings, careful —**consid'erately** *adv.* —**considera'tion** *n.* deliberation; point of importance; thoughtfulness; bribe, recompense

consign' [-īn'] *vt.* commit, hand over; entrust to carrier —**consignee'** *n.* —**consign'ment** *n.* goods consigned —**consign'or** *n.*

consist' *vi.* be composed of; (*with* in) have as basis; agree with, be compatible —**consist'ency, consist'ence** *n.* agreement; harmony; degree of firmness —**consist'ent** *a.* unchanging, constant; agreeing (with) —**consist'ently** *adv.*

consis'tory *n.* ecclesiastical court or council, *esp.* of Pope and Cardinals

console'[1] *vt.* comfort, cheer in distress —**consola'tion** *n.* —**consol'atory** *a.*

con'sole[2] *n.* bracket supporting shelf; keyboard, stops *etc.*, of organ; cabinet for television, radio *etc.*

consol'idate *vt.* combine into connected whole; make firm, secure —**consolida'tion** *n.*

consomm'é [-ā] *n.* clear meat soup

con'sonant *n.* sound making a syllable only with vowel; non-vowel —*a.* agreeing with, in accord —**con'sonance** *n.*

consort' *vi.* associate, keep company with —*n.* [kon'-] husband, wife, *esp.* of ruler; ship sailing with another —**consor'tium** *n.* association of banks, companies *etc.*

conspec'tus *n.* a comprehensive view or survey of subject; synopsis

conspic'uous *a.* striking, noticeable, outstanding; prominent; eminent —**conspic'uously** *adv.*

conspire' *vi.* combine for evil purpose; plot , devise —**conspir'acy** *n.* —**conspir'ator** *n.* —**conspirator'ial** *a.*

con'stable [kun'-] *n.* policeman of the lowest rank; *Hist.* officer of the peace —**constab'ulary** *n.* police force

con'stant *a.* fixed, unchanging; steadfast; always duly happening or continuing —*n.* quantity that does not vary —**con'stancy** *n.* steadfastness; loyalty —**con'stantly** *adv.*

constella'tion *n.* group of stars

consterna'tion *n.* alarm, dismay, panic —**con'sternate** *v.*

constipa'tion *n.* difficulty in emptying bowels —**con'stipate** *vt.* affect with this disorder

constit'uent *a.* going towards making up whole; having power to make, alter constitution of state; electing representative —*n.* component part; element; elector —**constit'uency** *n.* body of electors; parliamentary division

con'stitute *vt.* compose, set up, establish, form; make into, found, give form to —**constitu'tion** *n.* structure, composition; health; character, disposition; principles on which state is governed —**constitu'tional** *a.* pert. to constitution; in harmony with political constitution —*n.* walk taken for health's sake —**constitu'tionally** *adv.*

constrain' *vt.* force, compel —**constraint'** *n.* compulsion; restraint; embarrassment, tension

constric'tion *n.* compression, squeezing together —**constrict'** *vt.* —**constric'tive** *a.* —**constrict'or** *n.* that which constricts; *see also* BOA

construct' *vt.* make, build, form; put together; compose —**con'struct** *n.* —**construc'tion** *n.* —**construct'ive** *a.* serving to improve; positive —**construc'tively** *adv.*

construe' *vt.* interpret; deduce; analyse grammatically

con'sul *n.* officer appointed by a government to represent it in a foreign country; in ancient Rome, one of the chief magistrates —**con'sular** [-syoo-] *a.* —**con'sulate** *n.* —**con'sulship** *n.*

consult' *v.* seek counsel, advice, information from —**consul'tant** *n.* specialist, expert; **UK** senior hospital physician or surgeon —**consulta'tion** *n.* consulting; appointment to seek professional advice, *esp.* of doctor, lawyer —**consult'ative** *a.* having privilege of consulting, but not of voting; advisory

consume' [-syōōm'] *vt.* eat or drink; engross, possess; use up; destroy —**consu'mer** *n.* buyer or user of commodity; one who consumes —**consump'tion** *n.* using up; destruction; wasting disease, *esp.* tuberculosis of the lungs —**consump'tive** *a./n.* —**consump'tiveness** *n.*

con'summate *vt.* perfect; fulfil; complete (*esp.* marriage by sexual intercourse) —*a.* [-sum'-] of greatest perfection or completeness —**consum'mately** *adv.* —**consumma'tion** *n.*

cont. continued

con'tact *n.* touching; being in touch; junction of two or more electrical conductors; useful acquaintance —*vt.* —**contact lens** lens fitting over eyeball to correct defect of vision

conta'gion [-jən] *n.* passing on of disease by touch, contact; contagious disease; harmful physical or moral influence —**conta'gious** *a.* communicable by contact, catching

contain' *vt.* hold; have room for; include, comprise; restrain (oneself) —**contain'er** *n.* box *etc.* for holding; large cargo-carrying standard-sized receptacle for different modes of transport

contam'inate *vt.* stain, pollute, infect; make radioactive —**contamina'tion** *n.* pollution

con'template *vt.* reflect, meditate on; gaze upon; intend —**contempla'tion** *n.* thoughtful consideration; spiritual meditation —**con'templative** [*or* -tem'-] *a./n.* (one) given to contemplation

contem'porary *a.* existing or lasting at same time; of same age; present-day —*n.* one existing at same time as another —**contempora'neous** *a.*

contempt' *n.* feeling that something is worthless, despicable *etc.*; expression of this feeling; state of being despised, disregarded; wilful disrespect of authority

contend' *vi.* strive, fight; dispute —*vt.* maintain (that) —**conten'tion** *n.* strife; debate; subject matter of dispute —**conten'tious** *a.* quarrelsome; causing dispute —**conten'tiously** *adv.*

con'tent[1] *n.* that contained; holding capacity —*pl.* that contained; index of topics in book

content'[2] *a.* satisfied; willing (to) —*vt.* satisfy —*n.* satisfaction —**content'ed** *a.* —**content'ment** *n.*

conter'minous, conter'minal *a.* of the same extent (in time *etc.*); meeting along a common boundary; meeting end to end

con'test *n.* competition; conflict —*vt.* [-test'] dispute, debate; fight or compete for —**contest'able** *a.* —**contest'ant** *n.*

con'text *n.* words coming before, after a word or passage; conditions and circumstances of event, fact *etc.* —**contex'tual** *a.*

contig'uous *a.* touching, near —**contigu'ity** *n.*

con'tinent[1] *n.* large continuous mass of land —**continent'al** *a.*

con'tinent[2] *a.* able to control one's urination and defecation; sexually chaste —**con'tinence** *n.*

contin'gent [-j-] *a.* depending (on); possible; accidental —*n.* group (of troops, sportsmen *etc.*) part of or representative of a larger group —**contin'gency** *n.* —**contin'gently** *adv.*

contin'ue *v.* remain, keep in existence; carry on, last, go on; resume; prolong —**contin'ual** *a.* —**contin'ually** *adv.* —**continua'tion** *n.* extension, extra part; resumption; constant succession, prolongation —**continu'ity** *n.* logical sequence; state of being continuous —**contin'uous** *a.* —**contin'uously** *adv.*

contort' *vt.* twist out of normal shape —**contor'tion** *n.* —**contor'tionist** *n.* one who contorts his body to entertain

con'tour [-oor] *n.* outline, shape, *esp.* mountains, coast *etc.* —**contour line** line on map drawn through places of same height —**contour map**

contra- (*comb. form*) against, as in *contradistinc'tion, contraposi'tion etc.* Such words are omitted where the meaning may easily be inferred from the simple word

con'traband *n.* smuggled goods; illegal traffic in such goods —*a.* prohibited by law

contracep'tion *n.* prevention of conception usu. by artificial means, birth control —**contracep'tive** *a./n.*

contract' *v.* make or become smaller, shorter; [*or* kon'-] enter into agreement; agree upon —*vt.* incur, become affected by —*n.* [kon'-] bargain, agreement; formal document recording agreement; agreement enforceable by law —**contract'ed** *a.* drawn together —**contrac'tile** *a.* tending to contract —**contrac'tion** *n.* —**contract'or** *n.* one making contract, *esp.* builder —**contract'ual** *a.*

contradict' *vt.* deny; be at variance or inconsistent with —**contradic'tion** *n.* —**contradic'tory** *a.*

contral'to *n.* lowest of three female voices (*pl.* **-s**)

contrap'tion *n.* gadget; device; construction, device often overelaborate or eccentric

contrapun'tal *a. Mus.* pert. to counterpoint

con'trary *a.* opposed; opposite, other; [kən-trār'-] perverse, obstinate —*n.* something the exact opposite of another —*adv.* in opposition —**contrari'ety** *n.* —**contra'rily** *adv.* —**con'trariwise** *adv.* conversely

contrast' [-ah-] *vt.* bring out differences; set in opposition for comparison —*vi.* show great difference —*n.* [kon'-] striking difference; *Television* sharpness of image

contravene' *vt.* transgress, infringe; conflict with; contradict —**contraven'tion** *n.*

con'tretemps [kon'trə-tahn] *n.* unexpected and embarrassing event or mishap

contrib'ute *v.* give, pay to common fund; help to occur; write for the press —**contribu'tion** *n.* —**contrib'utive** *a.* —**contrib'utor** *n.* one who writes articles for newspapers *etc.*; one who donates —**contrib'utory** *a.* partly responsible; giving to pension fund *etc.*

con'trite [*or* -trīt'] *a.* remorseful for wrongdoing, penitent —**con'tritely** *adv.* —**contri'tion** *n.*

contrive' *vt.* manage; devise, invent, design —**contri'vance** *n.* artifice or device —**contrived'** *a.* obviously planned, artificial —**contri'ver** *n.*

control' [-ōl'] *vt.* command, dominate; regulate; direct, check, test (**-ll-**) —*n.* power to direct or determine; curb, check; standard of comparison in experiment —*pl.n.* system of instruments to control automobile, aircraft *etc.* —**control'lable** *a.* —**controll'er** *n.* one who controls; official controlling expenditure —**control tower** tower in airfield from which take-offs and landings are directed

con'troversy [*or* -trov'-] *n.* dispute, debate, *esp.* over public issues —**controver'sial** *a.* —**controver'sialist** *n.* —**con'trovert** *vt.* deny; argue —**controvert'ible** *a.*

con'tumacy [-tyoo-] *n.* stubborn disobedience —**contuma'cious** *a.*

con'tumely [-tyoom-i-li] *n.* insulting language or treatment —**contume'lious** *a.* abusive, insolent

contu'sion [-yōō'zh-] *n.* bruise —**contuse'** *vt.* bruise

conun'drum *n.* riddle, *esp.* with punning answer

conurba'tion *n.* densely populated urban sprawl formed by spreading of towns

convalesce' [-es'] *vi.* recover health after illness, operation *etc.* —**convales'cence** *n.* —**convales'cent** *a./n.*

convec'tion *n.* transmission, *esp.* of heat, by currents in liquids or gases —**convec'tor** *n.*

convene' *vt.* call together, assemble, convoke —**conven'tion** *n.* assembly; treaty, agreement; rule; practice based on agreement; accepted usage —**conven'tional** *a.* (slavishly) observing customs of society; customary; (of weapons, war *etc.*) not nuclear —**conventional'ity** *n.* —**conven'tionally** *adv.*

conve'nient *a.* handy; favourable to needs, comfort; well-adapted to one's purpose —**conve'nience** *n.* ease, comfort, suitability; **UK** a (public) lavatory —*a.* (of food) quick to prepare —**conve'niently** *adv.*

con'vent *n.* religious community, *esp.* of nuns; their building —**conven'tual** *a.*

converge' *vi.* approach, tend to meet —**conver'gence, -gency** *n.* —**conver'gent** *a.*

conver'sant *a.* acquainted, familiar (with), versed in

conversa'tion *see* CONVERSE[1]

converse'[1] *vi.* talk (with) —*n.* [kon'-] talk —**conversa'tion** *n.* —**conversa'tional** *a.* —**conversa'tionalist** *n.*

con'verse[2] *a.* opposite, turned round, reversed —*n.* the opposite, contrary

convert' *vt.* apply to another purpose; change; transform; cause to adopt (another) religion, opinion; *Football, rugby* make a convert or conversion —*n.* [kon'-] converted person; *Football* score made after a touchdown by kicking ball over crossbar —**conver'sion** *n.* change of state; unauthorized appropriation; change of opinion, religion, or party; *Rugby* score made after a try by kicking ball over crossbar —**convert'er** *n.* one who, that which converts; electrical machine for changing alternating current into direct current; vessel in which molten metal is refined —**conver'tible** *n.* automobile with folding roof —*a.*

con'vex [*or* -veks'] *a.* curved outwards; of a rounded form —**convex'ity** *n.*

convey' *vt.* carry, transport; impart, communicate; *Law* make over, transfer —**convey'ance** *n.* carrying; vehicle; act by which title to property is transferred —**convey'ancer** *n.* one skilled in legal forms of transferring property —**convey'ancing** *n.* this work —**conveyor belt** continuous moving belt for transporting things, *esp.* in factory

convict' *vt.* prove or declare guilty —*n.* [kon'-] person found guilty of crime; criminal serving prison sentence —**convic'tion** *n.* verdict of guilty; being convinced, firm belief, state of being sure

convince' *vt.* firmly persuade, satisfy by evidence or argument —**convin'cing** *a.* capable of compelling belief, effective

conviv'ial *a.* sociable, festive, jovial —**convivial'ity** *n.*

convoke' *vt.* call together —**convoca'tion** *n.* calling together, assembly, *esp.* of clergy, university graduates *etc.*

con'volute [-lo͞ot] *vt.* twist, coil, tangle —**con'voluted** *a.* —**convolu'tion** *n.*

convol'vulus *n.* genus of plants with twining stems

con'voy *n.* party (of ships, troops, lorries *etc.*) travelling together for protection —*vt.* escort for protection

convulse' *vt.* shake violently; affect with violent involuntary contractions of muscles —**convul'sion** *n.* violent upheaval —*pl.* spasms; fits of laughter or hysteria —**convuls'ive** *a.* —**convul'sively** *adv.*

co'n(e)y *n.* rabbit

coo *n.* cry of doves —*vi.* make such cry (**cooed** [ko͞od], **coo'ing**)

cook *vt.* prepare (food) for table, *esp.* by heat; *inf.* falsify (accounts *etc.*) —*vi.* undergo cooking; act as cook —*n.* one who prepares food for table —**cook'er** *n.* cooking apparatus; cooking apple —**cook'ery** *n.* —**cook'ie** *n.* dry, small, thin variety of cake —**cook up** *inf.* invent, plan; prepare meal

cool *a.* moderately cold; unexcited, calm; lacking friendliness or interest; *inf.* calmly insolent; *inf.* sophisticated, elegant —*v.* make, become cool —*n.* cool time, place *etc.*; *inf.* calmness, composure —**cool'ant** *n.* fluid used for cooling tool, machinery *etc.* —**cool'er** *n.* vessel in which liquids are cooled; *sl.* prison —**cool'ly** *adv.*

cool'ie *n.* (*oft. offens.*) cheaply hired oriental unskilled labour

coomb [ko͞om] *n.* valley

coon *n. sl. offens.* coloured person

coop[1] *n.* cage or pen for fowls —*vt.* shut up in a coop; confine

co'op[2], **co-op** [kō'op] *n.* cooperative society or shop run by one

coop'er *n.* one who makes casks

coop'erate [kō-op'-] *vi.* work together —**coopera'tion** *n.* —**coop'erative** *a.* willing to cooperate; (of an enterprise) owned collectively and managed for joint economic benefit (*also n.*) —**co-op'erator** *n.*

coopt' [kō-opt'] *vt.* bring on (committee *etc.*) as member, colleague, without election by larger body choosing first members

coord'inate [kō-awrd'-] *vt.* bring into order as parts of whole; place in same rank; put into harmony —*n. Maths* any of set of numbers defining location of point —*a.* equal in degree, status *etc.* —**coordina'tion** *n.* —**coord'inative** *a.*

coot *n.* small black water fowl; *sl.* silly (old) person

cop *sl. vt.* catch; (*usu. with* it) be punished (**-pp-**) —*n.* policeman; a capture

co'pal *n.* resin used in varnishes

copart'ner *n.* joint partner —**copart'nership** *n.*

cope[1] *vi.* deal successfully (with)

cope[2] *n.* ecclesiastical vestment like long cloak

Coper'nican *a.* pert. to Copernicus, Polish astronomer (1473-1543), or to his system

co'ping *n.* top course of wall, usu. sloping to throw off rain

co'pious *a.* abundant; plentiful; full, ample —**co'piously** *adv.* —**co'piousness** *n.*

copp'er[1] *n.* reddish-brown malleable ductile metal; bronze money, coin; large washing vessel —*vt.* cover with copper —**copp'erplate** *n.* plate of copper for engraving, etching; print from this; copybook writing; first-class handwriting —**copp'ersmith** *n.* one who works with copper

copp'er[2] *n. sl.* policeman

copp'ice, copse *n.* wood of small trees

cop'ra *n.* dried coconut kernels

cop'ula *n.* word, *esp.* verb acting as connecting link in sentence; connection, tie (*pl.* **-las**)

cop'ulate *vi.* unite sexually —**copula'tion** *n.* —**cop'ulative** *a.*

cop'y *n.* imitation; single specimen of book; matter for printing —*vt.* make copy of, imitate; transcribe; follow an example (**cop'ied, cop'ying**) —**cop'yist** *n.* —**cop'yright** *n.* legal exclusive right to print and publish book, article, work of art *etc.* —*vt.* protect by copyright —**cop'ywriter** *n.* one who composes advertisements

coquette' [-ket'] *n.* woman who flirts —**co'quetry** *n.* —**coquett'ish** *a.*

cor'acle [ko'rə-] *n.* boat of wicker covered with skins

cor'al [ko'rəl] *n.* hard substance made by sea polyps and forming growths, islands, reefs; ornament of coral —*a.* made of coral; of deep pink colour —**cor'alline** *a.*

cor ang'lais [kor-ong'glā] *n.* oboe set a fifth lower than ordinary oboe

corb'el *n.* stone or timber projection from wall to support something

cord *n.* thin rope or thick string; flexible insulated electric cable; rib on cloth; ribbed fabric —*vt.* fasten with cord —**cord'age** *n.*

cord'ate *a.* heart-shaped

cord'ial *a.* hearty, sincere, warm —*n.* sweet, fruit-flavoured drink —**cordial'ity** *n.* —**cord'ially** *adv.*

cor'dite *n.* explosive compound

cord'on *n.* chain of troops or police; fruit tree grown as single stem —*vt.* form cordon around

cordon bleu' [-blə'] *a.* (*esp.* of food preparation) of highest standard

cor'duroy [-də-] *n.* cotton fabric with velvety, ribbed surface

core *n.* horny seed case of apple and other fruits; central or innermost part of anything —*vt.* take out the core

co-respond'ent *n.* one cited in divorce case, alleged to have committed adultery with the respondent

cor'gi *n.* a small Welsh dog

corian'der *n.* herb

Corin'thian [-th-] *a.* of Corinth; of Corinthian order of architecture, ornate Greek

cork *n.* bark of an evergreen Mediterranean oak tree; piece of it or other material, *esp.* used as stopper for bottle *etc.* —*vt.* stop up with cork —**cork'age** *n.* charge for opening wine bottles in restaurant —**cork'screw** *n.* tool for pulling out corks

corm *n.* underground stem like a bulb, but more solid

cor'morant *n.* large voracious sea bird

corn[1] *n.* tall grass having edible grains growing on a spike or cob; grains of this plant used for food or fodder; grain, fruit of cereals; grain of all kinds; oversentimental, trite quality in play, movie *etc.* —*vt.* preserve (meat) with salt —**corn'y** *a. inf.* trite, oversentimental, hackneyed —**corn'flakes** *pl.n.* breakfast cereal —**corn'flower** *n.* blue flower growing in cornfields —**corn'starch** *n.* finely ground corn

corn[2] *n.* painful horny growth on foot or toe

corn'ea *n.* transparent membrane covering front of eye

corne'lian *n.* precious stone, kind of chalcedony

corn'er *n.* part of room where two sides meet; remote or humble place; point where two walls, streets *etc.* meet; angle, projection; *Business* buying up of whole existing stock of commodity —*vt.* drive into position of difficulty, or leaving no escape; establish monopoly —*vi.* move round corner —**corn'ered** *a.* —**corn'erstone** *n.* indispensable part, basis

corn'et *n.* trumpet with valves

corn'ice *n.* projection near top of wall; ornamental, carved moulding below ceiling

cornuco'pia *n.* symbol of plenty, consisting of goat's horn, overflowing with fruit and flowers

coroll'a *n.* flower's inner envelope of petals

coroll'ary *n.* inference from a preceding statement; deduction; result

coro'na *n.* halo around heavenly body; flat projecting part of cornice; top or crown (*pl.* **-s, -nae** [-nē]) —**cor'onal** [ko'rə-] *a.*

cor'onary [ko'rə-] *a.* of blood vessels surrounding heart —*n.* coronary thrombosis —**coronary thrombosis** disease of the heart

corona'tion *n.* ceremony of crowning a sovereign

cor'oner [ko'rə-] *n.* officer who holds inquests on bodies of persons supposed killed by violence, accident *etc.* —**cor'onership** *n.*

cor'onet [ko'rə-] *n.* small crown

corp'oral[1] *a.* of the body; material, not spiritual —**corporal punishment** (flogging *etc.*) of physical nature

corp'oral[2] *n.* noncommissioned officer below sergeant; in RCMP, noncommissioned officer below staff sergeant

corpora'tion *n.* association, body of persons legally authorized to act as an individual; authorities of town or city —**corp'orate** *a.*

corpor'eal *a.* of the body, material; tangible

corps [kawr] *n.* military force, body of troops; any organized body of persons (*pl.* **corps** [kawrz])

corpse *n.* dead body

corp'ulent *a.* fat —**corp'ulence** *n.*

cor'pus *n.* collection or body of works, *esp.* by single author; main part or body of something

corp'uscle [-usl] *n.* minute organism or particle, *esp.* red and white corpuscles of blood

corral' [-rahl'] *n.* enclosure for cattle, or for defence

correct' *vt.* set right; indicate errors in; rebuke, punish; counteract, rectify —*a.* right, exact, accurate; in accordance with facts or standards —**correc'tion** *n.* —**correct'ive** *n./a.* —**correct'ly** *adv.* —**correct'ness** *n.*

corr'elate *vt.* bring into reciprocal relation —*n.* either of two things or words necessarily implying the other —**correla'tion** *n.* —**correl'ative** *a./n.*

correspond' *vi.* be in agreement, be consistent with; be similar (to); exchange letters —**correspond'ence** *n.* agreement, corresponding; similarity; exchange of letters; letters received —**correspond'ent** *n.* writer of letters; one employed by newspaper *etc.* to report on particular topic, country *etc.*

corr'idor *n.* passage in building, railway train *etc.*; strip of territory (or air route) not under control of state through which it passes

corrigen'dum [-jen'-] *n.* thing to be corrected (*pl.* **-da**)

corrob'orate *vt.* confirm, support (statement *etc.*) —**corrobora'tion** *n.* —**corrob'orative** *a.*

corrode' *vt.* eat, wear away, eat into (by chemical action, disease *etc.*) —**corro'sion** *n.* —**corro'sive** *a.*

corr'ugate *v.* wrinkle, bend into wavy ridges —**corr'ugated** *a.* —**corruga'tion** *n.*

corrupt' *a.* lacking integrity; open to, or involving, bribery; wicked; spoilt by mistakes, altered for the worse (of words, literary passages *etc.*) —*vt.* make evil, pervert; bribe; make rotten —**corruptibil'ity** *n.* —**corrupt'ible** *a.* —**corrup'tion** *n.* —**corrupt'ly** *adv.*

corsage' [-sahzh'] *n.* (flower, spray, worn on) bodice of woman's dress

cors'air *n.* pirate (ship)

cors'et *n.* close-fitting undergarment stiffened to give support or shape to the body

cors(e)'let *n.* piece of armour to cover the trunk

cortege' [-tāzh'] *n.* formal (funeral) procession

cor'tex *n. Anat.* outer layer; bark; sheath (*pl.* **cor'tices** [-ti-sēz]) —**cor'tical** *a.*

cor'tisone *n.* synthetic hormone used in the treatment of a variety of diseases

corun'dum *n.* native crystalline aluminium oxide, used as abrasive

corvette' *n.* lightly armed warship for escort and antisubmarine duties

cosh *n.* blunt weapon —*vt.* strike with one

co'sine *n.* in a right-angled triangle, the ratio of a side adjacent to a given angle and the hypotenuse

cosmet'ic [-z-] *n.* preparation to beautify or improve skin, hair *etc.* —*a.* designed to improve appearance only

cos'mic [koz'-] *a.* relating to the universe; of the vastness of the universe —**cosmog'rapher** *n.* —**cosmograph'ic** *a.* —**cosmog'raphy** *n.* description or mapping of the universe —**cosmolog'ical** *a.* —**cosmol'ogy** *n.* the science or study of the universe

cosmic rays high-energy electromagnetic rays from space

cos'monaut [-z'-] *n.* Soviet astronaut

cosmopol'itan [-z-] *n.* person who has lived and travelled in many countries *a.* familiar with many countries; sophisticated; free from national prejudice —**cosmopol'itanism** *n.* —**cosmop'olite** *n.*

cos'mos[1] [-z'-] *n.* the world or universe considered as an ordered system

cos'mos[2] [-z'-] *n.* plant cultivated for brightly coloured flowers (*pl.* **-mos, -moses**)

Coss'ack *n.* member of tribe in SE Russia

coss'et *vt.* pamper, pet

cost *n.* price; expenditure of time, labour *etc.* —*pl.* expenses of lawsuit —*vt.* have as price; entail payment, or loss, or sacrifice of —**cost'ing** *n.* system of calculating cost of production —**cost'liness** *n.* —**cost'ly** *a.* valuable; expensive —**cost (price)** price at which article is bought by one intending to resell it

cos'tal *a.* pert. to side of body or ribs —**cos'tate** *a.* ribbed

cos'tume *n.* style of dress of particular place or time, or for particular activity; theatrical clothes —**costu'mier** [-mi-ər] *n.* dealer in costumes —**costume jewellery** artificial jewellery

co'sy [-z-] *a.* snug, comfortable, sheltered —*n.* covering to keep teapot *etc.* hot —**co'sily** *adv.*

cot *n.* **UK** crib; swinging bed on ship —**cot death UK** crib death

cote *n.* shelter, shed for animals or birds, *eg* dovecot(e)

co'terie *n.* exclusive group of people with common interests; social clique

cotill'(i)on [-til'yən] *n. Hist.* lively dance

cotoneas'ter [-tō-ni-as'-] *n.* garden shrub with red berries

cott'age *n.* small house; small house, as at resort, used for holidays —**cott'ager** *n.* —**cottage cheese** mild, soft cheese —**cottage industry** industry in which workers work in their own homes

cott'er *n.* pin, wedge *etc.* to prevent relative motion of two parts of machine *etc.*

cott'on *n.* plant; white downy fibrous covering of its seeds; thread or cloth made of this —**cotton to** take a liking to

cotyle'don [kot-i-lē'-] *n.* primary leaf of plant embryos

couch *n.* piece of furniture for reclining on by day, sofa —*vt.* put into (words), phrase; cause to lie down —**couch'ant** *a. Heraldry* lying down

couch grass [*or* -ōō-] type of creeping grass

cou'gar [kōō'-] *n.* puma

cough [kof] *vi.* expel air from lungs with sudden effort and noise, often to remove obstruction —*n.* act of coughing

could *pt. of* CAN[1]

cou'lomb [kōō'lom] *n.* unit of quantity of electricity

coul'ter [-ō-] *n.* sharp blade or disc at front of plough

coun'cil *n.* deliberative or administrative body; one of its meetings ; local governing authority of township *etc.* —**coun'cillor** *n.* member of council

coun'sel *n.* advice, deliberation or debate; barrister or barristers ; plan, policy —*vt.* advise, recommend (**-ll-**) —**coun'sellor** *n.* adviser —**keep one's counsel** keep a secret

count[1] *vt.* reckon, calculate, number; include; consider to be —*vi.* be reckoned in; depend (on); be of importance —*n.* reckoning; total number reached by counting; item in list of charges or indictment; act of counting —**count'less** *a.* too many to be counted —**counting house** room or building for bookkeeping

count[2] *n.* nobleman corresponding to British earl —**count'ess** *n. fem.* wife or widow of count or earl

count'enance *n.* face, its expression; support, approval —*vt.* give support, approve

count'er[1] *n.* horizontal surface in bank, shop *etc.*, on which business is transacted; disc, token used for counting or scoring, *esp.* in board games

count'er[2] *adv.* in opposite direction; contrary —*vi.* oppose, contradict; *Fencing* parry —*n.* parry

counter- (*comb. form*) reversed, opposite, rival, retaliatory, as in **count'erclaim** *n.* —**counterclock'wise** *adv./a.* —**counterirr'itant** *n.* —**count'ermarch** *vi.* —**count'ermine** *vi.*

—**counter-revolu'tion** *n. etc.* Such words are not given here where the meaning may be inferred from the simple word

counteract' *vt.* neutralize or hinder —**counterac'tion** *n.*

count'erattack *v./n.* attack after enemy's advance

count'erbalance *n.* weight balancing or neutralizing another

count'erfeit [-fit] *a.* sham, forged —*n.* imitation, forgery —*vt.* imitate with intent to deceive; forge —**count'erfeiter** *n.*

countermand' [-mahnd'] *vt.* cancel (previous order)

count'erpane *n.* top cover for bed

count'erpart *n.* thing so like another as to be mistaken for it; something complementary to or correlative of another

count'erpoint *n.* melody added as accompaniment to given melody; art of so adding melodies

Counter-Reforma'tion *n.* reform movement in Catholic Church in 16th and early 17th cent.

count'ersign [-sīn] *vt.* sign document already signed by another; ratify

count'ersink *v.* enlarge upper part of hole (drilled in timber *etc.*) to take head of screw, bolt *etc.* below surface

count'ess *n. see* COUNT[2]

coun'try [kun'-] *n.* region, district; territory of nation; land of birth, residence *etc.*; rural districts as opposed to town; nation —**coun'trified** *a.* rural in manner or appearance —**coun'tryman** *n.* rustic; compatriot —**country music** popular music based on Amer. White folk music —**coun'tryside** *n.* rural district; its inhabitants

count'y *n.* division of country, province *etc.*

coup [ko͞o] *n.* successful stroke, move or gamble; (*short for* **coup d'état**) sudden, violent seizure of government

cou'pé [ko͞o'pā] *n.* sporty style of automobile, *usu.* with two doors

coup'le [kup'l] *n.* two, pair; brace; husband and wife; any two persons —*vt.* connect, fasten together; associate, connect in the mind —*vi.* join, associate —**coup'ler** *n.* connection, esp. between railway cars —**coup'let** *n.* two lines of verse, *esp.* rhyming and of equal length —**coup'ling** *n.*

cou'pon [ko͞o'-] *n.* ticket or voucher entitling holder to discount, gift *etc.*; detachable slip used as order form; (in betting *etc.*) printed form on which to forecast results

cour'age [ku-] *n.* bravery, boldness —**coura'geous** *a.* —**coura'geously** *adv.*

coureur de bois' [ko͞o-rer-də-bwah'] *n.* French Canadian or Métis woodsman (*pl.* **coureurs de bois** [ko͞o-rer-])

courgette' [-zhet'] *n.* **UK** zucchini

cour'ier [koor'-] *n.* express messenger; person who looks after, guides travellers

course [-aw-] *n.* movement in space or time; direction of movement; successive development, sequence; line of conduct or action; series of lectures, exercises *etc.*; any of successive parts of meal; continuous line of masonry at particular level in building; area where golf is played; track or ground on which a race is run —*vt.* hunt —*vi.* run swiftly, gallop about; (of blood) circulate —**cours'er** *n.* *Poet.* swift horse

court [-aw-] *n.* space enclosed by buildings, yard; area marked off or enclosed for playing various games; retinue and establishment of sovereign; body with judicial powers, place where it meets, one of its sittings; attention, homage, flattery —*vt.* woo, try to win or attract; seek, invite —**court'ier** *n.* one who frequents royal court —**court'liness** *n.* —**court'ly** *a.* ceremoniously polite; characteristic of a court —**court card** king, queen or jack at cards —**court martial** court of naval or military officers for trying naval or military offences (*pl.* **court martials, courts martial**) —**court'yard** *n.* paved space enclosed by buildings or walls

courtesan' [kawr-ti-zan'] *obs. n.* court mistress; high-class prostitute

cour'tesy [kur'-] *n.* politeness, good manners; act of civility —**court'eous** [kurt'-] *a.* polite —**court'eously** *adv.*

court'ship [-aw-] *n.* wooing

cous'in [kuz'n] *n.* son or daughter of uncle or aunt; formerly, any kinsman —**cous'inly** *a.*

cove *n.* small inlet of coast, sheltered bay

cov'en [ku-] *n.* gathering of witches

cov'enant [ku-] *n.* contract, mutual agreement; compact *—v.* agree to a covenant —**cov'enanter** *n.*

cov'er [ku-] *vt.* place or spread over; extend, spread; bring upon (oneself); screen, protect; travel over; include; be sufficient; *Journalism etc.* report; point a gun at *—n.* lid, wrapper, envelope, binding, screen, anything which covers —**cov'erage** *n.* amount, extent covered —**cov'erlet** *n.* top covering of bed

cov'ert [ku-] *a.* secret, veiled, concealed, sly *—n.* thicket, place sheltering game —**cov'ertly** *adv.*

cov'et [ku-] *vt.* long to possess, *esp.* what belongs to another —**cov'etous** *a.* avaricious —**cov'etousness** *n.*

cov'ey [ku-] *n.* brood of partridges or quail (*pl.* **-eys**)

cow[1] *n.* the female of the bovine and of certain other animals (*eg* elephant, whale) (*pl.* **cows**) —**cow'boy** *n.* herdsman in charge of cattle on western plains of U.S.; *inf.* ruthless or unscrupulous operator in business *etc.* —**cow'man** *n.* man who owns cattle, rancher —**cow'pox** *n.* disease of cows, source of vaccine

cow[2] *vt.* frighten into submission, overawe, subdue

cow'ard *n.* one who lacks courage, shrinks from danger —**cow'ardice** *n.* —**cow'ardly** *a.*

cow'er *vi.* crouch, shrink in fear

cowl *n.* monk's hooded cloak; its hood; hooded top for chimney, ship's funnel *etc.*

cow'ling *n.* covering for aircraft engine

cow'rie *n.* brightly-marked sea shell

cow'slip *n.* yellow-flowered plant that grows in swampy places; wild species of primrose

cox'comb *n. obs.* one given to showing off

cox'swain [kok'sən], **cox** *n.* steersman of boat —**cox** *v.* act as cox

coy *a.* (pretending to be) shy, modest —**coy'ly** *adv.* —**coy'ness** *n.*

coyo'te [-ō'ti] *n.* N Amer. prairie wolf

coy'pu [-pōō] *n.* aquatic rodent, orig. from S Amer., yielding nutria fur

coz'en [ku-] *vt.* flatter in order to cheat, beguile

CP Canadian Pacific; Communist Party

Cpl. Corporal

Cr *Chem.* chromium

crab[1] *n.* edible crustacean with ten legs, noted for sidelong and backward walk; type of louse *—vi.* catch crabs; move sideways —**crabb'ed** *a.* of handwriting, hard to read —**catch a crab** *Rowing* dig oar too deeply for clean retrieval

crab[2] *n.* irritable person *—vi.* find fault, grumble —**crabb'y** *a.* bad-tempered

crab apple wild sour apple

crack *vt.* break, split partially; break with sharp noise; cause to make sharp noise, as of whip, rifle *etc.*; break down, yield; *inf.* tell (joke); solve, decipher *—vi.* make sharp noise; split, fissure; of the voice, lose clearness when changing from boy's to man's *—n.* sharp explosive noise; split, fissure; flaw; *inf.* joke, *esp.* sarcastic; chat; *sl.* pure, highly addictive form of cocaine *—a. inf.* special, smart, of great reputation for skill or fashion —**crack'er** *n.* decorated paper tube, pulled apart with a bang, containing paper hat, motto, toy *etc.*; explosive firework; thin dry biscuit —**crac'kle** *n.* sound of repeated small cracks *—vi.* make this sound —**crack'ling** *n.* crackle; crisp skin of roast pork —**cracks'man** *n.* burglar, *esp.* safe-breaker

cra'dle *n.* infant's bed (on rockers); *fig.* earliest resting-place or home; supporting framework *—vt.* hold or rock as in a cradle; cherish —**cra'dling** *n.*

craft[1] [-ah-] *n.* skill, ability, *esp.* manual ability; cunning; skilled trade; members of a trade —**craft'ily** *adv.* —**craft'y** *a.* cunning, shrewd —**crafts'man** *n.* —**crafts'manship** *n.*

craft[2] [-ah-] *n.* vessel; ship

crag *n.* steep rugged rock —**cragg'y** *a.* rugged

crake *n.* any of various birds of rail family

cram *vt.* fill quite full; stuff, force; pack tightly; feed to excess; prepare quickly for examination (**-mm-**) *—n.*

cramp *n.* painful muscular contraction; clamp for holding masonry, timber *etc.* together *—pl.* severe abdominal pain *—vt.* restrict or hamper; hem in, keep within too narrow limits

cramp'on *n.* spike in shoe for mountain climbing *esp.* on ice

cran'berry *n.* edible red berry of dwarf evergreen shrub

crane *n.* wading bird with long legs,

neck, and bill; machine for moving heavy weights —*vi.* stretch neck to see

crane fly insect with long spindly legs

cranes'bill *n.* plant with pink or purple flowers and beaked fruits

craniom'etry [krā-] *n.* the study of the measurements of the human head

cra'nium *n.* skull (*pl.* **-niums, -nia**) —**cra'nial** *a.*

crank *n.* arm at right angles to axis, for turning main shaft, changing reciprocal into rotary motion *etc.*; *inf.* eccentric person, faddist; bad-tempered person —*v.* start (engine) by turning crank —**crank'y** *a.* eccentric; bad-tempered; shaky —**crank'shaft** *n.* principal shaft of engine

crann'y *n.* small opening, chink —**cran'nied** *a.*

crap, craps *n.* gambling game played with two dice

crape *n.* crepe, *esp.* when used for mourning clothes

crash *v.* (cause to) make loud noise; (cause to) fall with crash —*vi.* break, smash; collapse, fail, *esp.* financially; cause (aircraft) to hit land or water; collide with (another automobile *etc.*); move noisily or violently —*n.* loud, violent fall or impact; collision, *esp.* between vehicles; sudden, uncontrolled descent of aircraft to land; sudden collapse or downfall; bankruptcy —*a.* requiring, using, great effort to achieve results quickly —**crash helmet** helmet worn by motorcyclists *etc.* to protect head —**crash-land** *v.* land aircraft in emergency, *esp.* with damage to craft

crass *a.* grossly stupid —**crass'ness** *n.* —**crass'ly** *adv.*

crate *n.* large (*usu.* wooden) container for packing goods

cra'ter *n.* mouth of volcano; bowl-shaped cavity, *esp.* one made by explosion of large shell, bomb, mine *etc.*

cravat' *n.* man's neckcloth

crave *v.* have very strong desire for, long for —*vt.* ask humbly; beg —**cra'ving** *n.*

cra'ven *a.* cowardly, abject, spineless —*n.* coward

craw *n.* bird's or animal's stomach; bird's crop

crawl *vi.* move on belly or on hands and knees; move very slowly; ingratiate oneself, cringe; swim with crawl-stroke; be overrun (with) —*n.* crawling motion; very slow walk; racing stroke at swimming —**crawl'er** *n.*

cray'fish, craw'fish *n.* edible freshwater crustacean like lobster

cray'on *n.* stick or pencil of coloured chalk, wax *etc.*

craze *n.* short-lived current fashion; strong desire or passion, mania; madness —**crazed** *a.* demented; (of porcelain) having fine cracks —**cra'zy** *a.* insane; very foolish; madly eager (for)

creak *n.* harsh grating noise —*vi.* make creaking sound

cream *n.* fatty part of milk; various foods, dishes, resembling cream; cosmetic *etc.* with creamlike consistency; yellowish-white colour; best part of anything —*vt.* take cream from; take best part from; beat to creamy consistency —**cream'y** *a.*

crease [-s] *n.* line made by folding; wrinkle; *Hockey* small area in front of each goal cage; superficial bullet wound —*v.* make, develop creases

create' [krē-āt'] *vt.* bring into being; give rise to; make —*vi. inf.* make a fuss —**crea'tion** *n.* —**crea'tive** *a.* —**crea'tor** *n.*

creat'ure [krēch'-] *n.* living being; thing created; dependant —**creature comforts** bodily comforts

crèche [kresh, krāsh] *n.* day nursery for very young children

cre'dence *n.* belief, credit; side-table for elements of the Eucharist before consecration

creden'tials *pl.n.* testimonials; letters of introduction, *esp.* those given to ambassador

cred'ible *a.* worthy of belief; trustworthy —**credibil'ity** *n.* —**cred'ibly** *adv.*

cred'it *n.* commendation, approval; source, cause, of honour; belief, trust; good name; influence, honour or power based on trust of others; system of allowing customers to take goods for later payment; money at one's disposal in bank *etc.*; side of book on which such sums are entered; reputation for financial reliability —*pl.* list of those responsible for production of motion picture —*vt.* attribute, believe that person has;

believe; put on credit side of account —**cred'itable** *a.* bringing honour —**cred'itably** *adv.* —**cred'itor** *n.* one to whom debt is due

cred'ulous *a.* too easy of belief, easily deceived or imposed on, gullible —**credu'lity** *n.* —**cred'ulousness** *n.*

creed *n.* formal statement of Christian beliefs; statement, system of beliefs or principles

creek *n.* narrow inlet on seacoast

creel *n.* angler's fishing basket

creep *vi.* make way along ground, as snake; move with stealthy, slow movements; crawl; act in servile way; of skin or flesh, feel shrinking, shivering sensation, due to fear, or repugnance (**crept** *pt./pp.*) —*n.* creeping; *sl.* repulsive person —*pl.* feeling of fear or repugnance —**creep'er** *n.* creeping or climbing plant, *eg* ivy —**creep'y** *inf. a.* uncanny, unpleasant; causing flesh to creep

crema'tion *n.* burning as means of disposing of corpses —**cremate'** *vt.* —**cremato'rium** *n.* place for cremation

cren'ellated *a.* having battlements

cre'ole *n.* hybrid language; (**C-**) native born W Indian, Latin American, of European descent

cre'osote *n.* oily antiseptic liquid distilled from coal or wood tar, used for preserving wood —*vt.* coat or impregnate with creosote

crepe [krāp] *n.* fabric with crimped surface; crape —**crepe rubber** rough-surfaced rubber used for soles of shoes

crept *pt./pp. of* CREEP

Cres. Crescent

crescen'do [-sh-] *n.* gradual increase of loudness, *esp.* in music —*a./adv.*

cres'cent [krez'ənt] *n.* (shape of) moon as seen in first or last quarter; any figure of this shape; row of houses built on curve

cress *n.* various plants with edible pungent leaves

crest *n.* comb or tuft on bird's or animal's head; plume on top of helmet; top of mountain, ridge, wave *etc.*; badge above shield of coat of arms, also used separately on seal, plate *etc.* —*vi.* crown —*vt.* reach top of —**crest'fallen** *a.* cast down by failure, dejected

creta'ceous [-shəs] *a.* chalky

cret'in *n.* person afflicted with cretinism; *inf.* stupid person —**cret'inism** *n.* deficiency in thyroid gland causing physical and mental retardation

cretonne' *n.* unglazed cotton cloth printed in coloured patterns

crevasse' *n.* deep open chasm, *esp.* in glacier

crev'ice [-is] *n.* cleft, fissure, chink

crew [-o͞o] *n.* ship's, boat's or aircraft's company, excluding passengers; *inf.* gang or set —*v.* serve as crew —**crew cut** man's closely cropped haircut

crew'el [kro͞o'-] *n.* fine worsted yarn, used in fancy work and embroidery

crib *n.* child's bed usu. with barred sides; barred rack used for fodder; plagiarism; translation used by students, sometimes illicitly —*vt.* confine in small space; copy unfairly (**-bb-**) —**crib death** unexplained death of baby while asleep

cribb'age *n.* card game for two, three, or four players

crick *n.* spasm or cramp in muscles, *esp.* in neck

crick'et[1] *n.* chirping insect

crick'et[2] *n.* outdoor game played with bats, ball and wickets by teams of eleven a side —**crick'eter** *n.*

crime *n.* violation of law (usu. a serious offence); wicked or forbidden act; *inf.* something to be regretted —**crim'inal** *a./n.* —**criminal'ity** *n.* —**crim'inally** *adv.* —**criminol'ogy** *n.* study of crime and criminals

crimp *vt.* pinch into tiny parallel pleats; wrinkle

crim'son [-z-] *a./n.* (of) rich deep red —*v.* turn crimson

cringe *vi.* shrink, cower; behave obsequiously

crin'kle [-ng'k-] *v./n.* wrinkle

crin'oline [-lin] *n.* hooped petticoat or skirt

crip'ple *n.* one not having normal use of limbs, disabled or deformed person —*vt.* maim, disable, impair; weaken, lessen efficiency of

cri'sis *n.* turning point or decisive moment, *esp.* in illness; time of acute danger or difficulty (*pl.* **cri'ses** [-sēz])

crisp *a.* brittle but firm; brisk, decided; clear-cut; fresh, invigorating; crackling; of hair, curly —*n.* **UK** potato chip —**crisp'er** *n.* refrigerator compartment for storing salads *etc.* —**crisp'y** *a.*

crite'rion [krī-] *n.* standard of judgment (*pl.* **-ria**)

crit'ical *a.* fault-finding; discerning; skilled in or given to judging; of great importance, crucial, decisive —**crit'ic** *n.* one who passes judgment; writer expert in judging works of literature, art *etc.* —**crit'ically** *adv.* —**crit'icism** *n.* —**crit'icize** *vt.* —**critique'** [-ēk'] *n.* critical essay, carefully written criticism

croak *v.* utter deep hoarse cry, as raven, frog; talk dismally —*vi. sl.* die —*n.* deep hoarse cry —**croak'er** *n.* —**croak'y** *a.* hoarse

cro'chet [-shā] *n.* kind of handicraft like knitting, done with small hooked needle —*v.* do, make such work

crock *n.* earthenware jar or pot; broken piece of earthenware; old broken-down thing or person —**crock'ery** *n.* earthenware dishes, utensils *etc.*

croc'odile [krok'-] *n.* large amphibious reptile; line of children walking two by two —**crocodil'ian** *a.* —**crocodile tears** insincere grief

cro'cus *n.* small bulbous plant with yellow, white or purple flowers (*pl.* **-cuses**)

croft *n.* (*esp. in Scot.*) small piece of arable land, smallholding —**crof'ter** *n.* one who works croft

croiss'ant [krwahs'ong] *n.* crescent-shaped roll of yeast dough like pastry

crom'lech [-lek] *n.* prehistoric structure, monument of flat stone resting on two upright ones

crone *n.* witchlike old woman

cro'ny *n.* intimate friend

crook *n.* hooked staff; any hook, bend, sharp turn; *inf.* swindler, criminal —**crook'ed** *a.* bent, twisted; deformed; dishonest

croon *v.* hum, sing in soft, low tone —**croon'er** *n.*

crop *n.* produce of cultivation of any plant or plants; harvest, *lit. or fig.*; pouch in bird's gullet; stock of whip; hunting whip; short haircut —*v.* cut short; raise, produce or occupy land with crop; (of animals) bite, eat down; poll or clip (**-pp-**) —**cropp'er** *inf. n.* heavy fall; disastrous failure —**crop-dusting** *n.* spreading fungicide *etc.* on crops from aircraft —**crop up** *inf.* happen unexpectedly

cro'quet [-kā] *n.* lawn game played with balls, wooden mallets and hoops

croquette' [-ket'] *n.* fried ball of minced meat, fish *etc.*

cro'sier, cro'zier [-zhər] *n.* bishop's or abbot's staff

cross *n.* structure or symbol of two intersecting lines or pieces (at right angles); such a structure of wood as means of execution by tying or nailing victim to it; symbol of Christian faith; any thing or mark in the shape of cross; misfortune, annoyance, affliction; intermixture of breeds, hybrid —*v.* move or go across (something); intersect; meet and pass —*vt.* mark with lines across; (*with* out) delete; place or put in form of cross; make sign of cross on or over; modify breed of animals or plants by intermixture; thwart; oppose —*a.* out of temper, angry; peevish, perverse; transverse; intersecting; contrary; adverse —**cross'ing** *n.* intersection of roads, rails *etc.*; part of street where pedestrians are expected to cross —**cross'ly** *adv.* —**cross'ways, cross'wise** *adv./a.* —**cross'bill** *n.* bird whose mandibles cross when closed —**cross'bow** *n.* bow fixed across wooden shoulder stock —**cross'breed** *n.* breed produced from parents of different breeds —**cross country** long race held over open ground —**cross-examine** *vt.* examine witness already examined by other side —**cross-eyed** *a.* having eye(s) turning inward —**cross-fertilization** *n.* fertilization of one plant by pollen of another —**cross-grained** *a.* perverse —**cross-ply** *a.* (of tyre) having fabric cords in outer casing running diagonally —**cross-reference** *n.* reference within text to another part of text —**cross'road** *n.* —**cross'roads** *n.* —**cross section** transverse section; group of people fully representative of a nation, community *etc.* —**cross'walk** *n.* place marked where pedestrians may cross road —**crossword puzzle** puzzle built up of intersecting words, of which some letters are common, the words being indicated by clues —**The Cross** cross on which Jesus Christ was executed; model or picture of this

crotch *n.* angle between legs, genital area; fork

crotch'et *n.* UK quarter note
crotch'ety *a.* peevish; irritable
crouch *vi.* bend low; huddle down close to ground; stoop servilely, cringe —*n.*
croup[1] [-ōō-] *n.* throat disease of children, with cough
croup[2] [-ōō-] *n.* hindquarters of horse; place behind saddle
croup'ier [-ōō-] *n.* person dealing cards, collecting money *etc.* at gambling table
crow[1] [-ō] *n.* large black carrion-eating bird —**crow's-foot** *n.* wrinkle at corner of eye —**crow's-nest** *n.* lookout platform high on ship's mast
crow[2] [-ō] *vi.* utter cock's cry; boast one's happiness or superiority —*n.* cock's cry
crow'bar [-ō-] *n.* iron bar, usu. beaked, for levering
crowd *n.* throng, mass —*vi.* flock together —*vt.* cram, force, thrust, pack; fill with people —**crowd out** exclude by excess already in
crown *n.* monarch's headdress; wreath for head; monarch; monarchy; royal power; formerly, British coin of five shillings; top of head; summit, top; completion or perfection of thing —*vt.* put crown on; confer title; occur as culmination of series of events; *inf.* hit on head —**crown land** public land —**crown prince** heir to throne
cru'cial [krōō'shəl] *a.* decisive, critical; *inf.* very important
cru'ciate [-ōō-] *a.* cross-shaped
cru'cible [-ōō-] *n.* small melting-pot
cru'cify [-ōō-] *vt.* put to death on cross; treat cruelly; *inf.* ridicule (**cru'cified, cru'cifying**) —**cru'cifix** *n.* cross; image of (Christ on the) Cross (*pl.* **-es**) —**crucifix'ion** *n.* —**cru'ciform** *a.*
crude [-ōō-] *a.* lacking taste, vulgar; in natural or raw state, unrefined; rough, unfinished —**crude'ly** *adv.* —**cru'dity** *n.*
cru'el [-ōō-] *a.* delighting in others' pain; causing pain or suffering —**cru'elly** *adv.* —**cru'elty** *n.*
cru'et [-ōō-] *n.* small container for salt, pepper, vinegar, oil *etc.*; stand holding such containers
cruise [-ōōz] *vi.* travel about in a ship for pleasure *etc.*; (of vehicle, aircraft) travel at safe, average speed —*n.* cruising voyage, *esp.* organized for holiday purposes —**cruis'er** *n.* ship that cruises; warship lighter and faster than battleship —**cruise missile** subsonic missile guided throughout its flight —**cruis'erweight** *n.* *Boxing* light-heavyweight
crumb [krum] *n.* small particle, fragment, *esp.* of bread —*vt.* reduce to, break into, cover with crumbs —**crumb'y** *a.*
crum'ble *v.* break into small fragments, disintegrate, crush; perish, decay —*vi.* fall apart or away —*n.* pudding covered with crumbly mixture —**crum'bly** *a.*
crumm'y *a.* *sl.* inferior, contemptible; truck that carries loggers to work from their camp
crump *vi.* thud, explode with dull sound —*n.*
crum'pet *n.* flat, soft cake eaten with butter
crum'ple *v.* (cause to) collapse; make or become crushed, wrinkled, creased —**crum'pled** *a.*
crunch *n.* sound made by chewing crisp food, treading on gravel, hard snow *etc.*; *inf.* critical moment or situation —*v.* make crunching sound
crupp'er *n.* strap holding back of saddle in place by passing round horse's tail; horse's hindquarters
crusade' *n.* medieval Christian war to recover Holy Land; campaign against something believed to be evil; concerted action to further a cause —*vi.* —**crusa'der** *n.*
cruse [-ōōz] *n.* small earthenware jug or pot
crush[1] *vt.* compress so as to break, bruise, crumple; break to small pieces; defeat utterly, overthrow —*n.* act of crushing; crowd of people *etc.*
crush[2] *n.* *inf.* infatuation
crust *n.* hard outer part of bread; similar hard outer casing on anything —*v.* cover with, form, crust —**crust'ily** *adv.* —**crust'y** *a.* having, or like, crust; short-tempered
crusta'cean [-shən] *n.* hard-shelled animal, *eg* crab, lobster —**crusta'ceous** [-shəs] *a.*
crutch *n.* staff with crosspiece to go under armpit of lame person; support
crux *n.* that on which a decision turns; anything that puzzles very much (*pl.* **crux'es, cru'ces** [krōō'sēz])
cry *vi.* weep; wail; utter call; shout;

clamour or beg (for) —*vt.* utter loudly, proclaim (**cried, cry'ing**) —*n.* loud utterance; scream, wail, shout; call of animal; fit of weeping; watchword

cryogen'ics [-jen'-] *n.* branch of physics concerned with phenomena at very low temperatures —**cryogen'ic** *a.*

crypt [kript] *n.* vault, *esp.* under church —**cryp'tic** *a.* secret, mysterious —**cryp'tically** *adv.* —**cryp'togram** *n.* piece of writing in code —**cryptog'raphy** *n.* art of writing, decoding ciphers

cryp'togam *n.* nonflowering plant, *eg* fern, moss *etc.*

crys'tal *n.* clear transparent mineral; very clear glass; cut-glass ware; characteristic form assumed by many substances, with definite internal structure and external shape of symmetrically arranged plane surfaces —**crys'talline, crys'talloid** *a.* —**crystalliza'tion** *n.* —**crys'tallize** *v.* form into crystals; become definite —**crystallog'rapher** *n.* —**crystallog'raphy** *n.* science of the structure, forms and properties of crystals

CST Central Standard Time

CTV Canadian Television (Network Ltd.)

Cu *Chem.* copper

cu. cubic

cub *n.* young of fox and other animals; C-) Cub Scout —*v.* bring forth cubs (**-bb-**) —**Cub Scout** member of junior branch of the Scout Association

cubb'yhole *n.* small, enclosed space or room

cube [kyoob] *n.* regular solid figure contained by six equal square sides; cube-shaped block; product obtained by multiplying number by itself twice —*vt.* multiply thus —**cu'bic(al)** *a.* —**cu'bism** *n.* style of art in which objects are presented as assemblage of geometrical shapes —**cu'bist** *n./a.*

cu'bicle *n.* partially or totally enclosed section of room, as in dormitory

cu'bit *n.* old measure of length, about 18 inches

cuck'old *n.* man whose wife has committed adultery —*vt.*

cuck'oo [kook'oo] *n.* migratory bird which deposits its eggs in the nests of other birds; its call —*a. sl.* crazy

cu'cumber *n.* plant with long fleshy green fruit; the fruit, used in salad

cud *n.* food which ruminant animal brings back into mouth to chew again —**chew the cud** reflect, meditate

cud'dle *vt.* hug —*vi.* lie close and snug, nestle —*n.*

cudd'y *n.* small cabin in boat

cudg'el *n.* short thick stick —*vt.* beat with cudgel (**-ll-**)

cue[1] [kyoo] *n.* last words of actor's speech *etc.* as signal to another to act or speak; signal, hint, example for action

cue[2] [kyoo] *n.* long tapering rod used in billiards; pigtail

cuff[1] *n.* ending of sleeve; turned-up fold at bottom of trouser leg; wristband —**off the cuff** *inf.* without preparation

cuff[2] *vt.* strike with open hand —*n.* blow with hand

cuirass' [kwi-] *n.* metal or leather armour of breastplate and backplate

cuisine' [kwi-zēn'] *n.* style of cooking; menu, food offered by restaurant *etc.*

cul'-de-sac *n.* street, lane open only at one end; blind alley (*pl.* **culs-de-sac**)

cul'inary *a.* of, for, suitable for, cooking or kitchen

cull *vt.* gather, select; take out selected animals from herd —*n.* act of culling

cul'minate *vi.* reach highest point; come to climax, to a head —**culmina'tion** *n.*

culottes' [kyoo-] *pl.n.* flared trousers (*esp.* for women) cut to look like skirt

cul'pable *a.* blameworthy —**culpabil'ity** *n.* —**cul'pably** *adv.*

cul'prit *n.* one guilty of usu. minor offence

cult *n.* system of religious worship; pursuit of, devotion to, some person, thing, or activity

cul'tivate *vt.* till and prepare (ground) to raise crops; develop, improve, refine; devote attention to, cherish; practise; foster —**cultiva'tion** *n.* —**cul'tivator** *n.*

cul'ture *n.* state of manners, taste, and intellectual development at a time or place; cultivating; artificial rearing; set of bacteria so reared —**cul'tural** *a.* —**cul'tured** *a.* refined, showing culture —**cultured pearl** pearl artificially induced to grow in oyster shell

cul'vert *n.* tunnelled drain for passage of water under road, railway *etc.*

cum *Lat.* with

cum'bersome *a.* awkward, unwieldy

cum(m)'in *n.* herb
cumm'erbund *n.* broad sash worn round waist
cum'quat [-kwot] *n. see* KUMQUAT
cu'mulative [-iv] *a.* becoming greater by successive additions; representing the sum of many items
cu'mulus *n.* cloud shaped in rounded white woolly masses (*pl.* **cu'muli**)
cu'neiform [kyōō'ni-] *a.* wedge-shaped, *esp.* of ancient Babylonian writing
cunn'ing *a.* crafty, sly; ingenious *—n.* skill in deceit or evasion; skill, ingenuity **—cunn'ingly** *adv.*
cup *n.* small drinking vessel with handle at one side; any small drinking vessel; contents of cup; various cup-shaped formations, cavities, sockets *etc.*; cup-shaped trophy as prize; portion or lot; iced drink of wine and other ingredients *—vt.* shape as cup (hands *etc.*) **—cup'ful** *n.* (*pl.* **cup'fuls**) **—cup'board** [kub'ərd] *n.* piece of furniture, recess in room, with door, for storage
cu'pel *n.* small vessel used in refining metals
Cu'pid *n.* god of love
cupid'ity *n.* greed for possessions; covetousness
cu'pola *n.* dome
cu'preous, cu'pric, cu'prous *a.* of, containing, copper
cur *n.* dog of mixed breed; surly, contemptible, or mean person
cu'raçao [kyoor'ə-sō] *n.* liqueur flavoured with bitter orange peel
curar'e, curar'i *n.* poisonous resin of S Amer. tree, now used as muscle relaxant in medicine
cu'rate [kyoor'ət] *n.* parish priest's appointed assistant **—cu'racy** *n.* his office
cu'rative [kyoor'-] *a.* tending to cure disease *—n.*
cura'tor [kyoo-rā'-] *n.* custodian, *esp.* of museum, library *etc.*
curb *n.* stone edging to sidewalk; check, restraint; chain or strap passing under horse's lower jaw and giving powerful control with reins *—vt.* restrain; apply curb to
curd *n.* coagulated milk **—cur'dle** *v.* turn into curd, coagulate **—curd'y** *a.* **—blood'curdling** *a.* terrifying, making blood appear to curdle
cure [kyoor] *vt.* heal, restore to health; remedy; preserve (fish, skins *etc.*) *—n.* remedy; course of medical treatment; successful treatment, restoration to health **—curabil'ity** *n.* **—cu'rable** *a.* **—cure of souls** care of parish or congregation
curet(te)' [kyoor-] *n.* surgical instrument for removing dead tissue *etc.* from some body cavities **—curettage'** [-tahzh'] *n.*
cur'few *n.* official regulation restricting or prohibiting movement of people, *esp.* at night; time set as deadline by such regulation
cu'rie [kyoor'-] *n.* standard unit of radium emanation
cu'rio [kyoor'-] *n.* rare or curious thing of the kind sought for collections (*pl.* **cu'rios**)
cu'rious [kyoor'-] *a.* eager to know, inquisitive; prying; puzzling, strange, odd **—curios'ity** *n.* eagerness to know; inquisitiveness; strange or rare thing **—cu'riously** *adv.*
cu'rium *n.* element produced from plutonium
curl *vi.* take spiral or curved shape or path *—vt.* bend into spiral or curved shape *—n.* spiral lock of hair; spiral, curved state, form or motion **—curl'ing** *n.* game played with large rounded stones on ice **—cur'ly** *a.* **—curling iron** heated, metal, scissor-like device for curling hair
cur'lew *n.* large long-billed wading bird
curmudg'eon *n.* surly or miserly person
curr'ant *n.* dried type of grape; fruit of various plants allied to gooseberry; the plants
curr'ent *a.* of immediate present, going on; up-to-date, not yet superseded; in circulation or general use *—n.* body of water or air in motion; tendency, drift; transmission of electricity through conductor **—curr'ency** *n.* money in use; state of being in use; time during which thing is current **—curr'ently** *adv.*
curric'ulum *n.* specified course of study (*pl.* **-lums, -la**)
curr'y[1] *n.* highly-flavoured, pungent condiment, preparation of turmeric; dish flavoured with it *—vt.* prepare, flavour dish with curry (**curr'ied, curr'ying**)
curr'y[2] *vt.* groom (horse) with comb;

dress (leather) (**curr'ied, curr'ying**) —**curry comb** metal comb for grooming horse —**curry favour** try to win favour unworthily, ingratiate oneself

curse *n.* profane or obscene expression of anger *etc.*; utterance expressing extreme ill will towards some person or thing; affliction, misfortune, scourge —*v.* utter curse, swear (at); afflict —**curs'ed** *a.* hateful; wicked; deserving of, or under, a curse —**curs'edly** *adv.* —**curs'edness** *n.*

curs'ive *a.* written in running script, with letters joined

curs'ory *a.* rapid, hasty, not detailed, superficial —**curs'orily** *adv.*

curt *a.* short, rudely brief, abrupt —**curt'ly** *adv.* —**curt'ness** *n.*

curtail' *vt.* cut short, diminish —**curtail'ment** *n.*

cur'tain [-tən] *n.* hanging drapery at window *etc.*; cloth hung as screen; screen separating audience and stage in theatre; end to act or scene *etc.* —*vt.* provide, cover with curtain —**curtain call** return to stage by performers to acknowledge applause —**curtain-raiser** *n.* short play coming before main one; any preliminary event

curt's(e)y *n.* woman's bow or respectful gesture made by bending knees and lowering body —*vi.*

curve *n.* line of which no part is straight; bent line or part —*v.* bend into curve —**curva'ceous** *a. inf.* shapely —**cur'vature** *n.* a bending; bent shape —**curvilin'ear** *a.* of bent lines

cush'ion [-oo-] *n.* bag filled with soft stuffing or air, to support or ease body; any soft pad or support; resilient rim of billiard table —*vt.* provide, protect with cushion; lessen effects of

cush'y [-oo-] *a. inf.* soft, comfortable, pleasant, light, well-paid

cusp *n.* pointed end, *esp.* of tooth —**cus'pid** *n.* pointed tooth —**cus'pidal** *a.* ending in point; of, or like, cusp

cus'pidor *n.* spittoon

cus'tard *n.* dish made of eggs and milk

cus'tody *n.* safe-keeping, guardianship, imprisonment —**custo'dian** *n.* keeper, caretaker, curator

cus'tom *n.* habit; practice; fashion, usage; business patronage; toll, tax —*pl.* duties levied on imports; government department which collects these; area in airport *etc.* where customs officials examine baggage for dutiable goods —**cus'tomarily** *adv.* —**cus'tomary** *a.* usual, habitual —**cus'tomer** *n.* one who enters shop to buy, *esp.* regularly; purchaser —**customs duties** taxes laid on imported or exported goods —**customs house** building where customs are collected

cut *vt.* sever, penetrate, wound, divide, or separate with pressure of edge or edged instrument; pare, detach, trim, or shape by cutting; divide; intersect; reduce, decrease; abridge; *inf.* ignore (person); strike (with whip *etc.*); *Sport* hit ball with downward slicing stroke; *inf.* deliberately stay away from (**cut, cutt'ing**) —*n.* act of cutting; stroke; blow, wound (of knife, whip *etc.*); reduction, decrease; fashion, shape; incision; engraving; piece cut off; division; *inf.* share, *esp.* of profits —**cut'ter** *n.* one who, that which, cuts; warship's rowing and sailing boat; small sloop-rigged vessel with straight running bowsprit —**cutt'ing** *n.* act of cutting, thing cut off or out, *esp.* excavation (for road, canal *etc.*) through high ground; shoot, twig of plant; piece cut from newspaper *etc.* —*a.* sarcastic, unkind —**cut'throat** *a.* merciless —*n.* murderer —**cut dead** refuse to recognize an acquaintance —**cut in** drive in front of another's vehicle so as to affect his driving; interrupt (in conversation); intrude

cuta'neous [kyōō-] *a.* of skin

cute [kyōōt] *a.* appealing, attractive, pretty; *inf.* affecting cleverness or prettiness

cu'ticle *n.* dead skin, *esp.* at base of fingernail

cut'lass *n.* short broad-bladed sword

cut'lery *n.* knives, forks, spoons *etc.* —**cut'ler** *n.* one who makes, repairs, deals in knives and cutting implements

cut'let *n.* small piece of meat grilled or fried

cut'tle *n.* sea mollusc like squid

CV curriculum vitae (outline of person's educational and professional history); Cross of Valour

Cwlth. Commonwealth

cwt. hundredweight

cy'anide [sī'-] *n.* extremely poisonous chemical compound —**cyan'ogen** *n.*

poisonous gas composed of nitrogen and carbon

cyano'sis [sī-] *n.* blueness of the skin

cybernet'ics [sī-] *pl.n.* (*with sing. v.*) comparative study of control mechanisms of electronic and biological systems

cyc'lamen [sik'-] *n.* plant with flowers having turned-back petals

cy'cle [sī'-] *n.* recurrent series or period; rotation of events; complete series or period; development following course of stages; series of poems *etc.*; bicycle —*vi.* move in cycles; ride bicycle —**cy'clic(al)** *a.* —**cy'clist** *n.* bicycle rider —**cyclom'eter** *n.* instrument for measuring circles or recording distance travelled by wheel, *esp.* of bicycle

cy'clone [sī'-] *n.* system of winds moving round centre of low pressure; circular storm —**cyclon'ic** *a.*

cyclope'dia *see* ENCYCLOPEDIA

cy'clostyle [sī'-] *vt.* produce (pamphlets *etc.*) in large numbers for distribution —*a./n.* (of) machine, method for doing this

cy'clotron [sī'-] *n.* powerful apparatus which accelerates the circular movement of subatomic particles in a magnetic field, used for work in nuclear disintegration *etc.*

cyg'net [sig'-] *n.* young swan

cyl'inder [sil'-] *n.* roller-shaped solid or hollow body, of uniform diameter; piston-chamber of engine —**cylin'drical** *a.* —**cyl'indroid** *a.*

cym'bal [sim'-] *n.* one of pair of two brass plates struck together to produce ringing or clashing sound in music

Cym'ric [kim'-] *a.* Welsh

cyn'ic [sin'-] *n.* one who expects, believes, the worst about people, their motives, or outcome of events —**cyn'ical** *a.* —**cyn'icism** *n.* being cynical

cyn'osure [sin'əz-yoor *or* sīn'-] *n.* centre of attraction

cy'pher *see* CIPHER

cy'press *n.* coniferous tree with very dark foliage

cyst [si-] *n.* sac containing liquid secretion or pus —**cys'tic** *a.* of cysts; of the bladder —**cysti'tis** *n.* inflammation of bladder

cytol'ogy [sī-] *n.* study of plant and animal cells

Czar, Tzar, Tsar [zahr] *n.* emperor, king, *esp.* of Russia 1547-1917 —**Czari'na** [-rē'-], **Czarit'sa, Tsarit'sa, Tzarit'sa** *n.* wife of Czar

Czech [chek] *n.* member of western branch of Slavs

D

D Democratic; *Chem.* deuterium

d *Physics* density

d. day; denarius (*Lat.*, penny); departs; diameter; died

dab[1] *vt.* apply with momentary pressure, *esp.* anything wet and soft; strike feebly —*n.* smear; slight blow or tap; small mass —**dab'chick** *n.* small grebe

dab[2] *n.* small flatfish

dab'ble *vi.* splash about; be desultory student or amateur (in) —**dabb'ler** *n.*

dace *n.* small freshwater fish

dachs'hund [daks'hoond] *n.* short-legged long-bodied dog

dac'tyl *n.* metrical foot of one long followed by two short syllables

dad, dadd'y *n. inf.* father —**daddy-longlegs** *n.* arachnid having small rounded body and very long thin legs

da'do [dā'dō] *n.* lower part of room wall when lined or painted separately (*pl.* **-do(e)s**)

daff'odil *n.* spring flower, yellow narcissus

daft [-ah-] *a.* foolish, crazy

dagg'er *n.* short, edged stabbing weapon

da'go *n. offens.* Italian or other Latin (*pl.* **-(e)s**)

daguerre'otype [-ger'-] *n.* early photographic process; photograph by it

dahl'ia [dāl'-] *n.* garden plant of various colours

Dáil, Dáil Éir'eann [doil-ā'rən] *n.* lower chamber of parliament in the Irish Republic

dail'y *a.* done, occurring, published every day —*adv.* every day —*n.* daily newspaper

dain'ty *a.* delicate; elegant, choice; pretty and neat; fastidious —*n.* delicacy —**dain'tily** *adv.* —**dain'tiness** *n.*

dair'y *n.* place for processing milk and its products —**dair'ying** *n.* —**dair'y-maid** *n.* —**dair'yman** *n.*

da'is [dā'-] *n.* raised platform, usually at end of hall

dais'y [-z-] *n.* flower with yellow centre and white petals

Dal'ai Lam'a [-ī-lahm'-] *n.* head of Buddhist hierarchy in Tibet

dale *n.* valley

dalles [dalz] *pl.n.* river rapids flowing between high rock walls

dall'y *vi.* trifle, spend time in idleness or amusement; loiter (**dall'ied, dall'ying**) —**dall'iance** *n.*

Dalma'tian *n.* large dog, white with black spots

dam[1] *n.* barrier to hold back flow of waters; water so collected —*vt.* hold with or as with dam (**-mm-**)

dam[2] *n.* female parent (used of animals)

dam'age *n.* injury, harm, loss —*pl.* sum claimed or adjudged in compensation for injury —*vt.* harm

dam'ask *n.* figured woven material of silk or linen, *esp.* white table linen with design shown up by light; colour of damask rose, velvety red —**dam'ascene, dam'askeen** *vt.* decorate (steel *etc.*) with inlaid gold or silver

dame *n. obs.* lady; (**D-**) title of lady in Order of the British Empire; *sl.* woman

damn [-m] *vt.* condemn to hell; be the ruin of; give hostile reception to —*vi.* curse (**damned** [damd], **damn'ing** [dam'ing]) —*interj.* expression of annoyance, impatience *etc.* —**dam'nable** *a.* deserving damnation; hateful, annoying —**damna'tion** *n.* —**dam'natory** *a.*

damp *a.* moist; slightly moist —*n.* diffused moisture; in coal mines, dangerous gas —*vt.* make damp; (*often with* down) deaden, discourage —**damp'en** *v.* make, become damp —*vt.* stifle, deaden —**damp'er** *n.* anything that discourages or depresses; plate in a flue to control draught

dam'sel [-z-] *n. obs.* girl

dam'son [-z-] *n.* small dark-purple plum; tree bearing it; its colour

Dan. Daniel

dance [-ah-] *vi.* move with measured rhythmic steps, usu. to music; be in lively movement; bob up and down —*vt.* perform (dance); cause to dance —*n.* lively, rhythmical movement; arrangement of such movements; tune for them; social gathering for the purpose of dancing —**danc'er** *n.* —**danseuse'** [-sәz'] *n.* female dancer (*pl.* **-s**)

D & C dilation and curettage (of womb)

dan'delion *n.* yellow-flowered wild plant

dan'der *n. inf.* temper, fighting spirit

dan'druff *n.* dead skin in small scales among the hair

dan'dy *n.* man excessively concerned with smartness of dress —*a. inf.* excellent —**dan'dyism** *n.*

dan'ger [dān'j-] *n.* liability or exposure to harm; risk, peril —**dan'gerous** *a.* —**dan'gerously** *adv.*

dan'gle [-ng'gәl] *v.* hang loosely and swaying; hold suspended; tempt with

dank *a.* unpleasantly damp and chilly —**dank'ness** *n.*

dapp'er *a.* neat and precise, *esp.* in dress, spruce

dap'ple *v.* mark with spots —**dap'pled** *a.* spotted; mottled; variegated —**dapple-grey** *a.* (of horse) grey marked with darker spots

dare [dār] *vt.* venture, have courage (to); challenge —*n.* challenge —**da'ring** *a.* bold —*n.* adventurous courage —**dare'-devil** *a./n.* reckless (person)

dark *a.* without light; gloomy; deep in tint; dim, secret; unenlightened; wicked —*n.* absence of light or colour or knowledge —**dark'en** *v.* —**dark'ly** *adv.* —**dark'ness** *n.* —**dark horse** somebody, something, *esp.* competitor in race, about whom little is known —**dark'-room** *n.* darkened room for processing film

dar'ling *a./n.* much loved or very lovable (person)

darn[1] *vt.* mend by filling (hole) with interwoven yarn —*n.* place so mended —**darn'ing** *n.*

darn[2] *interj.* mild expletive

dart *n.* small light pointed missile; darting motion; small seam or intake in garment —*pl.* indoor game played with numbered target and miniature darts —*vt.* cast, throw rapidly (dart glance *etc.*) —*vi.* go rapidly or abruptly

Darwin'ian *a.* pert. to Charles Darwin or his theory of evolution

dash *vt.* smash, throw, thrust, send with violence; cast down; tinge, flavour, mix —*vi.* move, go with great speed or violence —*n.* rush; vigour; smartness; small quantity, tinge; stroke (—) between words; short race —**dash'er** *n.* ledge along top of boards at ice hockey rink —**dash'ing** *a.* spirited, showy —**dash'-board** *n.* in automobile *etc.*, instrument panel in front of driver

das'tard *n. obs.* contemptible, sneaking coward —**das'tardly** *a.*

dat. dative

da'ta *pl.n.* (*oft. with sing. v.*) series of observations, measurements, or facts; information —**data base** systematized collection of data that can be manipulated by data-processing system for specific purpose —**data pen** device for scanning magnetically coded data on labels, packets, *etc.* —**data processing** handling of data by computer

date[1] *n.* day of the month; statement on document of its time of writing; time of occurrence; period of work of art *etc.*; engagement, appointment; *inf.* person, esp. of opposite sex, with whom one has social engagement —*vt.* mark with date; refer to date; reveal age of; *inf.* accompany on social outing —*vi.* exist (from); betray time or period of origin, become old-fashioned; be regular companion for social outings —**date'less** *a.* without date; immemorial

date[2] *n.* sweet, single-stone fruit of palm; the palm

da'tive [-tiv] *n.* noun case indicating indirect object *etc.*

da'tum *n.* thing given, known, or assumed as basis for reckoning, reasoning *etc.* (**da'ta** *pl.*)

daub *vt.* coat, plaster, paint coarsely or roughly —*n.* rough picture; smear —**daub'er** *n.*

daught'er [dawt'-] *n.* one's female child —**daught'erly** *a.* —**daughter-in-law** *n.* son's wife

daunt *vt.* frighten, *esp.* into giving up purpose —**daunt'less** *a.* intrepid, fearless

dau'phin [daw'fin] *n.* formerly (1349-1830) eldest son of French king

dav'enport *n.* large couch or settee

dav'it *n.* crane, usu. one of pair, at ship's side for lowering and hoisting boats

Davy Jones's locker sea, considered as sailors' grave

Da'vy lamp miner's safety lamp

daw *n. obs.* jackdaw

daw'dle *vi.* idle, waste time, loiter —**daw'dler** *n.*

dawn *n.* first light, daybreak; first gleam or beginning of anything —*vi.* begin to grow light; appear, begin; (begin to) be understood —**dawn'ing** *n.*

day *n.* period of 24 hours; time when sun is above horizon; point or unit of time; daylight; part of day occupied by certain activity, time period; special or designated day —**day'book** *n.* book in which day's sales *etc.* are entered for later transfer to ledger —**day'break** *n.* dawn —**daycare** *n.* care of preschool children during the day —**daycare centre** place for this —**day'dream** *n.* idle fancy —*vi.* —**day'light** *n.* natural light; dawn —**day'lights** *pl.n.* consciousness, wits —**daylight saving** in summer, time set one hour ahead of local standard time, giving extra daylight in evenings —**day'spring** *n.* dawn —**day'star** *n.* morning star —**day'time** *n.* time between sunrise and sunset

daze *vt.* stupefy, stun, bewilder —*n.* stupefied or bewildered state —**dazed** *a.*

daz'zle *vt.* blind, confuse or overpower with brightness, light, brilliant display or prospects —*n.* brightness that dazzles the vision —**daz'zlement** *n.*

dB decibel(s)

DBE Dame Commander of the British Empire

DBS Direct Broadcasting by Satellite

DC direct current

DD Doctor of Divinity

D-day day selected for start of something, *esp.* Allied invasion of Europe in 1944

D.D.T. *n.* hydrocarbon compound used as an insecticide

de- (*comb. form*) removal of, from, reversal of, as in **delouse, desegregate** Such words are omitted where their meaning may easily be inferred from the simple word

dea'con [dē'kən] *n.* one in lowest degree of holy orders; one who superintends secular affairs of Presbyterian church (**dea'coness** *fem.*)

dead [ded] *a.* no longer alive; obsolete; numb, without sensation; no longer functioning, extinguished; lacking lustre or movement or vigour; sure, complete —*n.* dead person or persons (*oft. in pl.*, **the dead**) —*adv.* utterly —**dead'en** *vt.* —**dead'ly** *a.* fatal; deathlike —*adv.* as if dead —**dead-and-alive** *a.* dull —**dead'beat** *n. inf.* lazy, useless person —**dead'head** *n. inf.* person who does not pay on bus, at game, *etc.*; *sl.* dull unenterprising person; train, bus *etc.* travelling empty; log sticking out of water as hindrance to navigation —**dead heat** race in which competitors finish exactly even —**dead letter** law no longer observed; letter which post office cannot deliver —**dead'line** *n.* limit of time allowed —**dead'lock** *n.* standstill —**deadly nightshade** plant with poisonous black berries —**dead'pan** *a.* expressionless —**dead reckoning** calculation of ship's position from log and compass, when observations cannot be taken —**dead set** absolutely; resolute attack —**dead of night** time of greatest stillness and darkness

deaf [def] *a.* wholly or partly without hearing; unwilling to listen —**deaf'en** *vt.* make deaf —**deaf'ness** *n.*

deal[1] *vt.* distribute, give out; inflict —*vi.* act; treat; do business (with, in) (**dealt** *pt./pp.*) —*n.* agreement; treatment; share; business transaction —**deal'er** *n.* one who deals (*esp.* cards); trader —**deal'ings** *pl.n.* transactions or relations with others —**deal with** handle, act towards

deal[2] *n.* (plank of) fir or pine wood

dean *n.* university or college official; head of cathedral chapter —**dean'ery** *n.* cathedral dean's house or appointment

dear *a.* beloved; precious; costly, expensive —*n.* beloved one —*adv.* at a high price —**dear'ly** *adv.* —**dear'ness** *n.*

dearth [derth] *n.* scarcity

death [deth] *n.* dying; end of life; end, extinction; annihilation; (**D-**) personification of death, as skeleton —**death'less** *a.* immortal —**death'ly** *a./adv.* like death —**death duty** tax on property left at death —**death mask** cast of person's face taken after death —**deathwatch beetle** beetle that bores into wood

debac'le [dā-bahk'l] *n.* utter collapse, rout, disaster

debar' *vt.* shut out from; stop; prohibit; preclude (**-rr-**)

debark' *v.* disembark

debase' *vt.* lower in value, quality or character; adulterate coinage —**debase'ment** *n.*

debate' *v.* argue, discuss, *esp.* in a formal assembly; consider —*n.* discussion; controversy —**deba'table** *a.* —**deba'ter** *n.*

debauch' [-bawch'] *vt.* lead into a life of depraved self-indulgence —*n.* bout of sensual indulgence —**debauchee'** *n.* dissipated person —**debauch'ery** *n.*

deben'ture *n.* bond of company or corporation

debil'ity *n.* feebleness, *esp.* of health; languor —**debil'itate** *vt.* weaken, enervate

deb'it *Accounting n.* entry in account of sum owed; side of book in which such sums are entered —*vt.* charge, enter as due

debonair' *a.* suave, genial, affable

debouch' *vi.* move out from narrow place to wider one —**debouch'ment** *n.*

debrief' *v.* of soldier *etc.*, report to superior on result of mission

de'bris [dā'brē, deb'-] *n. sing. and pl.* fragments, rubbish

debt [det] *n.* what is owed; state of owing —**debt'or** *n.*

debunk' *vt.* expose falseness, pretentiousness of, *esp.* by ridicule

de'but [dā'byōō] *n.* first appearance in public —**deb'utante** *n.* girl making official debut into society

Dec. December

deca- (*comb. form*) ten, as in **dec'alitre**

dec'ade *n.* period of ten years; set of ten

dec'adent *a.* declining, deteriorating; morally corrupt —**dec'adence** *n.*

decaff'einated [-in-āt-əd] *a.* (of coffee) with the caffeine removed

dec'agon *n.* figure of 10 angles —**decag'onal** *a.*

decahe'dron *n.* solid of 10 faces —**decahe'dral** *a.*

decal'cify *vt.* deprive of lime, as bones or teeth of their calcareous matter (**-fied, -fying**)

Dec'alogue [-log] *n.* the Ten Commandments

decamp' *vi.* make off, break camp, abscond

deca'nal *a.* of dean, deanery

decant' *vt.* pour off (liquid, as wine) to leave sediment —**decant'er** *n.* stoppered bottle for wine or spirits

decap'itate *vt.* behead —**decapita'tion** *n.* —**decap'itator** *n.*

decar'bonize *vt.* remove deposit of carbon, as from motor cylinder —**decarboniza'tion** *n.*

dec'asyllable *n.* ten-syllabled line —**decasyllab'ic** *a.*

decath'lon [-kath-] *n.* athletic contest with ten events

decay' *v.* rot, decompose; fall off, decline —*n.* rotting; a falling away, break up

decease' [-sēs'] *n.* death —*vi.* die —**deceased'** *a.* dead —*n.* person lately dead

deceive' [-sēv'] *vt.* mislead, delude, cheat —**deceit'** *n.* fraud; duplicity —**deceit'ful** *a.* —**deceiv'er** *n.*

decel'erate [-sel'-] *vi.* slow down

Decem'ber *n.* twelfth and last month of year

decenn'ial [-sen'-] *a.* of period of ten years —**decenn'ially** *adv.*

de'cent *a.* respectable; fitting, seemly; not obscene; adequate; *inf.* kind —**de'cency** *n.* —**de'cently** *adv.*

decen'tralize *vt.* divide (government, organization) among local centres

decep'tion *n.* deceiving; illusion; fraud; trick —**decep'tive** *a.* misleading; apt to mislead

dec'ibel [des'-] *n.* unit for measuring intensity of a sound

decide' *vt.* settle, determine, bring to resolution; give judgment —*vi.* come to a decision, conclusion —**deci'ded** *a.* unmistakable; settled; resolute —**deci'dedly** *adv.* certainly, undoubtedly —**deci'sion** [-zhən] *n.* —**deci'sive** *a.* —**deci'sively** *adv.*

decid'uous *a.* of trees, losing leaves annually; of antlers, teeth *etc.* being shed at the end of a period of growth

dec'imal [des'-] *a.* relating to tenths; proceeding by tens —*n.* decimal fraction —**decimaliza'tion** *n.* —**decimalize'**

vt. convert into decimal fractions or system —**decimal system** system of weights and measures, or coinage, in which value of each denomination is ten times the one below it —**dec'igram** *n.* tenth of gram —**dec'ilitre** *n.* tenth of litre —**dec'imetre** *n.* tenth of metre

dec'imate *vt.* destroy or kill a tenth of, large proportion of —**decima'tion** *n.* —**dec'imator** *n.*

deci'pher *vt.* make out meaning of; decode —**deci'pherable** *a.*

deck *n.* platform or floor, *esp.* one covering whole or part of ship's hull; turntable of record player; part of tape recorder supporting tapes —*vt.* array, decorate —**deck chair** folding chair made of canvas suspended in wooden frame

declaim' *v.* speak dramatically, rhetorically or passionately; protest loudly —**declama'tion** *n.* —**declam'atory** *a.*

declare' *vt.* announce formally; state emphatically; show; name (as liable to customs duty) —*vi.* take sides (for) —**declara'tion** *n.* —**declar'ative, declar'atory** *a.* —**decla'rer** *n. Bridge* person who names trumps or calls "No trumps"

decline' *vi.* refuse; slope, bend or sink downwards; deteriorate gradually; grow smaller, diminish; list the case endings of nouns —*n.* gradual deterioration; movement downwards; diminution; downward slope —**declen'sion** *n.* group of nouns; falling off; declining —**decli'nable** *a.* —**declina'tion** *n.* sloping away, deviation; angle

decliv'ity *n.* downward slope —**decliv'itous** *a.*

declutch' *vt.* disengage clutch of automobile *etc.*

decoc'tion *n.* extraction of essence by boiling down; such essence —**decoct'** *vt.* boil down

decode' *vt.* put in intelligible terms a message in code or secret alphabet

décolle'té [dā-kol'tā] *a.* (of women's garment) having a low-cut neckline

decompose' [-ōz'] *v.* separate into elements; rot —**decomposi'tion** *n.* decay

decompress' *vt.* free from pressure; return to condition of normal atmospheric pressure —**decompress'ion** *n.*

decongest'ant [-j-] *a./n.* (drug) relieving (*esp.* nasal) congestion

decontam'inate *vt.* free from contamination *eg* from poisons, radioactive substances —**decontamina'tion** *n.*

decontrol' *vt.* release from state control (**-ll-**)

dé'cor, de'cor [dā'-] *n.* decorative scheme of a room *etc.*; stage decoration, scenery

dec'orate *vt.* beautify by additions; paint or wallpaper room *etc.*; to invest (with an order, medal *etc.*) —**decora'tion** *n.* —**dec'orative** *a.* —**dec'orator** *n.*

decor'um *n.* seemly behaviour, propriety, decency —**dec'orous** *a.* —**dec'orously** *adv.*

de'coy *n.* something used to entrap others or to distract their attention; bait, lure —*v.* [di-koi'] lure, be lured as with decoy

decrease' *v.* diminish, lessen —*n.* [dē'-] lessening

decree' *n.* order having the force of law; edict —*v.* determine judicially; order

dec'rement *n.* act or state of decreasing; quantity lost by decrease

decrep'it *a.* old and feeble; broken down, worn out —**decrep'itude** *n.*

decry' *vt.* disparage (**decried', decry'ing**)

ded'icate *vt.* commit wholly to special purpose or cause; inscribe or address (book *etc.*); devote to God's service —**dedica'tion** *n.* —**ded'icatory** *a.*

deduce' *vt.* draw as conclusion from facts —**deduct'** *vt.* take away, subtract —**deduct'ible** *a.* —**deduc'tion** *n.* deducting; amount subtracted; conclusion deduced; inference from general to particular —**deduct'ive** *a.* —**deduct'ively** *adv.*

deed *n.* action or fact; exploit; legal document —*vt.* convey (property) by deed

deem *vt.* judge, consider, regard

deep *a.* extending far down, in or back; at, of given depth; profound; heartfelt; hard to fathom; cunning; engrossed, immersed; of colour, dark and rich; of sound, low and full —*n.* deep place; the sea —*adv.* far down *etc.* —**deep'en** *vt.* —**deep'ly** *adv.* —**deepfreeze'** *n.* refrigerator storing frozen food

deer *n.* family of ruminant animals typically with antlers in male (*pl.* **deer**)

—**deer'hound** *n.* large rough-coated dog —**deer'stalker** *n.* one who stalks deer; kind of cloth hat with peaks

deface' *vt.* spoil or mar surface; disfigure —**deface'ment** *n.*

de fac'to [dā-fak'tō] *Lat.* existing in fact, whether legally recognized or not

defame' *vt.* speak ill of, dishonour by slander or rumour —**defama'tion** *n.* —**defam'atory** *a.*

default' *n.* failure, neglect to act, appear or pay —*v.* fail (to pay) —**default'er** *n. esp.* soldier guilty of military offence —**in default of** in the absence of

defeat' *vt.* overcome, vanquish; thwart —*n.* overthrow; lost battle or encounter; frustration —**defeat'ism** *n.* attitude tending to accept defeat —**defeat'ist** *n./a.*

def'ecate *vt.* empty the bowels; clear of impurities —**defeca'tion** *n.*

de'fect [*or* -fekt'] *n.* lack, blemish, failing —*vi.* [-fekt'] desert one's country, cause *etc., esp.* to join opponents —**defec'tion** *n.* abandonment of duty or allegiance —**defect'ive** *a.* incomplete; faulty

defend' *vt.* protect, ward off attack; support by argument, evidence; (try to) maintain (title *etc.*) against challenger —**defence'**, *esp.* **US de'fense** *n.* a defending against attack; protection; justification; *Law* (argument of) defendant; *Sport* [dē'-] defending team, player, play —**defend'ant** *n.* person accused in court —**defend'er** *n.* —**defensibil'ity** *n.* —**defen'sible** *a.* —**defens'ive** *a.* serving for defence —*n.* position or attitude of defence

defer'[1] *vt.* put off, postpone (**-rr-**) —**defer'ment** *n.*

defer'[2] *vi.* submit to opinion or judgment of another (**-rr-**) —**def'erence** *n.* respect for another inclining one to accept his views *etc.* —**deferen'tial** *a.* —**deferen'tially** *adv.*

defi'ance *n.*, **defi'ant** *a. see* DEFY

defi'cient [-ish'ənt] *a.* lacking or falling short in something, insufficient —**defi'ciency** *n.* —**def'icit** *n.* amount by which sum of money is too small

defile'[1] *vt.* make dirty, pollute, soil; sully; desecrate —**defile'ment** *n.*

de'file[2] *n.* narrow pass or valley —*vi.* march in file

define' *vt.* state contents or meaning of; show clearly the form; lay down clearly, fix; mark out —**defi'nable** *a.* —**defini'tion** *n.* —**def'inite** [-it] *a.* exact, defined; clear, specific; certain, sure —**def'initely** *adv.* —**defin'itive** *a.* conclusive, to be looked on as final —**defin'itively** *adv.*

deflate' *v.* (cause to) collapse by release of gas from; take away (person's) self-esteem; *Economics* cause deflation —**defla'tion** *n.* deflating; *Economics* reduction of economic and industrial activity —**defla'tionary** *a.*

deflect' *v.* (cause to) turn from straight course —**deflec'tion** *n.*

deflow'er *vt.* deprive of virginity, innocence *etc.* —**deflora'tion** *n.*

defo'liate *v.* (cause to) lose leaves, *esp.* by action of chemicals —**defo'liant** *n.* —**defolia'tion** *n.*

defor'est *vt.* clear of trees —**deforesta'tion** *n.*

deform' *vt.* spoil shape of; make ugly; disfigure —**deforma'tion** *n.* —**deformed'** *a.* —**deform'ity** *n.*

defraud' *vt.* cheat, swindle

defray' *vt.* provide money for (expenses *etc.*)

defrock' *vt.* deprive (priest, minister) of ecclesiastical status

defrost' *v.* make, become free of frost, ice; thaw

deft *a.* skilful, adroit —**deft'ly** *adv.* —**deft'ness** *n.*

defunct' *a.* dead, obsolete

defuse' *vt.* remove fuse of bomb, *etc.*; remove tension (from situation *etc.*)

defy' *vt.* challenge, resist successfully; disregard (**defied', defy'ing**) —**defi'ance** *n.* resistance —**defi'ant** *a.* openly and aggressively hostile; insolent —**defi'antly** *adv.*

degauss' *vt.* equip (ship) with apparatus which prevents it detonating magnetic mines

degen'erate *vi.* deteriorate to lower mental, moral, or physical level —*a.* fallen away in quality —*n.* degenerate person —**degen'eracy** *n.* —**degenera'tion** *n.* —**degen'erative** *a.*

degrade' *vt.* dishonour; debase; reduce to lower rank —*vi.* decompose chemically —**degra'dable** *a.* capable of chemical, biological decomposition —**degra'd-**

ed *a.* shamed, humiliated —**degrada'tion** *n.*

degree' *n.* step, stage in process, scale, relative rank, order, condition, manner, way; university rank; unit of measurement of temperature or angle —**third degree** severe, lengthy examination, *esp.* of accused person by police, to extract information, confession

dehis'cent [-his'ənt] *a.* opening, as capsule of plant —**dehisce'** *vi.* burst open —**dehis'cence** *n.*

dehumid'ify *vt.* to extract moisture from

dehy'drate *vt.* remove moisture from —**dehydra'tion** *n.*

de-ice' *vt.* to dislodge ice from (*eg* windshield) or prevent its forming

de'ify [*or* dā'-] *vt.* make god of, treat, worship as god (**de'ified, de'ifying**) —**deifica'tion** *n.*

deign [dān] *vt.* condescend, stoop; think fit

de'ism [*or* dā'-] *n.* belief in god but not in revelation —**de'ist** *n.* —**deis'tic** *a.* —**de'ity** *n.* divine status or attributes; a god

déjà vu' [dā-zha-vo͞o'] *Fr.* experience of perceiving new situation as if it had occurred before

deject' *vt.* dishearten, cast down, depress —**deject'ed** *a.* —**dejec'tion** *n.*

de jur'e [dā-joor'ā] *Lat.* in law, by right

delay' *vt.* postpone, hold back —*vi.* be tardy, linger (**delayed', delay'ing**) —*n.* act or instance of delaying; interval of time between events

delect'able *a.* delightful —**delecta'tion** *n.* pleasure

del'egate *n.* person chosen to represent another —*vt.* send as deputy; commit (authority, business *etc.*) to a deputy —**del'egacy** *n.* —**delega'tion** *n.*

delete' *vt.* remove, cancel, erase —**dele'tion** *n.*

delete'rious *a.* harmful, injurious

delib'erate [-it] *a.* intentional; well-considered; without haste, slow —*v.* [-āt] consider, debate —**delib'erately** *adv.* —**delibera'tion** *n.* —**delib'erative** *a.*

del'icate *a.* exquisite; not robust, fragile; sensitive; requiring tact; deft —**del'icacy** *n.* —**del'icately** *adv.*

delicatess'en *n.* shop selling *esp.* imported or unusual foods

deli'cious [-ish'əs] *a.* delightful, pleasing to senses, *esp.* taste —**deli'ciously** *adv.*

delight' *vt.* please greatly —*vi.* take great pleasure (in) —*n.* great pleasure —**delight'ful** *a.* charming

delimita'tion *n.* assigning of boundaries —**delim'it** *vt.*

delin'eate *vt.* portray by drawing or description —**delinea'tion** *n.* —**delin'eator** *n.*

delin'quent *n.* someone, *esp.* young person, guilty of delinquency —*a.* —**delin'quency** *n.* (minor) offence or misdeed

deliquesce' [-kwes'] *vi.* become liquid —**deliques'cence** *n.* —**deliques'cent** *a.*

delir'ium *n.* disorder of the mind, *esp.* in feverish illness; violent excitement —**delir'ious** *a.* raving; light-headed, wildly excited

deliv'er *vt.* carry (goods *etc.*) to destination; hand over; release; give birth or assist in birth (of); utter or present (speech *etc.*) —**deliv'erance** *n.* rescue —**deliv'erer** *n.* —**deliv'ery** *n.*

dell *n.* wooded hollow

Del'phic *a.* pert. to Delphi or to the oracle of Apollo

delphin'ium *n.* garden plant with tall spikes of usu. blue flowers

del'ta *n.* alluvial tract where river at mouth breaks into several streams; Greek letter (Δ); shape of this letter

delude' [-o͞od'] *vt.* deceive; mislead —**delu'sion** *n.* —**delu'sive** *a.*

del'uge *n.* flood, great flow, rush, downpour, cloudburst —*vt.* flood, overwhelm

de luxe [-looks'] *a.* rich, sumptuous; superior in quality

delve *v.* (*with* into) search intensively; dig

demag'netize *vt.* deprive of magnetic polarity

dem'agogue [-og] *n.* mob leader or agitator —**demagog'ic** *a.* —**dem'agogy** *n.*

demand' [-ah-] *vt.* ask as giving an order; ask as by right; call for as due, right or necessary —*n.* urgent request, claim, requirement; call for (specific commodity) —**deman'ding** *a.* requiring great skill, patience *etc.*

de'marcate *vt.* mark boundaries or limits of —**demarca'tion** *n.*

démarche' [dā-mahsh'] *n.* step or manoeuvre, *esp.* in diplomacy

demean' *vt.* degrade, lower, humiliate

demean'o(u)r *n.* conduct, bearing, behaviour

dement'ed *a.* mad, crazy; beside oneself —**demen'tia** [-shə] *n.* form of insanity

demera'ra *n.* kind of brown cane sugar

demer'it *n.* bad point; undesirable quality; mark against person for failure or misconduct

demesne' [-ān', -ēn'] *n.* estate, territory; sphere of action —**hold in demesne** have unrestricted possession of

demi- (*comb. form*) half, as in **demigod** Such words are not given here where meaning may be inferred from the simple word

dem'ijohn *n.* large (wicker-cased) bottle

demil'itarize *vt.* prohibit military presence or function in (an area) —**demilitariza'tion** *n.*

demimonde' *n.* class of women of doubtful reputation

demise' [-īz'] *n.* death; conveyance by will or lease; transfer of sovereignty on death or abdication —*vt.* convey to another by will; lease

dem'iurge [dem'i-ərj] *n.* name given in some philosophies (*esp.* Platonic) to the creator of the world and man

dem'o *n. inf. short for* DEMONSTRATION

demo'bilize *vt.* disband (troops); discharge (soldier) —**demobiliza'tion** *n.*

democ'racy *n.* government by the people or their elected representatives; state so governed —**dem'ocrat** *n.* advocate of democracy —**democrat'ic** *a.* connected with democracy; favouring popular rights —**democrat'ically** *adv.* —**democratiza'tion** *n.* —**democ'ratize** *vt.*

demog'raphy *n.* study of population statistics, as births, deaths, diseases —**demog'rapher** *n.* —**demograph'ic** *a.*

demol'ish *vt.* knock to pieces; destroy utterly; overthrow —**demoli'tion** *n.*

de'mon *n.* devil, evil spirit; very cruel or malignant person; person very good at or devoted to a given activity —**demo'niac** *n.* one possessed with a devil —**demoni'acal** *a.* —**demon'ic** *a.* of the nature of a devil —**demonol'ogy** *n.* study of demons

dem'onstrate *vt.* show by reasoning, prove; describe, explain by specimens or experiments —*vi.* make exhibition of support, protest *etc.* by public parade, rally; make show of armed force —**demon'strable** *a.* —**demon'strably** *adv.* —**demonstra'tion** *n.* making clear, proving by evidence; exhibition and description; organized expression of public opinion; display of armed force —**demon'strative** *a.* expressing feelings, emotions easily and unreservedly; pointing out; conclusive —**dem'onstrator** *n.* one who demonstrates equipment, products *etc.*; one who takes part in a public demonstration; professor's assistant in laboratory *etc.*

demor'alize *vt.* deprive of courage and discipline; undermine morally —**demoraliza'tion** *n.*

demote' *vt.* reduce in status or rank —**demo'tion** *n.*

demur' [-mur'] *vi.* make difficulties, object (**-rr-**) —*n.* raising of objection; objection raised —**demurr'er** *n. Law* exception taken to opponent's point

demure' [-myoor'] *a.* reserved, quiet —**demure'ly** *adv.*

demurr'age *n.* charge for keeping ship *etc.* beyond time agreed for unloading

den *n.* cave or hole of wild beast; lair; small room, *esp.* study; site, haunt

denat'ionalize *vt.* return (an industry) from public to private ownership —**denationaliza'tion** *n.*

dena'ture *vt.* deprive of essential qualities, adulterate —**denatured alcohol** spirit made undrinkable

den'gue [deng'gi] *n.* an infectious tropical fever

deni'al *see* DENY

den'ier *n.* unit of weight of silk, rayon and nylon yarn

den'igrate *vt.* belittle or disparage character of

den'im *n.* strong cotton drill for pants, overalls *etc.*

den'izen *n.* inhabitant

denom'inate *vt.* give name to —**denomina'tion** *n.* distinctly named church or sect; name, *esp.* of class or group

—**denomina'tional** *a.* —**denom'inator** *n.* divisor in vulgar fraction

denote' *vt.* stand for, be the name of; mark, indicate, show —**denota'tion** *n.*

denoue'ment [dā-nōō'mon] *n.* unravelling of dramatic plot; final solution of mystery

denounce' *vt.* speak violently against; accuse; terminate (treaty) —**denuncia'tion** *n.* denouncing —**denun'ciatory** *a.*

dense *a.* thick, compact; stupid —**dense'ly** *adv.* —**dens'ity** *n.* mass per unit of volume

dent *n.* hollow or mark left by blow or pressure —*vt.* make dent in; mark with dent

dent'al *a.* of, pert. to teeth or dentistry; pronounced by applying tongue to teeth —**dent'ate** *a.* toothed —**dent'ifrice** [-is] *n.* powder, paste, or wash for cleaning teeth —**dent'ist** *n.* surgeon who attends to teeth —**dent'istry** *n.* art of dentist —**denti'tion** [-ish'ən] *n.* teething; arrangement of teeth —**dent'ure** *n.* (*usu. pl.*) set of false teeth —**dental floss** soft thread, oft. waxed, for cleaning teeth

dent'ine [-ēn] *n.* the hard bonelike part of a tooth

denude' *vt.* strip, make bare; expose (rock) by erosion of plants, soil *etc.* —**denuda'tion** *n.*

denuncia'tion *see* DENOUNCE

deny' *vt.* declare untrue; contradict; reject, disown; refuse to give; refuse; (*reflex.*) abstain from (**denied', deny'ing**) —**deni'able** *a.* —**deni'al** *n.*

deo'dorize *vt.* rid of smell or mask smell of —**deo'dorant** *n.* —**deodoriza'tion** *n.* —**deo'dorizer** *n.*

De'o volen'te [dā'ō-vo-len'ti] *Lat.* God willing

deox'idize *vt.* deprive of oxygen —**deoxidiza'tion** *n.*

dep. depart(s); departure; deposed; deposit; deputy

depart' *vi.* go away; start out, set forth; deviate, vary; die —**depart'ure** *n.*

depart'ment *n.* division; branch; province —**department'al** *a.* —**departmen'tally** *adv.* —**department store** large shop selling all kinds of goods

depend' *vi.* (*usu. with* on) rely entirely; live; be contingent, await settlement or decision —**depend'able** *a.* reliable —**depend'ant** *n.* one for whose maintenance another is responsible —**depend'ent** *a.* depending on —**depend'ence** *n.* —**depend'ency** *n.* subject territory

depict' *vt.* give picture of; describe in words —**depic'tion** *n.*

depil'atory *n.* substance that removes hair —*a.*

deplete' *vt.* empty; reduce; exhaust —**deple'tion** *n.*

deplore' *vt.* lament, regret; deprecate, complain of —**deplor'able** *a.* lamentable; disgraceful

deploy' *v.* of troops, ships, (cause to) adopt battle formation; arrange —**deploy'ment** *n.*

depo'larize *vt.* deprive of polarity —**depolariza'tion** *n.*

depo'nent *a.* of verb, having passive form but active meaning —*n.* deponent verb; one who makes statement on oath; deposition

depop'ulate *v.* (cause to) be reduced in population —**depopula'tion** *n.*

deport' *vt.* expel from foreign country, banish —**deporta'tion** *n.*

deport'ment *n.* behaviour, conduct, bearing —**deport'** *v.* behave, carry (oneself)

depose' *vt.* remove from office, *esp.* of sovereign —*vi.* make statement on oath, give evidence —**depo'sable** *a.* —**depo'sal** *n.* removal from office; statement made on oath

depos'it [-poz'-] *vt.* set down, *esp.* carefully; give into safe keeping, *esp.* in bank; let fall (as sediment) —*n.* thing deposited; money given in part payment or as security; sediment —**depos'itary** *n.* person with whom thing is deposited —**deposi'tion** *n.* statement written and attested; act of deposing or depositing —**depos'itor** *n.* —**depos'itory** *n.* place for safe-keeping

dep'ot [-ō] *n.* storehouse; building for storage and servicing of buses, railway engines *etc.*; [dē'pō] bus or railway station

deprave' *vt.* make bad, corrupt, pervert —**deprav'ity** *n.* wickedness, viciousness

dep'recate *vt.* express disapproval of; advise against —**depreca'tion** *n.* —**dep'recatory** *a.*

depre'ciate [-shi-] *vt.* lower price, value or purchasing power of; belittle —*vi.*

fall in value —**deprecia'tion** *n.* —**depre'ciator** *n.* —**depre'ciatory** *a.*

depreda'tion *n.* plundering, pillage —**dep'redate** *vt.* plunder, despoil —**dep'redator** *n.*

depress' *vt.* affect with low spirits; lower, in level or activity —**depress'ion** *n.* hollow; low spirits, dejection, despondency; low state of trade, slump —**depres'sant** *n.* —**depress'ive** *a.*

deprive' *vt.* strip, dispossess —**depriva'tion** *n.* —**deprived'** *a.* lacking adequate food, care, amenities *etc.*

dept. department

depth *n.* (degree of) deepness; deep place, abyss; intensity (of colour, feeling); profundity (of mind) —**depth charge** bomb for use against submarines

depute' [-pyo͞ot'] *vt.* allot; appoint as an agent or substitute —*a./n.* [dep'-] in Scotland, assistant —**deputa'tion** *n.* persons sent to speak for others —**dep'utize** *vi.* act for another —*vt.* depute —**dep'uty** *n.* assistant; substitute, delegate

derail' *v.* (cause to) go off the rails, as train *etc.* —**derail'ment** *n.*

deraill'eur [-yər] *a./n.* (of) gear-change mechanism for bicycles

derange' *vt.* put out of place, out of order; upset; make insane —**derange'ment** *n.*

der'by *n.* horserace, *esp.* (**D-**) famous horserace at Epsom, England; contest between local teams; man's low-crowned stiff felt hat

dereg'ulate *vt.* remove regulations or controls from

der'elict *a.* abandoned, forsaken; falling into ruins, dilapidated —*n.* social outcast, vagrant; abandoned property, ship *etc.* —**derelic'tion** *n.* neglect (of duty); abandoning

deride' *vt.* speak of or treat with contempt, ridicule —**deris'ion** [-zh-] *n.* ridicule —**deri'sive** *a.* —**deri'sory** *a.* mocking, ridiculing

de rigueur' [-gər'] *Fr.* required by etiquette or fashion

derive' *vt.* deduce, get from; show origin of —*vi.* issue, be descended (from) —**deriva'tion** *n.* —**deriv'ative** *a./n.*

dermati'tis *n.* inflammation of skin

dermatol'ogy *n.* science of skin —**dermatol'ogist** *n.* physician specializing in skin diseases

derog'atory *a.* disparaging, belittling, intentionally offensive

derr'ick *n.* hoisting machine; framework over oil well *etc.*

derr'ing-do *n.* (act of) spirited bravery, boldness

derr'inger [-j-] *n.* small pistol with large bore

der'vish *n.* member of Muslim ascetic order, noted for frenzied, whirling dance

des'cant *n. Mus.* decorative variation sung as accompaniment to basic melody —*vi.* [-kant'] talk about in detail; dwell (on) at length

descend' [-send'] *vi.* come or go down; slope down; stoop, condescend; spring from (ancestor *etc.*); pass to heir, be transmitted; swoop on or attack —*vt.* go or come down —**descend'ant** *n.* person descended from an ancestor —**descent'** *n.*

describe' *vt.* give detailed account of; pronounce or label; trace out (geometrical figure *etc.*) —**descrip'tion** *n.* detailed account; marking out; kind, sort, species —**descript'ive** *a.*

descry' *vt.* make out, catch sight of, *esp.* at a distance, espy (**descried', descry'ing**)

des'ecrate *vt.* violate sanctity of; profane; convert to evil use —**desecra'tion** *n.*

des'ert[1] [-z-] *n.* uninhabited and barren region —*a.* barren, uninhabited, desolate

desert'[2] [-z-] *vt.* abandon, forsake, leave —*vi.* run away from service, *esp.* of soldiers *etc.* —**desert'er** *n.* —**deser'tion** *n.*

desert'[3] [-z-] *n.* (*usu. pl.*) what is due as reward or punishment; merit, virtue

deserve' [-z-] *vt.* show oneself worthy of; have by conduct a claim to —**deserv'edly** [-id-li] *adv.* —**deserv'ing** *a.* worthy (of reward *etc.*)

deshabille' [dā-za-bēl'] *n. see* DISHABILLE

des'iccate *v.* dry; dry up —**desicca'tion** *n.*

desiderat'um [-raht'-] *n.* something lacked and wanted

design' [-zīn'] *vt.* make working drawings for; sketch; plan out; intend, select for —*n.* outline sketch; working plan; art of making decorative patterns *etc.*; project, purpose, mental plan —**design'edly**

[-id-li] *adv.* on purpose —**design'er** *n.* *esp.* one who draws designs for manufacturers —**design'ing** *a.* crafty, scheming

des'ignate [dez'ig-] *vt.* name, pick out, appoint to office —*a.* appointed but not yet installed —**designa'tion** *n.* name, appellation

desire' [-zīr'] *vt.* wish, long for; ask for, entreat —*n.* longing, craving; expressed wish, request; sexual appetite; something wished for or requested —**desirabil'ity** *n.* —**desi'rable** *a.* worth desiring —**desi'rous** *a.* filled with desire

desist' [-zist'] *vi.* cease, stop

desk *n.* table or other piece of furniture designed for reading or writing; counter; editorial section of newspaper *etc.* covering specific subject

des'olate *a.* uninhabited; neglected, barren, ruinous; solitary; dreary, dismal, forlorn —*vt.* depopulate, lay waste; overwhelm with grief —**desola'tion** *n.*

despair' *vi.* lose hope —*n.* loss of all hope; cause of this; despondency

despatch' *see* DISPATCH

des'perate *a.* reckless from despair; difficult or dangerous; frantic; hopelessly bad; leaving no room for hope —**despera'do** [-rahd'-] *n.* reckless, lawless person (*pl.* **-do(e)s**) —**des'perately** *adv.* —**despera'tion** *n.*

despise' [-īz'] *vt.* look down on as contemptible, inferior —**des'picable** [*or* -spik'-] *a.* base, contemptible, vile —**des'picably** *adv.*

despite' *prep.* in spite of

despoil' *vt.* plunder, rob, strip of —**despolia'tion** *n.*

despond'ent *a.* dejected, depressed —**despond'** *vi.* —**despond'ency** *n.* —**despon'dently** *adv.*

des'pot *n.* tyrant, oppressor —**despot'ic** *a.* —**despot'ically** *adv.* —**des'potism** *n.* autocratic government, tyranny

dessert' [-z-] *n.* sweet course, or fruit, served at end of meal

destina'tion *n.* place a person or thing is bound for; goal; purpose

des'tine [-tin] *vt.* ordain or fix beforehand; set apart, devote

des'tiny *n.* course of events or person's fate; the power which foreordains

des'titute *a.* in absolute want; in great need, devoid (of); penniless —**destitu'tion** *n.*

destroy' *vt.* ruin; pull to pieces; undo; put an end to; demolish; annihilate —**destroy'er** *n.* one who destroys; small, swift, heavily armed warship —**destruct'** *vt.* destroy (one's own missile *etc.*) for safety —**destruct'ible** *a.* —**destruc'tion** *n.* ruin, overthrow; death —**destruct'ive** *a.* destroying; negative, not constructive —**destruc'tively** *adv.* —**destruct'or** *n.* that which destroys, *esp.* incinerator

desu'etude [-syōō'i-tyōōd] *n.* disuse, discontinuance

des'ultory *a.* passing, changing fitfully from one thing to another; aimless; unmethodical

detach' *vt.* unfasten, disconnect, separate —**detach'able** *a.* —**detached'** *a.* standing apart, isolated; impersonal, disinterested —**detach'ment** *n.* aloofness; detaching; a body of troops detached for special duty

de'tail *n.* particular; small or unimportant part; treatment of anything item by item; party or man assigned for duty in army —*vt.* relate in full; appoint for duty

detain' *vt.* keep under restraint; hinder; keep waiting —**deten'tion** *n.* confinement; arrest; detaining

detect' *vt.* find out or discover existence, presence, nature or identity of —**detec'tion** *n.* —**detect'ive** *n.* policeman or private agent employed in detecting crime —*a.* employed in detection —**detect'or** *n.* *esp.* mechanical sensing device or device for detecting radio signals

détente' [dā-tahnt'] *n.* lessening of tension in political or international affairs

deten'tion *n.* *see* DETAIN

deter' *vt.* discourage, frighten; hinder, prevent (**-rr-**) —**deterr'ent** *a./n.*

deter'gent *n.* cleansing, purifying substance —*a.* having cleansing power —**deterge'** *vt.*

dete'riorate *v.* become or make worse —**deteriora'tion** *n.*

deter'mine *vt.* make up one's mind, decide; fix as known; bring to a decision; be deciding factor in; *Law* end —*vi.* come to an end; come to a decision —**deter'minable** *a.* —**deter'minant** *a./n.* —**deter'minate** *a.* fixed in scope or nature —**determina'tion** *n.* determining; firm or resolute conduct or purpose;

resolve **—deter'mined** *a.* resolute **—deter'minism** *n.* theory that human action is settled by forces independent of will **—deter'minist** *n./a.*

detest' *vt.* hate, loathe **—detest'able** *a.* **—detest'ably** *adv.* **—detesta'tion** *n.*

dethrone' *vt.* remove from throne, depose **—dethrone'ment** *n.*

det'onate *v.* of bomb, mine, explosives *etc.*, (cause to) explode **—detona'tion** *n.* **—det'onator** *n.* mechanical, electrical device, or small amount of explosive, used to set off main explosive charge

de'tour *n.* course which leaves main route to rejoin it later; roundabout way *—vi.*

detract' *v.* take away (a part) from, diminish **—detrac'tion** *n.* **—detrac'tive** *a.* **—detrac'tor** *n.*

det'riment *n.* harm done, loss, damage **—detriment'al** *a.* damaging, injurious **—detriment'ally** *adv.*

detri'tus *n.* worn-down matter such as gravel, or rock debris **—detri'tal** *a.* **—detri'tion** [-trish'-] *n.* wearing away from solid bodies by friction

de trop [dətrō'] *Fr.* not wanted, superfluous

detrude' *vt.* to thrust down **—detru'sion** *n.*

deuce [dyo͞os] *n.* two; card with two spots; *Tennis* forty all; in exclamatory phrases, the devil **—deu'ced** *a. inf.* excessive

Deut. Deuteronomy

deute'rium [dyo͞o-] *n.* form of hydrogen twice as heavy as the normal gas **—deu'teron** *n.* nucleus of this gas

Deut'sche Mark [doi'chə-] monetary unit of W Germany

deval'ue, deval'uate *v.* (of currency) reduce or be reduced in value; reduce the value or worth of **—devalua'tion** *n.*

dev'astate *vt.* lay waste; ravage; *inf.* overwhelm **—devasta'tion** *n.*

devel'op *vt.* bring to maturity; elaborate; bring forth, bring out; evolve; treat photographic plate or film to bring out image; improve value or change use of (land) by building *etc.* *—vi.* grow to maturer state (**devel'oped, devel'oping**) **—devel'oper** *n.* one who develops land; chemical for developing film **—devel'opment** *n.*

de'viate *vi.* leave the way, turn aside, diverge **—de'viant** *n./a.* (person) deviating from normal *esp.* in sexual practices **—devia'tion** *n.* **—de'viator** *n.* **—de'vious** *a.* deceitful, underhand; roundabout, rambling; erring

device' *n.* contrivance, invention; apparatus; stratagem; scheme, plot; heraldic or emblematic figure or design

dev'il *n.* personified spirit of evil; superhuman evil being; person of great wickedness, cruelty *etc.*; *inf.* fellow; *inf.* something difficult or annoying; energy, dash, unconquerable spirit; *inf.* rogue, rascal; one who devils for lawyer or author *—vt.* do work that passes for employer's, as for lawyer or author; grill with hot condiments **—dev'ilish** *a.* like, of the devil; evil *—adv. inf.* very, extremely **—dev'ilment** *n.* wickedness; wild and reckless mischief, revelry, high spirits **—dev'ilry** *n.* **—devil-may-care** *a.* happy-go-lucky **—devil's advocate** one who advocates opposing, unpopular view, *usu.* for sake of argument; *RC Church* one appointed to state disqualifications of person whom it is proposed to make a saint

de'vious *a. see* DEVIATE

devise' [-īz'] *vt.* plan, contrive; invent; plot; leave by will **—devisee'** *n.* **—devi'sor** *n.*

devitrifica'tion *n.* loss of glassy or vitreous condition **—devit'rify** *vt.* deprive of character or appearance of glass (**-fied, -fying**)

devoid' *a.* (*usu. with* of) empty, lacking, free from

devolve' *vi.* pass or fall (to, upon) *—vt.* throw (duty *etc.*) on to another **—devolu'tion** [-lo͞o'-] *n.* devolving, *esp.* transfer of authority from central to regional government

devote' *vt.* set apart, give up exclusively (to person, purpose *etc.*) **—devo'ted** *a.* loving, attached **—devotee'** *n.* ardent enthusiast; zealous worshipper **—devo'tion** *n.* deep affection, loyalty; dedication; religious earnestness *—pl.* prayers, religious exercises **—devo'tional** *a.*

devour' *vt.* eat greedily; consume, destroy; read, gaze at eagerly **—devour'er** *n.*

devout' *a.* earnestly religious, pious; sincere, heartfelt **—devout'ly** *adv.*

dew *n.* moisture from air deposited as

small drops on cool surface between nightfall and morning; any beaded moisture *—vt.* wet with or as with dew **—dew'iness** *n.* **—dew'y** *a.* **—dew'-claw** *n.* partly developed inner toe of dogs **—dew'lap** *n.* fold of loose skin hanging from neck **—dew-worm** *n.* large earthworm used as bait **—dewy-eyed** *a.* naive, innocent

dew'berry *n.* bramble with blue-black fruits

dexter'ity *n.* manual skill, neatness, deftness, adroitness **—dex'ter** *a. Heraldry* on the bearer's right-hand side of a shield **—dex'terous** *a.* showing dexterity, skilful

dex'trose *n.* white, soluble, sweet-tasting crystalline solid, occurring naturally in fruit, honey, animal tissue

DF Defender of the Faith

DFC Distinguished Flying Cross

DFM Distinguished Flying Medal

dg decigram

dhow *n.* lateen-rigged Arab sailing vessel

dia- [dī-ə-] (*comb. form*) through

diabe'tes [-bē'tēz] *n.* various disorders characterized by excretion of abnormal amount of urine, *esp.* **d. melli'tus**, in which body fails to store and utilize glucose **—diabet'ic** *n./a.*

diabol'ic(al) *a.* devilish; *inf.* very bad **—diabol'ically** *adv.* **—diab'olism** *n.* devil-worship

diab'olo *n.* game in which top is spun into air from string attached to two sticks

diac'onal *a.* pert. to deacon **—diac'onate** *n.* office, rank of deacon; body of deacons

diacrit'ic *n.* sign above letter or character indicating special phonetic value *etc.* **—diacrit'ic(al)** *a.* of a diacritic; showing a distinction

di'adem *n.* a crown

diaer'esis *see* DIERESIS

diagno'sis *n.* identification of disease from symptoms (*pl.* **diagno'ses**) **—di'agnose** *vt.* **—diagnos'tic** *a.*

diag'onal *a.* from corner to corner; oblique *—n.* line from corner to corner **—diag'onally** *adv.*

di'agram *n.* drawing, figure in lines, to illustrate something being expounded **—diagrammat'ic** *a.* **—diagrammat'ically** *adv.*

di'al *n.* face of clock *etc.*; plate marked with graduations on which a pointer moves (as on a meter, weighing machine *etc.*); numbered disc on front of telephone; **UK** *sl.* face *—vt.* operate telephone; indicate on dial (**-ll-**)

di'alect *n.* characteristic speech of district; local variety of a language **—dialec'tal** *a.*

dialect'ic *n.* art of arguing **—dialec'tic(al)** *a.* **—dialect'ically** *adv.* **—dialecti'cian** *n.* logician; reasoner

di'alogue *n.* conversation between two or more (persons); representation of such conversation in drama, novel *etc.*; discussion between representatives of two states, countries *etc.*

dial'ysis *n. Med.* filtering of blood through membrane to remove waste products

diaman'té *n.* (fabric covered with) glittering particles **—diaman'tine** *a.* like diamond

diam'eter *n.* (length of) straight line from side to side of figure or body (*esp.* circle) through centre; thickness **—diamet'rical** *a.* opposite **—diamet'rically** *adv.*

di'amond *n.* very hard and brilliant precious stone, also used in industry; rhomboid figure; suit at cards; playing field in baseball **—diamond jubilee, wedding** 60th (sometimes 75th) anniversary

dian'thus *n.* genus of herbaceous flowers, *eg* pinks and carnations

diapa'son [-pā'z-] *n.* fundamental organ stop; compass of voice or instrument

di'aper *n.* towelling cloth or other material placed around waist, between legs, of baby to absorb its excrement; fabric with small diamond pattern; pattern of that kind **—di'apered** *a.*

diaph'anous *a.* transparent

diaphoret'ic *n.* drug promoting perspiration *—a.*

di'aphragm [-am] *n.* muscular partition dividing two cavities of body, midriff; plate or disc wholly or partly closing tube or opening; any thin dividing or covering membrane **—diaphragmat'ic** [-frag-] *a.*

diarrh(o)e'a [-rē'ə] *n.* excessive looseness of the bowels

di'ary *n.* daily record of events or thoughts; book for this; book for noting engagements, memoranda *etc.* —**di'a-rist** *n.* writer of diary

di'astase [-as-tās] *n.* enzyme that converts starch into sugar

dias'tole [-tə-li] *n.* dilation of the chambers of the heart

di'athermy *n.* heating of body tissues with electric current for medical or surgical purposes

di'atom *n.* one of order of microscopic algae —**diatom'ic** *a.* of two atoms

diaton'ic *a. Mus.* pert. to regular major and minor scales; (of melody) composed in such a scale

di'atribe *n.* violently bitter verbal attack, invective, denunciation

dib'ble *n.* pointed tool for making holes in soil for seeds or plants

dice *pl.n.* (*also functions as sing., orig. sing.* **die**) cubes each with six sides marked one to six for games of chance —*vi.* gamble with dice —*vt. Cookery* cut vegetables into small cubes —**di'cer** *n.* —**di'cey** *a. inf.* dangerous, risky

diceph'alous [dī-sef'-] *a.* two-headed

dichot'omy [-kot'-] *n.* division into two parts

di'chroism [-krō-] *n.* property possessed by some crystals of exhibiting different colours when viewed from different directions —**dichro'ic** *a.*

dick *n. sl.* detective

dick'y, dick'ey *n.* detachable false shirt front; child's bib or pinafore; *inf.* small bird (*pl.* **dick'ies, dick'eys**)

Dic'taphone *n.* **R** tape recorder, used *esp.* for dictation

dictate' *v.* say or read for another to transcribe; prescribe, lay down; impose (as terms) —*n.* [dik'-] bidding —**dicta'tion** *n.* —**dicta'tor** *n.* absolute ruler —**dictator'ial** *a.* despotic; overbearing —**dictator'ially** *adv.* —**dicta'torship** *n.*

dic'tion *n.* choice and use of words; enunciation

dic'tionary *n.* book setting forth, alphabetically, words of language with meanings *etc.*; reference book with items in alphabetical order

dic'tum *n.* pronouncement, saying, maxim (*pl.* **dic'ta**)

did *pt. of* DO[1]

didac'tic *a.* designed to instruct; (of people) opinionated, dictatorial —**didac'ticism** *n.*

did'dle *vt. inf.* cheat

die[1] [dī] *vi.* cease to live; come to an end; stop functioning; *inf.* be nearly overcome (with laughter *etc.*); *inf.* look forward (to) (**died, dy'ing**) —**die'hard** *n.* one who resists (reform *etc.*) to the end

die[2] [dī] *see* DICE

die[3] [dī] *n.* shaped block of hard material to form metal in forge, press *etc.*; tool for cutting thread on pipe *etc.*

dielec'tric [dī-ə-lek'-] *n.* substance through or across which electric induction takes place; nonconductor; insulator

dier'esis, diaer'esis [dī-er'-] *n.* mark (¨) placed over vowel to show that it is sounded separately from preceding one (*eg* in Noël) (*pl.* **di(a)er'eses**)

die'sel [dē'zl] *a.* pert. to internal-combustion engine using oil as fuel —*n.* this engine; vehicle powered by it; the fuel

di'et[1] *n.* restricted or regulated course of feeding; kind of food lived on; food —*vi.* follow a dietary regimen, as to lose weight —**di'etary** *a.* relating to diet —*n.* a regulated diet; system of dieting —**dietet'ic** *a.* —**dietet'ics** *pl.n.* science of diet —**dieti'cian, -tian** [-tish'-] *n.* one skilled in dietetics —**dietary fibre** fibrous substances in fruit and vegetables, consumption of which aids digestion (*also* **roughage**)

di'et[2] *n.* parliament of some countries; formal assembly

diff'er *vi.* be unlike; disagree —**dif'ference** *n.* unlikeness; degree or point of unlikeness; disagreement; remainder left after subtraction —**diff'erent** *a.* unlike —**diff'erently** *adv.*

differen'tial *a.* varying with circumstances; special; *Math.* pert. to an infinitesimal change in variable quantity; *Physics etc.* relating to difference between sets of motions acting in the same direction or between pressures *etc.* —*n. Math.* infinitesimal difference between two consecutive states of variable quantity; mechanism in automobile *etc.* allowing back wheels to revolve at different speeds when rounding corner; difference between rates of pay for different types of labour —**differen'tially** *adv.* —**differen'tiate** *vt.* serve to distinguish between, make different —*vi.* discriminate —**differentia'tion** *n.* —**differential calculus** method of calculating relative rate of change for continuously varying quantities

diff'icult *a.* requiring effort, skill *etc.* to do or understand, not easy; obscure —**dif'ficulty** *n.* being difficult; difficult task, problem; embarrassment; hindrance; obscurity; trouble

diff'ident *a.* lacking confidence, timid, shy —**diff'idence** *n.* shyness —**dif'fidently** *adv.*

diffract' *vi.* break up, *esp.* of rays of light, sound-waves —**diffrac'tion** *n.* deflection of ray of light, electromagnetic wave caused by an obstacle

diffuse' [-fyōōz'] *vt.* spread abroad —*a.* [-fyōōs'] widely spread; loose, verbose, wordy —**diffuse'ly** *adv.* loosely; wordily —**diffu'sible** *a.* —**diffu'sion** *n.* —**diffu'sive** *a.* —**diffu'sively** *adv.*

dig *vi.* work with spade; search, investigate —*vt.* turn up with spade; hollow out, make hole in; excavate; thrust into; discover by searching (**dug, digg'ing**) —*n.* piece of digging; (archaeological) excavation; thrust; jibe, taunt —*pl.* **UK** *inf.* lodgings (*also* **digg'ings**) —**digg'er** *n.* one who digs; gold-miner; Aust. or N.Z. soldier (oft. term of address)

digest' [-j-] *vt.* prepare (food) in stomach *etc.* for assimilation; bring into handy form by sorting, tabulating, summarizing; reflect on; absorb —*vi.* of food, undergo digestion —*n.* [dī'-] methodical summary, *esp.* of laws; magazine containing condensed version of articles *etc.* already published elsewhere —**digest'ible** *a.* —**diges'tion** *n.* digesting —**digest'ive** *a.*

dig'it [-j-] *n.* finger or toe; any of the numbers 0 to 9 —**dig'ital** *a.* of, resembling digits; performed with fingers; displaying information (time *etc.*) by numbers rather than by pointer on dial —**dig'itate(d)** *a.* having separate fingers, toes —**digital recording** sound recording process that converts audio signals into pulses corresponding to voltage level

digita'lis, -lin [-j-] *n.* drug made from foxglove

dig'nity *n.* stateliness, gravity; worthiness, excellence, repute; honourable office or title —**dig'nify** *vt.* give dignity to (**-fied, -fying**) —**dig'nified** *a.* stately, majestic —**dig'nitary** *n.* holder of high office

digress' [dī-] *vi.* turn from main course, *esp.* to deviate from subject in speaking or writing —**digress'ion** *n.* —**digres'sive** *a.*

dihe'dral [dī-] *a.* having two plane faces or sides

dike *n.* embankment to prevent flooding; ditch

dik'tat *n.* arbitrary decree

dilap'idated *a.* in ruins; decayed —**dilapida'tion** *n.*

dilate' [dī-] *vt.* widen, expand —*vi.* expand; talk or write at length (on) —**dil(a-t)a'tion** *n.*

dil'atory *a.* tardy, slow, belated —**dil'atorily** *adv.* —**dil'atoriness** *n.* delay

dilemm'a *n.* position in fact or argument offering choice only between unwelcome alternatives; predicament

dilettan'te [-tahn'ti] *n.* person with taste and knowledge of fine arts as pastime; dabbler (*pl.* **dilettan'ti**) —*a.* amateur, desultory —**dilettan'tism** *n.*

dil'igent *a.* unremitting in effort, industrious, hard-working —**dil'igence** *n.*

dill *n.* yellow-flowered herb with medicinal seeds

dilly-dall'y *vi. inf.* loiter; vacillate

dilute' [-lōōt'] *vt.* reduce (liquid) in strength, *esp.* by adding water; thin; reduce in force, effect *etc.* —*a.* weakened thus —**dil'uent** [-yoo-] *a./n.* —**dilu'tion** *n.*

dilu'vial, -vian [-lōō'-] *a.* of, connected with, a deluge or flood, *esp.* the Flood of the Book of Genesis

dim *a.* indistinct, faint, not bright; mentally dull; unfavourable (**dimm'er** *comp.*, **dimm'est** *sup.*) —*v.* make, grow dim —*vt.* switch (headlights of vehicle) to low beam for short-range visibility (**-mm-**) —**dim'ly** *adv.* —**dim'mer** *n.* device for dimming electric lights —**dim'ness** *n.*

dime *n.* 10-cent piece, coin of US and Canada

dimen'sion *n.* measurement, size; aspect —**dimen'sional** *a.* —**fourth dimension** *Physics* time; supernatural, fictional dimension additional to those of length, breadth, thickness

dimin'ish *v.* lessen —**diminu'tion** *n.* —**dimin'utive** *a.* very small —*n.* derivative word, affix implying smallness

diminuen'do *a./adv. Mus.* of sound, dying away

dim'ity *n.* strong cotton fabric

dim'ple *n.* small hollow in surface of skin, *esp.* of cheek; any small hollow —*v.* mark with, show dimples

din *n.* continuous roar of confused noises —*vt.* repeat to weariness, ram (fact, opinion *etc.*) into (**-nn-**)

dine *vi.* eat dinner —*vt.* give dinner to —**di'ner** *n.* one who dines; small *usu.* cheap restaurant; dining car —**dining car** railway restaurant-car —**dining room**

ding *v.* ring (*esp.* with tedious repetition); make (imitation of) sound of bell —*n.* this sound

din'ghy [ding'gi] *n.* small open boat; collapsible rubber boat

din'gle [ding'gəl] *n.* dell

din'go [-ng'gō] *n.* Aust. wild dog

din'gy [-j-] *a.* dirty-looking, dull —**din'giness** *n.*

dinn'er *n.* chief meal of the day; official banquet

di'nosaur *n.* extinct reptile, often of gigantic size —**dinosaur'ian** *a.*

dint *n.* dent, mark —**by dint of** by means of

di'ocese [dī'ə-sis] *n.* district, jurisdiction of bishop —**dioc'esan** [-os'-] *a.* —*n.* bishop, clergyman, people of diocese

di'ode *n. Electronics* device for converting alternating current to direct current

diop'tre [dī-] *n.* unit for measuring refractive power of lens —**diop'trics** *pl.n.* (*with sing. v.*) that part of the science of optics which deals with refraction of light

dioram'a [dī-ə-rahm'ə] *n.* miniature three-dimensional scene, *esp.* as museum exhibit

diox'ide [dī-] *n.* oxide with two parts of oxygen to one of the other constituents

diox'in [dī-] *n.* extremely toxic byproduct of the manufacture of certain herbicides and bactericides

dip *vt.* put partly or for a moment into liquid; immerse, involve; lower and raise again; take up in ladle, bucket *etc.* —*vi.* plunge partially or temporarily; go down, sink; slope downwards (**-pp-**) —*n.* act of dipping; bathe; liquid chemical in which livestock are immersed to treat insect pests *etc.*; downward slope; hollow; creamy (savoury) mixture in which chips *etc.* are dipped before being eaten; lottery —**dip into** glance at

diphthe'ria [dip-thē'-] *n.* infectious disease of throat with membranous growth —**diphtherit'ic** *a.*

diph'thong [dif'-] *n.* union of two vowel sounds in single compound sound

diplo'ma *n.* document vouching for person's proficiency; title to degree, honour *etc.*

diplo'macy *n.* management of international relations; skill in negotiation; tactful, adroit dealing —**dip'lomat** *n.* one engaged in official diplomacy —**diplomat'ic** *a.* —**diplomat'ically** *adv.* —**diplo'matist** *n.* diplomat; tactful person

diplo'pia *n.* double vision

dipo'lar [dī-] *a.* having two poles

di'pole *n.* type of radio and television aerial

dipp'er *n.* long-handled utensil similar to ladle; bird (water ouzel)

dipsoma'nia *n.* uncontrollable craving for alcohol —**dipsoma'niac** *n.* victim of this

dip'tych [-ik] *n.* ancient tablet hinged in the middle, folding together like a book; painting, carving on two hinged panels

dire *a.* terrible; urgent

direct' *vt.* control, manage, order; point out the way; aim, point, turn; address (letter *etc.*); supervise actors *etc.* in play or motion picture —*a.* frank, straightforward; straight; going straight to the point; immediate; lineal —**direc'tion** *n.* directing; aim, course of movement; address, instruction —**direct'ive** *a./n.* —**direct'ly** *adv.* —**direct'ness** *n.* —**direc'tor** *n.* one who directs, *esp.* a motion picture; member of board managing company (**direct'ress** *fem.*) —**direc'torate** *n.* body of directors; office of director —**direct'orship** *n.* —**direc'tory** *n.* book of names, addresses, streets *etc.*; (**D-**) French revolutionary government 1795-9 —**direction finder** radio receiver that determines the direction of incoming waves

dirge *n.* song of mourning

dir'igible [-ij-] *a.* steerable —*n.* balloon or airship

dirk *n.* short dagger orig. carried by Scottish clansmen

dirn'dl [durn'-] *n.* full, gathered skirt

dirt *n.* filth; soil, earth; obscene material; contamination **—dirt'iness** *n.* **—dirt'y** *a.* unclean, filthy; obscene; unfair; dishonest **—dirt track** loose-surfaced track (*eg* for motorcycle racing)

dis- (*comb. form*) negation, opposition, deprivation; in many verbs indicates undoing of the action of simple verb In the list below, the meaning may be inferred from the word to which *dis-* is prefixed

disa'ble *vt.* make unable; cripple, maim **—disabil'ity** *n.* incapacity; drawback

disabuse' [-byōōz'] *vt.* undeceive, disillusion; free from error

disadvant'age [-vahnt'-] *n.* drawback; hindrance; detriment *—vt.* handicap **—disadvan'taged** *a.* deprived, discriminated against, underprivileged **—disadvanta'geous** *a.*

disaffect'ed *a.* ill-disposed, alienated, estranged **—disaffec'tion** *n.*

disagree' *vt.* be at variance; conflict; (of food *etc.*) have bad effect on **—disagree'ment** *n.* difference of opinion; discord; discrepancy **—disagree'able** *a.* unpleasant

disallow' *vt.* reject as untrue or invalid **—disallow'ance** *n.*

disappear' *vi.* vanish; cease to exist; be lost **—disappear'ance** *n.*

disappoint' *vt.* fail to fulfil (hope), frustrate **—disappoint'ment** *n.*

disarm' *v.* deprive of arms or weapons; reduce country's war weapons; win over **—disarm'ament** *n.* **—disarm'ing** *a.* removing hostility, suspicion

disarray' *vt.* throw into disorder, derange *—n.* disorderliness, *esp.* of clothing

disas'ter [-zahs'-] *n.* calamity, sudden or great misfortune **—disas'trous** *a.* calamitous

disbar' *vt. Law* expel from the bar

disbud' *vt.* remove superfluous buds, shoots from

disburse' *vt.* pay out money **—disburse'ment** *n.*

disc *see* DISK

discard' *v.* reject; give up; cast off, dismiss

discern' [-sern'] *vt.* make out; distinguish **—discern'ible** *a.* **—discern'ing** *a.* discriminating; penetrating **—discern'ment** *n.* insight

discharge' *vt.* release; dismiss; emit; perform (duties), fulfil (obligations); let go; fire off; unload; pay *—n.* discharging; being discharged; release; matter emitted; document certifying release, payment *etc.*

disci'ple [-sī'-] *n.* follower, one who takes another as teacher and model **—disci'pleship** *n.*

dis'cipline [-si-plin] *n.* training that produces orderliness, obedience, self-control; result of such training in order, conduct *etc.*; system of rules, *etc.* *—vt.* train; punish **—disciplina'rian** *n.* one who enforces rigid discipline **—dis'ciplinary** *a.*

disclaim' *vt.* deny, renounce **—disclaim'er** *n.* repudiation, denial

disaffil'iate	**disembark'**	**disloy'al**
disapproba'tion	**disengage'**	**disloy'alty**
disappro'val	**disengage'ment**	**dismount'**
disapprove'	**disentang'le**	**disorganiza'tion**
disarrange'	**disentang'lement**	**disor'ganize**
disassoc'ciate	**disestab'lish**	**dispropor'tion**
disavow'	**disestab'lishment**	**disprove'**
disband'	**disfa'vo(u)r**	**disrep'utable**
disbelief'	**disfran'chise**	**disrepute'**
discompose'	**dishar'mony**	**disrespect'(ful)**
discompo'sure	**disheart'en**	**dissatisfac'tion**
disconnect'	**disheart'enment**	**dissat'isfy**
discontent'	**dishon'est**	**dissim'ilar**
discontent'ment	**dishon'esty**	**dissimilar'ity**
discontin'ue	**dishon'o(u)rable**	**dissymm'etry**
discourt'eous	**disinter'**	**distrust'**
discourt'esy	**disjoin'**	**disunite'**

disclose' [-ōz'] *vt.* allow to be seen; make known —**disclo'sure** [-zhə] *n.* revelation

dis'co *n. short for* DISCOTHEQUE

discol'o(u)r [-kul'-] *vt.* alter colour of, stain —**discolo(u)ra'tion** *n.*

discom'fit [-um'-] *vt.* embarrass, disconcert, baffle —**discom'fiture** *n.*

discommode' *vt.* put to inconvenience; disturb —**discommo'dious** *a.*

disconcert' *vt.* ruffle, confuse, upset, embarrass

discon'solate *a.* unhappy, downcast, forlorn

dis'cord *n.* strife; difference, dissension; disagreement of sounds —**discord'ance** *n.* —**discord'ant** *a.* —**discord'antly** *adv.*

dis'cotheque [-tek] *n.* club *etc.* for dancing to recorded music

dis'count [*or* -kount'] *vt.* consider as possibility but reject as unsuitable, inappropriate *etc.*; deduct (amount, percentage) from usual price; sell at reduced price —*n.* [dis'-] amount deducted from cost, expressed as cash amount or percentage

discount'enance *vt.* abash; discourage; frown upon

discour'age [-kur'-] *vt.* reduce confidence of; deter; show disapproval of —**discour'agement** *n.*

dis'course *n.* conversation; speech, treatise, sermon —*vi.* [-kaws'] speak, converse, lecture

discov'er [-kuv'-] *vt.* (be the first to) find out, light upon; make known —**discov'erable** *a.* —**discov'erer** *n.* —**discov'ery** *n.*

discred'it *vt.* damage reputation of; cast doubt on; reject as untrue —*n.* disgrace; doubt —**discred'itable** *a.*

discreet' *a.* prudent, circumspect —**discreet'ly** *adv.* —**discreet'ness** *n.*

discrep'ancy *n.* conflict, variation, as between figures —**discrep'ant** *a.*

discrete' *a.* separate, disunited, discontinuous

discre'tion [-kresh'ən] *n.* quality of being discreet; prudence; freedom to act as one chooses —**discre'tionary** *a.*

discrim'inate *vi.* single out for special favour or disfavour; distinguish between; be discerning —**discrimina'tion** *n.*

discurs'ive *a.* passing from subject to subject, rambling

dis'cus *n.* disc-shaped object thrown in athletic competition

discuss' *vt.* exchange opinions about; debate —**discuss'ion** *n.*

disdain' *n.* scorn, contempt —*vt.* scorn —**disdain'ful** *a.* —**disdain'fully** *adv.*

disease' *n.* illness; disorder of health —**diseased'** *a.*

disembod'ied *a.* (of spirit) released from bodily form

disembow'el *vt.* take out entrails of

disenchan'ted [-ah-] *a.* disillusioned

disfig'ure *vt.* mar appearance of —**disfigura'tion** *n.* —**disfig'urement** *n.* blemish, defect

disgorge' *vt.* vomit; give up —**disgorge'ment** *n.*

disgrace' *n.* shame, loss of reputation, dishonour —*vt.* bring shame or discredit upon —**disgrace'ful** *a.* shameful —**disgrace'fully** *adv.*

disgrun'tled *a.* vexed; put out

disguise' [-gīz'] *vt.* change appearance of, make unrecognizable; conceal, cloak; misrepresent —*n.* false appearance; device to conceal identity

disgust' *n.* violent distaste, loathing, repugnance —*vt.* affect with loathing

dish *n.* shallow vessel for food; portion or variety of food; contents of dish; *sl.* attractive person —*vt.* put in dish; serve (up)

dishabille' [di-sa-bēl'] *n.* state of being partly or carelessly dressed

dishev'elled [-sh-] *a.* with disordered hair; ruffled, untidy, unkempt

disillu'sion [-loo'-] *vt.* destroy ideals, illusions, or false ideas of —*n.*

disinfect'ant *n.* substance that prevents or removes infection —**disinfect'** *vt.*

disinforma'tion *n.* false information intended to deceive or mislead

disingen'uous *a.* not sincere or frank

disinher'it *vt.* to deprive of inheritance

disin'tegrate *v.* break up, fall to pieces —**disintegra'tion** *n.*

disin'terest *n.* freedom from bias or involvement —**disin'terested** *a.*

disjoint' *vt.* put out of joint; break the natural order or logical arrangement of —**disjoint'ed** *a.* (of discourse) incoherent; disconnected

disk, disc *n.* thin, flat, circular object like a coin; phonograph record —**disk harrow** harrow which cuts soil with inclined disks —**disk jockey** announcer playing records, oft. on radio

dis'locate *vt.* put out of joint; disrupt, displace —**disloca'tion** *n.*

dislodge' *vt.* drive out or remove from hiding place or previous position —**dislodge'ment** *n.*

dis'mal [-z-] *a.* depressing; depressed; cheerless, dreary, gloomy —**dis'mally** *adv.*

disman'tle *vt.* take apart

dismay' *vt.* dishearten, daunt —*n.* consternation, horrified amazement; apprehension

dismem'ber *vt.* tear or cut limb from limb; divide, partition —**dismem'berment** *n.*

dismiss' *vt.* remove, discharge from employment; send away; reject —**dismis'sal** *n.*

disobey' [-bā'] *v.* refuse or fail to obey —**disobe'dience** *n.* —**disobe'dient** *a.*

disoblige' *vt.* disregard the wishes, preferences of

disord'er *n.* disarray, confusion, disturbance; upset of health, ailment —*vt.* upset order of; disturb health of —**disor'derly** *a.* untidy; unruly

disor'ientate *vt.* cause (someone) to lose his bearings, confuse

disown' *vt.* refuse to acknowledge

dispar'age [-pa'rij] *vt.* speak slightingly of; belittle —**dispar'agement** *n.*

dis'parate *a.* essentially different, unrelated —**dispar'ity** *n.* inequality; incongruity

dispass'ionate *a.* unswayed by passion; calm, impartial

dispatch', despatch' *vt.* send off to destination or on an errand; send off; finish off, get done with speed; *inf.* eat up; kill —*n.* sending off; efficient speed; official message, report

dispel' *vt.* clear, drive away, scatter (**-ll-**)

dispense' *vt.* deal out; make up (medicine); administer (justice); grant exemption from —**dispens'able** *a.* —**dispen'sary** *n.* place where medicine is made up —**dispensa'tion** *n.* act of dispensing; licence or exemption; provision of nature or providence —**dispens'er** *n.* —**dispense with** do away with; manage without

disperse' *vt.* scatter —**dispersed'** *a.* scattered; placed here and there —**disper'sal, disper'sion** *n.*

dispir'ited *a.* dejected, disheartened —**dispir'itedly** *adv.* —**dispir'iting** *a.*

displace' *vt.* move from its place; remove from office; take place of —**displace'ment** *n.* displacing; weight of liquid displaced by a solid in it —**displaced person** person forced from his home country, *esp.* by war *etc.*

display' *vt.* spread out for show; show, expose to view —*n.* displaying; parade; show, exhibition; ostentation

displease' *v.* offend; annoy —**displeas'ure** *n.* anger, vexation

disport' *v.refl.* gambol, amuse oneself, frolic

dispose' [-ōz'] *vt.* arrange; distribute; incline; adjust —*vi.* determine —**dispo'sable** *a.* designed to be thrown away after use —**dispo'sal** *n.* —**disposi'tion** *n.* inclination; temperament; arrangement; plan —**dispose of** sell, get rid of; have authority over, deal with

dispossess' *vt.* cause to give up possession (of)

dispute' *vi.* debate, discuss —*vt.* call in question; debate, argue; oppose, contest —**dispu'table** *a.* —**dispu'tant** *n.* —**disputa'tion** *n.* —**disputa'tious** *a.* argumentative; quarrelsome

disqual'ify *vt.* make ineligible, unfit for some special purpose

disqui'et *n.* anxiety, uneasiness —*vt.* cause (someone) to feel this

disquisi'tion [-zish'ən] *n.* learned or elaborate treatise, discourse or essay

disrepair' *n.* state of bad repair, neglect

disrobe' *v.* undress; divest of robes

disrupt' *vt.* interrupt; throw into turmoil or disorder —**disrup'tion** *n.* —**disrup'tive** *a.*

dissect' *vt.* cut up (body, organism) for detailed examination; examine or criticize in detail —**dissec'tion** *n.* —**dissec'tor** *n.* anatomist

dissem'ble *v.* conceal , disguise (feelings *etc.*); act the hypocrite —**dissem'bler** *n.*

dissem'inate *vt.* spread abroad, scatter —**dissemina'tion** *n.* —**dissem'inator** *n.*

dissent' *vi.* differ in opinion; express such difference; disagree with doctrine *etc.* of established church —*n.* such disagreement —**dissen'sion** *n.* —**dissent'er** *n.* —**dissen'tient** *a./n.*

disserta'tion *n.* written thesis; formal discourse —**dis'sertate** *vi.* hold forth

disser'vice *n.* ill turn, wrong, injury

diss'ident *n./a.* (one) not in agreement, *esp.* with government —**diss'idence** *n.* dissent; disagreement

dissim'ulate *v.* pretend not to have; practise deceit —**dissimula'tion** *n.* —**dissim'ulator** *n.*

diss'ipate *vt.* scatter; waste, squander —**diss'ipated** *a.* indulging in pleasure without restraint, dissolute; scattered, wasted —**dissipa'tion** *n.* scattering; frivolous, dissolute way of life

disso'ciate *v.* separate, sever; disconnect —**dissocia'tion** *n.*

diss'olute *a.* lax in morals

dissolu'tion [-lōō'-] *n.* break up; termination of parliament, meeting or legal relationship; destruction; death

dissolve' [-z-] *vt.* absorb or melt in fluid; break up, put an end to, annul —*vi.* melt in fluid; disappear, vanish; break up, scatter —**dissol'vable, dissol'uble** *a.* capable of being dissolved —**dissol'vent** *n.* thing with power to dissolve

diss'onant *a.* jarring, discordant —**dis'sonance** *n.*

dissuade' [-sw-] *vt.* advise to refrain, persuade not to —**dissua'sion** *n.* —**dissua'sive** *a.*

dissyll'able, disyll'able [dī-] *n.* word or metrical foot having two syllables —**dis(s)yllab'ic** *a.*

dis'taff [-ahf] *n.* cleft stick to hold wool *etc.*, for spinning —**distaff side** maternal side; female line

dis'tance *n.* amount of space between two things; remoteness; aloofness, reserve —*vt.* hold or place at distance —**dis'tant** *a.* far off, remote; haughty, cold —**dis'tantly** *adv.*

distaste' *n.* dislike of food or drink; aversion, disgust —**distaste'ful** *a.* unpleasant, displeasing to feelings —**distaste'fully** *adv.* —**distaste'fulness** *n.*

distem'per *n.* disease of dogs; method of painting on plaster without oil; paint used for this —*vt.* paint with distemper

distend' *v.* swell out by pressure from within, inflate —**disten'sible** *a.* —**disten'sion** *n.*

dis'tich [-ik] *n.* couplet

distil' *vt.* vaporize and recondense a liquid; purify, separate, concentrate liquids by this method; *fig.* extract quality of —*vi.* trickle down (**-ll-**) —**dist'illate** *n.* distilled liquid, *esp.* as fuel for some engines —**distill'er** *n.* one who distils, *esp.* manufacturer of alcoholic spirits —**distill'ery** *n.*

distinct' *a.* clear, easily seen; definite; separate, different —**distinc'tion** *n.* point of difference; act of distinguishing; eminence, repute, high honour, high quality —**distinct'ive** *a.* characteristic —**distinct'ly** *adv.* —**distinct'ness** *n.*

distin'guish [-ng'gw-] *vt.* make difference in; recognize, make out; honour; make prominent or honoured (*usu. refl.*); class —*vi.* (*usu. with* between *or* among) draw distinction, grasp difference —**distin'guishable** *a.* —**distin'guished** *a.* noble, dignified; famous, eminent

distort' *vt.* put out of shape, deform; misrepresent; garble, falsify —**distor'tion** *n.*

distract' *vt.* draw attention of (someone) away from work *etc.*; divert; perplex, bewilder, drive mad —**distrac'tion** *n.*

distraint' *n.* legal seizure of goods to enforce payment —**distrain'** *vt.* —**distrain'ment** *n.*

distrait' [-trā'] *a.* absent-minded; abstracted

distraught' [-awt'] *a.* bewildered, crazed with grief; frantic, distracted

distress' *n.* severe trouble, mental pain; severe pressure of hunger, fatigue or want; *Law* distraint —*vt.* afflict, give mental pain —**distress'ful** *a.*

distrib'ute *vt.* deal out, dispense; spread, dispose at intervals; classify —**distribu'tion** *n.* —**distrib'utive** *a.* —**distrib'utor** *n.* rotary switch distributing electricity in automobile engine

dis'trict *n.* region, locality; portion of territory

disturb' *vt.* trouble, agitate, unsettle, derange —**disturb'ance** *n.* —**disturb'er** *n.*

disuse' [-s'] *n.* state of being no longer used —**disused'** [-zd'] *a.*

disyll'able [dī-] *n. see* DISSYLLABLE

ditch *n.* long narrow hollow dug in ground for drainage *etc.* —*v.* make, repair ditches; run automobile *etc.* into ditch —*vt. sl.* abandon, discard

dith'er *vi.* be uncertain or indecisive —*n.* this state

dith'yramb [-i-ram] *n.* ancient Greek hymn sung in honour of Dionysus —**dithyram'bic** *a.*

ditt'o *n. It.* same, aforesaid (used to avoid repetition in lists *etc.*) —**do.** *abbrev.*

ditt'y *n.* simple song

diuret'ic [dī-yoo-] *a.* increasing the discharge of urine —*n.* substance with this property

diur'nal [dī-ur'-] *a.* daily; in or of daytime; taking a day

diva'lent [dī-] *a.* capable of combining with two atoms of hydrogen or their equivalent

divan' *n.* bed, couch without back or head; low cushioned seat by wall

dive *vi.* plunge under surface of water; descend suddenly; disappear; go deep down into; reach quickly —*n.* act of diving; *sl.* disreputable bar or club —**di'ver** *n.* one who descends into deep water; kinds of diving bird —**dive bomber** aircraft which attacks after diving steeply

diverge' [dī-] *vi.* get farther apart; separate —**diver'gence** *n.* —**diver'gent** *a.*

di'vers [-z] *a. obs.* some, various

diverse' [dī-] *a.* different, varied —**diver'sify** *vt.* make diverse or varied; give variety to (**-ified, -ifying**) —**diverse'ly** *adv.* —**diversifica'tion** *n.* —**diver'sity** *n.*

divert' [dī-] *vt.* turn aside, ward off; amuse, entertain —**diver'sion** *n.* a diverting; official detour for traffic when main route is closed; amusement —**divert'ing** *a.*

divest' [dī-] *vt.* unclothe, strip; dispossess, deprive

divide' *vt.* make into two or more parts, split up, separate; distribute, share; diverge in opinion; classify —*vi.* become separated; part into two groups for voting —*n.* watershed —**div'idend** *n.* share of profits, of money divided among creditors *etc.*; number to be divided by another —**divi'ders** *pl.n.* measuring compasses

divine' *a.* of, pert. to, proceeding from, God; sacred; heavenly —*n.* theologian; clergyman —*v.* guess; predict, foresee, tell by inspiration or magic —**divina'tion** *n.* divining —**divine'ly** *adv.* —**divi'ner** *n.* —**divin'ity** *n.* quality of being divine; god; theology —**divining rod** (forked) stick said to move when held over ground where water is present

divis'ion [-vizh'-] *n.* act of dividing; part of whole; barrier; section; political constituency; difference in opinion *etc.*; *Math.* method of finding how many times one number is contained in another; army unit; separation, disunion —**divi'sible** *a.* capable of division —**divi'sional** *a.* —**divi'sive** *a.* causing disagreement —**divi'sor** *n. Math.* number which divides dividend

divorce' *n.* legal dissolution of marriage; complete separation, disunion —*vt.* dissolve marriage; separate; sunder —**divorcee'** *n.*

div'ot *n.* piece of turf

divulge' [dī-] *vt.* reveal, let out (secret) —**divul'gence** *n.*

divv'y *inf. vt.* (*esp. with* up) divide and share —*n.* share, portion

dix'ie *n. inf.* (military) cooking utensil or mess tin; (**D-**) southern states of USA

dizz'y *a.* feeling dazed, unsteady, as if about to fall; causing or fit to cause dizziness, as speed *etc.*; *inf.* silly —*vt.* make dizzy (**dizz'ied, dizz'ying**) —**diz'zily** *adv.* —**dizz'iness** *n.*

DJ dinner jacket; disc jockey

dl decilitre

dm decimetre

DNA *n. abbrev. for* **deoxyribonucleic acid**, main constituent of the chromosomes of all organisms

do[1] [doo] *vt.* perform, effect, transact, bring about, finish; work at; work out, solve; suit; cover (distance); provide, prepare; *sl.* cheat, swindle; frustrate; look after —*vi.* act; manage; work; fare; serve, suffice; happen —*v. aux.* makes negative and interrogative sentences and expresses emphasis (**did, done, do'ing**) —*n. inf.* celebration, festivity —**do away with** destroy —**do up** fasten; renovate

—**do with** need; make use of —**do without** deny oneself

do[2] *see* DOH

do. ditto

do'cile *a.* willing to obey, submissive —**docil'ity** *n.*

dock[1] *n.* artificial enclosure near harbour for loading or repairing ships —*v.* of vessel, put or go into dock; of spacecraft, link or be linked together in space —**dock'yard** *n.* enclosure with docks, for building or repairing ships

dock[2] *n.* solid part of tail; cut end, stump —*vt.* cut short, *esp.* tail; curtail, deduct (an amount) from

dock[3] *n.* enclosure in criminal court for prisoner

dock[4] *n.* coarse weed

dock'et *n.* piece of paper sent with package *etc.* with details of contents, delivery instructions *etc.* —*vt.* fix docket to

doc'tor *n.* medical practitioner; one holding university's highest degree in any faculty —*vt.* treat medically; repair, mend; falsify (accounts *etc.*); *inf.* castrate or spay —**doc'toral** *a.* —**doc'torate** *n.*

doc'trine [-in] *n.* what is taught; teaching of church, school, or person; belief, opinion, dogma —**doctrinaire'** *a.* stubbornly insistent on applying theory without regard for circumstances —*n.* —**doctri'nal** *a.*

doc'udrama *n.* TV dramatization of true events

doc'ument *n.* piece of paper *etc.* providing information or evidence —*vt.* furnish with proofs, illustrations, certificates —**document'ary** *a./n. esp.* (of) type of motion picture dealing with real life, not fiction —**documenta'tion** *n.*

dodd'er *vi.* totter or tremble, as with age —**dodd'erer** *n.* feeble or inefficient person

dodge [doj] *v.* avoid or attempt to avoid (blow, discovery *etc.*) as by moving quickly; evade questions by cleverness —*n.* trick, artifice; ingenious method; act of dodging —**dodg'er** *n.* shifty person

do'do *n.* large extinct bird (*pl.* **do'do(e)s**)

doe [dō] *n.* female of deer, hare, rabbit

does [duz] *third pers. sing., pres. ind. active of* DO[1]

doff *vt.* take off (hat, clothing); discard, lay aside

dog *n.* domesticated carnivorous four-legged mammal; male of wolf, fox and other animals; person (in contempt, abuse or playfully); name given to various mechanical contrivances acting as holdfasts; device with tooth which penetrates or grips object and detains it; andiron or firedog —*vt.* follow steadily or closely (**-gg-**) —**dogg'ed** *a.* persistent, resolute, tenacious —**dogg'y** *a.* —**dog'-like** *a.* —**dog'cart** *n.* open vehicle with crosswise back-to-back seats —**dog days** hot season of the rising of Dog Star; period of inactivity —**dog-ear** *n.* turned-down corner of page in book —*vt.* turn down corners of pages —**dog-end** *inf. n.* cigarette end; rejected piece of anything —**dog'fight** *n.* skirmish between fighter planes; savage contest characterized by disregard of rules —**dog'fish** *n.* very small species of shark —**doggy bag** bag in which diner may take leftovers for dog —**dog'house** *n.* house, shelter for dog; *inf.* disfavour, *as* **in the doghouse** —**dog'leg** *n.* sharp bend or angle —**dog rose** wild rose —**dogs'body** *n. inf.* drudge —**dog'sled** *n.* sled drawn by dogs —**Dog Star** star Sirius —**dog train** sled drawn by dog team —**dog'watch** *n.* in ships, short half-watch, 4-6, 6-8 p.m. —**dog'wood** *n.* any of various shrubs having red shoots in winter —**go to the dogs** degenerate

doge [dōj] *n.* formerly, chief magistrate in Venice

dogg'erel *n.* slipshod, unpoetic or trivial verse

do'gie, do'g(e)y [-gi] *n.* motherless calf (*pl.* **-gies** *or* **-geys**)

dog'ma *n.* article of belief, *esp.* one laid down authoritatively by church; body of beliefs (*pl.* **-s, -ata**) —**dogmat'ic** *a.* asserting opinions with arrogance; relating to dogma —**dogmat'ically** *adv.* —**dog'matism** *n.* arrogant assertion of opinion —**dog'matist** *n.* —**dog'matize** *vi.*

doh, do *n.* first sol-fa note

doi'ly, doy'l(e)y *n.* small cloth, paper, piece of lace to place under cake, dish *etc.*

Dol'by R system used in tape recording to reduce unwanted noise

dol'ce [-chē] *a. Mus.* sweet

dol'drums *pl.n.* state of depression, dumps; region of light winds and calms near the equator

dole *n.* charitable gift; *inf.* payment under unemployment insurance —*vt.* (*usu. with* out) deal out sparingly

dole'ful *a.* dreary, mournful —**dole'fully** *adv.*

doll *n.* child's toy image of human being; *sl.* attractive girl or woman —*v.* dress (up) in latest fashion or smartly

doll'ar *n.* standard monetary unit of many countries, *esp.* USA, Canada and (since 1966) Aust.

doll'op *n. inf.* semisolid lump

doll'y *n.* doll; wheeled support for motion-picture, TV camera; various metal devices used as aids in hammering, riveting

dol'men *n.* kind of cromlech; stone table

dol'omite *n.* a type of limestone

dol'o(u)r *n.* grief, sadness, distress —**dol'orous** *a.* —**dol'orously** *adv.*

dol'phin *n.* sea mammal, smaller than whale, with beaklike snout

dolt [-ō-] *n.* stupid fellow —**dolt'ish** *a.*

domain' *n.* lands held or ruled over; sphere, field of influence; province

dome *n.* a rounded vault forming a roof; something of this shape

Domes'day Book [do͞omz'-] record of survey of England in 1086

domes'tic *a.* of, in the home; homeloving; (of animals) tamed, kept by man; of, in one's own country, not foreign —*n.* house servant —**domes'ticate** *vt.* tame (animals); accustom to home life; adapt to an environment —**domestica'tion** *n.* —**domestic'ity** [-tis'-] *n.*

dom'icile *n.* person's regular place of abode —**dom'iciled** *a.* living —**domicil'iary** *a.* of a dwelling place

dom'inate *vt.* rule, control, sway; of heights, overlook —*vi.* control, be the most powerful or influential member or part of something —**dom'inant** *a.* —**domina'tion** *n.* —**domineer'** *vi.* act imperiously, tyrannize

Domin'ican *n.* friar or nun of the order of St. Dominic —*a.* pert. to this order

domin'ion *n.* sovereignty, rule; territory of government

Dominion Day *see* CANADA DAY

dom'inoes *pl.n.* game played with 28 oblong flat pieces marked on one side with 0 to 6 spots on each half of the face —*sing.* one of these pieces; cloak with eye mask for masquerading

don[1] *vt.* put on (clothes) (**-nn-**)

don[2] *n.* fellow or tutor of college; Spanish title, Sir

donate' [dō-] *vt.* give —**dona'tion** *n.* gift to fund —**do'nor** *n.*

done *pp. of* DO[1]

don'jon *see* DUNGEON

donk'ey *n.* ass (*pl.* **-eys**) —**donkey engine** auxiliary engine —**donkey-work** *n.* drudgery

donned *pt./pp. of* DON

doo'dle *vi.* scribble absent-mindedly —*n.*

doom *n.* fate, destiny; ruin; judicial sentence, condemnation; the Last Judgment —*vt.* sentence, condemn; destine to destruction or suffering —**dooms'day** *n.* the day of the Last Judgment

door [dawr] *n.* hinged or sliding barrier to close any entrance —**door'way** *n.* entrance with or without door —**door'yard** *n.* yard by door of house

dope *n.* kind of varnish; drug, *esp.* illegal, narcotic drug; *inf.* information; *inf.* stupid person —*vt.* drug (*esp.* of racehorses) —**do'p(e)y** *a. inf.* foolish; drugged; half-asleep

Dor'ic [do'rik] *n.* dialect of Dorians; style of Greek architecture; rustic dialect —*a.* —**Dor'ian** [dawr'-] *a./n.* (member) of early Greek race

dorm'ant *a.* not active, in state of suspension; sleeping —**dorm'ancy** *n.*

dorm'er *n.* upright window set in sloping roof

dorm'itory *n.* sleeping room with many beds

dor'mouse *n.* small hibernating mouse-like rodent

dor'sal *a.* of, on back

dor'y *n.* flat-bottomed boat with high bow and stern

dose *n.* amount (of drug *etc.*) administered at one time; *inf.* instance or period of something unpleasant, *esp.* disease —*vt.* give doses to —**do'sage** *n.*

doss *inf. n.* temporary bed —*vi.* sleep in dosshouse; sleep —**doss'house** *n.* cheap lodging house

doss'ier [-i-ā, -yə] *n.* set of papers on some particular subject or event

dot[1] *n.* small spot, mark —*vt.* mark with dots; sprinkle; *sl.* hit —**dott'y** *a. sl.* crazy; *sl.* extremely fond of; marked with dots

dot[2] *n.* dowry

dote *vi.* (*with* on *or* upon) be passionately fond of; be silly or weak-minded —**do'tage** *n.* senility —**do'tard** *n.* —**do'ting** *a.* blindly affectionate

doub'le [dub'əl] *a.* of two parts, layers *etc.*, folded; twice as much or many; of two kinds; designed for two users; ambiguous; deceitful —*adv.* twice; to twice the amount or extent; in a pair —*n.* person or thing exactly like, or mistakable for, another; quantity twice as much as another; sharp turn; running pace —*v.* make, become double; increase twofold; fold in two; turn sharply; get round, sail round —**doub'ly** *adv.* —**double agent** spy employed simultaneously by two opposing sides —**double bass** largest and lowest-toned instrument in violin form —**double-cross** *v.* work for two sides at once, cheating each to betray another's trust —**double-crosser** *n.* —**double-dealing** *n.* artifice, duplicity —**double Dutch** *inf.* incomprehensible talk, gibberish —**double glazing** two panes of glass in a window to insulate against cold, sound *etc.* —**double knitting** medium thickness of knitting wool —**double-knitting** *a.* —**double-quick** *a./adv.* very fast —**double take** delayed reaction to a remark, situation *etc.*

double enten'dre [dub-əl-ahn-tahn'-drə] *n.* word or phrase with two meanings, one usu. indelicate

doub'let [dub'-] *n.* close-fitting body garment formerly worn by men; one of two words from same root but differing in form and usu. in meaning, as *warden* and *guardian*; false gem of thin layer of gemstone fused onto base of glass *etc.*

doubloon' [dub-] *n.* ancient Spanish gold coin

doubt [dowt] *vt.* hesitate to believe; call in question; suspect —*vi.* be wavering or uncertain in belief or opinion —*n.* uncertainty, wavering in belief; state of affairs giving cause for uncertainty —**doubt'er** *n.* —**doubt'ful** *a.* —**doubt'fully** *adv.* —**doubt'less** *adv.*

douche [dōōsh] *n.* jet or spray of water applied to (part of) body —*vt.* give douche to

dough [dō] *n.* flour or meal kneaded with water; *sl.* money —**dough'y** *a.* —**dough'nut** *n.* sweetened and fried ball or ring-shaped piece of dough

dought'y [dowt'-] *a.* valiant —**dough'tily** *adv.* —**dought'iness** *n.* boldness

dour [dōōr] *a.* grim, stubborn, severe

douse [dows] *vt.* thrust into water; extinguish (light)

dove [duv] *n.* bird of pigeon family; person opposed to war —**dove'cot(e)** *n.* house for doves —**dove'tail** *n.* joint made with fan-shaped tenon —*v.* fit closely, neatly, firmly together

dow'ager [-j-] *n.* widow with title or property derived from deceased husband

dow'dy *a.* unattractively or shabbily dressed —*n.* woman so dressed

dow'el *n.* wooden, metal peg, *esp.* joining two adjacent parts

dow'er *n.* widow's share for life of husband's estate —*vt.* endow —**dow'ry** *n.* property wife brings to husband at marriage; any endowment

down[1] *adv.* to, in, or towards, lower position; below the horizon; (of payment) on the spot, immediate —*prep.* from higher to lower part of; at lower part of; along —*a.* depressed, miserable —*vt.* knock, pull, push down; *inf.* drink, *esp.* quickly —*n.* descent; poor period; *Football* chance to move ball forward —**down'ward** *a./adv.* —**down'wards** *adv.* —**down-and-out** *a.* finished, defeated —**down'cast** *a.* dejected; looking down —**down'grade** *n.* downward slope —**down'hill'** *a.* going or sloping down —*adv.* downwards —**down'pour** *n.* heavy fall of rain —**down'right** *a.* plain, straightforward —*adv.* quite, thoroughly —**down'stage** *a./adv.* at, to front of stage —**down'town** *n./a./adv.* (of, in, to) central or main commercial area of city —**down under** *inf.* Australia and New Zealand —**go downhill** *inf.* decline, deteriorate —**have a down on** *inf.* have grudge against

down[2] *n.* soft underfeathers, hair or fibre; fluff —**down'y** *a.*

down'land *n.* open high land: *also* **downs** *pl.n.*

dow'ry *see* DOWER

dowse *vi.* use divining rod —**dow'ser** *n.* water diviner

doxol'ogy *n.* short hymn of praise to God

doy'en *n.* senior member of a body or profession (**-enne'** *fem.*)

doy'ley *see* DOILY

doz. dozen

doze *vi.* sleep drowsily, be half-asleep —*n.* nap —**do'zy** *a.* drowsy; *inf.* stupid

doz'en [duz'-] *n.* (set of) twelve

Dr. Doctor; Drive

drab *a.* dull, monotonous; of a dingy brown colour —*n.* mud colour

drachm [dram] *n.* unit of weight, 1/8 of fluid ounce, 1/16 of avoirdupois ounce

drach'ma [-k-] *n.* monetary unit of Greece (*pl.* **-mas** *or* **-mae** [-mē])

Draco'nian *a.* (*also* **d-**) like the laws of Draco; very harsh, cruel

draft[1] [-ah-] *n.* design, sketch; rough copy of document; order for money; detachment of men, *esp.* troops, reinforcements —*vt.* make sketch, plan, or rough design of; make rough copy (of writing *etc.*); send detached party

draft[2], **UK draught** *n.* current of air between apertures in room *etc.*; act or action of drawing; dose of medicine; act of drinking; quantity drunk at once; inhaling; depth of ship in water; the drawing in of, or fish taken in, net; **US** selection for compulsory military service —*a.* for drawing; drawn —**draft'y** *a.* full of air currents —**draft horse** horse for vehicles carrying heavy loads —**drafts'man** *n.* one who makes drawings, plans *etc.* —**drafts'manship** *n.*

drag *vt.* pull along with difficulty or friction; trail, go heavily; sweep with net or grapnels; protract —*vi.* lag, trail; be tediously protracted (**-gg-**) —*n.* check on progress; checked motion; iron shoe to check wheel; type of carriage; lure for hounds to hunt; kind of harrow; sledge, net, grapnel, rake; *inf.* tedious person or thing; *sl.* women's clothes worn by (transvestite) man —**drag'ster** *n.* car designed, modified for drag racing —**drag'net** *n.* fishing net to be dragged along sea floor; comprehensive search, *esp.* by police for criminal *etc.* —**drag race** motor car race where cars are timed over measured distance

dragée' [-zhā'] *n.* sugar-coated sweet, nut or pill

drag'on *n.* mythical fire-breathing monster, like winged crocodile; type of large lizard —**drag'onfly** *n.* long-bodied insect with gauzy wings

dragoon' *n.* cavalryman of certain regiments —*vt.* oppress; coerce

drain *vt.* draw off (liquid) by pipes, ditches *etc.*; dry; drink to dregs; empty, exhaust —*vi.* flow off or away; become rid of liquid —*n.* channel for removing liquid; sewer; depletion, strain —**drain'age** *n.*

drake *n.* male duck

dram *n.* small draught of strong drink; drachm

dram'a [-ahm'-] *n.* stage play; art or literature of plays; playlike series of events —**dramat'ic** *a.* pert. to drama; suitable for stage representation; with force and vividness of drama; striking; tense; exciting —**dram'atist** *n.* writer of plays —**dramatiza'tion** *n.* —**dram'atize** *vt.* adapt novel for acting

dram'aturgy *n.* the technique of writing and producing plays —**dram'aturgist** *n.* a playwright —**dramatur'gic** *a.*

drape *vt.* cover, adorn with cloth; arrange in graceful folds —*pl.n.* hanging drapery at window —**dra'per** *n.* dealer in cloth, linen *etc.* —**dra'pery** *n.*

dras'tic *a.* extreme, forceful; severe

draught [drahft] *n. see* DRAFT[2] —*pl.* **UK** checkers

draw *vt.* pull, pull along, haul; inhale; entice; delineate, portray with pencil *etc.*; frame, compose, draft, write; attract; bring (upon, out *etc.*); get by lot; of ship, require (depth of water); take from (well, barrel *etc.*); receive (money); bend (bow) —*vi.* pull, shrink; attract; make, admit current of air; make pictures with pencil *etc.*; finish game with equal points, goals *etc.*, tie; write orders for money; come, approach (near) (**drew** *pt.*, **drawn** *pp.*) —*n.* act of drawing; casting of lots; unfinished game, tie —**draw'able** *a.* —**draw'er** *n.* one who or that which draws; sliding box in table or chest —*pl.* two-legged undergarment —**draw'ing** *n.* art of depicting in line; sketch so done; action of verb —**draw'back** *n.* anything that takes away from satisfaction; snag —**draw'bridge** *n.* hinged bridge to pull up —**drawing room** living room, sitting room —**draw near** approach —**draw out** lengthen —**draw up** arrange; stop

drawl *v.* speak slowly —*n.* such speech —**drawl'ingly** *adv.*

drawn *pp. of* DRAW

dray *n.* low cart without sides for heavy loads

dread [dred] *vt.* fear greatly —*n.* awe, terror —*a.* feared, awful —**dread'ful** *a.* disagreeable, shocking or bad —**dread'locks** *pl.n.* Rastafarian hairstyle of long matted or tightly curled strands —**dread'nought** *n.* large battleship mounting heavy guns

dream [drēm] *n.* vision during sleep; fancy, reverie, aspiration; very pleasant idea, person, thing —*vi.* have dreams —*vt.* see, imagine in dreams; think of as possible (**dreamt** [dremt] *or* **dreamed** [drēmd] *pt./pp.*) —**dream'er** *n.* —**dream'less** *a.* —**dream'y** *a.* given to daydreams, unpractical, vague; *inf.* wonderful

drear'y *a.* dismal, dull —**drear** *a.* —**drear'ily** *adv.* —**drear'iness** *n.* gloom

dredge[1] *v.* bring up mud *etc.*, from sea bottom; deepen channel by dredge; search for, produce obscure, remote, unlikely material —*n.* form of scoop or grab —**dredg'er** *n.* ship for dredging

dredge[2] *vt.* sprinkle with flour *etc.* —**dredg'er** *n.*

dregs *pl.n.* sediment, grounds; worthless part

drench *vt.* wet thoroughly, soak; make (an animal) take dose of medicine —*n.* soaking; dose for animal

dress *vt.* clothe; array for show; trim, smooth, prepare surface of; prepare (food) for table; put dressing on (wound); align (troops) —*vi.* put on one's clothes; form in proper line —*n.* one-piece garment for woman; clothing; clothing for ceremonial evening wear —**dress'er** *n.* one who dresses, *esp.* actors or actresses; surgeon's assistant; kitchen sideboard —**dress'ing** *n.* something applied to something else, as sauce to food, ointment to wound, manure to land, stiffening to linen *etc.*; seasoned mixture for inserting into or serving with poultry *etc.*; *inf.* scolding, as in **dressing down** —**dress'y** *a.* stylish; fond of dress —**dress circle** first gallery in theatre —**dress coat** cutaway coat worn by men as evening dress —**dressing gown** —**dressing room** —**dressing table** —**dress'maker** *n.*

dress'age [-ahzh] *n.* method of training horse in special manoeuvres to show obedience

drew *pt. of* DRAW

drey *n.* squirrel's nest

drib'ble *v.* flow in drops, trickle; run at the mouth; *Football* work ball forward with short kicks —*n.* trickle, drop —**drib'let** *n.* small portion or instalment

drift *vi.* be carried as by current of air, water; move aimlessly or passively —*n.* process of being driven by current; slow current or course; deviation from course; tendency; speaker's meaning; wind-heaped mass of snow, sand *etc.*; material driven or carried by water —**drif'ter** *n.* one who, that which drifts; *inf.* aimless person with no fixed job *etc.* —**drift'wood** *n.* wood washed ashore by sea

drill[1] *n.* boring tool or machine; exercise of soldiers or others in handling of arms and manoeuvres; routine teaching —*vt.* bore, pierce hole; exercise in military and other routine —*vi.* practise routine

drill[2] *n.* machine for sowing seed; small furrow for seed; row of plants —*vt.* sow seed in drills or furrows

drill[3] *n.* coarsely woven twilled fabric

drill[4] *n.* W Afr. monkey

drink *v.* swallow liquid; absorb; take intoxicating liquor, *esp.* to excess (**drank** *pt.*, **drunk** *pp.*) —*n.* liquid for drinking; portion of this; act of drinking; intoxicating liquor; excessive use of it —**drink'able** *a.* —**drink'er** *n.* —**drink to, drink the health of** express good wishes *etc.* by drinking a toast to

drip *v.* fall or let fall in drops (**-pp-**) —*n.* act of dripping; drop; *Med.* intravenous administration of solution; *inf.* dull, insipid person —**dripp'ing** *n.* melted fat that drips from roasting meat —*a.* very wet —**drip-dry** *a.* (of fabric) drying free of creases if hung up while wet —**drip'stone** *n.* projection over window or door to stop dripping of water

drive *vt.* urge in some direction; make move and steer (vehicle, animal *etc.*); urge, impel; fix by blows, as nail; chase;

convey in vehicle; hit a ball with force as in golf, tennis —*vi.* keep machine, animal, going, steer it; be conveyed in vehicle; rush, dash, drift fast (**drove, driv'en, dri'ving**) —*n.* act, action of driving; journey in vehicle; private road leading to house; capacity for getting things done; united effort, campaign; energy; forceful stroke in cricket, golf, tennis —**dri'ver** *n.* one that drives; golf club —**drive-in** *n.* movie theatre, bank *etc.* designed to be used by patrons in their automobiles —**driving belt** belt that communicates motion to machinery

driv'el *vi.* run at the mouth or nose; talk nonsense —*n.* silly nonsense —**driv'eller** *n.*

driz'zle *vi.* rain in fine drops —*n.* fine, light rain

drogue [drōg] *n.* any funnel-like device, *esp.* of canvas, used as sea anchor; small parachute; wind indicator; windsock towed behind target aircraft; funnel-shaped device on end of refuelling hose of tanker aircraft to receive probe of aircraft being refuelled

droll [-ō-] *a.* funny, odd, comical —**droll'ery** *n.* —**droll'y** *adv.*

drom'edary *n.* one-humped camel bred *esp.* for racing

drone *n.* male of honey bee; lazy idler; deep humming; bass pipe of bagpipe; its note —*v.* hum; talk in monotonous tone

dron'go [-ng'g-] *n.* black, tropical bird

drool *vi.* to slaver, drivel

droop *vi.* hang down; wilt, flag —*vt.* let hang down —*n.* drooping condition —**droop'y** *a.*

drop *n.* globule of liquid; very small quantity; fall, descent; distance through which thing falls; thing that falls, as gallows platform; slot through which object can be dropped —*vt.* let fall; let fall in drops; utter casually; set down, unload; discontinue —*vi.* fall; fall in drops; lapse; come or go casually (**-pp-**) —**drop'let** *n.* —**dropp'ings** *pl.n.* dung of rabbits, sheep, birds *etc.* —**drop'out** *n.* person who fails to complete course of study or one who rejects conventional society

drop'sy *n.* disease causing watery fluid to collect in the body —**drop'sical** *a.*

dross *n.* scum of molten metal; impurity, refuse; anything of little or no value

drought [-owt] *n.* long spell of dry weather

drove[1] *pt. of* DRIVE

drove[2] *n.* herd, flock, crowd, *esp.* in motion —*v.* drive cattle *etc.*, *esp.* a long distance —**dro'ver** *n.* driver of cattle

drown *v.* die or be killed by immersion in liquid; get rid of as by submerging in liquid; make sound inaudible by louder sound

drow'sy [-z-] *a.* half-asleep; lulling; dull —**drowse** *vi.* —**drow'sily** *adv.* —**drow'siness** *n.*

drub *vt.* thrash, beat (**-bb-**) —**drub'bing** *n.* beating

drudge *vi.* work at menial or distasteful tasks, slave —*n.* one who drudges, hack —**drudg'ery** *n.*

drug *n.* medical substance; narcotic; commodity which is unsaleable because of overproduction —*vt.* mix drugs with; administer drug to, *esp.* one inducing unconsciousness (**-gg-**) —**drugg'ist** *n.* person who sells medicines *etc.*; pharmacist —**drug'store** *n.* pharmacy where wide variety of goods is available

drugg'et *n.* coarse woollen fabric, *esp.* for carpeting

dru'id [-ōō'-] *n.* (*also* **D-**) member of ancient order of Celtic priests; Eisteddfod official —**druid'ic(al)** *a.* —**dru'idism** *n.*

drum *n.* percussion instrument of skin stretched over round hollow frame, played by beating with sticks; various things shaped like drum; part of ear —*v.* play drum; tap, thump continuously (**-mm-**) —**drumm'er** *n.* one who plays drum —**drum'fire** *n.* heavy continuous rapid artillery fire —**drum'head** *n.* part of drum that is struck —**drumhead court-martial** summary one held at war front —**drum major** leader of military band —**drum'stick** *n.* stick for beating drum; lower joint of cooked fowl's leg —**drum out** expel from club *etc.*

drunk *a.* overcome by strong drink; *fig.* under influence of strong emotion —*pp. of* DRINK —**drunk'ard** *n.* one given to excessive drinking —**drunk'en** *a.* drunk; caused by, showing intoxication —*archaic pp. of* DRINK —**drunk'enly** *adv.* —**drunk'enness** *n.*

dry *a.* without moisture; rainless; not

yielding milk, or other liquid; cold, unfriendly; caustically witty; having prohibition of alcoholic drink; uninteresting; needing effort to study; lacking sweetness (as wines) —*vt.* remove water, moisture —*vi.* become dry; evaporate (**dried, dry'ing**) —*n. inf.* prohibitionist —**dri'ly** *adv.* —**dry'ness** *n.* —**dry'er, dri'er** *n.* person or thing that dries; apparatus for removing moisture —**dry battery** electric battery without liquid —**dry-clean** *v.* clean clothes with solvent other than water —**dry-cleaner** *n.* —**dry farming** methods of producing crops in areas of low rainfall —**dry ice** solid carbon dioxide —**dry point** needle for engraving without acid; engraving so made —**dry rot** fungoid decay in wood —**dry run** practice, rehearsal in simulated conditions

dry'ad *n.* wood nymph

DSC Distinguished Service Cross

DSc Doctor of Science

DSO Distinguished Service Order

D.T.'s *inf. short for* **delir'ium tre'mens**, disordered mental state produced by advanced alcoholism

du'al *a.* twofold; of two, double, forming pair —**du'alism** *n.* recognition of two independent powers or principles, *eg* good and evil, mind and matter —**dual'ity** *n.*

dub[1] *vt.* confer knighthood on; give title to; provide (motion picture) with soundtrack not in original language; smear with grease, dubbin (**-bb-**) —**dubb'in, dubb'ing** *n.* grease for making leather supple

dub[2] *n. inf.* clumsy person

du'bious *a.* causing doubt, not clear or decided; of suspect character —**dubi'ety** *n.* uncertainty, doubt

du'cal *a.* of, like a duke

duc'at [duk'-] *n.* former gold coin of Italy *etc.*

duch'ess *n.* duke's wife or widow

duch'y *n.* territory of duke, dukedom

duck[1] *n.* common swimming bird (**drake** *masc.*) —*v.* plunge (someone) under water; bob down —**duck'ling** *n.* —**duckbilled platypus** *see* PLATYPUS —**duck'weed** *n.* plant that floats on ponds *etc.*

duck[2] *n.* strong linen or cotton fabric —*pl.* trousers of it

duck[3], **DUKW** *n.* amphibious vehicle used in World War II

duct *n.* channel, tube —**duct'ile** *a.* capable of being drawn into wire; flexible and tough; docile —**ductil'ity** *n.* —**duct'less** *a.* (of glands) secreting directly certain substances essential to health

dud *n.* futile, worthless person or thing; shell that fails to explode —*a.* worthless

dude *n.* tourist, *esp.* in ranch district; dandy —**dude ranch** ranch serving as guesthouse and showplace

dudg'eon [-j'ən] *n.* anger, indignation, resentment

duds *pl.n. inf.* clothes

due *a.* owing; proper to be given, inflicted *etc.*; adequate, fitting; under engagement to arrive, be present; timed for —*adv.* (with points of compass) exactly —*n.* person's right; (*usu. pl.*) charge, fee *etc.* —**du'ly** *adv.* properly; fitly; rightly; punctually —**due to** attributable to; caused by

du'el *n.* arranged fight with deadly weapons, between two persons; keen two-sided contest —*vi.* fight in duel (**-ll-**) —**du'ellist** *n.*

duenn'a [dyōō-] *n.* Spanish lady-in-waiting; elderly governess, guardian, chaperon

duet' [dyōō-] *n.* piece of music for two performers —**duett'ist** *n.*

duff[1] *n.* kind of boiled pudding

duff[2] *vt.* manipulate, alter article so as to make it look like new; mishit, *esp.* at golf —*a. sl.* bad, useless

duff'el, duf'fle *n.* coarse woollen cloth; coat of this; equipment, esp. for camping

duff'er *n.* stupid inefficient person

dug[1] *pt./pp. of* DIG

dug[2] *n.* udder, teat of animal

du'gong *n.* whalelike mammal of tropical seas

dug'out *n.* covered excavation to provide shelter for troops *etc.*; canoe of hollowed-out tree; *Sport* covered bench for players when not on the field

duke *n.* peer of rank next below prince; sovereign of small state called duchy (**duch'ess** *fem.*) —**duke'dom** *n.*

dukes *pl.n. sl.* fists

dul'cet [-sit] *a.* (of sounds) sweet, melodious

dul'cimer [-sim-] *n.* stringed instrument played with hammers, ancestor of piano

dull *a.* stupid; insensible; sluggish; tedious; lacking liveliness or variety; gloomy, overcast —*v.* make or become dull —**dull'ard** *n.* —**dull'y** *adv.*

du'ly *see* DUE

dumb [dum] *a.* incapable of speech; silent; *inf.* stupid —**dumb'ly** *adv.* —**dumb'ness** *n.* —**dumb'bell** *n.* weight for exercises; *sl.* fool —**dumbfound'** *vt.* confound into silence —**dumb show** acting without words

dum'dum *n.* soft-nosed expanding bullet

dumm'y *n.* tailor's or dressmaker's model; imitation object; *Cards* hand exposed on table and played by partner; *Sports* feigned move or pass; UK pacifier; *sl.* stupid person —*a.* sham, bogus —**dummy run** practice or rehearsal

dump *vt.* throw down in mass; deposit; unload; send (low-priced goods) for sale abroad —*n.* rubbish heap; *inf.* dirty, unpleasant place; temporary depot of stores or munitions —*pl.* low spirits, dejection —**dump'ling** *n.* small round pudding of dough, often fruity —**dump'y** *a.* short, stout —**dumpy level** surveyor's levelling instrument

dun[1] *vt.* persistently demand payment of debts (**-nn-**) —*n.* one who duns

dun[2] *a.* of dull greyish brown —*n.* this colour; dun horse

dunce *n.* slow learner, stupid pupil

dun'derhead *n.* blockhead —**dun'derheaded** *a.*

dune *n.* sandhill on coast or desert

dung *n.* excrement of animals; manure —*vt.* manure (ground)

dungaree' *n.* coarse cotton fabric —*pl.* overalls of this material

dun'geon [-jən] *n.* underground cell or vault for prisoners, donjon; formerly, tower or keep of castle

dunk *vt.* dip bread *etc.* in liquid before eating it; submerge

dun'lin *n.* small sandpiper

dunn'age *n.* material for packing cargo

du'o *n.* pair of performers

duodec'imal [-des'-] *a.* computed by twelves; twelfth —**duode'nary** *a.* twelvefold

duodec'imo [-des'-] *n.* size of book in which each sheet is folded into 12 leaves; book of this size (*pl.* **-mos** [-mōz]) —*a.* of this size

duode'num *n.* upper part of small intestine —**duode'nal** *a.*

dupe *n.* victim of delusion or sharp practice —*vt.* deceive for advantage, impose upon

du'plex *a.* twofold —*n.* house divided into two separate dwellings; either dwelling

du'plicate *vt.* make exact copy of; double —*a.* double; exactly the same as something else —*n.* exact copy —**duplica'tion** *n.* —**du'plicator** *n.* machine for making copies —**duplic'ity** [-plis'-] *n.* deceitfulness, double-dealing, bad faith

du'rable *a.* lasting, resisting wear —**durabil'ity** *n.* —**du'rably** *adv.*

du'rance *n. obs.* imprisonment

dura'tion *n.* time thing lasts

duress' [dyoo-] *n.* compulsion by use of force or threats

du'ring *prep.* throughout, in the time of, in the course of

durst *obs. pt. of* DARE

dusk *n.* darker stage of twilight; partial darkness —**dusk'ily** *adv.* —**dusk'y** *a.* dark; dark-coloured

dust *n.* fine particles, powder of earth or other matter, lying on surface or blown along by wind; ashes of the dead —*vt.* sprinkle with powder; rid of dust —**dust'er** *n.* cloth for removing dust —**dust'y** *a.* covered with dust —**dust'bin** *n.* UK garbage can —**dust'bowl** *n.* area in which dust storms have carried away the top soil

Dutch *a.* pert. to the Netherlands, its inhabitants, its language —**Dutch courage** drunken bravado —**Dutch treat** one where each person pays his own share

du'ty *n.* moral or legal obligation; that which is due; tax on goods; military service; one's proper employment —**du'teous** *a.* —**du'tiable** *a.* liable to customs duty —**du'tiful** *a.*

du'vet [dōō'vā] *n.* quilt filled with down or artificial fibre

DV Deo volente

dwarf *n.* very undersized person; mythological, small, manlike creature (*pl.* **dwarfs, dwarves**) —*a.* unusually small, stunted —*vt.* make seem small by contrast; make stunted —**dwarf'ish** *a.*

dwell *vi.* live, make one's abode (in); fix one's attention, write or speak at length (on) (**dwelt** *pt./pp.*) —**dwell'er** *n.* —**dwell'ing** *n.* house

dwin'dle *vi.* grow less, waste away, decline

dye [dī] *vt.* impregnate (cloth *etc.*) with colouring matter; colour thus (**dyed** [dīd], **dye'ing** [dī'ing]) —*n.* colouring matter in solution or which may be dissolved for dyeing; tinge, colour —**dy'er** *n.*

dyke *n. see* DIKE

dynam'ics [dī-] *pl.n.* (*with sing. v.*) branch of physics dealing with force as producing or affecting motion; physical forces —**dynam'ic** *a.* of, relating to motive force, force in operation; energetic and forceful —**dynam'ical** *a.* —**dynam'ically** *adv.*

dy'namite *n.* high explosive mixture —*vt.* blow up with this —**dy'namiter** *n.*

dy'namo *n.* machine to convert mechanical into electrical energy, generator of electricity (*pl.* **-mos**) —**dynamom'eter** *n.* instrument to measure energy expended

dyn'asty [din'-] *n.* line, family, succession of hereditary rulers —**dyn'ast** *n.* —**dynast'ic** *a.* of dynasty

dyne *n.* cgs unit of force

dys'entery *n.* infection of intestine causing severe diarrhoea

dysfunc'tion [dis-] *n.* abnormal, impaired functioning, *esp.* of bodily organ

dyslex'ia [dis-] *n.* impaired ability to read, caused by brain disorder —**dyslex'ic** *a.*

dyspep'sia [dis-] *n.* indigestion —**dyspep'tic** *a./n.*

dys'trophy *n.* wasting of body tissues, *esp.* muscles

E

E Earl; East; Eastern; English

each *a./pron.* every one taken separately

ea'ger [ē'-] *a.* having a strong wish (for something); keen, impatient —**ea'gerly** *adv.* —**ea'gerness** *n.*

ea'gle [ē'-] *n.* large bird with keen sight which preys on small birds and animals; *Golf* score of two strokes under par for a hole —**ea'glet** *n.* young eagle

ear[1] *n.* organ of hearing, *esp.* external part of it; sense of hearing; sensitiveness to sounds; attention —**ear'ache** *n.* acute pain in ear —**ear'mark** *vt.* assign, reserve for definite purpose; make identification mark on ear of sheep *etc.* —*n.* this mark —**ear'phone** *n.* receiver for radio *etc.* held to or put in ear —**ear'ring** *n.* ornament for lobe of the ear —**ear'shot** *n.* hearing distance —**ear'wig** *n.* small insect with pincer-like tail

ear[2] *n.* spike, head of corn

earl [erl] *n.* British nobleman ranking next below marquis —**earl'dom** *n.* his domain, title

earl'y [erl'-] *a./adv.* before expected or usual time; in first part, near or nearer beginning of some portion of time

earn [ern] *vt.* obtain by work or merit; gain —**earn'ings** *pl.n.*

earn'est[1] [ern'-] *a.* serious, ardent, sincere —**earn'estly** *adv.* —**in earnest** serious, determined

earn'est[2] [ern'-] *n.* money paid over in token to bind bargain, pledge; foretaste

earth [er-] *n.* planet or world we live on; ground, dry land; mould, soil, mineral; fox's hole —*vt.* cover with earth —**earth'en** *a.* made of clay or earth —**earth'ly** *a.* possible, feasible —**earth'y** *a.* of earth; uninhibited; vulgar —**earth'enware** *n.* (vessels of) baked clay —**earth'quake** *n.* convulsion of earth's surface —**earth'work** *n.* bank of earth in fortification —**earth'worm** *n.*

ease [ēz] *n.* comfort; freedom from constraint, annoyance, awkwardness, pain or trouble; idleness —*v.* reduce burden; give bodily or mental ease to; slacken; (cause to) move carefully or gradually; relieve of pain —**ease'ment** *n.* *Law* right of way *etc.*, over another's land —**eas'ily** *adv.* —**eas'y** *a.* not difficult; free from pain, care, constraint or anxiety; compliant; characterized by low demand; fitting loosely; *inf.* having no preference for any particular course of action —**easy-going** *a.* not fussy; indolent

eas'el [ēz'l] *n.* frame to support picture *etc.*

east *n.* part of horizon where sun rises; eastern lands, orient —*a.* on, in, or near, east; coming from east —*adv.* from, or to, east —**east'erly** *a./adv.* from, or to, east —**east'ern** *a.* of, dwelling in, east —**east'erner** *n.* —**east'ing** *n.* distance eastwards of a point from a given meridian —**east'ward** *a./n.* —**east'ward(s)** *adv.*

East'er *n.* movable festival of the Resurrection of Christ

eas'y *see* EASE

eat *v.* chew and swallow; consume, destroy; gnaw; wear away (**ate** *pt.*, **eat'en** *pp.*) —**eat'able** *a.*

eau de Cologne' [ō-də-kə-lōn'] *Fr.* a light perfume

eaves [ēvz] *pl.n.* overhanging edges of roof —**eaves'drop** *v.* listen secretly —**eaves'dropper** *n.* —**eaves'dropping** *n.*

ebb *vi.* flow back; decay —*n.* flowing back of tide; decline, decay —**ebb tide**

eb'ony *n.* hard black wood —*a.* made of, black as ebony —**eb'onite** *n.* vulcanite —**eb'onize** *vt.* make colour of ebony

ebull'ient *a.* exuberant; boiling —**ebul'lience** *n.* —**ebulli'tion** *n.* boiling; effervescence; outburst

eccen'tric [eks-] *a.* odd, unconventional; irregular; not placed, or not having axis placed, centrally; not circular (in orbit) —*n.* odd, unconventional person; mechanical contrivance to change circular into to-and-fro movement —**eccen'trically** *adv.* —**eccentric'ity** [-is'-] *n.*

Eccles. Ecclesiastes

ecclesias'tic [-klēz-] *n.* clergyman —*a.* of, relating to the Christian Church —**ecclesias'tical** *a.* —**ecclesiol'ogy** *n.* science of church building and decoration

ECG electrocardiogram; electrocardiograph

ech'elon [esh'-] *n.* level, grade, of responsibility or command; formation of troops, planes *etc.* in parallel divisions each slightly to left or right of the one in front

ech'o [ek'ō] *n.* repetition of sounds by reflection; close imitation (*pl.* **ech'oes**) —*vt.* repeat as echo, send back the sound of; imitate closely —*vi.* resound; be repeated (**ech'oed, ech'oing**) —**echo sounder** —**echo sounding** system of ascertaining depth of water by measuring time required to receive an echo from sea bottom or submerged object

éclair' [ā-klār'] *n.* finger-shaped, iced cake filled with cream

éclat' [ā-klah'] *n.* splendour, renown, acclamation

eclec'tic *a.* selecting; borrowing one's philosophy from various sources —*n.* —**eclec'ticism** *n.*

eclipse' *n.* blotting out of sun, moon *etc.* by another heavenly body; obscurity —*vt.* obscure, hide; surpass —**eclip'tic** *a.* of eclipse —*n.* apparent path of sun

ec'logue [-og] *n.* short poem, *esp.* pastoral dialogue

ecol'ogy *n.* science of plants and animals in relation to their environment —**ecolog'ical** *a.* —**ecol'ogist** *n.* specialist in or advocate of ecological studies

econ'omy *n.* careful management of resources to avoid unnecessary expenditure or waste; sparing, restrained or efficient use; system of interrelationship of money, industry and employment in a country —**econom'ic** *a.* of economics; profitable; economical —**econom'ical** *a.* not wasteful of money, time, effort *etc.*; frugal —**econom'ically** *adv.* —**econom'ics** *pl.n.* (*with sing. v.*) study of economies of nations; (*used as pl.*) financial aspects —**econ'omist** *n.* specialist in economics —**econ'omize** *v.* limit or reduce expense, waste *etc.*

ec'ru [ek'ro͞o, ā'-] *n./a.* (of) colour of unbleached linen

ec'stasy *n.* exalted state of feeling, mystic trance; frenzy —**ecstat'ic** *a.* —**ecstat'ically** *adv.*

ec'toplasm *n.* in spiritualism, supposedly a semiluminous plastic substance which exudes from medium's body

ecumen'ic(al) [ē-kyoo-] *a.* of the Christian Church throughout the world, *esp.* with regard to its unity —**ecumen'icism** *n.*

ec'zema *n.* skin disease

E'dam *n.* round Dutch cheese with red rind

Edd'a *n.* collection of old Icelandic myths

edd'y *n.* small whirl in water, smoke *etc.* —*vi.* move in whirls (**edd'ied, edd'ying**)

e'delweiss [ā'dl-vīs] *n.* white-flowered alpine plant

ede'ma [i-dē'-] *n.* swelling in body tissues, due to accumulation of fluid

E'den *n.* garden in which Adam and Eve were placed at the Creation; any delightful, happy place or state

edge *n.* border, boundary; cutting side of blade; sharpness; advantage; acrimony, bitterness —*vt.* sharpen, give edge or border to; move gradually —*vi.* advance sideways or gradually —**edge'ways, edge'wise** *adv.* —**edg'ing** *n.* —**edg'y** *a.* irritable, sharp or keen in temper —**on edge** nervy, irritable; excited

ed'ible *a.* eatable, fit for eating —**edibil'ity** *n.*

e'dict *n.* order proclaimed by authority, decree

ed'ifice [-fis] *n.* building, *esp.* big one

ed'ify *vt.* improve morally, instruct (**-fied, -fying**) —**edifica'tion** *n.* improvement of the mind or morals

ed'it *vt.* prepare book, movie *etc.* for publication or broadcast —**edi'tion** *n.* form in which something is published; number of copies of new publication printed at one time —**ed'itor** *n.* —**edito'rial** *a.* of editor —*n.* article stating opinion of newspaper *etc.*

EDT Eastern Daylight Time

ed'ucate *vt.* provide schooling for; teach; train mentally and morally; train; improve, develop —**educa'tion** *n.* —**educa'tional** *a.* —**educa'tionally**

adv. —**educa'tion(al)ist** *n.* one versed in theory and practice of education —**ed'ucative** *a.* —**ed'ucator** *n.*

educe' *vt.* bring out, elicit, develop; infer, deduce —**edu'cible** *a.* —**educ'tion** *n.*

EEC European Economic Community

EEG electroencephalogram

eel *n.* snakelike fish

ee'rie, ee'ry *a.* weird, uncanny; causing superstitious fear

efface' *vt.* wipe or rub out —**efface'able** *a.* —**efface'ment** *n.*

effect' *n.* result, consequence; efficacy; impression; condition of being operative —*pl.* property; lighting, sounds *etc.* to accompany movie, broadcast *etc.* —*vt.* bring about, accomplish —**effect'ive** *a.* having power to produce effects; in effect, operative; serviceable; powerful; striking —**effect'ively** *adv.* —**effec'tual** *a.* successful in producing desired effect; satisfactory; efficacious —**effec'tually** *adv.* —**effect'uate** *vt.*

effem'inate *a.* womanish, unmanly —**effem'inacy** *n.*

eff'erent *a.* conveying outward or away

effervesce' [-es'] *vi.* give off bubbles; be in high spirits —**efferves'cence** *n.* —**efferves'cent** *a.*

effete' *a.* worn-out, feeble

effica'cious *a.* producing or sure to produce desired effect; effective; powerful; adequate —**eff'icacy** *n.* potency; force; efficiency

effi'cient [-fish'ənt] *a.* capable, competent, producing effect —**effi'ciency** *n.* —**effi'ciently** *adv.*

eff'igy *n.* image, likeness

effloresce' [-es'] *vt.* burst into flower —**efflores'cence** *n.* —**efflores'cent** *a.*

eff'luent *n.* liquid discharged as waste; stream flowing from larger stream, lake *etc.* —*a.* flowing out —**eff'luence** *n.* —**efflu'vium** *n.* something flowing out invisibly, *esp.* affecting lungs or sense of smell (*pl.* **-ia**) —**eff'lux** *n.*

eff'ort *n.* exertion, endeavour, attempt or something achieved —**eff'ortless** *a.*

effront'ery [-un-] *n.* brazen impudence

efful'gent *a.* radiant, shining brightly —**efful'gence** *n.*

effu'sion *n.* (unrestrained) outpouring —**effuse'** *vt.* pour out, shed —**effu'sive** *a.* gushing, demonstrative —**effu'sively** *adv.* —**effu'siveness** *n.*

Eftpos, EFTPOS electronic funds transfer at point of sale

e.g. exempli gratia (*Lat.*, for example)

egalita'rian *a.* believing that all people should be equal; promoting this ideal —*n.* —**egalita'rianism** *n.*

egg[1] *n.* oval or round object produced by female of bird *etc.*, from which young emerge, *esp.* egg of domestic hen, used as food —**egg cup** —**egg'plant** *n.* plant bearing egg-shaped purple fruit eaten as vegetable

egg[2] *vt.* —**egg on** encourage, urge; incite

eg'lantine *n.* sweet brier

eg'o [*or* ē'-] *n.* the self; the conscious thinking subject; one's image of oneself; morale —**e'goism** *n.* systematic selfishness; theory that bases morality on self-interest —**eg'oist** *n.* —**egois'tic(al)** *a.* —**eg'otism** *n.* selfishness; self-conceit —**eg'otist** *n.* —**egotis'tic(al)** *a.* —**egocen'tric** *a.* self-centred; egoistic; centred in the ego

egre'gious [-jəs] *a.* outstandingly bad, blatant; absurdly obvious, *esp.* of mistake *etc.*

e'gress *n.* way out; departure

e'gret *n.* lesser white heron; down of dandelion

ei'der [ī'-] *n.* Arctic duck —**ei'derdown** *n.* its breast feathers; quilt (stuffed with feathers)

eight [āt] *n.* cardinal number one above seven; eight-oared boat; its crew —*a.* —**eight'een'** *a./n.* eight more than ten —**eight'eenth'** *a./n.* —**eight'eenth'ly** *adv.* —**eighth** [āt-th] *a./n.* ordinal number —**eighth'ly** *adv.* —**eight'ieth** *a./n.* —**eight'y** *a./n.* ten times eight —**eighth note** musical note half length of quarter note —**figure of eight** a skating figure; any figure shaped as 8

Ei're [ā'rə] *n.* the Republic of Ireland

eistedd'fod [ī-sted'fəd] *n.* annual congress of Welsh bards; local gathering for competition in music and other performing arts

ei'ther [ī'-, ē'-] *a./pron.* one or the other; one of two; each —*adv./conj.* bringing in first of alternatives or strengthening an added negation

ejac'ulate *v.* eject (semen); exclaim,

utter suddenly —**ejacula'tion** *n.* —**ejac'ulatory** *a.*

eject' *vt.* throw out; expel, drive out —**ejec'tion** *n.* —**eject'ment** *n.* —**ejec'tor** *n.*

eke out make (supply) last, *esp.* by frugal use; supply deficiencies of; make with difficulty (a living *etc.*)

elab'orate [-it] *a.* carefully worked out, detailed; complicated —*vi.* [-āt] expand (upon) —*vt.* work out in detail; take pains with —**elabora'tion** *n.* —**elab'orator** *n.*

élan' [ā-lahn'] *n.* dash; ardour; impetuosity

e'land *n.* largest S Afr. antelope, resembling elk

elapse' *vi.* of time, pass

elas'tic *a.* resuming normal shape after distortion, springy; flexible —*n.* tape, fabric, containing interwoven strands of flexible rubber; something made of elastic, as rubber band —**elas'ticated** *a.* —**elastic'ity** [-is'-] *n.*

ela'tion *n.* high spirits; pride —**elate'** *vt.* (*usu. passive* be elated *etc.*) raise the spirits of; make happy; exhilarate

el'bow [-bō] *n.* joint between fore and upper parts of arm (*esp.* outer part of it); part of sleeve covering this —*vt.* shove, strike with elbow —**elbow grease** hard work —**elbow'room** *n.* sufficient room

el'der[1] *a.* older, senior —*comp. of* OLD —*n.* person of greater age; old person; official of certain churches —**el'derly** *a.* growing old —**el'dest** *a.* oldest —*sup. of* OLD

el'der[2] *n.* white-flowered tree

El Dorad'o [-ahd'-] *n.* fictitious country rich in gold

eld'ritch *a.* hideous; weird; uncanny; haggish

elect' *vt.* choose by vote; choose —*a.* appointed but not yet in office; chosen, select, choice —**elec'tion** *n.* choosing, *esp.* by voting —**electioneer'** *vi.* busy oneself in political elections —**elect'ive** *a.* appointed, filled, or chosen by election —**elect'or** *n.* one who elects —**elec'toral** *a.* —**elect'orate** *n.* body of electors —**elect'orship** *n.*

electric'ity [-is'-] *n.* form of energy associated with stationary or moving electrons or other charged particles; electric current or charge; science dealing with electricity —**elec'tric** *a.* derived from, produced by, producing, transmitting or powered by electricity; excited, emotionally charged —**elec'trical** *a.* —**electri'cian** *n.* one trained in installation *etc.* of electrical devices —**electrifica'tion** *n.* —**elec'trify** *vt.* (**-fied, -fying**) —**electric chair** chair in which criminals sentenced to death are electrocuted —**electric organ** *Mus.* organ in which sound is produced by electric devices instead of wind

electro- (*comb. form*) by, caused by electricity, as in **electrother'apy** *n.* Such words are not given here where the meaning may easily be inferred from the simple word

electrocar'diograph *n.* instrument for recording electrical activity of heart —**electrocar'diogram** *n.* tracing produced by this

elec'trocute *vt.* execute, kill by electricity —**electrocu'tion** *n.*

elec'trode *n.* conductor by which electric current enters or leaves battery, vacuum tube *etc.*

electrodynam'ics *n.* dynamics of electricity

electroenceph'alograph [-sef'-] *n.* instrument for recording electrical activity of brain —**electroenceph'alogram** *n.* tracing produced by this

elec'trolyse *vt.* decompose by electricity —**electrol'ysis** *n.*

elec'trolyte *n.* solution, molten substance that conducts electricity

electromag'net *n.* magnet containing coil of wire through which electric current is passed —**electromagnet'ic** *a.*

elec'tron *n.* one of fundamental particles of matter identified with unit of charge of negative electricity and essential component of the atom —**electron'ic** *a.* of electrons or electronics; using devices, such as semiconductors, transistors or valves, dependent on action of electrons —**electron'ics** *pl.n.* (*with sing. v.*) technology concerned with development of electronic devices and circuits; science of behaviour and control of electrons —**electron volt** unit of energy used in nuclear physics

elec'troplate *vt.* coat with silver *etc.* by electrolysis —*n.* articles electroplated

elec'troscope *n.* instrument to show presence or kind of electricity

elec'trotype *n.* art of producing copies of type *etc.*, by electric deposition of copper upon mould; copy so produced

elec'trum *n.* alloy of gold and silver used in jewellery *etc.*

eleemos'ynary [el-ē-mos'i-] *a.* charitable; dependent on charity

el'egant *a.* graceful, tasteful; refined —**el'egance** *n.*

el'egy [-ji] *n.* lament for the dead in poem or song —**elegi'ac** *a.* suited to elegies; plaintive —**elegi'acs** *pl.n.* elegiac verses

el'ement *n.* substance which cannot be separated into other substances by ordinary chemical techniques; component part; small amount, trace; heating wire in electric kettle, stove *etc.*; proper abode or sphere —*pl.* powers of atmosphere; rudiments, first principles —**element'al** *a.* fundamental; of powers of nature —**elemen'tary** *a.* rudimentary, simple —**elementary school** school in which instruction is given for first six to eight years

el'ephant *n.* huge four-footed, thick-skinned animal with ivory tusks and long trunk —**elephanti'asis** *n.* disease with hardening of skin and enlargement of legs *etc.* —**elephant'ine** *a.* unwieldy, clumsy, heavily big

el'evate *vt.* raise, lift up, exalt —**eleva'tion** *n.* raising; height, *esp.* above sea level; angle above horizon, as of gun; drawing of one side of building *etc.* —**el'evator** *n.* cage raised and lowered in vertical shaft to transport people or goods; tall, narrow granary, *esp.* as found on the prairies

elev'en *n.* number next above 10; team of 11 persons —*a.* —**elev'enfold** *a./adv.* —**elev'enth** *a.* the ordinal number —**eleventh hour** latest possible time

elf *n.* fairy; woodland sprite (*pl.* **elves**) —**elf'in, elf'ish, elv'ish, elf'like** *a.* roguish, mischievous

elic'it [-is'-] *vt.* draw out, evoke; bring to light

elide' *vt.* omit in pronunciation a vowel or syllable —**eli'sion** [-izh'ən] *n.*

el'igible *a.* fit or qualified to be chosen; suitable, desirable —**eligibil'ity** *n.*

elim'inate *vt.* remove, get rid of, set aside —**elimina'tion** *n.* —**elim'inator** *n.* one who, that which, eliminates

eli'sion *see* ELIDE

elite' [i-lēt', ā-] *n.* choice or select body; the pick or best part of society; typewriter typesize (12 letters to inch) —*a.* —**elit'ism** *n.*

elix'ir [-ik'sə] *n.* preparation sought by alchemists to change base metals into gold, or to prolong life; sovereign remedy

elk *n.* large deer

ellipse' *n.* oval —**ellip'tic(al)** *a.* —**ellip'tically** *adv.*

ellip'sis *n. Grammar* omission of parts of word or sentence (*pl.* **-ses** [sēz])

elm *n.* tree with serrated leaves; its wood

elocu'tion *n.* art of public speaking, voice management —**elocu'tionist** *n.* teacher of this; specialist in verse speaking

e'longate *vt.* lengthen, extend, prolong —**elonga'tion** *n.*

elope' *vi.* run away from home with lover —**elope'ment** *n.*

el'oquence *n.* fluent, powerful use of language —**el'oquent** *a.* —**el'oquently** *adv.*

else *adv.* besides, instead; otherwise —**elsewhere'** *adv.* in or to some other place

elu'cidate [-loo'-] *vt.* throw light upon, explain —**elucida'tion** *n.* —**elu'cidatory** *a.*

elude' [-lood'] *vt.* escape, slip away from, dodge; baffle —**elu'sion** *n.* act of eluding; evasion —**elu'sive** *a.* difficult to catch hold of, deceptive —**elus'ively** *adv.* —**elu'sory** *a.*

el'ver *n.* young eel

elves, elv'ish *see* ELF

em *n. Printing* the square of any size of type

em- *prefix see* EN-

ema'ciate *v.* make or become abnormally thin —**emacia'tion** *n.*

em'anate *vi.* issue, proceed from, originate —**emana'tion** *n.* —**em'anative** *a.*

eman'cipate *vt.* set free —**emancipa'tion** *n.* act of setting free, *esp.* from social, legal restraint; state of being set free —**emancipa'tionist** *n.* advocate of emancipation of slaves, women *etc.* —**eman'cipator** *n.* —**eman'cipatory** *a.*

emas'culate *vt.* castrate; enfeeble,

weaken —**emascula'tion** *n.* —**emas'culative** *a.*

embalm' *vt.* preserve corpse from decay by use of chemicals, herbs *etc.* —**embalm'ment** *n.*

embank'ment *n.* artificial mound carrying road, railway, or serving to dam water

embar'go *n.* order stopping movement of ships; suspension of commerce; ban (*pl.* **-goes**) —*vt.* put under embargo; requisition

embark' *v.* put, go, on board ship, aircraft *etc.*; (*with* on *or* upon) commence new project, venture *etc.* —**embarka'tion** *n.*

embarr'ass *vt.* perplex, disconcert; abash; confuse; encumber —**embar'rassment** *n.*

em'bassy *n.* office, work or official residence of ambassador; deputation

embed', imbed' *vt.* fix fast in something solid

embell'ish *vt.* adorn, enrich —**embel'lishment** *n.*

em'ber *n.* glowing cinder —*pl.* red-hot ashes

Ember days days appointed by Church for fasting in each quarter

embez'zle *vt.* divert fraudulently, misappropriate (money in trust *etc.*) —**embez'zlement** *n.* —**embezz'ler** *n.*

embitt'er *vt.* make bitter —**embit'terment** *n.*

embla'zon *vt.* to adorn richly, *esp.* heraldically

em'blem *n.* symbol; badge, device —**emblemat'ic** *a.* —**emblemat'ically** *adv.*

embod'y *vt.* give body, concrete expression to; represent, include, be expression of (**embod'ied, embod'ying**) —**embod'iment** *n.*

embold'en *vt.* make bold

em'bolism *n. Med.* obstruction of artery by blood clot or air bubble

emboss' *vt.* mould, stamp or carve in relief

embrace' *vt.* clasp in arms, hug; seize, avail oneself of, accept; comprise —*n.*

embra'sure [-zhə] *n.* opening in wall for cannon; bevelling of wall at sides of window

embroca'tion *n.* lotion for rubbing limbs *etc.* to relieve pain —**em'brocate** *vt.*

embroi'der *vt.* ornament with needlework; embellish, exaggerate (story) —**embroi'dery** *n.*

embroil' *vt.* bring into confusion; involve in hostility —**embroil'ment** *n.*

em'bryo [-bri-ō] *n.* unborn or undeveloped offspring, germ; undeveloped thing (*pl.* **-os**) —**embryol'ogist** *n.* —**embryol'ogy** *n.* —**embryon'ic** *a.*

embus' *v.* (*esp.* of troops) put into, mount bus (**-ss-**)

emend' *vt.* to remove errors from, correct —**emenda'tion** *n.* —**e'mendator** *n.*

em'erald *n.* bright green precious stone —*a.* of the colour of emerald

emerge' *vi.* come up, out; rise to notice; come into view; come out on inquiry —**emer'gence** *n.* —**emer'gent** *a.*

emer'gency *n.* sudden unforeseen thing or event needing prompt action; difficult situation; exigency, crisis

emer'itus *a.* retired, honourably discharged but retaining one's title (*eg* professor) on honorary basis

em'ery *n.* hard mineral used for polishing —**emery cloth** cloth or paper coated with finely powdered emery

emet'ic *n./a.* (medicine) causing vomiting

em'igrate *vt.* go and settle in another country —**em'igrant** *n.* —**emigra'tion** *n.*

ém'igré [em'i-grā] *n.* emigrant, *esp.* one forced to leave his country for political reasons (*pl.* **-s**)

em'inent *a.* distinguished, notable —**em'inence** *n.* distinction; height; rank; fame; rising ground; (**E-**) title of cardinal —**em'inently** *adv.*

em'issary *n.* agent, representative (*esp.* of government) sent on mission

emit' *vt.* give out, put forth (**-tt-**) —**emis'sion** *n.* —**emitt'er** *n.*

emoll'ient *a.* softening, soothing —*n.* ointment or other softening application

emol'ument *n.* salary, pay, profit from work

emo'tion *n.* mental agitation, excited state of feeling, as joy, fear *etc.* —**emo'tional** *a.* given to emotion; appealing to the emotions —**emo'tive** *a.* tending to arouse emotion

em'pathy *n.* power of understanding, imaginatively entering into, another's feelings

em'peror *n.* ruler of an empire (**em'press** *fem.*)

em'phasis *n.* importance attached; stress on words; vigour of speech, expression (*pl.* **-ses** [-sēz]) —**em'phasize** *vt.* —**emphat'ic** *a.* forceful, decided; stressed —**emphat'ically** *adv.*

em'pire *n.* large territory, *esp.* aggregate of states under supreme ruler, supreme control

empir'ical *a.* relying on experiment or experience, not on theory —**empir'ic** *a.* empirical —*n.* one who relies solely on experience and observation —**empir'ically** *adv.* —**empir'icism** [-s-] *n.*

emplace'ment *n.* putting in position; gun platform

employ' *vt.* provide work for (a person) in return for money, hire; keep busy; use (**employed'**, **employ'ing**) —**employ'ee** *n.* —**employ'er** *n.* —**employ'ment** *n.* an employing, being employed; work, trade; occupation

empor'ium *n.* large general shop; centre of commerce (*pl.* **-riums, -ria**)

empow'er *vt.* enable, authorize

em'press *see* EMPEROR

emp'ty *a.* containing nothing; unoccupied; senseless; vain, foolish —*v.* make, become devoid of content; discharge (contents) into (**emp'tied, emp'tying**) —**emp'ties** *pl.n.* empty boxes, bottles *etc.* —**emp'tiness** *n.*

e'mu [ē'myōō] *n.* large Aust. flightless bird like ostrich

em'ulate *vt.* strive to equal or excel; imitate —**emula'tion** *n.* rivalry; competition —**em'ulative** *a.* —**em'ulator** *n.* —**em'ulous** *a.* eager to equal or surpass another or his deeds

emul'sion *n.* light-sensitive coating of film; milky liquid with oily or resinous particles in suspension; paint *etc.* in this form —**emul'sifier** *n.* —**emul'sify** *vt.* (**emul'sified, emul'sifying**) —**emul'sive** *a.*

en *n. Printing* unit of measurement, half an em

en- (*also* **em-** *before labials*) (*comb. form*) put in, into, on, as **enrage'** *vt.* Such words are not given here where the meaning may easily be inferred from the simple word

ena'ble *vt.* make able, authorize, empower, supply with means (to do something)

enact' *vi.* make law; act part —**enact'ment** *n.*

enam'el *n.* glasslike coating applied to metal *etc.* to preserve surface; coating of teeth; any hard outer coating —*vt.* (**-ll-**)

enam'o(u)r *vt.* inspire with love; charm; bewitch

en bloc' [on-blok'] *Fr.* in a lump or block; all together

encamp' *v.* set up (in) camp —**encamp'ment** *n.* camp

encap'sulate *vt.* enclose in capsule; put in concise or abridged form

encaus'tic [-kos'-] *a.* with colours burnt in —*n.* art of ornament by burnt-in colours

enceph'alogram [-sef'-] *n.* x-ray photograph of brain

enchant' [-ah-] *vt.* bewitch, delight —**enchant'er** *n.* (**-tress** *fem.*) —**enchant'ment** *n.*

encir'cle *vt.* surround; enfold; go round so as to encompass —**encir'clement** *n.*

en'clave *n.* portion of territory entirely surrounded by foreign land

enclit'ic *a.* pronounced as part of (another word) —*n.*

enclose' *vt.* shut in; surround; envelop; place in with something else (in letter *etc.*) —**enclo'sure** [-zhə] *n.* —**enclosed order** Christian religious order whose members do not go into the outside world

enco'mium *n.* formal praise; eulogy —**enco'miast** *n.* one who composes encomiums —**encomias'tic** *a.* —**encomias'tically** *adv.*

encom'pass *vt.* surround, encircle, contain

en'core [ong'kawr] *interj.* again, once more —*n.* call for repetition of song *etc.*; the repetition —*vt.* ask to repeat

encount'er *vt.* meet unexpectedly; meet in conflict; be faced with (difficulty) —*n.*

encour'age [-kur'-] *vt.* hearten, animate, inspire with hope; embolden —**encour'agement** *n.*

encroach' *vi.* intrude (on) as usurper; trespass —**encroach'ment** *n.*

encrust', incrust' *v.* cover with or form a crust, or hard covering

encum'ber *vt.* hamper; burden —**encum'brance** *n.* impediment, burden

encyc'lical [-sik'-] *a.* sent to many persons or places —*n.* circular letter, *esp.* from Pope to all R.C. bishops

encyclop(a)e'dia [-pēd'-] *n.* book, set of books of information on all subjects, or on every branch of subject, usu. arranged alphabetically —**encyclop(a)e'dic** *a.* —**encyclop(a)e'dist** *n.*

end *n.* limit; extremity; conclusion, finishing; fragment; latter part; death; event, issue; purpose, aim; *Sport* either of the defended areas of a playing field *etc.*; *Football* player at extremity of playing line —*v.* put an end to; come to an end, finish —**end'ing** *n.* —**end'less** *a.* —**end'ways** *adv.* —**end'papers** *pl.n.* blank pages at beginning and end of book —**end zone** *Football* area between either goal line and boundary behind it —**end of steel** (town at) point to which railway tracks have been laid

endear' *vt.* to make dear or beloved —**endear'ing** *a.* —**endear'ingly** *adv.* —**endear'ment** *n.* loving word; tender affection

endeav'o(u)r [-dev'ər] *vi.* try, strive after —*n.* attempt, effort

endem'ic *a.* regularly occurring in a country or district —*n.* endemic disease

end'ive *n.* curly-leaved chicory used as salad

endo- (*comb. form*) within, as in *endocardium, endocrine etc.* Such words are not given here where the meaning may easily be inferred from the simple word

endocar'dium *n.* lining membrane of the heart

en'docrine [-īn] *a.* of those glands (thyroid, pituitary *etc.*) which secrete hormones directly into bloodstream

endorse' *vt.* sanction; confirm; write (*esp.* sign name) on back of —**endorsa'tion** *n.* approval, support —**endorse'ment** *n.*

endow' *vt.* provide permanent income for; furnish (with) —**endow'ment** *n.*

endue' *vt.* invest, furnish (with quality *etc.*)

endure' *vt.* undergo; tolerate, bear —*vi.* last —**endu'rable** *a.* —**endu'rance** *n.* act or power of enduring

en'ema *n.* medicine, liquid injected into rectum

en'emy *n.* hostile person; opponent; armed foe; hostile force

en'ergy *n.* vigour, force, activity; source(s) of power, as oil, coal *etc.*; capacity of machine, battery *etc.* for work or output of power —**energet'ic** *a.* —**energet'ically** *adv.* —**en'ergize** *vt.* give vigour to

en'ervate *vt.* weaken, deprive of vigour —**enerva'tion** *n.* lassitude, weakness

enfee'ble *vt.* weaken, debilitate —**enfee'blement** *n.*

enfilade' [-lād'] *n.* fire from artillery, sweeping line from end to end

enforce' *vt.* compel obedience to; impose (action) upon; drive home —**enforce'able** *a.* —**enforce'ment** *n.*

enfran'chise *vt.* give right of voting to; give parliamentary representation to; set free —**enfran'chisement** *n.*

Eng. England; English

engage' [-gāj'] *vt.* employ; reserve, hire; bind by contract or promise; order; pledge oneself; betroth; undertake; attract; occupy; bring into conflict; interlock —*vi.* employ oneself (in); promise; begin to fight —**engaged'** *a.* betrothed; in use; occupied, busy —**engage'ment** *n.* —**engag'ing** *a.* charming

engen'der [-jen'-] *vt.* give rise to; beget; rouse

en'gine [-jin] *n.* any machine to convert energy into mechanical work, as steam or gasoline engine; railway locomotive —**engineer'** *n.* one who is in charge of engines, machinery *etc.* or construction work (*eg* roads, bridges) or installation of plant; driver of locomotive; one who originates, organizes something —*vt.* construct as engineer; contrive —**engineer'ing** *n.*

Eng'lish [ing'gl-] *n.* the language of Britain, the U.S., most parts of the Commonwealth and certain other countries; the people of England —*a.* relating to England

engraft' [-ah-] *vt.* graft on; plant deeply; incorporate

engrain' *vt. see* INGRAIN

engrave' *vt.* cut in lines on metal for printing; carve, incise; impress deeply —**engra'ver** *n.* —**engra'ving** *n.* copy of picture printed from engraved plate

engross' [-ō-] *vt.* absorb (attention); occupy wholly; write out in large letters or in legal form; corner —**engross'ment** *n.*

engulf' *vt.* swallow up

enhance' [-ah-] *vt.* heighten, intensify, increase value or attractiveness —**enhance'ment** *n.*

enig'ma *n.* puzzling thing or person; riddle —**enigmat'ic(al)** *a.* —**enigmat'ically** *adv.*

enjamb'ment [-zham'-] *n.* in verse, continuation of sentence beyond end of line

enjoin' *vt.* command; impose, prescribe

enjoy' *vt.* delight in; take pleasure in; have use or benefit of —*v. refl.* be happy —**enjoy'able** *a.* —**enjoy'ment** *n.*

enlarge' *vt.* make bigger; reproduce on larger scale, as photograph —*vi.* grow bigger; talk, write about, in greater detail; be capable of reproduction on larger scale —**enlarge'able** *a.* —**enlarge'ment** *n.* —**enlarg'er** *n.* optical instrument for enlarging photographs

enlight'en *vt.* give information to; instruct, inform, shed light on —**enlight'enment** *n.*

enlist' *v.* engage as soldier or helper —**enlist'ment** *n.*

enli'ven *vt.* brighten, make more lively, animate

en masse' [on-mas'] *adv.* in a group, body; all together

enmesh' *vt.* entangle

en'mity *n.* ill will, hostility

enno'ble *vt.* make noble, elevate —**enno'blement** *n.*

en'nui [on'wē] *n.* boredom —**en'nuied, ennuyé** *a.*

enor'mous *a.* very big, vast —**enor'mity** *n.* a gross offence; great wickedness; *inf.* great size

enough' [i-nuf'] *a.* as much or as many as need be; sufficient —*n.* sufficient quantity —*adv.* (just) sufficiently

enounce' *vt.* state; enunciate, proclaim —**enounce'ment** *n.*

en passant' [on-pa-song'] *Fr.* in passing, by the way

enquire' *see* INQUIRE

enrap'ture *vt.* delight excessively; charm —**enrapt', enrap'tured** *a.* entranced

enrich' *vt.* make rich; add to —**enrich'ment** *n.*

enrol' [-ōl'] *vt.* write name of on roll or list; engage, enlist, take in as member; enter, record (**-ll-**) —*vi.* become member —**enrol'ment** *n.*

en route' [on-ro͞ot'] *Fr.* on the way

ensconce' *vt.* place snugly; establish in safety

ensem'ble [on-som'bəl] *n.* whole; all parts taken together; woman's complete outfit; company of actors, dancers *etc.*; *Mus.* group of soloists performing together; *Mus.* concerted passage; general effect

enshrine' *vt.* set in shrine, preserve with great care and sacred affection

en'sign [-sīn] *n.* naval or military flag; badge

en'silage *see* SILAGE

enslave' *vt.* make into slave —**enslave'ment** *n.* bondage —**ensla'ver** *n.*

ensnare' *vt.* capture in snare or trap; trick into false position; entangle

ensue' *vi.* follow, happen after

en suite' [on-swēt'] *adv.* forming a set or single unit

ensure' *vt.* make safe or sure; make certain to happen; secure

entail' *vt.* involve as result, necessitate; *Law* restrict ownership of property to designated line of heirs

entan'gle *vt.* ensnare; perplex —**entan'glement** *n.*

entente' [on-tont'] *n.* friendly understanding between nations

en'ter *vt.* go, come into; penetrate; join; write in, register —*vi.* go, come in, join, begin —**en'trance** *n.* going, coming in; door, passage to enter; right to enter; fee paid for this —**en'trant** *n.* one who enters, *esp.* contest —**en'try** *n.* entrance; entering; item entered, *eg* in account, list

enter'ic *a.* of or relating to the intestines —**enteri'tis** *n.* bowel inflammation

en'terprise *n.* bold or difficult undertaking; bold spirit; force of character in launching out; business, company —**en'terprising** *a.*

entertain' *vt.* amuse, divert; receive as guest; maintain; consider favourable, take into consideration —**entertain'er** *n.* —**entertain'ment** *n.*

enthral' *vt.* captivate, thrill, hold spellbound (**-ll-**) —**enthral'ment** *n.*

enthu'siasm *n.* ardent eagerness, zeal —**enthuse'** *v.* (cause to) show enthusiasm —**enthu'siast** *n.* ardent supporter of —**enthusias'tic** *a.* —**enthusias'tically** *adv.*

entice' *vt.* allure, attract, inveigle, tempt —**entice'ment** *n.* —**entic'ing** *a.* alluring

entire' *a.* whole, complete, unbroken —**entire'ly** *adv.* —**enti'rety** *n.*

enti'tle *vi.* give claim to; qualify; give title to; style

en'tity *n.* thing's being or existence; reality; thing having real existence

entomol'ogy *n.* study of insects —**entomolog'ical** *a.* —**entomol'ogist** *n.* —**entomol'ogize** *vi.*

entourage' [on-too-rahzh'] *n.* associates, retinue; surroundings

entozo'on *n.* internal parasite (*pl.* **entozo'a**) —**entozo'ic** *a.*

en'trails *pl.n.* bowels, intestines; inner parts

en'trance[1] *see* ENTER

entrance'[2] [-ah-] *vt.* delight; throw into a trance

entreat' *vt.* ask earnestly; beg, implore —**entreat'y** *n.* earnest request

en'trée [on'trā] *n.* right of access, admission; (dish served before) main course of meal

entrench' *vt.* establish in fortified position with trenches; establish firmly —**entrench'ment** *n.*

entrepreneur' [on-trə-prə-nur'] *n.* person who attempts to profit by risk and initiative

en'tropy *n.* unavailability of the heat energy of a system for mechanical work; measurement of this

entrust' *vt.* commit, charge with; put into care or protection of

entwine' *vt.* plait, interweave; wreathe with; embrace

enu'merate *vt.* mention one by one; count; compile or enter in voting list —**enumera'tion** *n.* —**enu'merative** *a.* —**enu'merator** *n.*

enun'ciate *vt.* state clearly; proclaim; pronounce —**enuncia'tion** *n.* —**enun'ciative** *a.* —**enun'ciator** *n.*

envel'op *vt.* wrap up, enclose, surround; encircle —**envel'opment** *n.*

en'velope *n.* folded, gummed cover of letter; covering, wrapper

enven'om *vt.* put poison, venom in; embitter

envi'ron *vt.* surround —**envi'ronment** *n.* surroundings; conditions of life or growth —**environmen'tal** *a.* —**environmen'talist** *n.* ecologist —**envi'rons** *pl.n.* districts round (town *etc.*), outskirts

envis'age [-z'-] *vt.* conceive of as possibility; visualize

en'voy *n.* messenger; diplomatic minister of rank below ambassador

en'vy *vt.* grudge another's good fortune, success or qualities; feel jealous of (**en'vied, en'vying**) —*n.* bitter contemplation of another's good fortune; jealousy; object of this feeling —**en'viable** *a.* arousing envy —**en'vious** *a.* full of envy

en'zyme [-zīm] *n.* any of group of complex proteins produced by living cells and acting as catalysts in biochemical reactions

e'olith [ē'ō-] *n.* early flint implement —**eolith'ic** *a.* of the period before stone age

e'on [ē'-] *n.* age, very long period of time; eternity

ep-, eph-, epi- (*comb. form*) upon, during, as in *ephemeral, epitaph, epoch etc.* Such words are not given here where the meaning may easily be inferred from the simple word

ep'aulette *n.* shoulder ornament on uniform

Eph. Ephesians

ephem'eral *a.* short-lived, transient —**ephem'eron** *n.* ephemeral thing (*pl.* **-rons, -ra**) *Also* **ephem'era** (*pl.* **-ras, -rae**) —**ephem'erous** *a.*

ep'ic *n.* long poem or story telling of achievements of hero or heroes; movie *etc.* about heroic deeds —*a.* of, like, an epic; impressive, grand

ep'icene [-sēn] *a.* common to both sexes

ep'icentre *n.* focus of earthquake —**epicen'tral** *a.*

ep'icure *n.* one delighting in eating and drinking —**epicure'an** [-ē'-] *a.* of Epicurus, who taught that pleasure, in the shape of practice of virtue, was highest good; given to refined sensuous enjoyment —*n.* such person or philosopher —**epicure'anism** *n.* —**ep'icurism** *n.*

ep'icycle *n.* circle whose centre moves on circumference of greater circle

epidem'ic *a.* (*esp.* of disease) prevalent and spreading rapidly; widespread *—n.* —**epidem'ical** *a.*

epider'mis *n.* outer skin

epidur'al [-dyo͞or'-] *n./a.* (of) spinal anaesthetic used for relief of pain during childbirth

epiglott'is *n.* cartilage that covers opening of larynx in swallowing —**epiglot'tic** *a.*

ep'igram *n.* concise, witty poem or saying —**epigrammat'ic(al)** *a.* —**epigrammat'ically** *adv.* —**epigram'matist** *n.*

ep'igraph *n.* inscription

ep'ilepsy *n.* disorder of nervous system causing fits and convulsions —**epilep'tic** *n.* sufferer from this *—a.* of, subject to, this

ep'ilogue [-og] *n.* short speech or poem at end, *esp.* of play

Epiph'any [-pif'-] *n.* festival of the announcement of Christ to the Magi, celebrated 6 Jan.

epis'copal *a.* of bishop; ruled by bishops —**epis'copacy** *n.* government by body of bishops —**Episcopa'lian** *a.* of branch of Anglican church *—n.* member, adherent of Episcopalian church —**epis'copate** *n.* bishop's office, see, or duration of office; body of bishops

ep'isode *n.* incident; section of (serialized) book, television programme *etc.* —**episod'ic(al)** *a.*

epistemol'ogy *n.* study of source, nature and limitations of knowledge —**epistemolog'ical** *a.* —**epistemol'ogist** *n.*

epis'tle [-sl] *n.* letter, *esp.* of apostle; poem in letter form —**epis'tolary** *a.* —**epis'toler** *n.*

ep'itaph *n.* memorial inscription on tomb

ep'ithet *n.* additional, descriptive word or name —**epithet'ic(al)** *a.*

epit'ome [-ə-mi] *n.* typical example; summary (*pl.* **-s**) —**epit'omist** *n.* —**epit'omize** *vt.* typify

e'poch [-ok] *n.* beginning of period; period, era, *esp.* one of notable events —**e'pochal** *a.*

ep'ode *n.* third, or last, part of lyric ode

EPOS electronic point of sale

eq'uable *a.* even-tempered, placid; uniform, not easily disturbed —**equabil'ity** *n.* —**eq'uably** *adv.*

e'qual *a.* the same in number, size, merit *etc.*; identical; fit or qualified; evenly balanced *—n.* one equal to another *—vt.* be equal to —**equal'ity** [-ol'-] *n.* state of being equal; uniformity —**equaliza'tion** *n.* —**e'qualize** *v.* make, become, equal —**e'qually** *adv.* —**equal opportunity** nondiscrimination as to sex, race *etc.* in employment, pay *etc.*

equanim'ity *n.* calmness, composure, steadiness

equate' *vt.* make equal; bring to a common standard —**equa'tion** *n.* equating of two mathematical expressions; balancing

equa'tor *n.* imaginary circle round earth equidistant from the poles —**equato'rial** *a.*

equerr'y *n.* officer in attendance on sovereign; officer in royal household in charge of horses

eques'trian *a.* of, skilled in, horseriding; mounted on horse *—n.* rider

equi- (*comb. form*) equal, at equal, as in **equidis'tant** *a.* Such words are not given here where the meaning can easily be inferred from the simple word

equian'gular *a.* having equal angles

equilat'eral *a.* having equal sides

equilib'rium *n.* state of steadiness, equipoise or stability (*pl.* **-riums, -ria**)

eq'uine *a.* of, like a horse

e'quinox *n.* time when sun crosses equator and day and night are equal *—pl.* points at which sun crosses equator —**equinoc'tial** *a.*

equip' *vt.* supply, fit out, array (**-pp-**) —**eq'uipage** *n.* carriage, horses and attendants; *obs.* outfit, requisites —**equip'ment** *n.*

eq'uipoise *n.* perfect balance; counterpoise; equanimity *—vt.* counterbalance

eq'uity *n.* fairness; use of principles of justice to supplement law; system of law so made —**eq'uitable** *a.* fair, reasonable, just —**eq'uitably** *adv.*

equiv'alent *a.* equal in value; having the same meaning or result; tantamount; corresponding —**equiv'alence** *n.* —**equiv'alency** *n.*

equiv'ocal *a.* of double or doubtful

meaning; questionable; liable to suspicion —**equivocal'ity** *n.* —**equiv'ocate** *vi.* use equivocal words to mislead —**equivoca'tion** *n.* —**equiv'ocator** *n.*

ER Elizabeth Regina

e'ra *n.* system of time in which years are numbered from particular event; time of the event; memorable date, period

erad'icate *vt.* wipe out, exterminate; root out —**erad'icable** *a.* —**eradica'tion** *n.* —**erad'icative** *a./n.* —**erad'icator** *n.*

erase' *vt.* rub out; remove, *eg* recording from magnetic tape —**era'ser** *n.* —**era'sure** *n.*

ere [ār] *prep./conj. Poet.* before; sooner than

erect' *a.* upright —*vt.* set up; build —**erec'tile** *a.* —**erec'tion** *n. esp.* an erect penis —**erect'or** *n.*

erg *n.* cgs unit of work or energy

ergonom'ics *pl.n.* (*with sing. v.*) study of relationship between workers and their environment —**ergon'omist** *n.*

er'got *n.* disease of grain; diseased seed used as drug —**erg'otism** *n.* disease caused by eating ergot-infested bread

er'mine [-min] *n.* stoat in northern regions, *esp.* in winter; its white winter fur

erode' *vt.* wear away; eat into —**ero'sion** *n.* —**ero'sive** *a.*

erog'enous [-jə-] *a.* sensitive to sexual stimulation

erot'ic *a.* relating to, or treating of, sexual pleasure —**erot'ica** *pl.n.* sexual literature or art —**erot'icism** *n.*

err *vi.* make mistakes; be wrong; sin —**errat'ic** *a.* irregular in movement, conduct *etc.* —**errat'ically** *adv.* —**erra'tum** [-aht'-] *n.* printing mistake noted for correction (*pl.* **-ta**) —**erro'neous** *a.* mistaken, wrong —**err'or** *n.* mistake; wrong opinion; sin

err'and *n.* short journey for simple business; the business, mission of messenger; purpose —**errand boy**

err'ant *a.* wandering in search of adventure; erring —**err'ancy** *n.* erring state or conduct —**err'antry** *n.* state or conduct of knight errant

er'satz [-zats] *a.* substitute; imitation

erst, erst'while *adv.* of old, formerly

er'udite *a.* learned —**erudi'tion** *n.* learning

erupt' *vi.* burst out —**erup'tion** *n.* bursting out, *esp.* volcanic outbreak; rash on the skin —**erupt'ive** *a.*

erysip'elas *n.* acute skin infection

erythe'ma *n.* patchy inflammation of skin —**erythemat'ic, erythe'matous** *a.*

es'calate *v.* increase, be increased, in extent, intensity *etc.*

es'calator *n.* moving staircase

escall'op *see* SCALLOP

escape' *vi.* get free; get off safely; go unpunished; find way out —*vt.* elude; be forgotten by —*n.* escaping —**es'capade** [*or* -pād'] *n.* wild (mischievous) adventure —**esca'pism** *n.* taking refuge in fantasy to avoid facing disagreeable facts —**escapol'ogist** *n.* entertainer specializing in freeing himself from confinement

escarp' *n.* steep bank under rampart —**escarp'ment** *n.* steep hillside, escarp

eschatol'ogy [-k-] *n.* study of death, judgment and last things —**eschatolog'ical** *a.*

eschew' *vt.* avoid, abstain from, shun

es'cort *n.* armed guard for traveller *etc.*; person or persons accompanying another —**escort'** *vt.*

escritoire' [-twah'] *n.* type of writing desk

es'culent *a.* edible

escutch'eon [-kuch'ən] *n.* shield with coat of arms; ornamental plate round keyhole *etc.*

Es'kimo *n.* one of aboriginal race inhabiting N Amer., Greenland *etc.*; their language (*pl.* **-mos**)

esoph'agus [ē-] *n.* canal from mouth to stomach, gullet (*pl.* **-gi** [-gī]) —**esophage'al** *a.*

esoter'ic [-ō-] *a.* abstruse, obscure; secret; restricted to initiates

ESP extrasensory perception

espal'ier [-yə] *n.* shrub, (fruit) tree trained to grow flat, as against wall *etc.*; trellis for this

espar'to *n.* kind of grass yielding fibre used for making rope *etc.*

espec'ial [is-pesh'əl] *a.* pre-eminent, more than ordinary; particular —**espe'cially** *adv.*

Esperan'to *n.* artificial language designed for universal use —**Esperant'ist** *n.* one who uses Esperanto

es'pionage [-nahzh] *n.* spying; use of secret agents

esplanade' *n.* level space, *esp.* one used as public promenade

espouse' [-owz'] *vt.* support, embrace (cause *etc.*); *obs.* marry —**espous'al** *n.*

espress'o *n.* strong coffee made by forcing steam through ground coffee beans

esprit' [-prē'] *n.* spirit; animation —**esprit de corps** [-kawr] attachment, loyalty to the society *etc.*, one belongs to

espy' *vt.* catch sight of (**espied', espy'ing**) —**espi'al** *n.* observation

Esq. Esquire

esquire' *n.* gentleman's courtesy title used on letters; formerly, a squire

ess'ay *n.* prose composition; short treatise; attempt —**essay'** *vt.* try, attempt; test (**essayed', essay'ing**) —**es'sayist** *n.*

ess'ence *n.* all that makes thing what it is; existence, being; entity, reality; extract got by distillation —**essen'tial** *a.* necessary, indispensable; inherent; of, constituting essence of thing —*n.* indispensable element; chief point —**essential'ity** *n.*

EST Eastern Standard Time

estab'lish *vt.* make secure; set up; settle; prove —**estab'lishment** *n.* permanent organized body, full number of regiment *etc.*; household; business; public institution —**Established Church** church officially recognized as national institution —**the Establishment** group, class of people holding authority within a society

estate' *n.* landed property; person's property; class as part of nation; rank, state, condition of life

esteem' *vt.* think highly of; consider —*n.* favourable opinion, regard, respect

es'ter *n. Chem.* organic compound produced by reaction between acid and alcohol

es'timate *vt.* form approximate idea of (amounts, measurements *etc.*); form opinion of; quote probable price for —*n.* approximate judgment of amounts *etc.*; amount *etc.*, arrived at; opinion; price quoted by contractor —**es'timable** *a.* worthy of regard —**estima'tion** *n.* opinion, judgment, esteem

es'tivate *vi.* spend the summer, *esp.* in dormant condition —**estiva'tion** *n.*

estrange' *vt.* lose affection of; alienate —**estrange'ment** *n.*

es'trogen *n.* hormone in females *esp.* controlling changes, cycles in reproductive organs

es'tuary *n.* tidal mouth of river, inlet —**es'tuarine** *a.*

ETA estimated time of arrival

etc., &c. et cetera

et cet'era [-set'-] *Lat.* and the rest, and others, and so on (abbrevs. *etc., &c.*)

etch *vt.* make engraving by eating away surface of metal plate with acids *etc.*; imprint vividly —**etch'er** *n.* —**etch'ing** *n.*

eter'nal *a.* without beginning or end; everlasting; changeless —**eter'nally** *adv.* —**eter'nity** *n.*

e'ther [-th-] *n.* colourless volatile liquid used as anaesthetic; intangible fluid formerly supposed to fill all space; the clear sky, region above clouds —**ethe'real** *a.* light, airy; heavenly, spiritlike —**ethereal'ity** *n.*

eth'ic(al) *a.* relating to morals —**eth'ically** *adv.* —**eth'ics** *pl.n.* science of morals; moral principles, rules of conduct

eth'nic *a.* of race or relating to classification of humans into social, cultural *etc.*, groups —**ethnograph'ic** *a.* —**ethnog'raphy** *n.* description of races of men —**ethnolog'ical** *a.* —**ethnol'ogy** *n.* the study of human races

e'thos *n.* distinctive character, spirit *etc.* of people, culture *etc.*

eth'yl [*or* ē'thīl] *n.* (C_2H_5) radical of ordinary alcohol and ether —**eth'ylene** *n.* poisonous gas used as anaesthetic and fuel

etiol'ogy [ē-ti-] *n.* study of causes, *esp.* inquiry into origin of disease —**etiolog'ical** *a.*

et'iquette [-ket] *n.* conventional code of conduct or behaviour

é'tude [ā'- *or* -tyo͞od'] *n.* short musical composition, study, intended often as technical exercise

etymol'ogy *n.* tracing, account of, formation of word's origin, development; science of this —**etymolog'ical** *a.* —**etymolog'ically** *adv.* —**etymol'ogist** *n.*

eu-, ev- (*comb. form*) well, as in *eugenic, euphony, evangelist etc.*

eu'calypt, eucalypt'us *n.* mostly Aust. genus of tree, the gum tree, yielding timber and oil, used medicinally from leaves

Eu'charist [-k-] *n.* Christian sacrament of the Lord's Supper; the consecrated elements —**Eucharis'tic** *a.*

eu'chre [-kər] *n.* card game for two, three or four players using poker pack —*vt.* prevent (player) from making his contracted tricks

eugen'ic [-j-] *a.* relating to, or tending towards, production of fine offspring —**eugen'icist** *n.* —**eugen'ics** *pl.n.* (*with sing. v.*) this science

eu'logy *n.* speech or writing in praise of person; praise —**eu'logist** *n.* —**eulogis'tic** *a.* —**eulogis'tically** *adv.* —**eu'logize** *vt.*

eu'nuch [-k] *n.* castrated man, *esp.* formerly one employed in harem

eu'phemism *n.* substitution of mild term for offensive or hurtful one; instance of this —**eu'phemist** *n.* —**euphemis'tic** *a.* —**euphemis'tically** *adv.* —**eu'phemize** *vt.*

eu'phony *n.* pleasantness of sound —**euphon'ic** *a.* —**eupho'nious** *a.* pleasing to ear —**eupho'nium** *n.* brass musical instrument, bass-tenor tuba

euphor'ia *n.* sense of well-being or elation —**euphor'ic** [-o'-] *a.*

eu'phuism *n.* affected high-flown manner of writing, *esp.* in imitation of Lyly's *Euphues* (1580) —**euphuis'tic** *a.*

Eura'sian *a.* of mixed European and Asiatic descent; of Europe and Asia —*n.* one of this descent

eure'ka [yoo-rē'-] *interj.* exclamation of triumph at finding something

Europe'an *n./a.* (native) of Europe —**European Economic Community** association of a number of European nations for trade

Eusta'chian tube passage leading from pharynx to middle ear

euthana'sia *n.* gentle, painless death; putting to death in this way, *esp.* to relieve suffering

euthen'ics *pl.n.* (*with sing. v.*) science of the relation of environment to human beings

evac'uate *vt.* empty; withdraw from; discharge —**evacua'tion** *n.* —**evacuee'** *n.* person moved from danger area *esp.* in time of war

evade' *vt.* avoid, escape from; elude —**eva'sion** *n.* subterfuge; excuse; equivocation —**eva'sive** *a.* elusive, not straightforward —**eva'sively** *adv.*

eval'uate *vt.* find or judge value of —**evalua'tion** *n.*

evanesce' [-es'] *vi.* fade away —**evanes'cence** *n.* —**evanes'cent** *a.* fleeting, transient

evangel'ical [-jel'-] *a.* of, or according to, gospel teaching; of Protestant sect which maintains salvation by faith —*n.* member of evangelical sect —**evangel'icalism** *n.* —**evan'gelism** *n.* —**evan'gelist** *n.* writer of one of the four gospels; ardent, zealous preacher of the gospel; revivalist —**evangeliza'tion** *n.* —**evan'gelize** *vt.* preach gospel to; convert

evap'orate *vi.* turn into, pass off in, vapour —*vt.* turn into vapour —**evapora'tion** *n.* —**evap'orative** *a.* —**evap'orator** *n.*

eva'sion *see* EVADE

eve [ēv] *n.* evening before (festival *etc.*); time just before (event *etc.*); *obs.* evening —**e'ven** *n. obs.* evening —**e'vensong** *n.* evening prayer

e'ven *a.* flat, smooth; uniform in quality, equal in amount, balanced; divisible by two; impartial —*vt.* make even; smooth; equalize —*adv.* equally; simply; notwithstanding; (used to express emphasis)

e'vening [-vn-] *n.* the close of day or early part of night; decline, end

event' *n.* happening; notable occurrence; issue, result; any one contest in series in sporting programme —**event'ful** *a.* full of exciting events —**event'ual** *a.* resulting in the end; ultimate; final —**eventual'ity** *n.* possible event —**even'tually** *adv.* —**event'uate** *vi.* turn out; happen; end

ev'er *adv.* always; constantly; at any time —**ev'ergreen** *n./a.* (tree or shrub) bearing foliage throughout year —**evermore'** *adv.*

ev'ery [-vri] *a.* each of all; all possible —**ev'erybody** *n.* —**ev'eryday** *a.* usual, ordinary —**ev'eryone** *n.* —**ev'erything** *n.* —**ev'erywhere** *adv.* in all places

evict' *vt.* expel by legal process, turn out —**evic'tion** *n.* —**evic'tor** *n.*

ev'ident *a.* plain, obvious —**ev'idence** *n.* ground of belief; sign, indication; testimony —*vt.* indicate, prove —**eviden'tial** *a.* —**ev'idently** *adv.* —**in evidence** conspicuous

e'vil *a.* bad, harmful —*n.* what is bad or harmful; sin —**e'villy** *adv.* —**e'vildoer** *n.* sinner

evince' *vt.* show, indicate

evoke' *vt.* draw forth; call to mind —**evoca'tion** *n.* —**evoc'ative** *a.*

evolve' *v.* develop or cause to develop gradually —*vi.* undergo slow changes in process of growth —**evolu'tion** [-lōō'-] *n.* evolving; development of species from earlier forms —**evolu'tional** *a.* —**evolu'tionary** *a.* —**evolu'tionist** *n.* —**evol'utive** *a.*

ewe [yōō] *n.* female sheep

ew'er [yōō'-] *n.* pitcher, water jug for washstand

Ex. Exodus

ex [eks] *n. inf.* ex-wife, ex-husband *etc.*

ex. example; except(ed); extra

ex-, e-, ef- (*comb. form*) out from, from, out of, formerly, as in *exclaim, evade, effusive, exodus* Such words are not given here where the meaning may easily be inferred from the simple word

exac'erbate [ig-zas'-] *vt.* aggravate, embitter, make worse —**exacerba'tion** *n.*

exact' [igz-] *a.* precise, accurate, strictly correct —*vt.* demand, extort; insist upon; enforce —**exact'ing** *a.* making rigorous or excessive demands —**exac'tion** *n.* act of exacting; that which is exacted, as excessive work *etc.*; oppressive demand —**exact'itude** *n.* —**exact'ly** *adv.* —**exact'ness** *n.* accuracy; precision —**exac'tor** *n.*

exagg'erate [ig-zaj'-] *vt.* magnify beyond truth, overstate; enlarge; overestimate —**exaggera'tion** *n.* —**exag'gerative** *a.* —**exagg'erator** *n.*

exalt' [igz-awlt'] *vt.* raise up; praise; make noble, dignify —**exalta'tion** *n.* an exalting; elevation in rank, dignity or position; rapture

exam' *n. short for* examination

exam'ine [-gz-] *vt.* investigate; look at closely; ask questions of; test knowledge or proficiency of; inquire into —**examina'tion** *n.* —**examinee'** *n.* —**exam'iner** *n.*

exam'ple [ig-zahm'-] *n.* thing illustrating general rule; specimen; model; warning, precedent, instance

exas'perate [ig-zahs'-] *vt.* irritate, enrage; intensify, make worse —**exaspera'tion** *n.*

ex'cavate *vt.* hollow out; make hole by digging; unearth —**excava'tion** *n.* —**ex'cavator** *n.*

exceed' *vt.* be greater than; do more than authorized; go beyond; surpass —**exceed'ingly** *adv.* very; greatly

excel' *vt.* surpass, be better than —*vi.* be very good, pre-eminent (-**ll**-) —**ex'cellence** *n.* —**ex'cellency** *n.* title borne by viceroys, ambassadors —**ex'cellent** *a.* very good

except' *prep.* not including; but —*conj. obs.* unless —*vt.* leave or take out; exclude —**except'ing** *prep.* not including —**excep'tion** *n.* thing excepted, not included in a rule; objection —**excep'tionable** *a.* open to objection —**excep'tional** *a.* not ordinary, *esp.* much above average —**excep'tionally** *adv.*

ex'cerpt *n.* quoted or extracted passage from book *etc.* —**excerpt'** *vt.* extract, quote (passage from book *etc.*) —**excerp'tion** *n.*

excess' *n.* an exceeding; amount by which thing exceeds; too great amount; intemperance or immoderate conduct —**excess'ive** *a.* —**excess'ively** *adv.*

exchange' *vt.* give (something) in return for something else; barter —*n.* giving one thing and receiving another; giving or receiving coin, bills *etc.*, of one country for those of another; thing given for another; building where merchants meet for business; central telephone office where connections are made *etc.* —**exchangeabil'ity** *n.* —**exchange'able** *a.*

excheq'uer [-k'ər] *n.* government department in charge of revenue

ex'cise[1] [-īz] *n.* duty charged on home goods during manufacture or before sale

excise'[2] [-īz'] *vt.* cut out, cut away —**exci'sion** [-si'zhən] *n.*

excite' *vt.* arouse to strong emotion, stimulate; rouse up, set in motion; *Electricity* magnetize poles of —**excitabil'ity** *n.* —**exci'table** *a.* —**exci'tably** *adv.*

—**excita'tion** *n.* —**excite'ment** *n.* —**exci'ting** *a.* thrilling; rousing to action

exclaim' *v.* speak suddenly, cry out —**exclama'tion** *n.* —**exclam'atory** *a.*

exclude' *vt.* shut out; debar from; reject, not consider —**exclu'sion** *n.* —**exclu'sive** *a.* excluding; inclined to keep out (from society *etc.*); sole, only; select —*n.* something exclusive, *esp.* story appearing only in one newspaper —**exclu'sively** *adv.*

excommu'nicate *vt.* to cut off from the sacraments of the Church —**excommunica'tion** *n.*

ex'crement *n.* waste matter from body, *esp.* from bowels; dung —**excre'ta** *pl.n.* (*usu. used as sing.*) excrement —**excrete'** *vi.* discharge from the system —**excre'tion** *n.* —**excre'tory** *a.*

excres'cent *a.* growing out of; redundant —**excres'cence** *n.* unnatural outgrowth

excru'ciate [-krōō'shi-] *vt.* torment acutely, torture in body or mind —**excru'ciating** *a.* —**excrucia'tion** *n.*

ex'culpate *vt.* free from blame, acquit —**exculpa'tion** *n.* —**excul'patory** *a.*

excur'sion *n.* journey, ramble, trip for pleasure; digression —**excur'sus** *n.* digression (*pl.* **-es, -sus** *rare*)

excuse' [-skyōōz'] *vt.* forgive, overlook; try to clear from blame; gain exemption; set free, remit —*n.* [-skyōōs'] that which serves to excuse; apology —**excu'sable** [-z-] *a.*

ex'ecrable *a.* abominable, hatefully bad

ex'ecute *vt.* inflict capital punishment on, kill; carry out, perform; make, produce; sign (document) —**exec'utant** *n.* performer, *esp.* of music —**execu'tion** *n.* —**execu'tioner** *n.* one employed to execute criminals —**exec'utive** *n.* person in administrative position; executive body; committee carrying on business of society *etc.* —*a.* carrying into effect, *esp.* of branch of government enforcing laws —**exec'utor** *n.* person appointed to carry out provisions of a will (**exec'utrix** *fem.*)

exege'sis [-jē'-] *n.* explanation, *esp.* of Scripture (*pl.* **-ge'ses** [-sēz]) —**exeget'ic(al)** *a.*

exem'plar *n.* model type —**exem'plarily** *adv.* —**exem'plary** *a.* fit to be imitated, serving as example; commendable; typical

exem'plify *vt.* serve as example of; illustrate; exhibit; make attested copy of (**-fied, -fying**) —**exemplifica'tion** *n.*

exempt' [igz-] *vt.* free from; excuse —*a.* freed from, not liable for; not affected by —**exemp'tion** *n.*

ex'equies [-kwiz] *pl.n.* funeral rites or procession

ex'ercise [-z] *vt.* use, employ; give exercise to; carry out, discharge; trouble, harass —*vi.* take exercise —*n.* use of limbs for health; practice for training; task for training; lesson; employment; use (of limbs, faculty *etc.*) —*pl.* formal routine, ceremony, *esp.* at school or college

exert' [igz-] *vt.* apply (oneself) diligently, make effort; bring to bear —**exer'tion** *n.* effort, physical activity

ex'eunt *Theatre* they leave the stage: stage direction

exfo'liate *v.* peel in scales, layers

ex gra'tia [-grā'shə] *adj.* given as favour, *esp.* where no legal obligation exists

exhale' *v.* breathe out; give, pass off as vapour

exhaust' [ig-zawst'] *vt.* tire out; use up; empty; draw off; treat, discuss thoroughly —*n.* used steam or fluid from engine; waste gases from internal combustion engine; passage for, or coming out of this —**exhaustibil'ity** *n.* —**exhaust'ible** *a.* —**exhaus'tion** *n.* state of extreme fatigue; limit of endurance —**exhaust'ive** *a.* comprehensive

exhib'it [igz-] *vt.* show, display; manifest; show publicly (often in competition) —*n.* thing shown, *esp.* in competition or as evidence in court —**exhibi'tion** [eks-] *n.* display, act of displaying; public show (of works of art *etc.*) —**exhibi'tionist** *n.* one with compulsive desire to draw attention to himself or to expose genitals publicly —**exhib'itor** *n.* one who exhibits, *esp.* in show —**exhib'itory** *a.*

exhil'arate [igz-] *vt.* enliven, gladden —**exhilara'tion** *n.* high spirits, enlivenment

exhort' [igz-] *vt.* urge, admonish earnestly —**exhorta'tion** *n.* —**exhort'er** *n.*

exhume' [-hyōōm'] *vt.* unearth what has been buried, disinter —**exhuma'tion** *n.*

ex'igent [-j-] *a.* exacting; urgent, pressing —**ex'igence, ex'igency** *n.* pressing need; emergency —**ex'igible** *a.* liable to be exacted or demanded

exig'uous [ig-zig'-] *a.* scanty, meagre

ex'ile [egz'-] *n.* banishment, expulsion from one's own country; long absence abroad; one banished or permanently living away from his home or country —*vt.* banish, expel

exist' [igz-] *vi.* be, have being, live —**exist'ence** *n.* —**exist'ent** *a.*

existen'tialism [egz-] *n.* philosophy stressing importance of personal responsibility and the free agency of the individual in a seemingly meaningless universe

ex'it *n.* way out; going out; death; actor's departure from stage —*vi.* go out

ex li'bris [-lē'-] *Lat.* from the library of

ex'ocrine [-in] *a.* of gland (*eg* salivary, sweat) secreting its products through ducts

ex'odus *n.* departure, *esp.* of crowd; (**E-**) second book of Old Testament

ex offic'io [-fish'-] *Lat.* by right of position or office

exon'erate *vt.* free, declare free, from blame; exculpate; acquit —**exonera'tion** *n.* —**exon'erative** *a.*

exorb'itant [igz-] *a.* very excessive, inordinate, immoderate —**exorb'itance** *n.* —**exorb'itantly** *adv.*

ex'orcise [-z] *vt.* cast out (evil spirits) by invocation; free person of evil spirits —**ex'orcism** *n.* —**ex'orcist** *n.*

exord'ium *n.* introductory part of a speech or treatise (*pl.* **-s, -ia**) —**exor'dial** *a.*

exoter'ic [-ō-te'rik] *a.* understandable by the many; ordinary, popular

exot'ic [igz-] *a.* brought in from abroad, foreign; rare, unusual, having strange or bizarre allure —*n.* exotic plant *etc.* —**exot'ica** *pl.n.* (*usu. with sing. v.*) (collection of) exotic objects —**exot'icism** *n.*

expand' *v.* increase, spread out, dilate, develop —**expand'able, -ible** *a.* —**expanse'** *n.* wide space; open stretch of land —**expansibil'ity** *n.* —**expan'sible** *a.* —**expan'sion** *n.* —**expan'sive** *a.* wide; extensive; friendly, talkative

expa'tiate [-shi-] *vi.* speak or write at great length (on); enlarge (upon) —**expatia'tion** *n.*

expat'riate *vt.* banish; exile; withdraw (oneself) from one's native land —*a./n.* —**expatria'tion** *n.*

expect' *vt.* regard as probable; look forward to; await, hope —**expect'ancy** *n.* state or act of expecting; that which is expected; hope —**expect'ant** *a.* looking or waiting for, *esp.* for birth of child —**expect'antly** *adv.* —**expecta'tion** *n.* act or state of expecting; prospect of future good; what is expected; promise; value of something expected —*pl.* prospect of fortune or profit by will

expect'orate *v.* spit out (phlegm *etc.*) —**expect'orant** *Med. a.* promoting secretion, liquefaction, or explosion of sputum from respiratory passages —*n.* expectorant drug or agent —**expectora'tion** *n.*

expe'dient *a.* fitting, advisable; politic; suitable; convenient —*n.* something suitable, useful, *esp.* in emergency —**expe'diency** *n.* —**expe'diently** *adv.*

ex'pedite [-īt] *vt.* help on, hasten; dispatch —**expedi'tion** [-ish'-] *n.* journey for definite (often scientific or military) purpose; people, equipment comprising expedition; excursion; promptness —**expedi'tionary** *a.* —**expedi'tious** *a.* prompt, speedy

expel' *vt.* drive, cast out; exclude; discharge (**-ll-**) —**expul'sion** *n.* —**expul'sive** *a.*

expend' *vt.* spend, pay out; use up —**expend'able** *a.* likely, or meant, to be used up or destroyed —**expend'iture** *n.* —**expense'** *n.* cost; (cause of) spending —*pl.* charges, outlay incurred —**expen'sive** *a.*

expe'rience *n.* observation of facts as source of knowledge; being affected consciously by event; the event; knowledge, skill, gained from life, by contact with facts and events —*vt.* undergo, suffer, meet with —**expe'rienced** *a.* skilled, expert, capable —**experien'tial** *a.*

exper'iment [-pe'ri-] *n.* test, trial, something done in the hope that it may succeed, or to test theory —*vi.* make experiment —**experiment'al** *a.* —**experimen'talist** *n.* —**experiment'ally** *adv.*

ex'pert *n.* one skilful, knowledgeable, in something; authority —*a.* practised, skilful —**expertise'** [-tēz'] *n.*

ex'piate *vt.* pay penalty for; make

amends for —**expia'tion** *n.* —**ex'piator** *n.* —**ex'piatory** *a.*

expire' *vi.* come to an end; give out breath; die —*vt.* breathe out —**expira'tion** *n.* —**expi'ratory** *a.* —**expi'ry** *n.* end

explain' *vt.* make clear, intelligible; interpret; elucidate; give details of; account for —**explana'tion** *n.* —**explan'atory, explan'ative** *a.*

exple'tive *n.* exclamation; oath —*a.* serving only to fill out sentence *etc.*

explic'able [*or* ex'-] *a.* explainable —**ex'plicate** *vt.* develop, explain —**expli'cative** *a.* —**ex- plic'atory** *a.*

explic'it [-is'-] *a.* stated in detail; stated, not merely implied; outspoken; clear, plain; unequivocal

explode' *vi.* go off with bang; burst violently; (of population) increase rapidly —*vt.* make explode; discredit, expose (a theory *etc.*) —**explo'sion** *n.* —**explo'sive** *a./n.*

ex'ploit *n.* brilliant feat, deed —*vt.* [-ploit'] turn to advantage; make use of for one's own ends —**exploita'tion** *n.* —**exploit'er** *n.*

explore' *vt.* investigate; examine; scrutinize; examine (country *etc.*) by going through it —**explora'tion** *n.* —**explo'ratory** [-plo'-] *a.* —**explor'er** *n.*

explo'sion *see* EXPLODE

ex'po *n. inf.* exposition, large international exhibition

expo'nent *see* EXPOUND

export' *vt.* send (goods) out of the country —**ex'port** *n./a.* —**exporta'tion** *n.* —**export'er** *n.*

expose' [-ōz'] *vt.* exhibit; disclose, reveal; lay open (to); leave unprotected; expose photographic plate or film to light —**exposed'** *a.* not concealed; without shelter from the elements; vulnerable —**expo'sure** *n.*

expo'sé [-zā] *n.* newspaper article *etc.*, disclosing scandal, crime *etc.*

exposi'tion *see* EXPOUND

expos'tulate *vi.* remonstrate; reason with (in a kindly manner) —**expostula'tion** *n.* —**expos'tulatory** *a.*

expound' *vt.* explain, interpret —**expo'nent** *n.* one who expounds or promotes (idea, cause *etc.*); performer, executant; *Math.* small, raised number showing the power of a factor —**exponen'tial** *a.* —**exposi'tion** *n.* explanation, description; exhibition of goods *etc.* —**expos'itor** *n.* one who explains, interpreter —**expos'itory** *a.* explanatory

express' *vt.* put into words; make known or understood by words, behaviour *etc.*; squeeze out —*a.* definitely stated; specially designed; clear; positive; speedy; of messenger, specially sent off; of train, fast and making few stops —*adv.* specially; on purpose; with speed —*n.* express train or messenger; rapid parcel delivery service —**express'ible** *a.* —**expres'sion** *n.* expressing; word, phrase; look, aspect; feeling; utterance —**express'ionism** *n.* theory that art depends on expression of artist's creative self, not on mere reproduction —**expres'sive** *a.* —**express'ly** *adv.* —**express'way** *n.* highway for fast-moving traffic, with limited access

expro'priate *vt.* dispossess; take out of owner's hands —**expropria'tion** *n.* —**expro'priator** *n.*

expulsion *see* EXPEL

expunge' *vt.* strike out, erase —**expunc'tion** *n.*

ex'purgate *vt.* remove objectionable parts (from book *etc.*), purge —**expurga'tion** *n.* —**ex'purgator** *n.* —**expur'gatory** *a.*

exquis'ite [-kwiz'- *or* eks'-] *a.* of extreme beauty or delicacy; keen, acute; keenly sensitive —**exquis'itely** *adv.*

extant' *a.* still existing

extem'pore [-pə-ri] *a./adv.* without previous thought or preparation —**extempora'neous** *a.* —**extem'porary** *a.* —**extemporiza'tion** *n.* —**extem'porize** *vt.* speak without preparation; devise for the occasion

extend' *vt.* stretch out, lengthen; prolong in duration; widen in area, scope; accord, grant —*vi.* reach; cover area; have range or scope; become larger or wider —**exten'dible, -dable, exten'sible** *a.* —**exten'sile** *a.* that can be extended —**exten'sion** *n.* stretching out, prolongation or enlargement; expansion; continuation, additional part, as of telephone *etc.* —**exten'sive** *a.* wide, large, comprehensive —**exten'sor** *n.* straightening muscle —**extent'** *n.* space or degree to which thing is extended; size; compass; volume

exten'uate *vt.* make less blameworthy, lessen; mitigate —**extenua'tion** *n.* —**exten'uatory** *a.*

exte'rior *n.* the outside; outward appearance —*a.* outer, outward, external

exterm'inate *vt.* destroy utterly, annihilate, root out, eliminate —**extermina'tion** *n.* —**exterm'inator** *n.* destroyer

extern'al *a.* outside, outward —**exter'nally** *adv.*

extinct' *a.* having died out or come to an end; no longer existing; quenched, no longer burning —**extinc'tion** *n.*

extin'guish [-ng'gw-] *vt.* put out, quench; wipe out —**extin'guishable** *a.* —**extin'guisher** *n.* device, *esp.* spraying liquid or foam, used to put out fires

ex'tirpate *vt.* root out, destroy utterly —**extirpa'tion** *n.* —**ex'tirpator** *n.*

extol' [-tōl'] *vt.* praise highly (**-ll-**)

extort' *vt.* get by force or threats; wring out; exact —**extor'tion** *n.* —**extor'tionate** *a.* of prices *etc.*, excessive, exorbitant —**extor'tioner** *n.*

ex'tra *a.* additional; larger, better, than usual —*adv.* additionally; more than usually —*n.* extra thing; something charged as additional; *Movies* actor hired for crowd scenes in motion picture

extra- (*comb. form*) beyond, as in *extradition, extramural, extraterritorial etc.* Such words are not given here where the meaning may easily be inferred from the simple word

extract' *vt.* take out, *esp.* by force; obtain against person's will; get by pressure, distillation *etc.*; deduce, derive; copy out, quote —*n.* [eks'-] passage from book, movie *etc.*; matter got by distillation; concentrated solution —**extrac'tion** *n.* extracting, *esp.* of tooth; ancestry —**extract'or** *n.*

extracurric'ular *a.* taking place outside regular course of study

extradi'tion [-dish'-] *n.* delivery, under treaty, of foreign fugitive from justice to authorities concerned —**ex'tradite** *vt.* give or obtain such delivery —**extradi't-able** *a.*

extramur'al [-myoor'-] *a.* connected with but outside normal courses *etc.* of university or college; situated outside walls or boundaries of a place

extra'neous *a.* not essential; irrelevant; added from without, not belonging

extraord'inary [-trawd'-] *a.* out of the usual course; additional; unusual, surprising, exceptional —**extraord'inarily** *adv.*

extrap'olate *vt.* infer something not known from known facts; *Maths.* estimate a value beyond known values

extrasen'sory *a.* of perception apparently gained without use of known senses

extraterrest'rial *a.* of, or from outside the earth's atmosphere

extrav'agant *a.* wasteful; exorbitant; wild, absurd —**extrav'agance** *n.* —**extrav'agantly** *adv.* —**extravagan'za** *n.* elaborate, lavish, entertainment, display *etc.*

ex'travert *see* EXTROVERT

extreme' *a.* of high or highest degree; severe; going beyond moderation; at the end; outermost —*n.* utmost degree; thing at one end or the other, first and last of series —**extreme'ly** *adv.* —**extre'mist** *n.* advocate of extreme measures —*a.* of immoderate or excessive actions, opinions etc. —**extrem'ity** *n.* end —*pl.* hands and feet; utmost distress; extreme measures

ex'tricate *vt.* disentangle, unravel, set free —**ex'tricable** *a.* —**extrica'tion** *n.*

extrin'sic *a.* accessory, not belonging, not intrinsic —**extrin'sically** *adv.*

ex'trovert *n.* one who is interested in other people and things rather than his own feelings —**extrover'sion** *n.*

extrude' *vt.* squeeze, force out; (*esp.* of molten metal or plastic *etc.*) shape by squeezing through suitable nozzle or die

exu'berant [ig-zyōō'-] *a.* high-spirited, vivacious, prolific, abundant, luxurious —**exu'berance** *n.* —**exu'berantly** *adv.*

exude' [ig-zyōōd'] *vi.* ooze out —*vt.* give off (moisture) —**exuda'tion** *n.* —**exu'dative** *a.*

exult' [igz-] *vi.* rejoice, triumph —**exult'ancy** *n.* —**exult'ant** *a.* triumphant —**exulta'tion** *n.*

eye [ī] *n.* organ of sight; look, glance; attention; aperture; view; judgment; watch, vigilance; thing, mark resembling eye; slit in needle for thread —*vt.* look at; observe —**eye'less** *a.* —**eye'ball** *n.* ball of eye —**eye'brow** *n.* fringe of hair above eye —**eye'glass** *n.* glass to assist sight; monocle —**eye'lash** *n.* hair fringing eyelid —**eye'let** *n.* small hole for rope *etc.* to pass through —**eye'lid** *n.* lid or cover of eye —**eye'opener** *n.* surprising news; revealing statement —**eye'-piece** *n.* lens or lenses in optical instrument nearest eye of observer —**eye shadow** coloured cosmetic put on around the eyes —**eye'sore** *n.* ugly object; thing that annoys one to see —**eye'-strain** *n.* fatigue of eyes, resulting from excessive use or uncorrected defects of vision—**eye'tooth** *n.* canine tooth —**eye'wash** *n. inf.* deceptive talk *etc.*, nonsense —**eye'witness** *n.* one who saw something for himself

ey'rie [ēr'-, īr'-] *n.* nest of bird of prey, *esp.* eagle; high dwelling place

F

F Fahrenheit; farad; Fellow; *Chem.* fluorine

f. feminine; folio; following; *Mus.* forte

fa *see* FAH

fa'ble *n.* short story with moral, *esp.* one with animals as characters; tale; legend; fiction or lie —*vt.* invent, tell fables about —**fab'ulist** *n.* writer of fables —**fab'ulous** *a.* amazing; *inf.* extremely good; told of in fables; unhistorical

fab'ric *n.* cloth; texture; frame, structure —**fab'ricate** *vt.* build; frame; construct; invent (lie *etc.*); forge (document) —**fabrica'tion** *n.* —**fab'ricator** *n.*

façade' [fə-sahd'] *n.* front of building; *fig.* outward appearance

face [fās] *n.* front of head; distorted expression; outward appearance; front, upper surface, or chief side of anything; dial of a clock *etc.*; dignity —*vt.* look or front towards; meet (boldly); give a covering surface —*vi.* turn —**fac'et** [fas'-] *n.* one side of many-sided body, *esp.* cut gem; one aspect —**fa'cial** [fā'shl] *a.* pert. to face —*n.* cosmetic treatment for face —**fa'cings** *pl.n.* lining for decoration or reinforcement, sewn on collar, cuff *etc.*; collar, cuffs *etc.* of uniform —**face'less** *a.* without a face; anonymous —**face card** in playing cards, the king, queen or jack —**face-lifting** *n.* operation to tighten skin of face to remove wrinkles —**face-off** *n. Hockey* method of starting play in which referee drops puck between two opposing players

face'tious [fə-sē'shəs] *a.* (sarcastically) witty; humorous, given to jesting, *esp.* at inappropriate time

fa'cia [-sh-] *n. see* FASCIA

fac'ile [fas'-] *a.* easy; working easily; easy-going; superficial, silly —**facil'itate** [-sil'-] *vt.* make easy, help —**facilita'tion** *n.* —**facil'itator** *n.* —**facil'ity** *n.* easiness, dexterity —*pl.* opportunities, good conditions; means, equipment for doing something

facsim'ile [fak-sim'i-li] *n.* an exact copy

fact *n.* thing known to be true; deed; reality —**fac'tual** *a.*

fac'tion[1] *n.* (dissenting) minority group within larger body; dissension —**fac'tious** *a.* of or producing factions

faction[2] *n.* novel, motion picture or TV programme presenting dramatized version of actual events

facti'tious [-ish'-] *a.* artificial; specially made up; unreal

fac'tor *n.* something contributing to a result; one of numbers which multiplied together give a given number; agent, dealer —**facto'tum** *n.* man-of-all-work —**factor 8** protein that participates in clotting of blood

fac'tory *n.* building where things are manufactured

fac'ulty *n.* inherent power; power of the mind; ability, aptitude; department of university; administrative and teaching staff at a college, school *etc.*; members of profession; authorization —**fac'ultative** *a.* optional, contingent

fad *n.* short-lived fashion; whim —**fad'dish** *a.* —**fadd'ism** *n.* —**fadd'ist** *n.* —**fadd'y** *a.*

fade *vi.* lose colour, strength; wither; grow dim; disappear gradually —*vt.* cause to fade —**fade'less** *a.* —**fade-in, -out** *n. Radio* variation in strength of signals; *TV, Cinema* gradual appearance and disappearance of picture

fae'ces [fē'sēz] *pl.n.* excrement, waste matter —**fae'cal** [fē'kəl] *a.*

fag *n. inf.* boring task; **UK** *sl.* cigarette; *sl.* homosexual (*abbrev. of* FAGGOT) —*v. inf.* (*esp. with* out) tire; do menial tasks for a senior boy in school (**-gg-**) —**fag end** last part, inferior remnant

fagg'ot *n.* bundle of sticks for fuel *etc.*; ball of chopped liver *etc.*; *sl.* male homosexual

fah, fa *n.* fourth sol-fa note

Fah'renheit [fa'rən-hīt] *a.* measured

by thermometric scale with freezing point of water 32°, boiling point 212°

faïence' [fī-ahns'] *n.* glazed earthenware or china

fail *vi.* be unsuccessful; stop operating or working; be below the required standard; be insufficient; run short; be wanting when in need; lose power; die away; become bankrupt *—vt.* disappoint, give no help to; neglect, forget to do; judge (candidate) to be below required standard **—fail'ing** *n.* deficiency; fault *—prep.* in default of **—fail'ure** *n.* **—fail-safe** *a.* of device ensuring safety or remedy of malfunction in machine, weapon *etc.* **—without fail** in spite of every difficulty; certainly

fain *obs. a.* glad, willing, constrained to *—adv.* gladly

faint *a.* feeble, dim, pale; weak; dizzy, about to lose consciousness *—vi.* lose consciousness temporarily

fair[1] *a.* just, impartial; according to rules, legitimate; blond; beautiful; ample; of moderate quality or amount; unblemished; plausible; middling; (of weather) favourable *—adv.* honestly **—fair'ing** *n. Aviation* streamlined casing, or any part so shaped that it provides streamline form **—fair'ish** *a.* **—fair'ly** *adv.* **—fair'ness** *n.* **—fair'way** *n.* navigable channel; *Golf* trimmed turf between rough

fair[2] *n.* **UK** travelling entertainment with sideshows, amusements *etc.*; large exhibition of commercial or industrial products; periodical market often with amusements **—fair'ground** *n.*

fair'y *n.* imaginary small creature with powers of magic; *sl.* male homosexual *—a.* of fairies; like fairy, beautiful and delicate, imaginary **—fairy lamp** small coloured lamp for decorations **—fair'yland** *n.* **—fairy ring** circle of darker colour in grass **—fairy-tale** *a.* of or like fairy tale **—fairy tale** story of imaginary beings and happenings, *esp.* as told to children

fait accom'pli [fe-ta-kon'pli] *Fr.* something already done that cannot be altered

faith *n.* trust; belief; belief without proof; religion; promise; loyalty, constancy **—faith'ful** *a.* constant, true **—faith'fully** *adv.* **—faith'less** *a.*

fake *vt.* conceal defects of by artifice; touch up; counterfeit *—n.* fraudulent object, person, act *—a.* **—fa'ker** *n.* one who deals in fakes; swindler

fa'kir *n.* member of Islamic religious order; Hindu ascetic

fal'chion [fawl'chən] *n.* a broad curved medieval sword

fal'con [fawl'-, faw'-] *n.* small bird of prey, *esp.* trained in hawking for sport **—fal'coner** *n.* one who keeps, trains, or hunts with, falcons **—fal'conry** *n.* hawking

fall [fawl] *vi.* drop, come down freely; become lower; decrease; hang down; come to the ground, cease to stand; perish; collapse; be captured; revert; lapse; be uttered; become; happen (**fell** *pt.*, **fall'en** *pp.*) *—n.* falling; amount that falls; amount of descent; decrease; collapse, ruin; drop; (*oft. pl.*) cascade; cadence; yielding to temptation; the season after summer; rope of hoisting tackle **—fall'out** *n.* radioactive particles spread as result of nuclear explosion **—fall for** *inf.* fall in love with; *inf.* be taken in by

fall'acy [fal'-] *n.* incorrect, misleading opinion or argument; flaw in logic; illusion **—falla'cious** *a.* **—fallibil'ity** *n.* **—fall'ible** *a.* liable to error **—fall'ibly** *adv.*

fall'en *pp. of* FALL

Fallo'pian tube either of a pair of tubes through which egg cells pass from ovary to womb

fall'ow[1] [fal'ō] *a.* ploughed and harrowed but left without crop; uncultivated; neglected

fall'ow[2] *a.* brown or reddish yellow **—fallow deer** deer of this colour

false [-aw-] *a.* wrong, erroneous; deceptive; faithless; sham, artificial **—false'ly** *adv.* **—false'ness** *n.* faithlessness **—falsifica'tion** *n.* **—fal'sify** *vt.* alter fraudulently; misrepresent; disappoint (hopes *etc.*) (**fal'sified, fal'sifying**) **—fal'sity** *n.* **—false'hood** *n.* lie

falsett'o *n.* forced voice above natural range (*pl.* **-os**)

Falstaff'ian [fawl-stahf'-] *a.* like Shakespeare's Falstaff; fat; convivial; boasting

fal'ter [-aw-] *vi.* hesitate; waver; stumble **—fal'teringly** *adv.*

fame *n.* reputation; renown **—famed** *a.* **—fa'mous** *a.* widely known; excellent

famil'iar *a.* well-known; frequent, customary; intimate; closely acquainted; unceremonious; impertinent, too friendly *—n.* familiar friend; familiar demon **—familiar'ity** *n.* **—familiariza'tion** *n.* **—famil'iarize** *vt.* **—famil'iarly** *adv.*

fam'ily *n.* group of parents and children, or near relatives; person's children; all descendants of common ancestor; household; group of allied objects **—famil'ial** *a.*

fam'ine [-in] *n.* extreme scarcity of food; starvation **—fam'ish** *vi.* be very hungry

fa'mous *see* FAME

fan[1] *n.* instrument for producing current of air, *esp.* for ventilating or cooling; folding object of paper *etc.*, used, *esp.* formerly, for cooling the face; outspread feathers of a bird's tail *—vt.* blow or cool with fan *—v.* spread out like fan (**-nn-**)

fan[2] *n. inf.* devoted admirer; an enthusiast, particularly for sport *etc.*

fanat'ic *a.* filled with abnormal enthusiasm, *esp.* in religion *—n.* fanatic person **—fanat'ical** *a.* **—fanat'ically** *adv.* **—fanat'icism** *n.* **—fanat'icize** *v.*

fan'cy *a.* ornamental, not plain; of whimsical or arbitrary kind *—n.* whim, caprice; liking, inclination; imagination; mental image *—vt.* imagine; be inclined to believe; *inf.* have a liking for (**fan'cied, fan'cying**) **—fan'cier** *n.* one with liking and expert knowledge (respecting some specific thing) **—fan'ciful** *a.* **—fan'cifully** *adv.*

fandan'go *n.* lively Spanish dance with castanets; music for this dance (*pl.* **-goes**)

fan'fare *n.* a flourish of trumpets or bugles; ostentatious display

fang *n.* snake's poison tooth; long, pointed tooth

fan'tail *n.* kind of bird (*esp.* pigeon) with fan-shaped tail

fan'tasy *n.* power of imagination, *esp.* extravagant; mental image; fanciful invention or design **—fanta'sia** [-z-] *n.* fanciful musical composition **—fan'tasize** *v.* **—fantas'tic** *a.* quaint, grotesque, extremely fanciful, wild; *inf.* very good; *inf.* very large **—fantas'tically** *adv.*

far *adv.* at or to a great distance, or advanced point; at or to a remote time; by very much (**far'ther, fur'ther** *comp.*, **far'thest, fur'thest** *sup.*) *—a.* distant; more distant **—far-fetched** *a.* incredible **—Far North** Arctic and sub-Arctic regions

far'ad [fa'rəd] *n.* unit of electrical capacity **—farada'ic** *a.*

farce *n.* comedy of boisterous humour; absurd and futile proceeding **—far'cical** *a.* ludicrous **—far'cically** *adv.*

fare *n.* charge for passenger's transport; passenger; food *—vi.* get on; happen; travel, progress **—farewell'** *interj.* goodbye *—n.* leave-taking

farina'ceous *a.* mealy, starchy

farm *n.* tract of land for cultivation or rearing livestock; unit of land, water, for growing or rearing a particular crop, animal *etc.* *—v.* cultivate (land); rear livestock (on farm) **—farm'er** *n.* **—farm'house** *n.* **—farm'stead** [-sted] *n.* **—farm'yard** *n.* **—farm out** rent (land, a business *etc.*) for fixed payment

fa'ro *n.* card game

farrag'o [-rahg'-] *n.* medley, hotchpotch (*pl.* **-gos**)

farr'ier *n.* one who shoes, cares for, horses **—farr'iery** *n.* his art

farr'ow *n.* litter of pigs *—v.* produce this

fart *vulg. n.* (audible) emission of gas from anus *—vi.*

far'ther [-TH-] *adv./a.* further; *comp. of* FAR **—far'thest** *adv./a.* furthest; *sup. of* FAR

far'thing [-TH-] *n.* formerly, coin worth a quarter of a penny

far'thingale [-TH-] *n. Hist.* hoop worn under skirts

fas'ces [fas'ēz] *pl.n.* bundle of rods bound together round axe, forming Roman badge of authority; emblem of Italian fascists

fa'scia, fa'cia [-sh-] *n.* flat surface above shop window; *Architecture* long flat surface between mouldings under eaves; face of wood or stone in a building (*pl.* **fa'(s)ciae** [-ē])

fas'cinate *vt.* attract and delight by rousing interest and curiosity; render motionless, as with a fixed stare **—fascina'tion** *n.*

fas'cism [-sh'-] *n.* authoritarian political system opposed to democracy and liberalism; behaviour (*esp.* by those in authority) supposedly typical of this system —**fasc'ist** *a./n.*

fash'ion *n.* (latest) style, *esp.* of dress *etc.*; manner, mode; form, type —*vt.* shape, make —**fash'ionable** *a.* —**fash'ionably** *adv.*

fast[1] [-ah-] *a.* (capable of) moving quickly; permitting, providing, rapid progress; ahead of true time; *obs.* dissipated; firm, steady; permanent —*adv.* rapidly; tightly —**fast'ness** *n.* fast state; fortress, stronghold —**fast'back** *n.* automobile with back forming continuous slope from roof to rear —**fast food** food, *esp.* hamburgers *etc.*, prepared and served very quickly

fast[2] [-ah-] *vi.* go without food, or some kinds of food —*n.* —**fast'ing** *n.*

fast'en [fahs'n] *vt.* attach, fix, secure —*vi.* become joined; seize (upon)

fastid'ious *a.* hard to please; discriminating; particular

fat *n.* oily animal substance; fat part —*a.* having too much fat; containing fat, greasy; profitable; fertile (**fatt'er** *comp.*, **fatt'est** *sup.*) —*vt.* feed (animals) for slaughter (**-tt-**) —**fat'ness** *n.* —**fatt'en** *v.* —**fatt'y** *a.* —**fat'head** *n. inf.* dolt, idiot

fate *n.* power supposed to predetermine events; goddess of destiny; destiny; person's appointed lot or condition; death or destruction —*vt.* preordain —**fa'tal** *a.* deadly, ending in death; destructive; disastrous; inevitable —**fa'talism** *n.* belief that everything is predetermined; submission to fate —**fa'talist** *n.* —**fatalis'tic** *a.* —**fatalis'tically** *adv.* —**fatal'ity** *n.* accident resulting in death; person killed in war, accident —**fa'tally** *adv.* —**fate'ful** *a.* fraught with destiny, prophetic

fath'er [fahTH'-] *n.* male parent; forefather, ancestor; (**F-**) God; originator, early leader; priest, confessor; oldest member of a society —*vt.* beget; originate; pass as father or author of; act as father to —**fath'erhood** *n.* —**fa'therless** *a.* —**fath'erly** *a.* —**father-in-law** *n.* husband's or wife's father

fath'om [faTH'-] *n.* measure of six feet of water —*vt.* sound (water); get to bottom of, understand —**fath'omable** *a.* —**fath'omless** *a.* too deep to fathom

fatigue' [-tēg'] *n.* weariness; toil; weakness of metals *etc.*, subjected to stress; soldier's nonmilitary duty —*vt.* weary

fat'uous *a.* very silly, idiotic —**fatu'ity** *n.*

fau'cet [faw'sit] *n.* tap

fault *n.* defect; flaw; misdeed; blame, culpability; blunder; mistake; *Tennis* ball wrongly served; *Geology* break in strata —*v.* find fault in; (cause to) undergo or commit fault —**fault'ily** *adv.* —**fault'less** *a.* —**fault'lessly** *adv.* —**fault'y** *a.*

faun *n.* mythological woodland being with tail and horns

faun'a *n.* animals of region or period collectively (*pl.* **-s, -ae** [-ē])

faux pas' [fō-pah'] *n.* social blunder or indiscretion

fa'vo(u)r [-vər] *n.* goodwill; approval; especial kindness; partiality; badge or knot of ribbons —*vt.* regard or treat with favour; oblige; treat with partiality; aid; support; resemble —**fa'vo(u)rable** *a.* —**fa'vo(u)rably** *adv.* —**fa'vo(u)rite** [-it] *n.* favoured person or thing; horse *etc.* expected to win race —*a.* chosen, preferred —**fa'vo(u)ritism** *n.* practice of showing undue preference

fawn[1] *n.* young deer —*a.* light yellowish brown

fawn[2] *vi.* of person, cringe, court favour servilely; *esp.* of dog, show affection by wagging tail and grovelling

faze *vt. inf.* disconcert

FBI Federal Bureau of Investigation

Fe *Chem.* iron

fe'alty *n.* fidelity of vassal to his lord; loyalty

fear *n.* dread, alarm, anxiety, unpleasant emotion caused by coming evil or danger —*vi.* have this feeling, be afraid —*vt.* regard with fear; hesitate, shrink from; revere —**fear'ful** *a.* —**fear'fully** *adv.* —**fear'less** *a.* intrepid —**fear'lessly** *adv.* —**fear'some** *a.*

fea'sible [-z-] *a.* able to be done; likely —**feasibil'ity** *n.* —**fea'sibly** *adv.*

feast *n.* banquet, lavish meal; religious anniversary; something very pleasant, sumptuous —*vi.* partake of banquet, fare sumptuously —*vt.* regale with feast; provide delight for —**feast'er** *n.*

feat *n.* notable deed; surprising or striking trick

feath'er [feTH'-] *n.* one of the barbed shafts which form covering of birds; anything resembling this —*vt.* provide, line with feathers —*vi.* grow feathers —*v.* turn (oar) edgeways —**feath'ery** *a.* —**feath'erweight** *n.* very light person or thing —**feather one's nest** enrich oneself —**the white feather** cowardice

fea'ture *n.* (*usu. pl.*) part of face; characteristic or notable part of anything; main or special item —*vt.* portray; present in leading role in a motion picture; give prominence to —*vi.* be prominent (in) —**fea'tureless** *a.* without striking features

Feb. February

fe'brile *a.* of fever

Feb'ruary *n.* second month of year (normally containing 28 days; in leap year, 29)

feck'less *a.* spiritless, weak, irresponsible

fe'cund [*or* fek'-] *a.* fertile, fruitful, fertilizing —**fe'cundate** *vt.* fertilize, impregnate —**fecunda'tion** *n.* —**fecund'ity** [fi-] *n.*

fed *pt./pp. of* FEED

fed'eral *a.* of, or like, the government of states which are united but retain internal independence —**fed'eralism** *n.* —**fed'eralist** *n.* —**fed'erate** *v.* form into, become, a federation —**federa'tion** *n.* league; federal union

fee *n.* payment for professional and other services

fee'ble *a.* weak; lacking strength or effectiveness, insipid —**fee'bly** *adv.*

feed *vt.* give food to; supply, support —*vi.* take food (**fed** *pt./pp.*) —*n.* feeding; fodder, pasturage; allowance of fodder; material supplied to machine; part of machine taking in material —**feed'er** *n.* one who or that which feeds; animal being fattened for slaughter —**feed'back** *n.* return of part of output of electrical circuit or loudspeakers; information received in response to enquiry *etc.* —**feed'lot** *n.* area, building where cattle are fattened for market

feel *v.* perceive, examine by touch; experience; proceed, find (one's way) cautiously; be sensitive to; show emotion (for); believe, consider (**felt** *pt./pp.*) —*n.* act or instance of feeling; quality or impression of something perceived by feeling; sense of touch —**feel'er** *n.* special organ of touch in some animals; proposal put forward to test others' opinion; that which feels —**feel'ing** *n.* sense of touch; ability to feel; physical sensation; emotion; sympathy, tenderness; conviction or opinion not solely based on reason —*pl.* susceptibilities —*a.* sensitive, sympathetic, heartfelt —**feel like** have an inclination for

feet *see* FOOT

feign [fān] *v.* pretend, sham

feint [fānt] *n.* sham attack or blow meant to deceive opponent; semblance, pretence —*vi.* make feint

felic'ity [-is'-] *n.* great happiness, bliss; appropriateness of wording —**felic'itate** *vt.* congratulate —**felicita'tion** *n.* (*usu. in pl.*) —**felic'itous** *a.* apt, well-chosen; happy

fe'line *a.* of cats; catlike

fell[1] *pt. of* FALL

fell[2] *vt.* knock down; cut down (tree) —*n.* timber felled in one season —**fell'er** *n.*

fell[3] *a. obs.* fierce, terrible

fell[4] *n.* skin or hide with hair

fell[5] *n.* mountain, stretch of moorland

fell'oe [-ō], **fell'y** *n.* outer part (or section) of wheel

fell'ow *n. inf.* man, boy; person; comrade, associate; counterpart; like thing; member (of society, college *etc.*) —*a.* of the same class, associated —**fel'lowship** *n.* fraternity; friendship; (in university *etc.*) research post or special scholarship

fel'on *n.* one guilty of felony —**felo'nious** *a.* —**fel'ony** *n.* serious crime

fel(d)'spar *n.* crystalline mineral found in granite *etc.* —**fel(d)spath'ic** *a.*

felt[1] *pt./pp. of* FEEL

felt[2] *n.* soft, matted fabric made by bonding fibres chemically and by pressure; thing made of this —*vt.* make into, or cover with, felt —*vi.* become matted like felt —**felt-tip pen** pen with writing point made from pressed fibres

fem. feminine

fe'male *a.* of sex which bears offspring; relating to this sex —*n.* one of this sex

fem'inine [-in] *a.* of women; womanly; class or type of grammatical inflection in some languages —**fem'inism** *n.* advocacy of equal rights for women —**fem'inist** *n./a.* —**feminin'ity** *n.*

fem'oral *a.* of the thigh

fe'mur [fē'mə] *n.* thigh-bone

fen *n.* tract of marshy land, swamp —**fenn'y** *a.*

fence *n.* structure of wire, wood *etc.* enclosing an area; (machinery) guard, guide; *sl.* dealer in stolen property —*v.* erect fence; enclose; fight (as sport) with swords; avoid question *etc.*; *sl.* deal in stolen property —**fen'cing** *n.* art of swordplay

fend *vt.* ward off, repel —*vi.* provide (for oneself *etc.*) —**fend'er** *n.* cover over wheel of automobile *etc.* to prevent mud, water *etc.* being splashed; low metal frame in front of fireplace; name for various protective devices; frame; edge; buffer

fenestra'tion *n.* arrangement of windows in a building

fenn'el *n.* yellow-flowered fragrant herb

fe'ral[1] *a.* wild, uncultivated

fe'ral[2] *a. obs.* funereal, gloomy

fer'ment *n.* leaven, substance causing thing to ferment; excitement, tumult —*v.* [-ment'] (cause to) undergo chemical change with effervescence, liberation of heat and alteration of properties, *eg* process set up in dough by yeast; (cause to) become excited —**fermenta'tion** *n.*

fern *n.* plant with feathery fronds —**fern'ery** *n.* place for growing ferns —**fern'y** *a.* full of ferns

fero'cious [-shəs] *a.* fierce, savage, cruel —**feroc'ity** *n.*

ferr'et *n.* tamed animal like weasel, used to catch rabbits, rats *etc.* —*vt.* drive out with ferrets; search out —*vi.* search about, rummage

ferr'ic, ferr'(e)ous *a.* pert. to, containing, iron —**ferrif'erous** *a.* yielding iron —**ferru'ginous** [-ro͞o'-] *a.* containing iron; reddish-brown —**ferrocon'crete** *n.* concrete strengthened by framework of metal

ferr'is wheel in fairground, large, vertical wheel with seats for riding

ferr'ule *n.* metal cap to strengthen end of stick *etc.*

ferr'y *n.* boat *etc.* for transporting people, vehicles, across body of water, *esp.* as repeated or regular service; place for ferrying —*v.* carry, travel, by ferry (**fer'ried, ferr'ying**) —**ferr'yman** *n.*

fer'tile *a.* (capable of) producing offspring, bearing crops *etc.*; fruitful, producing abundantly; inventive —**fertil'ity** *n.* —**fertiliza'tion** *n.* —**fer'tilize** *vt.* make fertile —**fer'tilizer** *n.*

fer'vent, fer'vid *a.* ardent, vehement, intense —**fer'vency** *n.* —**fer'vently** *adv.* —**fer'vo(u)r** [-vər] *n.*

fes'cue *n.* grass used as pasture, with stiff narrow leaves

fes'tal *a.* of feast or holiday; merry, gay —**fes'tally** *adv.*

fes'ter *v.* (cause to) form pus —*vi.* rankle; become embittered

fes'tival *n.* day, period, set aside for celebration, *esp.* of religious feast; organized series of events, performances *etc.* *usu.* in one place —**fes'tive** *a.* joyous, merry; of feast —**festiv'ity** *n.* gaiety, mirth; rejoicing —*pl.* festive proceedings

festoon' *n.* chain of flowers, ribbons *etc.* hung in curve between two points —*vt.* form, adorn with festoons

fetch *vt.* go and bring; draw forth; be sold for; attract —*n.* trick —**fetch'ing** *a.* attractive —**fetch up** *inf.* arrive at; run onto, into

fete, fête [fāt] *n.* gala, bazaar *etc.*, *esp.* one held out of doors; festival, holiday, celebration —*vt.* feast; honour with festive entertainment

fet'id, foet'id [-ē-] *a.* stinking

fet'ish *n.* (inanimate) object believed to have magical powers; excessive attention to something; object, activity, to which excessive devotion is paid

fet'lock *n.* projection behind and above horse's hoof, or tuft of hair on this

fett'er *n.* chain or shackle for feet; check, restraint —*pl.* captivity —*vt.* chain up; restrain, hamper

fet'tle *n.* condition, state of health

fe'tus, foe'tus *n.* fully-developed young in womb or egg —**fe'tal** *a.*

feud [fyo͞od] *n.* bitter, lasting, mutual hostility, *esp.* between two families or tribes; vendetta —*vi.* carry on feud

feu'dal [fyo͞o'-] *a.* of, like, medieval social and economic system based on holding land from superior in return for service; *inf.* very old-fashioned —**feu'dalism** *n.*

fe'ver *n.* condition of illness with high body temperature; intense nervous excitement —**fe'vered** *a.* —**fe'verish** *a.* having fever; accompanied by, caused by, fever; in a state of restless excitement —**fe'verishly** *adv.* —**fever pitch** very fast pace; intense excitement

few *a.* not many —*n.* small number —**good few, quite a few** several

fez *n.* red, brimless, orig. Turkish tasselled cap (*pl.* **fezz'es**)

ff *Mus.* fortissimo

ff. folios; following

fian'cé [-on'sā] *n.* man engaged to be married (**fian'cée** *fem.*)

fias'co *n.* breakdown, total failure (*pl.* **-co(e)s**)

fi'at *n.* decree; official permission

fib *n.* trivial lie, falsehood —*vt.* tell fib (**-bb-**) —**fibb'er** *n.*

fi'bre *n.* filament forming part of animal or plant tissue; substance that can be spun (*eg* wool, cotton) —**fibrosi'tis** *n.* inflammation of tissues of muscle sheaths —**fi'brous** *a.* made of fibre —**fi'breboard** *n.* building material of compressed plant fibres —**fi'breglass** *n.* material made of fine glass fibres —**fibre optics** *pl.n.* (*with sing. v.*) use of bundles of long transparent glass fibres in transmitting light

fib'rin *n.* insoluble protein in blood, causing coagulation

fib'ula *n.* slender outer bone of lower leg —**fib'ular** *a.*

fic'kle *a.* changeable, inconstant —**fic'kleness** *n.*

fic'tion *n.* prose, literary works of the imagination; invented statement or story —**fic'tional** *a.* —**ficti'tious** *a.* not genuine, false; imaginary; assumed

fid'dle *n.* violin; triviality; *inf.* illegal, fraudulent arrangement —*vi.* play fiddle; make idle movements, fidget, trifle —*v. sl.* cheat, contrive —**fidd'ling** *a.* trivial —**fidd'ly** *a.* small, awkward to handle —**fid'dlehead** *n.* edible coiled tip of young fern frond —**fid'dlesticks** *interj.* nonsense

fi'dei defen'sor [fi'di-ī] *Lat.* defender of the faith

fidel'ity *n.* faithfulness; quality of sound reproduction

fidg'et *vi.* move restlessly; be uneasy —*n.* (*oft. pl.*) nervous restlessness, restless mood; one who fidgets —**fidg'ety** *a.*

fidu'ciary [-sh-] *a.* held, given in trust; relating to trustee —*n.* trustee

fief [fēf] *n. Hist.* land held of a superior in return for service

field *n.* area of (farming) land; enclosed piece of land; tract of land rich in specified product (*eg goldfield*); players in a game or sport collectively; all competitors but the favourite; battlefield; area over which electric, gravitational, magnetic force can be exerted; surface of shield, coin *etc.*; sphere of knowledge; range, area of operation —*v. Baseball etc.* stop and return ball; send player, team, on to sportsfield —**field'er** *n.* —**field day** day of manoeuvres, outdoor activities; important occasion —**field events** throwing and jumping events in athletics —**field glasses** binoculars —**field hockey** hockey played on field, as distinct from ice hockey —**field marshal** army officer of highest rank —**field'work** *n.* research, practical work, conducted away from the classroom, laboratory *etc.* —**field of view** area covered in telescope, camera *etc.*

fiend *n.* demon, devil; wicked person; person very fond of or addicted to something *eg fresh-air fiend, drug fiend* —**fiend'ish** *a.* wicked, difficult, unpleasant

fierce *a.* savage, wild, violent; rough; severe; intense —**fierce'ly** *adv.* —**fierce'ness** *n.*

fi'ery *a.* consisting of fire; blazing, glowing, flashing; irritable; spirited (**fi'erier** *comp.*, **fi'eriest** *sup.*) —**fi'erily** *adv.*

fies'ta *n.* (religious) celebration, carnival

fife *n.* high-pitched flute —*v.* play on fife —**fi'fer** *n.*

fif'teen', fifth, fif'ty *see* FIVE

fig *n.* soft, pear-shaped fruit; tree bearing it —**full fig** full dress

fight [fīt] *v.* contend with in battle or in single combat; maintain against opponent; settle by combat (**fought** *pt./pp.*) —*n.* —**fight'er** *n.* one who fights; *Mil.* aircraft designed for destroying other aircraft —*a.*

fig'ment *n.* invention, purely imaginary thing

fig'ure [-ər] *n.* numerical symbol; amount, number; form, shape; bodily shape; appearance, *esp.* conspicuous appearance; space enclosed by lines, or surfaces; diagram, illustration; likeness; image; pattern, movement in dancing, skating, *etc.*; abnormal form of expression for effect in speech, *eg* metaphor —*vt.* calculate, estimate; *inf.* think, conclude or consider; represent by picture or diagram; ornament —*vi.* (*oft. with* in) show, appear, be conspicuous, be included —**fig'urative** *a.* metaphorical; full of figures of speech —**fig'uratively** *adv.* —**figurine'** [-ēn'] *n.* statuette —**fig'urehead** *n.* nominal leader; ornamental figure under bowsprit of ship

fil'ament *n.* fine wire in electric light bulb and radio valve which is heated by electric current; threadlike body

filch *vt.* steal, pilfer

file[1] *n.* box, folder, clip *etc.* holding papers for reference; papers so kept; information about specific person, subject; orderly line, as of soldiers, one behind the other —*vt.* arrange (papers *etc.*) and put them away for reference; *Law* place on records of a court; bring suit in lawcourt —*vi.* march in file —**fi'ling** *n.* —**single** (*or* **Indian**) **file** single line of people one behind the other

file[2] *n.* roughened tool for smoothing or shaping —*vt.* apply file to, smooth, polish —**fi'ling** *n.* action of using file; scrap of metal removed by file

fil'ial *a.* of, befitting, son or daughter —**fil'ially** *adv.*

fil'ibuster *n.* process of obstructing legislation by using delaying tactics —*vi.*

fil'igree *n.* fine tracery or openwork of metal, usu. gold or silver wire

fill *vt.* make full; occupy completely; hold, discharge duties of; stop up; satisfy; fulfil; supply —*vi.* become full —*n.* full supply; as much as desired; soil *etc.*, to bring area of ground up to required level —**fill'ing** *n.* —**fill out** complete (form *etc.*) —**fill the bill** *inf.* supply all that is wanted

fill'et *n.* boneless slice of meat, fish; narrow strip —*vt.* cut into fillets, bone —**fill'eted** *a.*

fill'ip *n.* stimulus; sudden release of finger bent against thumb; snap so produced —*vt.* stimulate; give fillip to

fill'y *n.* female horse under four years old

film *n.* motion picture; sensitized celluloid roll used in photography, cinematography; thin skin or layer; dimness on eyes; slight haze —*a.* connected with cinema —*vt.* photograph with movie camera; make motion picture of (scene, story *etc.*) —*v.* cover, become covered, with film —**film'y** *a.* membraneous; gauzy

fil'ter *n.* cloth or other material, or a device, permitting fluid to pass but retaining solid particles; anything performing similar function —*v.* act as filter, or as if passing through filter —*vi.* pass slowly (through) —**fil'trate** *n.* filtered gas or liquid

filth [-th] *n.* disgusting dirt; pollution; obscenity —**filth'ily** *adv.* —**filth'iness** *n.* —**filth'y** *a.* unclean; foul

fin *n.* propelling or steering organ of fish; anything like this, *eg* stabilizing plane of airplane

fi'nal *a.* at the end; conclusive —*n.* game, heat, examination *etc.*, coming at end of series —**final'e** [fi-nahl'i] *n.* closing part of musical composition, opera *etc.*; termination —**final'ity** *n.* —**fi'nalize** *v.* —**fi'nally** *adv.*

finance' [fi-, fī-, *or* fī'-] *n.* management of money; money resources (*also pl.*) —*vt.* find capital for —**finan'cial** *a.* of finance —**finan'cially** *adv.* —**finan'cier** *n.*

finch *n.* one of family of small singing birds

find [fī-] *vt.* come across; light upon, obtain; recognize; experience, discover; discover by searching; ascertain; supply (as funds); *Law* give a verdict (**found** *pt./pp.*) —*n.* finding; (valuable) thing found —**find'er** *n.* —**find'ing** *n.* judicial verdict

fine[1] *a.* choice, of high quality; delicate, subtle; pure; in small particles; slender; excellent; handsome; showy; *inf.* healthy, at ease, comfortable; free from rain —*vt.* make clear or pure; refine; thin —**fine'ly** *adv.* —**fine'ness** *n.* —**fi'nery** *n.* showy dress —**finesse'** [fin-] *n.* elegant, skilful management —**fine art** art produced for its aesthetic value —**fine-tune** *vt.* make fine adjustments to for optimum performance

fine[2] *n.* sum fixed as penalty —*vt.* punish by fine —**in fine** in conclusion; in brief

fin'ger [-ng'g-] *n.* one of the jointed branches of the hand; various things like this —*vt.* touch or handle with fingers —**fin'gering** *n.* manner or act of touching; choice of fingers, as in playing musical instrument; indication of this —**fin'gerboard** *n.* part of musical instrument on which fingers are placed —**fin'gerprint** *n.* impression of tip of finger, *esp.* as used for identifying criminals

fi'nial *n. Architecture* ornament at apex of gables, spires *etc.*

fin'icking, fin'icky *a.* fastidious, fussy; too fine

fin'is *Lat.* end, *esp.* of book

fin'ish *v.* (*mainly tr.*) bring, come to an end, conclude; complete; perfect; kill —*n.* end; way in which thing is finished, as an *oak finish*, of furniture; final appearance —**fin'isher** *n.*

fi'nite *a.* bounded, limited

fiord, fjord *n.* (*esp.* in Norway) long, narrow inlet of sea

fir *n.* kind of coniferous resinous tree; its wood

fire *n.* state of burning, combustion, flame, glow; mass of burning fuel; destructive burning, conflagration; device for heating a room *etc.*; ardour, keenness, spirit; shooting of firearms —*vt.* discharge (firearm); propel from firearm; *inf.* dismiss from employment; bake; make burn; supply with fuel; inspire; explode —*vi.* discharge firearm; begin to burn; become excited —**fire'arm** *n.* gun, rifle, pistol *etc.* —**fire'brand** *n.* burning piece of wood; energetic (troublesome) person —**fire'break** *n.* strip of cleared land to arrest progress of bush or grass fire —**fire brigade** organized body of men and appliances to put out fires and rescue those in danger —**fire'bug** *n. inf.* person who intentionally sets fire to buildings *etc.* —**fire'damp** *n.* explosive hydrocarbon gas forming in mines —**fire drill** rehearsal of procedures for escape from fire —**fire engine** vehicle with apparatus for extinguishing fires —**fire escape** means, *esp.* stairs, for escaping from burning buildings —**fire'fly** *n.* insect giving off phosphorescent glow —**fire'guard, fire screen** *n.* protective grating in front of fire —**fire hall** building housing fire brigade —**fire irons** tongs, poker and shovel —**fire'man** *n.* member of fire brigade; stoker; assistant to locomotive driver —**fire'place** *n.* recess in room for fire —**fire ship** burning vessel sent drifting against enemy ships —**fire station** fire hall —**fire'warden** *n.* officer responsible for fire prevention, *esp.* in forest —**fire'work** *n.* (*oft. pl.*) device to give spectacular effects by explosions and coloured sparks —*pl.* outburst of temper, anger —**firing party, firing squad** detachment sent to fire volleys at military funeral, or to shoot criminal

fir'kin *n.* small cask; **UK** measure of 9 gallons

firm *a.* solid, fixed, stable; steadfast; resolute; settled —*v.* make, become firm —*n.* commercial enterprise; partnership

firm'ament *n.* expanse of sky, heavens

first *a.* earliest in time or order; foremost in rank or position; most excellent; highest, chief —*n.* beginning; first occurrence of something; first-class honours degree at university —*adv.* before others in time, order *etc.* —**first'ly** *adv.* —**first aid** help given to injured person before arrival of doctor —**first-hand** *a.* obtained directly from the first source —**first mate, first officer** officer of merchant vessel immediately below captain —**first-rate** *a.* of highest class or quality —**first-strike** *a.* (of a nuclear missile) for use in an opening attack to destroy enemy nuclear weapons

firth, frith *n.* (*esp.* in Scotland) arm of the sea, river estuary

fis'cal *a.* of government finances

fish *n.* vertebrate cold-blooded animal with gills, living in water; its flesh as food (*pl.* **fish, fish'es**) —*v.* (attempt to) catch fish; search (for); try to get information indirectly —**fish'er** *n.* —**fish'ery** *n.* business of fishing; fishing ground —**fish'y** *a.* of, like, or full of fish; dubious, open to suspicion; unsafe —**fish'erman** *n.* one who catches fish for a living or for pleasure —**fish'monger** [-mung-] *n.* (*esp.* in Brit.) seller of fish —**fish stick** small piece of fish covered in breadcrumbs —**fish'wife** *n.* coarse, scolding woman

fish'plate *n.* piece of metal holding rails together

fiss'ure [-sh'-] *n.* cleft, split, cleavage —**fiss'ile** [fis'-] *a.* capable of splitting; tending to split —**fiss'ion** *n.* splitting; reproduction by division of living cells with two parts, each of which becomes complete organism; splitting of atomic nucleus with release of large amount of energy —**fiss'ionable** *a.* capable of undergoing nuclear fission —**fissip'arous** *a.* reproducing by fission

fist *n.* clenched hand —**fist'icuffs** *pl.n.* fighting

fist'ula *n.* pipelike ulcer (*pl.* **-las, -lae** [-lē])

fit[1] *vt.* be suited to; be properly adjusted to; arrange, adjust, apply, insert; supply, furnish —*vi.* be correctly adjusted or adapted; be of right size (**-tt-**) —*a.* well-suited, worthy; qualified; proper, becoming; ready; in good condition or health (**fitt'er** *comp.*, **fitt'est** *sup.*) —*n.* way anything fits, its style; adjustment —**fit'ly** *adv.* —**fit'ment** *n.* piece of furniture —**fit'ness** *n.* —**fitt'er** *n.* one who, that which, makes fit; one who supervises making and fitting of garments; mechanic skilled in fitting up metal work —**fit'ting** *a.* appropriate, suitable; proper —*n.* fixture; apparatus; action of fitting

fit[2] *n.* seizure with convulsions, spasms, loss of consciousness *etc.*, as of epilepsy, hysteria *etc.*; sudden passing attack of illness; passing state, mood —**fit'ful** *a.* spasmodic, capricious —**fit'fully** *adv.*

five *a./n.* cardinal number after four —**fifth** *a./n.* ordinal number —**fifth'ly** *adv.* —**fives** *pl.n.* (*with sing. v.*) ball game played with hand or bat in a court —**fif'teen'** *a./n.* ten plus five —**fif'teenth'** *a./n.* —**fif'tieth** *a./n.* —**fif'ty** *a./n.* five tens —**fifth column** organization spying for enemy within country at war —**five'pins** *pl.n.* (*with sing. v.*) bowling game in which heavy bowls are rolled down long lane to knock over five target pins at other end

fix *vt.* fasten, make firm or stable; set, establish; appoint, assign, determine; make fast; repair; *inf.* arrange; *inf.* prepare; *inf.* influence the outcome of unfairly or by deception; bribe; *sl.* give someone his just deserts —*vi.* become firm or solidified; determine —*n.* difficult situation; position of ship, aircraft ascertained by radar, observation *etc.*; *sl.* dose of narcotic drug —**fixa'tion** *n.* act of fixing; preoccupation, obsession; situation of being set in some way of acting or thinking —**fix'ative** *a.* capable of, or tending to fix —*n.* —**fix'edly** [-id-li] *adv.* intently —**fix'ings** *pl.n.* equipment; trimmings —**fix'ity** *n.* —**fix'ture** *n.* thing fixed in position; thing attached to house; date for sporting event; the event —**fix up** arrange; *inf.* repair —**fix (someone) up** attend to person's needs

fizz *vi.* hiss, splutter —*n.* hissing noise; effervescent liquid as soda water, champagne —**fiz'zle** *vi.* splutter weakly —*n.* fizzling noise; fiasco —**fizzle out** *inf.* come to nothing, fail

fjord [fyord] *see* FIORD

flabb'ergast [-gahst] *vt.* overwhelm with astonishment

flabb'y *a.* hanging loose, limp; out of condition, too fat; feeble; yielding —**flab** *n. inf.* unsightly fat on the body —**flab'biness** *n.*

flacc'id [flas'-, flak's-] *a.* flabby, lacking firmness —**flaccid'ity** *n.*

flag[1] *n.* banner, piece of bunting attached to staff or halyard as standard or signal; small paper emblem sold on flag days —*vt.* inform by flag signals (**-gg-**) —**flag'ship** *n.* admiral's ship; most important ship of fleet —**flag'staff** *n.* pole for flag

flag[2] *n.* water plant with sword-shaped leaves, *esp.* the iris —**flagg'y** *a.*

flag[3] *n.* flagstone —*vt.* (**-gg-**) —**flag'stone** *n.* flat slab of stone

flag[4] *vi.* droop, fade; lose vigour (**-gg-**)

flag'ellate [-aj'-] *vt.* scourge, flog —**flag'ellant** *n.* one who scourges himself, *esp.* in religious penance —**flagella'tion** *n.* —**flag'ellator** *n.*

flageolet' [flaj-ə-let'] *n.* small flutelike instrument

flag'on *n.* large bottle of wine *etc.*

fla'grant *a.* glaring, scandalous, blatant —**fla'grancy** *n.* —**fla'grantly** *adv.*

flail *n.* instrument for threshing corn by hand —*v.* beat with, move as, flail

flair *n.* natural ability; elegance

flak *n.* anti-aircraft fire; *inf.* adverse criticism

flake *n.* small, thin piece, *esp.* particle of snow; piece chipped off —*v.* (cause to) peel off in flakes —**fla'ky** *a.* —**flake out** *inf.* collapse, sleep from exhaustion

flamboy'ant *a.* florid, gorgeous, showy; exuberant, ostentatious

flame *n.* burning gas, *esp.* above fire; visible burning; passion, *esp.* love; *inf.*

sweetheart —*vi.* give out flames, blaze; shine; burst out

flamen'co *n.* Spanish dance to guitar

flamin'go [-ng'g-] *n.* large pink bird with long neck and legs (*pl.* **-s, -es**)

flamm'able *a.* liable to catch fire

flan *n.* **UK** open sweet or savoury tart

flange [-anj] *n.* projecting flat rim, collar, or rib —*v.* provide with or take form of flange

flank *n.* part of side between hips and ribs; side of anything, *eg* body of troops —*vt.* guard or strengthen on flank; attack or take in flank; be at, move along either side of

flann'el *n.* soft woollen fabric for clothing, *esp.* trousers —**flannelette'** *n.* cotton fabric imitating flannel —**flann'elly** *a.*

flap *v.* move (wings, arms *etc.*) as bird flying; (cause to) sway; strike with flat object; *inf.* be agitated, flustered (**-pp-**) —*n.* act of flapping; broad piece of anything hanging from hinge or loosely from one side; movable part of aircraft wing; *inf.* state of excitement or panic

flare [-ār] *vi.* blaze with unsteady flame; *inf.* (*with* up) suddenly burst into anger; spread outwards, as bottom of skirt —*n.* instance of flaring; signal light

flash *n.* sudden burst of light or flame; sudden short blaze; very short time; brief news item; ribbon or badge; display —*vi.* break into sudden flame; gleam; burst into view; move very fast; appear suddenly —*vt.* cause to gleam; emit (light *etc.*) suddenly —**flash, flash'y** *a.* showy, sham —**flash'er** *n.* —**flash'back** *n.* break in continuity of book, play or motion picture, to introduce what has taken place previously —**flash'bulb** *n.* *Photography* small glass light bulb triggered, usu. electrically, to produce bright flash of light —**flash'light** *n.* portable hand light containing electric battery and bulb; *Photography* brief light emitted by flashbulb or electronic flash —**flash point** temperature at which a vapour ignites

flask [-ah-] *n.* long-necked bottle for scientific use; pocket bottle; container packed with sand to form mould in foundry

flat[1] *a.* level; spread out; at full length; smooth; downright; dull, lifeless; *Mus.* below true pitch; (of tyre) deflated, punctured; (of battery) fully discharged, dead (**flatt'er** *comp.*, **flatt'est** *sup.*) —*n.* what is flat; *Mus.* note half tone below natural pitch —**flat'ly** *adv.* —**flat'ness** *n.* —**flatt'en** *vt.* —**flat'fish** *n.* type of fish which swims along sea floor on one side of body with both eyes on uppermost side —**flat rate** the same in all cases —**flat out** at, with maximum speed or effort

flat[2] *n.* **UK** apartment

flatt'er *vt.* fawn on; praise insincerely; inspire unfounded belief; gratify (senses); represent too favourably —**flatt'erer** *n.* —**flatt'ery** *n.*

flat'ulent *a.* suffering from, generating (excess) gases in intestines; pretentious —**flat'ulence** *n.* flatulent condition; verbosity, emptiness

flaunt *v.* show off; wave proudly —**flaunt'y** *a.*

flaut'ist *n.* flute player

flaves'cent *a.* yellowish, turning yellow

fla'vo(u)r [-vər] *n.* mixed sensation of smell and taste; distinctive taste, savour; undefinable characteristic, quality of anything —*vt.* give flavour to; season —**fla'vo(u)ring** *n.*

flaw *n.* crack; defect, blemish —*vt.* make flaw in —**flaw'less** *a.* perfect

flax *n.* plant grown for its textile fibre and seeds; its fibres, spun into linen thread —**flax'en** *a.* of flax; light yellow or straw-coloured

flay *vt.* strip skin off; criticize severely

flea [-ē] *n.* small, wingless, jumping, blood-sucking insect —**flea'bite** *n.* insect's bite; trifling injury; trifle —**flea-bitten** *a.* bitten by flea; mean, worthless; scruffy —**flea market** market for cheap goods

fleck *n.* small mark, streak, or particle —*vt.* mark with flecks

fled *pt./pp. of* FLEE

fledged *a.* (of birds) able to fly; experienced, trained —**fledg(e)'ling** *n.* young bird; inexperienced person

flee *v.* run away from (**fled, flee'ing**)

fleece *n.* sheep's wool —*vt.* rob —**flee'cy** *a.*

fleet[1] *n.* number of warships organized as unit; number of ships, automobiles *etc.* operating together

fleet[2] *a.* swift, nimble —**fleet'ing** *a.* passing, transient —**fleet'ingly** *adv.*

flense *vt.* strip (*esp.* whale) of flesh

flesh *n.* soft part, muscular substance, between skin and bone; in plants, pulp; fat; sensual appetites —**flesh'ily** *adv.* —**flesh'ly** *a.* carnal, material —**flesh'y** *a.* plump, pulpy —**flesh'pots** *pl.n.* (places catering for) self-indulgent living —**in the flesh** in person, actually present

fleur-de-lis' [flur-də-lē'] *n.* heraldic lily with three petals; iris (*pl.* **fleurs-de-lis'**)

flew *pt. of* FLY[1]

flex *n.* **UK** electric cord —*v.* bend, be bent —**flexibil'ity** *n.* —**flex'ible** *a.* easily bent; manageable; adaptable —**flex'ibly** *adv.* —**flex'ion, flec'tion** *n.* bending; bent state —**flex'(i)time** *n.* system permitting variation in starting and finishing times of work, providing an agreed number of hours is worked over a specified period

flibb'ertigibb'et *n.* flighty, gossiping person

flick *vt.* strike lightly, jerk —*n.* light blow; jerk; *sl.* movie

flick'er *vi.* burn, shine, unsteadily; waver, quiver —*n.* unsteady light or movement

flight [-īt] *n.* act or manner of flying through air; number flying together, as birds; journey in aircraft; Air Force unit of command; power of flying; swift movement or passage; sally; distance flown; stairs between two landings; running away —**flight recorder** electronic device in aircraft storing information about its flight

flight'y *a.* frivolous, erratic

flim'sy [-zi] *a.* frail, weak, thin; easily destroyed —**flim'sily** *adv.*

flinch *vi.* shrink, draw back, wince

fling *v.* (*mainly tr.*) throw, send, move, with force (**flung** *pt./pp.*) —*n.* throw; hasty attempt; spell of indulgence; vigorous dance

flint *n.* hard steel-grey stone; piece of this; hard substance used (as flint) for striking fire —**flint'ily** *adv.* —**flint'y** *a.* like or consisting of flint; hard, cruel

flip *v.* throw or flick lightly; turn over (**-pp-**) —*n.* instance, act, of flipping; drink with beaten egg —**flipp'ancy** *n.* —**flipp'ant** *a.* treating serious things lightly —**flipp'antly** *adv.* —**flipp'er** *n.* limb, fin for swimming —*pl.* fin-shaped rubber devices worn on feet to help in swimming

flirt *vi.* toy, play with another's affections; trifle, toy (with) —*n.* person who flirts —**flirta'tion** *n.* —**flirta'tious** *a.*

flit *vi.* pass lightly and rapidly; dart; *inf.* go away hastily, secretly (**-tt-**)

flitch *n.* side of bacon

float *vi.* rest, drift on surface of liquid; be suspended freely; move aimlessly —*vt.* of liquid, support, bear alone; in commerce, get (company) started; obtain loan —*n.* anything small that floats (*esp.* to support something else, *eg* fishnet); small delivery vehicle, *esp.* one powered by batteries; motor vehicle carrying tableau *etc.* in parade; sum of money used to provide change or for minor expenses —*pl.* footlights —**flota'tion** *n.* act of floating, *esp.* floating of company

flocc'ulent *a.* like tufts of wool

flock[1] *n.* number of animals of one kind together; *fig.* body of people; religious congregation —*vi.* gather in a crowd

flock[2] *n.* lock, tuft of wool *etc.*; wool refuse for stuffing cushions *etc.* —**flock'y** *a.*

floe [-ō] *n.* sheet of floating ice

flog *vt.* beat with whip *etc.* (**-gg-**)

flood [flud] *n.* inundation, overflow of water; rising of tide; outpouring; flowing water —*vt.* inundate; cover, fill with water; arrive, move *etc.* in great numbers —**flood'gate** *n.* gate, sluice for letting water in or out —**flood'light** *n.* broad, intense beam of artificial light —**flood'lit** *a.* —**flood tide** the rising tide; *fig.* peak of prosperity

floor [flawr] *n.* lower surface of room; set of rooms on one level, storey; flat space; (right to speak in) legislative hall —*vt.* supply with floor; knock down; confound —**floor'ing** *n.* material for floors —**floor show** entertainment in nightclub *etc.*

flop *vi.* bend, fall, collapse loosely, carelessly; fall flat on floor, on water *etc.*; *inf.* go to sleep; *inf.* fail (**-pp-**) —*n.* flopping movement or sound; *inf.* failure —**flop'pily** *adv.* —**flopp'iness** *n.* —**flopp'y** *a.* limp, unsteady —**floppy disk** *Computers* flexible magnetic disk that stores information

flor'a *n.* plants of a region; list of them (*pl.* **-ras, -rae** [-rē]) —**flor'al** *a.* of flowers —**flores'cence** *n.* state or time of flowering —**flor'et** *n.* small flower forming part of composite flower —**floribun'da** *n.* type of rose whose flowers grow in large clusters —**floricul'tural** *a.* —**flor'iculture** *n.* cultivation of flowers —**floricul'turist** *n.* —**flor'ist** [-o-] *n.* dealer in flowers

flor'id [-o-] *a.* with red, flushed complexion; ornate

flor'in [-o-] *n.* formerly, British silver two-shilling piece

floss *n.* mass of fine, silky fibres, *eg* of cotton, silk; fluff —**floss'y** *a.* light and downy; *sl.* showy

flota'tion *see* FLOAT

flotill'a *n.* fleet of small vessels; group of destroyers

flot'sam *n.* floating wreckage; discarded waste objects

flounce[1] *vi.* go, move abruptly and impatiently —*n.* fling, jerk of body or limb

flounce[2] *n.* ornamental gathered strip on woman's garment

floun'der[1] *vi.* plunge and struggle, *esp.* in water or mud; proceed in bungling, hesitating manner —*n.* act of floundering

floun'der[2] *n.* flatfish

flour *n.* powder prepared by sifting and grinding wheat *etc.*; fine soft powder —*vt.* sprinkle with flour —**flour'iness** *n.* —**flour'y** *a.*

flour'ish [flu'-] *vi.* thrive; be in the prime —*vt.* brandish, display; wave about —*n.* ornamental curve; showy gesture in speech *etc.*; waving of hand, weapon *etc.*; fanfare (of trumpets)

flout *vt.* show contempt for, mock; defy

flow [flō] *vi.* glide along as stream; circulate, as the blood; move easily; move in waves; hang loose; be present in abundance —*n.* act, instance of flowing; quantity that flows; rise of tide; ample supply —**flow chart** diagram showing sequence of operations in industrial *etc.* process

flow'er *n.* coloured (not green) part of plant from which fruit is developed; bloom, blossom; ornamentation; choicest part, pick —*pl.* chemical sublimate —*vi.* produce flowers; bloom; come to prime condition —*vt.* ornament with flowers —**flow'eret** *n.* small flower —**flow'ery** *a.* abounding in flowers; full of fine words, ornamented with figures of speech

flown [-ō-] *pp. of* FLY[1]

fl. oz. fluid ounce(s)

flu *n. short for* INFLUENZA

fluc'tuate *v.* vary, rise and fall, undulate —**fluctua'tion** *n.*

flue [flōō] *n.* passage or pipe for smoke or hot air, chimney

flu'ent [flōō'-] *a.* speaking, writing a given language easily and well; easy, graceful

fluff *n.* soft, feathery stuff; down; *inf.* mistake —*v.* make or become soft, light; *inf.* make mistake —**fluff'y** *a.*

flu'id [flōō'-] *a.* flowing easily, not solid —*n.* gas or liquid —**fluid'ity** *n.* —**fluid ounce** unit of capacity 1/20 of pint

fluke[1] [flōōk] *n.* flat triangular point of anchor —*pl.* whale's tail

fluke[2] [flōōk] *n.* stroke of luck, accident —*vt.* gain, make, hit by accident or by luck —**flu'ky** *a.* uncertain, got by luck

fluke[3] [flōōk] *n.* flatfish; parasitic worm

flume [flōōm] *n.* narrow (artificial) channel for water

flumm'ery *n.* nonsense, idle talk, humbug; dish of milk, flour, eggs *etc.*

flumm'ox *vt.* bewilder, perplex

flung *pt./pp. of* FLING

flunk *v. inf.* fail

flunk'ey *n.* servant, *esp.* liveried manservant; servile person

fluores'cence *n.* emission of light or other radiation from substance when bombarded by particles (electrons *etc.*) or other radiation, as in fluorescent lamp —**fluoresce'** *vi.* —**fluores'cent** *a.*

fluor'ite [flōōr'-] *n.* mineral containing fluorine (*also* **fluorspar**) —**fluor'ide** *n.* salt containing fluorine, *esp.* as added to domestic water supply as protection against tooth decay —**fluor'idate** *vt.* —**fluorida'tion** *n.* —**fluor'ine** *n.* nonmetallic element, yellowish gas

flurr'y *n.* squall, gust; bustle, commotion; death-struggle of whale; fluttering (as of snowflakes) —*vt.* agitate, bewilder, fluster (**flur'ried, flur'rying**)

flush[1] *vi.* blush; of skin, redden; flow suddenly or violently; be excited —*vt.* cleanse (*eg* toilet) by rush of water; excite —*n.* reddening, blush; rush of water; excitement; elation; glow of colour;

freshness, vigour —*a.* full, in flood; well supplied; level with surrounding surface

flush[2] *v.* (cause to) leave cover and take flight

flush[3] *n.* set of cards all of one suit

flus'ter *v.* make or become nervous, agitated —*n.*

flute [flōōt] *n.* wind instrument of tube with holes stopped by fingers or keys and blowhole in side; groove, channel —*vi.* play on flute —*vt.* make grooves in —**flu'ted** *a.* —**flu'ting** *n.*

flutt'er *v.* flap (as wings) rapidly without flight or in short flights; quiver; be or make excited, agitated —*n.* flapping movement; nervous agitation

flu'vial [flōō'-] *a.* of rivers

flux *n.* discharge; constant succession of changes; substance mixed with metal to clean, aid adhesion in soldering *etc.*; measure of strength in magnetic field

fly[1] *v.* move through air on wings or in aircraft; pass quickly (through air); float loosely; spring, rush; flee, run away —*vt.* operate aircraft; cause to fly; set flying —*vi.* run from (**flew** *pt.*, **flown** *pp.*) —*n.* (zipper or buttons fastening) opening in trousers; flap in garment or tent; flying —**fly'ing** *a.* hurried, brief —**fly'fish** *v.* fish with artificial fly as lure —**flying boat** airplane fitted with floats instead of landing wheels —**flying buttress** *Architecture* arched or slanting structure attached at only one point to a mass of masonry —**flying colours** conspicuous success —**flying fish** fish with winglike fins used for gliding above the sea —**flying fox** large fruit-eating bat —**flying saucer** unidentified (disc-shaped) flying object, supposedly from outer space —**fly'leaf** *n.* blank leaf at beginning or end of book (*pl.* **-leaves**) —**fly'wheel** *n.* heavy wheel regulating speed of machine

fly[2] *n.* two-winged insect, *esp.* common housefly —**fly'blown** *a.* infested with larvae of blowfly —**fly'catcher** *n.* small insect-eating songbird

FM Field Marshal; frequency modulation

FO Flying Officer

foal *n.* young of horse, ass *etc.* —*v.* bear (foal)

foam *n.* collection of small bubbles on liquid; froth of saliva or sweat; light cellular solid used for insulation, packing *etc.* —*v.* (cause to) produce foam; be very angry —**foam'y** *a.*

fob *n.* short watch chain; small pocket in waistband of trousers or waistcoat

fob off ignore, dismiss someone or something in offhand (insulting) manner; dispose of (**-bb-**)

fo'c'sle [fōk'səl] *n. contracted form of* FORECASTLE

fo'cus *n.* point at which rays meet after being reflected or refracted; state of optical image when it is clearly defined; state of instrument producing such image; point of convergence; point on which interest, activity is centred (*pl.* **fo'cuses, fo'ci** [-sī]) —*vt.* bring to focus, adjust; concentrate —*vi.* come to focus; converge (**fo'cused, fo'cusing**) —**fo'cal** *a.* of, at focus

fodd'er *n.* bulk food for livestock

foe [fō] *n.* enemy

FoE, FOE Friends of the Earth

foe'tus [-ē-] *n. see* FETUS

fog *n.* thick mist; dense watery vapour in lower atmosphere; cloud of anything reducing visibility —*vt.* cover in fog; puzzle (**-gg-**) —**fogg'y** *a.* —**fog'horn** *n.* instrument to warn ships in fog

fo'g(e)y *n.* old-fashioned person

foi'ble *n.* minor weakness, idiosyncrasy

foil[1] *vt.* baffle, defeat, frustrate —*n.* blunt sword, with button on point for fencing —**foil'able** *a.* —**foil'er** *n.*

foil[2] *n.* metal in thin sheet; anything which sets off another thing to advantage

foist *vt.* (*usu. with* off *or* on) sell, pass off inferior or unwanted thing as valuable

fold[1] [-ō-] *vt.* double up, bend part of; interlace (arms); wrap up; clasp (in arms); *Cooking* mix gently —*vi.* become folded; admit of being folded; *inf.* fail —*n.* folding; coil; winding; line made by folding; crease; foldlike geological formation —**fold'er** *n.* binder, file for loose papers

fold[2] [-ō-] *n.* enclosure for sheep; body of believers, church

fo'liage *n.* leaves collectively, leafage —**folia'ceous** [-shəs] *a.* of or like leaf —**fo'liate** *a.* leaflike, having leaves

fo'lio *n.* sheet of paper folded in half to make two leaves of book; book of largest common size made up of such sheets; page numbered on one side only; page number (*pl.* **fo'lios**)

folk [fōk] *n.* people in general; —*pl.*

family, relatives; race of people —**folk'sy** *a. inf.* of or like ordinary people; friendly; of or relating to folk art —**folk dance** —**folk'lore** *n.* tradition, customs, beliefs popularly held —**folk song** music originating among a people

foll'icle *n.* small sac; seed vessel —**follic'ular** *a.*

foll'ow *v.* go or come after —*vt.* accompany, attend on; keep to (path *etc.*); take as guide, conform to; engage in; have a keen interest in; be consequent on; grasp meaning of —*vi.* come next; result —**fol'lower** *n.* disciple, supporter —**fol'lowing** *a.* about to be mentioned —*n.* body of supporters —**follow-through** *n.* in ball games, continuation of stroke after impact with ball —**follow-up** *n.* something done to reinforce initial action

foll'y *n.* foolishness; foolish action, idea *etc.*; useless, extravagant structure

foment' *vt.* foster, stir up; bathe with hot lotions —**fomenta'tion** *n.*

fond *a.* tender, loving; *obs.* credulous; *obs.* foolish —**fond'ly** *adv.* —**fond'ness** *n.* —**fond of** having liking for

fon'dant *n.* soft sugar mixture for sweets; sweet made of this

fon'dle *vt.* caress

fon'due [-dyōō] *n.* Swiss dish of sauce (*esp.* cheese) into which pieces of bread *etc.* are dipped

font[1] *n.* bowl for baptismal water usu. on pedestal

font[2] *n.* complete set of printing type of one style and size

fontanel(le)' *n.* soft, membraneous gap between bones of baby's skull

food [-ōō-] *n.* solid nourishment; what one eats; mental or spiritual nourishment —**food additive** natural or synthetic substance added to commercially processed food as preservative or to add colour, flavour *etc.* —**food processor** electric domestic appliance for automatic chopping, blending *etc.* of foodstuffs —**food'stuff** *n.* food

fool [-ōō-] *n.* silly, empty-headed person; dupe; simpleton; *Hist.* jester, clown —*vt.* delude; dupe —*vi.* act as fool —**fool'ery** *n.* habitual folly; act of playing the fool; absurdity —**fool'hardiness** *n.* —**fool'hardy** *a.* foolishly adventurous —**fool'ish** *a.* ill-considered, silly, stupid —**fool'ishly** *adv.* —**fool'proof** *a.* proof against failure —**fool's cap** jester's or dunce's cap; this as watermark —**fools'cap** *n.* size of paper which formerly had this mark

foot [-oo-] *n.* lowest part of leg, from ankle down; lowest part of anything, base, stand; end of bed *etc.*; infantry; measure of twelve inches; division of verse (*pl.* **feet**) —*v.* (*usu. tr.*) dance; walk (*esp.* **foot it**); pay cost of (*esp. in* **foot the bill**) —**foot'age** *n.* length in feet; length, extent, of film used —**foot'ing** *n.* basis, foundation; firm standing, relations, conditions —*pl.* (concrete) foundations for walls of buildings —**foot-and-mouth disease** infectious viral disease in sheep, cattle *etc.* —**foot'ball** *n.* game played by two teams competing to kick, carry *etc.* ball into each other's goal *etc.* —**foot'baller** *n.* —**foot brake** brake operated by pressure on foot pedal —**foot fault** *Tennis* fault of overstepping base line while serving —**foot'hold** *n.* place affording secure grip for the foot; secure position from which progress may be made —**foot'lights** *pl.n.* lights across front of stage —**foot'loose** *a.* free from any ties —**foot'man** *n.* liveried servant —**foot'note** *n.* note of reference or explanation printed at foot of page —**foot-pound** *n.* unit of measurement of work in fps system —**foot'print** *n.* mark left by foot —**foot'slog** *vi.* walk, go on foot —**foot'slogger** *n.*

fop *n.* man excessively concerned with fashion —**fopp'ery** *n.* —**fopp'ish** *a.* —**fop'pishly** *adv.*

for *prep.* intended to reach, directed or belonging to; because of; instead of; towards; on account of; in favour of; respecting; during; in search of; in payment of; in the character of; in spite of —*conj.* because

for- (*comb. form*) from, away, against, as in *forswear*, *forbid* Such words are not given here where the meaning may easily be inferred from the simple word

for'age [fo'rij] *n.* food for cattle and horses —*vi.* collect forage; make roving search —**forage cap** soldier's undress cap

forasmuch' *conj.* (*with* as) as, seeing that, since

for'ay [fo'rā] *n.* raid, inroad —*vi.* make one —**for'ayer** *n.*

for(e)'bear [-bār] *n.* ancestor

forbear' [-bār'] *v.* (*esp. with* from) cease; refrain (from); be patient (**forbore'** *pt.*, **forborne'** *pp.*) —**forbear'ance** *n.* self-control, patience —**forbear'ing** *a.*

forbid' *vt.* prohibit; refuse to allow (**forbade'** [-bad'] *pt.*, **forbidd'en** *pp.*, **forbid'ding** *pr.p.*) —**forbidd'ing** *a.* uninviting, threatening

force *n.* strength, power; compulsion; that which tends to produce a change in a physical system; mental or moral strength; body of troops, police *etc.*; group of people organized for particular task or duty; effectiveness, operative state; violence —*vt.* constrain, compel; produce by effort, strength; break open; urge, strain; drive; hasten maturity of —**forced** *a.* accomplished by great effort; compulsory; unnatural; strained; excessive —**force'ful** *a.* powerful, persuasive —**for'cible** *a.* done by force; efficacious, compelling, impressive; strong —**for'cibly** *adv.*

for'ceps *pl.n.* surgical pincers

ford *n.* shallow place where river may be crossed —*vt.* —**ford'able** *a.*

fore[1] *a.* in front (**form'er, fur'ther** *comp.*, **fore'most, first, fur'thest** *sup.*) —*n.* front part

fore[2] *interj.* golfer's warning

fore- (*comb. form*) previous, before, front

fore-and-aft *a.* placed in line from bow to stern of ship

fore'arm *n.* arm between wrist and elbow —*vt.* [-arm'] arm beforehand

forebode' *vt.* indicate in advance —**forebo'ding** *n.* anticipation of evil

fore'cast *vt.* estimate beforehand (*esp.* weather); prophesy —*n.* prediction

fore'castle [fōk'səl] *n.* forward raised part of ship; sailors' quarters

foreclose' *vt.* take away power of redeeming (mortgage); prevent, shut out, bar —**foreclo'sure** *n.*

fore'court *n.* courtyard, open space, in front of building

fore'father *n.* ancestor

fore'finger *n.* finger next to thumb

foregath'er *see* FORGATHER

forego'[1] *vt.* precede in time, place (**-went'** *pt.*, **-gone'** *pp.*, **-go'ing** *pr.p.*) —**forego'ing** *a.* going before, preceding —**fore'gone** *a.* determined beforehand; preceding —**foregone conclusion** result that might have been foreseen

forego[2] *vt.* go without; give up (**-went'** *pt.*, **-gone'** *pp.*, **-go'ing** *pr.p.*) (*also* **forgo**)

fore'ground *n.* part of view, *esp.* in picture, nearest observer

fore'hand *a.* of stroke in racquet games made with inner side of wrist leading

fore'head [*or* fo'rid] *n.* part of face above eyebrows and between temples

for'eign [fo'rin] *a.* not of, or in, one's own country; relating to, or connected with other countries; irrelevant; coming from outside; unfamiliar, strange —**for'eigner** *n.*

fore'lock *n.* lock of hair above forehead

fore'man *n.* one in charge of work; leader of jury

fore'mast *n.* mast nearest bow

fore'most *a./adv.* first in time, place, importance *etc.*

fore'noon *n.* morning

foren'sic *a.* of courts of law —**forensic medicine** application of medical knowledge in legal matters

fore'play *n.* sexual stimulation before intercourse

fore'runner *n.* one who goes before, precursor

foresee' *vt.* see beforehand (**-saw'** *pt.*, **-seen'** *pp.*)

foreshad'ow *vt.* show, suggest beforehand, be a type of

fore'shore *n.* part of shore between high and low tide marks

foreshort'en *vt.* draw (object) so that it appears shortened; make shorter

fore'sight *n.* foreseeing; care for future

fore'skin *n.* skin that covers the glans penis

for'est [fo'rist] *n.* area with heavy growth of trees and plants; these trees; *fig.* something resembling forest —*vt.* plant, create forest (in an area) —**for'ester** *n.* one skilled in forestry —**for'estry** *n.* study, management of forest planting and maintenance

forestall' *vt.* anticipate; prevent, guard against in advance

fore'taste *n.* anticipation; taste beforehand

foretell' *vt.* prophesy (**foretold'**

pt./pp.)

fore'thought *n.* thoughtful consideration of future events

forev'er *adv.* always; eternally; *inf.* for a long time

forewarn' *vt.* warn, caution in advance

forewent' *see* FOREGO

fore'word *n.* preface

for'feit [-fit] *n.* thing lost by crime or fault; penalty, fine —*a.* lost by crime or fault —*vt.* lose by penalty —**for'feiture** *n.*

for(e)gath'er [-TH-] *vi.* meet together, assemble, associate

forge[1] [-j] *n.* place where metal is worked, smithy; furnace, workshop for melting or refining metal —*vt.* shape (metal) by heating in fire and hammering; make, shape, invent; make a fraudulent imitation of thing; counterfeit —**for'ger** *n.* —**for'gery** *n.* forged document, banknote *etc.*; the making of it

forge[2] [-j] *vi.* advance steadily

forget' *vt.* lose memory of, neglect, overlook (**forgot'** *pt.*, **forgott'en** *or obs.* **forgot'** *pp.*, **forgett'ing** *pr.p.*) —**forget'ful** *a.* liable to forget —**forget'fully** *adv.* —**forget-me-not** *n.* plant with small blue flower

forgive' [-giv'] *v.* cease to blame or hold resentment against; pardon —**forgive'ness** *n.*

forgo' *see* FOREGO[2]

forgot', forgott'en *see* FORGET

fork *n.* pronged instrument for eating food; pronged tool for digging or lifting; division into branches; point of this division; one of the branches —*vi.* branch —*vt.* dig, lift, throw, with fork; make fork-shaped —**fork out** *inf.* pay (reluctantly)

forlorn' *a.* forsaken; desperate —**forlorn hope** anything undertaken with little hope of success

form *n.* shape, visible appearance; visible person or animal; structure; nature; species, kind; regularly drawn up document, *esp.* printed one with blanks for particulars; condition, good condition; class in school; customary way of doing things; set order of words; long seat without back, bench; hare's nest; *Printing* frame for type —*vt.* shape, mould, arrange, organize; train, shape in the mind, conceive; go to make up, make part of —*vi.* come into existence or shape —**forma'tion** *n.* forming; thing formed; structure, shape, arrangement; military order —**for'mative** *a.* of, relating to, development; serving or tending to form; used in forming —**form'less** *a.*

for'mal *a.* ceremonial, according to rule; of outward form or routine; of, for, formal occasions; according to rule that does not matter; precise; stiff —*n.* dance party requiring formal clothes; gown worn at this —**for'malism** *n.* quality of being formal; exclusive concern for form, structure, technique in an activity, *eg* art —**for'malist** *n.* —**formal'ity** *n.* observance required by custom or etiquette; condition or quality of being formal; conformity to custom; conventionality, mere form; in art, precision, stiffness, as opposed to originality —**for'mally** *adv.*

formal'dehyde *n.* colourless, poisonous, pungent gas, used in making antiseptics and in chemistry —**form'alin** *n.* solution of formaldehyde in water, used as disinfectant, preservative *etc.*

for'mat *n.* size and shape of book; organization of television show *etc.*

for'mer *a.* earlier in time; of past times; first named —*pron.* first named thing or person or fact —**for'merly** *adv.* previously

Formi'ca R type of laminated sheet used to make heat-resistant surfaces

for'mic acid acid found in insects (*esp.* ants) and some plants

for'midable *a.* to be feared; overwhelming, terrible, redoubtable; likely to be difficult, serious —**for'midably** *adv.*

for'mula [-myoo-] *n.* set form of words setting forth principle, method or rule for doing, producing something; substance so prepared; specific category of car in motor racing; recipe; *Science, Math.* rule, fact expressed in symbols and figures (*pl.* **-ulae** [-ē], **-s**) —**for'mulary** *n.* collection of formulas —**for'mulate** *vt.* reduce to, express in formula, or in definite form; devise —**formula'tion** *n.* —**for'mulator** *n.*

fornica'tion *n.* sexual intercourse outside marriage —**for'nicate** *vi.*

forsake' *vt.* abandon, desert; give up (**forsook'**, **forsa'ken, forsa'king**)

forsooth' *adv. obs.* in truth

forswear' *vt.* renounce, deny *—refl.* perjure (**-swore'** *pt.*, **-sworn'** *pp.*)

forsy'thia *n.* widely cultivated shrub with yellow flowers

fort *n.* fortified place, stronghold

forte[1] [*or* for'tā] *n.* one's strong point, that in which one excels

for'te[2] [-ti] *adv. Mus.* loudly **—fortis'simo** *sup.*

forth *adv.* onwards, into view **—forthcom'ing** *a.* about to come; ready when wanted; willing to talk, communicative **—forthwith'** *adv.* at once, immediately

forth'right *a.* direct; outspoken

for'tieth *see* FOUR

for'tify *vt.* strengthen; provide with defensive works (**for'tified, for'tifying**) **—fortifica'tion** *n.*

for'titude *n.* courage in adversity or pain, endurance

fort'night [-nīt] *n.* two weeks **—fort'nightly** *adv.*

FORTRAN *Computers* a programming language for mathematical and scientific purposes

fort'ress *n.* fortified place, *eg* castle, stronghold

fortu'itous *a.* accidental, by chance **—fortu'itously** *adv.* **—fortu'ity** *n.*

for'tune *n.* good luck, prosperity; wealth; stock of wealth; chance, luck **—for'tunate** *a.* **—for'tunately** *adv.* **—fortune-hunter** *n.* person seeking fortune, *esp.* by marriage **—fortune-teller** *n.* one who predicts a person's future

for'ty *see* FOUR

for'um *n.* (place or medium for) meeting, assembly for open discussion or debate

for'ward *a.* lying in front of; onward; presumptuous, impudent; advanced, progressive; relating to the future *—n.* player placed in forward position in various team games, *eg* football *—adv.* towards the future; towards the front, to the front, into view; at, in fore part of ship; onward, so as to make progress *—vt.* help forward; send, dispatch **—for'wardly** *adv.* pertly **—for'wardness** *n.* **—for'wards** *adv.*

fosse *n.* ditch or moat

foss'il *n.* remnant or impression of animal or plant, *esp.* prehistoric one, preserved in earth; *inf.* person, idea *etc.* that is outdated and incapable of change *—a.* **—foss'ilize** *v.* turn into fossil; petrify

fos'ter *vt.* promote growth or development of; bring up child, *esp.* not one's own **—foster brother** one related by upbringing not blood; thus, **—foster father, mother, parent, child**

fought [fawt] *pt./pp. of* FIGHT

foul *a.* loathsome, offensive; stinking; dirty; unfair; wet, rough; obscene, disgustingly abusive; charged with harmful matter, clogged, choked *—n.* act of unfair play; the breaking of a rule *—adv.* unfairly *—v.* (*mainly tr.*) make, become foul; jam; collide with **—foul'ly** *adv.*

found[1] *pt./pp. of* FIND

found[2] *vt.* establish, institute; lay base of; base, ground **—founda'tion** *n.* basis; base, lowest part of building; founding; endowed institution *etc.* **—found'er** *n.* (**found'ress** *fem.*) **—foundation stone** one of stones forming foundation of building, *esp.* stone laid with public ceremony

found[3] *vt.* melt and run into mould; cast **—found'er** *n.* **—found'ry** *n.* place for casting; art of this

found'er *vi.* collapse; sink; become stuck as in mud *etc.*

found'ling *n.* deserted infant

fount *n.* fountain; source

foun'tain [-in] *n.* jet of water, *esp.* ornamental one; spring; source **—foun'tainhead** *n.* source **—fountain pen** pen with ink reservoir

four [-aw-] *n./a.* cardinal number next after three **—fourth** *a.* the ordinal number **—fourth'ly** *adv.* **—for'tieth** *a.* **—for'ty** *n./a.* four tens **—four'teen'** *n./a.* four plus ten **—four'teenth'** *a.* **—four-cycle** *a.* of internal-combustion engine firing once every four strokes of piston **—four'some** *n.* group of four people; game or dance for four people *—a.* **—four'square** *a.* firm, steady **—on all fours** on hands and knees

fowl *n.* domestic cock or hen; bird, its flesh *—vi.* hunt wild birds **—fowl'er** *n.* **—fowling piece** light gun

fox *n.* red bushy-tailed animal; its fur; cunning person *—vt.* perplex; discolour (paper) with brown spots; mislead *—vi.* act craftily; sham **—fox'y** *a.* **—fox'glove** *n.* tall flowering plant **—fox'hole** *n. sl.* in war, small trench giving protection **—fox'hound** *n.* dog bred for hunting foxes —**fox terrier** small dog now mainly kept as a pet —**fox'trot** *n.* (music for) ballroom dance —*v.*

foy'er [-ā] *n.* entrance-hall in theatres, hotels *etc.*

fps feet per second; foot-pound-second

Fr. Father; Frater (*Lat.* brother); French; Friday

frac'as [-k'ah] *n.* noisy quarrel; uproar, brawl

frac'tion *n.* numerical quantity not an integer; fragment, piece —**frac'tional** *a.* constituting a fraction; forming but a small part; insignificant

frac'tious [-shəs] *a.* unruly, irritable

frac'ture *n.* breakage, part broken; breaking of bone; breach, rupture —*v.* break

frag'ile [-aj'-] *a.* breakable; frail; delicate —**fragil'ity** *n.*

frag'ment *n.* piece broken off; small portion, incomplete part —*v.* [-ment'] —**frag'mentary** *a.*

fra'grant *a.* sweet-smelling —**fra'grance** *n.* scent —**fra'grantly** *adv.*

frail *a.* fragile, delicate; infirm; in weak health; morally weak —**frail'ly** *adv.* —**frail'ty** *n.*

frame *n.* that in which thing is set, as square of wood round picture *etc.*; structure; build of body; constitution; mood; individual exposure on strip of film —*vt.* put together, make; adapt; put into words; put into frame; bring false charge against —**frame-up** *n. sl.* plot, manufactured evidence —**frame'work** *n.* structure into which completing parts can be fitted; supporting work

franc [-angk] *n.* monetary unit of France, Switzerland and other countries

fran'chise *n.* right of voting; citizenship; privilege or right, *esp.* right to sell certain goods

Francis'can *n.* monk or nun of the order founded by St. Francis of Assisi —*a.*

Fran'cophone *n.* native speaker of French

frangipan'i [-ji-pahn'i] *n.* tropical American shrub

frank *a.* candid, outspoken; sincere —*n.* official mark on letter either cancelling stamp or ensuring delivery without stamp —*vt.* mark letter thus —**frank'ly** *adv.* candidly —**frank'ness** *n.*

Frank'enstein's monster [-īn] creation or monster that brings disaster and is beyond the control of its creator

frank'furter *n.* smoked sausage

frank'incense *n.* aromatic gum resin burned as incense

fran'tic *a.* distracted with rage, grief, joy *etc.*; frenzied —**fran'tically** *adv.*

frater'nal *a.* of brother, brotherly —**frater'nally** *adv.* —**frater'nity** *n.* brotherliness; brotherhood; college society —**fraterniza'tion** *n.* —**frat'ernize** *vi.* to associate, make friends —**fratrici'dal** *a.* —**frat'ricide** [-sīd] *n.* killing, killer of brother or sister

fraud *n.* criminal deception; swindle, imposture —**fraud'ulence** *n.* —**fraud'ulent** *a.*

fraught [-awt] *a.* filled (with), involving

fray[1] *n.* fight; noisy quarrel

fray[2] *v.* wear through by rubbing; make, become ragged at edge

fra'zil *n.* broken spikes of ice formed in turbulent water

fraz'zle *inf. v.* make or become exhausted; make or become irritated —*n.* exhausted state

freak *n.* abnormal person, animal, thing —*a.* —**freak'ish,** (*inf.*) **freak'y** *a.* —**freak out** *inf.* (cause to) hallucinate, be wildly excited *etc.*

frec'kle *n.* light brown spot on skin, *esp.* caused by sun; any small spot —*v.* bring, come out in freckles —**freck'led** *a.*

free *a.* able to act at will, not under compulsion or restraint; not restricted or affected by; not subject to cost or tax; independent; not exact or literal; generous; not in use; (of person) not occupied, having no engagement; loose, not fixed —*vt.* set at liberty; remove (obstacles, pain *etc.*); rid (of) (**freed, free'ing**) —**free'dom** *n.* —**free'ly** *adv.* —**free-for-all** *n.* brawl —**free'hand** *a.* drawn without guiding instruments —**free'hold** *n.* tenure of land without obligation of service or rent; land so held —**free'lance** [-ah-] *a./n.* (of) self-employed, unattached person —**Free'mason** *n.* member of secret fraternity for mutual help —**free-range** *a.* kept, produced in natural, nonintensive conditions —**free space** region that has no gravitational and electromagnetic fields —**free speech** right to express opinions publicly —**freethink'er** *n.* sceptic who forms his own opinions, *esp.* in religion —**free trade** international trade free of protective tariffs —**free'way** *n.* **US** expressway

free'sia [-zi-ə] *n.* plant with fragrant, tubular flowers

freeze *v.* change (by reduction of temperature) from liquid to solid, as water to ice —*vt.* preserve (food *etc.*) by extreme cold, as in freezer; fix (prices *etc.*) —*vi.* feel very cold; become rigid as with fear; stop (**froze, fro'zen, free'zing**) —**free'zer** *n.* insulated cabinet for long-term storage of perishable foodstuffs —**fro'zen** *a.* of credits *etc.*, unrealizable —**freezing point** temperature at which liquid becomes solid

freight [-āt] *n.* commercial transport (*esp.* by railway, ship); cost of this; goods so carried —*vt.* send as or by freight —**freight'age** *n.* money paid for freight —**freight'er** *n.*

French *n.* language spoken by people of France —*a.* of, or pertaining to France —**French doors** pair of glass doors opening in middle —**French dressing** salad dressing —**French fried potatoes** thin strips of potato, fried (*also* **French fries**) —**French horn** musical wind instrument —**French leave** unauthorized leave —**French polish** varnish for wood made from shellac dissolved in alcohol —**French window** window extended to floor level and used as door

frenet'ic *a.* frenzied

fren'zy *n.* violent mental derangement; wild excitement —**fren'zied** *a.*

fre'quent *a.* happening often; common; numerous —*vt.* [-kwent'] go often to —**fre'quency** *n.* rate of occurrence; in radio *etc.* cycles per second of alternating current —**frequent'ative** *a.* expressing repetition —**fre'quently** *adv.*

fres'co *n.* method of painting in water colour on plaster of wall before it dries; painting done thus (*pl.* **-co(e)s**)

fresh *a.* not stale; new; additional; different; recent; inexperienced; pure; not pickled, frozen *etc.*; not faded or dimmed; not tired; of wind, strong; *inf.* impudent; arrogant —**fresh'en** *v.* —**fresh'et** *n.* rush of water at river mouth; flood of river water —**fresh'ly** *adv.* —**fresh'man** *n.* first-year student —**fresh'ness** *n.*

fret[1] *v.* be irritated, worry (**-tt-**) —*n.* irritation —**fret'ful** *a.* irritable, (easily) upset

fret[2] *n.* repetitive geometrical pattern; small bar on fingerboard of guitar *etc.* —*vt.* ornament with carved pattern (**-tt-**) —**fret saw** saw with narrow blade and fine teeth, used for fretwork —**fret'work** *n.* carved or open woodwork in ornamental patterns and devices

Freu'dian [-oi'-] *a.* pert. to Austrian psychologist Sigmund Freud, or his theories

fri'able *a.* easily crumbled —**friabil'ity, fri'ableness** *n.*

fri'ar *n.* member of mendicant religious order —**fri'ary** *n.* house of friars

fricassee' [*or* frik'-] *n.* dish of pieces of chicken or meat, fried or stewed and served with rich sauce —*vt.* cook thus

fric'tion *n.* rubbing; resistance met with by body moving over another; clash of wills *etc.*, disagreement —**fric'tional** *a.*

Fri'day *n.* the sixth day of the week —**Good Friday** the Friday before Easter

fridge *n. inf.* refrigerator

fried *pt./pp. of* FRY[1]

friend [frend] *n.* one well known to another and regarded with affection and loyalty; intimate associate; supporter; (**F-**) Quaker —**friend'less** *a.* —**friend'liness** *n.* —**friend'ly** *a.* having disposition of a friend, kind; favourable —**friend'ship** *n.*

frieze[1] [frēz] *n.* ornamental band, strip (on wall)

frieze[2] [frēz] *n.* kind of coarse woollen cloth

frig'ate *n.* old (sailing) warship corresponding to modern cruiser; fast destroyerlike warship equipped for escort and antisubmarine duties —**frigate bird** bird of tropical and subtropical seas, with wide wingspan

fright [frīt] *n.* sudden fear; shock; alarm; grotesque or ludicrous person or thing —*vt. obs.* frighten —**fright'en** *vt.* cause fear, fright in —**fright'ful** *a.* terrible, calamitous; shocking; *inf.* very great, very large —**fright'fully** *adv. inf.* terribly; very —**fright'fulness** *n.*

frig'id [-ij'-] *a.* formal, dull; (sexually) unfeeling; cold —**frigid'ity** *n.* —**frig'idly** *adv.*

frill *n.* fluted strip of fabric gathered at one edge; ruff of hair, feathers around neck of dog, bird *etc.*; fringe; unnecessary words, politeness; superfluous thing; adornment —*vt.* make into, decorate with frill

fringe *n.* ornamental edge of hanging threads, tassels *etc.*; anything like this; hair cut in front and falling over brow; edge, limit —*vt.* adorn with, serve as, fringe —*a.* (of theatre *etc.*) unofficial, unconventional, extra

fripp'ery *n.* finery; trivia

frisk *vi.* move, leap, playfully —*vt.* wave briskly; *inf.* search (person) for concealed weapons *etc.* —*n.* —**frisk'ily** *adv.* —**frisk'y** *a.*

fritill'ary *n.* plant with purple or white bell-shaped flowers

fritt'er[1] *vt.* waste —**fritter away** throw away, waste

fritt'er[2] *n.* piece of food fried in batter

friv'olous *a.* not serious, unimportant; flippant —**frivol'ity** *n.*

frizz *vt.* crisp, curl into small curls —*n.* frizzed hair —**frizz'y** *a.* crimped

friz'zle *v.* fry, toast or grill with sizzling sound

fro *adv.* away, from (*only in* **to and fro**)

frock *n.* woman's dress; various similar garments —*vt.* invest with office of priest

frog[1] *n.* tailless amphibious animal developed from tadpole —**frog'man** *n.* swimmer equipped for swimming, working, underwater

frog[2] *n.* military-style coat fastening of button and loop; attachment to belt to carry sword

frol'ic *n.* merrymaking —*vi.* behave playfully (**frol'icked, frol'icking**) —**frol'icsome** *a.*

from *prep.* expressing point of departure, source, distance, cause, change of state *etc.*

frond *n.* plant organ consisting of stem and foliage, usually with fruit forms, *esp.* in ferns

front [-unt] *n.* fore part; position directly before or ahead; land bordering lake, street *etc.*; battle line or area; *Meteorology* dividing line between two air masses of different characteristics; outward aspect, bearing; *inf.* something serving as a respectable cover for another, *usu.* criminal, activity; field of activity; group with common goal —*v.* look, face; *inf.* be a cover for —*a.* of, at, the front —**front'age** *n.* façade of building; extent of front —**front'al** *a.* —**front'ier** *n.* edge of settled area of country; part of country which borders on another —**fron'tispiece** *n.* illustration facing title page of book

frost *n.* frozen dew or mist; act or state of freezing; weather in which temperature falls below point at which water turns to ice —*v.* cover, be covered with frost or something similar in appearance, as icing or frosting on cakes; give slightly roughened surface —**frost'ily** *adv.* —**frost'ing** *n.* mixture of sugar and water *etc.* used to decorate cakes —**frost'y** *a.* accompanied by frost; chilly; cold; unfriendly —**frost'bite** *n.* destruction by cold of tissue, *esp.* of fingers, ears *etc.*

froth [-th] *n.* collection of small bubbles, foam; scum; idle talk —*v.* (cause to) foam —**froth'ily** *adv.* —**froth'y** *a.*

frown *vi.* wrinkle brows —*n.*

frow'zy *a.* dirty, unkempt

froze *pt.* —**fro'zen** *pp. of* FREEZE

fruc'tify *v.* (cause to) bear fruit (**fruc'tified, fruc'tifying**) —**fructifica'tion** *n.*

fru'gal [froo͞'-] *a.* sparing; thrifty, economical; meagre —**frugal'ity** *n.* —**fru'gally** *adv.*

fruit [-o͞o-] *n.* seed and its envelope, *esp.* edible one; vegetable product; (*usu. in pl.*) result, benefit —*vi.* bear fruit —**fruit'erer** *n.* dealer in fruit —**fruit'ful** *a.* —**frui'tion** [-o͞o-ish'-] *n.* enjoyment; realization of hopes —**fruit'less** *a.* —**fruit'y** *a.*

frump *n.* dowdy woman —**frump'ish, frump'y** *a.*

frustrate' *vt.* thwart, balk; baffle, disappoint —**frustra'tion** *n.*

fry[1] *vt.* cook with fat —*vi.* be cooked thus (**fried, fry'ing**) —*n.* fried meat; dish of anything fried; social occasion, oft. outdoors, at which fried food is eaten

fry[2] *n.* young fishes —**small fry** young or insignificant beings

ft. feet; foot; fort

fu'chsia [fyōō'shə] *n.* ornamental shrub with purple-red flowers

fud'dle *v.* (cause to) be intoxicated, confused —*n.* this state

fudd'y-dudd'y *n. inf.* (elderly) dull person

fudge[1] *n.* soft, variously flavoured sweet

fudge[2] *vt.* make, do carelessly or dishonestly; fake

fu'el *n.* material for burning as source of heat or power; something which nourishes —*vt.* provide with fuel

fug *n.* stuffy indoor atmosphere —**fug'gy** *a.*

fu'gitive *n.* one who flees, *esp.* from arrest or pursuit —*a.* fleeing, elusive

fugue [fyōōg] *n.* musical composition in which themes are repeated in different parts

Führ'er [fyoor'-] *n.* leader, title of German dictator, *esp.* Hitler

ful'crum *n.* point on which a lever is placed for support (*pl.* **ful'cra**)

fulfil' [fool-] *vi.* satisfy; carry out; obey; satisfy (desire *etc.*) (**-ll-**) —**fulfil'ment** *n.*

full [fool] *a.* containing as much as possible; abundant; complete; ample; plump; (of garment) of ample cut —*adv.* very; quite; exactly —**full'y** *adv.* —**full'ness, ful'ness** *n.* —**ful'some** *a.* excessive —**fullblown'** *a.* fully developed

ful'mar [fool'-] *n.* Arctic sea bird

ful'minate *vi.* (*esp. with* against) criticize harshly —*n.* chemical compound exploding readily —**fulmina'tion** *n.*

ful'some *see* FULL

fum'ble *v.* grope about; handle awkwardly —*n.* awkward attempt

fume [fyōōm] *vi.* be angry; emit smoke or vapour —*n.* smoke; vapour —**fu'migate** *vt.* apply fumes or smoke to, *esp.* for disinfection —**fumiga'tion** *n.* —**fu'migator** *n.*

fun *n.* anything enjoyable, amusing *etc.* —**funn'ies** *pl.n. inf.* comic strips in newspaper —**funn'ily** *adv.* —**funn'y** *a.* comical; odd; difficult to explain

func'tion [-ngk'-] *n.* work a thing is designed to do; (large) social event; duty; profession; *Math.* quantity whose value depends on varying value of another —*vi.* operate, work —**func'tional** *a.* having a special purpose; practical, necessary; capable of operating —**func'tionary** *n.* official

fund *n.* stock or sum of money; supply, store —*pl.* money resources —*vt.* (in financial, business dealings) provide or obtain fund(s) in various ways

fundament'al *a.* of, affecting, or serving as, the base; essential, primary —*n.* basic rule or fact —**fund'ament** *n.* buttocks; foundation —**fundament'alism** *n.* —**fundament'alist** *n.* one laying stress on belief in literal and verbal inspiration of Bible and other traditional creeds

fu'neral *n.* (ceremony associated with) burial or cremation of dead —**fune'real** [-nē'-] *a.* like a funeral; dark; gloomy

fun'gus [-ng'g-] *n.* plant without leaves, flowers, or roots, as mushroom, mould (*pl.* **-gi** [-jī, -gī, -ji], **-guses**) —**fun'gal, fun'gous** *a.* —**fun'gicide** *n.* fungus destroyer

funic'ular [fyōō-] *n.* cable railway on mountainside with two counterbalanced cars

funk *n.* panic (*esp.* **blue funk**)

funn'el *n.* cone-shaped vessel or tube; chimney of locomotive or ship; ventilating shaft —*v.* (cause to) move as through funnel; concentrate, focus

funn'y *see* FUN

fur *n.* soft hair of animal; garment *etc.* of dressed skins with such hair; furlike coating —*vt.* cover with fur (**-rr-**) —**furr'ier** *n.* dealer in furs —**fur'ry** *a.* of, like fur

fur'bish *vt.* clean up

fur'cate(d) *a.* forked, branching

fur'ious [fyoor'-] *a.* extremely angry; violent —**fur'iously** *adv.* —**fu'riousness** *n.*

furl *vt.* roll up and bind (sail, umbrella *etc.*)

fur'long *n.* eighth of mile

fur'lough [-lō] *n.* leave of absence, *esp.* to soldier

fur'nace *n.* apparatus for applying great heat to metals; closed fireplace for heating boiler *etc.*; hot place

fur'nish *vt.* fit up house with furniture; equip; supply, yield —**fur'nishings** *pl.n.* furniture and accessories of house; articles of dress and accessories —**fur'niture** *n.* movable contents of a house or room

furor'e [fyoo-] *n.* public outburst, *esp.* of protest; sudden enthusiasm

furr'ow [-ō] *n.* trench as made by plough; groove —*vt.* make furrows in

fur'ther [-TH-] *adv.* more; in addition; at or to a greater distance or extent —*a.* more distant; additional —*comp. of* FAR, FORE[1] —*vt.* help forward; promote —**fur'therance** *n.* —**fur'therer** *n.* —**fur'thermore** *adv.* besides —**fur'thermost** *a.* —**fur'thest** *a. sup. of* FAR, FORE[1] —*adv.*

fur'tive *a.* stealthy, sly, secret —**fur'tively** *adv.*

fur'y [fyoor'-] *n.* wild rage, violent anger; violence of storm *etc.*; (*usu. pl.*) snake-haired avenging deity

furze *n.* prickly shrub, gorse

fus'cous [-kəs] *a.* dark-coloured

fuse [fyo͞oz] *v.* blend by melting; melt with heat; amalgamate; (cause to) fail as a result of blown fuse —*n.* soft wire, with low melting point, used as safety device in electrical systems; device (*orig.* combustible cord) for igniting bomb *etc.* —**fu'sible** *a.* —**fu'sion** *n.* melting; state of being melted; union of things, as atomic nuclei, as if melted together

fu'selage [-ahzh] *n.* body of aircraft

fusilier' [fyo͞o-zi-] *n.* soldier of certain regiments —**fusillade'** *n.* continuous discharge of firearms

fuss *n.* needless bustle or concern; complaint; objection —*vi.* make fuss —**fuss'ily** *adv.* —**fuss'iness** *n.* —**fuss'y** *a.* particular; faddy; overmeticulous; overelaborate

fus'tian *n.* thick cotton cloth; inflated language

fus'ty *a.* mouldy; smelling of damp; old-fashioned —**fus'tily** *adv.* —**fus'tiness** *n.*

fu'tile *a.* useless, ineffectual, trifling —**futil'ity** *n.*

fu'ton [fo͞o'-] *n.* Japanese padded quilt, laid on floor as bed

fu'ture *n.* time to come; what will happen; tense of verb indicating this; likelihood of development —*a.* that will be; of, relating to, time to come —**fu'turism** *n.* movement in art marked by revolt against tradition —**fu'turist** *n./a.* —**futuris'tic** *a.* ultra-modern —**futur'ity** *n.*

fuzz *n.* fluff; fluffy or frizzed hair; blur; *sl.* police(man) —**fuzz'y** *a.* fluffy, frizzy; blurred, indistinct

fwd. forward

G

g gram(s); (acceleration due to) gravity

gab'ble *v.* talk, utter inarticulately or too fast (**gab'bled, gab'bling**) —*n.* such talk —**gab** *inf. n./v.* talk, chatter —**gab'by** *a. inf.* talkative

gab'erdine, gab'ardine [-ēn] *n.* fine twill cloth like serge used *esp.* for raincoats; *Hist.* loose upper garment worn by Jews

ga'ble *n.* triangular upper part of wall at end of ridged roof —**gable end**

gad *vi.* (*esp. with* about) go around in search of pleasure (**-dd-**) —**gad'about** *n.* pleasure-seeker

gad'fly *n.* cattle-biting fly; worrying person

gadg'et *n.* small mechanical device; object valued for its novelty or ingenuity —**gadg'etry** *n.*

Gael [gāl] *n.* one who speaks Gaelic —**Gae'lic** *n.* language of Ireland and Scottish Highlands —*a.* of Gaels, their language or customs

gaff *n.* stick with iron hook for landing fish; spar for top of fore-and-aft sail —*vt.* seize (fish) with gaff

gaffe *n.* blunder; tactless remark

gaff'er *n.* old man

gag[1] *vt.* stop up (person's mouth) with cloth *etc.* —*vi. sl.* retch, choke (**-gg-**) —*n.* cloth *etc.* put into, tied across mouth

gag[2] *n.* joke, funny story, gimmick

ga'ga [gah'gah] *sl. a.* senile; crazy

gage[1] [gāj] *n.* pledge, thing given as security; challenge, or something symbolizing one

gage[2] [gāj] *see* GAUGE

gag'gle *n.* flock of geese; *inf.* disorderly crowd

gai'ety *see* GAY

gain *vt.* obtain, secure; obtain as profit; win; earn; reach —*vi.* increase, improve; get nearer; (of watch, machine *etc.*) operate too fast —*n.* profit; increase, improvement —**gain'fully** *adv.* profitably; for a wage, salary

gainsay' *vt.* deny, contradict (**gainsaid, gainsaying**)

gait [gāt] *n.* manner of walking; pace

gait'er *n.* covering of leather, cloth *etc.* for lower leg

Gal. Galatians

gal'a [gahl'ə] *n.* festive occasion; show

gal'axy *n.* system of stars bound by gravitational forces; splendid gathering, *esp.* of famous people —**galac'tic** *a.*

gale *n.* strong wind; *inf.* loud outburst, *esp.* of laughter

gale'na *n.* sulphide of, and principal ore of lead

gal(l)'ivant, gal'avant *vi.* gad about

gall[1] [gawl] *n. inf.* impudence; bitterness —**gall bladder** sac attached to liver, reservoir for bile —**gall'stone** *n.* hard secretion in gall bladder or ducts leading from it

gall[2] [gawl] *n.* painful swelling, *esp.* on horse; sore caused by chafing —*vt.* make sore by rubbing; vex, irritate

gall[3] [gawl] *n.* abnormal outgrowth on trees *etc.*

gall'ant *a.* fine, stately, brave; [*also* -lant'] chivalrous, very attentive to women —*n.* [*also* -lant'] lover, suitor; dashing, fashionable young man —**gall'antly** *adv.* —**gall'antry** *n.*

gall'eon *n.* large, high-built sailing ship of war

gall'ery *n.* covered walk with side openings, colonnade; platform or projecting upper floor in church, theatre *etc.*; group of spectators; long, narrow platform on outside of building; room or rooms for special purposes, *eg* showing works of art; passage in wall, open to interior of building; horizontal passage in mining

gall'ey *n.* one-decked vessel with sails and oars, usu. rowed by slaves or criminals; kitchen of ship or aircraft; large rowing boat; printer's tray for composed type —**galley proof** printer's proof in long slip form —**galley slave** one condemned to row in galley; drudge

Gall'ic *a.* of ancient Gaul; French —**gal'licism** *n.* French word or idiom

gall'ium *n.* soft, grey metal of great fusibility

gall'on *n.* **C, UK** liquid measure equal to 277.42 cu.in. (**US** 231 cu.in.)

gall'op *v.* go, ride at gallop; move fast —*n.* horse's fastest pace with all four feet off ground together in each stride; ride at this pace —**gall'oper** *n.* —**gall'oping** *a.* at a gallop; speedy, swift

gall'ows [-ōz] *n.* structure, usu. of two upright beams and crossbar, *esp.* for hanging criminals

Gall'up poll *n.* method of finding out public opinion by questioning a cross section of the population

galoot' *n. inf.* silly, clumsy person

galore' *adv.* in plenty

galosh'es *pl.n.* waterproof overshoes

galvan'ic *a.* of, producing, concerning electric current, *esp.* when produced chemically; *inf.* resembling effect of electric shock, startling —**gal'vanize** *vt.* stimulate to action; excite, startle; cover (iron *etc.*) with protective zinc coating

gam'bit *n. Chess* opening involving offer of a pawn; any opening manoeuvre, comment *etc.* intended to secure an advantage

gam'ble *vi.* play games of chance to win money; act on expectation of something —*n.* risky undertaking; bet, wager —**gam'bler** *n.*

gamboge' [-ōzh'] *n.* gum resin used as yellow pigment

gam'bol *vi.* skip, jump playfully (-**ll**-) —*n.*

game[1] *n.* diversion, pastime; jest; contest for amusement; scheme, strategy; animals or birds hunted; their flesh —*a.* brave; willing —*vi.* gamble —**game'ster** *n.* gambler —**game'cock** *n.* fowl bred for fighting —**game'keeper** *n.* man employed to breed game, prevent poaching

game[2], **gamm'y** *a.* lame, crippled

gam'ete [-ēt] *n. Biology* a sexual cell that unites with another for reproduction or the formation of a new individual

gamm'a *n.* third letter of the Greek alphabet —**gamma ray** a very penetrative electromagnetic ray

gamm'on *n.* cured or smoked ham; bottom piece of flitch of bacon

gamm'y *a. see* GAME[2]

gam'ut *n.* whole range or scale (*orig.* of musical notes)

gan'der *n.* male goose; *inf.* a quick look

gang *n.* (criminal) group; organized group of workmen —*vi.* (*esp. with* together) form gang —**gang up (on)** *inf.* combine against

gan'gling [-ng'g-] *a.* lanky, awkward in movement

gan'glion [-ng'g-] *n.* nerve nucleus

gang'plank *n.* portable bridge for boarding or leaving vessel

gan'grene [-ng'g-] *n.* death or decay of body tissue as a result of disease or injury —**gan'grenous** *a.*

gang'ster *n.* member of criminal gang; notorious or hardened criminal

gang'way *n.* bridge from ship to shore; anything similar; passage between row of seats —*interj.* make way, please!

gann'et *n.* predatory sea bird

gan'oid *a./n.* (fish) with smooth, hard, enamelled, bony scales, *eg* sturgeon

gan'try *n.* structure to support crane, railway signals *etc.*; framework beside rocket on launching pad

gaol [jāl] *n.* **UK** *see* JAIL

gap *n.* breach, opening, interval; cleft; empty space

gape *vi.* stare in wonder; open mouth wide, as in yawning; be, become wide open —*n.*

gar'age [ga'rahzh, -rij] *n.* (part of) building to house automobiles; refuelling and repair centre for automobiles —*vt.* leave automobile in garage

garb *n.* dress; fashion of dress —*vt.* dress, clothe

gar'bage [-ij] *n.* refuse, waste material —**garbage can** container for household waste

gar'ble *vt.* jumble or distort story, account *etc.*

gar'den *n.* ground for growing flowers, fruit, or vegetables —*vi.* cultivate garden —**gar'dener** *n.* —**gar'dening** *n.*

garde'nia [-ē-] *n.* (sub)tropical shrub, with fragrant white or yellow flowers

gar'(fish) *n.* elongated bony fish

gargan'tuan *a.* immense, enormous, huge

gar'gle *vi.* wash throat with liquid kept moving by the breath —*vt.* wash (throat) thus —*n.* gargling; preparation for this purpose

gar'goyle *n.* carved (grotesque) face on waterspout, *esp.* on Gothic church
ga'rish *a.* showy; gaudy
gar'land *n.* wreath of flowers worn or hung as decoration —*vt.* decorate with garlands
gar'lic *n.* (bulb of) plant with strong smell and taste, used in cooking and seasoning
gar'ment *n.* article of clothing —*pl.* clothes
gar'ner *vt.* store up, collect, as if in granary
gar'net *n.* red semiprecious stone
gar'nish *vt.* adorn, decorate (*esp.* food) —*n.* material for this
garr'et *n.* room on top floor, attic
garr'ison *n.* troops stationed in town, fort *etc.*; fortified place —*vt.* furnish or occupy with garrison
garrotte' *n.* Spanish capital punishment by strangling; apparatus for this —*vt.* execute, kill thus —**garrott'er** *n.*
garr'ulous *a.* (frivolously) talkative —**garru'lity** *n.* loquacity
gar'ter *n.* band or strap worn round leg to hold up sock or stocking
gas *n.* air-like substance, *esp.* one that does not liquefy or solidify at ordinary temperatures; fossil fuel in form of gas, used for heating or lighting; gaseous anaesthetic; poisonous or irritant substance dispersed through atmosphere in warfare *etc.*; gasoline; *inf.* idle, boastful talk (*pl.* **-es**) —*vt.* project gas over; poison with gas —*vi. inf.* talk idly, boastfully (**-ss-**) —**gas'eous** *a.* of, like gas —**gas'sy** *a.* —**gas'bag** *n. sl.* person who talks idly —**gas mask** mask with chemical filter to guard against poisoning by gas —**gasom'eter** *n.* tank for storing coal gas *etc.* —**gas station** garage selling oil, gasoline *etc.*
gash *n.* gaping wound, slash —*vt.* cut deeply
gas'ket *n.* rubber, asbestos *etc.* used as seal between metal faces, *esp.* in engines
gas'oline, -ene [-ēn] *n.* refined petroleum used in automobiles *etc.*
gasp [-ah-] *vi.* catch breath with open mouth, as in exhaustion or surprise —*n.* convulsive catching of breath
gas'tric *a.* of stomach —**gastronom'ical** *a.* —**gastron'omy** *n.* art of good eating
gastroenteri'tis *n.* inflammation of stomach and intestines
gas't(e)ropod *n.* mollusc, *eg* snail, with disc-like organ of locomotion on ventral surface
gate *n.* opening in wall, fence *etc.*; barrier for closing it; sluice; any entrance or way out; (entrance money paid by) those attending sporting event —**gate-crash** *v.* enter meeting, social function *etc.* uninvited
gât'eau [-ō] *n.* **UK** elaborate, rich cake (*pl.* **-x**)
gath'er [gaTH'-] *v.* (cause to) assemble; increase gradually; draw together —*vt.* collect; learn, understand; draw material into small tucks or folds —**gath'ering** *n.* assembly
gauche [gōsh] *a.* tactless, blundering —**gauch'erie** *n.* awkwardness, clumsiness
gauch'o [gowch'-] *n.* S Amer. cowboy
gaud [-aw-] *n.* showy ornament —**gaud'ily** *adv.* —**gaud'iness** *n.* —**gaud'y** *a.* showy in tasteless way
gauge [gāj] *n.* standard measure, as of diameter of wire, thickness of sheet metal *etc.*; distance between rails of railway; capacity, extent; instrument for measuring such things as wire, rainfall, height of water in boiler *etc.* —*vt.* measure; estimate
gaunt [-aw-] *a.* lean, haggard
gaunt'let [-aw-] *n.* armoured glove; glove covering part of arm —**run the gauntlet** formerly, run as punishment between two lines of men striking at runner with sticks *etc.*; be exposed to criticism or unpleasant treatment; undergo ordeal —**throw down the gauntlet** offer challenge
gauss [gows] *n.* unit of density of magnetic field
gauze [-aw-] *n.* thin transparent fabric of silk, wire *etc.* —**gauz'y** *a.*
gave *pt. of* GIVE
gav'el *n.* mallet of presiding officer or auctioneer
gavotte' *n.* lively dance; music for it
gawk *vi.* stare stupidly —**gaw'ky** *a.* clumsy, awkward
gay *a.* merry; lively; cheerful; bright; light-hearted; showy; given to pleasure; *inf.* homosexual —**gai'ety** *n.* —**gai'ly** *adv.*

gaze *vi.* look fixedly *—n.*

gaze'bo [-ē] *n.* summer-house, turret on roof, with extensive view

gazelle' *n.* small graceful antelope

gazette' *n.* official newspaper for announcements of government appointments *etc.*; newspaper title *—vt.* publish in gazette **—gazetteer'** *n.* geographical dictionary

GB Great Britain

GC George Cross

GDP gross domestic product

gear *n.* set of wheels working together, *esp.* by engaging cogs; connection by which engine, motor *etc.* is brought into work; arrangement by which driving wheel of cycle, automobile *etc.* performs more or fewer revolutions relative to pedals, pistons *etc.*; equipment; clothing; goods, utensils; apparatus, tackle, tools; rigging; harness *—vt.* adapt (one thing) so as to conform with another; provide with gear; put in gear **—gear'box** *n.* case protecting gearing of bicycle, automobile *etc.* **—gear'shift** *n.* lever used to move gears, *esp.* in motor vehicle **—in gear** connected up and ready for work **—out of gear** disconnected, out of working order

geese *pl. of* GOOSE

gee'zer *n. inf.* (old, eccentric) man

Gei'ger counter [gī'-] *n.* instrument for detecting radioactivity, cosmic radiation and charged atomic particles

gei'sha [gā'-] *n.* in Japan, professional female companion for men

gel [jel] *n.* jelly-like substance; such substance applied to hair before styling to retain shape *—vi.* form a gel (**-ll-**) *Also* **jell**

gel'atin(e) [jel'-] *n.* substance prepared from animal bones *etc.*, producing edible jelly; anything resembling this **—gelat'inous** *a.* like gelatin or jelly

geld *vt.* castrate **—geld'ing** *n.* castrated horse

gel'id [jel'-] *a.* very cold

gel'ignite [jel'-] *n.* powerful explosive consisting of dynamite in gelatin form

gem *n.* precious stone, *esp.* when cut and polished; treasure *—vt.* adorn with gems (**-mm-**)

gem'inate *vt.* double, pair, repeat **—gemina'tion** *n.*

Gem'ini *n.* (the twins) 3rd sign of the zodiac, operative May 21-June 20

gems'bok [-buk] *n.* S Afr. oryx

Gen. General; Genesis

gen [j-] *n. inf.* information

gen. gender; general; genitive; genus

gendarme' [zhon-] *n.* policeman in France

gen'der [j-] *n.* sex, male or female; grammatical classification of nouns, according to sex (actual or attributed)

gene [jēn] *n.* biological factor determining inherited characteristics

geneal'ogy [jē-] *n.* account of descent from ancestors; pedigree; study of pedigrees **—genealog'ical** *a.* **—geneal'ogist** *n.*

gen'era [j-] *pl. of* GENUS

gen'eral [j-] *a.* common, widespread; not particular or specific; applicable to all or most; not restricted to one department; usual, prevalent; miscellaneous; dealing with main element only; vague, indefinite *—n.* army officer of rank above colonel **—general'ity** *n.* general principle; vague statement; indefiniteness **—generaliza'tion** *n.* general conclusion from particular instance; inference **—gen'eralize** *vt.* reduce to general laws *—vi.* draw general conclusions **—gen'erally** *adv.* **—general practitioner** nonspecialist doctor with practice serving particular local area

gen'erate [j-] *vt.* bring into being; produce **—genera'tion** *n.* bringing into being; all persons born about same time; average time between two such generations (about 30 years) **—gen'erative** *a.* **—gen'erator** *n.* apparatus for producing (steam, electricity *etc.*); begetter

gener'ic [ji-ne'rik] *a.* belonging to, characteristic of class or genus **—gener'ically** *adv.*

gen'erous [j-] *a.* liberal, free in giving; abundant **—generos'ity** *n.* **—gen'erously** *adv.*

gen'esis [j-] *n.* origin; mode of formation; (**G-**) first book of Bible (*pl.* **-eses**)

gen'et [j-] *n.* catlike mammal of Afr. and S Europe

genet'ics [j-] *pl.n.* (*with sing. v.*) scientific study of heredity and variation in organisms **—genet'ic** *a.*

ge'nial [jē'-] *a.* cheerful, warm in behaviour; mild, conducive to growth —**geni'al'ity** *n.* —**ge'nially** *adv.*

ge'nie [jē'-] *n.* in fairy tales, servant appearing by, and working, magic (*pl.* **ge'nii**)

gen'ital [j-] *a.* relating to sexual organs or reproduction —**gen'itals** *pl.n.* the sexual organs

gen'itive [j-] *a./n.* possessive (case) —**geniti'val** *a.*

ge'nius [jē'-] *n.* (person with) exceptional power or ability, *esp.* of mind; distinctive spirit or nature (of nation *etc.*)

gen'ocide [j-] *n.* murder of a nationality or ethnic group

genre [zhahn'rə] *n.* kind; sort; style; painting of homely scene

gent [j-] *inf. n.* gentleman

genteel' [j-] *a.* well-bred; stylish; affectedly proper —**genteel'ly** *adv.*

gen'tian [jen'shən] *n.* plant, usu. with blue flowers

gen'tile [j-] *a.* of race other than Jewish; heathen —*n.*

gen'tle [j-] *a.* mild, quiet, not rough or severe; soft and soothing; courteous; moderate; gradual; noble; well-born —**gentil'ity** *n.* noble birth; respectability, politeness —**gen'tleness** *n.* quality of being gentle; tenderness —**gent'ly** *adv.* —**gent'ry** *n.* people of social standing next below nobility —**gen'tleman** *n.* chivalrous well-bred man; man of good social position; man (used as a mark of politeness) —**gen'tlemanly, gen'tlemanlike** *a.* —**gentleman's agreement** agreement binding by honour but not valid in law —**gen'tlewoman** *n.*

gen'uflect [j-] *vi.* bend knee, *esp.* in worship —**genuflec'tion, genuflex'ion** *n.*

gen'uine [j-] *a.* real, true, not sham, authentic; sincere; pure

ge'nus [jē'-] *n.* class, order, group (*esp.* of insects, animals *etc.*) with common characteristics usu. comprising several species (*pl.* **gen'era**)

geocen'tric [jē-ō-sen'-] *a.* *Astronomy* measured, seen from the earth; having the earth as centre —**geocen'trically** *adv.*

ge'ode [jē'-] *n.* cavity lined with crystals; stone containing this

geodes'ic [jē-] *a.* of geometry of curved surfaces —**geodesic dome** light but strong hemispherical construction formed from set of polygons

geod'esy [ji-od'-] *n.* science of measuring the earth's surface

geog'raphy [j-] *n.* science of earth's form, physical features, climate, population *etc.* —**geog'rapher** *n.* —**geograph'ic(al)** *a.* —**geograph'ically** *adv.*

geol'ogy [j-] *n.* science of earth's crust, rocks, strata *etc.* —**geolog'ical** *a.* —**geolog'ically** *adv.* —**geol'ogist** *n.*

geom'etry [j-] *n.* science of properties and relations of lines, surfaces *etc.* —**geomet'rical** *a.* —**geomet'rically** *adv.* —**geometri'cian** *n.*

geophys'ics [j-] *n.* science dealing with physics of the earth —**geophys'ical** *a.* —**geophys'icist** *n.*

georgette' [jawr-jet'] *n.* fine, silky, semitransparent fabric

Georg'ian [jawrj'-] *a.* of the times of the four Georges (1714-1830) or of George V (1910-36)

georg'ic [jawrj'-] *n.* poem on rural life, *esp.* one by Virgil

geosta'tionary *a.* (of satellite) in orbit around earth so it remains over same point on surface

gera'nium [j-] *n.* common cultivated plant with red, pink or white flowers, pelargonium; strong pink colour

ger'bil [j-] *n.* burrowing, desert rodent of Asia and Africa

ger'ent [je'r-] *n.* ruler, governor, director

geria'trics, gerontol'ogy [j-] *n.* branch of science dealing with old age and its diseases —**geriat'ric** *a./n.* old (person)

germ [j-] *n.* microbe, *esp.* causing disease; elementary thing; rudiment of new organism, of animal or plant —**germici'dal** *a.* —**germ'icide** *n.* substance for destroying disease germs

Ger'man [j-] *n./a.* (language or native) of Germany —**German measles** rubella, mild disease with symptoms like measles —**German shepherd** large dog of wolfhound breed

ger'man [j-] *a.* of the same parents; closely akin (*only in* **brother-, sister-, cousin-german**)

germane' [j-] *a.* relevant, pertinent

germ'inate [j-] *v.* (cause to) sprout or begin to grow —**germina'tion** *n.*

gerr'ymander [j-] *vt.* manipulate constituency so as to favour one side —*n.*

ger'und [jer'-] *n.* noun formed from verb, *eg* living

Gestap'o [-ahp'o] *n.* secret state police in Nazi Germany

gesta'tion [j-] *n.* carrying of young in womb between conception and birth; this period

gestic'ulate [j-] *vi.* use expressive movements of hands and arms when speaking —**gesticula'tion** *n.*

ges'ture [j-] *n.* movement to convey meaning; indication of state of mind —*vi.* make such a movement

get *vt.* obtain, procure; contract; catch; earn; cause to go or come; bring into position or state; induce; engender; be in possession of, have (to do); *inf.* understand; learn by study —*vi.* succeed in coming or going; reach, attain; become (**got, gett'ing**) —**get'away** *n.* escape —**get across** be understood —**get at** gain access to; annoy; criticize; influence

gey'ser [gē'z-] *n.* hot spring throwing up spout of water from time to time; apparatus for heating water and delivering it from a tap

ghast'ly [gah-] *a. inf.* unpleasant; deathlike, pallid; *inf.* unwell; horrible —*adv.* sickly

gher'kin [ger'-] *n.* small cucumber used in pickling

ghett'o [get'-] *n.* densely populated (*esp.* by one racial group) slum area (*pl.* **-tos**)

g(h)ill'ie *n.* in Scotland, attendant for hunting or fishing

ghost [gō-] *n.* spirit, dead person appearing again; spectre; semblance; faint trace; one who writes work to appear under another's name —*v.* write another's work, speeches *etc.* —**ghost'ly** *a.*

ghoul [gōōl] *n.* malevolent spirit; person with morbid interests; fiend —**ghoul'ish** *a.* of or like ghoul; horrible

GHQ General Headquarters

G.I. *short for* **Government Issue**, stamped on US military equipment —*n. inf.* US soldier

gi'ant [jī'-] *n.* mythical being of superhuman size; very tall person, plant *etc.* —*a.* huge —**gigan'tic** *a.* enormous, huge

gibb'er [j-] *vi.* make meaningless sounds with mouth, jabber, chatter —**gib'berish** *n.* meaningless speech or words

gibb'et [j-] *n.* gallows; post with arm on which executed criminal was hung; death by hanging —*vt.* hang on gibbet; hold up to scorn

gibb'on *n.* type of ape

gibe [j-], **jibe** *v.* utter taunts; mock; jeer —*n.*

gib'lets [j-] *pl.n.* internal edible parts of fowl, as liver, gizzard *etc.*

gidd'y *a.* dizzy, feeling as if about to fall; liable to cause this feeling; flighty, frivolous —**gidd'ily** *adv.* —**gidd'iness** *n.*

gift *n.* thing given, present; faculty, power —*vt.* present (with); endow, bestow —**gift'ed** *a.* talented

gig *n.* light, two-wheeled carriage; *inf.* single booking of musicians to play at concert *etc.*; cluster of fish-hooks

gigan'tic [jī-] *see* GIANT

gig'gle *vi.* laugh nervously, foolishly —*n.* such a laugh; joke

gig'olo [zhig'-] *n.* man kept, paid, by (older) woman to be her escort, lover (*pl.* **-s**)

gild[1] *vt.* put thin layer of gold on; make falsely attractive (**gilded** *pt.* —**gilt** *or* **gilded** *pp.*) —**gilt** *a.* gilded —*n.* thin layer of gold put on; superficial appearance

gild[2] *see* GUILD

gill[1] [g-] *n.* breathing organ in fish (*usu. pl.*)

gill[2] [j-] *n.* liquid measure, quarter of pint (0.142 litres)

gill'yflower *n.* fragrant flower

gim'bals [j-] *pl.n.* pivoted rings, for keeping things, *eg* compass, horizontal at sea

gim'let *n.* boring tool, usu. with screw point

gimm'ick *n.* clever device, stratagem *etc., esp.* designed to attract attention or publicity

gimp *n.* narrow fabric or braid used as edging or trimming

gin[1] [j-] *n.* spirit flavoured with juniper berries

gin[2] [j-] *n.* primitive engine in which vertical shaft is turned to drive horizontal beam in a circle; machine for separating cotton from seeds; snare, trap

gin'ger [j-] *n.* plant with hot-tasting spicy root used in cooking *etc.*; the root;

inf. spirit, mettle; light reddish-yellow colour —*vt.* stimulate —**gin'gery** *a.* of, like ginger; hot; high-spirited; reddish —**ginger ale** ginger-flavoured soft drink —**ginger beer** effervescing beverage made by fermenting ginger —**gin'gerbread** *n.* cake flavoured with ginger

gin'gerly [j-] *adv.* cautiously, warily, reluctantly —*a.*

ging'ham [-ng'əm] *n.* cotton cloth, usu. checked, woven from dyed yarn

gink'go *n.* ornamental Chinese tree (*pl.* **-oes**)

gin'seng *n.* (root of) plant believed to have tonic and energy-giving properties

Gip'sy *n. see* GYPSY

giraffe' [ji-rahf'] *n.* Afr. ruminant animal, with spotted coat and very long neck and legs

gird *vt.* put belt round; fasten clothes thus; equip with, or belt on, a sword; prepare (oneself); encircle (**girt, gird'ed** *pt./pp*) —**gird'er** *n.* large beam, *esp.* of steel

gir'dle *n.* corset; waistband; anything that surrounds, encircles; griddle —*vt.* surround, encircle

girl *n.* female child; young (unmarried) woman —**girl'hood** *n.* —**girl'ish** *a.*

girt *pt./pp. of* GIRD

girth *n.* measurement round thing; UK cinch

gist [j-] *n.* substance, main point (of remarks *etc.*)

give [giv] *vt.* bestow, confer ownership of, make present of; deliver; impart; assign; yield, supply; utter; emit; be host of (party *etc.*); make over; cause to have —*vi.* yield, give way, move (**gave, giv'en, giv'ing**) —*n.* yielding, elasticity —**give'away** *n.* betrayal or disclosure, *esp.* when unintentional; something given, *esp.* with articles on sale, to increase sales, attract publicity —**give up** acknowledge defeat; abandon

gizz'ard *n.* part of bird's stomach

gla'brous, gla'brate *a.* smooth; without hairs or any unevenness

glac'é [glas'i] *a.* crystallized, candied, iced; glossy

glac'ier [-as'-, -ā'-] *n.* river of ice, slow-moving mass of ice formed by accumulated snow in mountain valleys —**gla'cial** *a.* of ice, or of glaciers; very cold —**gla'ciated** *a.* —**glacia'tion** *n.*

glad *a.* pleased; happy, joyous; giving joy —**gladd'en** *vt.* make glad —**glad'ly** *adv.* —**glad'ness** *n.* —**glad'rags** *pl.n.* *sl.* clothes for special occasions

glade *n.* clear, grassy space in wood or forest

glad'iator *n.* trained fighter in Roman arena

gladio'lus *n.* kind of iris, with sword-shaped leaves —**glad** *inf.* gladiolus

Glad'stone (bag) *n.* travelling bag

glair *n.* white of egg; sticky substance —*vt.* smear with white of egg —**glair'y** *a.*

glam'our *n.* alluring charm, fascination —**glam'orize** *vt.* make appear glamorous —**glam'orous** *a.*

glance [-ah-] *vi.* look rapidly or briefly; allude, touch; glide off something struck; pass quickly —*n.* brief look; flash; gleam; sudden (deflected) blow

gland *n.* one of various small organs controlling different bodily functions by chemical means —**gland'ers** *n.* contagious horse disease —**gland'ular** *a.*

glare [-ār] *vi.* look fiercely; shine brightly, intensely; be conspicuous —*n.* —**gla'ring** *a.*

glass [-ah-] *n.* hard transparent substance made by fusing sand, soda, potash *etc.*; things made of it; tumbler; its contents; lens; mirror; telescope; barometer; microscope —*pl.* spectacles —**glass'ily** *adv.* —**glass'iness** *n.* —**glass'y** *a.* like glass; expressionless —**glass'house** *n.* greenhouse; *inf.* army prison —**glass wool** insulating fabric

glauco'ma *n.* eye disease

glaze *vt.* furnish with glass; cover with glassy substance —*vi.* become glassy —*n.* transparent coating; substance used for this; glossy surface —**gla'zier** *n.* one who glazes windows

gleam *n.* slight or passing beam of light; faint or momentary show —*vi.* give out gleams

glean *v.* pick up (facts *etc.*); gather, pick up (*orig.*) after reapers in cornfields —**glean'er** *n.*

glebe *n.* land belonging to parish church or benefice

glee *n.* mirth, merriment; musical composition for three or more voices —**glee'ful** *a.* —**glee'fully** *adv.* —**glee club** a club for singing part songs

glen *n.* narrow valley, usu. wooded and with a stream, *esp.* in Scotland

glengarr'y *n.* Scottish woollen boat-shaped cap with ribbons hanging down back

glib *a.* fluent but insincere or superficial; plausible **—glib'ly** *adv.* **—glib'ness** *n.*

glide *vi.* pass smoothly and continuously; of airplane, move without use of engines *—n.* smooth, silent movement; *Mus.* sounds made in passing from tone to tone **—gli'der** *n.* aircraft without engine which moves in air currents **—gli'ding** *n.* sport of flying gliders

glimm'er *vi.* shine faintly, flicker *—n.* **—glimm'ering** *n.* faint gleam of light; faint idea, notion

glimpse *n.* brief or incomplete view *—vt.* catch glimpse of

glint *v.* flash, glance, glitter; reflect *—n.*

glissade' [-ahd'] *n.* gliding dance step; slide, usu. on feet down slope of ice *—vi.*

glis'ten [-is'n] *vi.* gleam by reflecting light

glitt'er *vi.* shine with bright quivering light, sparkle; be showy *—n.* lustre; sparkle; ice formed from freezing rain

gloa'ming [-ō'-] *n.* evening twilight

gloat *vi.* regard, dwell on with smugness or malicious satisfaction

glob *n.* soft lump or mass

globe *n.* sphere with map of earth or stars; heavenly sphere, *esp.* the earth; ball, sphere **—glo'bal** *a.* of globe; relating to whole world **—glob'ular** *a.* globe-shaped **—glob'ule** *n.* small round particle; drop **—glob'ulin** *n.* kind of simple protein **—globe'trotter** *n.* (habitual) worldwide traveller

glock'enspiel [-spēl] *n.* percussion instrument of metal bars which are struck with hammers

gloom *n.* darkness; melancholy, depression **—gloom'ily** *adv.* **—gloom'y** *a.*

glor'y *n.* renown, honourable fame; splendour; exalted or prosperous state; heavenly bliss *—vi.* take pride (in) (**glo'ried, glor'ying**) **—glorifica'tion** *n.* **—glo'rify** *vt.* make glorious; invest with glory (**-ified, -ifying**) **—glor'ious** *a.* illustrious; splendid; excellent; delightful **—glor'iously** *adv.*

gloss[1] *n.* surface shine, lustre *—vt.* put gloss on; (*esp. with* over) (try to) cover up, pass over (fault, error) **—gloss'iness** *n.* **—gloss'y** *a.* smooth, shiny *—n.* magazine printed on shiny paper

gloss[2] *n.* marginal interpretation of word; comment, explanation *—vt.* interpret; comment; explain away **—glos'sary** *n.* dictionary, vocabulary of special words

glott'is *n.* human vocal apparatus, larynx **—glott'al, glott'ic** *a.*

glove [-uv] *n.* covering for the hand *—vt.* cover with, or as with glove

glow [-ō] *vi.* give out light and heat without flames; shine; experience feeling of wellbeing or satisfaction; be or look hot; burn with emotion *—n.* shining heat; warmth of colour; feeling of wellbeing; ardour **—glow-worm** *n.* female insect giving out green light

glow'er [-ow'-] *vi.* scowl

gloxin'ia *n.* tropical plant with large bell-shaped flowers

glu'cose [gloo͞'-] *n.* type of sugar found in fruit *etc.*

glue [-o͞o] *n.* any natural or synthetic adhesive; any sticky substance *—vt.* fasten with glue **—glu'ey** *a.* **—glue-sniffer** *n.* **—glue-sniffing** *n.* practice of inhaling fumes of glue for intoxicating or hallucinatory effects

glum *a.* sullen, moody, gloomy

glut *n.* surfeit, excessive amount *—vt.* feed, gratify to the full or to excess; overstock (**-tt-**)

glu'ten [gloo͞'-] *n.* protein present in cereal grain **—glu'tinous** *a.* sticky, gluey

glutt'on[1] *n.* greedy person; one with great liking or capacity for something **—glutt'onous** *a.* like glutton, greedy **—glutt'ony** *n.*

glutt'on[2] *n.* wolverine

glyc'erin(e), glyc'erol [glis'-] *n.* colourless sweet liquid with wide application in chemistry and industry

glyp'tic *a.* pert. to carving, *esp.* on precious stones

GM George Medal

gm gram

GMT Greenwich Mean Time

gnarled [narld] *a.* knobby, rugged, twisted

gnash [n-] *v.* grind (teeth) together as in anger or pain

gnat [n-] *n.* small, biting, two-winged fly

gnaw [n-] *v.* bite or chew steadily; (*esp. with* at) cause distress to

gneiss [nīs] *n.* coarse-grained metamorphic rock

gnome [n-] *n.* legendary creature like small old man; international financier

gno'mic [nō'-] *a.* of or like an aphorism

gnos'tic [n-] *a.* of, relating to knowledge, *esp.* spiritual knowledge

GNP Gross National Product

gnu [noo] *n.* S Afr. antelope somewhat like ox

go *vi.* move along, make way; be moving; depart; function; make specified sound; fail, give way, break down; elapse; be kept, put; be able to be put; result; contribute to result; tend to; be accepted, have force; become (**went** *pt.*, **gone** *pp.*) —*n.* going; energy, vigour; attempt; turn —**go-cart** *n.* small wagon for child to ride in or pull; light frame on wheels for baby learning to walk (*also* **go-kart**) —**go-go dancer** dancer, *usu.* scantily dressed, who performs rhythmic and oft. erotic modern dance routines, *esp.* in nightclub

goad *n.* spiked stick for driving cattle; anything that urges to action; incentive —*vt.* urge on; torment

goal *n.* end of race; object of effort; posts through which ball is to be driven in football *etc.*; the score so made

goat *n.* four-footed animal with long hair, horns and beard —**goat'ee** *n.* beard like goat's —**goat-herd** *n.* —**goat'sucker** *n.* nocturnal bird with harsh cry —**get (someone's) goat** *sl.* annoy (someone)

gob *n.* lump —**gobb'et** *n.* lump (of food) —**gob'ble** *vt.* eat hastily, noisily or greedily

gob'ble *n.* throaty, gurgling cry of the turkey-cock —*vi.* make such a noise

gob'bledegook, gob'bledygook *n.* pretentious language, *esp.* as used by officials

gob'let *n.* drinking cup

gob'lin *n. Folklore* small, usu. malevolent being

god *n.* superhuman being worshipped as having supernatural power; object of worship, idol; (**G-**) in monotheistic religions, the Supreme Being, creator and ruler of universe (**godd'ess** *fem.*) —**god'like** *a.* —**god'liness** *n.* —**god'ly** *a.* devout, pious —**god'child** *n.* one considered in relation to **godparent** *n.* —**god'father** *n.* sponsor at baptism (*fem.* **god'mother**) —**god-fearing** *a.* religious, good —**god'forsaken** *a.* hopeless, dismal —**god'head** *n.* divine nature or deity —**god'send** *n.* something unexpected but welcome

gog'gle *vi.* (of eyes) bulge; stare —*pl.n.* protective spectacles

goi'tre [-tə] *n.* neck swelling due to enlargement of thyroid gland

go-kart (*or* **cart**) *n.* miniature, low-powered racing car

gold [-ō-] *n.* yellow precious metal; coins of this; wealth; beautiful or precious thing; colour of gold —*a.* of, like gold —**gold'en** *a.* —**gold-digger** *n.* person who prospects or mines for gold; *inf.* woman skilful in extracting money from men —**golden mean** middle way between extremes —**goldenrod'** *n.* tall plant with golden flower spikes —**golden rule** important principle —**golden wedding** fiftieth wedding anniversary —**gold'field** *n.* place where gold deposits are known to exist —**gold'finch** *n.* bird with yellow feathers —**gold'fish** *n.* any of various ornamental pond or aquarium fish —**gold standard** financial arrangement whereby currencies of countries accepting it are expressed in fixed terms of gold

golf *n.* outdoor game in which small hard ball is struck with clubs into a succession of holes —*vi.* play this game —**golf'er** *n.*

goll'iwog *n.* black-faced doll

gon'ad *n.* gland producing gametes

gon'dola *n.* Venetian canal boat; low open flat-bottomed railway freight car; broadcasting booth built close to roof over hockey arena —**gondolier'** *n.* rower of gondola

gone [gon] *pp. of* GO

gong *n.* metal plate with turned rim which resounds as bell when struck with soft mallet; anything used thus

gonorrhoe'a [-rē'ə] *n.* a venereal disease

good *a.* commendable; right; proper; excellent; beneficial; well-behaved; virtuous; kind; safe; adequate; sound; valid (**bett'er** *comp.*, **best** *sup.*) —*n.* benefit; wellbeing; profit —*pl.* property; wares —**good'ly** *a.* large, considerable —**good'ness** *n.* —**good will** kindly feeling, heartiness; value of a business in reputation *etc.* over and above its tangible assets —**the goods** *sl.* incriminating evidence

goodbye' *interj./n.* form of address on parting

goo'ey *a. inf.* sticky, soft

goof *inf. n.* mistake; stupid person —*vi.* make mistake —**goof'y** *a.* silly, sloppy

goo'gly *n. Cricket* ball which changes direction unexpectedly on the bounce

goon *n. inf.* stupid fellow

goose *n.* web-footed bird; its flesh; simpleton (*pl.* **geese**) —**goose flesh** bristling of skin due to cold, fright —**goose step** formal parade step

goose'berry [gooz'-] *n.* thorny shrub; its hairy fruit; *inf.* unwelcome third party

go'pher *n.* various species of Amer. burrowing rodents

gore[1] *n.* (dried) blood from wound —**go'rily** *adv.* —**go'ry** *a.*

gore[2] *vt.* pierce with horns

gore[3] *n.* triangular piece inserted to shape garment —*vt.* shape thus

gorge [-j] *n.* ravine; disgust, resentment —*vi.* feed greedily —**gor'get** [-jit] *n.* armour, ornamentation or clothing for throat

gor'geous [-jəs] *a.* splendid, showy, dazzling; *inf.* extremely pleasing

gor'gon *n.* terrifying or repulsive woman

gorill'a *n.* largest anthropoid ape, found in Afr.

gor'mandize *vt.* eat hurriedly or like a glutton

gorse *n.* prickly shrub

gory *see* GORE[1]

gos'hawk *n.* large hawk

gos'ling [-z-] *n.* young goose

gos'pel *n.* unquestionable truth; (**G-**) any of first four books of New Testament

goss'amer *n.* filmy substance like spider's web; thin gauze or silk fabric

goss'ip *n.* idle (malicious) talk about other persons, *esp.* regardless of fact; one who talks thus —*vi.* engage in gossip; chatter

got *see* GET

Goth'ic *a. Architecture* of the pointed arch style common in Europe from twelfth-sixteenth century; of Goths; barbarous; gloomy; grotesque; (of type) German black letter

gouge [gowj] *vt.* scoop out; force out; *inf.* extort from —*n.* chisel with curved cutting edge

gou'lash [gōō'-] *n.* stew of meat and vegetables seasoned with paprika

gourd [goord] *n.* trailing or climbing plant; its large fleshy fruit; its rind as vessel

gour'mand [goor'-] *n.* glutton

gour'met [goor'mā] *n.* connoisseur of wine, food; epicure

gout [-ow-] *n.* disease with inflammation, *esp.* of joints —**gout'y** *a.*

Gov. Government; Governor

gov'ern [guv-] *vt.* rule, direct, guide, control; decide or determine; be followed by (grammatical case *etc.*) —**gov'ernable** *a.* —**gov'ernance** *n.* act of governing —**gov'erness** *n.* woman teacher, *esp.* in private household —**gov'ernment** *n.* exercise of political authority in directing a people, state *etc.*; system by which community is ruled; body of people in charge of government of state; ministry; executive power; control; direction; exercise of authority —**governmen'tal** *a.* —**gov'ernor** *n.* one who governs, *esp.* one invested with supreme authority in state *etc.*; chief administrator of an institution; member of committee responsible for an organization or institution; regulator for speed of engine —**governor general** representative of the Crown in certain independent countries of the Commonwealth

gown *n.* loose flowing outer garment; woman's (long) dress; official robe, as in university *etc.*

goy *n. sl.* derogatory Jewish term for a non-Jew (*pl.* **goy'im, goys**)

GP General Practitioner

grab *vt.* grasp suddenly; snatch (**-bb-**) —*n.* sudden clutch; quick attempt to seize; device or implement for clutching

grace *n.* charm, elegance; accomplishment; goodwill, favour; sense of propriety; postponement granted; short thanksgiving before or after meal; title of duke or archbishop —*vt.* add grace to, honour —**grace'ful** *a.* —**grace'fully** *adv.* —**grace'less** *a.* shameless, depraved —**gra'cious** *a.* favourable; kind; pleasing; indulgent, beneficent, condescending —**gra'ciously** *adv.* —**grace note** *Mus.* melodic ornament

grade *n.* step, stage; degree of rank *etc.*; school class; mark, rating; slope or degree of slope *—vt.* arrange in classes; assign grade to; level ground, move earth with grader **—grada'tion** *n.* series of degrees or steps; each of them; arrangement in steps; in painting, gradual passing from one shade *etc.* to another **—gra'der** *n. esp.* machine with wide blade used in road making **—grade crossing** point where railroad and highway intersect **—make the grade** succeed

gra'dient *n.* (degree of) slope

grad'ual *a.* taking place by degrees; slow and steady; not steep **—grad'ually** *adv.*

grad'uate *vi.* take university degree *—vt.* divide into degrees; mark, arrange according to scale; confer degree, diploma *etc.* upon *—n.* holder of university degree; student who has completed course in high school and received diploma; container marked to indicate capacity **—gradua'tion** *n.*

graffi'ti [-fē'tē] *pl.n.* (*sing.* **graffi'to**) (oft. obscene) writing, drawing on walls

graft[1] [-ah-] *n.* shoot of plant set in stalk of another; the process; surgical transplant of skin, tissue *—vt.* insert (shoot) in another stalk; transplant (living tissue in surgery)

graft[2] [-ah-] *inf. n.* self-advancement, profit by unfair means, *esp.* through official or political privilege; bribe; swindle **—graft'er** *n.*

gra'ham [gra'əm] *a.* made from unsifted whole-wheat flour

grail *n.* (*usu.* **Holy Grail**) cup or dish used by Christ at the Last Supper

grain *n.* seed, fruit of cereal plant; wheat and allied plants; small hard particle; unit of weight, 1/7000th of pound avoirdupois (0.0648 gram); texture; arrangement of fibres; any very small amount; natural temperament or disposition **—grain'y** *a.*

gram(me) *n.* unit of weight in metric system, one thousandth of a kilogram

gramm'ar *n.* science of structure and usages of language; book on this; correct use of words **—gramma'rian** *n.* **—grammat'ical** *a.* according to grammar **—grammat'ically** *adv.* **—grammar school UK** *esp.* formerly, state-maintained secondary school providing education with strong academic bias; public school with grades between primary and high school

gram'ophone *n.* **UK** recordplayer

gram'pus *n.* type of dolphin

gran'ary *n.* storehouse for grain; rich grain growing region

grand *a.* imposing; magnificent; majestic; noble; splendid; eminent; lofty; chief, of chief importance; final (total) *—n. sl.* thousand dollars **—gran'deur** [-jə] *n.* nobility; magnificence; dignity **—grandil'oquence** *n.* **—grandil'oquent** *a.* pompous in speech **—grandil'oquently** *adv.* **—grand'iose** *a.* imposing; affectedly grand; striking **—grand'child** [-n'ch-] *n.* child of one's child (**grand'son** *or* **grand'daughter**) **—grand'parent** [-n(d)'-] *n.* parent of parent (**grand'father** *or* **grand'mother**) **—grand piano** large harp-shaped piano with horizontal strings **—grand'stand** [-n(d)'-] *n.* structure with tiered seats for spectators

grange [-j] *n.* country house with farm buildings

gran'ite [-it] *n.* hard crystalline igneous rock **—granit'ic** *a.*

graniv'orous *a.* feeding on grain or seeds

grann'ie, grann'y *n. inf.* grandmother

grant [-ah-] *vt.* consent to fulfil (request); permit; bestow; admit *—n.* sum of money provided by government for specific purpose, as education; gift; allowance, concession **—grantee'** *n.* **—grantor'** *n.*

gran'ule *n.* small grain **—gran'ular** *a.* of or like grains **—gran'ulate** *vt.* form into grains *—vi.* take form of grains **—granula'tion** *n.*

grape *n.* fruit of vine **—grape'shot** *n.* bullets scattering when fired **—grape'vine** *n.* grape-bearing vine; *inf.* unofficial means of conveying information

grape'fruit *n.* subtropical citrus fruit

graph *n.* drawing depicting relation of different numbers, quantities *etc.*

graph'ic *a.* vividly descriptive; of, in, relating to, writing, drawing, painting *etc.* **—graph'icacy** *n.* ability to understand and use maps, plans *etc.* **—graph'ically** *adv.* **—graph'ite** *n.* form of carbon (used in pencils) **—graphol'ogy** *n.* study of handwriting

grap'nel *n.* hooked iron instrument for seizing anything; small anchor with several flukes

grap'ple *v.* come to grips with, wrestle; cope or contend —*n.* grappling; grapnel

grasp [-ah-] *v.* (try, struggle to) seize hold; understand —*n.* act of grasping; grip; comprehension —**grasp'ing** *a.* greedy, avaricious

grass [-ah-] *n.* common type of plant with jointed stems and long narrow leaves (including cereals, bamboo *etc.*); such plants grown as lawn; pasture; *sl.* marijuana; **UK** *sl.* informer, *esp.* criminal who betrays others to police —*vt.* cover with grass; **UK** inform (on) —**grass hockey** hockey played on field —**grass'hopper** *n.* jumping, chirping insect —**grass roots** fundamentals —**grass'roots** *a.* coming from ordinary people, the rank-and-file —**grass widow** wife whose husband is absent

grate[1] *n.* framework of metal bars for holding fuel in fireplace —**gra'ting** *n.* framework of parallel or latticed bars covering opening

grate[2] *vt.* rub into small bits on rough surface —*vi.* rub with harsh noise; have irritating effect —**gra'ter** *n.* utensil with rough surface for reducing substance to small particles —**gra'ting** *a.* harsh; irritating

grate'ful *a.* thankful; appreciative; pleasing —**grate'fully** *adv.* —**grate'fulness** *n.* —**grat'itude** *n.* sense of being thankful for favour

grat'ify *vt.* satisfy; please; indulge —**gratifica'tion** *n.*

gratin' [gra-tan'] *n.* method of cooking to form light crust; dish so cooked

gra'tis [-ā'-, -a'-, -ah'-] *adv./a.* free, for nothing

gratu'itous *a.* given free; uncalled for —**gratu'itously** *adv.* —**gratu'ity** *n.* gift of money for services rendered; donation

grave[1] *n.* hole dug to bury corpse; death —**grave'stone** *n.* monument on grave —**grave'yard** *n.*

grave[2] *a.* serious, weighty; dignified, solemn; plain, dark in colour; deep in note —**grave'ly** *adv.*

grave[3] [-ah-] *n.* accent (`) over vowel to indicate special sound quality

grave[4] *vt.* clean (ship's bottom) by scraping (**graved** *pt./pp.*) —**graving dock** dry dock

grav'el *n.* small stones; coarse sand —*vt.* cover with gravel —**grav'elly** *a.*

gra'ven *a.* carved, engraved

grav'itate *vi.* move by gravity; tend (towards) centre of attraction; sink, settle down —**gravita'tion** *n.*

grav'ity *n.* force of attraction of one body for another, *esp.* of objects to the earth; heaviness; importance; seriousness; staidness

gra'vy *n.* juices from meat in cooking; sauce for food made from these —**gravy train** *sl.* job, situation giving rich rewards for little effort

gray *a. alt., esp. US, spelling of* GREY —**gray'ling** *n.* fish of salmon family

graze[1] *v.* feed on grass, pasture —**gra'zier** *n.* one who raises cattle for market

graze[2] *vt.* touch lightly in passing, scratch, scrape —*n.* grazing; abrasion

grease [-ēs] *n.* soft melted fat of animals; thick oil as lubricant —*vt.* [*or* -ēz] apply grease to —**greas'er** *n.* —**grea'sily** *adv.* —**grea'siness** *n.* —**grea'sy** *a.* —**grease gun** appliance for injecting oil or grease into machinery —**grease'paint** *n.* theatrical make-up

great [-āt] *a.* large, big; important; preeminent, distinguished; *inf.* excellent —*prefix* indicates a degree further removed in relationship, *eg* **great-grand'father** *n.* —**great'ly** *adv.* —**great'ness** *n.* —**great'coat** *n.* overcoat, *esp.* military —**Great Dane** breed of very large dog

greave *n.* armour for leg below knee

grebe *n.* aquatic bird

Gre'cian *a.* of (ancient) Greece

greed *n.* excessive consumption of, desire for, food, wealth —**greed'y** *a.* gluttonous; eagerly desirous; voracious; covetous —**greed'ily** *adv.* —**greed'iness** *n.* voracity of appetite

Greek *n.* native language of Greece —*a.* of Greece or Greek

green *a.* of colour between blue and yellow; grass-coloured; emerald; unripe; uncooked (*esp.* prawns); (of bacon) unsmoked; inexperienced; gullible; envious —*n.* colour; area of grass, *esp.* for playing bowls *etc.* —*pl.* green vegetables —**green'ery** *n.* vegetation —**green'fly** *n.* aphid, small green garden pest

—**green'gage** *n.* kind of plum —**green'grocer** *n.* UK dealer in vegetables and fruit —**green'grocery** *n.* —**green'horn** *n.* inexperienced person, newcomer —**green'house** *n.* glasshouse for rearing plants —**green'room** *n.* room for actors when offstage —**green'sward** *n.* turf —**green thumb** talent for gardening

greet *vt.* meet with expressions of welcome; accost, salute; receive —**greet'ing** *n.*

grega'rious *a.* fond of company, sociable; living in flocks —**grega'riousness** *n.*

grem'lin *n.* imaginary being blamed for mechanical and other troubles

grenade' *n.* explosive shell or bomb, thrown by hand or shot from rifle —**grenadier'** *n.* soldier of Grenadier Guards; formerly, grenade thrower

grenadine' [-ēn'] *n.* syrup made from pomegranate juice, for sweetening and colouring drinks

grew [gro͞o] *pt. of* GROW

grey [grā] *a.* between black and white, as ashes or lead; clouded; dismal; turning white; aged; intermediate, indeterminate —*n.* grey colour; grey or white horse

grey'hound *n.* swift slender dog used in coursing and racing

grid *n.* network of horizontal and vertical lines, bars *etc.*; any interconnecting system of links; national network of electricity supply

grid'dle, gir'dle *n.* flat iron plate for cooking

grid'iron *n.* frame of metal bars for grilling; (field of play for) American football

grief [-ēf] *n.* deep sorrow —**grie'vance** *n.* real or imaginary ground of complaint —**grieve** *vi.* feel grief —*vt.* cause grief to —**grie'vous** *a.* painful, oppressive; very serious

griff'in, griff'on, gryph'on *n.* fabulous monster with eagle's head and wings and lion's body

grill *n.* device on cooker to radiate heat downwards; food cooked under grill; gridiron —*v.* cook (food) under grill, broil; subject to severe questioning —**grill'ing** *a.* very hot —*n.* severe cross-examination —**grill'room** *n.* where grilled food is served

grill(e) *n.* grating, crosswork of bars over opening

grim *a.* stern; of stern or forbidding aspect, relentless; joyless —**grim'ly** *adv.*

grimace' *n.* wry face —*vi.* pull wry face

grime *n.* ingrained dirt, soot —*vt.* soil; dirty; blacken —**gri'my** *a.*

grin *vi.* show teeth, as in laughter (**-nn-**) —*n.* grinning smile

grind [-ī-] *vt.* crush to powder; oppress; make sharp, smooth; grate —*vi.* perform action of grinding; *inf.* work (*esp.* study) hard; grate (**ground** *pt./pp.*) —*n. inf.* hard work; action of grinding —**grind'er** *n.* —**grind'stone** *n.* stone used for grinding

grin'go [-ng'g-] *n.* in Mexico, contemptuous name for foreigner, esp. Englishman or Amer. (*pl.* **-s**)

grip *n.* firm hold, grasp; grasping power; mastery; handle; suitcase or travelling bag —*vt.* grasp or hold tightly; hold interest or attention of (**-pp-**)

gripe *vi. inf.* complain (persistently) —*n.* intestinal pain (*esp.* in infants); *inf.* complaint

gris'ly [-z-] *a.* grim, causing terror, ghastly

grist *n.* corn to be ground —**grist for one's mill** something which can be turned to advantage

gris'tle [gris'l] *n.* cartilage, tough flexible tissue

grit *n.* rough particles of sand; coarse sandstone; courage; (**G-**) *inf. n./a.* Liberal —*pl.* wheat *etc.* coarsely ground —*vt.* clench, grind (teeth) (**-tt-**) —**gritt'iness** *n.* —**gritt'y** *a.*

griz'zle[1] *v.* make, become grey —**griz'zled** *a.* —**griz'zly** (**bear**) large Amer. bear

griz'zle[2] *inf.* UK *vi.* grumble, whine, complain —**griz'zly** *a.*

groan *vi.* make low, deep sound of grief or pain; be in pain or overburdened —*n.*

groat *Hist.* *n.* fourpenny piece; *orig.* various European coins

gro'cer *n.* dealer in foodstuffs —**gro'ceries** *pl.n.* commodities sold by a grocer —**gro'cery** *n.* trade, premises of grocer

grog *n.* spirit (*esp.* rum) and water —**grogg'y** *a. inf.* unsteady, shaky, weak

groin *n.* fold where legs meet abdomen;

edge made by intersection of two vaults —*vt.* build with groins

groom *n.* person caring for horses; bridegroom; officer in royal household —*vt.* tend or look after; brush or clean (*esp.* horse); train (someone for something) —**grooms'man** *n.* friend attending bridegroom —**well-groomed** *a.* neat, smart

groove *n.* narrow channel, hollow, *esp.* cut by tool; rut, routine —*vt.* cut groove in —**groo'vy** *a. sl.* fashionable, exciting

grope *vi.* feel about, search blindly

gro'per [grō'-] *n. see* GROUPER

gros'beak [grōs'-] *n.* finch with large powerful bill

gross [-ōs] *a.* very fat; total, not net; coarse; indecent; flagrant; thick, rank —*n.* twelve dozen —**gross'ly** *adv.*

grotesque' [-tesk'] *a.* (horribly) distorted; absurd —*n.* decorative style using distorted human, animal and plant forms; grotesque person, thing —**grotesque'ly** *adv.*

grott'o *n.* cave (*pl.* **-o(e)s**)

grott'y *a. inf.* dirty, untidy, unpleasant

grouch *inf. n.* persistent grumbler; discontented mood —*vi.* grumble, be peevish

ground[1] *n.* surface of earth; soil, earth; reason, motive; coating to work on with paint; background, main surface worked on in painting, embroidery *etc.*; special area; bottom of sea; wire connecting electrical apparatus to earth —*pl.* dregs; enclosed land round house —*vt.* establish; instruct (in elements); place on ground; connect electrically with earth —*vi.* run ashore —**groun'ded** *a.* of aircraft, unable or not permitted to fly —**ground'ing** *n.* basic general knowledge of a subject —**ground'less** *a.* without reason —**ground'hog** *n.* Amer. burrowing marmot —**ground'nut** *n.* earthnut; peanut —**ground'sheet** *n.* waterproof sheet on ground under tent *etc.* —**ground'speed** *n.* aircraft's speed in relation to ground

ground[2] *pt./pp. of* GRIND

ground'sel *n.* yellow flowered plant

group [-ōō-] *n.* number of persons or things near together, or placed or classified together; small musical band of players or singers; class; two or more figures forming one artistic design —*v.* place, fall into group

group'er [-ōō-] *n.* large, edible sea fish

grouse[1] [-ows] *n.* game bird; its flesh (*pl.* **grouse**)

grouse[2] [-ows] *vi.* grumble, complain —*n.* complaint —**grous'er** *n.* grumbler

grout *n.* thin fluid mortar —*vt.* fill up with grout

grove *n.* small group of trees; road lined with trees

grov'el *vi.* abase oneself; lie face down (**-ll-**)

grow [-ō] *vi.* develop naturally; increase in size, height *etc.*; be produced; become by degrees —*vt.* produce by cultivation (**grew** *pt.*, **grown** *pp.*) —**growth** *n.* growing; increase; what has grown or is growing —**grown-up** *a./n.* adult

growl *vi.* make low guttural sound of anger; rumble; murmur, complain —*n.* —**growl'er** *n.* person or animal that growls; small iceberg broken off from larger iceberg or glacier

groyne *n.* wall or jetty built out from riverbank or shore to control erosion

grub *vt.* dig superficially; root up —*vi.* dig, rummage; plod (**-bb-**) —*n.* larva of insect; *sl.* food —**grubb'y** *a.* dirty —**grub'stake** *n. inf.* supplies provided for prospector on condition of having stake in any finds —*vt.* supply (someone) in this way

grudge *vt.* be unwilling to give, allow —*n.* ill will

gru'el [grōō'-] *n.* food of oatmeal *etc.*, boiled in milk or water —**gru'elling** *a./n.* exhausting, severe (experience)

grue'some [grōō'-] *a.* fearful, horrible, grisly —**grue'someness** *n.*

gruff *a.* rough in manner or voice, surly —**gruff'ly** *adv.*

grum'ble *vi.* complain; rumble, murmur; make growling sounds —*n.* complaint; low growl —**grum'bler** *n.*

grump'y *a.* ill-tempered, surly —**grump'ily** *adv.*

grunt *vi.* make sound characteristic of pig —*n.* pig's sound; gruff noise

gryph'on *n. see* GRIFFIN

G-string *n.* very small covering for genitals; *Mus.* string tuned to G

guan'o [gwahn'-] *n.* sea bird manure (*pl.* **-nos**)

guarantee' [ga-] *n.* formal assurance (*esp.* in writing) that product *etc.* will meet certain standards, last for given time *etc.* —*vt.* give guarantee of, for something; secure (against risk *etc.*) (**guaranteed'**, **guarantee'ing**) —**guarantor'** *n.* one who undertakes fulfilment of another's promises

guard [gah-] *vt.* protect, defend —*vi.* be careful, take precautions (against) —*n.* person, group that protects, supervises, keeps watch; sentry; soldiers protecting anything; official in charge of train; protection; screen for enclosing anything dangerous; protector; posture of defence —*pl.* (**G-**) certain British regiments —**guard'ian** *n.* keeper, protector; person having custody of infant *etc.* —**guard'ianship** *n.* care —**guard'-house, -room** *n.* place for stationing those on guard or for prisoners —**Guards'man** *n.* soldier in Guards

guav'a [gwahv'-] *n.* tropical tree with fruit used to make jelly

gudge'on *n.* small freshwater fish

guer'don [gur'-] *n.* reward

guer(r)ill'a [gə-] *n.* member of irregular armed force, *esp.* fighting established force, government *etc.* —*a.*

guern'sey [gurn'-] *n.* breed of cattle; close-fitting knitted jumper

guess [ges] *vt.* estimate without calculation; conjecture, suppose; consider, think —*vi.* form conjectures —*n.*

guest [gest] *n.* one entertained at another's house; one living in hotel

guff *n. sl.* silly talk

guffaw' *n.* burst of boisterous laughter —*vi.*

guide [gīd] *n.* one who shows the way; adviser; book of instruction or information; contrivance for directing motion —*vt.* lead, act as guide to; arrange —**gui'dance** *n.* —**Girl Guide** member of **Girl Guides' Association**, organization for girls similar to that of Scouts —**guided missile** missile whose flight path is controlled by radio or preprogrammed homing mechanism

g(u)ild [gi-] *n.* organization, club; society for mutual help, or with common object; *Hist.* society of merchants or tradesmen —**guild'hall** *n.* meeting place of guild or corporation

guile [gīl] *n.* cunning, deceit —**guile'ful** *a.* —**guile'fully** *adv.* —**guile'less** *a.*

guill'emot [gil'i-] *n.* species of sea bird

guill'otine [gil'ə-tēn] *n.* machine for beheading; machine for cutting paper; in parliament *etc.* method of restricting length of debate by fixing time for taking vote —*vt.* behead; use guillotine on; limit debate by guillotine

guilt [gilt] *n.* fact, state of having done wrong; responsibility for criminal or moral offence —**guilt'iness** *n.* —**guilt'ily** *adv.* —**guilt'less** *a.* innocent —**guilt'y** *a.* having committed an offence

guin'ea [gin'i] *n.* **UK** formerly, sum of 21 shillings; gold coin of this value —**guinea fowl** bird allied to pheasant —**guinea pig** rodent originating in S Amer.; *inf.* person or animal used in experiments

guise [gīz] *n.* external appearance, *esp.* one assumed

guitar' [git-] *n.* 6-stringed instrument played by plucking or strumming —**guitar'ist** *n.* player of the guitar

gulch *n.* ravine; gully

gulf *n.* large inlet of the sea; chasm; large gap

gull[1] *n.* long-winged web-footed sea bird

gull[2] *n.* dupe, fool —*vt.* dupe, cheat —**gullibil'ity** *n.* —**gull'ible** *a.* easily imposed on, credulous

gull'et *n.* food passage from mouth to stomach

gull'y *n.* channel or ravine worn by water

gulp *vt.* swallow eagerly —*vi.* gasp, choke —*n.*

gum[1] *n.* firm flesh in which teeth are set —**gumm'y** *a.* toothless

gum[2] *n.* sticky substance issuing from certain trees; an adhesive; chewing gum; gumtree, eucalypt —*vt.* stick with gum (**-mm-**) —**gumm'y** *a.* —**gum'boots** *pl.n.* boots of rubber —**gum'shoe** *n.* waterproof overshoe; *sl.* detective —**gum'tree** *n.* any species of eucalypt —**gum up the works** *inf.* impede progress

gum'bo *n.* sticky pods of okra; soup thickened with okra pods; fine soil in prairies that becomes sticky when wet (*pl.* **-bos**)

gump'tion *n.* resourcefulness; shrewdness, sense

gun *n.* weapon with metal tube from which missiles are discharged by explosion; cannon, pistol *etc.* —*v.* shoot; pursue, as with gun; race engine (of automobile) —**gunn'er** *n.* —**gunn'ery** *n.* use or science of large guns —**gun'boat** *n.* small warship —**gun dog** (breed of) dog used to retrieve *etc.* game —**gun'man** *n.* armed criminal —**gun'metal** *n.* alloy of copper and tin or zinc, formerly used for guns —**gun'powder** *n.* explosive mixture of saltpetre, sulphur, charcoal —**gun'room** *n.* in warship, mess room of junior officers —**gun'shot** *n.* shot or range of gun —*a.* caused by missile from gun —**gun'wale** [gun'əl], **gunn'el** *n.* upper edge of ship's side

gunk *n. inf.* any dirty, oily matter

gunn'y *n.* strong, coarse sacking made from jute

gupp'y *n.* small colourful aquarium fish

gur'gle *n.* bubbling noise —*vi.* utter, flow with gurgle

gur'nard, gur'net *n.* spiny armour-headed sea fish

gur'u [goo'roo] *n.* a spiritual teacher, *esp.* in India

gush *vi.* flow out suddenly and copiously, spurt —*n.* sudden and copious flow; effusiveness —**gush'er** *n.* gushing person; oil well

guss'et *n.* triangle or diamond-shaped piece of material let into garment —**gus'seted** *a.*

gust *n.* sudden blast of wind; burst of rain, anger, passion *etc.* —**gust'y** *a.*

gust'o *n.* enjoyment, zest

gut *n.* (*oft. pl.*) entrails, intestines; material made from guts of animals, *eg* for violin strings *etc.* —*pl. inf.* essential, fundamental part; courage —*vt.* remove guts from (fish *etc.*); remove, destroy contents of (house) —**gut'sy** *a. inf.* greedy; courageous

gutta-percha *n.* (tropical tree producing) whitish rubber substance

gutt'er *n.* shallow trough for carrying off water from roof or side of street —*vt.* make channels in —*vi.* flow in streams; of candle, melt away by wax forming channels and running down —**gutter press** journalism that relies on sensationalism —**gutt'ersnipe** *n.* neglected slum child; mean vindictive person

gutt'ural *a.* of, relating to, or produced in, the throat —*n.* guttural sound or letter

guy[1] [gī] *n.* **UK** effigy of Guy Fawkes burnt on Nov. 5th; *inf.* person (*usu.* male) —*vt.* make fun of; ridicule —**wise guy** *inf., usu. disparaging* clever person

guy[2] [gī] *n.* rope, chain to steady, secure something, *eg* tent —*vt.* keep in position by guy —**guy'rope** *n.*

guz'zle *v.* eat or drink greedily —*n.*

gybe [jīb] *v.* (of boom of fore-and-aft sail) swing over to other side with following wind; alter course thus

gym [jim] *n. short for* GYMNASIUM *or* GYMNASTICS

gymna'sium [jim-] *n.* place equipped for muscular exercises, athletic training (*pl.* **-s, -na'sia**) —**gym'nast** *n.* expert in gymnastics —**gymnas'tics** *pl.n.* muscular exercises, with or without apparatus, *eg* parallel bars

gynaecol'ogy [gīn-] *n.* branch of medicine dealing with functions and diseases of women —**gynaecolog'ical** *a.* —**gynaecol'ogist** *n.*

gypsoph'ila [jip-] *n.* garden plant with small white or pink flowers

gyp'sum [jip'-] *n.* crystalline sulphate of lime, a source of plaster

Gyp'sy [jip'-] *n.* one of wandering race originally from NW India, Romany

gyrate' [jī-] *vi.* move in circle, spirally, revolve —**gyra'tion** *n.* —**gyra'tional** *a.* —**gy'ratory** *a.* revolving, spinning

gyr'falcon, ger'falcon [jer-] *n.* large, rare falcon

gy'rocompass [jī'-] *n.* compass using gyroscope

gy'roscope [jī'-] *n.* disc or wheel so mounted as to be able to rotate about any axis, *esp.* to keep disc (with compass *etc.*) level despite movement of ship *etc.* —**gyroscop'ic** *a.*

gyrosta'bilizer [jī-] *n.* gyroscopic device to prevent rolling of ship or airplane

H

H (of pencils) hard; *Chem.* hydrogen

ha'beas cor'pus [hā'bi-əs-] *n.* writ issued to produce prisoner in court

hab'erdasher *n.* dealer in articles of dress, ribbons, pins, needles *etc.* —**hab'erdashery** *n.*

habil'iments *pl.n.* dress

hab'it *n.* settled tendency or practice; constitution; customary apparel *esp.* of nun or monk; woman's riding dress —**habit'ual** *a.* formed or acquired by habit; usual, customary —**habit'ually** *adv.* —**habit'uate** *vt.* accustom; frequent —**habitua'tion** *n.* —**habit'ué** [-yoo-ā] *n.* constant visitor

hab'itable *a.* fit to live in —**hab'itant** *n.* (descendant of) original French settler —**hab'itat** *n.* natural home (of animal *etc.*) —**habita'tion** *n.* dwelling place

hacien'da [ha-si-en'-] *n.* ranch or large estate in Sp. Amer.

hack[1] *vt.* cut, chop (at) violently; *inf.* utter harsh, dry cough; *sl.* tolerate, cope with —*n.* —**hack'er** *n. sl.* computer fanatic who through personal computer breaks into computer system of company or government

hack[2] *n.* horse for ordinary riding; drudge, *esp.* writer of inferior literary works —**hack work** dull, repetitive work

hac'kle *n.* neck feathers of turkey *etc.* —*pl.* hairs on back of neck of dog and other animals which are raised in anger

hack'ney *n.* harness horse, carriage, coach kept for hire (*pl.* **-neys**)

hack'neyed *a.* (of words *etc.*) stale, trite because of overuse

hack'saw *n.* handsaw for cutting metal

had *pt./pp. of* HAVE

hadd'ock *n.* large, edible seafish

Ha'des [hā'dēz] *n.* abode of the dead; underworld; hell

haema-, haemo- (*comb. form*) blood

hae'matite [hē'-] *n.* ore of iron

haemoglo'bin [hē-] *n.* colouring and oxygen-bearing matter of red blood corpuscles

haemophil'ia [hē-] *n.* hereditary tendency to intensive bleeding as blood fails to clot —**haemophil'iac** *n.*

haem'orrhage [hem'ə-rij] *n.* profuse bleeding

haem'orrhoids [hem'ə-roidz] *pl.n.* swollen veins in rectum (*also called* **piles**)

haft [-ah-] *n.* handle (of knife *etc.*) —*vt.* fit with one

hag *n.* ugly old woman; witch —**hag-ridden** *a.* troubled, careworn

hagg'ard *a.* wild-looking; anxious, careworn —*n. Falconry* untamed hawk

hagg'is *n.* Scottish dish made from sheep's heart, lungs, liver, chopped with oatmeal, suet, onion *etc.*, and boiled in the stomach-bag

hag'gle *vi.* bargain, wrangle over price —*n.*

hagiol'ogy [hag-] *n.* literature of the lives of saints —**hagiog'rapher** *n.* —**hagiog'raphy** *n.* writing of this

hail[1] *n.* (shower of) pellets of ice; intense shower, barrage —*v.* pour down as shower of hail —**hail'stone** *n.*

hail[2] *vt.* greet (*esp.* enthusiastically); acclaim, acknowledge; call —*vi.* come (from)

hair *n.* filament growing from skin of animal, as covering of man's head; such filaments collectively —**hair'iness** *n.* —**hair'y** *a.* —**hair'do** *n.* way of dressing hair —**hair'dresser** *n.* one who attends to and cuts hair, *esp.* women's hair —**hair'line** *a./n.* very fine (line) —**hair'pin** *n.* pin for keeping hair in place —**hair'splitting** *n.* making of over-fine distinctions —**hair'spring** *n.* very fine, delicate spring in timepiece —**hair trigger** trigger operated by light touch

hake *n.* edible fish of the cod family

hal'berd *n.* combined spear and battle-axe

hal'cyon [-si-ən] *n.* bird fabled to calm the sea and to breed on floating nest, kingfisher

hale *a.* robust, healthy, *esp. in* **hale and hearty**

half [hahf] *n.* either of two equal parts of thing (*pl.* **halves** [hahvz]) *—a.* forming half *—adv.* to the extent of half **—half'-back** *n. Sport* man behind forwards **—half-baked** *a.* underdone; *inf.* immature, silly **—half-breed, half-caste** *n.* person with parents of different races **—half-brother, -sister** *n.* brother (sister) by one parent only **—half-cocked** *a.* ill-prepared **—half-hearted** *a.* unenthusiastic **—half-life** *n.* time taken for half the atoms in radioactive material to decay **—half-nelson** *n.* hold in wrestling **—half-note** *n.* musical note half length of whole note **—half'penny** [hā'pni] *n.* formerly, half British penny; half British new penny (*pl.* **-pence** *or* **-pennies**) *Also inf.* **half —half step** *Mus.* difference in pitch between adjacent notes on scale **—half-time** *n. Sport* rest period between two halves of a game **—half'-tone** *n.* illustration printed from relief plate, showing lights and shadows by means of minute dots **—half volley** striking of a ball the moment it bounces **—half'wit** *n.* mentally-retarded person

hal'ibut *n.* large edible flatfish

halito'sis *n.* bad-smelling breath

hall [hawl] *n.* (entrance) passage; large room or building belonging to particular group or used for particular purpose *esp.* public assembly **—hall'way** *n.* (entrance) passage

hallelu'jah [-loo'yə] *n./interj.* exclamation of praise to God

hall'mark *n.* mark used to indicate standard of tested gold and silver; mark of excellence; distinguishing feature

hallo' *interj. see* HELLO

halloo' *n.* call to spur on hunting dogs *—v.* shout loudly to

hall'ow [-ō] *vt.* make, or honour as holy **—Hallowe'en'** [-ō-ēn'] *n.* the evening of Oct. 31st, the day before All Hallows' or All Saints' day

hallu'cinate [-lōō'si-] *vi.* suffer illusions **—hallucina'tion** *n.* illusion **—hallu'cinatory** *a.* **—hallu'cinogen** *n.* drug inducing hallucinations

ha'lo *n.* circle of light round moon, sun *etc.*; disc of light round saint's head in picture; ideal glory attaching to person (*pl.* **-lo(e)s**) *—vt.* surround with halo

halt[1] [hawlt] *n.* interruption or end to progress *etc.* (*esp.* as command to stop marching) *—v.* (cause to) stop

halt[2] [hawlt] *vi.* falter, fail **—halt'ing** *a.* hesitant, lame

hal'ter [hawl't-] *n.* rope or strap with headgear to fasten horses or cattle; low-cut dress style with strap passing behind neck; noose for hanging person *—vt.* put halter on, fasten with one

halve [hahv] *vt.* cut in half; reduce to half; share

hal'yard, hall'iard *n.* rope for raising sail, signal flags *etc.*

ham *n.* meat (*esp.* salted or smoked) from thigh of pig; actor adopting exaggerated, unconvincing style (*also a. and v.*); amateur radio enthusiast **—ham-fisted, -handed** *a.* clumsy **—ham'-string** *n.* tendon at back of knee *—vt.* cripple by cutting this

ham'burger *n.* fried cake of minced beef, *esp.* served in bread roll

ham'let *n.* small village

hamm'er *n.* tool usu. with heavy head at end of handle, for beating, driving nails *etc.*; machine for same purposes; contrivance for exploding charge of gun; auctioneer's mallet; metal ball on wire thrown in sports *—v.* strike with, or as with, hammer **—hamm'erhead** *n.* shark with wide, flattened head **—hamm'ertoe** *n.* deformed toe **—hammer out** solve problem by full investigation of difficulties

hamm'ock *n.* bed of canvas *etc.*, hung on cords

hamp'er[1] *n.* large covered basket

hamp'er[2] *vt.* impede, obstruct movements of

ham'ster *n.* type of rodent, sometimes kept as pet

ham'strung *a.* crippled; thwarted

hand *n.* extremity of arm beyond wrist; side, quarter, direction; style of writing; cards dealt to player; measure of four inches; manual worker; sailor; help, aid; pointer on dial; applause *—vt.* pass; deliver; hold out **—hand'ful** *n.* small quantity or number; *inf.* person, thing causing problems (*pl.* **-fuls**) **—hand'ily** *adv.* **—hand'iness** *n.* dexterity; state of being near, available —**hand'y** *a.* convenient; clever with the hands —**hand'bag** *n.* woman's bag for personal articles, purse; bag for carrying in hand —**hand'bill** *n.* small printed notice —**hand'book** *n.* small reference or instruction book —**hand'cuff** *n.* fetter for wrist, usu. joined in pair —*vt.* secure thus —**hand'i-craft** *n.* manual occupation or skill —**hand'iwork** *n.* thing done by particular person —**hand'kerchief** [hang'kə-chif] *n.* small square of fabric carried in pocket for wiping nose *etc.*; neckerchief —**hand-out** *n.* money, food *etc.* given free; pamphlet giving news, information *etc.* —**hands-on** *a.* involving practical experience of equipment —**hand'stand** *n.* act of supporting body in upside-down position by hands alone —**hand'writing** *n.* way person writes —**hand'yman** *n.* man employed to do various tasks; man skilled in odd jobs —**hand down** pass on; deliver (verdict) —**hand in glove** very intimate

hand'icap *n.* something that hampers or hinders; race, contest in which chances are equalized by starts, weights carried *etc.*; condition so imposed; any physical disability —*vt.* hamper; impose handicaps on (**-pp-**)

han'dle *n.* part of thing to hold it by —*vi.* touch, feel with hands; manage; deal with; trade —**han'dlebars** *pl.n.* curved metal bar used to steer bicycle, motorbike *etc.*

hand'some [han's-] *a.* of fine appearance; generous; ample —**hand'somely** *adv.*

hang *vt.* suspend; kill by suspension by neck (**hanged** *pt./pp.*); attach, set up (wallpaper, doors *etc.*) —*vi.* be suspended, cling (**hung** *pt./pp.*) —**hang'er** *n.* frame on which clothes *etc.* can be hung —**hang'bird** *n.* bird, as oriole, that builds hanging nest —**hang'dog** *a.* sullen, dejected —**hang-glider** *n.* glider like large kite, with pilot hanging in frame below —**hang-gliding** *n.* —**hang'man** *n.* executioner —**hang'-over** *n.* after-effects of too much drinking —**hang out** *inf.* reside, frequent —**hang-up** *n. inf.* persistent emotional problem

hang'ar *n.* large shed for aircraft

hank *n.* coil, skein, length, *esp.* as measure of yarn

hank'er *vi.* crave

han'ky, han'kie *n. short for* HANDKERCHIEF

hank'y-pank'y *inf. n.* trickery; illicit sexual relations

Han'sard *n.* official printed record of speeches, debates *etc.* in Brit., Aust., Canad. and other parliaments

han'som *n.* two-wheeled horse-drawn cab for two to ride inside with driver mounted up behind

haphaz'ard *a.* random, careless

hap'less *a.* unlucky

happ'en *vi.* come about, occur; chance to do —**happ'ening** *n.* occurrence, event —**happ'enstance** *n. inf* chance occurrence

happ'y *a.* glad, content; lucky, fortunate; apt —**happ'ily** *adv.* —**happ'iness** *n.* —**happy-go-lucky** *a.* casual, light-hearted

harakir'i *n.* in Japan, ritual suicide by disembowelling

harangue' [-ang'] *n.* vehement speech; tirade —*v.*

har'ass [ha'rəs] *vt.* worry, trouble, torment —**har'assment** *n.*

harb'inger [-j-] *n.* one who announces another's approach; forerunner, herald

har'bo(u)r [-bər] *n.* shelter for ships; shelter —*v.* give shelter, protection to; maintain (secretly) *esp.* grudge *etc.*

hard *a.* firm, resisting pressure; solid; difficult to understand; harsh, unfeeling; difficult to bear; practical, shrewd; heavy; strenuous; of water, not making lather well with soap; of drugs, highly addictive —*adv.* vigorously; with difficulty; close —**hard'en** *v.* —**hard'ly** *adv.* unkindly, harshly; scarcely, not quite; only just —**hard'ness** *n.* —**hard'ship** *n.* ill-luck; severe toil, suffering; instance of this —**hard'board** *n.* thin stiff sheet made of compressed sawdust and woodchips —**hard-boiled** *a.* boiled so long as to be hard; *inf.* of person, experienced, unemotional, unsympathetic —**hard-headed** *a.* shrewd; stubborn —**hard'rock** *a.* (of mining) concerned with extracting minerals (other than coal) from solid rock —*n. sl.* tough man, player *etc.* —**hard'-ware** *n.* tools, implements; necessary (parts of) machinery; *Computers* mechanical and electronic parts —**hard'-wood** *n.* wood from deciduous trees —**hard of hearing** rather deaf —**hard up** very short of money

hard'y *a.* robust, vigorous; bold; of plants, able to grow in the open all the year round —**hard'ihood** *n.* extreme boldness, audacity —**hard'ily** *adv.* —**har'diness** *n.*

hare *n.* animal like large rabbit, with longer legs and ears, noted for speed —**hare'bell** *n.* round-leaved bell-flower —**hare'brained** *a.* rash, wild —**hare'-lip** *n.* fissure of upper lip

ha'rem [*or* hah-rēm'] *n.* women's part of Mohammedan dwelling; one man's wives

har'icot [ha'ri-kō] *n.* type of French bean that can be dried

hark *vi.* listen —**hark back** return to previous subject of discussion

har'lequin *n.* stock comic character, *esp.* masked clown in diamond-patterned costume —**harlequinade'** *n.* scene in pantomime; buffoonery

har'lot *n.* whore, prostitute —**har'lot-ry** *n.*

harm *n.* damage, injury —*vt.* cause harm to —**harm'ful** *a.* —**harm'fully** *adv.* —**harm'less** *a.* unable or unlikely to hurt —**harm'lessly** *adv.*

harm'ony *n.* agreement; concord; peace; combination of notes to make chords; melodious sound —**harmon'ic** *a.* of harmony —*n.* tone or note whose frequency is a multiple of its pitch —**harmon'ics** *pl.n.* science of musical sounds; harmonious sounds —**harmon'i-ca** *n.* various musical instruments, but *esp.* mouth organ —**harmo'nious** *a.* —**harmo'niously** *adv.* —**har'monist** *n.* —**harmo'nium** *n.* small organ —**har-moniza'tion** *n.* —**har'monize** *vt.* bring into harmony; cause to agree; reconcile —*vi.* be in harmony

harn'ess *n.* equipment for attaching horse to cart, plough *etc.;* any such equipment —*vt.* put on, in harness; utilize energy or power of (waterfall *etc.*)

harp *n.* musical instrument of strings played by hand —*vi.* play on harp; dwell on continuously —**harp'er, harp'ist** *n.* —**harp'sichord** *n.* stringed instrument like piano

harpoon' *n.* barbed spear with rope attached for catching whales —*vt.* catch, kill with this —**harpoon'er** *n.* —**har-poon gun** gun for firing harpoon in whaling

harp'y *n.* monster with body of woman and wings and claws of bird; cruel, grasping person

harr'idan *n.* shrewish old woman, hag

harr'ier *n.* hound used in hunting hares; falcon

harr'ow [-ō] *n.* implement for smoothing, levelling or stirring up soil —*vt.* draw harrow over; distress greatly —**har'-rowing** *a.* heart-rending; distressful

harr'y *vt.* harass; ravage (**harr'ied, harr'ying**)

harsh *a.* rough, discordant; severe; unfeeling —**harsh'ly** *adv.*

hart *n.* male deer —**harts'horn** *n.* material made from harts' horns, formerly the chief source of ammonia

harte'beest *n.* Afr. antelope

ha'rum-sca'rum *a.* reckless, wild; giddy

harv'est *n.* (season for) gathering in grain; gathering; crop; product of action —*vt.* reap and gather in —**harv'ester** *n.*

has *third person sing. pres. indicative of* HAVE

hash *n.* dish of hashed meat *etc.*; *inf. short for* HASHISH —*vt.* cut up small, chop; mix up

hash'ish [-ēsh], **hash'eesh** *n.* resinous extract of Indian hemp, *esp.* used as hallucinogen

hasp [-ah-] *n.* clasp passing over a staple for fastening door *etc.* —*vt.* fasten, secure with hasp

has'sle *inf. n.* quarrel; a lot of bother, trouble —*v.*

hass'ock *n.* kneeling-cushion; tuft of grass

hast *obs. second person sing. pres. indicative of* HAVE

haste [hāst] *n.* speed, quickness, hurry —*vi.* hasten —**ha'sten** [-sən] *v.* (cause to) hurry, increase speed —**ha'stily** *adv.* —**ha'sty** *a.*

hat *n.* head-covering, usu. with brim —**hat'ter** *n.* dealer in, maker of hats —**hat trick** any three successive achievements, *esp.* in sport

hatch[1] *v.* of young, *esp.* of birds, (cause to) emerge from egg; contrive, devise —**hatch'ery** *n.*

hatch[2] *n.* hatchway; trapdoor over it;

opening in wall or door, as service hatch, to facilitate service of meals *etc.*, between two rooms; lower half of divided door —**hatch'back** *n.* automobile with single lifting door in rear —**hatch'way** *n.* opening in deck of ship *etc.*

hatch[3] *vt.* engrave or draw lines on for shading; shade with parallel lines

hatch'et *n.* small axe —**hatchet job** malicious verbal or written attack —**hatchet man** *inf.* person carrying out unpleasant assignments for another; hired murderer —**bury the hatchet** make peace

hate *vt.* dislike strongly; bear malice towards —*n.* this feeling; that which is hated —**hate'ful** *a.* detestable —**hate'fully** *adv.* —**ha'tred** *n.* extreme dislike, active ill will

haught'y [hawt'-] *a.* proud, arrogant —**haught'ily** *adv.* —**haught'iness** *n.*

haul *vt.* pull, drag with effort —*vi.* of wind, shift —*n.* hauling; what is hauled; catch of fish; acquisition; distance (to be) covered —**haul'age** *n.* carrying of loads; charge for this —**haul'er** *n.* firm, person that transports goods by road —**haul off** *inf.* draw back in preparation (esp. to strike or fight)

haunch *n.* human hip or fleshy hindquarter of animal; leg and loin of venison

haunt *vt.* visit regularly; visit in form of ghost; recur to —*n. esp.* place frequently visited —**haunt'ed** *a.* frequented by ghosts; worried

hauteur' [ō-tur'] *n.* haughty spirit

Havan'a, Havann'ah *n.* fine quality of cigar

have [hav] *vt.* hold, possess; be possessed, affected with; be obliged (to do); cheat, outwit; engage in, obtain; contain; allow; cause to be done; give birth to; (as auxiliary, forms perfect and other tenses) (*pres. tense:* I *have,* thou *hast,* he *has,* we, you, they *have*) (**had, hav'ing**)

ha'ven *n.* place of safety

hav'ersack *n.* canvas bag for provisions *etc.* carried on back or shoulder when hiking *etc.*

hav'oc *n.* devastation, ruin; *inf.* confusion, chaos

hawk[1] *n.* bird of prey smaller than eagle; supporter, advocate, of warlike policies —*vi.* hunt with hawks; attack like hawk

hawk[2] *vt.* offer (goods) for sale, as in street —**hawk'er** *n.*

hawk[3] *vi.* clear throat noisily

hawse [-z] *n.* part of ship's bows with holes for cables

haw'ser [-z-] *n.* large rope or cable

haw'thorn *n.* thorny shrub or tree

hay *n.* grass mown and dried —**hay fever** allergic reaction to pollen, dust *etc.* —**hay'seed** *n.* seeds of grass; *inf. offens.* yokel —**hay'stack** *n.* large pile of hay —**hay'wire** *a.* crazy; disorganized

haz'ard *n.* chance; risk, danger —*vt.* expose to risk; run risk of —**haz'ardous** *a.* risky

haze[1] *n.* mist, often due to heat; obscurity —**ha'zy** *a.* misty; obscured; vague

haze[2] *vt.* subject (fellow students) to ridicule —**ha'zer** *n.*

ha'zel *n.* bush bearing nuts; yellowish-brown colour of the nuts —*a.* light brown

HBC Hudson's Bay Company

H bomb *short for* HYDROGEN BOMB

HE high explosive; His Eminence; His (*or* Her) Excellency

He *Chem.* helium

he *pron.* (*third person masculine pronoun*) person, animal already referred to; (*comb. form*) male, as **he-goat**

head [hed] *n.* upper part of man's or animal's body, containing mouth, sense organs and brain; upper part of anything; chief of organization, school *etc.*; chief part; aptitude, capacity; crisis; leader; section of chapter; title; headland; person, animal considered as unit; white froth on beer *etc.* —*a.* chief, principal; of wind, contrary —*vt.* be at the top, head of; lead, direct; provide with head; hit (ball) with head —*vi.* make for; form a head —**head'er** *n.* plunge headfirst; brick laid with end in face of wall; action of striking ball with head —**head'ing** *n.* title —**heads** *adv. inf.* with obverse side (of coin) uppermost —**head'y** *a.* apt to intoxicate or excite —**head'ache** [-āk] *n.* continuous pain in head; worrying circumstance —**head'board** *n.* vertical board at head of bed —**head'cheese** *n.* seasoned jellied loaf made from head and sometimes feet of pig —**head'land** *n.* promontory —**head'light** *n.* powerful lamp carried on front of locomotive, motor vehicle *etc.* —**head'line** *n.* news summary, in large type in newspaper

—**head'long** *adv.* head foremost, in rush —**head'quarters** *pl.n.* residence of commander-in-chief; centre of operations —**head'stone** *n.* gravestone —**head'-strong** *a.* self-willed —**head'way** *n.* advance, progress

heal *v.* make or become well —**health** [helth] *n.* soundness of body; condition of body; toast drunk in person's honour —**health'ily** *adv.* —**health'iness** *n.* —**health'y** *a.* of strong constitution; of or producing good health, wellbeing *etc.*; vigorous —**health food** vegetarian food, organically grown, eaten for dietary value

heap *n.* pile of things lying one on another; great quantity —*vt.* pile, load with

hear *vt.* perceive by ear; listen to; *Law* try (case); heed —*vi.* perceive sound; learn (**heard** [herd] *pt./pp.*) —**hear'er** *n.* —**hear'ing** *n.* ability to hear; earshot; judicial examination —**hear! hear!** *interj.* exclamation of approval, agreement —**hear'say** *n.* rumour —*a.*

hear'ken [hahr'-] *vi.* listen

hearse [hurs] *n.* funeral carriage for casket

heart [-ah-] *n.* organ which makes blood circulate; seat of emotions and affections; mind, soul, courage; central part; playing card marked with figure of heart; one of these marks —**heart'en** *v.* make, become cheerful —**heart'ily** *adv.* —**heart'less** *a.* unfeeling —**heart'y** *a.* friendly; vigorous; in good health; satisfying the appetite —**heart attack** sudden severe malfunction of heart —**heart'-burn** *n.* pain in higher intestine —**heart-rending** *a.* overwhelming with grief; agonizing —**heart-throb** *n. sl.* object of infatuation —**by heart** by memory

hearth [-ah-] *n.* part of room where fire is made; home

heat *n.* hotness; sensation of this; hot weather or climate; warmth of feeling, anger *etc.*; sexual excitement caused by readiness to mate in female animals; one of many races *etc.* to decide persons to compete in finals —*v.* make, become hot —**heat'ed** *a. esp.* angry —**heat'edly** *adv.*

heath *n.* tract of waste land; low-growing evergreen shrub

hea'then [-TH-] *a.* not adhering to a religious system; pagan; barbarous; unenlightened —*n.* heathen person (*pl.* **hea'-thens, hea'then**) —**hea'thendom** *n.* —**hea'thenish** *a.* of or like heathen; rough; barbarous —**hea'thenism** *n.*

heath'er [heTH'-] *n.* shrub growing on heaths and mountains —**heath'ery** *a.*

heave *vt.* lift with effort; throw (something heavy); utter (sigh) —*vi.* swell, rise; feel nausea —*n.*

heav'en [hev'n] *n.* abode of God; place of bliss; sky (*also pl.*) —**heav'enly** *a.* lovely, delightful, divine; beautiful; of or like heaven

heav'y [hev'-] *a.* weighty, striking, falling with force; dense; sluggish; difficult, severe; sorrowful; serious; dull —**heav'i-ly** *adv.* —**heav'iness** *n.* —**heavy industry** basic, large scale industry producing metal, machinery *etc.* —**heavy metal** rock music with strong beat and amplified instrumental effects —**heavy water** deuterium oxide, water in which normal hydrogen content has been replaced by deuterium

Heb. Hebrew; Hebrews

He'brew *n.* member of an ancient Semitic people; their language; its modern form, used in Israel —*a.*

hec'kle [hek'l] *v.* interrupt or try to annoy (speaker) by questions, taunts *etc.*

hect-, hecto- (*comb. form*) one hundred, *esp.* in metric system, as in **hec'to-litre, hec'tometre**

hec'tare [-tahr] *n.* one hundred ares or 10 000 square metres (2.471 acres)

hec'tic *a.* rushed, busy

hec'tor *v.* bully, bluster —*n.* blusterer

hed'dle *n. Weaving* one of set of frames of vertical wires

hedge *n.* fence of bushes —*vt.* surround with hedge; obstruct; hem in; bet on both sides —*vi.* make or trim hedges; be evasive; secure against loss —**hedge'-hog** *n.* small animal covered with spines —**hedge'row** *n.* bushes forming hedge —**hedge sparrow** small brownish songbird

he'donism *n.* doctrine that pleasure is the chief good —**he'donist** *n.* —**hedon-is'tic** *a.*

heed *vt.* take notice of, care for —**heed'ful** *a.* —**heed'less** *a.* careless

heel[1] *n.* hinder part of foot; part of shoe

supporting this; *sl.* undesirable person —*vt.* supply with heel; touch ground, ball, with heel

heel[2] *v.* of ship, (cause to) lean to one side —*n.* heeling, list

hef'ty *a.* bulky; weighty; strong

hegem'ony *n.* leadership, political domination —**hegemon'ic** *a.*

heif'er [hef'-] *n.* young cow

height [hīt] *n.* measure from base to top; quality of being high; elevation; highest degree; (*oft. pl.*) hilltop —**height'en** *vt.* make higher; intensify —**height of land** watershed

hei'nous [hā'-] *a.* atrocious, extremely wicked, detestable

heir [ār] *n.* person entitled to inherit property or rank (**heir'ess** *fem.*) —**heir'loom** *n.* thing that has been in family for generations

held *pt./pp. of* HOLD[1]

hel'ical *a.* spiral

hel'icopter *n.* aircraft made to rise vertically by pull of airscrew revolving horizontally —**hel'iport** *n.* airport for helicopters

helio- (*comb. form*) sun

he'liograph *n.* signalling apparatus employing a mirror to reflect sun's rays

he'liostat *n.* astronomical instrument used to reflect the light of the sun in a constant direction

heliother'apy [hē-] *n.* therapeutic use of sunlight

he'liotrope *n.* plant with purple flowers; colour of the flowers —**heliotrop'ic** *a.* growing, turning towards source of light

he'lium *n.* very light, nonflammable gaseous element

hell *n.* abode of the damned; abode of the dead generally; place or state of wickedness, or misery, or torture —**hell'ish** *a.*

hell'ebore *n.* plant with white flowers that bloom in winter, Christmas rose

Hellen'ic *a.* pert. to inhabitants of Greece —**Hell'enist** *n.*

hello' (*also* **hallo'**, **hullo'**) *interj.* expression of greeting or surprise

helm *n.* tiller, wheel for turning ship's rudder

helm'et *n.* defensive or protective covering for head *Also* **helm**

help *vt.* aid, assist; support; succour; remedy, prevent —*n.* —**help'er** *n.* —**help'ful** *a.* —**help'ing** *n.* single portion of food taken at a meal —**help'less** *a.* useless, incompetent; unaided; unable to help —**help'lessly** *adv.* —**help'mate, -meet** *n.* helpful companion; husband or wife

hel'ter-skel'ter *adv./a./n.* (in) hurry and confusion

hem *n.* border of cloth, *esp.* one made by turning over edge and sewing it down —*vt.* sew thus; confine, shut in (**-mm-**) —**hem'stitch** *n.* ornamental stitch —*vt.*

hemi- (*comb. form*) half

hem'isphere *n.* half sphere; half of celestial sphere; half of the earth —**hemispher'ical** *a.*

hem'istich [-ik] *n.* half a line of verse

hem'lock *n.* poisonous plant; poison extracted from it; evergreen of pine family

hemp *n.* Indian plant; its fibre used for rope *etc.*; any of several narcotic drugs made from varieties of hemp —**hemp'en** *a.* made of hemp or rope

hen *n.* female of domestic fowl and others —**hen'peck** *vt.* (of a woman) harass (a man, *esp.* husband) by nagging

hence *adv.* from this point; for this reason —**hencefor'ward, hence'forth** *adv.* from now onwards

hench'man *n.* trusty follower

henn'a *n.* flowering shrub; reddish dye made from it

henothe'ism *n.* belief in one god (of several) as special god of one's family, tribe *etc.*

hen'ry *n.* SI unit of electrical inductance

hepat'ic *a.* pert. to the liver —**hepati'tis** *n.* inflammation of the liver

hepta- (*comb. form*) seven

hept'agon *n.* figure with seven angles —**heptag'onal** *a.*

hep'tarchy [-ki] *n.* rule by seven

her *a.* objective and possessive case of SHE —**hers** *pron.* of her —**herself'** *pron.*

her'ald [he'rəld] *n.* messenger, envoy; officer who makes royal proclamations, arranges ceremonies, regulates armorial bearings *etc.* —*vt.* announce; proclaim approach of —**herald'ic** *a.* —**her'aldry** *n.* study of (right to have) heraldic bearings

herb *n.* plant with soft stem which dies down after flowering; plant of which parts are used in cookery or medicine —**herba'ceous** [-shəs] *a.* of, like herbs; perennial flowering —**herb'age** *n.* herbs; grass; pasture —**herb'al** *a.* of herbs —*n.* book on herbs —**herb'alist** *n.* writer on herbs; dealer in medicinal herbs —**herba'rium** *n.* collection of dried plants (*pl.* **-iums, -ia**) —**herb'icide** *n.* chemical which destroys plants —**herbiv'orous** *a.* feeding on plants

Her'cules [-kyoo-lēz] *n.* mythical hero noted for strength —**hercule'an** *a.* requiring great strength, courage

herd *n.* company of animals, *usu.* of same species, feeding or travelling together; herdsman —*v.* crowd together —*vt.* tend (herd) —**herds'man** *n.*

here *adv.* in this place; at or to this point —**hereaf'ter** *adv.* in time to come —*n.* future existence —**heretofore'** *adv.* before

hered'ity *n.* tendency of organism to transmit its nature to its descendants —**heredit'ament** *n.* *Law* property that can be inherited —**hered'itarily** *adv.* —**hered'itary** *a.* descending by inheritance; holding office by inheritance; that can be transmitted from one generation to another

her'esy [he'rə-] *n.* opinion contrary to orthodox opinion or belief —**her'etic** *n.* one holding opinions contrary to orthodox faith —**heret'ical** *a.* —**heret'ically** *adv.*

her'itage [he'ri-] *n.* what may be or is inherited; anything from past, *esp.* owned or handed down by tradition —**her'itable** *a.* that can be inherited

hermaph'rodite *n.* person, animal with characteristics, or reproductive organs, of both sexes

hermet'ic *a.* sealed so as to be airtight —**hermet'ically** *adv.*

her'mit *n.* one living in solitude, *esp.* from religious motives —**her'mitage** *n.* his abode

hern'ia *n.* projection of (part of) organ through lining encasing it (*pl.* **-ias, -iae** [-i-ē]) —**hern'ial** *a.*

he'ro *n.* one greatly regarded for achievements or qualities; principal character in poem, play, story; illustrious warrior; demigod (*pl.* **he'roes** —**her'oine** *fem.*) —**hero'ic** [hi-] *a.* of, like hero; courageous, daring —**hero'ically** *adv.* —**hero'ics** *pl.n.* extravagant behaviour —**her'oism** [he'rō-] *n.* qualities of hero; courage, boldness —**hero worship** admiration of heroes or of great men; excessive admiration of others

her'oin [he'rō-] *n.* white crystalline derivative of morphine, a highly addictive narcotic

her'on [he'rən] *n.* long-legged wading bird —**her'onry** *n.* place where herons breed

her'pes [-pēz] *n.* any of several skin diseases, including shingles and cold sores

herr'ing *n.* important food fish of northern hemisphere

herr'ingbone *n.* stitch, or pattern of zigzag lines

hertz *n.* SI unit of frequency (*pl.* **hertz**)

hes'itate [hez'-] *vi.* hold back; feel, or show indecision; be reluctant —**hes'itancy, hesita'tion** *n.* wavering; doubt; stammering —**hes'itant** *a.* undecided, pausing —**hes'itantly** *adv.*

hess'ian *n.* coarse jute cloth

hest *n.* behest, command

hetero- (*comb. form*) other or different

het'erodox *a.* not orthodox —**het'erodoxy** *n.*

heteroge'neous *a.* composed of diverse elements —**heterogene'ity** *n.*

heterosex'ual *n.* person sexually attracted to members of the opposite sex —**heterosexual'ity** *n.*

heuris'tic [hyoo-] *a.* serving to find out or to stimulate investigation

hew *v.* chop, cut with axe; conform (to code *etc.*) (**hewn, hewed** *pp.*) —**hew'er** *n.*

hex *vt. inf.* bewitch —*n.* evil spell

hex-, hexa- (*comb. form*) six

hex'agon *n.* figure with six angles —**hexag'onal** *a.*

hexam'eter *n.* line of verse of six feet

hey'day *n.* bloom, prime

HF high frequency

Hg *Chem.* mercury

HH His (*or* Her) Highness; His Holiness

hia'tus [hī-ā'-] *n.* break or gap where something is missing (*pl.* **hia'tuses, hia'tus**)

hi'bernate *vi.* pass the winter, *esp.* in a torpid state —**hiberna'tion** *n.* —**hi'bernator** *n.*

Hiber'nian *a./n.* Irish (person)

hibis'cus *n.* flowering (sub-)tropical shrub

hicc'up, hicc'ough [hik'up] *n.* spasm of the breathing organs with an abrupt cough-like sound —*vi.* have this

hick *a. inf.* rustic; unsophisticated —*n.* person like this

hick'ory *n.* N Amer. nut-bearing tree; its tough wood

hide[1] *vt.* put, keep out of sight; conceal, keep secret —*vi.* conceal oneself (**hid** *pt.*, **hidd'en** *or* **hid** *pp.*, **hi'ding** *pr.p.*) —**hide-out** *n.* hiding place

hide[2] *n.* skin of animal —**hi'ding** *n. sl.* thrashing —**hide'bound** *a.* restricted, *esp.* by petty rules *etc.*; narrow-minded

hid'eous *a.* repulsive, revolting —**hid'eously** *adv.*

hie [hī] *v. obs.* hasten (**hied** [hīd] *pt./pp.*, **hy'ing** *or* **hie'ing** *pr.p.*)

hi'erarchy [-ki] *n.* system of persons or things arranged in graded order —**hierar'chical** *a.*

hieroglyph'ic *a.* of a system of picture writing, as used in ancient Egypt —*n.* symbol representing object, concept or sound; symbol, picture, difficult to decipher —**hi'eroglyph** *n.*

hi'-fi [hī'fī] *a. short for* HIGH-FIDELITY —*n.* high-fidelity equipment

hig'gledy-pig'gledy *adv./a.* in confusion

high [hī] *a.* tall, lofty; far up; of meat, tainted; of season, well advanced; of sound, acute in pitch; expensive; of great importance, quality, or rank; *inf.* in state of euphoria, *esp.* induced by drugs; *inf.* bad-smelling —*adv.* far up; strongly, to a great extent; at, to a high pitch; at a high rate —**high'ly** *adv.* —**high'ness** *n.* quality of being high; (**H-**) title of prince and princess —**High Arctic** regions of Canada, *esp.* northern islands within Arctic Circle —**high'boy** *n.* tall chest of drawers —**high'brow** *n. sl.* intellectual, *esp.* intellectual snob —*a.* intellectual; difficult; serious —**High Church** party within Anglican Communion emphasizing authority of bishops and importance of sacraments, rituals and ceremonies —**high-fidelity** *a.* of high-quality sound reproducing equipment —**high-flown** *a.* extravagant, bombastic —**high-handed** *a.* domineering, dogmatic —**high hat** top hat —**high-hat** *a. inf.* snobbish —*vt.* treat in snobbish way —**high'land(s)** *n.(pl.)* relatively high ground —**High'land** *a.* of, from the Highlands of Scotland —**high'light** *n.* lightest or brightest area in painting, photograph *etc.*; outstanding feature —*vt.* bring into prominence —**high-rise** *a.* of building that has many storeys —**high school** school above elementary or public school, secondary school —**high-sounding** *a.* pompous, imposing —**high-strung** *a.* excitable, nervous —**high'tail** *vi. inf.* go or move in great hurry —**high tech** interior design using features of industrial equipment —**high-tech** *a.* —**high time** latest possible time —**high'way** *n.* main road; ordinary route —**high'wayman** *n.* (formerly) robber on road, *esp.* mounted

hi'jack *vt.* divert or wrongfully take command of a vehicle (*esp.* aircraft) or its contents; rob —**hi'jacker** *n.*

hike *vi.* walk a long way (for pleasure) in country —*vt.* pull (up), hitch —*n.* —**hi'ker** *n.*

hilar'ity [-la'ri-] *n.* cheerfulness, gaiety —**hila'rious** *a.*

hill *n.* natural elevation, small mountain; mound —**hill'ock** *n.* little hill —**hill'y** *a.* —**hill'billy** *n.* unsophisticated (country) person

hilt *n.* handle of sword *etc.*

him *pron.* objective case of pronoun HE —**himself'** *pron.* emphatic form of HE

hind[1] [hīnd] *n.* female of deer

hind[2] [hīnd], **hind'er** *a.* at the back, posterior

hin'der *vt.* obstruct, impede, delay —**hin'drance** *n.*

Hin'di *n.* language of N central India —**Hin'du** [-ōō] *n.* person who adheres to **Hinduism**, the dominant religion of India

hinge [-j] *n.* movable joint, as that on which door hangs —*vt.* attach with, or as with, hinge —*vi.* turn, depend on

hint *n.* slight indication or suggestion —*v.* give hint of

hint'erland *n.* district lying behind coast, or near city, port *etc.*

hip[1] *n.* either side of body below waist and above thigh; angle formed where sloping sides of roof meet; fruit of rose, *esp.* wild

hip[2] *a. sl.* aware of, following latest trends in music, fashion *etc.*; (*oft. with* to) informed (about)

hipp'ie, -y *n.* (young) person whose behaviour, dress *etc.* implies rejection of conventional values

hipp'odrome *n.* music hall; variety theatre; circus

hippopot'amus *n.* large Afr. animal living in rivers (*pl.* **-amuses, -ami** [-mī])

hire *vt.* obtain temporary use of by payment; engage for wage —*n.* hiring or being hired; payment for use of thing —**hire'ling** *n.* one who serves for wages —**hire-purchase** *n.* **UK** instalment plan

hir'sute [-syo͞ot] *a.* hairy

his *pron./a.* belonging to him

his'pid *a.* rough with bristles or minute spines; bristly, shaggy —**hispid'ity** *n.*

hiss *vi.* make sharp sound of letter S, *esp.* in disapproval —*vt.* express disapproval, deride thus —*n.* —**hiss'ing** *n.*

hist'amine [-ēn] *n.* substance released by body tissues, sometimes creating allergic reactions

histog'eny [-toj'-] *n.* formation and development of organic tissues

histol'ogy *n.* science that treats of minute structure of organic tissues —**histol'ogist** *n.*

his'tory *n.* record of past events; study of these; past events; train of events, public or private; course of life or existence; systematic account of phenomena —**histor'ian** *n.* writer of history —**histor'ic** [-to'rik] *a.* noted in history —**histor'ical** *a.* of, based on, history; belonging to past —**histor'ically** *adv.* —**historic'ity** [-ris'-] *n.* historical authenticity —**historiog'rapher** *n.* official historian; one who studies historical method

histrion'ic *a.* excessively theatrical, insincere, artificial in manner —**histrion'ics** *pl.n.* behaviour like this

hit *vt.* strike with blow or missile; affect injuriously; find —*vi.* strike; light (upon) (**hit, hitt'ing**) —*n.* blow; success —**hit'ter** *n.* —**hit man** *sl.* hired assassin —**hit it off** get along with (person) —**hit or miss** haphazard(ly) —**hit the hay** *sl.* go to bed —**hit the trail, hit the road** *inf.* proceed on journey; leave

hitch *vt.* fasten with loop *etc.*; raise, move with jerk —*vi.* be caught or fastened —*n.* difficulty; knot, fastening; jerk —**hitch'(hike)** *vi.* travel by begging free rides

hith'er [hiTH'-] *adv.* to or towards this place —*a. obs.* situated on this side —**hitherto'** *adv.* up to now or to this time

hive *n.* structure in which bees live or are housed; *fig.* place swarming with busy occupants —*v.* gather, place bees, in hive —**hive away** store, keep —**hive off** transfer; dispose of

hives *pl.n.* eruptive skin disease

HM His (*or* Her) Majesty

HMCS His (*or* Her) Majesty's Canadian Ship

HMS His (*or* Her) Majesty's Service *or* Ship

hoard [-aw-] *n.* stock, store, *esp.* hidden away —*vt.* amass and hide away; store

hoard'ing [-aw-] *n.* temporary wooden fence round building or piece of ground; **UK** billboard

hoarse [-aw-] a. rough, harsh sounding, husky —**hoarse'ly** *adv.* —**hoarse'ness** *n.*

hoar'y [hawr'-] *a.* grey with age; greyish-white; of great antiquity; venerable —**hoar'frost** *n.* frozen dew

hoax [hōks] *n.* practical joke; deceptive trick —*vt.* play trick upon; deceive —**hoax'er** *n.*

hob *n.* flat-topped casing of fireplace —**hob'nail** *n.* large-headed nail for boot soles

hob'ble *vi.* walk lamely —*vt.* tie legs together (of horse *etc.*) —*n.* straps or ropes put on an animal's legs to prevent it straying; limping gait

hob'bledehoy *n. obs.* rough, ill-mannered clumsy youth

hobb'y *n.* favourite occupation as pastime —**hobb'yhorse** *n.* toy horse; favourite topic, preoccupation

hobgob'lin *n.* mischievous fairy

hob'nob *vi.* drink together; be familiar (with) (**-bb-**)

ho'bo *n.* shiftless, wandering person (*pl.* **-bo(e)s**)

hock[1] *n.* backward-pointing joint on leg of horse *etc.*, corresponding to human ankle —*vt.* disable by cutting tendons of hock

hock[2] *n.* dry white wine

hock[3] *vt. inf.* pawn —*n.* state of being in pawn

hock'ey *n.* team game played on ice with puck and curved sticks; field hockey

ho'cus-po'cus *n.* trickery; mystifying jargon

hod *n.* small trough on a staff for carrying mortar, bricks *etc.;* tall, narrow coal scuttle

hodge'podge *n.* jumbled mixture

hoe *n.* tool for weeding, breaking ground *etc.* —*vt.* (**hoed, hoe'ing**)

hoe'down *n.* boisterous square dance; party with such dances

hog *n.* pig, *esp.* castrated male for fattening; greedy, dirty person —*vt. inf.* eat, use (something) selfishly —**hogs'head** *n.* large cask; liquid measure of 52½ or 54 imperial gallons —**hog'wash** *n.* nonsense; pig food

Hogmanay' *n.* in Scotland, last day of year

hoi polloi' *n.* the common mass of people; the masses

hoist *vt.* raise aloft, raise with tackle *etc.*

ho'kum *n. sl.* claptrap

hold[1] [-ō-] *vt.* keep fast, grasp; support in or with hands *etc.*; maintain in position; have capacity for; own, occupy; carry on; detain; celebrate; keep back; believe —*vi.* cling; not to give away; abide (by); keep (to); last, proceed, be in force; occur (**held** *pt./pp.*) —*n.* grasp; influence —**hold'er** *n.* —**hold'ing** *n.* (*oft. pl.*) property, as land or stocks and shares —**hold'all** *n.* **UK** carryall —**hold'fast** *n.* clamp —**hold'up** *n.* armed robbery; delay

hold[2] [-ō-] *n.* space in ship or aircraft for cargo

hole *n.* hollow place, cavity; perforation; opening; *inf.* unattractive place; *inf.* difficult situation —*v.* make holes in; go into a hole; drive into a hole —**ho'ley** *a.*

hol'iday *n.* day or other period of rest from work *etc., esp.* spent away from home, vacation

holl'and *n.* linen fabric —**holl'ands** *n.* spirit, gin

holl'ow [-ō] *a.* having a cavity, not solid; empty; false; insincere; not full-toned —*n.* cavity, hole, valley —*vt.* make hollow, make hole in; excavate

holl'y *n.* evergreen shrub with prickly leaves and red berries

holl'yhock *n.* tall plant bearing many large flowers

holm oak evergreen Mediterranean oak tree

hol'ocaust *n.* great destruction of life, *esp.* by fire

hol'ograph *n.* document wholly written by the signer

holog'raphy *n.* science of using lasers to produce a photographic record (**hologram**) which can reproduce a three-dimensional image

hol'ster [hōl'-] *n.* leather case for pistol, hung from belt *etc.*

holt [-ō-] *n.* wood, wooded hill

ho'ly *a.* belonging, devoted to God; free from sin; divine; consecrated —**ho'lily** *adv.* —**ho'liness** *n.* sanctity; (**H-**) Pope's title —**holy day** day of religious festival —**Holy Communion** service of the Eucharist —**Holy Week** that before Easter

hom'age *n.* tribute, respect, reverence; formal acknowledgment of allegiance

home *n.* dwelling-place; residence; native place; institution for the elderly, infirm *etc.* —*a.* of, connected with, home; native —*adv.* to, at one's home; to the point —*v.* direct or be directed onto a point or target —**home'less** *a.* —**home'ly** *a.* plain —**home'ward** *a./adv.* —**home'wards** *adv.* —**home-brew** *n.* alcoholic drink made at home —**home'maker** *n.* person who manages a home —**home run** *Baseball* hit that enables batter to run round all four bases (*also* **ho'mer**) —**home'sick** *a.* depressed by absence from home —**home'sickness** *n.* —**home'spun** *a.* domestic; simple —*n.* cloth made of homespun yarn —**home'stead** [-sted] *n.* house with outbuildings, *esp.* on farm; house and land occupied by owner and exempt from seizure and forced sale for debt —**home'steader** *n.* —**home'work** *n.* school work done usu. at home —**bring home to** impress deeply upon

hom'icide *n.* killing of human being; killer —**homici'dal** *a.*

hom'ily *n.* sermon; religious discourse —**homilet'ic** *a.* of sermons —**homilet'ics** *pl.n.* art of preaching

Ho'mo *n.* genus to which modern man belongs

homo- (*comb. form*) same, as in *homeopathy, homosexual etc.* Such words are not given here where the meaning may easily be inferred from the simple word

hom(o)eop'athy [hō-mi-op'-] *n.* treatment of disease by small doses of what would produce symptoms in healthy person —**ho'moeopath** *n.* one who believes in or practises homoeopathy —**homoeopath'ic** *a.* —**homoeopath'ically** *adv.*

homoge'neous [-j-] *a.* formed of uniform parts; similar, uniform; of the same nature —**homogene'ity** *n.* —**homog'enize** *vt.* break up fat globules in milk and cream to distribute them evenly

homol'ogous *a.* having the same relation, relative position *etc.* —**hom'ologue** *n.* homologous thing

hom'onym *n.* word of same form as another, but of different sense —**homon'ymous** *a.*

homosex'ual *n.* person sexually attracted to members of the same sex —*a.* —**homosexual'ity** *n.* —**homopho'bia** *n.* hate or fear of homosexuals and homosexuality —**ho'mophobe** *n.*

Hon. Honourable; (*also* **h-**) honorary

hone *n.* whetstone —*vt.* sharpen on one

hon'est [on'-] *a.* not cheating, lying, stealing *etc.*; genuine; without pretension —**hon'estly** *adv.* —**hon'esty** *n.* quality of being honest; plant with silvery seed pods

hon'ey [hun'i] *n.* sweet fluid made by bees; term of endearment —**hon'eycomb** *n.* wax structure in hexagonal cells in which bees place honey, eggs *etc.* —*vt.* fill with cells or perforations —**hon'eydew** *n.* sweet sticky substance found on plants; type of sweet melon —**hon'eymoon** *n.* holiday taken by newly-wedded pair —**hon'eysuckle** *n.* climbing plant

honk *n.* call of wild goose; any sound like this, *esp.* sound of automobile horn —*vi.* make this sound —**honk'er** *n.* person or thing that honks; *inf.* Canada goose —**honky-tonk** *n.* cheap disreputable nightclub, bar *etc.*; ragtime style of piano-playing

hon'o(u)r [on'ə] *n.* personal integrity; renown; reputation; sense of what is right or due; chastity; high rank or position; source, cause of honour; pleasure, privilege —*pl.* mark of respect; distinction in examination —*vt.* respect highly; confer honour on; accept or pay (bill *etc.*) when due —**hon'o(u)rable** *a.* —**hon'o(u)rably** *adv.* —**honora'rium** *n.* a fee (*pl.* **-ria**) —**hon'orary** *a.* conferred for the sake of honour only; holding position without pay or usual requirements; giving services without pay —**honorif'ic** *a.* conferring honour

hood[1] *n.* covering for head and neck, often part of cloak or gown; hood-like thing as (adjustable) top of automobile, perambulator *etc.*; cover of automobile engine —**hood'ed** *a.* covered with or shaped like a hood —**hood'wink** *vt.* deceive

hood[2] *n. sl.* hoodlum

hood'lum [-ōō-] *n.* gangster, bully

hoo'doo *n.* cause of bad luck

hoof [-ōō-] *n.* horny casing of foot of horse *etc.* (*pl.* **hoofs** *or* **hooves**) —**on the hoof** (of livestock) alive

hook *n.* bent piece of metal *etc.*, for catching hold, hanging up *etc.*; something resembling hook in shape or function; curved cutting tool; *Boxing* blow delivered with bent elbow —*vt.* grasp, catch, hold, as with hook; fasten with hook; *Golf etc.* drive (ball) widely to the left —**hooked** *a.* shaped like hook; caught; *sl.* addicted to —**hook'er** *n. sl.* prostitute; *Rugby* player who uses feet to get ball in scrum —**hook'y** *n. inf.* unofficial absence, *esp.* from school —**hook-up** *n.* linking of radio, television stations —**hook'worm** *n.* parasitic worm infesting humans and animals —**play hooky** *inf.* be absent without permission

hook'ah *n.* oriental pipe in which smoke is drawn through water and long tube

hoo'ligan *n.* violent, irresponsible (young) person —**hoo'liganism** *n.*

hoop [-ōō-] *n.* rigid circular band of metal, wood *etc.*; such a band used for binding barrel *etc.*, for use as a toy, or for jumping through as in circus acts —*vt.* bind with hoops; encircle

hoop'la [hōōp'lah] *n. sl.* noise, bustle; ballyhoo

hoop'oe [hōō'pō] *n.* bird with large crest

hoot [-ōō-] *n.* owl's cry or similar sound; cry of disapproval or derision; *inf.* funny person or thing —*vi.* utter hoot (*esp.* in derision); sound automobile horn; *inf.* laugh

hoote'nanny *n.* informal performance by folk singers

hop[1] *vi.* spring on one foot; *inf.* move quickly —*vt.* travel by means of (aircraft, bus *etc.*) (**-pp-**) —*n.* leap, skip; one stage of journey —**hop'scotch** *n.* children's game of hopping in pattern drawn on ground

hop[2] *n.* climbing plant with bitter cones used to flavour beer *etc.* —*pl.* the cones

hope *n.* expectation of something desired; thing that gives, or object of, this feeling —*v.* feel hope (for) —**hope'ful** *a.* —**hope'fully** *adv.* (*esp. now*) *inf.* it is hoped —**hope'less** *a.* —**young hopeful** promising boy or girl

hopp'er *n.* one who hops; device for feeding material into mill or machine or grain into railway wagon *etc.*

hor'al, hor'ary *a. obs.* pert. to an hour; hourly

horde *n.* large crowd (*esp.* moving together)

hore'hound *n.* plant with bitter juice formerly used medicinally

hori'zon *n.* boundary of part of the earth seen from any given point; lines where earth and sky seem to meet; boundary of mental outlook —**horizon'tal** *a.* parallel with horizon, level —**horizon'tally** *adv.*

hor'mone *n.* substance secreted by certain glands which stimulates organs of the body; synthetic substance with same effect

horn *n.* hard projection on heads of certain animals, *eg* cows; substance of it; various things made of, or resembling it; wind instrument *orig.* made of a horn; device (*esp.* in automobile) emitting sound as alarm, warning *etc.* —**horned** *a.* having horns —**horn'y** *a.* —**horn'beam** *n.* tree with smooth grey bark —**horn'bill** *n.* type of bird with horny growth on large bill —**horn'pipe** *n.* lively dance, *esp.* associated with sailors

horn'blende *n.* mineral consisting of silica, with magnesia, lime, or iron

horn'et *n.* large insect of wasp family

hor'ologe [ho'rə-loj] *n.* any timepiece —**horol'ogy** *n.* art or science of clock-making and measuring time

hor'oscope [ho'rə-] *n.* observation of, or scheme showing disposition of planets *etc.*, at given moment, *esp.* birth, by which character and abilities of individual are predicted; telling of person's fortune by this method

horren'dous *a.* horrific

horr'or *n.* terror; loathing, fear of; its cause —**horr'ible** *a.* exciting horror, hideous, shocking —**horr'ibly** *adv.* —**hor'rid** *a.* unpleasant, repulsive; *inf.* unkind —**horr'ify** *vt.* move to horror (**-ified, -ifying**) —**horrif'ic** *a.* particularly horrible

hors d'oeu'vre [aw-dur'vr] *n.* small dish served before main meal

horse *n.* four-footed animal used for riding and draught; cavalry; vaulting-block; frame for support *etc.*, *esp.* for drying clothes —*vt.* provide with horse or horses —**hors'y** *a.* having to do with horses; devoted to horses or horse racing —**horse'back** *n./a.* (on) horse's back —**horse chestnut** tree with conical clusters of white or pink flowers and large nuts —**horse'fly** *n.* large, blood-sucking fly —**horse laugh** harsh boisterous laugh —**horse'man** *n.* (**horse'-woman** *fem.*) rider on horse —**horse'-power** *n.* unit of power of engine *etc.* 550 foot-pounds per second —**horse'radish** *n.* plant with pungent root —**horse'shoe** *n.* protective U-shaped piece of iron nailed to horse's hoof; thing so shaped —**horse'tail** *n.* green flowerless plant with erect, jointed stem —**horse about** (*or* **around**) *inf.* play roughly, boisterously

hor'ticulture *n.* art or science of gardening —**horticul'tural** *a.* —**horticul'-turist** *n.*

Hos. Hosea

hosann'a [-z-] *n.* cry of praise, adoration

hose *n.* flexible tube for conveying liquid or gas; stockings or socks —*vt.* water with hose —**ho'sier** *n.* dealer in stockings *etc.* —**ho'siery** *n.* stockings *etc.*

hos'pice [-is] *n. obs.* traveller's house of rest kept by religious order

hos'pital *n.* institution for care of sick —**hospitaliza'tion** *n.* —**hos'pitalize** *vt.* to place for care in a hospital

hospital'ity *n.* friendly and liberal reception of strangers or guests —**hos'pitable** *a.* welcoming, kindly —**hos'pitably** *adv.*

host[1] [hō-] *n.* (**host'ess** *fem.*) one who entertains another; innkeeper; compere of show; animal, plant on which parasite lives —*vt.* act as a host

host[2] [hō-] *n.* large number

Host [hō-] *n.* consecrated bread of the Eucharist

hos'tage *n.* person taken or given as pledge or security

hos'tel *n.* building providing accommodation at low cost for particular category of people, as students, or the homeless —**hos'telry** *n. obs.* inn —**hostel school** government boarding school for Indian and Inuit students

hos'tile *a.* opposed, antagonistic; warlike; of an enemy; unfriendly —**hostil'ity** *n.* enmity —*pl.* acts of warfare

hot *a.* of high temperature, very warm, giving or feeling heat; angry; severe; recent, new; much favoured; spicy; *sl.* good, quick, smart; *sl.* stolen (**hott'er** *comp.*, **hott'est** *sup.*) —**hot'ly** *adv.* —**hot'ness** *n.* —**hot air** *inf.* boastful, empty talk —**hot'bed** *n.* bed of earth heated by manure and grass for young plants; any place encouraging growth —**hot-blooded** *a.* passionate, excitable —**hot dog** hot sausage (*esp.* frankfurter) in split bread roll —**hot'foot** *v./adv.* (go) quickly —**hot'head** *n.* hasty, intemperate person —**hot'house** *n.* forcing house for plants; heated building for cultivating tropical plants in cold or temperate climates —**hot line** direct communication link between heads of governments *etc.* —**hot'plate** *n.* heated plate on electric cooker; portable device for keeping food warm

hotch'potch *n.* hodgepodge

hotel' [hō-] *n.* commercial establishment providing lodging and meals —**hotel keeper, hotel'ier** [-yā] *n.*

Hott'entot *n.* member of a native S Afr. race, now nearly extinct

hough [hok] *n. same as* HOCK[1]

hound *n.* hunting dog —*vt.* chase, urge, pursue

hour [owr] *n.* twenty-fourth part of day; sixty minutes; time of day; appointed time —*pl.* fixed periods for work, prayers *etc.*; book of prayers —**hour'ly** *adv.* every hour; frequently —*a.* frequent; happening every hour —**hour'glass** *n.* sandglass running an hour

hou'ri [hōō'ri] *n.* beautiful nymph of the Muslim paradise (*pl.* **-ris**)

house [-s] *n.* building for human habitation; building for other specified purpose; legislative, or other assembly; family; business firm; theatre audience, performance —*vt.* [-z] give or receive shelter, lodging or storage; cover or contain —**hous'ing** *n.* (providing of) houses; part or structure designed to cover, protect, contain —**house'boat** *n.* boat for living in on river *etc.* —**house'breaker** *n.* burglar —**house'coat** *n.* woman's long loose garment for casual wear at home —**house'hold** *n.* inmates of house collectively —**house'holder** *n.* occupier of house as his dwelling; head of household —**house'keeper** *n.* person managing affairs of household —**house'keeping** *n.* (money for) running household —**house'maid** *n.* maidservant who cleans rooms *etc.* —**house-warming** *n.* party to celebrate entry into new house —**house'wife** *n.* woman who runs a household, homemaker

hov'el *n.* mean dwelling

hov'er *vi.* hang in the air (of bird *etc.*); loiter; be in state of indecision —**hov'ercraft** *n.* type of craft which can travel over both land and sea on a cushion of air

how *adv.* in what way; by what means; in what condition; to what degree; (in direct or dependent question) —**howev'er** *conj.* nevertheless —*adv.* in whatever way, degree; all the same

how'dah *n.* (canopied) seat on elephant's back

how'itzer *n.* short gun firing shells at high elevation

howl *vi.* utter long loud cry —*n.* such cry —**how'ler** *n.* one that howls; *inf.* stupid mistake

hoy'den *n.* wild, boisterous girl, tomboy

HP high pressure; (*also* **hp**) horsepower

HQ headquarters

HRH His (*or* Her) Royal Highness

HRT hormone replacement therapy

hub *n.* middle part of wheel, from which spokes radiate; central point of activity

hubb'ub *n.* confused noise of many voices; uproar

huck'ster *n.* person using aggressive or questionable methods of selling —*vt.* sell goods thus

hud'dle *n.* crowded mass; *inf.* impromptu conference —*v.* heap, crowd together; hunch

hue [hyo͞o] *n.* colour, complexion

hue and cry public uproar, outcry; loud outcry usually in pursuit of wrongdoer

huff *n.* passing mood of anger —*v.* make or become angry, resentful —*vi.* blow, puff heavily —**huff'ily** *adv.* —**huff'y** *a.*

hug *vt.* clasp tightly in the arms; cling; keep close to (**-gg-**) —*n.* fond embrace

huge *a.* very big —**huge'ly** *adv.* very much

hu'la [ho͞o'-] *n.* native dance of Hawaii

Hula-Hoop R hoop of plastic *etc.* swung round body by wriggling hips

hulk *n.* body of abandoned vessel; *offens.* large, unwieldy person or thing —**hulk'ing** *a.* unwieldy, bulky

hull *n.* frame, body of ship; calyx of strawberry , raspberry, or similar fruit; shell, husk —*vt.* remove shell, hull; send shot into hull

hullabaloo' *n.* uproar, clamour, row

hum *vi.* make low continuous sound as bee; *sl.* be very active —*vt.* sing with closed lips (**-mm-**) —*n.* humming sound; *sl.* great activity; in radio, disturbance affecting reception —**humm'ingbird** *n.* very small bird whose wings make humming noise

hu'man *a.* of man, relating to, characteristic of, man's nature —**humane'** *a.* benevolent, kind; merciful —**hu'manism** *n.* belief in human effort rather than religion; interest in human welfare and affairs; classical literary culture —**hu'manist** *n.* —**humanita'rian** *n.* philanthropist —*a.* —**human'ity** *n.* human nature; human race; kindliness —*pl.* study of literature, philosophy, the arts —**hu'manize** *vt.* make human; civilize —**hu'manly** *adv.* —**hu'mankind** *n.* whole race of man

hum'ble *a.* lowly, modest —*vt.* bring low, abase, humiliate —**hum'bly** *adv.*

hum'bug *n.* impostor; sham, nonsense, deception; sweet of boiled sugar —*vt.* deceive; defraud (**-gg-**)

hum'dinger *n. sl.* excellent person or thing

hum'drum *a.* commonplace, dull, monotonous

hu'meral *a.* of shoulder —**hu'merus** *n.* long bone of upper arm (*pl.* **-eri** [-ī])

hu'mid *a.* moist, damp —**humid'ifier** *n.* device for increasing amount of water vapour in air in room *etc.* —**humid'ify** *vt.* —**humid'ity** *n.*

humil'iate [hyo͞o-] *vt.* lower dignity of, abase, mortify —**humilia'tion** *n.*

humil'ity [hyo͞o-] *n.* state of being humble; meekness

humm'ock *n.* low knoll, hillock; ridge of ice

hu'mo(u)r *n.* faculty of saying or perceiving what excites amusement; state of mind, mood; temperament; *obs.* fluids of body —*vt.* gratify, indulge —**hu'morist** *n.* person who acts, speaks, writes humorously —**hu'morous** *a.* funny; amusing —**hu'morously** *adv.*

hump *n.* normal or deforming lump, *esp.* on back; hillock —*vt.* make hump-shaped; *sl.* carry or heave —**hump'back** *n.* person with hump —**hump'backed** *a.* having a hump

hu'mus *n.* decayed vegetable and animal mould

hunch *n. inf.* intuition or premonition; hump —*vt.* thrust, bend into hump —**hunch'back** *n.* humpback

hun'dred *n./a.* cardinal number, ten times ten —**hun'dredth** *a.* the ordinal number —**hun'dredfold** *a./adv.* —**hun'dredweight** *n.* weight of 100 lbs. (45.4kg); **UK** weight of 112 lbs. (50.8 kg), 20th part of ton

hung *pt./pp. of* HANG —*a.* (of jury *etc.*) unable to decide; not having majority —**hung-over** *a. inf.* suffering from after-effects of excessive drinking —**hung up** *inf.* emotionally disturbed

hun'ger *n.* discomfort, exhaustion from lack of food; strong desire —*vi.* —**hun'grily** *adv.* —**hun'gry** *a.* having keen appetite —**hunger strike** refusal of all food, as a protest

hunk *n.* thick piece

hunk'y-dor'y *a. inf.* very satisfactory

hunt *v.* seek out to kill or capture for sport or food; search (for) —*n.* chase, search; track of country hunted over; (party organized for) hunting; pack of hounds; hunting district or society —**hun'ter** *n.* one who hunts (**hunt'ress** *fem.*); horse, dog bred for hunting —**hunter-killer** *a.* denoting submarine designed to pursue and destroy enemy craft —**hunts'man** *n.* man in charge of pack of hounds

hur'dle *n.* portable frame of bars for

temporary fences or for jumping over; obstacle —*pl.* race over hurdles —*vi.* race over hurdles —**hurd'ler** *n.* one who races over hurdles

hur'dy-gur'dy *n.* mechanical (musical) instrument, *eg* barrel organ

hurl *vt.* throw violently —**hurly-burly** *n.* loud confusion

hurrah', hurray' *interj.* exclamation of joy or applause

hurr'icane *n.* very strong, potentially destructive wind or storm

hurr'y *v.* (cause to) move or act in great haste (**hurr'ied, hurr'ying**) —*n.* undue haste; eagerness —**hurr'iedly** *adv.*

hurt *vt.* injure, damage, give pain to, wound feelings of; distress —*vi. inf.* feel pain (**hurt** *pt./pp.*) —*n.* wound, injury, harm —**hurt'ful** *a.*

hur'tle *vi.* move rapidly; rush violently; whirl

hus'band [-z-] *n.* married man —*vt.* economize; use to best advantage —**hus'bandry** *n.* farming; economy

hush *v.* make or be silent —*n.* stillness; quietness —**hush'hush** *a. inf.* secret —**hush up** suppress rumours, information, make secret

husk *n.* dry covering of certain seeds and fruits; worthless outside part —*vt.* remove husk from —**husk'y** *a.* rough in tone; hoarse; dry as husk, dry in the throat; of, full of, husks; *inf.* big and strong

hus'ky *n.* Arctic sled dog; *sl.* Inuit

hussar' [-z-] *n.* light armed cavalry soldier

huss'y *n.* cheeky girl or young woman

hust'ings *pl.n.* UK platform from which parliamentary candidates were nominated; political campaigning

hus'tle [hus'l] *v.* push about, jostle, hurry —*vi. sl.* solicit —*n.* —**hus'tler** *n.*

hut *n.* any small house or shelter, usu. of wood or metal

hutch *n.* box-like pen for rabbits *etc.*

hy'acinth *n.* bulbous plant with bell-shaped flowers, *esp.* purple-blue; this blue; orange gem jacinth

hy(a)e'na [hī-ē'nə] *n.* wild animal related to dog

hy'aline [-lin] *a.* clear, translucent

hy'brid *n.* offspring of two plants or animals of different species; mongrel —*a.* crossbred —**hy'bridism** *n.* —**hy'bridize** *v.* make hybrid; cross-breed

hy'datid *a./n.* (of) watery cyst, resulting from development of tapeworm larva causing serious disease (in man)

hy'dra *n.* fabulous many-headed water serpent; any persistent problem; freshwater polyp —**hydra-headed** *a.* hard to root out

hydrang'ea [-rānj'ə] *n.* ornamental shrub with pink, blue, or white flowers

hy'drant *n.* water-pipe with nozzle for hose

hydraul'ic *a.* concerned with, operated by, pressure transmitted through liquid in pipe —**hydraul'ics** *pl.n.* science of mechanical properties of liquid in motion

hy'dro *n.* hydroelectric power; electricity as supplied to residence, business *etc.*; (**H-**) hydroelectric power company

hydro- (*comb. form*) water, as *hydroelectric*; presence of hydrogen, as *hydrocarbon*

hydrocar'bon *n.* compound of hydrogen and carbon

hydrochlor'ic acid [-klo'-] strong colourless acid used in many industrial and laboratory processes

hydrodynam'ics *n.* science of the motions of system wholly or partly fluid

hydroelec'tric *a.* pert. to generation of electricity by use of water

hy'drofoil *n.* fast, light vessel with hull raised out of water at speed by vanes in water

hy'drogen *n.* colourless gas which combines with oxygen to form water —**hydrogen bomb** atom bomb of enormous power in which hydrogen nuclei are converted into helium nuclei —**hydrogen peroxide** colourless liquid used as antiseptic and bleach

hydrog'raphy *n.* description of waters of the earth —**hydrog'rapher** *n.* —**hydrograph'ic** *a.*

hydrol'ysis *n.* decomposition of chemical compound reacting with water

hydrom'eter *n.* device for measuring relative density of liquid

hydropho'bia *n.* aversion to water, esp. as symptom of rabies

hy'drophone *n.* instrument for detecting sound through water

hy'droplane *n.* light skimming motorboat; seaplane; vane controlling motion of submarine *etc.*

hydropon'ics *pl.n.* science of cultivating plants in water without using soil

hydrother'apy *n. Med.* treatment of disease by external application of water

hy'drous *a.* containing water

hy'giene [hī'jēn] *n.* principles and practice of health and cleanliness; study of these principles —**hygie'nic** *a.* —**hygie'nically** *adv.* —**hy'gienist** *n.*

hygrom'eter *n.* instrument for measuring humidity of air

hygroscop'ic *a.* readily absorbing moisture from the atmosphere

hy'men *n.* membrane partly covering vagina of virgin; (**H-**) Greek god of marriage

hymn [him] *n.* song of praise, *esp.* to God —*vt.* praise in song —**hym'nal** *a.* of hymns —*n.* book of hymns *Also* **hymn book** —**hym'nodist** *n.* —**hym'nody** *n.* singing or composition of hymns

hype[1] *sl. n.* hypodermic syringe; drug addict —*v.* (*with* up) inject (oneself) with drug

hype[2] *sl. n.* deception, racket; intensive publicity —*v.* promote (a product) using intensive publicity

hyper- (*comb. form*) over, above, excessively, as in **hyperac'tive** *etc.* Such words are not given here where the meaning may easily be inferred from the simple word

hyper'bola *n.* curve produced when cone is cut by plane making larger angle with the base than the side makes

hyper'bole [-bə-li] *n.* rhetorical exaggeration —**hyperbol'ic(al)** *a.*

hyperbor'ean *a./n.* (inhabitant) of extreme north

hypercrit'ical *a.* too critical —**hypercrit'icism** *n.*

hypersen'sitive *a.* unduly vulnerable emotionally or physically

hyperten'sion *n.* abnormally high blood pressure

hy'phen *n.* short line (-) indicating that two words or syllables are to be connected —**hy'phenate** *vt.* —**hy'phenated** *a.* joined by a hyphen

hypno'sis [hip-] *n.* induced state like deep sleep in which subject acts on external suggestion —**hypnot'ic** *a.* of hypnosis or of the person or thing producing it —**hyp'notism** *n.* —**hyp'notist** *n.* —**hyp'notize** *vt.* affect with hypnosis

hy'po *n. short for* hyposulphite (sodium thiosulphate), used as fixer in developing photographs

hypo-, hyph-, hyp- (*comb. forms*) under, below, less, as in *hypocrite, hyphen etc.* Such words are not given here where meaning may easily be inferred from simple word

hypoallergen'ic *a.* (of cosmetics *etc.*) not likely to cause allergic reaction

hy'pocaust *n.* ancient Roman underfloor heating system

hypochon'dria [hī-pō-kon'-] *n.* morbid depression, without cause, about one's own health —**hypochon'driac** *a./n.* —**hypochondri'acal** *a.*

hypoc'risy [hip-] *n.* assuming of false appearance of virtue; insincerity —**hyp'ocrite** *n.* —**hypocrit'ical** *a.* —**hypocrit'ically** *adv.*

hypoderm'ic [hī-] *a.* introduced, injected beneath the skin —*n.* hypodermic syringe or needle

hypogas'tric [hī-] *a.* relating to, situated in, lower part of abdomen

hypot'enuse [hī-] *n.* side of a right-angled triangle opposite the right angle

hypother'mia *n.* condition of having body temperature reduced to dangerously low level

hypoth'esis [hī-] *n.* suggested explanation of something; assumption as basis of reasoning (*pl.* **-eses** [-sēz]) —**hypothet'ical** *a.* —**hypothet'ically** *adv.* —**hypoth'esize** *v.*

hypso- (*comb. form*) height, as in *hypsometry*

hypsog'raphy *n.* branch of geography dealing with altitudes

hy'rax *n.* genus of hoofed but rodent-like animals

hyss'op [his'-] *n.* small aromatic herb

hysterec'tomy [his-] *n.* surgical operation for removing the uterus

hystere'sis [his-] *n. Physics* lag or delay in changes in variable property of a system

hyste'ria [his-] *n.* mental disorder with emotional outbursts; any frenzied emotional state; fit of crying or laughing —**hyster'ical** [-te'ri-] *a.* —**hyster'ically** *adv.* —**hyster'ics** *pl.n.* fits of hysteria

Hz hertz

I

I *Chem.* iodine

I *pron.* the pronoun of the first person singular

iam'bus, i'amb [ī-] *n.* metrical foot of short and long syllable (*pl.* **-uses, -bi** [-bī], **i'ambs**) —**iam'bic** *a.*

IATA International Air Transport Association

iat'ric, iat'rical [ī-] *a.* of medicine or physicians, *esp.* as suffix **-iatrics, -iatry**, as in *paediatrics, psychiatry*

Ibe'rian [ī-] *a.* of Iberia, *ie* Spain and Portugal

i'bex *n.* wild goat with large horns (*pl.* **i'bexes, ib'ices** [-sēz])

ibid' *short for* ibidem (*Lat.* in the same place)

i'bis *n.* storklike bird

ICBM intercontinental ballistic missile

ice *n.* frozen water; frozen confection, ice cream —*v.* cover, become covered with ice; cool with ice; cover with icing —**i'cicle** *n.* tapering spike of ice hanging where water has dripped —**i'cily** *adv.* —**i'ciness** *n.* —**i'cing** *n.* mixture of sugar and water *etc.* used to decorate cakes —**i'cy** *a.* covered with ice; cold; chilling —**ice'berg** *n.* large floating mass of ice —**ice cream** sweetened frozen dessert made from cream, eggs *etc.* —**ice floe** sheet of floating ice —**ice hockey** team game played on ice with puck

ichneu'mon [ik-nyōō'-] *n.* greyish brown mongoose —**ichneumon fly** insect laying its eggs on larvae of other insects

ichthyol'ogy [ik-thi-] *n.* scientific study of fish —**ichthyosaur'us** *n.* a prehistoric marine animal (*pl.* **-i**)

i'cicle *see* ICE

i'con *n.* image, representation, *esp.* of religious figure —**icon'oclasm** *n.* —**icon'oclast** *n.* one who attacks established principles *etc.*; breaker of icons —**iconoclas'tic** *a.* —**iconog'raphy** *n.* icons collectively; study of icons

id *n. Psychoanalysis* the mind's instinctive energies

ide'a *n.* notion in the mind; conception; vague belief; plan, aim —**ide'al** *n.* conception of something that is perfect; perfect person or thing —*a.* perfect; visionary; existing only in idea —**ide'alism** *n.* tendency to seek perfection in everything; philosophy that mind is the only reality —**ide'alist** *n.* one who holds doctrine of idealism; one who strives after the ideal; impractical person —**idealis'tic** *a.* —**idealiza'tion** *n.* —**ide'alize** *vt.* portray as ideal —**ide'ally** *adv.*

i'dem *Lat.* the same

ident'ity *n.* individuality; being the same, exactly alike —**ident'ical** *a.* very same —**ident'ically** *adv.* —**iden'tifiable** *a.* —**identifica'tion** *n.* —**iden'tify** *v.* establish identity of; associate (oneself) with; treat as identical (**ident'ified, ident'ifying**)

id'eograph *n.* picture, symbol, figure *etc.*, suggesting an object without naming it *Also* **id'eogram** —**ideog'raphy** *n.* representation of things by ideographs

ideol'ogy [ī-di-] *n.* body of ideas, beliefs of group, nation *etc.* —**ideolog'ical** *a.*

ides [īdz] *pl.n.* the 15th of March, May, July and Oct. and the 13th of other months of the Ancient Roman calendar

id'iocy *see* IDIOT

id'iom *n.* way of expression natural or peculiar to a language or group; characteristic style of expression —**idiomat'ic** *a.* using idioms; colloquial —**idiomat'ically** *adv.*

idiosyn'crasy *n.* peculiarity of mind, temper or disposition in a person

id'iot *n.* mentally deficient person; foolish, senseless person —**id'iocy** *n.* —**idiot'ic** *a.* utterly senseless or stupid —**idiot'ically** *adv.*

i'dle *a.* unemployed; lazy; useless, vain, groundless —*vi.* be idle; (of engine) run slowly with gears disengaged —*vt.* (*esp. with* away) waste; cause (person or thing) to be unemployed —**i'dleness** *n.* —**i'dler** *n.* —**i'dly** *adv.*

i'dol *n.* image of deity as object of worship; object of excessive devotion —**idol'ater** *n.* worshipper of idols (**idol'atress** *fem.*) —**idol'atrous** *a.* —**idol'atry** *n.* —**i'dolize** *vt.* love or venerate to excess; make an idol of

id'yll *n.* short descriptive poem of picturesque or charming scene or episode, *esp.* of rustic life —**idyll'ic** *a.* of, like, idyll; delightful —**idyll'ically** *adv.*

i.e. *Lat. id est*, that is

if *conj.* on condition or supposition that; whether; although —*n.* uncertainty or doubt (*esp. in* **ifs and buts**) —**if'fy** *a. inf.* dubious

ig'loo *n.* dome-shaped Inuit house of snow and ice

ig'neous *a. esp.* of rocks, formed as molten rock cools and hardens

ignite' *v.* (cause to) burn —**igni'tion** *n.* act of kindling or setting on fire; in internal-combustion engine, means of firing explosive mixture, usu. electric spark

igno'ble *a.* mean, base; of low birth —**igno'bly** *adv.*

ig'nominy *n.* dishonour, disgrace; shameful act —**ignomin'ious** *a.* —**ignomin'iously** *adv.*

ignore' *vt.* disregard, leave out of account —**ignora'mus** *n.* ignorant person (*pl.* **-muses**) —**ig'norance** *n.* lack of knowledge —**ig'norant** *a.* lacking knowledge; uneducated; unaware —**ig'norantly** *adv.*

iguan'a [i-gwahn'ə] *n.* large tropical American lizard

iguan'odon [-gwahn'-] *n.* gigantic extinct herbivorous reptile

il- (*comb. form*) for *in-* before *l*: *see* IN- and listed words

il'eum *n.* lower part of small intestine —**il'eac** *a.*

ilk *a.* same —**of that ilk** of the same type or class

ill *a.* not in good health; bad, evil; faulty; unfavourable —*n.* evil, harm; mild disease —*adv.* badly; hardly, with difficulty —**ill'ness** *n.* —**ill-advised** *a.* imprudent; injudicious —**ill-fated** *a.* unfortunate —**ill-favo(u)red** *a.* ugly, deformed —**ill-gotten** *a.* obtained dishonestly —**ill-mannered** *a.* boorish, uncivil —**ill-omened** *a.* unlucky, inauspicious —**ill-timed** *a.* inopportune —**ill-treat** *vt.* treat cruelly —**ill will** unkind feeling, hostility

ill. illustrated; illustration

illegit'imate [-jit'-] *a.* born out of wedlock; unlawful; not regular —*n.* bastard —**illegit'imacy** *n.*

illic'it [-lis'-] *a.* illegal; prohibited, forbidden

illim'itable *a.* that cannot be limited, boundless, unrestricted, infinite —**illim'itableness** *n.*

illit'erate *a.* not literate; unable to read or write —*n.* illiterate person —**illit'eracy** *n.*

illu'minate [-lōō'-] *vt.* light up; clarify; decorate with lights; decorate with gold and colours —**illu'minant** *n.* agent of lighting —**illumina'tion** *n.* —**illu'minative** *a.* —**illu'mine** *vt. Poet.* illuminate

illu'sion [-lōō'-] *n.* deceptive appearance or belief —**illu'sionist** *n.* conjurer —**illu'sive** *a.* false —**illu'sory** *a.*

ill'ustrate *vt.* provide with pictures or examples; exemplify —**illustra'tion** *n.* picture, diagram; example; act of illustrating —**ill'ustrative** *a.* providing explanation —**ill'ustrator** *n.*

illus'trious *a.* famous; distinguished; exalted

im- (*comb. form*) for *in-* before *m*, *b*, and *p*: *see* IN- and listed words

im'age *n.* representation or likeness of person or thing; optical counterpart, as in mirror; double, copy; general impression; mental picture created by words, *esp.* in literature —*vt.* make image of; reflect —**im'agery** *n.* images collectively, *esp.* in literature

imag'ine [-maj'-] *vt.* picture to oneself; think; conjecture —**imag'inable** *a.* —**imag'inary** *a.* existing only in fancy —**imagina'tion** *n.* faculty of making mental images of things not present; fancy —**imag'inative** *a.* —**imag'inatively** *adv.*

ima'go *n.* last, perfected state of insect life; image (*pl.* **-es, imag'ines** [i-maj'ə-nēz])

imam' [-mahm'] *n.* Islamic minister or priest

imbal'ance *n.* lack of balance, proportion

im'becile [-sēl] *n.* idiot —*a.* idiotic —**imbecil'ity** *n.*
imbibe' *vt.* drink in; absorb —*vi.* drink
im'bricate(d) *a.* lying over each other in regular order, like tiles or shingles on roof —**imbrica'tion** *n.*
imbrogl'io [-brōl'yō] *n.* complicated situation, plot (*pl.* **-ios**)
imbrue' *vt.* stain (*esp.* with blood); permeate —**imbrue'ment** *n.*
imbue' [-byōō'] *vt.* inspire; imbrue; saturate, dye
IMF International Monetary Fund
im'itate *vt.* take as model; mimic, copy —**im'itable** *a.* —**imita'tion** *n.* act of imitating; copy of original; likeness; counterfeit —**im'itative** *a.* —**im'itator** *n.*
immac'ulate *a.* spotless; pure; unsullied
imm'anent *a.* abiding in, inherent —**im'manence** *n.*
immate'rial *a.* unimportant, trifling; not consisting of matter; spiritual
imme'diate *a.* occurring at once; direct, not separated by others —**imme'diacy** *n.* —**imme'diately** *adv.*
immemor'ial *a.* beyond memory —**immemo'rially** *adv.*
immense' *a.* huge, vast —**immense'ly** *adv.* —**immen'sity** *n.* vastness
immerse' *vt.* dip, plunge, into liquid; involve; engross —**immer'sion** *n.* immersing
imm'igrate *vi.* come into country as settler —**imm'igrant** *n./a.* —**immigra'tion** *n.*
imm'inent *a.* liable to happen soon; close at hand —**imm'inence** *n.* —**imm'inently** *adv.*
imm'olate *vt.* kill, sacrifice —**immola'tion** *n.*
immor'al [-mo'rəl] *a.* corrupt; promiscuous; indecent; unethical —**immoral'ity** *n.*
immor'tal *a.* deathless; famed for all time —*n.* immortal being; god; one whose fame will last —**immortal'ity** *n.* —**immor'talize** *vt.*
immune' [-myōōn'] *a.* proof (against a disease *etc.*); secure, exempt —**immu'nity** *n.* state of being immune; freedom from prosecution, tax *etc.* —**immuniza'tion** *n.* process of making immune to disease —**imm'unize** *vt.* make immune —**immunol'ogy** *n.* branch of biology concerned with study of immunity
immure' *vt.* imprison, wall up
immu'table *a.* unchangeable
imp *n.* little devil; mischievous child
imp. imperative; imperfect
im'pact *n.* collision; profound effect —**impact'** *vt.* drive, press
impair' *vt.* weaken, damage —**impair'ment** *n.*
impa'la [-pah'-] *n.* antelope of Southern Africa
impale' *vt.* pierce with sharp instrument; combine (two coats of arms) by placing them side by side with line between —**impale'ment** *n.*
impart' *vt.* communicate (information *etc.*); give
impar'tial *a.* not biased or prejudiced; fair —**impartial'ity** *n.*
impass'able *a.* not capable of being passed; blocked, as mountain pass
impasse' [-pahs'] *n.* deadlock; place, situation, from which there is no outlet
impass'ioned [-sh'-] *a.* deeply moved, ardent
impass'ive *a.* showing no emotion; calm —**impassiv'ity** *n.*
impeach' *vt.* charge with crime; call to account; denounce —**impeach'able** *a.* —**impeach'ment** *n.*
impecc'able *a.* without flaw or error —**impeccabil'ity** *n.*
impecu'nious *a.* poor —**impecunios'ity** *n.*
impede' *vt.* hinder —**impe'dance** *n.* *Electricity* measure of opposition offered to flow of alternating current —**imped'iment** *n.* obstruction; defect
impel' *vt.* induce, incite; drive, force (**-ll-**) —**impell'er** *n.*
impend' *vi.* threaten; be imminent; hang over —**impen'ding** *a.*
imper'ative [-pe'rə-] *a.* necessary; peremptory; expressing command —*n.* imperative mood —**imper'atively** *adv.*
impe'rial *a.* of empire, or emperor; majestic; denoting weights and measures established by law in Brit. —**impe'rialism** *n.* extension of empire; belief in colonial empire —**impe'rialist** *n.* —**imperialis'tic** *a.*
imper'il [-pe'ril] *vt.* bring into peril, endanger (**-ll-**)
impe'rious *a.* domineering; haughty

impers. impersonal
imper'sonal *a.* objective, having no personal significance; devoid of human warmth, personality *etc.*; (of verb) without personal subject —**impersonal'ity** *n.*
imper'sonate *vt.* pretend to be (another person); play the part of —**imperson'tion** *n.* —**imper'sonator** *n.*
impert'inent *a.* insolent, rude —**imper'tinence** *n.* —**impert'inently** *adv.*
impertur'bable *a.* calm, not excitable —**impertur'bably** *adv.*
imper'vious *a.* not affording passage; impenetrable (to feeling, argument *etc.*) —**imper'viously** *adv.* —**imper'viousness** *n.*
impeti'go [-tī'-] *n.* contagious skin disease
impet'uous *a.* likely to act without consideration, rash —**impet'uously** *adv.* —**impetuos'ity** *n.*
im'petus *n.* force with which body moves; impulse
impinge' *vi.* encroach (upon); collide (with) —**impinge'ment** *n.*
im'pious *a.* irreverent, profane, wicked
implac'able *a.* not to be appeased; unyielding —**implacabil'ity** *n.*
implant' [-ah-] *vt.* insert, fix
im'plement *n.* tool, instrument, utensil —*vt.* carry out (instructions *etc.*); put into effect
im'plicate *vt.* involve, include; entangle; imply —**implica'tion** *n.* something implied —**implic'it** [-plis'-] *a.* implied but not expressed; absolute and unreserved —**implic'itly** *adv.*
implore' *vt.* entreat earnestly —**implor'ingly** *adv.*
imply' *vt.* indicate by hint, suggest; mean (**implied'**, **imply'ing**)
import' *vt.* bring in, introduce (*esp.* goods from foreign country); imply —*n.* [im'-] thing imported; meaning; importance; *sl.* sportsman not native to area where he plays —**import'able** *a.* —**importa'tion** *n.* —**import'er** *n.*
import'ant *a.* of great consequence; momentous; pompous —**import'ance** *n.* —**import'antly** *adv.*
impor'tune *vt.* request, demand persistently —**impor'tunate** *a.* persistent —**impor'tunately** *adv.* —**importu'nity** *n.*
impose' *vt.* levy (tax, duty *etc.*, upon) —*vi.* take advantage (of), practise deceit on —**impos'ing** *a.* impressive —**imposi'tion** *n.* that which is imposed; tax; burden; deception —**im'post** *n.* duty, tax on imports
imposs'ible *a.* incapable of being done or experienced; absurd; unreasonable —**impossibil'ity** *n.* —**imposs'ibly** *adv.*
impos'tor *n.* deceiver, one who assumes false identity —**impos'ture** *n.*
im'potent *a.* powerless; (of males) incapable of sexual intercourse —**im'potence** *n.* —**im'potently** *adv.*
impound' *vt.* take legal possession of and, often, place in a pound (automobiles, animals *etc.*); confiscate
impov'erish *vt.* make poor or weak —**impov'erishment** *n.*
impreca'tion *n.* invoking of evil; curse —**im'precate** *vt.*
impreg'nable *a.* proof against attack; unassailable; unable to be broken into —**impregnabil'ity** *n.* —**impreg'nably** *adv.*
im'pregnate *vt.* saturate, infuse; make pregnant —**impregna'tion** *n.*
impresar'io *n.* organizer of public entertainment; manager of opera, ballet *etc.* (*pl.* **-s**)
impress'[1] *vt.* affect deeply, usu. favourably; imprint, stamp; fix —*n.* [im'-] act of impressing; mark impressed —**impressibil'ity** *n.* —**impress'ible** *a.* —**impres'sion** *n.* effect produced, *esp.* on mind; notion, belief; imprint; a printing; total of copies printed at once; printed copy —**impressionabil'ity** *n.* —**impres'sionable** *a.* susceptible to external influences —**impress'ionism** *n.* art style that renders general effect without detail —**impress'ionist** *n.* —**impressionis'tic** *a.* —**impress'ive** *a.* making deep impression
impress'[2] *vt.* press into service —**impress'ment** *n.*
imprest' *vt.* advance on loan by government —*n.* money advanced by government
imprima'tur *n.* licence to print book *etc.*
im'print *n.* mark made by pressure; characteristic mark —*vt.* [im-print'] produce mark; stamp; fix in mind

impris'on [-z'-] *vt.* put in prison —**impris'onment** *n.*

impromp'tu [-tyōō] *adv./a.* extempore; unrehearsed —*n.* improvisation

improve' [-ōōv'] *v.* make or become better in quality, standard, value *etc.* —**improv'able** *a.* —**improve'ment** *n.* —**improv'er** *n.*

improv'ident *a.* thriftless; negligent; imprudent —**improv'idence** *n.*

im'provise *v.* make use of materials at hand; compose, utter without preparation —**improvisa'tion** *n.*

im'pudent [-pyoo-] *a.* disrespectful, impertinent —**im'pudence** *n.* —**im'pudently** *adv.*

impugn' [-pyōōn'] *vt.* call in question, challenge

im'pulse *n.* sudden inclination to act; sudden application of force; motion caused by it; stimulation of nerve moving muscle —**impul'sion** *n.* impulse, usu. in the first sense —**impul'sive** *a.* given to acting without reflection, rash —**impul'sively** *adv.*

impu'nity *n.* freedom, exemption from injurious consequences or punishment

impute' *vt.* ascribe, attribute to —**imputabil'ity** *n.* —**imputa'tion** *n.* that which is imputed as a charge or fault; reproach, censure

in *prep.* expresses inclusion within limits of space, time, circumstance, sphere *etc.* —*adv.* in or into some state, place *etc.*; *inf.* in vogue *etc.* —*a. inf.* fashionable

in. inch(es)

in- (*comb. form*) with its forms **il-, im-, ir-** negatives the idea of the simple word: also forms compounds with the meaning of in, into, upon, as *inter, impend, irrigate.* The list below contains some compounds that will be understood if *not* or *lack of* is used with the meaning of the simple word

inadvert'ent *a.* not attentive; negligent; unintentional —**inadvert'ence, inadvert'ency** *n.* —**inadvert'ently** *adv.*

inane' *a.* foolish, silly, vacant —**inani'tion** *n.* exhaustion; silliness —**inan'ity** *n.*

inan'imate *a.* lacking qualities of living beings; appearing dead; lacking vitality

inasmuch' *adv.* seeing that (*only in* **inasmuch as**)

inaug'urate [-yoo-rāt] *vt.* begin, initiate the use of, *esp.* with ceremony; admit to office —**inaug'ural** *a.* —**inaug'urally** *adv.* —**inaugura'tion** *n.* act of inaugurating; ceremony to celebrate the initiation or admittance of

inauspi'cious [-spish'-] *a.* not auspicious; unlucky; unfavourable —**inauspi'ciously** *adv.*

in'board *a.* inside hull or bulwarks

in'born *a.* existing from birth; inherent

inbreed' *vt.* breed from union of closely related individuals (**inbred'** *pp.*) —**inbred'** *a.* produced as result of inbreeding; inborn, ingrained —**inbreed'ing** *n.*

inc. inclusive; incorporated; increase

incal'culable *a.* beyond calculation; very great

in cam'era in secret or private session

incandes'cent *a.* glowing with heat, shining; of artificial light, produced by glowing filament —**incandesce'** *vi.* glow —**incandes'cence** *n.*

incanta'tion *n.* magic spell or formula, charm

incapac'itate [-pas'-] *vt.* disable; make unfit; disqualify —**incapac'ity** *n.*

incar'cerate *vt.* imprison —**incarcera'tion** *n.* —**incar'cerator** *n.*

incarn'ate *vt.* embody in flesh, *esp.* in human form —*a.* embodied in flesh, in human form; typified —**incarna'tion** *n.*

incen'diary *a.* of malicious setting on fire of property; creating strife, violence *etc.*; designed to cause fires —*n.* fire

ille'gal	**impa'tient**	**impure'**	**incom'petent**
illeg'ible	**impercep'tible**	**inabil'ity**	**incomplete'**
illog'ical	**imper'fect**	**inacc'urate**	**inconsid'erate**
immature'	**impolite'**	**inad'equate**	**inconsist'ent**
immo'bile	**imprac'ticable**	**inappro'priate**	**inconve'nience**
immod'erate	**imprac'tical**	**inca'pable**	**incorrect'**
immod'est	**improb'able**	**incom'parable**	**incu'rable**
immov(e)'able	**impropri'ety**	**incompat'ible**	**inde'cent**

raiser; agitator; bomb filled with inflammatory substance —**incen'diarism** *n.*

incense'[1] *vt.* enrage

in'cense[2] *n.* gum, spice giving perfume when burned; its smoke —*vt.* burn incense to; perfume with it

incen'tive *n.* something that arouses to effort or action; stimulus

incep'tion *n.* beginning —**incep'tive** *a.* —**incep'tor** *n.*

incess'ant *a.* unceasing

in'cest *n.* sexual intercourse between two people too closely related to marry —**incest'uous** *a.*

inch *n.* one twelfth of foot, or 0.0254 metre —*v.* move very slowly

incho'ate [-kō'-] *a.* just begun; undeveloped

in'cident *n.* event, occurrence —*a.* naturally attaching to; striking, falling (upon) —**in'cidence** *n.* degree, extent or frequency of occurrence; a falling on, or affecting —**incident'al** *a.* occurring as a minor part or an inevitable accompaniment or by chance —**incident'ally** *adv.* by chance; by the way —**inciden'tals** *pl.n.* accompanying items

incin'erate *vt.* burn up completely; reduce to ashes —**incinera'tion** *n.* —**incin'erator** *n.*

incip'ient *a.* beginning

incise' [-sīz'] *vt.* cut into; engrave —**inci'sion** [-sizh'-] *n.* —**inci'sive** *a.* keen or biting (of remark *etc.*); sharp —**inci'sor** *n.* cutting tooth

incite' *vt.* urge, stir up —**incita'tion, incite'ment** *n.*

inclem'ent *a.* of weather, stormy, severe, cold —**inclem'ency** *n.*

incline' *v.* lean, slope; (cause to) be disposed; bend or lower (the head *etc.*) —*n.* [in'-] slope —**inclina'tion** *n.* liking, tendency or preference; sloping surface; degree of deviation

include' [-klōōd'] *vt.* have as (part of) contents; comprise; add in; take in —**inclu'sion** *n.* —**inclu'sive** *a.* including (everything) —**inclu'sively** *adv.*

incogni'to [-nē'- *or* in-kog'-] *adv./a.* under assumed identity —*n.* assumed identity (*pl.* **-tos**)

incohe'rent *a.* lacking clarity, disorganized; inarticulate —**incohe'rence** *n.* —**incohe'rently** *adv.*

in'come *n.* amount of money, *esp.* annual, from salary, investments *etc.*; receipts —**income tax** personal tax levied on annual income

in'coming *a.* coming in; about to come into office; next

incommode' *vt.* trouble, inconvenience; disturb —**incommo'dious** *a.* cramped; inconvenient

incommunicad'o [-kahd'ō] *a./adv.* deprived (by force or by choice) of communication with others

incon'gruous [-ng'g-] *a.* not appropriate; inconsistent, absurd —**incongru'ity** *n.* —**incon'gruously** *adv.*

in'connu *n.* whitefish of N Canad. waters

incon'sequent, inconsequen'tial *a.* illogical; irrelevant, trivial

incontrover'tible *a.* undeniable; indisputable

incorp'orate *vt.* include; unite into one body; form into corporation —**incorpora'tion** *n.*

incorr'igible *a.* beyond correction or reform; firmly rooted —**incorrigibil'ity** *n.*

increase' *v.* make or become greater in size, number *etc.* —*n.* [in'-] growth, enlargement, profit —**increas'ingly** *adv.* more and more

incred'ible *a.* unbelievable; *inf.* marvellous, amazing

incred'ulous *a.* unbelieving —**incredu'lity** *n.*

in'crement *n.* increase, *esp.* one of a series

indeci'sive
indef'inite
indirect'
indiscreet'
ineffic'ient
inexpen'sive
inexper'ienced
infer'tile
infor'mal
infre'quent
ingrat'itude
inhospit'able
inoffen'sive
insan'itary
insen'sitive
insignif'icant
insincere'
insol'vent
insuffic'ient
intan'gible
intol'erable
inval'id
inva'riable
invis'ible
invul'nerable
irrat'ional
irreg'ular
irrel'evant
irreplace'able
irresist'ible
irres'olute
irrespon'sible

incrim'inate *vt.* imply guilt of; charge with crime —**incrim'inatory** *a.*

incrust' *see* ENCRUST

in'cubate [-kyoo-] *vt.* provide (eggs, embryos, bacteria *etc.*) with heat or other favourable condition for development —*vi.* develop in this way —**incuba'tion** *n.* —**in'cubator** *n.* apparatus for artificially hatching eggs, for rearing premature babies

in'cubus [-kyoo-] *n.* nightmare or obsession; (*orig.*) demon believed to afflict sleeping person (*pl.* **-bi** [-bī], **-buses**)

in'culcate *vt.* impress on the mind —**inculca'tion** *n.* —**in'culcator** *n.*

incumb'ent *a.* lying, resting (on) —*n.* holder of office, *esp.* church benefice —**incumb'ency** *n.* obligation; office or tenure of incumbent —**it is incumbent on** it is the duty of

incur' *vt.* fall into, bring upon oneself (**-rr-**) —**incur'sion** *n.* invasion, penetration

incuse' *vt.* impress by striking or stamping —*a.* hammered —*n.* impression made by stamping

ind. independent; index; indicative

indebt'ed [-det'-] *a.* owing gratitude for help, favours *etc.*; owing money —**indebt'edness** *n.*

indeed' *adv.* in truth; really; in fact; certainly —*interj.* denoting surprise, doubt *etc.*

indefat'igable *a.* untiring —**indefat'igably** *adv.*

indefeas'ible [-fēz'-] *a.* that cannot be lost or annulled —**indefeasibil'ity** *n.*

indefen'sible *a.* not justifiable or defensible —**indefen'sibly** *adv.*

indel'ible *a.* that cannot be blotted out, effaced or erased; producing such a mark —**indelibil'ity** *n.* —**indel'ibly** *adv.*

indel'icate *a.* coarse, embarrassing, tasteless

indem'nity *n.* compensation; security against loss —**indemnifica'tion** *n.* —**indem'nify** *vt.* give indemnity to; compensate (**indem'nified, indem'nifying**)

indent' *v.* set in (from margin *etc.*); make notches, holes in; draw up document in duplicate; make an order (upon someone for); place order for by indent —*n.* [in'-] notch; order, requisition —**indenta'tion** *n.* —**inden'ture** *n.* indented document; contract, *esp.* one binding apprentice to master —*vt.* bind thus

indepen'dent *a.* not subject to others; self-reliant; free; valid in itself; politically of no party —**indepen'dence, indepen'dency** *n.* being independent; self-reliance; self-support —**indepen'dently** *adv.*

indescri'bable *a.* beyond description; too intense *etc.* for words —**indescri'bably** *adv.*

indeterm'inate *a.* uncertain; inconclusive; incalculable

in'dex *n.* alphabetical list of references, usu. at end of book; pointer, indicator; *Math.* exponent; forefinger (*pl.* **in'dexes,** *Math.* **in'dices** [-sēz]) —*vt.* provide book with index; insert in index

India ink very dark black (drawing) ink

In'dian *n.* native of India; aboriginal American —*a.* —**Indian corn** corn —**Indian hemp** cannabis —**Indian list** *inf.* list of people to whom spirits may not be sold

in'dicate *vt.* point out; state briefly; signify —**indica'tion** *n.* sign; token; explanation —**indic'ative** *a.* pointing to; *Grammar* stating fact —**in'dicator** *n.* one who, that which, indicates; on vehicle, flashing light showing driver's intention to turn

indict' [-dīt'] *vt.* accuse, *esp.* by legal process —**indict'able** *a.* —**indict'ment** *n.*

indiff'erent *a.* uninterested; unimportant; neither good nor bad; inferior; neutral —**indiff'erence** *n.* —**indif'ferently** *adv.*

indig'enous [-dij'-] *a.* born in or natural to a country —**in'digene** *n.* aborigine; native

in'digent [-j-] *a.* poor, needy —**in'digence** *n.* poverty

indigest'ion [-jest'-] *n.* (discomfort, pain caused by) difficulty in digesting food —**indigest'ible** *a.*

indig'nant *a.* moved by anger and scorn; angered by sense of injury or injustice —**indig'nantly** *adv.* —**indigna'tion** *n.* —**indig'nity** *n.* humiliation, insult, slight

in'digo *n.* blue dye obtained from plant; the plant (*pl.* **-go(e)s**) —*a.* deep blue

indiscrim'inate *a.* lacking discrimination; jumbled

indispens'able *a.* necessary; essential

indisposi'tion [-zish'-] *n.* sickness; disinclination —**indispose'** *vt.* —**indisposed'** *a.* unwell, not fit; disinclined

indissol'uble *a.* permanent

in'dium *n.* soft silver-white metallic element

individ'ual *a.* single; characteristic of single person or thing; distinctive —*n.* single person or thing —**individ'ualism** *n.* principle of asserting one's independence —**individ'ualist** *n.* —**individualis'tic** *a.* —**individual'ity** *n.* distinctive character; personality —**individ'ualize** *vt.* make (or treat as) individual —**individ'ually** *adv.* singly

indoc'trinate *vt.* implant beliefs in the mind of

in'dolent *a.* lazy —**in'dolence** *n.* —**in'dolently** *adv.*

indom'itable *a.* unyielding —**indom'itably** *adv.*

in'door *a.* within doors; under cover —**indoors'** *adv.*

indorse' *see* ENDORSE

indu'bitable *a.* beyond doubt; certain —**indu'bitably** *adv.*

induce' *vt.* persuade; bring on; cause; produce by induction —**induce'ment** *n.* incentive, attraction

induct' *vt.* install in office —**induc'tion** *n.* an inducting; general inference from particular instances; production of electric or magnetic state in body by its being near (not touching) electrified or magnetized body; in internal-combustion engine, part of the piston's action which draws gas from carburettor —**induc'tance** *n.* —**induc'tive** *a.* —**induc'tively** *adv.* —**induc'tor** *n.*

indulge' *vt.* gratify; give free course to; pamper; spoil —**indul'gence** *n.* an indulging; extravagance; something granted as a favour or privilege; *RC Ch.* remission of temporal punishment due after absolution —**indul'gent** *a.* —**indul'gently** *adv.*

in'dustry *n.* manufacture, processing *etc.* of goods; branch of this; diligence; habitual hard work —**indus'trial** *a.* of industries, trades —**indus'trialize** *vt.* —**indus'trious** *a.* diligent

ine'briate *vt.* make drunk; intoxicate —*a.* drunken —*n.* habitual drunkard —**inebria'tion, inebri'ety** *n.* drunkenness

ined'ible *a.* not eatable; unfit for food —**inedibil'ity** *n.*

ined'ucable *a.* incapable of being educated, *esp.* through mental retardation

ineff'able *a.* too great or sacred for words; unutterable —**ineffabil'ity** *n.* —**inef'fably** *adv.*

inel'igible [-ji-] *a.* not fit or qualified (for something) —**ineligibil'ity** *n.*

inept' *a.* absurd; out of place; clumsy —**inept'itude** *n.*

inert' *a.* without power of action or resistance; slow, sluggish; chemically unreactive —**iner'tia** [-shə] *n.* inactivity; property by which matter continues in its existing state of rest or motion in straight line, unless that state is changed by external force —**inert'ly** *adv.* —**inert'ness** *n.*

ines'timable *a.* too good, too great, to be estimated

inev'itable *a.* unavoidable; sure to happen —**inevitabil'ity** *n.* —**inev'itably** *adv.*

inex'orable *a.* relentless —**inex'orably** *adv.*

inexplic'able *a.* impossible to explain

in extre'mis *Lat.* at the point of death

inf. infinitive; information

infall'ible *a.* unerring; not liable to fail; certain, sure —**infallibil'ity** *n.* —**infal'libly** *adv.*

in'famous *a.* notorious; shocking —**in'famously** *adv.* —**in'famy** *n.*

in'fant *n.* very young child —**in'fancy** *n.* —**infant'icide** *n.* murder of newborn child; person guilty of this —**in'fantile** *a.* childish

in'fantry *n.* foot soldiers

infat'uate *vt.* inspire with folly or foolish passion —**infat'uated** *a.* foolishly enamoured —**infatua'tion** *n.*

infect' *vt.* affect (with disease); contaminate —**infec'tion** *n.* —**infec'tious** *a.* catching, spreading, pestilential

infer' *vt.* deduce, conclude (**-rr-**) —**in'ference** *n.* —**inferen'tial, infer'able** *a.* deduced

infe'rior *a.* of poor quality; lower —*n.* one lower (in rank *etc.*) —**inferior'ity** *n.* —**inferiority complex** *Psychoanalysis* repressed sense of inferiority

infern'al *a.* devilish; hellish; *inf.* irritating, confounded —**infern'ally** *adv.*

infer'no *n.* region of hell; conflagration

infest' *vt.* inhabit or overrun in dangerously or unpleasantly large numbers —**infesta'tion** *n.*

infidel'ity *n.* unfaithfulness; religious disbelief; disloyalty; treachery —**in'fidel** *n.* unbeliever —*a.*

in'filtrate *v.* trickle through; cause to pass through pores; gain access surreptitiously —**infiltra'tion** *n.*

in'finite [-it] *a.* boundless —**in'finitely** *adv.* exceedingly —**infinites'imal** *a.* extremely, infinitely small —**infin'ity** *n.* unlimited and endless extent

infin'itive *a. Grammar* in mood expressing notion of verb without limitation of tense, person, or number —*n.* verb in this mood; the mood

infirm' *a.* physically weak; mentally weak; irresolute —**infirm'ary** *n.* hospital, sick-quarters —**infirm'ity** *n.*

inflame' *v.* rouse to anger, excitement; cause inflammation in; become inflamed —**inflammabil'ity** *n.* —**inflamm'able** *a.* easily set on fire; excitable —**inflamma'tion** *n.* infection of part of the body, with pain, heat, swelling, and redness —**inflamm'atory** *a.*

inflate' *v.* blow up with air, gas; swell; cause economic inflation; raise price, *esp.* artifically —**infla'table** *a.* —**infla'tion** *n.* increase in prices and fall in value of money —**infla'tionary** *a.*

inflect' *vt.* modify (words) to show grammatical relationships; bend inwards —**inflec'tion** *n.* modification of word; modulation of voice

inflex'ible *a.* incapable of being bent; stern —**inflexibil'ity** *n.* —**inflex'ibly** *adv.*

inflict' *vt.* impose, deliver forcibly —**inflic'tion** *n.* inflicting; punishment

inflores'cence *n.* the unfolding of blossoms; botanical term for arrangement of flowers on stem

in'fluence *n.* effect of one person or thing on another; power of person or thing having an effect; thing, person exercising this —*vt.* sway; induce; affect —**influen'tial** *a.* —**influen'tially** *adv.*

influen'za *n.* contagious feverish catarrhal virus disease

in'flux *n.* a flowing in; inflow

in'fo *n. inf.* information

inform' *vt.* tell; animate —*vi.* give information (about) —**inform'ant** *n.* one who tells —**informa'tion** *n.* what is told, knowledge —**inform'ative** *a.* —**inform'er** *n.*

in'fra *adv.* below; under; after —**infra dig** *inf.* beneath one's dignity —**infrared'** *a.* denoting rays below red end of visible spectrum

infrac'tion *n. see* INFRINGE

in'frastructure *n.* basic structure or fixed-capital items of an organization or economic system

infringe' *vt.* transgress, break —**infrac'tion** *n.* breach; violation —**infringe'ment** *n.*

infur'iate [-fyoor'-] *vt.* enrage

infuse' *v.* soak to extract flavour *etc.*; instil, charge —**infu'sion** *n.* an infusing; liquid extract obtained

inge'nious [-jē'-] *a.* clever at contriving; cleverly contrived —**inge'niously** *adv.* —**ingenu'ity** *n.*

ingénue' [an-zhā-nyo͞o'] *n.* artless girl or young woman; actress playing such a part

ingen'uous [-jen'-] *a.* frank; naive, innocent —**ingen'uously** *adv.*

ingest'ion [-jest'-] *n.* act of introducing food into the body

in'glenook [ing'g-] *n.* corner by a fireplace

in'got [ing'g-] *n.* brick of cast metal, *esp.* gold

ingrain', engrain' *vt.* implant deeply; *obs.* dye, infuse deeply —**ingrained', engrained'** *a.* deep-rooted; inveterate

ingra'tiate *v. refl.* get (oneself) into favour —**ingra'tiatingly** *adv.*

ingre'dient *n.* component part of a mixture

in'gress *n.* entry, means, right of entrance

inhab'it *vt.* dwell in —**inhab'itable** *a.* —**inhab'itant** *n.* —**inhabita'tion** *n.*

inhale' *v.* breathe in (air *etc.*) —**inhala'tion** *n. esp.* medical preparation for inhaling —**inha'ler** *n.* device producing, and assisting inhalation of therapeutic vapours

inhere' *vi.* of qualities, exist (in); of rights, be vested (in person) —**inhe'rence, inhe'rency** *n.* —**inhe'rent** *a.*

existing as an inseparable part —**inhe'rently** *adv.*

inher'it [-he'rit] *vt.* receive as heir; derive from parents —*vi.* succeed as heir —**inher'itance** *n.* —**inher'itor** *n.* heir; one who inherits (**-ress, -rix** *fem.*)

inhib'it *vt.* restrain (impulse, desire *etc.*); hinder (action); forbid —**inhibi'tion** *n.* repression of emotion, instinct; a stopping or retarding —**inhib'itory** *a.*

inhu'man *a.* cruel, brutal; not human —**inhuman'ity** *n.*

inhume' [-hyōōm'] *vt.* bury, inter —**inhuma'tion** *n.*

inim'ical *a.* unfavourable (to); unfriendly; hostile

inim'itable *a.* defying imitation —**inim'itably** *adv.*

iniq'uity *n.* gross injustice; wickedness, sin —**iniq'uitous** *a.* unfair, sinful, unjust; *inf.* outrageous

ini'tial [-ish'-] *a.* of, occurring at the beginning —*n.* initial letter, *esp.* of person's name —*vt.* mark, sign with one's initials (**-ll-**)

ini'tiate [-ish'-] *vt.* originate; begin; admit into closed society; instruct in elements (of) —*n.* initiated person —**initia'tion** *n.* —**ini'tiative** *n.* first step, lead; ability to act independently —*a.* originating —**ini'tiatory** *a.*

inject' *vt.* introduce (*esp.* fluid, medicine *etc.* with syringe) —**injec'tion** *n.* —**injec'tor** *n.*

injunc'tion *n.* judicial order to restrain; authoritative order

in'jury *n.* physical damage or harm; wrong —**in'jure** *vt.* do harm or damage to —**injur'ious** *a.* —**injur'iously** *adv.*

injus'tice *n.* want of justice; wrong; injury; unjust act

ink *n.* fluid used for writing or printing —*vt.* mark with ink; cover, smear with it —**ink'er** *n.* —**ink'y** *a.* —**ink'stand** *n.* —**ink'well** *n.* vessel for holding ink

ink'ling *n.* hint, slight knowledge or suspicion

inlaid' *see* INLAY

in'land *n.* interior of country —*a.* in this; away from the sea; within a country —*adv.* in or towards the inland

in'-law *n.* relative by marriage

inlay' *vt.* embed; decorate with inset pattern (**inlaid'** *pt./pp.*) —*n.* [in'-] inlaid piece or pattern

in'let *n.* entrance; mouth of creek; piece inserted

in lo'co paren'tis *Lat.* in place of a parent

in'mate *n.* occupant, *esp.* of prison, hospital *etc.*

in'most *a.* most inward, deepest —*sup. of* IN

inn *n.* public house providing food and accommodation; hotel —**inn'keeper** *n.*

inn'ards (*orig.* **in'wards**) *pl.n. inf.* internal organs or working parts

innate' *a.* inborn; inherent

inn'er *a.* lying within —*n.* ring next to the bull's-eye on target —**inn'ermost** *a.* —**inner tube** rubber air tube of pneumatic tyre

inn'ings *n. Sport* player's or side's turn of batting; spell, turn

inn'ocent *a.* pure; guiltless; harmless —*n.* innocent person, *esp.* young child —**inn'ocence** *n.* —**inn'ocently** *adv.*

innoc'uous *a.* harmless —**innoc'uously** *adv.*

inn'ovate *vt.* introduce changes, new things —**innova'tion** *n.* —**in'novator** *n.*

innuen'do *n.* allusive remark, hint; indirect accusation (*pl.* **-does**)

innu'merable *a.* countless; very numerous —**innu'merably** *adv.*

inoc'ulate *vt.* immunize by injecting vaccine —**inocula'tion** *n.*

inop'erable *a.* unworkable; *Med.* that cannot be operated on —**inop'erative** *a.* not operative; ineffective

inopp'ortune *a.* badly timed

inord'inate *a.* excessive

inorgan'ic *a.* not having structure or characteristics of living organisms; of substances without carbon —**inorgan'ically** *adv.*

in'patient *n.* patient that stays in hospital

in'put *n.* act of putting in; that which is put in, as resource needed for industrial production *etc.*; data *etc.* fed into a computer

in'quest *n.* legal or judicial inquiry presided over by a coroner; detailed inquiry or discussion

inquire', enquire' *vi.* seek information —**inqui'rer, enqui'rer** *n.* —**inqui'ry, enqui'ry** *n.* question; investigation

inquisi'tion [-zish'-] *n.* searching investigation, official inquiry; *Hist.* (**I-**) tribunal for suppression of heresy —**inquis'itor** *n.* —**inquisitor'ial** *a.*

inquis'itive *a.* curious; prying —**inquis'itively** *adv.*

in'road *n.* incursion

ins. inches; insurance

insane' *a.* mentally deranged; crazy, senseless —**insane'ly** *adv.* like a lunatic, madly; excessively —**insan'ity** *n.*

insa'tiable *a.* incapable of being satisfied

inscribe' *vt.* write, engrave (in or on something); mark; dedicate; trace (figure) within another —**inscrip'tion** *n.* inscribing; words inscribed on monument *etc.*

inscru'table *a.* mysterious, impenetrable; affording no explanation —**inscrutabil'ity** *n.* —**inscru'tably** *adv.*

in'sect *n.* small invertebrate animal with six legs, usu. segmented body and two or four wings —**insect'icide** *n.* preparation for killing insects —**insectiv'orous** *a.* insect-eating

insecure' [-kyoor'] *a.* not safe or firm; anxious, not confident

insem'inate *vt.* implant semen into —**artificial insemination** impregnation of the female by artificial means

insen'sate *a.* without sensation, unconscious; unfeeling

insen'sible *a.* unconscious; without feeling; not aware; not perceptible —**insensibil'ity** *n.* —**insen'sibly** *adv.* imperceptibly

insert' *vt.* introduce; place or put (*in, into, between*) —*n.* [in'-] something inserted —**inser'tion** *n.*

in'set *n.* something extra inserted, *esp.* as decoration —**inset'** *vt.*

in'shore *adv./a.* near shore

inside' [*or* in'-] *n.* inner side, surface, or part —*a.* of, in, or on, inside —*adv.* in or into the inside; *sl.* in prison —*prep.* within, on inner side

insid'ious *a.* stealthy, treacherous; unseen but deadly —**insid'iously** *adv.*

in'sight [-sīt] *n.* mental penetration, discernment

insig'nia *pl.n.* badges, emblems of honour or office

insin'uate *vt.* hint; work oneself into favour; introduce gradually or subtly —**insinua'tion** *n.*

insip'id *a.* dull, tasteless, spiritless —**insipid'ity** *n.*

insist' *vi.* demand persistently; maintain; emphasize —**insist'ence** *n.* —**insist'ent** *a.* —**insist'ently** *adv.*

in sit'u [-yōō] *Lat.* in its original position

in'solent *a.* arrogantly impudent —**in'solence** *n.* —**in'solently** *adv.*

insom'nia *n.* sleeplessness —**insom'niac** *a./n.*

insomuch' *adv.* to such an extent

insou'ciant [-sōō'si-] *a.* indifferent, careless, unconcerned —**insou'ciance** *n.*

inspect' *vt.* examine closely or officially —**inspec'tion** *n.* —**inspec'tor** *n.* one who inspects; high-ranking police officer —**inspector'ial** *a.*

inspire' *vt.* animate, invigorate; arouse, create feeling, thought; give rise to; breathe in, inhale —**inspira'tion** *n.* good idea; creative influence or stimulus

inspir'it *vt.* animate, put spirit into, encourage

inst. (*instant*) of the current month

instal(l)' [-awl'] *vt.* have (apparatus) put in; establish; place (person in office *etc.*) with ceremony —**installa'tion** *n.* act of installing; that which is installed

instal'ment [-awl'-] *n.* payment of part of debt; any of parts of a whole delivered in succession —**instalment plan** system by which thing becomes hirer's after stipulated number of payments

in'stance *n.* example; particular case; request; stage in proceedings —*vt.* cite

in'stant *n.* moment, point of time —*a.* immediate; urgent; (of foods) requiring little preparation —**instanta'neous** *a.* happening in an instant —**instanta'neously** *adv.* —**instant'er** *adv. Law* at once —**in'stantly** *adv.* at once

instead' [-ed'] *adv.* in place (of); as a substitute

in'step *n.* top of foot between toes and ankle

in'stigate *vt.* incite, urge; bring about —**instiga'tion** *n.* —**in'stigator** *n.*

instil' *vt.* implant; inculcate (**-ll-**) —**instilla'tion** *n.* —**instil'ment** *n.*

in'stinct *n.* inborn impulse or propensity; unconscious skill; intuition —**instinc'tive** *a.* —**instinct'ively** *adv.*

in'stitute *vt.* establish, found; appoint; set going —*n.* society for promoting some public object, *esp.* scientific; its building —**institu'tion** *n.* an instituting; establishment for care or education, hospital, college *etc.*; an established custom or law or (*inf.*) figure —**institu'tional** *a.* of institutions; routine —**institu'tionalize** *vt.* subject to (adverse) effects of confinement in institution; place in an institution; make or become an institution —**in'stitutor** *n.*

instruct' *vt.* teach; inform; order; brief (solicitor, barrister) —**instruc'tion** *n.* teaching; order —*pl.* directions —**instruc'tive** *a.* informative; useful —**instruc'tively** *adv.* —**instruc'tor** *n.* teacher; university teacher of lowest rank (**instruc'tress** *fem.*)

in'strument *n.* tool, implement, means, person, thing used to make, do, measure *etc.*; mechanism for producing musical sound; legal document —**instrumen'tal** *a.* acting as instrument or means; helpful; belonging to, produced by musical instruments —**instrumen'talist** *n.* player of musical instrument —**instrumental'ity** *n.* agency, means —**instrumen'tally** *adv.* —**instrumenta'tion** *n.* arrangement of music for instruments

insubor'dinate *a.* not submissive; mutinous, rebellious —**insubordina'tion** *n.*

in'sular [-syoo-] *a.* of an island; remote, detached; narrow-minded or prejudiced —**insular'ity** *n.*

in'sulate [-syoo-] *vt.* prevent or reduce transfer of electricity, heat, sound *etc.*; isolate, detach —**insula'tion** *n.* —**in'sulator** *n.*

in'sulin [-syoo-] *n.* pancreatic hormone used in treating diabetes

insult' *vt.* behave rudely to; offend —*n.* [in'-] offensive remark; affront —**insult'ing** *a.* —**insult'ingly** *adv.*

insu'perable [-sōō'-] *a.* that cannot be got over or surmounted; unconquerable —**insuperabil'ity** *n.* —**insu'perably** *adv.*

insure' *v.* contract for payment in event of loss, death *etc.*, by payment of premiums; make such contract about; make safe (against) —**insur'able** *a.* —**insur'ance** *n.* —**insur'er** *n.* —**insurance policy** contract of insurance

insur'gent *a.* in revolt —*n.* rebel —**insur'gence, insurrec'tion** *n.* revolt

int. interest; interior; internal; international

intact' *a.* untouched; uninjured

intagl'io [-tahl'-] *n.* engraved design; gem so cut (*pl.* **-ios, -i** [-yē]) —**intag'liated** *a.*

in'take *n.* what is taken in; quantity taken in; opening for taking in; in automobile, air passage into carburettor

in'teger [-j-] *n.* whole number; whole of anything

in'tegral [-g-] *a.* constituting an essential part of a whole —**in'tegrate** *vt.* combine into one whole; unify diverse elements (of community *etc.*) —**integra'tion** *n.* —**integral calculus** branch of mathematics of changing quantities which calculates total effects of the change —**integrated circuit** tiny electronic circuit, usu. on silicon chip

integ'rity *n.* honesty; original perfect state

integ'ument *n.* natural covering, skin, rind, husk

in'tellect *n.* power of thinking and reasoning —**intellec'tual** *a.* of, appealing to intellect; having good intellect —*n.* one endowed with intellect and attracted to intellectual things —**intellectual'ity** *n.*

intell'igent *a.* having, showing good intellect; quick at understanding; informed —**intell'igence** *n.* quickness of understanding; mental power or ability; intellect; information, news, *esp.* military information —**intell'igently** *adv.* —**intelligent'sia** *n.* intellectual or cultured classes —**intelligibil'ity** *n.* —**intel'ligible** *a.* understandable —**intell'igibly** *adv.*

intemp'erate *a.* drinking alcohol to excess; immoderate; unrestrained —**intem'perance** *n.*

intend' *vt.* propose, mean (to do, say *etc.*) —**intend'ed** *a.* planned, future —*n.* *inf.* proposed spouse

intense' *a.* very strong or acute; emotional —**intensifica'tion** *n.* —**inten'sify** *v.* make or become stronger; increase (**intens'ified, intens'ifying**) —**inten'sity** *n.* intense quality; strength —**inten'sive** *a.* characterized by intensity or emphasis on specified factor —**in·ten'sively** *adv.*

intent' *n.* purpose —*a.* concentrating (on); resolved, bent; preoccupied, absorbed —**inten'tion** *n.* purpose, aim —**inten'tional** *a.* —**intent'ly** *adv.* —**intent'ness** *n.*

inter' *vt.* bury (**-rr-**) —**inter'ment** *n.*

inter- (*comb. form*) between, among, mutually, *eg* **intergla'cial, interrela'tion** Such words are not given here where the meaning may easily be inferred from the simple word

interact' *vi.* act on each other —**interac'tion** *n.* —**interac'tive** *a.*

in'ter a'lia *Lat.* among other things

interbreed' *v.* breed within a related group

intercede' *vi.* plead in favour of, mediate —**intercess'ion** *n.* —**interces'sor** *n.*

intercept' *vt.* cut off; seize, stop in transit —*n. Sport* act of intercepting opponent's pass —**intercep'tion** *n.* —**intercep'tor, -er** *n.* one who, that which intercepts; fast fighter plane, missile *etc.*

interchange' *v.* (cause to) exchange places —*n.* [in'-] expressway junction —**interchange'able** *a.* able to be exchanged in position or use

in'tercom *n.* internal telephonic system

intercontinen'tal *a.* connecting continents; (of missile) able to reach one continent from another

in'tercourse *n.* mutual dealings; communication; sexual joining of two people; copulation

in'terdict *n.* decree of Pope restraining clergy from performing divine service; formal prohibition —**interdict'** *vt.* prohibit, forbid; restrain —**interdic'tion** *n.* —**interdict'ory** *a.*

in'terest *n.* concern, curiosity; thing exciting this; sum paid for use of borrowed money (*also fig.*); legal concern; right, advantage, share —*vt.* excite, cause to feel interest —**in'teresting** *a.* —**in'terestingly** *adv.*

in'terface *n.* area, surface, boundary linking two systems

interfere' *vi.* meddle, intervene; clash —**interfe'rence** *n.* act of interfering; *Radio* interruption of reception by atmospherics or by unwanted signals

interfe'ron *n.* a cellular protein that stops the development of an invading virus

in'terim *n.* meantime —*a.* temporary, intervening

inte'rior *a.* inner; inland; indoor —*n.* inside; inland region

interject' *vt.* interpose (remark *etc.*) —**interjec'tion** *n.* exclamation; interjected remark

interlace' *vt.* unite, as by lacing together —**interlace'ment** *n.*

interlard' *v.* intersperse

interleave' *vt.* insert, as blank leaves in book, between other leaves —**in'terleaf** *n.* extra leaf

interlock' *v.* lock together firmly —*a.* knitted with close, small stitches

interloc'utor *n.* one who takes part in conversation —**interlocu'tion** *n.* dialogue —**interloc'utory** *a.*

in'terloper *n.* one intruding in another's affairs; intruder

in'terlude *n.* interval (in play *etc.*); something filling an interval

intermarr'y *vi.* (of families, races, religions) become linked by marriage; marry within one's family —**intermar'riage** *n.*

interme'diate *a.* coming between; interposed —**interme'diary** *n.*

intermezz'o [-mets'-] *n.* short performance between acts of play or opera (*pl.* **-os, -mezz'i** [-ē])

interm'inable *a.* endless —**inter'minably** *adv.*

intermit' *v.* stop for a time (**-tt-**) —**intermis'sion** *n.* —**intermitt'ent** *a.* occurring at intervals

intern'[1] *vt.* confine to special area or camp —**intern'ment** *n.*

in'tern[2] *n.* junior doctor who is a resident member of staff of hospital

inter'nal *a.* inward; interior; within (a country, organization) —**inter'nally** *adv.* —**internal combustion** process of exploding mixture of air and fuel in piston-fitted cylinder

interna'tional [-nash'-] *a.* of relations between nations —*n.* game or match between teams of different countries —**Interna'tionale** *n.* socialistic hymn —**interna'tionally** *adv.*

interne'cine *a.* mutually destructive; deadly
in'ternode *n.* space between two nodes or leaf joints —**interno'dal** *a.*
inter'pellate *vt.* interrupt business of the day to demand explanation from (minister) —**interpella'tion** *n.*
interplan'etary *a.* of, linking planets
in'terplay *n.* action and reaction of two things, sides *etc.*, upon each other; interaction; reciprocation
inter'polate *vt.* insert new (*esp.* misleading) matter (in book *etc.*); interject (remark); *Maths.* estimate a value between known values —**interpola'tion** *n.*
interpose' *vt.* insert; say as interruption; put in the way —*vi.* intervene; obstruct —**interposi'tion** *n.*
inter'pret *v.* explain; translate, *esp.* orally; *Art* render, represent —**interpreta'tion** *n.* —**inter'preter** *n.*
interreg'num *n.* interval between reigns; gap in continuity (*pl.* **-na, -nums**)
interr'ogate *vt.* question, *esp.* closely or officially —**interroga'tion** *n.* —**interrog'ative** *a.* questioning —*n.* word used in asking question —**interr'ogator** *n.* —**interrog'atory** *a.* of inquiry —*n.* question, set of questions
interrupt' *v.* break in (upon); stop the course of; block —**interrup'tion** *n.*
intersect' *vt.* divide by passing across or through —*vi.* meet and cross —**intersec'tion** *n.* point where lines, roads cross
intersperse' *vt.* sprinkle (something with *or* something among or in) —**intersper'sion** *n.*
in'terstate *a.* between, involving two or more states
interstell'ar *a.* (of the space) between stars
inter'stice *n.* chink, gap , crevice —**intersti'tial** *a.*
intertwine' *v.* twist together, entwine
in'terval *n.* intervening time or space; pause, break; short period between parts of play, concert *etc.*; difference (of pitch)
intervene' *vi.* come into a situation in order to change it; be, come between or among; occur in meantime; interpose —**interven'tion** *n.*
in'terview *n.* meeting, *esp.* formally arranged and involving questioning of a person —*vt.* have interview with —**interviewee'** *n.* —**in'terviewer** *n.*
intest'ate *a.* not having made a will —*n.* person dying intestate —**intes'tacy** *n.*
intest'ine *n.* (*usu. pl.*) lower part of alimentary canal between stomach and anus —**intest'inal** *a.* of bowels
in'timate[1] [-it] *a.* closely acquainted, familiar; private; extensive; having sexual relations (with) —*n.* intimate friend —**in'timacy** *n.*
in'timate[2] [-āt] *vt.* announce; imply —**intima'tion** *n.* notice
intim'idate *vt.* frighten into submission; deter by threats —**intimida'tion** *n.* —**intim'idator** *n.*
in'to *prep.* expresses motion to a point within; indicates change of state; indicates coming up against, encountering; indicates arithmetical division
intone' *vt.* chant; recite in monotone —**intona'tion** *n.* modulation of voice; intoning; accent
intox'icate *vt.* make drunk; excite to excess —**intox'icant** *a./n.* intoxicating (liquor) —**intoxica'tion** *n.*
intra- (*comb. form*) within
intract'able *a.* difficult to influence; hard to control
intramur'al *a. Education* in or for those in single establishment
intran'sigent *a.* uncompromising, obstinate
intrau'terine [-ə-yōō'-] *a.* within the womb: *see* IUD
intrave'nous *a.* into a vein
intrep'id *a.* fearless, undaunted —**intrepid'ity** *n.*
in'tricate *a.* involved, puzzlingly entangled —**in'tricacy** *n.* —**in'tricately** *adv.*
intrigue' [-trēg'] *n.* underhand plot; secret love affair —*vi.* carry on intrigue —*vt.* interest, puzzle —**intri'guer** *n.*
intrin'sic *a.* inherent, essential —**intrin'sically** *adv.*
intro- (*comb. form*) into, within, as in *introduce, introvert etc.*
introduce' *vt.* make acquainted; present; bring in; bring forward; bring into practice; insert —**introduc'tion** *n.* an introducing; presentation of one person to another; preliminary section or treatment —**introduc'tory** *a.* preliminary

in'troit *n. Eccles.* anthem sung as priest approaches altar

introspec'tion *n.* examination of one's own thoughts —**introspec'tive** *a.* —**introspec'tively** *adv.*

in'trovert *n. Psychoanalysis* one who looks inward rather than at the external world —**introver'sible** *a.* —**introver'sion** *n.* —**introver'sive** *a.* —**in'troverted** *a.*

intrude' *v.* thrust (oneself) in uninvited —**intru'der** *n.* —**intru'sion** *n.* —**intru'sive** *a.*

intui'tion [-ish'-] *n.* immediate mental apprehension without reasoning; immediate insight —**intu'it** *v.* —**intu'itive** *a.* —**intu'itively** *adv.*

In'uit [in'yo͞o-it] *n.* Eskimo of N Amer. or Greenland

Inuk'titut [i-nook'tə-toot] *n.* language of Inuit, Eskimo

in'undate *vt.* flood; overwhelm —**inunda'tion** *n.*

inure' *vt.* accustom, *esp.* to hardship, danger *etc.*

invade' *vt.* enter by force with hostile intent; overrun; pervade —**inva'der** *n.* —**inva'sion** *n.*

in'valid [-lēd] *n.* one suffering from chronic ill health —*a.* ill, suffering from sickness or injury —*v.* become an invalid; retire from active service because of illness *etc.*

inval'uable *a.* priceless

In'var R steel containing 30 per cent nickel, with low coefficient of expansion

inva'sion *see* INVADE

inveigh' [-vā'] *vi.* speak violently (against) —**invec'tive** *n.* abusive speech or writing, vituperation

invei'gle [-vē'-, -vā'-] *vt.* entice, seduce, wheedle —**invei'glement** *n.*

invent' *vt.* devise, originate; fabricate (falsehoods *etc.*) —**inven'tion** *n.* that which is invented; ability to invent; contrivance; deceit; lie —**invent'ive** *a.* resourceful; creative —**invent'ively** *adv.* —**invent'or** *n.*

in'ventory *n.* detailed list of goods *etc.* —*vt.* make list of

invert' *vt.* turn upside down; reverse position, relations of —**inverse'** [*or* in'-] *a.* inverted; opposite —*n.* —**inverse'ly** *adv.* —**inver'sion** *n.*

inver'tebrate *n.* animal having no vertebral column —*a.* spineless

invest' *vt.* lay out (money, time, effort *etc.*) for profit or advantage; install; endow; *obs.* clothe; *Poet.* cover as with garment —**invest'iture** *n.* formal installation of person in office or rank —**invest'ment** *n.* investing; money invested; stocks and shares bought —**invest'or** *n.*

invest'igate *vt.* inquire into; examine —**investiga'tion** *n.* —**invest'igator** *n.*

invet'erate *a.* deep-rooted; long established, confirmed —**invet'eracy** *n.*

invid'ious *a.* likely to cause ill will or envy —**invid'iously** *adv.*

invig'ilate [-vij'-] *vi.* supervise examination candidates

invig'orate *vt.* give vigour to, strengthen

invin'cible *a.* unconquerable —**invincibil'ity** *n.*

invi'olable *a.* not to be profaned; sacred; unalterable —**invi'olate** *a.* unhurt; unprofaned; unbroken

invite' *vt.* request the company of; ask courteously; ask for; attract, call forth —*n.* [in'-] *inf.* invitation —**invita'tion** *n.*

in'voice *n.* a list of goods or services sold, with prices —*vt.* make or present an invoice

invoke' *vt.* call on; appeal to; ask earnestly for; summon —**invoca'tion** *n.*

invol'untary *a.* not done voluntarily; unintentional; instinctive —**invol'untarily** *adv.*

in'volute *a.* complex; coiled spirally; rolled inwards (*also* **involu'ted**) —*n. Maths.* a type of curve —**involu'tion** *n.*

involve' *vt.* include; entail; implicate (person); concern; entangle —**involu'tion** *n.* —**involved'** *a.* complicated; concerned (in)

in'ward *a.* internal; situated within; spiritual, mental —*adv.* (*also* **in'wards**) towards the inside; into the mind —*pl.n. see* INNARDS —**in'wardly** *adv.* in the mind; internally

i'odine [-ēn] *n.* nonmetallic element found in seaweed and used in antiseptic tincture, photography, and dyeing —**i'odize** *vt.* treat or react with iodine —**io'doform** *n.* antiseptic

i'on *n.* electrically charged atom or group of atoms —**ion'ic** *a.* —**ioniza'tion** *n.* —**i'onize** *vt.* change into ions

—**ion'osphere** *n.* region of atmosphere 60 to 100 km above earth's surface

Ion'ic [ī-] *a. Architecture* distinguished by scroll-like decoration on columns

io'ta [ī-ō'-] *n.* the Greek letter *i*; (*usu. with* not) very small amount

I.O.U. *n.* signed paper acknowledging debt

IPA International Phonetic Alphabet

ipecacuan'ha [-an'ə] *n.* S Amer. plant yielding an emetic (**ip'ecac**)

ip'so fac'to *Lat.* by that very fact

IQ intelligence quotient

ir- (*comb. form*) for *in-* before *r*: *see* IN- and listed words

IRA Irish Republican Army

ire *n.* anger, wrath —**irascibil'ity** [i-] *n.* —**iras'cible** *a.* hot-tempered —**iras'cibly** *adv.* —**irate'** [ī-] *a.* angry

irides'cent *a.* exhibiting changing colours like those of the rainbow —**irides'cence** *n.*

irid'ium *n.* very hard, corrosion-resistant metal

i'ris *n.* circular membrane of eye containing pupil; plant with sword-shaped leaves and showy flowers

irk *vt.* irritate, vex —**irk'some** *a.* tiresome

i'ron *n.* metallic element, much used for tools *etc.*, and the raw material of steel; tool *etc.*, of this metal; appliance used, when heated, to smooth cloth; metal-headed golf club —*pl.* fetters —*a.* of, like, iron; inflexible, unyielding; robust —*v.* smooth, cover, fetter *etc.*, with iron or an iron —**iron age** era of iron implements —**i'ronclad** *a.* protected with or as with iron —**iron curtain** any barrier that separates communities or ideologies —**iron lung** apparatus for administering artificial respiration —**i'ronmonger** *n.* UK dealer in hardware —**i'ronwood** *n.* various S Afr. trees

i'rony *n.* (*usu.* humorous or mildly sarcastic) use of words to mean the opposite of what is said; event, situation opposite of that expected —**iron'ic(al)** *a.* of, using, irony

irra'diate *vt.* treat by irradiation; shine upon, throw light upon, light up —**irradia'tion** *n.* impregnation by x-rays, light rays

irrefrang'ible *a.* inviolable; in optics, not susceptible to refraction

irref'utable *a.* that cannot be refuted, disproved

irreg. irregular(ly)

irrep'arable *a.* not able to be repaired or remedied

irrespec'tive *a.* without taking account (of)

irrev'ocable *a.* not able to be changed, undone, altered

irr'igate *vt.* water by artificial channels, pipes *etc.* —**irriga'tion** *n.* —**ir'rigator** *n.*

irr'itate *vt.* annoy; inflame; stimulate —**irr'itable** *a.* easily annoyed —**ir'ritably** *adv.* —**irr'itant** *a./n.* (person or thing) causing irritation —**irrita'tion** *n.*

irrupt' *vi.* enter forcibly; increase suddenly —**irrup'tion** *n.*

Is. Isaiah

is third person singular, *present indicative of* BE

ISBN International Standard Book Number

i'singlass [ī'zing-glahs] *n.* kind of gelatin obtained from some freshwater fish

Is'lam [iz'lahm] *n.* Mohammedan faith or world —**Islam'ic** *a.*

i'sland [ī'lənd] *n.* piece of land surrounded by water; anything like this —**i'slander** *n.* inhabitant of island

isle [īl] *n.* island —**i'slet** [ī'lit] *n.* little island

i'sobar *n.* line on map connecting places of equal mean barometric pressure —**isobar'ic** *a.*

i'solate *vt.* place apart or alone —**isola'tion** *n.* —**isola'tionism** *n.* policy of not participating in international affairs —**isola'tionist** *n.*

i'somer *n.* substance with same molecules as another but different atomic arrangement —**isomer'ic** *a.* —**isom'erism** *n.*

isomet'ric *a.* having equal dimensions; relating to muscular contraction without movement —**isomet'rics** *pl.n.* system of isometric exercises

isos'celes [ī-sos'i-lēz] *a.* of triangle, having two sides equal

i'sotherm *n.* line on map connecting points of equal mean temperature

i'sotope *n.* atom of element having a different nuclear mass and atomic weight from other atoms in same element —**isotop'ic** *a.* —**isot'opy** *n.* existence in the form of isotopes

iss'ue [i'shyōō] *n.* sending or giving out officially or publicly; number or amount so given out; discharge; offspring, children; topic of discussion; question, dispute; outcome, result —*vi.* go out; result in; arise (from) —*vt.* emit, give out, send out; distribute, publish

isth'mus [is'məs] *n.* neck of land between two seas

it *pron.* neuter pronoun of the third person —**its** *a.* belonging to it —**it's** *contraction of* it is —**itself'** *pron.* emphatic form of *it*

IT information technology

ital. italic (type)

Ital'ian *n.* language or native of Italy —*a.* of Italy

ital'ic *a.* of type, sloping —**ital'icize** *vt.* put in italics —**ital'ics** *pl.n.* this type, now used for emphasis *etc.*

itch *vi./n.* (feel) irritation in the skin —**itch'y** *a.*

i'tem *n.* single thing in list, collection *etc.*; piece of information; entry in account *etc.* —*adv.* also —**i'temize** *vt.*

it'erate *vt.* repeat —**itera'tion** *n.* —**it'erative** *a.*

itin'erant [i-, ī-] *a.* travelling from place to place; working for a short time in various places; travelling on circuit —**itin'eracy** *n.* —**itin'erary** *n.* record, line of travel; route; guidebook

IUD intrauterine device (for contraception)

i'vory *n.* hard white substance of the tusks of elephants *etc.* —**ivory tower** seclusion, remoteness

i'vy *n.* climbing evergreen plant —**i'vied** *a.* covered with ivy

J

jab *vt.* poke roughly; thrust, stab abruptly (**-bb-**) —*n.* poke

jabb'er *v.* chatter; utter, talk rapidly, incoherently —**jabb'er-wocky** *n.* nonsense, *esp.* in verse

jab'ot [zhab'ō] *n.* frill, ruffle at throat or breast of garment

jacaran'da *n.* S Amer. tree with fern-like leaves and pale purple flowers

jac'inth [jas'-] *n.* reddish-orange precious stone

jack *n.* fellow, man; *inf.* sailor; male of some animals; device for lifting heavy weight, *esp.* automobile; various mechanical appliances; lowest court card, with picture of page-boy; *Bowls* ball aimed at; socket-and-plug connection in electronic equipment; small flag, *esp.* national, at sea —*vt.* (*usu. with* up) lift (an object) with a jack

jack'al [-awl] *n.* wild, gregarious animal of Asia and Africa closely allied to dog

jack'ass *n.* the male of the ass; blockhead —**laughing jackass** the Aust. kookaburra

jack'boot *n.* large riding boot coming above knee

jack'daw *n.* small kind of crow

jack'et *n.* outer garment, short coat; outer casing, cover

jack'hammer *n.* hand-held hammer drill

jack'knife *n.* clasp knife; dive with sharp bend at waist in midair —*v.* bend sharply, *eg* a tractor-trailer *etc.* forming a sharp angle with its trailer

jack'pot *n.* large prize, accumulated stake, as pool in poker

jack rabbit N Amer. hare

Jacobe'an [-bē'ən] *a.* of the reign of James I

Jac'obite *n.* adherent of Stuarts after overthrow of James II

Jac'quard [zhak'ard] *n.* fabric in which design is incorporated into the weave

Jacu'zzi [jə-kōō'zi] R device that swirls water in a bath; bath with this device

jade[1] *n.* ornamental semiprecious stone, usu. dark green; this colour

jade[2] *n.* sorry or worn-out horse; *obs. offens.* woman —**ja'ded** *a.* tired; off colour

jae'ger [yā'gər] *n.* type of skua

jag *n.* sharp or ragged projection —**jag'ged** *a.*

jag'uar *n.* large S Amer. spotted animal of cat tribe

jail *n.* building for confinement of criminals or suspects —*vt.* send to, confine in prison —**jail'er** *n.* —**jail'bird** *n.* hardened criminal

jalop'y *n. inf.* old automobile

jam *vt.* pack together; (cause to) stick together and become unworkable; apply fiercely; squeeze; *Radio* block (another station) with impulses of equal wavelength (**-mm-**) —*n.* fruit preserved by boiling with sugar; crush; holdup of traffic; awkward situation —**jam-packed** *a.* filled to capacity —**jam session** (improvised) jazz session

jamb [jam] *n.* side post of door, fireplace *etc.*

jamboree' *n.* large gathering or rally of Boy Scouts; spree, celebration

Jan. January

jan'gle [-ng'gl] *v.* (cause to) sound harshly, as bell; (of nerves) irritate —*n.* harsh sound

jan'itor *n.* caretaker (**jan'itress** *fem.*)

Jan'uary *n.* first month

japan' *n.* very hard *usu.* black varnish —*vt.* cover with this (**-nn-**)

jape *n./vi.* joke

japon'ica *n.* shrub with red flowers

jar[1] *n.* round vessel of glass, earthenware *etc.*

jar[2] *v.* (cause to) vibrate suddenly, violently; have disturbing, painful effect on (**-rr-**) —*n.* jarring sound; shock *etc.*

jardinière' [zhah-din-yār'] *n.* ornamental pot for growing plants

jar'gon *n.* specialized language concerned with particular subject; pretentious or nonsensical language

Jas. James

jas'min(e), jess'amin(e) *n.* flowering shrub

jas'per *n.* red, yellow, dark green or brown quartz

jaun'dice *n.* disease marked by yellowness of skin; bitterness, ill humour; prejudice —*v.* make, become prejudiced, bitter *etc.*

jaunt *n.* short pleasure excursion —*vi.* make one

jaunt'y *a.* sprightly; brisk; smart, trim —**jaunt'ily** *adv.*

jav'elin *n.* spear, *esp.* for throwing in sporting events

jaw *n.* one of bones in which teeth are set —*pl.* mouth; *fig.* narrow opening of a gorge or valley; gripping part of vice *etc.* —*vi. sl.* talk lengthily

jay *n.* noisy bird of brilliant plumage —**jay'walk** *vi.* —**jay'walker** *n.* careless pedestrian

jazz *n.* syncopated music and dance —**jazz'y** *a.* flashy, showy —**jazz up** play as jazz; make more lively, appealing

jeal'ous [jel'-] *a.* distrustful of the faithfulness (of); envious; suspiciously watchful —**jeal'ously** *adv.* —**jeal'ousy** *n.*

jeans *pl.n.* casual pants, *esp.* of denim

Jeep R light four-wheel-drive motor utility vehicle

jeer *v.* scoff, deride —*n.* scoff, taunt, gibe

Jeho'vah [jihō'və] *n.* God

jejune' [ji-jo͞on'] *a.* simple, naive; meagre

jell *v.* congeal; *inf.* assume definite form

jell'y *n.* semitransparent food made with gelatin, becoming softly stiff as it cools; anything of the consistency of this —**jell'yfish** *n.* jellylike small sea animal

jenn'y *n.* female ass; female wren

jeop'ardy [jep'-] *n.* danger —**jeop'ardize** *vt.* endanger

Jer. Jeremiah

jerbo'a *n.* small Afric. burrowing rodent animal resembling a mouse; desert rat

jerk *n.* sharp, abruptly stopped movement; twitch; sharp pull; *sl.* stupid person —*v.* move or throw with a jerk —**jerk'ily** *adv.* —**jerk'iness** *n.* —**jerk'y** *a.* uneven, spasmodic

jer'kin *n.* sleeveless jacket, *esp.* of leather

jerk'water *a. sl.* inferior and insignificant

jerr'y-built *a.* of flimsy construction with bad materials —**jerry-builder** *n.*

jer'sey [-z-] *n.* knitted sweater; machine-knitted fabric; (**J-**) breed of cow

jess'amine *see* JASMINE

jest *n./vi.* joke —**jest'er** *n.* joker, *esp. Hist.* court fool

Jes'uit [jez'-] *n.* member of Society of Jesus, Order founded by Ignatius Loyola in 1534 —**jesuit'ical** *a.* of Jesuits

jet[1] *n.* stream of liquid, gas *etc.*, *esp.* shot from small hole; the small hole; spout, nozzle; aircraft driven by jet propulsion —*v.* throw out; shoot forth (**-tt-**) —**jet lag** fatigue caused by crossing time zones in jet aircraft —**jet-propelled** *a.* —**jet propulsion** propulsion by thrust provided by jet of gas or liquid

jet[2] *n.* hard black mineral capable of brilliant polish —**jet-black** *a.* glossy black

jet'sam *n.* goods thrown out to lighten ship and later washed ashore —**jett'ison** *vt.* abandon; throw overboard

jett'y *n.* small pier, wharf

Jew *n.* one of Hebrew religion or ancestry —**Jew'ess** *n.fem.* —**Jew'ish** *a.* —**Jew'ry** *n.* the Jews —**jew's-harp** *n.* small musical instrument held between teeth and played by finger

jew'el *n.* precious stone; ornament containing one; precious thing —**jew'eller** *n.* dealer in jewels —**jew'ellery** *n.*

jew'fish *n.* large fish of tropical and temperate waters

jib *n.* triangular sail set forward of mast; projecting arm of crane or derrick —*vi.* object to proceeding; of horse, person, stop and refuse to go on (**-bb-**) —**jibb'er** *n.* —**jib boom** spar from end of bowsprit

jibe *see* GYBE *and* GIBE

jiff'y *n. inf.* very short period of time

jig *n.* lively dance; music for it; small mechanical device; guide for cutting *etc.*; *Angling* any of various lures —*vi.* dance jig; make jerky up-and-down movements (**-gg-**) —**jigg'er** *n.* person who jigs; small glass for spirits; fishing jig; device used in fishing beneath ice; flat railway car driven by handle pumped up and down; *inf.* device whose name is unknown or forgotten —**jig'saw** *n.* machine fretsaw —**jigsaw puzzle** picture stuck on board and cut into interlocking pieces with jigsaw

jigg'ery-po'kery *n. inf.* trickery, nonsense

jig'gle *v.* move (up and down *etc.*) with short jerky movements

jilt *vt.* cast off (lover)

jimm'y *n.* short steel crowbar used *esp.* by burglars to force doors *etc.*

jim'son weed poisonous plant of nightshade family

jin'gle [-ng'gl] *n.* mixed metallic noise, as of shaken chain; catchy, rhythmic verse, song *etc.* —*v.* (cause to) make jingling sound

jin'goism [-ng'g-] *n.* chauvinism —**jingois'tic** *a.*

jinks *pl.n.* —**high jinks** boisterous merrymaking

jinx *n.* force, person, thing bringing bad luck —*v.*

jitt'ers *pl.n.* worried nervousness, anxiety —**jitt'ery** *a.* nervous

jiu'jitsu *n. see* JUJITSU

jive *n.* (dance performed to) rock-and-roll music, *esp.* of 1950's —*vi.*

job *n.* piece of work, task; post, office; *inf.* difficult task —**jobb'er** *n.* stockjobber —**jobb'ing** *a.* doing single, particular jobs for payment —**job'less** *a./pl.n.* unemployed (people) —**job lot** assortment sold together; miscellaneous collection

jock'ey *n.* professional rider in horse races (*pl.* **-eys**) —*v.* (*esp. with* for) manoeuvre (**jock'eyed, jock'eying**)

jocose' *a.* waggish, humorous —**jocose'ly** *adv.* —**jocos'ity** *n.* —**joc'ular** *a.* joking; given to joking —**jocular'ity** *n.*

joc'und *a.* merry, cheerful —**jocun'dity** *n.*

jodh'purs [jod'pərz] *pl.n.* tight-legged riding breeches

jog[1] *vi.* run slowly or move at trot, *esp.* for physical exercise —*vt.* jar, nudge; remind, stimulate (**-gg-**) —*n.* jogging —**jog'ger** *n.* —**jogg'ing** *n.* —**jog trot** slow regular trot

jog[2] *n.* sharp protruding point; sudden change in direction

jog'gle *v.* move to and fro in jerks; shake —*n.*

John *n.* name —**John Bull** typical Englishman —**John Dory** *see* DORY

john *n. inf.* toilet

Johnn'y Canuck' *inf.* a Canadian; Canada

joie de vi'vre [zhwad vēv'r] *Fr.* enjoyment of life, ebullience

join *vt.* put together, fasten, unite; become a member (of) —*vi.* become united, connected; (*with* up) enlist; take part (in) —*n.* joining; place of joining —**join'er** *n.* maker of finished woodwork; one who joins —**join'ery** *n.* joiner's work

joint *n.* arrangement by which two things fit together, rigidly or loosely; place of this; UK meat for roasting, oft. with bone; *inf.* house, place *etc.*; *sl.* disreputable bar or nightclub; *sl.* marijuana cigarette —*a.* common; shared by two or more —*vt.* connect by joints; divide at the joints —**joint'ly** *adv.* —**out of joint** dislocated; disorganized

join'ture *n.* property settled on wife for her use after husband's death

joist *n.* one of the parallel beams stretched from wall to wall on which to fix floor or ceiling —**joist'ed** *a.*

joke *n.* thing said or done to cause laughter; something not in earnest, or ridiculous —*vi.* make jokes —**jo'ker** *n.* one who jokes; *sl.* fellow; extra card in pack, counting as highest card in some games

joll'y *a.* jovial; festive, merry —*vt.* (*esp. with* along) (try to) make person, occasion *etc.* happier (**joll'ied, joll'ying**) —**jollifica'tion** *n.* merrymaking —**jol'lity** *n.*

Joll'y Rog'er pirates' flag, black, with white skull and crossbones

jolt [-ō-] *n.* sudden jerk; bump; shock —*v.* move, shake with jolts —**jolt'y** *a.*

jon'quil *n.* fragrant yellow or white narcissus —*a.* pale yellow

josh *v. sl.* tease, banter

joss *n.* Chinese idol —**joss house** Chinese temple —**joss stick** stick of Chinese incense

jos'tle [-sl] *v.* knock or push against

jot *n.* small amount, whit —*vt.* write briefly; make note of (**-tt-**) —**jott'ing** *n.* memorandum

joule [jo͞ol] *n. Electricity* unit of work or energy

jour'nal [jur'nəl] *n.* daily newspaper or other periodical; daily record; logbook; part of axle or shaft resting on the bearings —**journalese'** *n.* journalist's jargon; high-flown style, full of clichés —**jour'nalism** *n.* editing, writing in periodicals —**jour'nalist** *n.* —**journalis'tic** *a.*

jour'ney [jur'-] *n.* going to a place, excursion; distance travelled —*vi.* travel

jour'neyman *n.* craftsman or artisan employed by another

joust *Hist. n.* encounter with lances between two mounted knights —*vi.* engage in joust

jo'vial *a.* convivial, merry, gay —**jovial'ity** *n.*

jowl *n.* cheek, jaw; outside of throat when prominent

joy *n.* gladness, pleasure, delight; cause of this —**joy'ful** *a.* —**joy'less** *a.* —**joy ride** trip, *esp.* in stolen automobile —**joy'stick** *n. inf.* control column of aircraft

JP Justice of the Peace

Jr. Junior

ju'bilate *vi.* rejoice —**ju'bilant** *a.* exultant —**ju'bilantly** *adv.* —**jubila'tion** *n.*

ju'bilee *n.* time of rejoicing, *esp.* 25th or 50th anniversary

Jud. Judges

Juda'ic [jo͞o-] *a.* Jewish —**Ju'daism** *n.* —**Ju'daize** [-dā-īz] *vt.* make Jewish; follow Jewish custom

Ju'das tree small tree with pinkish-purple flowers

judd'er *vi.* shake, vibrate —*n.*

judge [juj] *n.* officer appointed to try cases in law courts; one who decides in a dispute, contest *etc.*; one able to form a reliable opinion, arbiter; umpire; in Jewish history, ruler —*vi.* act as judge —*vt.* act as judge of; try, estimate; decide —**judg(e)'ment** *n.* faculty of judging; sentence of court; opinion; misfortune regarded as sign of divine displeasure

ju'dicature *n.* administration of justice; body of judges —**judic'ial** [-ish'-] *a.* of, or by, a court or judge; proper to a judge; discriminating —**judi'cially** *adv.* —**judi'ciary** *n.* system of courts and judges —**judi'cious** *a.* well-judged, sensible, prudent —**judi'ciously** *adv.*

ju'do *n.* modern sport derived from jujitsu

jug *n.* vessel for liquids, with handle and small spout; its contents; *sl.* prison —*vt.* stew (*esp.* hare) in jug (**-gg-**)

jugg'ernaut *n.* any irresistible, destructive force

jug'gle *v.* throw and catch (several objects) so most are in the air simultaneously; manage, manipulate (accounts *etc.*) to deceive —*n.* —**jugg'ler** *n.* —**jug'glery** *n.*

jug'ular vein one of three large veins of the neck returning blood from the head

juice [jo͞os] *n.* liquid part of vegetable, fruit, or meat; *inf.* electric current; *inf.* gasoline; vigour, vitality —**juic'y** *a.* succulent

jujit'su, jujut'su, jiujit'su *n.* the Japanese art of wrestling and self-defence

ju'jube *n.* lozenge of gelatin, sugar *etc.*; a fruit; shrub producing it

juke'box *n.* automatic, coin-operated record player

ju'lep *n.* sweet drink; medicated drink

Ju'lian *a.* of Julius Caesar —**Julian calendar** calendar as adjusted by Julius Caesar in 46 B.C., in which the year was made to consist of 365 days, 6 hours, instead of 365 days

julienne' *n.* kind of clear soup

July' *n.* the seventh month

jum'ble *vt.* mingle, mix in confusion —*n.* confused heap, muddle

jum'bo *n. inf.* elephant; anything very large

jump *v.* (cause to) spring, leap (over); move hastily; pass or skip (over) —*vi.* move hastily; rise steeply; parachute from aircraft; start, jerk (with astonishment *etc.*); of faulty film *etc.*, make abrupt movements —*vt.* come off (tracks, rails *etc.*); *inf.* attack without warning —*n.* act of jumping; obstacle to be jumped; distance, height jumped; sudden nervous jerk or start; sudden rise in prices —**jump'er** *n.* one who, that which jumps; dress with bib top —**jump'y** *a.* nervous —**jumper cables** electric cables to connect discharged automobile battery to external battery to aid starting of engine —**jump suit** one-piece garment of pants and top

junc'tion *n.* railway station *etc.* where lines, routes join; place of joining ; joining

junc'ture *n.* state of affairs

June [jōōn] *n.* the sixth month

jun'gle [-ng'gl] *n.* tangled vegetation of equatorial forest; land covered with it; tangled mass; condition of intense competition, struggle for survival —**jun'gly** *a.*

ju'nior *a.* younger; of lower standing —*n.* junior person —**junior college** college providing first two years of university course

ju'niper *n.* evergreen shrub with berries yielding oil of juniper, used for medicine and gin making

junk[1] *n.* discarded, useless objects; *inf.* nonsense; *sl.* narcotic drug —*vt. inf.* discard as junk —**junk'ie, junk'y** *n. sl.* drug addict —**junk food** food, oft. of low nutritional value, eaten in addition to or instead of regular meals —**junk'man** *n.* man who buys and sells discarded furniture, clothing *etc.*

junk[2] *n.* Chinese sailing vessel

junk'et *n.* curdled milk flavoured and sweetened; excursion, *esp.* for pleasure, at public expense —*vi.* feast, picnic; go on excursion —**junk'eting** *n.*

jun'ta *n.* group of military officers holding power in a country

Ju'piter *n.* Roman chief of gods; largest of the planets

jurisdic'tion [joor-] *n.* administration of justice; authority; territory covered by it —**jurispru'dence** *n.* science of, skill in, law —**ju'rist** *n.* one skilled in law —**juris'tic** *a.* —**juris'tical** *a.*

jur'y [joor'i] *n.* body of persons sworn to render verdict in court of law; body of judges of competition —**jur'or, jur'yman** *n.* one of jury —**jury box**

just *a.* fair; upright, honest; proper, right, equitable —*adv.* exactly; barely; at this instant; merely, only; really —**just'ice** [-s] *n.* quality of being just; fairness; judicial proceedings; judge, magistrate —**jus'tify** *vt.* prove right, true or innocent; vindicate; excuse (**-ified, ifying**) —**just'ifiable** *a.* —**just'ifiably** *adv.* —**justifica'tion** *n.* —**just'ly** *adv.*

jut *vi.* project, stick out (**-tt-**) —*n.* projection

jute *n.* fibre of certain plants, used for rope, canvas *etc.*

ju'venile *a.* young; of, for young children; immature —*n.* young person, child —**juvenes'cence** *n.* —**juvenes'cent** *a.* becoming young —**juvenil'ia** *pl.n.* works produced in author's youth —**juvenil'ity** *n.* —**juvenile court** court dealing with young offenders —**juvenile delinquent** young person guilty of some offence, antisocial behaviour *etc.*

juxtapose' [-pōz'] *vt.* put side by side —**juxtaposi'tion** *n.* contiguity, being side by side

K

K Kelvin; *Chess* king; *Chem.* potassium

k knit

kaf'tan *n.* long coatlike Eastern garment; imitation of it, *esp.* as woman's long, loose dress with sleeves

kale, kail *n.* type of cabbage

kalei'doscope [-lī'-] *n.* optical toy for producing changing symmetrical patterns by multiple reflections of coloured glass chips *etc.*, in inclined mirrors enclosed in tube; any complex, frequently changing pattern —**kaleidoscop'ic** *a.* swiftly changing

kamikaz'e [-kahz'-] *n.* suicidal attack, *esp.* as in World War II, by Japanese pilots

kangaroo' *n.* Aust. marsupial with very strongly developed hind legs for jumping —**kangaroo court** irregular, illegal court

ka'olin *n.* a fine white clay used for porcelain and medicinally

ka'pok *n.* tropical tree; fibre from its seed pods used to stuff cushions *etc.*

kaput' *a. inf.* ruined, broken, no good

kar'at *n.* proportional measure of twenty-fourths used to state fineness of gold

karat'e [-raht'-] *n.* Japanese system of unarmed combat using feet, hands, elbows *etc.* as weapons in a variety of ways

kar'ma *n. Buddhism & Hinduism* person's actions affecting his fate for his next reincarnation

katab'olism *n. see* CATABOLISM

kau'ri [-ow'-] *n.* large N.Z. pine giving valuable timber

kav'a [-ah-] *n.* the beverage derived from a Polynesian plant of the pepper family

kay'ak [kī'-] *n.* Inuit canoe made of sealskins stretched over frame; any canoe of this design

kazoo' *n.* cigar-shaped musical instrument producing nasal sound

KB Knight of the Bath

KBE Knight Commander (of the Order) of the British Empire

KC King's Counsel

KCB Knight Commander (of the Order) of the Bath

kebab' *n.* dish of small pieces of meat, tomatoes *etc.* grilled on skewers (*also* **shish kebab**)

kedge *n.* small anchor —*vt.* move (ship) by cable attached to kedge

kedg'eree *n.* dish of fish cooked with rice, eggs *etc.*

keel *n.* lowest longitudinal support on which ship is built —**keel'haul** *vt.* formerly, punish by hauling under keel of ship; rebuke severely —**keel'son** [kel'-] *n.* line of timbers or plates bolted to keel —**keel over** turn upside down; *inf.* collapse suddenly

keen[1] *a.* sharp; acute; eager; shrewd, strong; *sl.* very good —**keen'ly** *adv.* —**keen'ness** *n.*

keen[2] *n.* funeral lament —*vi.* wail over the dead

keep *vt.* retain possession of, not lose; store; cause to continue; take charge of; maintain, detain; provide upkeep; reserve —*vi.* remain good; remain; continue (**kept** *pt./pp.*) —*n.* living or support; charge or care; central tower of castle, stronghold —**keep'er** *n.* —**keep'ing** *n.* harmony, agreement; care, charge, possession —**keep fit** exercises designed to promote physical fitness —**keep'sake** *n.* thing treasured for sake of giver

keg *n.* small barrel; metal container for beer

kelp *n.* large seaweed; its ashes, yielding iodine

Kel'vin *a.* of thermometric scale starting at absolute zero (-273.15° Celsius) —*n.* SI unit of temperature

ken *n.* range of knowledge —*vt.* (in Scotland) know

ken'do *n.* Japanese form of fencing, using wooden staves

kenn'el *n.* UK doghouse —*pl.* place for breeding, boarding dogs —*vt.* put into kennel (**-ll-**)

ke'no [-ē] *n.* game of chance similar to bingo

kent'ledge *n. Naut.* scrap metal used as ballast

kepi' *n.* military cap with circular top and horizontal peak (*pl.* **-s**)

kept *pt./pp. of* KEEP

kerb *n.* UK curb

ker'chief [-chif] *n.* head-cloth; handkerchief

kerm'es [-iz] *n.* an insect used for red dyestuff

kern'el *n.* inner seed of nut or fruit stone; central, essential part

ker'osene *n.* paraffin oil distilled from petroleum or coal and shale used as fuel, solvent *etc.*

kes'trel *n.* small falcon

ketch *n.* two-masted sailing vessel

ketch'up *n.* sauce of vinegar, tomatoes *etc.*

ket'tle *n.* metal vessel with spout and handle, *esp.* for boiling water —**ket'tledrum** *n.* musical instrument made of membrane stretched over copper hemisphere —**a fine kettle of fish** awkward situation, mess

key *n.* instrument for operating lock, winding clock *etc.*; something providing control, explanation, means of achieving an end *etc.*; *Mus.* set of related notes; operating lever of typewriter, piano, organ *etc.*; spanner; mode of thought —*vt.* provide symbols on map *etc.* to assist identification of positions on it; scratch plaster surface to provide bond for plaster or paint —*a.* vital; most important —**key'board** *n.* set of keys on piano *etc.* —**key'hole** *n.* small opening in door or lock into which key is inserted —**key'note** *n.* dominant idea; basic note of musical key —**key'pad** *n.* small keyboard with push buttons —**key'stone** *n.* central stone of arch which locks all other stones in position

kg kilogram(s)

khak'i [kahk'-] *a.* dull yellowish-brown —*n.* khaki cloth; military uniform

Khmer [kmer] *n.* member of a people of Kampuchea

kHz kilohertz

kib'ble *vt.* grind into small pieces

kibbutz' [-oo-] *n.* Jewish communal agricultural settlement in Israel

ki'bosh *n.* —**put the kibosh on** *sl.* silence; get rid of; defeat

kick *vi.* strike out with foot; score with a kick; be recalcitrant; recoil —*vt.* strike or hit with foot; *inf.* free oneself of (habit *etc.*) —*n.* foot blow; recoil; excitement, thrill —**kick'back** *n.* strong reaction; money paid illegally for favours done *etc.* —**kick off** start game of football; *inf.* begin (discussion *etc.*)

kid *n.* young goat; leather of its skin; *inf.* child —*vt. inf.* tease, deceive —*vi. inf.* behave, speak in fun (**-dd-**)

kid'nap *vt.* seize and hold to ransom (**-pp-**) —**kid'napper** *n.*

kid'ney *n.* either of the pair of organs which secrete urine; animal kidney used as food; nature, kind (*pl.* **-neys**) —**kidney bean** dwarf French bean; scarlet runner

kill *vt.* deprive of life; destroy; neutralize; pass (time); weaken or dilute; *inf.* exhaust; *inf.* cause to suffer pain; *inf.* quash, defeat, veto —*n.* act or time of killing; animals *etc.* killed in hunt —**kill'er** *n.* one who, that which, kills —**kill'ing** *inf. a.* very tiring; very funny —*n.* sudden success, *esp.* on stock market —**killer whale** ferocious toothed whale most common in cold seas —**kill-joy** *n.* person who spoils other people's pleasure

kiln *n.* furnace, oven

ki'lo [kē'-] *n. short for* KILOGRAM(ME)

kilo- (*comb. form*) one thousand, as in **kil'olitre** *n.*, **kil'ometre** [*or* -lom'-] *n.*

kil'ogram(me) *n.* weight of 1000 grams

kil'ohertz *n.* one thousand cycles per second

kil'owatt *n. Electricity* one thousand watts

kilt *n.* short, usu. tartan, skirt, deeply pleated, worn orig. by Scottish Highlanders —**kilt'ed** *a.*

kil'ter *n.* —**out of kilter** not in working order

kimo'no *n.* loose, wide-sleeved Japanese robe, fastened with sash; European garment like this

kin *n.* family, relatives —*a.* related by blood —**kin'dred** *n.* relationship; relatives —*a.* similar; related —**kins'folk** *n.*

(*also* **kin'folk**) —**kin'ship** *n.* —**kins'man** *n.* (**kins'woman** *fem.*)

kind [kīnd] *n.* genus, sort, class —*a.* sympathetic, considerate; good, benevolent; gentle —**kind'liness** *n.* —**kind'ly** *a.* kind, genial —*adv.* —**kind'ness** *n.* —**kind-hearted** *a.* kindly, readily sympathetic —**in kind** (of payment) in goods rather than money; with something similar

kin'dergarten *n.* class, school for children of about five years old

kin'dle *vt.* set on fire; inspire, excite —*vi.* catch fire —**kind'ling** *n.* small wood to kindle fires

kine *obs. pl. of* COW

kinemat'ic [ki-] *a.* of motion without reference to mass or force —**kinemat'ics** *pl.n.* science of this —**kinematog'rapher** *see* CINEMATOGRAPHER

kinet'ic *a.* of motion in relation to force —**kinet'ics** *pl.n.* science of this

king *n.* male sovereign ruler of independent state; monarch; piece in game of chess; highest court card, with picture of a king; *Checkers* two pieces on top of one another, allowed freedom of movement —**king'ly** *a.* royal; appropriate to a king —**king'ship** *n.* —**king'dom** *n.* state ruled by king; realm; sphere —**king'fisher** *n.* small bird with bright plumage which dives for fish —**king'pin** *n.* swivel pin; central or front pin in bowling; *inf.* chief thing or person —**king post** beam in roof framework rising from tie beam to the ridge —**king-size(d)** *a. inf.* large; larger than standard size

kink *n.* tight twist in rope, wire, hair *etc.*; crick, as of neck; *inf.* eccentricity —*v.* make, become kinked; put, make kink in; twist —**kink'y** *a.* full of kinks; *inf.* eccentric, *esp.* given to deviant (sexual) practices

ki'osk [kē'-] *n.* small, sometimes movable construction used as bus shelter, newsstand or telephone booth

kip *n./vi. inf.* sleep

kipp'er *vt.* cure (fish) by splitting open, rubbing with salt, and drying or smoking —*n.* kippered fish

kirk *n.* in Scotland, church

kirsch *n.* brandy made from cherries

kis'met [kiz'-] *n.* fate, destiny

kiss *n.* touch or caress with lips; light touch —*v.* —**kiss'er** *n.* one who kisses; *sl.* mouth or face —**kiss of life** mouth-to-mouth resuscitation

kit *n.* outfit, equipment; personal effects, *esp.* of traveller; set of pieces of equipment sold ready to be assembled —**kit'bag** *n.* bag for holding soldier's or traveller's kit

kitch'en *n.* room used for cooking —**kitchenette'** *n.* small room (or part of larger room) used for cooking —**kitchen garden** garden for raising vegetables, herbs *etc.* —**kitchen sink** *n.* sink in kitchen —*a.* sordidly domestic

kite *n.* light papered frame flown in wind; *sl.* airplane; large hawk

kith *n.* acquaintance, kindred (*only in* **kith and kin**)

kitsch [kitch] *n.* vulgarized, pretentious art, literature *etc.*, usu. with popular, sentimental appeal

kitt'en *n.* young cat —**kitt'enish** *a.* like kitten, lively; (of woman) flirtatious, esp. coyly

kitt'iwake *n.* type of seagull

kitt'y *n. short for* KITTEN; in some card games, pool; communal fund

ki'wi [kē'-] *n.* any N.Z. flightless bird of the genus *Apteryx*; *inf.* New Zealander —**kiwi fruit** fuzzy fruit of Asian climbing plant, the Chinese gooseberry

klax'on *n.* formerly, a powerful electric motor horn

kleptoma'nia *n.* compulsive tendency to steal for the sake of theft —**kleptoma'niac** *n.*

km kilometre(s)

knack [n-] *n.* acquired facility or dexterity; trick; habit

knap'sack [n-] *n.* soldier's or traveller's bag to strap to the back, rucksack

knap'weed *n.* plant having purplish thistlelike flowers

knave [nā-] *n.* jack at cards; *obs.* rogue —**kna'very** *n.* villainy —**kna'vish** *a.*

knead [nē-] *vt.* work (flour) into dough; work, massage —**knead'er** *n.*

knee [n-] *n.* joint between thigh and lower leg; part of garment covering knee; lap —*vt.* strike, push with knee —**knee'cap** *n.* bone in front of knee

kneel [n-] *vi.* fall, rest on knees (**knelt** *pt./pp.*)

knell [n-] *n.* sound of a bell, *esp.* at funeral or death; portent of doom

knew *pt. of* KNOW

knick'erbockers [n-] *pl.n.* knickers

knick'ers [n-] *pl.n.* loose-fitting trousers gathered in at knee

knick'-knack [nik'nak] *n.* trifle, trinket

knife [n-] *n.* cutting blade, *esp.* one in handle, used as implement or weapon (*pl.* **knives**) —*vt.* cut or stab with knife —**knife edge** critical, possibly dangerous situation

knight [nīt] *n.* man of rank below baronet, having right to prefix *Sir* to his name; member of medieval order of chivalry; champion; piece in chess —*vt.* confer knighthood on —**knight'hood** *n.* —**knight'ly** *a.*

knit [n-] *v.* form (garment *etc.*) by putting together series of loops in wool, or other yarn; draw together; unite (**knit'ted, knit** *pt./pp.* —**knitt'ing** *pr.p.*) —**knit'ter** *n.* —**knitt'ing** *n.* knitted work; act of knitting —**knit'wear** *n.* knitted clothes, esp. sweaters

knob [n-] *n.* rounded lump, *esp.* at end or on surface of anything —**knobb'(l)y** *a.*

knock [n-] *vt.* strike, hit; *inf.* disparage; rap audibly; (of engine) make metallic noise, pink —*n.* blow, rap —**knock'er** *n.* metal appliance for knocking on door; who or what knocks —**knock-kneed** *a.* having incurved legs —**knock'out** *n.* blow *etc.* that renders unconscious; *inf.* person or thing overwhelmingly attractive —**knocked up** *inf.* exhausted, tired, worn out —**knock off** *inf.* cease work; *inf.* make something hurriedly; *inf.* kill —**knock out** *inf.* render opponent unconscious; overwhelm, amaze

knoll [nōl] *n.* small rounded hill, mound

knot[1] [n-] *n.* fastening of strands by looping and pulling tight; cockade, cluster; small closely knit group; tie, bond; hard lump, *esp.* of wood where branch joins or has joined in; measure of ship's speed, *eg* **ten knots** means ten nautical miles per hour; difficulty —*vt.* tie with knot, in knots (**-tt-**) —**knott'y** *a.* full of knots; puzzling, difficult —**knot'hole** *n.* hole in wood where knot has been

knot[2] *n.* small northern sandpiper with grey plumage

know [nō] *vt.* be aware of, have information about, be acquainted with, recognize, have experience, understand —*vi.* have information or understanding (**knew** *pt.*, **known** *pp.*) —**know'able** *a.* —**know'ing** *a.* cunning, shrewd —**know'ingly** *adv.* shrewdly; deliberately —**knowl'edge** [nol-] *n.* knowing; what one knows; learning —**knowl'edg(e)able** *a.* intelligent, well-informed —**know-how** *n. inf.* practical knowledge, experience, aptitude —**in the know** *inf.* informed

knuc'kle [nuk'l] *n.* bone at finger joint; knee joint of calf or pig —*vt.* strike with knuckles —**knuckle-duster** *n.* metal appliances worn on knuckles to add force to blow —**knuckle down** get down (to work) —**knuckle under** yield, submit

knur, nur [n-] *n.* knot in wood; hard lump

knurled [n-] *a.* serrated; gnarled

KO knockout

koal'a [kō-ahl'ə] *n.* marsupial Aust. animal, native bear

kohl [kōl] *n.* powdered antimony used orig. in Eastern countries for darkening the eyelids

kohlra'bi [kōl-rah'bi] *n.* type of cabbage with edible stem

kokan'ee [-ē] *n.* salmon of N Amer. lakes

ko'matik *n.* Inuit sled with wooden runners

kook'aburra *n.* large Aust. kingfisher with cackling cry (*also called* **laughing jackass**)

ko'pe(c)k, co'peck *n.* Soviet monetary unit, one hundredth of rouble

Koran' [-ahn'] *n.* sacred book of Muslims

ko'sher *a.* permitted, clean, good, as of food *etc.*, conforming to the Jewish dietary law; *inf.* legitimate, authentic —*n.* kosher food

kow'tow *n.* former Chinese custom of touching ground with head in respect; submission —*vi.* (*esp. with* to) prostrate oneself; be obsequious, fawn on

kraal [-ah-] *n.* S Afr. village with fence; corral

krak'en [-ah-] *n.* mythical Norwegian sea monster

kraut [-owt] *a./n. sl. offens.* German

Krem'lin *n.* central government of Soviet Union

krill *n.* small shrimplike marine animal (*pl.* **krill**)

kryp'ton [krip'-] *n.* rare gaseous element, present in atmosphere

ku'dos [kyōō'-] *n.* fame; credit

ku'du [kōō'-dōō] *n.* Afr. antelope with spiral horns

kuk'ri [koo-] *n.* heavy, curved Gurkha knife

ku'ku, kuku'pa *n.* New Zealand fruit-eating pigeon

ku'lak [kōō'-] *n.* independent well-to-do Russian peasant

küm'mel *n.* cumin flavoured German liqueur

kum'quat [-kwot] *n.* small Chinese tree; its round orange fruit

kung fu [fōō] *n.* Chinese martial art combining techniques of judo and karate

kW kilowatt

ky'mograph [kī'-] *n.* instrument for recording on graph pressure, oscillations, sound waves

L

L Latin

l litre

l. lake; left; line

la *see* LAH

lab *n. inf. short for* LABORATORY

la'bel *n.* slip of paper, metal *etc.*, fixed to object to give information about it; brief, descriptive phrase or term —*vt.* (**-ll-**)

la'bial *a.* of the lips; pronounced with the lips —*n.*

la'bo(u)r [lā'bər] *n.* exertion of body or mind; task; workers collectively; effort, pain, of childbirth or time taken for this —*vi.* work hard; strive; maintain normal motion with difficulty; (*esp.* of ship) be tossed heavily —*vt.* elaborate; stress to excess —**la'bo(u)red** *a.* uttered, done, with difficulty —**la'bo(u)rer** *n.* one who labours, *esp.* man doing manual work for wages —**labor'ious** *a.* tedious —**labo'riously** *adv.*

labor'atory [-bo'-] *n.* place for scientific investigations or for manufacture of chemicals

lab'rador *n.* breed of large, smooth-coated retriever dog

labur'num *n.* tree with yellow hanging flowers

lab'yrinth *n.* network of tortuous passages, maze; inexplicable difficulty; perplexity —**labyrin'thine** [-th-] *a.*

lac[1] *n.* resinous substance secreted by some insects

lac[2]**, lakh** *n.* one hundred thousand (of rupees)

lace *n.* fine patterned openwork fabric; cord, usu. one of pair, to draw edges together, *eg* to tighten shoes *etc.*; ornamental braid —*vt.* fasten with laces; flavour with spirit —**lac'y** *a.* fine, like lace

la'cerate [las'-] *vt.* tear, mangle; distress —**lac'erable** *a.* —**lacera'tion** *n.*

lac'hrymal, lac'rimal [lak'ri-] *a.* of tears —**lac'hrymatory** *a.* causing tears or inflammation of eyes —**lac'hrymose** *a.* tearful

lack *n.* deficiency, need —*vt.* need, be short of —**lack'lustre** *a.* lacking brilliance or vitality

lackadai'sical [-dā'z-] *a.* languid, listless; lazy, careless

lack'ey *n.* servile follower; footman (*pl.* **-eys**) —*vt.* be, or play, the lackey; to wait upon

lacon'ic [lə-kon'-] *a.* using, expressed in few words; brief, terse; offhand, not caring —**lacon'ically** *adv.* —**lacon'icism** *n.*

lac'quer [lak'ər] *n.* hard varnish —*vt.* coat with this

lacrosse' *n.* ball game played with long-handled racket or crosse

lac'tic, lac'teal *a.* of milk —**lac'tate** *vi.* secrete milk —**lacta'tion** *n.* —**lac-to'meter** *n.* instrument for measuring purity and density of milk —**lac'tose** *n.* white crystalline substance occurring in milk

lacu'na [-kyōō'-] *n.* gap, missing part, *esp.* in document or series (*pl.* **-nae** [-nē], **-nas**)

lad *n.* boy, young fellow

ladd'er *n.* frame of two poles connected by cross-bars called rungs, used for climbing; flaw in stockings, sweaters *etc.*, caused by running of torn stitch

lade *vt.* load; ship; burden, weigh down (**la'den** *pp.*) —**la'ding** *n.* cargo, freight

la'dle *n.* spoon with long handle and large bowl —*vt.* serve out liquid with a ladle

la'dy *n.* female counterpart of gentleman; *polite term for* a woman; title of some women of rank —**la'dybug** *n.* small beetle, usu. red with black spots —**Lady Day** Feast of the Annunciation, 25th March —**la'dylike** *a.* gracious; well-mannered —**la'dyship** *n.* title of a lady —**lady's-slipper** *n.* orchid with reddish or purple flowers —**Our Lady** the Virgin Mary

lag[1] *vi.* go too slowly, fall behind (**-gg-**) —*n.* lagging, interval of time between events —**lagg'ard** *n.* one who lags —**lag'ging** *a.* loitering, slow

lag[2] *vt.* wrap boiler, pipes *etc.* with insulating material (**-gg-**) —**lagg'ing** *n.* this material

lag'er [lahg'-] *n.* a light-bodied type of beer

lagoon' *n.* saltwater lake, enclosed by atoll, or separated by sandbank from sea

lah, la *n.* sixth sol-fa note

la'ic *a.* secular, lay —**laiciza'tion** *n.* —**la'icize** *vt.* render secular or lay

laid *pt./pp. of* LAY[2] —**laid-back** *a. inf.* relaxed

lain *pp. of* LIE[1]

lair *n.* resting place, den of animal

laird *n.* Scottish landowner —**laird'ship** *n.* estate

laissez-faire' [les-ā-fer'] *n.* principle of nonintervention, *esp.* by government in commercial affairs; indifference

la'ity *n.* laymen, the people as opposed to clergy

lake[1] *n.* expanse of inland water —**lake'let** *n.* —**lake herring** cisco

lake[2] *n.* red pigment

lam *n.* —**on the lam** *sl.* making escape

Lam. Lamentations

la'ma [lahm'-] *n.* Buddhist priest in Tibet or Mongolia —**la'masery** *n.* monastery of lamas

lamb [lam] *n.* young of the sheep; its meat; innocent or helpless creature —*vi.* (of sheep) give birth to lamb —**lamb'like** *a.* meek, gentle

lambast(e)' [-bāst'] *vt.* beat, reprimand

lam'bent *a.* (of flame) flickering softly; glowing

lame *a.* crippled in a limb, *esp.* leg; limping; (of excuse *etc.*) unconvincing —*vt.* cripple —**lame duck** disabled, weak person or thing

lam'é [lahm'ā] *n./a.* (fabric) interwoven with gold or silver thread

lamell'a *n.* thin plate or scale (*pl.* **-ae** [-ē]) —**lamell'ar, -ate** *a.*

lament' *v.* feel, express sorrow (for) —*n.* passionate expression of grief; song of grief —**lam'entable** *a.* deplorable —**lamenta'tion** *n.*

lam'ina *n.* thin plate, scale, flake (*pl.* **-nae** [-nē], **-nas**) —**lam'inate** *v.* make (sheet of material) by bonding together two or more thin sheets; split, beat, form into thin sheets; cover with thin sheet of material —*n.* laminated sheet —**lamina'tion** *n.*

Lamm'as *n.* 1st August, formerly a harvest festival

lamp *n.* any of various appliances (*esp.* electrical) that produce light, heat, radiation *etc.*; formerly, vessel holding oil burned by wick for lighting —**lamp'black** *n.* pigment made from soot —**lamp'light** *n.* —**lamp'post** *n.* post supporting lamp in street —**lamp'shade** *n.*

lampoon' *n.* satire ridiculing person, literary work *etc.* —*vt.* satirize, ridicule —**lampoo'ner, -ist** *n.*

lamp'rey *n.* fish like an eel with a sucker mouth

lance' [-ah-] *n.* horseman's spear —*vt.* pierce with lance or lancet —**lan'ceolate** *a.* lance-shaped, tapering —**lan'cer** *n.* formerly, cavalry soldier armed with lance —**lan'cet** *n.* pointed two-edged surgical knife —**lance corporal, lance sergeant** *n.* noncommissioned officer in army

land *n.* solid part of earth's surface; ground, soil; country; property consisting of land —*pl.* estates —*vi.* come to land, disembark; bring an aircraft from air to land or water; alight, step down; arrive on ground; be legally admitted as immigrant —*vt.* bring to land; bring to some point or condition; *inf.* obtain; catch; *inf.* strike —**land'ed** *a.* possessing, consisting of lands —**land'ing** *n.* act of landing; platform between flights of stairs; a landing stage —**land'ward** *a./adv.* —**land'wards** *adv.* —**land'fall** *n.* ship's approach to land at end of voyage —**land grant** grant of public land to college, railway *etc.* —**land-holder** *n.* person who owns or occupies land —**landing gear** wheels, struts *etc.* under aircraft —**landing stage** platform for embarkation and disembarkation —**land'locked** *a.* enclosed by land; (*esp.* of certain salmon) living in fresh water that is permanently isolated from sea —**land'lord** *n.*, **land'lady** *fem.* person who lets land or houses *etc.*; master or mistress of inn, boarding house *etc.* —**land'lubber** *n.* person ignorant of the sea and ships —**land'mark** *n.* boundary mark, conspicuous object, as guide for direction *etc.*; event, decision *etc.* considered as important stage in development of something —**land office** office administering sale of public land —**land'scape** *n.* piece of inland scenery; picture of it; prospect —*v.* create, arrange, garden, park *etc.* —**landscape gardening** —**landscape painter** —**land'slide, land'slip** *n.* falling of soil, rock *etc.* down mountainside; overwhelming electoral victory

lan'dau [-daw] *n.* four-wheeled carriage with folding top

lane *n.* narrow road or street; specified route followed by shipping or aircraft; area of road for one stream of traffic

lan'guage [lang'gwij] *n.* system of sounds, symbols *etc.* for communicating thought; specialized vocabulary used by a particular group; style of speech or expression

lan'guish [-ng'gw-] *vi.* be or become weak or faint; be in depressing or painful conditions; droop, pine —**lan'guid** *a.* lacking energy, interest; spiritless, dull —**lan'guidly** *adv.* —**lan'guor** [-gər] *n.* want of energy or interest; faintness; tender mood; softness of atmosphere —**lan'guorous** *a.*

lan'iary *a.* lacerating or tearing (*esp.* of teeth)

lank *a.* lean and tall; greasy and limp —**lank'y** *a.*

lan'olin *n.* grease from wool used in ointments *etc.*

lanta'na *n.* tropical shrub

lan'tern *n.* transparent case for lamp or candle; erection on dome or roof to admit light —**lant'horn** *n. obs.* lantern

lan'thanum *n.* silvery-white ductile metallic element

lan'yard *n.* short cord for securing knife or whistle; short nautical rope; cord for firing cannon

lap[1] *n.* the part between waist and knees of a person when sitting; *fig.* place where anything lies securely; single circuit of racecourse, track; stage or part of journey; single turn of wound thread *etc.* —*vt.* enfold, wrap round; overtake opponent to be one or more circuits ahead (**-pp-**) —**lapp'et** *n.* flap, fold —**lap'dog** *n.* small pet dog

lap[2] *vt.* drink by scooping up with tongue; (of waves *etc.*) beat softly (**-pp-**)

lapel' *n.* part of front of a coat folded back towards shoulders

lap'idary *a.* of stones; engraved on stone —*n.* cutter, engraver of stones

lap'is laz'uli [-yoo-lī] *n.* bright blue stone or pigment

lapse *n.* fall (in standard, condition, virtue *etc.*); slip; mistake; passing (of time *etc.*) —*vi.* fall away; end, *esp.* through disuse

lap'wing *n.* type of plover

lar'board *n./a. old term for* port (side of ship)

lar'ceny *n.* theft

larch *n.* deciduous coniferous tree

lard *n.* prepared pig's fat —*vt.* insert strips of bacon in (meat); intersperse, decorate (speech with strange words *etc.*) —**lard'y** *a.*

lard'er *n.* storeroom for food

large *a.* broad in range or area; great in size, number *etc.*; liberal; generous —*adv.* in a big way —**large'ly** *adv.* —**largess(e)'** *n.* bounty; gift; donation —**at large** free, not confined; in general; fully

lar'go *adv. Mus.* in a slow and dignified manner

lar'iat [la'ri-] *n.* lasso; rope for tethering animals

lark[1] *n.* small, brown singing-bird, skylark —**lark'spur** *n.* plant with spikes of blue, pink, or white flowers

lark[2] *n.* frolic, spree —*vi.* indulge in lark —**lark'y** *a.*

larr'igan *n.* knee-high moccasin boot worn by trappers *etc.*

lar'va *n.* insect in immature but active stage (*pl.* **-ae** [-ē]) —**lar'val** *a.* —**lar'viform** *a.*

lar'ynx [la'ringks] *n.* part of throat containing vocal cords (*pl.* **laryn'ges** [-jēz]) —**laryngi'tis** *n.* inflammation of this

lasagn'e [lə-zan'yə] *n.* pasta formed in wide, flat sheets

las'car *n.* E Indian seaman

lasciv'ious [lə-siv'-] *a.* lustful

la'ser [lā'z-] *n.* device for concentrating electromagnetic radiation or light of mixed frequencies into an intense, narrow, concentrated beam

lash[1] *n.* stroke with whip; flexible part of whip; eyelash —*vt.* strike with whip, thong *etc.*; dash against (as waves); attack verbally, ridicule; flick, wave sharply to and fro —*vi.* (*with* out) hit, kick

lash[2] *vt.* fasten or bind tightly with cord *etc.*

lash'ings *pl.n. inf.* abundance

lass, lass'ie *n.* girl

lass'itude *n.* weariness

lasso' [-ōō'] *n.* rope with noose for catching cattle *etc.* (*pl.* **lasso(e)s'**) —*vt.* (**lassoed'** [la-sōōd'], **lasso'ing**)

last[1] [-ah-] *a./adv.* after all others, coming at the end; most recent(ly) —*a.* only remaining —*sup.* of LATE —*n.* last person or thing —**last'ly** *adv.* finally

last[2] [-ah-] *vi.* continue, hold out, remain alive or unexhausted, endure

last[3] [-ah-] *n.* model of foot on which shoes are made, repaired

latch *n.* fastening for door, consisting of bar, catch for it, and lever to lift it; small lock with spring action —*vt.* fasten with latch

late *a.* coming after the appointed time; delayed; that was recently but now is not; recently dead; recent in date; of late stage of development (**la'ter** *comp.*, **la'test, last** *sup.*) —*adv.* after proper time; recently; at, till late hour —**late'ly** *adv.* not long since

lateen' (sail) *a.* triangular sail on long yard hoisted to head of mast

la'tent *a.* existing but not developed; hidden

lat'eral *a.* of, at, from the side —**lat'erally** *adv.*

lat'erite *n.* brick-coloured rock or clay formed by weathering of rock in tropical regions

la'tex *n.* sap or fluid of plants, *esp.* of rubber tree —**laticif'erous** [lat-i-sif'-] *a.* bearing or containing latex or sap

lath [lahth] *n.* thin strip of wood (*pl.* **-s**) —**lath'ing** *n.* —**lath'y** *a.* like a lath; tall and thin

lathe [lāTH] *n.* machine for turning object while it is being shaped

lath'er [lahTH'-] *n.* froth of soap and water; frothy sweat —*v.* make frothy; *inf.* beat

Lat'in *n.* language of ancient Romans —*a.* of ancient Romans, of, in their language; speaking a language descended from theirs —**Lat'inism** *n.* word, idiom imitating Latin —**Latin'ity** *n.* manner of writing Latin; Latin style

lat'itude *n.* angular distance on meridian reckoned N or S from equator; deviation from a standard; freedom from restriction; scope —*pl.* regions —**latitu'dinal** *a.* —**latitudinar'ian** *a.* claiming, showing latitude of thought, *esp.* in religion —**latitudinar'ianism** *n.*

latrine' [-ēn'] *n.* in army *etc.*, lavatory

latt'er *a.* second of two; later; more recent —**latt'erly** *adv.*

latt'ice *n.* structure of strips of wood, metal *etc.* crossing with spaces between; window so made —**latt'iced** *a.*

laud *n.* praise, song of praise —*vt.* —**laudabil'ity** *n.* —**laud'able** *a.* praiseworthy —**laud'ably** *adv.* —**lauda'tion** *n.* praise; honour paid —**laud'atory** *a.* expressing, containing, praise

laud'anum *n.* tincture of opium

laugh [lahf] *vi.* make sounds instinctively expressing amusement, merriment, or scorn —*n.* —**laugh'able** *a.* ludicrous —**laugh'ably** *adv.* —**laugh'ter** *n.* —**laughing gas** nitrous oxide as anaesthetic —**laughing hyena** spotted hyena, so called from its cry —**laughing jackass** *see* KOOKABURRA —**laughing stock** object of general derision

launch[1] *vt.* set afloat; set in motion; begin; propel (missile, spacecraft) into space; hurl, send —*vi.* enter on course —**launch'er** *n.* installation, vehicle, device for launching rockets, missiles *etc.*

launch[2] *n.* large power-driven boat

laun'dry *n.* place for washing clothes, *esp.* as a business; clothes *etc.* for washing —**laun'der** *vt.* wash and iron —**Laun'dromat** R shop with coin-operated washing, drying machines

lau'reate [law'ri-ət] *a.* crowned with laurels —**lau'reateship** *n.* post of poet laureate —**poet laureate** poet with appointment to Royal Household, nominally to compose verses on occasions of national importance

lau'rel [lo'-] *n.* glossy-leaved shrub, bay tree —*pl.* its leaves, emblem of victory or merit

lav'a [lahv'-] *n.* molten matter thrown out by volcanoes, solidifying as it cools

lav'atory *n.* toilet, water closet

lave *vt.* wash, bathe

lav'ender *n.* shrub with fragrant flowers; colour of the flowers, pale lilac

lav'ish *a.* giving or spending profusely;

very, too abundant —*vt.* spend, bestow, profusely

law *n.* rule binding on community; system of such rules; legal science; knowledge, administration of it; *inf.* (member of) police force; general principle deduced from facts; invariable sequence of events in nature —**law'ful** *a.* allowed by law —**law'fully** *adv.* —**law'less** *a.* ignoring laws; violent —**law'lessly** *adv.* —**law'yer** *n.* professional expert in law —**law-abiding** *a.* obedient to laws; well-behaved —**law'giver** *n.* one who makes laws —**law'suit** *n.* prosecution of claim in court

lawn[1] *n.* stretch of carefully tended turf in garden *etc.* —**lawn mower** —**lawn tennis** tennis played on grass court

lawn[2] *n.* fine linen

lawyer *see* LAW

lax *a.* not strict; lacking precision; loose, slack —**lax'ative** *a.* having loosening effect on bowels —*n.* —**lax'ity, lax'ness** *n.* slackness; looseness of (moral) standards —**lax'ly** *adv.*

lay[1] *pt. of* LIE[1] —**lay'about** *n.* lazy person, loafer

lay[2] *vt.* deposit, set, cause to lie (**laid, lay'ing**) —**lay'er** *n.* single thickness of some substance, as stratum or coating on surface; laying hen; shoot of plant pegged down or partly covered with earth to encourage root growth —*vt.* propagate plants by making layers —**lay'out** *n.* arrangement, *esp.* of matter for printing —**lay off** dismiss staff during slack period (**lay-off** *n.*) —**lay on** provide, supply; apply; strike —**lay out** display; expend; prepare for burial; plan copy for printing *etc.*; *sl.* knock out —**lay waste** devastate

lay[3] *n.* minstrel's song

lay[4] *a.* not clerical or professional; of, or done by, persons not clergymen —**lay'man** *n.* ordinary person

layette' [lā-et'] *n.* clothes for newborn child

lay figure jointed figure of the body used by artists; nonentity

laz'ar *n.* leper

la'zy *a.* averse to work, indolent —**laze** *vi.* indulge in laziness —**la'zily** *adv.* —**la'ziness** *n.*

lb. pound

l.b.w. leg before wicket

lea [lē] *n. Poet.* piece of meadow or open ground

lead[1] [lēd] *vt.* guide, conduct; persuade; direct; conduct people —*vi.* be, go, play first; result; give access to (**led, lead'ing**) —*n.* leading; that which leads or is used to lead; example; front or principal place, role *etc.*; cable bringing current to electric instrument —**lead'er** *n.* one who leads; something offered at low price to attract customers; leading article —**lead'ership** *n.* —**leading article** *see* EDITORIAL —**leading case** legal decision used as precedent —**leading question** question worded to prompt answer desired —**lead time** time between design of product and its production

lead[2] [led] *n.* soft heavy grey metal; plummet, used for sounding depths of water; graphite —*pl.* lead-covered piece of roof; strips of lead used to widen spaces in printing *etc.* —*vt.* cover, weight or space with lead (**lead'ed, lead'ing**) —**lead'en** *a.* of, like lead; heavy; dull

leaf *n.* organ of photosynthesis in plants, consisting of a flat, usu. green blade on stem; two pages of book *etc.*; thin sheet; flap, movable part of table *etc.* (*pl.* **leaves**) —*vt.* turn through (pages *etc.*) cursorily —**leaf'less** *a.* —**leaf'let** *n.* small leaf; single sheet, often folded, of printed matter for distribution, handbill —**leaf'y** *a.*

league[1] [lēg] *n.* agreement for mutual help; parties to it; federation of clubs *etc.*; *inf.* class, level —*vi.* form an alliance; combine in an association —**leag'uer** *n.* member of league

league[2] [lēg] *n. obs.* measure of distance, about three miles

leak *n.* hole, defect, that allows escape or entrance of liquid, gas, radiation *etc.*; disclosure —*vi.* let fluid *etc.* in or out; (of fluid *etc.*) find its way through leak —*vt.* let escape —*v.* (allow to) become known little by little —**leak'age** *n.* leaking; gradual escape or loss —**leak'y** *a.*

lean[1] *a.* lacking fat; thin; meagre; (of mixture of fuel and air) with too little fuel —*n.* lean part of meat, mainly muscular tissue

lean[2] *v.* rest against; bend, incline; tend (towards); depend, rely (on) (**leaned** [lēnd] or **leant** [lent] *pt./pp.*) —**lean'ing**

n. tendency —**lean-to** *n.* room, shed built against existing wall

leap *vi.* spring, jump —*vt.* spring over (**leaped** [lēpt] or **leapt** [lept] *pt./pp.*) —*n.* jump —**leap'frog** *n.* game in which player vaults over another bending down —**leap year** year with February 29th as extra day, occurring every fourth year

learn [lern] *vt.* gain skill, knowledge by study, practice or teaching —*vi.* gain knowledge; be taught; find out (**learnt, learned** [lernd] *pt./pp.*) —**learn'ed** *a.* erudite, deeply read; showing much learning —**learn'edly** *adv.* —**learn'er** *n.* —**learn'ing** *n.* knowledge got by study

lease *n.* contract by which land or property is rented for stated time by owner to tenant —*vt.* let, rent by, take on lease —**lease'hold** *a.* held on lease

leash *n.* thong for holding a dog; set of three animals held in leash —*vt.* hold in leash

least *a.* smallest —*sup. of* LITTLE —*n.* smallest one —*adv.* in smallest degree

leath'er [leTH'-] *n.* prepared skin of animal —**leath'ery** *a.* like leather, tough —**leath'erjacket** *n.* crane fly grub —**leath'erwood** *n.* N Amer. tree with tough, leathery bark

leave[1] *vt.* go away from; deposit; allow to remain; depart from; entrust; bequeath —*vi.* go away, set out (**left, lea'ving**)

leave[2] *n.* permission; permission to be absent from work, duty; period of such absence; formal parting

leav'en [lev'-] *n.* yeast; *fig.* transforming influence —*vt.* raise with leaven; taint; influence; modify

lech'er *n.* man given to lewdness —**le(t)ch** *vi. inf.* behave lecherously —**lech'erous** *a.* lewd; provoking lust; lascivious —**lech'erously** *adv.* —**lech'erousness** *n.* —**lech'ery** *n.*

lec'tern *n.* reading desk, *esp.* in church

lec'tion *n.* difference in copies of manuscript or book; reading —**lec'tionary** *n.* book, list of scripture lessons for particular days —**lec'tor** *n.* reader

lec'ture *n.* instructive discourse; speech of reproof —*vi.* deliver discourse —*vt.* reprove —**lec'turer** *n.* —**lec'tureship** *n.* appointment as lecturer

LED light-emitting diode

ledge *n.* narrow shelf sticking out from wall, cliff *etc.*; ridge, rock below surface of sea

ledg'er *n.* book of debit and credit accounts, chief account book of firm; flat stone —**ledger line** *Mus.* short line, above or below stave

lee *n.* shelter; side of anything, *esp.* ship, away from wind —**lee'ward** *a./n.* (on) lee side —*adv.* towards this side —**lee'way** *n.* leeward drift of ship; room for free movement within limits; loss of progress

leech[1] *n.* species of bloodsucking worm; *Hist.* physician

leech[2] *n.* edge of a sail

leek *n.* plant like onion with long bulb and thick stem

leer *vi.* glance with malign, sly, or lascivious expression —*n.* such glance

lees [-z] *pl.n.* sediment of wine *etc.*; dregs of liquor

left[1] *a.* denotes the side that faces west when the front faces north; opposite to the right —*n.* the left hand or part; *Politics* reforming or radical party (*also* **left wing**) —*adv.* on or towards the left —**left'ist** *n./a.* (person) of the political left —**lef'ty** *n. inf.* left-handed person

left[2] *pt./pp. of* LEAVE[1]

leg *n.* one of limbs on which person or animal walks, runs, stands; part of garment covering leg; anything which supports, as leg of table; stage of journey —**legg'ings** *pl.n.* covering of leather or other material for legs —**legg'y** *a.* long-legged; (of plants) straggling —**leg'man** *n.* newsman who reports from scene; person running errands, collecting information *etc.* —**leg'warmer** *n.* one of pair of long knitted footless socks worn over tights when exercising

leg'acy *n.* anything left by will, bequest; thing handed down to successor

le'gal *a.* of, appointed or permitted by, or based on, law —**legal'ity** *n.* —**legaliza'tion** *n.* —**le'galize** *vt.* make legal —**le'gally** *adv.*

leg'ate *n.* ambassador, *esp.* papal —**leg'ateship** *n.* —**lega'tion** *n.* diplomatic minister and his staff; his residence

legatee' *n.* recipient of legacy

lega'to [-gah'tō] *adv. Mus.* smoothly

leg'end [lej'-] *n.* traditional story or myth; traditional literature; famous, renowned, person or event; inscription —**leg'endary** *a.*

leg'erdemain [lej'-] *n.* juggling, conjuring, sleight of hand, trickery

leg'horn *n.* kind of straw; hat made of it; [le-gorn'] breed of fowls

leg'ible [lej'-] *a.* easily read —**legibil'ity** *n.* —**leg'ibly** *adv.*

le'gion [lē'jən] *n.* body of infantry in Roman army; various modern military bodies; association of veterans; large number —**le'gionary** *a./n.* —**legionnaire's disease** serious bacterial disease similar to pneumonia

leg'islator [lej'-] *n.* maker of laws —**leg'islate** *vi.* make laws —**legisla'tion** *n.* act of legislating; laws which are made —**leg'islative** *a.* —**leg'islature** *n.* body that makes laws of a state —**legislative assembly** single-chamber legislature in most Canad. provinces

legit'imate [-j-] *a.* born in wedlock; lawful, regular; fairly deduced —**legit'imacy** *n.* —**legit'imate, legit'imize** *vt.* make legitimate —**legit'imateness** *n.* —**legitima'tion** *n.* —**legit'imism** *n.* —**legit'imist** *n.* supporter of hereditary title to monarchy

Leg'o R construction toy of plastic bricks fitted together by studs

legu'minous [-gyōō'-] *a.* (of plants) pod-bearing

lei [lā] *n.* garland of flowers

lei'sure [lezh'ər] *n.* freedom from occupation; spare time —**lei'sured** *a.* with plenty of spare time —**lei'surely** *a.* deliberate, unhurried —*adv.* slowly

leit'motif [līt'mō-tēf] *n. Mus.* recurring theme associated with some person, situation, thought

lemm'ing *n.* rodent of arctic regions

lem'on *n.* pale yellow acid fruit; tree bearing it; its colour; *sl.* useless or defective person or thing —**lemonade'** *n.* drink made from lemon juice

le'mur [lē'mər] *n.* nocturnal animal like monkey

lend *vt.* give temporary use of; let out for hire or interest; give, bestow (**lent, lend'ing**) —**lend'er** *n.* —**lends itself to** is suitable for

length *n.* quality of being long; measurement from end to end; duration; extent; piece of a certain length —**length'en** *v.* make, become, longer; draw out —**length'ily** *adv.* —**length'wise** *a./adv.* —**length'y** *a.* (over)long —**at length** in full detail; at last

le'nient *a.* mild, tolerant, not strict —**le'nience, le'niency** *n.* —**le'niently** *adv.*

len'itive *n.* soothing or mildly laxative drug

len'ity *n.* mercy; clemency

le'no *n.* thin linen or cotton cloth like muslin

lens [-z] *n.* piece of glass or similar material with one or both sides curved, used to converge or diverge light rays in cameras, spectacles, telescopes *etc.* (*pl.* **lens'es**)

lent *pt./pp. of* LEND

Lent *n.* period of fasting from Ash Wednesday to Easter Eve —**Lent'en** *a.* of, in, or suitable to Lent

lent'il *n.* edible seed of leguminous plant —**lentic'ular** *a.* like lentil

len'to *adv. Mus.* slowly

Le'o *n.* (the lion) 5th sign of the zodiac, operative *c.* July 22-Aug. 21

le'onine *a.* like a lion

leop'ard [lep'-] *n.* large, spotted, carnivorous animal of cat family, like panther (**leop'ardess** *fem.*)

le'otard [lē'ō-] *n.* tight-fitting garment covering most of body, worn by acrobats, dancers *etc.*

lep'er *n.* one suffering from leprosy; person ignored or despised —**lep'rosy** *n.* disease attacking nerves and skin resulting in loss of feeling in affected parts —**lep'rous** *a.*

lepidop'tera *pl.n.* order of insects with four wings covered with fine gossamer scales, as moths, butterflies —**lepidop'terous** *a.*

lep'rechaun [-kawn] *n.* mischievous elf of Irish folklore

les'bian *n.* a homosexual woman —**les'bianism** *n.*

lèse-maj'esté [lāz-maj'es-tā] *Fr. n.* treason; taking of liberties

le'sion *n.* injury, injurious change in texture or action of an organ of the body

less *a. comp. of* LITTLE; not so much —*n.* smaller part, quantity; a lesser amount —*adv.* to a smaller extent or degree —*prep.* after deducting, minus —**less'en** *vt.* diminish; reduce —**less'er** *a.* less; smaller; minor

lessee' *n.* one to whom lease is granted

less'on *n.* instalment of course of instruction; content of this; experience that teaches; portion of Scripture read in church

less'or *n.* grantor of a lease

lest *conj.* in order that not; for fear that

let[1] *vt.* allow, enable, cause; allow to escape; grant use of for rent, lease —*vi.* be leased —*v. aux.* used to express a proposal, command, threat, assumption (**let, lett'ing**)

let[2] *n.* hindrance; in some games, minor infringement or obstruction of ball requiring replaying of point

le'thal [lē'-] *a.* deadly

leth'argy *n.* apathy, want of energy or interest; unnatural drowsiness —**lethar'gic** *a.* —**lethar'gically** *adv.*

lett'er *n.* alphabetical symbol; written message; strict meaning, interpretation —*pl.* literature, knowledge of books —*vt.* mark with, in, letters —**lett'ered** *a.* learned —**lett'erpress** *n.* printed matter as distinct from illustrations *etc.* —**letters patent** document under seal of state, granting exclusive right, privilege

lett'uce [-tis] *n.* plant grown for use in salad

leu'cocyte [lyōō'kō-sīt] *n.* one of white blood corpuscles

leuco'ma [lyōō-kō'-] *n.* disorder of the eye, characterized by opacity of the cornea

leukae'mia [lyōō-kē'-] *n.* a progressive blood disease

Lev. Leviticus

lev'ee[1] *n.* British sovereign's reception for men only; *Hist.* reception held by sovereign on rising

lev'ee[2] *n.* river embankment, natural or artificial; landing-place

lev'el *a.* horizontal; even in surface; consistent in style, quality *etc.* —*n.* horizontal line or surface; instrument for showing, testing horizontal plane; position on scale; standard, grade; horizontal passage in mine —*vt.* make level; bring to same level; knock down; aim (gun, or, *fig.*, accusation *etc.*) —*vi. inf.* (*esp. with* with) be honest, frank —**lev'eller** *n.* advocate of social equality —**levelheaded** *a.* not apt to be carried away by emotion

le'ver *n.* rigid bar pivoted about a fulcrum to transfer a force with mechanical advantage; handle pressed, pulled *etc.* to operate something —*vt.* prise, move, with lever —**le'verage** *n.* action, power of lever; influence; power to accomplish something; advantage

lev'eret *n.* young hare

levi'athan *n.* sea monster; anything huge or formidable

lev'igate *Chem. vt.* smooth; grind to fine powder

levita'tion *n.* the power of raising a solid body into the air supernaturally —**lev'itate** *v.* (cause to) do this

lev'ity *n.* inclination to make a joke of serious matters, frivolity; facetiousness

lev'y *vt.* impose (tax); raise (troops) (**lev'ied, lev'ying**) —*n.* imposition or collection of taxes; enrolling of troops; amount, number levied

lewd *a.* lustful; indecent —**lewd'ly** *adv.* —**lewd'ness** *n.*

lex'icon *n.* dictionary —**lex'ical** *a.* —**lexicog'rapher** *n.* writer of dictionaries —**lexicog'raphy** *n.*

li'able *a.* answerable; exposed (to); subject (to); likely (to) —**liabil'ity** *n.* state of being liable, obligation; hindrance, disadvantage —*pl.* debts

liai'son [lē-ā'zon] *n.* union; connection; intimacy, *esp.* secret —**liaise'** *vi.* —**liaison officer** officer who keeps units of troops in touch

lian'a, liane' [-ah-] *n.* climbing plant in tropical forests

liar *n. see* LIE[2]

Lib. Liberal

lib *n. inf. short for* LIBERATION

liba'tion [lī-] *n.* drink poured as offering to the gods

li'bel *n.* published statement falsely damaging person's reputation —*vt.* defame falsely (**-ll-**) —**li'bellous** *a.* defamatory

lib'eral *a.* generous; tolerant; abundant; (of education) designed to develop general cultural interests; (**L-**) of or belonging to Liberal Party —*n.* one who has liberal ideas or opinions —**lib'eralism** *n.* principles of Liberal Party —**liberal'ity** *n.* munificence —**lib'eralize** *vt.* —**lib'erally** *adv.* —**Liberal Party** major political party with viewpoints between those of Progressive-Conservative Party and New Democratic Party

lib'erate *vt.* set free —**libera'tion** *n.* —**lib'erator** *n.*

libertar'ian *n.* believer in freedom of thought *etc.*, or in free will —*a.* —**libertar'ianism** *n.*

lib'ertine [-ēn] *n.* morally dissolute person —*a.* dissolute —**lib'ertinism** *n.*

lib'erty *n.* freedom —*pl.* rights, privileges —**at liberty** free; having the right —**take liberties (with)** be presumptuous

libi'do [-bē'-] *n. Psychoanalysis* emotional or mental drive or energy behind all human activities; emotional craving, *esp.* of sexual origin —**libid'inous** *a.* lustful

Li'bra [lī'-] *n.* (the balance) 7th sign of the zodiac, operative *c.* Sept. 22-Oct. 22; *Hist.* a pound weight

li'brary *n.* room, building where books are kept; collection of books, gramophone records *etc.*; reading, writing room in house —**librar'ian** *n.* keeper of library —**librar'ianship** *n.*

li'brate *v.* vibrate as scales before attaining balance; quiver, oscillate; poise —**libra'tion** *n.* —**li'bratory** *a.* vibrating

librett'o *n.* words of an opera (*pl.* **-os, -i**) —**librett'ist** *n.*

lice *pl.n. see* LOUSE

li'cence, *esp.* **US li'cense** *n.* (document, certificate, giving) leave, permission; excessive liberty; dissoluteness; writer's, artist's transgression of rules of his art (*often* **poetic licence**) —**li'cense** *vt.* grant licence to —**licensee'** *n.* holder of licence —**licen'tiate** *n.* one licensed to practise art, profession —**licence plate** plate mounted on front and back of motor vehicle bearing registration number

licen'tious [lī-] *a.* dissolute; sexually immoral —**licen'tiously** *adv.*

li'chen [līk'-, lich'-] *n.* small flowerless plants forming crust on rocks, trees *etc.* —**li'chened** *a.* —**lichenol'ogy** *n.*

lich'gate, lych'gate *n.* roofed gate of churchyard

lick *vt.* pass the tongue over; touch lightly; *sl.* defeat; *sl.* flog, beat —*n.* act of licking; small amount (*esp.* of paint *etc.*); block or natural deposit of salt or other chemical licked by cattle *etc.*; *inf.* speed —**lick'ing** *n. sl.* beating

lick'ety-split' *adv. inf.* very quickly

lic'orice *n.* black substance used in medicine and as a sweet; (root of) plant from which it is obtained

lid *n.* movable cover; cover of the eye; *sl.* hat

li'do [lē'-] *n.* pleasure centre with swimming and boating

lie[1] *vi.* be horizontal, at rest; be situated; remain, be in certain state or position; exist, be found; recline (**lay, lain, lying**) —*n.* state (of affairs *etc.*); direction

lie[2] *vi.* make false statement (**lied, ly'ing**) —*n.* deliberate falsehood —**li'ar** *n.* person who tells lies —**white lie** untruth said without evil intent —**give the lie to** disprove

liege [lēj] *a.* bound to render or receive feudal service; faithful —*n.* lord; vassal, subject

li'en [lē'ən] *n.* right to hold another's property until claim is met

lieu [lyōō] *n.* place —**in lieu of** instead of

lieuten'ant [lef-] *n.* deputy; *Army* rank below captain; *Navy* rank equivalent to captain; **US** [lōō-ten'-] police officer —**lieutenant-governor** *n.* representative of the Crown in province

life *n.* active principle of existence of animals and plants, animate existence; time of its lasting; history of such existence; way of living; vigour, vivacity (*pl.* **lives**) —**life'less** *a.* dead; inert; dull —**life'long** *a.* lasting a lifetime —**life belt, jacket, preserver** buoyant device to keep afloat person in danger of drowning —**life style** particular attitudes, habits *etc.* of person or group —**life-support** *a.* of equipment or treatment necessary to keep a person alive —**life'time** *n.* length of time person, animal, or object lives or functions

lift *vt.* raise in position, status, mood, volume *etc.*; take up and remove; exalt spiritually; *inf.* steal —*vi.* rise —*n.* raising apparatus; **UK** elevator; act of lifting; ride in automobile *etc.* as passenger; force of air acting at right angles on aircraft wing, so lifting it; *inf.* feeling of cheerfulness, uplift

lig'ament *n.* band of tissue joining

bones —**lig'ature** *n.* anything which binds; thread for tying up artery

light[1] [līt] *a.* of, or bearing, little weight; not severe; gentle; easy, requiring little effort; trivial; (of industry) producing small, usu. consumer goods, using light machinery —*adv.* in light manner —*vi.* alight (from vehicle *etc.*); come by chance (upon) (**light'ed, lit** *pt./pp.*) —**light'en** *vt.* reduce, remove (load *etc.*) —**light'ly** *adv.* —**light'ness** *n.* —**lights** *pl.n.* lungs of animals —**light-headed** *a.* dizzy, inclined to faint; delirious —**light-hearted** *a.* carefree —**light-minded** *a.* frivolous —**light'weight** *n./a.* (person) of little weight or importance

light[2] [līt] *n.* electromagnetic radiation by which things are visible; source of this, lamp; window; mental vision; light part of anything; means or act of setting fire to; understanding —*a.* bright; pale, not dark —*vt.* set burning; give light to —*vi.* take fire; brighten (**light'ed** or **lit** *pt./pp.*) —**light'en** *vt.* give light to —**light'ing** *n.* apparatus for supplying artificial light —**light'ning** *n.* visible discharge of electricity in atmosphere —**light'house** *n.* tower with a light to guide ships —**light year** *Astronomy* distance light travels in one year, about six million million miles

light'er *n.* device for lighting cigarettes *etc.*; flat-bottomed boat for unloading ships

lig'neous *a.* of, or of the nature of, wood —**lig'nite** *n.* woody or brown coal

lig'nin *n.* organic substance which forms characteristic part of all woody fibres

lig'num vi'tae [vī'ti] *Lat.* tropical tree; its extremely hard wood

like[1] *a.* resembling; similar; characteristic of —*adv.* in the manner of —*pron.* similar thing —**like'lihood** *n.* probability —**like'ly** *a.* probable; hopeful, promising —*adv.* probably —**li'ken** *vt.* compare —**like'ness** *n.* resemblance; portrait —**like'wise** *adv.* in like manner

like[2] *vt.* find agreeable, enjoy, love —**like'able** *a.* —**lik'ing** *n.* fondness; inclination, taste

li'lac *n.* shrub bearing pale mauve or white flowers; pale mauve colour —*a.* of lilac colour

Lillipu'tian *a.* diminutive —*n.* midget, pygmy

lilt *v.* sing merrily; move lightly —*n.* rhythmical effect in music, swing —**lilt'ing** *a.*

lil'y *n.* bulbous flowering plant —**lily-white** *a.* —**lily of the valley** small garden plant with fragrant, white bell-like flowers

limb[1] [lim] *n.* arm or leg; wing; branch of tree

limb[2] [lim] *n.* edge of sun or moon; edge of sextant

lim'ber[1] *n.* detachable front of gun carriage

lim'ber[2] *a.* pliant, lithe —**limber up** loosen stiff muscles by exercises

lim'bo[1] *n.* supposed region intermediate between Heaven and Hell for the unbaptized; intermediate, indeterminate place or state (*pl.* **-bos**)

lim'bo[2] *n.* West Indian dance in which dancers pass under a bar (*pl.* **-bos**)

lime[1] *n.* any of certain calcium compounds used in making fertilizer, cement —*vt.* treat (land) with lime —**lime'light** *n.* formerly, intense white light obtained by heating lime; glare of publicity —**lime'stone** *n.* sedimentary rock used in building

lime[2] *n.* small acid fruit like lemon —**lime-juice** *n.* juice of lime prepared as drink

lime[3] *n.* tree, the linden

lim'erick *n.* self-contained, nonsensical, humorous verse of five lines

li'mey *n. sl.* British person

lim'it *n.* utmost extent or duration; boundary —*vt.* restrict, restrain, bound —**lim'itable** *a.* —**limita'tion** *n.* —**lim'ited** *a.* restricted; narrow; checked, as by law; (of train) stopping only at certain stations and having set number of cars —**lim'itless** *a.* —**limited company** one whose shareholders' liability is restricted

limn [lim] *vt.* paint, depict, draw —**lim'ner** *n.*

lim'ousine [-zēn] *n.* large, luxurious automobile

limp[1] *a.* without firmness or stiffness —**limp'ly** *adv.*

limp[2] *vi.* walk lamely —*n.* limping gait

limp'et *n.* shellfish which sticks tightly to rocks

limp'id *a.* clear; translucent —**limpid'ity** *n.* —**limp'idly** *adv.*

linch'pin *n.* pin to hold wheel on its axle; essential person or thing

linc'tus *n.* syrupy cough medicine

lind'en *n.* deciduous tree, with fragrant flowers; the lime

line *n.* long narrow mark; stroke made with pen *etc.*; continuous length without breadth; row; series, course; telephone connection; progeny; province of activity; system of travel or transportation; railway track; any class of goods; cord; string; wire; advice, guidance —*vt.* cover inside; mark with lines; bring into line; be, form border, edge —**lin'eage** [-i-ij] *n.* descent from, descendants of an ancestor —**lin'eal** *a.* of lines; in direct line of descent —**lin'eament** [-i-ə-mənt] *n.* feature —**lin'ear** *a.* of, in lines —**li'ner** *n.* large ship or aircraft of passenger line —**line'man** *n.* person who installs and maintains telephone and power lines; *Sport* player on forward line; *Surveying* person who carries the chain —**lines'man** *n.* in some sports, official who helps referee, umpire —**get a line on** obtain all relevant information about

lin'en *a.* made of flax —*n.* cloth made of flax; linen articles collectively; sheets, tablecloths *etc.*, or shirts (orig. made of linen)

ling[1] *n.* slender food fish

ling[2] *n.* heather

lin'ger [-ng'g-] *vi.* delay, loiter; remain long

lin'gerie [lan'zhə-rē] *n.* women's underwear or nightwear

ling'o *n. inf.* language, speech *esp.* applied to dialects

lin'gua fran'ca *It.* language used for communication between people of different mother tongues

lin'gual [-ng'gw-] *a.* of the tongue or language —*n.* sound made by the tongue, as *d, l, t* —**lin'guist** *n.* one skilled in languages or language study —**linguis'tic** *a.* of languages or their study —**linguis'tics** *pl.n.* (*with sing. v.*) study, science of language

lin'iment *n.* embrocation

li'ning *n.* covering for the inside of garment *etc.*

link *n.* ring of a chain; connection; measure, 1/100th part of chain —*vt.* join with, as with, link; intertwine —*vi.* be so joined —**link'age** *n.*

links *pl.n.* **UK** golf course

linn'et *n.* songbird of finch family

li'nocut *n.* design cut in relief on block of linoleum; print from this

lino'leum *n.* floor covering of hessian with smooth, hard, decorative coating of powdered cork, linseed oil *etc.*

Li'notype R typesetting machine which casts lines of words in one piece

lin'seed *n.* seed of flax plant

lint *n.* soft material for dressing wounds

lin'tel *n.* top piece of door or window

li'on *n.* large animal of cat family (**li'oness** *fem.*) —**li'onize** *vt.* treat as celebrity —**lion-hearted** *a.* brave

lip *n.* either edge of the mouth; edge or margin; *sl.* impudence —**lip gloss** cosmetic to give lips sheen —**lip-reading** *n.* method of understanding spoken words by interpreting movements of speaker's lips —**lip service** insincere tribute or respect —**lip'stick** *n.* cosmetic preparation in stick form, for colouring lips

liqueur' [li-kyoor'] *n.* alcoholic liquor flavoured and sweetened

liq'uid *a.* fluid, not solid or gaseous; flowing smoothly; (of assets) in form of money or easily converted into money —*n.* substance in liquid form —**liquefac'tion** *n.* —**liq'uefy, liq'uidize** *v.* make or become liquid (**liq'uefied, liq'uefying**) —**liques'cence** *n.* —**liques'cent** *a.* tending to become liquid —**liquid'ity** *n.* state of being able to meet financial obligations —**liq'uidizer** *n.* —**liquid air, gas** air, or gas, reduced to liquid state on application of increased pressure at low temperature

liq'uidate *vt.* pay (debt); arrange affairs of, and dissolve (company); wipe out, kill —**liquida'tion** *n.* process of clearing up financial affairs; state of being bankrupt —**liq'uidator** *n.* official appointed to liquidate business

liq'uor [lik'ər] *n.* liquid, *esp.* an alcoholic one

liq'uorice [-kər-is] *n. see* LICORICE

lir'a [lē-] *n.* monetary unit of Italy and Turkey (*pl.* **-re, -ras**)

lisle [līl] *n.* fine hand-twisted cotton thread

lisp *v.* speak with faulty pronunciation of 's' and 'z'; speak falteringly *—n.*

liss'om *a.* supple, agile

list[1] *n.* inventory, register; catalogue; edge of cloth *—pl.* field for combat *—vt.* place on list

list[2] *vi.* (of ship) lean to one side *—n.* inclination of ship

list'en [lis'ən] *vi.* try to hear, attend to **—list'ener** *n.*

list'er *n.* plough that throws soil to both sides of central furrow

list'less *a.* indifferent, languid **—list'lessly** *adv.*

lit *pt./pp. of* LIGHT[1], LIGHT[2]

lit'any *n.* prayer with responses from congregation

lit'eral *a.* according to sense of actual words, not figurative; exact in wording; of letters **—lit'erally** *adv.*

lit'erate *a.* able to read and write; educated *—n.* literate person **—lit'eracy** *n.* **—litera'ti** [-ah'-] *pl.n.* scholarly, literary people

lit'erature *n.* books and writings of a country, period or subject **—lit'erary** *a.* of or learned in literature **—lit'erarily** *adv.*

lithe [līTH] *a.* supple, pliant **—lithe'some** *a.* lissom, supple

lith'ium *n.* one of the lightest alkaline metals

lithog'raphy *n.* method of printing from metal or stone block using the antipathy of grease and water **—lith'ograph** *n.* print so produced *—vt.* print thus **—lithog'rapher** *n.* **—lithograph'ic** *a.*

lit'igate *vt.* contest in law *—vi.* carry on a lawsuit **—lit'igant** *n./a.* (person) conducting a lawsuit **—litiga'tion** *n.* lawsuit **—litig'ious** [-tij'-] *a.* given to engaging in lawsuits; disputatious

lit'mus *n.* blue dye turned red by acids and restored to blue by alkali **—litmus paper**

li'totes [lī'tō-tēz] *n.* ironical understatement for rhetorical effect

li'tre [lē'tər] *n.* measure of volume of fluid, one cubic decimetre, about 1.75 pints

litt'er *n.* untidy refuse; odds and ends; young of animal produced at one birth; straw *etc.* as bedding for animals; portable couch; kind of stretcher for wounded *—vt.* strew with litter; bring forth

lit'tle *a.* small, not much (**less, least**) *—n.* small quantity *—adv.* slightly

litt'oral *a.* pert. to the seashore *—n.* coastal district

lit'urgy *n.* prescribed form of public worship **—litur'gical** *a.*

live[1] [liv] *v.* have life; pass one's life; continue in life; continue, last; dwell; feed **—liv'able** *a.* suitable for living in; tolerable **—liv'ing** *n.* action of being in life; people now alive; way of life; means of living; church benefice

live[2] [līv] *a.* living, alive, active, vital; flaming; (of rail *etc.*) carrying electric current; (of broadcast) transmitted during the actual performance **—live'liness** *n.* **—live'ly** *a.* brisk, active, vivid **—li'ven** *vt.* (*esp. with* up) make (more) lively **—live-axle** *n.* driving shaft in automobile's back axle **—live'stock** *n.* domestic animals **—live wire** wire carrying electric current; able, very energetic person

live'lihood *n.* means of living; subsistence, support

live'long [liv-] *a.* lasting throughout the whole day

liv'er *n.* organ secreting bile; animal liver as food **—liv'erish** *a.* unwell, as from liver upset; cross, touchy, irritable

liv'ery *n.* distinctive dress of person or group, *esp.* servant(s); allowance of food for horses; a livery stable **—livery stable** stable where horses are kept at a charge or hired out

liv'id *a.* of a bluish pale colour; discoloured, as by bruising; *inf.* angry, furious

liz'ard *n.* four-footed reptile

LJ Lord Justice

llam'a [lahm'ə] *n.* woolly animal used as beast of burden in S Amer.

LL.B. Bachelor of Laws

loach *n.* carplike freshwater fish

load *n.* burden; amount usu. carried at once; actual load carried by vehicle; resistance against which engine has to work; amount of electrical energy drawn from a source *—vt.* put load on or into; charge (gun); weigh down **—load'ed** *a.* carrying a load; (of dice) dishonestly weighted; biased; (of question) containing hidden trap or implication; *sl.* wealthy; *sl.* drunk

load'star, -stone *n. see* LODE

loaf[1] *n.* mass of bread as baked; shaped mass of food (*pl.* **loaves**)

loaf[2] *vi.* idle, loiter —**loaf'er** *n.* idler; moccasin-like casual shoe

loam *n.* fertile soil

loan *n.* act of lending; thing lent; money borrowed at interest; permission to use —*vt.* lend, grant loan of

lo(a)th [-th] *a.* unwilling, reluctant (to) —**loath'ly** *a./adv.* —**loathe** [-TH] *vt.* hate, abhor —**loath'ing** *n.* disgust; repulsion —**loath'some** *a.* disgusting

lob *n.* in tennis *etc.*, shot pitched high in air —*v.* throw, pitch shot thus (**-bb-**)

lobb'y *n.* corridor into which rooms open; passage or room in legislative building, *esp.* houses of parliament of Britain, Canada and Aust., to which the public has access; group which tries to influence members of law-making assembly —**lobb'ying** *n.* frequenting lobby to collect news or influence members —**lob'byist** *n.*

lobe *n.* any rounded projection; subdivision of body organ; soft, hanging part of ear —**lobed** *a.* —**lobot'omy** *n.* surgical incision into lobe of organ, *esp.* brain

lobe'lia [lō-bē'-] *n.* garden plant with blue, red or white flowers

lob'ster *n.* shellfish with long tail and claws, turning red when boiled

lob'worm *n.* lugworm

lo'cal *a.* of, existing in particular place; confined to a definite spot, district or part of the body; of place; (of bus *etc.*) stopping at all stops —*n.* person belonging to a district; local or regional branch of association; item of local interest in newspaper —**locale'** [-ahl'] *n.* scene of event —**local'ity** *n.* place, situation; district —**lo'calize** *vt.* assign, restrict to definite place —**lo'cally** *adv.*

locate' *vt.* attribute to a place; find the place of; situate —*vi.* become established or settled —**loca'tion** *n.* placing; situation; site of movie production away from studio —**loc'ative** *a./n.* grammatical case denoting "place where"

loch [loH, lok] *n.* Scottish lake or long narrow bay

lock[1] *n.* appliance for fastening door, lid *etc.*; mechanism for firing gun; enclosure in river or canal for moving boats from one level to another; extent to which vehicle's front wheels will turn; appliance to check the revolution of a wheel; interlocking; block, jam —*vt.* fasten, make secure with lock; place in locked container; join firmly; cause to become immovable; embrace closely —*vi.* become fixed or united; become immovable —**lock'er** *n.* small cupboard with lock —**lock'jaw** *n.* tetanus —**lock'out** *n.* exclusion of workmen by employers as means of coercion —**lock'smith** *n.* one who makes and mends locks —**lock'up** *n.* prison

lock[2] *n.* tress of hair

lock'et *n.* small hinged pendant for portrait *etc.*

lo'co cita'to *Lat.* at the place quoted (*usu.* **loc. cit.**)

locomo'tive [lō-] *n.* engine for pulling carriages on railway tracks —*a.* having power of moving from place to place —**locomo'tion** *n.* action, power of moving

lo'cum te'nens *Lat.* (*usu. shortened to* **lo'cum**) substitute, *esp.* for doctor or clergyman during absence —**lo'cum te'nency**

lo'cus *n.* exact place or locality; curve made by all points satisfying certain mathematical condition, or by point, line or surface moving under such condition (*pl.* **lo'ci** [-sī])

lo'cust *n.* destructive winged insect —**locust tree** false acacia; the carob —**locust bean** its bean-shaped fruit

locu'tion *n.* a phrase; speech; mode or style of speaking

lode *n.* a vein of ore —**lode'star** *n.* Pole Star —**lode'stone** *n.* magnetic iron ore

lodge *n.* house, cabin used seasonally or occasionally, *eg* for hunting, skiing; gatekeeper's house; meeting place of branch of club *etc.*; the branch —*vt.* house; deposit; bring (a charge *etc.*) against someone —*vi.* live in another's house at fixed charge; come to rest (in, on) —**lodg'er** *n.* —**lodg(e)'ment** *n.* lodging, being lodged —**lodg'ings** *pl.n.* rented room(s) in another person's house

loft *n.* space between top storey and roof; gallery in church *etc.* —*vt.* send (golf ball *etc.*) high —**loft'ily** *adv.* haughtily —**loft'iness** *n.* —**loft'y** *a.* of great height; elevated; haughty

log[1] *n.* portion of felled tree stripped of

branches; detailed record of voyages, time travelled *etc.* of ship, aircraft *etc.*; apparatus used formerly for measuring ship's speed —*vt.* keep a record of; travel (specified distance, time) (**-gg-**) —**log'ger** *n.* —**logg'ing** *n.* cutting and transporting logs to river —**log'book** *n.* —**log jam** blockage caused by mass of floating logs

log[2] *n.* logarithm

lo'gan *n. see* BOGAN

lo'ganberry *n.* trailing prickly plant, cross between raspberry and blackberry; its purplish-red fruit

log'arithm [-THəm] *n.* one of series of arithmetical functions tabulated for use in calculation —**logarith'mic** *a.*

logg'erhead *n.* —**at loggerheads** quarrelling, disputing

lo'ggia [lō'jə] *n.* covered, arcaded gallery (*pl.* **lo'ggias, lo'ggie**)

log'ic [loj'-] *n.* art or philosophy of reasoning; reasoned thought or argument; coherence of various facts, events *etc.* —**log'ical** *a.* of logic; according to reason; reasonable; apt to reason correctly —**log'ically** *adv.* —**logi'cian** *n.*

logis'tics *pl.n.* (*with sing. or pl. v.*) the transport, housing and feeding of troops; organization of any project, operation —**logis'tical** *a.*

lo'go *n.* company emblem or similar device (*pl.* **-os**)

Log'os *n.* the Divine Word incarnate, Christ

loin *n.* part of body between ribs and hip; cut of meat from this —*pl.* hips and lower abdomen —**loin'cloth** *n.* garment covering loins only

loi'ter *vi.* dawdle, hang about; idle —**loi'terer** *n.*

loll *vi.* sit, lie lazily; (*esp.* of the tongue) hang out —*vt.* hang out (tongue)

loll'ipop *n.* piece of hard candy, *esp.* on small wooden stick

lone *a.* solitary —**lone'liness** *n.* —**lone'ly** *a.* sad because alone; unfrequented; solitary, alone —**lo'ner** *n. inf.* one who prefers to be alone —**lone'some** *a.*

long[1] *a.* having length, *esp.* great length, in space or time; extensive; protracted —*adv.* for a long time —**long'hand** *n.* writing of words, letters *etc.* in full —**long'playing** *a.* (of record) lasting for 10 to 30 minutes because of its fine grooves —**long-range** *a.* of the future; able to travel long distances without refuelling; (of weapons) designed to hit distant target —**long shot** competitor, undertaking, bet *etc.* with small chance of success —**long ton UK** the imperial ton (2240 lb) —**long-winded** *a.* tediously loquacious

long[2] *vi.* have keen desire, yearn (for) —**long'ing** *n.* yearning

lon'geron [-jər-] *n.* long spar running fore and aft in body of aircraft

longev'ity [-j-] *n.* long existence or life —**longe'val** *a.*

lon'gitude [-j-] *n.* distance east or west from standard meridian —**longitu'dinal** *a.* of length or longitude; lengthwise

long'shoreman *n.* wharf labourer

loo *n.* **UK** *inf.* lavatory

loo'fah *n.* pod of plant used as sponge; the plant

look *vi.* direct, use eyes; face; seem; search (for); hope (for); (*with* after) take care of —*n.* looking; view; search; (*oft. pl.*) appearance —**good looks** beauty —**look'alike** *n.* person who is double of another —**looking glass** mirror —**look'out** *n. inf.* worry, concern —**look after** tend —**look down on** despise

loom[1] *n.* machine for weaving; middle part of oar

loom[2] *vi.* appear dimly; seem ominously close; assume great importance

loon[1] *n. inf.* stupid, foolish person —**loo'ny** *a./n.*

loon[2] *n.* diving bird

loop *n.* figure made by curved line crossing itself; similar rounded shape in cord or rope *etc.* crossed on itself; aerial manoeuvre in which aircraft describes complete circle —*v.* form loop

loop'hole *n.* means of escape, of evading rule without infringing it; vertical slit in wall, *esp.* for defence

loose *a.* not tight, fastened, fixed, or tense; slack; vague; dissolute —*vt.* free; unfasten; slacken —*vi.* (*with* off) shoot, let fly —**loose'ly** *adv.* —**loos'en** *vt.* make loose —**loose'ness** *n.* —**on the loose** free; *inf.* on a spree

loot *n./vt.* plunder

lop[1] *vt.* cut away twigs and branches; chop off (**-pp-**)

lop[2] *vi.* hang limply (**-pp-**) —**lop'eared**

a. having drooping ears —**lopsi'ded** *a.* with one side lower than the other, badly balanced

lope *vi.* run with long, easy strides

loqua'cious *a.* talkative —**loquac'ity** [-kwas'-] *n.*

lo'quat [lō'kwot] *n.* Japanese plum tree; its fruit

lord *n.* British nobleman, peer of the realm; feudal superior; one ruling others; owner; God —*vi.* domineer —**lord'liness** *n.* —**lord'ly** *a.* imperious, proud; fit for a lord —**lord'ship** *n.* rule, ownership; domain; title of some noblemen

lore *n.* learning; body of facts and traditions

lorgnette' [lor-nyet'] *n.* pair of eyeglasses mounted on long handle

lor'ikeet *n.* small parrot

lor'is *n.* tree-dwelling, nocturnal Asian animal

lorn *a. poet.* abandoned; desolate

lor'ry *n.* long, flat wagon without sides; **UK** truck

lose [lo͞oz] *vt.* be deprived of, fail to retain or use; let slip; fail to get; (of clock *etc.*) run slow (by specified amount); be defeated in —*vi.* suffer loss (**lost** *pt./pp.* —**los'ing** [lo͞oz'ing] *pr.p.*) —**loss** *n.* a losing; what is lost; harm or damage resulting from losing —**lost** *a.* unable to be found; unable to find one's way; bewildered; not won; not utilized

lot *pron.* great number —*n.* collection; large quantity; share; fate; destiny; item at auction; one of a set of objects used to decide something by chance, as in **cast lots**; area of land, plot —*pl. inf.* great numbers or quantity —*adv. inf.* a great deal

loth *see* LOATH

lo'tion *n.* liquid for washing wounds, improving skin *etc.*

lott'ery *n.* method of raising funds by selling tickets and prizes by chance; gamble

lott'o *n.* game of chance like bingo

lo'tus *n.* legendary plant whose fruits induce forgetfulness when eaten; Egyptian water lily —**lotus position** seated cross-legged position used in yoga *etc.*

loud *a.* strongly audible; noisy; obtrusive —**loud'ly** *adv.* —**loudspeak'er** *n.* instrument for converting electrical signals into sound audible at a distance

lough [loH, lok] *n.* in Ireland, loch

lounge *vi.* sit, lie, walk, or stand in a relaxed manner —*n.* **UK** parlour; general waiting, relaxing area in airport, hotel *etc.* —**loung'er** *n.* loafer —**lounge suit** man's suit for daytime wear

lour *see* LOWER

louse [lows] *n.* a parasitic insect (*pl.* **lice**) —**lous'y** [-z'-] *a. sl.* nasty, unpleasant; *sl.* (too) generously provided, thickly populated (with); *sl.* bad, poor; having lice

lout *n.* crude, oafish person —**lout'ish** *a.*

lou'vre [lo͞o'vər] *n.* one of a set of boards or slats set parallel and slanted to admit air but not rain; ventilating structure of these

love [luv] *n.* warm affection; benevolence; charity; sexual passion; sweetheart; *Tennis etc.* score of nothing —*vt.* admire passionately; delight in —*vi.* be in love —**lov'(e)able** *a.* —**love'less** *a.* —**love'liness** *n.* —**love'lorn** *a.* forsaken by, pining for a lover —**love'ly** *a.* beautiful, delightful —**lov'er** *n.* —**lov'ing** *a.* affectionate; tender —**lov'ingly** *adv.* —**love'bird** *n.* small parrot —**love letter** —**loving cup** bowl formerly passed round at banquet —**make love (to)** have sexual intercourse (with)

low[1] [lō] *a.* not tall, high or elevated; humble; commonplace; coarse, vulgar; dejected; ill; not loud; moderate; cheap —**low'er** *vt.* cause, allow to descend; move down; diminish, degrade —*a.* below in position or rank; at an early stage, period of development —**low'liness** *n.* —**low'ly** *a.* modest, humble —**low'boy** *n.* table with drawers and short legs —**low'brow** *n.* one with no intellectual or cultural interests —*a.* —**Low Church** section of Anglican Church stressing evangelical beliefs and practices —**low'-down** *n. inf.* inside information —**low-down** *a. inf.* mean, shabby, dishonourable —**low frequency** in electricity, any frequency of alternating current from about 30 to 10,000 cycles; frequency within audible range —**low-key** *a.* subdued, restrained, not intense —**low'land** *n.* low-lying country —**Low'lander** *n.* —**Low'lands** *pl.n.* less mountainous parts of Scotland —**low-tension** *a.* carrying, operating at low voltage

low[2] [lō] *vi.* of cattle, utter their cry, bellow —*n.* cry of cattle, bellow

low'er, lour [low'ər] *vi.* look gloomy or threatening, as sky; scowl —*n.* scowl, frown

loy'al *a.* faithful, true to allegiance —**loy'alist** *n.* —**Loy'alist** *n.* United Empire Loyalist —**loy'ally** *adv.* —**loy'alty** *n.*

loz'enge *n.* small sweet or tablet of medicine; rhombus, diamond figure

LP longplaying (record)

LPG liquefied petroleum gas

LSD lysergic acid diethylamide (hallucinogenic drug); librae, solidi, denarii (*Lat.*, pounds, shillings, pence)

Lt. Lieutenant

Ltd. Limited (Liability)

lubb'er *n.* clumsy fellow; unskilled seaman

lu'bricate [lōō'-] *vt.* oil, grease; make slippery —**lu'bricant** *n.* substance used for this —**lubrica'tion** *n.* —**lu'bricator** *n.* —**lubric'ity** [-bris'-] *n.* slipperiness, smoothness; lewdness

lu'cent [lōō'-] *a.* bright, shining

lucerne' [lōō-] *n.* fodder plant like clover, alfalfa

lu'cid [lōō'sid] *a.* clear; easily understood; sane —**lucid'ity, lu'cidness** *n.* —**lu'cidly** *adv.*

Lu'cifer [lōō'-] *n.* Satan; Venus as the morning star; *obs.* match

luck *n.* fortune, good or bad; good fortune; chance —**luck'ily** *adv.* fortunately —**luck'less** *a.* having bad luck —**luck'y** *a.* having good luck

lu'cre [lōō'kər] *n.* (*usu. facetious*) money, wealth —**lu'crative** *a.* very profitable —**filthy lucre** *inf.* money

lu'dicrous [lōō'-] *a.* absurd, laughable, ridiculous

lu'do [lōō'-] *n.* **UK** game played with dice and counters on board

luff *n.* the part of fore-and-aft sail nearest mast —*v.* sail (ship) into wind so that sails flap; (of sails) flap

lug[1] *vt.* drag with effort —*vi.* pull hard (**-gg-**)

lug[2] *n.* projection, tag serving as handle or support; *Scot. inf.* ear

lugg'age *n.* traveller's trunks and other baggage

lugg'er *n.* working boat (*eg* fishing, prawning lugger) orig. fitted with lugsail

lug'sail *n.* oblong sail fixed on yard which hangs slanting on mast

lugu'brious [lōō-gōō'-] *a.* mournful, doleful, gloomy —**lugu'briously** *adv.*

lug'worm *n.* large worm used as bait, lobworm

luke'warm [lōōk'-] *a.* moderately warm, tepid; indifferent

lull *vt.* soothe, sing to sleep; make quiet —*vi.* become quiet, subside —*n.* brief time of quiet in storm *etc.* —**lull'aby** [-bī] *n.* lulling song, *esp.* for children

lum'bar *a.* relating to body between lower ribs and hips —**lumba'go** *n.* rheumatism in the lower part of the back

lum'ber *n.* sawn timber —*vi.* move heavily —*vt. inf.* burden with something unpleasant —**lum'bering** *n.* business of cutting and transporting timber —**lum'berjack** *n.* man who fells trees and prepares logs for transport to mill —**lum'beryard** *n.* establishment where lumber is stored and sold

lu'men *n.* SI unit of luminous flux (*pl.* **-mens, -mina**)

lu'minous [lōō'-] *a.* bright; shedding light; glowing; lucid —**lu'minary** *n.* learned person; heavenly body giving light —**lumines'cence** *n.* emission of light at low temperatures by process (*eg* chemical) not involving burning —**luminos'ity** *n.*

lump *n.* shapeless piece or mass; swelling; large sum —*vt.* throw together in one mass or sum —*vi.* move heavily —**lump'ish** *a.* clumsy; stupid —**lump'y** *a.* full of lumps; uneven —**lump it** *inf.* put up with

lu'nar [lōō'-] *a.* relating to the moon

lu'natic [lōō'-] *a.* insane —*n.* insane person —**lu'nacy** *n.* —**lunatic fringe** extreme, radical section of group *etc.*

lunch *n.* meal taken in the middle of the day —*v.* eat, entertain to lunch —**lunch'eon** [-shən] *n.* a lunch —**luncheonette'** *n.* café where light meals or snacks are served —**lunch'room** *n.* room where employees *etc.* may eat lunch

lung *n.* one of the two organs of respiration in vertebrates —**lung'fish** *n.* type of fish with air-breathing lung —**lung'worm** *n.* parasitic worm infesting lungs of some animals —**lung'wort** *n.* flowering plant

lunge *vi.* thrust with sword *etc.* —*n.* such thrust; sudden movement of body, plunge

lu'pin [lōō'-] *n.* leguminous plant with tall spikes of flowers

lu'pine [lōō'-] *a.* like a wolf

lu'pus [lōō'-] *n.* skin disease

lurch *n.* sudden roll to one side —*vi.* stagger —**leave in the lurch** leave in difficulties

lurch'er *n.* crossbred dog trained to hunt silently

lure [lyōōr] *n.* something which entices; bait; power to attract —*vt.* entice; attract

lu'rid *a.* vivid in shocking detail, sensational; pale, wan; lit with unnatural glare —**lu'ridly** *adv.*

lurk *vi.* lie hidden —**lurk'ing** *a.* (of suspicion) not definite

lus'cious [-shəs] *a.* sweet, juicy; extremely pleasurable or attractive

lush[1] *a.* (of grass *etc.*) luxuriant and juicy, fresh

lush[2] *n. sl.* heavy drinker; alcoholic —**lush'y** *a.*

lust *n.* strong desire for sexual gratification; any strong desire —*vi.* have passionate desire —**lust'ful** *a.* —**lust'ily** *adv.* —**lust'y** *a.* vigorous, healthy

lustra'tion *n.* purification by sacrifice —**lus'tral** *a.* used in lustration —**lus'trate** *vt.*

lus'tre *n.* gloss, sheen; splendour; renown; glory; glossy material; metallic pottery glaze —**lus'trous** *a.* shining, luminous

lute[1] [lōōt] *n.* old stringed musical instrument played with the fingers —**lu'tenist, lu'tist** *n.*

lute[2] [lōōt] *n.* composition to make joints airtight (*also* **lu'ting**) —*vt.* close with lute

lux *n.* SI unit of illumination (*pl.* **lux**)

lux'ury *n.* possession and use of costly, choice things for enjoyment; enjoyable but not necessary thing; comfortable surroundings —**luxu'riance** *n.* abundance, proliferation —**luxu'riant** *a.* growing thickly; abundant —**luxu'riantly** *adv.* —**luxu'riate** *vi.* indulge in luxury; flourish profusely; take delight (in) —**luxu'rious** *a.* fond of luxury; self-indulgent; sumptuous —**luxu'riously** *adv.*

lyce'um [lī-sē'-] *n.* public building for concerts *etc.*

lych'gate *see* LICHGATE

lydd'ite *n.* powerful explosive used in shells

lye *n.* water made alkaline with wood ashes *etc.* for washing

ly'ing *pr.p. of* LIE[1], LIE[2]

lymph *n.* colourless bodily fluid, mainly of white blood cells —**lymphat'ic** *a.* of lymph; flabby, sluggish —*n.* vessel in the body conveying lymph

lynch *vt.* put to death without trial —**lynch law** procedure of self-appointed court trying and executing accused

lynx *n.* animal of cat family

lyre [līr] *n* instrument like harp —**lyr'ic(al)** [lir'-] *a.* of short personal poems expressing emotion; of lyre; meant to be sung —**lyr'ic** *n.* lyric poem —*pl.* words of popular song —**lyr'icist** *n.* —**lyr'ist** *n.* [lir'-] lyric poet; [lī'-] player on lyre —**lyre'bird** *n.* Aust. bird, the male of which displays tail shaped like a lyre —**wax lyrical** express great enthusiasm

M

M Medieval; Monsieur; **UK** Motorway

m metre(s)

m. male; married; masculine; mile; minute

MA Master of Arts

macab're [-kahb'ər] *a.* gruesome, ghastly

macad'am *n.* road surface made of pressed layers of small broken stones —**macad'amize** *vt.* pave road with this

macaro'ni *n.* pasta in long, thin tubes (*pl.* **-ni(e)s**)

macaroon' *n.* small cake, biscuit containing almonds

macaw' *n.* kind of parrot

mace[1] *n.* staff with metal head; staff of office

mace[2] *n.* spice made of the husk of the nutmeg

mac'erate [mas'-] *vt.* soften by soaking; cause to waste away —**macera'tion** *n.*

Mach (number) [mah, mak] *n.* the ratio of the air speed of an aircraft to the velocity of sound under given conditions

machet'e [mə-shet'i] *n.* broad, heavy knife used for cutting or as a weapon

Machiavell'ian [mak-] *a.* politically unprincipled, crafty, perfidious, subtle, deep-laid

machina'tion [-kin-] *n.* (*usu. pl.*) plotting, intrigue —**mach'inate** *vi.* lay, devise plots; conspire

machine' [-shēn'] *n.* apparatus combining action of several parts to apply mechanical force; controlling organization; mechanical appliance; vehicle —*vt.* sew, print, shape *etc.* with machine —**machin'ery** *n.* parts of machine collectively; machines —**machin'ist** *n.* one who makes or works machines —**machine gun** gun firing repeatedly and continuously with an automatic loading and firing mechanism

machis'mo [-kiz'-] *n.* strong or exaggerated masculine pride or masculinity —**mach'o** [-ch'-] *a.* denoting or exhibiting such pride in masculinity —*n.* (*pl.* **-os**)

mack'erel *n.* edible sea fish with blue and silver stripes

Mack'inaw (coat) *n.* thick, short plaid coat

mack'intosh *n.* waterproof raincoat of rubberized cloth; any raincoat

macram'é [-krahm'i] *n.* ornamental work of knotted cord

macrobiot'ics *pl.n.* (*with sing. v.*) dietary system advocating grain and vegetables grown without chemical additives

mac'rocosm *n.* the universe; any large, complete system

mad *a.* suffering from mental disease, insane; wildly foolish; very enthusiastic (about); excited; *inf.* furious, angry —**mad'den** *vt.* make mad —**mad'ly** *adv.* —**mad'man** *n.* —**mad'ness** *n.* insanity; folly

mad'am *n.* polite form of address to a woman ; *inf.* precocious or conceited girl

mad'cap *n.* reckless person —*a.*

madd'er *n.* climbing plant; its root; red dye made from this

made *pt./pp. of* MAKE

Madeir'a [-dēr'ə] *n.* rich sherry wine

Madonn'a *n.* the Virgin Mary; picture or statue of her

madrepore' *n.* kind of coral

mad'rigal *n.* unaccompanied part song; short love poem or song

mael'strom [māl'-] *n.* great whirlpool; turmoil

mae'nad [mē'-] *n.* *Class. Literature* frenzied female worshipper of Dionysus

maesto'so [mī-stō'zō] *adv. Mus.* grandly, in majestic manner

mae'stro [mī'-] *n.* outstanding musician, conductor; man regarded as master of any art

Mae West [mā] *sl.* inflatable life jacket

Maf'ia *n.* international secret criminal organization, *orig.* Italian

magazine' [-zēn'] *n.* periodical publication with stories and articles by different writers; appliance for supplying cartridges automatically to gun; storehouse for explosives or arms

magent'a [-j-] *a./n.* (of) deep purplish-red colour

magg'ot *n.* grub, larva —**magg'oty** *a.* infested with maggots

Ma'gi [mā'jī] *pl.n.* priests of ancient Persia; the wise men from the East at the Nativity

mag'ic [-j'-] *n.* art of supposedly invoking supernatural powers to influence events *etc.*; any mysterious agency or power; witchcraft, conjuring —*a.* —**mag'ical** *a.* —**mag'ically** *adv.* —**magi'cian** *n.* one skilled in magic, wizard, conjurer, enchanter —**magic lantern** early form of projector using slides

mag'istrate [maj'-] *n.* civil officer administering law; justice of the peace —**magiste'rial** *a.* of, referring to magistrate; dictatorial —**mag'istracy** *n.* office of magistrate; magistrates collectively

mag'ma *n.* paste, suspension; molten rock inside earth's crust

magnan'imous *a.* noble, generous, not petty —**magnanim'ity** *n.*

mag'nate *n.* influential or wealthy person

magne'sium *n.* metallic element —**magne'sia** *n.* white powder compound of this used in medicine

mag'net *n.* piece of iron, steel having properties of attracting iron, steel and pointing north and south when suspended; lodestone —**magnet'ic** *a.* with properties of magnet; exerting powerful attraction —**magnet'ically** *adv.* —**mag'netism** *n.* magnetic phenomena; science of this; personal charm or power of attracting others —**magnetiza'tion** *n.* —**mag'netize** *vt.* make into a magnet; attract as if by magnet; fascinate —**magne'to** *n.* apparatus for ignition in internal-combustion engine (*pl.* **-tos**) —**magnetom'eter** *n.* instrument used to measure magnetic force —**magnetic tape** long coated plastic strip for recording sound or video signals

Magnif'icat *n.* hymn of Virgin Mary in *Luke* 1. 46-55, used as canticle

magnif'icent *a.* splendid; stately, imposing; excellent —**magnif'icence** *n.* —**magnif'icently** *adv.*

mag'nify [-fī] *vt.* increase apparent size of, as with lens; exaggerate; make greater (**-fied, -fying**) —**magnifica'tion** *n.*

magnil'oquent *a.* speaking pompously; grandiose —**magnil'oquence** *n.*

mag'nitude *n.* importance; greatness, size

magno'lia *n.* shrub or tree with large white, sweet-scented flowers

mag'num *n.* large wine bottle (approx. 52 fluid ounces)

mag'pie *n.* black-and-white bird

Mag'yar *n.* member of prevailing race in Hungary; native speech of Hungary —*a.* pert. to Magyars; *Dressmaking* cut with sleeves and bodice of garment in one piece

mahara'jah [mah-hə-rah'-] *n.* former title of some Indian princes (**mahara'nee** *fem.*)

mahari'shi [mah-hah-rē'-] *n.* Hindu religious teacher or mystic

mahat'ma *n.* *Hinduism* man of saintly life with supernatural powers; one endowed with great wisdom and power

mahjong(g)' *n.* Chinese table game for four, played with pieces called tiles

mahl'stick *n.* *see* MAULSTICK

mahog'any *n.* tree yielding reddish-brown wood

maid'en *n.* *Literary* young unmarried woman —*a.* unmarried; of, suited to maiden; first; having blank record —**maid** *n.* *Literary* young unmarried woman; woman servant —**maid'enly** *a.* modest —**maid'enhair** *n.* fern with delicate stalks and fronds —**maid'enhead** *n.* virginity —**maid'enhood** *n.* —**maiden name** woman's surname before marriage —**maid of honour** principal unmarried attendant of bride

mail[1] *n.* letters *etc.* transported and delivered by the post office; letters *etc.* conveyed at one time; the postal system; train, ship *etc.* carrying mail —*vt.* send by post —**mail'er** *n.* person who mails letters; machine used for stamping and addressing mail; container for mailing —**mail'box** *n.* public box into which letters are put for collection and delivery; private box outside house where occupant's mail is delivered —**mail drop** receptacle or chute for mail

—**mail'man** *n.* person who collects or delivers mail —**mail order** referring to goods ordered through post

mail[2] *n.* armour of interlaced rings or overlapping plates —**mailed** *a.* covered with mail

maim *vt.* cripple, mutilate

main *a.* chief, principal, leading —*n.* principal pipe, line carrying water, electricity *etc.*; chief part; strength, power; *obs.* open sea —**main'ly** *adv.* for the most part, chiefly —**main force** physical strength —**main'frame** *Computers* *a.* denoting a high-speed general-purpose computer —*n.* such a computer; the central processing unit of a computer —**main'land** *n.* stretch of land which forms main part of a country —**main'mast** *n.* chief mast in ship —**main'sail** *n.* lowest sail of mainmast —**main'spring** *n.* chief spring of watch or clock; chief cause or motive —**main'stay** *n.* rope from mainmast; chief support —**main'streeting** *n.* (of politician) walking streets to gain votes and greet supporters

maintain' *vt.* carry on; preserve; support; sustain; keep up; keep supplied; affirm; support by argument; defend —**maintain'able** *a.* —**main'tenance** *n.* maintaining; means of support; upkeep of buildings *etc.*; provision of money for separated or divorced spouse

maisonette' [mā-zən-et'] *n.* apartment usu. on two floors fitted as self-contained dwelling

maître d'hôtel' [met-rə dō-tel'] *Fr.* restaurant manager

maize *n.* corn, Indian corn

maj'esty *n.* stateliness; sovereignty; grandeur —**majes'tic** *a.* splendid; regal —**majes'tically** *adv.*

ma'jor *n.* army officer ranking next above captain; scale in music; principal field of study at university *etc.* (*also vi.*); person of legal majority —*a.* greater in number, quality, extent ; significant, serious —**major'ity** *n.* greater number; larger party voting together; excess of the vote on one side; coming of age; rank of major —**major-do'mo** *n.* house-steward (*pl.* **-s**) —**major league** league of highest classification in baseball, football or hockey —**the majors** major leagues

make *vt.* construct; produce; create; establish; appoint; amount to; cause to do something; accomplish; reach; earn —*vi.* tend; contribute (**made, ma'king**) —*n.* brand, type, or style —**ma'king** *n.* creation —*pl.* necessary requirements or qualities —**make'shift** *n.* temporary expedient —**make-up** *n.* cosmetics; characteristics; layout —**make'weight** *n.* trifle added to make something stronger or better —**make up** compose; compile; complete; compensate; apply cosmetics; invent —**on the make** *inf.* intent on gain

mak'o [mahk'ō] *n.* type of shark (*pl.* **-s**)

mal-, male- (*comb. form*) ill, badly, as in **malforma'tion** *n.*, —**malfunc'tion** *n./vi.*

malacc'a *n.* brown cane used for walking-stick

mal'achite [-kīt] *n.* green mineral

maladjust'ed *a.* *Psychol.* unable to meet the demands of society; badly adjusted —**maladjust'ment** *n.*

maladministra'tion *n.* inefficient or dishonest administration

maladroit' *a.* clumsy, awkward

mal'ady *n.* disease

malaise' [-āz'] *n.* vague, unlocated feeling of bodily discomfort

mal'apropism *n.* ludicrous misuse of word

malapropos' [-pō'] *a./adv.* inappropriate(ly)

mala'ria *n.* infectious disease caused by bite of some mosquitoes —**mala'rial** *a.*

Malay' *n.* native of Malaysia or Indonesia; language of this people —**Malay'an** *a./n.*

mal'content *a.* actively discontented —*n.* malcontent person

male *a.* of sex producing gametes which fertilize female gametes; of men or male animals —*n.* male person or animal

maledic'tion *n.* curse

mal'efactor *n.* criminal

malef'icent *a.* harmful, hurtful —**malef'icence** *n.*

malev'olent *a.* full of ill will —**malev'olence** *n.*

malfea'sance [-fē'z-] *n.* illegal action; official misconduct —**malfea'sant** *a./n.*

mal'ice *n.* ill will; spite —**malic'ious** *a.* intending evil or unkindness; spiteful; moved by hatred —**malic'iously** *adv.*

malign' [-līn'] *a.* evil in influence or

effect —*vt.* slander, misrepresent —**malig'nancy** *n.* —**malig'nant** *a.* feeling extreme ill will; (of disease) resistant to therapy —**malig'nantly** *adv.* —**malig'nity** *n.* malignant disposition

maling'er [-ng'g-] *vi.* feign illness to escape duty —**maling'erer** *n.*

mall [mawl, mal] *n.* level, shaded walk; street, shopping area closed to vehicles

mall'ard *n.* wild duck

mall'eable *a.* capable of being hammered into shape; adaptable —**malleabil'ity** *n.*

mall'et *n.* (wooden) hammer; croquet or polo stick

mall'ow *n.* wild plant with purple flowers

malm'sey [mahm'zi] *n.* strong sweet wine

malnutri'tion [-trish'-] *n.* inadequate nutrition

malo'dorous *a.* evil-smelling

malprac'tice *n.* immoral, illegal or unethical conduct

malt [mawlt] *n.* grain used for brewing —*vt.* make into malt —**malt'ster** *n.* maker of malt

maltreat' *vt.* treat badly, handle roughly —**maltreat'ment** *n.*

mam'ba *n.* deadly S Afr. snake

mam'bo *n.* Latin Amer. dance like rumba

mamm'al *n.* animal of type that suckles its young —**mamma'lian** *a.*

mamm'ary *a.* of, relating to breast or milk-producing gland

mamm'on *n.* wealth regarded as source of evil; (**M-**) false god of covetousness —**mamm'onism** *n.* —**mam'monist** *n.*

mamm'oth *n.* extinct animal like an elephant —*a.* colossal

man *n.* human being; person; human race; adult male; manservant; piece used in chess *etc.* (*pl.* **men**) —*vt.* supply (ship *etc.*) with necessary men; fortify (**-nn-**) —**man'ful** *a.* brave, vigorous —**man'fully** *adv.* —**man'like** *a.* —**man'liness** *n.* —**man'ly** *a.* —**mann'ish** *a.* like a man —**man'handle** *vt.* treat roughly —**man'hole** *n.* opening through which man may pass to a drain, sewer *etc.* —**man'hood** *n.* —**mankind'** *n.* human beings in general —**man(n)'ikin** *n.* little man; model of human body; lay figure —**man'power** *n.* power of human effort; available number of workers —**man'slaughter** *n.* culpable homicide without malice aforethought

Man. Manitoba

man'acle *n.* fetter, handcuff —*vt.* shackle

man'age *vt.* be in charge of, administer; succeed in doing; control; handle, cope with; conduct, carry on; persuade —**man'ageable** *a.* —**man'agement** *n.* those who manage, as board of directors *etc.*; administration; skilful use of means; conduct —**man'ager** *n.* (**manageress'** *fem.*) one in charge of business, institution, actor *etc.*; one who manages efficiently —**manage'rial** *a.* —**man'aging** *a.* having administrative control

manatee' *n.* large, plant-eating aquatic mammal

man'ciple *n.* steward who buys provisions for college *etc.*

manda'mus *n.* writ from superior court to inferior, conveying order

man'darin *n.* *Hist.* Chinese high-ranking bureaucrat; *fig.* any high government official; Chinese variety of orange

man'date *n.* command of, or commission to act for, another; commission from United Nations to govern a territory; instruction from electorate to representative or government —**man'dated** *a.* committed to a mandate —**man'datory, -tary** *n.* holder of a mandate —**man'datory** *a.* compulsory

man'dible *n.* lower jawbone; either part of bird's beak —**mandib'ular** *a.* of, like mandible

man'dolin(e) *n.* stringed musical instrument

man'drake, mandrag'ora *n.* narcotic plant

man'drel *n.* axis on which material is supported in a lathe; rod round which metal is cast or forged

man'drill *n.* large blue-faced baboon

mane *n.* long hair on neck of horse, lion *etc.* —**maned** *a.*

man'ganese [-ng'g-] *n.* metallic element; black oxide of this

mange [mānj] *n.* skin disease of dogs *etc.* —**ma'ngy** *a.* scruffy, shabby

man'gelwurzel [mang'gəl-] *n.* variety of beet used as cattle food: also **man'goldwurzel**

man'ger [mān'jər] *n.* eating trough in stable
man'gle[1] [mang'gəl] *n.* machine for rolling clothes *etc.* to remove water *—vt.* press in mangle
man'gle[2] [mang'gəl] *vt.* mutilate, spoil, hack
man'go [-ng'gō] *n.* tropical fruit; tree bearing it (*pl.* **-go(e)s**)
man'grove *n.* tropical tree which grows on muddy banks of estuaries
ma'nia *n.* madness; prevailing craze **—ma'niac, mani'acal, man'ic** *a.* affected by mania **—ma'niac** *inf. n.* mad person; crazy enthusiast
man'icure *n.* treatment and care of fingernails and hands *—vt.* apply such treatment **—man'icurist** *n.* one doing this professionally
man'ifest *a.* clearly revealed, visible, undoubted *—vt.* make manifest *—n.* list of cargo for customs **—manifesta'tion** *n.* **—man'ifestly** *adv.* clearly **—manifes'to** *n.* declaration of policy by political party, government, or movement (*pl.* **-to(e)s**)
man'ifold *a.* numerous and varied *—n.* in internal combustion engine, pipe with several outlets *—vt.* make copies of (document)
man(n)'ikin *see* MAN
manil(l)'a *n.* fibre used for ropes; tough paper
manip'ulate *vt.* handle; deal with skilfully; manage; falsify **—manipula'tion** *n.* act of manipulating, working by hand; skilled use of hands **—manip'ulative** *a.* **—manip'ulator** *n.*
man'ito(u) *n.* spirit of good or evil among Amer. Indians
mann'a *n.* food of Israelites in the wilderness; nourishment
mann'equin [-i-kin] *n.* woman who models clothes, *esp.* at fashion shows
mann'er *n.* way thing happens or is done; sort, kind; custom; style *—pl.* social behaviour **—mann'erism** *n.* person's distinctive habit, trait **—mann'erly** *a.* polite
manoeu'vre [-ōō'vər] *n.* contrived, complicated, perhaps deceptive plan or action; skilful management *—v.* employ stratagems, work adroitly; (cause to) perform manoeuvres
manom'eter *n.* gauge of gas pressure
man'or *n. Hist.* land belonging to a lord; feudal unit of land **—manor'ial** *a.* **—manor house** residence of lord of manor
man'sard roof roof with break in its slope, lower part being steeper than upper
manse *n.* house of minister in some religious denominations
man'sion *n.* large house
man'tel *n.* structure round fireplace **—mantel shelf, man'telpiece** *n.* shelf at top of mantel
mantill'a *n.* in Spain, (lace) scarf worn as headdress
man'tis *n.* genus of insects including the stick-insects and leaf insects (*pl.* **man'-tes** [-tēz])
man'tle *n.* loose cloak; covering; incandescent gauze round gas jet *—vt.* cover; conceal
man'ual *a.* of, or done with, the hands; by human labour, not automatic *—n.* handbook; textbook; organ keyboard
manufac'ture *vt.* process, make (materials) into finished articles; produce (articles); invent, concoct *—n.* making of articles, materials, *esp.* in large quantities; anything produced from raw materials **—manufac'turer** *n.* owner of factory
manumit' *vt.* free from slavery (**-tt-**) **—manumiss'ion** *n.*
manure' *vt.* enrich land *—n.* dung or chemical fertilizer used to enrich land
man'uscript *n.* book, document, written by hand; copy for printing *—a.* handwritten
Manx *a.* of Isle of Man *—n.* Manx language **—Manx'man** *n.* **—Manx cat** tailless breed of cat
man'y [men'i] *a.* numerous (**more** *comp.*, **most** *sup.*) *—n.* large number
Mao'ism [mow'-] *n.* form of Marxism advanced by Mao Tse-Tung in China **—Mao'ist** *n./a.*
Mao'ri [mow'ri] *n.* New Zealand native race; their language
map *n.* flat representation of the earth or some part of it, or of the heavens *—vt.* make a map of; (*with* out) plan (**-pp-**)
ma'ple *n.* tree of the sycamore family, a variety of which yields sugar **—maple leaf** leaf of maple, *esp.* as Canadian emblem **—maple sugar** sugar made

from sap of sugar maple —**maple syrup** very sweet syrup made from sap of sugar maple

ma'quis [ma'kē] *n.* scrubby undergrowth of Mediterranean countries; name adopted by French underground resistance movement in WWII

mar *vt.* spoil, impair (**-rr-**)

Mar. March

mar'abou [ma-] *n.* kind of stork; its soft white lower tail feathers, used to trim hats *etc.*; kind of silk

marac'a [-ak'-] *n.* percussion instrument of gourd containing dried seeds *etc.*

maraschi'no [mar-ə-skē'-] *n.* liqueur made from cherries

mar'athon [ma-] *n.* long-distance race; endurance contest

maraud' *v.* make raid for plunder; pillage —**maraud'er** *n.*

mar'ble *n.* kind of limestone capable of taking polish; slab of, sculpture in this; small ball used in children's game —**mar'bled** *a.* having mottled appearance, like marble —**mar'bly** *a.*

March *n.* third month

march[1] *vi.* walk with military step; go, progress —*vt.* cause to march —*n.* action of marching; distance marched in day; tune to accompany marching

march[2] *n.* border or frontier —*vi.* border

mar'chioness [-shən-] *n.* wife, widow of marquis

Mar'di Gras' [-grah'] *n.* festival of Shrove Tuesday; revelry celebrating this

mare *n.* female horse —**mare's nest** supposed discovery which proves worthless

mar'garine [-j-, -g-] *n.* butter substitute made from vegetable fats (*inf.* **marge** [-j])

mar'gin [-j-] *n.* border, edge; space round printed page; amount allowed beyond what is necessary —**mar'ginal** *a.*

marguerite' [-ēt'] *n.* large daisy

mar'igold [ma-] *n.* plant with yellow flowers

marijua'na, marihua'na [mar-i-hwah'nə] *n.* dried flowers and leaves of hemp plant, used as narcotic

mari'na [-rē'-] *n.* mooring facility for yachts and pleasure boats

marinade' *n.* seasoned, flavoured liquid used to soak fish, meat *etc.* before cooking —**mar'inate** *vt.*

marine' [-ēn'] *a.* of the sea or shipping; used at, found in sea —*n.* shipping, fleet; soldier trained for land or sea combat —**mar'iner** *n.* sailor

marionette' [ma-] *n.* puppet worked with strings

mar'ital [ma'-] *a.* relating to a husband or to marriage

mar'itime [ma'-] *a.* connected with seafaring; naval; bordering on the sea

mar'joram *n.* aromatic herb

mark[1] *n.* line, dot, scar *etc.*; sign, token; inscription; letter, number showing evaluation of schoolwork *etc.*; indication; target —*vt.* make a mark on; be distinguishing mark of; indicate; notice; watch; assess, *eg* examination paper; stay close to sporting opponent to hamper his play —*vi.* take notice —**mark'er** *n.* one who, that which keeps score at games; counter used at card playing *etc.* —**marks'man** *n.* skilled shot

mark[2] *n.* German coin

mark'et *n.* assembly, place for buying and selling; demand for goods; centre for trade —*vt.* offer or produce for sale —**mark'etable** *a.*

marl *n.* clayey soil used as fertilizer —*vt.* fertilize with it

mar'line [-in] *n.* two-strand cord —**mar'linespike** *n.* pointed hook *esp.* for unravelling rope to be spliced

mar'malade *n.* preserve usually made of oranges, lemons *etc.*

marmor'eal *a.* of or like marble

mar'moset *n.* small bushy-tailed monkey

mar'mot *n.* burrowing rodent

maroon'[1] *n.* brownish-crimson; firework —*a.* of the colour

maroon'[2] *vt.* leave (person) on deserted island or coast; isolate, cut off by any means

marquee' [-kē'] *n.* large tent; canopy over entrance to theatre, hotel *etc.*

mar'quetry [-kit-] *n.* inlaid work, wood mosaic

mar'quis, -quess *n.* nobleman of rank below duke —**mar'quisate** *n.*

marr'ow [-rō] *n.* fatty substance inside bones; vital part; vegetable marrow —**mar'rowy** *a.* —**marr'owfat** *n.* large pea

marr'y *v.* join as husband and wife; unite closely (**marr'ied, marr'ying**) —**marr'iage** [-ij] *n.* state of being married; wedding —**marr'iageable** *a.*

Mars *n.* Roman god of war; planet nearest but one to earth —**Mar'tian** *n.* supposed inhabitant of Mars —*a.* of Mars

Marsal'a [-sahl'-] *n.* a sweet wine

Marseillaise' [mah-sā-yāz'] *n.* the French national anthem

marsh *n.* low-lying wet land —**marsh'y** *a.* —**marshmall'ow** *n.* spongy sweet orig. made from root of **marsh mallow**, shrubby plant growing near marshes

mar'shal *n.* high officer of state; **US** law enforcement officer —*vt.* arrange in due order; conduct with ceremony —**field marshal** (in certain countries) military officer of the highest rank

marsu'pial *n.* animal that carries its young in pouch, *eg* kangaroo —*a.*

mart *n.* place of trade; market

martell'o tow'er round fort, for coast defence

mar'ten *n.* weasellike animal; its fur

mar'tial [-shəl] *a.* relating to war; warlike, brave —**court martial** *see* COURT —**martial law** law enforced by military authorities in times of danger or emergency

mar'tin *n.* species of swallow

martinet' *n.* strict disciplinarian —**martinet'ish** *a.*

mar'tingale [-ng-g-] *n.* strap to prevent horse from throwing up its head

marti'ni [-tē'-] *n.* cocktail containing *esp.* vermouth, gin, bitters; (**M-**) **R** Italian vermouth

Mar'tinmas *n.* feast of St. Martin, 11th November

mart'let *n.* *Heraldry* bird without feet

mar'tyr [-tər] *n.* one put to death for his beliefs; one who suffers in some cause; one in constant suffering —*vt.* make martyr of —**mar'tyrdom** *n.* —**martyrol'ogy** *n.* list, history of Christian martyrs

mar'vel *vi.* wonder (**-ll-**) —*n.* wonderful thing —**mar'vellous** *a.* amazing; wonderful

Marx'ism [marks'izm] *n.* state socialism as conceived by Karl Marx —**Marx'ian** *a.* —**Marx'ist** *n./a.*

mar'zipan *n.* paste of almonds, sugar *etc.* used in sweets, cakes *etc.*

masc. masculine

mascar'a *n.* cosmetic for darkening eyelashes

mas'cot *n.* thing supposed to bring luck

mas'culine [-lin] *a.* relating to males; manly; of the grammatical gender to which names of males belong

mash *n.* meal mixed with warm water; warm food for horses *etc.*; **UK** *inf.* mashed potatoes —*vt.* make into a mash; crush into soft mass or pulp

mash'ie *n.* *Golf* iron club with deep sloping blade for lob shots

mask [-ah-] *n.* covering for face; *Surgery* covering for nose and mouth; disguise, pretence —*vt.* cover with mask; hide, disguise

mas'ochism [-kizm] *n.* abnormal condition where pleasure (*esp.* sexual) is derived from pain, humiliation *etc.* —**mas'ochist** *n.* —**masochis'tic** *a.*

ma'son *n.* worker in stone; (**M-**) Freemason —**Mason'ic** *a.* of Freemasonry —**ma'sonry** *n.* stonework; (**M-**) Freemasonry

masque [mahsk] *n.* *Hist.* form of theatrical performance —**masquerade'** *n.* masked ball —*vi.* appear in disguise

Mass *n.* service of the Eucharist, *esp.* in R.C. Church

mass *n.* quantity of matter; dense collection of this; large quantity or number —*v.* form into a mass —**mass'ive** *a.* large and heavy —**mass'y** *a.* solid, weighty —**mass-produce** *vt.* produce standardized articles in large quantities —**mass production** —**the masses** the populace

mass'acre [-kər] *n.* indiscriminate, large-scale killing, *esp.* of unresisting people —*vt.* kill indiscriminately

mass'age [-ahzh] *n.* rubbing and kneading of muscles *etc.* as curative treatment —*vt.* apply this treatment to —**masseur'** *n.* one who practises massage (**masseuse'** *fem.*)

massasau'ga [-saw'-] *n.* N Amer. rattlesnake

massé' [-sā'] *n.* *Billiards* stroke with cue upright

mas'sif [-sēf] *n.* compact group of mountains

mast[1] [-ah-] *n.* pole for supporting ship's sails; tall upright support for aerial *etc.*

mast[2] [-ah-] *n.* fruit of beech, oak *etc.* used as pig fodder

mastec'tomy *n.* surgical removal of a breast

mas'ter [mah'-] *n.* one in control; employer; head of household; owner; document *etc.* from which copies are made; captain of merchant ship; expert; great artist; teacher —*vt.* overcome; acquire knowledge of or skill in —**mas'terful** *a.* imperious, domineering —**mas'terly** *a.* showing great competence —**mas'tery** *n.* full understanding (of); expertise; authority; victory —**master key** one that opens many different locks —**mas'termind** *vt.* plan, direct —*n.* —**mas'terpiece** *n.* outstanding work

mas'tic *n.* gum got from certain trees; puttylike substance

mas'ticate *vt.* chew —**mastica'tion** *n.* —**mas'ticatory** *a.*

mas'tiff *n.* large dog

mas'toid *a.* nipple-shaped —*n.* prominence on bone behind human ear —**mastoidi'tis** *n.* inflammation of this area

mas'turbate *v.* stimulate (one's own) genital organs —**masturba'tion** *n.*

mat[1] *n.* small rug; piece of fabric to protect another surface or to wipe feet on *etc.*; thick tangled mass —*v.* form into such mass (**-tt-**)

mat[2] *a.* dull, lustreless, not shiny

mat'ador *n.* man who slays bull in bullfights

match[1] *n.* contest, game; equal; person, thing exactly corresponding to another; marriage; person regarded as eligible for marriage —*vt.* get something corresponding to (colour, pattern *etc.*); oppose, put in competition (with); join (in marriage) —*vi.* correspond —**match'less** *a.* unequalled —**match'board** *n.* boards fitted into each other by tongue and groove —**match'maker** *n.* one who schemes to bring about a marriage

match[2] *n.* small stick with head which ignites when rubbed; fuse —**match'box** *n.* —**match'lock** *n.* early musket fired by fuse —**match'wood** *n.* small splinters

mate[1] *n.* comrade; husband, wife; one of pair; officer in merchant ship; *inf.* common Brit. and Aust. term of address, *esp.* between males —*v.* marry; pair

mate[2] *n./vt. Chess* checkmate

mate'rial *n.* substance from which thing is made; cloth, fabric —*a.* of matter or body; affecting physical wellbeing; unspiritual; important, essential —**mate'rialism** *n.* excessive interest in, desire for money and possessions; doctrine that nothing but matter exists, denying independent existence of spirit —**mate'rialist** *a./n.* —**materialis'tic** *a.* —**mate'rialize** *vi.* come into existence or view —*vt.* make material —**mate'rially** *adv.* appreciably

mater'nal *a.* of, related through mother —**matern'ity** *n.* motherhood

math *n. inf.* mathematics

mathemat'ics *pl.n.* (*with sing. v.*) science of number, quantity, shape and space —**mathemat'ical** *a.* —**mathemat'ically** *adv.* —**mathemati'cian** [-tish'-] *n.*

mat'inée [-nā] *n.* afternoon performance in theatre

mat'ins *pl.n.* morning prayers

ma'triarch [-k] *n.* mother as head and ruler of family —**ma'triarchal** *a.* —**ma'triarchy** *n.* society with matriarchal government and descent reckoned in female line

mat'ricide *n.* the crime of killing one's mother; one who does this

matric'ulate *v.* enrol, be enrolled in a college or university —**matricula'tion** *n.*

mat'rimony *n.* marriage —**matrimo'nial** *a.*

ma'trix *n.* substance, situation in which something originates, takes form, or is enclosed; mould for casting; *Math.* rectangular array of elements set out in rows and columns (*pl.* **ma'trices** [-sēz])

ma'tron *n.* married woman; woman who superintends domestic arrangements of public institution, boarding school *etc.* —**ma'tronly** *a.* sedate

Matt. Matthew

matt *see* MAT[2]

matt'er *n.* substance of which thing is made; physical or bodily substance; affair, business; cause of trouble; substance of book *etc.*; pus —*vi.* be of importance, signify

matt'ock *n.* tool like pick with ends of blades flattened for cutting, hoeing

matt'ress *n.* stuffed flat case, often

with springs, or foam rubber pad, used as part of bed; underlay

mature' *a.* ripe, completely developed; grown-up —*v.* bring, come to maturity —*vi.* (of bill) fall due —**matura'tion** *n.* process of maturing —**matu'rity** *n.* full development

maud'lin *a.* weakly or tearfully sentimental

maul *vt.* handle roughly; beat or bruise —*n.* heavy wooden hammer

maul'stick *n.* light stick with ball at one end, held in left hand to support right hand while painting

maund'er *vi.* talk, act aimlessly, dreamily

maun'dy *n.* foot-washing ceremony on Thursday before Easter (cf. *John* xiii, 14); royal alms given on that day

mausole'um *n.* stately building as a tomb (*pl.* **-le'ums, -le'a**)

mauve [mōv] *a./n.* (of) pale purple colour

mav'erick *n.* unbranded steer, strayed cow; independent, unorthodox person

maw *n.* stomach, crop

mawk'ish *a.* weakly sentimental, maudlin; sickly

maxill'a *n.* jawbone —**maxill'ary** *a.* of the jaw

max'im *n.* general truth, proverb; rule of conduct, principle

max'imum *n.* greatest size or number; highest point —*a.* greatest —**max'imize** *vt.*

May *n.* fifth month; (**m-**) hawthorn or its flowers —**may'fly** *n.* short-lived flying insect, found near water —**may'pole** *n.* pole set up for dancing round on **May Day**, first day of May

may *v. aux.* expresses possibility, permission, opportunity *etc.* (**might** *pt.*) —**may'be** *adv.* perhaps; possibly

May'day *n.* international radiotelephone distress signal

may'hem *n.* depriving person by violence of limb, member or organ, or causing mutilation of body; any violent destruction; confusion

mayonnaise' *n.* creamy sauce of egg yolks *etc.*, *esp.* for salads

mayor [mãr] *n.* head of municipality —**mayor'al** *a.* —**mayor'alty** *n.* (time of) office of mayor —**mayor'ess** *n.* mayor's wife; lady mayor

maze *n.* labyrinth; network of paths, lines; state of confusion

maz(o)ur'ka *n.* lively Polish dance like polka; music for it

MB Bachelor of Medicine; Medal of Bravery

MBE Member of the Order of the British Empire

MC Master of Ceremonies; Military Cross

MCP male chauvinist pig

MD Doctor of Medicine

MDT Mountain Daylight Time

me[1] *pron.* objective case singular of first personal pronoun I

me[2], **mi** *n.* third sol-fa note

me'a cul'pa [mā'ah-kul'pah] *Lat.* my fault

mead *n.* alcoholic drink made from honey

mead'ow [med'-] *n.* piece of grassland —**mead'owsweet** *n.* plant with dense heads of small fragrant flowers

mea'gre [mē'gər] *a.* lean, thin, scanty, insufficient

meal[1] *n.* occasion when food is served and eaten; the food

meal[2] *n.* grain ground to powder —**meal'y** *a.* —**mealy-mouthed** *a.* euphemistic, insincere in what one says

mean[1] *vt.* intend; signify —*vi.* have a meaning; have the intention of behaving (**meant** [ment] *pt./pp.*, **mean'ing** *pr.p.*) —**mean'ing** *n.* sense, significance —*a.* expressive —**mean'ingful** *a.* of great meaning or significance —**mean'ingless** *a.*

mean[2] *a.* ungenerous, petty; miserly, niggardly; unpleasant; callous; shabby; ashamed; *inf.* bad-tempered —**mean'ly** *adv.* —**mean'ness** *n.*

mean[3] *n.* thing which is intermediate; middle point —*pl.* that by which thing is done; money; resources —*a.* intermediate in time, quality *etc.*; average —**mean'time, mean'while** *adv./n.* (during) time between one happening and another —**by all means** certainly —**by no means** not at all

meand'er [mē-and'-] *vi.* flow windingly; wander aimlessly

meas'les [mēz'lz] *n.* infectious disease producing rash of red spots —**meas'ly** *a.* *inf.* poor, wretched, stingy; of measles

meas'ure [mezh'ər] *n.* size, quantity; vessel, rod, line *etc.* for ascertaining size or quantity; unit of size or quantity; course, plan of action; law; poetical rhythm; musical time; *Poet.* tune; *obs.* dance —*vt.* ascertain size, quantity of; be (so much) in size or quantity; indicate measurement of; estimate; bring into competition (against) —**meas'urable** *a.* —**meas'ured** *a.* determined by measure; steady; rhythmical; carefully considered —**meas'urement** *n.* measuring; size —*pl.* dimensions

meat *n.* animal flesh as food; food —**meat'y** *a.* (tasting) of, like meat; brawny; full of import or interest

Mecc'a *n.* holy city of Islam; place that attracts visitors

mechan'ic [-k-] *n.* one employed in working with machinery; skilled workman —*pl.* scientific theory of motion —**mechan'ical** *a.* concerned with machines or operation of them; worked, produced (as though) by machine; acting without thought —**mechan'ically** *adv.* —**mechani'cian** [-nish'-] *n.*

mech'anism [mek'-] *n.* structure of machine; piece of machinery —**mechaniza'tion** *n.* —**mech'anize** *vt.* equip with machinery; make mechanical, automatic; *Mil.* equip with armoured vehicles —**mech'anized** *a.*

med. medical; medicine; medieval; medium

med'al *n.* piece of metal with inscription *etc.* used as reward or memento —**medall'ion** *n.* large medal; various things like this in decorative work —**med'allist** *n.* winner of a medal; maker of medals

med'dle *vi.* interfere, busy oneself with unnecessarily —**med'dlesome** *a.*

me'dia *n., pl. of* MEDIUM, used *esp.* of the mass media, radio, television *etc.* —**media event** event staged for or exploited by mass media

mediae'val *see* MEDIEVAL

me'dial *a.* in the middle; pert. to a mean or average —**me'dian** *a./n.* middle (point or line)

me'diate *vi.* intervene to reconcile —*vt.* bring about by mediation —*a.* depending on mediation —**media'tion** *n.* intervention on behalf of another; act of going between —**me'diator** *n.*

med'icine [-sin] *n.* drug or remedy for treating disease; science of preventing, diagnosing, alleviating, or curing disease —**med'ical** *a.* —**med'ically** *adv.* —**medic'ament** *n.* remedy —**med'icate** *vt.* impregnate with medicinal substances —**medica'tion** *n.* —**med'icative** *a.* healing —**medic'inal** *a.* curative —**medicine ball** heavy ball for physical training —**medicine man** witch doctor

medie'val, mediae'val *a.* of Middle Ages —**medie'valism** *n.* spirit of Middle Ages; cult of medieval ideals —**medie'valist** *n.* student of the Middle Ages

medio'cre [mē-dē-ō'kər] *a.* neither bad nor good, ordinary, middling; second-rate —**medioc'rity** *n.*

med'itate *vi.* be occupied in thought; reflect deeply on spiritual matters —*vt.* think about; plan —**medita'tion** *n.* thought; absorption in thought; religious contemplation —**med'itative** *a.* thoughtful; reflective —**med'itatively** *adv.*

me'dium *a.* between two qualities, degrees *etc.*, average —*n.* middle quality, degree; intermediate substance conveying force; means, agency of communicating news *etc.* to public, as radio, newspapers *etc.*; person through whom communication can supposedly be held with spirit world; surroundings; environment (*pl.* **me'diums, me'dia**) —**medium frequency** *Radio* frequencies between 300-3000 kilohertz

med'lar *n.* tree with fruit like small apple; the fruit, eaten when decayed

med'ley *n.* miscellaneous mixture (*pl.* **-leys**)

medull'a *n.* marrow, pith, inner tissue —**medull'ary** *a.*

Medu'sa [-dyōō'zə] *n. Myth.* Gorgon whose head turned beholders into stone; (**m-**) jellyfish (*pl.* **-sae** [-zē])

meek *a.* submissive, humble —**meek'ly** *adv.* —**meek'ness** *n.*

meer'schaum [-shəm] *n.* white substance like clay; tobacco pipe bowl of this

meet[1] *vt.* come face to face with, encounter; satisfy; pay —*vi.* come face to face; converge at specified point; assemble; come into contact (**met** *pt./pp.*) —*n.* meeting, *esp.* for sports —**meet'ing** *n.* assembly; encounter

meet[2] *a. obs.* fit, suitable

meg'abit *n. Computers* one million bits; 2^{20} bits

meg'aflop *n. Computers* measure of processing speed consisting of one million floating-point operations a second

meg'alith *n.* great stone —**megalith'ic** *a.*

megaloma'nia *n.* desire for, delusions of grandeur, power *etc.* —**megaloma'niac** *a./n.*

meg'aphone *n.* cone-shaped instrument to amplify voice

meg'aton *n.* one million tons; explosive power of 1 000 000 tons of TNT

meg'ohm *n. Electricity* one million ohms

mel'ancholy [-k-] *n.* sadness, dejection, gloom —*a.* gloomy, dejected —**melancho'lia** *n.* mental disease accompanied by depression —**melanchol'ic** *a.*

melange' [-lahnzh'] *n.* mixture

mel'anin *n.* dark pigment found in hair, skin *etc.* of man

mêl'ée [mel'ā] *n.* mixed fight, or crowd

me'liorate *v.* improve —**meliora'tion** *n.* —**me'liorism** *n.* doctrine that the world may be improved by human effort —**me'liorist** *n.*

mellif'luous, -luent *a.* (of sound) smooth, sweet —**mellif'luence** *n.*

mell'ow *a.* ripe; softened by age, experience; soft, not harsh; genial, gay —*v.* make, become mellow

mel'odrama *n.* play full of sensational and startling situations, often highly emotional; overdramatic behaviour, emotion —**melodramat'ic** *a.*

mel'ody *n.* series of musical notes which make tune; sweet sound —**melo'dious** *a.* pleasing to the ear; tuneful —**mel'odist** *n.* singer; composer

mel'on *n.* large, fleshy, juicy fruit

melt *v.* (cause to) become liquid by heat; dissolve; soften; waste away; blend (into); disappear (**melt'ed** *pt./pp.*, **mol'ten** [mōl'tən] *pp.*) —**melt'ing** *a.* softening; languishing; tender —**melt'down** *n.* in nuclear reactor, melting of fuel rods, with possible release of radiation

mem'ber *n.* any of individuals making up body or society; limb; any part of complex whole —**mem'bership** *n.*

mem'brane *n.* thin flexible tissue in plant or animal body

memen'to *n.* thing serving to remind, souvenir (*pl.* **-to(e)s**)

mem'o *n. short for* MEMORANDUM

mem'oir [-wahr] *n.* autobiography, personal history, biography; record of events

mem'ory *n.* faculty of recollecting, recalling to mind; recollection; thing remembered; length of time one can remember; commemoration; part or faculty of computer which stores information —**memor'ial** *a.* of, preserving memory —*n.* thing, *esp.* a monument, which serves to keep in memory —**mem'orable** *a.* worthy of remembrance, noteworthy —**mem'orably** *adv.* —**memoran'dum** *n.* note to help the memory *etc.*; informal letter; note of contract (*pl.* **-dums, -da**) —**memor'ialist** *n.* —**memo'rialize** *vt.* commemorate —**mem'orize** *vt.* commit to memory

men *n. pl. of* MAN

men'ace *n.* threat —*vt.* threaten, endanger

ménage' [me-nahzh', mā-] *n.* persons of a household

menag'erie [-j-] *n.* exhibition, collection of wild animals

mend *vt.* repair, patch; reform, correct, put right —*vi.* improve, *esp.* in health —*n.* repaired breakage, hole —**on the mend** regaining health

menda'cious *a.* untruthful —**mendac'ity** *n.* (tendency to) untruthfulness

mend'icant *a.* begging —*n.* beggar —**men'dicancy, mendic'ity** *n.* begging

men'hir *n.* single, upright monumental stone, monolith

me'nial *a.* of work requiring little skill; of household duties or servants; servile —*n.* servant; servile person

meningi'tis [-jī'-] *n.* inflammation of the membranes of the brain

menis'cus *n.* curved surface of liquid; curved lens

men'opause *n.* final cessation of menstruation

menstrua'tion *n.* approximately monthly discharge of blood and cellular debris from womb of nonpregnant woman —**men'strual** *a.* —**men'struate** *vi.*

mensura'tion [-shə-rā'-] *n.* measuring, *esp.* of areas

ment'al *a.* of, done by the mind; *inf.* feeble-minded, mad —**mental'ity** *n.* state or quality of mind —**ment'ally** *adv.*

men'thol *n.* organic compound found in peppermint, used medicinally

men'tion *vt.* refer to briefly, speak of —*n.* acknowledgment; reference to or remark about (person or thing) —**men'tionable** *a.* fit or suitable to be mentioned

men'tor *n.* wise, trusted adviser, guide

men'u *n.* list of dishes to be served, or from which to order

mer'cantile [-k-] *a.* of, engaged in trade, commerce

Merca'tor projection method of map making with all parallels and meridians as straight lines

mer'cenary [-s-] *a.* influenced by greed; working merely for reward —*n.* hired soldier

mer'cer *n. esp.* formerly, dealer in fabrics —**mer'cery** *n.* his trade, goods

mer'cerize *vt.* give lustre to cotton fabrics by treating with chemicals —**mer'cerized** *a.*

mer'chant *n.* one engaged in trade; retail trader —**mer'chandise** *n.* his wares —**mer'chantman** *n.* trading ship

mer'cury [-kyoor-] *n.* silvery metal, liquid at ordinary temperature, quicksilver; (**M-**) Roman god of eloquence; planet nearest to sun —**mercu'rial** *a.* relating to, containing mercury; lively, changeable

mer'cy *n.* refraining from infliction of suffering by one who has right, power to inflict it, compassion —**mer'ciful** *a.* —**mer'ciless** *a.*

mere[1] [mēr] *a.* only; not more than; nothing but —**mere'ly** *adv.*

mere[2] [mēr] *n. obs.* lake

meretric'ious [-ish'-] *a.* superficially or garishly attractive; insincere

mergan'ser *n.* large, crested diving duck

merge *v.* (cause to) lose identity or be absorbed —**mer'ger** [-j-] *n.* combination of business firms into one; absorption into something greater

merid'ian *n.* circle of the earth passing through poles; imaginary circle in sky passing through celestial poles; highest point reached by star *etc.*; period of greatest splendour —*a.* of meridian; at peak of something

meringue' [mə-rang'] *n.* baked mixture of white of eggs and sugar; cake of this

meri'no [-ē'-] *n.* breed of sheep originating in Spain (*pl.* **-os**)

mer'it *n.* excellence, worth; quality of deserving reward —*pl.* excellence —*vt.* deserve —**meritor'ious** *a.* deserving praise

mer'lin *n.* small falcon

mer'maid *n.* imaginary sea creature with upper part of woman and lower part of fish

merr'y *a.* joyous, cheerful —**merr'ily** *adv.* —**merr'iment** *n.* —**merry-go-round** *n.* revolving circular platform on which people ride for amusement

mesh *n.* (one of the open spaces of, or wires *etc.* forming) network, net —*v.* entangle, become entangled; (of gears) engage —*vi.* coordinate (with)

mes'merism [-z-] *n. former term for* HYPNOTISM —**mesmer'ic** *a.* —**mes'merist** *n.* —**mes'merize** *vt.* hypnotize; fascinate, hold spellbound

me'son [-z-] *n.* elementary atomic particle

mess *n.* untidy confusion; trouble, difficulty; group in armed services who regularly eat together; place where they eat —*vi.* make mess; potter (about); *Mil.* eat in a mess —*vt.* muddle —**mess'y** *a.*

mess'age *n.* communication sent; meaning, moral; errand —**mess'enger** *n.* bearer of message

Messi'ah *n.* Jews' promised deliverer; Christ —**messian'ic** *a.*

Messrs. [mes'əz] *pl. of* Mr.

met *pt./pp. of* MEET[1], MEET[2]

meta- (*comb. form*) change, as in *metamorphose, metathesis etc.*

metab'olism *n.* chemical process of living body —**metabol'ic** *a.* —**metab'olize** *vt.*

met'al *n.* mineral substance, opaque, fusible and malleable, capable of conducting heat and electricity; broken stone for macadamized roads —**metal'lic** *a.* —**metall'urgist** *n.* —**metal'lurgy** *n.* scientific study of extracting, refining metals, and their structure and properties

metamor'phosis *n.* change of shape, character *etc.* (*pl.* **-phoses** [-ēz]) —**metamor'phic** *a.* (*esp.* of rocks) changed in texture, structure by heat, pressure *etc.* —**metamor'phose** *vt.* transform

met'aphor *n.* figure of speech in which term is transferred to something it does not literally apply to; instance of this —**metaphor'ical** [-fo'ri-] *a.* figurative —**metaphor'ically** *adv.*

metaphys'ics *pl.n.* (*with sing. v.*) branch of philosophy concerned with being and knowing —**metaphys'ical** *a.* —**metaphysi'cian** *n.*

metath'esis *n.* transposition, *esp.* of letters in word, *eg* Old English *bridd* gives modern *bird* (*pl.* **-eses** [-ēz])

mete *vt.* measure —**mete out** distribute; allot as punishment

me'teor *n.* small, fast-moving celestial body, visible as streak of incandescence if it enters earth's atmosphere —**meteor'ic** [-o'rik] *a.* of, like meteor; brilliant but short-lived —**me'teorite** *n.* fallen meteor

meteorol'ogy *n.* study of earth's atmosphere, esp. for weather forecasting —**meteorolog'ical** *a.* —**meteorol'ogist** *n.*

me'ter *n.* that which measures; instrument for recording consumption of gas, electricity *etc.*

me'thane *n.* inflammable gas, compound of carbon and hydrogen

meth'anol *n.* colourless, poisonous liquid used as solvent and fuel (*also* **methyl alcohol**)

methinks' *v. impers. obs.* it seems to me (**methought'** *pt.*)

meth'od *n.* way, manner; technique; orderliness, system —**method'ical** *a.* orderly —**meth'odize** *vt.* reduce to order —**methodol'ogy** *n.* particular method or procedure

Meth'odist *n.* member of any of the churches originated by Wesley and his followers —*a.* —**Meth'odism** *n.*

meth'yl [meth'-, mē'-] *n.* (compound containing) a saturated hydrocarbon group of atoms —**meth'ylate** *vt.* combine with methyl; mix with methanol —**methylated spirits** alcoholic mixture denatured with methanol

metic'ulous *a.* (over)particular about details

mét'ier [māt'yā] *n.* profession, vocation; one's forte

Métis' [me-tēs'] *n.* person of mixed (*esp.* French and Amer. Indian) parentage

meton'ymy *n.* figure of speech in which thing is replaced by another associated with it, *eg* 'the Crown' for 'the king' —**metonym'ical** *a.*

me'tre *n.* unit of length in decimal system; SI unit of length; rhythm of poem —**met'ric** *a.* of system of weights and measures in which metre is a unit —**met'rical** *a.* of measurement of poetic metre

Met'ro *n.* metropolitan city administration

met'ronome *n.* instrument which marks musical time by means of ticking pendulum

metrop'olis *n.* chief city of a country, region (*pl.* **-lises**) —**metropol'itan** *a.* of metropolis —*n.* bishop with authority over other bishops of a province

met'tle *n.* courage, spirit —**met'tlesome** *a.* high-spirited

mew *n.* cry of cat, gull —*vi.* utter this cry

mews *pl.n.* (*used as sing.*) **UK** yard, street orig. of stables, now oft. converted to houses

mezz'anine [met'sə-nēn, mez'ə-] *n.* intermediate storey, balcony between two main storeys, *esp.* between first and second floors; *Theatre* (front of) first balcony

mezz'o-sopra'no [met'sō-] *n.* voice, singer between soprano and contralto (*pl.* **-nos**)

mezz'otint [met'sō-] *n.* method of engraving by scraping roughened surface; print so made

Mg *Chem.* magnesium

mg milligram(s)

MHz megahertz

mi *see* ME[2]

MI Military Intelligence

mias'ma [-z-] *n.* unwholesome or foreboding atmosphere (*pl.* **-mata, -mas**) —**miasmat'ic** *a.*

mi'ca *n.* mineral found as glittering scales, plates

Mich'aelmas [mik'əl-] *n.* **UK** feast of Archangel St. Michael, 29th September

mi'crobe *n.* minute organism; disease germ —**micro'bial** *a.*

mi'crochip *n.* small wafer of silicon *etc.* containing electronic circuits, chip

microcompu'ter *n.* computer having a central processing unit contained in one or more silicon chips

mi'crocopy *n.* minute photographic

replica useful for storage because of its small size

mi'crocosm *n.* miniature representation, model *etc.* of some larger system; man as epitome of universe —**microcos'mic** *a.*

mi'crodot *n.* extremely small microcopy

mi'crofiche [-fēsh] *n.* microfilm in sheet form

mi'crofilm *n.* miniaturized recording of manuscript, book on roll of film

mi'crogroove *n.* narrow groove of long-playing gramophone record —*a.*

mi'crolight *n.* small, light, private aircraft used in pleasure flying and racing

microm'eter [mī-] *n.* instrument for measuring very small distances or angles

mi'cron *n.* unit of length, one millionth of a metre

microor'ganism [-ō-or'-] *n.* organism of microscopic size

mi'crophone *n.* instrument for amplifying, transmitting sounds

micropro'cessor *n.* integrated circuit acting as central processing unit in small computer

mi'croscope *n.* instrument by which very small body is magnified and made visible —**microscop'ic** *a.* of microscope; very small —**micros'copy** *n.* use of microscope

mi'crowave *n.* electromagnetic wave with wavelength of a few centimetres, used in radar, cooking *etc.*

mid *a.* intermediate, in the middle of —**mid'day** *n.* noon —**mid'land** *n.* middle part of country —**mid'night** *n.* twelve o'clock at night —**mid'shipman** *n.* naval officer of lowest commissioned rank —**midsumm'er** *n.* summer solstice; middle of summer —**mid'way** *a./adv.* halfway —*n.* place in fair where sideshows and amusements are located —**midwin'ter** *n.*

midd'en *n.* dunghill; refuse heap

mid'dle *a.* equidistant from two extremes; medium, intermediate —*n.* middle point or part —**mid'dling** *a.* mediocre; moderate —*adv.* —**Middle Ages** period from end of Roman Empire to Renaissance, roughly A.D. 500-1500 —**middle class** social class of businessmen, professional people *etc.* —**middle-class** *a.* —**mid'dleman** *n.* trader between producer and consumer

midge *n.* gnat or similar insect

midg'et [mij'it] *n.* very small person or thing

mid'riff *n.* middle part of body

midst *prep.* in the middle of —*n.* middle —**in the midst of** surrounded by, among

mid'wife *n.* trained person who assists at childbirth —**mid'wifery** [-wif-əri] *n.* art, practice of this

mien [mēn] *n.* person's bearing, demeanour or appearance

might[1] [mīt] *see* MAY

might[2] [mīt] *n.* power, strength —**might'ily** *adv.* strongly; powerfully —**might'y** *a.* of great power; strong; valiant; important —*adv. inf.* very

mignonette' [min-yən-] *n.* grey-green plant with sweet-smelling flowers

mi'graine [mē'grān] *n.* severe headache, often with nausea and other symptoms

migrate' [mī-] *vi.* move from one place to another —**mi'grant** *n./a.* —**migra'tion** *n.* act of passing from one place, condition to another; number migrating together —**mi'gratory** *a.* of, capable of migration; (of animals) changing from one place to another according to season

mike *n. inf.* microphone

milch *a.* giving, kept for milk

mild [-ī-] *a.* not strongly flavoured; gentle, merciful; calm or temperate —**mild'ly** *adv.* —**mild'ness** *n.*

mil'dew *n.* destructive fungus on plants or things exposed to damp —*v.* become tainted, affect with mildew

mile *n.* measure of length, 1760 yards, 1.609 km —**mile'age** *n.* distance in miles; travelling expenses per mile; miles travelled (per gallon of gasoline) —**mile'stone** *n.* stone marker showing distance; significant event, achievement

mil'foil *n.* yarrow

mi'lieu [mē'lyə] *n.* environment, condition in life

mil'itary *a.* of, for, soldiers, armies or war —*n.* armed services —**mil'itancy** *n.* —**mil'itant** *a.* aggressive, vigorous in support of cause; prepared, willing to fight —**mil'itarism** *n.* enthusiasm for military force and methods —**mil'itarist** *n.* —**mil'itarize** *vt.* convert to military use —**mili'tia** [-ish'ə] *n.* military force of citizens for home service

mil'itate *vi.* (*esp. with* against) have strong influence, effect on

milk *n.* white fluid with which mammals feed their young; fluid in some plants —*vt.* draw milk from —**milk'y** *a.* containing, like milk; (of liquids) opaque, clouded —**milk bar** snack bar specializing in milk drinks —**milk'maid** *n. esp.* formerly, woman working with cows or in dairy —**milk'sop** *n.* effeminate fellow —**milk teeth** first set of teeth in young mammals —**Milky Way** luminous band of stars *etc.* stretching across sky, the galaxy

mill[1] *n.* factory; machine for grinding, pulverizing corn, paper *etc.* —*vt.* put through mill; cut fine grooves across edges of (*eg* coins) —*vi.* move in confused manner, as cattle or crowds of people —**mill'er** *n.* —**mill'race** *n.* current of water driving mill wheel —**mill'stone** *n.* flat circular stone for grinding

mill[2] *n.* one thousandth of dollar

millenn'ium *n.* period of a thousand years during which some claim Christ is to reign on earth; period of a thousand years; period of peace, happiness (*pl.* **-iums, -ia**)

mill'epede, mill'ipede *n.* small animal with jointed body and many pairs of legs

mill'et *n.* a cereal grass

milli- (*comb. form*) thousandth, as in **mill'igram** *n.* thousandth part of a gram —**mill'ilitre** *n.* —**mill'imetre** *n.*

mill'ibar *n.* unit of atmospheric pressure

mill'iner *n.* maker of, dealer in women's hats, ribbons *etc.* —**mill'inery** *n.* his goods or work

mill'ion *n.* 1000 thousands —**millionaire'** *n.* owner of a million pounds, dollars *etc.*; very rich man —**mill'ionth** *a./n.*

milque'toast [milk'-] *n.* meek, timid person

milt *n.* spawn of male fish

mime *n.* acting without the use of words —*v.* act in mime

mim'ic *vt.* imitate (person, manner *etc.*) *esp.* for satirical effect (**mim'icked, mim'icking**) —*n.* one who, or animal which does this, or is adept at it —*a.* —**mim'icry** *n.* mimicking

mimo'sa *n.* genus of plants with fluffy, yellow flowers and sensitive leaves

min. minim; minimum; minute

minaret' *n.* tall slender tower of mosque

mince *vt.* cut, chop small; soften or moderate (words *etc.*) —*vi.* walk, speak in affected manner —*n.* minced meat —**min'cer** *n.* —**min'cing** *a.* affected in manner —**mince'meat** *n.* mixture of currants, spices, suet *etc.* —**mince pie** pie containing mincemeat or mince

mind [-ī-] *n.* thinking faculties as distinguished from the body, intellectual faculties; memory, attention; intention; taste; sanity —*vt.* take offence at; care for; attend to; be cautious, careful about (something); be concerned, troubled about —*vi.* be careful; heed —**mind'ful** *a.* heedful; keeping in memory —**mind'less** *a.* stupid, careless

mine[1] *pron.* belonging to me

mine[2] *n.* deep hole for digging out coal, metals *etc.*; in war, hidden deposit of explosive to blow up ship *etc.*; profitable source —*vt.* dig from mine; make mine in or under; place explosive mines in, on —*vi.* make, work in mine —**mi'ner** *n.* one who works in a mine —**mine'field** *n.* area of land or sea containing mines —**mine'layer** *n.* ship for laying mines —**mine'sweeper** *n.* ship for clearing away mines

min'eral *n.* naturally occurring inorganic substance, *esp.* as obtained by mining —*a.* —**min'eralist** *n.* —**mineralog'ical** *a.* —**mineral'ogy** *n.* science of minerals —**mineral water** water containing some mineral, *esp.* natural or artificial kinds for drinking

minestro'ne [-ō'ni] *n.* type of soup containing pasta

min'gle [-ng'g-] *v.* mix, blend, unite, merge

min'i *n.* something small or miniature; short skirt —*a.*

min'iature [-it-] *n.* small painted portrait; anything on small scale —*a.* small-scale, minute —**min'iaturist** *n.*

min'ibus *n.* small bus for about ten passengers

min'im *n.* unit of fluid measure, one sixtieth of a drachm

min'imize *vt.* bring to, estimate at smallest possible amount —**min'imal** *a.* —**min'imum** *n.* lowest size or quantity —*a.* least possible (*pl.* **-mums, -ma**)
min'ion *n.* favourite; servile dependant
min'iseries *n.* TV programme in several parts, shown on consecutive days
min'ister *n.* person in charge of department of State; diplomatic representaiive; clergyman —*vi.* attend to needs of, take care of —**ministe'rial** *a.* —**ministe'rialist** *n.* supporter of government —**min'istrant** *a./n.* —**ministra'tion** *n.* rendering help, *esp.* to sick —**min'istry** *n.* office of clergyman; body of ministers forming government; act of ministering
min'iver *n.* a white fur used in ceremonial costumes
mink *n.* variety of weasel; its (brown) fur
minn'ow [-ō] *n.* small freshwater fish
mi'nor *a.* lesser; under age —*n.* person below age of legal majority; scale in music; subsidiary subject of college or university student —**minor'ity** *n.* lesser number; smaller party voting together; ethical or religious group in a minority in any state; state of being a minor —**minor league** any professional league in baseball *etc.* other than major league
Mi'notaur [-tawr] *n.* fabled monster, half bull, half man
min'ster *n. Hist.* monastery church; cathedral, large church
min'strel *n.* medieval singer, musician, poet —*pl.* performers of negro songs —**min'strelsy** *n.* art, body of minstrels; collection of songs
mint[1] *n.* place where money is coined —*vt.* coin, invent
mint[2] *n.* aromatic plant
minuet' *n.* stately dance; music for it
mi'nus *prep./a.* less, with the deduction of, deprived of; lacking; negative —*n.* the sign of subtraction (-)
minute'[1] [mī-nyōōt'] *a.* very small; precise —**minute'ly** *adv.* —**minu'tiae** [-shi-ē] *pl.n.* trifles, precise details
min'ute[2] [min'it] *n.* 60th part of hour or degree; moment; memorandum —*pl.* record of proceedings of meeting *etc.* —*vt.* make minute of; record in minutes
minx *n.* bold, flirtatious woman
mir'acle *n.* supernatural event; marvel —**mirac'ulous** *a.* —**mirac'ulously** *adv.* —**miracle play** drama (*esp.* medieval) based on sacred subject
mir'age [-ahzh] *n.* deceptive image in atmosphere, *eg* of lake in desert
mire *n.* swampy ground, mud —*vt.* stick in, dirty with mud
mirr'or *n.* glass or polished surface reflecting images —*vt.* reflect
mirth *n.* merriment, gaiety —**mirth'ful** *a.* —**mirth'less** *a.*
mis- (*comb. form*) wrong(ly), bad(ly), as in the following

misbehave'	**misplace'**
miscal'culate	**mis'print**
miscon'duct	**mispronounce'**
mis'deed	**missha'pen**
misfor'tune	**misspell'**
misinform'	**misspent'**
misjudge'	**misunderstand'**
misman'agement	**misuse'**

misadven'ture *n.* unlucky chance
mis'anthrope, misan'thropist *n.* hater of mankind —**misanthrop'ic** *a.* —**misan'thropy** *n.*
misappro'priate *vt.* put to dishonest use; embezzle —**misappropria'tion** *n.*
miscarr'y *vi.* bring forth young prematurely; go wrong, fail —**miscarr'iage** *n.*
miscast' *v.* distribute acting parts wrongly; assign to unsuitable role —*a.*
miscella'neous *a.* mixed, assorted —**miscel'lany** *n.* collection of assorted writings in one book; medley
mischance' *n.* unlucky event
mis'chief [-chif] *n.* annoying behaviour; inclination to tease, disturb; harm; source of harm or annoyance —**mis'chievous** *a.* of a child, full of pranks; disposed to mischief; having harmful effect
mis'cible *a.* capable of mixing
misconcep'tion *n.* wrong idea, belief
mis'creant *n.* wicked person, evildoer, villain
misdemea'no(u)r *n.* formerly, offence less grave than a felony; minor offence
mi'ser *n.* hoarder of money; stingy person —**mi'serliness** *n.* —**mi'serly** *a.* avaricious; niggardly
mis'erable [-z-] *a.* very unhappy, wretched; causing misery; worthless;

squalid —**mis'ery** *n.* great unhappiness; distress; poverty

misfire' *vi.* fail to fire, start, function successfully

mis'fit *n. esp.* person not suited to his environment or work

misgiv'ing *n.* (*oft. pl.*) feeling of fear, doubt *etc.*

misgui'ded *a.* foolish, unreasonable

mis'hap *n.* minor accident

mislay' *vt.* put in place which cannot later be remembered

mislead' *vt.* give false information to; lead astray (**misled'** *pp.*) —**mislead'ing** *a.* deceptive

misno'mer *n.* wrong name or term; use of this

misog'amy [-og'-] *n.* hatred of marriage —**misog'amist** *n.*

misog'yny [-oj'-] *n.* hatred of women —**misog'ynist** *n.*

misrepresent' *vt.* portray in wrong or misleading light

Miss *n.* title of unmarried woman; (**m-**) girl

miss *vt.* fail to hit, reach, find, catch, or notice; not to be in time for; omit; notice or regret absence of; avoid —*vi.* (of engine) misfire —*n.* fact, instance of missing —**miss'ing** *a.* lost; absent

miss'al *n.* book containing prayers *etc.* of the Mass

miss'ile *n.* that which may be thrown, shot, homed to damage, destroy —**guided missile** *see* GUIDE

miss'ion [mish'ən] *n.* specific task or duty; calling in life; delegation; sending or being sent on some service; those sent —**miss'ionary** *n.* one sent to a place, society to spread religion —*a.*

miss'ive [-iv] *n.* letter

mist *n.* water vapour in fine drops —**mist'ily** *adv.* —**mis'ty** *a.* full of mist; dim; obscure

mistake' *n.* error, blunder —*vt.* fail to understand; form wrong opinion about; take (person or thing) for another —*vi.* be in error

mis'ter *n.* title of courtesy to man (*abbrev.* **Mr.**)

mis'tletoe [mis'əl-] *n.* evergreen parasitic plant with white berries which grows on trees

mis'tral *n.* strong, dry, N wind in France

mis'tress *n.* object of man's illicit love; woman with mastery or control; woman owner; woman teacher; *obs.* title given to married woman (*abbrev.* **Mrs.** [mis'iz])

mite *n.* very small insect; anything very small; small but well-meant contribution

mit'igate *vt.* make less severe —**mitiga'tion** *n.*

mi'tre [-tər] *n.* bishop's headdress; joint between two pieces of wood *etc.* meeting at right angles —*vt.* join with, shape for a mitre joint; put mitre on

mitt *n.* glove leaving fingers bare; baseball catcher's glove; *sl.* hand

mitt'en *n.* glove with two compartments, one for thumb and one for fingers

mix *vt.* put together, combine, blend, mingle —*vi.* be mixed; associate —**mixed** *a.* composed of different elements, races, sexes *etc.* —**mix'er** *n.* one who, that which mixes —**mix'ture** *n.* —**mixed-up** *a. inf.* confused —**mix-up** *n.* confused situation

miz(z)'en *n.* lowest fore-and-aft sail on aftermost mast of ship —**miz(z)'enmast** *n.* aftermost mast on full-rigged ship

ml millilitre(s)

MLA Member of the Legislative Assembly

mm millimetre(s)

MMM Member of the Order of Military Merit

Mn *Chem.* manganese

MNA Member of the National Assembly (of Quebec)

mnemon'ic [n-] *a.* helping the memory —*n.* something intended to help the memory

MO Medical Officer

moan *n.* low murmur, usually of pain —*v.* utter with moan, lament

moat *n.* deep wide ditch *esp.* round castle —*vt.* surround with moat

mob *n.* disorderly crowd of people; mixed assembly —*vt.* attack in mob, hustle or ill-treat (**-bb-**)

mo'bile *a.* capable of movement; easily moved or changed —*n.* hanging structure of card, plastic *etc.* designed to move in air currents —**mobil'ity** *n.*

mo'bilize *v.* (of armed services) prepare for military service —*vt.* organize for a purpose —**mobiliza'tion** *n.* in war time, calling up of men and women for active service

mocc'asin *n.* Amer. Indian soft shoe, usu. of deerskin

moch'a [mok'-] *n.* type of strong, dark coffee; this flavour

mock *vt.* make fun of, ridicule; mimic —*vi.* scoff —*n.* act of mocking; laughing stock —*a.* sham, imitation —**mock'er** *n.* —**mock'ery** *n.* derision; travesty —**mocking bird** N Amer. bird which imitates songs of others —**mock orange** shrub with white fragrant flowers —**mock-up** *n.* scale model

mod. moderate; modern

mode *n.* method, manner; prevailing fashion —**mo'dish** *a.* in the fashion

mod'el *n.* miniature representation; pattern; person or thing worthy of imitation; person employed by artist to pose, or by dress designer to display clothing —*vt.* make model of; mould; display (clothing) for dress designer (**-ll-**)

mod'erate [-ər-it] *a.* not going to extremes, temperate, medium —*n.* person of moderate views —*v.* [-ər-āt] make, become less violent or excessive; preside over meeting *etc.* —**modera'tion** *n.* —**mod'erator** *n.* mediator; president of Presbyterian body; arbitrator

mod'ern *a.* of present or recent times; in, of current fashion —*n.* person living in modern times —**mod'ernism** *n.* (support of) modern tendencies, thoughts *etc.* —**mod'ernist** *n.* —**modern'ity** *n.* —**moderniza'tion** *n.* —**mod'ernize** *vt.* bring up to date

mod'est *a.* not overrating one's qualities or achievements; shy; moderate, not excessive; decorous, decent —**mod'estly** *adv.* —**mod'esty** *n.*

mod'icum *n.* small quantity

mod'ify [-fī] *v.* (*mainly tr.*) change slightly; tone down (**-fied, -fying**) —**modifica'tion** *n.* —**mod'ifier** *n. esp.* word qualifying another

mod'ulate *vt.* regulate; vary in tone —*vi.* change key of music —**modula'tion** *n.* modulating; *Electronics* superimposing signals on to high-frequency carrier —**mod'ulator** *n.*

mod'ule *n.* (detachable) unit, section, component with specific function

mo'dus operan'di *Lat.* method of operating, tackling task

mo'gul *n.* important or powerful person

mo'hair *n.* fine cloth of goat's hair; hair of Angora goat

Mohamm'ed *n.* prophet and founder of Islam —**Mohamm'edan** *a./n.* Muslim

moi'ety *n.* a half

moist *a.* damp, slightly wet —**moist'en** [moi'sən] *v.* —**mois'ture** *n.* liquid, *esp.* diffused or in drops —**moist'urize** *vt.* add, restore moisture to (skin *etc.*)

mo'lar *a.* (of teeth) for grinding —*n.* molar tooth

molass'es [-iz] *n.* syrup, by-product of process of sugar refining

mole[1] *n.* small dark protuberant spot on the skin

mole[2] *n.* small burrowing animal

mole[3] *n.* pier or breakwater; causeway; harbour within this

mole[4] *n.* SI unit of amount of substance

mol'ecule *n.* simplest freely existing chemical unit, composed of two or more atoms; very small particle —**molec'ular** *a.* of, inherent in molecules

molest' *vt.* pester, interfere with so as to annoy or injure —**molesta'tion** *n.*

moll *n. sl.* gangster's female accomplice; prostitute

moll'ify *vt.* calm down, placate, soften (**-fied, -fying**) —**mollifica'tion** *n.*

moll'usc [-əsk] *n.* soft-bodied, usu. hard-shelled animal, *eg* snail, oyster

moll'ycoddle *v.* pamper

Mol'otov cock'tail home-made incendiary device consisting of bottle filled with gasoline

molten *see* MELT

molyb'denum [-lib'-] *n.* silver-white metallic element

mom *n. inf.* mother

mo'ment *n.* very short space of time; (present) point in time —**mo'mentarily** *adv.* temporarily; very soon —**mo'mentary** *a.* lasting only a moment

momen'tous *a.* of great importance

momen'tum *n.* force of a moving body; impetus gained from motion (*pl.* **-ta, -tums**)

mon'arch [-k] *n.* sovereign ruler of a state —**monarch'ic** *a.* —**mon'archist** *n.* supporter of monarchy —**mon'archy** *n.* state ruled by sovereign; his rule

mon'astery *n.* house occupied by a religious order —**monas'tic** *a.* relating to monks, nuns, or monasteries —*n.* monk, recluse —**monas'ticism** *n.*

Mon'day [mun'di] *n.* second day of the week, or first of working week

mon'ey [mun'i] *n.* banknotes, coin *etc.*, used as medium of exchange (*pl.* **-eys, -ies**) —**mon'etarism** *n.* theory that inflation is caused by increase in money supply —**mon'etarist** *n./a.* —**mon'etary** *a.* —**monetiza'tion** *n.* —**mon'etize** *vt.* make into, recognize as money —**mon'eyed, mon'ied** *a.* rich —**money order** written order, available at post office, for payment of sum of money

mon'golism [-ng'g-] *n.* form of physical and mental retardation —**mon'gol** *n./a.* (one) afflicted with this

mon'goose [-ng'g-] *n.* small animal of Asia and Africa noted for killing snakes (*pl.* **-gooses**)

mon'grel [mung'g-] *n.* animal, *esp.* dog, of mixed breed; hybrid —*a.*

mon'itor *n.* person or device which checks, controls, warns or keeps record of something; pupil assisting teacher with odd jobs in school; television set used in a studio for checking programme being transmitted; type of large lizard —*vt.* watch, check on —**moni'tion** *n.* warning —**mon'itory** *a.*

monk [mungk] *n.* one of a religious community of men living apart under vows —**monk'ish** *a.* —**monks'hood** *n.* poisonous plant with hooded flowers

monk'ey [mungk'i] *n.* long-tailed primate; mischievous child —*vi.* meddle, fool (with) —**monkey wrench** spanner with movable jaw

mono- (*comb. form*) single, as in **monosyllab'ic** *a.*

mon'ochrome *n.* representation in one colour —*a.* of one colour —**monochromat'ic** *a.*

mon'ocle *n.* single eyeglass

monoc'ular *a.* one-eyed

monog'amy *n.* custom of being married to one person at a time

mon'ogram *n.* design of letters interwoven

mon'ograph *n.* short book on single subject

mon'olith *n.* monument consisting of single standing stone

mon'ologue [-log] *n.* dramatic composition with only one speaker; long speech by one person

monoma'nia *n.* excessive preoccupation with one thing

mon'oplane *n.* airplane with one pair of wings

monop'oly *n.* exclusive possession of trade, privilege *etc.* —**monop'olist** *n.* —**monop'olize** *vt.* claim, take exclusive possession of

mon'orail *n.* railway with cars running on or suspended from single rail

mon'otheism *n.* belief in only one God —**mon'otheist** *n.*

mon'otone *n.* continuing on one note —**monot'onous** *a.* lacking in variety, dull, wearisome —**monot'ony** *n.*

Mon'otype ® type set as individual letters

monsoon' *n.* seasonal wind of SE Asia; very heavy rainfall season

mon'ster *n.* fantastic imaginary beast; misshapen animal or plant; very wicked person; huge person, animal or thing —*a.* huge —**monstros'ity** *n.* monstrous being; deformity; distortion —**mon'strous** *a.* of, like monster; unnatural; enormous; horrible —**mon'strously** *adv.*

mon'strance *n. R.C.Ch.* vessel in which consecrated Host is exposed for adoration

montage' [-ahzh'] *n.* elements of two or more pictures imposed upon a single background to give a unified effect; method of editing a movie

month [munth] *n.* one of twelve periods into which the year is divided; period of moon's revolution —**month'ly** *a.* happening or payable once a month —*adv.* once a month —*n.* magazine published every month

mon'ument *n.* anything that commemorates, *esp.* a building or statue —**monument'al** *a.* vast, lasting; of or serving as monument

moo *n.* cry of cow —*vi.* make this noise, low

mooch *vi. sl.* loaf, slouch; steal; get (something) by begging

mood[1] *n.* state of mind and feelings —**mood'y** *a.* gloomy, pensive; changeable in mood

mood[2] *n. Grammar* form indicating function of verb

moon *n.* satellite which takes lunar month to revolve round earth; any secondary planet —*vi.* go about dreamily

—**moon'light** *n.* —**moon'shine** *n.* whisky illicitly distilled; nonsense —**moon'stone** *n.* transparent semiprecious stone —**moon'struck** *a.* deranged

Moor *n.* member of race in Morocco and adjoining parts of N W Africa

moor[1] *n.* tract of open uncultivated land, often hilly and heather-clad —**moor'hen** *n.* water bird

moor[2] *v.* secure (ship) with chains or ropes —**moor'age** *n.* place, charge for mooring —**moor'ings** *pl.n.* ropes *etc.* for mooring; something providing stability, security

moose *n.* N Amer. deer, like elk

moot *a.* that is open to argument, debatable —*vt.* bring for discussion —*n.* meeting

mop *n.* bundle of yarn, cloth *etc.* on end of stick, used for cleaning; tangle (of hair *etc.*) —*vt.* clean, wipe with mop or other absorbent stuff (**-pp-**)

mope *vi.* be gloomy, apathetic

mo'ped *n.* light motorized bicycle

moraine' *n.* accumulated mass of debris, earth, stones *etc.*, deposited by glacier

mor'al [mo'-] *a.* pert. to right and wrong conduct; of good conduct —*n.* practical lesson, *eg* of fable —*pl.* habits with respect to right and wrong, *esp.* in matters of sex —**mor'alist** *n.* teacher of morality —**moral'ity** *n.* good moral conduct; moral goodness or badness; kind of medieval drama, containing moral lesson —**mor'alize** *vi.* write, think about moral aspect of things —*vt.* interpret morally —**mor'ally** *adv.* —**moral victory** triumph that is psychological rather than practical

morale' [-ahl'] *n.* degree of confidence, hope of person or group

morass' *n.* marsh; mess

morator'ium *n.* act authorizing postponement of payments *etc.*; delay (*pl.* **-ria**)

mor'ay [mo'-] *n.* large, voracious eel

mor'bid *a.* unduly interested in death; gruesome; diseased

mord'ant *a.* biting; corrosive; scathing —*n.* substance that fixes dyes

more *a.* greater in quantity or number —*comp. of* MANY *and* MUCH —*adv.* to a greater extent; in addition —*pron.* greater or additional amount or number —**moreo'ver** *adv.* besides, further

morganat'ic marr'iage marriage of king or prince in which wife does not share husband's rank or possessions and children do not inherit from father

morgue [mawrg] *n.* mortuary

mor'ibund [mo'ri-] *a.* dying; stagnant

Mor'mon *n.* member of religious sect founded in U.S.A. —**Mor'monism** *n.*

mor'nay *a.* denoting cheese sauce used in various dishes

morn'ing *n.* early part of day until noon —**morn** *n. Poet.* morning —**morning-glory** *n.* plant with trumpet-shaped flowers which close in late afternoon

morocc'o *n.* goatskin leather

mor'on *n.* mentally deficient person; *inf.* fool —**moron'ic** *a.*

morose' [-ōs'] *a.* sullen, moody

morph'ia, morph'ine *n.* narcotic extract of opium; drug used to induce sleep and relieve pain

morphol'ogy *n.* science of structure of organisms; form and structure of words of a language —**morpholog'ical** *a.*

morr'is dance *n.* English folk dance

morr'ow [mo'rō] *n. Poet.* next day

Morse *n.* system of telegraphic signalling in which letters of alphabet are represented by combinations of dots and dashes, or short and long flashes

mor'sel *n.* fragment, small piece

mor'tal *a.* subject to death; causing death —*n.* mortal creature —**mortal'ity** *n.* state of being mortal; great loss of life; death rate —**mor'tally** *adv.* fatally; deeply, intensely —**mortal sin** *R.C.Ch.* sin meriting damnation

mor'tar *n.* mixture of lime, sand and water for holding bricks and stones together; small cannon firing over short range; vessel in which substances are pounded —**mor'tarboard** *n.* square academic cap

mort'gage [mawr'gij] *n.* conveyance of property as security for debt with provision that property be reconveyed on payment within agreed time —*vt.* convey by mortgage; pledge as security —**mortgagee'** *n.* —**mort'gagor, -ger** *n.*

morti'cian *n.* **US** undertaker

mort'ify *vt.* humiliate; subdue by self-denial —*vi.* (of flesh) be affected with gangrene (**-fied, -fying**) —**mortifica'tion** *n.*

mor'tise [-tis] *n.* hole in piece of wood *etc.* to receive the tongue (tenon) and end of another piece —*vt.* make mortise in; fasten by mortise and tenon —**mortise lock** one embedded in door

mor'tuary *n.* building where corpses are kept before burial —*a.* of, for burial

Mosa'ic [mō-zā'ik] *a.* of Moses

mosa'ic [mō-zā'ik] *n.* picture or pattern of small bits of coloured stone, glass *etc.*; this process of decoration

Moselle' [mō-zel'] *n.* light white wine

mo'sey *vi. inf.* amble

Mos'lem *n. see* MUSLIM

mosque [mosk] *n.* Muslim temple

mosqui'to [-kē'tō] *n.* various kinds of flying, biting insects (*pl.* **-toes**)

moss *n.* small plant growing in masses on moist surfaces —**moss'y** *a.* covered with moss —**moss agate** agate with mosslike markings —**moss'back** *n.* old turtle that has growth of algae on its back; *inf.* conservative person

most [mō-] *a.* greatest in size, number, or degree —*sup. of* MUCH *and of* MANY —*n.* greatest number, amount, or degree —*adv.* in the greatest degree; *abbrev. of* ALMOST —**most'ly** *adv.* for the most part, generally, on the whole

motel' [mō-] *n.* roadside hotel with accommodation for motorists and vehicles

motet' [mō-] *n.* short sacred vocal composition

moth *n.* usu. nocturnal insect like butterfly; its grub —**moth'y** *a.* infested with moths —**moth'ball** *n.* small ball of camphor or naphthalene to repel moths from stored clothing *etc.* —*vt.* put in mothballs; store, postpone *etc.* —**moth'eaten** *a.* eaten, damaged by grub of moth; decayed, scruffy

moth'er [muTH'-] *n.* female parent; head of religious community of women —*a.* natural, native, inborn —*vt.* act as mother to —**moth'erhood** *n.* —**moth'erly** *a.* —**mother-in-law** *n.* mother of one's wife or husband —**mother of pearl** iridescent lining of certain shells

motif' [mō-tēf'] *n.* dominating theme; recurring design

mo'tion *n.* process or action or way of moving; proposal in meeting; application to judge; **UK** evacuation of bowels —*vt.* direct by sign —**mo'tionless** *a.* still, immobile —**motion picture** sequence of images projected on screen, creating illusion of movement

mo'tive *n.* that which makes person act in particular way; inner impulse —*a.* causing motion —**mo'tivate** *vt.* instigate; incite —**motiva'tion** *n.*

mot'ley *a.* miscellaneous, varied; multicoloured —*n.* motley colour or mixture; jester's particoloured dress

mo'tocross *n.* motorcycle race over rough course

mo'tor *n.* that which imparts movement; machine to supply motive power; motorcar —*vi.* travel by automobile —**mo'toring** *n.* —**mo'torist** *n.* user of motorcar —**mo'torize** *vt.* equip with motor; provide with motor transport —**mo'torbike, mo'torcycle, mo'torboat, mo'torcar, motor scooter** *n.* vehicles driven by motor

mot'tle *vt.* mark with blotches, variegate —*n.* arrangement of blotches; blotch on surface

mott'o *n.* saying adopted as rule of conduct; short inscribed sentence; word or sentence on heraldic crest (*pl.* **-es**)

mou'f(f)lon [mōō'-] *n.* wild mountain sheep

mould[1] [mōld] *n.* hollow object in which metal *etc.* is cast; pattern for shaping; character; shape, form —*vt.* shape or pattern —**mould'ing** *n.* moulded object; ornamental edging; decoration

mould[2] [mōld] *n.* fungoid growth caused by dampness —**mould'y** *a.* stale, musty

mould[3] [mōld] *n.* loose or surface earth —**mould'er** *vi.* decay into dust

moult [mōlt] *v.* cast or shed fur, feathers *etc.* —*n.* moulting

mound *n.* heap of earth or stones; small hill

mount *vi.* rise; increase; get on horseback —*vt.* get up on; frame (picture); fix, set up; provide with horse —*n.* that on which thing is supported or fitted; horse; hill

moun'tain *n.* hill of great size; surplus —**mountaineer'** *n.* one who lives among or climbs mountains —**mountaineer'ing** *n.* —**moun'tainous** *a.* very high, rugged

moun'tebank [-ti-] *n.* charlatan, fake

Mount'ie *n. inf.* member of Royal Canadian Mounted Police

mourn [-aw-] *v.* feel, show sorrow (for) —**mourn'er** *n.* —**mourn'ful** *a.* sad; dismal —**mourn'fully** *adv.* —**mourn'ing** *n.* grieving; conventional signs of grief for death; clothes of mourner

mouse *n.* small rodent (*pl.* **mice**) —*vi.* catch, hunt mice; prowl —**mous'er** *n.* cat used for catching mice —**mous'y** *a.* like mouse, *esp.* in colour; meek, shy

mousse [mo͞os] *n.* sweet dish of flavoured cream whipped and frozen

moustache' [mə-stahsh'] *n.* hair on the upper lip

mouth [-th; *pl.* -THz] *n.* opening in head for eating, speaking *etc.*; opening into anything hollow; outfall of river; entrance to harbour *etc.* —*vt.* [-TH] declaim, *esp.* in public; form (words) with lips without speaking; take, move in mouth —**mouth'piece** *n.* end of anything placed between lips, *eg* pipe; spokesman

move [mo͞ov] *vt.* change position of; stir emotions of; incite; propose for consideration —*vi.* change places; change one's dwelling *etc.*; take action —*n.* a moving; motion towards some goal —**mov(e)'able** *a./n.* —**move'ment** *n.* process, action of moving; moving parts of machine; division of piece of music —**moving picture** motion picture

mo'vie [mo͞o'-] *inf. n.* motion picture —**movie camera** camera for taking moving pictures

mow [mō] *v.* cut (grass *etc.*) (**mown** *pp.*) —**mow'er** *n.* man or machine that mows

MP Member of Parliament; Military Police; Mounted Police

mpg miles per gallon

mph miles per hour

Mr. mister

Mrs. title of married woman

Ms [miz] title used instead of Miss or Mrs.

MS(S) manuscript(s)

MSc Master of Science

MST Mountain Standard Time

Mt. Mount

much *a.* existing in quantity (**more** *comp.*, **most** *sup.*) —*n.* large amount; a great deal; important matter —*adv.* in a great degree; nearly

mu'cilage *n.* gum, glue

muck *n.* cattle dung; unclean refuse —**muck'y** *a.* dirty; messy; unpleasant

mu'cus *n.* viscid fluid secreted by mucous membrane —**mucos'ity** *n.* —**mu'cous** *a.* resembling mucus; secreting mucus; slimy —**mucous membrane** lining of canals and cavities of the body

mud *n.* wet and soft earth; *inf.* slander —**mudd'y** *a.* —**mud'guard** *n.* **UK** fender on automobile —**mud'pack** *n.* cosmetic paste to improve complexion

mud'dle *vt.* (*esp. with* up) confuse; bewilder; mismanage —*n.* confusion; tangle

mues'li [myo͞oz'-] *n.* mixture of grain, dried fruit *etc.* eaten with milk

muezz'in [myo͞o-ez'-] *n.* crier who summons Muslims to prayer

muff[1] *n.* tube-shaped covering to keep the hands warm

muff[2] *vt.* miss, bungle, fail in

muff'in *n.* small cup-shaped sweet bread roll

muf'fle *vt.* wrap up, *esp.* to deaden sound —**muff'ler** *n.* scarf; device to reduce noise of engine exhaust, firearm

muf'ti *n.* plain clothes as distinguished from uniform, *eg* of soldier

mug[1] *n.* drinking cup

mug[2] *n. sl.* face —*vt.* rob violently —**mug'ger** *n.*

mugg'y *a.* damp and stifling

muk'luk *n.* Inuit's soft (sealskin) boot

mulatt'o [myo͞o-] *n.* child of one European and one Negro parent (*pl.* **-o(e)s**)

mul'berry *n.* tree whose leaves are used to feed silkworms; its purplish fruit

mulch *n.* straw, leaves *etc.*, spread as protection for roots of plants —*vt.* protect thus

mulct *vt.* defraud; fine

mule *n.* animal which is cross between horse and ass; hybrid; spinning machine —**muleteer'** [myo͞o-li-] *n.* mule driver —**mu'lish** *a.* obstinate

mull *vt.* heat (wine) with sugar and spices; think (over), ponder

mull'ah *n.* Muslim theologian

mull'e(i)n [-lin] *n.* plant with tall spikes of yellow flowers

mull'et *n.* edible sea fish

mull'igan *n.* stew made from scraps of food

mulligataw'ny *n.* soup made with curry powder

mull'ion *n.* upright dividing bar in window —**mull'ioned** *a.*

multi-, mult- (*comb. form*) many, as in **multira'cial** *a.*, **multistor'ey** *a.* Such words are omitted where the meaning may easily be found from the simple word

multifa'rious *a.* of various kinds or parts —**multifa'riously** *adv.*

mul'tiple *a.* having many parts —*n.* quantity which contains another an exact number of times —**multiplicand'** *n.* *Math.* number to be multiplied —**multiplica'tion** *n.* —**multiplic'ity** [-plis'-] *n.* variety, greatness in number —**mul'tiply** *v.* (cause to) increase in number, quantity, or degree —*vt.* combine (two numbers or quantities) by multiplication —*vi.* increase in number by reproduction (**-plied, -plying**)

mul'tiplex *a.* *Telecommunications* capable of transmitting numerous messages over same wire or channel

mul'titude *n.* great number; great crowd; populace —**multitu'dinous** *a.* very numerous

mum *n. inf.* mother

mum'ble *v.* speak indistinctly, mutter

mumm'er *n.* actor in dumb show —**mum** *a.* silent —**mum(m)** *v.* act in mime (**-mm-**) —**mumm'ery** *n.* dumb show acting

mumm'y *n.* embalmed body —**mum'mify** *vt.* (**-fied, -fying**)

mumps *pl.n.* infectious disease marked by swelling in the glands of the neck

munch *v.* chew noisily and vigorously; crunch

mundane' *a.* ordinary, everyday; belonging to this world, earthly

munic'ipal [myo͞o-nis'-] *a.* belonging to affairs of city, town, or other municipality —**municipal'ity** *n.* city, town, county, district, township or other area with local self-government; its governing body

munif'icent [myo͞o-] *a.* very generous —**munif'icence** *n.* bounty

mu'niments *pl.n.* title deeds, documents verifying ownership

muni'tion [myo͞o-nish'-] *n.* (*usu. pl.*) military stores

mur'al [myoor'-] *n.* painting on a wall —*a.* of or on a wall

mur'der *n.* unlawful premeditated killing of human being —*vt.* kill thus —**mur'derer** *n.* (**mur'deress** *fem.*) —**mur'derous** *a.*

murk *n.* thick darkness —**murk'y** *a.* gloomy

mur'mur *n.* low, indistinct sound —*vi.* make such a sound; complain —*vt.* utter in a low voice

murr'ain [-in] *n.* cattle plague

mus. museum; music(al)

mus'cat *n.* musk-flavoured grape; raisin —**muscatel'** *n.* muscat; strong wine made from it

mus'cle [mus'əl] *n.* part of body which produces movement by contracting; system of muscles —**mus'cular** *a.* with well-developed muscles; strong; of, like muscle —**muscle-bound** *a.* with muscles stiff through over-development —**muscular dystrophy** [dis'trə-fi] disease with wasting of muscles —**muscle in** *inf.* force one's way into

Muse [myo͞oz] *n.* one of the nine goddesses inspiring learning and the arts

muse [myo͞oz] *vi.* ponder; consider meditatively; be lost in thought —*n.* state of musing or abstraction; reverie

muse'um [myo͞o-zē'-] *n.* (place housing) collection of natural, artistic, historical or scientific objects

mush[1] *n.* soft pulpy mass; *inf.* cloying sentimentality —**mush'y** *a.*

mush[2] *interj.* order to dogs in sled team to advance —*v.* travel by or drive dogsled —*n.* journey with dogsled

mush'room *n.* fungoid growth, typically with stem and cap structure, some species edible —*vi.* shoot up rapidly; expand

mu'sic [-z-] *n.* art form using melodious and harmonious combination of notes; laws of this; composition in this art —**mu'sical** *a.* of, like music; interested in, or with instinct for, music; pleasant to ear —*n.* show, film in which music plays essential part —**mu'sically** *adv.* —**musi'cian** [-zish'ən] *n.* —**musicale'** [-kahl'] *n.* social evening with music —**musicol'ogist** *n.* —**musicol'ogy** *n.* scientific study of music —**musical comedy** light dramatic entertainment of songs, dances *etc.* —**music hall UK** vaudeville

musk *n.* scent obtained from gland of **musk deer**; various plants with similar scent —**musk'y** *a.* —**musk ox** ox of Arctic Amer. —**musk'rat** *n.* N Amer. rodent found near water; its fur

mus'keg *n.* bog, swamp

mus'kellunge *n.* N Amer. freshwater game fish
mus'ket *n. Hist.* infantryman's gun —**musketeer'** *n.* —**musk'etry** *n.* (use of) firearms
Mus'lim *n.* follower of religion of Islam —*a.* of religion, culture *etc.* of Islam
mus'lin [-z-] *n.* fine cotton fabric —**mus'lined** *a.*
mus'quash *n.* muskrat
muss *vt./n. inf.* muddle
muss'el *n.* bivalve shellfish
must[1] *v. aux.* be obliged to, or certain to —*n.* something one must do
must[2] *n.* newly-pressed grape juice; unfermented wine
mus'tang *n.* wild horse
mus'tard *n.* powder made from the seeds of a plant, used in paste as a condiment; the plant —**mustard gas** poisonous gas causing blistering
mus'ter *v.* assemble —*n.* assembly, *esp.* for exercise, inspection
must'y *a.* mouldy, stale —**must, must'iness** *n.*
mutate' [myōō-] *v.* (cause to) undergo mutation —**mu'table** *a.* liable to change —**mu'tant** *n.* mutated animal, plant *etc.* —**muta'tion** *n.* change, *esp.* genetic change causing divergence from kind or racial type
mute *a.* dumb; silent —*n.* dumb person; *Mus.* contrivance to soften tone of instruments —**mu'ted** *a.* (of sound) muffled; (of light) subdued —**mute'ly** *adv.*
mu'tilate *vt.* deprive of a limb or other part; damage; deface —**mutila'tion** *n.* —**mu'tilator** *n.*
mu'tiny *n.* rebellion against authority, esp. against officers of disciplined body —*vi.* commit mutiny (**mu'tinied, mu'tinying**) —**mutineer'** *n.* —**mu'tinous** *a.* rebellious
mutt *inf. n.* stupid person; dog
mutt'er *vi.* speak with mouth nearly closed, indistinctly; grumble —*vt.* utter in such tones —*n.* act of muttering
mutt'on *n.* flesh of sheep used as food
mu'tual *a.* done, possessed *etc.*, by each of two with respect to the other; reciprocal; *inf.* common to both or all —**mu'tually** *adv.*
Mu'zak R recorded light music played in shops *etc.*
muz'zle *n.* mouth and nose of animal; cover for these to prevent biting; open end of gun —*vt.* put muzzle on; silence, gag
MV motor vessel
MW megawatt(s)
mW milliwatt(s)
my *a.* belonging to me —**myself'** *pron.* emphatic or reflexive form of I or ME
myal'gia *n.* pain in a muscle
mycol'ogy *n.* science of fungi
my'na(h) *n.* Indian bird related to starling
myo'pia *n.* short-sightedness —**myop'ic** *a.*
myr'iad [mir'-] *a.* innumerable —*n.* large indefinite number
myrrh [mer] *n.* aromatic gum, formerly used as incense
myr'tle [mer'-] *n.* flowering evergreen shrub
myself' *see* MY
mys'tery [mis'-] *n.* obscure or secret thing; anything strange or inexplicable; religious rite; in Middle Ages, biblical play —**myste'rious** *a.* —**myste'riously** *adv.*
mys'tic [mis'-] *n.* one who seeks divine, spiritual knowledge, *esp.* by prayer, contemplation *etc.* —*a.* of hidden meaning, *esp.* in religious sense —**myst'ical** *a.* —**myst'icism** *n.*
myst'ify [mis'-] *vt.* bewilder, puzzle (**-fied, -fying**) —**mystifica'tion** *n.*
mystique' [mis-tēk'] *n.* aura of mystery, power *etc.*
myth [mith] *n.* tale with supernatural characters or events; invented story; imaginary person or object —**myth'ical** *a.* —**mytholog'ical** *a.* —**mythol'ogist** *n.* —**mythol'ogy** *n.* myths collectively; study of them
myxomato'sis [miks-] *n.* contagious, fatal disease of rabbits caused by a virus

N

N *Chess* knight; *Chem.* nitrogen; *Physics* newton; north(ern)

n. neuter; noun; number

Na *Chem.* sodium

nab *inf. vt.* arrest criminal; catch suddenly (**-bb-**)

na'cre [-kər] *n.* mother-of-pearl; shellfish

na'dir *n.* point opposite the zenith; lowest point

naeve, nae'vus [nēv'-] *n.* congenital mark on skin; birthmark, mole

nag[1] *v.* scold or annoy constantly; cause pain to constantly (**-gg-**) *—n.* nagging; one who nags

nag[2] *n. inf.* horse; small horse for riding

nai'ad [nī-] *n.* water nymph

nail [nāl] *n.* horny shield at ends of fingers, toes; claw; small metal spike for fixing wood *etc.* *—vt.* fix, stud with nails; *inf.* catch

naive', naïve' [nah-ēv', nī-] *a.* simple, unaffected, ingenuous **—naiveté', naive'ty** *n.*

na'ked *a.* without clothes; exposed, bare; undisguised **—na'kedly** *adv.* **—na'kedness** *n.* **—naked eye** the eye unassisted by any optical instrument

nam'by-pam'by *a.* weakly; sentimental; insipid *—n.*

name *n.* word by which person, thing *etc.* is denoted; reputation; title; credit; family; famous person *—vt.* give name to; call by name; entitle; appoint; mention; specify **—name'less** *a.* without a name; indescribable; too dreadful to be mentioned; obscure **—name'ly** *adv.* that is to say **—name'sake** *n.* person with same name as another

nann'y *n.* child's nurse **—nanny goat** she-goat

na'nook *n.* polar bear

nap[1] *vi.* take short sleep, *esp.* in daytime (**-pp-**) *—n.* short sleep

nap[2] *n.* downy surface on cloth made by projecting fibres

nap[3] *n.* card game

na'palm [nā'pahm, nap'-] *n.* jellied petrol, highly inflammable, used in bombs *etc.*

nape *n.* back of neck

naph'tha [naf'-, nap'-] *n.* inflammable oil distilled from coal *etc.* **—naph'thalene** *n.* white crystalline product distilled from coal tar, used in disinfectants, mothballs *etc.*

nap'kin *n.* cloth, paper for wiping fingers or lips at table, serviette; small towel; diaper

napp'y *n.* **UK** baby's diaper

narciss'us *n.* genus of bulbous plants including daffodil, jonquil, *esp.* one with white flowers (*pl.* **-ciss'i** [-ī]) **—nar'cissism** *n.* abnormal love and admiration of oneself **—nar'cissist** *n.*

narcot'ic *n.* any of a group of drugs, including morphine and opium, producing numbness and stupor, used medicinally but addictive *—a.* **—narco'sis** *n.* effect of narcotic

narrate' *vt.* relate, recount, tell (story) **—narra'tion** *n.* **—narr'ative** *n.* account, story *—a.* relating **—narra'tor** *n.*

narr'ow [-ō] *a.* of little breadth, *esp.* in comparison to length; limited; barely adequate or successful *—v.* make, become narrow **—narr'ows** *pl.n.* narrow part of straits **—narr'owly** *adv.* **—nar'rowness** *n.* **—narrow-minded** *a.* illiberal; bigoted **—narrow-mindedness** *n.* prejudice, bigotry

nar'whal *n.* arctic whale with long spiral tusk

NASA US National Aeronautics and Space Administration

na'sal [-z-] *a.* of nose *—n.* sound partly produced in nose **—na'salize** *vt.* make nasal in sound **—na'sally** *adv.*

nas'cent *a.* just coming into existence; springing up

nastur'tium [-shəm] *n.* genus of plants which includes the watercress; trailing garden plant with red or orange flowers

nas'ty [nah-] *a.* foul, disagreeable, unpleasant —**nas'tily** *adv.* —**nas'tiness** *n.*

nat. national; native; natural

na'tal *a.* of birth

na'tant *a.* floating

na'tion [-shən] *n.* people or race organized as a state; people of same descent —**nat'ional** [nash'-] *a.* belonging or pert. to a nation; public, general —*n.* member of a nation —**nat'ionalism** *n.* loyalty, devotion to one's country; movement for independence of state, people, ruled by another —**nat'ionalist** *n./a.* —**national'ity** *n.* national quality or feeling; fact of belonging to particular nation —**nationaliza'tion** *n.* acquisition and management of industries by the State —**na'tionalize** *vt.* convert (private industry, resources *etc.*) to state control —**na'tionally** *adv.* —**National Assembly** legislative assembly of Quebec

na'tive *a.* inborn; born in particular place; found in pure state; that was place of one's birth —*n.* one born in a place; member of indigenous race of a country; species of plant, animal *etc.* originating in a place

nativ'ity *n.* birth; time, circumstances of birth; (**N-**) birth of Christ

NATO North Atlantic Treaty Organization

natt'er *vi. inf.* talk idly

natt'y *a.* neat and smart; spruce —**nat'tily** *adv.*

na'ture *n.* innate or essential qualities of person or thing; class, sort; life force; (*oft.* **N-**) power underlying all phenomena in material world; material world as a whole; natural unspoilt scenery or countryside, and plants and animals in it; disposition; temperament —**nat'ural** *a.* of, according to, occurring in, provided by, nature; inborn; normal; unaffected; illegitimate —*n.* something, somebody well suited for something; *Mus.* character (♮) used to remove effect of sharp or flat preceding it —**nat'uralist** *n.* student of natural history —**naturalis'tic** *a.* of or imitating nature in effect or characteristics —**naturaliza'tion** *n.* —**nat'uralize** *vt.* admit to citizenship; accustom to new climate —**nat'urally** *adv.* of or according to nature; by nature; of course —**na'turism** *n.* nature-worship; nudism —**na'turist** *n.* —**natural history** study of animals and plants

naught [nawt] *n. obs.* nothing; nought —**set at naught** defy, disregard

naught'y *a.* disobedient, not behaving well; *inf.* mildly indecent —**naught'ily** *adv.*

nau'sea [-si-ə, -zi-ə] *n.* feeling that precedes vomiting —**nau'seate** *vt.* sicken —**nau'seous** *a.* disgusting; causing nausea

nau'tical *a.* of seamen or ships; marine —**nautical mile** 1852 metres

nau'tilus *n.* univalvular shellfish (*pl.* **-tiluses, -tili** [-ī])

na'val *see* NAVY

nave[1] *n.* main part of church

nave[2] *n.* hub of wheel

na'vel *n.* umbilicus, small scar, depression in middle of abdomen where umbilical cord was attached

nav'igate *v.* plan, direct, plot path or position of ship *etc.*; travel —**nav'igable** *a.* —**naviga'tion** *n.* science of directing course of seagoing vessel, or of aircraft in flight; shipping —**nav'igator** *n.* one who navigates

navv'y *n.* UK labourer employed on roads, railways *etc.*

na'vy *n.* fleet; warships of country with their crews and organization —*a.* navy-blue —**na'val** *a.* of the navy —**navy-blue** *a.* very dark blue

nay *adv. obs.* no

Na'zi [naht'si] *n.* member of the National Socialist political party in Germany, 1919-45; one who thinks, acts, like a Nazi —*a.* —**Naz'(i)ism** *n.* Nazi doctrine

NB nota bene

N.B. New Brunswick

Nb *Chem.* niobium

NCO noncommissioned officer

NDP New Democratic Party

NDT Newfoundland Daylight Time

NE northeast(ern)

Ne *Chem.* neon

Nean'derthal [ni-an'dər-tahl] *a.* of a type of primitive man

neap *a.* low —**neap tide** the low tide at the first and third quarters of the moon

near *prep.* close to —*adv.* at or to a short distance —*a.* close at hand; closely related; narrow, so as barely to escape; stingy; (of vehicles, horses *etc.*) left —*v.* approach —**near'by** *a.* adjacent —**near'ly** *adv.* closely; almost —**near'ness** *n.*

neat *a.* tidy, orderly; efficient; precise, deft; cleverly worded; undiluted; simple and elegant; *sl.* very good —**neat'ly** *adv.* —**neat'ness** *n.*

neb'ula *n. Astronomy* diffuse cloud of particles, gases (*pl.* **-ulae** [-lē]) —**neb'ulous** *a.* cloudy; vague, indistinct

nec'essary [nes'-] *a.* needful, requisite, that must be done; unavoidable, inevitable —**nec'essarily** *adv.* —**neces'sitate** *vt.* make necessary —**neces'sitous** *a.* poor, needy, destitute —**neces'sity** *n.* something needed, requisite; constraining power or state of affairs; compulsion; poverty

neck *n.* part of body joining head to shoulders; narrower part of a bottle *etc.*; narrow piece of anything between wider parts —*vi. sl.* embrace, cuddle —**neck'erchief** [-chif] *n.* kerchief for the neck —**neck'lace** *n.* ornament round the neck —**neck'let** *n.* neck ornament, piece of fur *etc.*

nec'romancy *n.* magic, *esp.* by communication with dead —**nec'romancer** *n.* wizard

necrop'olis *n.* cemetery (*pl.* **-olises, -oleis** [-lās])

nec'tar *n.* honey of flowers; drink of the gods —**nec'tary** *n.* honey gland of flower

nec'tarine [-rin] *n.* variety of peach

née, nee [nā] *a.* indicating maiden name of married woman

need *vt.* want, require —*n.* (state, instance of) want; requirement; necessity; poverty —**need'ful** *a.* necessary, requisite —**need'less** *a.* unnecessary —**needs** *adv.* of necessity (*esp. in* **needs must** *or* **must needs**) —**need'y** *a.* poor, in want

nee'dle *n.* pointed pin with an eye and no head, for sewing; long, pointed pin for knitting; pointer of gauge, dial; magnetized bar of compass; stylus for record player; leaf of fir or pine; obelisk; *inf.* hypodermic syringe —*vt. inf.* goad, provoke —**nee'dlecord** *n.* corduroy fabric with narrow ribs —**nee'dlework** *n.* embroidery, sewing

ne'er [nār] *adv. Literary* never —**ne'er-do-well** *n.* worthless person

nefar'ious [-ār'-] *a.* wicked

negate' *vt.* deny, nullify —**nega'tion** *n.* contradiction, denial

neg'ative *a.* expressing denial or refusal; lacking enthusiasm, energy, interest; not positive; of electrical charge having the same polarity as the charge of an electron —*n.* negative word or statement; *Photography* picture made by action of light on chemicals in which lights and shades are reversed —*vt.* disprove, reject

neglect' *vt.* disregard, take no care of; fail to do; omit through carelessness —*n.* fact of neglecting or being neglected —**neglect'ful** *a.*

neg'ligee, -gé(e) [-zhā] *n.* woman's light, gauzy nightdress or dressing gown

neg'ligence [-jəns] *n.* neglect; carelessness —**neg'ligent** *a.* —**neg'ligible** *a.* able to be disregarded; very small or unimportant

nego'tiate *vi.* discuss with view to mutual settlement —*vt.* arrange by conference; transfer (bill, cheque *etc.*); get over, past, around (obstacle) —**nego'tiable** *a.* —**negotia'tion** *n.* treating with another on business; discussion; transference (of bill, cheque *etc.*) —**nego'tiator** *n.*

Ne'gro *n.* member of black orig. Afr. race (*pl.* **-es,** *fem.* **Ne'gress**) —**Ne'groid** *a.* of or like Negro

neigh [nā] *n.* cry of horse —*vi.* utter this cry

neigh'bo(u)r [nā'bər] *n.* one who lives near another —**neigh'bo(u)rhood** *n.* district; people of a district; region round about —**neigh'bo(u)ring** *a.* situated nearby —**neigh'bo(u)rly** *a.* as or befitting a good or friendly neighbour; friendly; sociable; helpful

nei'ther [nī'-, nē'-] *a./pron.* not the one or the other —*adv.* not on the one hand; not either —*conj.* not yet

nem. con. (*Lat.*, nemine contradicente) unanimously

Nem'esis *n.* retribution; the goddess of vengeance

ne'o- (*comb. form*) new, later, revived in modified form, based upon

neolith'ic *a.* of the later Stone Age

neol'ogism [-j-] *n.* new-coined word or phrase —**neol'ogize** *vi.*

ne'on *n.* one of the inert constituent

gases of the atmosphere, used in illuminated signs and lights

ne'ophyte *n.* new convert; beginner, novice

neph'ew [nev'-, nef'-] *n.* brother's or sister's son

nephri'tis [-frī'-] *n.* inflammation of a kidney

nep'otism *n.* undue favouritism towards one's relations

Nep'tune *n.* god of the sea; planet second farthest from sun

neptu'nium *n.* synthetic metallic element

nerve *n.* sinew, tendon; fibre or bundle of fibres conveying feeling, impulses to motion *etc.* to and from brain and other parts of body; assurance; coolness in danger; audacity —*pl.* irritability, unusual sensitiveness to fear, annoyance *etc.* —*vt.* give courage or strength to —**nerve'less** *a.* without nerves; useless; weak; paralysed —**nerv'ous** *a.* excitable; timid, apprehensive, worried; of the nerves —**nerv'ously** *adv.* —**nerv'ousness** *n.* —**nerv'y** *a. inf.* brash or cheeky —**nervous breakdown** condition of mental, emotional disturbance, disability

nes'cient [-si-ənt] *a.* ignorant; agnostic —**nes'cience** *n.*

ness *n.* headland, cape

nest *n.* place in which bird lays and hatches its eggs; animal's breeding place; snug retreat —*vi.* make, have a nest —**nest egg** (fund of) money in reserve

nes'tle [-sl] *vi.* settle comfortably, usu. pressing in or close to something

nest'ling *n.* bird too young to leave nest

net[1] *n.* openwork fabric of meshes of cord *etc.*; piece of it used to catch fish *etc.* —*vt.* cover with, or catch in, net (-tt-) —**nett'ing** *n.* string or wire net

net[2] *a.* left after all deductions; free from deduction —*vt.* gain, yield as clear profit

neth'er [-TH-] *a.* lower

net'tle *n.* plant with stinging hairs on the leaves —*vt.* irritate, provoke

net'work *n.* system of intersecting lines, roads *etc.*; interconnecting group of people or things; in broadcasting, group of stations connected to transmit same programmes simultaneously

neu'ral [nyoo'-] *a.* of the nerves

neural'gia [nyoor-] *n.* pain in, along nerves, *esp.* of face and head —**neural'gic** *a.*

neuri'tis [nyoor-] *n.* inflammation of nerves

neurol'ogy [nyoor-] *n.* science, study of nerves —**neurol'ogist** *n.*

neuro'sis [nyoor-] *n.* relatively mild mental disorder —**neurot'ic** *a.* suffering from nervous disorder; abnormally sensitive —*n.* neurotic person

neut'er [nyōōt'-] *a.* neither masculine nor feminine —*n.* neuter word; neuter gender —*vt.* castrate, spay (domestic animals)

neu'tral [nyōō'-] *a.* taking neither side in war, dispute *etc.*; without marked qualities; belonging to neither of two classes —*n.* neutral nation or a subject of one; neutral gear —**neutral'ity** *n.* —**neu'tralize** *vt.* make ineffective; counterbalance —**neutral gear** in vehicle, position of gears that leaves transmission disengaged

neu'tron [nyōō'-] *n.* electrically neutral particle of the nucleus of an atom —**neutron bomb** nuclear bomb designed to destroy people but not buildings

nev'er *adv.* at no time —**nev'ertheless'** *adv.* for all that, notwithstanding

never-never *n.* UK *inf.* hire-purchase

new *a.* not existing before, fresh; that has lately come into some state or existence; unfamiliar, strange —*adv.* (*usu.* **new'ly**) recently, fresh —**new'ly** *adv.* —**new'ness** *n.* —**new'comer** *n.* recent arrival —**new'fang'led** [-ng'gld] *a.* of new fashion —**New Democratic Party** major political party with policies to left of Liberal and Progressive-Conservative Parties

new'el *n.* central pillar of winding staircase; post at top or bottom of staircase rail

news *n.* report of recent happenings, tidings; interesting fact not previously known —**news'y** *a.* full of news —**news'agent** *n.* shopkeeper who sells and distributes newspapers —**news'cast** *n.* news broadcast —**news'caster** *n.* —**news'flash** *n.* brief news item, *oft.* interrupting programme —**news'paper** *n.* periodical publication containing news —**news'print** *n.* paper of the kind used for newspapers *etc.* —**news'reel** *n.* cinema or television motion picture giving news —**news'room** *n.* room where news is received and prepared for publication or broadcast —**news'worthy** *a.* sufficiently interesting or important to be reported as news

newt *n.* small, tailed amphibious creature

new'ton *n.* SI unit of force

next *a./adv.* nearest; immediately following —**next-of-kin** *n.* nearest relative

nex'us *n.* tie; connection, link (*pl.* **nex'-us**)

Nfld. Newfoundland

Ni *Chem.* nickel

nib *n.* (split) pen point; bird's beak —*pl.* crushed cocoa beans

nib'ble *v.* take little bites of —*n.* little bite

nibs *n.* mock title of respect, as **his nibs**

nice *a.* pleasant; friendly, kind; attractive; subtle, fine; careful, exact; difficult to decide —**nice'ly** *adv.* —**ni'cety** [-si-ti] *n.* minute distinction or detail; subtlety; precision

niche [nich, nēsh] *n.* recess in wall; suitable place in life, public estimation *etc.*

nick *vt.* make notch in, indent —*n.* notch; exact point of time

nick'el *n.* silver-white metal much used in alloys and plating; five cent piece

nickelo'deon *n. Hist.* cheap cinema; jukebox

nick'name *n.* familiar name added to or replacing an ordinary name

nic'otine [-ēn] *n.* poisonous oily liquid in tobacco —**nic'otinism** *n.* tobacco poisoning

niece *n.* brother's or sister's daughter

nif'ty *inf. a.* neat, smart; quick

nigg'ard *n.* mean, stingy person —**nig'-gardly** *a./adv.*

nigg'er *n. offens.* Negro

nig'gle *vi.* find fault continually; annoy —**nig'gling** *a.* petty; irritating and persistent

nigh [nī] *a./adv./prep. Obs. or poet.* near

night [nīt] *n.* time of darkness between sunset and sunrise; end of daylight; dark —**night'ie, night'y** *n.* woman's nightdress —**night'ly** *a.* happening, done every night; of the night —*adv.* every night; by night —**night'cap** *n.* cap worn in bed; late-night (alcoholic) drink —**night'club** *n.* establishment for dancing, music *etc.* opening late at night —**night'dress** *n.* woman's loose robe worn in bed —**night'ingale** [-ng-g-] *n.* small bird which sings *usu.* at night —**night'mare** *n.* very bad dream; terrifying experience —**night'shade** *n.* various plants of potato family, some of them with very poisonous berries —**night-time** *n.*

ni'hilism [nī'il-] *n.* rejection of all religious and moral principles; opposition to all constituted authority, or government —**ni'hilist** *n.* —**nihilist'ic** *a.*

nil *n.* nothing, zero

nim'ble *a.* agile, active, quick, dexterous —**nim'bly** *adv.*

nim'bus *n.* rain or storm cloud; cloud of glory, halo (*pl.* **-bi** [-bī], **-buses**)

nin'compoop *n.* fool, simpleton

nine *a./n.* cardinal number next above eight —**ninth** [-ī-] *a.* —**ninth'ly** *adv.* —**nine'teen'** *a./n.* nine more than ten —**nine'teenth'** *a.* —**nine'ty** *a./n.* nine tens —**nine'tieth** *a.* —**nine'pins** *pl.n.* game where wooden pins are set up to be knocked down by rolling ball, skittles

ninn'y *n.* fool, simpleton

nip *vt.* pinch sharply; detach by pinching, bite; check growth (of plants) thus; *sl.* steal —*vi. inf.* hurry (**-pp-**) —*n.* pinch; check to growth; sharp coldness of weather; short drink —**nipp'er** *n.* thing (*eg* crab's claw) that nips; **UK** *inf.* small child —*pl.* pincers —**nipp'y** *a. inf.* cold —**nip and tuck** even or level in race or competition

nip'ple *n.* point of a breast, teat; anything like this

Nipp'on *n.* Japan

nirvan'a [-vahn'ə] *n. Buddhism* absolute blessedness; *Hinduism* merging of individual in supreme spirit

ni'si *a.* (of decree) coming into effect within a certain time, unless cause is shown for rescinding it (*esp.* in divorce cases)

nit *n.* egg of louse or other parasite; *inf. short for* nitwit —**nit-picking** *a. inf.* overconcerned with detail, *esp.* to find fault —**nit'wit** *n. inf.* fool —**nitty-gritty** *n. inf.* basic facts, details

ni'trogen *n.* one of the gases making up the air —**ni'trate** *n.* compound of nitric acid and an alkali —**ni'tric, ni'trous** *a.* —**nitrog'enous** [-j-] *a.* of, containing nitrogen —**nitrogly'cerin(e)** [-s-] *n.* explosive liquid

nix *n. sl.* nothing —*adv.* no —*vt.* veto

NNE north-northeast

NNW north-northwest

no *a.* not any, not a; not at all —*adv.* expresses negative reply to question or request —*n.* refusal; denial; negative vote or voter (*pl.* **noes**) —**no-one, no one** nobody —**no-man's-land** waste or unclaimed land; contested land between two opposing forces

no. number

nob *sl. n.* member of upper classes; the head

nob'ble *sl. vt.* disable (*esp.* racehorse with drugs); secure dishonestly; catch criminal; cheat, swindle

nobe'lium *n.* synthetic element produced from curium

No'bel Prize prize awarded annually since 1901 for outstanding achievement in various fields

no'ble *a.* of the nobility; showing, having high moral qualities; impressive, excellent —*n.* member of the nobility —**nobil'ity** *n.* class holding special rank, usu. hereditary, in state; being noble —**no'bleman** *n.* —**no'bly** *adv.*

no'body *n.* no person; person of no importance

noctur'nal *a.* of, in, by, night; active by night

noc'turne *n.* dreamy piece of music; night scene

nod *v.* bow head slightly and quickly in assent, command *etc.*; let head droop with sleep (**-dd-**) —*n.* act of nodding —**nodding acquaintance** slight knowledge of person or subject —**nod off** *inf.* fall asleep

nod'dle *n. inf.* the head

nodd'y *n.* a fool

node *n.* knot or knob; point at which curve crosses itself —**no'dal** *a.* —**nod'ical** *a.*

nod'ule *n.* little knot; rounded irregular mineral mass

Noel', Nowel(l)' [nō-el'] *n.* Christmas; Christmas carol

nog *n.* peg or block; stump —**nogg'ing** *n.* horizontal timber member in framed construction

nogg'in *n.* small amount of liquor; small mug; *inf.* head

noise *n.* any sound, *esp.* disturbing one; clamour, din; loud outcry; talk or interest —*vt.* rumour —**noise'less** *a.* without noise, quiet, silent —**nois'ily** *adv.* —**nois'y** *a.* making much noise; clamorous

noi'some *a.* disgusting

no'mad *n.* member of tribe with no fixed dwelling place; wanderer —**nomad'ic** *a.*

nom de plume *Fr.* writer's assumed name; pen name; pseudonym

nomen'clature *n.* terminology of particular science *etc.*

nom'inal *a.* in name only; (of fee *etc.*) small, insignificant; of a name or names —**nom'inally** *adv.* in name only; not really

nom'inate *vt.* propose as candidate; appoint to office —**nomina'tion** *n.* —**nom'inative** *a./n.* (of) case of nouns, pronouns when subject of verb —**nom'inator** *n.* —**nominee'** *n.* candidate

non- (*comb. form*) negatives the idea of the simple word, as in list below

nonagena'rian [nōn-] *a.* aged between ninety and ninety-nine —*n.* person of such age

non'agon *n.* plane figure of nine sides

nonaligned' *a.* (of states *etc.*) not part of a major alliance or power bloc

nonce *n.* —**for the nonce** for the occasion only; for the present

non'chalant [-sh-] *a.* casually unconcerned, indifferent, cool —**non'chalance** *n.* —**non'chalantly** *adv.*

noncom'batant *n.* civilian during war; member of army who does not fight *eg* doctor

noncommiss'ioned off'icer *Mil.* subordinate officer, risen from the ranks

nonaggress'ion
nonalcohol'ic
nonbeliev'er
nonbreak'able
noncombust'ible
noncompet'itive
nonconduc'tive
noncontrib'utory
noncontrover'sial
nondenomina'tional
nondrink'er
nonevent'
nonexist'ent
nonfic'tion
noninterven'tion
noni'ron
nonmem'ber
non-nego'tiable

noncommitt'al *a.* avoiding definite preference or pledge

non com'pos men'tis *Lat.* of unsound mind

nonconform'ist *n.* dissenter, *esp.* from Established Church —**nonconform'ity** *n.*

non'descript *a.* lacking distinctive characteristics, indeterminate

none [nun] *pron.* no-one, not any —*a.* no —*adv.* in no way —**nonetheless'** *adv.* despite that, however

nonen'tity *n.* insignificant person, thing; nonexistent thing

nonflamm'able *a.* incapable of burning; not easily set on fire

non'pareil [-rəl] *a.* unequalled, matchless —*n.* person or thing unequalled or unrivalled

nonplus' *vt.* disconcert, confound, or bewilder completely (**-ss-**)

non'sense *n.* lack of sense; absurd language; absurdity; silly conduct —**nonsen'sical** *a.* ridiculous; meaningless; without sense

non se'quitur [-sek'wit-] *Lat.* statement with little or no relation to what preceded it

noo'dle[1] *n.* strip of pasta served in soup *etc.*

noo'dle[2] *n.* simpleton, fool; *sl.* head

nook *n.* sheltered corner, retreat —**nook'y** *a.*

noon [-ōō-] *n.* midday, twelve o'clock —**noon'day** *n.* noon —**noon'tide** *n.* the time about noon

noose [-ōō-] *n.* running loop; snare —*vt.* catch, ensnare in noose, lasso

nor *conj.* and not

Nor'dic *a.* pert. to peoples of Germanic stock

norm *n.* average level of achievement; rule or authoritative standard; model; standard type or pattern —**nor'mal** *a.* ordinary; usual; conforming to type —*n.* *Geom.* perpendicular —**normal'ity** *n.* —**nor'mally** *adv.*

north [-th] *n.* direction to the right of person facing the sunset; part of the world, of country *etc.* towards this point —*adv.* towards or in the north —*a.* to, from, or in the north —**nor'therly** [-TH-] *a.* —*n.* wind from the north —**nor'thern** *a.* —**nor'therner** *n.* person from the north —**north'wards** *adv.*

nos. numbers

nose *n.* organ of smell, used also in breathing; any projection resembling a nose, as prow of ship, aircraft *etc.* —*v.* (cause to) move forward slowly and carefully —*vt.* touch with nose; smell, sniff —*vi.* smell; pry —**no's(e)y** *a. inf.* inquisitive —**nose dive** downward sweep of aircraft —**nose'gay** *n.* bunch of flowers

nosh *sl. n.* food —*v.* eat

nostal'gia [-j-] *n.* longing for return of past events; homesickness —**nostal'gic** *a.*

nos'tril *n.* one of the two external openings of the nose

nos'trum *n.* quack medicine; secret remedy

not *adv.* expressing negation, refusal, denial

no'ta be'ne [-ni] *Lat.* note well

no'table *a.* worthy of note, remarkable —*n.* person of distinction —**notabil'ity** *n.* an eminent person —**no'tably** *adv.*

no'tary *n.* person authorized to draw up deeds, contracts

nota'tion *n.* representation of numbers, quantities, by symbols; set of such symbols; footnote, memorandum

notch *n.* V-shaped cut or indentation; narrow pass or gorge; *inf.* step, grade —*vt.* make notches in

note *n.* brief comment or record; short letter; banknote; symbol for musical sound; single tone; sign; indication, hint; fame; notice; regard —*pl.* brief jottings written down for future reference —*vt.* observe, record; heed —**no'ted** *a.* well-known —**note'book** *n.* small book with blank pages for writing —**note'worthy** *a.* worth noting, remarkable

noth'ing [nuth'-] *n.* no thing, not any-

nonpart'y
nonpay'ment
non-profit-making
nonread'er
nonres'ident
nonreturn'able
nonselec'tive
nonshrink'able
nonslip'
nonsmo'ker
nonstan'dard
nonstart'er
nonstick'
nonstop'
nontax'able
nontech'nical
nontox'ic
nonvi'olent

thing, nought —*adv.* not at all, in no way —**noth'ingness** *n.*

no'tice [-tis] *n.* observation; attention, consideration; warning, intimation, announcement; advance notification of intention to end a contract *etc.*, as of employment; review —*vt.* observe, mention; give attention to —**no'ticeable** *a.* conspicuous; attracting attention; appreciable

no'tify *vt.* report; give notice of or to (**-fied, -fying**) —**notifi'able** *a.* —**notifica'tion** *n.*

no'tion *n.* concept; opinion; whim —*pl.* pins, needles, thread *etc.* —**no'tional** *a.* speculative, imaginary, abstract

notor'ious *a.* known for something bad; well-known —**notori'ety** *n.* discreditable publicity

notwithstand'ing *prep.* in spite of —*adv.* all the same —*conj.* although

nou'gat [noo'gah, nug'ət] *n.* chewy sweet containing nuts, fruit *etc.*

nought [nawt] *n.* nothing; cipher 0

noun [nown] *n.* word used as name of person, idea, or thing, substantive

nour'ish [nu'-] *vt.* feed; nurture; tend; encourage —**nour'ishment** *n.*

nous [nows] *n.* mind, intellect; common sense

Nov. November

no'va *n.* star that suddenly becomes brighter then loses brightness through months or years (*pl.* **-vae** [-vē], **-vas**)

nov'el[1] *n.* fictitious tale in book form —**novelette'** *n.* short novel —**nov'elist** *n.* writer of novels

nov'el[2] *a.* new, recent; strange —**nov'elty** *n.* newness; something new or unusual; small ornament, trinket

Novem'ber *n.* the eleventh month

nove'na [nō-vē'-] *n.* *R.C. Church* prayers, services, lasting nine consecutive days

nov'ice *n.* one new to anything; beginner; candidate for admission to religious order —**novi'tiate, novi'ciate** [-vish'-] *n.* probationary period; part of religious house for novices; novice

now *adv.* at the present time; immediately; recently (*oft. with* just) —*conj.* seeing that, since —**now'adays** *adv.* in these times, at present

now'el *n.* inner part of large mould used for castings

Nowel(l)' *n. see* NOEL

no'where *adv.* not in any place or state

no'wise *adv.* not in any manner or degree

nox'ious [-k'shəs] *a.* poisonous, harmful

noz'zle *n.* pointed spout, *esp.* at end of hose

N.S. Nova Scotia

NST Newfoundland Standard Time

NT New Testament

nuance' [nyoo-ahns', nyoo'-] *n.* delicate shade of difference, in colour, tone of voice *etc.*

nub *n.* small lump; main point (of story *etc.*) —**nubb'in** *n.* something small and undeveloped, *esp.* ear of corn or fruit

nu'bile *a.* marriageable

nu'cleus *n.* centre, kernel; beginning meant to receive additions; core of the atom (*pl.* **-lei** [-li-ī]) —**nu'clear** [-i-ər] *a.* of, pert. to atomic nucleus —**nucleon'ics** *pl.n.* (*with sing. v.*) branch of physics dealing with applications of nuclear energy —**nuclear energy** energy released by nuclear fission —**nuclear fission** disintegration of the atom —**nuclear reaction** change in structure and energy content of atomic nucleus by interaction with another nucleus, particle —**nuclear reactor** *see* REACTOR —**nuclear winter** period of extremely low temperatures and little light after nuclear war

nude [nyood] *n.* state of being naked; (picture, statue *etc.* of) naked person —*a.* naked —**nu'dism** *n.* practice of nudity —**nu'dist** *n.* —**nu'dity** *n.*

nudge *vt.* touch slightly with elbow —*n.* such touch

nu'gatory *a.* trifling, futile

nugg'et *n.* rough lump of native gold

nui'sance [nyoo'-] *n.* something or someone harmful, offensive, annoying or disagreeable

nuke [nyook] *vt. sl.* attack or destroy with nuclear weapons

null *a.* of no effect, void —**null'ify** *vt.* cancel; make useless or ineffective (**-fied, -fying**) —**null'ity** *n.* state of being null and void

Num. Numbers

numb [num] *a.* deprived of feeling, *esp.* by cold —*vt.* make numb; deaden

num'ber *n.* sum or aggregate; word or symbol saying how many; single issue of a paper *etc.*, issued in regular series; classification as to singular or plural; song, piece of music; performance; company, collection; identifying number, as of particular house, telephone *etc.*; *sl.* measure, correct estimation of —*vt.* count; class, reckon; give a number to; amount to —**num'berless** *a.* countless —**number crunching** *Computers* large-scale processing of numerical data

nu'meral *n.* sign or word denoting a number —**nu'merate** *a.* able to use numbers in calculations —*vt.* count —**numera'tion** *n.* —**nu'merator** *n.* top part of fraction, figure showing how many of the fractional units are taken —**numer'ical** *a.* of, in respect of, number or numbers —**nu'merous** *a.* many

numismat'ic [nyoo-miz-] *a.* of coins —**numismat'ics** *pl.n.* (*with sing. v.*) the study of coins —**numis'matist** *n.*

num'skull *n.* dolt, dunce

nun *n.* woman living (in convent) under religious vows —**nunn'ery** *n.* convent of nuns

nunn'y bag small sealskin haversack

nup'tial *a.* of, relating to marriage —**nup'tials** *pl.n.* marriage; wedding ceremony

nurse *n.* person trained for care of sick or injured; woman tending another's child —*vt.* act as nurse to; suckle; pay special attention to; harbour (grudge *etc.*) —**nur'sery** *n.* room for children; rearing place for plants —**nur'seryman** *n.* one who raises plants for sale —**nursery slope** gentle slope for beginners in skiing

nur'ture *n.* bringing up; education; rearing; nourishment —*vt.* bring up; educate

nut *n.* fruit consisting of hard shell and kernel; hollow metal collar into which a screw fits; *inf.* head; *inf.* eccentric or crazy person (*also* **nutt'er**) —*vi.* gather nuts (**-tt-**) —**nutt'y** *a.* of, like nut; pleasant to taste and bite; *sl.* insane, crazy (*also* **nuts**) —**nut'hatch** *n.* small songbird —**nut'meg** *n.* aromatic seed of Indian tree

nu'tria *n.* fur of coypu

nu'trient *a.* nourishing —*n.* something nutritious

nu'triment *n.* nourishing food —**nutri'tion** [-trish'-] *n.* receiving foods; act of nourishing —**nutri'tious, nu'tritive** *a.* nourishing; promoting growth

nux vom'ica *n.* seed of tree which yields strychnine

nuz'zle *vi.* burrow, press with nose; nestle

NW northwest(ern)

N.W.T. Northwest Territories

ny'lon *n.* synthetic material used for fabrics, bristles, ropes *etc.* —*pl.* stockings made of this

nymph *n.* legendary semidivine maiden of sea, woods, mountains *etc.*

nymph'et *n.* sexually precocious young girl

nymphoma'nia *n.* abnormally intense sexual desire in women

NZ New Zealand

O

O *Chem.* oxygen
oaf *n.* lout; dolt
oak *n.* common, deciduous forest tree —**oak'en** *a.* of oak —**oak apple** round gall on oak trees
oak'um *n.* loose fibre got by unravelling old rope
oar *n.* wooden lever with broad blade worked by the hands to propel boat; oarsman —*v.* row —**oar'lock** *n.* appliance on gunwale of boat serving as point of leverage for oar —**oars'man** *n.* —**oars'manship** *n.* skill in rowing
oa'sis [ō-ā'-] *n.* fertile spot in desert (*pl.* **oa'ses** [-sēz])
oast *n.* kiln for drying hops
oat *n.* (*usu. pl.*) grain of cereal plant; the plant —**oat'en** *a.* —**oat'meal** *n.*
oath *n.* confirmation of truth of statement by naming something sacred; curse
ob'durate *a.* stubborn, unyielding —**ob'duracy** *n.*
OBE Officer of the Order of the British Empire
obe'dience *n.* submission to authority —**obe'dient** *a.* willing to obey; compliant; dutiful —**obe'diently** *adv.*
obeis'ance [-bās'-, -bēs'-] *n.* a bow or curtsey
ob'elisk *n.* tapering rectangular stone column, with pyramidal apex
obese' *a.* very fat, corpulent —**obe'sity** *n.*
obey' [-bā'] *vt.* do the bidding of; act in accordance with —*vi.* do as ordered; submit to authority
ob'fuscate *vt.* perplex; darken
obit'uary *n.* notice, record of death; biographical sketch of deceased person, *esp.* in newspaper (*also inf.* **ob'it**) —**obi'tuarist** *n.*
obj. object; objective
ob'ject[1] *n.* material thing; that to which feeling or action is directed; end or aim; *Grammar* word dependent on verb or preposition —**object lesson** lesson with practical and concrete illustration —**no object** not an obstacle or hindrance
object'[2] *vt.* state in opposition —*vi.* feel dislike or reluctance to something —**objec'tion** *n.* —**objec'tionable** *a.* disagreeable; justly liable to objection —**objec'tor** *n.*
objec'tive *a.* external to the mind; impartial —*n.* thing or place aimed at —**objectiv'ity** *n.*
objure' *vt.* charge under oath —**objura'tion** *n.*
ob'jurgate *vt.* scold, reprove —**objurga'tion** *n.*
ob'late *a.* of a sphere, flattened at the poles
obla'tion *n.* offering —**ob'late** *n.* person dedicated to religious work —**obla'tional** *a.*
ob(b)liga'to [-ah'-] *n.* an essential part of a musical score (*pl.* **-tos**)
oblige' *vt.* bind morally or legally to do service to; compel —**ob'ligate** *vt.* bind *esp.* by legal contract; put under obligation —**obliga'tion** *n.* binding duty, promise; debt of gratitude —**oblig'atory** *a.* required; binding —**obli'ging** *a.* ready to serve others, civil, helpful, courteous
oblique' [-lēk'] *a.* slanting; indirect —**oblique'ly** *adv.* —**obliq'uity** [-lik'wit-i] *n.* slant; dishonesty —**oblique angle** one not a right angle
oblit'erate *vt.* blot out, efface, destroy completely —**oblitera'tion** *n.*
obliv'ion *n.* forgetting or being forgotten —**obliv'ious** *a.* forgetful; unaware
ob'long *a.* rectangular, with adjacent sides unequal —*n.* oblong figure
ob'loquy [-kwi] *n.* reproach, abuse; disgrace; detraction
obnox'ious [-nok'shəs] *a.* offensive, disliked, odious
o'boe [-bō] *n.* woodwind instrument, hautboy —**o'boist** *n.*
obscene' *a.* indecent, lewd, repulsive —**obscen'ity** *n.*
obscure' *a.* unclear, indistinct; unex-

plained; dark, dim; humble *—vt.* make unintelligible; dim; conceal **—obscu'rant** *n.* one who opposes enlightenment or reform **—obscurant'ism** *n.* **—obscu'rity** *n.* indistinctness; lack of intelligibility; darkness; obscure, *esp.* unrecognized, place or position; retirement

ob'secrate *vt.* beseech

ob'sequies [-iz] *pl.n.* funeral rites **—obse'quial** *a.*

obse'quious *a.* servile, fawning

observe' [-z-] *vt.* notice, remark; watch; note systematically; keep, follow *—vi.* make a remark **—observ'able** *a.* **—observ'ably** *adv.* **—observ'ance** *n.* paying attention; keeping **—observ'ant** *a.* quick to notice **—observa'tion** *n.* action, habit of observing; noticing; remark **—observ'atory** *n.* place for watching stars *etc.* **—observ'er** *n.*

obsess' *vt.* haunt, fill the mind **—obses'sion** *n.* fixed idea; domination of the mind by one idea **—obsess'ive** *a.*

obsid'ian *n.* fused volcanic rock, forming hard, dark, natural glass

ob'solete *a.* disused, out of date **—obsoles'cent** [-ənt] *a.* going out of use

ob'stacle *n.* hindrance; impediment, barrier, obstruction

obstet'rics *pl.n.* (*with sing. v.*) branch of medicine concerned with childbirth and care of women before and after childbirth **—obstet'ric** *a.* **—obstetri'cian** *n.*

ob'stinate *a.* stubborn; self-willed; unyielding; hard to overcome or cure **—ob'stinacy** *n.* **—ob'stinately** *adv.*

obstrep'erous *a.* unruly, noisy, boisterous

obstruct' *vt.* block up; hinder; impede **—obstruc'tion** *n.* **—obstruc'tionist** *n.* one who deliberately opposes transaction of business **—obstruc'tive** *a.*

obtain' *vt.* get; acquire; procure by effort *—vi.* be customary **—obtain'able** *a.* procurable

obtrude' *vt.* thrust forward unduly **—obtru'sion** *n.* **—obtru'sive** *a.* forward, pushing **—obtru'sively** *adv.*

obtuse' [-tyo͞os'] *a.* dull of perception; stupid; greater than right angle; not pointed **—obtuse'ly** *adv.*

ob'verse *n.* a fact, idea *etc.* which is the complement of another; side of coin, medal *etc.* that has the principal design *—a.*

ob'viate *vt.* remove, make unnecessary

ob'vious *a.* clear, evident; wanting in subtlety

ocari'na [-rē'-] *n.* small, egg-shaped wind instrument made of terracotta

occa'sion *n.* time when thing happens; reason, need; opportunity; special event *—vt.* cause **—occa'sional** *a.* happening, found now and then; produced for some special event, as *occasional music* **—occa'sionally** *adv.* sometimes, now and then

Oc'cident [ok'si-] *n.* the West **—Occiden'tal** *a.*

oc'ciput [ok'si-] *n.* back of head **—occip'ital** *a.*

occlude' [-klo͞od'] *vt.* shut in or out **—occlu'sion** *n.* **—occlu'sive** *a.* serving to occlude

occult' *a.* secret, mysterious; supernatural *—n.* esoteric knowledge *—vt.* hide from view **—occulta'tion** *n.* eclipse **—oc'cultism** *n.* study of supernatural **—occult'ness** *n.* mystery

occ'upy *vt.* inhabit, fill; employ; take possession of (**-pied, -pying**) **—oc'cupancy** *n.* fact of occupying; residing **—occ'upant** *n.* **—occupa'tion** *n.* employment; pursuit; fact of occupying; seizure **—occupa'tional** *a.* pert. to occupation, *esp.* of diseases arising from a particular occupation; pert. to use of occupations, *eg* craft, hobbies *etc.* as means of rehabilitation **—occ'upier** *n.* tenant

occur' *vi.* happen; come to mind (**-rr-**) **—occurr'ence** *n.* happening

o'cean [ō'shən] *n.* great body of water; large division of this; the sea **—ocean'ic** [ō-shi-, ō-si-] *a.* **—oceanol'ogy** *n.* branch of science which relates to ocean

o'celot [ō'si-, os'i-] *n.* Amer. leopard

o'chre [ō'kər] *n.* various earths used as yellow or brown pigments **—o'chr(e)ous** *a.*

o'clock' *adv.* by the clock

oct-, octa-, octo- (*comb. form*) eight

oc'tagon *n.* plane figure with eight angles **—octag'onal** *a.*

octahe'dron *n.* solid figure with eight sides

oc'tane *n.* ingredient of motor fuel **—octane rating** measure of quality or type of gasoline

oc'tant *n.* the eighth part of a circle; instrument for measuring angles having arc of 45°

oc'tave *n. Mus.* eighth note above or below given note; this space; eight lines of verse

octa'vo *n.* book in which each sheet is folded three times forming eight leaves (*pl.* **-vos**)

octenn'ial *a.* lasting, happening every eight years

octet' *n.* group of eight; music for eight instruments or singers

Octo'ber *n.* the tenth month (Roman eighth)

octogena'rian *n.* person aged between eighty and ninety *—a.*

oc'topus *n.* mollusc with eight arms covered with suckers **—oc'topod** *n./a.* (mollusc) with eight feet

oc'tosyllable *n.* word, line of verse of eight syllables

oc'ular *a.* of eye or sight **—oc'ularly** *adv.*

OD *Med.* overdose

odd *a.* strange, queer; incidental, random; that is one in addition when the rest have been divided into equal groups; not even; not part of a set **—odds** *pl.n.* advantage conceded in betting; likelihood **—odd'ity** *n.* odd person or thing; quality of being odd **—odd'ments** *pl.n.* remnants; trifles **—odds and ends** odd fragments or scraps

ode *n.* lyric poem on particular subject

o'dium *n.* hatred, widespread dislike **—o'dious** *a.* hateful, repulsive, obnoxious

odom'eter *n.* device that records distance vehicle has travelled

odontol'ogy *n.* science of dentistry

o'do(u)r *n.* smell **—odorif'erous** *a.* spreading an odour **—o'dorize** *vt.* fill with scent **—o'dorous** *a.* fragrant; scented **—o'do(u)rless** *a.*

Od'yssey *n.* Homer's epic describing Odysseus' return from Troy; any long adventurous journey

OECD Organization for Economic Cooperation and Development

oesoph'agus [ē-] *n. see* ESOPHAGUS

of *prep.* denotes removal, separation, ownership, attribute, material, quality

off *adv.* away *—prep.* away from *—a.* not operative; cancelled or postponed; bad, sour *etc.*; distant; of horses, vehicles *etc.*, right **—off'ing** *n.* part of sea visible to observer on ship or shore **—off colour** slightly ill **—offhand'** *a./adv.* without previous thought; curt **—off-licence** *n.* **UK** place where alcoholic drinks are sold for consumption elsewhere **—off'set** *n.* that which counterbalances, compensates; method of printing **—offset'** *vt.* **—off'spring** *n.* children, issue **—in the offing** likely to happen soon

off. office; officer; official

off'al *n.* edible entrails of animal; refuse

offend' *vt.* hurt feelings of, displease *—vi.* do wrong **—offence'**, *esp.* **US o'ffense** *n.* wrong; crime; insult; *Sport* [o'-] attacking team, players, play **—offend'er** *n.* **—offen'sive** *a.* causing displeasure; aggressive *—n.* position or movement of attack

off'er *vt.* present for acceptance or refusal; tender; propose; attempt *—vi.* present itself *—n.* offering, bid **—off'erer** *n.* **—off'ertory** *n.* offering of the bread and wine at the Eucharist; collection in church service

off'ice *n.* room(s), building, in which business, clerical work *etc.* is done; commercial or professional organization; official position; service; duty; form of worship *—pl.* task; service **—off'icer** *n.* one in command in army, navy, ship *etc.*; official

offic'ial [-fish'-] *a.* with, by, authority *—n.* one holding office, *esp.* in public body **—offic'ialdom** *n.* officials collectively, or their attitudes, work, usu. in contemptuous sense

offic'iate [-fish'-] *vi.* perform duties of office; perform ceremony

offic'ious [-fish'əs] *a.* importunate in offering service; interfering

offside' *a./adv. Sport* illegally forward

of'ten [of'n] *adv.* many times, frequently (*Poet.* **oft**)

o'gee arch pointed arch with S-shaped curve on both sides

o'gle *v.* stare, look (at) amorously *—n.* this look **—o'gler** *n.*

o'gre [-gər] *n. Folklore* man-eating giant; monster (**o'gress** *fem.*)

oh [ō] *interj.* exclamation of surprise, pain *etc.*

ohm *n.* unit of electrical resistance **—ohm'meter** *n.* **—ohm'ic** *a.*

OHMS On His (*or* Her) Majesty's Service

oil *n.* any of a number of viscous liquids with smooth, sticky feel and wide variety of uses; petroleum; any of variety of petroleum derivatives, *esp.* as fuel or lubricant —*vt.* lubricate with oil; apply oil to —**oil'y** *a.* —**oil'skin** *n.* cloth treated with oil to make it waterproof

oint'ment *n.* greasy preparation for healing or beautifying the skin

o.k., okay' *inf. a./adv.* all right —*n.* approval —*vt.* approve

okap'i [-kahp'-] *n.* Afr. animal like short-necked giraffe

o'kra [ō'krə] *n.* tropical plant of mallow family bearing edible sticky green pods; pod of this plant eaten in soups *etc.*, gumbo

old [ōld] *a.* aged, having lived or existed long; belonging to earlier period (**old'er, eld'er** *comp.*, **old'est, eld'est** *sup.*) —**old'en** *a.* old —**old'ish** *a.* —**old-fashioned** *a.* in style of earlier period, out of date; fond of old ways —**old-line** *a.* conservative; traditional —**old maid** elderly spinster

oleag'inous [ō-lē-aj'-] *a.* oily, producing oil; unctuous, fawning —**oleag'inousness** *n.*

olean'der [ō-lē-an'-] *n.* evergreen flowering shrub, poisonous, *esp.* to cattle

oleas'ter [ō-lē-as'-] *n.* wild olive; yellow-flowered shrubs like it

olfac'tory *a.* of smelling

ol'igarchy [-ki] *n.* government by a few —**ol'igarch** *n.* —**oligarch'ic** *a.*

ol'ive [-iv] *n.* evergreen tree; its oil-yielding fruit; its wood —*a.* greyish-green

Olym'piad *n.* four-year period between Olympic Games

OM Order of Merit

om'budsman [-boodz-] *n.* official who investigates citizens' complaints against government *etc.*

o'mega [ō'-] *n.* last letter of Greek alphabet; end

om'elet(te) *n.* dish of eggs beaten up and fried with seasoning

o'men *n.* prophetic object or happening —**om'inous** *a.* boding evil, threatening

omit' *vt.* leave out, neglect; leave undone (**-tt-**) —**omiss'ion** *n.* —**omiss'ive** *a.*

OMM Officer of the Order of Military Merit

omni- (*comb. form*) all

om'nibus *n.* large road vehicle travelling on set route and taking passengers at any stage (*also* **bus**); book containing several works —*a.* serving, containing several objects

omnidirec'tional *a.* in radio, denotes transmission, reception in all directions

omnip'otent *a.* all-powerful —**omnip'otence** *n.*

omnipres'ent *a.* present everywhere —**omnipres'ence** *n.*

omnis'cient [-nis'i-ənt] *a.* knowing everything —**omnis'cience** *n.*

omniv'orous *a.* devouring all foods; not fastidious

on *prep.* above and touching, at, near, towards *etc.*; attached to; concerning; performed upon; during; taking regularly —*a.* operating; taking place —*adv.* so as to be on; forwards; continuously *etc.*; in progress

on- (*comb. form*) on, as **on'looker**

o'nanism *n.* masturbation

once [wuns] *adv.* one time; formerly; ever —**once-over** *n. inf.* quick examination —**at once** immediately; simultaneously

on'cogene [ong'kō-jēn] *n.* any of several genes that when abnormally activated can cause cancer

one [wun] *a.* lowest cardinal number; single; united; only, without others; identical —*n.* number or figure 1; unity; single specimen —*pron.* particular but not stated person; any person —**one'ness** *n.* unity; uniformity; singleness —**oneself'** *pron.* —**one-sided** *a.* partial; uneven —**one-way** *a.* denotes system of traffic circulation in one direction only; denoting ticket for train *etc.* valid for outward journey only

on'erous *a.* burdensome

on'ion [un'yən] *n.* edible bulb of pungent flavour

on'ly [ō-] *a.* being the one specimen —*adv.* solely, merely, exclusively —*conj.* but then, excepting that

onomas'tics *pl.n.* study of proper names

onomatopoe'ia [-pē'ə] *n.* formation of a word by using sounds that resemble or suggest the object or action to be named

—**onomatopoe'ic, onomatopoet'ic** [-pō-et'-] *a.*

on'set *n.* violent attack; assault; beginning

on'slaught [-slawt] *n.* attack

Ont. Ontario

on'to *prep.* on top of; aware of

ontol'ogy *n.* science of being or reality —**ontolog'ical** *a.* —**ontol'ogist** *n.*

o'nus *n.* responsibility, burden

on'ward *a.* advanced or advancing —*adv.* in advance, ahead, forward —**on'wards** *adv.*

on'yx [on'iks] *n.* variety of chalcedony

Ook'pik R sealskin doll resembling owl

ool'ogy [ō-ol'-] *n.* study of eggs, and of birds during the nesting season

ooze *vi.* pass slowly out, exude (moisture) —*n.* sluggish flow; wet mud, slime —**ooz'y** *a.*

op. opera; operation; opus

o'pal *n.* glassy gemstone displaying variegated colours —**opales'cent** *a.*

opaque' [ō-pāk'] *a.* not allowing the passage of light, not transparent —**opac'ity** [-pas'-] *n.*

op. cit. (*Lat.* opere citato) in the work cited

OPEC Organization of Petroleum Exporting Countries

o'pen *a.* not shut or blocked up; without lid or door; bare; undisguised; not enclosed, covered or exclusive; spread out, accessible; frank, sincere —*vt.* set open, uncover, give access to; disclose, lay bare; begin; make a hole in —*vi.* become open; begin —*n.* clear space, unenclosed country; *Sport* competition in which all may enter —**o'pening** *n.* hole, gap; beginning; opportunity —*a.* first; initial —**o'penly** *adv.* without concealment —**o'pencast** *a.* of coal, mined from the surface, not underground —**open-handed** *a.* generous —**open-hearted** *a.* frank, magnanimous —**open-minded** *a.* unprejudiced —**open verdict** coroner's verdict not stating cause (of death) —**o'penwork** *n.* pattern with interstices

op'era *n.* musical drama —**operat'ic** *a.* of opera —**operett'a** *n.* light, comic opera

opera'tion *n.* working, way things work; scope; act of surgery; military action —**op'erate** *vt.* cause to function; effect —*vi.* work; produce an effect; perform act of surgery; exert power —**opera'tional** *a.* of operation(s); working —**op'erative** *a.* working —*n.* worker, *esp.* with a special skill —**op'erator** *n.*

oper'culum [ō-per'-] *n.* lid or cover (*pl.* **-lums, -la**)

ophid'ian [ō-fid'-] *a./n.* (reptile) of the order including snakes

ophthal'mic [of-thal'-] *a.* of eyes —**ophthalmol'ogist** *n.* —**ophthalmol'ogy** *n.* study of eye and its diseases —**ophthal'moscope** *n.* instrument for examining interior of eye —**ophthalmic optician** one qualified to prescribe spectacles *etc.*

o'piate *see* OPIUM

opin'ion *n.* what one thinks about something; belief, judgment —**opine'** *vt.* think; utter opinion —**opin'ionated** *a.* stubborn in one's opinions; dogmatic

o'pium *n.* sedative-narcotic drug made from poppy —**o'piate** *n.* drug containing opium; narcotic —*a.* inducing sleep; soothing

oposs'um *n.* small Amer. and Aust. marsupial animal

oppo'nent *n.* adversary, antagonist

opp'ortune *a.* seasonable, well-timed —**opportu'nism** *n.* policy of doing what is expedient at the time regardless of principle —**opportu'nist** *n./a.* —**opportu'nity** *n.* favourable time or condition; good chance

oppose' [-z] *vt.* resist, withstand; contrast; set against —**oppo'ser** *n.* —**op'posite** [-zit] *a.* contrary; facing; diametrically different; adverse —*n.* the contrary —*prep./adv.* facing; on the other side —**opposi'tion** [-ish'-] *n.* antithesis; resistance; obstruction; hostility; group opposing another; party opposing that in power

oppress' *vt.* govern with tyranny; weigh down —**oppress'ion** *n.* act of oppressing; severity; misery —**oppress'ive** *a.* tyrannical; hard to bear; heavy; hot and tiring (of weather) —**oppress'ively** *adv.* —**oppress'or** *n.*

oppro'brium *n.* disgrace —**oppro'brious** *a.* reproachful; shameful; abusive

oppugn' [ə-pyo͞on'] *vt.* call into question, dispute

op'sonin *n.* substance in blood assisting destruction of invading bacteria —**opsonic index** a standard by which the power of resistance to disease is estimated

opt *vi.* make a choice —**op'tative** *a.* expressing wish or desire —*n.* mood of verb expressing wish

opt. optical; optional

op'tic *a.* of eye or sight —*n.* eye —*pl.* (*with sing. v.*) science of sight and light —**op'tical** *a.* —**opti'cian** [-ish'-] *n.* maker of, dealer in spectacles, optical instruments

op'timism *n.* disposition to look on the bright side; doctrine that good must prevail in the end; belief that the world is the best possible world —**op'timist** *n.* —**optimis'tic** *a.* —**optimis'tically** *adv.*

op'timum *a./n.* the best, the most favourable

op'tion *n.* choice; preference; thing chosen; in business, purchased privilege of either buying or selling things at specified price within specified time —**op'tional** *a.* leaving to choice

optom'etrist *n.* person *usu.* not medically qualified, testing eyesight, prescribing corrective lenses *etc.* —**optom'etry** *n.*

op'ulent *a.* rich; copious —**op'ulence** *n.* riches, wealth

o'pus *n.* work; musical composition (*pl.* **op'era**)

or *conj.* introduces alternatives; if not

or'acle [o'rə-] *n.* divine utterance, prophecy, *oft.* ambiguous, given at shrine of god; the shrine; wise or mysterious adviser —**orac'ular** *a.* of oracle; prophetic; authoritative; ambiguous

or'al *a.* spoken; by mouth —*n.* spoken examination —**or'ally** *adv.*

or'ange [o'rinj] *n.* bright reddish-yellow round fruit; tree bearing it; fruit's colour

orang-outang', orang-utan' *n.* large E. Indian ape

or'ator [o'rə-] *n.* maker of speech; skilful speaker —**ora'tion** *n.* formal speech —**orator'ical** *a.* of orator or oration —**or'atory** *n.* speeches; eloquence; small private chapel

orator'io *n.* semi-dramatic composition of sacred music (*pl.* **-rios**)

orb *n.* globe, sphere —**orbic'ular** *a.*

orb'it *n.* track of planet, satellite, comet *etc.*, around another heavenly body; field of influence, sphere; eye socket —*v.* move in, or put into, an orbit

orch'ard *n.* area for cultivation of fruit trees; the trees

or'chestra [-k-] *n.* band of musicians; place for such band in theatre *etc.*; main floor of theatre —**orches'tral** *a.* —**or'chestrate** *vt.* compose or arrange music for orchestra; organize, arrange —**orchestra'tion** *n.*

or'chid, or'chis [-k-] *n.* genus of various flowering plants

ordain' *vt.* admit to Christian ministry; confer holy orders upon; decree, enact; destine —**ordina'tion** *n.*

ordeal' *n.* severe, trying experience; *Hist.* form of trial by which accused underwent severe physical test

or'der *n.* regular or proper arrangement or condition; sequence; peaceful condition of society; rank, class; group; command; request for something to be supplied; mode of procedure; instruction; monastic society —*vt.* command; request (something) to be supplied or made; arrange —**or'derliness** *n.* —**or'derly** *a.* tidy; methodical; well-behaved —*n.* hospital attendant; soldier following officer to carry orders —**or'dinal** *a.* showing position in a series —*n.* ordinal number —**Order of Canada** order awarded to Canadians for outstanding achievement

or'dinance *n.* decree, rule; rite, ceremony

or'dinary *a.* usual, normal; common; plain; commonplace —*n.* bishop in his province —**or'dinarily** *adv.*

ord'nance *n.* big guns, artillery; military stores

or'dure *n.* dung; filth

ore *n.* naturally occurring mineral which yields metal

oregan'o [o-ri-gahn'ō] *n.* herb, variety of marjoram

or'gan *n.* musical wind instrument of pipes and stops, played by keys; member of animal or plant carrying out particular function; means of action; medium of information, *esp.* newspaper —**organ'ic** *a.* of, derived from, living organisms; of bodily organs; affecting bodily organs; having vital organs; *Chem.* of compounds formed from carbon; grown with fertilizers derived from animal or vegetable matter; organized, systematic —**organ'ically** *adv.* —**or'ganist** *n.* organ player

or'gandie *n.* light, transparent muslin

or'ganize *vt.* give definite structure; get up, arrange; put into working order; unite in a society —**or'ganism** *n.* organized body or system; plant, animal —**organiza'tion** *n.* act of organizing; body of people; society —**or'ganizer** *n.*

or'gasm *n.* sexual climax

or'gy [-ji] *n.* drunken or licentious revel, debauch; act of immoderation, overindulgence

or'iel *n.* projecting part of an upper room with a window; the window

or'ient *n.* (**O-**) East; lustre of best pearls —*a.* rising; (**O-**) Eastern —*vt.* place so as to face East; take bearings; determine one's position (*lit.* or *fig.*) —**orien'tal** *a./n.* —**orien'talist** *n.* expert in Eastern languages and history —**or'ientate** *vt.* orient —**orienta'tion** *n.* —**orientee'ring** *n.* competitive sport involving compass and map-reading skills

or'ifice [o'ri-] *n.* opening, mouth of a cavity, *eg* pipe

origam'i [o-ri-gahm'i] *n.* Japanese art of paper folding

or'igin [o'ri-j-] *n.* beginning; source; parentage

orig'inal [-j-] *a.* primitive, earliest; new, not copied or derived; thinking or acting for oneself; eccentric —*n.* pattern, thing from which another is copied; unconventional or strange person —**original'ity** *n.* power of producing something individual to oneself —**orig'inally** *adv.* at first; in the beginning

orig'inate *v.* come or bring into existence, begin —**origina'tion** *n.* —**orig'inator** *n.*

or'iole *n.* tropical thrushlike bird

Ori'on *n.* bright constellation

or'ison [o'ri-zən] *n.* prayer

or'molu [-lo͞o] *n.* gilded bronze; gold-coloured alloy; articles of these

or'nament *n.* any object used to adorn or decorate; decoration —*vt.* adorn —**ornamen'tal** *a.* —**ornamenta'tion** *n.*

ornate' *a.* highly decorated or elaborate

or'nery *a. inf., dial.* stubborn; treacherous

ornithol'ogy *n.* science of birds —**ornitholog'ical** *a.* —**ornithol'ogist** *n.*

orog'raphy, orol'ogy *n.* geography of mountains

or'otund [o'rō-] *a.* full, clear, and musical; pompous

or'phan *n.* child bereaved of one or both parents —**or'phanage** *n.* institution for care of orphans —**or'phanhood** *n.*

orr'ery *n.* mechanical model of solar system to show revolutions, planets *etc.*

orr'is, orr'ice *n.* kind of iris —**orris root** violet-scented perfume from root of kinds of iris

ortho- (*comb. form*) right, correct

or'thodox *a.* holding accepted views; conventional —**or'thodoxy** *n.*

orthog'raphy *n.* correct spelling

orthop(a)ed'ic [-pēd'-] *a.* for curing deformity, disorder of bones

orthop'tics *n.* the science and study of correcting ocular deviation, by exercising the eye muscles —**orthop'tist** *n.*

ort'olan *n.* a small bird, *esp.* as table delicacy

or'yx *n.* large Afr. antelope

os'cillate *vi.* swing to and fro; waver; fluctuate (regularly) —**oscilla'tion** *n.* —**os'cillator** *n.* —**os'cillatory** *a.* —**oscil'loscope** *n.* electronic instrument producing visible representation of rapidly changing quantity

o'sier [-z-] *n.* species of willow used for basketwork

os'mium [oz'-] *n.* heaviest known of metallic elements

osmo'sis [oz-] *n.* percolation of fluids through porous partitions —**osmot'ic** *a.*

os'prey *n.* fishing hawk; plume

oss'eous *a.* of, like bone; bony —**ossifica'tion** *n.* —**oss'ify** *v.* turn into bone; grow rigid (**-fied, -fying**)

osten'sible *a.* apparent; professed —**osten'sibly** *adv.*

ostenta'tion *n.* show, pretentious display —**ostenta'tious** *a.* given to display; showing off —**ostenta'tiously** *adv.*

osteop'athy *n.* art of treating disease by removing structural derangement by manipulation, *esp.* of spine —**os'teopath** *n.* one skilled in this art, bonesetter

os'tler [-sl-] *n. Hist.* stableman at an inn

os'tracize *vt.* exclude, banish from society, exile —**os'tracism** *n.* social boycotting

os'trich *n.* large swift-running flightless Afr. bird

oth'er [uTH'-] *a.* not this; not the same;

alternative, different *—pron.* other person or thing **—oth'erwise** *adv.* differently; in another way *—conj.* else, if not

o'tiose *a.* superfluous; useless

ott'er *n.* furry aquatic fish-eating animal

Ott'oman *a.* Turkish *—n.* Turk; (**o-**) cushioned, backless seat, storage box

ouananiche' [wah-nə-nēsh'] *n.* variety of Atlantic salmon found only in lakes

oubliette' *n.* dungeon entered by trapdoor

ouch *interj.* exclamation of sudden pain

ought [awt] *v. aux.* expressing duty or obligation or advisability; be bound

Oui'ja [wē'-] **R** board with letters and symbols used to obtain messages at seances

ounce *n.* a weight, sixteenth of avoirdupois pound (28.4 grams), twelfth of troy pound (31.1 grams)

our *a.* belonging to us **—ours** *pron.* **—ourself'** *pron.* myself, used in regal, or formal style **—ourselves'** *pl.pron.* emphatic or reflexive form of WE

oust *vt.* put out, expel

out *adv.* from within, away; wrong; on strike *—a.* not worth considering; not allowed; unfashionable; unconscious; not in use, operation *etc.*; at an end; not burning; *Sport* dismissed **—out'er** *a.* away from the inside **—out'ermost, out'most** *a.* on extreme outside **—out'-ing** *n.* pleasure excursion **—out'ward** *a./adv.* **—out'wardly** *adv.* **—out'wards** *adv.*

out- (*comb. form*) beyond, in excess, as **outclass'** *vt.*, **outdist'ance** *vt.*, **out'-size** *a.* Such compounds are not given here where the meaning may easily be inferred from the simple word

out'back *n.* **A** remote, sparsely populated country

outbal'ance *vt.* outweigh; exceed in weight

out'board *a.* of boat's engine, mounted on, outside stern

out'break *n.* sudden occurrence, *esp.* of disease or strife

out'burst *n.* bursting out, *esp.* of violent emotion

out'cast *n.* someone rejected *—a.*

outclass' *vt.* excel, surpass

out'come *n.* result

out'crop *n. Geology* rock coming out of stratum to the surface *—vi.* come out to the surface (**-pp-**)

outdoors' *adv.* in the open air **—out'-door** *a.*

out'fall *n.* mouth of river

out'fit *n.* equipment; clothes and accessories; *inf.* group or association regarded as a unit **—out'fitter** *n.* one who deals in outfits

outflank' *vt.* to get beyond the flank (of enemy army); circumvent

out'going *a.* departing; friendly, sociable

outgrow' *vt.* become too large or too old for; surpass in growth (**outgrew', outgrown', outgrow'ing**)

out'house *n.* outdoor toilet; shed *etc.* near main building

outland'ish *a.* queer, extravagantly strange

out'law *n.* one beyond protection of the law; exile, bandit *—vt.* make (someone) an outlaw; ban **—out'lawry** *n.*

out'lay *n.* expenditure

out'let *n.* opening, vent; means of release or escape; market for product or service

out'line *n.* rough sketch; general plan; lines enclosing visible figure *—vt.* sketch; summarize

out'look *n.* point of view; probable outcome; view

out'lying *a.* distant, remote

outmo'ded *a.* no longer fashionable or accepted

out'port *n.* isolated fishing village, *esp.* in Newfoundland

out'put *n.* quantity produced; *Computers* information produced

out'rage *n.* violation of others' rights; gross or violent offence or indignity; anger arising from this *—vt.* offend grossly; insult; injure, violate **—outra'geous** *a.*

ou'tré [o͞o'trā] *a.* extravagantly odd; bizarre

out'rigger *n.* frame, *esp.* with float attached, outside boat's gunwale; frame on rowing boat's side with rowlock; boat with one

out'right *a.* undisputed; downright; positive *—adv.* completely; once for all; openly

out'set *n.* beginning

outside' *n.* exterior; (in North) settled

parts of Canada *—adv.* not inside; in the open air *—a.* on exterior; remote, unlikely; greatest possible, probable **—outsid'er** *n.* person outside specific group; person not living in Arctic regions; contestant thought unlikely to win

out'skirts *pl.n.* outer areas, districts, *esp.* of city

outspo'ken *a.* frank, candid

outstand'ing *a.* excellent; remarkable; unsettled, unpaid

outstrip' *vt.* outrun, surpass

out-take *n.* unreleased take from recording, motion picture or television programme

outwit' *vt.* get the better of by cunning

out'work *n.* part of fortress outside main wall

ou'zel, ou'sel [ōō'-] *n.* type of thrush; kind of diving bird

o'val *a.* egg-shaped, elliptical *—n.* something of this shape

o'vary *n.* female egg-producing organ **—ova'rian** *a.*

ova'tion *n.* enthusiastic burst of applause

ov'en [uv'-] *n.* heated chamber for baking in

o'ver *adv.* above, above and beyond, going beyond, in excess, too much, past, finished, in repetition, across, downwards *etc. —prep.* above; on, upon; more than, in excess of, along *etc. —a.* upper, outer *—n. Cricket* delivery of agreed number of balls from one end (usu. 6)

over- (*comb. form*) too, too much, in excess, above, as in

overawe'	**overlap'**
overbal'ance	**o'verlord**
o'vercoat	**overpow'er**
overcrowd'	**overreact'**
overdo'	**overrule'**
o'verdose	**overrun'**
overdue'	**overshoot'**
overflow'	**o'verspill**

o'verall *n.* loose, hard-wearing work trousers, usu. with a part that covers the chest; UK loose garment worn as protection against dirt *etc.* (*also pl.*) *—a.* total

overbear'ing *a.* domineering

overblown' *a.* excessive, bombastic

o'verboard *adv.* from a vessel into the water

o'vercast *a.* covered over, *esp.* by clouds

overcome' *vt.* conquer; surmount; make powerless

o'verdraft *n.* withdrawal of money in excess of credit balance on bank account

overhaul' *vt.* examine and set in order, repair; overtake *—n.* [ō'-] thorough examination, *esp.* for repairs

overhead' *a.* over one's head, above *—adv.* aloft, above **—o'verheads** *pl.n.* expenses of running a business, over and above cost of manufacturing and of raw materials

o'verkill *n.* capacity, advantage greater than required

o'verland *a./adv.* by land

overlook' *vt.* fail to notice; disregard; look over

override' *vt.* set aside, disregard; cancel; trample down

o'verseas *a.* foreign *—a./adv.* to, from place over the sea

o'verseer *n.* supervisor **—oversee'** *vt.* supervise

o'versight *n.* failure to notice; mistake

o'vert *a.* open, unconcealed **—o'vertly** *adv.*

overtake' *vt.* move past (vehicle, person) travelling in same direction; come up with in pursuit; catch up

overtax' *vt.* tax too heavily; impose too great a strain on

overthrow' *vt.* upset, overturn; defeat (**overthrew', overthrown', overthrow'ing**) *—n.* [ō'-] ruin; defeat; fall

o'vertime *n.* time at work, outside normal working hours; payment for this time

o'vertone *n.* additional meaning, nuance

o'verture *n. Mus.* orchestral introduction; opening of negotiations; formal offer

overween'ing *a.* thinking too much of oneself

overwhelm' *vt.* crush; submerge, engulf **—overwhelm'ing** *a.* decisive; irresistible **—overwhelm'ingly** *adv.*

overwrought' *a.* overexcited; too elaborate

o'viform *a.* egg-shaped

o'vine [-ī-] *a.* of, like, sheep

ovip'arous *a.* laying eggs

o'void *a.* egg-shaped

ov'ule *n.* unfertilized seed —**ov'ulate** *vi.* produce, discharge (egg) from ovary —**ovula'tion** *n.*

o'vum *n.* female egg-cell, in which development of fetus takes place (*pl.* **o'va**)

owe [ō] *vt.* be bound to repay, be indebted for —**ow'ing** *a.* owed, due —**owing to** caused by, as result of

owl *n.* night bird of prey —**owl'et** *n.* young owl —**owl'ish** *a.* solemn and dull

own [ōn] *a.* emphasizes possession —*vt.* possess; acknowledge —*vi.* to confess —**own'er** *n.* —**own'ership** *n.* possession

ox *n.* large cloven-footed and usu. horned farm animal; bull or cow (*pl.* **ox'en**) —**ox'bow** *n.* U-shaped harness collar of ox; lake formed from deep bend of river —**ox'eye** *n.* daisylike plant

ox'alis *n.* genus of plants —**oxal'ic acid** poisonous acid derived from oxalis

ox'ide *n.* compound of oxygen and one other element —**oxidiza'tion** *n.* —**ox'idize** *v.* (cause to) combine with oxide, rust

ox'ygen *n.* gas in atmosphere essential to life, combustion *etc.* —**ox'ygenate, ox'ygenize** *vt.* combine or treat with oxygen —**oxyacet'ylene** *a.* denoting flame used for welding produced by mixture of oxygen and acetylene

oxymor'on *n.* figure of speech in which two ideas of opposite meaning are combined to form an expressive phrase or epithet, *eg* "cruel kindness"

oyez' [ō-yes'] *n.* call, uttered three times by public crier or court official

oy'ster [oi'-] *n.* edible bivalve mollusc or shellfish —**oy'stercatcher** *n.* shore bird

oz. ounce

o'zone *n.* form of oxygen with pungent odour —**o'zonize** *vt.*

P

P *Chess* pawn; *Chem.* phosphorus; pressure

p page; **UK** pence; **UK** penny; *Mus.* piano (softly)

PA public-address system

p.a. per annum

pace *n.* step; its length; rate of movement; walk, gait —*vi.* step —*vt.* set speed for; cross, measure with steps —**pa'cer** *n.* one who sets the pace for another —**pace'maker** *n. esp.* electronic device surgically implanted in those with heart disease

pach'yderm [pak'-] *n.* thick-skinned animal, *eg* elephant —**pachyder'matous** *a.* thick-skinned, stolid

pac'ify [pas'-] *vt.* calm; establish peace (**-ified, -ifying**) —**pac'ifier** *n.* rubber teat for baby to suck on —**pacif'ic** *a.* peaceable; calm, tranquil —**pacifica'tion** *n.* —**pacif'icatory** *a.* tending to make peace —**pac'ifism** *n.* —**pac'ifist** *n.* advocate of abolition of war; one who refuses to help in war

pack *n.* bundle; band of animals; large set of people or things; set of, container for, retail commodities; set of playing cards; mass of floating ice; rucksack or backpack —*vt.* put together in suitcase *etc.*; make into a bundle; press tightly together, cram; fill with things; fill (meeting *etc.*) with one's own supporters; order off; carry (goods) on one's back —**pack'age** *n.* parcel; set of items offered together —*vt.* —**pack'et** *n.* small parcel —**pack'et (boat)** *n.* boat that transports mail, passengers *etc.* on fixed short route —**pack'horse** *n.* horse for carrying goods —**pack ice** loose floating ice which has been compacted together —**pack'sack** *n.* traveller's bag to strap to the back —**pack saddle** one to carry goods

pact *n.* covenant, agreement, compact —**pac'tional** *a.*

pad[1] *n.* piece of soft stuff used as a cushion, protection *etc.*; block of sheets of paper; foot or sole of various animals; place for launching rockets; *sl.* residence —*vt.* make soft, fill in, protect *etc.*, with pad or padding (**-dd-**) —**padd'ing** *n.* material used for stuffing; literary matter put in simply to increase quantity

pad[2] *vi.* walk with soft step; travel slowly (**-dd-**) —*n.* sound of soft footstep

pad'dle[1] *n.* short oar with broad blade at one or each end —*v.* move by, as with, paddles; row gently —*vt.* spank —**paddle wheel** wheel with crosswise blades striking water successively to propel ship

pad'dle[2] *vt.* walk with bare feet in shallow water —*n.*

padd'ock *n.* small grass field or enclosure

padd'y *n.* rice growing or in the husk —**paddy field** field where rice is grown

pad'lock *n.* detachable lock with hinged hoop to go through staple or ring —*vt.* fasten thus

pad're [pahd'ri] *n.* chaplain with the armed forces

pae'an [pē'-] *n.* song of triumph or thanksgiving

pa'gan *a./n.* heathen —**pa'ganism** *n.*

page[1] *n.* one side of leaf of book *etc.*

page[2] *n.* boy servant or attendant; young person employed in legislative chamber to run errands —*v.* summon by loudspeaker announcement

pag'eant [paj'ənt] *n.* show of persons in costume in procession, dramatic scenes *etc.*, usu. illustrating history; brilliant show —**pag'eantry** *n.*

pag'inate [paj'-] *vt.* number pages of —**pagina'tion** *n.*

pago'da *n.* pyramidal temple or tower of Chinese or Indian type

paid *pt. of* PAY

pail *n.* bucket —**pail'ful** *n.*

paill'asse *n. see* PALLIASSE

pain *n.* bodily or mental suffering; penalty or punishment —*pl.* trouble, exertion —*vt.* inflict pain upon —**pain'ful** *a.*

—**pain'fully** adv. —**pain'less** *a.* —**pain'lessly** *adv.* —**pain'killer** *n.* drug, as aspirin, that reduces pain —**pains'taking** *a.* diligent, careful

paint *n.* colouring matter spread on a surface with brushes, roller, spray gun *etc.* —*vt.* portray, colour, coat, or make picture of, with paint; apply make-up; describe —**paint'er** *n.* —**paint'ing** *n.* picture in paint

paint'er *n.* line at bow of boat for tying it up

pair *n.* set of two, *esp.* existing or generally used together —*v.* arrange in twos; group or be grouped in twos

pais'ley [pāz'-] *n.* pattern of small curving shapes

pajam'as *pl.n. see* PYJAMAS

pal *n. inf.* friend

pal'ace *n.* residence of king, bishop *etc.*; stately mansion —**pala'tial** *a.* like a palace; magnificent —**pal'atine** *a.* with royal privileges

pal'adin *n. Hist.* knight errant

pal'ate *n.* roof of mouth; sense of taste —**pal'atable** *a.* agreeable to eat —**pal'atal, pal'atine** *a.* of the palate; made by placing tongue against palate —*n.* palatal sound

pala'tial, pal'atine *see* PALACE

palav'er [-ahv'-] *n.* fuss; conference, discussion

pale[1] *a.* wan, dim, whitish —*vi.* whiten; lose superiority or importance

pale[2] *n.* stake, boundary —**pa'ling** *n.* upright plank making up fence

pal(a)eog'raphy [-li-og'-] *n.* study of ancient writings

pal(a)eolith'ic [pal-i-ō-] *a.* of the old Stone Age

pal(a)eontol'ogy [-li-on-] *n.* study of past geological periods and fossils —**pal(a)eontolog'ical** *a.*

pal'ette *n.* artist's flat board for mixing colours on

pal'indrome *n.* word, verse or sentence that is the same when read backwards or forwards

palisade' *n.* fence of stakes —*pl.* high cliffs in line, oft. along river, like palisade —*vt.* to enclose or protect with palisade

pall[1] [pawl] *n.* cloth spread over a coffin; depressing, oppressive atmosphere —**pall'bearer** *n.* one carrying, attending coffin at funeral

pall[2] [pawl] *vi.* become tasteless or tiresome; cloy

pall'et[1] *n.* straw mattress; small bed

pall'et[2] *n.* portable platform for storing and moving goods

pall'iasse [pal'i-as] *n.* straw mattress

pall'iate *vt.* relieve without curing; excuse —**pallia'tion** *n.* —**pall'iative** *a.* giving temporary or partial relief —*n.* that which excuses, mitigates or alleviates

pall'id *a.* pale, wan, colourless —**pall'or** *n.* paleness

palm [pahm] *n.* inner surface of hand; tropical tree; leaf of the tree as symbol of victory —*vt.* conceal in palm of hand; pass off by trickery —**palm'ist** *n.* —**palm'istry** *n.* fortune-telling from lines on palm of hand —**palm'y** *a.* flourishing, successful —**Palm Sunday** Sunday before Easter

palomi'no [-mē'-] *n.* golden horse with white mane and tail (*pl.* **-nos**)

pal'pable *a.* obvious; certain; that may be touched or felt —**pal'pably** *adv.*

pal'pate *vt. Med.* examine by touch

pal'pitate *vi.* throb; pulsate violently —**palpita'tion** *n.* throbbing; violent, irregular beating of heart

pal'sy [pawl'zi] *n.* paralysis —**pal'sied** *a.* affected with palsy

pal'try [pawl'-] *a.* worthless, contemptible, trifling

pam'pas *pl.n.* vast grassy treeless plains in S Amer.

pam'per *vt.* overindulge, spoil by coddling

pamph'let *n.* thin unbound book usu. on some topical subject —**pamphleteer'** *n.* writer of these

pan[1] *n.* broad, shallow vessel; **UK** bowl of lavatory; depression in ground, *esp.* where salt forms —*vt.* wash gold ore in pan; *inf.* criticize harshly (**-nn-**) —**pan'tile** *n.* curved roofing tile —**pan out** *vi.* result

pan[2] *v.* move movie camera slowly while filming to cover scene, follow moving object *etc.* (**-nn-**)

pan-, pant-, panto- (*comb. form*) all, as in *panacea, pantomime* Such words are not given here where the meaning may easily be inferred from simple word

panace'a [-sē'ə] *n.* universal remedy, cure for all ills

panache' [-ash'] *n.* dashing style

panama' [-mah'] *n.* straw hat

pan'cake *n.* thin cake of batter fried in pan —*vi. Aviation* make flat landing by dropping in a level position

panchromat'ic *a. Photography* sensitive to light of all colours

pan'creas [-ng'-kri-əs] *n.* digestive gland behind stomach —**pancreat'ic** *a.*

pan'da *n.* large black and white bearlike mammal of China

pandem'ic *a.* (of disease) occurring over wide area

pandemo'nium *n.* scene of din and uproar

pan'der *v.* (*esp. with* to) give gratification to (weakness or desires) —*n.* pimp

P & O Peninsular and Oriental (Steamship Company)

p & p postage and packing

pane *n.* single piece of glass in a window or door

panegyr'ic [-i-jir'-] *n.* speech of praise —**panegyr'ical** *a.* laudatory —**panegyr'ist** *n.*

pan'el *n.* compartment of surface, usu. raised or sunk, *eg* in door; any distinct section of something, *eg* of automobile body; strip of material inserted in garment; group of persons as team in quiz game *etc.*; list of jurors, doctors *etc.*; thin board with picture on it —*vt.* adorn with panels (**-ll-**) —**pan'elling** *n.* panelled work —**pan'ellist** *n.* member of panel

pang *n.* sudden pain, sharp twinge; compunction

pan'ic *n.* sudden and infectious fear; extreme fright; unreasoning terror —*a.* of fear *etc.* —*v.* feel or cause to feel panic (**-icked, -icking**) —**pan'icky** *a.* inclined to panic; nervous —**panic button** button or switch that operates safety device, for use in emergency —**pan'icmonger** *n.* one who starts panic —**panic-stricken, -struck** *a.*

pann'ier *n.* basket carried by beast of burden, bicycle, or on person's shoulders

pann'ikin *n. obs.* small metal drinking cup

pan'oply *n.* complete, magnificent array —**pan'oplied** *a.*

panoram'a [-ahm'-] *n.* wide or complete view; picture arranged round spectator or unrolled before him —**panora'mic** [-ram'-] *a.*

pan'sy [-zi] *n.* flower, species of violet; *inf.* effeminate man

pant *vi.* gasp for breath; yearn; long; throb —*n.* gasp

pantaloon' *n.* in pantomime, foolish old man who is the butt of clown —*pl. inf. Hist.* close-fitting trousers

pantech'nicon [-tek'-] *n.* large van, *esp.* for carrying furniture

pan'theism *n.* identification of God with the universe —**pan'theist** *n.* —**pantheis'tic** *a.* —**pan'theon** *n.* temple of all gods

pan'ther *n.* variety of leopard

pan'ties *pl.n.* women's undergarment

pan'tihose *n. see* PANTYHOSE

pan'tograph *n.* instrument for copying maps *etc.*, to any scale —**pantograph'ic** *a.*

pan'tomime *n.* theatrical show, usu. produced at Christmas time, often founded on a fairy tale; dramatic entertainment in dumbshow

pan'try *n.* room for storing food or utensils

pants *pl.n.* two-legged outer garment with legs reaching ankles; panties

pan'tyhose *n.* woman's garment consisting of sheer stockings knitted in one piece with pantie-like top

pap[1] *n.* soft food for infants, invalids *etc.*; pulp, mash

pap[2] *n.* breast; nipple

pa'pacy *n.* office of Pope; papal system —**pa'pal** *a.* of, relating to, the Pope —**pa'pist** *n.* —**papist'ic** *a.*

paparaz'zo [papərat'sō] *n.* freelance photographer specializing in candid camera shots of famous people (*pl.* **-raz'zi** [-rat'sē])

pa'paw [paw'paw] *n.* tree bearing melon-shaped fruit; its fruit (*also* **papa'ya** [pə-pī'ə])

pa'per *n.* material made by pressing pulp of rags, straw, wood *etc.*, into thin, flat sheets; printed sheet of paper; newspaper; article, essay; set of examination questions —*pl.* documents *etc.* —*vt.* cover, decorate with paper —**pa'perback** *n.* book with flexible covers

papier-mâch'é [pap-yā- mash'ā] *n.* pulp from rags or paper mixed with size, shaped by moulding and dried hard

papoose' *n.* N Amer. Indian child

pap'rika *n.* (powdered seasoning prepared from) type of red pepper

papy'rus *n.* species of reed; (manuscript written on) kind of paper made from this plant (*pl.* **papy'ri** [-rī])

par *n.* equality of value or standing; face value (of stocks and shares); *Golf* estimated standard score —**par'ity** [pa'ri-] *n.* equality; analogy

par. paragraph; parallel; parenthesis

par'a-, par-, pa- (*comb. form*) beside, beyond, as in *paradigm, parallel, parody*

par'able [pa'rə-] *n.* allegory, story with a moral lesson

parab'ola [pə-] *n.* section of cone cut by plane parallel to the cone's side

parace'tamol *n.* mild drug used as alternative to aspirin

par'achute [pa'rə-shōōt] *n.* apparatus extending like umbrella used to retard the descent of a falling body —*v.* land or cause to land by parachute —**par'achutist** *n.*

parade' *n.* display; muster of troops; parade ground; public walk —*v.* march; display

par'adigm [pa'rə-dīm] *n.* example; model —**paradigmat'ic** [-dig-mat'-] *a.*

par'adise [pa'rə-] *n.* Heaven; state of bliss; Garden of Eden

par'adox [pa'rə-] *n.* statement that seems absurd or self-contradictory but may be true —**paradox'ical** *a.*

par'affin [pa'rə-] *n.* waxlike hydrocarbon mixture used in candles *etc.*; **UK** kerosene

par'agliding *n.* sport of cross-country gliding using a specially designed parachute

par'agon [pa'rə-] *n.* pattern or model of excellence

par'agraph [pa'rə-] *n.* section of chapter or book; short notice, as in newspaper —*vt.* arrange in paragraphs —**paragraph'ic** *a.*

par'akeet [pa'rə-] *n.* small kind of parrot

par'allax [pa'rə-] *n.* apparent difference in object's position or direction as viewed from different points

par'allel [pa'rə-] *a.* continuously at equal distances; precisely corresponding —*n.* line equidistant from another at all points; thing exactly like another; comparison; line of latitude —*vt.* represent as similar, compare —**par'allelism** *n.* —**parallel'ogram** *n.* four-sided plane figure with opposite sides parallel

paral'ysis *n.* incapacity to move or feel, due to damage to nervous system (*pl.* **-yses** [-sēz]) —**par'alyse** [pa'rə-] *vt.* affect with paralysis; cripple; make useless or ineffectual —**paralyt'ic** *a./n.* (person) affected with paralysis —**infantile paralysis** poliomyelitis

paramed'ical *a.* of persons working in various capacities in support of medical profession

param'eter *n.* any constant limiting factor

paramil'itary *a.* of civilian group organized on military lines or in support of the military

par'amount [pa'rə-] *a.* supreme, eminent, pre-eminent, chief

par'amour [pa'rə-] *n. esp.* formerly, illicit lover, mistress

par'ang *n.* heavy Malay knife

paranoi'a [pa-rə-] *n.* mental disease with delusions of fame, grandeur, persecution —**paranoi'ac** *a./n.* —**par'anoid** *a.* of paranoia; *inf.* exhibiting fear of persecution *etc.* —*n.*

par'apet [pa'rə-] *n.* low wall, railing along edge of balcony, bridge *etc.*

paraphernа'lia *pl.n.* (*used as sing.*) personal belongings; odds and ends of equipment

par'aphrase [pa'rə-] *n.* expression of meaning of passage in other words; free translation —*vt.* put into other words

paraple'gia [-j-] *n.* paralysis of lower half of body —**paraple'gic** *n./a.*

parapsychol'ogy *n.* study of subjects pert. to extrasensory perception, *eg* telepathy

par'asite [pa'rə-] *n.* animal or plant living in or on another; self-interested hanger-on —**parasit'ic** *a.* of the nature of, living as, parasite —**par'asitism** *n.* —**parasitol'ogy** *n.* study of animal and vegetable parasites, *esp.* as causes of disease

par'asol [pa'rə-] *n.* sunshade

paratax'is *n.* arrangement of sentences which omits connecting words

par'atroops, -troopers [pa'rə-] *pl.n.* troops trained to descend by parachute

paraty'phoid *n.* an infectious disease similar to but distinct from typhoid fever

par'boil *vt.* boil until partly cooked

par'cel *n.* packet of goods, *esp.* one enclosed in paper; quantity dealt with at one time; piece of land —*vt.* wrap up; divide into parts (**-ll-**)

parch *v.* dry by heating; make, become hot and dry; scorch; roast slightly

parch'ment *n.* sheep, goat, calf skin prepared for writing; manuscript of this

par'don *vt.* forgive, excuse —*n.* forgiveness; release from punishment —**par'donable** *a.* —**par'donably** *adv.*

pare *vt.* trim, cut edge or surface of; decrease bit by bit —**pa'ring** *n.* piece pared off, rind

pa'rent *n.* father or mother —**pa'rentage** *n.* descent, extraction —**parent'al** *a.* —**pa'renthood** *n.*

paren'thesis *n.* word or sentence inserted in passage independently of grammatical sequence and usu. marked off by brackets, dashes, or commas —**paren'theses** [-sēz] *pl.n.* round brackets, ( ), used for this —**parenthet'ical** *a.*

par'fleche [-sh] *n.* rawhide that has been dried after soaking in lye and water to remove hair; bag, *etc.* made of this

par'get [-jit] *n.* rough plaster; gypsum —*vt.* cover with plaster

pari'ah *n.* social outcast

pari'etal *a.* of the walls of bodily cavities, *eg* skull

pari-mu'tuel [-'tyo͞oel] *n.* system of betting in which betters on winners share total amount wagered, less percentage for management (*pl.* **-uels, paris-mutuels**)

par'ish [pa'-] *n.* district under one clergyman; subdivision of county —**parish'ioner** *n.* inhabitant of parish

par'ity *see* PAR

park *n.* large area of land in natural state preserved for recreational use; large enclosed piece of ground, usu. with grass or woodland, attached to country house or for public use; space in camp for military supplies —*vt.* leave for a short time; manoeuvre (automobile) into a suitable space; arrange or leave in a park —**park'way** *n.* wide road planted with trees —**parking lot** area, building where vehicles may be left for a time

park'a *n.* warm waterproof coat, often with hood

parl'ance *n.* way of speaking, conversation; idiom

parl'ay [-li] *vt.* stake (winnings from one bet) on subsequent wager; exploit (one's talent) —*n.* such bet

parl'ey *n.* meeting between leaders or representatives of opposing forces to discuss terms (*pl.* **-leys**) —*vi.* hold discussion about terms

parl'iament *n.* the legislature of Canada; the legislature of the United Kingdom; any similar legislative assembly —**parliamenta'rian** *n.* member of parliament —**parliament'ary** *a.*

parl'o(u)r *n.* sitting room, room for receiving company in small house; room or shop as business premises, *esp.* hairdresser *etc.* —**parlo(u)r car** *see* CLUB CAR

parl'ous *a. obs.* perilous

Parmesan' *n.* hard dry Italian cheese

paro'chial [-k-] *a.* narrow, provincial; of a parish —**paro'chialism** *n.*

par'ody [pa'rə-] *n.* composition in which author's style is made fun of by imitation; travesty —*vt.* write parody of (**-odied, -odying**) —**par'odist** *n.*

parole' [-rōl'] *n.* early freeing of prisoner on condition he is of good behaviour; word of honour —*vt.* place on parole

par'oxysm [pa'rəks-] *n.* sudden violent attack of pain, rage, laughter

par'quet [-kā] *n.* flooring of wooden blocks arranged in pattern —*vt.* lay a parquet —**par'quetry** [-kit-] *n.*

parr'akeet *n. see* PARAKEET

parr'icide *n.* murder or murderer of a parent

parr'ot *n.* bird with short hooked beak, some varieties of which can imitate speaking; unintelligent imitator

parr'y *vt.* ward off, turn aside (**par'ried, par'rying**) —*n.* act of parrying, *esp.* in fencing

parse [-z] *vt.* describe (word); analyse (sentence) in terms of grammar

par'sec *n.* unit of length used in expressing distance of stars

par'simony *n.* stinginess; undue economy —**parsimo'nious** *a.* sparing

par'sley *n.* herb used for seasoning, garnish *etc.*

par'snip *n.* edible yellow root vegetable

par'son *n.* clergyman of parish or church; clergyman —**par'sonage** *n.* parson's house

part *n.* portion, section, share; division;

actor's role; duty; (*oft. pl.*) region; interest; division between sections of hair on head —*v.* divide; separate —**part'ing** *n.* separation; leave-taking —**part'ly** *adv.* in part —**part song** song for several voices singing in harmony

partake' *v.* take or have share in; take food or drink (**partook', -ta'ken, -ta'king**)

parterre' [-tār'] *n.* ornamental arrangement of beds in a flower garden; the pit of a theatre

par'tial [-shəl] *a.* not general or complete; prejudiced; fond of —**partial'ity** *n.* favouritism; fondness for —**par'tially** *adv.* partly

partic'ipate [-tis'-] *v.* share in; take part in —**partic'ipant** *n.* —**participa'tion** *n.* —**partic'ipator** *n.*

part'iciple *n.* adjective made by inflection from verb and keeping verb's relation to dependent words —**particip'ial** *a.*

part'icle *n.* minute portion of matter; least possible amount; minor part of speech in grammar, prefix, suffix

par'ti-coloured *a.* differently coloured in different parts, variegated

partic'ular *a.* relating to one, not general; distinct; minute; very exact; fastidious —*n.* detail, item —*pl.* detailed account; items of information —**particular'ity** *n.* —**partic'ularize** *vt.* mention in detail —**partic'ularly** *adv.*

Parti Quebecois [par-tē'kā-bek-wah'] political party in Quebec originally advocating separation of Quebec from rest of country

partisan' [-zan'] *n.* adherent of a party; guerilla, member of resistance movement —*a.* adhering to faction; prejudiced

parti'tion [-tish'-] *n.* division; interior dividing wall —*vt.* divide, cut into sections

part'ner *n.* ally or companion; a member of a partnership; one that dances with another; a husband or wife; *Golf, Tennis etc.* one who plays with another against opponents —*v.* (cause to) be a partner of —**part'nership** *n.* association of persons for business *etc.*

part'ridge *n.* Old World game bird of the grouse family; any of various related N Amer. birds

parturi'tion [-yoo-rish'-] *n.* act of bringing forth young; childbirth

part'y *n.* social assembly; group of persons travelling or working together; group of persons united in opinion; side; person —*a.* of, belonging to, a party or faction —**party line** telephone line serving two or more subscribers; policies of political party —**party wall** common wall separating adjoining premises

par'venu [-nyo͞o] *n.* one newly risen into position of notice, power, wealth; upstart

pas'cal *n.* SI unit of pressure

pas'chal [-kəl] *a.* of the Passover or Easter

pass [-ah-] *vt.* go by, beyond, through *etc.*; exceed; be accepted by; undergo successfully; spend; transfer; exchange; disregard —*v.* go; be transferred from one state or person to another; elapse; undergo examination successfully; bring into force, sanction a parliamentary bill *etc.* —*n.* way, *esp.* a narrow and difficult way; permit, licence, authorization; successful result from test; condition; *Sport* transfer of ball —**pass'able** *a.* (just) acceptable —**pass'ing** *a.* transitory; cursory, casual —**pass up** ignore, neglect, reject

pass'age *n.* channel, opening; way through, corridor; part of book *etc.*; journey, voyage, fare; enactment of law by parliament *etc.*; conversation, dispute

pass'é [pas'-, pahs'-] *a.* out-of-date; past the prime

pass'enger *n.* traveller, *esp.* by public conveyance

pass'erine *a.* of the order of perching birds

pass'im *Lat.* everywhere, throughout

pass'ion [-sh'-] *n.* ardent desire, *esp.* sexual; any strongly felt emotion; suffering (*esp.* that of Christ) —**pass'ionate** *a.* (easily) moved by strong emotions —**pass'ionflower** *n.* tropical Amer. plant —**passion fruit** edible fruit of passionflower

pass'ive *a.* unresisting; submissive; inactive; denoting grammatical mood of verb in which the action is suffered by the subject —**passiv'ity** *n.* —**passive smoking** inhalation of smoke from others' cigarettes by nonsmoker

Pass'over [-ah-] *n.* Jewish spring festival

pass'port [-ah-] *n.* official document granting permission to pass, travel abroad *etc.*

pass'word [-ah-] *n.* word, phrase, to distinguish friend from enemy; countersign

past [-ah-] *a.* ended; gone by; elapsed —*n.* bygone times —*adv.* by; along —*prep.* beyond; after

pas'ta *n.* any of several variously shaped edible preparations of dough, *eg* spaghetti

paste *n.* soft composition, as toothpaste; soft plastic mixture or adhesive; fine glass to imitate gems —*vt.* fasten with paste —**pa'sty** *a.* like paste; white; sickly —**paste'board** *n.* stiff thick paper

pas'tel *n.* coloured crayon; art of drawing with crayons; pale, delicate colour —*a.* delicately tinted

pas'teurize *vt.* sterilize by heat —**pasteuriza'tion** *n.*

pastiche' [-tēsh'] *n.* literary, musical, artistic work composed of parts borrowed from other works and loosely connected together; work imitating another's style

pas'til(le) *n.* lozenge; aromatic substance burnt as fumigator

pas'time [-ah-] *n.* that which makes time pass agreeably; recreation

pas'tor [-ah-] *n.* clergyman in charge of a congregation —**pas'toral** *a.* of, or like, shepherd's or rural life; of office of pastor —*n.* poem describing rural life —**pas'torate** *n.* office, jurisdiction of pastor

pa'stry *n.* article of food made chiefly of flour, fat and water

pas'ture [-ah-] *n.* grass for food of cattle; ground on which cattle graze —*v.* (cause to) graze —**pas'turage** *n.* (right to) pasture

pas'ty *n.* small pie of meat and crust, baked without a dish

pat[1] *vt.* tap (**-tt-**) —*n.* light, quick blow; small mass, as of butter, beaten into shape

pat[2] *adv.* exactly; fluently; opportunely; glib; exactly right —**stand pat** refuse to abandon belief, decision *etc.*

pat. patent(ed)

patch *n.* piece of cloth sewed on garment; spot; plot of ground; protecting pad for the eye; small contrasting area; short period —*vt.* mend; repair clumsily —**patch'y** *a.* of uneven quality; full of patches —**patch'work** *n.* work composed of pieces sewn together; jumble

patchou'li [-choo'-] *n.* Indian herb; perfume from it

pate *n.* head; top of head

pât'é [pat'ā] *n.* spread of finely minced liver *etc.*

patell'a *n.* kneecap (*pl.* **patell'ae** [-ē]) —**patell'ar** *a.*

pat'en *n.* plate for bread in the Eucharist

pa'tent *n.* deed securing to person exclusive right to invention —*a.* open; evident; manifest; open to public perusal, as **letters patent** —*vt.* secure a patent —**patentee'** *n.* one that has a patent —**pa'tently** *adv.* obviously —**patent leather** (imitation) leather processed to give hard, glossy surface

paterfamil'ias [pā-] *n.* father of a family (*pl.* **patresfamil'ias** [pā-trēz-])

pater'nal *a.* fatherly; of a father —**pater'nalism** *n.* authority exercised in a way that limits individual responsibility —**paternalis'tic** *a.* —**patern'ity** *n.* relation of a father to his offspring; fatherhood

paternos'ter *n.* Lord's Prayer; beads of rosary; type of lift

path [-ah-] *n.* way or track; course of action

pathet'ic *a.* affecting or moving tender emotions; distressingly inadequate —**pathet'ically** *adv.*

pathogen'ic [-jen'-] *a.* producing disease —**pathog'eny** *n.* mode of development of disease

pathol'ogy *n.* science of diseases —**patholog'ical** *a.* of the science of disease; due to disease; *inf.* compulsively motivated —**pathol'ogist** *n.*

pa'thos *n.* power of exciting tender emotions

pa'tient [-shənt] *a.* bearing trials calmly —*n.* person under medical treatment —**pa'tience** *n.* quality of enduring; card game for one

pat'ina *n.* fine layer on a surface; sheen of age on woodwork

pat'io *n.* paved area adjoining house

pat'ois [-wah] *n.* regional dialect

pa'triarch [-k-] *n.* father and ruler of family, *esp.* Biblical —**patriarch'al** *a.* venerable

patri'cian [-rish'-] *n.* noble of ancient Rome; one of noble birth —*a.* of noble birth

pat'ricide *n.* murder or murderer of father

pat'rimony *n.* property inherited from ancestors

pa'triot [*or* pat'-] *n.* one that loves his country and maintains its interests —**patriot'ic** [pat-] *a.* inspired by love of one's country —**pat'riotism** *n.* love of, loyalty to one's country

patrol' [-ōl'] *n.* regular circuit by guard; person, small group patrolling; unit of Boy Scouts or Girl Guides —*v.* go round on guard, or reconnoitring (**-ll-**) —**patrol wagon** police truck for transporting prisoners

pa'tron *n.* one who sponsors or aids artists, charities *etc.*; protector; regular customer; guardian saint; one that has disposition of church living *etc.* —**pat'ronage** *n.* support given by, or position of, a patron —**pat'ronize** *vt.* assume air of superiority towards; frequent as customer; encourage

patronym'ic *n.* name derived from that of parent or an ancestor

patt'en *n. Hist.* wooden clog, shoe, on raised platform

patt'er *vi.* make noise, as sound of quick, short steps; tap in quick succession; pray, talk rapidly —*n.* quick succession of taps; *inf.* glib, rapid speech

patt'ern *n.* arrangement of repeated parts; design; shape to direct cutting of cloth *etc.*; model; specimen —*vt.* (*with* on, after) model; decorate with pattern

patt'y *n.* a little pie

pau'city *n.* scarcity; smallness of quantity; fewness

paunch *n.* belly

pau'per *n.* poor person, *esp.* formerly, one supported by the public —**pau'perism** *n.* destitution; extreme poverty —**pauperiza'tion** *n.* —**pau'perize** *vt.* reduce to pauperism

pause *vi.* cease for a time —*n.* stop or rest

pave *vt.* form surface with stone or brick —**pave'ment** *n.* paved floor; **UK** sidewalk; material for paving

pavil'ion *n.* clubhouse on playing field *etc.*; building for housing exhibition *etc.*; large ornate tent

paw *n.* foot of animal —*v.* scrape with forefoot; handle roughly; stroke with the hands

pawn[1] *vt.* deposit (article) as security for money borrowed —*n.* article deposited —**pawn'broker** *n.* lender of money on goods pledged

pawn[2] *n.* piece in chess; *fig.* person used as mere tool

pay *vt.* give money *etc.*, for goods or services rendered; compensate; give or bestow; be profitable to; (*with* out) release bit by bit, as rope —*vi.* be remunerative; be profitable; (*with* out) spend; (**paid, pay'ing**) —*n.* wages; paid employment —**pay'able** *a.* justly due; profitable —**payee'** *n.* person to whom money is paid or due —**pay'ment** *n.* discharge of debt —**pay'load** *n.* part of cargo earning revenue; explosive power of missile *etc.* —**paying guest** boarder, lodger, *esp.* in private house

Pb *Chem.* lead

PC Police Constable; Privy Councillor; Progressive Conservative

p.c. per cent; postcard

PDT Pacific Daylight Time

pea *n.* fruit, growing in pods, of climbing plant; the plant —**pea-green** *a.* of shade of green like colour of green peas —**peasoup'er** *n. inf.* thick fog; *offens.* French Canadian

peace *n.* freedom from war; harmony; quietness of mind; calm; repose —**peace'able** *a.* disposed to peace —**peace'ably** *adv.* —**peace'ful** *a.* free from war, tumult; mild; undisturbed —**peace'fully** *adv.*

peach *n.* stone fruit of delicate flavour; *inf.* anything very pleasant; pinkish-yellow colour —**peach'y** *a.* like peach; *inf.* fine, excellent

pea'cock *n.* male of bird (**pea'fowl**) with fan-like tail, brilliantly coloured (**pea'hen** *fem.*) —*vt.* strut about or pose, like a peacock

peak *n.* pointed end of anything, *esp.* hill's sharp top; point of greatest development *etc.*; sharp increase; projecting piece on front of cap —*v.* (cause to) form, reach peaks —**peaked, peak'y** *a.* like, having a peak; sickly, wan, drawn

peal *n.* loud sound or succession of loud sounds; changes rung on set of bells; chime —*vi.* sound loudly

pea'nut *n.* pea-shaped nut that ripens underground —*pl. inf.* trifling amount of money

pear [pār] *n.* tree yielding sweet, juicy fruit; the fruit

pearl [purl] *n.* hard, lustrous structure found in several molluscs, *esp.* pearl oyster and used as jewel —**pear'ly** *a.* like pearls —**pearl barley** barley with skin ground off

peas'ant [pez'-] *n.* member of low social class, *esp.* in rural district —**peas'antry** *n.* peasants collectively

peat *n.* decomposed vegetable substance found in bogs; turf of it used for fuel

peavey' *n.* wooden lever with metal pointed end and hinged hook, used for handling logs

peb'ble *n.* small roundish stone; pale, transparent rock crystal; grainy, irregular surface —*vt.* pave, cover with pebbles

pecan' *n.* N Amer. tree, species of hickory, allied to walnut; its edible nut

pecc'able *a.* liable to sin —**pecc'ancy** *n.* —**pecc'ant** *a.* sinful; offensive

peccadill'o *n.* slight offence; petty crime (*pl.* **-es, -s**)

pecc'ary *n.* vicious Amer. animal allied to pig

peck[1] *n.* fourth part of bushel, 2 gallons; great deal

peck[2] *v.* pick, strike with or as with beak; nibble; *inf.* kiss quickly —*n.* —**peck'ish** *a.* **UK** *inf.* hungry

pec'tin *n.* gelatinizing substance obtained from ripe fruits —**pec'tic** *a.* congealing; denoting pectin

pec'toral *a.* of the breast —*n.* chest medicine; breastplate

pec'ulate *v.* embezzle; steal —**pecula'tion** *n.* —**pec'ulator** *n.*

pecu'liar *a.* strange; particular; belonging to —**peculiar'ity** *n.* oddity; characteristic; distinguishing feature

pecu'niary *a.* relating to, or consisting of, money

ped'agogue [-gog] *n.* schoolmaster; pedant —**pedagog'ic** *a.*

ped'al *n.* something to transmit motion from foot; foot lever to modify tone or swell of musical instrument; *Mus.* note, usu. bass, held through successive harmonies —*a.* of a foot —*v.* propel bicycle by using its pedals; use pedal (**-ll-**)

ped'ant *n.* one who overvalues, or insists on, petty details of book-learning, grammatical rules *etc.* —**pedant'ic** *a.* —**ped'antry** *n.*

ped'dle *vt.* go round selling goods —**ped'dler** *n.* one who sells; hawker

ped'erast *n.* man who has homosexual relations with boy —**ped'erasty** *n.*

ped'estal *n.* base of column, pillar

pedes'trian *n.* one who walks on foot —*a.* going on foot; commonplace; dull, uninspiring —**pedes'trianism** *n.* the practice of walking —**pedestrian crossing UK** crosswalk

pediat'rics [pē-] *pl.n.* (*with sing v.*) branch of medicine dealing with diseases and disorders of children —**pediatri'cian** *n.*

ped'icel [-s-] *n.* small, short stalk of leaf, flower or fruit

ped'icure *n.* medical or cosmetic treatment of feet

ped'igree *n.* register of ancestors; genealogy

ped'iment *n.* triangular part over Greek portico *etc.* —**pediment'al** *a.*

ped'lar *n.* peddler

pedom'eter *n.* instrument which measures the distance walked

pedun'cle *n.* flower stalk; stalklike structure

peek *vi./n.* peep, glance

peel *vt.* strip off skin, rind or any form of covering —*vi.* come off, as skin, rind —*n.* rind, skin —**peeled** *a. inf.* of eyes, watchful —**peel'ings** *pl.n.*

peep[1] *vi.* look slyly or quickly —*n.* such a look

peep[2] *vi.* cry, as chick; chirp —*n.* such a cry

peer[1] *n.* nobleman (**peer'ess** *fem.*); one of the same rank —**peer'age** *n.* body of peers; rank of peer —**peer'less** *a.* without match or equal

peer[2] *vi.* look closely and intently

peeved *a. inf.* sulky, irritated

peev'ish *a.* fretful; irritable —**peev'ishly** *adv.* —**peev'ishness** *n.* annoyance

pee'wit *n.* lapwing

peg *n.* nail or pin for joining, fastening, marking *etc.*; (mark of) level, standard *etc.* —*vt.* fasten with pegs; stabilize (prices); *inf.* throw —*vi.* (*with* away) persevere (**-gg-**)

P.E.I. Prince Edward Island

pei'gnoir [pā'nwahr] *n.* lady's dressing gown, jacket, wrapper

pejor'ative [pi-jo'rə- *or* pē'jər-] *a.* (of words *etc.*) with unpleasant, disparaging connotation

Pekin(g)ese' [-ēz'] *n.* small Chinese dog

pela'gian, pelag'ic *a.* of the deep sea

pelargo'nium *n.* plant with red, white or pink flowers

pel'ican *n.* large, fish-eating waterfowl with large pouch beneath its bill

pell'et *n.* little ball, pill

pell'icle *n.* thin skin, film

pell'-mell' *adv.* in utter confusion, headlong

pellu'cid [-lōō'-] *a.* translucent; clear —**pellucid'ity** *n.*

pelt[1] *vt.* strike with missiles —*vi.* throw missiles; rush; fall persistently, as rain

pelt[2] *n.* raw hide or skin

pel'vis *n.* bony cavity at base of human trunk (*pl.* **pel'vises, -ves** [-vēz]) —**pel'vic** *a.* pert. to pelvis

pen[1] *n.* instrument for writing —*vt.* compose; write (**-nn-**) —**pen name** author's pseudonym

pen[2] *n.* small enclosure, as for sheep —*vt.* put, keep in enclosure (**-nn-**)

pen[3] *n.* female swan

pen[4] *n. inf.* penitentiary

pe'nal *a.* of, incurring, inflicting, punishment —**pe'nalize** *vt.* impose penalty on; handicap —**pen'alty** *n.* punishment for crime or offence; forfeit; *Sports* handicap or disadvantage imposed for infringement of rule *etc.*

pen'ance *n.* suffering submitted to as expression of penitence; repentance

pence UK *n. pl. of* PENNY

pen'chant [*or* pahn'shahn] *n.* inclination, decided taste

pen'cil *n.* instrument as of graphite, for writing *etc.*; *Optics* narrow beam of light —*vt.* paint or draw; mark with pencil (**-ll-**)

pend'ant *n.* hanging ornament —**pen'dent** *a.* suspended; hanging; projecting

pend'ing *prep.* during, until —*a.* awaiting settlement; undecided; imminent

pend'ulous *a.* hanging, swinging —**pen'dulum** *n.* suspended weight swinging to and fro, *esp.* as regulator for clock

pen'etrate *vt.* enter into; pierce; arrive at the meaning of —**penetrabil'ity** *n.* quality of being penetrable —**pen'etrable** *a.* capable of being entered or pierced —**pen'etrating** *a.* sharp; easily heard; subtle; quick to understand —**penetra'tion** *n.* insight, acuteness —**pen'etrative** *a.* piercing; discerning —**pen'etrator** *n.*

pen'guin *n.* flightless, short-legged swimming bird

penicill'in [-sil'-] *n.* antibiotic drug effective against a wide range of diseases, infections

penin'sula *n.* portion of land nearly surrounded by water —**penin'sular** *a.*

pe'nis *n.* male organ of copulation (and of urination) in man and many mammals (*pl.* **pe'nises, pe'nes** [-nēz])

pen'itent *a.* affected by sense of guilt —*n.* one that repents of sin —**pen'itence** *n.* sorrow for sin; repentance —**peniten'tial** *a.* of, or expressing, penitence —**peniten'tiary** *a.* relating to penance, or to the rules of penance —*n.* prison

penn'ant *n.* long narrow flag; *Sport* flag as emblem of championship

penn'on *n.* small pointed or swallow-tailed flag

penn'y *n.* one cent; Brit. bronze coin, now 100th part of pound (*pl.* **pence, penn'ies**) —**penn'iless** *a.* having no money; poor

penol'ogy [pē-] *n.* study of punishment and prevention of crime

pen'sion[1] *n.* regular payment to retired people after long service, old people, soldiers *etc.* —*vt.* grant pension to —**pen'sioner** *n.*

pension'[2] [pahn-syon'] *n.* continental boarding house; (full) board

pen'sive *a.* thoughtful with sadness; wistful

pent *a.* shut up, kept in —**pent-up** *a.* not released, repressed

pent'agon *n.* plane figure having five angles —**pentag'onal** *a.*

Pent'agon *n.* military headquarters in USA

pentam'eter *n.* verse of five metrical feet

Pent'ateuch [-tyōōk] *n.* first five books of Old Testament

pentath'lon *n.* athletic contest of five events

Pent'ecost *n.* Whitsuntide; Jewish harvest festival on 50th day after Passover

pent'house *n.* apartment, flat or other structure on top, or top floor, of building

pen'tode *n.* *Electronics* five-electrode thermionic valve, having anode, cathode and three grids

pentste'mon *n.* bright-flowered garden plant

pen'ult [*or* -nult'] *n.* last syllable but one of word —**penul'timate** *a.* next before the last

penum'bra *n.* imperfect shadow; in an eclipse, the partially shadowed region which surrounds the full shadow —**penum'bral** *a.*

pen'ury *n.* extreme poverty; extreme scarcity —**penu'rious** *a.* niggardly, stingy; poor, scanty

pe'ony *n.* plant with showy red, pink, or white flowers

peo'ple [pē'pl] *pl.n.* persons generally; community, nation; race; family —*vt.* stock with inhabitants; populate

pep *n. inf.* vigour; energy; enthusiasm —*vt.* impart energy to; speed up (**-pp-**)

pepp'er *n.* fruit of climbing plant, which yields pungent aromatic spice; various slightly pungent vegetables *eg* capsicum —*vt.* season with pepper; sprinkle, dot; pelt with missiles —**pepp'ery** *a.* having the qualities of pepper; irritable —**pepp'ercorn** *n.* dried pepper berry; something trifling —**pepp'ermint** *n.* plant noted for aromatic pungent liquor distilled from it; a sweet flavoured with this —**pepper tree** ornamental, evergreen tree

pep'tic *a.* relating to digestion or digestive juices

Péquiste' [pā-kēst'] *n.* member or supporter of Parti Quebecois

per *prep.* for each; by; in manner of

per-, par-, pel-, pil- (*comb. form*) through, thoroughly, as in *perfect, pellucid*

peram'bulate *vt.* walk through or over; traverse —*vi.* walk about —**peram'bulator** *n.* pram

per ann'um *Lat.* by the year

percale' *n.* woven cotton used *esp.* for sheets

perceive' *vt.* obtain knowledge of through senses; observe; understand —**perceiv'able** *a.* —**perceptibil'ity** *n.* —**percep'tible** *a.* discernible, recognizable —**percep'tion** *n.* faculty of perceiving; intuitive judgment —**percep'tive** *a.*

percent'age *n.* proportion or rate per hundred —**per cent** in each hundred

percep'tion *n. see* PERCEIVE

perch[1] *n.* freshwater fish

perch[2] *n.* resting place, as for bird; formerly, measure of 5½ yards —*vt.* place, as on perch —*vi.* alight, settle on fixed body; roost; balance on

perchance' *adv. obs.* perhaps

percip'ient *a.* having faculty of perception; perceiving —*n.* one who perceives

per'colate *v.* pass through fine mesh as liquor; permeate; filter —**percola'tion** *n.* —**per'colator** *n.* coffeepot with filter

percuss'ion [-sh'-] *n.* collision; impact; vibratory shock —**percussion instrument** one played by being struck, *eg* drum, cymbals *etc.*

perdi'tion [-ish'-] *n.* spiritual ruin

per'egrinate [pe'ri-] *vi.* travel about; roam —**peregrina'tion** *n.*

per'egrine [pe'ri-] *n.* type of falcon

perempt'ory *a.* authoritative, imperious; forbidding debate; decisive

perenn'ial *a.* lasting through the years; perpetual, unfailing —*n.* plant lasting more than two years —**perenn'ially** *adv.*

per'fect *a.* complete; finished; whole; unspoilt; faultless; correct, precise; excellent; of highest quality —*n.* tense denoting a complete act —*vt.* [-fekt'] improve; finish; make skilful —**perfect'ible** *a.* capable of becoming perfect —**perfec'tion** *n.* state of being perfect; faultlessness —**per'fectly** *adv.*

per'fidy *n.* treachery, disloyalty —**perfid'ious** *a.*

per'forate *vt.* make holes in, penetrate —**perfora'tion** *n.* hole(s) made through thing

perforce' *adv.* of necessity

perform' *vt.* bring to completion; accomplish; fulfil; represent on stage —*vi.* function; act part; play, as on musical instrument —**perform'ance** *n.* —**perform'er** *n.*

per'fume *n.* agreeable scent; fragrance —*vt.* [-fyōōm'] imbue with an agreeable odour; scent —**perfu'mer** *n.* —**perfu'mery** *n.* perfumes in general

perfunct'ory *a.* superficial; hasty; done indifferently

per'gola *n.* area covered by plants growing on trellis; the trellis

perhaps' *adv.* possibly

peri- (*comb. form*) round, as in *perimeter, period, periphrasis*

pericar'dium *n.* membrane enclosing the heart —**pericar'diac, -dial** *a.* —**pericardi'tis** *n.* inflammation of this

perihe'lion *n.* point in orbit of planet or comet nearest to sun (*pl.* **-lia**)

per'il [pe'r-] *n.* danger; exposure to injury —**per'ilous** *a.* full of peril, hazardous

perim'eter *n.* outer boundary of an area; length of this

pe'riod *n.* particular portion of time; a series of years; single occurrence of menstruation; cycle; conclusion; punctuation mark (.) at the end of a sentence; complete sentence —*a.* of furniture, dress, play *etc.*, belonging to particular time in history —**period'ic** *a.* recurring at regular intervals —**period'ical** *a./n.* (of) publication issued at regular intervals —*a.* of a period; periodic —**periodic'ity** *n.*

peripatet'ic *a.* itinerant; walking, travelling about

periph'ery *n.* circumference; surface, outside —**periph'eral** *a.* minor, unimportant; of periphery

periph'rasis *n.* roundabout speech or phrase; circumlocution —**periphras'tic** *a.*

per'iscope [pe'ri-] *n.* instrument used *esp.* in submarines, for giving view of objects on different level —**periscop'ic** *a.*

per'ish [pe'r-] *vi.* die, waste away; decay, rot —**perishabil'ity** *n.* —**per'ishable** *a.* that will not last long —*pl.n.* perishable food

per'istyle [pe'ri-] *n.* range of pillars surrounding building, square *etc.*; court within this

peritone'um *n.* membrane lining internal surface of abdomen (*pl.* **-ne'a**) —**peritoni'tis** *n.* inflammation of it

per'iwig [pe'ri-] *n. Hist.* wig

per'iwinkle [pe'ri-] *n.* flowering plant; small edible shellfish (*also* **winkle**)

per'jure *vt.* be guilty of perjury —**per'jury** *n.* crime of false testimony on oath; false swearing

perk *n. inf. short for* PERQUISITE

per'ky *a.* lively, cheerful, jaunty, gay —**perk up** make, become cheerful

per'mafrost *n.* permanently frozen ground

per'manent *a.* continuing in same state; lasting —**per'manence, per'manency** *n.* fixedness —**permanent wave** (*abbrev.* **perm**) *n.* (treatment of hair producing) long-lasting style

permang'anate *n.* salt of an acid of manganese

per'meate *vt.* pervade, saturate; pass through pores of —**per'meable** *a.* admitting of passage of fluids

permit' *vt.* allow; give leave to (**-tt-**) —*n.* [per'-] warrant or licence to do something; written permission —**permis'sible** *a.* allowable —**permiss'ion** *n.* authorization; leave, liberty —**permis'sive** *a.* (too) tolerant, lenient, *esp.* sexually

permute' *vt.* interchange —**permuta'tion** *n.* mutual transference; *Maths.* arrangement of a number of quantities in every possible order

perni'cious [-nish'-] *a.* wicked or mischievous; extremely hurtful; having quality of destroying or injuring

pernick'ety *a. inf.* fussy; fastidious about trifles

perora'tion *n.* concluding part of oration —**per'orate** *vi.*

perox'ide *n.* oxide of a given base containing greatest quantity of oxygen; *short for* HYDROGEN PEROXIDE

perpendic'ular *a.* at right angles to the plane of the horizon; at right angles to given line or surface; exactly upright —*n.* line falling at right angles on another line or plane

per'petrate *vt.* perform or be responsible for (something bad) —**perpetra'tion** *n.* —**per'petrator** *n.*

perpet'ual *a.* continuous; lasting for ever —**perpet'ually** *adv.* —**perpet'uate** *vt.* make perpetual; not to allow to be forgotten —**perpetua'tion** *n.* —**perpetu'ity** *n.*

perplex' *vt.* puzzle; bewilder; make difficult to understand —**perplex'ity** *n.* puzzled or tangled state

per'quisite [-it] *n.* any incidental benefit from a certain type of employment; casual payment in addition to salary

perr'y *n.* fermented drink made from pears

per se [-sā'] *Lat.* by or in itself

per'secute *vt.* oppress because of race, religion *etc.*; subject to persistent ill-treatment —**persecu'tion** *n.* —**per'secutor** *n.*

persevere' *vi.* persist, maintain effort —**perseve'rance** *n.* persistence

per'siflage [-flahzh] *n.* idle talk; frivolous style of treating subject

persimm'on *n.* Amer. tree; its hard wood; its fruit

persist' *vi.* continue in spite of obstacles or objections —**persist'ence, persis'tency** *n.* —**persist'ent** *a.* persisting; steady; persevering; lasting

per'son *n.* individual (human) being; body of human being; *Grammar* classification, or one of the classes, of pronouns and verb forms according to the person speaking, spoken to, or spoken of —**perso'na** *n.* assumed character —**per'sonable** *a.* good-looking —**per'sonage** *n.* notable person —**per'sonal** *a.* individual, private, or one's own; of, relating to grammatical person —**personal'ity** *n.* distinctive character; a celebrity —**per'sonally** *adv.* in person —**per'sonalty** *n.* personal property —**per'sonate** *vt.* pass oneself off as —**persona'tion** *n.* —**personal property** *Law* all property except land and interests in land that pass to heir

person'ify *vt.* represent as person; typify (**-ified, -ifying**) —**personifica'tion** *n.*

personnel' *n.* staff employed in a service or institution

perspect'ive [-iv] *n.* mental view; art of drawing on flat surface to give effect of solidity and relative distances and sizes; drawing in perspective

perspica'cious *a.* having quick mental insight —**perspicac'ity** [-kas'-] *n.*

perspic'uous *a.* clearly expressed; lucid; plain; obvious —**perspicu'ity** *n.*

perspire' *v.* sweat —**perspira'tion** *n.* sweating

persuade' [-sw-] *vt.* bring (one to do something) by argument, charm *etc.*; convince —**persua'sion** *n.* art, act of persuading; way of thinking or belief —**persua'sive** *a.*

pert *a.* forward, saucy

pertain' *vi.* belong, relate, have reference (to); concern

pertina'cious [-shəs] *a.* obstinate, persistent —**pertinac'ity** [-as'-] *n.* doggedness, resolution

pert'inent *a.* to the point —**per'tinence** *n.* relevance

perturb' *vt.* disturb greatly; alarm —**perturb'able** *a.* —**perturba'tion** *n.* agitation of mind

peruke' [-ōōk'] *n. Hist.* wig

peruse' [-ōōz'] *vt.* read, *esp.* in slow and careful, or leisurely, manner —**peru'sal** *n.*

pervade' *vt.* spread through; be rife among —**perva'sion** *n.* —**perva'sive** *a.*

pervert' *vt.* turn to wrong use; lead astray —*n.* [per'-] one who shows unhealthy abnormality, *esp.* in sexual matters —**perverse'** *a.* obstinately or unreasonably wrong; self-willed; headstrong; wayward —**perverse'ly** *adv.* —**perver'sion** *n.* —**perver'sity** *n.*

per'vious *a.* permeable; penetrable, giving passage

pese'ta *n.* Sp. monetary unit

pesk'y *a. inf.* troublesome

pess'ary *n.* instrument used to support mouth and neck of uterus; appliance to prevent conception; medicated suppository

pess'imism *n.* tendency to see the worst side of things; theory that everything turns to evil —**pess'imist** *n.* —**pessimis'tic** *a.*

pest *n.* troublesome or harmful thing, person or insect; plague —**pest'icide** *n.* chemical for killing pests, *esp.* insects —**pestif'erous** *a.* troublesome; bringing plague

pest'er *vt.* trouble or vex persistently; harass

pes'tilence *n.* epidemic disease *esp.* bubonic plague —**pes'tilent** *a.* troublesome; deadly —**pestilen'tial** *a.*

pes'tle [pes'əl] *n.* instrument with which things are pounded in a mortar —*v.*

Pet. Peter

pet *n.* animal or person kept or regarded with affection —*vt.* make pet of; *inf.* hug, embrace, fondle (**-tt-**)

pet'al *n.* white or coloured leaflike part of flower —**pet'alled** *a.*
petard' *n.* formerly, an explosive device
pe'ter *vi.* —**peter out** *inf.* disappear, lose power gradually
pet'it [-i] *a. Law* small, petty
petite' [-tēt'] *a.* small, dainty
peti'tion [-ish'-] *n.* entreaty, request, *esp.* one presented to sovereign or parliament —*vt.* present petition to —**peti'tionary** *a.* —**peti'tioner** *n.*
pet'rel *n.* sea bird
pet'rify *vt.* turn to stone; *fig.* make motionless with fear; make dumb with amazement (**-ified, -ifying**) —**petrifac'tion, petrifica'tion** *n.*
petro'leum *n.* mineral oil —**pet'rol** *n.* UK gasoline
petrol'ogy *n.* study of rocks and their structure
pett'icoat *n.* women's undergarment worn under skirts, dresses *etc.*
pett'ifogger *n.* low-class lawyer; one given to mean dealing in small matters —**pett'ifog** *vi.* be, act like pettifogger
pett'y *a.* unimportant, trivial; small-minded, mean; on a small scale —**petty cash** cash kept by firm to pay minor incidental expenses —**petty officer** noncommissioned officer in Navy
pet'ulant *a.* given to small fits of temper; peevish —**pet'ulance** *n.* peevishness
petu'nia *n.* plant with funnel-shaped purple or white flowers
pew *n.* fixed seat in church
pe'wit *see* PEEWIT
pew'ter *n.* alloy of tin and lead; ware of this
phalan'ger *n.* any of various Aust. tree-dwelling marsupials, the Aust. possum
phal'anx *n.* body of men formed in close array (*pl.* **phal'anxes, phalan'ges** [-jēz])
phal'arope *n.* small wading bird
phall'us *n.* penis; symbol of it used in primitive rites —**phall'ic** *a.* —**phal'licism** *n.*
phan'tasm *n.* vision of absent person; illusion —**phantasmagor'ia** *n.* crowd of dim or unreal figures; exhibition of illusions —**phantas'mal** *a.* —**phan'tasy** *n.* *see* FANTASY
phan'tom *n.* apparition; spectre, ghost; fancied vision
Pha'raoh [fā'rō] *n.* title of ancient Egyptian kings
phar'isee [fa'ri-] *n.* sanctimonious person; hypocrite —**pharisa'ic(al)** *a.*
pharmaceut'ic [-syoot'-] *a.* of pharmacy —**pharmaceut'ics** *pl.n.* science of pharmacy —**pharmaceut'ical** *a* —**phar'macist** *n.* person qualified to dispense drugs —**pharmacol'ogy** *n* study of drugs —**pharmacopoe'ia** [-pē'-] *n.* official book with list and directions for use of drugs —**phar'macy** *n* preparation and dispensing of drugs; dispensary
phar'ynx [fa'ringks] *n.* cavity forming back part of mouth and terminating in gullet (*pl.* **pharyn'ges** [-jēz]) —**pharyn'geal** *a.* —**pharyngi'tis** [-jī'-] *n.* inflammation of pharynx
phase [-z] *n.* any distinct or characteristic period or stage in a development or chain of events —*vt.* arrange, execute in stages or to coincide with something else
PhD Doctor of Philosophy
pheas'ant [fez'-] *n.* game bird with bright plumage
phenac'etin [-nas'-] *n.* drug to relieve fever, used for headache *etc.*
phenobarb'itone [fē-nō-] *n.* drug inducing sleep
phe'nol *n.* carbolic acid
phenom'enon *n.* anything appearing or observed; remarkable person or thing (*pl.* **phenom'ena**) —**phenom'enal** *a.* relating to phenomena; remarkable; recognizable or evidenced by senses
phi'al *n.* small bottle for medicine *etc.*
Phil. Philippians
phil- (*comb. form*) loving, as in *philanthropy, philosophy*
philan'der *vi.* (of man) flirt with women
philan'thropy *n.* practice of doing good to one's fellow men; love of mankind —**philanthrop'ic** *a.* loving mankind; benevolent —**philan'thropist** *n.*
philat'ely *n.* stamp collecting —**philatel'ic** *a.* —**philat'elist** *n.*
philharmon'ic *a.* musical (only for titles of societies)
phil'istine *n.* ignorant, smug person —*a.* —**phil'istinism** *n.*
philoden'dron *n.* widely cultivated tropical Amer. climbing plant
philol'ogy *n.* science of structure and

development of languages —**philolog'i-cal** *a.* —**philol'ogist** *n.*

philos'ophy *n.* pursuit of wisdom; study of realities and general principles; system of theories on nature of things or on conduct; calmness of mind —**philos'o-pher** *n.* one who studies, possesses, or originates philosophy —**philosoph'i-c(al)** *a.* of, like philosophy; wise, learned; calm, stoical —**philos'ophize** *vi.* reason like philosopher; theorize; moralize

phil'tre [-tər] *n.* love potion

phlebi'tis *n.* inflammation of a vein

phlegm [flem] *n.* viscid substance formed by mucous membrane and ejected by coughing *etc.*; calmness, sluggishness —**phlegmat'ic** [fleg-] *a.* not easily agitated; composed

phlox *n.* flowering plant

pho'bia *n.* fear or aversion; unreasoning dislike

phoe'nix [fē'-] *n.* legendary bird; unique thing

phone *n./vi. inf.* telephone

phonet'ic *a.* of, or relating to, vocal sounds —**phonet'ics** *pl.n.* science of vocal sounds —**phoneti'cian** *n.*

phono- (*comb. form*) sounds, as in *phonology*

pho'nograph *n.* instrument recording and reproducing sounds —**phono-graph'ic** *a.*

phonol'ogy *n.* study of speech sounds and their development; system of sounds in a language —**phonolog'ic(al)** *a.* —**phonol'ogist** *n.*

pho'ny *a. inf.* counterfeit, sham, fraudulent; suspect

phos'gene [foz'jēn] *n.* lung-irritant poison gas used in warfare

phos'phorus *n.* toxic, flammable, nonmetallic element which appears luminous in the dark —**phos'phate** *n.*, **phos'phide** *n.*, **phos'phite** *n.* compounds of phosphorus —**phosphores'-cence** *n.* faint glow in the dark

pho'to *n. inf. short for* PHOTOGRAPH —**photo finish** photo taken at end of race to show placing of contestants

photo- (*comb. form*) light, as in *photometer, photosynthesis*

photochem'istry *n.* study of chemical action of light

pho'tocopy *n.* photographic reproduction —*vt.*

photoelectric'ity *n.* electricity produced or affected by action of light

photoelec'tron *n.* electron liberated from metallic surface by action of beam of light

photogen'ic *a.* capable of being photographed attractively

pho'tograph *n.* picture made by chemical action of light on sensitive film —*vt.* take photograph of —**photog'ra-pher** *n.* —**photograph'ic** *a.* —**photog'-raphy** *n.*

photogravure' *n.* process of etching, product of photography; picture so reproduced

photolithog'raphy *n.* art of printing from photographs transferred to stone or metal plate —**photolithograph'ic** *a.*

photom'eter *n.* instrument for measuring light's intensity —**photom'etry** *n.*

Pho'tostat R apparatus for obtaining direct, facsimile, photographic reproductions of documents, manuscripts, drawings *etc.*, without printing from negatives —*vt.* take photostat copies of

photosyn'thesis *n.* process by which green plant uses sun's energy to build up carbohydrate reserves

phrase [-z] *n.* group of words; pithy expression; mode of expression —*vt.* express in words —**phraseol'ogy** [frāz-i-] *n.* manner of expression, choice of words —**phrasal verb** phrase consisting of verb and preposition, often with meaning different to the parts (*eg* take in)

phrenol'ogy *n.* (formerly) study of skull's shape; theory that character and mental powers are indicated by shape of skull —**phrenolog'ical** *a.* —**phrenol'o-gist** *n.*

phut *n.* dull, heavy sound —**go phut** collapse

phylac'tery *n.* leather case containing religious texts worn by Jewish men

phys'ic [-iz'-] *n.* medicine, *esp.* cathartic —*pl.* science of properties of matter and energy —**phys'ical** *a.* bodily, as opposed to mental or moral; material; of physics of body —**phys'ically** *adv.* —**physi'-cian** *n.* qualified medical practitioner —**phys'icist** *n.* one skilled in, or student of, physics

physiogn'omy [-on'-] *n.* judging character by face; face; outward appearance of something

physiog'raphy *n.* science of the earth's surface —**physiog'rapher** *n.*

physiol'ogy *n.* science of normal function of living things —**physiol'ogist** *n.*

physiother'apy *n.* therapeutic use of physical means, as massage *etc.* —**physiother'apist** *n.*

physique' [-ēk'] *n.* bodily structure, constitution and development

pi *n. Maths.* ratio of circumference of circle to its diameter

pian'o *n.* (*orig.* **pianofor'te**) musical instrument with strings which are struck by hammers worked by keyboard (*pl.* **pian'os**) —*a./adv. Mus.* softly —**pi'anist** [pē'-] *n.* performer on piano —**Piano'la R** mechanically played piano

piazz'a [-at'sə] *n.* square, marketplace

pic *n. inf.* picture; illustration (*pl.* **pics, pix**)

pi'ca *n.* printing type of 6 lines to the inch; size of type, 12 point; typewriter typesize (10 letters to inch)

pic'ador *n.* mounted bullfighter with lance

picaresque' [-esk'] *a.* of fiction, *esp.* episodic and dealing with the adventures of rogues

picayune' [-yōōn'] *a. inf.* of small value; mean, petty

pic'caninny *n. offens.* small negro child

picc'olo *n.* small flute (*pl.* **-los**)

pick[1] *vt.* choose, select carefully; pluck, gather; peck at; pierce with something pointed; find occasion for —*n.* act of picking; choicest part —**pick'ings** *pl.n.* gleanings; odds and ends of profit —**pick'lock** *n.* instrument for opening locks —**pick'pocket** *n.* one who steals from another's pocket —**pick-up** *n.* device for conversion of mechanical energy into electric signals, as in record player *etc.*; small truck —**pick on** find fault with —**pick up** raise, lift; collect; improve, get better; accelerate

pick[2] *n.* tool with curved iron crossbar and wooden shaft, for breaking up hard ground or masonry —**pick'axe** *n.* pick

pick'aback *n.* ride on the back of man or animal, given to child

pick'erel *n.* young pike

pick'et *n.* prong, pointed stake; party of trade unionists posted to deter would-be workers during strike —*vt.* post as picket; beset with pickets; tether to peg —**picket fence** fence of pickets

pic'kle [pik'l] *n.* food preserved in brine, vinegar *etc.*; liquid used for preserving; cucumber preserved in pickling solution; awkward situation —*pl.* pickled vegetables —*vt.* preserve in pickle —**pick'led** *a. inf.* drunk

pic'nic *n.* pleasure excursion including meal out of doors —*vi.* take part in picnic (**pic'nicked, pic'nicking**)

pic'ric acid powerful acid used in dyeing, medicine, and as ingredient in certain explosives

Pict *n.* member of ancient race of NE Scotland —**Pict'ish** *a.*

pic'ture *n.* drawing or painting; mental image; beautiful or picturesque object —*pl.* UK cinema —*vt.* represent in, or as in, a picture —**pictor'ial** *a.* of, in, with, painting or pictures; graphic —*n.* newspaper with pictures —**pictor'ially** *adv.* —**picturesque'** [-esk'] *a.* such as would be effective in picture; striking, vivid

pidg'in *n.* language, not a mother tongue, made up of elements of two or more other languages

pie *n.* baked dish of meat, fruit *etc.*, usu. with pastry crust; *obs.* magpie

pie'bald *a.* irregularly marked with black and white; motley —*n.* piebald horse or other animal —**pied** *a.* piebald; variegated

piece [pēs] *n.* bit, part, fragment; single object; literary or musical composition *etc.*; small object used in checkers, chess *etc.* —*vt.* mend, put together —**piece'meal** *adv.* by, in, or into pieces, a bit at a time —**piece'work** *n.* work paid for according to quantity produced

pièce de résistance' [pyes-də-re-zis-tahns'] *Fr.* principal item

pier *n.* structure running into sea as landing stage; piece of solid upright masonry, *esp.* supporting bridge

pierce *vt.* make hole in; make a way through —**pierc'ing** *a.* keen; penetrating

pier'rot [pēr'ō] *n.* pantomime character, clown

pi'ety *n.* godliness; devoutness, goodness; dutifulness

pif'fle *n. inf.* rubbish, twaddle, nonsense, trash

pig *n.* wild or domesticated mammal

killed for pork, ham, bacon; *inf.* greedy, dirty person; oblong mass of smelted metal —*vi.* of sow, produce litter (**-gg-**) —**pigg'ery** *n.* place for keeping, breeding pigs; greediness —**pigg'ish, pigg'y** *a.* dirty; greedy; stubborn —**pig-headed** *a.* obstinate —**pig'pen** *n.* enclosure for pigs —**pig'tail** *n.* plait of hair hanging from back or either side of head

pig'eon [pij'in] *n.* bird of many wild and domesticated varieties, often trained to carry messages; *inf.* concern, responsibility —**pig'eonhole** *n.* compartment for papers in desk *etc.* —*vt.* defer; classify —**pigeon-toed** *a.* with feet, toes turned inwards

pigg'yback *n. see* PICKABACK

pig'ment *n.* colouring matter, paint or dye

pig'my *see* PYGMY

pike[1] *n.* various types of large, predatory freshwater fish

pike[2] *n.* spear formerly used by infantry

pilas'ter *n.* square column, usu. set in wall

pilau' [-low'], **pil'af(f)** *n.* Oriental dish of meat or fowl boiled with rice, spices *etc.*

pil'chard *n.* small sea fish like the herring

pile[1] *n.* heap; great mass of building —*vt.* heap (up), stack load —*vi.* (*with* in, out, off *etc.*) move in a group —**atomic pile** nuclear reactor

pile[2] *n.* beam driven into the ground, *esp.* as foundation for building in water or wet ground —**pile'driver** *n.* machine for driving down piles

pile[3] *n.* nap of cloth, *esp.* of velvet, carpet *etc.*; down

piles *pl.n.* tumours of veins of rectum, haemorrhoids

pil'fer *v.* steal in small quantities —**pil'ferage** *n.* —**pil'ferer** *n.*

pil'grim *n.* one who journeys to sacred place; wanderer, wayfarer —**pil'grimage** *n.*

pill *n.* small ball of medicine swallowed whole; anything disagreeable which has to be endured —**the pill** oral contraceptive —**pill'box** *n.* small box for pills; small concrete fort

pill'age *v.* plunder, ravage, sack —*n.* seizure of goods, *esp.* in war; plunder

pill'ar *n.* slender, upright structure, column; prominent supporter

pill'ion *n.* seat, cushion, for passenger behind rider of motorcycle or horse

pill'ory *n.* frame with holes for head and hands in which offender was confined and exposed to public abuse and ridicule —*vt.* expose to ridicule and abuse; set in pillory (**pill'oried, pil'lorying**)

pill'ow *n.* cushion for the head, *esp.* in bed —*vt.* lay on, or as on, pillow

pi'lot *n.* person qualified to fly an aircraft or spacecraft; one qualified to take charge of ship entering or leaving harbour, or where knowledge of local water is needed; steersman; guide —*a.* experimental and preliminary —*vt.* act as pilot to; steer —**pi'lotage** *n.* work, fee of pilot —**pilot fish** small fish which accompanies sharks, larger fish —**pilot light** small auxiliary flame lighting main one in gas appliance *etc.*; small electric light as indicator

Pils'(e)ner *n.* type of pale beer

pil'ule *n.* small pill

pimen'to *n.* allspice; sweet red pepper (*also* **pimien'to**) (*pl.* **-tos**)

pimp *n.* one who solicits for prostitute —*vi.* act as pimp

pim'pernel *n.* plant with small scarlet, blue, or white flowers closing in dull weather

pim'ple *n.* small pus-filled spot on the skin —**pim'ply** *a.*

pin *n.* short thin piece of stiff wire with point and head, for fastening; wooden or metal peg or rivet —*vt.* fasten with pin; seize and hold fast (**-nn-**) —**pin'ball** *n.* electrically operated table game, where small ball is shot through various hazards —**pin money** trivial sum —**pin'point** *vt.* mark exactly

pin'afore *n.* apron

pince-nez [pans'nā] *sing. n.* eyeglasses kept on nose by spring

pin'cers *pl.n.* tool for gripping, composed of two limbs crossed and pivoted; claws of lobster *etc.*

pinch *vt.* nip, squeeze; stint; *inf.* steal; *inf.* arrest —*n.* nip; as much as can be taken up between finger and thumb; stress; emergency

pinch'beck *n.* zinc and copper alloy —*a.* counterfeit, flashy

pinch-hit *vi. Baseball* bat as substitute batter; act as substitute —**pinch hitter**

pine[1] *n.* evergreen coniferous tree; its wood

pine[2] *vi.* yearn; waste away with grief *etc.*

pin'eal *a.* shaped like pine cone —**pineal gland** small cone-shaped gland situated at base of brain

pine'apple *n.* tropical plant with spiny leaves bearing large edible fruit; the fruit

ping'er *n.* device that makes ringing sound, *esp.* timer

Ping'-Pong R table tennis

pin'ion[1] *n.* bird's wing —*vt.* disable or confine by binding wings, arms *etc.*

pin'ion[2] *n.* small cogwheel

pink *n.* pale red colour; garden plant; best condition, fitness —*a.* of colour pink —*vt.* pierce; ornament with perforations or scalloped, indented edge —*vi.* of engine, knock —**pink'ie** *n.* little finger

pinn'acle *n.* highest pitch or point; mountain peak; pointed turret on buttress or roof

pint [-ī-] *n.* liquid measure, half a quart, 1/8 gallon

pin'tail *n.* type of duck

pin'tle *n.* pivot pin

pint'o *a.* marked with patches of white —*n.* pinto horse (*pl.* **-tos**)

pin'-up *n.* picture of sexually attractive person, *esp.* (partly) naked

pioneer' [pī-ə-] *n.* explorer; early settler; originator; one of advance party preparing road for troops —*vi.* act as pioneer or leader

pi'ous *a.* devout; righteous

pip[1] *n.* seed in fruit

pip[2] *n.* high-pitched sound used as time signal on radio; spot on playing cards, dice, or dominoes; *inf.* star on junior officer's shoulder showing rank

pip[3] *n.* disease of fowl —**give someone the pip** *sl.* annoy someone

pipe *n.* tube of metal or other material; tube with small bowl at end for smoking tobacco; musical instrument, whistle; wine cask —*pl.* bagpipes —*v.* play on pipe; utter in shrill tone; convey by pipe; ornament with a piping or fancy edging —**pi'per** *n.* player on pipe or bagpipes —**pi'ping** *n.* system of pipes; decoration of icing on cake; fancy edging or trimming on clothes; act or art of playing on pipe, *esp.* bagpipes —**pipe dream** fanciful, impossible plan *etc.* —**pipe'line** *n.* long pipe for transporting oil, water *etc.*; means of communications —**in the pipeline** yet to come; in process of completion *etc.*

pipette' *n.* slender glass tube to transfer fluids from one vessel to another

pip'it *n.* bird like lark

pipp'in *n.* kinds of apple

pi'quant [pē'kənt] *a.* pungent; stimulating —**pi'quancy** *n.*

pique [pēk] *n.* feeling of injury, baffled curiosity or resentment —*vt.* hurt pride of; irritate; stimulate

pi'qué [pē'kā] *n.* stiff ribbed cotton fabric

piquet' [pi-ket', -kā'] *n.* card game for two

piran'ha [-rahn'yə] *n.* small voracious freshwater fish of tropical Amer.

pi'rate *n.* sea robber; publisher *etc.*, who infringes copyright —*n./a.* (person) broadcasting illegally —*vt.* use or reproduce (artistic work *etc.*) illicitly —**pi'racy** *n.* —**pirat'ical** *a.* —**pirat'ically** *adv.*

pirouette' [pi-roo-] *n.* spinning round on the toe —*vi.* do this

Pi'sces [pī'sēz] *pl.n.* the Fishes, 12th sign of zodiac, operative *c.* Feb. 19-Mar. 20 —**pis'catory, piscator'ial** *a.* of fishing or fishes

pistach'io [-tahsh'-] *n.* small hard-shelled, sweet-tasting nut; tree producing it (*pl.* **-os**)

pist'il *n.* seed-bearing organ of flower

pist'ol *n.* small firearm for one hand —*vt.* shoot with pistol (**-ll-**)

pist'on *n.* in internal-combustion engine, steam engine *etc.*, cylindrical part propelled to and fro in hollow cylinder by pressure of gas *etc.* to convert reciprocating motion to rotation

pit[1] *n.* deep hole in ground; mine or its shaft; depression; part of theatre occupied by orchestra; enclosure where animals were set to fight; servicing, refuelling area on motor-racing track —*vt.* set to fight, match; mark with small dents or scars (**-tt-**) —**pit'fall** *n.* any hidden danger; covered pit for catching animals or men

pit[2] *n.* stone of cherry, plum *etc.* —*vt.* extract stone from (**-tt-**)

pitch[1] *vt.* cast or throw; set up; set the key of (a tune) —*vi.* fall headlong; of ship, plunge lengthwise —*n.* act of pitching; degree, height, intensity; slope; distance airscrew advances during one revolution; distance between threads of screw, teeth of saw *etc.*; acuteness of tone; part of ground where wickets are set up; *Sport* field of play; station of street vendor *etc.*; *inf.* persuasive sales talk —**pitch'er** *n.* *Baseball* player who delivers ball to batter —**pitch'fork** *n.* fork for lifting hay *etc.* —*vt.* throw with, as with, pitchfork

pitch[2] *n.* dark sticky substance obtained from tar or turpentine —*vt.* coat with this —**pitch'y** *a.* covered with pitch; black as pitch —**pitch-black, -dark** *a.* very dark —**pitch pine** resinous kind of pine

pitch'blende *n.* mineral composed largely of uranium oxide, yielding radium

pitch'er *n.* large jug

pith *n.* tissue in stems and branches of certain plants; essential substance, most important part —**pith'ily** *adv.* —**pith'less** *a.* —**pith'y** *a.* terse, cogent, concise; consisting of pith

pitt'ance *n.* small allowance; inadequate wages

pitu'itary *a.* of, pert. to, the endocrine gland at base of brain

pit'y *n.* sympathy, sorrow for others' suffering; regrettable fact —*vt.* feel pity for (**pit'ied, pit'ying**) —**pit'eous** *a.* deserving pity; sad, wretched —**pit'iable** *a.* —**pit'iably** *adv.* —**pit'iful** *a.* woeful; contemptible —**pit'iless** *a.* feeling no pity; hard, merciless

piv'ot *n.* shaft or pin on which thing turns —*vt.* furnish with pivot —*vi.* hinge on one —**piv'otal** *a.* of, acting as, pivot; of crucial importance

pix'y, pix'ie *n.* fairy

pizz'a [pēt'sə] *n.* dish, (*orig.* It.) of baked disc of dough covered with wide variety of savoury toppings —**pizzeri'a** [-rē'ə] *n.* place selling pizzas

pizzazz' [pə-] *n. inf.* sparkle, vitality, glamour

pizzicat'o [pit-si-caht'ō] *a./n.* *Mus.* (note, passage) played by plucking string of violin *etc.*, with finger

pl. place; plate; plural

plac'ard *n.* paper or card with notice on one side for posting up or carrying, poster —*vt.* post placards on; advertise, display on placards

placate' *vt.* conciliate, pacify, appease —**plac'atory** [*or* -kā'-] *a.*

place *n.* locality, spot; position; stead; duty; town, village, residence, buildings; office, employment; seat, space; *Horse racing* first or usu. second position at finish —*vt.* put in particular place; set; identify; make (order, bet *etc.*) —*vi.* *Sport* finish among first three in contest, *esp.* second

place'bo *n.* sugar pill *etc.* given to unsuspecting patient as active drug

placen'ta [-sen'-] *n.* organ formed in uterus during pregnancy, providing nutrients for foetus; afterbirth (*pl.* **-tas, -tae** [-tē]) —**placen'tal** *a.*

plac'id [plas'-] *a.* calm; equable —**placid'ity** *n.* mildness, quiet

plack'et *n.* opening at top of skirt *etc.* fastened with buttons, zip

pla'giarism [-jə-] *n.* taking ideas, passages *etc.* from an author and presenting them, unacknowledged, as one's own —**pla'giarize** *v.*

plague [plāg] *n.* highly contagious disease, *esp.* bubonic plague; *inf.* nuisance; affliction —*vt.* trouble, annoy —**pla'guily** *adv.* —**pla'gu(e)y** [plā'gi] *a. inf.* tiresome; annoying

plaice *n.* flat fish

plaid [plad, plād] *n.* long Highland cloak or shawl; checked or tartan pattern

plain *a.* flat, level; unobstructed, not intricate; clear, obvious; easily understood; simple; ordinary; without decoration; not beautiful —*n.* tract of level country —*adv.* clearly —**plain'ly** *adv.* —**plain'ness** *n.* —**plain clothes** civilian dress, as opposed to uniform —**plain sailing** unobstructed course of action —**plain speaking** frankness, candour

plaint *n.* *Law* statement of complaint; *obs.* lament —**plaint'iff** *n.* *Law* one who sues in court —**plaint'ive** *a.* sad, mournful, melancholy

plait [plat] *n.* braid of hair, straw *etc.* —*vt.* form or weave into plaits

plan *n.* scheme; way of proceeding; project, design; drawing of horizontal section; diagram, map —*vt.* make plan of; arrange beforehand (**-nn-**)

plan'chet [-ahn'-] *n.* disc of metal from which coin is stamped

planchette' [plahn-shet'] *n.* small board used in spiritualism

plane[1] *n.* smooth surface; a level; carpenter's tool for smoothing wood —*vt.* make smooth with one —*a.* perfectly flat or level —**pla'ner** *n.* planing machine

plane[2] *v.* of airplane, glide; of boat, rise and partly skim over water —*n.* wing of airplane; airplane

plane[3] *n.* tree with broad leaves

plan'et *n.* heavenly body revolving round the sun —**plan'etary** *a.* of planets

planeta'rium *n.* an apparatus that shows the movement of sun, moon, stars and planets by projecting lights on the inside of a dome; building in which the apparatus is housed

plan'gent [-j-] *a.* resounding

plank *n.* long flat piece of sawn timber —*vt.* cover with planks; cook on a board

plank'ton *n.* minute animal and vegetable organisms floating in ocean

plant [-ah-] *n.* living organism feeding on inorganic substances and without power of locomotion; such an organism that is smaller than tree or shrub; equipment or machinery needed for manufacture; building and equipment for manufacturing purposes —*vt.* set in ground, to grow; support, establish; stock with plants; *sl.* hide, *esp.* to deceive or observe —**plant'er** *n.* one who plants; ornamental pot or stand for house plants

plan'tain[1] [-tin] *n.* low-growing herb with broad leaves

plan'tain[2] [-tin] *n.* tropical plant like banana; its fruit

planta'tion *n.* estate for cultivation of tea, tobacco *etc.*; wood of planted trees; formerly, colony

plaque [plak] *n.* ornamental plate, tablet; plate of clasp or brooch; filmy deposit on surfaces of teeth, conducive to decay

plas'ma [-az'-] *n.* clear, fluid portion of blood —**plas'mic** *a.*

plast'er [-ah-] *n.* mixture of lime, sand *etc.* for coating walls *etc.*; piece of fabric spread with medicinal or adhesive substance —*vt.* apply plaster to; apply like plaster —**plast'erer** *n.*

plast'ic *n.* any of a group of synthetic products derived from casein, cellulose *etc.* which can be readily moulded into any form and are extremely durable —*a.* made of plastic; easily moulded, pliant; capable of being moulded; produced by moulding —**plastic'ity** [-s'-] *n.* ability to be moulded police in riot control —**plastic surgery** repair or reconstruction of missing or malformed parts of the body for medical or cosmetic reasons

Plast'icine R a modelling material like clay

plate *n.* shallow round dish; flat thin sheet of metal, glass *etc.*; utensils of gold or silver; device for printing; illustration in book; device used by dentists to straighten children's teeth; *inf.* set of false teeth —*vt.* cover with thin coating of gold, silver, or other metal —**plate'ful** *n.* —**pla'ter** *n.* —**plate glass** kind of thick glass used for mirrors, windows *etc.* —**plate tecton'ics** *Geol.* study of structure of earth's crust, *esp.* movement of layers of rocks

plat'eau [-ō] *n.* tract of level high land, tableland; period of stability

plat'en *n. Printing* plate by which paper is pressed against type; roller in typewriter

plat'form *n.* raised level surface or floor, stage; raised area in station from which passengers board trains; political programme

plat'inum *n.* white heavy malleable metal

plat'itude *n.* commonplace remark —**platitu'dinous** *a.*

Platon'ic *a.* of Plato or his philosophy; (**p-**) (of love) purely spiritual, friendly

platoon' *n.* body of soldiers employed as unit

platt'er *n.* flat dish

plat'ypus *n.* small Aust. egg-laying amphibious mammal, with dense fur, webbed feet and ducklike bill (*also* **duck-billed platypus**) (*pl.* **-puses**)

plau'dit *n.* act of applause, hand clapping

plau'sible [-z-] *a.* apparently fair or reasonable; fair-spoken —**plausibil'ity** *n.*

play [plā] *vi.* amuse oneself; take part in game; behave carelessly; act a part on the stage; perform on musical instrument; move with light or irregular motion, flicker *etc.* —*vt.* contend with in game; take part in (game); trifle; act the part of; perform (music); perform on (instrument); use, work (instrument) —*n.*

dramatic piece or performance; sport; amusement; manner of action or conduct; activity; brisk or free movement; gambling —**play'er** *n.* —**play'ful** *a.* lively —**play'house** *n.* theatre —**playing card** one of set of 52 cards used in card games —**play-off** (*also* **play-down**) *n. Sport* extra contest to decide winner when tied; contest between league leaders to determine championship —**play'thing** *n.* toy —**play'wright** *n.* author of plays

plaz'a [-ahz'ə] *n.* open space or square; complex of shops *etc.*

PLC, plc Public Limited Company

plea [plē] *n.* entreaty; statement of prisoner or defendant; excuse —**plead** *vi.* make earnest appeal; address court of law —*vt.* bring forward as excuse or plea (**plead'ed** *or* **pled, plead'ing**)

please [-z] *vt.* be agreeable to; gratify; delight —*vi.* like; be willing —*adv.* word of request —**pleas'ance** [plez'-] *n.* secluded part of garden —**pleas'ant** *a.* pleasing, agreeable —**pleas'antly** *adv.* —**pleas'antry** *n.* joke, humour —**pleas'urable** *a.* giving pleasure —**pleas'ure** *n.* enjoyment; satisfaction, will, choice

pleat *n.* any of various types of fold made by doubling material back on itself —*vi.* make, gather into pleats

plebe'ian [-bē'ən] *a.* belonging to the common people; low or rough —*n.* one of the common people (*also offens. sl.* **pleb**)

pleb'iscite *n.* decision by direct voting of the electorate

plec'trum *n.* small implement for plucking strings of guitar *etc.*

pledge *n.* promise; thing given over as security; toast —*vt.* promise formally; bind or secure by pledge; give over as security

plei'stocene [plī'stə-sēn] *a.* glacial period of formation

ple'nary *a.* complete, without limitations, absolute; of meeting *etc.*, with all members present

plenipoten'tiary *a./n.* (envoy) having full powers

plen'itude *n.* completeness, abundance, entirety

plent'y *n.* abundance; quite enough —**plen'teous** *a.* ample; rich; copious —**plent'iful** *a.* abundant

ple'num *n.* space as considered to be full of matter (opposed to vacuum); condition of fullness

ple'onasm *n.* use of more words than necessary —**pleonast'ic** *a.* redundant

pleth'ora *n.* oversupply —**plethor'ic** [-o'rik] *a.*

pleur'isy [ploor'-] *n.* inflammation of **pleura**, membrane lining the chest and covering the lungs

plex'us *n.* network of nerves or fibres (*pl.* **plex'us**)

pli'able *a.* easily bent or influenced —**pliabil'ity** *n.* —**pli'ancy** *n.* —**pli'ant** *a.* pliable

pli'ers *pl.n.* tool with hinged arms and jaws for gripping

plight[1] [plīt] *n.* distressing state; predicament

plight[2] [plīt] *vt.* promise, engage oneself to

Plim'soll line mark on ships indicating maximum draught permitted when loaded

plinth *n.* slab as base of column *etc.*

pli'ocene *n. Geol.* the most recent tertiary deposits

PLO Palestine Liberation Organization

plod *vi.* walk or work doggedly (**-dd-**)

plonk[1] *v.* drop, fall suddenly and heavily —*n.*

plonk[2] *n.* **UK** *inf.* alcoholic drink, *esp.* (cheap) wine

plop *n.* sound of object falling into water without splash —*v.*

plot[1] *n.* secret plan, conspiracy; essence of story, play *etc.* —*vt.* devise secretly; mark position of; make map of —*vi.* conspire (**-tt-**)

plot[2] *n.* small piece of land

plough, plow [plow] *n.* implement for turning up soil; similar implement for clearing snow *etc.* —*vt.* turn up with plough, furrow —*vi.* work at slowly —**plough'man** *n.* —**plough'share** *n.* blade of plough

plov'er [pluv'-] *n.* various shore birds, typically with round head, straight bill and long pointed wings

ploy *n.* stratagem; occupation; prank

pluck *vt.* pull, pick off; strip from; sound strings of (guitar *etc.*) with fingers, plectrum —*n.* courage; sudden pull or tug

—**pluck'ily** *adv.* —**pluck'y** *a.* courageous

plug *n.* thing fitting into and filling a hole; *Electricity* device connecting appliance to electricity supply; tobacco pressed hard; *inf.* recommendation, advertisement —*vt.* stop with plug; *inf.* advertise anything by constant repetition; *sl.* punch; *sl.* shoot —*vi. inf.* (*with* away) work hard (**-gg-**) —**plug in** connect (electrical appliance) with power source by means of plug

plum *n.* stone fruit; tree bearing it; choicest part, piece, position *etc.*; dark reddish-purple colour —*a.* choice; plum-coloured

plu'mage *see* PLUME

plumb [-m] *n.* ball of lead (**plumb bob**) attached to string used for sounding, finding the perpendicular *etc.* —*a.* perpendicular —*adv.* perpendicularly; exactly; *inf.* downright; honestly; exactly —*vt.* set exactly upright; find depth of; reach, undergo; equip with, connect to plumbing system —**plumb'er** *n.* worker who attends to water and sewage systems —**plumb'ing** *n.* trade of plumber; system of water and sewage pipes —**plumb'line** *n.* cord with plumb attached

plume [ploom] *n.* feather; ornament of feathers or horsehair —*vt.* furnish with plumes; pride oneself —**plu'mage** *n.* bird's feathers collectively

plumm'et *vi.* plunge headlong —*n.* plumbline

plump[1] *a.* of rounded form, moderately fat, chubby —*v.* make, become plump

plump[2] *vi.* sit, fall abruptly; choose, vote only for —*vt.* drop, throw abruptly —*adv.* suddenly; heavily; directly

plun'der *vt.* take by force; rob systematically —*vi.* rob —*n.* pillage; booty, spoils

plunge *vt.* put forcibly (into) —*vi.* throw oneself (into); enter, rush with violence; descend very suddenly —*n.* dive —**plun'ger** *n.* rubber suction cap to unblock drains; pump piston

plunk *v.* pluck (string of banjo *etc.*); drop suddenly

pluper'fect *a./n.* (tense) expressing action completed before past point of time

plur'al [ploor'-] *a.* of, denoting more than one person or thing —*n.* word in its plural form —**plur'alism** *n.* holding of more than one appointment, vote *etc.*; coexistence of different social groups *etc.*, in one society —**plur'alist** *n./a.* —**plural'ity** *n.* majority of votes *etc.*

plus *prep.* with addition of (*usu.* indicated by the sign +) —*a.* to be added; positive

plush *n.* fabric with long nap, long-piled velvet —*a.* luxurious

Plu'to *n.* Greek god of the underworld; farthest planet from the sun

plutoc'racy [ploo-] *n.* government by the rich; state ruled thus; wealthy class —**plu'tocrat** *n.* wealthy man —**plutocrat'ic** *a.*

Pluto'nian *a.* pert. to Pluto or the infernal regions, dark

pluto'nium *n.* radioactive metallic element used *esp.* in nuclear reactors and weapons

plu'vial [ploo'-] *a.* of, caused by the action of rain

ply[1] *vt.* wield; work at; supply pressingly; urge; keep busy —*vi.* go to and fro, run regularly (**plied, ply'ing**)

ply[2] *n.* fold or thickness; strand of yarn —**ply'wood** *n.* board of thin layers of wood glued together with grains at right angles

PM paymaster; postmaster; prime minister

pm, PM post meridiem (*Lat.*, after noon); post mortem

PMG Postmaster General('s Department)

PMS premenstrual syndrome

PMT premenstrual tension

pneumat'ic [nyoo-] *a.* of, worked by, inflated with wind or air

pneumo'nia [nyoo-] *n.* inflammation of the lungs

PO Petty Officer; Post Office

poach[1] *vt.* take (game) illegally; trample, make swampy or soft —*vi.* trespass for this purpose; encroach —**poach'er** *n.*

poach[2] *vt.* simmer (eggs, fish *etc.*) gently in water *etc.* —**poach'er** *n.*

pock *n.* pustule, as in smallpox *etc.* —**pock'marked** *a.*

pock'et *n.* small bag inserted in garment; cavity filled with ore *etc.*; socket, cavity, pouch or hollow; mass of water or air differing from that surrounding it;

isolated group or area —*vt.* put into one's pocket; appropriate, steal —*a.* small —**pock'etbook** *n.* small bag for money *etc.* carried in pocket; finances; small paperback book; *esp.* **US** woman's handbag —**pocket money** small, regular allowance given to children by parents; allowance for small, occasional expenses

pod *n.* long seed vessel, as of peas, beans *etc.* —*vi.* form pods —*vt.* shell (**-dd-**)

podg'y *a.* short and fat

po'dium *n.* small raised platform

po'em *n.* imaginative composition in rhythmic lines —**po'et** *n.* writer of poems (**po'etess** *fem.*) —**po'etry** *n.* art or work of poet, verse —**po'esy** [-zi] *n.* poetry —**poet'ic(al)** *a.* —**poet'ically** *adv.* —**poetast'er** *n.* would-be or inferior poet

pog'rom *n.* organized persecution and massacre, *esp.* of Jews in Russia

po'g(e)y *sl.n.* unemployment insurance; dole

poign'ant [poin'yənt] *a.* moving; biting, stinging; vivid; pungent —**poign'ancy** *n.*

poincian'a [-ahn'-] *n.* tropical tree with scarlet flowers

poinsett'ia *n. orig.* Amer. shrub, widely cultivated for its clusters of scarlet leaves, resembling petals

point *n.* dot, mark; punctuation mark; item, detail; unit of value; position, degree, stage; moment; gist of an argument; purpose; striking or effective part or quality; essential object or thing; sharp end; single unit in scoring; headland; one of direction marks of compass; fine kind of lace; act of pointing; power point; printing unit, one twelfth of a pica —*pl.* electrical contacts in distributor of engine —*vi.* show direction or position by extending finger; direct attention; (of dog) indicate position of game by standing facing it —*vt.* aim, direct; sharpen; fill up joints with mortar; give value to (words *etc.*) —**point'ed** *a.* sharp; direct, telling —**point'edly** *adv.* —**point'er** *n.* index; indicating rod *etc.*, used for pointing; indication; dog trained to point —**point'less** *a.* blunt; futile, irrelevant —**point-blank** *a.* aimed horizontally; plain, blunt —*adv.* with level aim (there being no necessity to elevate for distance); at short range —**point-to-point** *n.* steeplechase usu. for amateur riders only

poise *n.* composure; self-possession; balance, equilibrium, carriage (of body *etc.*) —*v.* (cause to be) balanced or suspended —*vt.* hold in readiness

poi'son [-z-] *n.* substance which kills or injures when introduced into living organism —*vt.* give poison to; infect; pervert, spoil —**poi'soner** *n.* —**poi'sonous** *a.* —**poison-pen letter** malicious anonymous letter

poke[1] *vt.* push, thrust with finger, stick *etc.*; thrust forward —*vi.* make thrusts; pry —*n.* act of poking —**po'ker** *n.* metal rod for poking fire —**pok(e)y** *a.* small, confined, cramped —*n. sl.* a jail

poke[2] —**pig in a poke** something bought *etc.* without previous inspection

po'ker *n.* card game

po'lar *a. see* POLE[2]

Po'laroid **R** type of plastic which polarizes light; camera that develops print very quickly inside itself

pol'der [*or* pōl'-] *n.* land reclaimed from the sea

pole[1] *n.* long rounded piece of wood *etc.* —*vt.* propel with pole

pole[2] *n.* each of the ends of axis of earth or celestial sphere; each of opposite ends of magnet, electric cell *etc.* —**po'lar** *a.* pert. to the N and S pole, or to magnetic poles; directly opposite in tendency, character *etc.* —**polar'ity** *n.* —**polariza'tion** *n.* —**po'larize** *vt.* give polarity to; affect light in order to restrict vibration of its waves to certain directions —**polar bear** white Arctic bear

pole'axe *n.* battle-axe —*vt.* hit, fell as with poleaxe

pole'cat *n.* small animal of weasel family

polem'ic *a.* controversial —*n.* war of words, argument —**polem'ical** *a.* —**polem'icize** *vt.*

police' [pə-lēs'] *n.* the civil force which maintains public order —*vt.* keep in order —**police'man** *n.* member of police force (**police'woman** *fem.*)

pol'icy[1] *n.* course of action adopted, *esp.* in state affairs; prudence

pol'icy[2] *n.* insurance contract

poliomyeli'tis [-mī-ə-lī'tis] *n.* disease of spinal cord characterized by fever and possibly paralysis (*abbrev.* **po'lio**)

pol'ish *vt.* make smooth and glossy; refine —*n.* shine; polishing; substance for polishing; refinement

polite' *a.* showing regard for others in manners, speech *etc.* refined, cultured —**polite'ly** *adv.* —**polite'ness** *n.* courtesy

pol'itic *a.* wise, shrewd, expedient, cunning —**pol'itics** *pl.n.* art of government; political affairs or life —**polit'ical** *a.* of the state or its affairs —**politi'cian** *n.* one engaged in politics —**pol'ity** *n.* form of government; organized state; civil government —**political economy** *former name for* ECONOMICS

pol'ka *n.* lively dance in 2/4 time; music for it —**polka dot** one of pattern of bold spots on fabric *etc.*

poll [pōl] *n.* voting; counting of votes; number of votes recorded; canvassing of sample of population to determine general opinion; (top of) head —*vt.* receive (votes); take votes of; lop, shear; cut horns from animals —*vi.* vote —**poll, polled** *a.* hornless —**poll'ster** *n.* one who conducts polls —**polling booth** voting place at election —**poll tax** (*esp.* formerly) tax on each person

poll'ack, poll'ock *n.* type of food fish

poll'ard *n.* hornless animal of normally horned variety; tree on which a close head of young branches has been made by polling —*vt.* make a pollard of

poll'en *n.* fertilizing dust of flower —**pol'linate** *vt.*

poll'iwog *n.* tadpole

pollute' [-lo͞ot'] *vt.* make foul; corrupt; desecrate —**pollu'tant** *n.* —**pollu'tion** *n.*

po'lo *n.* game like hockey played by teams of 4 players on horseback —**water polo** game played similarly by swimmers seven-a-side

polonaise' [-nāz'] *n.* Polish dance; music for it

pol'tergeist [-gīst] *n.* noisy mischievous spirit

poltroon' *n.* abject coward

poly- (*comb. form*) many, as in **polysyllab'ic** *a.*

polyan'dry *n.* polygamy in which woman has more than one husband

polyan'thus *n.* cultivated primrose

pol'ychrome *a.* many coloured —*n.* work of art in many colours —**polychromat'ic** *a.*

polyes'ter *n.* any of large class of synthetic materials used as plastics, textile fibres *etc.*

polyeth'ylene *n.* tough thermoplastic material

polyg'amy [-lig'-] *n.* custom of being married to several persons at a time —**polyg'amist** *n.*

pol'yglot *a.* speaking, writing in several languages

pol'ygon *n.* figure with many angles or sides —**polyg'onal** *a.*

polyg'yny [-lij'-] *n.* polygamy in which one man has more than one wife

polyhe'dron *n.* solid figure contained by many faces

pol'ymer *n.* compound, as polystyrene, that has large molecules formed from repeated units —**polymeriza'tion** *n.* —**pol'ymerize** *vt.*

pol'yp *n.* sea anemone, or allied animal; (*also* **pol'ypus**) tumour with branched roots

pol'yphase *a.* of alternating current of electricity, possessing number of regular sets of alternations

polysty'rene *n.* synthetic material used *esp.* as white rigid foam for packing *etc.*

polytech'nic *n.* college dealing mainly with various arts and crafts —*a.*

pol'ytheism *n.* belief in many gods —**pol'ytheist** *n.* —**polytheist'ic** *a.*

pol'ythene *n.* polyethylene

polyunsat'urated *a.* of group of fats that do not form cholesterol in blood

polyur'ethane [-yoor'-] *n.* class of synthetic materials, often in foam or flexible form

polyva'lent *a.* having more than one valency

poman'der *n.* (container for) mixture of sweet-smelling herbs *etc.*

pom'egranate *n.* tree; its fruit with thick rind containing many seeds in red pulp

Pomera'nian *n.* breed of small dog

pomm'el *n.* front of saddle; knob of sword hilt —*vt. see* PUMMEL

pomp *n.* splendid display or ceremony

pom'pon, pom'pom *n.* tuft of ribbon, wool, feathers *etc.*, decorating hat, shoe *etc.*

pomp'ous *a.* self-important; ostentatious; of language, inflated, stilted —**pompos'ity** *n.*

pon'cho *n.* loose circular cloak with hole for head (*pl.* **-s**)

pond *n.* small body, pool or lake of still water —**pond'weed** *n.* various water plants

pon'der *v.* muse, meditate, think over; consider, deliberate on

pond'erous *a.* heavy, unwieldy; boring —**pond'erable** *a.* able to be evaluated or weighed

pon'iard [-yəd] *n.* dagger —*vt.* stab with one

pon'tiff *n.* Pope; high priest; bishop —**pontif'ical** *a.* —**pontif'icate** *n.* dignity or office of pontiff —**pon'tify, pontif'icate** *vi.* speak bombastically; act as pontiff

pontoon'[1] *n.* flat-bottomed boat or metal drum for use in supporting temporary bridge

pontoon'[2] *n.* gambling card game (*also* **twenty-one**)

po'ny *n.* horse of small breed; very small glass

pooch *n. sl.* dog

poo'dle *n.* pet dog with long curly hair often clipped fancifully

poof *n.* **UK** *sl.* homosexual man

Pooh'-Bah' *n.* pompous official

pool[1] [-oo-] *n.* small body of still water; deep place in river or stream; puddle; swimming pool

pool[2] [-oo-] *n.* common fund or resources; group of people, *eg* typists, any of whom can work for any of several employers; collective stakes in various games; cartel; variety of billiards —*vt.* put in common fund

poop[1] [-oo-] *n.* ship's stern

poop[2] [-oo-] *v. sl.* make or become exhausted

poor *a.* having little money; unproductive; inadequate, insignificant; needy; miserable, pitiable; feeble; not fertile —**poor'ly** *adv./a.* not in good health —**poor'ness** *n.*

pop[1] *vi.* make small explosive sound; *inf.* go or come unexpectedly or suddenly —*vt.* cause to make small explosive sound; put or place suddenly (**-pp-**) —*n.* small explosive sound; *inf.* nonalcoholic fizzy drink —**popp'er** *n.* container for cooking popcorn in —**pop'corn** *n.* any kind of corn that puffs up when roasted; the roasted product

pop[2] *n. inf.* father

pop[3] *n.* music of general appeal, *esp.* to young people —*a. short for* POPULAR

pop. popular; population

Pope *n.* bishop of Rome and head of R.C. Church —**po'pery** *n. offens.* papal system, doctrines

pop'lar *n.* tree noted for its slender tallness

pop'lin *n.* corded fabric *usu.* of cotton

pop'over *n.* light hollow puffy muffin

popp'adom *n.* thin, round, crisp Indian bread

popp'y *n.* bright-flowered plant yielding opium

Pop'sicle **R** flavoured ice on stick

pop'ulace *n.* the common people; the masses

pop'ular *a.* finding general favour; of, by the people —**popular'ity** *n.* state or quality of being generally liked —**populariza'tion** *n.* —**pop'ularize** *vt.* make popular —**pop'ularly** *adv.*

pop'ulate *vt.* fill with inhabitants —**popula'tion** *n.* inhabitants; their number —**pop'ulous** *a.* thickly populated or inhabited

por'celain [-slin] *n.* fine earthenware, china —**porcelain clay** kaolin

porch *n.* covered approach to entrance of building; exterior roofed gallery, veranda

por'cine [-sin] *a.* of, like pig

porc'upine *n.* rodent covered with long, pointed quills

pore[1] *vi.* fix eye or mind upon; study closely

pore[2] *n.* minute opening, *esp.* in skin —**poros'ity** *n.* —**por'ous** *a.* allowing liquid to soak through; full of pores

pork *n.* pig's flesh as food —**pork'er** *n.* pig raised for food —**pork'y** *a.* fleshy, fat

porn, por'no *n. inf. short for* PORNOGRAPHY

pornog'raphy *n.* indecent literature, movies *etc.* —**pornog'rapher** *n.* —**pornograph'ic** *a.* —**pornograph'ically** *adv.*

porph'yry *n.* reddish stone with embedded crystals

por'poise [-pəs] *n.* blunt-nosed sea mammal like dolphin

porr'idge *n.* soft food of oatmeal *etc.* boiled in water

port[1] *n.* harbour, haven; town with harbour

port[2] *n.* larboard or left side of ship *—vt.* turn to left side of a ship

port[3] *n.* strong red wine

port[4] *n.* opening in side of ship **—port'-hole** *n.* small opening or window in side of ship

port[5] *vt. Mil.* carry rifle, *etc.* diagonally across body *—n.* this position

port'able *n./a.* (something) easily carried

port'age *n.* (cost of) transport

por'tal *n.* large doorway or imposing gate

portcull'is *n.* defence grating to raise or lower in front of castle gateway

portend' *vt.* foretell; be an omen of **—port'ent** *n.* omen, warning; marvel **—portent'ous** *a.* ominous; threatening; pompous

port'er *n.* person employed to carry burden, *eg* on railway; sleeping-car attendent **—port'erage** *n.* (charge for) carrying of supplies

portfo'lio *n.* flat portable case for loose papers; office of minister of state (*pl.* **-s**)

port'ico *n.* colonnade; covered walk (*pl.* **-os**)

portiere' [-ti-ār'] *n.* heavy door curtain

por'tion *n.* part, share, helping; destiny, lot *—vt.* divide into shares **—por'tionless** *a.*

port'ly *a.* bulky, stout

portman'teau [-tō] *n.* leather suitcase, *esp.* one opening into two compartments (*pl.* **-s, -x** [-ōz])

portray' *vt.* make pictures of, describe **—por'trait** [-trit] *n.* likeness of (face of) individual **—por'traiture** *n.* **—portray'al** *n.* act of portraying

Por'tuguese [-gēz] *a.* pert. to Portugal or its inhabitants **—Portuguese man-of-war** kind of jellyfish

pose *vt.* place in attitude; put forward *—vi.* assume attitude, affect or pretend to be a certain character *—n.* attitude, *esp.* one assumed for effect **—poseur'** *n.* one who assumes affected attitude to create impression

po'ser *n.* puzzling question

posh *a. inf.* smart, elegant, stylish

pos'it [poz'-] *vt.* lay down as principle

posi'tion [-zish'-] *n.* place; situation; location, attitude; status; state of affairs; employment; strategic point *—vt.* place in position

pos'itive [poz'-] *a.* certain; sure; definite, absolute, unquestionable; utter; downright; confident; not negative; greater than zero; *Electricity* having deficiency of electrons *—n.* something positive; *Photog.* print in which lights and shadows are not reversed **—pos'itively** *adv.* **—pos'itivism** *n.* philosophy recognizing only matters of fact and experience **—pos'itivist** *n.* believer in this

pos'itron [poz'-] *n.* positive electron

poss'e *n.* body of men, *esp.* for maintaining law and order; group of trained horsemen who perform at rodeos

possess' [-zes'] *vt.* own; (of evil spirit *etc.*) have mastery of **—possess'ion** *n.* act of possessing; thing possessed; ownership **—possess'ive** *a.* of, indicating possession; with excessive desire to possess, control *—n.* possessive case in grammar **—possess'or** *n.* owner

poss'ible *a.* that can, or may, be, exist, happen or be done; worthy of consideration *—n.* possible candidate **—possibil'ity** *n.* **—poss'ibly** *adv.* perhaps

poss'um *n. see* OPOSSUM **—play possum** pretend to be dead, asleep *etc.* to deceive opponent

post[1] [pōst] *n.* upright pole of timber or metal fixed firmly, usu. to support or mark something *—vt.* display; stick up (on notice board *etc.*) **—post'er** *n.* large advertising bill; one who posts bills **—poster paints, colours** lustreless paints suited for posters

post[2] [pōst] *n.* official carrying of letters or parcels; collection or delivery of these; office; situation; point, station, place of duty; place where soldier is stationed; place held by body of troops; fort *—vt.* put into official box for carriage by post; supply with latest information; station (soldiers *etc.*) in particular spot; transfer (entries) to ledger *—adv.* in haste **—post'age** *n.* charge for carrying letter **—post'al** *a.* **—post'card** *n.* stamped card sent by post **—postal code** *n.* system of letters and numbers used to aid sorting of mail **—post'man** *n.* mailman **—post'mark** *n.* official mark with name of office *etc.* stamped on letters **—post'-**

master, post'mistress *n.* official in charge of **post office**, place where postal business is conducted —**post paid** with the postage prepaid

post- (*comb. form*) after, behind, later than, *eg* **post'war** *a.* Such compounds are not given here where the meaning can easily be found from the simple word

postdate' *vt.* give date later than actual date

poste' restante' [post'ri-stant'] *Fr.* department of post office where traveller's letters are kept till called for

poste'rior [pos-] *a.* later, hinder —*n.* the buttocks

poster'ity [-te'ri-] *n.* later generations; descendants

pos'tern *n.* private entrance; small door, gate

postgrad'uate *a.* carried on after graduation —*n.*

pos'thumous [-tyoo-] *a.* occurring after death; born after father's death; published after author's death —**pos'thumously** *adv.*

postill'ion *n. Hist.* man riding one of pair of horses drawing a carriage

postmor'tem *n.* medical examination of dead body —*a.* taking place after death

post-o'bit *a.* taking effect after death

postpone' *vt.* put off to later time, defer —**postpone'ment** *n.*

postpran'dial *a.* after dinner

post'script *n.* addition to letter, book

post'ulant *n.* candidate for admission to religious order

pos'tulate *vt.* take for granted; lay down as self-evident; stipulate —*n.* proposition assumed without proof; prerequisite —**postula'tion** *n.*

pos'ture *n.* attitude, position of body —*v.* pose

po'sy *n.* bunch of flowers

pot *n.* round vessel; cooking vessel; trap, *esp.* for crabs, lobsters; *sl.* cannabis —*pl. inf.* a lot —*vt.* put into, preserve in pot (-tt-) —**pott'ed** *a.* preserved in a pot; *inf.* abridged —**pot'hole** *n.* pitlike cavity in rocks, usu. limestone, produced by faulting and water action; hole worn in road —**potluck'** *n.* whatever is to be had (to eat) —**pot'sherd** *n.* broken fragment of pottery —**pot shot** easy or random shot

po'table *a.* drinkable —**pota'tion** *n.* drink; drinking

pot'ash *n.* alkali used in soap *etc.*; crude potassium carbonate

potass'ium *n.* white metallic element

pota'to *n.* plant with tubers grown for food (*pl.* **-es**) —**potato chip** very thin slice of potato fried and eaten cold —**sweet potato** trailing plant; its edible sweetish tubers

po'tent *a.* powerful, influential; (of male) capable of sexual intercourse —**po'tency** *n.* physical or moral power; efficacy —**po'tently** *adv.*

po'tentate *n.* ruler

poten'tial *a.* latent, that may or might but does not now exist or act —*n.* possibility; amount of potential energy; *Electricity* level of electric pressure —**potential'ity** *n.*

po'tion *n.* dose of medicine or poison

potpourr'i [pō-poor'i] *n.* mixture of rose petals, spices *etc.*; musical, literary medley

pott'age *n.* soup or stew

pott'er[1] *n.* maker of earthenware vessels —**pott'ery** *n.* earthenware; where it is made; art of making it

pott'er[2] *vi. see* PUTTER

pott'y *a.* UK *inf.* (of person) mad; (of thing) silly, trivial

pouch *n.* small bag; pocket —*vt.* put into one

poult'ice [pōlt'is] *n.* soft composition of mustard, kaolin *etc.*, applied hot to sore or inflamed parts of the body

poul'try [pōl'-] *n.* domestic fowls —**poul'terer** *n.* dealer in poultry

pounce[1] *vi.* spring upon suddenly, swoop (upon) —*n.* swoop or sudden descent

pounce[2] *n.* fine powder used to prevent ink from spreading on unsized paper or in pattern making

pound[1] *vt.* beat, thump; crush to pieces or powder; walk, run heavily

pound[2] *n.* unit of troy weight; unit of avoirdupois weight equal to 0.454 kg; monetary unit in U.K.

pound[3] *n.* enclosure for stray animals or officially removed vehicles; confined space

pound'al *n.* a unit of force in the foot-pound-second system

pour [pawr] *vi.* come out in a stream,

crowd *etc.*; flow freely; rain heavily —*vt.* give out thus; cause to run out

pout[1] *v.* thrust out (lips), look sulky —*n.* act of pouting —**pout'er** *n.* pigeon with power of inflating its crop

pout[2] *n.* type of food fish

pov'erty *n.* state of being poor; poorness; lack of means; scarcity

POW prisoner of war

pow'der *n.* solid matter in fine dry particles; medicine in this form; gunpowder; facepowder *etc.* —*vt.* apply powder to; reduce to powder —**pow'dery** *a.*

pow'er *n.* ability to do or act; strength; authority; control; person or thing having authority; mechanical energy; electricity supply; rate of doing work; product from continuous multiplication of number by itself —**pow'ered** *a.* having or operated by mechanical or electrical power —**pow'erful** *a.* —**pow'erless** *a.* —**pow'erhouse, power station** *n.* installation for generating and distributing electric power

pow'wow *n.* conference —*vi.* confer

pox *n.* one of several diseases marked by pustular eruptions of skin; *inf.* syphilis

pp pages

PQ Parti Quebecois

PR proportional representation; public relations

pr. pair; present; price; pronoun

prac'tical *a.* given to action rather than theory; relating to action or real existence; useful; in effect though not in name; virtual —**prac'tically** *adv.* —**practicabil'ity** *n.* —**prac'ticable** *a.* that can be done, used *etc.* —**practi'tioner** *n.* one engaged in a profession

prac'tise, *esp.* **US prac'tice** *vt.* do repeatedly, work at to gain skill; do habitually; put into action —*vi.* exercise oneself; exercise profession —**prac'tice** *n.* habit; mastery or skill; exercise of art or profession; action, not theory

pragmat'ic *a.* concerned with practical consequence; of the affairs of state —**pragmat'ical** *a.* —**prag'matism** *n.* —**prag'matist** *n.*

prair'ie *n.* large treeless tract of grassland —**prairie dog** small Amer. rodent allied to marmot —**prairie oyster** cocktail —**prairie schooner** N Amer. covered wagon

praise *n.* commendation; fact, state of being praised —*vt.* express approval, admiration of; speak well of; glorify —**praise'worthy** *a.*

pral'ine [prahl'ēn] *n.* sweet composed of nuts and sugar

pram *n.* **UK** baby carriage

prance [-ah-] *vi.* swagger; caper; walk with bounds —*n.* prancing

pran'dial *a.* of dinner

prank *n.* mischievous trick or escapade, frolic

prase *n.* light green translucent chalcedony

prate *vi.* talk idly, chatter —*n.*

prat'tle *vi.* talk like child —*n.* trifling, childish talk —**prat'tler** *n.* babbler

prawn *n.* edible sea crustacean like a shrimp but larger

prax'is *n.* practice, *esp.* as opposed to theory

pray *vt.* ask earnestly; entreat —*vi.* offer prayers *esp.* to God —**prayer** [prār] *n.* action, practice of praying to God; earnest entreaty

pre- (*comb. form*) before, beforehand *eg* **prena'tal** *a.*, **prerecord'** *vt.*, **preshrunk'** *a.* Such compounds are not given here where the meaning can easily be found from the simple word

preach *vi.* deliver sermon; give moral, religious advice —*vt.* set forth in religious discourse; advocate —**preach'er** *n.*

pream'ble *n.* introductory part of story *etc.*

preb'end *n.* stipend of canon or member of cathedral chapter —**preb'endary** *n.* holder of this

preca'rious *a.* insecure, unstable, perilous

precau'tion *n.* previous care to prevent evil or secure good; preventive measure —**precau'tionary** *a.*

precede' *v.* go, come before in rank, order, time *etc.* —**prec'edence** [*or* prē-sē'-] *n.* priority in position, rank, time *etc.* —**prec'edent** *n.* previous case or occurrence taken as rule

precent'or *n.* leader of singing choir or congregation

pre'cept *n.* rule for conduct, maxim —**precept'or** *n.* instructor —**preceptor'rial** *a.*

precess'ion [-sesh'-] *n.* act of preceding; motion of spinning body (*eg* top, planet) wobbling so that axis of rotation marks out a cone

pre'cinct *n.* enclosed, limited area; **US** administrative area of city *—pl.* environs

prec'ious [presh'əs] *a.* beloved, cherished; of great value, highly valued; rare **—precios'ity** *n.* overrefinement in art or literature **—prec'iously** *adv.* **—pre'ciousness** *n.*

prec'ipice [pres'-] *n.* very steep cliff or rockface **—precip'itous** *a.* sheer

precip'itant *a.* hasty, rash; abrupt **—precip'itance, -ancy** *n.*

precip'itate [-āt] *vt.* hasten happening of; throw headlong; *Chem.* cause to be deposited in solid form from solution *—a.* [-it] too sudden; rash, impetuous *—n.* [-āt] substance chemically precipitated **—precip'itately** *adv.* **—precipita'tion** *n. esp.* rain, snow *etc.*

pré'cis [prā'sē] *n.* abstract, summary (*pl.* **pré'cis** [-sēz])

precise' *a.* definite; particular; exact, strictly worded; careful in observance; punctilious, formal **—precise'ly** *adv.* **—preci'sion** *n.* accuracy

preclude' *vt.* prevent from happening; shut out

preco'cious *a.* developed, matured early or too soon **—precoc'ity** [-os'-], **preco'ciousness** *n.*

preconceive' *vt.* form an idea beforehand **—preconcep'tion** *n.*

precondi'tion *n.* necessary or required condition

precur'sor *n.* forerunner **—precur'sive, precur'sory** *a.*

pred'atory *a.* hunting, killing other animals *etc.* for food; plundering **—pred'ator** *n.* predatory animal

pre'decessor *n.* one who precedes another in an office or position; ancestor

predes'tine [-tin] *vt.* decree beforehand, foreordain **—predestina'tion** *n.*

predic'ament *n.* perplexing, embarrassing or difficult situation

pred'icate *vt.* affirm, assert; base (on or upon) *—n.* that which is predicated; *Grammar* statement made about a subject **—predica'tion** *n.* **—predic'ative** *a.*

predict' *vt.* foretell, prophesy **—predict'able** *a.* **—predic'tion** *n.*

predilec'tion *n.* preference, liking, partiality

predispose' *vt.* incline, influence someone (towards); make susceptible (to)

predom'inate *vi.* be main or controlling element **—predom'inance** *n.* **—predom'inant** *a.* chief

pre-em'inent *a.* excelling all others, outstanding **—pre-em'inence** *n.* **—pre-em'inently** *adv.*

pre-empt' *vt.* acquire in advance or act in advance of or to exclusion of others **—pre-emp'tion** *n.* **—pre-emp'tive** *a.*

preen *vt.* trim (feathers) with beak, plume; smarten oneself

pref. preface; preference; prefix

prefab'ricate *vt.* manufacture buildings *etc.* in shaped sections, for rapid assembly on the site **—pre'fab** *n.* house so made

pref'ace [-is] *n.* introduction to book *etc.* *—vt.* introduce **—pref'atory** *a.*

pre'fect *n.* person put in authority; schoolchild in position of limited power over others **—pre'fecture** *n.* office, residence, district of a prefect

prefer' *vt.* like better; promote (**-rr-**) **—pref'erable** *a.* more desirable **—pref'erably** *adv.* **—pref'erence** *n.* **—preferen'tial** *a.* giving, receiving preference **—prefer'ment** *n.* promotion, advancement

prefig'ure *vt.* exhibit, suggest by previous types, foreshadow **—prefig'urative** *a.*

pre'fix *n.* preposition or particle put at beginning of word or title *—vt.* [-fiks'] put as introduction; put before word to make compound

preg'nant *a.* carrying foetus in womb; full of meaning, significance; inventive **—preg'nancy** *n.*

prehen'sile *a.* capable of grasping **—prehensil'ity** *n.*

prehistor'ic [-to'rik] *a.* before period in which written history begins **—prehis'tory** *n.*

prej'udice [-is] *n.* preconceived opinion; bias, partiality; injury likely to happen to person or his rights as a result of others' action or judgment *—vt.* influence; bias; injure **—prejudi'cial** *a.* injurious; disadvantageous

prel'ate *n.* bishop or other church dignitary of equal or higher rank **—prel'acy** *n.* his office **—prelat'ical** *a.*

prelim'inary *a.* preparatory, introductory —*n.* introductory, preparatory statement, action

prel'ude *n. Mus.* introductory movement; performance, event *etc.* serving as introduction —*v.* serve as prelude, introduce

premar'ital *a.* occurring before marriage

premature' [*or* prem'-] *a.* happening, done before proper time

premed'itate *vt.* consider, plan beforehand —**premedita'tion** *n.*

prem'ier *n.* prime minister; head of government of Aust. state —*a.* chief, foremost; first —**prem'iership** *n.* office of premier

première' [-mi-ār'] *n.* first performance of a play, movie *etc.*

prem'ise [-is] *n. Logic* proposition from which inference is drawn —*pl.* house, building with its belongings; *Law* beginning of deed —**premise'** [-īz'] *vt.* state by way of introduction —**prem'iss** *n.* (logical) premise

pre'mium *n.* bonus; sum paid for insurance; excess over nominal value; great value or regard (*pl.* **-iums**)

premoni'tion [-nish'-] *n.* presentiment, foreboding

preocc'upy [-pī] *vt.* occupy to the exclusion of other things —**preoccupa'tion** *n.* mental concentration or absorption

prep. preparation; preparatory; preposition

prepare' *vt.* make ready; make —*vi.* get ready —**prepara'tion** *n.* making ready beforehand; something that is prepared, as a medicine; at school, (time spent) preparing work for lesson —**prepar'atory** [-pa'rə-] *a.* serving to prepare; introductory —**prepa'redness** *n.* state of being prepared

prepay' *vt.* pay in advance (**prepaid'**, **prepay'ing**)

prepond'erate *vi.* be of greater weight or power —**prepond'erance** *n.* superiority of power, numbers *etc.*

preposi'tion [-zish'-] *n.* word marking relation between noun or pronoun and other words —**preposi'tional** *a.*

prepossess' [prē-] *vt.* impress, *esp.* favourably, beforehand; possess beforehand —**prepossess'ing** *a.* inviting favourable opinion, attractive, winning —**preposses'sion** *n.*

prepos'terous *a.* utterly absurd, foolish

prep'uce *n.* retractable fold of skin covering tip of penis, foreskin

prereq'uisite *n./a.* (something) required as prior condition

prerog'ative *n.* peculiar power or right, *esp.* as vested in sovereign —*a.* privileged

Pres. President

pres'age *n.* omen, indication of something to come —*vt.* foretell

presbyo'pia *n.* progressively diminishing ability of the eye to focus, *esp.* on near objects, longsightedness

pres'byter [prez'bi-tər] *n.* elder in early Christian church; priest; member of a presbytery —**Presbyte'rian** *a./n.* (member) of Protestant church governed by lay elders —**Presbyte'rianism** *n.* —**pres'bytery** *n.* church court composed of all ministers within a certain district and one ruling elder from each church; *R.C.Ch.* priest's house

pres'cience *n.* foreknowledge —**pres'cient** *a.*

prescribe' *v.* set out rules for; order; ordain; order use of (medicine) —**prescrip'tion** *n.* prescribing; thing prescribed; written statement of it —**prescrip'tive** *a.*

pres'ent[1] [-z-] *a.* that is here; now existing or happening —*n.* present time or tense —**pres'ence** *n.* being present; appearance, bearing —**pres'ently** *adv.* soon; at present

present'[2] [-z-] *vt.* introduce formally; show; give; offer; point, aim —**pres'ent** *n.* gift —**present'able** *a.* fit to be seen —**presenta'tion** *n.* —**present'er** *n.* person introducing TV or radio show, compere —**present'ment** *n.*

present'iment [-z-] *n.* sense of something (esp. evil) about to happen

preserve' [-z-] *vt.* keep from harm, injury or decay; maintain; pickle —*n.* special area; that which is preserved, as fruit *etc.*; place where game is kept for private fishing, shooting —**preserva'tion** *n.* —**preserv'ative** *n.* chemical put into perishable foods, drinks *etc.* to keep them from going bad —*a.* tending to preserve; having quality of preserving

preside' [-z-] *vi.* be chairman; superintend —**pres'ident** *n.* head of society, company, republic *etc.* —**pres'idency** *n.* —**presiden'tial** *a.*

press[1] *vt.* subject to push or squeeze; smooth by pressure or heat; urge steadily, earnestly —*vi.* bring weight to bear; throng; hasten —*n.* a pressing; machine for pressing, *esp.* printing machine; printing house; its work or art; newspapers collectively; reporters, journalists; crowd; stress; large cupboard —**press'ing** *a.* urgent; persistent —**press agent** person employed to advertise and secure press publicity for any person, enterprise *etc.* —**press'man** *n.* printer who attends to the press; journalist

press[2] *vt.* force to serve in navy or army —**press gang** formerly, body of men employed to press men into naval service —*vt.* force (someone to do something)

press'ure [presh'-] *n.* act of pressing; influence; authority; difficulties; *Physics* thrust per unit area —*vt.* compel, constrain —**pressuriza'tion** *n.* in aircraft, maintenance of normal atmospheric pressure at high altitudes —**press'urize** *vt.* —**pressure cooker** vessel like saucepan which cooks food rapidly by steam under pressure —**pressure group** organized group which exerts influence on policies, public opinion *etc.*

prestige' [-ēzh'] *n.* reputation; influence depending on it —**prestig'ious** [-tij'-] *a.*

pres'to *adv. Mus.* quickly

prestressed' *a.* (of concrete) containing stretched steel cables for strengthening

presume' [-zyōōm'] *vt.* take for granted —*vi.* take liberties —**presu'mably** *adv.* probably; doubtlessly —**presump'tion** *n.* forward, arrogant opinion or conduct; strong probability —**presump'tive** *a.* that may be assumed as true or valid until contrary is proved —**presump'tuous** *a.* forward, impudent, taking liberties —**presump'tuously** *adv.* —**heir presumptive** heir whose right may be defeated by birth of nearer relative

presuppose' *vt.* assume or take for granted beforehand —**presupposi'tion** *n.* previous supposition

pretend' *vt.* claim or allege (something untrue); make believe, as in play —*vi.* lay claim (to) —**pretence'**, *esp.* **US pretense'** *n.* simulation; pretext —**pretend'er** *n.* claimant (to throne) —**preten'sion** *n.* —**preten'tious** *a.* making claim to special merit or importance; given to outward show

preter- (*comb. form*) beyond, more than

pret'erite [-it] *a.* past; expressing past state or action —*n.* past tense

preternat'ural [prē-] *a.* out of ordinary way of nature; abnormal, supernatural

pre'text *n.* excuse; pretence

prett'y [prit'i] *a.* having beauty that is attractive rather than imposing; charming *etc.* —*adv.* fairly, moderately —**pret'tily** *adv.* —**prett'iness** *n.*

pret'zel [-səl] *n.* small, brittle, savoury biscuit

prevail' *vi.* gain mastery; triumph; be in fashion, generally established —**prevail'ing** *a.* widespread; predominant —**prev'alence** *n.* —**prev'alent** *a.* extensively existing, rife

prevar'icate [-va'ri-] *vi.* make evasive or misleading statements; quibble —**prevarica'tion** *n.* —**prevar'icator** *n.*

prevent' *vt.* stop, hinder —**prevent'able** *a.* —**preven'tion** *n.* —**preven'tive** *a./n.*

pre'view *n.* advance showing; a showing of scenes from a forthcoming movie

pre'vious *a.* earlier; preceding; happening before; *inf.* hasty —**pre'viously** *adv.* before

prey *n.* that is hunted and killed by carnivorous animals; victim —*vi.* seize for food; treat as prey; afflict, obsess (*with* upon)

price *n.* that for which thing is bought or sold; cost; value; reward; odds in betting —*vt.* fix, ask price for —**price'less** *a.* invaluable —**pri'c(e)y** *a. inf.* expensive

prick *vt.* pierce slightly with sharp point; cause to feel mental pain; mark by prick; erect (ears) —*n.* slight hole made by pricking; pricking or being pricked; sting; remorse; that which pricks; sharp point —**pric'kle** *n.* thorn, spike —*vi.* feel tingling or pricking sensation —**prick'ly** *a.* —**prickly heat** inflammation of skin with stinging pains

pride *n.* too high an opinion of oneself, inordinate self-esteem; worthy self-esteem; feeling of elation or great satisfaction; something causing this; group (of lions) *—v.refl.* take pride

priest *n.* official minister of religion, clergyman (**-ess** *fem.*) **—priest'hood** *n.* **—priest'ly** *a.*

prig *n.* self-righteous person who professes superior culture, morality *etc.* **—prig'gery** *n.* **—prigg'ish** *a.* **—prig'gism** *n.*

prim *a.* very restrained, formally prudish

pri'ma [prē'-] *a.* first **—prima donna** principal female singer in opera; *inf.* temperamental person (*pl.* **donnas**)

pri'macy *n.* state of being first in rank, grade *etc.*; office of archbishop

pri'ma fa'cie [-shi] *Lat.* at first sight

pri'mal *a.* of earliest age; first, original **—pri'marily** *adv.* **—pri'mary** *a.* chief; of the first stage, decision *etc.*; elementary

pri'mate[1] *n.* archbishop

pri'mate[2] *n.* one of order of mammals including monkeys and man

prime[1] *a.* fundamental; original; chief; best *—n.* first, best part of anything; youth; full health and vigour *—vt.* prepare (gun, engine, pump *etc.*) for use; fill up, *eg* with information, liquor **—pri'ming** *n.* powder mixture used for priming gun **—Prime Minister** leader of government

prime[2] *vt.* prepare for paint with preliminary coating of oil, size *etc.* **—pri'mer** *n.* paint *etc.* for priming

pri'mer *n.* elementary school book or manual

prim(a)e'val *a.* of the earliest age of the world

prim'itive *a.* of an early undeveloped kind, ancient; crude, rough

primogen'iture *n.* rule by which real estate passes to the first born son **—primogen'ital** *a.*

primor'dial *a.* existing at or from the beginning

prim'rose *n.* pale yellow spring flower; this colour *—a.* of this colour

prim'ula *n.* genus of plants, including primrose

Pri'mus R portable cooking stove, used *esp.* by campers (*pl.* **-ses**)

prince *n.* son or (in Britain) grandson of king or queen; ruler, chief (**princess'** *fem.*) **—prince'ly** *a.* generous, lavish; stately; magnificent

prin'cipal *a.* chief in importance *—n.* person for whom another is agent; head of institution, *esp.* school or college; sum of money lent and yielding interest; chief actor **—principal'ity** *n.* territory, dignity of prince

prin'ciple *n.* moral rule; settled reason of action; uprightness; fundamental truth or element

print *vt.* reproduce (words, pictures *etc.*), by pressing inked types on blocks to paper *etc.*; produce thus; write in imitation of this; impress; *Photog.* produce pictures from negatives; stamp (fabric) with coloured design *—n.* printed matter; printed lettering; written imitation of printed type; photograph; impression, mark left on surface by thing that has pressed against it; printed cotton fabric **—print'er** *n.* one engaged in printing **—printed circuit** electronic circuit with wiring printed on an insulating base **—print-out** *n.* printed information from computer, teleprinter *etc.* **—out of print** no longer available from publisher

pri'or *a.* earlier *—n.* chief of religious house or order (**-ess** *fem.*) **—prior'ity** [-o'ri-] *n.* precedence; something given special attention **—pri'ory** *n.* monastery, nunnery under prior, prioress **—prior to** before, earlier

prise *vt.* force open by levering; obtain (information *etc.*) with difficulty

prism [-zəm] *n.* transparent solid usu. with triangular ends and rectangular sides, used to disperse light into spectrum or refract it in optical instruments *etc.* **—prismat'ic** *a.* of prism shape; (of colour) such as is produced by refraction through prism, rainbowlike, brilliant

pris'on [-iz'-] *n.* jail **—pris'oner** *n.* one kept in prison; captive

priss'y *a. inf.* fussy, prim

prist'ine *a.* original, primitive, unspoiled, good

pri'vate *a.* secret, not public; reserved for, or belonging to, or concerning, an individual only; personal; secluded; denoting soldier of lowest rank; not controlled by State *—n.* private soldier **—pri'vacy** [*or* priv'-] *n.* **—pri'vately** *adv.*

privateer' *Hist. n.* privately owned armed vessel authorized by government to take part in war; captain of such ship —**privateer'ing** *n./a.*

priva'tion *n.* want of comforts or necessaries; hardship; act of depriving —**priv'ative** *a.* of privation or negation

priv'et *n.* bushy evergreen shrub used for hedges

priv'ilege [-lij] *n.* advantage or favour that only a few obtain; right, advantage belonging to person or class —**priv'ileged** *a.* enjoying special right or immunity

priv'y *a.* admitted to knowledge of secret —*n.* toilet, *esp.* outhouse; *Law* person having interest in an action —**priv'ily** *adv.* —**privy council** council of state of monarch

prize[1] *n.* reward given for success in competition; thing striven for; thing won, *eg* in lottery *etc.* —*a.* winning or likely to win a prize —*vt.* value highly —**prize'fight** *n.* boxing match for money —**prize'fighter** *n.* professional boxer

prize[2] *n.* ship, property captured in (naval) warfare

pro[1] *a./adv.* in favour of

pro[2] *n.* professional; prostitute —*a.* professional

pro- (*comb. form*) for, instead of, before, in front, as in *proconsul, pronoun, project* Such compounds are not given here where the meaning may easily be found from the simple word

prob'able *a.* likely —**probabil'ity** *n.* likelihood; anything that has appearance of truth —**prob'ably** *adv.*

pro'bate *n.* proving of authenticity of will; certificate of this —*vt.* establish validity of (a will)

proba'tion *n.* system of releasing law breakers, *esp.* juvenile ones, but placing them under supervision for stated period; testing of candidate before admission to full membership —**proba'tioner** *n.* person on probation

probe *vt.* search into, examine, question closely —*n.* that which probes, or is used to probe; thorough inquiry

pro'bity *n.* honesty, uprightness, integrity

prob'lem *n.* matter *etc.* difficult to deal with or solve; question set for solution; puzzle —**problemat'ic(al)** *a.* questionable; uncertain; disputable

probos'cis [-sis] *n.* trunk or long snout, *eg* of elephant (*pl.* **probos'cides** [-si-dēz])

proceed' *vi.* go forward, continue; be carried on; go to law —**pro'ceeds** *pl.n.* price or profit —**proce'dural** *a.* —**proce'dure** *n.* act, manner of proceeding; conduct —**proceed'ing** *n.* act or course of action; transaction —*pl.* minutes of meeting; methods of prosecuting charge, claim *etc.*

pro'cess *n.* series of actions or changes; method of operation; state of going on; action of law; outgrowth —*vt.* handle, treat, prepare by special method of manufacture *etc.* —**process'ion** *n.* regular, orderly progress; train of persons in formal order —**process'ional** *a.* —**pro'cessor** *n.*

proclaim' *vt.* announce publicly, declare —**proclama'tion** *n.*

procliv'ity *n.* inclination, tendency

procon'sul *n. Hist.* governor of province

procrast'inate *vi.* put off, delay —**procrastina'tion** *n.* —**procras'tinator** *n.*

pro'create *vt.* produce offspring, generate —**procrea'tion** *n.*

Procrust'ean *a.* compelling uniformity by violence

proc'tor *n.* university official with disciplinary powers

procure' *vt.* obtain, acquire; provide; bring about —*vi.* act as pimp —**procu'rable** *a.* —**procura'tion** *n.* —**proc'urator** *n.* one who manages another's affairs —**procure'ment** *n.* —**procu'rer** *n.* one who procures; pimp (**procu'ress** *fem.*)

prod *vt.* poke with something pointed (**-dd-**) —*n.* prodding; goad; pointed instrument

prod'igal *a.* wasteful; extravagant —*n.* spendthrift —**prodigal'ity** *n.* reckless extravagance

prod'igy [-ji] *n.* person with some marvellous gift; thing causing wonder —**prodi'gious** *a.* very great, immense; extraordinary —**prodig'iously** *adv.*

produce' *vt.* bring into existence; yield; make; bring forward; manufacture; exhibit; present on stage, screen, television; *Geom.* extend in length —*n.* [prod'-] that which is yielded or made —**produ'cer** *n.* person who produces, *esp.* play, movie *etc.* —**prod'uct** *n.* result of process of manufacture; number resulting from multiplication —**produc'tion** *n.* producing; things produced —**produc'tive** *a.* fertile; creative; efficient —**productiv'ity** *n.*

Prof. Professor

profane' *a.* irreverent, blasphemous; not sacred —*vt.* pollute, desecrate —**profana'tion** *n.* —**profan'ity** *n.* profane talk or behaviour, blasphemy

profess' *vt.* affirm belief in; confess publicly; assert; claim, pretend —**profess'edly** [-id-li] *adv.* avowedly —**profes'sion** *n.* calling or occupation, *esp.* learned, scientific or artistic; a professing; vow of religious faith on entering religious order —**profess'ional** *a.* engaged in a profession; engaged in a game or sport for money —*n.* paid player —**profess'or** *n.* teacher in university —**professor'ial** *a.* —**professor'iate** *n.* body of university professors —**profes'sorship** *n.*

proff'er *vt./n.* offer

profi'cient [-ish'-] *a.* skilled; expert —**profi'ciency** *n.*

pro'file *n.* outline, *esp.* of face, as seen from side; brief biographical sketch

prof'it *n.* money gained; benefit obtained —*v.* benefit —**prof'itable** *a.* yielding profit —**profiteer'** *n.* one who makes excessive profits at the expense of the public —*vi.* do this —**prof'itless** *a.*

prof'ligate *a.* dissolute; reckless, wasteful —*n.* dissolute person —**prof'ligacy** *n.*

pro for'ma *Lat.* prescribing a set form

profound' *a.* very learned; deep —**profun'dity** *n.*

profuse' [-fyōōs'] *a.* abundant, prodigal —**profu'sion** *n.*

prog'eny [proj'-] *n.* children —**progen'itor** *n.* ancestor

progest'erone [-jest'-] *n.* hormone which prepares uterus for pregnancy and prevents further ovulation

progna'thous *a.* with projecting lower jaw

progno'sis *n.* art of foretelling course of disease by symptoms; forecast —**prognos'tic** *a.* of, serving as prognosis —*n.* —**prognost'icate** *vt.* foretell —**prognostica'tion** *n.*

pro'gram(me) *n.* plan, detailed notes of intended proceedings; broadcast on radio or television; detailed instructions for a computer —*vt.* feed program into (computer); arrange detailed instructions for computer (**-mm-**) —**pro'grammer** *n.*

pro'gress *n.* onward movement; development —*vi.* [-gres'] go forward; improve —**progress'ion** *n.* moving forward; advance, improvement; increase or decrease of numbers or magnitudes according to fixed law; *Mus.* regular succession of chords —**progress'ive** *a.* progressing by degrees; favouring political or social reform —**Progressive-Conservative Party** major political party with conservative policies

prohib'it *vt.* forbid —**prohibi'tion** [-bish'-] *n.* act of forbidding; interdict; interdiction of supply and consumption of alcoholic drinks —**prohibi'tionist** *n.* person favouring prohibition of alcohol —**prohib'itive** *a.* tending to forbid or exclude; (of prices) very high —**prohib'itory** *a.*

proj'ect *n.* plan, scheme; design —*vt.* [-jekt'] plan; throw; cause to appear on distant background —*vi.* stick out, protrude —**project'ile** *n.* heavy missile, *esp.* shell or ball —*a.* for throwing —**projec'tion** *n.* —**projec'tionist** *n.* operator of film projector —**project'or** *n.* apparatus for projecting photographic images, films, slides on screen; one that forms scheme or design

pro'lapse, prolap'sus *n.* falling, slipping down of part of body from normal position

pro'late *a.* having polar diameter greater than the equatorial diameter

prolegom'ena *pl.n.* introductory remarks prefixed to a book, preface

proleta'riat *n.* lowest class of community, working class —**proleta'rian** *a./n.*

prolif'erate *v.* grow or reproduce rapidly —**prolifera'tion** *n.*

prolif'ic *a.* fruitful; producing much

pro'lix *a.* wordy, long-winded —**prolix'ity** *n.*

pro'logue [-log] *n.* preface, *esp.* speech before a play

prolong' *vt.* lengthen; protract —**prolonga'tion** *n.*

prom *n. inf.* formal dance at high school or college

promenade' [-ahd'] *n.* leisurely walk;

place made or used for this; ball or formal dance —*vi.* take leisurely walk; go up and down

prom'inent *a.* sticking out; conspicuous; distinguished —**prom'inence** *n.*

promis'cuous *a.* indiscriminate, *esp.* in sexual relations; mixed without distinction —**promiscu'ity** *n.*

prom'ise [-is] *v.* give undertaking or assurance —*vi.* be likely to —*n.* undertaking to do or not to do something; potential —**prom'ising** *a.* showing good signs, hopeful —**prom'issory** *a.* containing promise —**promissory note** written promise to pay sum to person named, at specified time

prom'ontory *n.* point of high land jutting out into the sea, headland

promote' *vt.* help forward; move up to higher rank or position; work for; encourage sale of —**promo'ter** *n.* —**promo'tion** *n.* advancement; preferment

prompt *a.* done at once; acting with alacrity; punctual; ready —*v.* urge, suggest; help out (actor or speaker) by reading or suggesting next words —**prompt'er** *n.* —**prompt'itude, prompt'ness** *n.* —**prompt'ly** *adv.*

prom'ulgate *vt.* proclaim, publish —**promulga'tion** *n.* —**prom'ulgator** *n.*

pron. pronoun; pronunciation

prone *a.* lying face or front downwards; inclined (to) —**prone'ness** *n.*

prong *n.* one spike of fork or similar instrument

prong'horn *n.* Amer. antelope

pro'noun *n.* word used to replace noun —**pronom'inal** *a.* pert. to, like pronoun

pronounce' *vt.* utter formally; form with organs of speech; speak distinctly; declare —*vi.* give opinion or decision —**pronounce'able** *a.* —**pronounced'** *a.* strongly marked, decided —**pronounce'ment** *n.* declaration —**pronuncia'tion** *n.* way word *etc.* is pronounced; articulation

pron'to *adv. inf.* at once, immediately, quickly

proof *n.* evidence; thing which proves; test, demonstration; trial impression from type or engraved plate; *Photog.* print from a negative; standard of strength of alcoholic drink —*a.* giving impenetrable defence against; of proved strength —**proof'read** *v.* read and correct proofs —**proof'reader** *n.* —**proof'reading** *n.*

prop[1] *vt.* support, sustain, hold up (**-pp-**) —*n.* pole, beam *etc.* used as support

prop[2] *n. short for* PROPELLER

prop[3] *n. short for* (theatrical) PROPERTY

propagand'a *n.* organized dissemination of information to assist or damage political cause *etc.* —**propagan'dist** *n.*

prop'agate *vt.* reproduce, breed, spread by sowing, breeding *etc.*; transmit —*vi.* breed, multiply —**propaga'tion** *n.* —**prop'agative** *a.*

pro'pane *n.* colourless, flammable gas from petroleum

propel' *vt.* cause to move forward (**-ll-**) —**propell'ant, -ent** *n.* something causing propulsion, *eg* rocket fuel —**propel'ler** *n.* revolving shaft with blades for driving ship or aircraft —**propul'sion** *n.* act of driving forward —**propul'sive, propul'sory** *a.* tending, having power to propel; urging on

propen'sity *n.* inclination or bent; tendency; disposition

prop'er *a.* appropriate; correct; conforming to etiquette, decorous; strict; (of noun) denoting individual person or place —**prop'erly** *adv.*

prop'erty *n.* that which is owned; estate whether in lands, goods, or money; quality, attribute of something; article used on stage in play *etc.*

proph'et *n.* inspired teacher or revealer of Divine Will; foreteller of future (**-tess** *fem.*) —**proph'ecy** [-si] *n.* prediction, prophetic utterance —**proph'esy** [-sī] *vi.* foretell —**prophet'ic** *a.* —**prophet'ically** *adv.*

prophylact'ic *n./a.* (something) done or used to ward off disease; condom —**prophylax'is** *n.*

propin'quity *n.* nearness, proximity, close kinship

propi'tiate [-ish'-] *vt.* appease, gain favour of —**propitia'tion** *n.* —**propi'tiatory** *a.* —**propi'tious** *a.* favourable, auspicious

propo'nent *n.* one who advocates something

propor'tion *n.* relative size or number; comparison; due relation between connected things or parts; share; relation

—*pl.* dimensions —*vt.* arrange proportions of —**propor'tionable** *a.* —**propor'tional, propor'tionate** *a.* having a due proportion; corresponding in size, number *etc.* —**propor'tionally** *adv.*

propose' *vt.* put forward for consideration; nominate; intend —*vi.* offer marriage —**propo'sal** *n.* —**propo'ser** *n.* —**proposi'tion** *n.* offer; statement, assertion; theorem; suggestion of terms; *inf.* thing to be dealt with

propound' *vt.* put forward for consideration or solution

propri'etor *n.* owner (**-tress, -trix** *fem.*) —**propri'etary** *a.* belonging to owner; made by firm with exclusive rights of manufacture

propri'ety *n.* properness, correct conduct, fitness

propul'sion *see* PROPEL

pro rat'a [-raht'-] *Lat.* in proportion

prorate' [-ō-] *v.* divide (something) proportionately

prorogue' [-rōg'] *vt.* dismiss (parliament) at end of session without dissolution

prosa'ic *a.* commonplace, unromantic —**prosa'ical** *a.*

prosce'nium [-sē'-] *n.* arch or opening framing stage (*pl.* **-nia**)

proscribe' *vt.* outlaw, condemn —**proscrip'tion** *n.*

prose *n.* speech or writing not verse —**pro'sily** *adv.* —**pro'siness** *n.* —**pro'sy** *a.* tedious, dull

pros'ecute *vt.* carry on, bring legal proceedings against —**prosecu'tion** *n.* —**pros'ecutor** *n.* (**-trix** *fem.*)

pros'elyte *n.* convert —**pros'elytize** *vt.* —**pros'elytism** *n.*

pros'ody *n.* system, study of versification —**pros'odist** *n.*

pros'pect *n.* expectation, chance for success; view, outlook; likely customer or subscriber; mental view —*v.* [*or* -pekt'] explore, *esp.* for gold —**prospect'ive** *a.* anticipated; future —**prospect'ively** *adv.* —**prospect'or** *n.* —**prospect'us** *n.* circular describing company, school *etc.*

pros'per *v.* (cause to) do well —**prosper'ity** [-pe'ri-] *n.* good fortune, well-being —**pros'perous** *a.* doing well, successful; flourishing, rich, well-off —**pros'perously** *adv.*

pros'tate *n.* gland accessory to male generative organs

pros'thesis *n.* (replacement of part of body with) artificial substitute

pros'titute *n.* one who offers sexual intercourse in return for payment —*vt.* make a prostitute of; put to unworthy use —**prostitu'tion** *n.*

pros'trate *a.* lying flat; crushed, submissive, overcome —*vt.* [-trāt'] throw flat on ground; reduce to exhaustion —**prostra'tion** *n.*

protag'onist *n.* leading character; principal actor; champion of a cause

prot'asis *n.* introductory clause of conditional sentence

prote'an *a.* variable; versatile

protect' *vt.* defend, guard, keep from harm —**protec'tion** *n.* —**protec'tionist** *n.* one who advocates protecting industries by taxing competing imports —**protect'ive** *a.* —**protect'or** *n.* one who protects; regent —**protect'orate** *n.* relation of state to territory it protects and controls; such territory; office, period of protector of a state

pro'tégé [-ti-zhā] *n.* one under another's care, protection or patronage (**-ée** *fem.*)

pro'tein [-tēn] *n.* kinds of organic compound which form most essential part of food of living creatures

pro tem'pore [-pə-ri] *Lat.* for the time being (*also* **pro tem**)

pro'test *n.* declaration or demonstration of objection —*vi.* [-test'] object; make declaration against; assert formally —**protesta'tion** *n.* strong declaration

Prot'estant *a.* belonging to any branch of the Western Church outside the Roman Catholic Church —*n.* member of such church —**Prot'estantism** *n.*

prothalam'ium, -ion *n.* bridal song

pro'tium *n.* most common isotope of hydrogen

proto-, prot- (*comb. form*) first, as in *prototype*

pro'tocol *n.* diplomatic etiquette; draft of terms signed by parties as basis of formal treaty

pro'ton *n.* positively charged particle in nucleus of atom

pro'toplasm *n.* substance that is living matter of all animal and plant cells —**protoplas'mic** *a.*

pro'totype *n.* original, or model, after which thing is copied; pattern

protozo'an *n.* minute animal of lowest and simplest class

protract' *vt.* lengthen; prolong; delay; draw to scale —**protract'ed** *a.* long drawn out; tedious —**protrac'tion** *n.* —**protract'or** *n.* instrument for measuring angles on paper

protrude' *v.* stick out, project —**protru'sion** *n.* —**protru'sive** *a.* thrusting forward —**protru'sively** *adv.* —**protru'siveness** *n.* —**protru'sile** *a.*

protu'berant *a.* bulging out —**protu'berance** *n.* bulge, swelling

proud *a.* feeling or displaying pride; arrogant; gratified; noble; self-respecting; stately —**proud'ly** *adv.* —**proud flesh** flesh growing around healing wound

Prov. Proverbs

prove [pro͞ov] *vt.* establish validity of; demonstrate, test —*vi.* turn out (to be *etc.*); (of dough) rise in warm place before baking (**proved, pro'ven** [pro͞o'-] *pp.*) —**pro'ven** [pro͞o'-] *a.* proved

prov'enance *n.* place of origin, source

prov'ender *n.* fodder

prov'erb *n.* short, pithy, traditional saying in common use —**proverb'ial** *a.*

provide' *vi.* make preparation —*vt.* supply, equip, prepare, furnish, give —**provi'der** *n.* —**provided that** on condition that

prov'ident *a.* thrifty; showing foresight —**prov'idence** *n.* kindly care of God or nature; foresight; economy —**providen'tial** *a.* strikingly fortunate, lucky —**providen'tially** *adv.*

prov'ince *n.* division of a country, district; sphere of action —*pl.* any part of country outside capital —**provin'cial** *a.* of a province; unsophisticated; narrow in outlook —*n.* unsophisticated person; inhabitant of province —**provin'cialism** *n.* narrowness of outlook; lack of refinement; idiom peculiar to province

provi'sion [-vizh'-] *n.* a providing, *esp.* for the future; thing provided —*pl.* food; *Law* articles of instrument or statute —*vt.* supply with food —**provi'sional** *a.* temporary; conditional

provi'so *n.* condition (*pl.* **-os**)

provoke' *vt.* irritate; incense; arouse; excite; cause —**provoca'tion** *n.* —**provoc'ative** *a.*

prov'ost *n.* one who superintends or presides; head of certain colleges; administrative head of Scottish burgh —**provost marshal** [prə-vō'] head of military police

prow *n.* bow of vessel

prow'ess *n.* bravery, fighting capacity; skill

prowl *vi.* roam stealthily, *esp.* in search of prey or booty —*n.* —**prowl'er** *n.*

prox'imate *a.* nearest, next, immediate —**proxim'ity** *n.* —**prox'imo** *adv.* in the next month

prox'y *n.* authorized agent or substitute; writing authorizing one to act as this

prude *n.* one who affects excessive modesty or propriety —**pru'dery** *n.* —**pru'dish** *a.*

pru'dent *a.* careful, discreet; sensible —**pru'dence** *n.* habit of acting with careful deliberation; wisdom applied to practice —**pruden'tial** *a.*

prune[1] *n.* dried plum

prune[2] *vt.* cut out dead parts, excessive branches *etc.*; shorten, reduce —**pruning hook**

prur'ient [pro͝or'-] *a.* given to, springing from lewd thoughts; having unhealthy curiosity or desire —**prur'ience, pru'riency** *n.*

pry *vi.* make furtive or impertinent inquiries; look curiously; force open; obtain (information *etc.*) (**pried, pry'ing**) —*n.* inquisitive person; lever

PS postscript

Ps. Psalm(s)

psalm [sahm] *n.* sacred song; (**P-**) any of the sacred songs making up the Book of Psalms in the Bible —**psalm'ist** *n.* writer of psalms —**psalm'ody** *n.* art, act of singing sacred music —**Psal'ter** [sawl'-] *n.* book of psalms; copy of the Psalms as separate book —**psal'tery** *n.* obsolete stringed instrument like lyre

psephol'ogy [se-] *n.* statistical study of elections

pseu'd(o) [syo͞o'-] *n./a. inf.* (something, somebody) sham, fake

pseudo- (*comb. form*) sham, as in **pseudo-Gothic, pseudomod'ern** *etc.* Such compounds are not given here where the meaning may easily be inferred from the simple word

pseu'donym [syo͞o'-] *n.* false, fictitious name; pen name —**pseudon'ymous** *a.*

psitt'acine [sit'ə-sīn] *a.* pert. to, like parrots —**psittaco'sis** [-kō'-] *n.* dangerous infectious disease, germ of which is carried by parrots

PST Pacific Standard Time

psychedel'ic *a.* of or causing hallucinations; like intense colours *etc.* experienced during hallucinations

psy'chic [sī'kik] *a.* sensitive to phenomena lying outside range of normal experience; of soul or mind; that appears to be outside region of physical law —**psy'chical** *a.* psychic —**psychi'atry** *n.* medical treatment of mental diseases —**psychoanal'ysis** *n.* method of studying and treating mental disorders —**psychoan'alyst** *n.* —**psycholog'ical** *a.* of psychology; of the mind —**psychol'ogist** *n.* —**psychol'ogy** *n.* study of mind; *inf.* person's mental make-up —**psychom'etry** *n.* measurement, testing of psychological processes; supposed ability to divine unknown person's qualities by handling object used or worn by him —**psy'chopath** *n.* person afflicted with severe mental disorder causing him to commit antisocial, often violent acts —**psychopath'ic** *a.* —**psycho'sis** *n.* severe mental disorder in which person's contact with reality becomes distorted —**psychosomat'ic** *a.* of physical disorders thought to have psychological causes —**psychother'apy** *n.* treatment of disease by psychological, not physical, means

psych up [sīk] prepare (oneself or another) psychologically for action, performance *etc.*

PT physical therapy; physical training

Pt *Chem.* platinum

Pt. Point; Port

pt. part; pint; point

PTA Parent-Teacher Association

ptar'migan [t-] *n.* bird of grouse family which turns white in winter

Pte. Private (soldier)

pterodact'yl [t-] *n.* extinct flying reptile with batlike wings

PTO please turn over

pto'maine [t-] *n.* kinds of poisonous alkaloid found in decaying matter

Pu *Chem.* plutonium

pub *n.* UK public house

pu'berty *n.* sexual maturity —**pu'bertal** *a.*

pu'bic *a.* of the lower abdomen

pub'lic *a.* of or concerning the public as a whole; not private; open to general observation or knowledge; accessible to all; serving the people —*n.* the community or its members —**pub'lican** *n.* UK keeper of public house —**pub'licly** *adv.* —**public house** inn, tavern or small hotel —**public relations** promotion of good relations of an organization or authority with the general public —**public school** elementary school; UK private independent fee-paying school —**public service** government employment —**public spirit** interest in and devotion to welfare of community

pub'licist *n.* writer on public concerns; journalist —**public'ity** [-lis'-] *n.* process of attracting public attention; attention thus gained —*a.* pert. to advertisement —**pub'licize** *vt.* advertise

pub'lish *vt.* prepare and issue for sale (books, music *etc.*); make generally known; proclaim —**publica'tion** *n.* —**pub'lisher** *n.*

puce *a./n.* purplish-brown (colour)

puck *n.* rubber disc used instead of ball in ice hockey

Puck *n.* mischievous sprite —**puck'ish** *a.*

puck'er *v.* gather into wrinkles —*n.* crease, fold

pudd'ing [pood'-] *n.* sweet, cooked dessert, often made from suet, flour *etc.*; sweet course of meal; soft savoury dish with pastry or batter; kind of sausage

pud'dle *n.* small muddy pool; rough cement for lining ponds *etc.* —*vt.* line with puddle; make muddy —**pudd'ling** *n.* method of converting pig iron to wrought iron by oxidizing the carbon

pu'dency *n.* modesty; chastity —**pu'dic** *a.*

puer'ile [pyoor'-] *a.* childish; foolish; trivial

puerpe'rium [pyo͞or-] *n.* period of about six weeks after childbirth —**puer'peral** [pyo͞o- er'-] *a.*

puff *n.* short blast of breath, wind *etc.*; its sound; type of pastry; laudatory notice or advertisement —*vi.* blow abruptly; breathe hard —*vt.* send out in a puff; blow out, inflate; advertise; smoke hard —**puff'y** *a.* short-winded; swollen —**puff'ball** *n.* ball-shaped fungus

puff'in *n.* sea bird with large brightly-coloured beak

pug *n.* small snub-nosed dog; *sl.* boxer —**pug nose** snub nose

pu'gilist [-j-] *n.* boxer —**pu'gilism** *n.* —**pugilist'ic** *a.*

pugna'cious *a.* given to fighting —**pugnac'ity** *n.*

pu'issant *a. Poet.* powerful, mighty —**pu'issance** [*or* pwē'-] *n.* show jumping competition over very high fences; *obs.* power —**puiss'antly** *adv.*

puke [pyo͞ok] *vi. sl.* vomit —*n. sl.* vomiting

pul'chritude *n.* beauty

pule [pyo͞ol] *vi.* whine; whimper

pull [pool] *vt.* exert force on object to move it towards source of force; strain or stretch; tear; propel by rowing —*n.* act of pulling; force exerted by it; draught of liquor; *inf.* power, influence —**pull in** (of train) arrive; *sl.* arrest —**pull off** *inf.* carry through to successful issue —**pull out** withdraw; extract; (of train) depart —**pull up** tear up; recover lost ground; improve; come to a stop; halt

pull'et [-oo-] *n.* young hen

pull'ey [-oo-] *n.* wheel with groove in rim for cord, used to raise weights by downward pull

Pull'man car railway saloon car

pull'over *n.* jersey, sweater without fastening, to be pulled over head

pul'monary *a.* of lungs

pulp *n.* soft, moist, vegetable or animal matter; flesh of fruit; any soft soggy mass —*vt.* reduce to pulp

pul'pit [-oo-] *n.* (enclosed) platform for preacher

pul'sar *n.* small dense star emitting radio waves

pulse[1] *n.* movement of blood in arteries corresponding to heartbeat, discernible to touch, *eg* in wrist; any regular beat or vibration —**pulsate'** *vi.* throb, quiver —**pulsa'tion** *n.*

pulse[2] *n.* edible seeds of pod-bearing plants, *eg* beans

pul'verize *vt.* reduce to powder; smash or demolish —**pulveriza'tion** *n.*

pu'ma *n.* large Amer. feline carnivore, cougar

pum'ice [-is] *n.* light porous variety of lava

pumm'el *vt.* strike repeatedly (**-ll-**)

pump[1] *n.* appliance in which piston and handle are used for raising water, or putting in or taking out air or liquid *etc.* —*vt.* raise, put in, take out *etc.* with pump; empty by means of a pump; extract information from —*vi.* work pump; work like pump —**pump iron** *sl.* do body-building exercises

pump[2] *n.* light shoe

pump'kin *n.* any of several varieties of gourd, eaten *esp.* as vegetable

pun *n.* play on words —*vi.* make one (**-nn-**) —**pun'ster** *n.*

punch[1] *n.* tool for perforating or stamping; blow with fist; *inf.* vigour —*vt.* stamp, perforate with punch; strike with fist —**punch-drunk,** *inf.* **punch'y** *a.* dazed, as by repeated blows

punch[2] *n.* drink of spirits or wine with fruit juice, spice *etc.*

Punchinell'o *n.* clown and chief character of Italian puppet show —**Punch** *n.* same character in English puppet show, called **Punch and Judy show**

punctil'ious *a.* making much of details of etiquette; very exact, particular

punc'tual *a.* in good time, not late, prompt —**punctual'ity** *n.* —**punc'tually** *adv.*

punc'tuate *vt.* put in punctuation marks; interrupt at intervals —**punctua'tion** *n.* marks, *eg* commas, colons *etc.* put in writing to assist in making sense clear

punc'ture *n.* small hole made by sharp object, *esp.* in tyre; act of puncturing —*vt.* prick hole in, perforate

pun'dit *n.* self-appointed expert

pun'gent [-j-] *a.* biting; irritant; piercing; tart; caustic —**pun'gency** *n.*

pun'ish *vt.* cause to suffer for offence; inflict penalty on; use or treat roughly —**pun'ishable** *a.* —**pun'ishment** *n.* —**pu'nitive** *a.* inflicting or intending to inflict punishment

punk *a./n.* inferior, rotten, worthless (person or thing); petty (hoodlum); (of) style of rock music

punn'et *n.* small (wooden) basket for fruit

punt[1] *n.* flat-bottomed square-ended boat, propelled by pushing with pole —*vt.* propel thus

punt[2] *vt. Sport* kick ball before it touches

ground, when let fall from hands —*n.* such a kick

punt[3] *vi.* gamble, bet —**punt'er** *n.* one who punts; professional gambler

pu'ny *a.* small and feeble

pup *n.* young of certain animals, *eg* dog, seal

pu'pa *n.* stage between larva and adult in metamorphosis of insect, chrysalis (*pl.* **pu'pae** [-pē]) —**pu'pal** *a.*

pu'pil *n.* person being taught; opening in iris of eye

pupp'et *n.* small doll or figure of person *etc.* controlled by operator's hand —**puppeteer'** *n.* —**pupp'etry** *n.* —**puppet show** show with puppets worked by hidden showman

pupp'y *n.* young dog

pur'blind *a.* dim-sighted

pur'chase *vt.* buy —*n.* buying; what is bought; leverage, grip —**pur'chaser** *n.*

pur'dah [-də] *n.* Muslim, Hindu custom of keeping women in seclusion; screen, veil to achieve this

pure [pyoor] *a.* unmixed, untainted; simple; spotless; faultless; innocent; concerned with theory only —**pure'ly** *adv.* —**purifica'tion** *n.* —**pur'ificatory** *a.* —**pur'ify** *vt.* make, become pure, clear or clean (**-ified, -ifying**) —**pur'ism** *n.* excessive insistence on correctness of language —**pur'ist** *n.* —**pur'ity** *n.* state of being pure

pur'ée [pyoor'ā] *n.* pulp of cooked fruit or vegetables —*vt.*

pur'fle, pur'fling *n.* ornamental border on edges of furniture, garments *etc.*

purg'atory *n.* place or state of torment, pain or distress, *esp.* temporary —**purgator'ial** *a.*

purge [-j] *vt.* make clean, purify; remove, get rid of; clear out —*n.* act, process of purging; removal of undesirable members from political party, army *etc.* —**purga'tion** [-gā'-] *n.* —**pur'gative** *a./n.*

Pur'itan [pyoor'-] *n. Hist.* member of extreme Protestant party; (**p-**) person of extreme strictness in morals or religion —**puritan'ic(al)** *a.* strict in the observance of religious and moral duties; overscrupulous —**pu'ritanism** *n.*

purl[1] *n.* stitch that forms ridge in knitting —*vi.* knit in purl

purl[2] *vi.* flow with burbling sound, swirl, babble

pur'lieus [-lyōōz] *pl.n.* outlying parts, outskirts

purloin' *vt.* steal; pilfer

pur'ple *n./a.* (of) colour between crimson and violet

purport' *vt.* claim to be (true *etc.*); signify, imply —*n.* [pur'-] meaning; apparent meaning; significance

pur'pose [-pəs] *n.* reason, object; design; aim, intention —*vt.* intend —**pur'posely** *adv.* —**on purpose** intentionally

purr *n.* pleased noise which cat makes —*vi.* utter this

purse *n.* small bag for money; woman's handbag; resources; money as prize —*vt.* pucker in wrinkles —*vi.* become wrinkled and drawn in —**pur'ser** *n.* ship's officer who keeps accounts

pursue' [-syōō'] *vt.* run after; chase; aim at; engage in; continue; follow —*vi.* go in pursuit; continue —**pursu'ance** *n.* carrying out —**pursu'ant** *adv.* accordingly —**pursu'er** *n.* —**pursuit'** [-syōōt'] *n.* running after, attempt to catch; occupation

pur'suivant [-siv-] *n.* officer of College of Arms below herald

pur'ulent *a. see* PUS

purvey' *vt.* supply (provisions) —**purvey'ance** *n.* —**purvey'or** *n.*

pur'view *n.* scope, range

pus *n.* yellowish matter produced by suppuration —**pur'ulence** *n.* —**pu'rulent** [pyoor'-] *a.* forming, discharging pus; septic

push [-oo-] *vt.* move, try to move away by pressure; drive or impel; *inf.* sell (*esp.* narcotic drugs) illegally —*vi.* make thrust; advance with steady effort —*n.* thrust; persevering self-assertion; big military advance; *sl.* dismissal —**push'er** *n.* —**push'ing,** *inf.* **push'y** *a.* given to pushing oneself —**push'cart** *n.* small wheeled handcart —**push'chair** *n.* **UK** baby carriage, stroller

pusillan'imous [pyōō-] *a.* cowardly —**pusillanim'ity** *n.*

puss [poos] *n.* cat (*also* **puss'y**)

puss'yfoot *vi. inf.* move stealthily; act indecisively, procrastinate

pust'ule *n.* pimple containing pus —**pus'tular** *a.*

put [poot] *vt.* place; set; express; throw

(*esp.* shot) (**put, putt'ing**) —*n.* throw —**put across** express, carry out successfully —**put off** postpone; disconcert; repel —**put up** erect; accommodate; nominate

pu'tative *a.* reputed, supposed —**pu'tatively** *adv.*

pu'trid *a.* decomposed; rotten —**pu'trefy** *v.* make or become rotten (**-efied, -efying**) —**putrefac'tion** *n.* —**putres'cence** *n.* —**putres'cent** *a.* becoming rotten —**putrid'ity** *n.*

putsch [pooch] *n.* surprise attempt to overthrow the existing power, political revolt

putt [put] *vt.* strike (golf ball) along ground in direction of hole —**putt'er** *n.* golf club for putting

putt'ee *n.* strip of cloth wound round leg like bandage, serving as gaiter

putt'er *vi.* work, act in feeble, unsystematic way

putt'y *n.* paste of whiting and oil as used by glaziers; jeweller's polishing powder —*vt.* fix, fill with putty (**-ied, -ying**)

puz'zle *v.* perplex or be perplexed —*n.* bewildering, perplexing question, problem or toy —**puz'zlement** *n.*

PVC polyvinyl chloride, synthetic thermoplastic material

pyae'mia [pī-ē'-] *n.* form of blood poisoning —**pyae'mic** *a.*

pyg'my, pig'my *n.* abnormally undersized person; (**P-**) member of one of dwarf peoples of Equatorial Africa —*a.* undersized

pyjam'as [pə-jahm'-] *pl.n.* sleeping suit of pants and jacket

py'lon *n.* towerlike erection *esp.* to carry electric cables

pyorrhoe'a [-rē'ə] *n.* inflammation of the gums with discharge of pus and loosening of teeth

pyr'amid *n.* solid figure with sloping sides meeting at apex; structure of this shape, *esp.* ancient Egyptian; group of persons or things highest in the middle —**pyram'idal** *a.*

pyre *n.* pile of wood for burning a dead body

pyre'thrum [pī-rē'-] *n.* type of cultivated chrysanthemum; insecticide made from it

Py'rex R glassware resistant to heat

pyri'tes *n.* sulphide of a metal, *esp.* iron pyrites

pyrogen'ic, pyrog'enous *a.* produced by or producing heat; causing or resulting from fever

pyroma'niac *n.* person with uncontrollable desire to set things on fire

pyrom'eter *n.* instrument for measuring very high temperature —**pyrom'etry** *n.*

pyrotech'nics [-k-] *n.* manufacture, display of fireworks —**pyrotech'nist** *n.*

Pyr'rhic victory [pi'rik] one won at high cost

py'thon *n.* large nonpoisonous snake that crushes its prey —**python'ic** *a.*

pyx [piks] *n.* box in Brit. Royal Mint holding specimen coins kept to be tested for weight; vessel in which consecrated Host is preserved

Q

Q *Chess* Queen; Question

q. quart; quarter; quarto; question

QED (*Lat.*, quod erat demonstrandum) which was to be proved

QM Quartermaster

qr. quarter; quire

qt. quart; quantity

qua [kwā] *prep.* in the capacity of

quack *n.* harsh cry of duck; pretender to medical or other skill —*vi.* (of duck) utter cry

quad [kwod] *short for* QUADRANGLE; QUADRANT; QUADRAPHONIC; QUADRUPLET

quadr-, quadri- (*comb. form*) four

Quadrages'ima [kwod-rə- jes'-] *n.* forty days of fast before Easter; Lent

quad'rangle [kwod'-] *n.* four-sided figure; four-sided courtyard in a building —**quadrang'ular** *a.*

quad'rant [kwod'-] *n.* quarter of circle; instrument for taking angular measurements —**quadrate'** *vt.* make square —**quadrat'ic** *a.* of equation, involving square of unknown quantity

quadraphon'ic [kwod-] *a.* of a sound system using four independent speakers

quadrilat'eral [kwod-] *a.* four-sided —*n.* four-sided figure

quadrille' [kwod-] *n.* square dance; music played for it; old card game

quadrill'ion [kwod-] *n.* **US, C** thousand trillions, 1×10^{15}; **UK** a million Brit. trillions, 1×10^{24}

quadru'manous [kwod-rōō'-] *a.* of apes *etc.* having four feet which can be used as hands

quad'ruped [kwod'-] *n.* four-footed animal —**quadru'pedal** [-rōō'-] *a.*

quad'ruple [kwod'-] *a.* fourfold —*v.* make, become four times as much —**quadru'plicate** *a.* fourfold

quad'ruplet [kwod'-] *n.* one of four offspring born at one birth

quaff [-o-, -ah-] *v.* drink heartily or in one draught

quag, quag'mire *n.* bog, swamp

quagg'a *n.* recently extinct member of horse family

quail[1] *n.* small bird of partridge family

quail[2] *vi.* flinch; cower

quaint *a.* interestingly old-fashioned or odd; curious; whimsical —**quaint'ly** *adv.* —**quaint'ness** *n.*

quake *vi.* shake, tremble

Qua'ker *n.* member of Christian sect, the **Society of Friends** (**Qua'keress** *fem.*)

qual'ify *vi.* make oneself competent —*vt.* moderate; limit; make competent; ascribe quality to; describe (**-fied, -fying**) —**qualifica'tion** *n.* thing that qualifies, attribute; restriction; qualifying

qual'ity [kwol'-] *n.* attribute, characteristic, property; degree of excellence; rank —**qual'itative** *a.* depending on quality

qualm [kwahm] *n.* misgiving; sudden feeling of sickness —**qualm'ish** *a.*

quan'dary [kwon'-] *n.* state of perplexity, puzzling situation, dilemma

quan'tity [kwon'-] *n.* size, number, amount; specified or considerable amount —**quant'ify** *vt.* discover, express quantity of —**quan'titative** *a.* —**quan'tum** *n.* desired or required amount (*pl.* **-ta**) —**quantum theory** theory that in radiation, energy of electrons is discharged not continuously but in discrete units or quanta

quar'antine [kwo'rən-tēn] *n.* isolation to prevent spreading of infection —*vt.* put, keep in quarantine

quark *n. Physics* any of several hypothetical particles thought to be fundamental units of matter

quarr'el[1] [kwo'r-] *n.* angry dispute; argument —*vi.* argue; find fault with (**-ll-**) —**quarr'elsome** *a.*

quarr'el[2] [kwo'r-] *n.* crossbow arrow; diamond-shaped pane

quarr'y[1] [kwo'ri] *n.* object of hunt or pursuit; prey

quarr'y^2 [kwo'ri] *n.* excavation where stone *etc.* is got from ground for building *etc.* —*v.* get from quarry (**quarr'ied, quarr'ying**)

quart [kwort] *n.* liquid measure, quarter of gallon or 2 pints

quart'er [kwort'-] *n.* fourth part; 25 cents; region, district; mercy —*pl.* lodgings —*vt.* divide into quarters; lodge —**quar'terly** *a.* happening, due *etc.* each quarter of year —*n.* quarterly periodical —**quartet'** *n.* group of four musicians; music for four performers —**quar'to** *n.* size of book in which sheets are folded into four leaves (*pl.* **-os**) —*a.* of this size —**quart'erback** *n. Football* player, positioned usu. behind centre, who directs attacking play —**quar'terdeck** *n.* after part of upper deck used *esp.* for official, ceremonial purposes —**quarter horse** small, powerful breed of horse —**quart'ermaster** *n.* officer responsible for stores —**quarter note** musical note, equal to half the length of a half note —**quart'erstaff** *n.* long staff for fighting

quartz [kworts] *n.* stone of pure crystalline silica —**quartz'ite** *n.* quartz rock —**quartz timepiece** watch or clock operated by a vibrating quartz crystal

qua'sar [-z-] *n.* extremely distant starlike object emitting powerful radio waves

quash [kwosh] *vt.* annul; reject; subdue forcibly

qua'si- [kwā'zī, kwahz'i] (*comb. form*) seemingly, resembling but not actually being, as in **quasi-scientific**

quass'ia [kwosh'ə] *n.* tropical Amer. tree

quater'nary *a.* of the number four; having four parts; *Geology* (**Q-**) of most recent period after Tertiary

quatrain' [kwot-] *n.* four-line stanza, *esp.* rhymed alternately

qua'ver *vt.* say or sing in quavering tones —*vi.* tremble, shake, vibrate —*n.* quavering trill

quay [kē] *n.* solid, fixed landing stage; wharf

Que. Quebec

queas'y *a.* inclined to, or causing, sickness

queen *n.* king's wife; female sovereign; piece in chess; fertile female bee, wasp *etc.*; court card with picture of a queen, ranking between king and jack; *inf.* male homosexual —**queen'ly** *adv.*

queer *a.* odd, strange; *inf.* homosexual (*also n.*) —*vt. inf.* spoil; interfere with

quell *vt.* crush, put down; allay; pacify

quench *vt.* slake; extinguish, put out, suppress

quern *n.* stone hand mill

quer'ulous [kwe'roo-] *a.* fretful, peevish, whining

que'ry *n.* question; mark of interrogation —*vt.* question, ask (**que'ried, que'rying**)

quest *n./vi.* search

ques'tion [-chən] *n.* sentence seeking for answer; that which is asked; interrogation; inquiry; problem; point for debate; debate, strife —*vt.* ask questions of, interrogate; dispute; doubt —**ques'tionable** *a.* doubtful, *esp.* not clearly true or honest —**questionnaire'** *n.* list of questions drawn up for formal answer

queue [kyo͞o] *n.* line of waiting persons, vehicles —*vi.* wait in queue (*with* up)

quib'ble *n.* trivial objection —*v.* make this

quiche [kēsh] *n.* open savoury pie

quick *a.* rapid, swift; keen; brisk; hasty —*n.* part of body sensitive to pain; sensitive flesh; *obs.* (*with* the) living people —*adv.* rapidly —**quick'en** *v.* make, become faster or more lively —**quick'ie** *n. inf.* a quick one —**quick'ly** *adv.* —**quick'lime** *n.* calcium oxide —**quick'sand** *n.* loose wet sand easily yielding to pressure and engulfing persons, animals *etc.* —**quick'silver** *n.* mercury —**quick'step** *n.* ballroom dance —*vi.* —**quick-tempered** *a.* irascible

quid *n.* UK *inf.* pound (sterling)

quid pro quo *Lat.* something given in exchange

quies'cent [kwi-es'-] *a.* at rest, inactive, inert; silent —**quies'cence, quies'cency** *n.*

qui'et *a.* with little or no motion or noise; undisturbed; not showy or obtrusive —*n.* state of peacefulness, absence of noise or disturbance —*v.* make, become quiet —**qui'eten** *v.* make, become quiet —**qui'etly** *adv.* —**qui'etness, qui'etude** *n.*

qui'etism *n.* passive attitude to life, *esp.* as form of religion —**qui'etist** *n.*

quill *n.* large feather; hollow stem of this; pen, plectrum made from feather; spine of porcupine

quilt *n.* padded coverlet *—vt.* stitch (two pieces of cloth) with pad between

quince *n.* acid pear-shaped fruit; tree bearing it

quinine' [-ēn'] *n.* bitter drug made from bark of tree, used to treat fever, and as tonic

Quinquages'ima [-jes'-] *n.* Sunday 50 days before Easter

quinquenn'ial *a.* occurring once in, or lasting, five years

quin'sy [-zi] *n.* inflammation of throat or tonsils

quint *n. short for* QUINTUPLET

quintess'ence *n.* purest form, essential feature; embodiment **—quintessen'tial** *a.*

quintet' *n.* set of five singers or players; composition for five voices, or instruments

quin'tuplet [-tyoo-] *n.* one of five offspring born at one birth

quip *n./v.* (utter) witty saying

quire *n.* 24 sheets of writing paper

quirk *n.* individual peculiarity of character; unexpected twist or turn

quis'ling [-iz'-] *n.* traitor who aids occupying enemy force

quit *vi.* stop doing a thing; depart *—vt.* leave, go away from; cease from (**quit** *or* **quitt'ed** *pt./pp.*) *—a.* free, rid **—quits** *a.* on equal or even terms by repayment *etc.* **—quitt'ance** *n.* discharge; receipt **—quitt'er** *n.* one lacking perseverance

quite *adv.* wholly, completely; very considerably; somewhat, rather *—interj.* exactly, just so

quiv'er[1] *vi.* shake or tremble *—n.* quivering; vibration

quiv'er[2] *n.* carrying case for arrows

quixot'ic *a.* unrealistically and impractically optimistic, idealistic, chivalrous

quiz *n.* entertainment in which general or specific knowledge of players is tested by questions; examination, interrogation *—vt.* question, interrogate; test (**-zz-**) **—quizz'ical** *a.* questioning; mocking

quoin *n.* external corner of building; small wedge for locking printing type into the form

quoit *n.* ring for throwing at peg as a game *—pl.* (*with sing. v.*) the game

Quonset hut R military shelter of corrugated sheet steel with rounded roof

quor'um *n.* least number that must be present in meeting to make its transactions valid

quo'ta *n.* share to be contributed or received; specified number, quantity, which may be imported or admitted (*pl.* **-s**)

quote *vt.* copy or repeat passages from; refer to, *esp.* to confirm view; state price for **—quo'table** *a.* **—quota'tion** *n.*

quoth [-ō-] *obs.* said

quotid'ian *a.* daily; everyday, commonplace

quo'tient [-shənt] *n.* number resulting from dividing one number by another

q.v. *quod vide* (*Lat.*, which see)

qwert'y *n.* standard typewriter keyboard layout

R

R radius; ratio; Regina (*Lat.* Queen); Rex (*Lat.* King); river; *Chess* rook

RA Rear Admiral; Royal Academy; Royal Artillery

Ra *Chem.* radium

rabb'i [-ī] *n.* Jewish learned man, spiritual leader (*pl.* **rabb'is** [-īz]) —**rabbin'ical** *a.* —**rabb'inism** *n.*

rabb'it *n.* small burrowing mammal —*vi.* hunt rabbits

rab'ble *n.* crowd of vulgar, noisy people; mob

rab'id *a.* relating to or having rabies; furious; mad; fanatical —**rab'idly** *adv.* —**rab'idness** *n.*

ra'bies *n.* acute infectious viral disease transmitted by dogs *etc.*

raccoon' *n.* small N Amer. mammal

race[1] *n.* contest of speed, as in running, swimming *etc.*; contest, rivalry; strong current of water, *esp.* leading to water wheel —*pl.* meeting for horse racing —*vt.* cause to run rapidly —*vi.* run swiftly; of engine, pedal *etc.*, to move rapidly and erratically, *esp.* on removal of resistance —**ra'cer** *n.* person, vehicle, animal that races

race[2] *n.* group of people of common ancestry with distinguishing physical features (skin colour *etc.*); species; type —**ra'cial** *a.* —**ra'cialism, ra'cism** *n.* belief in innate superiority of particular race; antagonism towards members of different race based on this belief —**ra'cialist, ra'cist** *a./n.*

raceme' *n.* cluster of flowers along a central stem, as in the foxglove

rack[1] *n.* framework for displaying or holding baggage, books, hats, bottles *etc.*; *Mechanics* straight bar with teeth on its edge, to work with pinion; instrument of torture by stretching —*vt.* stretch on rack or wheel; torture; stretch, strain —**rack'ing** *a.* agonizing (pain)

rack[2] *n.* destruction *esp. in* **rack and ruin**

rack[3] *n.* thin, flying clouds

rack[4] *vt.* clear wine, beer *etc.* by drawing off from dregs

rack[5] *n.* neck or rib section of mutton, lamb, pork

rack'et[1] *n.* loud noise, uproar; occupation by which money is made illegally —**racketeer'** *n.* one making illegal profits —**racketeer'ing** *n.* —**rack'ety** *a.* noisy

rack'et[2] *n.* bat used in tennis *etc.* —*pl.* ball game played in paved, walled court

raconteur' [-kon-] *n.* skilled storyteller

rac'quet *see* RACKET[2]

ra'cy *a.* spirited; lively; having strong flavour; spicy; piquant —**ra'cily** *adv.* —**ra'ciness** *n.*

ra'dar *n.* device for finding range and direction by ultrahigh frequency point-to-point radio waves, which reflect back to their source and reveal position and nature of objects sought

ra'dial *see* RADIUS

ra'diate *v.* emit, be emitted in rays; spread out from centre —**ra'diance** *n.* brightness; splendour —**ra'diant** *a.* beaming; shining; emitting rays —*n. Geometry* straight line from point about which it is imagined to revolve —**radia'tion** *n.* transmission of heat, light *etc.* from one body to another; particles, rays, emitted in nuclear decay; act of radiating —**ra'diator** *n.* that which radiates, *esp.* heating apparatus for rooms; cooling apparatus of car engine

rad'ical *a.* fundamental, thorough; extreme; of root —*n.* person of extreme (political) views; radicle; number expressed as root of another; group of atoms of several elements which remain unchanged in a series of chemical compounds —**rad'icalism** *n.*

rad'icle *n.* root

ra'dio *n.* use of electromagnetic waves for broadcasting, communication *etc.*; electronic device for receiving, amplifying radio signals; broadcasting, content of radio programmes (*pl* **-os**) —*vt.* transmit message *etc.* by means of radio waves

radio- (*comb. form*) of rays, of radiation, of radium, as in *radiology*

radioact'ive *a.* emitting invisible rays that penetrate matter **—radioactiv'ity** *n.*

radiog'raphy *n.* production of image on film or plate by radiation **—radiog'rapher** *n.*

radiol'ogy *n.* science of use of rays in medicine **—radiol'ogist** *n.*

radiother'apy *n.* diagnosis and treatment of disease by x-rays

rad'ish *n.* pungent root vegetable

ra'dium *n.* radioactive metallic element

ra'dius *n.* straight line from centre to circumference of circle; outer of two bones in forearm (*pl.* **ra'dii** [-di-ī], **ra'diuses**) **—ra'dial** *a.* arranged like radii of circle; of ray or rays; of radius

ra'don *n.* radioactive gaseous element

RAF UK Royal Air Force

raff'ia *n.* prepared palm fibre for making mats *etc.*

raff'ish *a.* disreputable

raf'fle *n.* lottery in which an article is assigned by lot to one of those buying tickets —*vt.* dispose of by raffle

raft [-ah-] *n.* floating structure of logs, planks *etc.*

raft'er [-ah-] *n.* one of the main beams of a roof

rag[1] *n.* fragment of cloth; torn piece; *inf.* newspaper *etc.*, *esp.* one considered worthless; piece of ragtime music —*pl.* tattered clothing **—ragg'ed** *a.* shaggy; torn; clothed in torn clothes; lacking smoothness **—rag'bag** *n.* confused assortment **—rag'time** *n.* style of jazz piano music

rag[2] *vt.* tease; torment; play practical jokes on —*n.* UK period of carnival with procession *etc.* organized by students to raise money for charities

rag'amuffin *n.* ragged, dirty person or boy

rage *n.* violent anger or passion; fury —*vi.* speak, act with fury; proceed violently and without check (as storm, battle *etc.*); be widely and violently prevalent **—all the rage** very popular

rag'lan *a.* of sleeves that continue to the neck so that there are no shoulder seams

ragout' [-gōō'] *n.* highly seasoned stew of meat and vegetables

raid *n.* rush, attack; foray —*vt.* make raid on **—raid'er** *n.*

rail[1] *n.* horizontal bar, *esp.* as part of fence, track *etc.* **—rail'ing** *n.* fence, barrier made of rails supported by posts **—rail'head** *n.* farthest point to which railway line extends **—rail'way, rail'road** *n.* track of iron rails on which trains run; company operating railway (*also pl.*)

rail[2] *vi.* utter abuse; scoff; scold; reproach **—raill'ery** *n.* banter

rail[3] *n.* kinds of marsh bird

rai'ment [rā'-] *n. obs.* clothing

rain *n.* moisture falling in drops from clouds; fall of such drops —*vi.* fall as rain —*vt.* pour down like rain **—rain'y** *a.* **—rain'bow** *n.* arch of prismatic colours in sky **—rain check** ticket stub for baseball or other game that allows readmission on future date if event is cancelled because of rain; deferral of acceptance of offer **—rain'coat** *n.* light water-resistant overcoat **—rain gauge** instrument for measuring rainfall

raise [-z] *vt.* lift up; set up; build; increase; elevate; promote; heighten, as pitch of voice; breed into existence; levy, collect; end (siege) —*n.* increase, *esp.* of wages **—raise Cain** *inf.* be riotous, angry *etc.*

rai'sin [-z-] *n.* dried grape

raison d'être' [rā-zon-detr'] *Fr.* reason or justification for existence

raj [rahj] *n.* rule, sway, *esp.* in India **—raj'ah** *n.* Indian prince or ruler

rake[1] *n.* tool with long handle and crosspiece with teeth for gathering hay, leaves *etc.* —*vt.* gather, smooth with rake; sweep, search over; sweep with shot **—rake-off** *n. inf.* monetary commission, *esp.* illegal

rake[2] *n.* dissolute or dissipated man

rake[3] *n.* slope, *esp.* backwards, of ship's funnel *etc.* —*v.* incline from perpendicular **—ra'kish** *a.* appearing dashing or speedy

rall'y *vt.* bring together, *esp.* what has been scattered, as routed army or dispersed troops —*vi.* come together; regain health or strength, revive (**rall'ied, ral'lying**) —*n.* act of rallying; assembly, *esp.* outdoor, of any organization; *Tennis* lively exchange of strokes

ram *n.* male sheep; hydraulic machine; battering engine —*vt.* force, drive; strike against with force; stuff; strike with ram (**-mm-**)

Ramadan' [-dahn'] *n.* 9th Mohammedan month; strict fasting observed during this time

ram'ble *vi.* walk without definite route; wander; talk incoherently; spread in random fashion —*n.* rambling walk —**ram'bler** *n.* climbing rose; one who rambles

ram'ekin *n.* small fireproof dish; savoury food baked in it

ram'ify *v.* spread in branches, subdivide; become complex (**-ified, -ifying**) —**ramifica'tion** *n.* branch, subdivision; process of branching out; consequence

ra'mose *a.* branching

ramp *n.* gradual slope joining two level surfaces

rampage' *vi.* dash about violently —*n.* [ram'-] angry or destructive behaviour —**rampa'geous** *a.*

ram'pant *a.* violent; rife; rearing

ram'part *n.* mound, wall for defence —*vt.* defend with one

ram'pike *n.* tall tree, burnt or bare of branches

ram'shackle *a.* tumbledown, rickety, makeshift

ran *pt. of* RUN

ranch [-ah-] *n.* Amer. cattle farm —*vi.* manage one —**ranch'er** *n.*

ran'cherie *n.* Indian village or settlement

ran'cid *a.* smelling or tasting offensively, like stale fat —**rancid'ity** *n.*

ran'co(u)r [rang'kər] *n.* bitter, inveterate hate —**ran'corous** *a.* malignant; virulent

rand *n.* monetary unit of S Africa

ran'dom *a.* made or done by chance, without plan —**at random** haphazard(ly)

rand'y *a.* **UK** *sl.* sexually aroused

rang *pt. of* RING[2]

range *n.* limits; row; scope, sphere; tract of open land on which livestock can graze; distance missile can travel; distance of mark shot at; place for shooting practice or rocket testing; rank; kitchen stove —*vt.* set in row; classify; roam —*vi.* extend; roam; pass from one point to another; fluctuate (as prices) —**rang'er** *n.* official in charge of or patrolling park *etc.*; (**R-**) member of senior branch of Guides —**rang'y** [rān'ji] *a.* with long, slender limbs; spacious —**range'finder** *n.* instrument for finding distance away of given object

rank[1] *n.* row, line; order; social class; status; relative place or position —*pl.* common soldiers; great mass or majority of people (*also* **rank and file**) —*vt.* draw up in rank, classify —*vi.* have rank, place; have certain distinctions —**rank'ing** *a.* prominent

rank[2] *a.* growing too thickly, coarse; offensively strong; rancid; vile; flagrant —**rank'ly** *adv.*

ran'kle [-ng'kl] *vi.* fester, continue to cause anger, resentment or bitterness

ran'sack *vt.* search thoroughly; pillage, plunder

ran'som *n.* release from captivity by payment; amount paid —*vt.* pay ransom for

rant *vi.* rave in violent, high-sounding language —*n.* noisy, boisterous speech; wild gaiety —**ran'ter** *n.*

ranun'culus *n.* kinds of plant, *eg* buttercup

rap[1] *n.* smart slight blow —*v.* give rap to —*vt.* utter abruptly —*vi.* perform rhythmic monologue to music (**-pp-**) —**take the rap** *sl.* suffer punishment (for) whether guilty or not

rap[2] *n.* —**not care a rap** *inf.* not care at all

rapa'cious *a.* greedy; grasping —**rapac'ity** [-pas'-] *n.*

rape[1] *vt.* force (woman) to submit unwillingly to sexual intercourse —*n.* act of raping; any violation or abuse —**ra'pist** *n.*

rape[2] *n.* plant with oil-yielding seeds, also used as fodder

rap'id *a.* quick, swift —*n.* (*esp. in pl.*) part of river with fast, turbulent current —**rapid'ity** *n.* —**rap'idly** *adv.*

ra'pier *n.* fine-bladed sword for thrusting only

rap'ine *n.* plunder

rapport' [-pawr'] *n.* harmony, agreement

rapproche'ment [-prosh'mong] *n.* re-establishment of friendly relations, *esp.* between nations

rapscall'ion *n.* rascal, rogue

rapt *a.* engrossed, spellbound —**rap'ture** *n.* ecstasy —**rap'turous** *a.*

raptor'ial *a.* predatory; of the order of birds of prey

rare[1] [rār] *a.* uncommon; infrequent; of uncommon quality; of atmosphere, having low density, thin —**rare'ly** *adv.* seldom —**ra'rity** *n.* anything rare; rareness

rare[2] [rār] *a.* (of meat) lightly cooked

rare'bit [rār'-] *n.* savoury cheese dish

ra'refy *v.* make, become thin, rare, or less dense; refine (**-fied, -fying**) —**rarefac'tion** *n.*

ra'ring *a.* enthusiastically willing, ready

ras'cal *n.* rogue; naughty (young) person —**rascal'ity** *n.* roguery, baseness —**ras'cally** *a.*

rash[1] *a.* hasty, reckless, incautious —**rash'ly** *adv.*

rash[2] *n.* skin eruption; outbreak, series of (unpleasant) occurrences

rash'er *n.* thin slice of bacon or ham

rasp [-ah-] *n.* harsh, grating noise; coarse file —*v.* scrape with rasp; make scraping noise; speak in grating voice; grate upon; irritate

rasp'berry [rahz'b-] *n.* red, juicy edible berry; plant which bears it; *inf.* spluttering noise with tongue and lips to show contempt

Rastafa'rian (*oft. shortened to* **Ras'ta**) *n.* member of Jamaican cult regarding Haile Selassie as God —*a.*

rat *n.* small rodent; *inf.* contemptible person, *esp.* deserter, informer *etc.* —*vi.* inform (on); betray; desert, abandon; hunt rats (**-tt-**) —**ratt'y** *sl. a.* shabby, dilapidated —**rat-catcher** *n.* —**rat race** continual hectic competitive activity

rat'chet *n.* set of teeth on bar or wheel allowing motion in one direction only

rate[1] *n.* proportion between two things; charge; degree of speed *etc.* —*pl.* local tax on property —*vt.* value; estimate value of; assess for local taxation —**rat(e)'able** *a.* that can be rated; liable to pay rates —**rate'payer** *n.*

rate[2] *vt.* scold, chide

rath'er [rahTH'-] *adv.* to some extent; preferably; more willingly

rat'ify *vt.* confirm (**-ified, -ifying**) —**ratifica'tion** *n.*

ra'ting *n.* valuing or assessing; fixing a rate; classification, *esp.* of ship; sailor (**naval rating**)

ra'tio [-shi-ō] *n.* proportion; quantitative relation

ratioc'inate [-ti-os'-] *vi.* reason —**ratiocina'tion** *n.*

ra'tion [rash'ən] *n.* fixed allowance of food *etc.* —*vt.* supply with, limit to certain amount

ra'tional [rash'ən-] *a.* reasonable, sensible; capable of thinking, reasoning —**rationale'** [-ahl'] *n.* reasons given for actions *etc.* —**ra'tionalism** *n.* philosophy which regards reason as only guide or authority —**ra'tionalist** *n.* —**rational'ity** *n.* —**rationaliza'tion** *n.* —**ra'tionalize** *vt.* justify by plausible reasoning; reorganize to improve efficiency *etc.* —**ra'tionally** *adv.*

rattan' *n.* climbing palm with jointed stems; cane of this

rat'tle *vi.* give out succession of short sharp sounds; clatter —*vt.* shake briskly causing a sharp clatter of sounds; *inf.* confuse, fluster —*n.* such sound; instrument for making it; set of horny rings in rattlesnake's tail —**rat'tlesnake** *n.* poisonous snake

rau'cous [-aw'-] *a.* hoarse; harsh

raunch'y *a. sl.* earthy, sexy

rav'age *vt.* lay waste, plunder —*n.* destruction

rave *vi.* talk wildly in delirium or enthusiastically —*n.*

rav'el *vt.* entangle; fray out; disentangle (**-ll-**)

ra'ven[1] *n.* black bird like crow

rav'en[2] *v.* seek prey, plunder —**rav'enous** *a.* very hungry

ravine' [-ēn'] *n.* narrow steep-sided valley worn by stream, gorge

ravio'li *pl.n.* small, thin pieces of dough filled with highly seasoned, chopped meat and cooked

rav'ish *vt.* enrapture; commit rape upon —**rav'ishing** *a.* lovely, entrancing

raw *a.* uncooked; not manufactured or refined; skinned; inexperienced, unpractised, as recruits; sensitive; chilly —**raw deal** unfair or dishonest treatment —**raw'hide** *n.* untanned hide; whip of this

ray[1] *n.* single line or narrow beam of light, heat *etc.*; any of set of radiating lines —*vi.* come out in rays; radiate

ray[2] *n.* marine fish, often very large, with winglike pectoral fins and whiplike tail

ray[3], **re** *n.* second sol-fa note

ray'on *n.* (fabric of) synthetic fibre

raze *vt.* destroy completely; wipe out, delete; level

ra'zor *n.* sharp instrument for shaving or for cutting hair —**ra'zorbill** *n.* N Atlantic auk

razz *vt. sl.* make fun of

RC Red Cross; Roman Catholic

RCAF Royal Canad. Air Force

RCMP Royal Canad. Mounted Police

RCN Royal Canad. Navy

Rd. Road

re[1] *see* RAY[3]

re[2] *prep.* with reference to, concerning

re-, red-, ren- (*comb. form*) again In the list below, the meaning may be inferred from the word to which *re-* is prefixed

reach *vt.* arrive at; extend; succeed in touching; attain to —*vi.* stretch out hand; extend —*n.* act of reaching; power of touching; grasp, scope; range; stretch of river between two bends

react' *vi.* act in return, opposition or towards former state —**reac'tance** *n. Electricity* resistance in coil, apart from ohmic resistance, due to current reacting on itself —**reac'tion** *n.* any action resisting another; counter or backward tendency; *inf.* response; chemical or nuclear change, combination or decomposition —**reac'tionary** *n./a.* (person) opposed to change, *esp.* in politics *etc.* —**reac'tive** *a.* chemically active —**reac'tor** *n.* apparatus in which nuclear reaction is maintained and controlled to produce nuclear energy

read [rēd] *vt.* look at and understand written or printed matter; learn by reading; interpret mentally; read and utter; interpret; study; understand any indicating instrument; (of instrument) register —*vi.* be occupied in reading; find mentioned in reading (**read** [red] *pt./pp.*) —**readabil'ity** *n.* —**read'able** *a.* that can be read, or read with pleasure —**read'er** *n.* one who reads; **UK** university lecturer; school textbook; one who reads manuscripts submitted to publisher; one who reads printer's proofs —**read'ing** *n.*

read'y [red'i] *a.* prepared for use or action; willing, prompt —**read'ily** *adv.* promptly; willingly —**read'iness** *n.*

rea'gent [rē-ā'jənt] *n.* chemical substance that reacts with another and is used to detect presence of the other —**rea'gency** *n.*

real *a.* existing in fact; happening; actual; genuine; (of property) consisting of land and houses —**re'alism** *n.* regarding things as they are; artistic treatment with this outlook —**re'alist** *n.* —**realis'tic** *a.* —**real'ity** *n.* real existence —**re'ally** *adv.* —**real'tor** *n.* agent, *esp.* accredited one who sells houses *etc.* for others —**re'alty** *n.* real estate —**real ale** beer allowed to ferment in the barrel and served without using carbon dioxide —**real estate** landed property

re'alize *vt.* apprehend, grasp significance of; make real; convert into money —**realiza'tion** *n.*

realm [relm] *n.* kingdom, province, domain, sphere

ream[1] *n.* twenty quires of paper, generally 480 sheets —*pl. inf.* large quantity of written matter

ream[2] *vt.* enlarge, bevel out, as hole in metal —**ream'er** *n.* tool for this

reap *v.* cut and gather harvest; receive as fruit of previous activity —**reap'er** *n.*

rear[1] *n.* back part; part of army, procession *etc.* behind others —**rear admiral** lowest flag rank in certain navies —**rear'guard** *n.* troops protecting rear of army —**rear'most** *a.*

rear[2] *vt.* care for and educate (children); breed; erect —*vi.* rise, *esp.* on hind feet

readjust'
readmiss'ion
reappear'
rearm'
rearrange'
reborn'
rebuild'
recap'ture
reconnect'
reconsid'er
reconstruct'
reconvene'
re-cov'er
re-create'
redec'orate
redevel'op
rediscov'er
re-ech'e
re-elect'
re-em'phasize
refill'
re-form'
reheat'
remarr'y
reo'pen
reprint'
reroute'
reset'
reshuf'fle
restrain'
reunite'
rewind'

reas'on [rēz'-] *n.* ground, motive; faculty of thinking; sanity; sensible or logical thought or view —*vi.* think logically in forming conclusions —*vt.* (*usu. with* with) persuade by logical argument into doing *etc.* —**reas'onable** *a.* sensible, not excessive; suitable; logical

reassure' *vt.* restore confidence to

re'bate[1] *n.* discount, refund —*vt.* [-bāt'] deduct

re'bate[2] *n.* recess, groove cut into piece of timber to join with matching piece —*vt.* cut rebate in

rebel' *vi.* revolt, resist lawful authority, take arms against ruling power (**-ll-**) —*n.* [reb'-] one who rebels; insurgent —*a.* in rebellion —**rebell'ion** *n.* organized open resistance to authority, revolt —**rebel'lious** *a.* —**rebell'iously** *adv.*

re'bore, rebor'ing *n.* boring of cylinder to regain true shape

rebound' *vi.* spring back; misfire, *esp.* so as to hurt perpetrator (of plan, deed *etc.*) —*n.* [rē'-] act of springing back or recoiling; return

rebuff' *n.* blunt refusal; check —*vt.* repulse, snub

rebuke' *vt.* reprove, reprimand, find fault with —*n.*

re'bus *n.* riddle in which names of things *etc.* are represented by pictures standing for syllables *etc.* (*pl.* **-es**)

rebut' *vt.* refute, disprove (**-tt-**) —**rebut'tal** *n.*

recal'citrant *a./n.* wilfully disobedient (person) —**recal'citrance** *n.*

recall' *vt.* recollect, remember; call, summon, order back; annul, cancel; revive, restore —*n.* summons to return; ability to remember

recant' *vt.* withdraw statement, opinion *etc.* —**recanta'tion** *n.*

re'cap *v./n. short for* RECAPITULATE, RECAPITULATION

recapit'ulate *vt.* state again briefly; repeat —**recapitula'tion** *n.*

recede' *vi.* go back; become distant; slope backwards; start balding

receipt' [-sēt'] *n.* written acknowledgment of money received; receiving or being received —*vt.* acknowledge payment of in writing

receive' [-sēv'] *vt.* take, accept, get; experience; greet (guests) —**receiv'able** *a.* —**receiv'er** *n.* officer appointed to take public money; one who takes stolen goods knowing them to have been stolen; equipment in telephone, radio or television that converts electrical signals into sound and light

re'cent *a.* that has lately happened; new —**re'cently** *adv.*

recep'tacle *n.* vessel, place or space, to contain anything

recep'tion *n.* receiving; manner of receiving; welcome; formal party; area for receiving guests, clients *etc.*; in broadcasting, quality of signals received —**recep'tionist** *n.* person who receives guests, clients *etc.*

recep'tive *a.* able, quick, willing to receive new ideas, suggestions *etc.* —**receptiv'ity** *n.*

recess' *n.* niche, alcove; hollow; secret, hidden place; remission or suspension of business; break between classes at school; vacation, holiday

recess'ion [-sesh'-] *n.* period of reduction in trade; act of receding —**reces'sive** *a.* receding

recess'ional *n.* hymn sung while clergy retire

recher'ché [-sher'shā] *a.* of studied elegance; exquisite; choice

recid'ivist *n.* one who relapses into crime

rec'ipe [res'i-pi] *n.* directions for cooking a dish; prescription; expedient

recip'ient *a.* that can or does receive —*n.* one who, that which receives —**recip'ience** *n.*

recip'rocal *a.* complementary; mutual; moving backwards and forwards; alternating —**recip'rocally** *adv.* —**recip'rocate** *vt.* give and receive mutually; return —*vi.* move backwards and forwards —**reciproca'tion** *n.* —**reciproc'ity** [-os'-] *n.*

recite' *vt.* repeat aloud, *esp.* to audience —**reci'tal** *n.* musical performance, usu. by one person; act of reciting; narration of facts *etc.*; story; public entertainment of recitations *etc.* —**recita'tion** *n.* recital, usu. from memory, of poetry or prose; recountal —**recitative'** [-ēv'] *n.* musical declamation —**reci'ter** *n.*

reck'less *a.* heedless, incautious —**reck'lessness** *n.*

reck'on *v.* count; include; consider;

think, deem; make calculations —**reck'oner** *n.*

reclaim' *vt.* make fit for cultivation; bring back; reform; demand the return of —**reclaim'able** *a.* —**reclama'tion** *n.*

recline' *vi.* sit, lie back or on one's side

recluse' [-kloos'] *n.* hermit —*a.* living in complete retirement —**reclu'sive** *a.* —**reclu'sion** *n.*

rec'ognize *vt.* know again; treat as valid; notice, show appreciation of; grant (person) right to speak in debate —**recogni'tion** *n.* —**recogni'zable** *a.* —**recog'nizance** *n.* avowal; bond by which person undertakes before court to observe some condition; *obs.* recognition

recoil' *vi.* draw back in horror *etc.*; go wrong so as to hurt the perpetrator; rebound (*esp.* of gun when fired) —*n.* [*or* re'-] backward spring; retreat; recoiling

recollect' *vt.* call back to mind, remember —**recollec'tion** *n.*

recommend' *vt.* advise, counsel; praise, commend; make acceptable —**recommenda'tion** *n.*

rec'ompense *vt.* reward; compensate, make up for —*n.* compensation; reward; requital

rec'oncile *vt.* bring back into friendship; adjust, settle, harmonize —**rec'oncilable** *a.* —**rec'oncilement** *n.* —**reconcilia'tion** *n.*

recon'dite *a.* obscure, abstruse, little known

recondi'tion [-dish'-] *vt.* restore to good condition, working order

reconnoi'tre [-tər] *vt.* make preliminary survey of; survey position of enemy —*vi.* make reconnaissance —**recon'naissance** *n.* examination or survey for military or engineering purposes; scouting

recon'stitute *vt.* restore (food) to former state *esp.* by addition of water to a concentrate

rec'ord *n.* being recorded; document or other thing that records; disk with indentations which gramophone transforms into sound; best recorded achievement; known facts about person's past —*vt.* [-kord'] put in writing; register —*v.* preserve (sound, TV programmes *etc.*) on plastic disk, magnetic tape *etc.* for reproduction on playback device —**record'er** *n.* one who, that which records; type of flute; judge in certain courts —**record'ing** *n.* process of making records from sound; something recorded, *eg* radio or TV programme —**record player** instrument for reproducing sound on disks —**off the record** not for publication

recount' *vt.* tell in detail —**recount'al** *n.*

recoup' *vt.* recompense, compensate; recover what has been expended or lost

recourse' *n.* (resorting to) source of help; *Law* right of action or appeal

recov'er [-kuv'-] *vt.* regain, get back —*vi.* get back health —**recov'erable** *a.* —**recov'ery** *n.*

rec'reant *a.* cowardly, disloyal —*n.* recreant person; renegade —**rec'reancy** *n.*

recrea'tion *n.* agreeable or refreshing occupation, relaxation, amusement —**rec'reative** *a.* —**rec room** room in house for relaxation —**recreation room** rec room; room in hospital, hotel *etc.* for social gatherings

recrim'inate *vi.* make countercharge or mutual accusation —**recrimina'tion** *n.* mutual abuse and blame —**recrim'inative, recrim'inatory** *a.*

recrudesce' [-kroo-des'] *vi.* break out again —**recrudes'cence** *n.* —**recrudes'cent** *a.*

recruit' [-oot'] *n.* newly-enlisted soldier; one newly joining society *etc.* —*vt.* enlist fresh soldiers *etc.* —**recruit'ment** *n.*

rect'angle *n.* oblong four-sided figure with four right angles —**rectang'ular** *a.* shaped thus

rect'ify *vt.* put right, correct, remedy, purify (**-fied, -fying**) —**rectifica'tion** *n.* act of setting right; refining by repeated distillation; *Electricity* conversion of alternating current into direct current —**rect'ifier** *n.* thing that rectifies

rectilin'eal, rectilin'ear *a.* in straight line; characterized by straight lines

rect'itude *n.* moral uprightness; honesty of purpose

rect'o *n.* right-hand page of book, front of leaf (*pl.* **-tos**)

rec'tor *n.* clergyman with care of parish; head of certain institutions, chiefly academic —**rec'torship** *n.* —**rec'tory** *n.* rector's house

rect'um *n.* final section of large intestine (*pl.* **-ta**) —**rect'al** *a.*

recum'bent *a.* lying down —**recum'bency** *n.*

recu'perate [-koo'-] *v.* restore, be restored from illness, losses *etc.*; convalesce —**recupera'tion** *n.*

recur' *vi.* happen again; return again and again; go or come back in mind (-**rr**-) —**recurr'ence** *n.* repetition —**recur'rent** *a.*

rec'usant *n.* one who refused to conform to rites of Established Anglican Church —*a.* obstinate in refusal

recy'cle *vt.* reprocess a manufactured substance for use again; reuse

red *a.* of colour varying from crimson to orange and seen in blood, rubies, glowing fire *etc.* —*n.* the colour; *inf.* communist —**redd'en** *v.* make red; become red; flush —**redd'ish** *a.* —**red-blooded** *a.* vigorous; virile —**red'cap** *n.* porter at railway station —**red'coat** *n. obs.* soldier; *inf* Mountie —**Red Cross** international humanitarian organization providing medical care for war casualties, famine relief *etc.* —**red'fish** *n.* various types of fish —**red flag** emblem of communist party; (**R- F-**) their song; danger signal —**red-handed** *a. inf.* (caught) in the act —**red herring** topic introduced to divert attention from main issue —**Red Indian** *offens.* N Amer. Indian —**red tape** excessive adherence to official rules —**red'wood** *n.* giant coniferous tree of California —**in the red** *inf.* in debt —**see red** *inf.* be angry

redeem' *vt.* buy back; set free; free from sin; make up for —**redemp'tion** *n.* —**redeem'able** *a.* —**The Redeemer** Jesus Christ

red'olent *a.* smelling strongly, fragrant; reminiscent (of) —**red'olence** *n.*

redoub'le [-dub'-] *v.* increase, multiply, intensify; double a second time

redoubt' [-dowt'] *n.* detached outwork in fortifications

redoubt'able [-dowt'-] *a.* dreaded, formidable

redound' *vt.* contribute (to); recoil

redress' *vt.* set right; make amends for —*n.* compensation, amends

reduce' *vt.* bring down, lower; lessen, weaken; bring by force or necessity to some state or action; slim; simplify; dilute; *Chem.* separate substance from others with which it is combined —**reduc'ible** *a.* —**reduc'tion** *n.* —**reducing agent** substance used to deoxidize or lessen density of another substance

redun'dant *a.* superfluous; (of worker) deprived of job because no longer needed —**redun'dancy** *n.*

reed *n.* various marsh or water plants; tall straight stem of one; *Mus.* vibrating cane or metal strip of certain wind instruments —**reed'y** *a.* full of reeds; like reed instrument, harsh and thin in tone —**reed'bird** *n.* bobolink

reef *n.* ridge of rock or coral near surface of sea; vein of ore; part of sail which can be rolled up to reduce area —*vt.* take in a reef of —**reef'er** *n.* sailor's jacket; *sl.* hand-rolled cigarette, *esp.* with cannabis

reek *n.* strong (unpleasant) smell —*vi.* emit fumes; smell

reel *n.* spool on which film is wound; portion of motion-picture film; winding apparatus; bobbin; thread wound on this; lively dance; music for it; act of staggering —*vt.* wind on reel; draw (in) by means of reel —*vi.* stagger, sway, rock —**reel off** recite, write fluently, quickly

reeve[1] *n.* president of local (*esp.* rural) council; *Hist.* manorial steward or official

reeve[2] *vt.* pass (rope) through hole, in block *etc.*

ref. referee; reference; reformed

refec'tory *n.* room for meals in college *etc.* —**refec'tion** *n.* meal

refer' *vi.* relate (to), allude —*vt.* send to for information; trace, ascribe to; submit for decision (-**rr**-) —**refer(r)'able** *a.* —**referr'al** *n.* act, instance of referring —**referee'** *n.* arbitrator; person willing to testify to someone's character *etc.*; umpire —*v.* act as referee —**ref'erence** *n.* act of referring; citation or direction in book; appeal to judgment of another; testimonial; one to whom inquiries as to character *etc.* may be made —**referen'dum** *n.* submitting of question to electorate (*pl.* **-dums, -da**)

refine' *vt.* purify —**refine'ment** *n.* subtlety; improvement, elaboration; fineness of feeling, taste or manners —**refi'ner** *n.* —**refi'nery** *n.* place where sugar, oil *etc.* is refined

refla'tion *n.* (steps taken to produce) increase in economic activity of country *etc.*

reflect' *vt.* throw back, *esp.* rays of light; cast (discredit *etc.*) upon —*vi.* meditate —**reflec'tion, reflex'ion** *n.* act of reflecting; return of rays of heat, light, or waves of sound, from surface; image of object given back by mirror *etc.*; conscious thought; meditation; expression of thought —**reflect'ive** *a.* meditative, quiet, contemplative; throwing back images —**reflec'tor** *n.* polished surface for reflecting light *etc.*

re'flex *n.* reflex action; reflected image; reflected light, colour *etc.* —*a.* (of muscular action) involuntary; reflected; bent back —**reflex'ive** *a.* *Grammar* describes verb denoting agent's action on himself —**reflex action** involuntary response to (nerve) stimulation

re'flux *n.* flowing back, ebb —**ref'luence** *n.* —**ref'luent** *a.* returning, ebbing

reform' *v.* improve; abandon evil practices; reconstruct —*n.* improvement —**reforma'tion** *n.* —**reform'atory** *n.* institution for reforming juvenile offenders —*a.* reforming —**reform'er** *n.*

refract' *vi.* change course of light *etc.* passing from one medium to another —**refrac'tion** *n.* —**refract'ive** *a.*

refract'ory *a.* unmanageable; difficult to treat or work; *Med.* resistant to treatment; resistant to heat

refrain'[1] *vi.* abstain (from)

refrain'[2] *n.* chorus

refran'gible *a.* that can be refracted —**refrangibil'ity** *n.*

refresh' *vt.* give freshness to; revive; renew; brighten; provide with refreshment —**refresh'er** *n.* that which refreshes —**refresh'ment** *n.* that which refreshes, *esp.* food, drink; restorative

refrig'erate [-frij'-] *vt.* freeze; cool —**refrig'erant** *n.* refrigerating substance —*a.* —**refrigera'tion** *n.* —**refrig'erator** *n.* apparatus in which foods, drinks are kept cool

ref'uge *n.* shelter, protection, retreat, sanctuary —**refugee'** *n.* one who seeks refuge, *esp.* in foreign country

reful'gent [-j-] *a.* shining, radiant —**reful'gence** *n.* —**reful'gency** *n.* splendour

refund' *vt.* pay back —*n.* [rē'-]

refur'bish *vt.* furbish, furnish or polish anew

refuse'[1] [-z] *v.* decline, deny, reject —**refu'sal** *n.* denial of anything demanded or offered; option

ref'use[2] [-yōōs] *n.* useless matter, waste

refute' *vt.* disprove —**refu'table** *a.* —**refuta'tion** *n.*

re'gal *a.* of, like a king —**rega'lia** *pl.n.* insignia of royalty, as used at coronation *etc.*; emblems of high office, an order *etc.* —**regal'ity** *n.* —**re'gally** *adv.*

regale' *vt.* give pleasure to; feast —**regale'ment** *n.*

regard' *vt.* look at; consider; relate to; heed —*n.* look; attention; particular respect; esteem —*pl.* expression of good will —**regard'ful** *a.* heedful, careful —**regard'less** *a.* heedless —*adv.* in spite of everything

regatt'a *n.* meeting for yacht or boat races

regen'erate [-jen'-] *v.* cause spiritual rebirth; reform morally; reproduce, recreate; reorganize —*a.* born anew —**regenera'tion** *n.* —**regen'erative** *a.* —**regen'erator** *n.*

re'gent *n.* ruler of kingdom during absence, minority *etc.*, of its monarch; member of governing body of certain schools and colleges —*a.* ruling —**re'gency** *n.* status, (period of) office of regent

regg'ae [-gā] *n.* style of popular West Indian music with strong beat

reg'icide [rej'-] *n.* one who kills a king; this crime

regime' [rā-zhēm'] *n.* system of government, administration

reg'imen [rej'-] *n.* prescribed system of diet *etc.*; rule

reg'iment [rej'-] *n.* organized body of troops as unit of army —*vt.* discipline, organize rigidly or too strictly —**regimen'tal** *a.* of regiment —**regiment'als** *pl.n.* uniform

re'gion [-jən] *n.* area, district; stretch of country; part of the body; sphere, realm; (*oft.* **R-**) administrative division of a country —**re'gional** *a.*

reg'ister [rej'-] *n.* list; catalogue; roll; device for registering; written record; range of voice or instrument —*v.* show, be shown on meter, face *etc.* —*vt.* enter in register; record; show; set down in writing; *Printing, Photography* cause to correspond precisely —**registrar'** *n.* keeper of a register; **UK** senior hospital doctor, junior to consultant —**registra'tion** *n.* —**reg'istry** *n.* registering; place where registers are kept, *esp.* of births, marriages, deaths

reg'nal *a.* pert. to reign of a sovereign —**reg'nancy** *n.* rule; predominance —**reg'nant** *a.* reigning

regorge' *v.* vomit up

regress' *vi.* return, revert to former place, condition *etc.* —*n.* [rē'-] —**regres'sion** *n.* act of returning; retrogression —**regress'ive** *a.* falling back —**regres'sively** *adv.*

regret' *vt.* feel sorry, distressed for loss of or on account of (**-tt-**) —*n.* sorrow, distress for thing done or left undone or lost —**regret'ful** *a.* —**regrett'able** *a.*

reg'ular *a.* normal; habitual; done, occurring, according to rule; periodical; straight, level; living under rule; belonging to standing army; *inf.* likeable, dependable —*n.* regular soldier; *inf.* regular customer —**regular'ity** *n.* —**reg'ularize** *vt.*

reg'ulate *vt.* adjust; arrange; direct; govern; put under rule —**regula'tion** *n.* —**reg'ulator** *n.* contrivance to produce uniformity of motion, as fly wheel, governor *etc.*

regur'gitate [-gur'ji-] *v.* vomit; bring back (swallowed food) into mouth —**regurgita'tion** *n.*

rehabil'itate [rē-] *vt.* help (person) to readjust to society after a period of illness, imprisonment *etc.*; restore to reputation or former position; make fit again; reinstate —**rehabilita'tion** *n.*

rehash' *vt.* rework, reuse —*n.* old materials presented in new form

rehearse' [-hurs'] *vt.* practise (play *etc.*); repeat aloud; say over again; train, drill —**rehears'al** *n.*

reign [rān] *n.* period of sovereign's rule —*vi.* be sovereign; be supreme

reimburse' [rē-im-] *vt.* refund; pay back —**reimburse'ment** *n.*

rein [rān] *n.* narrow strap attached to bit to guide horse; instrument for governing —*vt.* check, manage with reins; control —**give rein to** remove restraints

reincarna'tion [rē-in-] *n.* rebirth of soul in successive bodies; one of series of such transmigrations —**rein'carnate** *vt.*

rein'deer [rān'-] *n.* deer of cold regions, *eg* Lapland

reinforce' [rē-in-] *vt.* strengthen with new support, material, force; strengthen with additional troops, ships *etc.* —**reinforce'ment** *n.* —**reinforced concrete** concrete strengthened internally by steel bars; ferroconcrete

reinstate' [rē-in-] *vt.* replace, restore, re-establish —**reinstate'ment** *n.*

reit'erate [rē-it'-] *vt.* repeat again and again —**reitera'tion** *n.* repetition —**reit'erative** *a.*

reject' *vt.* refuse to accept; put aside; discard; renounce —*n.* [rē'-] person or thing rejected as not up to standard —**rejec'tion** *n.* refusal

rejoice' *v.* make or be joyful, merry; gladden; exult

rejoin' *vt.* reply; join again —**rejoin'der** *n.* answer, retort

reju'venate *vt.* restore to youth —**rejuvena'tion** *n.*

relapse' *vi.* fall back into evil, illness *etc.* —*n.*

relate' *vt.* narrate, recount; establish relation between; have reference or relation to —*vi.* (*with* to) form sympathetic relationship

rela'tion *n.* relative quality or condition; connection by blood or marriage; connection between things; act of relating; narrative —**rela'tionship** *n.* —**rel'ative** *a.* dependent on relation to something else, not absolute; having reference or relation (to) —*n.* one connected by blood or marriage; relative word or thing —**rel'atively** *adv.* —**relativ'ity** *n.* state of being relative; subject of two theories of Albert Einstein, dealing with relationships of space, time and motion, and acceleration and gravity

relax' *vt.* make loose or slack —*vi.* become loosened or slack; ease up from effort or attention; become more friendly, less strict —**relaxa'tion** *n.* relaxing recreation; alleviation; abatement

re'lay *n.* fresh set of people or animals relieving others; *Electricity* device for making or breaking local circuit; *Radio, Television* broadcasting station receiving programmes from another station —*vt.* [-lā'] pass on, as message (**relayed', re'laying**) —**relay race** race between teams of which each runner races part of distance

release' *vt.* give up, surrender, set free; permit public showing of (motion picture *etc.*) *—n.* setting free; releasing; written discharge; permission to show publicly; motion picture, record *etc.* newly issued

rel'egate *vt.* banish, consign; demote **—relega'tion** *n.*

relent' *vi.* give up harsh intention, become less severe **—relent'less** *a.* pitiless; merciless

rel'evant *a.* having to do with the matter in hand, to the point **—rel'evance** *n.*

reli'able, reli'ance *see* RELY

rel'ic *n.* thing remaining, *esp.* as memorial of saint; memento *—pl.* remains, traces; *obs.* dead body **—rel'ict** *n. obs.* widow

relief' *n.* alleviation, end of pain, distress *etc.*; money, food given to victims of disaster, poverty *etc.*; release from duty; one who relieves another; bus, plane *etc.* that carries passengers when a scheduled service is full; freeing of besieged city *etc.*; projection of carved design from surface; distinctness, prominence **—relieve'** *vt.* bring or give relief to **—relief map** map showing elevations and depressions of country in relief

relig'ion [-lij'-] *n.* system of belief in, worship of a supernatural power or god **—relig'ious** *a.* pert. to religion; pious; conscientious **—relig'iously** *adv.* in religious manner; scrupulously; conscientiously

relin'quish *vt.* give up, abandon **—relin'quishment** *n.*

rel'iquary [-kwər-i] *n.* case or shrine for holy relics

rel'ish *v.* enjoy, like *—n.* liking, gusto; savoury taste; taste or flavour; sauce, pickle

reluct'ant *a.* unwilling, loath, disinclined **—reluct'ance** *n*

rely' *vi.* depend (on); trust **(relied', rely'ing) —reliabil'ity** *n.* **—reli'able** *a* trustworthy, dependable **—reli'ance** *n.* trust; confidence; dependence **—reli'ant** *a.* confident

remain' *vi.* stay, be left behind; continue; abide; last **—remains'** *pl.n.* relics, *esp.* of ancient buildings; dead body **—remain'der** *n.* rest, what is left after subtraction *—vt.* offer (end of consignment of goods, material *etc.*) at reduced prices

remand' [-ah-] *vt.* send back, *esp.* into custody *—n.* act of remanding

remark' *vi.* make casual comment (on) *—vt.* comment, observe; say; take notice of *—n.* observation, comment **—remark'able** *a.* noteworthy, unusual **—remark'ably** *adv.* exceedingly; unusually

rem'edy *n.* means of curing, counteracting or relieving disease, trouble *etc.* *—vt.* put right **(-edied, -edying) —reme'diable** *a.* **—reme'dial** *a.* designed, intended to correct specific disability, handicap *etc.*

remem'ber *vt.* retain in, recall to memory *—vi.* have in mind **—remem'brance** *n.* memory; token; souvenir; reminiscence

remind' [-mīnd'] *vt.* cause to remember; put in mind (of) **—remind'er** *n.*

reminisce' [-is'] *vi.* talk, write of past times, experiences *etc.* **—reminis'cence** *n.* remembering; thing recollected *—pl.* memoirs **—reminis'cent** *a.* reminding or suggestive (of)

remiss' *a.* negligent, careless **—remiss'ly** *adv.*

remit' *v.* send money for goods, services *etc.*, *esp.* by post; refrain from exacting; give up; restore, return; slacken; *obs.* forgive **—remiss'ible** *a.* **—remiss'ion** *n.* abatement; reduction in length of prison term; pardon, forgiveness **—remit'tance** *n.* sending of money; money sent

rem'nant *n.* fragment or small piece remaining; oddment

rem'onstrate *vi.* protest, reason with, argue **—remon'strance** *n.*

remorse' *n.* regret and repentance **—remorse'ful** *a.* **—remorse'fully** *adv.* **—remorse'less** *a.* pitiless

remote' *a.* far away, distant; aloof; slight **—remote'ly** *adv.* **—remote control** control of apparatus from a distance by electrical device

remove' [-mo͞ov'] *vt.* take away or off; transfer; withdraw *—vi.* go away, change residence *—n.* degree of difference **—remo'vable** *a.* **—remo'val** [-o͞o-] *n.*

remu'nerate *vt.* reward, pay **—remunera'tion** *n.* **—remu'nerative** *a.*

renaissance' [-əsahns', -nā'səns] *n.* revival, rebirth, *esp.* **(R-)** revival of learning in 14th to 16th centuries (*also* **renascence'**)

re'nal *a.* of the kidneys

renas'cent *a.* springing up again into being

rend *v.* tear, wrench apart; burst, break, split (**rent, rend'ing**)

rend'er *vt.* submit, present; give in return, deliver up; cause to become; portray, represent; melt down; cover with plaster

rend'ezvous [rond'i-voo] *n.* meeting place; appointment; haunt; assignation —*vi.* meet, come together

rendi'tion [-dish'-] *n.* performance; translation

ren'egade *n.* deserter; outlaw; rebel —*a.*

renege' [-nēg'] *vi.* (*usu. with* on) go back on (promise *etc.*)

renew' *vt.* begin again; reaffirm; make valid again; make new; revive; restore to former state; replenish —*vi.* be made new; grow again —**renewabil'ity** *n.* quality of being renewable —**renew'able** *a.* —**renew'al** *n.* revival, restoration; regeneration

renn'et *n.* preparation for curdling milk

renounce' *vt.* give up, cast off, disown; abjure; resign, as title or claim —**renuncia'tion** *n.*

ren'ovate *vt.* restore, repair, renew, do up —**renova'tion** *n.*

renown' *n.* fame

rent[1] *n.* payment for use of land, buildings, machines *etc.* —*vt.* hold by lease; hire; let —**rent'al** *n.* sum payable as rent —**for rent** available for use subject to payment of rent

rent[2] *n.* tear; fissure —*pt./pp. of* REND

renuncia'tion *see* RENOUNCE

rep[1] *n.* fabric with corded surface for upholstery *etc.*

rep[2] *a./n. short for* REPERTORY (COMPANY)

rep[3] *n. short for* REPRESENTATIVE

repaid' *pt./pp. of* REPAY

repair'[1] *vt.* make whole, sound again; mend; patch; restore —*n.* —**repair'able** *a.* —**repara'tion** *n.* repairing; amends, compensation

repair'[2] *vi.* resort (to), go

repartee' *n.* witty retort; interchange of them

repast' [-ah-] *n.* meal

repat'riate *vt.* send (someone) back to his own country —**repatria'tion** *n.*

repay' *vt.* pay back, refund; make return for (**repaid', repay'ing**) —**repay'able** *a.* —**repay'ment** *n.*

repeal' *vt.* revoke, annul, cancel —*n.* act of repealing

repeat' *vt.* say, do again; reproduce; recur —*vi.* recur —*n.* act, instance of repeating, *esp.* TV show broadcast again —**repeat'edly** [-id-li] *adv.* again and again; frequently —**repeat'er** *n.* firearm that may be discharged many times without reloading; watch that strikes hours —**repeti'tion** *n.* act of repeating; thing repeated; piece learnt by heart and repeated —**repeti'tious** *a.* repeated unnecessarily —**repet'itive** *a.* repeated

repel' *vt.* drive back, ward off, refuse; be repulsive to (**-ll-**) —**repell'ent** *a.* distasteful; resisting water *etc.* —*n.* that which repels, esp. chemical to repel insects

repent' *vi.* wish one had not done something; feel regret for deed or omission —*vt.* feel regret for —**repent'ance** *n.* contrition —**repent'ant** *a.*

repercuss'ion [-kush'-] *n.* indirect effect, oft. unpleasant; recoil; echo

rep'ertory *n.* repertoire, collection; store —**rep'ertoire** [-twahr] *n.* stock of plays, songs *etc.* that player or company can give —**repertory (theatre, company, group)** (theatre *etc.* with) permanent company producing succession of plays

repeti'tion, repeti'tious, repet'itive *see* REPEAT

repine' *vi.* fret, complain

replace' *vt.* substitute for; put back —**replace'ment** *n.*

re'play *n.* immediate reshowing on T.V. of incident in sport, *esp.* in slow motion (*also* **action replay**); replaying of a match —*vt.* [-plā']

replen'ish *vt.* fill up again —**replen'ishment** *n.*

replete' *a.* filled, gorged —**reple'tion** *n.* complete fullness

rep'lica *n.* exact copy; facsimile, duplicate —**rep'licate** *vt.* make, be a copy of

reply' *v.* answer (**replied', reply'ing**) —*n.*

report' *n.* account, statement; rumour; repute; bang —*vt.* announce, relate;

make, give account of; take down in writing; complain about —*vi.* make report; act as reporter; present oneself (to) —**report'er** *n.* one who reports, *esp.* for newspaper

repose' *n.* peace; composure; sleep —*vi.* rest —*vt.* lay at rest; place; rely, lean (on) —**repos'itory** *n.* place where valuables are deposited for safekeeping; store

repouss'é [rə-pōōs'ā] *a.* embossed; hammered into relief from reverse side —*n.* metal work so produced

reprehend' *vt.* find fault with —**reprehen'sible** *a.* deserving censure; unworthy —**reprehen'sion** *n.* censure

represent' [-zent'] *vt.* stand for; deputize for; act, play; symbolize; make out to be; call up by description or portrait —**representa'tion** *n.* —**represent'ative** *n.* one chosen to stand for group —*a.* typical

repress' *vt.* keep down or under, quell, check —**repress'ion** *n.* restraint —**repres'sive** *a.*

reprieve' *vt.* suspend execution of (condemned person); give temporary relief (to) —*n.* postponement or cancellation of punishment; respite; last-minute intervention

rep'rimand [-mahnd] *n.* sharp rebuke —*vt.* rebuke sharply

repri'sal [-zəl] *n.* retaliation

reproach' *vt.* blame, rebuke —*n.* scolding, upbraiding; expression of this; thing bringing discredit —**reproach'ful** *a.*

rep'robate *a.* depraved; cast off by God —*n.* depraved or disreputable person —*vt.* disapprove of, reject —**reproba'tion** *n.*

reproduce' [rē-] *vt.* produce copy of; bring new individuals into existence; re-create, produce anew —*vi.* propagate; generate —**reprodu'cible** *a.* —**reproduc'tion** *n.* process of reproducing; that which is reproduced; facsimile, as of painting *etc.* —**reproduct'ive** *a.*

reprove' [-ōōv'] *vt.* censure, rebuke —**reproof'** *n.*

rep'tile *n.* cold-blooded, air breathing vertebrate with horny scales or plates, as snake, tortoise *etc.* —**reptil'ian** *a.*

repub'lic *n.* state without monarch in which supremacy of people or their elected representatives is formally acknowledged —**repub'lican** *a./n.* —**repub'licanism** *n.*

repu'diate *vt.* reject authority or validity of; cast off, disown —**repudia'tion** *n.*

repug'nant *a.* offensive; distasteful; contrary —**repug'nance** *n.* dislike, aversion; incompatibility

repulse' *vt.* drive back; rebuff; repel —*n.* driving back, rejection, rebuff —**repul'sion** *n.* distaste, aversion; *Physics* force separating two objects —**repul'sive** *a.* loathsome, disgusting

repute' *vt.* reckon, consider —*n.* reputation, credit —**rep'utable** *a.* of good repute; respectable —**reputa'tion** *n.* estimation in which person is held; character; good name

request' *n.* asking; thing asked for —*vt.* ask

Req'uiem [rek'wi-əm] *n.* Mass for the dead; music for this

require' *vt.* want, need; demand —**require'ment** *n.* essential condition; specific need; want

req'uisite [-zit] *a.* necessary; essential —*n.*

requisi'tion [-zish'-] *n.* formal demand, *eg* for materials or supplies —*vt.* demand (supplies); press into service

requite' *vt.* repay —**requi'tal** *n.*

rere'dos [rēr'dos] *n.* ornamental screen behind altar

rescind' [-sind'] *vt.* cancel, annul —**rescis'sion, rescind'ment** *n.*

res'cue *vt.* save, deliver, extricate —*n.* —**res'cuer** *n.*

research' *n.* investigation, *esp.* scientific study to discover facts —*v.* carry out investigations (on, into) —**research'er** *n.*

resem'ble [-z-] *vt.* be like; look like —**resem'blance** *n.*

resent' [-z-] *vt.* show, feel indignation at; retain bitterness about —**resent'ful** *a.* —**resent'ment** *n.*

reserve' [-z-] *vt.* hold back, set aside, keep for future use —*n.* (*also pl.*) something, *esp.* money, troops *etc.* kept for emergencies; area of land reserved for particular purpose or for use by particular group of people *etc.* (*also* **reservation**); reticence, concealment of feelings or friendliness —**reserva'tion** *n.* reserving; thing reserved; doubt; exception or limitation —**reserved'** *a.* not showing feelings, lacking cordiality —**reserv'ist** *n.* one serving in reserve

res'ervoir [rez'ər-vwahr] *n.* enclosed area for storage of water, *esp.* for community supplies; receptacle for liquid, gas *etc.*; place where anything is kept in store

reside' [-z-] *vi.* dwell permanently —**res'idence** *n.* home; house —**res'idency** *n.* official dwelling *esp.* formerly of British government agent; period during which physician undergoes further clinical training —**res'ident** *a./n.* —**residen'tial** *a.* (of part of town) consisting mainly of residences; of, connected with residence; providing living accommodation —**residential school** boarding school for children from sparsely populated settlements

res'idue [rez'-] *n.* what is left, remainder —**resid'ual** *a.* —**resid'uary** *a.*

resign' [-zīn'] *vt.* give up —*vi.* give up office, employment *etc.*; reconcile (oneself) to —**resigna'tion** [-zig-nā'-] *n.* resigning; being resigned, submission —**resigned'** *a.* content to endure

resil'ient [-z-] *a.* capable of returning to normal after stretching *etc.*, elastic; (of person) recovering quickly from shock *etc.* —**resil'ience, -ency** *n.*

res'in [rez'-] *n.* sticky substance formed in and oozing from plants, *esp.* firs and pines —**res'inous** *a.* of, like resin

resist' [-z-] *v.* withstand, oppose —**resis'tance** *n.* act of resisting; opposition; hindrance; *Electricity* opposition offered by circuit to passage of current through it —**resist'ant** *a.* —**resist'ible** *a.* —**resistiv'ity** *n.* measure of electrical resistance —**resist'or** *n.* component of electrical circuit producing resistance

res'olute [rez'ə-lo͞ot] *a.* determined —**res'olutely** *adv.* —**resolu'tion** *n.* resolving; firmness; purpose or thing resolved upon; decision of court, or vote of assembly

resolve' [-z-] *vt.* make up one's mind; decide with effort of will; form by resolution of vote; separate component parts of; make clear —*n.* resolution; fixed purpose —**resolv'able** *a.* —**resolv'ent** *a./n.* —**resolv'er** *n.*

res'onance [rez'-] *n.* echoing, *esp.* in deep tone; sound produced by body vibrating in sympathy with neighbouring source of sound —**res'onant** *a.* —**res'onate** *vi.* —**res'onator** *n.*

resort' [-z-] *vi.* have recourse; frequent —*n.* place of recreation *eg* beach; recourse; frequented place; haunt

resound' [-z-] *vi.* echo, ring, go on sounding —**resound'ing** *a.* echoing; thorough

resource' [-zawrs', -sawrs'] *n.* capability, ingenuity; that to which one resorts for support; expedient —*pl.* source of economic wealth; stock that can be drawn on; means of support, funds —**resource'ful** *a.* —**resource'fully** *adv.* —**resource'fulness** *n.*

respect' *n.* deference, esteem; point or aspect; reference, relation —*vt.* treat with esteem; show consideration for —**respectabil'ity** *n.* —**respect'able** *a.* worthy of respect, decent; fairly good —**respect'er** *n.* —**respect'ful** *a.* —**respect'ing** *prep.* concerning —**respec'tive** *a.* relating separately to each of those in question; several, separate —**respec'tively** *adv.*

respire' *v.* breathe —**respi'rable** *a.* —**respira'tion** *n.* —**res'pirator** *n.* apparatus worn over mouth and breathed through as protection against dust, poison gas *etc.* or to provide artificial respiration —**res'piratory** *a.*

res'pite *n.* pause; interval; suspension of labour; delay; reprieve

resplend'ent *a.* brilliant, splendid; shining —**resplend'ence, -ency** *n.*

respond' *vi.* answer; act in answer to any stimulus; react —**respond'ent** *a.* replying —*n.* one who answers; defendant —**response'** *n.* answer —**respon'sive** *a.* readily reacting to some influence —**respon'siveness** *n.*

respon'sible *a.* liable to answer for; accountable; dependable; involving responsibility; of good credit or position —**responsibil'ity** *n.* state of being answerable; duty; charge; obligation

rest[1] *n.* repose; freedom from exertion *etc.*; that on which anything rests or leans; pause, *esp.* in music; support —*vi.* take rest; be supported —*vt.* give rest to; place on support —**rest'ful** *a.* —**rest'less** *a.* —**rest room** room in public building having toilets, washing facilities *etc.*

rest[2] *n.* remainder; others —*vi.* remain; continue to be

rest'aurant [-tə-rong, -ront] *n.* commercial establishment serving food **—restaurateur'** *n.* keeper of one

restitu'tion *n.* giving back or making up; reparation, compensation

rest'ive *a.* restless; resisting control, impatient

restore' *vt.* build up again, repair, renew; re-establish; give back **—restora'tion** *n.* **—restor'ative** *a.* restoring *—n.* medicine to strengthen *etc.* **—restor'er** *n.*

restrain' *vt.* check, hold back; prevent; confine **—restraint'** *n.* restraining, control, *esp.* self-control

restrict' *vt.* limit, bound **—restric'tion** *n.* limitation; restraint; rule **—restric'tive** *a.*

result' [-z-] *vi.* follow as consequence; happen; end *—n.* effect, outcome **—result'ant** *a.* arising as result

resume' [-z-] *vt.* begin again **—rés'umé** [rez'yoo-mā] *n.* summary, abstract **—resump'tion** [-z-] *n.* resuming; fresh start **—resump'tive** *a.*

resur'gence *n.* rising again **—resur'gent** *a.*

resurrect' *vt.* restore to life, resuscitate; use once more (something discarded *etc.*) **—resurrec'tion** *n.* rising again (*esp.* from dead); revival

resus'citate *vt.* revive to life, consciousness **—resuscita'tion** *n.*

re'tail *n.* sale in small quantities *—adv.* by retail *—v.* sell, be sold, retail; [-tāl'] recount **—re'tailer** *n.*

retain' *vt.* keep; engage services of **—retain'er** *n.* fee to retain professional adviser, *esp.* barrister; *Hist.* follower of nobleman *etc.* **—reten'tion** *n.* **—reten'tive** *a.* capable of retaining, remembering

retal'iate *v.* repay in kind; revenge **—retalia'tion** *n.* **—retal'iatory** *a.*

retard' *vt.* make slow or late; keep back; impede development of **—retarda'tion** *n.* **—retard'ed** *a.* underdeveloped, *esp.* mentally

retch *vi.* try to vomit

ret'icent *a.* reserved in speech; uncommunicative **—ret'icence** *n.*

retic'ulate [-lit], **retic'ular** *a.* made or arranged like a net **—retic'ulate** [-lāt] *v.* make, be like net **—reticula'tion** *n.*

ret'ina *n.* light-sensitive membrane at back of eye

ret'inue *n.* band of followers or attendants

retire' *vi.* give up office or work; go away; withdraw; go to bed *—vt.* cause to retire **—retired'** *a.* that has retired from office *etc.* **—retire'ment** *n.* **—reti'ring** *a.* unobtrusive, shy

retort' *vt.* reply; repay in kind, retaliate; hurl back (charge *etc.*) *—vi.* reply with countercharge *—n.* vigorous reply or repartee; vessel with bent neck used for distilling

retouch' *vt.* touch up, improve by new touches, *esp.* of paint *etc.*

retrace' *vt.* go back over (a route *etc.*) again

retract' *v.* draw back, recant **—retract'able, -ible** *a.* **—retrac'tion** *n.* drawing or taking back, *esp.* of statement *etc.* **—retrac'tor** *n.* muscle; surgical instrument

retread' [-tred'] *vt.* renovate worn rubber tire *—n.* [rē'-] renovated tire

retreat' *vi.* move back from any position; retire *—n.* act of, or military signal for, retiring, withdrawal; place to which anyone retires; refuge; sunset call on bugle

retrench' *vt.* reduce expenditure, *esp.* by dismissing staff; cut down **—retrench'ment** *n.*

retribu'tion *n.* recompense, *esp.* for evil deeds; vengeance **—retrib'utive** *a.*

retrieve' *vt.* fetch back again; restore; rescue from ruin; recover, *esp.* information from computer; regain **—retriev'able** *a.* **—retriev'al** *n.* **—retriev'er** *n.* dog trained to retrieve game

ret'roact *vi.* react; act in opposite direction **—retroact'ive** *a.* applying or referring to the past **—retroact'ively** *adv.*

ret'roflex *a.* bent, curved backwards

ret'rograde *a.* going backwards, reverting; reactionary **—retrogress'ion** *n.* **—retrogress'ive** *a.*

ret'rorocket *n.* rocket engine to slow or reverse spacecraft *etc.*

ret'rospect *n.* looking back, survey of past **—retrospec'tion** *n.* **—retrospec'tive** *a.*

retrouss'é [-trōōs'ā] *a.* turned upwards, pug

retsi'na [-sē'-] *n.* Greek wine

return' *vi.* go, come back —*vt.* give, send back; report officially; elect —*n.* returning, being returned; profit; official report; return ticket —**returning officer** one conducting election

reu'nion *n.* gathering of people who have been apart

Rev. Revelation(s); Reverend

rev *inf. n.* revolution (of engine) —*v.* (*oft. with* up) increase speed of revolution (of engine)

reval'ue *v.* adjust exchange value of currency upwards —**revalua'tion** *n.*

revamp' *vt.* renovate, restore

reveal' *vt.* make known; show —**revela'tion** *n.*

reveill'e [-val'i] *n.* morning bugle call *etc.* to waken soldiers

rev'el *vi.* take pleasure (in); make merry (-ll-) —*n.* (*usu. pl.*) merrymaking —**rev'eller** *n.* —**rev'elry** *n.* festivity

rev'enant *n.* something, *esp.* ghost, that returns

revenge' *n.* retaliation for wrong done; act that satisfies this; desire for this —*vt.* avenge; make retaliation for —*v.refl.* avenge oneself —**revenge'ful** *a.* vindictive; resentful

rev'enue *n.* income, *esp.* of state, as taxes *etc.*

rever'berate *v.* echo, resound, throw back (sound *etc.*) —**reverbera'tion** *n.*

revere' [-vēr'] *vt.* hold in great regard or religious respect —**rev'erence** *n.* revering; awe mingled with respect and esteem; veneration —**rev'erend** *a.* (*esp.* as prefix to clergyman's name) worthy of reverence —**rev'erent** *a.* showing reverence —**reveren'tial** *a.* marked by reverence

rev'erie *n.* daydream, absent-minded state

revers' [-vēr'] *n.* part of garment which is turned back, *eg* lapel

reverse' *v.* (of vehicle) (cause to) move backwards —*vt.* turn upside down or other way round; change completely —*n.* opposite, contrary; side opposite, obverse; defeat; reverse gear —*a.* opposite, contrary —**revers'al** *n.* —**revers'ible** *a.* —**reverse gear** mechanism enabling vehicle to move backwards

revert' *vi.* return to former state; come back to subject; refer to a second time; turn backwards —**rever'sion** *n.* (of property) rightful passing to owner or designated heir *etc.* —**revert'ed** *a.* —**revert'ible** *a.*

revet'ment *n.* facing of stone, sand bags *etc.* for wall

review' [-vyōō'] *vt.* examine; look back on; reconsider; hold, make, write review of —*n.* general survey; critical notice of book *etc.*; periodical with critical articles; inspection of troops; relearning of notes, subject for examination —**review'er** *n.* writer of reviews

revile' *vt.* be viciously scornful of, abuse —**revi'ler** *n.*

revise' [-vīz'] *vt.* look over and correct; restudy (work done previously) in preparation for an examination; change, alter —**revi'ser** *n.* —**revi'sion** *n.* reexamination for purpose of correcting; revised copy

revive' *v.* bring, come back to life, vigour, use *etc.* —**revi'val** *n.* reviving, *esp.* of religious fervour —**revi'valist** *n.* organizer of religious revival

revoke' *vt.* take back, withdraw; cancel —**rev'ocable** *a.* —**revoca'tion** *n.* repeal

revolt' [-ō-] *n.* rebellion —*vi.* rise in rebellion; feel disgust —*vt.* affect with disgust —**revolt'ing** *a.* disgusting, horrible

revolve' *vi.* turn round, rotate; be centred on —*vt.* rotate —**revolu'tion** [-lōō'-] *n.* violent overthrow of government; great change; complete rotation, turning or spinning round —**revolu'tionary** *a./n.* —**revolu'tionize** *vt.* change considerably; bring about revolution in

revol'ver *n.* repeating pistol with revolving magazine

revue' *n.* theatrical entertainment with topical sketches and songs

revul'sion *n.* sudden violent change of feeling; marked repugnance or abhorrence

reward' *vt.* pay, make return for service, conduct *etc.* —*n.* —**reward'ing** *a.* giving personal satisfaction, worthwhile

rhap'sody *n.* enthusiastic or high-flown (musical) composition or utterance —**rhapsod'ic** *a.* —**rhap'sodist** *n.* —**rhap'sodize** *v.*

rhe'a *n.* S Amer. three-toed ostrich

rheol'ogy *n.* science of the study of the

deformation and flow of matter —**rhe·ol'ogist** *n.*

rhe'ostat *n.* instrument for regulating the value of the resistance in an electric circuit

rhe'sus *n.* small, long-tailed monkey of S Asia —**rhesus factor** (*also* **Rh factor**) feature distinguishing different types of human blood

rhet'oric *n.* art of effective speaking or writing; artificial or exaggerated language —**rhetor'ical** [-o'ri-] *a.* (of question) not requiring an answer —**rhetori'cian** *n.*

rheum [ro͞om] *n.* watery discharge, mucus; catarrh —**rheum'y** *a.*

rheum'atism [ro͞om'-] *n.* painful inflammation of joints or muscles —**rheumat'ic** *a./n.* —**rheu'matoid** *a.* of, like rheumatism

Rh factor *see* RHESUS

rhinoc'eros [-os'-] *n.* large thick-skinned animal with one or two horns on nose

rho'dium *n.* hard metal like platinum —**rho'dic** *a.*

rhododen'dron *n.* evergreen flowering shrub

rhom'bus, rhomb [rom] *n.* equilateral but not right-angled parallelogram, diamond-shaped figure —**rhom'boid** *a.*

rhon'chus [-kəs] *n.* rattling or wheezing sound, as of disordered respiration

rhu'barb *n.* garden plant of which the fleshy stalks are cooked and used as fruit; laxative from root of allied Chinese plant; *sl.* heated discussion or quarrel

rhyme, rime *n.* identity of sounds at ends of lines of verse, or in words; word or syllable identical in sound to another; verse marked by rhyme —*vt.* make rhymes —**rhy'mer, ri'mer** *n.*

rhythm [riTH'əm] *n.* measured beat or flow, *esp.* of words, music *etc.* —**rhyth'mic(al)** *a.* —**rhyth'mically** *adv.*

rib[1] *n.* one of curved bones springing from spine and forming framework of upper part of body; cut of meat including rib(s); curved timber of framework of boat; raised series of rows in knitting *etc.* —*vt.* furnish, mark with ribs; knit to form a rib pattern (**-bb-**) —**ribb'ing** *n.*

rib[2] *vt. inf.* tease, ridicule

rib'ald *a.* irreverent, scurrilous; indecent —*n.* ribald person —**rib'aldry** *n.* vulgar, indecent talk

ribb'on *n.* narrow band of fabric used for trimming, tying *etc.*; long strip or line of anything

ribofla'vin [rī-] *n.* form of vitamin B

rice *n.* Eastern cereal plant; its seeds as food —**ri'cer** *n.* kitchen utensil with small holes through which cooked potatoes *etc.* are pressed to form coarse mash —**rice paper** fine, edible Chinese paper

rich *a.* wealthy; fertile; abounding; valuable; (of food) containing much fat or sugar; mellow; amusing —*n.* the wealthy classes —**rich'es** *pl.n.* wealth —**rich'ly** *adv.*

rick[1] *n.* stack of hay *etc.*

rick[2] *vt./n.* sprain, wrench

rick'ets *n.* disease of children marked by softening of bones, bow legs *etc.*, caused by vitamin D deficiency —**rick'ety** *a.* shaky, insecure, unstable; suffering from rickets

rick'shaw *n.* light two-wheeled man-drawn Asian vehicle

ric'ochet [-shā] *vi.* (of bullet) rebound or be deflected by solid surface or water —*n.* bullet or shot to which this happens

rid *vt.* clear, relieve of; free; deliver (**rid, ridd'ing**) —**ridd'ance** *n.* clearance; act of ridding; deliverance; relief

ridd'en *pp. of* RIDE —*a.* (*in combination*) afflicted, affected, as **disease-ridden**

rid'dle[1] *n.* question made puzzling to test one's ingenuity; enigma; puzzling thing, person —*vi.* speak in, make riddles

rid'dle[2] *vt.* pierce with many holes —*n.* coarse sieve for gravel *etc.* —**riddled with** full of, *esp.* holes

ride *v.* sit on and control or propel (horse, bicycle *etc.*); be carried on or across —*vi.* go on horseback or in vehicle; lie at anchor —*vt.* travel over; cause to be carried (**rode, ridd'en, ri'ding**) —*n.* journey on horse *etc.*, or in any vehicle; riding track —**ri'der** *n.* one who rides; supplementary clause; addition to a document; mathematical problem on given proposition —**ri'derless** *a.*

ridge *n.* long narrow hill; long, narrow elevation on surface; line of meeting of two sloping surfaces —*vt.* form into ridges

ridic'ulous *a.* deserving to be laughed at, absurd, foolish —**rid'icule** *n.* treatment of person or thing as ridiculous —*vt.* laugh at, deride

ri'ding *n.* electoral constituency

ries'ling [rēz'-] *n.* dry white wine; type of grape used to make it

rife *a.* prevalent, common

rif'fle *n.* a rapid in stream; rocky shoal; ripple in water —*v.* flick through (pages *etc.*) quickly

riff'raff *n.* rabble, disreputable people

ri'fle *vt.* search and rob; ransack; make spiral grooves in (gun barrel *etc.*) —*n.* firearm with long barrel —**ri'fling** *n.* arrangement of grooves in gun barrel; pillaging

rift *n.* crack, split, cleft

rig *vt.* provide (ship) with spars, ropes *etc.*; equip; set up, *esp.* as makeshift; arrange in dishonest way (**-gg-**) —*n.* way ship's masts and sails are arranged; apparatus for drilling for oil and gas; truck, *esp.* tractor-trailer; style of dress —**rig'ger** *n.* —**rigg'ing** *n.* ship's spars and ropes

right [rīt] *a.* just; in accordance with truth and duty; true; correct; proper; of side that faces east when front is turned to north; *Politics* conservative or reactionary (*also* **right wing**); straight; upright; of outer or more finished side of fabric —*vt.* bring back to vertical position; do justice to —*vi.* come back to vertical position —*n.* claim, title *etc.* allowed or due; what is right, just or due; conservative political party; punch, blow with right hand —*adv.* straight; properly; very; on or to right side —**right'ful** *a.* —**right'ly** *adv.* —**right angle** angle of 90 degrees —**right of way** *Law* right to pass over someone's land; path used

right'eous [rī'chəs] *a.* just, upright; godly; virtuous; good; honest —**right'eousness** *n.*

rig'id [rij'-] *a.* inflexible; harsh, stiff —**rigid'ity** *n.*

rig'marole *n.* meaningless string of words; long, complicated procedure

ri'gor [*or* rig'-] *n.* sudden coldness attended by shivering —**rigor mortis** stiffening of body after death

rig'o(u)r *n.* harshness, severity, strictness; hardship —**rig'orous** *a.* stern, harsh, severe

rile *vt.* agitate (water *etc.*); anger, annoy

rill *n.* small stream

rim *n.* edge, border, margin; outer ring of wheel —**rimmed** *a.* bordered, edged

rime *n.* hoarfrost —**ri'my** *a.*

rind [-ī-] *n.* outer coating of fruits *etc.*

rin'derpest *n.* malignant infectious disease of cattle

ring[1] *n.* circle of gold *etc.*, *esp.* for finger; any circular band, coil, rim *etc.*; circle of persons; enclosed area, *esp.* roped-in square for boxing —*vt.* put ring round; mark (bird *etc.*) with ring —**ring'er** *n.* one who rings bells; *sl.* (*esp. in* **dead ringer**) person, thing apparently identical to another —**ring'bark** *vt.* kill tree by cutting bark round trunk —**ring'leader** *n.* instigator of mutiny, riot *etc.* —**ring'let** *n.* curly lock of hair —**ring road** *chiefly* **UK** main road that bypasses a town (centre) —**ring'worm** *n.* fungal skin disease in circular patches

ring[2] *vi.* give out clear resonant sound, as bell; resound —*vt.* cause (bell) to sound; telephone (**rang** *pt.*, **rung** *pp.*) —*n.* a ringing; telephone call

rink *n.* sheet of ice for skating or curling; floor for roller skating

rinse [-s] *vt.* remove soap (from washed clothes, hair *etc.*) by applying clean water; wash lightly —*n.* a rinsing; liquid to tint hair

ri'ot *n.* tumult, disorder; loud revelry; disorderly, unrestrained disturbance; profusion —*vi.* make, engage in riot —**ri'otous** *a.* unruly, rebellious, wanton —**riot shield** rectangular shield used by police or servicemen during a riot

RIP requiescat in pace (*Lat.*, rest in peace)

rip[1] *vt.* cut, tear away, slash, rend (**-pp-**) —*n.* rent, tear —**rip'cord** *n.* cord pulled to open parachute —**rip'saw** *n.* handsaw with coarse teeth (used for cutting wood along grain) —**rip off** *sl.* steal; *sl.* overcharge —**rip-off** *n. sl.* act of stealing, overcharging *etc.*

rip[2] *n.* strong current, *esp.* one moving away from the shore

ripa'rian [rī-] *a.* of, on banks of river

ripe *a.* ready to be reaped, eaten *etc.*; matured; (of judgment *etc.*) sound —**ri'pen** *v.* grow ripe; mature

riposte' *n.* verbal retort; counterstroke; *Fencing* quick lunge after parry

rip'ple *n.* slight wave, ruffling of surface; sound like ripples of water —*vi.* flow, form into little waves; (of sounds) rise and fall gently —*vt.* form ripples on

rise [rīz] *vi.* get up; move upwards; appear above horizon; reach higher level; increase in value or price; rebel; adjourn; have its source (**rose, ris'en, ri'sing**) —*n.* rising; upslope —**ri'ser** *n.* one who rises, esp. from bed; vertical part of step —**ri'sing** *n.* revolt —*a.* increasing in rank, maturity

ris'ible [riz'-] *a.* inclined to laugh; laughable —**risibil'ity** *n.*

risk *n.* chance of disaster or loss —*vt.* venture; put in jeopardy; take chance of —**risk'ily** *adv.* —**risk'y** *a.* dangerous; hazardous

risott'o [-zot'-] *n.* dish of rice cooked in stock with various other ingredients

ris'qué [-kā] *a.* suggestive of indecency

riss'ole *n.* dish of fish or meat minced, coated with egg and breadcrumbs and fried

rite *n.* formal practice or custom, *esp.* religious —**rit'ual** *n.* prescribed order or book of rites; regular, stereotyped action or behaviour —*a.* concerning rites —**rit'ualism** *n.* practice of ritual —**rit'ualist** *n.*

ri'val *n.* one that competes with another for favour, success *etc.* —*vt.* vie with (**-ll-**) —*a.* in position of rival —**ri'valry** *n.* keen competition

riv'en *a.* split

riv'er *n.* large natural stream of water; copious flow

riv'et *n.* bolt for fastening metal plates, the end being put through holes and then beaten flat —*vt.* fasten with rivets; cause to be fixed or held firmly, *esp.* (*fig.*) in surprise, horror *etc.* —**riv'eter** *n.*

riv'ulet *n.* small stream

rly. railway

RM Rural Municipality

RN Royal Navy

roach *n.* freshwater fish

road *n.* track, way prepared for passengers, vehicles *etc.*; direction, way; street —**road'ie** *n. inf.* person who transports and sets up equipment for band or group —**road'block** *n.* barricade across road to stop traffic for inspection *etc.* —**road hog** selfish, aggressive driver —**road'house** *n.* restaurant on country route —**road metal** broken stones used in macadamizing roads —**road sense** sound judgment in driving road vehicles —**road'side** *n./a.* —**road'ster** *n. obs.* touring automobile; kind of bicycle —**road'works** *pl.n.* repairs to road, *esp.* blocking part of road —**road'worthy** *a.* (of vehicle) mechanically sound

roam *v.* wander about, rove —**roam'er** *n.*

roan *a.* (of horses) having coat in which main colour is thickly interspersed with another, *esp.* bay, sorrel or chestnut mixed with white or grey —*n.* roan horse

roar [rawr] *v.* make or utter loud deep hoarse sound as of lion, thunder, voice in anger *etc.* —*n.* such a sound —**roar'ing** *a. inf.* brisk and profitable —*adv.* noisily

roast *v.* bake, cook in closed oven; cook by exposure to open fire; make, be very hot; *inf.* ridicule or criticize severely —*n.* roasted joint; picnic at which food is cooked over open fire —*a.* roasted

rob *vt.* plunder, steal from; pillage, defraud (**-bb-**) —**robb'er** *n.* —**robb'ery** *n.*

robe *n.* long outer garment, often denoting rank or office —*vt.* dress —*vi.* put on robes, vestments

rob'in *n.* large Amer. thrush with red breast; small brown European bird with red breast

ro'bot *n.* automated machine, *esp.* performing functions in human manner; person of machine-like efficiency —**robot'ics** *n.* science of designing and using robots; (*also* **robot dancing**) body popping

robust' *a.* sturdy, strong —**robust'ness** *n.*

roc [rok] *n.* monstrous bird of Arabian mythology

roch'et *n.* garment like surplice, with tight sleeves, worn by bishops

rock[1] *n.* stone; large rugged mass of stone —**rock'ery** *n.* mound or grotto of stones or rocks for plants in a garden —**rock'y** *a.* having many rocks; rugged —**rock bottom** lowest possible level —**rock candy** sugar in large hard crystals —**rock tripe** any of various edible lichens that grow on rocks

rock[2] *v.* (cause to) sway to and fro —*n.* style of pop music derived from rock-and-roll —**rock'er** *n.* curved piece of wood *etc.* on which thing may rock;

rocking chair —**rock-and-roll** *n.* popular dance rhythm

rock'et *n.* self-propelling device powered by burning of explosive contents (used as firework, for display, signalling, line carrying, weapon *etc.*); vehicle propelled by rocket engine, as weapon or carrying spacecraft —*vi.* move fast, *esp.* upwards, as rocket —**rock'etry** *n.*

roco'co [rə-kō'kō] *a.* of furniture, architecture *etc.* having much conventional decoration in style of early 18th cent. work in France; tastelessly florid

rod *n.* slender straight bar, stick; cane; old measure (5½ yards)

rode *pt. of* RIDE

ro'dent *n.* gnawing animal, *eg* rat

ro'deo [*or* -dā'ō] *n.* display of skills, competition, with bareback riding, cattle handling techniques *etc.*

roe[1] *n.* small species of deer

roe[2] *n.* mass of eggs in fish

roent'gen [ront'-] *n.* measuring unit of radiation dose

Roga'tion Days three days preceding Ascension day

rogue [rōg] *n.* rascal, knave, scoundrel; mischief-loving person or child; wild beast of savage temper, living apart from herd —**ro'guish** [-gish] *a.* —**ro'guery** *n.*

rois'ter *vi.* be noisy, boisterous, bragging —**rois'terer** *n.* reveller

role, rôle *n.* actor's part; specific task or function

roll [rōl] *v.* move by turning over and over —*vt.* wind round; smooth out with roller —*vi.* move, sweep along; undulate; of ship, swing from side to side; of aircraft, turn about a line from nose to tail in flight —*n.* act of lying down and turning over and over or from side to side; piece of paper *etc.* rolled up; any object thus shaped, as *meat roll, Swiss roll, etc.*; list, catalogue; bread baked into small oval or round; continuous sound, as of drums, thunder *etc.* —**roll'er** *n.* cylinder of wood, stone, metal *etc.* used for pressing, crushing, smoothing, supporting thing to be moved, winding thing on *etc.*; long wave of sea —**roll call** act, time of calling over list of names, as in schools or army —**rolled gold** metal coated with a thin layer of gold —**roller bearings** bearings of hardened steel rollers —**roller skate** skate with wheels instead of runner —**roller skating** —**roller towel** loop of towel on roller —**rolling pin** cylindrical roller for pastry or dough —**rolling stock** locomotives, cars *etc.* of railway —**roll-top** *a./n.* in desk, flexible lid sliding in grooves —**roll up** *inf.* appear, turn up

roll'icking *a.* boisterously jovial and merry

ro'ly-po'ly *n.* pudding of suet pastry covered with jam and rolled up —*a.* round, plump

ROM *Computers* read only memory

Rom. Romans

romaine' *n.* type of lettuce with long crisp leaves

Ro'man *a.* of Rome or Church of Rome —**Roman Catholic** member of that section of Christian Church which acknowledges supremacy of the Pope —**Roman numerals** letters I, V, X, L, C, D, M used to represent numbers in manner of Romans —**roman type** plain upright letters, ordinary style of printing

Romance' *a.* of vernacular language of certain countries, developed from Latin, as French, Spanish *etc.* —*n.*

romance' *n.* love affair, *esp.* intense and happy one; mysterious or exciting quality; tale of chivalry; tale with scenes remote from ordinary life; literature like this; picturesque falsehood —*vi.* exaggerate, fantasize —**romanc'er** *n.* —**roman'tic** *a.* characterized by romance; of or dealing with love; of literature *etc.*, preferring passion and imagination to proportion and finish —*n.* —**roman'ticism** *n.* —**roman'ticist** *n.* —**roman'ticize** *vi.*

romanesque' [-esk'] *a./n.* (in) style of round-arched vaulted architecture of period between Classical and Gothic

Rom'any *n.* gypsy; gypsy language —*a.* gypsy

romp *vi.* run, play wildly, joyfully —*n.* spell of romping —**rom'pers** *pl.n.* child's overall —**romp home** win easily

ron'deau [-dō] *n.* short poem with opening words used as refrain (*pl.* **-x**) —**ron'del** *n.* extended rondeau —**ron'delet** *n.* short rondeau

ron'do *n.* piece of music with leading theme to which return is continually made

Ro'neo R duplicating machine —*v.* duplicate letters *etc.* by this means

rönt'gen *n. see* ROENTGEN

rood [rōōd] *n.* the Cross; crucifix; quarter of acre —**rood screen** one separating nave from choir

roof [rōōf] *n.* outside upper covering of building; top, covering part of anything —*vt.* put roof on, over

rook[1] *n.* bird of crow family —*vt. sl.* swindle, cheat —**rook'ery** *n.* colony of rooks

rook[2] *n.* piece at chess (*also* **castle**)

rook'ie *n. inf.* recruit, *esp.* in army

room [rōōm] *n.* space; space enough; division of house; scope, opportunity —*pl.* lodgings —**room'y** *a.* spacious —**roomette'** *n.* small self-contained compartment in railway sleeping car —**rooming house** house with furnished rooms for rent

roost [-ōō-] *n.* perch for fowls —*vi.* perch —**roost'er** *n.* domestic cock

root[1] [rōōt] *n.* part of plant that grows down into earth and conveys nourishment to plant; plant with edible root, *eg* carrot; vital part; source, origin, original cause of anything; *Anatomy* embedded portion of tooth, nail, hair *etc.*; primitive word from which other words are derived; factor of a quantity which, when multiplied by itself the number of times indicated, gives the quantity —*v.* (cause to) take root; pull by roots; dig, burrow —**root beer** effervescent drink made from extracts of various roots

root[2] [rōōt] *vi. inf.* cheer; applaud; encourage —**root'er** *n.*

rope *n.* thick cord —*vt.* secure, mark off with rope —**ro'piness** *n.* —**ro'py** *a. inf.* inferior, inadequate; *inf.* not well; (of liquid) sticky and stringy —**rope in** trick or entice into some activity

ro'sary *n.* series of prayers; string of beads for counting these prayers as they are recited; rose garden

rose[1] *n.* shrub, climbing plant *usu.* with prickly stems and fragrant flowers; the flower; perforated flat nozzle for hose *etc.*; pink colour —*a.* of this colour —**ro'seate** *a.* rose-coloured, rosy —**rosette'** *n.* rose-shaped bunch of ribbon; rose-shaped architectural ornament —**ro'sy** *a.* flushed; hopeful, promising —**rose-coloured** *a.* having colour of rose; unwarrantably optimistic —**rose window** circular window with series of mullions branching from centre —**rose'wood** *n.* fragrant wood —**rose of Sharon** low, spreading shrub with yellow flowers

rose[2] *pt. of* RISE

ro'sé [-zā] *n.* pink wine

rose'mary *n.* evergreen fragrant flowering shrub

Rosicru'cian [rōz-] *n.* member of secret order devoted to occult law —*a.* —**Rosicru'cianism** *n.*

ros'in [roz'-] *n.* resin

ros'ter *n.* list or plan showing turns of duty

ros'trum *n.* platform, stage, pulpit; beak or bill of a bird (*pl.* **-trums, -tra**)

rot *v.* decompose naturally; corrupt (**-tt-**) —*n.* decay, putrefaction; any disease producing decomposition of tissue; *inf.* nonsense —**rott'en** *a.* decomposed, putrid; corrupt

ro'ta *n.* roster, list

ro'tary *a.* (of movement) circular; operated by rotary movement —*n.* traffic circle —**rotate'** *v.* (cause to) move round centre or on pivot —**rota'tion** *n.* rotating; regular succession —**ro'tatory** *a.* —**Rotary Club** one of international association of businessmen's clubs —**Rota'rian** *n.* member of such

rote *n.* mechanical repetition —**by rote** by memory

rotiss'erie *n.* (electrically driven) rotating spit for cooking meat

ro'tor *n.* revolving portion of a dynamo motor or turbine

rott'en *see* ROT

rotund' *a.* round; plump; sonorous —**rotun'dity** *n.*

rou'ble [rōō'-] *n.* Russian monetary unit

rouge [rōōzh] *n.* red powder, cream used to colour cheeks —*v.* colour with rouge

rough [ruf] *a.* not smooth, of irregular surface; violent, stormy, boisterous; rude; uncivil; lacking refinement; approximate; in preliminary form —*vt.* make rough; plan out approximately; (*with* it) live without usual comforts *etc.* —*n.* rough state or area; sketch —**rough'en** *vt.* —**rough'ly** *adv.* —**rough'age** *n.* unassimilated portion of food promoting proper intestinal action —**rough'cast** *a.* coated with mixture of lime and gravel —*n.* such mixture —*vt.* coat with it

—**rough diamond** trustworthy but unsophisticated person —**rough-hew** *vt.* shape roughly —**rough'house** *n./v. sl.* fight, row

roulette' [roo-] *n.* game of chance played with revolving wheel and ball

round [-ow-] *a.* spherical, cylindrical, circular, curved; full, complete; roughly correct; large, considerable; plump; positive —*adv.* with circular or circuitous course —*n.* thing round in shape; recurrent duties; stage in competition; customary course, as of milkman; game (of golf); one of several periods in boxing match *etc.*; cartridge for firearm; rung; movement in circle —*prep.* about; on all sides of —*v.* make, become round —*vt.* move round —**round'ly** *adv.* plainly; thoroughly —**round'about** *n.* **UK** merry-go-round; **UK** traffic circle —*a.* not straightforward —**round robin** petition signed with names in circle to conceal order; tournament in which each player plays every other —**round-trip ticket** one allowing passengers to travel to and from a place —**round up** drive (cattle) together; collect and arrest criminals

round'el [-ow-] *n.* rondeau; small disc —**round'elay** *n.* simple song with refrain

rouse [rowz] *vt.* wake up, stir up, excite to action; cause to rise —*vi.* waken —**roust'about** [rowst'-] *n.* unskilled labourer

rout [rowt] *n.* overwhelming defeat, disorderly retreat; noisy rabble —*vt.* scatter and put to flight

route [root] *n.* road, chosen way —**route'march** *n.* long march undertaken for training purposes

routine' [roo-tēn'] *n.* regularity of procedure, unvarying round; regular course —*a.* ordinary, regular

roux [roo] *n.* fat and flour cooked together as basis for sauces

rove *v.* wander, roam —**ro'ver** *n.* one who roves; pirate

row[1] [rō] *n.* number of things in a straight line; rank; file; line; one of a strip of houses forming one building

row[2] [rō] *v.* propel boat by oars —*n.* spell of rowing —**row'boat** *n.*

row[3] *inf. n.* dispute; disturbance —*vi.* quarrel noisily

row'an [*or* rō'-] *n.* native British tree producing bright red berries, mountain ash

rowd'y *a.* disorderly, noisy and rough —*n.* person like this

row'el *n.* small wheel with points on spur

row'lock [rol'ək] *n.* **UK** oarlock

roy'al *a.* of, worthy of, befitting, patronized by, king or queen; splendid —**roy'alist** *n.* supporter of monarchy —**roy'alty** *n.* royal dignity or power; royal persons; payment to owner of land for right to work minerals, or to inventor for use of his invention; payment to author depending on sales

rpm revolutions per minute

RR Rural Route

RSVP répondez s'il vous plaît (*Fr.* please reply)

rub *vt.* apply pressure to with circular or backwards and forwards movement; clean, polish, dry, thus; pass hand over; abrade, chafe; remove by friction —*vi.* come into contact accompanied by friction; become frayed or worn by friction (**-bb-**) —*n.* rubbing; impediment

rubb'er[1] *n.* coagulated sap of rough, elastic consistency, of certain tropical trees; piece of rubber *etc.* used for erasing; thing for rubbing; person who rubs; overshoe made of rubber —*a.* of rubber —**rubb'erize** *vt.* coat, impregnate, treat with rubber —**rubb'ery** *a.* —**rubber stamp** device for imprinting dates *etc.*; automatic authorization

rubb'er[2] *n.* series of odd number of games or contests at various games; two out of three games won

rubb'ish *n.* garbage; anything worthless; trash, nonsense —**rubb'ishy** *a.* valueless

rub'ble *n.* fragments of stone *etc.*; builders' waste materials

rubell'a *n.* mild contagious viral disease, German measles

ru'bicund [roo'-] *a.* ruddy

ru'bric [roo'-] *n.* title, heading; direction in liturgy; instruction

ru'by [roo'-] *n.* precious red gem; its colour —*a.* of this colour

ruck[1] *n.* crowd; common herd; rank and file

ruck[2] *n.* crease —*v.* make, become wrinkled

ruck'sack *n.* pack carried on back, knapsack

ruck'us *n. inf.* uproar, disturbance

ruc'tion *n. inf.* noisy disturbance

rudd'er *n.* flat piece hinged to boat's stern or rear of aircraft to steer by

rudd'y *a.* of fresh or healthy red colour; rosy; florid

rude *a.* impolite; coarse; vulgar; primitive; roughly made; uneducated; sudden, violent —**rude'ly** *adv.*

ru'diments [rōō'-] *pl.n.* elements, first principles —**rudimen'tary** *a.*

rue[1] [rōō] *v.* grieve for; regret; deplore; repent —*n. obs.* repentance —**rue'ful** *a.* sorry; regretful; dejected; deplorable —**rue'fully** *adv.*

rue[2] [rōō] *n.* plant with evergreen bitter leaves

ruff[1] *n.* starched and frilled collar; natural collar of feathers, fur *etc.* on some birds and animals —**ruf'fle** *vt.* rumple, disorder; annoy, put out; frill, pleat —*n.* frilled trimming

ruff[2] *n./v. Cards* trump

ruff'ian *n.* violent, lawless person —**ruf'fianism** *n.* —**ruff'ianly** *a.*

rug *n.* small, *oft.* shaggy or thick-piled floor mat; thick woollen wrap, coverlet

rug'by *n.* form of football in which the ball may be carried in the hands (*also inf.* **rugg'er**)

rugg'ed *a.* rough; broken; unpolished; harsh, austere; sturdy or strong

ru'in [rōō'-] *n.* decay, destruction; downfall; fallen or broken state; loss of wealth, position *etc.* —*pl.* ruined buildings *etc.* —*vt.* reduce to ruins; bring to decay or destruction; spoil; impoverish —**ruina'tion** *n.* —**ru'inous** *a.* causing or characterized by ruin or destruction —**ru'inously** *adv.*

rule *n.* principle; precept; authority; government; what is usual; control; measuring stick —*vt.* govern; decide; mark with straight lines; draw (line) —**ru'ler** *n.* one who governs; stick for measuring or ruling lines

rum *n.* spirit distilled from sugar cane

rum'ba *n.* rhythmic dance, *orig.* Cuban; music for it

rum'ble *vi.* make noise as of distant thunder, heavy vehicle *etc.* —*n.* such noise

rumbust'ious *a.* boisterous, unruly

ru'minate [rōō'-] *vi.* chew cud; ponder over; meditate —**ru'minant** *a./n.* cud-chewing (animal) —**rumina'tion** *n.* quiet meditation and reflection —**ru'minative** *a.*

rumm'age *v.* search thoroughly —*n.* —**rummage sale** sale of miscellaneous items, old clothes *etc.* in aid of charity

rumm'y *n.* card game

ru'mo(u)r [rōō'mə] *n.* hearsay, common talk, unproved statement —*vt.* put round as, by way of, rumour

rump *n.* tail end; buttocks

rum'ple *v./n.* crease, wrinkle

rum'pus *n.* disturbance; noise and confusion —**rumpus room** room used for noisy activities, as parties or children's games

run *vi.* move with more rapid gait than walking; go quickly; flow; flee; compete in race, contest, election; revolve; continue; function; travel according to schedule; fuse; melt; spread over; have certain meaning —*vt.* cross by running; expose oneself (to risk *etc.*); cause to run; (of newspaper) print, publish; land and dispose of (smuggled goods); manage; operate (**ran** *pt.*, **run** *pp.*, **runn'ing** *pr.p.*) —*n.* act, spell of running; rush; tendency, course; period; sequence; heavy demand; enclosure for domestic fowls, animals; ride in car; series of unravelled stitches, ladder; score of one at cricket; steep snow-covered course for skiing —**run'ner** *n.* racer; messenger; curved piece of wood on which sleigh slides; any similar appliance; slender stem of plant running along ground forming new roots at intervals; strip of cloth, carpet —**runn'ing** *a.* continuous; consecutive; flowing; discharging; effortless; entered for race; used for running —*n.* act of moving or flowing quickly; management —**runn'y** *a.* tending to flow or exude moisture —**run'down** *n.* summary —**run-down** *a.* exhausted —**run down** stop working; reduce; exhaust; denigrate —**run'way** *n.* level stretch where aircraft take off and land —**in the running** having fair chance in competition

rune *n.* character of earliest Germanic alphabet; magic sign —**ru'nic** *a.*

rung[1] *n.* crossbar or spoke, *esp.* in ladder

rung[2] *pp. of* RING[2]

runn'el *n.* gutter; small brook or rivulet

runn'ing *see* RUN

runt *n.* small animal, below usual size of species; *offens.* undersized person

rupee' *n.* monetary unit of India and Pakistan

rup'ture *n.* breaking, breach; hernia —*v.* break; burst, sever

rur'al [roor'-] *a.* of the country; rustic —**rur'alize** *v.* —**rural route** mail service in rural area

ruse [-z] *n.* stratagem, trick

rush[1] *vt.* impel, carry along violently and rapidly; take by sudden assault; make concerted effort to secure participation of (person) —*vi.* cause to hurry; move violently or rapidly —*n.* rushing, charge; hurry; eager demand for; heavy current (of air, water *etc.*) —*a.* done with speed; characterized by speed —**rush hour** period at beginning and end of day when many people are travelling to and from work

rush[2] *n.* marsh plant with slender pithy stem; the stems as material for baskets —**rush'y** *a.* full of rushes

rusk *n.* kind of biscuit, *esp.* used for feeding babies

russ'et *a.* reddish-brown —*n.* the colour

rust *n.* reddish-brown coating formed on iron by oxidation; disease of plants —*v.* contract, affect with rust —**rust'y** *a.* coated with rust, of rust colour; out of practice —**rust'proof** *a.*

rust'ic *a.* of, or as of, country people; rural; of rude manufacture; made of untrimmed branches —*n.* countryman, peasant —**rust'icate** *vt.* banish from university —*vi.* live a country life —**rustica'tion** *n.* —**rustic'ity** *n.*

rus'tle[1] [-sl] *vi.* make sound as of blown dead leaves *etc.* —*n.* this sound

rus'tle[2] [-sl] *vt.* steal (cattle) —*vi. inf.* move swiftly and energetically —**rus'tler** *n.* cattle thief

rut[1] *n.* furrow made by wheel; settled habit or way of living; groove —**rutt'y** *a.*

rut[2] *n.* periodic sexual excitement among animals —*vi.* be under influence of this (**-tt-**)

rutaba'ga [ro͞otəbā'gə] *n.* yellow variety of turnip

ruth'less [ro͞oth'-] *a.* pitiless, merciless —**ruth'lessly** *adv.*

rye *n.* grain used for fodder and bread; plant bearing it; whisky made from rye

rye-grass *n.* kinds of grass cultivated for fodder

S

S Saint; South(ern); *Chem.* sulphur
s second(s); shilling; singular
SA Salvation Army; South Africa; South Australia
Sabb'ath *n.* Saturday, devoted to worship and rest from work in Judaism and certain Christian Churches; Sunday, observed by Christians as day of worship and rest —**sabbat'ical** *a./n.* (denoting) leave granted to university staff *etc.* for study
sa'ble *n.* small weasellike Arctic animal; its fur; black —*a.* black
sab'ot [-bō] *n.* shoe made of wood, or with wooden sole
sab'otage [-tahzh] *n.* intentional damage done to roads, machines *etc.*, *esp.* secretly in war —*v.* —**saboteur'** *n.*
sa'bre [-bər] *n.* curved cavalry sword
sac *n.* pouchlike structure in an animal or vegetable body
sacc'harin [sak'ə-] *n.* artificial sweetener —**sacc'harine** *a. lit./fig.* excessively sweet
sacerdo'tal [sas-] *a.* of priests
sach'et [sash'ā] *n.* small envelope or bag, *esp.* one holding liquid, as shampoo
sack *n.* large bag, *orig.* of coarse material; pillaging; *inf.* dismissal; *sl.* bed —*vt.* pillage (captured town); *inf.* dismiss —**sack'ing** *n.* material for sacks —**sack'cloth** *n.* coarse fabric used for sacks
sac'rament *n.* one of certain ceremonies of Christian Church *esp.* Eucharist —**sacrament'al** *a.*
sa'cred *a.* dedicated, regarded as holy; set apart, reserved; inviolable; connected with, intended for religious use —**sa'credly** *adv.*
sac'rifice *n.* giving something up for sake of something else; act of giving up; thing so given up; making of offering to a god; thing offered —*vt.* offer as sacrifice; give up; sell at very cheap price —**sacrifi'cial** [-fish'-] *a.*
sac'rilege [-lij] *n.* misuse, desecration of something sacred —**sacrileg'ious** *a.* profane; desecrating
sac'ristan *n.* official in charge of vestments and sacred vessels of church —**sac'risty** *n.* room where sacred vessels *etc.* are kept
sac'rosanct *a.* preserved by religious fear against desecration or violence; inviolable —**sacrosanc'tity** *n.*
sa'crum *n.* five vertebrae forming compound bone at base of spinal column
sad *a.* sorrowful; unsatisfactory, deplorable —**sadd'en** *vt.* make sad —**sad'ly** *adv.* —**sad'ness** *n.*
sad'dle *n.* rider's seat to fasten on horse, bicycle *etc.*; anything resembling a saddle; joint of mutton or venison; ridge of hill —*vt.* put saddle on; lay burden, responsibility on —*a.* resembling a saddle, as in **sadd'leback** —**sadd'ler** *n.* maker of saddles *etc.* —**sadd'lery** *n.*
sa'dism *n.* form of (sexual) perversion marked by love of inflicting pain —**sa'dist** *n.* —**sadist'ic** *a.*
safar'i *n.* (party making) overland (hunting) journey, *esp.* in Africa
safe *a.* secure, protected; uninjured, out of danger; not involving risk; trustworthy; sure, reliable; cautious —*n.* strong lockable container; ventilated cupboard for meat *etc.*; *sl.* condom —**safe'ly** *adv.* —**safe'ty** *n.* —**safe-conduct** *n.* passport, permit to pass somewhere —**safe'guard** *n.* protection —*vt.* protect —**safety glass** unsplinterable glass
saff'lower *n.* thistlelike plant with flowers used for dye, oil
saff'ron *n.* crocus; orange coloured flavouring obtained from it; the colour —*a.* orange
sag *vi.* sink in middle; hang sideways; curve downwards under pressure; give way; tire; (of clothes) hang loosely (**-gg-**) —*n.* droop
sag'a [sahg'ə] *n.* legend of Norse heroes; any long (heroic) story
saga'cious *a.* wise —**saga'ciously**

adv. —**sagac'ity** [-gas'-] *n.*

sage[1] *n.* very wise man —*a.* wise —**sage'ly** *adv.*

sage[2] *n.* aromatic herb

Sagitta'rius [saj-] *n.* (the Archer) 9th sign of zodiac, operative *c.* Nov. 22-Dec. 20

sa'go *n.* starchy cereal from powdered pith of sago palm

said [sed] *pt./pp. of* SAY

sail *n.* piece of fabric stretched to catch wind for propelling ship *etc.*; act of sailing; journey upon the water; ships collectively; arm of windmill —*vi.* travel by water; move smoothly; begin voyage —*vt.* navigate —**sail'or** *n.* seaman; one who sails —**sail'board** *n.* craft used for windsurfing like surfboard with mast and single sail

saint *n.* (title of) person formally recognized (*esp.* by R.C. Church) after death, as having gained by holy deeds a special place in heaven; exceptionally good person —**saint'ed** *a.* canonized; sacred —**saint'liness** *n.* holiness —**saint'ly** *a.*

sake[1] *n.* cause, account; end, purpose —**for the sake of** in behalf of; to please or benefit

sak'e[2] [sahk'i] *n.* Japanese alcoholic drink made of fermented rice

salaam' [-lahm'] *n.* bow of salutation, mark of respect in East —*vt.* salute

sala'cious *a.* excessively concerned with sex, lewd —**salac'ity** *n.*

sal'ad *n.* mixed vegetables, or fruit, used as food without cooking —*a.* —**salad dressing** oil, vinegar, herbs *etc.* mixed together as sauce for salad

sal'amander *n.* variety of lizard; mythical lizardlike fire spirit

salam'i [-lahm'-] *n.* variety of highly-spiced sausage

sal'ary *n.* fixed regular payment to persons employed usu. in nonmanual work —**sal'aried** *a.*

sale *n.* selling; selling of goods at unusually low prices; auction —**sale'able** *a.* capable of being sold —**sales'clerk** *n.* shop assistant —**sales'man** *n.* shop assistant; one travelling to sell goods, *esp.* as representative of firm —**sales'manship** *n.* art of selling or presenting goods in most effective way

sal'icin *n.* substance obtained from poplars and used in medicine —**salicyl'ic** *a.*

sa'lient *a.* prominent, noticeable; jutting out —*n.* salient angle, *esp.* in fortification —**sa'lience** *n.* —**sa'liently** *adv.*

sa'line *a.* containing, consisting of a chemical salt, *esp.* common salt; salty —**salin'ity** *n.*

sali'va *n.* liquid which forms in mouth, spittle —**sali'vary** *a.* —**sal'ivate** *v.*

Salk vaccine [sawlk] vaccine against poliomyelitis

sall'ow[1] *a.* of unhealthy pale or yellowish colour

sall'ow[2] *n.* tree or low shrub allied to the willow

sall'y *n.* rushing out, *esp.* by troops; outburst; witty remark —*vi.* rush; set out (**sall'ied, sall'ying**)

salm'on [sam'-] *n.* large silvery fish with orange-pink flesh valued as food; colour of its flesh —*a.* of this colour

salmonell'a *pl.n.* bacteria causing disease (*esp.* food poisoning)

sal'on *n.* (reception room for) guests in fashionable household; commercial premises of hairdressers, beauticians *etc.*

saloon' *n.* place where alcoholic drink is sold and consumed; principal cabin or sitting room in passenger ship; public room for specified use, *eg* billiards; **UK** sedan

salpigloss'is *n.* plant with bright funnel-shaped flowers

sal'sify [-fi] *n.* purple-flowered plant with edible root

SALT Strategic Arms Limitation Talks *or* Treaty

salt [sawlt] *n.* white powdery or granular crystalline substance consisting mainly of sodium chloride, used to season or preserve food; chemical compound of acid and metal; wit —*vt.* season, sprinkle with, preserve with salt —**salt'less** *a.* —**salt'ness** *n.* —**salt'y** *a.* of, like salt —**old salt** sailor —**salt'cellar** *n.* small vessel for salt at table —**salt lick** deposit, block of salt licked by game, cattle *etc.* —**salt'pan** *n.* depression encrusted with salt after draining away of water —**saltpe'tre** [-tər] *n.* potassium nitrate used in gunpowder —**salt'water** *a.* —**with a pinch, grain, of salt** allowing for exaggeration —**worth one's salt** efficient

sal'tant *a.* leaping; dancing —**sal'tatory** *a.* —**salta'tion** *n.*

salu'brious [-loo'-] *a.* favourable to health, beneficial —**salu'brity** *n.*

Salu'ki *n.* tall hound with silky coat

sal'utary *a.* wholesome, resulting in good —**sal'utarily** *adv.*

salute' [-loot'] *vt.* greet with words or sign; acknowledge with praise —*vi.* perform military salute —*n.* word, sign by which one greets another; motion of arm as mark of respect to superior *etc.* in military usage; firing of guns as military greeting of honour —**saluta'tion** [-yoo-tā'-] *n.*

sal'vage *n.* act of saving ship or other property from danger of loss; property so saved —*vt.*

salva'tion *n.* fact or state of being saved, *esp.* of soul

salve [*or* sahv] *n.* healing ointment —*vt.* anoint with such, soothe

sal'ver *n.* (silver) tray for presentation of food, letters *etc.*

sal'via *n.* plant with blue or red flowers

sal'vo *n.* simultaneous discharge of guns *etc.* (*pl.* **-vo(e)s**)

sal volat'ile [-il-i] *n.* preparation of ammonia used to revive persons who faint *etc.*

SAM surface-to-air missile

Sam. Samuel

Samar'itan [-ma'ri-] *n.* native of ancient Samaria; benevolent person

sam'ba *n.* dance of S Amer. origin; music for it

same *a.* identical, not different, unchanged; uniform; just mentioned previously —**same'ness** *n.* similarity; monotony

sam'ite *n.* rich silk cloth

sam'ovar *n.* Russian tea urn

Samoyed' *n.* dog with thick white coat and tightly curled tail

sam'pan *n.* small oriental boat

sam'phire *n.* herb found on rocks by seashore

sam'ple [sah'-] *n.* specimen —*vt.* take, give sample of; try; test; select —**sam'pler** *n.* beginner's exercise in embroidery —**sam'pling** *n.* the taking of samples; sample

sam'urai [-oo-rī] *n.* member of ancient Japanese warrior caste

sanator'ium *n.* hospital, *esp.* for chronically ill; health resort (*pl.* **-riums, -ria**) —**san'atory, san'ative** *a.* curative

sanc'tify *vt.* set apart as holy; free from sin (**-fied, -fying**) —**sanctifica'tion** *n.* —**sanc'tity** *n.* saintliness; sacredness; inviolability —**sanc'tuary** *n.* holy place; part of church nearest altar; place where fugitive was safe from arrest or violence; place protected by law where animals *etc.* can live without interference —**sanc'tum** *n.* sacred place or shrine; person's private room

sanctimo'nious *a.* making a show of piety, holiness —**sanc'timony, sanctimo'niousness** *n.*

sanc'tion *n.* permission, authorization; penalty for breaking law —*pl.* boycott or other coercive measure *esp.* by one state against another regarded as having violated a law, right *etc.* —*vt.* allow, authorize, permit

sand *n.* substance consisting of small grains of rock or mineral, *esp.* on beach or in desert —*pl.* stretches or banks of this, usually forming seashore —*vt.* polish, smooth with sandpaper; cover, mix with sand —**sand'er** *n.* power tool for smoothing surfaces —**sand'y** *a.* like sand; sand-coloured; consisting of, covered with sand —**sand'bag** *n.* bag filled with sand or earth, used as protection against gunfire, floodwater *etc.* and as weapon —*vt.* beat, hit with sandbag —**sand'blast** *n.* jet of sand blown from a nozzle under pressure for cleaning, grinding *etc.* —*vt.* —**sand'box** *n.* box containing sand for children to play in —**sand'paper** *n.* paper with sand stuck on it for scraping or polishing wood *etc.* —**sand'piper** *n.* various kinds of shore birds —**sand'stone** *n.* rock composed of sand —**sandtrap** sandy hollow on golf course

san'dal *n.* shoe consisting of sole attached by straps

san'dalwood *n.* sweet-scented wood

sand'wich [san'wij] *n.* two slices of bread with meat or other substance between —*vt.* insert between two other things

sane *a.* of sound mind; sensible, rational —**san'ity** *n.*

San'forize R preshrink (fabric) using a patented process

sang *pt. of* SING

sang-froid' [sahn-frwah'] *n.* composure; indifference; self-possession

san'guine [-ng'gwin] *a.* cheerful, confident; ruddy in complexion —**san'guinary** *a.* accompanied by bloodshed; bloodthirsty —**san'guinely** *adv.* hopefully, confidently

san'itary *a.* helping protection of health against dirt *etc.* —**sanita'tion** *n.* measures, apparatus for preservation of public health —**san'itize** *vt.* make sanitary or hygenic

sank *pt. of* SINK

San'skrit, San'scrit *n.* ancient language of India

sap[1] *n.* moisture which circulates in plants; energy —*v.* drain off sap (**-pp-**) —**sap'less** *a.* —**sap'ling** *n.* young tree

sap[2] *v.* undermine; destroy insidiously; weaken (**-pp-**) —*n.* trench dug in order to approach or undermine enemy position —**sapp'er** *n.* soldier in engineering unit

sap[3] *n. inf.* foolish, gullible person —**sap'py** *a.*

sa'pient *a.* (*usu. ironical*) wise; discerning; shrewd; knowing —**sa'pience** *n.*

Sapph'ic [saf'-] *a.* of Sappho, a Grecian poetess; denoting a kind of verse —*n.* Sapphic verse —**sapph'ism** *n.* lesbianism

sapph'ire [saf'-] *n.* (usu. blue) precious stone; deep blue —*a.*

sar'aband(e) [sa'rə-] *n.* slow, stately Spanish dance; music for it

Sar'acen [sa'rə-] *n.* Arabian; adherent of Mohammedanism in Syria and Palestine; infidel

sar'casm *n.* bitter or wounding ironic remark; such remarks; taunt; sneer; irony; use of such expressions —**sarcast'ic** *a.* —**sarcast'ically** *adv.*

sarcoph'agus [-kof'-] *n.* stone coffin

sard *n.* precious stone, variety of chalcedony

sardine' [-dēn'] *n.* small fish of herring family, usu. preserved in oil

sardon'ic *a.* characterized by irony, mockery or derision

sar'donyx [-də-niks] *n.* gemstone, variety of chalcedony

sargass'um, sargass'o *n.* gulfweed, type of floating seaweed

sar'i *n.* Hindu woman's robe

sarong' *n.* skirtlike garment worn in Asian and Pacific countries

sarsaparill'a *n.* (flavour of) drink, *orig.* made from root of plant

sartor'ial *a.* of tailor, tailoring, or men's clothes

sash[1] *n.* decorative belt, ribbon, wound around the body

sash[2] *n.* wooden window frame opened by moving up and down in grooves

Sask. Saskatchewan

saskatoon' *n.* N Amer. shrub with purplish berries

sass *n. inf.* impudent talk or behaviour —*vi.* talk or answer back in such a way —*vt.* talk impudently to

sass'afras *n.* laurellike tree with aromatic bark used medicinally

sat *pt./pp. of* SIT

Sa'tan *n.* the devil —**satan'ic(al)** *a.* devilish, fiendish —**satan'ically** *adv.*

sat'chel *n.* small bag, *esp.* for school books

sate *vt.* satisfy a desire or appetite fully or excessively

sat'ellite *n.* celestial body or man-made projectile orbiting planet; person, country *etc.* dependent on another

sa'tiate [-shi-āt] *vt.* satisfy to the full; surfeit —**sa'tiable** *a.* —**satia'tion** *n.* —**sati'ety** [sə-tī'-] *n.* feeling of having had too much

sat'in *n.* fabric (of silk, rayon *etc.*) with glossy surface on one side —**sat'iny** *a.* of, like satin —**sat'inwood** *n.* various tropical trees yielding hard satiny wood

sat'ire *n.* composition in which vice, folly or foolish person is held up to ridicule; use of ridicule or sarcasm to expose vice and folly —**satir'ic(al)** [-ti'ri-] *a.* of nature of satire; sarcastic; bitter —**sat'irist** *n.* —**sat'irize** *vt.* make object of satire; censure thus

sat'isfy *vt.* content, meet wishes of; pay; fulfil, supply adequately; convince (**-fied, -fying**) —**satisfac'tion** *n.* —**satisfac'tory** *a.*

satsu'ma [-sōō'-] *n.* kind of small orange

sat'urate *vt.* soak thoroughly; cause to absorb maximum amount; *Chem.* cause substance to combine to its full capacity with another; shell or bomb heavily —**satura'tion** *n.* act, result of saturating

Sat'urday *n.* seventh day of week, after Friday

Sat'urn *n.* Roman god; one of planets —**sat'urnine** *a.* gloomy; sluggish in temperament, dull, morose —**Saturna'lia** *n.* ancient festival of Saturn; (*also* **s-**) noisy revelry, orgy

sat'yr [-ər] *n.* woodland deity, part man, part goat; lustful man

sauce *n.* liquid added to food to enhance flavour; stewed fruit; *inf.* impudence —*vt.* add sauce to; *inf.* be cheeky, impudent to —**sau'cily** *adv.* —**sauc'y** *a.* impudent —**sauce'pan** *n.* cooking pot with long handle

sau'cer *n.* curved plate put under cup; shallow depression

sau'erkraut [sow'ər-krowt] *n.* German dish of finely shredded and pickled cabbage

sault [so͞o] *n.* rapids, waterfall

sau'na *n.* steam bath, *orig.* Finnish

saun'ter *vi.* walk in leisurely manner, stroll —*n.* leisurely walk or stroll

sau'rian *n.* one of the order of reptiles including the alligator, lizard *etc.*

saus'age [sos'-] *n.* minced meat enclosed in thin tube of animal intestine or synthetic material —**sausage roll UK** pastry cylinder filled with sausage

sau'té [sō'tā] *a.* fried quickly with little fat

Sauternes' [sō-tern'] *n.* sweet white Fr. wine

sav'age *a.* wild; ferocious; brutal; uncivilized, primitive —*n.* member of savage tribe, barbarian —*vt.* attack ferociously —**sav'agely** *adv.* —**sav'agery** *n.*

savann'a(h) *n.* extensive open grassy plain

sav'ant *n.* man of learning

save *vt.* rescue, preserve; protect; secure; keep for future, lay by; prevent need of; spare; except —*vi.* lay by money —*prep. obs.* except —*conj. obs.* but —**sa'ving** *a.* frugal; thrifty; delivering from sin; excepting; compensating —*prep.* excepting —*n.* economy —*pl.* money, earnings put by for future use

sa'vio(u)r *n.* person who rescues another; (**S-**) Christ

sav'oir-faire' [sav'wahr-fer'] *Fr. n.* ability to do, say, the right thing in any situation

sa'vo(u)r [-vər] *n.* characteristic taste; flavour; odour; distinctive quality —*vi.* have particular smell or taste; have suggestion (of) —*vt.* give flavour to; have flavour of; enjoy, appreciate —**sa'vo(u)ry** *a.* attractive to taste or smell; not sweet —*n.* savoury snack (before meal)

sa'vory *n.* aromatic herb used in cooking

savoy' *n.* variety of cabbage

savv'y *sl. vt.* understand —*n.* wits, intelligence

saw[1] *n.* tool for cutting wood *etc.* by tearing it with toothed edge —*vt.* cut with saw —*vi.* make movements of sawing (**sawed, sawn, saw'ing**) —**saw'yer** *n.* one who saws timber —**saw'buck** *n.* sawhorse; *sl.* ten-dollar bill —**saw'dust** *n.* fine wood fragments made in sawing —**saw'fish** *n.* fish armed with toothed snout —**saw'horse** *n.* stand for timber during sawing —**saw'mill** *n.* mill where timber is sawn into planks *etc.* —**saw'off** *n. sl.* compromise, settlement

saw[2] *pt. of* SEE

saw[3] *n.* wise saying, proverb

sax *n. inf. short for* SAXOPHONE

saxe *n.* shade of blue

sax'horn *n.* instrument of trumpet class

sax'ifrage *n.* Alpine or rock plant

Sax'on *n.* member of West Germanic people who settled widely in Europe in the early Middle Ages —*a.*

sax'ophone *n.* keyed wind instrument

say *vt.* speak; pronounce; state; express; take as example or as near enough; form and deliver opinion (**said** [sed] *pt./pp.*, **say'ing** *pr.p.*, **says** *3rd pers. sing. pres. ind.*) —*n.* what one has to say; chance of saying it; share in decision —**say'ing** *n.* maxim, proverb

SC Star of Courage

scab *n.* crust formed over wound; skin disease; disease of plants; *offens.* one who works during strike —**scabb'y** *a.*

scabb'ard *n.* sheath for sword or dagger

sca'bies [skā'-] *n.* contagious skin disease —**sca'bious** *a.* having scabies, scabby

sca'bious *n.* plant with pink, white or blue flowers

sca'brous *a.* having rough surface; thorny; indecent; risky

scaff'old *n.* temporary platform for

workmen; gallows —**scaff'olding** *n.* (material for building) scaffold

sca'lar *n.* variable quantity, *eg* time, having magnitude but no direction —*a.*

scald [skawld] *vt.* burn with hot liquid or steam; clean, sterilize with boiling water; heat (liquid) almost to boiling point —*n.* injury by scalding

scale[1] *n.* one of the thin, overlapping plates covering fishes and reptiles; thin flake; incrustation which forms in boilers *etc.* —*vt.* remove scales from —*vi.* come off in scales —**sca'ly** *a.* resembling or covered in scales —**scale insect** plant pest which lives under scale

scale[2] *n.* (*chiefly in pl.*) weighing instrument —*vt.* weigh in scales; have weight of

scale[3] *n.* graduated table or sequence of marks at regular intervals used as reference or for fixing standards, as in making measurements, in music *etc.*; ratio of size between a thing and a model or map of it; (relative) degree, extent —*vt.* climb —*a.* proportionate —**scale up** *or* **down** increase or decrease proportionately in size

sca'lene *a.* (of triangle) with three unequal sides

scall'op [skol'-] *n.* edible shellfish; edging in small curves like edge of scallop shell —*vt.* shape like scallop shell; cook in scallop shell or dish like one

scalp *n.* skin and hair of top of head —*vt.* cut off scalp of

scal'pel *n.* small surgical knife

scamp *n.* mischievous person or child —*v.* skimp

scam'per *vi.* run about; run hastily from place to place —*n.*

scam'pi *pl.n.* kind of large prawn

scan *vt.* look at carefully, scrutinize; measure or read (verse) by metrical feet; examine, search by systematically varying the direction of a radar or sonar beam; glance over quickly —*vi.* (of verse) conform to metrical rules (**-nn-**) —*n.* scanning —**scann'er** *n.* device, *esp.* electronic, which scans —**scan'sion** *n.*

scan'dal *n.* action, event generally considered disgraceful; malicious gossip —**scan'dalize** *vt.* shock —**scan'dalous** *a.* outrageous, disgraceful

scant *a.* barely sufficient or not sufficient —**scant'ily** *adv.* —**scan'ty** *a.*

scape'goat *n.* person bearing blame due to others —**scape'grace** *n.* mischievous person

scap'ula *n.* shoulder blade (*pl.* **-lae** [-lē], **-las**) —**scap'ular** *a.* of scapula —*n.* part of habit of certain religious orders in R.C. Church

scar *n.* mark left by healed wound, burn or sore; change resulting from emotional distress —*v.* mark, heal with scar (**-rr-**) —**scarred** *a.*

scar'ab [ska'rəb] *n.* sacred beetle of ancient Egypt; gem cut in shape of this

scarce [skārs] *a.* hard to find; existing or available in insufficient quantity; uncommon —**scarce'ly** *adv.* only just; not quite; definitely or probably not —**scarce'ness, scarc'ity** *n.*

scare [skār] *vt.* frighten —*n.* fright, sudden panic —**scar'y** *a. inf.* —**scare'crow** *n.* thing set up to frighten birds from crops; badly dressed or miserable looking person —**scare'monger** *n.* one who spreads alarming rumours

scarf[1] *n.* long narrow strip, large piece of material to put round neck, head *etc.* (*pl.* **scarfs** *or* **scarves**)

scarf[2] *n.* part cut away from each of two pieces of timber to be jointed longitudinally; joint so made —*vt.* cut or join in this way —**scarf'ing** *n.*

sca'rify *vt.* scratch, cut slightly all over; lacerate; stir surface soil of; criticize mercilessly (**-fied, -fying**) —**scarifica'tion** *n.*

scar'let *n.* a brilliant red colour; cloth or clothing of this colour, *esp.* military uniform —*a.* of this colour; immoral, *esp.* unchaste —**scarlet fever** infectious fever with scarlet rash

scarp *n.* steep slope; inside slope of ditch in fortifications

scat *vi. inf.* (*usu. imp.*) go away

scathe [-āTH] (*usu. now as pp./a.* **scathed** & **unscathed'**) *n.* injury, harm, damage —*vt.* injure, damage —**sca'thing** *a.* harshly critical; cutting; damaging

scatt'er *vt.* throw in various directions; put here and there; sprinkle —*vi.* disperse —*n.* —**scatt'erbrain** *n.* silly, careless person

scav'enge *v.* search for (anything usable) *usu.* among discarded material

—**scav'enger** *n.* person who scavenges; animal, bird which feeds on refuse

ScD Doctor of Science

scene [sēn] *n.* place of action of novel, play *etc.*; place of any action; subdivision of play; view; episode; display of strong emotion —**sce'nery** *n.* natural features of district; constructions of wood, canvas *etc.* used on stage to represent a place where action is happening —**sce'nic** *a.* picturesque; of or on the stage —**scenar'io** *n.* summary of plot (of play *etc.*) or plan (*pl.* **-ios**)

scent [sent] *n.* distinctive smell, *esp.* pleasant one; trail, clue; perfume —*vt.* detect or track (by smell); suspect, sense; fill with fragrance

scep'tic [sk-], **skep'tic** *n.* one who maintains doubt or disbelief; agnostic; unbeliever —**scep'tical** *a.* —**scep'ticism** *n.*

scep'tre [sep'tər] *n.* ornamental staff as symbol of royal power; royal dignity

sched'ule [sk-, sh-] *n.* plan of procedure for a project; list; timetable —*vt.* enter in schedule; plan to occur at certain time —**on schedule** on time

sche'ma [skē'-] *n.* overall plan or diagram —**schemat'ic** *a.* presented as plan or diagram —**sche'matize** *v.*

scheme [sk-] *n.* plan, design; project; outline —*v.* devise, plan, *esp.* in underhand manner —**sche'mer** *n.*

scher'zo [sker'tso] *n. Mus.* light playful composition

schis'm [siz'm] *n.* (group resulting from) division in political party, church *etc.* —**schismat'ic** *n./a.*

schist [sh-] *n.* crystalline rock which splits into layers —**schist'ose** *a.*

schizophre'nia [skit-sō-frē'-] *n.* mental disorder involving deterioration of, confusion about personality —**schizophren'ic** *a./n.* —**schiz'oid** *a.* relating to schizophrenia

schmaltz [shm-] *n.* excessive sentimentality —**schmalt'zy** *a.*

schnap(p)s [shn-] *n.* spirit distilled from potatoes; *inf.* any strong spirit

schnit'zel [shn-] *n.* thin slice of meat, *esp.* veal, as *Wiener schnitzel*

schol'ar *n. see* SCHOOL[1]

scho'lium [sk-] *n.* marginal annotation; note; comment (*pl.* **-lia, -liums**) —**scho'liast** *n.* commentator or annotator —**scholias'tic** *a.* pert. to a scholiast or his pursuits

school[1] [sk-] *n.* institution for teaching children or for giving instruction in any subject; buildings of such institution; group of thinkers, writers, artists *etc.* with principles or methods in common —*vt.* educate; bring under control, train —**school board** local board of education —**school'man** *n.* medieval philosopher —**schol'ar** *n.* learned person; one taught in school; one quick to learn —**schol'arly** *a.* learned, erudite —**schol'arship** *n.* learning; prize, grant to student for payment of school or college fees —**scholas'tic** *a.* of schools or scholars, or education; pedantic

school[2] [sk-] *n.* shoal (of fish, whales *etc.*)

schoon'er [sk-] *n.* fore-and-aft rigged vessel with two or more masts; tall glass for beer

schottische' [sho-tēsh'] *n.* kind of dance; music for this

sciat'ica [sī-] *n.* neuralgia of hip and thigh; pain in sciatic nerve —**sciat'ic** *a.* of the hip; of sciatica

sci'ence [sī'-] *n.* systematic study and knowledge of natural or physical phenomena; any branch of study concerned with observed material facts —**scientif'ic** *a.* of the principles of science; systematic —**scientif'ically** *adv.* —**sci'entist** *n.* one versed in natural sciences —**science fiction** stories set in the future making imaginative use of scientific knowledge

Scientol'ogy [sī-] **R** religious cult

scim'itar [sim'-] *n.* oriental curved sword

scin'tillate [sin'-] *vi.* sparkle; be animated, witty, clever —**scintilla'tion** *n.*

sci'on [sī'-] *n.* descendant, heir; slip for grafting

sciss'ion [sish'-] *n.* act of cutting, dividing, splitting —**sciss'ile** *a.*

sciss'ors [siz'-] *pl.n.* (*esp.* **pair of scissors**) cutting instrument of two blades pivoted together —*n./a.* (with) scissor-like action of limbs in swimming, athletics *etc.*, *eg* **scissors kick**

sclero'sis *n.* a hardening of bodily organs, tissues *etc.*

scoff [sk-] *vt.* express derision for —*n.* derision; mocking words —**scoff'er** *n.*

scold [skō-] *v.* find fault; reprimand, be angry with —*n.* someone who does this —**scold'ing** *n.*

scoll'op *n. see* SCALLOP

sconce [sk-] *n.* bracket candlestick on wall

scone [skon] *n.* small plain cake baked on griddle or in oven

scoop [-ōō-] *n.* small shovellike tool for ladling, hollowing out *etc.*; *sl.* profitable deal; *Journalism* exclusive news item —*vt.* ladle out; hollow out, rake in with scoop; make sudden profit; beat (rival newspaper *etc.*)

scoot [-ōō-] *vi. sl.* move off quickly —**scoot'er** *n.* child's vehicle propelled by pushing on ground with one foot; (*also* **motor scooter**) light motorcycle

scope *n.* range of activity or application; room, opportunity

scorch *v.* burn, be burnt, on surface; parch; shrivel; wither —*n.* slight burn —**scorch'er** *n. inf.* very hot day

score *n.* points gained in game, competition; group of 20; a lot (*esp. pl.*); musical notation; mark or notch, *esp.* to keep tally; reason, account; grievance —*vt.* gain points in game; mark; cross out; arrange music (for); criticize harshly —*vi.* keep tally of points; succeed

scorn *n.* contempt, derision —*vt.* despise —**scorn'er** *n.* —**scorn'ful** *a.* derisive —**scorn'fully** *adv.*

Scor'pio *n.* (the scorpion) 8th sign of zodiac, operative *c.* Oct. 23 - Nov. 21

scor'pion *n.* small lobster-shaped animal with sting at end of jointed tail

Scot *n.* native of Scotland —**Scott'ish** *a.* (*also* **Scotch, Scots**) —**Scotch** *n.* Scotch whisky —**Scots'man** *n.*

scotch *vt.* put an end to; *obs.* wound

scot-free' *a.* without harm or loss

scoun'drel *n.* villain, blackguard —**scoun'drelly** *a.*

scour[1] *vt.* clean, polish by rubbing; clear or flush out

scour[2] *v.* move rapidly along or over (territory) in search of something

scourge [skurj] *n.* whip, lash; severe affliction; pest; calamity —*vt.* flog; punish severely

scout *n.* one sent out to reconnoitre; (**S-**) member of **Scout Association**, organization to develop character and responsibility —*vi.* go out, act as scout; reconnoitre —**Scout'er** *n.* leader of troop of Scouts

scow *n.* unpowered barge

scowl *vi.* frown gloomily or sullenly —*n.* angry or gloomy expression

scrabb'le *v.* scrape at with hands, claws in disorderly manner —*n.* (**S-**) ® word game

scrag *n.* lean person or animal; lean end of a neck of mutton —**scragg'y** *a.* thin, bony

scragg'ly *a.* untidy

scram[1] *v. inf.* (*oft. imp.*) go away hastily, get out

scram[2] *n.* emergency shutdown of nuclear reactor —*v.*

scram'ble *vi.* move along or up by crawling, climbing *etc.*; struggle with others (for); (of aircraft, aircrew) take off hurriedly —*vt.* mix up; cook (eggs) beaten up with milk; render (speech) unintelligible by electronic device —*n.* scrambling; rough climb; disorderly proceeding; motorcycle race over rough ground

scrap *n.* small piece or fragment; leftover material; *inf.* fight —*v.* break up, discard as useless —*vi. inf.* fight (**-pp-**) —**scrapp'y** *a.* unequal in quality; badly finished —**scrap'book** *n.* book in which newspaper cuttings *etc.* are kept

scrape *vt.* rub with something sharp; clean, smooth thus; grate; scratch; rub with harsh noise —*n.* act, sound of scraping; *inf.* awkward situation, *esp.* as result of escapade —**scra'per** *n.* instrument for scraping; contrivance on which mud is scraped from shoes *etc.*

scratch *vt.* score, make narrow surface wound with claws, nails, or anything pointed; make marks on with pointed instruments; scrape (skin) with nails to relieve itching; remove, withdraw from list, race *etc.* —*vi.* use claws or nails, *esp.* to relieve itching —*n.* wound, mark or sound made by scratching; line or starting point —*a.* got together at short notice; impromptu —**scratch'y** *a.*

scrawl *vt.* write, draw untidily —*n.* thing scrawled; careless writing

scraw'ny *a.* thin, bony

scream *vi.* utter piercing cry, *esp.* of fear, pain *etc.*; be very obvious —*vt.* utter in a scream —*n.* shrill, piercing cry; *inf.* very funny person or thing —**scream'er**

n. person or thing that screams; sensational headline

scree *n.* loose shifting stones; slope covered with these

screech *vi./n.* scream

screed *n.* long (tedious) letter, passage or speech; thin layer of cement

screen *n.* device to shelter from heat, light, draught, observation *etc.*; anything used for such purpose; mesh over doors, windows to keep out insects; white or silvered surface on which photographic images are projected; wooden or stone partition in church —*vt.* shelter, hide; protect from detection; show (movie); scrutinize; examine (group of people) for presence of disease, weapons *etc.*; examine for political motives; *Electricity* protect from stray electric or magnetic fields —**the screen** motion pictures generally

screw [-ōō] *n.* (naillike device or cylinder with) spiral thread cut to engage similar thread or to bore into material (wood *etc.*) to pin or fasten; anything resembling a screw in shape, esp. in spiral form; propeller; twist —*vt.* fasten with screw; twist around; *inf.* extort —**screw'y** *a. inf.* crazy, eccentric —**screw'ball** *n.* odd or eccentric person —*a.* odd, zany, eccentric —**screw'-driver** *n.* tool for turning screws —**screw up** distort; *inf.* bungle

scrib'ble *v.* write, draw carelessly; make meaningless marks with pen or pencil —*n.* something scribbled —**scrib'bly** *a.*

scribe *n.* writer; copyist —*v.* scratch a line with pointed instrument

scrimm'age *n.* scuffle; *Football* play in which two teams line up and ball is passed back from centre —*v.* take part in this play

scrimp *vt.* make too small or short; treat meanly —**scrim'py** *a.*

scrip *n.* written certificate *esp.* of holding stocks or shares

script *n.* (system or style of) handwriting; written characters; written text of motion picture, play, radio or television programme; answer paper in examination

scrip'ture *n.* sacred writings; the Bible —**script'ural** *a.*

scriv'ener *n. obs.* copyist, clerk

scrof'ula *n.* tuberculosis of lymphatic glands, *esp.* of neck —**scrof'ulous** *a.*

scroll [-ōl] *n.* roll of parchment or paper; list; ornament shaped thus

scro'tum *n.* pouch containing testicles (*pl.* **-ta**) —**scro'tal** *a.*

scrounge *v. inf.* get without cost, by begging —**scroun'ger** *n.*

scrub[1] *vt.* clean with hard brush and water; scour; *inf.* cancel, get rid of (**-bb-**) —*n.* scrubbing —**scrubbing brush**

scrub[2] *n.* stunted trees; brushwood; anything stunted or inferior; *Sport* player not in first team —*a.* small, stunted or inferior; *Sport* (of player) not in first team —**scrubb'y** *a.* covered with scrub; stunted; *inf.* messy

scruff *n.* nape (of neck)

scrum(mage) *n. Rugby* (*esp. Brit.*) restarting of play in which opposing packs of forwards push against each other to gain possession of the ball; crush, crowd

scru'ple *n.* doubt or hesitation about what is morally right; weight of 20 grains —*vi.* hesitate —**scru'pulous** *a.* extremely conscientious; thorough, attentive to small points —**scru'pulously** *adv.* —**scru'pulousness** *n.*

scru'tiny *n.* close examination; critical investigation; official examination of votes *etc.*; searching look —**scrutineer'** *n.* examiner of votes —**scru'tinize** *vt.* examine closely

scu'ba *n./a.* (relating to) *s*elf-*c*ontained *u*nderwater *b*reathing *a*pparatus

scud *vi.* run fast; run before wind (**-dd-**)

scuff *vi.* drag, scrape with feet in walking —*vt.* scrape with feet; graze —*n.* act, sound of scuffing —*pl.* thong sandals —**scuffed** *a.* (of shoes) scraped or slightly grazed

scuf'fle *vi.* fight in disorderly manner; shuffle —*n.*

scull *n.* oar used in stern of boat; short oar used in pairs —*v.* propel, move by means of scull(s)

scull'ery *n.* place for washing dishes *etc.* —**scull'ion** *n.* despicable person; *obs.* kitchen underservant

sculp'ture *n.* art of forming figures in relief or solid; product of this art —*vt.* represent by sculpture —**sculpt** *v.* —**sculp'tural** *a.* with qualities proper to sculpture —**sculp'tor** *n.* (**sculp'tress** *fem.*)

scum *n.* froth or other floating matter on liquid; waste part of anything; vile person(s) or thing(s) —**scumm'y** *a.*

scupp'er *n.* hole in ship's side level with deck to carry off water —*vt. inf.* ruin, destroy, kill

scurf *n.* flaky matter on scalp, dandruff —**scurf'y** *a.*

scurr'ilous *a.* coarse, indecently abusive —**scurril'ity** *n.*

scurr'y *vi.* run hastily (**scurr'ied, scur'rying**) —*n.* bustling haste; flurry

scur'vy *n.* disease caused by lack of vitamin C —*a.* afflicted with the disease; mean, contemptible

scut *n.* short tail of hare or other animal

scutch'eon *see* ESCUTCHEON

scut'tle[1] *n.* fireside container for coal

scut'tle[2] *vi.* rush away; run hurriedly —*n.*

scut'tle[3] *vt.* make hole in ship to sink it

scythe [sīTH] *n.* manual implement with long curved blade for cutting grass —*vt.* cut with scythe

SDI Strategic Defense Initiative

SE southeast(ern)

sea *n.* mass of salt water covering greater part of earth; broad tract of this; waves; swell; large quantity; vast expanse —**sea anemone** sea animal with suckers like petals —**sea'board** *n.* coast —**sea'faring** *a.* occupied in sea voyages —**sea gull** gull —**sea horse** fish with bony plated body and horselike head —**sea lion** kind of large seal —**sea'man** *n.* sailor —**sea'sickness** *n.* nausea caused by motion of ship —**sea'sick** *a.* —**sea'side** *n.* place, *esp.* holiday resort, on coast —**sea urchin** marine animal, echinus —**sea'weed** *n.* plant growing in sea —**sea'worthy** *a.* in fit condition to put to sea

seal[1] *n.* piece of metal or stone engraved with device for impression on wax *etc.*; impression thus made (on letters *etc.*); device, material preventing passage of water, air, oil *etc.* (also **seal'er**) —*vt.* affix seal to ratify, authorize; mark with stamp as evidence of some quality; keep close or secret; settle; make watertight, airtight *etc.*

seal[2] *n.* amphibious furred carnivorous mammal with flippers as limbs —*vi.* hunt seals —**seal'er** *n.* man or ship engaged in sealing —**seal'skin** *n.* skin, fur of seals

seam *n.* line of junction of two edges, *eg* of two pieces of cloth, or two planks; thin layer, stratum —*vt.* mark with furrows or wrinkles —**seam'less** *a.* —**seam'y** *a.* sordid; marked with seams —**seam'stress** [sem'-], **semp'stress** *n.* sewing woman

se'ance [sā'ons] *n.* meeting of spiritualists

sear *vt.* scorch, brand with hot iron; deaden

search [-ur-] *v.* look over or through to find something; probe into, examine —*n.* act of searching; quest —**search'er** *n.* —**search'ing** *a.* keen; thorough; severe —**search'light** *n.* powerful electric light with concentrated beam

seas'on [sēz'-] *n.* one of four divisions of year associated with type of weather and stage of agriculture; period during which thing happens, grows, is active *etc.*; proper time —*vt.* flavour with salt, herbs *etc.*; make reliable or ready for use; make experienced —**seas'onable** *a.* appropriate for the season; opportune; fit —**sea'sonal** *a.* depending on, varying with seasons —**seas'oning** *n.* flavouring —**season ticket** one for series of journeys, events *etc.* within a certain time

seat *n.* thing for sitting on; buttocks; base; right to sit (*eg* in council *etc.*); place where something is located, centred; locality of disease, trouble *etc.*; country house —*vt.* make to sit; provide sitting accommodation for; install firmly

SEATO Southeast Asia Treaty Organization

seba'ceous [-shəs] *a.* of, pert. to fat; secreting fat, oil

se'cant *n. Maths.* (secant of an angle) reciprocal of its cosine; line that intersects a curve

sec'ateurs [*or* -turz'] *pl.n.* small pruning shears

secede' [si-sēd'] *vi.* withdraw formally from federation, Church *etc.* —**seces'sion** *n.* —**secess'ionist** *n.*

seclude' *vt.* guard from, remove from sight, view, contact with others —**seclu'ded** *a.* remote; private —**seclu'sion** *n.*

sec'ond[1] *a.* next after first; alternate,

additional; of lower quality —*n.* person or thing coming second; attendant; sixtieth part of minute; SI unit of time; moment; (*esp. pl.*) inferior goods —*vt.* support; support (motion in meeting) so that discussion may be in order —**sec'onder** *n.* —**sec'ondly** *adv.* —**second-hand** *a.* bought after use by another; not original —**second sight** faculty of seeing events before they occur

second'[2] *vt.* transfer (employee, officer) temporarily

sec'ondary *a.* subsidiary, of less importance; developed from, or dependent on, something else; *Education* following elementary school —**sec'ondarily** *adv.*

se'cret *a.* kept, meant to be kept from knowledge of others; hidden; private —*n.* thing kept secret —**se'crecy** *n.* keeping or being kept secret —**se'cretive** *a.* given to having secrets; uncommunicative; reticent —**se'cretiveness** *n.* —**se'cretly** *adv.*

sec'retary *n.* one employed by individual or organization to deal with papers and correspondence, keep records, prepare business *etc.*; head of a state department —**secreta'rial** *a.* —**secreta'riat** *n.* body of secretaries; building occupied by secretarial staff

secrete' *vt.* hide; conceal; (of gland *etc.*) collect and supply particular substance in body —**secre'tion** *n.* —**secre'tory** *a.*

sect *n.* group of people (within religious body *etc.*) with common interest; faction —**secta'rian** *a.* of a sect; narrow-minded —**sect'ary** *n.*

sec'tion *n.* part cut off; division; portion; distinct part of city, country, people *etc.*; cutting; drawing of anything as if cut through; smallest military unit; area of land one mile square —**sec'tional** *a.*

sec'tor *n.* part or subdivision; part of circle enclosed by two radii and the arc which they cut off

sec'ular *a.* worldly; lay, not religious; not monastic; lasting for, or occurring once in, an age; centuries old —**sec'ularism** *n.* —**sec'ularist** *n.* one who believes that religion should have no place in civil affairs —**seculariza'tion** *n.* —**sec'ularize** *vt.* transfer from religious to lay possession or use

secure' [-kyoor'] *a.* safe; free from fear, anxiety; firmly fixed; certain; sure, confident —*vt.* gain possession of; make safe; free (creditor) from risk of loss; make firm —**secure'ly** *adv.* —**secur'ity** *n.* state of safety; protection; that which secures; assurance; anything given as bond, caution or pledge; one that becomes surety for another

sedan' *n.* closed automobile with 2 or 4 doors and 4-6 seats —**sedan chair** *Hist.* closed chair for one person, carried on poles by bearers

sedate'[1] *a.* calm, collected, serious —**sedate'ly** *adv.*

sedate'[2] *vt.* make calm by sedative —**seda'tion** *n.* —**sed'ative** *a.* having soothing or calming effect —*n.* sedative drug

sed'entary *a.* done sitting down; sitting much

sedge *n.* plant like coarse grass growing in swampy ground

sedi'lia *pl.n.* stone seats on south side of altar for priests

sed'iment *n.* matter which settles to the bottom of liquid; dregs, lees —**sedimen'tary** *a.*

sedi'tion [-dish'-] *n.* speech or action threatening authority of a state —**sedi'tious** *a.*

seduce' *vt.* persuade to commit some (wrong) deed, *esp.* sexual intercourse; tempt; attract —**seduc'tion** *n.* —**seduc'tive** *a.* alluring; winning —**sedu'cer** *n.* (**seduct'ress** *fem.*)

sed'ulous *a.* diligent; industrious; persevering, persistent —**sedu'lity** *n.*

se'dum *n.* rock plant

see[1] *vt.* perceive with eyes or mentally; observe; watch; find out; reflect; come to know; interview; make sure; accompany —*vi.* perceive; consider; understand (**saw, seen, see'ing**) —**see'ing** *conj.* since; in view of the fact that

see[2] *n.* diocese, office, or jurisdiction of bishop

seed *n.* reproductive germs of plants; one grain of this; such grains saved or used for sowing; origin; sperm; *obs.* offspring —*vt.* sow with seed; arrange draw for lawn tennis or other tournament, so that best players do not meet in early rounds —*vi.* produce seed —**seed'ling** *n.* young plant raised from seed —**seed'y** *a.* shabby; run to seed; *inf.* unwell, ill

seek *vt.* make search or enquiry for —*vi.* search (**sought** [sawt], **seek'ing**)

seem *vi.* appear (to be or to do); look; appear to one's judgment —**seem'ing** *a.* apparent but not real —**seem'ingly** *adv.*

seem'ly *a.* becoming and proper —**seem'liness** *n.*

seen *pp. of* SEE[1]

seep *vi.* trickle through slowly, as water, ooze

seer *n.* prophet

seer'sucker *n.* light cotton fabric with slightly crinkled surface

see'saw *n.* game in which children sit at opposite ends of plank supported in middle and swing up and down; plank used for this —*vi.* move up and down

seethe [-TH] *vi.* boil, foam; be very agitated; be in constant movement (as large crowd *etc.*) (**seethed, see'thing**)

seg'ment *n.* piece cut off; section —*v.* [-ment'] to divide into segments —**segmen'tal** *a.* —**segmenta'tion** *n.*

seg'regate *vt.* set apart from rest; dissociate; separate; isolate —**segrega'tion** *n.*

se'gue [sā'gwi] *vi.* proceed from one section or piece of music to another without break (**se'gued, se'gueing**) —*n.*

seine [sān] *n.* type of large fishing net

seis'mic [sīz'-] *a.* pert. to earthquakes —**seis'mograph** *n.* instrument to record earthquakes (*also* **seismom'eter**) —**seismolog'ic(al)** *a.* pert. to seismology —**seismol'ogist** *n.* one versed in seismology —**seismol'ogy** *n.* science of earthquakes

seize [sēz] *vt.* grasp; lay hold of; capture —*vi.* in machine, of bearing or piston, to stick tightly through overheating —**seiz'able** *a.* —**seiz'ure** *n.* act of taking, *esp.* by warrant, as goods; sudden onset of disease

sel'dom *adv.* not often, rarely

select' *vt.* pick out, choose —*a.* choice, picked; exclusive —**selec'tion** *n.* —**selec'tive** *a.* —**selectiv'ity** *n.* —**selec'tor** *n.*

sele'nium *n.* nonmetallic element with photoelectric properties —**sele'nic** *a.*

self *pron.*, used reflexively or to express emphasis (*pl.* **selves**) —*a.* (of colour) same throughout, uniform —*n.* one's own person or individuality —**self'ish** *a.* concerned unduly over personal profit or pleasure; lacking consideration for others; greedy —**self'ishly** *adv.* —**self'less** *a.* having no regard to self; unselfish

self- (*comb. form*) of oneself or itself, as in

self-addressed
self-assured
self-catering
self-centred
self-confident
self-contained
self-control
self-defence
self-denial
self-employed
self-evident
self-help
self-indulgent
self-interest
self-pity
self-raising
self-reliant
self-sacrifice
self-satisfied
self-supporting

self-con'scious *a.* unduly aware of oneself; conscious of one's acts or states

self'-determina'tion *n.* the right of person or nation to decide for itself

self-made' *a.* having achieved wealth, status *etc.* by one's own efforts

self-possessed' *a.* calm, composed —**self-possession** *n.*

self-respect' *n.* proper sense of one's own dignity and integrity

self-right'eous *a.* smugly sure of one's own virtue

self'same *a.* very same

self-seek'ing *a./n.* (having) preoccupation with one's own interests

self-ser'vice *a./n.* (of) shop or restaurant where customers serve themselves

self-suffi'cient *a.* sufficient in itself; relying on one's own powers

self-will' *n.* obstinacy; wilfulness —**self-willed** *a.* headstrong

sell *vt.* hand over for a price; stock, have for sale; make someone accept; *inf.* betray, cheat —*vi.* find purchasers (**sold, sell'ing**) —*n. inf.* disappointment; *inf.*

hoax —**sell'er** *n.* —**sell'out** *n.* disposing of completely by selling; betrayal

Selt'zer (water) [-sər] *n.* aerated mineral water

sel'vage, sel'vedge [-vij] *n.* finished, unfraying edge of cloth

seman'tic *a.* relating to meaning of words or symbols —**seman'tics** *pl.n.* study of linguistic meaning

sem'aphore *n.* post with movable arms for signalling; system of signalling by human or mechanical arms

sem'blance *n.* (false) appearance; image, likeness

se'men *n.* fluid carrying sperm of male animals; sperm

semes'ter *n.* half-year session in college, university

semi- (*comb. form*) half, partly, not completely, as in *semicircle*

sem'icircle *n.* half of circle —**semicir'cular** *a.*

semico'lon *n.* punctuation mark (;)

semidetached' *a./n.* (of) house joined to another on one side only

semifi'nal *n.* match, round *etc.* before final

sem'inal *a.* capable of developing; influential, important; rudimentary; of semen or seed

sem'inar *n.* meeting of group (of students) for discussion

sem'inary *n.* college for priests

semipre'cious [-presh'-] *a.* (of gemstones) having less value than precious stones

semiskilled' *a.* partly skilled, trained but not for specialized work

Se'mite *n.* member of race including Jews and Arabs —**Semit'ic** *a.* denoting a Semite; Jewish

sem'itone *n.* musical half step

semoli'na [-lē'-] *n.* hard grains left after sifting of flour, used for puddings *etc.*

sen'ate *n.* upper council of state, university *etc.* —**sen'ator** *n.* —**senator'ial** *a.*

send *vt.* cause to go or be conveyed; despatch; transmit (by radio) (**sent, send'ing**)

sen'eschal *n. Hist.* steward

se'nile *a.* showing weakness of old age —**senil'ity** *n.*

se'nior *a.* superior in rank or standing; older —*n.* superior; elder person —**senior'ity** [-o'ri-] *n.*

sen'na *n.* tropical plant; its dried leaves or pods used as laxative

señor' [se-nyawr'] *n. Sp.* title of respect, like Mr. —**señor'a** *n.* Mrs. —**señori'ta** [-rē'-] *n.* Miss

sensa'tion *n.* operation of sense, feeling, awareness; excited feeling, state of excitement; exciting event; strong impression; commotion —**sensa'tional** *a.* producing great excitement; melodramatic; of perception by senses —**sensa'tionalism** *n.* use of sensational language *etc.* to arouse intense emotional excitement; doctrine that sensations are basis of all knowledge

sense *n.* any of bodily faculties of perception or feeling; sensitiveness of any or all of these faculties; ability to perceive, mental alertness; consciousness; meaning; coherence, intelligible meaning; sound practical judgment —*vt.* perceive; understand —**sense'less** *a.* —**sense'lessly** *adv.*

sen'sible *a.* reasonable, wise; perceptible by senses; aware, mindful; considerable, appreciable —**sensibil'ity** *n.* ability to feel *esp.* emotional or moral feelings —**sen'sibly** *adv.*

sen'sitive *a.* open to, acutely affected by, external impressions; easily affected or altered; easily upset by criticism; responsive to slight changes —**sen'sitively** *adv.* —**sensitiv'ity, sen'sitiveness** *n.* —**sen'sitize** *vt.* make sensitive, *esp.* make (photographic film *etc.*) sensitive to light

sen'sor *n.* device that responds to stimulus

sen'sory *a.* relating to organs, operation, of senses

sen'sual *a.* of senses only and not of mind; given to pursuit of pleasures of sense; self-indulgent; licentious —**sen'sualism** *n.* —**sen'sualist** *n.* —**sensual'ity** *n.*

sen'suous *a.* stimulating, or apprehended by, senses *esp.* in aesthetic manner

sent *pt./pp. of* SEND

sen'tence *n.* combination of words, which is complete as expressing a thought; judgment passed on criminal by court or judge —*vt.* pass sentence on, condemn —**senten'tial** *a.* of sentence —**senten'tious** *a.* full of axioms and maxims; pithy; pompously moralizing

—**senten'tiously** *adv.* —**senten'tiousness** *n.*

sen'tient *a.* capable of feeling; feeling; thinking —**sen'tience, sen'tiency** *n.*

sent'iment *n.* tendency to be moved by feeling rather than reason; verbal expression of feeling; mental feeling, emotion; opinion —**sentiment'al** *a.* given to indulgence in sentiment and in its expression; weak; sloppy —**sentimen'talist** *n.* —**sentimental'ity** *n.* —**sentimen'talize** *v.*

sent'inel *n.* sentry

sen'try *n.* soldier on watch

sep'al *n.* leaf or division of the calyx of a flower

sep'arate [-āt] *vt.* part; divide; sever; put apart; occupy place between —*vi.* withdraw, become parted from —*a.* [-it] disconnected, apart, distinct, individual —**sep'arable** *a.* —**sep'arately** *adv.* —**separa'tion** *n.* disconnection; *Law* living apart of married people without divorce —**Sep'aratist** *n.* person who advocates secession of province, *esp.* Quebec, from Canada —**sep'arator** *n.* that which separates; apparatus for separating cream from milk —**separate school** school for a large religious minority

se'pia *n.* reddish-brown pigment made from a fluid secreted by the cuttle fish —*a.* of this colour

sep'sis *n.* presence of pus-forming bacteria in body

Sept. September

Septem'ber *n.* 9th month (7th in Roman calendar)

septenn'ial *a.* lasting, occurring every seven years

septet(te)' *n.* music for seven instruments or voices; group of seven performers

sep'tic *a.* of, caused by, sepsis; (of wound) infected —**septic(a)e'mia** [-sē'-] *n.* blood poisoning

septuagena'rian *a.* aged between seventy and eighty —*n.*

Septuages'ima [-jes'-] *n.* third Sunday before Lent

sep'ulchre [-kər] *n.* tomb; burial vault —**sepul'chral** *a.* of burial, or the grave; mournful; gloomy —**sep'ulture** *n.* burial

se'quel *n.* consequence; continuation, *eg* of story

se'quence *n.* arrangement of things in successive order; section, episode of motion picture —**se'quent, sequen'tial** *a.*

sequest'er *vt.* separate; seclude; put aside —**sequest'rate** *vt.* confiscate; divert or appropriate income of property to satisfy claims against its owner —**sequestra'tion** *n.*

se'quin *n.* small ornamental metal disc on dresses *etc.*; *orig.* Venetian gold coin

sequoi'a [si-kwoi'ə] *n.* giant Californian coniferous tree

seragl'io [-rahl'-] *n.* harem, palace, of Turkish sultan (*pl.* **-ios**)

ser'aph [se'rəf] *n.* member of highest order of angels (*pl.* **-s, ser'aphim**) —**seraph'ic** *a.*

serenade' *n.* sentimental piece of music or song of type addressed to woman by lover *esp.* at evening —*v.* sing serenade (to someone)

serendip'ity *n.* faculty of making fortunate discoveries by accident

serene' *a.* calm, tranquil; unclouded; quiet, placid —**serene'ly** *adv.* —**seren'ity** *n.*

serf *n.* one of class of medieval labourers bound to, and transferred with, land —**serf'dom** *n.*

Serg. Sergeant

serge *n.* strong hard-wearing twilled worsted fabric

serg'eant [sahrj'ənt] *n.* noncommissioned officer in army; police officer above constable (*also esp.* **UK ser'jeant**) —**sergeant major** highest noncommissioned officer in regiment —**sergeant at arms** an officer in a legislature or court who keeps order

se'ries *n.* sequence; succession, set (*eg* of radio, TV programmes with same characters, setting, but different stories) (*pl.* **se'ries**) —**se'rial** *n.* story or play produced in successive episodes or instalments; periodical publication —*a.* —**se'rialize** *v.* publish, present as serial —**seria'tim** *adv.* one after another

ser'if [se'rif] *n.* small line finishing off stroke of letter

se'rious *a.* thoughtful, solemn; earnest, sincere; of importance; giving cause for concern —**se'riously** *adv.*

ser'mon *n.* discourse of religious instruction or exhortation spoken or read from pulpit; any similar discourse

—**ser'monize** *vi.* talk like preacher; compose sermons

ser'pent *n. obs., biblical* snake —**ser'pentine** *a.* like, shaped like, serpent —*n.* green to black rock

serr'ate, serra'ted *a.* having notched, sawlike edge —**serra'tion** *n.*

serr'ied *a.* in close order, shoulder to shoulder

se'rum *n.* watery animal fluid, *esp.* thin part of blood as used for inoculation or vaccination

ser'val *n.* feline Afr. mammal

serve *v.* (*mainly vt.*) work for, under, another; attend (to customers) in shop *etc.*; provide; help to (food *etc.*); present (food *etc.*) in particular way; provide with regular supply of; be member of military unit; pay homage to; spend time doing; be useful, suitable enough; *Tennis etc.* put (ball) into play —*n. Tennis etc.* act of serving ball —**ser'vant** *n.* personal or domestic attendant —**ser'vice** *n.* the act of serving, helping, assisting; system organized to provide for needs of public; maintenance of vehicle; use; readiness, availability for use; department of State employ; employment of persons engaged in this; set of dishes *etc.*; form, session, of public worship —*pl.* armed forces —*vt.* overhaul —**ser'viceable** *a.* in working order, usable; durable —**ser'viceman** *n.* member of the armed forces —**service road** narrow road giving access to houses, shops *etc.* —**service station** place supplying fuel, oil, maintenance for motor vehicles

serviette' *n.* table napkin

ser'vile *a.* slavish, without independence; cringing; fawning; menial —**servil'ity** *n.*

ser'vitude *n.* bondage, slavery

ser'vomechanism *n.* device for converting small mechanical force into larger, *esp.* in steering mechanisms

ses'ame [-ə-mi] *n.* plant with seeds used as herbs and for making oil

sess'ion [sesh'-] *n.* meeting of court *etc.*; assembly; continuous series of such meetings; any period devoted to an activity; school or university term or year

set *v.* (*mainly tr.*) put or place in specified position or condition; cause to sit; fix, point, put up; make ready; become firm or fixed; establish; prescribe, allot; put to music; of hair, arrange while wet, so that it dries in position; of sun, go down; have direction (**set, sett'ing**) —*a.* fixed, established; deliberate; formal, arranged beforehand; unvarying —*n.* act or state of being set; bearing, posture; *Radio, Television* complete apparatus for reception or transmission; *Theatre, Television etc.* organized settings and equipment to form ensemble of scene; number of things, persons associated as being similar, complementary or used together; *Maths.* group of numbers, objects *etc.* with at least one common property —**set'back** *n.* anything that hinders or impedes —**set'up** *n.* position; organization —**set up** establish

settee' *n.* couch

sett'er *n.* various breeds of gun dog

sett'ing *n.* background; surroundings; scenery and other stage accessories; act of fixing; decorative metalwork holding precious stone *etc.* in position; tableware and cutlery for (single place at) table; descending below horizon of sun; music for song

set'tle *vt.* arrange, put in order; establish, make firm or secure or quiet; decide upon; end (dispute *etc.*); pay; bestow (property) by legal deed —*vi.* come to rest; subside; become clear; take up residence; subside, sink to bottom; come to agreement —**set'tlement** *n.* act of settling; place newly inhabited; money bestowed legally; subsidence (of building) —**sett'ler** *n.* colonist

sev'en *a./n.* cardinal number, next after six —**sev'enth** *a.* the ordinal number —**sev'enteen'** *a./n.* ten and seven —**sev'enty** *a./n.* ten times seven

sev'er *v.* separate, divide; cut off —**sev'erance** *n.* —**severance pay** compensation paid by a firm to an employee for loss of employment

sev'eral *a.* some, a few; separate; individual; various; different —*pron.* indefinite small number —**sev'erally** *adv.* apart from others

severe' [-ēr'] *a.* strict; rigorous; hard to do; harsh; austere; extreme —**severe'ly** *adv.* —**sever'ity** [-ve'ri-] *n.*

sew [sō] *v.* join with needle and thread; make by sewing (**sewed** *pt.*, **sewed, sewn** *pp.*, **sew'ing** *pr.p.*) —**sew'ing** *n.*

sew'age [so͞o'ij] *n.* refuse, waste matter,

excrement conveyed in sewer —**sew'er** *n.* underground drain to remove waste water and refuse —**sew'erage** *n.* arrangement of sewers; sewage

sex *n.* state of being male or female; males or females collectively; sexual intercourse —*a.* concerning sex —*vt.* ascertain sex of —**sex'ism** *n.* discrimination on basis of sex —**sex'ist** *n./a.* —**sex'ual** *a.* —**sex'ually** *adv.* —**sex'y** *a.* —**sexual intercourse** act of procreation in which male's penis is inserted into female's vagina

sexagena'rian *a./n.* (person) sixty years old

Sexages'ima [-jes'-] *n.* the second Sunday before Lent

sexenn'ial *a.* lasting, occurring every six years

sex'tant *n.* navigator's instrument for measuring elevations of heavenly body *etc.*

sextet(te)' *n.* (composition for) six singers or players; group of six

sex'ton *n.* official in charge of a church, often acting as gravedigger

sf science fiction

shabb'y *a.* faded, worn, ragged; poorly dressed; mean, dishonourable; stingy —**shab'bily** *adv.* —**shabb'iness** *n.*

shack *n.* rough hut —**shack up (with)** live (with)

shac'kle *n.* metal ring or fastening for prisoner's wrist or ankle; anything that confines —*vt.* fasten with shackles; hamper

shad *n.* various herring-like fish

shade *n.* partial darkness; shelter, place sheltered from light, heat *etc.*; darker part of anything; depth of colour; tinge; ghost; screen; anything used to screen; windowblind —*pl. sl.* sunglasses —*vt.* screen from light, darken; represent shades in drawing —**sha'dy** *a.* shielded from sun; dim; dubious; dishonest; dishonourable

shad'ow *n.* dark figure projected by anything that intercepts rays of light; patch of shade; slight trace; indistinct image; gloom; inseparable companion —*vt.* cast shadow over; follow and watch closely —**shad'owy** *a.*

shaft [-ah-] *n.* straight rod, stem, handle; arrow; ray, beam (of light); revolving rod for transmitting power; one of the bars between which horse is harnessed; entrance boring of mine

shag[1] *n.* matted wool or hair; long-napped cloth; coarse shredded tobacco —**shagg'y** *a.* covered with rough hair or wool; tousled; unkempt

shag[2] *n.* cormorant

shah *n.* formerly, ruler of Iran

shake *v.* (cause to) move with quick vibrations; tremble; grasp the hand (of another) in greeting; upset; wave, brandish —*vt.* escape from (**shook, sha'ken**) —*n.* act of shaking; vibration; jolt; *inf.* short period of time, jiffy —**sha'kily** *adv.* —**sha'ky** *a.* unsteady, insecure

shale *n.* flaky, sedimentary rock

shall *v. aux.* makes compound tenses or moods to express obligation, command, condition or intention (**should** *pt.*)

shallot' *n.* kind of small onion

shall'ow [-ō] *a.* not deep; having little depth of water; superficial; not sincere —*n.* shallow place —**shall'owness** *n.*

sham *a./n.* imitation, counterfeit —*v.* pretend, feign (**-mm-**)

sham'ble *vi.* walk in shuffling, awkward way

sham'bles *pl.n.* messy, disorderly thing or place

shame *n.* emotion caused by consciousness of guilt or dishonour in one's conduct or state; cause of disgrace; ignominy; pity, hard luck —*vt.* cause to feel shame; disgrace; force by shame (into) —**shame'ful** *a.* disgraceful —**shame'fully** *adv.* —**shame'less** *a.* with no sense of shame; indecent —**shame'faced** *a.* ashamed

shamm'y (leather) *inf.* chamois leather

shampoo' *n.* various preparations of liquid soap for washing hair, carpets *etc.*; this process —*vt.* use shampoo to wash

sham'rock *n.* clover leaf, *esp.* as Irish emblem

shan'dy *n. esp.* UK mixed drink, *esp.* beer diluted with soft drink

shanghai' [-hī'] *vt.* force, trick someone to do something

shank *n.* lower leg; shinbone; stem of thing

shantung' *n.* soft, natural Chinese silk

shant'y[1] *n.* temporary wooden building; crude dwelling

shan'ty[2], **chan'ty** *n.* sailor's song with chorus

shape *n.* external form or appearance; mould, pattern; *inf.* condition, *esp.* of physical fitness —*vt.* form, mould, fashion, make —*vi.* develop (**shaped, sha'ping**) —**shape'less** *a.* —**shape'ly** *a.* well-proportioned

shard *n.* broken fragment, *esp.* of earthenware

share[1] [shār] *n.* portion; quota; lot; unit of ownership in public company —*v.* give, take a share; join with others in doing, using, something —**share'holder** *n.*

share[2] [shār] *n.* blade of plough

shark *n.* large usu. predatory sea fish; person who cheats others

shark'skin *n.* stiff rayon fabric

sharp *a.* having keen cutting edge or fine point; keen; not gradual or gentle; brisk; clever; harsh; dealing cleverly but unfairly; shrill; strongly marked, *esp.* in outline —*adv.* promptly —*n. Mus.* note half a tone above natural pitch; *sl.* cheat, swindler —**sharp'en** *vt.* make sharp —**sharp'ly** *adv.* —**sharp'ness** *n.* —**sharp'shooter** *n.* marksman

shatt'er *v.* break in pieces; ruin (plans *etc.*); disturb (person) greatly

shave *v.* cut close, *esp.* hair of face or head; pare away; graze; reduce (**shaved, sha'ven, sha'ving**) —*n.* shaving —**sha'vings** *pl.n.* parings —**close, near shave** narrow escape

shawl *n.* piece of fabric to cover woman's shoulders or wrap baby

she *pron.* 3rd person singular feminine pronoun

sheaf *n.* bundle, *esp.* corn; loose leaves of paper (*pl.* **sheaves**)

shear *vt.* clip hair, wool from; cut through; fracture (**sheared** *pt.* —**shorn, sheared** *pp.* —**shear'ing** *pr.p.*) —**shear'er** *n.* —**shears** *pl.n.* large pair of scissors; mechanical shearing, cutting instrument

shear'water *n.* various sea birds

sheath *n.* close-fitting cover, *esp.* for knife or sword; scabbard; **UK** condom —**sheathe** *vt.* put into sheath

shebang' *n. sl.* situation, matter, *esp.* **whole shebang**

shed[1] *n.* roofed shelter used as store or workshop

shed[2] *vt.* (cause to) pour forth (*eg* tears, blood); cast off (**shed, shedd'ing**)

sheen *n.* gloss —**sheen'y** *a.*

sheep *n.* ruminant animal bred for wool and meat —**sheep'ish** *a.* embarrassed, shy —**sheep-dip** *n.* (deep trough containing) solution in which sheep are immersed to kill vermin and germs in fleece —**sheep'dog** *n.* dog of various breeds *orig.* for herding sheep —**sheep'skin** *n.* skin of sheep (with fleece) used for clothing, rug or without fleece for parchment

sheer[1] *a.* perpendicular; of material, very fine, transparent; absolute, unmitigated

sheer[2] *vi.* deviate from course; swerve; turn aside

sheet[1] *n.* large piece of cotton *etc.* to cover bed; broad piece of any thin material; large expanse —*vt.* cover with sheet

sheet[2] *n.* rope fastened in corner of sail —**sheet anchor** large anchor for emergency

sheik(h) [-āk, -ēk] *n.* Arab chief

shek'el *n.* Jewish weight and silver coin; money, cash

shelf *n.* board fixed horizontally (on wall *etc.*) for holding things; ledge (*pl.* **shelves**)

shell *n.* hard outer case (*esp.* of egg, nut *etc.*); husk; explosive projectile; outer part of structure left when interior is removed —*vt.* take shell from; take out of shell; fire at with shells —**shell'fish** *n.* mollusc; crustacean —**shell shock** nervous disorder caused by bursting of shells or bombs —**shell out** *inf.* pay up

shellac' *n.* lac in thin plates for use as varnish —*vt.* coat with shellac (**-lacked, -lacking**)

shel'ter *n.* place, structure giving protection; protection; refuge; haven —*vt.* give protection to; screen —*vi.* take shelter

shelve *vt.* put on a shelf; put off; cease to employ; defer indefinitely —*vi.* slope gradually

shenan'igan *n. sl.* frolicking; playing tricks *etc.*

shep'herd [shep'ərd] *n.* man who tends sheep (**shep'herdess** *fem.*) —*vt.* guide, watch over —**shepherd's-purse** *n.* plant with white flowers

sher'bet *n.* frozen dessert made from fruit juice, sugar, egg whites and milk
sher'iff [she'rif] *n.* municipal officer who enforces court orders *etc.;* **US** law enforcement officer; in England and Wales, chief executive representative of the crown in a county; in Scotland, chief judge of a district —**sher'iffdom** *n.*
Sher'pa *n.* member of a Tibetan people (*pl.* **-pas, -pa**)
sherr'y *n.* fortified wine
shew [shō] *vt. old form of* SHOW
shew'bread [shō'-] *n.* unleavened bread used in Jewish ritual
shibb'oleth *n.* custom, word *etc.* distinguishing people of particular class or group
shield *n.* piece of armour carried on arm; any protection used to stop blows, missiles *etc.*; any protective device; sports trophy —*vt.* cover, protect
shift *v.* (cause to) move, change position —*n.* relay of workers; time of their working; evasion; expedient; removal; woman's underskirt or dress —**shift'iness** *n.* —**shift'less** *a.* lacking in resource or character —**shift'y** *a.* evasive, of dubious character
shille'lagh [-lā'lə] *n.* (in Ireland) cudgel
shill'ing *n.* former Brit. coin, now 5p; monetary unit in various countries
shill'yshally *vi.* waver —*n.* wavering, indecision
shimm'er *vi.* shine with quivering light —*n.* such light; glimmer
shin *n.* front of lower leg —*vi.* climb with arms and legs —*vt.* kick on shin (**-nn-**) —**shin'bone** *n.* tibia
shin'dig, shin'dy *n. inf.* row; noisy disturbance
shine *vi.* give out, reflect light; perform very well, excel —*vt.* cause to shine by polishing (**shone** [shon], **shi'ning**) —*n.* brightness, lustre; polishing —**shi'ny** *a.*
shin'gle[1] [-ng'gl] *n.* wooden roof tile; small signboard fixed outside office of doctor, lawyer *etc.* —*vt.* cover with shingles
shin'gle[2] [-ng'gl] *n.* mass of pebbles
shin'gles [-ng'glz] *n.* disease causing inflammation along a nerve
shinn'y *n.* simple form of hockey played with ball and sticks curved at lower end; stick used in this game —*vi.* play shinny
Shin'to *n.* native Japanese religion —**Shin'toism** *n.*
ship *n.* large seagoing vessel —*vt.* put on or send (*esp.* by ship) —*vi.* embark; take service in ship (**-pp-**) —**ship'ment** *n.* act of shipping; goods shipped —**ship'ping** *n.* freight transport business; ships collectively —**ship'shape** *a.* orderly, trim —**ship'wreck** *n.* destruction of a ship through storm, collision *etc.* —*vt.* cause to undergo shipwreck —**ship'yard** *n.* place for building and repair of ships
shire *n. Brit.* county
shirk *vt.* evade, try to avoid (duty *etc.*) —**shirk'er** *n.*
shirr *vt.* gather (fabric) into parallel rows —*n.*
shirt *n.* garment for upper part of body
shiv'er[1] *vi.* tremble, usu. with cold or fear; shudder; vibrate —*n.* act, state, of shivering
shiv'er[2] *v.* splinter, break in pieces —*n.* splinter
shoal[1] *n.* stretch of shallow water; sandbank or bar —*v.* make, become, shallow
shoal[2] *n.* large number of fish swimming together —*vi.* form shoal
shock[1] *vt.* horrify, scandalize —*n.* violent or damaging blow; emotional disturbance; state of weakness, illness, caused by physical or mental shock; paralytic stroke; collision; effect on sensory nerves of electric discharge —**shock'er** *n.* person or thing which shocks or distresses —**shock absorber** device (*esp.* in automobiles) to absorb shocks
shock[2] *n.* group of corn sheaves placed together
shock[3] *n.* mass of hair —*a.* shaggy —**shock'headed** *a.*
shodd'y *a.* worthless, trashy, second-rate, of poor material
shoe [shōō] *n.* covering for foot, not enclosing ankle; metal rim or curved bar put on horse's hoof; various protective plates or undercoverings (*pl.* **shoes**) —*vt.* protect, furnish with shoe or shoes (**shod** *pt./pp.*, **shoe'ing** *pr.p.*) —**shoe'string** *a./n.* very small (amount of money *etc.*)
shone [shon] *pt./pp. of* SHINE
shoo *interj.* go away! —*vt.* drive away
shook *pt. of* SHAKE
shoot *v.* hit, wound, kill with missile

fired from weapon; discharge weapon; send, slide, push rapidly; photograph, film —*vi.* hunt; sprout (**shot, shoot'ing**) —*n.* young branch, sprout; shooting competition; hunting expedition —**shoot'er** *n.*

shop *n.* place for retail sale of goods and services; workshop, works building —*vi.* visit shops to buy —*vt. sl.* inform against (**-pp-**) —**shop'lifter** *n.* one who steals from shop —**shop steward** trade union representative of workers in factory *etc.* —**talk shop** talk of one's business *etc.* at unsuitable moments

shore[1] *n.* edge of sea or lake

shore[2] *vt.* prop (up)

shorn *pp. of* SHEAR

short *a.* not long; not tall; brief, hasty; not reaching quantity or standard required; wanting, lacking; abrupt, rude; friable —*adv.* suddenly, abruptly; without reaching end —*n.* **UK** drink of spirits, as opposed to beer *etc.*; short motion picture —*pl.* short pants; men's underpants —**short'age** *n.* deficiency —**short'en** *v.* —**short'ening** *n.* butter, lard *etc.* used in pastry, cakes to make mixture crumbly —**short'ly** *adv.* soon; briefly —**short'cake, short'bread** *n.* sweet, brittle cake made of butter, flour and sugar —**short circuit** *Electricity* connection, often accidental, of low resistance between two parts of circuit —**short'coming** *n.* failing; defect —**short'hand** *n.* method of rapid writing by signs or contractions —**short-handed** *a.* lacking the usual or necessary number of workers, helpers —**short shrift** summary treatment —**short ton** US ton (2000 lb.) —**short wave** radio wave between 10 and 50 metres

shot *n.* act of shooting; missile; lead in small pellets; marksman, shooter; try, attempt; photograph; short motion-picture sequence; dose; *inf.* injection —*a.* woven so that colour is different, according to angle of light —*pt./pp. of* SHOOT

should [-ood] *pt. of* SHALL

shoul'der [-ōl'-] *n.* part of body to which arm or foreleg is attached; anything resembling shoulder; side of road —*vt.* undertake; bear (burden); accept (responsibility); put on one's shoulder —*vi.* make way by pushing —**shoulder blade** shoulder bone

shout *n.* loud cry —*v.* utter (cry *etc.*) with loud voice

shove [-uv] *vt.* push; *inf.* put —*n.* push —**shove off** *inf.* go away

shov'el [-uv'-] *n.* instrument for scooping, lifting earth *etc.* —*vt.* lift, move (as) with shovel (**-ll-**)

show [-ō] *vt.* expose to view; point out; display; exhibit; explain; prove; guide; accord (favour *etc.*) —*vi.* appear; be noticeable (**showed, shown, show'ing**) —*n.* display, exhibition; spectacle; theatrical or other entertainment; indication; competitive event; ostentation; semblance; pretence —**show'ily** *adv.* —**show'y** *a.* gaudy; ostentatious —**show'down** *n.* confrontation; final test —**show'jumping** *n.* horse-riding competition to demonstrate skill in jumping obstacles —**show'man** *n.* one employed in, or owning, show at fair *etc.*; one skilled at presenting anything in effective way —**show off** exhibit to invite admiration; behave in this way —**show-off** *n.* —**show up** reveal; expose; **UK** *inf.* embarrass; *inf.* arrive

show'er *n.* short fall of rain; anything coming down like rain; kind of bath in which person stands while being sprayed with water; party to present gifts to a person, as a prospective bride —*vt.* bestow liberally —*vi.* take bath in shower —**show'ery** *a.*

shrank *pt. of* SHRINK

shrap'nel *n.* shell filled with pellets which scatter on bursting; shell splinters

shred *n.* fragment, torn strip; small amount —*vt.* cut, tear to shreds (**shred** *or* **shredd'ed, shredd'ing**)

shrew [-o͞o] *n.* animal like mouse; bad-tempered woman; scold —**shrew'ish** *a.* nagging

shrewd [-o͞od] *a.* astute, intelligent; crafty —**shrewd'ly** *adv.* —**shrewd'ness** *n.*

shriek *n.* shrill cry; piercing scream —*v.* screech

shrike *n.* bird of prey

shrill *a.* piercing, sharp in tone —*v.* utter in such tone —**shrill'y** *adv.*

shrimp *n.* small edible crustacean; *inf.* undersized person —*vi.* go catching shrimps

shrine *n.* place (building, tomb, alcove) of worship, usu. associated with saint

shrink *vi.* become smaller; retire, flinch, recoil *—vt.* make smaller (**shrank** *pt.*, **shrunk'en, shrunk** *pp.*, **shrink'ing** *pr.p.*) *—n. sl.* psychiatrist —**shrink'age** *n.*

shrive *vt.* give absolution to (**shrived, shrove** *pt.*, **shriv'en** *pp.*, **shri'ving** *pr.p.*) —**shrift** *n.* confession; absolution

shriv'el *vi.* shrink and wither (**-ll-**)

shroud *n.* sheet, wrapping, for corpse; anything which covers, envelops like shroud *—pl.* set of ropes to masthead *—vt.* put shroud on; screen, veil; wrap up

Shrove'tide *n.* the three days preceding Lent —**Shrove Tuesday** day before Ash Wednesday

shrub *n.* bushy plant —**shrubb'ery** *n.* plantation, part of garden, filled with shrubs —**shrubb'y** *a.*

shrug *vi.* raise shoulders, as sign of indifference, ignorance *etc. —vt.* move (shoulders) thus; (*with* off) dismiss as unimportant (**-gg-**) *—n.* shrugging

shrunk('en) *pp. of* SHRINK

shuck *n.* shell, husk, pod

shucks *interj.* exclamation of disgust, annoyance *etc.*

shudd'er *vi.* shake, tremble violently, *esp.* with horror *—n.* shuddering, tremor

shuf'fle *vi.* move feet without lifting them; act evasively *—vt.* mix (cards); (*with* off) evade, pass to another *—n.* shuffling; rearrangement —**shuff'ler** *n.*

shun *vt.* avoid; keep away from (**-nn-**)

shunt *vt.* push aside; divert; move (train) from one line to another

shut *v.* close; bar; forbid entrance to (**shut, shutt'ing**) —**shutt'er** *n.* movable window screen, usu. hinged to frame; device in camera admitting light as required to film or plate —**shut'out** *n. Sport* win in which defeated team has no score —**shut down** close or stop factory, machine *etc.* —**shut out** prevent (opponent) from scoring

shut'tle *n.* instrument which threads weft between threads of warp in weaving; similar appliance in sewing machine; plane, bus *etc.* travelling to and fro over short distance —**shut'tlecock** *n.* small, light cone with cork stub and fan of feathers used as a ball in badminton

shy[1] *a.* awkward in company; timid, bashful; reluctant; scarce, lacking (*esp.* in card games, not having enough money for bet *etc.*) *—vi.* start back in fear; show sudden reluctance (**shied, shy'ing**) *—n.* start of fear by horse —**shy'ly** *adv.* —**shy'ness** *n.*

shy[2] *vt./n.* throw (**shied, shy'ing**)

shy'ster *n. sl.* dishonest, deceitful person

SI *Fr.* Système International (d'Unités), international system of units of measurement based on units of ten

Si *Chem.* silicon

Siamese' *a.* of Siam, former name of Thailand —**Siamese cat** breed of cat with blue eyes —**Siamese twins** twins born joined to each other by some part of body

sib'ilant *a.* hissing *—n.* speech sound with hissing effect

sib'ling *n.* person's brother or sister *—a.*

sib'yl *n.* woman endowed with spirit of prophecy —**sib'ylline** *a.* occult

sic *Lat.* thus: oft. used to call attention to a quoted mistake

sick *a.* inclined to vomit, vomiting; not well or healthy, physically or mentally; *inf.* macabre, sadistic, morbid; *inf.* bored, tired; *inf.* disgusted —**sick'en** *v.* make, become, sick; disgust; nauseate —**sick'ly** *a.* unhealthy, weakly; inducing nausea —**sick'ness** *n.* —**sick'bay** *n.* place set aside for treating sick people, *esp.* in ships

sic'kle *n.* reaping hook

side *n.* one of the surfaces of object, *esp.* upright inner or outer surface; either surface of thing having only two; part of body that is to right or left; region nearer or farther than, or right or left of, dividing line *etc.*; region; aspect or part; one of two parties or sets of opponents; sect, faction; line of descent traced through one parent *—a.* at, in, the side; subordinate, incidental *—vi.* take up cause of (*usu. with* with) —**si'ding** *n.* short line of rails on which trains or wagons are shunted from main line —**side'board** *n.* piece of furniture for holding dishes *etc.* in dining room —**side'burns** *pl.n.* man's side whiskers —**side'car** *n.* small car attached to side of motorcycle —**side'-light** *n.* light from side; incidental information —**side'line** *n. Sport* boundary of playing area; subsidiary interest or activity —**side'long** *a.* lateral, not directly forward —*adv.* obliquely —**side'slip** *n.* skid —**sides'man** *n. Anglican Ch.* man elected to help parish churchwarden —**side'track** *n.* railway siding; a digression —*v.* switch (train) to siding; deviate from main topic —**side'walk** *n.* footpath beside road —**side'ways** *adv.* to or from the side; laterally

side'real [sī-dē'ri-əl] *a.* relating to, fixed by, stars

si'dle *vi.* move in furtive or stealthy manner; move sideways; fawn

SIDS sudden infant death syndrome (*see* CRIB DEATH)

siege [-j] *n.* besieging of town or fortified place

sienn'a [si-en'ə] *n.* (pigment of) brownish-yellow colour

sierr'a [si-er'ə] *n.* range of mountains with jagged peaks

siest'a [si-est'ə] *n.* rest, sleep in afternoon

sieve [siv] *n.* device with network or perforated bottom for sifting —*v.* sift; strain

sift *vt.* separate (*eg* with sieve) coarser portion from finer; examine closely —**sift'er** *n.*

sigh [sī] *v./n.* (utter) long audible breath —**sigh for** yearn for, grieve for

sight [sīt] *n.* faculty of seeing; seeing; thing seen; view; glimpse; device for guiding eye; spectacle; *inf.* pitiful or ridiculous object; *inf.* large number, great deal —*vt.* catch sight of; adjust sights of gun *etc.* —**sight'less** *a.* —**sight-read** *v.* play, sing music without previous preparation —**sight'see** *vt.* visit (place) to look at interesting sights —**sight'seeing** *n.* —**sight'seer** *n.*

sign [sīn] *n.* mark, gesture *etc.* to convey some meaning; (board, placard bearing) notice, warning *etc.*; symbol; omen; evidence —*vt.* put one's signature to; ratify —*vi.* make sign or gesture; affix signature —**sign'board** *n.* board carrying sign or notice

sig'nal *n.* sign to convey order or information, *esp.* on railway; that which in first place impels any action; *Radio etc.* sequence of electrical impulses transmitted or received —*a.* remarkable, striking —*vt.* make signals to —*vi.* give orders *etc.* by signals (**-ll-**) —**sig'nalize** *vt.* make notable —**sig'nally** *adv.*

sig'natory *n.* one of those who sign agreements, treaties

sig'nature *n.* person's name written by himself; act of writing it

sig'net *n.* small seal

signif'icant *a.* revealing; designed to make something known; important —**signif'icance** *n.* import, weight; meaning —**signif'icantly** *adv.* —**significa'tion** *n.* meaning

sig'nify *vt.* mean; indicate; denote; imply —*vi.* be of importance (**sig'nified, sig'nifying**)

sig'nor [sē'nyawr] *n.* Italian title of respect, like Mr. —**signor'a** *n.* Mrs. —**signori'na** [-rē'-] *n.* Miss

Sikh [sēk] *n.* member of Indian religious sect

si'lage *n.* fodder crop harvested while green and stored in state of partial fermentation

si'lence *n.* absence of noise; refraining from speech —*vt.* make silent; put a stop to —**si'lent** *a.*

silhouette' [-lōō-] *n.* outline of object seen against light; profile portrait in black

sil'ica *n.* naturally occurring dioxide of silicon —**sili'ceous, sili'cious** [-lish'-] *a.* —**silico'sis** *n.* lung disease caused by inhaling silica dust over a long period

sil'icon *n.* brittle metalloid element found in sand, clay, stone, widely used in chemistry, industry —**sil'icone** *n.* large class of synthetic substances, related to silicon and used in chemistry, industry, medicine

silk *n.* fibre made by larvae (**silkworm**) of certain moth; thread, fabric made from this —**silk'en** *a.* made of, like silk; soft; smooth; dressed in silk —**silk'ily** *adv.* —**silk'iness** *n.* —**silk'y** *a.*

sill *n.* ledge beneath window; bottom part of door or window frame

sill'y *a.* foolish; trivial; feeble-minded —**sill'iness** *n.*

si'lo *n.* pit, tower for storing fodder or grain; underground missile launching site (*pl.* **-los**)

silt *n.* mud deposited by water —*v.* fill, be choked with silt —**silta'tion** *n.* —**silt'y** *a.*

sil'van *a. see* SYLVAN

sil'ver *n.* white precious metal; things made of it; silver coins; cutlery —*a.* made of silver; resembling silver or its colour; having pale lustre, as moon; soft, melodious, as sound; bright *—vt.* coat with silver **—sil'very** *a.* **—silver birch** tree having silvery white peeling bark **—silver thaw** freezing rainstorm; glitter **—silver wedding** 25th wedding anniversary

sim'ian *a.* of, like apes

sim'ilar *a.* resembling, like **—similar'ity** *n.* likeness; close resemblance **—sim'ilarly** *adv.*

sim'ile [-i-li] *n.* comparison of one thing with another, using 'as' or 'like', *esp.* in poetry

simil'itude *n.* outward appearance, likeness; guise

simm'er *v.* keep or be just bubbling or just below boiling point; to be in state of suppressed anger or laughter

si'mony *n.* (sinful) buying, selling of church preferment

sim'per *vi.* smile, utter in silly or affected way *—n.*

sim'ple *a.* not complicated; plain; not combined or complex; ordinary, mere; guileless; stupid **—sim'pleton** *n.* foolish person **—simplic'ity** [-lis'-] *n.* simpleness, clearness, artlessness **—simplifica'tion** *n.* **—sim'plify** *vt.* make simple, plain or easy (**-plified, -plifying**) **—simplis'tic** *a.* very simple, naive **—sim'ply** *adv.* **—simple fraction** one in which both the numerator and the denominator are integers

sim'ulate *vt.* make pretence of; reproduce, copy, *esp.* conditions of particular situation **—simula'tion** *n.* **—sim'ulator** *n.*

simulta'neous *a.* occurring at the same time **—simultane'ity, simulta'neousness** *n.* **—simulta'neously** *adv.*

SIN Social Insurance Number

sin *n.* transgression of divine or moral law, *esp.* committed consciously; offence against principle or standard *—vi.* commit sin (**-nn-**) **—sin'ful** *a.* of nature of sin; guilty of sin **—sin'fully** *adv.* **—sin'ner** *n.*

since *prep.* during or throughout period of time after *—conj.* from time when; because *—adv.* from that time

sincere' *a.* not hypocritical, actually moved by or feeling apparent emotions; true, genuine; unaffected **—sincere'ly** *adv.* **—sincer'ity** [-se'ri-] *n.*

sine [-ī-] *n.* mathematical function, *esp.* ratio of length of hypotenuse to opposite side in right-angled triangle

si'necure *n.* office with pay but minimal duties

si'ne di'e *Lat.* with no date, indefinitely postponed

si'ne qua non' [sī'ni-kwā-non'] *Lat.* essential condition or requirement

sin'ew *n.* tough, fibrous cord joining muscle to bone *—pl.* muscles, strength **—sin'ewy** *a.* stringy; muscular

sing *vi.* utter musical sounds; hum, whistle, ring *—vt.* utter (words) with musical modulation; celebrate in song or poetry (**sang, sung, sing'ing**) **—sing'er** *n.* **—sing'song** *n.* informal singing session *—a.* monotonously regular in tone, rhythm

singe [-nj] *vt.* burn surface of (**singed, singe'ing**) *—n.* act or effect of singeing

sin'gle [-ng'gl] *a.* one only; alone, separate; unmarried; for one; formed of only one part, fold *etc.*; whole-hearted, straightforward *—n.* single thing; gramophone record with one short item on each side *—vt.* pick (out) **—sin'gly** *adv.* **—single file** persons, things arranged in one line **—single-handed** *a.* without assistance **—singles bar** bar or club that is social meeting place for single people

sing'let *n.* sleeveless undervest

sin'gular *a.* remarkable; unusual; unique; denoting one person or thing **—singular'ity** *n.* something unusual **—sin'gularly** *adv.* particularly; peculiarly

sin'ister *a.* threatening; evil-looking; wicked; unlucky; *Heraldry* on left-hand side

sink *vi.* become submerged (in water); drop, give way; decline in value, health *etc.*; penetrate (into) *—vt.* cause to sink; make by digging out; invest (**sank** *pt.*, **sunk, sunk'en** *pp.*, **sink'ing** *pr.p.*) *—n.* receptacle with pipe for carrying away waste water; cesspool; place of corruption, vice **—sink'er** *n.* weight for fishing line **—sinking fund** money set aside at intervals for payment of particular liability at fixed date

Sinn Fein [shin fān] Irish republican political movement

Sino- (*comb. form*) Chinese, of China

sin'uous *a.* curving, devious, lithe —**sin'uate** *a.* —**sinuos'ity** *n.* —**sin'u-ously** *adv.*

si'nus *n.* cavity, *esp.* air passages in bones of skull —**sinusi'tis** *n.* inflammation of sinus

sip *v.* drink in very small portions (**-pp-**) —*n.*

si'phon, sy'phon *n.* device, *esp.* bent tube, which uses atmospheric or gaseous pressure to draw liquid from container —*v.* draw off thus; draw off in small amounts

sir *n.* polite term of address for a man; (**S-**) title of knight or baronet

sire *n.* male parent, *esp.* of horse or domestic animal; term of address to king —*v.* beget

si'ren *n.* device making loud wailing noise, *esp.* giving warning of danger; legendary sea nymph who lured sailors to destruction; alluring woman

sir'loin *n.* prime cut of loin of beef

si'sal *n.* (fibre of) plant used in making ropes

siss'y *a./n.* weak, cowardly (person)

sis'ter *n.* daughter of same parents; woman fellow-member *esp.* of religious body; senior nurse —*a.* closely related, similar —**sis'terhood** *n.* relation of sister; order, band of women —**sis'terly** *a.* —**sister-in-law** *n.* sister of husband or wife; brother's wife

sit *v.* (*mainly intr.*) adopt posture or rest on buttocks, thighs; perch; incubate; pose for portrait; occupy official position; hold session; remain; take examination; keep watch over baby *etc.* —**sit in** protest by refusing to move from place —**sit-in** *n.*

sitar' *n.* stringed musical instrument, *esp.* of India

site *n.* place, location; space for, with, a building

sit'uate *v.* place, locate —**situa'tion** *n.* place, position; state of affairs; employment, post

six *a./n.* cardinal number one more than five —**sixth** *a.* ordinal number —*n.* sixth part —**six'teen'** *n./a.* six and ten —**six'ty** *n./a.* six times ten

size[1] *n.* bigness, dimensions; one of series of standard measurements of clothes *etc.*; *inf.* state of affairs —*vt.* arrange according to size —**siz(e)'able** *a.* quite large —**size up** *inf.* assess (person, situation *etc.*)

size[2] *n.* gluelike sealer, filler —*vt.* coat, treat with size

siz'zle *v./n.* (make) hissing, spluttering sound as of frying —**sizz'ler** *n. inf.* hot day

skald [-awl-] *n.* ancient Scandinavian poet

skate[1] *n.* steel blade attached to boot, for gliding over ice —*vi.* glide as on skates —**skate'board** *n.* small board mounted on roller-skate wheels

skate[2] *n.* large marine ray

skedad'dle *vi. inf.* scamper off

skein [-ā-] *n.* quantity of yarn, wool *etc.* in loose knot; flight of wildfowl

skel'eton *n.* bones of animal; bones separated from flesh and preserved in their natural position; very thin person; outline, draft, framework; nucleus —*a.* reduced to a minimum; drawn in outline; not in detail —**skel'etal** *a.* —**skeleton key** key filed down so as to open many different locks

sketch *n.* rough drawing; brief account; essay; short humorous play —*v.* make sketch (of) —**sketch'y** *a.* omitting detail; incomplete; inadequate

skew *vi.* move obliquely —*a.* slanting; crooked

skew'bald *a.* white and any other colour (except black) in patches (*esp.* of horse)

skew'er *n.* pin to fasten (meat) together —*v.* pierce or fasten with skewer

ski [skē] *n.* long runner fastened to foot for sliding over snow or water (*pl.* **skis** [-z]) —*v.* slide on skis (**skied, ski'ing**) —**ski lift** machine for carrying or pulling skiers to top of slope

skid *v.* slide (sideways), *esp.* vehicle out of control with wheels not revolving (**-dd-**) —*n.* instance of this; device to facilitate sliding, *eg* in moving heavy objects —**skid row** *sl.* dilapidated section of city inhabited by vagrants *etc.*

skidoo' *n.* snowmobile

skiff *n.* small boat

skill *n.* practical ability, cleverness, dexterity —**skilled** *a.* having, requiring knowledge, united with readiness and dexterity —**skil'ful** *a.* expert, masterly; adroit —**skil'fully** *adv.*

skill'et *n.* small frying pan

skim *vt.* remove floating matter from surface of liquid; glide over lightly and rapidly; read thus —*vi.* move thus (**-mm-**) —**skim(med) milk** milk from which cream has been removed

skimp *vt.* give short measure; do thing imperfectly —**skimp'y** *a.* meagre; scanty

skin *n.* outer covering of vertebrate body, lower animal or fruit; animal skin used as material or container; film on surface of cooling liquid *etc.*; complexion —*vt.* remove skin of (**-nn-**) —**skin'less** *a.* —**skinn'er** *n.* dealer in hides; furrier —**skinn'y** *a.* thin —**skin-deep** *a.* superficial; slight —**skin diving** underwater swimming using breathing apparatus —**skin'flint** *n.* miser, niggard —**skin graft** transplant of piece of healthy skin to wound to form new skin —**skin'tight** *a.* fitting close to skin

skip[1] *vi.* leap lightly; jump a rope as it is swung under one —*vt.* pass over, omit (**-pp-**) —*n.* act of skipping

skip[2] *n.* large open container for builders' rubbish *etc.*; large bucket, container for transporting men, materials in mines *etc.*

skipp'er *n.* captain of ship, plane or team —*vt.* captain

skirl *n.* sound of bagpipes

skirm'ish *n.* fight between small parties, small battle —*vi.* fight briefly or irregularly

skirt *n.* woman's garment hanging from waist; lower part of woman's dress, coat *etc.*; outlying part; *sl.* woman —*vi.* border; go round

skit *n.* satire, *esp.* theatrical burlesque

skitt'ish *a.* frisky, frivolous

skit'tles *pl.n.* ninepins

skivv'y *n.* **UK** female servant who does menial work

sku'a *n.* large predatory gull

skuldugg'ery *n. inf.* trickery

skulk *vi.* sneak out of the way; lurk —**skulk'er** *n.*

skull *n.* bony case that encloses brain —**skull'cap** *n.* close-fitting cap

skunk *n.* small N Amer. animal which emits evil-smelling fluid; *sl.* mean person

sky *n.* apparently dome-shaped expanse extending upwards from the horizon; outer space; heavenly regions (*pl.* **skies**) —*vt.* hit (cricket ball) high —**sky'diving** *n.* parachute jumping with delayed opening of parachute —**sky'light** *n.* window in roof or ceiling —**sky'scraper** *n.* very tall building

slab *n.* thick, broad piece

slack[1] *a.* loose; sluggish; careless, negligent; not busy —*n.* loose part, as of rope —*vi.* be idle or lazy —**slack'ly** *adv.* —**slack'en** *v.* become looser; become slower, abate

slack[2] *n.* coal dust, small pieces of coal

slacks *pl.n.* informal trousers worn by men or women

slag *n.* refuse of smelted metal

slain *pp. of* SLAY

slake *vt.* satisfy (thirst, desire *etc.*); combine (lime) with water to produce calcium hydroxide

slal'om [slahl'əm] *n./v.* (race over) winding course in skiing *etc.*

slam *v.* shut noisily; bang; hit; dash down; *inf.* criticize harshly (**-mm-**) —*n.* (noise of) this action —**grand slam** *Cards* winning of all tricks

slan'der [-ah-] *n.* false or malicious statement about person —*v.* utter such statement —**slan'derer** *n.* —**slan'derous** *a.*

slang *n.* colloquial language —*vt. sl.* scold, abuse violently

slant [-ah-] *v.* slope; put at angle; write, present (news *etc.*) with bias —*n.* slope; point of view; idea —*a.* sloping, oblique —**slant'wise** *adv.*

slap *n.* blow with open hand or flat instrument —*vt.* strike thus; *inf.* put on, down carelessly or messily (**-pp-**) —**slap'dash** *a.* careless and abrupt —**slap'stick** *n.* boisterous knockabout comedy

slash *vt.* gash; lash; cut, slit; criticize unmercifully —*n.* gash; cutting stroke

slat *n.* narrow strip of wood or metal as in blinds *etc.*

slate *n.* kind of stone which splits easily in flat sheets; piece of this for covering roof or, formerly, for writing on; list of candidates in election —*vt.* cover with slates; enter as candidate —**sla'ter** *n.* woodlouse —**sla'ting** *n.* severe reprimand

slath'er [-ahTH'-] *n. inf.* large quantity

slatt'ern *n.* slut —**slatt'ernly** *a.* slovenly, untidy

slaugh'ter [slaw'-] *n.* killing —*vt.* kill —**slaugh'terous** *a.* —**slaugh'terhouse** *n.* place for killing animals for food

slave *n.* captive, person without freedom or personal rights; one dominated by another or by a habit *etc.* —*vi.* work like slave —**sla'ver** *n.* person, ship engaged in slave traffic —**sla'very** *n.* —**sla'vish** *a.* servile

slav'er *vi.* dribble saliva from mouth; fawn —*n.* saliva running from mouth

slaw *n. short for* COLESLAW

slay *vt.* kill; *inf.* impress, *esp.* by being very funny (**slew, slain, slay'ing**) —**slay'er** *n.* killer

sleaz'y *a.* sordid —**sleaze** *n. inf.* sordidness

sled, sledge *n.* carriage on runners for sliding on snow; toboggan —*v.*

sledge, sledge'hammer *n.* heavy hammer with long handle

sleek *a.* glossy, smooth, shiny

sleep *n.* unconscious state regularly occurring in man and animals; slumber, repose; *inf.* dried particles *oft.* found in corners of eyes after sleeping —*vi.* take rest in sleep, slumber (**slept, sleep'ing**) —**sleep'er** *n.* one who sleeps; UK beam supporting rails of railway; railway sleeping car; *inf.* person or thing that achieves unexpected success —**sleep'ily** *adv.* —**sleep'iness** *n.* —**sleep'less** *a.* —**sleep'y** *a.* —**sleeping sickness** Afr. disease spread by tsetse fly

sleet *n.* rain and snow or hail falling together

sleeve *n.* part of garment which covers arm; case surrounding shaft; gramophone record cover —*vt.* furnish with sleeves —**sleeved** *a.* —**sleeve'less** *a.* —**have up one's sleeve** have something prepared secretly for emergency

sleigh [slā] *n.* sled

sleight [slīt] *n.* dexterity; trickery; deviousness —**sleight of hand** (manual dexterity in) conjuring, juggling; legerdemain

slen'der *a.* slim, slight; feeble

slept *pt./pp. of* SLEEP

sleuth [-ōō-] *n.* detective; tracking dog (*also* **sleuth'hound**) —*vt.* track

slew[1] *pt. of* SLAY

slew[2] *v.* swing round

slew[3] *n. inf.* great number or amount

slice *n.* thin flat piece cut off; share; flat culinary tool —*vt.* cut into slices; cut cleanly; hit with bat *etc.* at angle

slick *a.* smooth; smooth-tongued; flattering; superficially attractive; sly —*vt.* make glossy, smooth —*n.* slippery area; patch of oil on water

slide *v.* slip smoothly along; glide, as over ice; pass imperceptibly; deteriorate morally (**slid** *pt.*, **slid, slidd'en** *pp.*, **sli'ding** *pr.p.*) —*n.* sliding; surface, track for sliding; sliding part of mechanism; piece of glass holding object to be viewed under microscope; photographic transparency —**slide fastener** zipper —**slide rule** mathematical instrument of two parts, one of which slides upon the other, for rapid calculations —**sliding scale** schedule for automatically varying one thing (*eg* wages) according to fluctuations of another (*eg* cost of living)

slight [-īt] *a.* small, trifling; not substantial, fragile; slim, slender —*vt.* disregard; neglect —*n.* indifference; act of discourtesy —**slight'ly** *adv.*

slim *a.* thin; slight —*v.* reduce person's weight by diet and exercise (**-mm-**)

slime *n.* greasy, thick, liquid mud or similar substance —**sli'my** *a.* like slime; fawning

sling *n.* strap, loop with string attached at each end for hurling stone; bandage for supporting wounded limb; rope, belt *etc.* for hoisting, carrying weights —*vt.* throw; hoist, swing by rope (**slung, sling'ing**) —**sling'shot** *n.* small forked stick with elastic sling used for throwing stones

slink *vi.* move stealthily, sneak (**slunk, slink'ing**) —**slink'y** *a.* sinuously graceful; (of clothes *etc.*) figure-hugging

slip[1] *v.* (cause to) move smoothly, easily, quietly; pass out of (mind *etc.*); (of motor vehicle clutch) engage partially, fail —*vi.* lose balance by sliding; fall from person's grasp; make mistake (*usu. with* up); decline in health, morals —*vt.* put on or take off easily, quickly; let go (anchor *etc.*); dislocate (bone) (**-pp-**) —*n.* act or occasion of slipping; mistake; petticoat; small piece of paper; plant cutting; launching slope on which ships are built; covering for pillow —**slip'shod** *a.* slovenly, careless —**slip'stream** *n. Aviation* stream of air driven astern by engine

slip[2] *n.* clay mixed with water to creamy consistency, used for decorating ceramic ware

slipp'er *n.* light shoe for indoor use —**slipp'ered** *a.*

slipp'ery *a.* so smooth as to cause slipping or to be difficult to hold or catch; changeable; unreliable; crafty; wily

slit *vt.* make long straight cut in; cut in strips (**slit, slitt'ing**) —*n.*

slith'er [-TH'-] *vi.* slide unsteadily (down slope *etc.*)

sliv'er *n.* thin small piece torn off something; splinter

slob *n. inf.* stupid, coarse person

slobb'er *v.* slaver; be weakly and excessively demonstrative —*n.* running saliva; maudlin speech —**slobb'ery** *a.*

slob ice sludgy masses of floating ice

sloe *n.* blue-black, sour fruit of blackthorn

slog *vt.* hit vigorously, *esp.* at cricket —*vi.* work or study with dogged determination; move, work with difficulty (**-gg-**) —*n.*

slo'gan *n.* distinctive phrase (in advertising *etc.*)

sloop *n.* small one-masted vessel; *Hist.* small warship

slop *vi.* spill —*vt.* spill, splash (**-pp-**) —*n.* liquid spilt; liquid food; dirty liquid —*pl.* liquid refuse —**slopp'y** *a.* careless, untidy; sentimental; wet, muddy

slope *vt.* place slanting —*vi.* lie in, follow an inclined course; go furtively —*n.* slant; upward, downward inclination

slosh *n.* watery mud *etc.*; *sl.* heavy blow —*v.* splash; hit —**sloshed** *a. sl.* drunk

slot *n.* narrow hole or depression; slit for coins —*vt.* put in slot; sort; *inf.* place in series, organization (**-tt-**) —**slot machine** automatic machine worked by insertion of coin

sloth [-ō-] *n.* sluggish S Amer. animal; sluggishness —**sloth'ful** *a.* lazy, idle —**sloth'fully** *adv.*

slouch *vi.* walk, sit *etc.* in lazy or ungainly, drooping manner —*n.* —*a.* (of hat) with wide, flexible brim

slough[1] [-ow] *n.* bog; large hollow where water collects

slough[2] [-uf] *n.* skin shed by snake —*v.* shed (skin); drop off

slov'en [-uv'-] *n.* dirty, untidy person —**slov'enly** *a.* untidy; careless; disorderly —*adv.*

slow [-ō] *a.* lasting a long time; moving at low speed; behind the true time; dull —*v.* slacken speed (of) —**slow'ly** *adv.* —**slow'ness** *n.* —**slow'down** *n.* deliberate slackening of the rate of production as form of industrial protest —**slow-motion** *a.* (of motion picture) showing movement greatly slowed down —**slow'-poke** *n. inf.* person slow in moving, acting, deciding *etc.*

slow'worm [slō'-] *n.* small legless lizard, blindworm

sludge *n.* slush, ooze; sewage

slug[1] *n.* land snail with no shell; bullet —**slugg'ard** *n.* lazy, idle person —**slug'gish** *a.* slow; lazy, inert; not functioning well —**slugg'ishness** *n.*

slug[2] *v.* hit, slog (**-gg-**) —*n.* heavy blow; portion of spirits; metal token for use in slot machines —**slugg'er** *n.* hard-hitting boxer, slogger

sluice [-o͞os] *n.* gate, door to control flow of water —*vt.* pour water over, through

slum *n.* squalid street or neighbourhood —*vi.* visit slums (**-mm-**)

slum'ber *vi./n.* sleep —**slum'berer** *n.*

slump *v.* fall heavily; relax ungracefully; decline suddenly in value, volume or esteem —*n.* sudden decline; (of prices *etc.*) sharp fall; depression

slung *pt./pp. of* SLING

slunk *pt./pp. of* SLINK

slur *vt.* pass over lightly; run together (words, musical notes); disparage (**-rr-**) —*n.* slight, stigma; *Mus.* curved line above or below notes to be slurred

slurp *v. inf.* eat, drink noisily

slurr'y *n.* muddy liquid mixture as cement, mud *etc.*

slush *n.* watery, muddy substance; excess sentimentality —**slush fund** fund for financing bribery, corruption

slut *n.* dirty (immoral) woman —**slut'tish** *a.* —**slutt'ishness** *n.*

sly *a.* cunning, wily, knowing; secret, deceitful —**sly'ly** *adv.* —**sly'ness** *n.*

smack[1] *n.* taste, flavour; *sl.* heroin —*vi.* taste (of); suggest

smack[2] *vt.* slap; open and close (lips) with loud sound —*n.* smacking slap; crack; such sound; loud kiss —*adv. inf.* squarely; directly

smack[3] *n.* small sailing vessel, usu. for fishing
small [-awl] *a.* little, unimportant; petty; short; weak; mean —*n.* small slender part *esp.* of the back —**small'ness** *n.* —**small'holding** *n.* small area of farming land —**small hours** hours just after midnight —**small-minded** *a.* having narrow views; petty —**small'pox** *n.* contagious disease —**small talk** light, polite conversation
smarm *v.* UK *inf.* fawn —**smarm'y** *inf.* *a.* unpleasantly suave; fawning
smart *a.* astute; brisk; clever, witty; impertinent; trim, well dressed; fashionable; causing stinging pain —*v.* feel, cause pain —*n.* sharp pain —**smart'en** *vt.* —**smart'ly** *adv.* —**smart'ness** *n.* —**smart aleck** *inf.* conceited person, know-all
smash *vt.* break violently; strike hard; ruin; destroy —*vi.* break; dash violently against —*n.* heavy blow; collision (of vehicles *etc.*); total financial failure; *inf.* popular success —**smashed** *a. sl.* very drunk or affected by drugs
smatt'ering *n.* slight superficial knowledge
smear *vt.* rub with grease *etc.*; smudge, spread with dirt, grease *etc.* —*n.* mark made thus; sample of secretion for medical examination; slander —**smear'y** *a.* greasy
smell *vt.* perceive by nose; *fig.* suspect —*vi.* give out odour; use nose (**smelt** *or* **smelled, smell'ing**) —*n.* faculty of perceiving odours by nose; anything detected by sense of smell —**smell'y** *a.* with strong (unpleasant) smell
smelt[1] *vt.* extract metal from ore —**smel'tery** *n.*
smelt[2] *n.* fish of salmon family
smile *n.* curving or parting of lips in pleased or amused expression —*v.* wear, assume a smile; approve, favour
smirch *vt.* dirty, sully; disgrace, discredit —*n.* stain; disgrace
smirk *n.* smile expressing scorn, smugness —*v.*
smite *vt.* strike; attack; afflict; affect, *esp.* with love or fear (**smote, smitt'en, smi'ting**)
smith *n.* worker in iron, gold *etc.* —**smith'y** [-TH'-] *n.* blacksmith's workshop
smithereens' *pl.n.* small bits
smock *n.* loose, outer garment —*vt.* gather by sewing in honeycomb pattern —**smock'ing** *n.*
smog *n.* mixture of smoke and fog
smoke *n.* cloudy mass of suspended particles that rises from fire or anything burning; spell of tobacco smoking —*vi.* give off smoke; inhale and expel tobacco smoke —*vt.* use (tobacco) by smoking; expose to smoke (*esp.* in curing fish *etc.*) —**smo'ker** *n.* —**smo'kily** *adv.* —**smo'ky** *a.*
smooch *inf. v./n.* kiss, cuddle
smooth [-TH] *a.* not rough, even of surface or texture; sinuous; flowing; calm, soft, soothing; suave, plausible; free from jolts —*vt.* make smooth; quieten —**smooth'ly** *adv.*
smor'gasbord [-gəs-] *n.* buffet meal of assorted dishes
smote *pt. of* SMITE
smoth'er [-uTH'-] *v.* suffocate; envelop; suppress —*vi.* be suffocated
smoul'der [-ō-] *vi.* burn slowly without flame; (of feelings) exist in suppressed state
smudge *v.* make smear, stain, dirty mark (on) —*n.*
smug *a.* self-satisfied, complacent —**smug'ly** *adv.*
smug'gle *vt.* import, export without paying customs duties; conceal, take secretly —**smugg'ler** *n.*
smut *n.* piece of soot, particle of dirt; lewd or obscene talk *etc.*; disease of grain —*vt.* blacken, smudge (**-tt-**) —**smut'ty** *a.* soiled with smut, soot; obscene, lewd
Sn *Chem.* tin
snack *n.* light, hasty meal —**snack bar** bar at which snacks are served
snaf'fle *n.* light bit for horse —*vt. sl.* appropriate, scrounge; put snaffle on
snag *n.* difficulty; sharp protuberance; hole, loop in fabric caused by sharp object; obstacle (*eg* tree branch *etc.* in river bed) —*vt.* catch, damage on snag
snail *n.* slow-moving mollusc with shell; slow, sluggish person —**snail-like** *a.*
snake *n.* long scaly limbless reptile, serpent —*v.* move like snake —**sna'ky** *a.* of, like snakes
snap *v.* break suddenly; make cracking sound; bite (at) suddenly; speak suddenly,

angrily; *Football* pass (ball) back between legs from line of scrimmage *—n.* act of snapping; fastener; *inf.* snapshot; *inf.* easy task; brief period, *esp.* of cold weather; *Football* act of snapping; player (centre) who does this *—a.* sudden, unplanned, arranged quickly **—snapp'er** *n.* perch-like fish **—snapp'y** *a.* irritable; *sl.* quick; *sl.* well-dressed, fashionable **—snap'dragon** *n.* plant with flowers that can be opened like a mouth **—snap'shot** *n.* photograph

snare *n.* (noose used as) trap *—vt.* catch with one

snarl *n.* growl of angry dog; tangle, knot *—vi.* utter snarl; grumble **—snarl-up** *n. inf.* confusion, obstruction, *esp.* traffic jam

snatch *v.* make quick grab or bite (at); seize, catch *—n.* grab; fragment; short spell

snazz'y *a. inf.* stylish, flashy

sneak *vi.* slink; move about furtively; act in mean, underhand manner *—n.* mean, treacherous person; petty informer **—sneak'ing** *a.* secret but persistent

sneak'ers *pl.n.* flexible, informal sports shoes

sneer *n.* scornful, contemptuous expression or remark *—v.*

sneeze *vi.* emit breath through nose with sudden involuntary spasm and noise *—n.*

snick *n.* small cut or notch; nick *—vt.* cut; clip; nick

snick'er *n.* sly disrespectful laugh, *esp.* partly stifled *—v.*

snide *a.* malicious, supercilious

sniff *vi.* inhale through nose with sharp hiss; (*with* at) express disapproval *etc.* by sniffing *—vt.* take up through nose, smell *—n.* **—snif'fle** *vi.* sniff noisily through nose, *esp.* when suffering from a cold in the head; snuffle

snigg'er *n./v. same as* SNICKER

snip *vt.* cut, cut bits off (**-pp-**) *—n.* act, sound of snipping; bit cut off; small or insignificant person **—snipp'et** *n.* shred, fragment, clipping **—snips** *pl.n.* tool for cutting

snipe *n.* wading bird *—v.* shoot at enemy from cover; (*with* at) criticize, attack (person) slyly **—sni'per** *n.*

snitch *inf. vt.* steal *—vi.* inform *—n.* telltale

sniv'el *vi.* sniffle to show distress; whine (**-ll-**)

snob *n.* one who pretentiously judges others by social rank *etc.* **—snobb'ery** *n.* **—snobb'ish** *a.* of or like a snob **—snobb'ishly** *adv.*

snoo'ker *n.* game played on billiard table *—vt.* leave (opponent) in unfavourable position; place (someone) in difficult situation

snoop *v.* pry, meddle; peer into *—n.* one who acts thus; snooping **—snoop'er** *n.*

snoot'y *a. sl.* haughty

snooze *vi.* take short sleep, be half asleep *—n.* nap

snore *vi.* breathe noisily when asleep *—n.*

snor'kel *n.* tube for breathing underwater *—vi.* swim, fish using this

snort *vi.* make (contemptuous) noise by driving breath through nostrils *—n.*

snot *n. vulg.* mucus from nose

snout *n.* animal's nose

snow *n.* frozen vapour which falls in flakes; *sl.* cocaine *—v.* fall, sprinkle as snow; let fall, throw down like snow; cover with snow **—snow'y** *a.* of, like snow; covered with snow; very white **—snow'ball** *n.* snow pressed into hard ball for throwing *—v.* increase, expand rapidly; play, fight with snowballs **—snow'blindness** *n.* temporary blindness due to brightness of snow **—snow'blower** *n.* snow-clearing machine that draws snow in and blows it away **—snow'drift** *n.* bank of deep snow **—snow'drop** *n.* small, white, bell-shaped spring flower **—snow fence** fence erected in winter beside exposed road **—snow goose** white N Amer. goose **—snow line** elevation above which snow does not melt **—snow'man** *n.* figure shaped out of snow **—snow'-mobile** [-bēl] *n.* motor vehicle with caterpillar tracks and front skis **—snow'-plough, snow'plow** *n.* machine with large blade for clearing snow from streets *etc.* **—snow'shoes** *pl.n.* shoes like rackets for travelling on snow **—snow under** cover and block with snow; *fig.* overwhelm

snub *vt.* insult (*esp.* by ignoring) intentionally (**-bb-**) *—n. —a.* short and blunt **—snub-nosed** *a.*

snuff[1] *n.* powdered tobacco for inhaling

through nose —**snuff-dipping** *n.* practice of absorbing nicotine by retaining tobacco in mouth

snuff[2] *v.* extinguish (*esp.* candle *etc.*)

snuf'fle *vi.* breathe noisily, with difficulty

snug *a.* warm, comfortable —**snug'gle** *v.* lie close to, for warmth or affection —**snug'ly** *adv.*

snye *n.* side channel of river

so[1] *adv.* to such an extent; in such a manner; very; the case being such; accordingly —*conj.* therefore; in order that; with the result that —*interj.* well! —**so-called** *a.* called by but doubtfully deserving that name

so[2] *see* SOH

soak *v.* steep; absorb; drench; lie in liquid —*n.* soaking; *sl.* habitual drunkard

soap *n.* compound of alkali and oil used in washing —*vt.* apply soap to —**soap'y** *a.* —**soap opera** radio or television serial of domestic life

soar [sawr] *vi.* fly high; increase, rise (in price *etc.*)

sob *vi.* catch breath, *esp.* in weeping (**-bb-**) —*n.* sobbing —**sob story** tale of personal distress told to arouse sympathy

so'ber *a.* not drunk; temperate; subdued; dull, plain; solemn —*v.* make, become sober —**so'berly** *adv.* —**sobri'ety** *n.* state of being sober

so(u)'briquet [sō'bri-kā] *n.* nickname; assumed name

Soc. Society

socc'er *n.* game of football, with spherical ball

so'ciable *a.* friendly; convivial —**sociabil'ity** *n.* —**so'ciably** *adv.*

so'cial *a.* living in communities; relating to society; sociable —*n.* informal gathering —**so'cialite** *n.* member of fashionable society —**socializa'tion** *n.* —**so'cialize** *v.* —**so'cially** *adv.* —**social security** state provision for the unemployed, aged *etc.* —**social work** work to improve welfare of others

so'cialism *n.* political system which advocates public ownership of means of production, distribution and exchange —**so'cialist** *n./a.* —**socialist'ic** *a.*

soci'ety *n.* living associated with others; those so living; companionship; company; association; club; fashionable people collectively

sociol'ogy *n.* study of societies

sock[1] *n.* cloth covering for foot

sock[2] *sl. vt.* hit —*n.* blow

sock'et *n.* hole or recess for something to fit into

Socrat'ic *a.* of, like Greek philosopher Socrates

sod *n.* lump of earth with grass

so'da *n.* compound of sodium; soda water; fizzy drink —**soda fountain** counter that serves drinks, snacks *etc.*; apparatus dispensing soda water —**soda water** water charged with carbon dioxide

sodd'en *a.* soaked; drunk; heavy and doughy

so'dium *n.* metallic alkaline element —**sodium bicarbonate** white crystalline soluble compound (*also* **bicarbonate of soda**)

sod'omy *n.* anal intercourse —**sod'omite** *n.*

so'fa *n.* upholstered seat with back and arms, for two or more people

soft *a.* yielding easily to pressure, not hard; mild; easy; subdued; quiet, gentle; (too) lenient; oversentimental; feeble-minded; (of water) containing few mineral salts; (of drugs) not liable to cause addiction —**soft'en** [sof'n] *v.* make, become soft or softer; mollify; lighten; mitigate; make less loud —**soft'ly** *adv.* gently, quietly —**soft drink** one that is nonalcoholic —**soft option** easiest alternative —**soft soap** flattery —**soft'ware** *n.* computer programs, tapes *etc.* —**soft'wood** *n.* wood of coniferous tree

sogg'y *a.* soaked with liquid; damp and heavy

soh, so, sol *n.* fifth sol-fa note

soil[1] *n.* earth, ground; country, territory

soil[2] *v.* make, become dirty; tarnish, defile —*n.* dirt; sewage; stain

soir'ee [swahr'ā] *n.* private evening party *esp.* with music

soj'ourn [soj'ərn] *vi.* stay for a time —*n.* short stay —**soj'ourner** *n.*

sol *see* SOH

sol'ace *n./vt.* comfort in distress

so'lar *a.* of the sun —**solar plexus** network of nerves at pit of stomach

sola'rium *n.* room built mainly of glass to give exposure to sun

sold *pt./pp. of* SELL

sol'der *n.* easily-melted alloy used for joining metal —*vt.* join with it —**solder-**

ing iron

sol'dier [sōl'jər] *n.* one serving in army —*vi.* serve in army; (*with* on) persist doggedly —**sol'dierly** *a.* —**sol'diery** *n.* troops

sole[1] *a.* one and only, unique; solitary —**sole'ly** *adv.* alone; only; entirely

sole[2] *n.* underside of foot; underpart of boot *etc.* —*vt.* fit with sole

sole[3] *n.* small edible flatfish

sol'ecism *n.* breach of grammar or etiquette

sol'emn [-əm] *a.* serious; formal; impressive —**solem'nity** *n.* —**solemniza'tion** *n.* —**sol'emnize** *vt.* celebrate, perform; make solemn —**sol'emnly** *adv.*

so'lenoid *n.* coil of wire as part of electrical apparatus

sol-fa *n. Mus.* system of syllables sol, fa *etc.* sung in scale

solic'it [-lis'-] *vt.* request; accost; urge; entice —**solicita'tion** *n.* —**solic'itor** *n.* lawyer who prepares documents, advises clients, but represents them in lower courts only —**solic'itous** *a.* anxious; eager; earnest —**solic'itude** *n.*

sol'id *a.* not hollow; compact; composed of one substance; firm; massive; reliable, sound —*n.* body of three dimensions; substance not liquid or gas —**solidar'ity** [-da'ri-] *n.* unity of interests; united state —**solidifica'tion** *n.* —**solid'ify** *v.* make, become solid or firm; harden (**-ified, -ifying**) —**solid'ity** *n.* —**sol'idly** *adv.*

solil'oquy [-ə-kwi] *n.* (*esp.* in drama) thoughts spoken by person while alone —**solil'oquize** *vi.*

sol'ipsism *n.* doctrine that self is the only thing known to exist —**sol'ipsist** *n.*

sol'itary *a.* alone, single —*n.* hermit —**solitaire'** [*or* sol'-] *n.* game for one person played with pegs set in board; single precious stone set by itself —**sol'itude** *n.* state of being alone; loneliness

so'lo *n.* music for one performer; card game like whist (*pl.* **so'los**) —*a.* not concerted; unaccompanied, alone; piloting aeroplane alone —**so'loist** *n.*

sol'stice [-is] *n.* either shortest (winter) or longest (summer) day of year —**solsti'tial** [-stish'-] *a.*

solve *vt.* work out, explain; find answer to —**solubil'ity** *n.* —**sol'uble** *a.* capable of being dissolved in liquid; able to be solved or explained —**solu'tion** [-lōō'-] *n.* answer to problem; dissolving; liquid with something dissolved in it —**sol'vable** *a.* —**sol'vency** *n.* —**sol'vent** *a.* able to meet financial obligations —*n.* liquid with power of dissolving —**solvent abuse** deliberate inhalation of intoxicating fumes from certain solvents

som'bre *a.* dark, gloomy

sombre'ro [-ā'-] *n.* wide-brimmed hat (*pl.* **-ros**)

some [sum] *a.* denoting an indefinite number, amount or extent; one or other; amount of; certain; approximately —*pron.* portion, quantity —**some'body** *n.* some person; important person —**some'how** *adv.* by some means unknown —**some'place** *adv.* in, at, or to some unspecified place or region —**some'thing** *n.* thing not clearly defined; indefinite amount, quantity or degree —**some'time** *adv.* formerly; at some (past or future) time —*a.* former —**some'times** *adv.* occasionally; now and then —**some'what** *adv.* to some extent, rather —**some'where** *adv.*

som'ersault [sum'-] *n.* tumbling head over heels

somnam'bulist *n.* sleepwalker —**somnam'bulism** *n.* —**somnambulis'tic** *a.*

som'nolent *a.* drowsy; causing sleep —**som'nolence** *n.*

son *n.* male child —**son-in-law** *n.* daughter's husband

so'nar *n.* device like echo sounder

sonat'a [-naht'ə] *n.* piece of music in several movements —**sonati'na** [-tē'-] *n.* short sonata

son et lu'mière [son-ā- lōōm'yār] *Fr.* entertainment staged at night at famous place, building, giving dramatic history of it with lighting and sound effects

song *n.* singing; poem *etc.* for singing —**song'ster** *n.* singer; songbird (**song'stress** *fem.*)

son'ic *a.* pert. to sound waves —**sonic boom** explosive sound caused by aircraft travelling at supersonic speed

sonn'et *n.* fourteen-line poem with definite rhyme scheme —**sonneteer'** *n.* writer of this

sonor'ous *a.* giving out (deep) sound, resonant —**sonor'ously** *adv.* —**sonor'ity** [-o'ri-] *n.*

soon [-oo-] *adv.* in a short time; before long; early, quickly

soot [-oo-] *n.* black powdery substance formed by burning of coal *etc.* —**soot'y** *a.* of, like soot

sooth [-oo-] *n.* truth —**sooth'sayer** *n.* one who foretells future; diviner

soothe [-ooTH] *vt.* make calm, tranquil; relieve (pain *etc.*)

sop *n.* piece of bread *etc.* soaked in liquid; concession, bribe —*vt.* steep in water *etc.*; soak (up) (**-pp-**) —**sopp'ing** *a.* completely soaked —**sopp'y** *a. inf.* oversentimental

soph'ist *n.* fallacious reasoner, quibbler —**soph'ism** *n.* specious argument —**sophis'tical** *a.* —**soph'istry** *n.*

sophist'icate *vi.* make artificial, spoil, falsify, corrupt —*n.* sophisticated person —**sophis'ticated** *a.* having refined or cultured tastes, habits; worldly wise; superficially clever; complex —**sophistica'tion** *n.*

soph'omore *n.* student in second year at college

soporif'ic *a.* causing sleep (*esp.* by drugs)

sopran'o [-rahn'-] *n.* highest voice in women and boys; singer with this voice; musical part for it (*pl.* **-os**)

sor'cerer *n.* magician (**sor'ceress** *fem.*) —**sor'cery** *n.* witchcraft, magic

sor'did *a.* mean, squalid; ignoble, base —**sor'didly** *adv.* —**sor'didness** *n.*

sore *a.* painful; causing annoyance; severe; distressed; annoyed —*adv. obs.* grievously, intensely —*n.* sore place, ulcer, boil *etc.* —**sore'ly** *adv.* grievously; greatly —**sore'ness** *n.* —**sore'head** *n. inf.* peevish or disgruntled person

sor'ghum [-gəm] *n.* kind of grass cultivated for grain

sorr'el *n.* plant; reddish-brown colour; horse of this colour —*a.* of this colour

sorr'ow [-ō] *n.* pain of mind, grief, sadness —*vi.* grieve —**sorr'owful** *a.* —**sor'rowfully** *adv.*

sorr'y *a.* feeling pity or regret; distressed; miserable, wretched; mean, poor —**sorr'ily** *adv.* —**sorr'iness** *n.*

sort *n.* kind or class —*vt.* classify —**sort'er** *n.*

sort'ie *n.* sally by besieged forces

SOS *n.* international code signal of distress; call for help

so-so *a. inf.* mediocre

sot *n.* habitual drunkard

sott'o vo'ce [-chi] *It.* in an undertone

sou'fflé [soo'flā] *n.* dish of eggs beaten to froth, flavoured and baked

sough [sow] *n.* low murmuring sound as of wind in trees

sought [sawt] *pt./pp. of* SEEK

soul [sōl] *n.* spiritual and immortal part of human being; example, pattern; person; (*also* **soul music**) type of Black music combining urban blues with jazz, pop *etc.* —**soul'ful** *a.* full of emotion or sentiment —**soul'less** *a.* mechanical; lacking sensitivity or nobility; heartless, cruel

sound[1] *n.* what is heard; noise —*vi.* make sound; seem; give impression of —*vt.* cause to sound; utter —**sound barrier** *inf.* hypothetical barrier to flight at speed of sound waves —**sound track** recorded sound accompaniment of motion picture *etc.*

sound[2] *a.* in good condition; solid; of good judgment; legal; solvent; thorough; effective; watertight; deep —**sound'ly** *adv.* thoroughly

sound[3] *vt.* find depth of, as water; ascertain views of; probe —**sound'ings** *pl.n.* measurements taken by sounding

sound[4] *n.* channel; strait

soup [soop] *n.* liquid food made by boiling meat, vegetables *etc.* —**soup'y** *a.* like soup; murky; sentimental

sour *a.* acid; gone bad; rancid; peevish; disagreeable —*v.* make, become sour —**sour'ly** *adv.* —**sour'ness** *n.* —**sour'puss** *n.* sullen, sour-faced person

source [-aw-] *n.* origin, starting point; spring

souse *v.* plunge, drench; pickle —*n.* sousing; brine for pickling

soutane' [soo-tan'] *n.* priest's cassock

south *n.* cardinal point opposite north; region, part of country *etc.* lying to that side —*a./adv.* (that is) towards south —**south'erly** [suTH'-] *a.* towards south —*n.* wind from the south —**south'ern** [suTH'-] *a.* in south —**south'wards** *a./adv.* —**South'down** *n.* breed of sheep

souvenir' [soo-və-nēr'] *n.* keepsake, memento

sou'west'er [sow-] *n.* waterproof hat

sov'ereign [sov'rin] *n.* king, queen; former Brit. gold coin worth 20 shillings

—*a.* supreme; efficacious —**sov'ereignty** *n.* supreme power and right to exercise it; dominion; independent state

so'viet *n.* elected council at various levels of government in USSR; citizen of USSR —*a.* of, pert. to USSR, its people, government —**so'vietism** *n.*

sow[1] [sō] *vi.* scatter, plant seed —*vt.* scatter, deposit (seed); spread abroad (**sowed** *pt.*, **sown** *or* **sowed** *pp.*, **sow'ing** *pr.p.*) —**sow'er** *n.*

sow[2] *n.* female adult pig

soy'bean *n.* edible bean used as meat substitute, in making **soy(a) sauce** *etc.*

sozz'led [-əld] *a. sl.* drunk

spa [spah] *n.* medicinal spring; place, resort with one

space *n.* extent; room; period; empty place; area; expanse; region beyond earth's atmosphere —*vt.* place at intervals —**spa'cious** *a.* roomy, extensive —**space'craft, space'ship** *n.* vehicle for travel beyond earth's atmosphere —**Space Invaders R** game played on video screen in amusement arcades *etc.* involving destroying aliens from outer space —**space'man** *n.* —**space shuttle** vehicle for repeated space flights —**space'suit** *n.* sealed, pressurized suit worn by astronaut

spade[1] *n.* tool for digging —**spade work** arduous preparatory work

spade[2] *n.* leaf-shaped black symbol on playing card

spaghett'i [-get'-] *n.* pasta in form of long strings

spake *obs. pt. of* SPEAK

span *n.* space from thumb to little finger as measure; extent, space; stretch of arch *etc.*; *abbrev. of* **wingspan**, distance from wingtip to wingtip —*vt.* stretch over; measure with hand (**-nn-**)

span'gle [-ng'gl] *n.* small shiny metallic ornament —*vt.* decorate with spangles

span'iel *n.* breed of dog with long ears and silky hair

spank *vt.* slap with flat of hand, *esp.* on buttocks —*n.* —**spank'ing** *n.* series of spanks —*a.* quick, lively; large, fine

spann'er *n.* tool for gripping nut or bolt head

spar[1] *n.* pole, beam, *esp.* as part of ship's rigging

spar[2] *vi.* box; dispute, *esp.* in fun (**-rr-**) —*n.* sparring

spar[3] *n.* kinds of crystalline mineral

spare [-ār] *vt.* leave unhurt; show mercy; abstain from using; do without; give away —*a.* additional; in reserve; thin; lean; scanty —*n.* spare part (for machine) —**spa'ring** *a.* economical, careful

spark *n.* small glowing or burning particle; flash of light produced by electrical discharge; vivacity, humour; trace; in internal-combustion engines, electric spark (in spark plug) which ignites explosive mixture in cylinder —*v.* emit sparks; kindle, excite

spar'kle *vi.* glitter; effervesce; scintillate —*n.* small spark; glitter; flash; lustre —**spar'kling** *a.* flashing; glittering; brilliant; lively; (of wines) effervescent

sparr'ow [-ō] *n.* small brownish bird —**sparr'owhawk** *n.* hawk that hunts small birds

sparse *a.* thinly scattered

spar'tan *a.* hardy; austere; frugal

spasm [-zm] *n.* sudden convulsive (muscular) contraction; sudden burst of activity *etc.* —**spasmod'ic** *a.* occurring in spasms

spas'tic *a.* affected by spasms, suffering cerebral palsy —*n.*

spat[1] *pt. of* SPIT[1]

spat[2] *n.* short gaiter

spat[3] *n.* slight quarrel

spate *n.* rush, outpouring; flood

spathe *n.* large sheathlike leaf enclosing flower cluster

spa'tial *a.* of, in space

spatt'er *vt.* splash, cast drops over —*vi.* be scattered in drops —*n.* slight splash; sprinkling

spat'ula *n.* utensil with broad, flat blade for various purposes

spav'in *n.* injury to, growth on horse's leg —**spav'ined** *a.* lame, decrepit

spawn *n.* eggs of fish or frog; *oft. offens.* offspring —*vi.* (of fish or frog) cast eggs

spay *vt.* remove ovaries from (animal)

speak *vi.* utter words; converse; deliver discourse —*vt.* utter; pronounce; express; communicate in (**spoke, spo'ken, speak'ing**) —**speak'able** *a.* —**speak'er** *n.* one who speaks; one who specializes in speech making; (*oft.* **S-**) official chairman of many legislative bodies; loudspeaker

spear *n.* long pointed weapon; slender shoot, as of asparagus —*vt.* transfix, pierce, wound with spear —**spear'head** *n.* leading force in attack, campaign —*vt.*

spear'mint *n.* type of mint

spec'ial [spesh'əl] *a.* beyond the usual; particular, individual; distinct; limited —**spe'cialism** *n.* —**spec'ialist** *n.* one who devotes himself to special subject or branch of subject —**special'ity, spe'cialty** *n.* special product, skill, characteristic *etc.* —**specializa'tion** *n.* —**spe'cialize** *vi.* be specialist —*vt.* make special —**spec'ially** *adv.*

spe'cie [spē'shē] *n.* coined, as distinct from paper, money

spe'cies [-shēz] *n.* sort, kind, *esp.* animals *etc.*; class; subdivision (*pl.* **spe'cies**)

specif'ic *a.* definite; exact in detail; characteristic of a thing or kind —**specif'ically** *adv.* —**spec'ify** *vt.* state definitely or in detail (**-ified, -ifying**) —**specifica'tion** *n.* detailed description of something to be made, done —**specific gravity** ratio of density of substance to that of water

spec'imen [-es'-] *n.* part typifying whole; individual example

spe'cious *a.* deceptively plausible, but false —**spe'ciously** *adv.* —**spe'ciousness** *n.*

speck *n.* small spot, particle —*vt.* spot —**spec'kle** *n./vt.* speck

spec'tacle *n.* show; thing exhibited; ridiculous sight —*pl.* pair of lenses for correcting defective sight —**spectac'ular** *a.* impressive; showy; grand; magnificent —*n.* lavishly produced performance —**spectate'** *vi.* —**specta'tor** *n.* one who looks on

spec'tre *n.* ghost; image of something unpleasant —**spect'ral** *a.* ghostly

spec'trum *n.* band of colours into which beam of light can be decomposed *eg* by prism (*pl.* **spec'tra**) —**spec'troscope** *n.* instrument for producing, examining spectra

spec'ulate *vi.* guess, conjecture; engage in (risky) commercial transactions —**specula'tion** *n.* —**spec'ulative** *a.* given to, characterized by speculation —**spec'ulator** *n.*

spec'ulum *n.* mirror; reflector of polished metal, *esp.* in reflecting telescopes (*pl.* **-la, -lums**) —**spec'ular** *a.*

speech *n.* act, faculty of speaking; words, language; conversation; discourse; (formal) talk given before audience —**speech'ify** *vi.* make speech, *esp.* long and tedious one (**-ified, -ifying**) —**speech'less** *a.* dumb; at a loss for words

speed *n.* swiftness; rate of progress; degree of sensitivity of photographic film; *sl.* amphetamine —*vi.* move quickly; drive vehicle at high speed; *obs.* succeed —*vt.* further; expedite (**sped** *or* **speed'ed** *pt./pp.*) —**speed'ing** *n.* driving (vehicle) at high speed, *esp.* over legal limit —**speed'ily** *adv.* —**speed'y** *a.* quick; rapid; nimble; prompt —**speed'boat** *n.* light fast motorboat —**speedom'eter** *n.* instrument to show speed of vehicle —**speed'way** *n.* racetrack for automobiles; road for fast driving —**speed'well** *n.* plant with small *usu.* blue flowers

speleol'ogy [spē-li-] *n.* study, exploring of caves —**speleolog'ical** *a.*

spell[1] *vt.* give letters of in order; read letter by letter; indicate, result in (**spelled** *or* **spelt** *pt./pp.*, **spell'ing** *pr.p.*) —**spell'ing** *n.* —**spell out** make explicit

spell[2] *n.* magic formula; enchantment —**spell'bound** *a.* enchanted; entranced

spell[3] *n.* (short) period of time, work

spen'cer *obs. n.* overcoat; woman's undervest

spend *vt.* pay out; pass (time) on activity *etc.*; use up completely (**spent** *pt./pp.*, **spend'ing** *pr.p.*) —**spend'er** *n.* —**spend'thrift** *n.* wasteful person

sperm *n.* male reproductive cell; semen —**spermat'ic** *a.* of sperm —**sper'micide** *n.* drug *etc.* that kills sperm

spermacet'i [-set'-] *n.* white, waxy substance obtained from oil from head of sperm whale —**sperm whale** large, toothed whale

spew *v.* vomit

sphag'num [sfag'-] *n.* moss that grows in bogs

sphere [sfēr] *n.* ball, globe; range; field of action; status; position; province —**spher'ical** [sfe'ri-] *a.*

sphinc'ter *n.* ring of muscle surrounding opening of hollow bodily organ

sphinx *n.* statue in Egypt with lion's body and human head; (**S-**) monster, half woman, half lion; enigmatic person (*pl.* **-es, sphin'ges** [-jēz])

spice *n.* aromatic or pungent vegetable substance; spices collectively; anything that adds flavour, relish, piquancy, interest *etc.* —*vt.* season with spices, flavour —**spi'cily** *adv.* —**spi'cy** *a.* flavoured with spices; *inf.* slightly indecent, risqué

spick-and-span *a.* neat, smart, new-looking

spi'der *n.* small eight-legged creature which spins web to catch prey —**spi'dery** *a.* —**spider plant** hardy house plant with long thin leaves

spiel [shpēl] *inf. n.* glib (sales) talk —*vi.* deliver spiel, recite —**spiel'er** *n.*

spig'ot *n.* peg or plug

spike *n.* sharp point; sharp pointed object; long flower cluster with flowers attached directly to the stalk —*vt.* pierce, fasten with spike; render ineffective; add alcohol to (drink) —**spi'ky** *a.*

spill[1] *v.* (cause to) pour from, flow over, fall out, *esp.* unintentionally; upset; be lost or wasted (**spilt** *or* **spilled** *pt./pp.*) —*n.* fall; amount spilt —**spill'age** *n.*

spill[2] *n.* thin strip of wood, twisted paper *etc.* for lighting fires *etc.*

spin *v.* (cause to) revolve rapidly; whirl; twist into thread; prolong; *inf.* tell (a story); fish with lure (**spun,** *obs.* **span** *pt.*, **spun** *pp.*, **spinn'ing** *pr.p.*) —*n.* spinning; (of aircraft) descent in dive with continued rotation; rapid run or ride —**spinn'ing** *n.* act, process of drawing out and twisting into threads, as wool, cotton, flax *etc.* —**spinning wheel** household machine with large wheel turned by treadle for spinning wool *etc.* into thread —**spin dry** spin clothes in (washing) machine to remove excess water —**spin-dryer** *n.*

spin'ach [-ij, -ich] *n.* garden vegetable

spin'dle *n.* rod, axis for spinning —**spin'dly** *a.* long and slender; attenuated

spin'drift *n.* spray blown along surface of sea

spine *n.* backbone; thin spike, *esp.* on fish *etc.*; ridge; back of book —**spi'nal** *a.* —**spine'less** *a.* lacking spine; cowardly

spin'et [*or* -et'] *n.* keyboard instrument like harpsichord

spinn'aker *n.* large yacht sail

spinn'ey *n.* small wood

spin'ster *n.* unmarried woman

spirae'a [-rēə] *n.* shrub, plant with small white or pink flower sprays

spi'ral *n.* continuous curve drawn at ever increasing distance from fixed point; anything resembling this —*a.* —**spi'rally** *adv.*

spire *n.* pointed part of steeple; pointed stem

spir'it *n.* life principle animating body; disposition; liveliness; courage; frame of mind; essential character or meaning; soul; ghost; liquid got by distillation, alcohol —*pl.* emotional state; strong alcoholic drink *eg* whisky —*vt.* carry away mysteriously —**spir'ited** *a.* lively —**spir'itless** *a.* listless, apathetic —**spir'itual** *a.* given to, interested in things of the spirit —*n.* Negro sacred song, hymn —**spir'itualism** *n.* belief that spirits of the dead communicate with the living —**spir'itualist** *n.* —**spiritual'ity** *n.* —**spir'itually** *adv.* —**spir'ituous** *a.* alcoholic —**spirit level** glass tube containing bubble in liquid, used to check horizontal, vertical surfaces

spirt *n. see* SPURT

spit[1] *vi.* eject saliva —*vt.* eject from mouth (**spat, spit** *pt./pp.*, **spitt'ing** *pr.p.*) —*n.* spitting, saliva —**spit'tle** *n.* saliva —**spittoon'** *n.* vessel to spit into —**spit'fire** *n.* person with fiery temper

spit[2] *n.* sharp rod to put through meat for roasting; sandy point projecting into the sea —*vt.* thrust through (**-tt-**)

spite *n.* malice —*vt.* thwart spitefully —**spite'ful** *a.* —**spite'fully** *adv.* —**in spite of** *prep.* regardless of; notwithstanding

spiv *n.* smartly dressed man, *esp.* one who makes living by shady dealings

splake *n.* hybrid trout

splash *v.* scatter liquid about or on, over something; print, display prominently —*n.* sound of this; patch, *esp.* of colour; (effect of) extravagant display; small amount

splat *n.* wet, slapping sound

splatt'er *v./n.* spatter

splay *a.* spread out; slanting; turned outwards —*vt.* spread out; twist outwards —*n.* slant surface; spread —**splay'-footed** *a.* flat and broad (of foot)

spleen *n.* organ in the abdomen; anger; irritable or morose temper —**splenet'ic** *a.*

splen'did *a.* magnificent, brilliant, excellent —**splen'didly** *adv.* —**splen'do(u)r** *n.*

splice *vt.* join by interweaving strands; join (wood) by overlapping; *sl.* join in marriage —*n.* spliced joint

spline *n.* narrow groove, ridge, strip, *esp.* joining wood *etc.*

splint *n.* rigid support for broken limb *etc.*

splint'er *n.* thin fragment —*vi.* break into fragments, shiver —**splinter group** group that separates from main party, organization, *oft.* after disagreement

split *v.* break asunder; separate; divide (**split, splitt'ing**) —*n.* crack, fissure; dessert of fruit and ice cream

splotch, splodge *n./v.* splash, daub —**splotch'y, splodg'y** *a.*

splurge *v.* spend money extravagantly —*n.*

splutt'er *v.* make hissing, spitting sounds; utter incoherently with spitting sounds —*n.*

spoil *vt.* damage, injure; damage manners or behaviour of (*esp.* child) by indulgence; pillage —*vi.* go bad (**spoiled** *or* **spoilt** *pt./pp.*, **spoil'ing** *pr.p.*) —*n.* booty; waste material, *esp.* in mining (*also* **spoil'age**) —**spoil'er** *n.* slowing device on aircraft wing *etc.* —**spoiling for** eager for

spoke[1] *pt.*, **spo'ken** *pp. of* SPEAK —**spokes'man** *n.* one deputed to speak for others

spoke[2] *n.* radial bar of a wheel —**spoke'shave** *n.* tool for shaping wood

spolia'tion [spō-] *n.* act of spoiling; robbery; destruction —**spo'liate** *v.* despoil, plunder, pillage

spon'dee *n.* metrical foot consisting of two long syllables

sponge [-unj] *n.* marine animal; its skeleton, or a synthetic substance like it, used to absorb liquids; type of light cake —*vt.* wipe with sponge —*v.* live meanly at expense of others; cadge —**spong'er** *n. sl.* one who cadges, or lives at expense of others —**spong'y** *a.* spongelike; wet and soft

spon'sor *n.* one promoting, advertising something, *esp.* commercial organization that pays all or part of cost of putting on concert, sporting event *etc.*; one who agrees to give money to a charity on completion of specified activity by another; business that pays costs of radio or television program in return for advertising time; one taking responsibility (*esp.* for welfare of child at baptism, *ie* godparent); guarantor —*vt.* act as sponsor —**spon'sorship** *n.*

sponta'neous *a.* voluntary; natural; not forced; produced without external force —**spontane'ity** [*or* -ā'-] *n.* —**sponta'neously** *adv.* —**sponta'neousness** *n.*

spoof [-ōō-] *n.* mild satirical mockery; trick, hoax

spook [-ōō-] *n.* ghost —**spook'y** *a.*

spool [-ōō-] *n.* reel, bobbin

spoon [-ōō-] *n.* implement with shallow bowl at end of handle for carrying food to mouth *etc.* —*vt.* lift with spoon —**spoon'ful** *n.*

spoon'erism [-ōō-] *n.* amusing transposition of initial consonants, *eg* "half-warmed fish" for "half-formed wish"

spoor *n.* trail of wild animals —*v.* follow spoor

sporad'ic *a.* intermittent; scattered, single —**sporad'ically** *adv.*

spore *n.* minute reproductive organism of some plants and protozoans

sporr'an *n.* pouch worn in front of kilt

sport *n.* game, activity for pleasure, competition, exercise; enjoyment; mockery; cheerful person, good loser —*vt.* wear (*esp.* ostentatiously) —*vi.* frolic; play (sport) —**sport'ing** *a.* of sport; behaving with fairness, generosity —**spor'tive** *a.* playful —**sports car** fast (open) car —**sports'man** *n.* one who engages in sport; good loser

spot *n.* small mark, stain; blemish; pimple; place; (difficult) situation; *inf.* small quantity —*vt.* mark with spots; detect; observe (**-tt-**) —**spot'less** *a.* unblemished; pure —**spot'lessly** *adv.* —**spot'ty** *a.* with spots; uneven —**spot check** random examination —**spot'light** *n.* powerful light illuminating small area; centre of attention

spouse *n.* husband or wife —**spou'sal** *n.* marriage

spout *v.* pour out; *sl.* speechify —*n.* projecting tube or lip for pouring liquids; copious discharge

sprain *n./vt.* wrench or twist (of muscle *etc.*)

sprang *pt. of* SPRING
sprat *n.* small sea fish
sprawl *vi.* lie or sit about awkwardly; spread in rambling, unplanned way *—n.* sprawling
spray[1] *n.* (device for producing) fine drops of liquid *—vt.* sprinkle with shower of fine drops
spray[2] *n.* branch, twig with buds, flowers *etc.*; floral ornament, brooch *etc.* like this
spread [-ed] *v.* extend; stretch out; open out; scatter; distribute; unfold; cover (**spread, spread'ing**) *—n.* extent; increase; ample meal; food which can be spread on bread *etc.* **—spread-eagle(d)** *a.* with arms and legs outstretched
spree *n.* session of overindulgence; romp
sprig *n.* small twig; ornamental design like this; small nail
spright'ly [-rīt'-] *a.* lively, brisk **—spright'liness** *n.*
spring *vi.* leap; shoot up or forth; come into being; appear; grow; become bent or split *—vt.* produce unexpectedly; set off (trap) (**sprang, sprung, spring'ing**) *—n.* leap; recoil; piece of coiled or bent metal with much resilience; flow of water from earth; first season of year **—spring'y** *a.* elastic **—spring'board** *n.* flexible board for diving **—spring tide** high tide at new or full moon
spring'bok *n.* S Afr. antelope
sprin'kle [-ng'kl] *vt.* scatter small drops on, strew **—sprin'kler** *n.* **—sprin'kling** *n.* small quantity or number
sprint *vt.* run short distance at great speed *—n.* such run, race **—sprint'er** *n.* one who sprints
sprit *n.* small spar set diagonally across a fore-and-aft sail in order to extend it **—sprit'sail** *n.* sail extended by a sprit
sprite *n.* fairy, elf
sprock'et *n.* projection on wheel or capstan for engaging chain; wheel with these
sprout *vi.* put forth shoots, spring up *—n.* shoot **—Brussels sprout** kind of miniature cabbage
spruce[1] *n.* variety of fir
spruce[2] *a.* neat in dress
sprung *pp. of* SPRING
spry *a.* nimble, vigorous
spud *n. inf.* potato
spume *n./vi.* foam, froth
spun *pt./pp. of* SPIN
spunk *n.* courage, spirit
spur *n.* pricking instrument attached to horseman's heel; incitement; stimulus; projection on cock's leg; projecting mountain range; branch (road *etc.*) *—vt.* ride hard (**-rr-**)
spurge *n.* plant with milky sap
spur'ious [spyoor'-] *a.* not genuine
spurn *vt.* reject with scorn, thrust aside
spurt, spirt *v.* send, come out in jet; rush suddenly *—n.* jet; short sudden effort, *esp.* in race
sput'nik [-oo-] *n.* one of series of Russian satellites
sputt'er *v.* splutter
spu'tum *n.* spittle (*pl.* **-ta**)
spy *n.* one who watches (*esp.* in rival countries, companies *etc.*) and reports secretly *—vi.* act as spy *—vt.* catch sight of (**spied, spy'ing**) **—spy'glass** *n.* small telescope
Sq. Square
squab'ble [-ob'-] *vi.* engage in petty, noisy quarrel, bicker *—n.*
squad [-od] *n.* small party, *esp.* of soldiers; *Sports* team or part of team **—squad'ron** *n.* division of cavalry regiment, fleet or air force
squal'id [-ol'-] *a.* mean and dirty **—squal'or** *n.*
squall [-awl] *n.* harsh cry; sudden gust of wind; short storm *—vi.* yell
squan'der [-on'-] *vt.* spend wastefully, dissipate
square [-âr] *n.* equilateral rectangle; area of this shape; in town, open space (of this shape); product of a number multiplied by itself; instrument for drawing right angles *—a.* square in form; honest; straight, even; level, equal; denoting a measure of area; *inf.* old-fashioned, conservative *—vt.* make square; find square of; pay; bribe *—vi.* fit, suit **—square'ly** *adv.* **—square dance** any of various formation dances in which couples form squares **—square metre** *etc.* area equal to that of square with sides one metre *etc.* long **—square root** number that, multiplied by itself, gives number of which it is factor
squash [-osh] *vt.* crush flat; pulp; suppress; humiliate (person) *—n.* crowd; game played with rackets and soft balls in walled court; marrowlike plant

squat [-ot] *vi.* sit on heels; act as squatter (**-tt-**) —*a.* short and thick —**squatt'er** *n.* one who settles on land or occupies house without permission

squaw *n.* Amer. Indian woman

squawk *n.* short harsh cry, *esp.* of bird —*v.* utter this

squeak *v./n.* (make) short shrill sound

squeal *n.* long piercing squeak —*vi.* make one; *sl.* confess information (about another)

squeam'ish *a.* easily made sick; easily shocked; overscrupulous

squee'gee [-jē] *n.* tool with rubber blade for clearing water (from glass *etc.*), spreading wet paper *etc.* —*vt.* press, smooth with a squeegee

squeeze *vt.* press; wring; force; hug; subject to extortion —*n.* act of squeezing; period of hardship, difficulty caused by financial weakness

squelch *vi.* make, walk with wet sucking sound, as in walking through mud —*n.*

squib *n.* small (faulty) firework

squid *n.* type of cuttlefish

squig'gle *n.* wavy, wriggling mark —*vi.* wriggle; draw squiggle

squint *vi.* have the eyes turned in different directions; glance sideways —*n.* this eye disorder; glance

squire *n.* country gentleman

squirm *vi.* wriggle; be embarrassed —*n.*

squirr'el *n.* small graceful bushy-tailed tree animal

squirt *v.* (of liquid) force, be forced through narrow opening —*n.* jet; *inf.* short or insignificant person

squish *v./n.* (make) soft splashing sound

Sr *Chem.* strontium

Sr. Senior; Sister

SS steamship

St. Saint; Strait; Street

st. stone (weight)

stab *v.* pierce, strike (at) with pointed weapon (**-bb-**) —*n.* blow, wound so inflicted; sudden sensation, *eg* of fear; attempt

sta'bilize *vt.* make steady, restore to equilibrium, *esp.* of money values, prices and wages —**stabiliza'tion** *n.* —**sta'bilizer** *n.* device to maintain equilibrium of ship, aircraft *etc.*

sta'ble[1] *n.* building for horses; racehorses of particular owner, establishment; such establishment —*vt.* put into stable

sta'ble[2] *a.* firmly fixed; steadfast, resolute —**stabil'ity** *n.* steadiness; ability to resist change of any kind —**sta'bly** *adv.*

staccat'o [-kaht'-] *a. Mus.* with notes sharply separated; abrupt

stack *n.* ordered pile, heap; chimney —*vt.* pile in stack; control aircraft waiting to land so that they fly at different altitudes

sta'dium *n.* open-air arena for athletics *etc.* (*pl.* **-s, -ia**)

staff [-ah-] *n.* body of officers or workers; personnel; pole; five lines on which music is written (*pl.* **staffs, staves**) —*vt.* employ personnel; supply with personnel

stag *n.* male deer —*a.* for men only, as in **stag party**

stage *n.* period, division of development; raised floor or platform; (platform of) theatre; scene of action; stopping-place on road, distance between two of them; separate unit of space rocket, that can be jettisoned —*vt.* put (play) on stage; arrange, bring about —**sta'gy** *a.* theatrical —**stage whisper** loud whisper intended to be heard by audience

stagg'er *vi.* walk unsteadily —*vt.* astound; arrange in overlapping or alternating positions, times; distribute over a period —*n.* act of staggering —*pl.* form of vertigo; disease of horses —**stagg'ering** *a.* astounding

stag'nate [*or* -nāt'] *vi.* cease to flow or develop —**stag'nant** *a.* sluggish; not flowing; foul, impure —**stagna'tion** *n.*

staid *a.* of sober and quiet character, sedate —**staid'ly** *adv.* —**staid'ness** *n.*

stain *v.* spot, mark; apply liquid colouring to (wood *etc.*); bring disgrace upon —*n.* —**stain'less** *a.* —**stainless steel** rustless steel alloy

stairs *pl.n.* set of steps, *esp.* as part of house —**stair'case, stair'way** *n.* structure enclosing stairs; stairs

stake *n.* sharpened stick or post; money wagered or contended for —*vt.* secure, mark out with stakes; wager, risk

stal'actite *n.* lime deposit like icicle on roof of cave

stal'agmite *n.* lime deposit like pillar on floor of cave

stale *a.* old, lacking freshness; hackneyed; lacking energy, interest through monotony —**stale'mate** *n. Chess* draw through one player being unable to move; deadlock, impasse

stalk[1] [-awk] *n.* plant's stem; anything like this

stalk[2] [-awk] *v.* follow, approach stealthily; walk in stiff and stately manner —*n.* stalking —**stalking-horse** *n.* pretext

stall [-awl] *n.* compartment in stable *etc.*; erection for display and sale of goods; seat in chancel of church; **UK** front seat in theatre *etc.*; finger sheath —*v.* put in stall; stick fast; (motor engine) unintentionally stop; (aircraft) lose flying speed; delay; hinder; prevaricate

stall'ion *n.* uncastrated male horse, *esp.* for breeding

stal'wart [-awl'-] *a.* strong, brave; staunch —*n.* stalwart person

sta'men *n.* male organ of a flowering plant

stam'ina *n.* power of endurance, vitality

stamm'er *v.* speak, say with repetition of syllables, stutter —*n.* habit of so speaking —**stamm'erer** *n.*

stamp *vi.* put down foot with force —*vt.* impress mark on; affix postage stamp; fix in memory; reveal, characterize —*n.* stamping with foot; imprinted mark; appliance for marking; piece of gummed paper printed with device as evidence of postage *etc.*; character

stampede' *n.* sudden frightened rush, *esp.* of herd of cattle, crowd; rodeo —*v.* cause, take part in stampede

stance *n.* manner, position of standing; attitude; point of view

stanch [-ah-] *see* STAUNCH

stan'chion [stahn'shən] *n.* upright bar, support —*vt.* support

stand *v.* have, take, set in upright position; remain; be situated; remain firm or stationary; cease to move; endure; adhere to principles; offer oneself as a candidate; be symbol *etc.* of —*vt. inf.* provide free, treat to (**stood, stand'ing**) —*n.* holding firm; position; halt; something on which thing may be placed; structure from which spectators watch sport *etc.*; stop made by pop group *etc.* —**stand'ing** *n.* reputation, status; duration —*a.* erect; permanent, lasting; stagnant; performed from stationary position (as **standing jump**) —**stand in** deputize (for) (**stand-in** *n.*) —**stand over** watch closely; postpone

stand'ard *n.* accepted example of something against which others are judged; degree, quality; flag; weight or measure to which others must conform; post —*a.* usual, regular; average; of recognized authority, competence; accepted as correct —**standardiza'tion** *n.* —**stan'dardize** *vt.* regulate by a standard

stand'pipe *n.* vertical pipe up which water rises, providing supply *eg* outside a building

stand'point *n.* point of view, opinion; mental attitude

stank *pt. of* STINK

stann'ous *a.* of, containing tin

stan'za *n.* group of lines of verse (*pl.* **-zas**)

sta'ple *n.* U-shaped piece of metal with pointed ends to drive into wood for use as ring; paper fastener; main product; fibre; pile of wool *etc.* —*a.* principal; regularly produced or made for market —*vt.* fasten with staple; sort, classify (wool *etc.*) according to length of fibre —**sta'pler** *n.* small device for fastening papers together

star *n.* celestial body, seen as twinkling point of light; asterisk (*); celebrated player, actor ; medal, jewel *etc.* of apparent shape of star —*vt.* adorn with stars; mark (with asterisk); feature as star performer —*vi.* play leading role in movie *etc.* (**-rr-**) —*a.* leading, most important, famous —**starr'y** *a.* covered with stars —**star'dom** *n.* —**star'fish** *n.* small star-shaped sea creature —**Star Wars** U.S. proposed system of artificial satellites armed with lasers to destroy enemy missiles in space (*also* **SDI**)

star'board *n.* right-hand side of ship, looking forward —*a.* of, on this side

starch *n.* substance forming the main food element in bread, potatoes *etc.*, and used mixed with water, for stiffening linen *etc.* —*vt.* stiffen thus —**starch'y** *a.* containing starch; stiff; formal; prim

stare *vi.* look fixedly at; gaze with wide-open eyes; be obvious or visible to —*n.* staring, fixed gaze —**stare out** abash by staring at

stark *a.* blunt, bare; desolate; absolute *—adv.* completely

star'ling *n.* glossy black speckled songbird

start *vt.* begin; set going *—vi.* begin, *esp.* journey; make sudden movement *—n.* beginning; abrupt movement; advantage of a lead in a race **—start'er** *n.* electric motor starting automobile engine; competitor in, supervisor of, start of race

star'tle *vt.* give a fright to

starve *v.* (cause to) suffer or die from hunger **—starva'tion** *n.*

stash *sl. vt.* put away, hide *—n.* secret store or place where this is hidden

state *n.* condition; place, situation; politically organized people; government; rank; pomp *—vt.* express in words **—sta'ted** *a.* fixed; regular; settled **—state'ly** *a.* dignified, lofty **—state'ment** *n.* expression in words; account **—state'room** *n.* private cabin on ship; large room in palace, mansion, used for ceremonial occasions **—states'man** *n.* respected political leader **—states'manship** *n.* his art

stat'ic *a.* motionless, inactive; pert. to bodies at rest, or in equilibrium *—n.* electrical interference in radio reception *—pl.* branch of physics **—stat'ically** *adv.*

sta'tion *n.* place where thing stops or is placed; stopping place for railway trains; local office for police force, fire brigade *etc.*; place equipped for radio or television transmission; bus garage; post, employment; status; position in life *—vt.* put in position **—sta'tionary** *a.* not moving, fixed; not changing **—station wagon** automobile with rear door and baggage space behind rear seats

sta'tioner *n.* dealer in writing materials *etc.* **—sta'tionery** *n.*

statist'ics *pl.n.* (*with sing. v.*) numerical facts collected systematically and arranged; the study of them **—statis'tical** *a.* **—statist'ically** adv. **—statisti'cian** [-tish'-] *n.* one who compiles and studies statistics

stat'ue *n.* solid carved or cast image of person, animal *etc.* **—stat'uary** *n.* statues collectively **—statuesque'** [-esk'] *a.* like statue; dignified **—statuette'** *n.* small statue

stat'ure *n.* bodily height; greatness

sta'tus *n.* position, rank; prestige; relation to others **—status quo** existing state of affairs

stat'ute *n.* written law **—stat'utory** *a.* enacted, defined or authorized by statute

staunch [-aw-] *vt.* stop flow (of blood) from *—a.* trustworthy, loyal

stave *n.* one of the pieces forming barrel; verse, stanza; *Mus.* staff *—vt.* break hole in; ward (off) (**stove, staved** *pt./pp.*, **sta'ving** *pr.p.*)

stay[1] *vi.* remain; sojourn; pause; wait; endure *—vt.* stop; hinder; postpone (**stayed, stay'ing**) *—n.* remaining, sojourning; check; restraint; deterrent; postponement

stay[2] *n.* support, prop, rope supporting mast *etc.* *—pl.* formerly, laced corsets

stead [-ed] *n.* place **—in stead** in place (of) **—in good stead** of service

stead'y *a.* firm; regular; temperate; industrious; reliable *—vt.* make steady **—stead'ily** *adv.* **—stead'iness** *n.* **—stead'fast** *a.* firm, fixed, unyielding **—stead'fastly** *adv.* **—steady (on)** be careful!

steak [stāk] *n.* thick slice of meat, *esp.* beef; slice of fish

steal [-ēl] *vi.* rob; move silently *—vt.* take without right or leave (**stole, sto'len, steal'ing**) *—n. inf.* act of stealing; something stolen or acquired easily or at little cost

stealth [stelth] *n.* secret or underhand procedure, behaviour **—stealth'ily** *adv.* **—stealth'y** *a.*

steam *n.* vapour of boiling water; *inf.* power, energy *—vi.* give off steam; rise in vapour; move by steam power *—vt.* cook or treat with steam **—steam'er** *n.* steam-propelled ship; vessel for cooking or treating with steam **—steam-engine** *n.* engine worked or propelled by steam **—steam'roller** *n.* large roller, *orig.* moved by steam, for levelling road surfaces *etc.*; any great power used to crush opposition *—vt.* crush

steed *n. Poet.* horse

steel *n.* hard and malleable metal made by mixing carbon in iron; tool, weapon of steel; railway track, line *—vt.* harden **—steel'y** *a.*

steel'yard *n.* kind of balance with unequal arms

steep[1] *a.* rising, sloping abruptly; precipitous; *inf.* difficult; (of prices) very high or exorbitant; *inf.* unreasonable —**steep'en** *v.* —**steep'ly** *adv.*

steep[2] *v.* soak, saturate —*n.* act or process of steeping; the liquid used

stee'ple *n.* church tower with spire —**stee'plechase** *n.* horse race with ditches and fences to jump; foot race with hurdles *etc.* to jump —**stee'plejack** *n.* one who builds, repairs chimneys, steeples *etc.*

steer[1] *vt.* guide, direct course of vessel, motor vehicle *etc.* —*vi.* direct one's course —**steer'age** *n.* effect of a helm; formerly, cheapest accommodation on ship —**steering gear, wheel** *etc.* mechanism for steering

steer[2] *n.* castrated male ox

stein [stīn] *n.* earthenware beer mug

ste'le *n.* ancient carved stone pillar or slab

stell'ar *a.* of stars

stem[1] *n.* stalk, trunk; long slender part, as in tobacco pipe; part of word to which inflections are added; foremost part of ship

stem[2] *vt.* check, stop, dam up (**-mm-**)

stench *n.* evil smell

sten'cil *n.* thin sheet pierced with pattern which is brushed over with paint or ink, leaving pattern on surface under it; the pattern; the plate; pattern made —*vt.* (**-ll-**) —**sten'ciller** *n.*

stenog'raphy *n.* shorthand writing —**stenog'rapher** *n.* —**stenograph'ic** *a.*

stentor'ian *a.* (of voice) very loud

step *vi.* move and set down foot; proceed (in this way) —*vt.* measure in paces (**-pp-**) —*n.* act of stepping; sound made by stepping; mark made by foot; manner of walking; series of foot movements forming part of dance; gait; pace; measure, act, stage in proceeding; board, rung *etc.* to put foot on; degree in scale; mast socket; promotion —*pl.* (**pair of steps**) portable ladder with hinged prop attached, stepladder —**step'ladder** *n.* four-legged ladder having broad flat steps

step'child *n.* child of husband or wife by former marriage —**step'brother** *n.* —**step'father** *n.* —**step'mother** *n.* —**step'sister** *n.*

steppe *n.* extensive treeless plain in European and Asiatic Russia

stere *n.* cubic metre

stereophon'ic *a.* (of sound) giving effect of coming from many directions —**ster'eo** *a./n.* (of, for) stereophonic record player *etc.*

stereoscop'ic *a.* having three-dimensional effect

ster'eotype [ste'ri-] *n.* metal plate for printing cast from set-up type; something (monotonously) familiar, conventional, predictable —*vt.* make stereotype of

ster'ile [ste'rīl] *a.* unable to produce fruit, crops, young *etc.*; free from (harmful) germs —**steril'ity** *n.* —**steriliza'tion** *n.* process or act of making sterile —**ster'ilize** *vt.* render sterile —**ster'ilizer** *n.*

ster'ling *a.* genuine, true; of solid worth, dependable; in British money —*n.* British money

stern[1] *a.* severe, strict —**stern'ly** *adv.* —**stern'ness** *n.*

stern[2] *n.* rear part of ship

ster'num *n.* the breast bone

ster'ols [ster'olz] *pl.n.* class of complex organic alcohols, including ergosterol, cholesterol

ster'torous *a.* with sound of heavy breathing, hoarse snoring

stet *Lat.* let it stand (proofreader's direction to cancel alteration previously made)

steth'oscope *n.* instrument for listening to action of heart, lungs *etc.* —**stethoscop'ic** *a.*

stet'son *n.* type of broad-brimmed felt hat

ste'vedore *n.* one who loads or unloads ships

stew *n.* food cooked slowly in closed vessel; state of excitement, agitation or worry —*v.* cook by stewing

stew'ard *n.* one who manages another's property; official managing race meeting, assembly *etc.*; attendant on ship's or aircraft's passengers (**stew'ardess** *fem.*)

stick *n.* long, thin piece of wood; anything shaped like a stick; *inf.* person (as **good stick** *etc.*) —*vt.* pierce, stab; place, fasten, as by pins, glue; protrude; *inf.* tolerate, abide —*vi.* adhere; come to stop, jam; remain; be fastened; protrude (**stuck** *pt./pp.*) —**stick'er** *n. esp.* adhesive label, poster —**stick'y** *a.* covered with, like adhesive substance; (of weather) warm, humid; *inf.* difficult, unpleasant

stic'kleback [-kl-b-] *n.* small fish with sharp spines on back

stick'ler *n.* person who insists on something

stiff *a.* not easily bent or moved; rigid; awkward; difficult; thick, not fluid; formal; stubborn; unnatural; strong or fresh, as breeze; *inf.* excessive —*n. sl.* corpse —**stiff'en** *v.* —**stiff'ly** *adv.* —**stiff'ness** *n.* —**stiff-necked** *a.* obstinate, stubborn

sti'fle *vt.* smother, suppress

stig'ma *n.* distinguishing mark *esp.* of disgrace (*pl.* **stig'mas, stig'mata**) —**stig'matism** *n.* —**stig'matize** *vt.* mark with stigma

stile *n.* arrangement of steps for climbing a fence

stilett'o *n.* small dagger; small boring tool (*pl.* **-os**) —*a.* thin, pointed like a stiletto

still[1] *a.* motionless, noiseless, at rest —*vt.* quiet —*adv.* to this time; yet; even —*n.* photograph *esp.* of movie scene —**still'ness** *n.* —**still'born** *a.* born dead —**still life** painting of inanimate objects

still[2] *n.* apparatus for distilling

stilt *n.* pole with footrests for walking raised from ground; long post supporting building *etc.* —**stilt'ed** *a.* stiff in manner, pompous —**stilt'edly** *adv.*

stim'ulus *n.* something that rouses to activity; incentive (*pl.* **-uli** [-lī, -lē]) —**stim'ulant** *n.* drug *etc.* acting as a stimulus —**stim'ulate** *vt.* rouse up, spur —**stim'ulating** *a.* acting as stimulus —**stimula'tion** *n.* —**stim'ulative** *a.*

sting *vt.* thrust sting into; cause sharp pain to; *sl.* impose upon by asking for money, overcharge —*vi.* feel sharp pain (**stung, sting'ing**) —*n.* (wound, pain, caused by) sharp pointed organ, often poisonous, of certain insects and animals

stin'gy [-ji] *a.* mean; avaricious; niggardly —**stin'gily** *adv.* —**stin'giness** *n.*

stink *vi.* give out strongly offensive smell; *sl.* be abhorrent (**stank, stunk, stink'ing**) —*n.* such smell, stench; *inf.* fuss, bother

stint *vt.* be frugal, miserly to (someone) or with (something) —*n.* allotted amount of work or time; limitation, restriction

sti'pend *n.* salary, *esp.* of clergyman —**stipend'iary** *a.* receiving stipend

stip'ple *vt.* engrave, paint in dots —*n.* this process

stip'ulate *vi.* specify in making a bargain —**stipula'tion** *n.* proviso; condition —**stip'ulator** *n.*

stir *v.* (begin to) move; rouse; cause trouble —*vt.* set, keep in motion; excite (**-rr-**) —*n.* commotion, disturbance

stirr'up *n.* metal loop hung from strap for supporting foot of rider on horse

stitch *n.* movement of needle in sewing *etc.*; its result in the work; sharp pain in side; least fragment (of clothing) —*v.* sew

stoat *n.* small mammal with brown coat and black-tipped tail

stock *n.* goods, material stored, *esp.* for sale or later use; reserve, fund; financial shares in, or capital of, company *etc.*; standing, reputation; farm animals (livestock); plant, stem from which cuttings are taken; handle of gun, tool *etc.*; liquid broth produced by boiling meat *etc.*; flowering plant; lineage —*pl. Hist.* frame to secure feet, hands (of offender); frame to support ship during construction —*a.* kept in stock; standard, hackneyed —*vt.* keep, store; supply with livestock, fish *etc.* —**stock'y** *a.* thickset —**stock'broker** *n.* agent for buying, selling shares in companies —**stock car** ordinary automobile strengthened and modified for a form of racing in which automobiles often collide —**stock exchange** institution for buying and selling shares —**stock'jobber** *n.* dealer on a stock exchange —**stock'man** *n.* man experienced in driving, handling cattle, sheep —**stock'pile** *v.* acquire and store large quantity of (something) —**stock-still** *a.* motionless —**stock'taking** *n.* examination, counting and valuing of goods in a shop *etc.*

stockade' *n.* enclosure of stakes, barrier

stockinet' *n.* machine-knitted elastic fabric

stock'ing *n.* close-fitting covering for leg and foot —**stock'inged** *a.*

stodg'y *a.* heavy, dull —**stodge** *n.* heavy, solid food

sto'ic *a.* capable of much self-control,

great endurance without complaint —*n.* stoical person —**sto'ical** *a.* —**sto'icism** *n.*

stoke *v.* feed, tend fire or furnace —**sto'ker** *n.*

stole[1] *pt.* —**sto'len** *pp. of* STEAL

stole[2] *n.* long scarf or shawl

stol'id *a.* hard to excite; heavy, slow, apathetic —**stolid'ity** *n.* —**stol'idly** *adv.*

stom'ach [-um'ək] *n.* sac forming chief digestive organ in any animal; appetite; desire, inclination —*vt.* put up with

stomp *vi. inf.* stamp

stone *n.* (piece of) rock; gem; hard seed of fruit; hard deposit formed in kidneys, bladder; **UK** weight, 14 lbs. —*vt.* throw stones at; free (fruit) from stones —**stoned** *a. sl.* stupefied by alcohol or drugs —**sto'nily** *adv.* —**sto'ny** *a.* of, like stone; hard; cold —**stone-blind** *a.* completely blind —**stone'boat** *n.* type of sled used for moving stones from fields —**stone-broke** *a. sl.* with no money left —**stone deaf** *a.* completely deaf —**stonewall'** *vi.* obstruct business; play slow game, *esp.* in cricket —**stone'ware** *n.* heavy common pottery

stood *pt./pp. of* STAND

stooge [stōōj] *n. Theatre etc.* performer always the butt of another's jokes; *sl.* one taken advantage of by another

stook [-ōō-] *n.* group of sheaves set upright in field to dry

stool [-ōō-] *n.* backless chair; excrement

stoop[1] [-ōō-] *vi.* lean forward or down, bend; swoop; abase, degrade oneself —*n.* stooping carriage of the body

stoop[2] [-ōō-] *n.* small platform with steps up to it at entrance of building

stop *vt.* check, bring to halt; prevent; interrupt; suspend; desist from; fill up an opening —*vi.* cease, come to a halt; stay (-**pp**-) —*n.* stopping or becoming stopped; punctuation mark, *esp.* period; any device for altering or regulating pitch; set of pipes in organ having tones of a distinct quality —**stopp'age** *n.* —**stop'per** *n.* plug for closing bottle *etc.* —**stop'cock** *n.* valve to control or stop flow of fluid in pipe —**stop'gap** *n.* temporary substitute —**stop'off, stop'over** *n.* short break in journey —**stop'watch** *n.* one which can be stopped for exact timing of race

store *vt.* stock, furnish, keep —*n.* shop; abundance; stock; department store; place for keeping goods; warehouse —*pl.* stocks of goods, provisions —**stor'age** *n.* —**store cattle** cattle bought lean to be fattened for market

stor'ey *n.* horizontal division of a building

stork *n.* large wading bird

storm *n.* violent weather with wind, rain, hail, sand, snow *etc.*; assault on fortress; violent outbreak, discharge —*vt.* assault; take by storm —*vi.* rage —**storm'y** *a.* like storm; (emotionally) violent

stor'y *n.* (book, piece of prose *etc.*) telling about events, happenings; *inf.* lie; *same as* STOREY

stoup [-ōō-] *n.* small basin for holy water

stout *a.* fat; sturdy, resolute —*n.* kind of beer —**stout'ly** *adv.* —**stout'ness** *n.*

stove[1] *n.* apparatus for cooking, heating *etc.*

stove[2] *pt./pp. of* STAVE

stow [stō] *vt.* pack away —**stow'age** *n.* —**stow'away** *n.* one who hides in ship to obtain free passage

strad'dle *vt.* bestride; *inf.* be in favour of both sides of (something) —*vi.* spread legs wide —*n.*

strafe [-āf, -ahf] *vt.* attack (*esp.* with bullets, rockets) from air

strag'gle *vi.* stray, get dispersed, linger —**stragg'ler** *n.*

straight [strāt] *a.* without bend; honest; level; in order; (of spirits) undiluted, neat; expressionless; (of drama, actor *etc.*) serious; *sl.* heterosexual —*n.* straight state or part —*adv.* direct —**straight'en** *v.* —**straight'away** *adv.* immediately —**straightfor'ward** *a.* open, frank; simple; honest —**straightfor'wardly** *adv.*

strain[1] *vt.* stretch tightly; stretch to full or to excess; filter —*vi.* make great effort —*n.* stretching force; violent effort; injury from being strained; burst of music or poetry; great demand; (condition caused by) overwork, worry *etc.*; tone of speaking or writing —**strained** *a.* —**strain'er** *n.* filter, sieve

strain[2] *n.* breed or race; type (*esp.* in biology); trace, streak

strait *n.* channel of water connecting two larger areas of water —*pl.* position of difficulty or distress —*a.* narrow; strict

—**strait'en** *vt.* make strait, narrow; press with poverty —**strait'jacket** *n.* jacket to confine arms of violent person —**strait-laced** *a.* austere, strict; puritanical

strand[1] *v.* run aground; leave, be left in difficulties or helpless —*n. Poet.* shore

strand[2] *n.* one single string or wire of rope *etc.*

strange [-ānj] *a.* odd; queer; unaccustomed; foreign; uncommon; wonderful; singular —**stran'ger** *n.* unknown person; foreigner; one unaccustomed (to) —**strange'ly** *adv.* —**strange'ness** *n.*

stran'gle [-ng'gl] *vt.* kill by squeezing windpipe; suppress —**strangula'tion** *n.* strangling

strap *n.* strip, *esp.* of leather —*vt.* fasten, beat with strap (**-pp-**) —**strapped** *a. sl.* short of (money) —**strapp'ing** *a.* tall and well-made —**strap'hanger** *n.* in bus, train, one who has to stand, steadying himself with strap provided for this

strat'agem [-jəm] *n.* plan, trick —**strat'egy** *n.* art of war; overall plan —**strate'gic(al)** *a.* —**strat'egist** *n.*

strathspey' [-spā'] *n.* type of Scottish dance with gliding steps

strat'osphere *n.* upper part of the atmosphere approx. 11 km above earth's surface

strat'um [-aht'-] *n.* layer, *esp.* of rock; class in society (*pl.* **-ta**) —**strat'ify** [-at'-] *v.* form, deposit in layers (**-ified, -ifying**) —**stratifica'tion** *n.*

straw *n.* stalks of grain; single stalk; long, narrow tube used to suck up liquid —**straw'berry** *n.* creeping plant producing a red, juicy fruit; the fruit —**straw vote** unofficial vote to determine opinion of group

stray *vi.* wander; digress; get lost —*a.* strayed; occasional, scattered —*n.* stray animal

streak *n.* long line or band; element, trace —*vt.* mark with streaks —*vi.* move fast; *inf.* run naked in public —**streak'y** *a.* having streaks; striped

stream *n.* flowing body of water or other liquid; steady flow —*vi.* flow; run with liquid; float, wave in the air —**stream'er** *n.* (paper) ribbon, narrow flag

stream'lined *a.* (of automobile, plane *etc.*) built so as to offer least resistance to air

street *n.* road in town or village, usu. lined with houses —**street'car** *n.* vehicle (esp. electrically driven and for public transport) running on rails laid on roadway —**street'walker** *n.* prostitute —**street'wise** *a.* adept at surviving in urban, *oft.* criminal, environment (*also* **street-smart**)

strength *n.* quality of being strong; power; capacity for exertion or endurance; vehemence; force; full or necessary number of people —**strength'en** *v.* make stronger, reinforce —**on the strength of** relying on; because of

stren'uous *a.* energetic; earnest —**stren'uously** *adv.*

streptococc'us *n.* genus of bacteria (*pl.* **-cocc'i** [-kok'ī])

streptomy'cin *n.* antibiotic drug

stress *n.* emphasis; strain; impelling force; effort; tension —*vt.* emphasize; accent; put mechanical stress on

stretch *vt.* extend; exert to utmost; tighten, pull out; reach out —*vi.* reach; have elasticity —*n.* stretching, being stretched, expanse; spell —**stretch'er** *n.* person, thing that stretches; appliance on which disabled person is carried; bar linking legs of chair; bar in boat for rower's feet

strew [-rōō] *vt.* scatter over surface, spread (**strewed** *pt.*, **strewn** *or* **strewed** *pp.*, **strew'ing** *pr.p.*)

stri'a *n.* small channel or threadlike line in surface of shell or other object (*pl.* **stri'ae** [-ē]) —**stri'ate** [-it], **stria'ted** *a.* streaked, furrowed, grooved —**stria'tion** *n.*

strick'en *a.* seriously affected by disease, grief, famine; afflicted; *pp. of* STRIKE

strict *a.* stern, not lax or indulgent; defined; without exception —**strict'ly** *adv.* —**strict'ness** *n.*

stric'ture *n.* critical remark; constriction

stride *vi.* walk with long steps (**strode, stridd'en, stri'ding**) —*n.* single step; its length; regular pace

stri'dent *a.* harsh in tone; loud; urgent

strife *n.* conflict; quarrelling

strike *v.* hit (against); ignite; (of snake) bite; arrive at, come upon; of plants (cause to) take root; attack; hook (fish); sound (time) as bell in clock *etc.* —*vt.* affect; enter mind of; discover (gold, oil *etc.*); dismantle, remove; make (coin) —*vi.* cease work as protest or to make demands (**struck** *pt.*, **strick'en, struck** *pp.*, **stri'king** *pr.p.*) —*n.* act of striking —**stri'ker** *n.* —**stri'king** *a.* noteworthy, impressive —**strike pay** allowance paid by trade union to members on strike —**strike off** remove

string *n.* (length of) thin cord or other material; strand, row; series; fibre in plants —*pl.* conditions —*vt.* provide with, thread on string; form in line, series (**strung, string'ing**) —**stringed** *a.* (of musical instruments) furnished with strings —**string'y** *a.* like string; fibrous

strin'gent [-j-] *a.* strict, rigid, binding —**strin'gency** *n.* severity —**strin'gently** *adv.*

strip *vt.* lay bare, take covering off; dismantle; deprive (of) —*vi.* undress (**-pp-**) —*n.* long, narrow piece —**strip'per** *n.* —**strip(tease')** *n.* cabaret or theatre act in which person undresses

stripe *n.* narrow mark, band; chevron as symbol of military rank; sort, type —**stri'py** *a.*

strip'ling *n.* youth

strive *vi.* try hard, struggle, contend (**strove, striv'en, stri'ving**)

strobe *n.* apparatus which produces high-intensity flashing light

strode *pt. of* STRIDE

stroke *n.* blow; sudden action, occurrence; apoplexy; mark of pen, pencil, brush *etc.*; chime of clock; completed movement in series; act, manner of striking (ball *etc.*); style, method of swimming; rower sitting nearest stern setting the rate; act of stroking —*vt.* set time in rowing; pass hand lightly over

stroll [-ōl] *vi.* walk in leisurely or idle manner —*n.* —**stroll'er** *n.* person who strolls; chair-shaped carriage for baby

strong *a.* powerful, robust, healthy; difficult to break; noticeable; intense; emphatic; not diluted; having a certain number —**strong'ly** *adv.* —**strong'hold** *n.* fortress

stron'tium *n.* silvery-white chemical element —**strontium 90** radioactive isotope of strontium present in fallout of nuclear explosions

strop *n.* leather for sharpening razors —*vt.* sharpen on one (**-pp-**)

stro'phe *n.* division of ode —**stroph'ic** *a.*

strove *pt. of* STRIVE

struck *pt./pp. of* STRIKE

struc'ture *n.* (arrangement of parts in) construction, building *etc.*; form; organization —*v.* give structure to —**struc'tural** *a.*

strug'gle *vi.* contend; fight; proceed, work, move with difficulty and effort —*n.*

strum *v.* strike notes of guitar *etc.* (**-mm-**)

strum'pet *n. obs.* promiscuous woman

strung *pt./pp. of* STRING

strut *vi.* walk affectedly or pompously (**-tt-**) —*n.* brace; rigid support, usu. set obliquely; strutting gait

strych'nine [-ik'nēn] *n.* poison got from nux vomica seeds

stub *n.* remnant of anything, *eg* pencil, cigarette *etc.*; part of cheque, receipt *etc.* kept as record —*vi.* strike, as toes, against fixed object; extinguish by pressing against surface (**-bb-**) —**stubb'y** *a.* short, broad

stub'ble *n.* stumps of cut grain after reaping; short growth of beard —**stubble-jumper** *n. sl.* prairie grain farmer

stubb'orn *a.* unyielding, obstinate —**stub'bornly** *adv.* —**stub'bornness** *n.*

stucc'o *n.* plaster —**stucc'oed** *a.*

stuck *pt./pp. of* STICK

stud[1] *n.* nail with large head; removable double-headed button; vertical wall support —*vt.* set with studs (**-dd-**)

stud[2] *n.* set of horses kept for breeding —**stud'book** *n.* book giving pedigree of noted or thoroughbred animals, *esp.* horses —**stud farm**

stu'dio *n.* workroom of artist, photographer *etc.*; building, room where motion picture, television or radio shows are made, broadcast (*pl.* **-s**)

stud'y *vi.* be engaged in learning —*vt.* make study of; try constantly to do; consider; scrutinize (**stud'ied, stud'ying**) —*n.* effort to acquire knowledge; subject of this; room to study in; book, report *etc.* produced as result of study; sketch —**stu'dent** *n.* one who studies, *esp.* at university *etc.* —**stud'ied** *a.* carefully designed, premeditated —**stu'di·ous** *a.* fond of study; thoughtful; painstaking; deliberate —**stu'diously** *adv.*

stuff *v.* pack, cram, fill (completely); eat large amount; fill with seasoned mixture; fill (animal's skin) with material to preserve lifelike form —*n.* material, fabric; any substance —**stuff'ing** *n.* material for stuffing; **UK** dressing for poultry —**stuff'y** *a.* lacking fresh air; *inf.* dull, conventional —**do your stuff** *inf.* do what is required or expected of you

stult'ify *vt.* make ineffectual (**-ified, -ifying**) —**stultifica'tion** *n.*

stum'ble *vi.* trip and nearly fall; falter —*n.* —**stumbling block** obstacle

stump *n.* remnant of tree, tooth *etc.*, when main part has been cut away —*vt.* confuse, puzzle —*vi.* walk heavily, noisily —**stump'age** *n.* standing timber or its value; right to fell timber; tax payable on each tree felled —**stump'y** *a.* short and thickset —**on the stump** engaged in campaigning *esp.* by political speech-making

stun *vt.* knock senseless; amaze (**-nn-**) —**stunn'ing** *a.*

stung *pt./pp. of* STING

stunk *pp. of* STINK

stunt[1] *vt.* check growth of, dwarf —**stunt'ed** *a.* underdeveloped; undersized

stunt[2] *n.* feat of dexterity or daring; anything spectacular, unusual done to gain publicity

stu'pefy *vt.* make insensitive, lethargic; astound (**-efied, -efying**) —**stupefac'tion** *n.*

stupen'dous [styōō-] *a.* astonishing; amazing; huge

stu'pid *a.* slow-witted; silly; in a stupor —**stupid'ity** *n.* —**stu'pidly** *adv.*

stu'por *n.* dazed state; insensibility —**stu'porous** *a.*

stur'dy *a.* robust, strongly built; vigorous —**stur'dily** *adv.* —**stur'diness** *n.*

stur'geon [-jən] *n.* fish yielding caviare and isinglass

stutt'er *v.* speak with difficulty; stammer —*n.*

sty[1] *n.* place to keep pigs in; hovel, dirty place

sty[2], **stye** *n.* inflammation on edge of eyelid

Styg'ian [stij'-] *a.* of river Styx in Hades; gloomy; infernal

style *n.* manner of writing, doing *etc.*; designation; sort; elegance, refinement; superior manner, quality; design —*vt.* shape, design; adapt; designate —**sty'lish** *a.* fashionable —**sty'lishly** *adv.* —**sty'list** *n.* one cultivating style in literary or other execution; designer; hairdresser —**stylis'tic** *a.* —**styl'ize** *vt.* give conventional stylistic form to —**styling mousse** foamy substance applied to hair before styling to retain shape

sty'lus *n.* writing instrument; (in record player) tiny point running in groove of record (*pl.* **-li** [-lī], **-luses**)

sty'mie *vt.* hinder, thwart

styp'tic *a./n.* (designating) a substance that stops bleeding

sty'rene *n.* colourless liquid used in making synthetic rubber, plastics

suave [swahv] *a.* smoothly polite, affable, bland —**suav'ity** *n.*

sub *short for* subeditor, submarine, subscription, substitute —*n. inf.* **UK** advance payment of wages, salary —*inf. v.* serve as substitute; **UK** grant or receive advance payment; subedit (**-bb-**)

sub- (*comb. form*) under, less than, in lower position, subordinate, forming subdivision *etc.*, as in **subaqu'a** *a.*, **subed'itor** *n.*, **sub'heading** *n.*, **subnor'mal** *a.*, **sub'soil** *n.* Such words are not given here where the meaning may be easily inferred from the simple word

sub'altern [-əl-tən] *n.* army officer below rank of captain

sub'committee *n.* section of committee functioning separately from main body

subcon'scious *a.* acting, existing without one's awareness —*n.* *Psychology* that part of the human mind unknown, or only partly known to possessor

subcuta'neous *a.* under the skin

subdivide' *vt.* divide again; divide (land) into lots for sale —**subdivi'sion** [-vizh'-] *n.* division following upon earlier division; portion resulting from subdivision; tract of land for building; houses *etc.* built on such tract

subdue' *v.* overcome —**subdued'** *a.* cowed, quiet; not bright or intense

sub'ject *n.* theme, topic; that about

which something is predicated; conscious self; one under power of another —*a.* owing allegiance; subordinate; dependent; liable (to) —*vt.* [-jekt'] cause to undergo; make liable; subdue —**subjec'tion** *n.* act of bringing, or state of being, under control —**subject'ive** *a.* based on personal feelings, not impartial; of the self; existing in the mind; displaying artist's individuality —**subjectiv'ity** *n.*

subjoin' *vt.* add to end

sub ju'dice [-di-si] *Lat.* under judicial consideration

sub'jugate *vt.* force to submit; conquer —**subjuga'tion** *n.* —**sub'jugator** *n.*

subjunc'tive *n.* mood used mainly in subordinate clauses expressing wish, possibility —*a.* in, of, that mood

sublet' *vt.* (of tenant) let whole or part of what he has rented to another (**sublet', sublett'ing**)

sub'limate *vt. Psychology* direct energy (*esp.* sexual) into activities considered more socially acceptable; refine —*n. Chem.* material obtained when substance is sublimed —**sublima'tion** *n. Psychology* unconscious diversion of sexual impulses towards new aims and activities; *Chem.* process in which a solid changes directly into a vapour

sublime' *a.* elevated; eminent; majestic; inspiring awe; exalted —*v. Chem.* change or cause to change from solid to vapour —**sublime'ly** *adv.* —**sublim'ity** *n.*

sublim'inal *a.* resulting from processes of which the individual is not aware

sub-machine'-gun *n.* portable automatic gun with short barrel

sub'marine [*or* -rēn'] *n.* (war)ship which can travel (and attack from) below surface of sea and remain submerged for long periods —*a.* below surface of sea

submerge' *v.* place, go under water —**submer'sion** *n.*

submit' *vt.* surrender; put forward for consideration —*vi.* surrender; defer (**-tt-**) —**submiss'ion** *n.* —**submiss'ive** *a.* meek, obedient

subord'inate [-it] *a.* of lower rank or less importance —*n.* inferior; one under order of another —*vt.* [-āt] make, treat as subordinate —**subord'inately** *adv.* —**subordina'tion** *n.*

suborn' *vt.* bribe to do evil —**suborna'tion** *n.* —**suborn'er** *n.*

subpoe'na [-pē'nə] *n.* writ requiring attendance at court of law —*vt.* summon by such order (**-naed** [-nəd], **-naing**)

subscribe' *vt.* pay, promise to pay (contribution); write one's name at end of document —**subscri'ber** *n.* —**subscrip'tion** *n.* subscribing; money paid

sub'section *n.* division of a section

sub'sequent *a.* later, following or coming after in time —**sub'sequence** *n.* —**sub'sequently** *adv.*

subser'vient *a.* submissive, servile —**subser'vience** *n.* —**subser'viently** *adv.*

subside' *vi.* abate, come to an end; sink; settle; collapse —**subsi'dence** [*or* sub'si-] *n.*

subsid'iary *a.* supplementing; secondary; auxiliary —*n.*

sub'sidize *vt.* help financially; pay grant to —**sub'sidy** *n.* money granted

subsist' *vi.* exist, sustain life —**subsist'ence** *n.* the means by which one supports life; livelihood

subson'ic *a.* concerning speeds less than that of sound

sub'stance *n.* matter; particular kind of matter; chief part, essence; wealth —**substan'tial** *a.* considerable; of real value; solid, big, important; really existing —**substantial'ity** *n.* —**substan'tially** *adv.* —**substan'tiate** *vt.* bring evidence for, confirm, prove —**substantia'tion** *n.* —**sub'stantive** *a.* having independent existence; real, fixed —*n.* noun

sub'stitute *v.* put, serve in exchange (for) —*n.* thing, person put in place of another; deputy —**substitu'tion** *n.*

substrat'um [-raht'-] *n.* that which is laid or spread under; layer of earth lying under another; basis; subsoil (*pl.* **-ta, -tums**)

subsume' *vt.* incorporate (idea, case *etc.*) under comprehensive heading, classification

subtend' *vt.* be opposite to and delimit

sub'terfuge *n.* trick, lying excuse used to evade something

subterra'nean, subterra'neous *a.* underground

sub'title *n.* secondary title of book;

written translation of movie dialogue, superimposed on screen

subt'le [sut'l] *a.* not immediately obvious; ingenious, acute; crafty; intricate; delicate; making fine distinctions —**sub'tlety** *n.* —**subt'ly** *adv.*

subtract' *vt.* take away, deduct —**subtrac'tion** *n.*

subtrop'ical *a.* of regions bordering on the tropics

sub'urb *n.* residential area on outskirts of city —**suburb'an** *a.* —**suburb'ia** *n.* suburbs of a city

subven'tion *n.* subsidy

subvert' *vt.* overthrow; corrupt —**subver'sion** *n.* —**subver'sive** *a.*

sub'way *n.* underground passage; underground railway

succeed' [sək-sēd'] *vi.* accomplish purpose; turn out satisfactorily; follow —*vt.* follow, take place of —**success'** *n.* favourable accomplishment, attainment, issue or outcome; successful person or thing —**success'ful** *a.* —**success'fully** *adv.* —**success'ion** *n.* following; series; succeeding —**success'ive** *a.* following in order; consecutive —**success'ively** *adv.* —**success'or** *n.*

succinct' [sək-singkt'] *a.* terse, concise —**succinct'ly** *adv.* —**succinct'ness** *n.*

succ'o(u)r *vt./n.* help in distress

succ'otash [suk'ə-] *n.* mixture of cooked corn kernels and beans

succ'ubus *n.* female demon fabled to have sexual intercourse with sleeping men (*pl.* **-bi** [-bī])

succ'ulent *a.* juicy, full of juice; (of plant) having thick, fleshy leaves —*n.* such plant —**succ'ulence** *n.*

succumb' [-kum'] *vi.* yield, give way; die

such *a.* of the kind or degree mentioned; so great, so much; so made *etc.*; of the same kind —**such'like** *inf.* *a.* such —*pron.* other such things

suck *vt.* draw into mouth; hold (dissolve) in mouth; draw in —*n.* sucking —**suck'er** *n.* person, thing that sucks; organ, appliance which adheres by suction; shoot coming from root or base of stem of plant; *inf.* person easily deceived or taken in

suc'kle *v.* feed from the breast —**suck'ling** *n.* unweaned infant

suc'tion *n.* drawing or sucking of air or fluid; force produced by difference in pressure

sudd'en *a.* done, occurring unexpectedly; abrupt, hurried —**sudd'enly** *adv.* —**sud'denness** *n.*

sudorif'ic *a.* causing perspiration —*n.* medicine that produces sweat

suds *pl.n.* froth of soap and water, lather; *sl.* beer

sue *vt.* prosecute; seek justice from —*vi.* make application or entreaty; beseech

suede [swād] *n.* leather with soft, velvety finish

su'et [soo'it] *n.* hard animal fat from sheep, ox *etc.*

suff'er *v.* undergo, endure, experience (pain *etc.*); *obs.* allow —**suff'erable** *a.* —**suff'erance** *n.* toleration —**suf'ferer** *n.*

suffice' *v.* be adequate, satisfactory (for) —**suffi'ciency** [-fish'-] *n.* adequate amount —**suffi'cient** *a.* enough, adequate

suff'ix *n.* letter or word added to end of word —*vt.* add to end

suff'ocate *v.* kill, be killed by deprivation of oxygen; smother —**suffoca'tion** *n.*

suff'ragan *n.* bishop appointed to assist an archbishop or another bishop

suff'rage [-rij] *n.* vote or right of voting —**suff'ragist** *n.* one claiming a right of voting (**suffragette'** *fem.*)

suffuse *vt.* well up and spread over —**suffu'sion** *n.*

sug'ar [shoog'-] *n.* sweet crystalline vegetable substance —*vt.* sweeten, make pleasant (with sugar) —**sug'ary** *a.* —**sugar beet** varieties of common beet grown for sugar —**sugar cane** plant from whose juice sugar is obtained —**sugar daddy** *sl.* wealthy (elderly) man who pays for (*esp.* sexual) favours of younger person —**sugar maple** large N Amer. maple tree yielding sweet sap from which sugar and syrup are made

suggest' [-j-] *vt.* propose; call up the idea of —**suggestibil'ity** *n.* —**suggest'ible** *a.* easily influenced —**sugges'tion** *n.* hint; proposal; insinuation of impression, belief *etc.*, into mind —**sugges'tive** *a.* containing, open to suggestion, *esp.* of something indecent —**sugges'tively** *adv.*

su'icide [soo'-] *n.* (act of) one who kills

himself —**suici'dal** *a.* —**suici'dally** *adv.*

suit [soot] *n.* set of clothing; garment worn for particular event, purpose; one of four sets in pack of cards; action at law —*v.* make, be fit or appropriate for; be acceptable to (someone) —**suitabil'ity** *n.* —**suit'able** *a.* fitting, proper, convenient; becoming —**suit'ably** *adv.* —**suit'case** *n.* flat rectangular travelling case

suite [swēt] *n.* matched set *esp.* furniture; set of rooms; retinue

suit'or [soot'-] *n.* wooer; one who sues; petitioner

sulk *vi.* be silent, resentful, *esp.* to draw attention to oneself —*n.* this mood —**sulk'ily** *adv.* —**sulk'y** *a.*

sull'en *a.* unwilling to talk or be sociable, morose; dismal; dull —**sull'enly** *adv.*

sull'y *vt.* stain, tarnish, disgrace (**sul'lied, sull'ying**)

sul'phate *n.* salt formed by sulphuric acid in combination with any base

sulphon'amides *pl. n.* group of drugs used as internal germicides in treatment of many bacterial diseases

sul'phur, sul'fur [-fər] *n.* pale yellow nonmetallic element —**sulphur'ic** [-fyoor'-] *a.* —**sul'phurous** *a.*

sul'tan *n.* ruler of Muslim country —**sultan'a** [-tahn'-] *n.* sultan's wife; kind of raisin

sul'try *a.* (of weather) hot, humid; (of person) looking sensual

sum *n.* amount, total; problem in arithmetic —*v.* add up; make summary of main parts (**-mm-**)

su'mach [soo'mak] *n.* shrub with clusters of green flowers and red hairy fruits

summ'ary *n.* abridgment or statement of chief points of longer document, speech *etc.*; abstract —*a.* done quickly —**summ'arily** *adv.* speedily; abruptly —**summ'arize** *vt.* make summary of; present briefly and concisely —**summa'tion** *n.* adding up

summ'er *n.* second, warmest season —*vi.* pass the summer —**summ'ery** *a.* —**summer'time** *n.* daylight saving time, *ie* time shown by clocks *etc.* put forward one hour during certain period of year

summ'it *n.* top, peak —**summit conference** meeting of heads of governments

summ'on *vt.* demand attendance of; call on; bid witness appear in court; gather up (energies *etc.*) —**summ'ons** *n.* call; authoritative demand

sump *n.* place or receptacle (*esp.* as oil reservoir in engine) where fluid collects

sump'tuous *a.* lavish, magnificent; costly —**sump'tuously** *adv.* —**sump'tuousness** *n.* —**sump'tuary** *a.* pert. to or regulating expenditure

sun *n.* luminous body round which earth and other planets revolve; its rays —*vt.* expose to sun's rays (**-nn-**) —**sun'less** *a.* —**sunn'y** *a.* like the sun; warm; cheerful —**sun'bathing** *n.* exposure of whole or part of body to sun's rays —**sun'beam** *n.* ray of sun —**sun'burn** *n.* inflammation of skin due to excessive exposure to sun —**sun'down** *n.* sunset —**sun'fish** *n.* sea fish with large rounded body —**sun'flower** *n.* plant with large golden flowers —**sun'spot** *n.* dark patch appearing temporarily on sun's surface —**sun'stroke** *n.* illness caused by prolonged exposure to intensely hot sun —**sun'tan** *n.* colouring of skin by exposure to sun

sun'dae [-dā] *n.* ice cream topped with fruit *etc.*

Sun'day *n.* first day of the week; Christian Sabbath —**Sunday school** school for religious instruction of children

sun'der *vt.* separate, sever

sun'dry *a.* several, various —**sun'dries** *pl.n.* odd items not mentioned in detail

sung *pp. of* SING

sunk, sunk'en *pp. of* SINK

sup *vt.* take by sips —*vi.* take supper (**-pp-**) —*n.* mouthful of liquid

su'per [soo'-] *a. inf.* very good

super- (*comb. form*) above, greater, exceeding(ly), as in **superhu'man** *a.*, **su'perman** *n.*, **su'perstore** *n.*, **su'pertanker** *n.* Such compounds are not given here where the meaning may be inferred from the simple word

su'perable [soo'-] *a.* capable of being overcome; surmountable

superann'uate *vt.* pension off; discharge or dismiss as too old —**superan'nuated** *a.* —**superannua'tion** *n.* pension given on retirement; contribution by employee to pension

superb' *a.* splendid, grand, impressive —**superb'ly** *adv.*

su'percharge [soo'-] *vt.* charge, fill to excess —**su'percharged** *a.* —**su'percharger** *n.* (internal-combustion engine) device to ensure complete filling of cylinder with explosive mixture when running at high speed

supercil'ious *a.* displaying arrogant pride, scorn, indifference —**supercil'iously** *adv.* —**supercil'iousness** *n.*

superfi'cial [-fish'-] *a.* of or on surface; not careful or thorough; without depth, shallow —**superficial'ity** *n.*

super'fluous *a.* extra, unnecessary; excessive; left over —**superflu'ity** [-floo'-] *n.* superabundance; unnecessary amount —**super'fluously** *adv.*

superintend' *v.* have charge of; overlook; supervise —**superintend'ence** *n.* —**superintend'ent** *n.* person who directs and manages organization, office *etc.*; person in charge of premises

supe'rior *a.* greater in quality or quantity; upper, higher in position, rank or quality; showing consciousness of being so —**superior'ity** [-o'ri-] *n.* quality of being higher, greater, or more excellent

super'lative *a.* of, in highest degree or quality; surpassing; *Grammar* denoting form of adjective, adverb meaning 'most' —*n.* *Grammar* superlative degree of adjective or adverb

su'permarket *n.* large self-service store selling chiefly food and household goods

super'nal *a.* celestial

supernat'ural *a.* being beyond the powers or laws of nature; miraculous —**supernat'urally** *adv.*

supernu'merary *a.* in excess of normal number, extra —*n.* extra person or thing

superphos'phate *n.* chemical fertilizer

su'perscript *n./a.* (character) printed, written above the line

supersede' *vt.* take the place of; set aside, discard, supplant

superson'ic *a.* denoting speed greater than that of sound

supersti'tion [-stish'-] *n.* religion, opinion or practice based on belief in luck or magic —**supersti'tious** *a.* —**supersti'tiously** *adv.*

su'perstructure [soo'-] *n.* structure above foundations; part of ship above deck

su'pertax [soo'-] *n.* tax on large incomes in addition to usual income tax

supervene' *vi.* happen, as an interruption or change —**superven'tion** *n.*

su'pervise [soo'-] *vt.* oversee; direct; inspect and control; superintend —**supervi'sion** [-vizh'-] *n.* —**su'pervisor** *n.* —**supervi'sory** *a.*

supine' [*or* soo'-] *a.* lying on back with face upwards; indolent —*n.* [soo'-] Latin verbal noun

supp'er *n.* (light) evening meal —**sup'perless** *a.*

supplant' [-ahnt'] *vt.* take the place of, *esp.* unfairly; oust —**supplant'er** *n.*

sup'ple *a.* pliable; flexible; compliant —**sup'ply** *adv.*

supp'lement *n.* thing added to fill up, supply deficiency, *esp.* extra part added to book *etc.*; additional number of periodical, usu. on special subject; separate, often illustrated section published periodically with newspaper —*vt.* add to; supply deficiency —**supplement'ary** *a.* additional

supp'liant *a.* petitioning —*n.* petitioner

supp'licate *v.* beg humbly, entreat —**supplica'tion** *n.* —**supp'licatory** *a.*

supply' *vt.* furnish; make available; provide (**supplied', supply'ing**) —*n.* supplying, substitute; stock, store

support' *vt.* hold up; sustain; assist —*n.* supporting, being supported; means of support —**support'able** *a.* —**support'er** *n.* adherent —**support'ing** *a.* (of motion picture *etc.* role) less important —**support'ive** *a.*

suppose' [-ōz'] *vt.* assume as theory; take for granted; accept as likely; (in passive) be expected, obliged; ought —**supposed'** *a.* —**suppos'edly** [-id-li] *adv.* —**supposi'tion** [-zish'-] *n.* assumption; belief without proof; conjecture —**supposi'tious** *a.* —**suppositi'tious** *a.* sham; spurious; counterfeit

suppos'itory [-oz'-] *n.* medication (in capsule) for insertion in orifice of body

suppress' *vt.* put down, restrain ; crush, stifle; keep or withdraw from publication —**suppress'ion** [-esh'-] *n.*

supp'urate *vi.* fester, form pus —**suppura'tion** *n.*

supra- (*comb. form*) above, over, as in **supranat'ional** *a.* involving more than one nation Such words are not given here where the meaning may easily be inferred from the simple word

supreme' *a.* highest in authority or rank; utmost —**suprem'acy** *n.* position of being supreme —**supreme'ly** *adv.*

surcease' *v.* (cause to) cease, give respite —*n.* cessation

sur'charge *n.* additional charge —*vt.* make additional charge

sure [shoor] *a.* certain; trustworthy; without doubt —*adv. inf.* certainly —**sure'ly** *adv.* —**sure'ty** *n.* one who makes himself responsible for another's obligations

surf *n.* waves breaking on shore —*v.* swim in, ride surf —**surf'er** *n.* one who (often) goes surfing —**surf'board** *n.* board used in sport of riding over surf

sur'face [-fis] *n.* outside face of body; exterior; plane; top, visible side; superficial appearance, outward impression —*a.* involving the surface only; going no deeper than surface —*v.* (cause to) come to surface; put a surface on

sur'feit [-fit] *n.* excess; disgust caused by excess —*v.* feed to excess

surge *n.* wave; sudden increase; *Electricity* sudden rush of current in circuit —*vi.* move in large waves; swell, billow

sur'geon [-jən] *n.* medical expert who performs operations —**sur'gery** *n.* medical treatment by operation; room in which operations take place —**sur'gical** *a.* —**sur'gically** *adv.*

sur'ly *a.* gloomily morose; ill-natured; cross and rude —**sur'lily** *adv.* —**sur'liness** *n.*

surmise' *v./n.* guess, conjecture

surmount' *vt.* get over, overcome —**surmount'able** *a.*

sur'name *n.* family name

surpass' [-ahs'] *vt.* go beyond; excel; outstrip —**surpass'able** *a.* —**surpas'sing** *a.* excellent; exceeding others

sur'plice [-plis] *n.* loose white vestment worn by clergy and choristers

sur'plus *n.* what remains over in excess

surprise' [-īz'] *vt.* cause surprise to; astonish; take, come upon unexpectedly; startle (someone) into action thus —*n.* what takes unawares; something unexpected; emotion aroused by being taken unawares

surre'alism *n.* movement in art and literature emphasizing expression of the unconscious —**surre'al** *a.* —**surre'alist** *n./a.*

surren'der *vt.* hand over, give up —*vi.* yield; cease resistance; capitulate —*n.* act of surrendering

surrepti'tious [-tish'-] *a.* done secretly or stealthily; furtive —**surrepti'tiously** *adv.*

surr'ogate [-git] *n.* deputy, *esp.* of bishop; substitute —**surrogate mother** woman who bears child on behalf of childless couple

surround' *vt.* be, come all round, encompass; encircle; hem in —*n.* border, edging —**surround'ings** *pl.n.* conditions, scenery *etc.* around a person, place, environment

sur'tax *n.* additional tax

surveill'ance [sur-vāl'-] *n.* close watch, supervision

survey' *vt.* view, scrutinize; inspect, examine; measure, map (land) —*n.* [sur'-] a surveying; inspection; report incorporating results of survey —**survey'or** *n.*

survive' *vt.* outlive; come alive through —*vi.* continue to live or exist —**survi'val** *n.* continuation of existence of persons, things *etc.* —**survi'vor** *n.* one left alive when others have died

suscep'tible [sə-sep'-] *a.* yielding readily (to); capable (of); impressionable —**susceptibil'ity** *n.*

suspect' *vt.* doubt innocence of; have impression of existence or presence of; be inclined to believe that; mistrust —*a.* [sus'-] of suspected character —*n.* suspected person

suspend' *vt.* hang up; cause to cease for a time; debar from an office or privilege; keep inoperative; sustain in fluid —**suspend'ers** *pl.n.* straps worn over shoulders to hold up trousers; **UK** straps for supporting stockings

suspense' *n.* state of uncertainty, *esp.* while awaiting news, an event *etc.*; anxiety, worry —**suspen'sion** *n.* state of being suspended; springs on axle of body of vehicle —**suspen'sory** *a.*

suspi'cion [-spish'-] *n.* suspecting, being suspected; slight trace —**suspi'cious** *a.* —**suspi'ciously** *adv.*

sustain' *vt.* keep, hold up; endure; keep

alive; confirm —**sustain'able** *a.* —**sus'tenance** *n.* food

su'ture [sōō'-] *n.* act of sewing; sewing up of a wound; material used for this; a joining of the bones of the skull —**su'tural** *a.*

su'zerain [sōō'-] *n.* sovereign with rights over autonomous state; feudal lord —**su'zerainty** *n.*

svelte *a.* lightly built, slender; sophisticated

SW southwest(ern)

swab [-ob] *n.* mop; pad of surgical wool *etc.* for cleaning, taking specimen *etc.*; *sl.* low or unmannerly fellow —*vt.* clean with swab (**-bb-**) —**swabb'er** *n.*

swad'dle [-od'-] *vt.* swathe —**swaddling clothes** *Hist.* long strips of cloth for wrapping newborn baby

swag *n. sl.* stolen property

swagg'er *vi.* strut; boast —*n.* strutting gait; boastful, overconfident manner

swain *n.* rustic lover

swall'ow[1] [-ol'ō] *vt.* cause, allow to pass down gullet; engulf; suppress, keep back; *inf.* believe gullibly —*n.* act of swallowing

swall'ow[2] [-ol'ō] *n.* migratory bird with forked tail and skimming manner of flight

swam *pt. of* SWIM

swamp [-omp] *n.* bog —*vt.* entangle in swamp; overwhelm; flood —**swamp'y** *a.*

swan [-on] *n.* large, web-footed water bird with graceful curved neck —*vi. inf.* stroll idly (**-nn-**) —**swan song** fabled song of a swan before death; last act *etc.* before death —**swann'ery** *n.*

swank *vi. sl.* swagger; show off —**swank'y** *a. sl.* smart; showy

swap [-op], **swop** *inf. n./v.* exchange; barter (**-pp-**)

sward [-aw-] *n.* green turf

swarm[1] [-aw-] *n.* large cluster of insects; vast crowd —*vi.* (of bees) be on the move in swarm; gather in large numbers

swarm[2] [-aw-] *vi.* climb (rope *etc.*) by grasping with hands and knees

swar'thy [-aw-] *a.* dark-complexioned

swash'buckler [-osh'-] *n.* swaggering daredevil person —**swash'buckling** *a.*

swas'tika [-os'-] *n.* form of cross with arms bent at right angles, used as badge by Nazis

swat [swot] *vt.* hit smartly; kill, *esp.* insects (**-tt-**)

swath [-awth] *n.* line of grass or grain cut and thrown together by scythe; whole sweep of scythe (*also* **swathe** [-āTH])

swathe *vt.* cover with wraps or bandages

sway *v.* swing unsteadily; (cause to) vacillate in opinion *etc.* —*vt.* influence opinion *etc.* —*n.* control; power; swaying motion

swear [-ār] *vt.* promise on oath; cause to take an oath —*vi.* declare; curse (**swore, sworn, swear'ing**)

sweat [swet] *n.* moisture oozing from, forming on skin, *esp.* in humans —*v.* (cause to) exude sweat; toil; employ at wrongfully low wages; *inf.* worry (**sweat** *or* **sweat'ed** *pt./pp.*, **sweat'ing** *pr.p.*) —**sweat'y** *a.* —**sweat shirt** long-sleeved cotton jersey

sweat'er *n.* woollen jersey

Swede *n.* native of Sweden

sweep *vi.* effect cleaning with broom; pass quickly or magnificently; extend in continuous curve —*vt.* clean with broom; carry impetuously (**swept, sweep'ing**) —*n.* act of cleaning with broom; sweeping motion; wide curve; range; long oar; one who cleans chimneys —**sweep'ing** *a.* wide-ranging; without limitations, reservations —**sweep, sweep'stake** *n.* gamble in which winner takes stakes contributed by all

sweet *a.* tasting like sugar; agreeable; kind, charming; fresh, fragrant; in good condition; tuneful; gentle, dear, beloved —*n.* small piece of sweet food; sweet course served at end of meal —**sweet'en** *v.* —**sweet'ish** *a.* —**sweet'ly** *adv.* —**sweet'bread** *n.* animal's pancreas used as food —**sweet'brier** *n.* wild rose —**sweet'heart** *n.* lover —**sweet'meat** *n.* sweetened delicacy *eg* small cake, sweet —**sweet pea** plant of pea family with bright flowers —**sweet potato** trailing plant; its edible, sweetish, starchy tubers —**sweet-talk** *v. inf.* coax, flatter —**sweet william** garden plant with flat flower clusters

swell *v.* expand —*vi.* be greatly filled with pride, emotion (**swelled, swo'llen, swell'ing**) —*n.* act of swelling or being swollen; wave of sea; mechanism in organ to vary volume of sound; *sl.* person of high social standing —*a. sl.* smart, fine

swelt'er *vi.* be oppressed with heat

swept *pt./pp. of* SWEEP
swerve *vi.* swing round, change direction during motion; turn aside (from duty *etc.*) —*n.* swerving
swift *a.* rapid, quick, ready —*n.* bird like a swallow —**swift'ly** *adv.*
swig *n.* large swallow of drink —*v.* drink thus (**-gg-**)
swill *v.* drink greedily; pour water over or through —*n.* liquid pig foods; greedy drinking
swim *vi.* support and move oneself in water; float; be flooded; have feeling of dizziness —*vt.* cross by swimming; compete in by swimming (**swam, swum, swimm'ing**) —*n.* spell of swimming —**swimm'er** *n.* —**swimm'ingly** *adv.* successfully, effortlessly
swin'dle *n./v.* cheat —**swind'ler** *n.* —**swind'ling** *n.*
swine *n.* pig; contemptible person (*pl.* **swine**) —**swi'nish** *a.* —**swine'herd** *n.*
swing *v.* (cause to) move to and fro; (cause to) pivot, turn; hang; arrange, play music with (jazz) rhythm —*vi.* be hanged; hit out (at) (**swung** *pt./pp.*) —*n.* act, instance of swinging; seat hung to swing on; fluctuation (*esp. eg* in voting pattern); tour of particular area or region; train of freight sleds, canoes —**swing'er** *n. sl.* person regarded as modern, lively
swipe *v.* strike with wide, sweeping or glancing blow; *sl.* steal
swirl *v.* (cause to) move with eddying motion —*n.* such motion
swish *v.* (cause to) move with audible hissing sound —*n.* the sound
Swiss *n.* native of Switzerland —*a.* —**swiss roll UK** type of rolled-up sponge cake
switch *n.* mechanism to complete or interrupt electric circuit *etc.*; abrupt change; movable rail changing train to other track; flexible stick or twig; tufted end of animal's tail; tress of false hair —*vi.* shift, change; swing —*vt.* affect (current *etc.*) with switch; change abruptly; change (train) to other track; strike with switch —**switch'back** *n.* road, railway with steep rises and descents —**switch'blade** *n.* knife with retractable blade that springs out when button is pressed —**switch'board** *n.* installation for establishing or varying connections in telephone and electric circuits —**switch'man** *n.* person who operates railway switch
swiv'el *n.* mechanism of two parts which can revolve the one on the other —*v.* turn (on swivel) (**-ll-**)
swo'llen *pp. of* SWELL
swoon [-ōō-] *vi./n.* faint
swoop [-ōō-] *vi.* dive, as hawk —*n.* act of swooping; sudden attack
swop *vt. see* SWAP
sword [sawrd] *n.* weapon with long blade for cutting or thrusting —**sword'-fish** *n.* fish with elongated sharp upper jaw, like sword
swore *pt.* —**sworn** *pp. of* SWEAR
swot *inf. v.* study hard (**-tt-**) —*n.* one who works hard at lessons or studies
swum *pp. of* SWIM
swung *pt./pp. of* SWING
syb'arite *n.* person who loves luxury —**sybarit'ic** *a.*
syc'amore [sik'-] *n.* tree allied to plane tree and maple
syc'ophant [sik'-] *n.* one using flattery to gain favours —**sycophant'ic** *a.* —**syc'ophancy** *n.*
syll'able *n.* division of word as unit for pronunciation —**syllab'ic** *a.* —**syllab'i-fy** *vt.*
syll'abub, sill'abub *n.* sweet frothy dish of cream, sugar and wine; something insubstantial
syll'abus *n.* outline of a course of study; programme, list of subjects studied on course (*pl.* **-es, -bi** [-bī])
syll'ogism [-j-] *n.* form of logical reasoning consisting of two premisses and conclusion —**syllogist'ic** *a.* —**syllo-gis'tically** *adv.*
sylph [silf] *n.* slender, graceful woman; sprite
syl'van *a.* of forests, trees
sym- *see* SYN-, used before labial consonants
symbio'sis *n.* living together of two organisms of different kinds, *esp.* to their mutual benefit —**symbiot'ic** *a.*
sym'bol *n.* sign; thing representing or typifying something —**symbol'ic** *a.* —**symbol'ically** *adv.* —**sym'bolism** *n.* use of, representation by symbols; movement in art holding that work of art should express idea in symbolic form —**sym'bolist** *n./a.* —**sym'bolize** *vt.*
symm'etry *n.* proportion between

parts; balance of arrangement between two sides; order —**symmet'rical** *a.* having due proportion in its parts; harmonious; regular —**symmet'rically** *adv.*

sym'pathy *n.* feeling for another in pain *etc.*; compassion, pity; sharing of emotion, interest, desire *etc.*; fellow feeling —**sympathet'ic** *a.* —**sympathet'ically** *adv.* —**sym'pathize** *vi.*

sym'phony *n.* composition for full orchestra; harmony of sounds —**symphon'ic** *a.* —**sympho'nious** *a.* harmonious

sympo'sium *n.* conference, meeting; discussion, writings on a given topic

symp'tom *n.* change in body indicating its state of health or disease; sign, token —**symptomat'ic** *a.*

syn- [sin-, sing-] (*comb. form*) with, together, alike

syn'agogue [-gog] *n.* (place of worship of) Jewish congregation

syn'chromesh *a.* (of gearbox) having device that synchronizes speeds of gears before they engage

syn'chronize *vt.* make agree in time —*vi.* happen at same time —**syn'chronism** *n.* —**synchroniza'tion** *n.* —**syn'chronous** *a.* simultaneous

syn'chrotron [-krə-] *n.* device for acceleration of stream of electrons

syn'copate *vt.* accentuate weak beat in bar of music —**syncopa'tion** *n.*

syn'cope [-kə-pi] *n.* fainting; elision of letter(s) from middle of word

syn'dicate *n.* body of people, delegates associated for some enterprise —*v.* form syndicate —*vt.* publish in many newspapers at the same time —**syn'dicalism** *n.* economic movement aiming at combination of workers in all trades to enforce demands of labour

syn'drome *n.* combination of several symptoms in disease; symptom, set of symptoms or characteristics

synec'doche [-nek'də-ki] *n.* figure of speech by which whole of thing is put for part or part for whole, *eg sail* for *ship*

syn'od *n.* church council; convention

syn'onym *n.* word with same meaning as another —**synonym'ity** *n.* —**synon'ymous** *a.*

synop'sis *n.* summary, outline —**synop'size** *vt.* make synopsis of —**synop'tic** *a.* of, like synopsis; having same viewpoint

syn'tax *n.* part of grammar treating of arrangement of words in sentence —**syntac'tic** *a.* —**syntac'tically** *adv.*

syn'thesis *n.* putting together, combination (*pl.* **-theses** [-ēz]) —**syn'thesize** *v.* make artificially —**syn'thesizer** *n.* electronic keyboard instrument capable of reproducing a wide range of musical sounds —**synthet'ic** *a.* artificial; of synthesis —**synthet'ically** *adv.*

syph'ilis *n.* contagious venereal disease —**syphilit'ic** *a.*

syr'inge [si'rinj] *n.* instrument for drawing in liquid by piston and forcing it out in fine stream or spray; squirt —*vt.* spray, cleanse with syringe

syr'up [si'rəp] *n.* thick solution obtained in process of refining sugar; any liquid like this, *esp.* in consistency —**syr'upy** *a.*

sys'tem *n.* complex whole, organization; method; classification —**systemat'ic** *a.* methodical —**systemat'ically** *adv.* —**sys'tematize** *vt.* reduce to system; arrange methodically —**system'ic** *a.* affecting entire body or organism

sys'tole [-tə-li] *n.* contraction of heart and arteries for expelling blood and carrying on circulation —**systol'ic** *a.* contracting; of systole

T

T tablespoon; temperature; *Chem.* tritium —**to a T** precisely, to a nicety

t. tense; ton

t tonne

ta [tah] *interj. inf.* thank you

tab *n.* tag, label, short strap; bill, *esp.* for meal or drinks —**keep tabs on** *inf.* keep watchful eye on

tab'ard *n.* (herald's) short tunic open at sides

tabb'y *n./a.* (cat) with markings of stripes *etc.* on lighter background

tab'ernacle *n.* portable shrine of Israelites; *RC Ch.* receptacle containing consecrated Host; place of worship not called a church

ta'ble *n.* piece of furniture consisting of flat board supported by legs; food; set of facts, figures arranged in lines or columns —*vt.* lay on table; submit (motion *etc.*) for consideration by meeting —**ta'bleland** *n.* plateau, high flat area —**ta'blespoon** *n.* spoon used for serving food *etc.* —**table tennis** ball game played on table with small bats and light hollow ball

tab'leau [-lō] *n.* group of persons, silent and motionless, arranged to represent some scene; dramatic scene (*pl.* **-leaux** [-lō])

tab'le d'hôte' [tahb'l-dōt'] *Fr.* meal, with limited choice of dishes, at a fixed price

tab'let *n.* pill of compressed powdered medicinal substance; flattish cake of soap *etc.*; slab of stone, wood *etc.*, *esp.* used formerly for writing on

tab'loid *n.* illustrated popular small-sized newspaper with terse, sensational headlines

taboo' *a.* forbidden or disapproved of —*n.* prohibition resulting from social conventions *etc.*; thing prohibited —*vt.* place under taboo

tab'ular *a.* shaped, arranged like a table —**tab'ulate** *vt.* arrange (figures, facts *etc.*) in tables —**tabula'tion** *n.* —**tab'ulator** *n.*

tacho- (*comb. form*) speed

tachom'eter [-kom'-] *n.* device for measuring speed, *esp.* of revolving shaft (in car) and hence revolutions per minute

tac'it [tas'-] *a.* implied but not spoken; silent —**tac'itly** *adv.* —**tac'iturn** *a.* talking little; habitually silent —**taciturn'nity** *n.*

tack[1] *n.* small nail; long loose stitch; *Naut.* course of ship obliquely to windward; course, direction; *inf.* food —*vt.* nail with tacks; stitch lightly; append, attach; sail to windward

tack[2] *n.* riding harness for horses

tac'kle [-kəl] *n.* equipment, apparatus, *esp.* lifting appliances with ropes; *Sport* physical challenge of opponent —*vt.* take in hand; grip, grapple with; challenge

tack'y[1] *a.* sticky; not quite dry —**tack'iness** *n.*

tack'y[2] *a. inf.* shabby; ostentatious and vulgar

tact *n.* skill in dealing with people or situations; delicate perception of the feelings of others —**tact'ful** *a.* —**tact'fully** *adv.* —**tact'less** *a.* —**tact'lessly** *adv.*

tact'ics *pl.n.* art of handling troops, ships in battle; adroit management of a situation; plans for this —**tact'ical** *a.* —**tacti'cian** *n.*

tact'ile *a.* of, relating to the sense of touch

tad *n.* small boy; small bit or piece

tad'pole *n.* immature frog, in its first state before gills and tail are absorbed

taff'eta *n.* smooth, stiff fabric of silk, rayon *etc.*

taff'rail *n.* rail at stern of ship; flat ornamental part of stern

Taff'y *n. sl.* Welshman; (**t-**) chewy candy made of brown sugar or molasses and butter

tag[1] *n.* label identifying or showing price of (something); ragged, hanging end;

pointed end of shoelace *etc.*; trite quotation; any appendage —*vt.* append, add (on); trail (along) behind (**-gg-**) —**tag end** last part of something

tag[2] *n.* children's game where one being chased becomes the chaser upon being touched; *Baseball* act of touching runner with ball, putting him out —*vt.* touch (**-gg-**)

tail *n.* flexible prolongation of animal's spine; lower or inferior part of anything; appendage; rear part of aircraft; *inf.* person employed to follow another —*pl.* reverse side of coin; *inf.* tail coat —*vt.* remove tail of; *inf.* follow closely, trail —**tailed** *a.* —**tail'ings** *pl.n.* waste left over from some (*eg* industrial) process —**tail'less** *a.* —**tail'board** *n.* removable or hinged rear board on truck *etc.* —**tail coat** man's evening dress jacket —**tail end** last part —**tail'gate** *n.* tailboard, *esp.* on truck or station wagon —*vi.* follow too closely behind another vehicle —**tail'light** *n.* light carried at rear of vehicle —**tail'spin** *n.* spinning dive of aircraft —**turn tail** run away

tail'or *n.* maker of outer clothing, *esp.* for men —**tailor-made** *a.* made by tailor; well-fitting; appropriate

taint *v.* affect or be affected by pollution *etc.* —*n.* defect, flaw; infection, contamination

take *vt.* grasp, get hold of; get; receive, assume; adopt; accept; understand; consider; carry, conduct; use; capture; consume; subtract; require —*vi.* be effective; please; go (**took, ta'ken, ta'king**) —*n.* *esp.* (recording of) scene, sequence on film photographed without interruption —**ta'king** *a.* charming —**ta'kings** *pl.n.* earnings, receipts —**take-off** *n.* instant at which aircraft becomes airborne; commencement of flight; *inf.* parody —**take'out** *a./n.* (food, restaurant selling food) prepared for consumption elsewhere —**take after** resemble in face or character —**take down** write down; dismantle; humiliate —**take in** understand; make (garment *etc.*) smaller; deceive —**take in vain** blaspheme; be facetious —**take off** (of aircraft) leave ground; *inf.* go away; *inf.* mimic —**take to** become fond of

talc *n.* soft mineral of magnesium silicate; talcum powder —**talcum powder** powder, *usu.* scented, to absorb body moisture, deodorize *etc.*

tale *n.* story, narrative, report; fictitious story

tal'ent *n.* natural ability or power; ancient weight or money —**tal'ented** *a.* gifted

tal'isman [-iz-] *n.* object supposed to have magic power; amulet (*pl.* **-mans**) —**talisman'ic** *a.*

talk [tawk] *vi.* express, exchange ideas *etc.* in words —*vt.* express in speech, utter; discuss —*n.* speech, lecture; conversation; rumour —**talk'ative** *a.* fond of talking —**talk'er** *n.* —**talking-to** *n.* *inf.* reproof

tall [tawl] *a.* high; of great stature; incredible, untrue, as **tall story**; *inf.* difficult to accomplish

tall'ow [-ō] *n.* melted and clarified animal fat —*vt.* smear with this

tall'y *vi.* correspond one with the other; keep record (**tall'ied, tall'ying**) —*n.* record, account, total number —**tal'lier** *n.*

tally-ho' *interj.* huntsman's cry to urge on hounds

Tal'mud *n.* body of Jewish law —**Talmud'ic** *a.*

tal'on *n.* claw

tam'arind *n.* tropical tree; its pods containing sour brownish pulp

tam'arisk *n.* ornamental, evergreen tree or shrub with slender branches, very small leaves and spiky flowers

tambourine' [-rēn'] *n.* flat half-drum with jingling discs of metal attached

tame *a.* not wild, domesticated; subdued; uninteresting —*vt.* make tame —**tame'ly** *adv.* in a tame manner; without resisting —**ta'mer** *n.*

tam-o'-shant'er, tamm'y *n.* brimless wool cap with bobble in centre

tamp *vt.* pack, force down by repeated blows

tamp'er *vi.* interfere (with) improperly; meddle

tam'pon *n.* plug of lint, cotton *etc.* inserted in wound, body cavity, to stop flow of blood, absorb secretions *etc.*

tan *a./n.* (of) brown colour of skin after long exposure to rays of sun *etc.* —*v.* (cause to) go brown; (of animal hide) convert to leather by chemical treatment (**-nn-**) —**tann'er** *n.* —**tann'ery** *n.*

place where hides are tanned —**tann'ic** *a.* —**tann'in** *n.* vegetable substance used as tanning agent —**tan'bark** *n.* bark of certain trees, yielding tannin

tan'dem *n.* bicycle for two riders, one behind the other

tang *n.* strong pungent taste or smell; trace, hint; spike, barb —**tang'y** *a.*

tan'gent [-j-] *n.* line that touches a curve without cutting; divergent course —*a.* touching, meeting without cutting —**tangen'tial** *a.* —**tangen'tially** *adv.*

tangerine' [-rēn'] *n.* Asian citrus tree; its fruit, a variety of orange

tan'gible *a.* that can be touched; definite; palpable; concrete —**tangibil'ity** *n.*

tan'gle [-ng'gl] *n.* confused mass or situation —*vt.* twist together in muddle; contend

tan'go *n.* dance of S Amer. origin (*pl.* **-gos**)

tank *n.* storage vessel for liquids or gas; armoured motor vehicle moving on tracks; cistern; reservoir —**tank'er** *n.* ship, truck *etc.* for carrying liquid in bulk

tank'ard *n.* large drinking cup of metal or glass; its contents, *esp.* beer

tann'in *see* TAN

tan'sy [-zi] *n.* yellow-flowered aromatic herb

tan'talize *vt.* torment by appearing to offer something desired; tease

tan'tamount *a.* equivalent in value or signification; equal, amounting (to)

tan'trum *n.* childish outburst of temper

tap[1] *v.* strike lightly but with some noise (**-pp-**) —*n.* slight blow, rap

tap[2] *n.* valve with handle to regulate or stop flow of fluid in pipe *etc.*; stopper, plug permitting liquid to be drawn from cask *etc.*; steel tool for forming internal screw threads; connection for supply of electricity at intermediate point in supply line —*vt.* put tap in; draw off with or as with tap; make secret connection to telephone wire to overhear conversation on it; make connection for supply of electricity at intermediate point in supply line; form internal threads in (**-pp-**)

tape *n.* narrow long strip of fabric, paper *etc.*; magnetic recording of music *etc.* —*vt.* record (speech, music *etc.*) —**tape measure** tape of fabric, metal marked off in centimetres, inches *etc.* —**tape recorder** apparatus for recording sound on magnetized tape and playing it back —**tape'worm** *n.* long flat worm parasitic in animals and man

ta'per *vi.* become gradually thinner towards one end —*n.* thin candle; long wick covered with wax; a narrowing

tap'estry *n.* fabric decorated with designs in colours woven by needles, not in shuttles —**tap'estried** *a.*

tapio'ca *n.* beadlike starch made from cassava root, used *esp.* in puddings

ta'pir [-pər] *n.* Amer. animal with elongated snout, allied to pig

tapp'et *n.* in internal-combustion engine, short steel rod conveying movement imparted by the lift of a cam to the valve stem

tap'root *n.* large single root growing straight down

tar[1] *n.* thick black liquid distilled from coal *etc.* —*vt.* coat, treat with tar (**-rr-**)

tar[2] *n. inf.* sailor

tarantell'a *n.* lively Italian dance; music for it

taran'tula *n.* any of various large (poisonous) hairy spiders

tard'y *a.* slow, late —**tard'ily** *adv.*

tare[1] *n.* weight of wrapping, container for goods; unladen weight of vehicle

tare[2] *n.* vetch; weed

tar'get *n.* mark to aim at in shooting; thing aimed at; object of criticism; butt

tar'iff [ta'rif] *n.* tax levied on imports *etc.*; list of charges; method of charging for supply of services, *eg* electricity

Tar'mac **R** mixture of tar, bitumen and crushed stones rolled to give hard, smooth surface to road *etc.*; **UK** (**t-**) airport runway

tarn *n.* small mountain lake

tar'nish *v.* (cause to) become stained, lose shine or become dimmed or sullied —*n.* discoloration, blemish

tar'o *n.* plant of Pacific islands; its edible roots

tar'ot [ta'rō] *n.* one of special pack of cards now used mainly in fortune-telling

tarpaul'in *n.* (sheet of) heavy hard-wearing waterproof fabric

tarr'agon *n.* aromatic herb

tarr'y *vi.* linger, delay; stay behind (**tar'ried, tarr'ying**)

tart[1] *n.* small flan filled with fruit, jam *etc.*; *inf. offens.* promiscuous woman

tart[2] *a.* sour; sharp; bitter

tar'tan *n.* woollen cloth woven in pattern of coloured checks, *esp.* in colours, patterns associated with Scottish clans; such pattern

tar'tar[1] *n.* crust deposited on teeth; deposit formed during fermentation of wine —**tartar'ic** [-ta'rik] *a.*

tar'tar[2] *n.* vicious-tempered person, difficult to deal with

tar'trazine [-trə-zēn] *n.* artificial yellow dye widely used in food, soft drinks, drugs and to dye textiles

task [-ah-] *n.* piece of work (*esp.* unpleasant or difficult) set or undertaken —*vt.* assign task to; exact —**task force** naval or military unit dispatched to carry out specific undertaking —**task'master** *n.* overseer —**take to task** reprove

tass'el *n.* ornament of fringed knot of threads *etc.*; tuft

taste *n.* sense by which flavour, quality of substance is detected by the tongue; this act or sensation; (brief) experience of something; small amount; preference, liking; power of discerning, judging; discretion, delicacy —*v.* observe or distinguish the taste of a substance; take small amount into mouth; experience —*vi.* have specific flavour —**taste'ful** *a.* in good style; with, showing good taste —**taste'fully** *adv.* —**taste'less** *a.* —**ta'sty** *a.* pleasantly or highly flavoured —**taste bud** small organ of taste on tongue

tat *v.* make by tatting (**-tt-**) —**tatt'er** *n.* —**tatt'ing** *n.* type of handmade lace

tatt'er *v.* make or become ragged, worn to shreds —*n.* ragged piece

tat'tle *vi./n.* gossip, chatter —**tat'tletale** *n.* one who spreads gossip

tattoo'[1] *n.* beat of drum and bugle call; military spectacle or pageant

tattoo'[2] *vt.* mark skin in patterns *etc.* by pricking and filling punctures with indelible coloured inks (**tattooed', tattoo'ing**) —*n.* mark so made

tatt'y *a.* shabby, worn out —**tat'tiness** *n.*

taught *pt./pp. of* TEACH

taunt *vt.* provoke, deride with insulting words *etc.* —*n.* instance of this

Tau'rus [taw'-] *n.* (the bull) 2nd sign of the zodiac, operative *c.* Apr. 21-May 20

taut *a.* drawn tight; under strain —**taut'en** *vt.* make tight or tense

tautol'ogy *n.* repetition of same thing in other words in same sentence —**tautolog'ical** *a.*

tav'ern *n.* place licensed for sale and consumption of alcoholic drink; inn

taw *n.* large marble —*pl.* game of marbles

taw'dry *a.* showy, but cheap and without taste, flashy —**taw'drily** *adv.* —**taw'driness** *n.*

tawn'y *a./n.* (of) light (yellowish) brown

tax *n.* compulsory payments by wage earners, companies *etc.* imposed by government to raise revenue; heavy demand on something —*vt.* impose tax on; strain; accuse, blame —**tax'able** *a.* —**taxa'tion** *n.* levying of taxes —**tax'payer** *n.*

tax'i(cab) *n.* motor vehicle for hire with driver (*pl.* **tax'is** [-iz]) —*vi.* (of aircraft) run along ground under its own power; go in taxi (**tax'ied** *pt./pp.*, **tax'ying, tax'iing** *pr.p.*) —**taxi stand**

tax'idermy *n.* art of stuffing, mounting animal skins to give them lifelike appearance —**taxider'mal, taxider'mic** *a.* —**tax'idermist** *n.*

taxon'omy *n.* science, practice of classification, *esp.* of biological organisms

TB tuberculosis

te, ti *n.* seventh sol-fa note

tea *n.* dried leaves of plant cultivated *esp.* in (sub)tropical Asia; infusion of it as beverage; various herbal infusions; tea, cakes *etc.* as light afternoon meal; main evening meal —**tea bag** small porous bag of paper containing tea leaves —**tea'spoon** *n.* small spoon for stirring tea *etc.*

teach *vt.* instruct; educate; train; impart knowledge of —*vi.* act as teacher (**taught, teach'ing**) —**teach'er** *n.* —**teach'ing** *n.*

teak *n.* East Indian tree; very hard wood obtained from it

teal *n.* type of small duck; greenish-blue colour

team *n.* set of animals, players of game *etc.* associated in activity —*vi.* (*usu. with* up) (cause to) make a team —*vt.* drag or transport by team —**team'ster** *n.* driver of team of draught animals; truck driver —**team spirit** subordination of individual desire for good of team —**team'-**

work *n.* co-operative work by team acting as unit

tear[1] [tēr] *n.* drop of fluid appearing in and falling from eye —**tear'ful** *a.* inclined to weep; involving tears —**tear'less** *a.* —**tear'drop** *n.* —**tear gas** irritant gas causing abnormal watering of eyes, and temporary blindness —**tear-jerker** *n. inf.* excessively sentimental film *etc.*

tear[2] [tār] *vt.* pull apart, rend —*vi.* become torn; rush (**tore, torn, tear'ing**) —*n.* hole, cut or split

tease *vt.* tantalize, torment, irritate, bait; pull apart fibres of —*n.* one who teases —**teas'ing** *a.*

tea'sel, tea'zel *n.* plant with prickly leaves and head

teat *n.* nipple of female breast; rubber nipple of baby's feeding bottle

tech [tek] *a./n. inf. short for* technical (school or college)

tech. technical; technology

tech'nical *a.* of, specializing in industrial, practical or mechanical arts and applied sciences; skilled in practical and mechanical arts; belonging to particular art or science; according to letter of the law —**technical'ity** *n.* point of procedure; state of being technical —**tech'nically** *adv.* —**techni'cian** *n.* one skilled in technique of an art —**technique'** [-nēk'] *n.* method of performance in an art; skill required for mastery of subject —**technical school** school that gives training for agriculture, industry *etc.*

Tech'nicolor [tek'-] R colour photography, *esp.* in cinema

technoc'racy [tek-] *n.* government by technical experts; group of these experts

technol'ogy [tek-] *n.* application of practical, mechanical sciences to industry, commerce; technical methods, skills, knowledge —**technolog'ical** *a.* —**technol'ogist** *n.*

tecton'ic *a.* of construction or building —**tecton'ics** *pl.n.* (*used as sing.*) art, science of building

tedd'y (bear) child's soft toy bear

te'dious *a.* causing fatigue or boredom, monotonous —**te'dium** *n.* monotony

tee *n. Golf* slightly raised ground from which first stroke of hole is made; small peg supporting ball for this stroke; target in some games, *eg* quoits —**tee off** make first stroke of hole in golf

teem *vi.* abound with; swarm; be prolific; pour, rain heavily

teens *pl.n.* years of life from 13 to 19 —**teen'age** *a.* —**teen'ager** *n.* young person between 13 and 19

tee'pee *n. see* TEPEE

tee'ter *vi.* seesaw or make similar movements; vacillate

teeth *n., pl.* of TOOTH

teethe [-TH] *vi.* (of baby) grow first teeth —**teething troubles** problems, difficulties at first stage of something

teeto'tal *a.* pledged to abstain from alcohol —**teeto'talism** *n.* —**teeto'taller** *n.*

Tef'lon R polymer used to make nonstick coatings on cooking utensils

tel. telegram; telegraph; telephone

tele- (*comb. form*) at a distance, and from far off

tel'ecast *v./n.* (broadcast) television programme

telecommunica'tions *pl.n.* (*with sing. v.*) science and technology of communications by telephony, radio, television *etc.*

tel'egram *n.* message sent by telegraph

tel'egraph *n.* electrical apparatus for transmitting messages to a distance; any signalling device for transmitting messages —*v.* communicate by telegraph; cast votes illegally by impersonating registered voters —**telegraph'ic** *a.* —**telegraph'ically** *adv.* —**teleg'raphist** *n.* one who works telegraph —**teleg'raphy** *n.* science of telegraph; use of telegraph

teleol'ogy *n.* doctrine of final causes; belief that things happen because of the purpose or design that will be fulfilled by them —**teleolog'ic(al)** *a.*

telep'athy *n.* action of one mind on another at a distance —**telepath'ic** *a.* —**telepath'ically** *adv.*

tel'ephone *n.* apparatus for communicating sound to hearer at a distance —*v.* communicate, speak by telephone —**telephon'ic** *a.* —**teleph'onist** *n.* person operating telephone switchboard —**teleph'ony** *n.* —**telephone booth** kiosk for public telephone

telepho'to *a.* (of lens) producing magnified image of distant object

tel'eprinter *n.* apparatus, like typewriter, by which typed messages are sent and received by wire

Tel'eprompter R *Television* device to enable speaker to refer to his script out of sight of the cameras

tel'escope *n.* optical instrument for magnifying distant objects —*v.* slide or drive together, *esp.* parts designed to fit one inside the other; make smaller, shorter —**telescop'ic** *a.*

tel'etext *n.* electronic system which shows information, news on subscribers' television screens

Tel'etype R type of teleprinter

tel'evision *n.* system of producing on screen images of distant objects, events *etc.* by electromagnetic radiation; device for receiving this transmission and converting it to optical images; programmes *etc.* viewed on television set —**tel'evise** *vt.* transmit by television; make, produce as television programme

tel'ex *n.* international telegraph service using teleprinters —*v.*

Tel'idon R interactive viewdata service

tell *vt.* let know; order, direct; narrate, make known; discern; distinguish; count —*vi.* give account; be of weight, importance; *inf.* reveal secrets (**told, tell'ing**) —**tell'er** *n.* narrator; bank cashier —**tell'ing** *a.* effective, striking —**tell'-tale** *n.* sneak; automatic indicator —*a.* revealing

tellur'ian [-loor'-] *a.* of the earth —**tellu'rium** *n.* nonmetallic bluish-white element —**tellur'ic** *a.* —**tell'urous** *a.*

tell'y *n. inf.* television (set)

temer'ity [-me'ri-] *n.* boldness, audacity

temp *n. inf.* one employed on temporary basis

temp. temperature; temporary

temp'er *n.* frame of mind; anger, oft. noisy; mental constitution; degree of hardness of steel *etc.* —*vt.* restrain, qualify, moderate; harden; bring to proper condition

tem'pera *n.* emulsion used as painting medium

temp'erament *n.* natural disposition; emotional mood; mental constitution —**temperamen'tal** *a.* given to extremes of temperament, moody; of, occasioned by temperament —**temperamen'tally** *adv.*

temp'erate *a.* not extreme; showing, practising moderation —**temp'erance** *n.* moderation; abstinence, *esp.* from alcohol —**temp'erately** *adv.*

temp'erature *n.* degree of heat or coldness; *inf.* (abnormally) high body temperature

temp'est *n.* violent storm —**tempes'tuous** *a.* turbulent; violent, stormy —**tempes'tuously** *adv.*

tem'plate, tem'plet *n.* mould, pattern to help shape something accurately

tem'ple[1] *n.* building for worship; shrine

tem'ple[2] *n.* flat part on either side of forehead

tem'po *n.* rate, rhythm, *esp.* in music

temp'oral *a.* of time; of this life or world, secular —**temporal'ity** *n.*

temp'orary *a.* lasting, used only for a time —**temp'orarily** *adv.*

temp'orize *vi.* use evasive action; hedge; gain time by negotiation *etc.*; conform to circumstances —**tem'porizer** *n.*

tempt *vt.* try to persuade, entice, *esp.* to something wrong or unwise; dispose, cause to be inclined to —**tempta'tion** *n.* act of tempting; thing that tempts —**tempt'er** *n.* (**tempt'ress** *fem.*) —**tempt'ing** *a.* attractive, inviting

ten *n./a.* cardinal number next after nine —**tenth** *a./n.* ordinal number

ten'able *a.* able to be held, defended, maintained

tena'cious *a.* holding fast; retentive; stubborn —**tenac'ity** [-nas'-] *n.*

ten'ant *n.* one who holds lands, house *etc.* on rent or lease —**ten'ancy** *n.* —**ten'antry** *n.* body of tenants

tend[1] *vi.* be inclined; be conducive; make in direction of —**tend'ency** *n.* inclination, bent —**tenden'tious** *a.* having, showing tendency or bias, controversial

tend[2] *vt.* take care of, watch over; *inf.* pay attention —**tend'er** *n.* small boat carried by yacht or ship; carriage for fuel and water attached to steam locomotive; one who tends, *eg* **bartender**

tend'er[1] *a.* not tough or hard; easily injured; gentle, loving, affectionate; delicate, soft —**tend'erly** *adv.* —**ten'derness** *n.* —**tend'erize** *vt.* soften (meat) by pounding or by treating (it) with substance made for this purpose

—**tend'erfoot** *n.* newcomer, *esp.* to ranch *etc.*

tend'er[2] *vt.* offer —*vi.* make offer or estimate —*n.* offer; offer or estimate for contract to undertake specific work; what may legally be offered in payment

tend'on *n.* sinew attaching muscle to bone *etc.*

tend'ril *n.* slender curling stem by which climbing plant clings to anything; curl, as of hair

ten'ement *n.* building divided into separate apartments

ten'et [*or* tē'-] *n.* doctrine, belief

tenn'is *n.* game in which ball is struck with racket by players on opposite sides of net, lawn tennis —**tennis elbow** strained muscle as a result of playing tennis

ten'on *n.* tongue put on end of piece of wood *etc.*, to fit into a mortise —**tenon saw**

ten'or *n.* male voice between alto and bass; music for, singer with this; general course, meaning

ten'pins *pl.n.* (*with sing. v.*) bowling game in which heavy bowls are rolled down long lane to knock over ten target pins at the other end

tense[1] *n.* modification of verb to show time of action

tense[2] *a.* stretched tight; strained; taut; emotionally strained —*v.* make, become tense —**ten'sile** *a.* of, relating to tension; capable of being stretched —**ten'sion** *n.* stretching; strain when stretched; emotional strain or excitement; hostility, suspense; *Electricity* voltage

tent *n.* portable shelter of canvas

tent'acle *n.* elongated, flexible organ of some animals (*eg* octopus) used for grasping, feeding *etc.*

tent'ative *a.* done as a trial; experimental, cautious —**tent'atively** *adv.*

tent'erhooks *pl.n.* —**on tenterhooks** in anxious suspense

ten'uous *a.* flimsy, uncertain; thin, fine, slender —**tenu'ity** *n.*

ten'ure *n.* (length of time of) possession, holding of office, position *etc.*

te'pee *n.* N Amer. Indian cone-shaped tent of animal skins

tep'id *a.* moderately warm, lukewarm; half-hearted

tequi'la [-kē'-] *n.* Mexican alcoholic spirit

ter'bium *n.* rare metallic element

tercente'nary *a./n.* (of) three-hundredth anniversary

term *n.* word, expression; limited period of time; period during which courts sit, schools are open *etc.*; limit, end —*pl.* conditions; mutual relationship —*vt.* name, designate

term'inal *a.* at, forming an end; pert. to, forming a terminus; (of disease) ending in death —*n.* terminal part or structure; terminus; extremity; point where current enters, leaves electrical device (*eg* battery); device permitting operation of computer at some distance from it

term'inate *v.* bring, come to an end —**term'inable** *a.* —**termina'tion** *n.*

terminol'ogy *n.* set of technical terms or vocabulary; study of terms —**terminolog'ical** *a.*

term'inus *n.* finishing point; farthest limit; railway station, bus station *etc.* at end of long-distance line (*pl.* **-ni** [-nī])

ter'mite *n.* insect, some species of which feed on and damage wood (*also called* **white ant**)

tern *n.* sea bird like gull

tern'ary *a.* consisting of three; proceeding in threes

terr. terrace; territory

terr'ace *n.* raised level place; level cut out of hill —*vt.* form into, furnish with terrace

terr'a cott'a hard unglazed pottery; its colour, a brownish-red

terr'a fir'ma *Lat.* firm ground; dry land

terr'ain [*or* -ān'] *n.* area of ground, *esp.* with reference to its physical character

Terramy'cin R antibiotic allied to penicillin

terr'apin *n.* type of aquatic tortoise

terra'rium *n.* enclosed container in which small plants, animals are kept

terrazz'o [-ats'ō] *n.* floor, wall finish of chips of stone set in mortar and polished

terrest'rial *a.* of the earth; of, living on land

terr'ible *a.* serious; dreadful, frightful; excessive; causing fear —**terr'ibly** *adv.*

terr'ier *n.* small dog of various breeds, *orig.* for following quarry into burrow

terrif'ic *a.* very great; *inf.* good, excellent; terrible, awe-inspiring

terr'ify *vt.* fill with fear, dread

terr'itory *n.* region; geographical area under control of a political unit, *esp.* a sovereign state; area of knowledge —**territo'rial** *a.* of territory

terr'or *n.* great fear; *inf.* troublesome person or thing —**terr'orism** *n.* use of violence, intimidation to achieve ends; state of terror —**terr'orist** *n./a.* —**ter'rorize** *vt.* force, oppress by fear, violence

terr'y *n./a.* (pile fabric) with the loops uncut

terse *a.* expressed in few words, concise; abrupt

ter'tiary [-shər-i] *a.* third in degree, order *etc.* —*n.* (**T-**) geological period before Quaternary

Ter'ylene [te'rə-] R synthetic yarn; fabric made of it

tess'ellate *vt.* make, pave, inlay with mosaic of small tiles; (of identical shapes) fit together exactly —**tes'sellated** *a.* —**tessella'tion** *n.* —**tess'era** *n.* stone used in mosaic (*pl.* **-ae** [-ē])

test *vt.* try, put to the proof; carry out test(s) on —*n.* critical examination; means of trial —**test'ing** *a.* difficult —**test case** lawsuit viewed as means of establishing precedent —**test match** one of series of international sports contests, *esp.* cricket —**test tube** narrow cylindrical glass vessel used in scientific experiments —**test-tube baby** baby conceived in artificial womb

test'ament *n.* *Law* will; declaration; (**T-**) one of the two main divisions of the Bible —**testament'ary** *a.*

test'ate *a.* having left a valid will —**tes'tacy** *n.* state of being testate —**testa'tor** *n.* maker of will (**testa'trix** *fem.*)

test'icle *n.* either of two male reproductive glands

test'ify *v.* declare; bear witness (to) (**-ified, -ifying**)

test'imony *n.* affirmation; evidence —**testimo'nial** *n.* certificate of character, ability *etc.*; gift by person expressing regard for recipient

test'is *n.* testicle (*pl.* **test'es** [-ēz])

test'y *a.* irritable, short-tempered —**test'ily** *adv.*

tet'anus *n.* acute infectious disease producing muscular spasms, contractions (*also called* **lockjaw**)

tête-à-tête' [tāt-ə-tāt'] *Fr.* private conversation

teth'er [-TH-] *n.* rope or chain for fastening (grazing) animal —*vt.* tie up with rope —**be at the end of one's tether** have reached limit of one's endurance

tet'ragon *n.* figure with four angles and four sides —**tetrag'onal** *a.* —**tetrahe'dron** *n.* solid contained by four plane faces

Teuton'ic *a.* German; of ancient Teutons

text *n.* (actual words of) book, passage *etc.*; passage of Scriptures *etc.*, *esp.* as subject of discourse —**text'ual** *a.* of, in a text —**text'book** *n.* book of instruction on particular subject

tex'tile *n.* any fabric or cloth, *esp.* woven —*a.* of (the making of) fabrics

tex'ture *n.* character, structure ; consistency

thalid'omide *n.* drug formerly used as sedative, but found to cause abnormalities in developing foetus

thall'ium *n.* highly toxic metallic element —**thall'ic** *a.*

than [TH-] *conj.* introduces second part of comparison

thane *n.* *Hist.* nobleman holding lands in return for certain services

thank *vt.* express gratitude to; say thanks; hold responsible —**thanks** *pl.n.* words of gratitude —**thank'ful** *a.* grateful, appreciative —**thank'less** *a.* having, bringing no thanks; unprofitable —**Thanksgiving Day** in Canada, public holiday on second Monday in October; in US, public holiday on fourth Thursday in November

that [TH-] *a.* demonstrates or particularizes (*pl.* **those**) —*demonstrative pron.* particular thing meant (*pl.* **those**) —*adv.* as —*relative pron.* which, who —*conj.* introduces noun or adverbial clauses

thatch *n.* reeds, straw *etc.* used as roofing material —*vt.* to roof (a house) with reeds, straw *etc.* —**thatch'er** *n.*

thaw *v.* melt; (cause to) unfreeze; defrost; become warmer, or more genial —*n.* a melting (of frost *etc.*)

the [THə, THē] is the definite article

the'atre [-tər] *n.* place where plays *etc.*

are performed; drama, dramatic works generally; large room with (tiered) seats, used for lectures *etc.*; surgical operating room **—theat'rical** *a.* of, for the theatre; exaggerated, affected **—theat'rically** *adv.* **—theat'ricals** *pl.n.* amateur dramatic performances

thee [TH-] *pron. obs.* objective and dative of THOU

theft *n.* stealing

their [THār] *a./pron. of* THEM; *possessive of* THEY **—theirs** *poss. pron.* belonging to them

the'ism *n.* belief in creation of universe by one god **—the'ist** *n.* **—theist'ic** *a.*

them *pron.* objective case of THEY; those persons or things **—themselves'** *pron.* emphatic and reflexive form of THEY

theme *n.* main idea or topic of conversation, book *etc.*; subject of composition; recurring melody in music **—themat'ic** *a.* **—theme park** leisure area designed round one subject **—theme song** tune associated with particular program, person *etc.*

then [TH-] *adv.* at that time; next; that being so

thence [TH-] *adv. obs.* from that place, point of reasoning *etc.*

theoc'racy *n.* government by a deity or a priesthood **—theocrat'ic** *a.*

theod'olite *n.* transit for surveying

theol'ogy *n.* systematic study of religion(s) and religious belief(s) **—theolog'ical** *a.* **—theolog'ically** *adv.* **—theolo'gian** *n.*

the'orem *n.* proposition which can be demonstrated by argument **—theoremat'ic(al)** *a.*

the'ory *n.* supposition to account for something; system of rules and principles; rules and reasoning *etc.* as distinguished from practice **—theoret'ical** *a.* based on theory; speculative, as opposed to practical **—theoret'ically** *adv.* **—the'orist** *n.* **—the'orize** *vi.* form theories, speculate

theos'ophy *n.* any of various religious, philosophical systems claiming possibility of intuitive insight into divine nature

ther'apy [the'rə-] *n.* healing treatment: *usu.* in compounds as RADIOTHERAPY **—therapeu'tic** [-pyōō'-] *a.* of healing; serving to improve or maintain health **—therapeu'tics** *pl.n.* art of healing **—ther'apist** *n.*

there [TH-] *adv.* in that place; to that point **—thereby'** *adv.* by that means **—there'fore** *adv.* in consequence, that being so **—thereupon'** *conj.* at that point, immediately afterwards

therm *n.* unit of measurement of heat **—ther'mal, ther'mic** *a.* of, pert. to heat; hot, warm (*esp.* of spring *etc.*)

ther'mion *n.* ion emitted by incandescent body **—thermion'ic** *a.* pert. to thermion **—thermionic tube** electronic valve in which electrons are emitted from a heated rather than a cold cathode

thermo- (*comb. form*) related to, caused by or producing heat

thermodynam'ics *pl.n.* (*with sing. v.*) the science that deals with the interrelationship and interconversion of different forms of energy

thermoelectric'ity *n.* electricity developed by the action of heat

ther'mograph *n.* self-registering thermometer

thermom'eter *n.* instrument to measure temperature **—thermomet'ric** *a.*

thermonu'clear *a.* involving nuclear fusion

thermoplas'tic *n.* plastic that retains its properties after being melted and solidified *—a.*

Ther'mos R vacuum flask

ther'mostat *n.* apparatus for automatically regulating temperature **—thermostat'ic** *a.*

thesau'rus [-aw'-] *n.* book containing lists of synonyms and antonyms; dictionary of selected words, topics

these [TH-] *pron., pl. of* THIS

the'sis *n.* written work submitted for degree, diploma; theory maintained in argument (*pl.* **the'ses** [-sēz])

Thes'pian *a.* theatrical *—n.* actor, actress

they [THā] *pron.* the third person plural pronoun

thi'amine *n.* soluble white crystalline vitamin of B group

thick *a.* having great thickness, not thin; dense, crowded; viscous; (of voice) throaty; *inf.* stupid, insensitive; *inf.* friendly *—n.* busiest, most intense part **—thick'en** *v.* make, become thick; become more involved, complicated

—**thick'ly** *adv.* —**thick'ness** *n.* dimensions of anything measured through it, at right angles to length and breadth; state of being thick; layer —**thick'et** *n.* thick growth of small trees —**thickset'** *a.* sturdy and solid of body; set closely together

thief *n.* one who steals (*pl.* **thieves**) —**thieve** *v.* steal —**thiev'ish** *a.*

thigh [thī] *n.* upper part of leg

thim'ble *n.* cap protecting end of finger when sewing

thin *a.* of little thickness; slim; lean; of little density; sparse; fine; loose, not close-packed; *inf.* unlikely —*v.* make, become thin —**thin'ner** *n.* —**thin'ness** *n.*

thine [THīn] *pron./a. obs.* belonging to thee

thing *n.* material object; any possible object of thought

think *vi.* have one's mind at work; reflect, meditate; reason; deliberate; imagine; hold opinion —*vt.* conceive, consider in the mind; believe; esteem (**thought** [thawt], **think'ing**) —**think'able** *a.* able to be conceived, considered, possible, feasible —**think'er** *n.* —**think'ing** *a.* reflecting —**think-tank** *n.* group of experts studying specific problems

third *a.* ordinal number corresponding to *three* —*n.* third part —**third degree** *see* DEGREE —**third party** *Law, Insurance etc.* person involved by chance or only incidentally in legal proceedings *etc.* —**Third World** developing countries of Africa, Asia, Latin Amer.

thirst *n.* desire to drink; feeling caused by lack of drink; craving; yearning —*v.* feel lack of drink —**thirst'ily** *adv.* —**thirst'y** *a.*

thir'teen' *a./n.* three plus ten —**thir'ty** *n./a.* three times ten

this [TH-] *demonstrative a./pron.* denotes thing, person near, or just mentioned (*pl.* **these**)

this'tle [-sl] *n.* prickly plant with dense flower heads

thith'er [THiTH'-] *adv. obs.* to or towards that place

thong *n.* narrow strip of leather, strap

thor'ax *n.* part of body between neck and belly —**thorac'ic** [-as'-] *a.*

thor'ium *n.* radioactive metallic element

thorn *n.* prickle on plant; spine; bush noted for its thorns; *fig.* anything which causes trouble or annoyance —**thorn'y** *a.*

thor'ough [thur'ə] *a.* careful, methodical; complete, entire —**thor'oughly** *adv.* —**thor'oughbred** *a.* of pure breed —*n.* purebred animal, *esp.* horse —**thor'oughfare** *n.* road or passage open at both ends; right of way

those [TH-] *pron., pl. of* THAT; denoting, as a correlative of THESE, the former, as distinguished from the latter

thou [TH-] *pron. obs.* the second person singular pronoun (*pl.* **ye, you**)

though [THō] *conj.* in spite of the fact that, even if —*adv.* nevertheless

thought [thawt] *n.* process of thinking; what one thinks; product of thinking; meditation —*pt./pp. of* THINK —**thought'ful** *a.* considerate; showing careful thought; engaged in meditation; attentive —**thought'less** *a.* inconsiderate, careless, heedless

thou'sand [-z-] *n./a.* cardinal number, ten hundred

thrall [-awl] *n.* slavery; slave, bondsman —*vt.* enslave —**thral(l)'dom** *n.* bondage

thrash *vt.* beat, whip soundly; defeat soundly; thresh —*vi.* move, plunge (*esp.* arms, legs) in wild manner —**thrash out** argue about from every angle; solve by exhaustive discussion

thread [-ed] *n.* fine cord; yarn; ridge cut spirally on screw; theme, meaning —*vt.* put thread into; fit film, magnetic tape *etc.* into machine; put on thread; pick (one's way *etc.*) —**thread'bare** *a.* worn, with nap rubbed off; meagre; shabby

threat [-et] *n.* declaration of intention to harm, injure *etc.*; person or thing regarded as dangerous —**threat'en** *vt.* utter threats against; menace

three *n./a.* cardinal number, one more than two —**three-ply'** *a.* having three layers (as wood) or strands (as wool) —**three'some** *n.* group of three —**three-dimen'sional, 3-D** *a.* having three dimensions; simulating the effect of depth

thresh *v.* beat, rub (wheat, *etc.*) to separate grain from husks and straw; thrash

thresh'old [-ōld] *n.* bar of stone or wood forming bottom of doorway; entrance;

starting-point; point at which a stimulus is perceived, or produces a response

threw *pt. of* THROW

thrice *adv.* three times

thrift *n.* saving, economy; genus of plant, sea pink —**thrift'y** *a.* economical, frugal, sparing

thrill *n.* sudden sensation of excitement and pleasure —*v.* (cause to) feel a thrill; vibrate, tremble —**thrill'er** *n.* book *etc.* with story of mystery, suspense —**thrill'ing** *a.* exciting

thrive *vi.* grow well; flourish, prosper (**throve, thrived** *pt.*, **thriv'en, thrived** *pp.*, **thri'ving** *pr.p.*)

throat *n.* front of neck; either or both of passages through it —**throat'y** *a.* (of voice) hoarse

throb *vi.* beat, quiver strongly, pulsate (**-bb-**) —*n.* pulsation, beat; vibration

throes [-ōz] *pl.n.* condition of violent pangs, pain *etc.* —**in the throes of** *inf.* in the process of

thrombo'sis *n.* formation of clot of coagulated blood in blood vessel or heart

throne *n.* ceremonial seat, powers and duties of king or queen —*vt.* place on throne, declare king *etc.*

throng *n./v.* crowd

throt'tle *n.* device controlling amount of fuel entering engine and thereby its speed —*vt.* strangle; suppress; restrict (flow of liquid *etc.*)

through [thrōō] *prep.* from end to end, from side to side of; between the sides of; in consequence of; by means or fault of —*adv.* from end to end; to the end —*a.* completed; *inf.* finished; continuous; (of transport, traffic) not stopping —**throughout'** *adv./prep.* in every part (of) —**through'put** *n.* quantity of material processed, *esp.* by computer —**through ticket** ticket for whole of journey —**through train, bus** *etc.* train *etc.* which travels whole (unbroken) length of long journey —**carry through** accomplish

throve *pt. of* THRIVE

throw [-ō] *vt.* fling, cast; move, put abruptly, carelessly; give, hold (party *etc.*); cause to fall; shape on potter's wheel; move (switch, lever *etc.*); *inf.* baffle, disconcert (**threw, thrown, throw'ing**) —*n.* act or distance of throwing —**throw'back** *n.* one who, that which reverts to character of an ancestor; this process

thrush[1] *n.* songbird

thrush[2] *n.* fungal disease of mouth, *esp.* in infants; foot disease of horses

thrust *v.* push, drive; stab; push one's way (**thrust, thrust'ing**) —*n.* lunge, stab with pointed weapon *etc.*; cutting remark; propulsive force or power

thud *n.* dull heavy sound —*vi.* make thud (**-dd-**)

thug *n.* brutal, violent person —**thug'gery** *n.* —**thugg'ish** *a.*

thumb [-m] *n.* first, shortest, thickest finger of hand —*vt.* handle, dirty with thumb; signal for lift in vehicle; flick through (pages of book *etc.*) —**thumb'tack** *n.* tack with broad head for fastening papers to board *etc.*

thump *n.* dull heavy blow; sound of one —*vt.* strike heavily

thun'der *n.* loud noise accompanying lightning —*vi.* rumble with thunder; make noise like thunder —*vt.* utter loudly —**thun'derous** *a.* —**thun'dery** *a.* sultry —**thun'derbolt, thun'derclap** *n.* lightning flash followed by peal of thunder; anything totally unexpected and unpleasant —**thun'derstruck** *a.* amazed

Thurs'day *n.* fifth day of the week

thus [TH-] *adv.* in this way; therefore

thwack *vt./n.* whack

thwart [-awt] *vt.* foil, frustrate, baffle —*adv. obs.* across —*n.* seat across a boat

thy [THī] *a. obs.* belonging to thee —**thyself'** *pron.* emphasized form of THOU

thyme [tīm] *n.* aromatic herb

thy'mus *n.* small ductless gland in upper part of chest

thy'roid gland endocrine gland controlling body growth, situated (in man) at base of neck

ti *see* TE

Ti *Chem.* titanium

tiar'a *n.* jewelled head ornament, coronet

tib'ia *n.* thicker inner bone of lower leg (*pl.* **-biae** [-bi-ē], **-bias**) —**tib'ial** *a.*

tic *n.* spasmodic twitch in muscles, *esp.* of face

tick[1] *n.* slight tapping sound, as of watch movement; small mark (✓); *inf.* moment —*vt.* mark with tick —*vi.* make the sound —**ticker tape** continuous paper ribbon —**tick off** mark off; reprimand —**tick**

over (of engine) idle; continue to function smoothly

tick[2] *n.* small insectlike parasite living on and sucking blood of warm-blooded animals

tick[3] *n.* mattress case —**tick'ing** *n.* strong material for mattress covers

tick'et *n.* card, paper entitling holder to admission, travel *etc.*; label; **US** list of candidates of one party for election —*vt.* attach label to; issue tickets to

tic'kle *vt.* touch, stroke, poke (person, part of body *etc.*) to produce laughter *etc.*; please, amuse —*vi.* be irritated, itch —*n.* act, instance of this; narrow strait —**tick'lish** *a.* sensitive to tickling; requiring care or tact

tick-tack-toe *n.* game in which two players alternately mark circle or cross in one of nine squares, winner being first to fill three in a row

tid'bit *n.* tasty morsel of food; pleasing scrap (of scandal *etc.*) (*also* **titbit**)

tidd'lywinks *pl.n.* game of trying to flip small plastic discs into cup

tide *n.* rise and fall of sea happening twice each lunar day; stream; *obs.* season, time —**ti'dal** *a.* of, like tide —**tidal wave** great wave, *esp.* produced by earthquake —**tide over** help someone for a while, *esp.* by loan *etc.*

ti'dings *pl.n.* news

ti'dy *a.* orderly, neat; *inf.* of fair size —*n.* protective cover for back of chair *etc.* —*vt.* put in order

tie *v.* equal (score of) —*vt.* fasten, bind, secure; restrict (**tied, ty'ing**) —*n.* that with which anything is bound; restriction, restraint; long, narrow piece of material worn knotted round neck; bond; connecting link; beam supporting rails of railway; drawn game, contest; match, game in eliminating competition —**tie-dyeing** *n.* way of dyeing cloth in patterns by tying sections tightly so they will not absorb dye —**tie-up** *n.* stoppage of work as result of strike, of traffic as result of accident *etc*; *inf.* connection, relation

tier [tēr] *n.* row, rank, layer

tiff *n.* petty quarrel

ti'ger *n.* large carnivorous feline animal

tight [tīt] *a.* taut, tense; closely fitting; secure, firm; not allowing passage of water *etc.*; cramped; *inf.* mean; *inf.* drunk —**tights** *pl.n.* one-piece clinging garment covering body from waist to feet —**tight'en** *v.* —**tight'ly** *adv.* —**tight'-rope** *n.* rope stretched taut above the ground, on which acrobats perform —**tight'wad** *n. sl.* stingy person

tile *n.* flat piece of ceramic, plastic *etc.* material used for roofs, walls, floors, fireplaces *etc.* —*vt.* cover with tiles —**tiled** *a.* —**ti'ling** *n.*

till[1] *prep.* up to the time of —*conj.* to the time that

till[2] *vt.* cultivate —**till'age** *n.* —**till'er** *n.*

till[3] *n.* drawer for money in shop counter; cash register

till'er *n.* lever to move rudder of boat

tilt *v.* incline, slope, slant; tip up —*vi.* take part in medieval combat with lances; thrust, aim (at) —*n.* slope, incline; *Hist.* combat for mounted men with lances, joust

tilth *n.* tilled land; condition of soil

tim'ber *n.* trees, *esp.* when growing in forest, lumber; large piece of wood for use in building, beam —**tim'bered** *a.* made of wood; covered with trees —**timber limit** area to which rights of cutting trees are limited; timber line —**timber line** geographical limit beyond which trees will not grow

tim'bre [-bər, tam'brə] *n.* quality of musical sound, or sound of human voice

time *n.* existence as a succession of states; hour; duration; period; point in duration; opportunity; occasion; leisure; tempo —*vt.* choose time for; note time taken by —**time'ly** *a.* at opportune or appropriate time —**ti'mer** *n.* person, device for recording or indicating time —**time bomb** bomb designed to explode at prearranged time —**time-honoured** *a.* respectable because old —**time-lag** *n.* period of time between cause and effect —**time-out** *n. Sport* interruption in play; break during work —**time'piece** *n.* watch, clock —**time sharing** system of part ownership of holiday property for specified period each year; *Computers* system enabling users at different terminals to communicate with computer apparently at same time —**time'table** *n.* plan showing hours of work, times of arrival and departure *etc.* —**Greenwich Mean Time** world standard time, time as settled by passage of sun over the meridian at Greenwich

tim'id *a.* easily frightened; lacking self-confidence —**timid'ity** *n.* —**tim'idly** *adv.* —**tim'orous** *a.* timid; indicating fear

tim'pani, tym'pani *pl.n.* set of kettle-drums —**tim'panist** *n.*

tin *n.* malleable metal; container made of tin or tinned iron, can —*vt.* put in tin, *esp.* for preserving (food); coat with tin (**-nn-**) —**tinn'y** *a.* (of sound) thin, metallic; cheap, shoddy —**tin'foil** *n.* thin sheet of tin or aluminum

tinc'ture *n.* solution of medicinal substance in alcohol; colour, stain —*vt.* colour, tint

tin'der *n.* dry easily-burning material used to start fire

tine *n.* tooth, spike of fork, antler, harrow *etc.*

tin'ea *n.* fungal skin disease

ting *n.* sharp sound, as of bell; tinkling —*vi.* tinkle

tinge [-j] *n.* slight trace, flavour —*vt.* colour, flavour slightly

tin'gle [-ng'gl] *vi.* feel thrill or pricking sensation —*n.*

tin'ker *n.* formerly, travelling mender of pots and pans —*vi.* fiddle, meddle (*eg* with machinery) oft. inexpertly

tin'kle [-ng-k-] *v.* (cause to) give out series of light sounds like small bell —*n.* this sound or action

tin'sel *n.* glittering metallic substance for decoration; anything sham and showy

tint *n.* colour; shade of colour; tinge —*vt.* dye, give tint to

ti'ny *a.* very small, minute

tip[1] *n.* slender or pointed end of anything; piece of metal, leather *etc.* protecting an extremity —*vt.* put a tip on (**-pp-**)

tip[2] *n.* small present of money given for service rendered; helpful piece of information; warning, hint —*vt.* give tip to (**-pp-**) —**tip'ster** *n.* one who sells tips about races

tip[3] *vt.* tilt, upset; touch lightly —*vi.* topple over (**-pp-**)

tipp'et *n.* covering for the neck and shoulders

tip'ple *v.* drink (alcohol) habitually, *esp.* in small quantities —*n.* drink —**tip'-pler** *n.*

tip'sy *a.* drunk, partly drunk

tip'toe *vi.* walk on ball of foot and toes; walk softly

tiptop' *a.* of the best quality or highest degree

tirade' [tī-rād'] *n.* long speech, generally vigorous and hostile, denunciation

tire[1] *vt.* reduce energy of, *esp.* by exertion; bore; irritate —*vi.* become tired, wearied, bored —**ti'ring** *a.* —**tire'some** *a.* wearisome, irritating, tedious

tire[2] *n.* (inflated) rubber ring over rim of road vehicle; metal band on rim of cart wheel

ti'ro *n. see* TYRO

tiss'ue *n.* substance of animal body, plant *etc.*; fine, soft paper, *esp.* used as handkerchief *etc.*; fine woven fabric

tit[1] *n.* varieties of small birds, usu. in combination, *eg* **tomtit, bluetit, titmouse**

tit[2] *n. vulg. sl.* female breast; *sl.* despicable, stupid person

titan'ic [tī-] *a.* huge, epic

tita'nium [ti-] *n.* rare metal of great strength and rust-resisting qualities

tit'bit *n. see* TIDBIT

tit for tat blow for blow, retaliation

tithe [-TH] *n.* tenth part *esp. Hist.* of agricultural produce paid for the upkeep of the clergy or as tax —*vt.* exact tithes from

tit'ian [tish'-] *a.* (of hair) reddish-gold, auburn

tit'illate *vt.* tickle, stimulate agreeably —**titilla'tion** *n.*

tit'ivate *v.* dress or smarten up —**titiva'tion** *n.*

ti'tle *n.* name of book; heading; name; appellation denoting rank; legal right or document proving it; *Sport* championship —**ti'tled** *a.* of the aristocracy —**title deed** legal document as proof of ownership

titt'er *vi.* laugh in suppressed way —*n.* such laugh

tit'tle *n.* whit, detail

tit'tle-tattle *n./vi.* gossip

tit'ular *a.* pert. to title; nominal; held by virtue of a title —**tit'ularly** *adv.*

tizz, tizz'y *n. inf.* state of confusion, anxiety

T.N.T. *see* TRINITROTOLUENE

to *prep.* towards, in the direction of; as far as; used to introduce a comparison, ratio, indirect object, infinitive mood *etc.* —*adv.* to the required or normal state or position

toad *n.* animal like large frog —**toad'y** *n.* one who flatters, ingratiates himself —*vi.* do this (**toad'ied, toad'ying**) —**toad'stool** *n.* fungus like mushroom, but usu. poisonous

toast *n.* slice of bread crisped and browned on both sides by heat; tribute, proposal of health, success *etc.* made by company of people and marked by drinking together; one toasted —*vt.* crisp and brown (as bread); drink toast to; dry or warm at fire —**toast'er** *n.* electrical device for toasting bread

tobacc'o *n.* plant with leaves used for smoking; the prepared leaves (*pl.* **-cos**) —**tobacc'onist** *n.* one who sells tobacco products

tobogg'an *n.* sled for sliding down slope of snow —*vi.* slide on one

to'by jug mug in form of stout, seated man

tocca'ta [-ah'-] *n.* rapid piece of music for keyboard instrument

toc'sin [tok's-] *n.* alarm signal, bell

today' *n.* this day —*adv.* on this day; nowadays

tod'dle *vi.* walk with unsteady short steps; *inf.* stroll —*n.* toddling —**todd'ler** *n.* child beginning to walk

todd'y *n.* sweetened mixture of alcoholic spirit, hot water *etc.*

to-do' *n. inf.* fuss, commotion (*pl.* **-dos**)

toe *n.* digit of foot; anything resembling toe in shape or position —*vt.* reach, touch with toe —**toe the line** conform

toff *n. Brit. sl.* well-dressed or upper class person

toff'ee *n.* chewy sweet made of boiled sugar *etc.*

to'ga *n.* loose outer garment worn by ancient Romans

togeth'er [-TH'-] *adv.* in company, simultaneously; *inf.* (well) organized

tog'gle *n.* small wooden, metal peg fixed crosswise on cord, wire *etc.* and used for fastening as button; any similar device

togs *inf. pl.n.* clothes

toil *n.* heavy work or task —*vi.* labour —**toil'worn** *a.* weary with toil; hard and lined

toil'et *n.* sanitary convenience for bodily waste, flushed by water; process of washing, dressing; articles used for this

to'ken *n.* sign or object used as evidence; symbol; disc used as money; gift card, voucher exchangeable for goods of a certain value —*a.* nominal, slight

told *pt./pp. of* TELL

tol'erate *vt.* put up with; permit —**tol'erable** *a.* bearable; fair, moderate —**tol'erably** *adv.* —**tol'erance** *n.* (degree of) ability to endure stress, pain, radiation *etc.* —**tol'erant** *a.* disinclined to interfere with others' ways or opinions; forbearing; broad-minded —**tol'erantly** *adv.* —**tolera'tion** *n.*

toll[1] [tōl] *vt.* make (bell) ring slowly at regular intervals; announce death thus —*vi.* ring thus —*n.* tolling sound

toll[2] [tōl] *n.* tax, *esp.* for the use of bridge or road; loss, damage incurred through accident, disaster *etc.* —**toll call** long-distance telephone call

tom *n.* male of some animals, *esp.* cat

tom'ahawk *n.* fighting axe of N Amer. Indians —*vt.* strike, kill with one

toma'to [-ā'-] *n.* plant with red fruit; the fruit, used in salads *etc.* (*pl.* **-toes**)

tomb [tōōm] *n.* grave; monument over one —**tomb'stone** *n.* gravestone

tom'boy *n.* girl who acts, dresses in boyish way

tome [tōm] *n.* large book or volume

tomfool'ery *n.* nonsense, silly behaviour

tomm'y *n. sl.* private soldier in Brit. army —**Tommy gun** type of submachine-gun

tomorr'ow [-ō] *adv./n.* (on) the day after today

tom'-tom *n.* drum associated with N Amer. Indians or with Asia

ton [tun] *n.* **US, C** measure of weight, 907 kg (2000 lbs.) (*also* **short ton**); **UK** measure of weight, 1016 kg (2240 lbs.) (*also* **long ton**) —**tonn'age** *n.* carrying capacity; charge per ton; ships collectively

tone *n.* musical sound of definite frequency or pitch; quality of musical sound; quality of voice, colour *etc.*; general character, style; healthy condition —*vt.* give tone to; blend, harmonize (with) —**to'nal** *a.* —**tonal'ity** *n.* —**to'ner** *n.* substance that modifies colour or composition —**tone poem** orchestral work based on story, legend *etc.*

tongs [-z] *pl.n.* large pincers, *esp.* for handling coal, sugar

tongue [tung] *n.* muscular organ inside mouth, used for speech, taste *etc.*; various things shaped like this; language, speech, voice

ton'ic *n.* medicine to improve bodily tone or condition; *Mus.* keynote; first note of scale *—a.* invigorating, restorative; of tone **—tonic (water)** mineral water oft. containing quinine

tonight' [-nīt'] *n.* this night; the coming night *—adv.* on this night

tonne [tun, tun'i] *n.* metric ton, 1000 kg

ton'sil *n.* gland in throat **—ton'sillar** *a.* **—tonsilli'tis** *n.* inflammation of tonsils

ton'sure *n.* shaving of part of head as religious or monastic practice; part shaved *—vt.* shave thus

ton'tine [-ēn] *n.* fund, subscribers to which receive annuities increasing as number of subscribers decreases

too *adv.* also, in addition; in excess, overmuch; *inf.* indeed, most certainly

took *pt. of* TAKE

tool [-ōō-] *n.* implement or appliance for mechanical operations; servile helper; means to an end *—vt.* work on with tool, *esp.* chisel stone; indent design on leather book cover *etc.* **—tool'ing** *n.* decorative work; setting up *etc.* of tools, *esp.* for machine operation

toot [-ōō-] *n.* short sound of horn, trumpet *etc.*

tooth [-ōō-] *n.* bonelike projection in gums of upper and lower jaws of vertebrates; various pointed things like this; prong, cog (*pl.* **teeth**)

too'tle [-ōō'-] *inf. v.* toot

top[1] *n.* highest part, summit; highest rank; first in merit ; garment for upper part of body ; lid, stopper of bottle *etc.*; platform on ship's mast *—vt.* cut off, pass, reach, surpass top; provide top for (**-pp-**) **—top'less** *a.* (of costume, woman) with no covering for breasts **—top'most** *a.* supreme; highest **—topdress'** *vt.* spread soil, fertilizer *etc.* on surface of land **—top'dressing** *n.* **—top hat** man's hat with tall cylindrical crown **—top-heavy** *a.* unbalanced; with top too heavy for base **—top-notch** *a.* excellent, first-class **—top-secret** *a.* needing highest level of secrecy, security **—top'soil** *n.* surface layer of soil; more fertile soil spread on lawns *etc.*

top[2] *n.* toy which spins on tapering point

to'paz *n.* precious stone of various colours

to'piary *a.* (of shrubs) shaped by cutting or pruning, made ornamental by trimming or training *—n.* **—to'piarist** *n.*

top'ic *n.* subject of discourse, conversation *etc.* **—top'ical** *a.* up-to-date, having news value; of topic

topog'raphy *n.* (description of) surface features of a place **—topog'rapher** *n.* **—topograph'ic** *a.* **—topograph'ically** *adv.*

top'ple *v.* (cause to) fall over, collapse

top'sy-tur'vy *a.* upside down, in confusion

toque [tōk] *n.* small round hat; knitted cap

torch *n.* UK flashlight; burning brand *etc.*; any apparatus burning with hot flame, *eg* for welding **—torch'bearer** *n.*

tore *pt.* **—torn** *pp. of* TEAR[2]

tor'eador [to'ri-] *n.* bull fighter

torment' *v.* torture in body or mind; afflict; tease *—n.* [tor'-] suffering, torture, agony of body or mind **—torment'or, -er** *n.*

torna'do *n.* whirlwind; violent storm (*pl.* **-does**)

torpe'do *n.* cylindrical self-propelled underwater missile with explosive warhead, fired *esp.* from submarine (*pl.* **-does**) *—vt.* strike, sink with, as with, torpedo

tor'pid *a.* sluggish, apathetic **—tor'por** *n.* torpid state **—torpid'ity** *n.*

torque [-k] *n.* collar, similar ornament of twisted gold or other metal; *Mechanics* rotating or twisting forces

torr'ent *n.* a rushing stream; downpour **—torren'tial** *a.* resembling a torrent; overwhelming

torr'id *a.* parched, dried with heat; highly emotional **—torrid'ity, torr'idness** *n.* **—Torrid Zone** land between tropics

tor'sion *n.* twist, twisting

tor'so *n.* (statue of) body without head or limbs; trunk (*pl.* **-sos, -si** [-sē])

tort *n.* *Law* private or civil wrong

tortill'a [-tē'ə] *n.* thin Mexican pancake

tor'toise [-təs] *n.* land turtle **—tor'toiseshell** *n.* mottled brown shell of hawksbill turtle used commercially *—a.*

tor'tuous *a.* winding, twisting; involved, not straightforward **—tortuos'ity** *n.*

tor'ture *n.* infliction of severe pain *—vt.* subject to torture **—tor'turer** *n.*

Tor'y *n.* member of Brit., Canad. conservative party; politically reactionary person

toss *vt.* throw up, about *—vi.* be thrown, fling oneself about *—n.* act of tossing

tot *n.* very small child; **UK** small quantity, *esp.* of drink

to'tal *n.* whole amount; sum, aggregate *—a.* complete, entire, full, absolute *—vi.* amount to *—vt.* add up (**-ll-**) **—total'ity** *n.*

totalita'rian *a.* of dictatorial, one-party government

tote *vt.* haul, carry

to'tem *n.* tribal badge or emblem **—totem'ic** *a.* **—totem pole** post carved, painted with totems, *esp.* by Amer. Indians

tott'er *vi.* walk unsteadily; begin to fall

tou'can [too'kən] *n.* tropical Amer. bird with large bill

touch [tuch] *n.* sense by which qualities of object *etc.* are perceived by touching; characteristic manner or ability; touching; slight blow, stroke, contact, amount *etc.* *—vt.* come into contact with; put hand on; reach; affect emotions of; deal with, handle; eat, drink; *inf.* (try to) borrow from *—vi.* be in contact; (*with* on) refer to **—touch'ing** *a.* emotionally moving *—prep.* concerning **—touch'y** *a.* easily offended, sensitive **—touch'down** *n. Football* score gained by being in prossession of ball behind opponents' goal line **—touch'line** *n.* side line of pitch in some games **—touch'stone** *n.* criterion **—touch'wood** *n.* tinder **—touch and go** precarious (situation)

touché' [too͞-shā'] *interj.* acknowledgement that blow (*orig.* in fencing), remark *etc.* has been successful

tough [tuf] *a.* strong, resilient, not brittle; sturdy; able to bear hardship, strain; difficult; needing effort to chew; *sl.* rough; uncivilized; violent; *inf.* unlucky, unfair *—n. inf.* rough, violent person **—tough'en** *v.* **—tough'ness** *n.*

tou'pée [too͞'pā] *n.* hairpiece, wig

tour [toor] *n.* travelling round; journey to one place after another; excursion *—v.* make tour (of) **—tour'ism** *n.* tourist travel; this as an industry **—tour'ist** *n.* one who travels for pleasure

tour de force *Fr.* brilliant stroke, achievement

tour'maline [toor'-] *n.* crystalline mineral used for optical instruments and as gem

tour'nament [toor'-] *n.* competition, contest usu. with several stages to decide overall winner; *Hist.* contest between knights on horseback **—tour'ney** *n. Hist.* knightly tournament

tour'niquet [toor'ni-kā] *n.* bandage, surgical instrument to constrict artery and stop bleeding

tou'sle *vt.* tangle, ruffle; treat roughly *—n.*

tout *vi.* solicit custom (usu. in undesirable fashion); obtain and sell information about racehorses *—n.* one who touts

tow[1] [tō] *vt.* drag along behind, *esp.* at end of rope *—n.* towing or being towed; vessel, vehicle in tow **—tow'age** *n.* **—tow'path** *n.* path beside canal, river, orig. for towing

tow[2] [tō] *n.* fibre of hemp, flax **—tow-headed** *a.* with pale-coloured, or rumpled hair

toward' [tə-] *prep.* in direction of; with regard to; as contribution to (*also* **towards'**)

tow'el *n.* cloth for wiping off moisture after washing **—tow'elling** *n.* material used for making towels

tow'er *n.* tall strong structure often forming part of church or other large building; fortress *—vi.* stand very high; loom (over)

town *n.* collection of dwellings *etc.* larger than village and smaller than city **—town'ship** *n.* small town; land survey area **—town clerk** chief administrative officer of town **—town house** house that is part of a row **—towns'people** *n.*

tox'ic *a.* poisonous; due to poison **—tox(a)e'mia** [-sē'-] *n.* blood poisoning **—toxic'ity** [-is'-] *n.* strength of a poison **—toxicol'ogy** *n.* study of poisons **—tox'in** *n.* poison of bacterial origin

toy *n.* something designed to be played with; (miniature) replica *—a.* very small *—vi.* act idly, trifle

trace[1] *n.* track left by anything; indication; minute quantity *—vt.* follow course, track of; find out; make plan of; draw or copy exactly, *esp.* using tracing paper **—tra'cery** *n.* interlaced ornament , *esp.* stonework of Gothic window **—tra'cing** *n.* traced copy of drawing **—trace el-**

ement chemical element occurring in very small quantity in soil *etc.* —**tracer bullet, shell** *etc.* one which leaves visible trial so that aim can be checked —**tracing paper** transparent paper placed over drawing, map *etc.* to enable exact copy to be taken

trace[2] *n.* chain, strap by which horse pulls vehicle; *Angling* short piece of gut, nylon attaching hook or fly to line

trache'a [-kē'-] *n.* windpipe (*pl.* **trache'ae** [-kē'ē]) —**trache'al, -e'an** *a.* —**tracheot'omy** *n.* surgical incision into trachea

tracho'ma [-kō'-] *n.* contagious viral disease of eye —**trachom'atous** *a.*

track *n.* mark, line of marks, left by passage of anything; path; rough road; course; railway line; distance between two road wheels on one axle; circular jointed metal band driven by wheels as on tank, bulldozer *etc.*; course for running or racing; sports performed on a track; separate section on phonograph record —*vt.* follow trail or path of; find thus —**track meet** track-and-field contest —**track record** past accomplishments of person, company *etc.* —**track'-suit** *n.* warm, two-piece garment worn *esp.* by athletes —**track and field** athletics, including running and field events

tract[1] *n.* wide expanse, area; *Anat.* system of organs *etc.* with particular function

tract[2] *n.* treatise or pamphlet, *esp.* religious one —**tract'ate** *n.* short tract

tract'able *a.* easy to manage, docile, amenable

trac'tion *n.* action of drawing, pulling —**traction engine**

trac'tor *n.* motor vehicle for hauling, pulling *etc.* —**tractor-trailer** *n.* freight vehicle consisting of truck with engine and cab pulling open or closed trailer

trad. traditional

trade *n.* commerce, business; buying and selling; any profitable pursuit; those engaged in trade —*v.* engage in trade; buy and sell; barter —**tra'der** *n.* —**trade-in** *n.* used article given in part payment for new —**trade'mark, trade'name** *n.* distinctive mark (secured by legal registration) on maker's goods —**trades'man** *n.* shopkeeper; skilled worker —**trade-off** *n.* exchange, *esp.* as compromise —**trade union** society of workers for protection of their interests —**trade wind** wind blowing constantly towards equator in certain parts of globe

tradi'tion [-dish'-] *n.* unwritten body of beliefs, facts *etc.* handed down from generation to generation; custom, practice of long standing; process of handing down —**tradi'tional** *a.* —**tradi'tionally** *adv.*

traduce' *vt.* slander

traff'ic *n.* vehicles passing to and fro in street, town *etc.*; (illicit) trade —*vi.* trade, *esp.* in illicit goods, *eg* drugs (**traf'ficked, traff'icking**) —**traff'icker** *n.* trader —**traffic circle** road junction in which traffic circulates round central island —**traffic lights** set of coloured lights at road junctions *etc.* to control flow of traffic

trag'edy [-aj'-] *n.* sad or calamitous event; dramatic, literary work dealing with serious, sad topic and with ending marked by (inevitable) disaster —**trage'dian** *n.* actor in, writer of tragedies —**trag'ic** *a.* of, in manner of tragedy; disastrous; appalling —**trag'ically** *adv.* —**tragicom'edy** *n.* play with both tragic and comic elements

trail *vt.* drag behind one —*vi.* be drawn behind; hang, grow loosely —*n.* track or trace; thing that trails; rough ill-defined track in wild country —**trail'er** *n.* vehicle towed by another vehicle; large enclosed vehicle for living in, pulled by automobile *etc.*; advertisement of forthcoming movie or program; trailing plant

train *vt.* educate, instruct, exercise; cause to grow in particular way; aim (gun *etc.*) —*vi.* follow course of training, *esp.* to achieve physical fitness for athletics —*n.* line of railway vehicles joined to locomotive; succession, *esp.* of thoughts, events *etc.*; procession of animals, vehicles *etc.* travelling together; trailing part of dress; body of attendants —**train'ing** *n.* —**trainee'** *n.* one training to be skilled worker, *esp.* in industry

traipse *vi. inf.* walk wearily

trait [trāt, trā] *n.* characteristic feature

trait'or *n.* one who betrays or is guilty of treason —**trait'orous** *a.* disloyal; guilty of treachery —**trait'orously** *adv.*

trajec'tory *n.* line of flight, (curved) path of projectile

tram *n.* UK streetcar

tramm'el *n.* anything that restrains or holds captive; type of compasses *—vt.* restrain; hinder (**-ll-**)

tramp *vi.* travel on foot, *esp.* as vagabond or for pleasure; walk heavily *—n.* (homeless) person who travels about on foot; walk; tramping; vessel that takes cargo wherever shippers desire

tram'ple *vt.* tread on and crush under foot

tram'poline [-lin] *n.* tough canvas sheet stretched horizontally with elastic cords *etc.* to frame, for gymnastic, acrobatic use

trance [-ah-] *n.* unconscious or dazed state; state of ecstasy or total absorption

tran'quil [-ng'kw-] *a.* calm, quiet; serene —**tranquill'ity** *n.* —**tran'quillize** *vt.* make calm —**tran'quillizer** *n.* drug which induces calm, tranquil state —**tran'quilly** *adv.*

trans- (*comb. form*) across, through, beyond

transact' *vt.* carry through; negotiate; conduct (affair *etc.*) —**transac'tion** *n.* performing of any business; that which is performed; single sale or purchase *—pl.* proceedings; reports of a society

transceiv'er *n.* combined radio transmitter and receiver

transcend' *vt.* rise above; exceed, surpass —**transcend'ent** *a.* —**transcend'ence** *n.* —**transcenden'tal** *a.* surpassing experience; supernatural; abstruse —**transcendent'alism** *n.*

transcribe' *vt.* copy out; record for later broadcast; arrange (music) for different instrument —**tran'script** *n.* copy; official record of student's school progress

tran'sept *n.* transverse part of cruciform church; either of its arms

transfer' *vt.* move, send from one person, place *etc.* to another (**-rr-**) *—n.* [trans'-] removal of person or thing from one place to another; ticket allowing passenger to change routes; design which can be transferred from one surface to another by pressure, heat *etc.* —**transfer(r)'able** *a.* —**trans'ference** *n.* transfer

transfig'ure *vt.* alter appearance of —**transfigura'tion** *n.*

transfix' *vt.* astound, stun; pierce

transform' *vt.* change shape, character of —**transforma'tion** *n.* —**transform'er** *n. Electricity* apparatus for changing voltage of alternating current

transfuse' *vt.* convey from one vessel to another, *esp.* blood from healthy person to one injured or ill —**transfu'sion** *n.*

transgress' *vt.* break (law); sin —**transgres'sion** *n.* —**transgres'sor** *n.*

trans(s)hip' *vt.* move from one ship, train *etc.* to another

tran'sient [-z-] *a.* fleeting, not permanent —**trans'ience** *n.*

transis'tor *n. Electronics* small, semiconducting device used to amplify electric currents; portable radio using transistors

tran'sit *n.* passage, crossing; surveying instrument for measuring angles —**transi'tion** *n.* change from one state to another —**transi'tional** *a.* —**tran'sitive** *a.* (of verb) requiring direct object —**tran'sitory** *a.* not lasting long, transient

translate' *vt.* turn from one language into another; interpret —**transla'tion** *n.* —**transla'tor** *n.*

translit'erate *vt.* write in the letters of another alphabet —**translitera'tion** *n.*

translu'cent [-lōō'-] *a.* letting light pass through, semitransparent —**translu'cence** *n.*

transmigrate' *vi.* (of soul) pass into another body —**transmigra'tion** *n.*

transmit' *vt.* send, cause to pass to another place, person *etc.*; communicate; send out (signals) by means of radio waves; broadcast (radio, television programme) —**transmiss'ion** *n.* transference; gear by which power is communicated from engine to road wheels

transmog'rify *vt. inf.* change completely *esp.* into bizarre form

transmute' *vt.* change in form, properties, or nature —**transmuta'tion** *n.*

tran'som [-zəm] *n.* crosspiece; lintel

transpar'ent [-pa'rənt] *a.* letting light pass without distortion; that can be seen through distinctly; obvious —**transpar'ence** *n.* —**transpar'ency** *n.* quality of being transparent; photographic slide;

picture made visible by light behind it —**transpar'ently** *adv.*

transpire' *vi.* become known; *inf.* happen; (of plants) give off water vapour through leaves —**transpira'tion** *n.*

transplant' *vt.* move and plant again in another place; transfer organ surgically from one body to another —*n.* [trans'-] surgical transplanting of organ; anything transplanted —**transplanta'tion** *n.*

transport' *vt.* convey from one place to another; *Hist.* banish, as criminal, to penal colony; enrapture —*n.* [trans'-] means of conveyance; ships, aircraft *etc.* used in transporting stores, troops *etc.*; a ship *etc.* so used —**transporta'tion** *n.* transporting; *Hist.* deportation to penal colony

transpose' *vt.* change order of; interchange; put music into different key —**transpo'sal** *n.* —**transposi'tion** *n.*

transubstantia'tion *n.* doctrine that substance of bread and wine changes into substance of Christ's body when consecrated in Eucharist

transverse' *a.* lying across; at right angles

transvest'ite *n.* person seeking sexual pleasure by wearing clothes normally worn by opposite sex

trap *n.* snare, device for catching game *etc.*; anything planned to deceive, betray *etc.*; arrangement of pipes to prevent escape of gas; movable opening, *esp.* through ceiling *etc.*; *Hist.* two-wheeled carriage; *sl.* mouth —*vt.* catch, ensnare (**-pp-**) —**trapp'er** *n.* one who traps animals for their fur —**trap'door** *n.* door in floor or roof

trapeze' *n.* horizontal bar suspended from two ropes for use in gymnastics, acrobatic exhibitions *etc.*

trape'zium *n.* quadrilateral figure with no parallel sides (*pl.* **-ziums, -zia**) (**UK trap'ezoid**) —**trap'ezoid** *n.* quadrilateral with two sides only parallel (**UK trape'zium**)

trapp'ings *pl.n.* equipment, ornaments

Trapp'ist *n.* member of Cistercian order of monks who observe strict silence

trash *n.* garbage; nonsense; poor or worthless person or group —**trash'y** *a.* worthless, cheap —**trash can** garbage can

trau'ma [-aw'-] *n.* nervous shock; injury —**traumat'ic** *a.* of, causing, caused by trauma

trav'ail *vi./n.* labour, toil

trav'el *v.* go, move from one place to another (**-ll-**) —*n.* act of travelling, *esp.* as tourist; *Machinery* distance component is permitted to move —*pl.* (account of) travelling —**trav'eller** *n.* —**trav'elogue** [-log] *n.* film *etc.* about travels

trav'erse *vt.* cross, go through or over (of gun) move laterally —*n.* anything set across; partition; *Mountaineering* face steep slope to be crossed from side to side —*a.* being, lying across

trav'esty *n.* farcical, grotesque imitation; mockery —*vt.* make, be a travesty of (**-estied, -estying**)

travois' [-voi'] *n.* sled for dragging logs

trawl *n.* net dragged at deep levels behind special boat, to catch fish, prawns *etc.* —*vi.* fish with one —**trawl'er** *n.* trawling vessel

tray *n.* flat board, usu. with rim, for carrying things; any similar utensil

treach'ery [trech'-] *n.* deceit, betrayal —**treach'erous** *a.* disloyal; unreliable, dangerous —**treach'erously** *adv.*

trea'cle *n.* **UK** molasses

tread [tred] *vt.* set foot on; trample; oppress —*vi.* walk (**trod** *pt.*, **trodd'en** *or* **trod** *pp.*, **tread'ing** *pr.p.*) —*n.* treading; fashion of walking; upper surface of step; part of rubber tire in contact with ground —**tread'mill** *n. Hist.* cylinder turned by treading on steps projecting from it; dreary routine *etc.*

tread'le [tred'l] *n.* lever worked by foot to turn wheel

trea'son [-z-] *n.* violation by subject of allegiance to sovereign or state; treachery; disloyalty —**trea'sonable** *a.* constituting treason —**trea'sonably** *adv.* —**trea'sonous** *a.*

treas'ure [trezh'-] *n.* riches; stored wealth or valuables —*vt.* prize, cherish; store up —**treas'urer** *n.* official in charge of funds —**treas'ury** *n.* place for treasure; government department in charge of finance —**treasure-trove** *n.* treasure found hidden with no evidence of ownership

treat *n.* pleasure, entertainment given —*vt.* deal with, act towards; give medical treatment to; (*with* of) discourse on; entertain, *esp.* with food or drink —*vi.*

negotiate —**treat'ment** *n.* method of counteracting a disease; act or mode of treating; manner of handling an artistic medium

treat'ise [-iz] *n.* book discussing a subject, formal essay

treat'y *n.* signed contract between states *etc.*

treb'le [treb'l] *a.* threefold, triple; *Mus.* high-pitched —*n.* soprano voice; part of music for it; singer with such voice —*v.* increase threefold —**treb'ly** *adv.*

tree *n.* large perennial plant with woody trunk; beam; anything (*eg* genealogical chart) resembling tree, or tree's structure —*vt.* force, drive up tree; plant with trees; *inf.* force into difficult situation —**tree line** level on mountains above which trees will not grow; timber line —**up a tree** *inf.* in difficult situation

tref'oil *n.* plant with three-lobed leaf, clover; carved ornament like this

trek *vi./n.* (make) long difficult journey, *esp.* on foot —**trekk'er** *n.*

trell'is *n.* lattice or grating of light bars fixed crosswise —*vt.* screen, supply with one

trem'ble *vi.* quiver, shake; feel fear, anxiety —*n.* involuntary shaking; quiver; tremor

tremen'dous *a.* vast, immense; *inf.* exciting, unusual; *inf.* excellent

trem'olo *n.* quivering or vibrating effect in singing or playing

trem'or *n.* quiver; shaking; minor earthquake

trem'ulous *a.* quivering slightly; timorous, agitated

trench *n.* long narrow ditch, *esp.* as shelter in war —*vt.* cut grooves or ditches in —**trench coat** double-breasted waterproof coat

trench'ant *a.* cutting, incisive, biting

trench'er *n. Hist.* wooden plate on which food was served

trend *n.* direction, tendency, inclination, drift —**trend'y** *inf. a./n.* consciously fashionable (person) —**trend'iness** *n.*

trepan' *n. see* TREPHINE

trepang' *n.* edible sea slug or bêche-de-mer

trephine' [-fēn'] *n.* instrument for cutting circular pieces, *esp.* from skull —*vt.*

trepida'tion *n.* fear, anxiety

tres'pass *vi.* intrude (on) property *etc.* of another; *obs.* transgress, sin —*n.* wrongful entering on another's land; wrongdoing

tress *n.* long lock of hair

tres'tle [-sl] *n.* board fixed on pairs of spreading legs and used as support

tri- (*comb. form*) three

tri'ad *n.* group of three; *Chem.* element, radical with valency of three

tri'al *n.* act of trying, testing; experimental examination; *Law* investigation of case before judge; thing, person that strains endurance or patience

tri'angle *n.* figure with three angles; percussion musical instrument —**trian'gular** *a.*

tribe *n.* race; subdivision of race of people —**tri'bal** *a.*

tribula'tion *n.* misery, trouble, affliction, distress; cause of this

trib'une *n.* person or institution upholding public rights —**tribu'nal** *n.* lawcourt

trib'utary *n.* stream flowing into another —*a.* auxiliary; contributory; paying tribute

trib'ute *n.* sign of honour or recognition; tax paid by one state to another

trice *n.* moment —**in a trice** instantly

trichi'na [-kī'-] *n.* minute parasitic worm —**trichino'sis** *n.* disease caused by this

trick *n.* deception; prank; mannerism; illusion; feat of skill or cunning; knack; cards played in one round; spell of duty —*vt.* cheat; hoax; deceive —**trick'ery** *n.* —**trick'ster** *n.* —**trick'y** *a.* difficult, needing careful handling; crafty

tric'kle *v.* (cause to) run, flow, move in thin stream or drops

tric'olour *a.* three coloured —*n.* tricolour flag, *eg* of France

tri'cycle *n.* three-wheeled cycle

tri'dent *n.* three-pronged fork or spear

trienn'ial *a.* happening every, or lasting, three years

tri'fle *n.* insignificant thing or matter; small amount; pudding of spongecake, whipped cream *etc.* —*vi.* toy (with); act, speak idly —**tri'fler** *n.*

trig *n./a. short for* TRIGONOMETRY, TRIGONOMETRICAL

trigg'er *n.* catch which releases spring esp. to fire gun —*vt.* (*oft. with* off) start, set in action *etc.* —**trigger-happy** *a.* tending to irresponsible, ill-considered behaviour, *esp.* in use of firearms

trigonom'etry *n.* branch of mathematics dealing with relations of sides and angles of triangles —**trigonomet'rical** *a.*

trihe'dron *n.* figure formed by intersection of three planes —**trihe'dral** *a.*

trilat'eral *a.* having three sides —**trilat'erally** *adv.*

trill *vi.* sing with quavering voice; sing lightly; warble —*n.* such singing or sound

trill'ion *n.* **US, C** one million million, 10^{12}; **UK** one million million million, 10^{18}

tril'ogy [-ji] *n.* series of three related (literary) works

trim *a.* neat, smart; slender; in good order —*vt.* shorten slightly by cutting; prune; decorate; adjust; put in good order; adjust balance of (ship, aircraft) (**-mm-**) —*n.* decoration; order, state of being trim; haircut that neatens existing style; upholstery, accessories in car; edging material, as inside woodwork round doors, windows *etc.* —**trimm'ing** *n.* (*oft. pl.*) decoration, addition

tri'maran *n.* three-hulled vessel

trimes'ter *n.* period of three months; (in some U.S. & Canad. universities or schools) any of the three academic sessions

trinitrotol'uene *n.* a high explosive derived from toluene

trin'ity *n.* the state of being threefold; (**T-**) the three persons of the Godhead —**trinita'rian** *n./a.*

trink'et *n.* small ornament, trifle —**trin'ketry** *n.*

tri'o [-ē'ō] *n.* group of three; music for three parts (*pl.* **-s**)

tri'ode *n.* *Electronics* three-electrode valve

trip *n.* (short) journey for pleasure; stumble; switch; *inf.* hallucinatory experience caused by drug —*v.* (cause to) stumble; (cause to) make false step, mistake —*vi.* run lightly; skip; dance; *inf.* take hallucinatory drugs —*vt.* operate (switch) (**-pp-**)

tripart'ite *a.* having, divided into three parts

tripe *n.* stomach of cow *etc.* prepared for food; *inf.* nonsense

tri'plane *n.* airplane with three wings one above the other

trip'le [trip'l] *a.* threefold —*v.* treble —**trip'let** *n.* three of a kind; one of three offspring born at one birth —**trip'lex** *a.* threefold —**trip'ly** *adv.*

trip'licate [-it] *a.* threefold —*vt.* [-āt] make threefold —*n.* state of being triplicate; one of set of three copies —**triplica'tion** *n.*

tri'pod *n.* stool, stand *etc.* with three feet

trip'tych [-tik] *n.* carving, set of pictures (*esp.* altarpiece) on three panels hinged side by side

trite *a.* hackneyed, banal

trit'ium *n.* radioactive isotope of hydrogen

tri'umph *n.* great success; victory; exultation —*vi.* achieve great success or victory; prevail; exult —**triumph'al** *a.* —**triumph'ant** *a.* victorious

trium'virate [trī-] *n.* joint rule by three persons

triv'et *n.* metal bracket or stand for pot or kettle

triv'ia *pl.n.* petty, unimportant things, details —**triv'ial** *a.* of little consequence; commonplace —**trivial'ity** *n.*

tro'chee [trō'kē] *n.* in verse, foot of two syllables, first long and second short —**trocha'ic** *a.*

trod *pt.*, **trodd'en, trod** *pp. of* TREAD

trog'lodyte *n.* cave dweller

Tro'jan *a./n.* (inhabitant) of ancient Troy; steadfast or persevering (person)

troll[1] [-ō-] *vt.* fish for by dragging baited hook or lure through water

troll[2] [-ō-] *n.* supernatural being in Scandinavian mythology and folklore

troll'ey *n.* device that collects current from overhead wires, third rail *etc.* to drive motor of electric vehicle; truck, cage or basket suspended from overhead track or cable for carrying loads —**trolley car** electric streetcar powered by trolley

troll'op *n.* promiscuous or slovenly woman

trombone' *n.* deep-toned brass wind instrument with sliding tube —**trombo'nist** *n.*

troop *n.* group or crowd of persons or animals; unit of cavalry —*pl.* soldiers —*vi.* move in a troop, flock —**troop'er** *n.* cavalry soldier

trope *n.* figure of speech

tro'phy *n.* prize, award, as shield, cup; memorial of victory, hunt *etc.*

trop'ic *n.* either of two lines of latitude at 23½° N (**tropic of Cancer**) or 23½° S (**tropic of Capricorn**) —*pl.* area of earth's surface between these lines —**trop'ical** *a.* pert. to, within tropics; (of climate) very hot

trot *vi.* (of horse) move at medium pace, lifting feet in diagonal pairs; (of person) run easily with short strides (**-tt-**) —*n.* trotting, jog —**trott'er** *n.* horse trained to trot in race; foot of certain animals, *esp.* pig

troth [-ō-] *n. obs.* fidelity, truth

trou'badour [trōō'-] *n.* one of school of early poets and singers

troub'le [trub'l] *n.* state or cause of mental distress, pain, inconvenience *etc.*; care, effort —*vt.* be trouble to —*vi.* be inconvenienced, concerned (about); be agitated; take pains, exert oneself —**trou'blesome** *a.*

trough [trof] *n.* long open vessel, *esp.* for animals' food or water; hollow between two waves; *Meteorology* area of low pressure

trounce *vt.* beat thoroughly, thrash

troupe [-ōō-] *n.* company of performers —**troup'er** *n.*

trou'sers *pl.n.* pants (outer garment)

trou'sseau [trōō'sō] *n.* bride's outfit of clothing

trout *n.* freshwater sport and food fish

trow'el *n.* small tool like spade for spreading mortar, lifting plants *etc.*

troy weight system of weights used for gold, silver and gems

tru'ant [trōō'-] *n.* one absent without leave, *esp.* child so absenting himself or herself from school —*a.* —**tru'ancy** *n.*

truce *n.* temporary cessation of fighting; respite, lull

truck[1] *n.* motor vehicle for transporting goods by road; wheeled (motor) vehicle for moving goods —*vi.* drive truck —**truck'er** *n.* truck driver

truck[2] *n.* vegetables grown for market; barter; dealing, *esp.* in **have no truck with**; payment of workmen in goods —**truck'er** *n.* truck farmer; peddler —**truck farm** farm where vegetables are grown for market

truck'le *vi.* yield weakly (to)

truc'ulent *a.* aggressive, defiant

trudge *vi.* walk laboriously —*n.* laborious or wearisome walk

true [trōō] *a.* in accordance with facts; faithful; exact, correct; genuine —**tru'ism** *n.* self-evident truth —**tru'ly** *adv.* exactly; really; sincerely —**truth** [-ōō-] *n.* state of being true; something that is true —**truth'ful** *a.* accustomed to speak the truth; accurate, exact —**truth'fully** *adv.*

truf'fle *n.* edible fungus growing underground; sweet resembling this

tru'ism *n. see* TRUE

trump[1] *n.* card of suit temporarily ranking above others —*vt.* take trick with a trump —**trump up** invent, concoct —**turn up** *or* **out trumps** turn out (unexpectedly) well, successfully

trump[2] *n.* trumpet; blast on trumpet

trum'pery *a.* showy but worthless —*n.* worthless finery; trash, rubbish

trum'pet *n.* metal wind instrument like horn —*vi.* blow trumpet; make sound like one, as elephant —*vt.* proclaim, make widely known

truncate' *vt.* cut short

trun'cheon *n.* short thick club or baton; staff of office or authority —*vt.* cudgel

trun'dle *vt.* roll, as a thing on little wheels

trunk *n.* main stem of tree; person's body without or excluding head and limbs; box for clothes *etc.*; elephant's proboscis; baggage receptacle in automobile —*pl.* man's swimming costume —**trunk line** main line of railway, canal, telephone *etc.*

truss *vt.* fasten up, tie up —*n.* support; medical device of belt *etc.* to hold hernia in place; cluster of flowers at end of single stalk

trust *n.* confidence; firm belief; reliance; combination of producers to reduce competition and keep up prices; care, responsibility; property held for another —*vt.* rely on; believe in; expect, hope; consign for care —**trustee'** *n.* one legally holding property on another's behalf —**trustee'ship** *n.* —**trust'ful** *a.* inclined to trust; credulous —**trust'worthy** *a.* reliable; dependable; honest; safe —**trust'y** *a.* faithful; reliable

truth *see* TRUE

try *vi.* attempt, endeavour —*vt.* attempt; test; make demands upon; investigate (case); examine (person) in court of law;

purify or refine (as metals) (**tried, try'ing**) —*n.* attempt, effort; *Rugby* score gained by touching ball down over opponent's goal line —**tried** *a.* proved; afflicted —**try'ing** *a.* upsetting, annoying; difficult —**try'out** *n.* trial or test as of athlete or actor

tryst *n.* appointment to meet; place appointed

tsar *see* CZAR

tset'se *n.* Afr. bloodsucking fly whose bite transmits various diseases to man and animals

T-shirt, tee-shirt *n.* informal (short-sleeved) sweater, *usu.* of cotton

T-square *n.* T-shaped ruler for drawing parallel lines, right angles *etc.*

TT teetotal; tuberculin tested

tub *n.* open wooden vessel like bottom half of barrel; small round container; bathtub; washtub; *inf.* bath; *inf.* old, slow ship *etc.*

tu'ba *n.* valved brass wind instrument of low pitch

tube *n.* long, narrow, hollow cylinder; flexible cylinder with cap to hold liquids, pastes; tunnel as for subway; *inf.* subway —**tu'bular** *a.* like tube

tu'ber *n.* fleshy underground stem of some plants, *eg* potato —**tu'berous** *a.*

tu'bercle *n.* any small rounded nodule on skin *etc.*; small lesion of tissue, *esp.* produced by tuberculosis —**tuber'cular** *a.* —**tuber'culin** *n.* extraction from bacillus used to test for and treat tuberculosis —**tuberculo'sis** *n.* communicable disease, *esp.* of lungs

tuck *vt.* push, fold into small space; gather, stitch in folds; draw, roll together —*n.* stitched fold; **UK** *inf.* food —**tuck'er** *n.* strip of linen or lace formerly worn across bosom by women

tuck'er *vt. inf.* (*oft. with* out) weary or tire completely

Tu'dor *a.* of the English royal house ruling 1485-1603; in, resembling style of this period, *esp.* of architecture

Tues'day *n.* third day of the week

tu'fa *n.* porous rock formed as deposit from springs *etc.*

tuft *n.* bunch of feathers, threads *etc.*

tug *vt.* pull hard or violently; haul; jerk forward (**-gg-**) —*n.* violent pull; ship used to tow other vessels —**tug of war** contest in which two teams pull against one another on a rope

tui'tion [tyo͞o-ish'ən] *n.* teaching, instruction; private coaching —**tui'tional** *a.*

tu'lip *n.* plant with bright cup-shaped flowers

tulle [tyo͞ol] *n.* kind of fine thin silk or lace

tull'ibee *n.* Canad. whitefish

tum'ble *v.* (cause to) fall or roll, twist *etc.* (*esp.* in play); rumple, disturb —*n.* fall; somersault —**tum'bler** *n.* stemless drinking glass; acrobat; spring catch in lock —**tumble-down** *a.* dilapidated —**tumble(r) drier** machine that dries clothes *etc.* by tumbling in warm air —**tumble to** *inf.* realize, understand

tum'brel, tum'bril *n.* open cart for taking victims of French Revolution to guillotine

tu'mefy *v.* (cause to) swell —**tumes'cence** *n.* —**tumes'cent** *a.* (becoming) swollen

tumm'y *n. inf.* childish word for stomach

tu'mo(u)r *n.* abnormal growth in or on body

tu'mult *n.* violent uproar, commotion —**tumult'uous** *a.*

tu'mulus *n.* burial mound, barrow (*pl.* **-li** [-lī])

tun *n.* large cask; measure of liquid

tu'na *n. see* TUNNY

tun'dra *n.* vast treeless zone between ice cap and timber line of N America and Eurasia

tune *n.* melody; quality of being in pitch; adjustment of musical instrument; concord; frame of mind —*vt.* put in tune; adjust machine to obtain most efficient running; adjust radio circuit —**tune'ful** *a.* —**tune'fully** *adv.* —**tu'ner** *n.* —**tune in** adjust (radio, television) to receive (a station, programme)

tung'sten *n.* greyish-white metal, used in lamp filaments, some steels *etc.*

tu'nic *n.* close-fitting jacket forming part of uniform; loose hip-length or knee-length garment

tunn'el *n.* underground passage, *esp.* as track for railway line; burrow of a mole *etc.* —*v.* make tunnel (through) (**-ll-**) —**tunn'eller** *n.*

tunn'y *n.* large marine food and game fish
tu'pik [tōō'-] *n.* tent used as summer shelter by Inuit
tuque [took] *n.* knitted cap with tapering end
tur'ban *n.* in certain countries, man's headdress, made by coiling length of cloth round head or a cap; woman's hat like this
tur'bid *a.* muddy, not clear; disturbed —**turbid'ity** *n.*
tur'bine *n.* rotary engine driven by steam, gas, water or air playing on blades
turbo- (*comb. form*) of, relating to, or driven by a turbine
tur'bot *n.* large European flatfish
tur'bulent *a.* in commotion; swirling; riotous —**tur'bulence** *n. esp.* instability of atmosphere causing gusty air currents *etc.*
tureen' *n.* serving dish for soup
turf *n.* short grass with earth bound to it by matted roots; grass, *esp.* as lawn (*pl.* **turfs, turves**) —*vt.* lay with turf —**the turf** horse racing; racecourse —**turf out** *inf.* dismiss, throw out
tur'gid *a.* swollen, inflated; bombastic —**turges'cent** *a.* —**turgid'ity** *n.*
tur'key *n.* large bird reared for food; *inf.* dramatic production that fails; *sl.* stupid or incompetent person —**talk turkey** discuss frankly and practically
Turk'ish *a.* of, pert. to Turkey, the Turks —**Turkish bath** steam bath —**Turkish delight** gelatin flavoured and coated with powdered sugar
tur'meric *n.* Asian plant; powdered root of this used as dye, medicine and condiment
tur'moil *n.* confusion and bustle, commotion
turn *v.* move around, rotate; change, reverse, alter position or direction (of); (*oft. with* into) change in nature, character *etc.* —*vt.* make, shape on lathe —*n.* act of turning; inclination *etc.*; period, spell; turning; short walk; (part of) rotation; performance —**turn'er** *n.* —**turn'ing** *n.* road, path leading off main route —**turn'coat** *n.* one who forsakes his party or principles —**turn'out** *n.* number of people appearing for some purpose, occasion; way in which person is dressed, equipped —**turn'over** *n.* total sales made by business over certain period; rate at which staff leave and are replaced; small pasty —**turn'pike** *n. Hist.* (gate across) road where toll was paid —**turn'stile** *n.* revolving gate for controlling admission of people —**turn'table** *n.* revolving platform —**turn down** refuse —**turn up** appear; be found; increase (flow, volume)
turn'ip *n.* plant with globular root used as food
turp'entine *n.* resin got from certain trees; oil, spirits made from this —**turps** *n. short for* turpentine
turp'itude *n.* depravity
tur'quoise *n.* bluish-green precious stone; this colour
turr'et *n.* small tower; revolving armoured tower for guns on warship, tank *etc.*
tur'tle *n.* any of various four-footed reptiles covered with shell of horny plates
tusk *n.* long pointed side tooth of certain animals, *eg* elephant, wild boar *etc.* —**tusk'er** *n.* animal with tusks fully developed
tus'sle *n./v.* fight, wrestle, struggle
tuss'ock *n.* clump of grass; tuft
tu'telage *n.* act, office of tutor or guardian —**tu'telary** *a.*
tu'tor *n.* one teaching individuals or small groups —*v.* teach thus —**tutor'ial** *n.* period of instruction with tutor
tu'tu [tōō'tōō] *n.* short, stiff skirt worn by ballerinas
tux *n. inf.* tuxedo
tuxe'do *n.* man's semiformal black evening jacket
TV television —**TV game** game like tennis played on domestic TV screen using special attachment
twad'dle [twod'l] *n.* silly talk
twain *n. obs.* two —**in twain** asunder
twang *n.* vibrating metallic sound; nasal speech —*v.* (cause to) make such sounds
tweak *vt.* pinch and twist or pull —*n.*
tweed *n.* rough-surfaced cloth used for clothing —*pl.* suit of tweed
tweet *n./vi.* chirp —**tweet'er** *n.* loudspeaker reproducing high-frequency sounds
tweez'ers *pl.n.* small forceps or tongs
twelve *n./a.* cardinal number two more

than ten —**twelfth** *a.* the ordinal number —*n.*

twent'y *n./a.* cardinal number, twice ten —**twent'ieth** *a.* the ordinal number —*n.*

twerp, twirp *n. inf.* silly person

twice *adv.* two times

twid'dle *v.* fiddle; twist

twig[1] *n.* small branch, shoot

twig[2] *v. inf.* notice, understand (**-gg-**)

twi'light *n.* soft light after sunset

twill *n.* fabric woven so as to have surface of parallel ridges

twin *n.* one of pair, *esp.* of two children born together —*a.* being a twin —*v.* pair, be paired

twine *v.* twist, coil round —*n.* string, cord

twinge *n.* momentary sharp, shooting pain; qualm

twin'kle *vi.* shine with dancing or quivering light, sparkle —*n.* twinkling; flash; gleam of amusement in eyes —**twin'kling** *n.* very brief time

twirl *vt.* turn or twist round quickly; whirl; twiddle

twist *v.* make, become spiral, by turning with one end fast; distort, change; wind —*n.* thing twisted —**twist'er** *n. inf.* tornado; person or thing that twists —**twist'y** *a.*

twit *n. inf.* foolish person; *inf.* nervous or excitable state —*vt.* taunt (**-tt-**)

twitch *v.* give momentary sharp pull or jerk (to) —*n.* such pull or jerk; spasmodic jerk, spasm

twitt'er *vi.* (of birds) utter succession of tremulous sounds —*n.* such succession of notes

two [tōō] *n./a.* cardinal number, one more than one —**two'fold** *a./adv.* —**two-cycle** *a.* (of internal-combustion engine) making one explosion to every two strokes of piston —**two-faced** *a.* double-dealing, deceitful; with two faces

tycoon' [tī-] *n.* powerful, influential businessman

tyke, tike *inf. n.* small, cheeky child; small (mongrel) dog

tym'pani *see* TIMPANI

type *n.* class; sort; model; pattern; characteristic build; specimen; block bearing letter used for printing; such pieces collectively —*vt.* print with typewriter; typify; classify —**type'script** *n.* typewritten document or copy —**type'write** *v.* —**type'writer** *n.* keyed writing machine —**ty'pist** *n.* one who operates typewriter —**ty'po** *n. inf.* error in typing

ty'phoid *n.* acute infectious disease, affecting *esp.* intestines —*a.* —**ty'phus** *n.* infectious disease

typhoon' *n.* violent tropical storm or cyclone —**typhon'ic** *a.*

typ'ical *a.* true to type; characteristic —**typ'ically** *adv.*

typ'ify *vt.* serve as type or model of (**-ified, -ifying**)

typog'raphy [tī-] *n.* art of printing; style of printing —**typograph'ical** *a.* —**typog'rapher** *n.*

ty'rant [tī'-] *n.* oppressive or cruel ruler; one who forces his will on others cruelly and arbitrarily —**tyrann'ical** [ti-] *a.* despotic; ruthless —**tyrann'ically** *adv.* —**tyran'nicide** *n.* slayer of tyrant; his deed —**tyr'annize** *v.* exert ruthless or tyrannical authority (over) —**tyr'annous** *a.* —**tyr'anny** *n.* despotism

tyre *n. see* TIRE[2]

ty'ro [tī'-] *n.* novice, beginner

U

U Union; United; *Chem.* uranium

ubiq'uitous [yōō-bik'w-] *a.* everywhere at once; omnipresent —**ubiq'uity** *n.*

udd'er *n.* milk-secreting organ of cow *etc.*

UFO unidentified flying object

ug'ly *a.* unpleasing, repulsive to the sight, hideous; ill-omened; threatening —**ug'lify** *vt.* —**ug'liness** *n.*

UHF ultrahigh frequency

UK United Kingdom

ukule'le [yōō-kə-lā'li] *n.* small four-stringed guitar

ul'cer *n.* open sore on skin, mucous membrane that is slow to heal —**ul'cerate** *v.* make, form ulcer(s) —**ul'cerated** *a.* —**ulcera'tion** *n.* —**ul'cerous** *a.*

ul'na *n.* longer of two bones of forearm (*pl.* **ul'nae** [-nē])

ult. ultimate; ultimo

ulte'rior *a.* lying beneath, beyond what is revealed or evident (*eg* motives); situated beyond

ult'imate *a.* last; highest; most significant; fundamental —**ult'imately** *adv.* —**ultima'tum** *n.* final proposition; final terms offered (*pl.* **-s, -ta**) —**ult'imo** *adv.* in last month

ultra- (*comb. form*) beyond, excessively, as in **ultramod'ern** *a.*

ultrahigh frequency (band of) radio waves of very short wavelength

ultramarine' [-ēn'] *n.* blue pigment

ultrason'ic *a.* of sound waves beyond the range of human ear

ultravi'olet *a.* of electromagnetic radiation (*eg* of sun *etc.*) beyond limit of visibility at violet end of spectrum

um'bel *n.* umbrella-like flower cluster with stalks springing from central point —**umbellif'erous** *a.*

um'ber *n.* dark brown pigment

umbil'ical *a.* of (region of) navel —**umbilical cord** cordlike structure connecting fetus with placenta of mother; cord joining astronaut to spacecraft *etc.*

um'brage *n.* offence, resentment

umbrell'a *n.* folding circular cover of nylon *etc.* on stick, carried in hand to protect against rain, heat of sun; anything shaped or functioning like an umbrella

u'miak [ōō'-] *n.* Inuit boat made of skins

um'pire *n.* person chosen to decide question, or to decide disputes and enforce rules in a game —*v.* act as umpire (in)

umpteen' *inf. a.* many —**umpteenth'** *a.*

UN United Nations

un- (*comb. form*) indicating not, contrary to, opposite of, reversal of an action, removal from, release or deprivation The list below contains some of the more common compounds

unaccount'able *a.* that cannot be explained

unan'imous [yōō-] *a.* in complete agreement; agreed by all —**unanim'ity** *n.*

unassu'ming *a.* not pretentious, modest

unaccept'able
unaccom'panied
unaccus'tomed
unaffect'ed
unapproach'able
unattached'
unattrac'tive
unauth'orized
unbear'able
unbeliev'able
unbi'as(s)ed
unbreak'able
uncer'tain
uncharacteris'tic
unchar'itable
uncom'fortable
uncommitt'ed
uncomm'only
uncondi'tional
unconstitu'tional
unconven'tional
uncoor'dinated
uncrit'ical
undeci'ded
undemand'ing
undeserved'
undesi'rable
undeterred'
undifferen'tiated
undimin'ished
undis'ciplined
undiscov'ered
undisturbed'
undrink'able
unearned'
uneat'able
uneconom'ic
uned'ucated
unemo'tional
unend'ing
une'qualled
unequiv'ocal
uneth'ical
unevent'ful
unexpect'ed
unexplained'
unfail'ing
unfair'
unfamil'iar
unfa'vo(u)rable
unfeel'ing

unavail'ing *a.* useless, futile

unaware' *a.* not aware, uninformed —**unawares'** *adv.* without previous warning; unexpectedly

unbos'om [-booz'-] *vt.* tell or reveal (one's secrets *etc.*)

uncann'y *a.* weird, mysterious

unc'le *n.* brother of father or mother; husband of aunt

uncomplimen'tary *a.* not complimentary; insulting, derogatory

uncon'scionable *a.* unscrupulous, unprincipled; excessive

uncon'scious *a.* insensible; not aware; not knowing; of thoughts, memories *etc.* of which one is not normally aware —*n.* these thoughts —**uncon'sciously** *adv.* —**uncon'sciousness** *n.*

uncouth' [-ōōth'] *a.* clumsy, boorish; without ease or polish

unc'tion [ungk'shən] *n.* anointing; excessive politeness; soothing words or thoughts —**unc'tuous** *a.* slippery, greasy; oily in manner, gushing

undeceive' *vt.* reveal truth to (someone mistaken, misled)

un'der *prep.* below, beneath; bound by, included in; less than; subjected to; known by; in the time of —*adv.* in lower place or condition —*a.* lower

under- (*comb. form*) beneath, below, lower, as in *underground*

un'derarm *a.* (of measurement) from armpit to wrist; *Sport* (of bowling *etc.*) with hand swung below shoulder level

un'derbrush *n.* small trees, bushes *etc.* growing beneath taller trees, undergrowth

un'dercarriage *n.* landing gear of aircraft

undercharge' *vt.* charge less than proper amount —*n.* too low a charge

un'dercoat *n.* coat of paint applied before top coat

undercut' *v.* charge less than (competitor); cut away the under part of (something); *Golf etc.* hit (ball) to give backspin —*n.* act, instance of cutting underneath; notch cut in tree to ensure clean break in felling

undergo' *vt.* experience, endure, sustain (**-went'**, **-gone'**, **-go'ing**)

undergrad'uate *n.* student member of university or college who has not taken degree

un'derground *a.* under the ground; secret —*adv.* secretly —*n.* secret but organized resistance to government in power; UK subway

un'derhand *a.* secret, sly; *Sport* underarm

underline' *vt.* put line under; emphasize

un'derling *n.* subordinate

undermine' *vt.* wear away base, support of; weaken insidiously

underneath' *adv.* below —*prep.* under —*a.* lower —*n.*

un'derpass *n.* section of road passing under another road, railway line *etc.*

un'dershirt *n.* undergarment for the trunk

understand' *v.* know and comprehend;

unfeigned'
unfin'ished
unfit'
unfold'
unforgett'able
unfor'tunate
unfound'ed
ungov'ernable
ungra'cious
ungrammat'ical
unguard'ed
unhapp'y
unharmed'
unhealth'y
unheat'ed
unhelp'ful
unhurr'ied
unhurt'
unhygie'nic
uniden'tified
unimag'inative
unimpaired'
unimpor'tant
unimpressed'
uninhab'ited
uninhib'ited
uninspired'
uninsured'
unintell'igible
uninten'tional
unin'teresting
uninterrupt'ed
uninvi'ted
unjus'tified
unla'belled
unlaw'ful
unlim'ited
unlined'
unlocked'
unluck'y
unman'ageable
unmarr'ied
unmen'tionable
unmer'ited
unmistak(e)'able
unmoved'
unmu'sical
unnamed'
unnat'ural
unnec'essary
unno'ticed

realize —*vt.* infer; take for granted (**-stood'**, **-stand'ing**) —**understand'able** *a.* —**understand'ably** *adv.* —**understand'ing** *n.* intelligence; opinion; agreement —*a.* sympathetic

un'derstudy *n.* one prepared to take over theatrical part from performer if necessary —*vt.*

undertake' *vt.* make oneself responsible for; enter upon; promise (**-took'**, **-ta'ken**, **-ta'king**) —**un'dertaker** *n.* one who arranges funerals —**un'dertaking** *n.* that which is undertaken; project; guarantee

un'dertone *n.* quiet, dropped tone of voice; underlying tone or suggestion

un'dertow *n.* backwash of wave; current beneath surface moving in different direction from surface current

un'derwear *n.* garments worn next to skin (*also* **un'derclothes**)

un'derworld *n.* criminals and their associates; *Myth.* abode of the dead

un'derwrite *vt.* agree to pay; accept liability in insurance policy (**-wrote**, **-written**, **-writing**) —**un'derwriter** *n.* agent for insurance

undo' [-doo'] *vt.* untie, unfasten; reverse; cause downfall of (**-did'**, **-done'**, **-do'ing**) —**undo'ing** *n.* —**undone'** *a.* ruined; not performed

un'dulate [-dyoo-] *v.* move up and down like waves —**undula'tion** *n.* —**un'dulatory** *a.*

unearth' *vt.* dig up; discover

uneas'y *a.* anxious; uncomfortable

unemployed' *a.* having no paid employment, out of work —**unemploy'ment** *n.*

unerr'ing *a.* not missing the mark; consistently accurate

UNESCO United Nations Educational, Scientific and Cultural Organization

ungain'ly *a.* awkward, clumsy

un'guent [ung'gwənt] *n.* ointment

uni- (*comb. form*) one, as in *unicorn, uniform etc.* Such words are not given here where the meanings may easily be inferred from the simple word

UNICEF United Nations International Children's Emergency Fund

u'nicorn *n.* mythical horselike animal with single long horn

u'niform *n.* identifying clothes worn by members of same group *eg* soldiers, nurses *etc.* —*a.* not changing, unvarying; regular, consistent; conforming to same standard or rule —**uniform'ity** *n.* sameness —**u'niformly** *adv.*

u'nify *v.* make or become one (**-ified**, **-ifying**) —**unifica'tion** *n.*

unilat'eral [yoo-] *a.* one-sided; (of contract) binding one party only —**unilat'erally** *adv.*

u'nion *n.* joining into one; state of being joined; result of being joined; federation, combination of societies *etc.*; trade union —**u'nionism** *n.* —**u'nionist** *n.* supporter of union —**u'nionize** *v.* organize (workers) into trade union —**Union Jack** national flag of United Kingdom

unique' [yoo-nēk'] *a.* being only one of its kind; unparalleled

u'nison *n. Mus.* singing *etc.* of same

unobser'vant
unobtain'able
unobtru'sive
unoffi'cial
uno'pened
unopposed'
unor'thodox
unpaid'
unpar'donable
unpleas'ant
unpop'ular
unprec'edented
unprepared'
unques'tionably
unrealis'tic
unrea'sonable
unrelent'ing
unrepresent'ative
unrequi'ted
unresolved'
unrestrained'
unri'valled
unroll'
unruf'fled
unsafe'
unsale'able
unsatisfac'tory
unsched'uled
unselfcon'scious
unshak(e)'able
unsolic'ited
unspec'ified
unspo'ken
unsuccess'ful
unsuit'able
unsweet'ened
unsympathet'ic
unsystemat'ic
untrained'
untrust'worthy
untyp'ical
unu'sable
unu'sual
unutt'erable
unwant'ed
unwarr'anted
unwhole'some
unwill'ing
unwind'
unwise'
unwrap'

note as others; agreement, harmony, concord

u'nit *n.* single thing or person; standard quantity; group of people or things with one purpose —**unita'rian** *n.* member of Christian body that denies doctrine of the Trinity —**unita'rianism** *n.* —**u'nitary** *a.*

unite' [yōō-] *vt.* join into one, connect; associate; cause to adhere —*vi.* become one; combine —**u'nity** *n.* state of being one; harmony; agreement, uniformity; combination of separate parts into connected whole; *Maths* the number one —**United Empire Loyalist** American colonist who settled in Canada in War of Amer. Independence from loyalty to Britain —**United Nations Organization** an organization formed in 1945 to promote peace and international cooperation

u'niverse *n.* all existing things considered as constituting systematic whole; the world —**univer'sal** *a.* relating to all things or all people; applying to all members of a community —**universal'ity** *n.* —**univer'sally** *adv.*

univer'sity [yōō-] *n.* educational institution for study, examination and conferment of degrees in various branches of learning

unkempt' *a.* of rough or uncared-for appearance

unless' *conj.* if not, except

UNO United Nations Organization

unrav'el *vt.* undo, untangle

unremitt'ing *a.* never slackening or stopping

unru'ly [-rōō'-] *a.* badly behaved, ungovernable, disorderly

unsa'vo(u)ry *a.* distasteful, disagreeable

unsight'ly *a.* ugly

unten'able *a.* (of theories *etc.*) incapable of being maintained, defended

unthink'able *a.* out of the question; inconceivable; unreasonable

until' *conj.* to the time that; (with a negative) before —*prep.* up to the time of

un'to *prep. obs.* to

untouched' *a.* not touched; not harmed —**untouch'able** *a.* not able to be touched —*n. esp.* formerly, non-caste Hindu, forbidden to be touched by one of caste

untoward' *a.* awkward, inconvenient

untram'melled *a.* not confined, not constrained

unwell' *a.* not well, ill

unwield'y *a.* awkward, big, heavy to handle; clumsy

unwitt'ing *a.* not knowing; not intentional

up *prep.* from lower to higher position; along —*adv.* in or to higher position, source, activity *etc.*; indicating completion (**upp'er** *comp.*, **upp'ermost** *sup.*) —**up'ward** *a./adv.* —**up'wards** *adv.* —**up against** confronted with

up- (*comb. form*) up, upper, upwards as in *uproot, upgrade etc.* Such words are not given here where the meaning may easily be found from the simple word

upbraid' *vt.* scold, reproach

up'bringing *n.* rearing and education of children

update' *vt.* bring up to date

upfront' *a. inf.* open, frank —*a./adv.* (of money) paid out at beginning of business arrangement

upgrade' *vt.* promote to higher position; improve —*n.* [up'-] upward slope —*a.* going or sloping upward —**on the upgrade** improving or progressing

upheav'al *n.* sudden or violent disturbance

uphold' *vt.* maintain, support *etc.* (**upheld'**, **uphold'ing**)

upholst'er [-ō-] *vt.* fit springs, padding and coverings on chairs *etc.* —**uphol'sterer** *n.* one who fits coverings *etc.* —**upholst'ery** *n.*

up'keep *n.* act, process or cost of keeping something in good repair

up'land *n.* high land

uplift' *vt.* raise aloft —*n.* [up'-] a lifting up; mental, social or emotional improvement

upon' *prep.* on

upp'er *a.* higher, situated above —*comp. of* UP —*n.* upper part of boot or shoe —**upp'ercut** *n.* short-arm upward blow —**upp'ermost** *a. sup. of* UP

upp'ish, upp'ity *inf. a.* self-assertive; arrogant; affectedly superior

up'right *a.* erect; honest, just —*adv.* vertically —*n.* thing standing upright, *eg* post in framework

up'rising *n.* rebellion, revolt

up'roar *n.* tumult, disturbance —**up-**

roar'ious *a.* rowdy —**uproar'iously** *adv.*

upset' *vt.* overturn; distress; disrupt; make ill (**upset', upsett'ing**) —*n.* [up'-] unexpected defeat; confusion; trouble

up'shot *n.* outcome, end

up'side *n.* upper surface or part —**upside down** turned over completely; *Inf.* confused, topsy-turvy

up'stage' *a.* of back of stage —*vt. inf.* draw attention away from another to oneself

up'start *n.* one suddenly raised to wealth, power *etc.*

up'stream *a./adv.* in, towards higher part of stream, against current

up'thrust *n.* upward push or thrust; *Geology* violent upheaval of earth's surface

uptight' *inf. a.* displaying tense nervousness, irritability; repressed

up'town' *a./adv.* toward, in or of part of town away from centre —*n.* such part of town

ura'nium [yoo-] *n.* white radioactive metallic element, used as chief source of nuclear energy

Ura'nus *n.* Greek god, personification of sky; seventh planet from the sun

ur'ban *a.* relating to town or city —**ur'banize** *vt.* change countryside to residential or industrial area

urbane' *a.* elegant, sophisticated —**urban'ity** *n.*

urch'in *n.* mischievous, unkempt child

ur'ea [yoor'-] *n.* substance occurring in urine

ure'thra [yoor-] *n.* canal conveying urine from bladder out of body

urge *vt.* exhort earnestly; entreat; drive on —*n.* strong desire —**ur'gency** *n.* —**ur'gent** *a.* pressing; needing attention at once —**ur'gently** *adv.*

u'rine *n.* fluid excreted by kidneys to bladder and passed as waste from body —**u'ric** *a.* —**uri'nal** *n.* (place with) sanitary fitting(s) used by men for urination —**u'rinary** *a.* —**u'rinate** *vi.* discharge urine —**urina'tion** *n.*

urn *n.* vessel like vase, *esp.* for ashes of the dead; large container with tap for making and dispensing tea, coffee *etc.*

ur'sine *a.* of, like a bear

US, USA United States (of America)

us *pron. pl.* the objective case of the pronoun WE

use [yōōz] *vt.* employ, avail oneself of; exercise; exploit; consume; partake of (drugs *etc.*) —*n.* [yōōs] employment, application to a purpose; need to employ; serviceableness; profit; habit —**u'sable** [-z-] *a.* fit for use —**u'sage** [-s-] *n.* act of using; custom; customary way of using —**used** [-z-] *a.* second-hand, not new —**use'ful** [-s-] *a.* of use; helpful; serviceable —**use'fully** *adv.* —**use'fulness** *n.* —**use'less** *a.* —**use'lessly** *adv.* —**use'lessness** *n.* —**used to** [-s-] *a.* accustomed to —*vt.* did so formerly —**user friendly** (of computer *etc.*) easily understood and operated

ush'er *n.* doorkeeper, one showing people to seats *etc.* (**usherette'** *fem.*) —*vt.* introduce, announce; inaugurate

USSR Union of Soviet Socialist Republics

u'sual *a.* habitual, ordinary —**u'sually** *adv.* as a rule; generally, commonly

u'surer *n.* person who lends money at extremely high rate of interest

usurp' [yōō-z-] *vt.* seize wrongfully —**usurpa'tion** *n.* violent or unlawful seizing of power —**usurp'er** *n.*

u'sury [-zhə-] *n.* lending of money at excessive interest; such interest —**u'surer** *n.* money lender —**usur'ious** [-zhoor'-] *a.*

uten'sil [yōō-] *n.* vessel, implement, *esp.* in domestic use

u'terus *n.* womb (*pl.* **u'teri** [-ī]) —**u'terine** *a.*

util'idor *n.* above ground insulated casing for pipes

util'ity [yōō-] *n.* usefulness; benefit; useful thing —*a.* made for practical purposes —**utilita'rian** *a.* useful rather than beautiful —**utilita'rianism** *n.* doctrine that morality of actions is to be tested by their utility, *esp.* that the greatest good of the greatest number should be the sole end of public action —**u'tilizable** *a.* —**utiliza'tion** *n.* —**u'tilize** *vt.* make worthwhile use of

ut'most *a.* to the highest degree; extreme, furthest —*n.* greatest possible amount

Uto'pia [yōō-] *n.* imaginary state with perfect political and social conditions, or constitution —**uto'pian** *a.* ideally perfect but impracticable

utt'er[1] *vt.* express, emit audibly, say; put in circulation (forged banknotes, counterfeit coin) —**utt'erance** *n.* act of speaking; expression in words; spoken words

utt'er[2] *a.* complete, total, absolute —**ut'terly** *adv.*

utt'ermost *a.* farthest out; utmost —*n.* highest degree

U-turn *n.* U-shaped turn by vehicle in order to go in opposite direction; reversal of political policy

UV ultraviolet

u'vula [-vyoo-] *n.* pendent fleshy part of soft palate —**u'vular** *a.* —**uvuli'tis** *n.* inflammation of uvula

uxor'ious *a.* excessively fond of one's wife

V

V *Chem.* vanadium

v volt

v. verb; verso; versus; very; vide

va'cant *a.* without thought, empty; unoccupied —**va'cancy** *n.* state of being unoccupied; unfilled post, accommodation *etc.* —**va'cantly** *adv.*

vacate' *vt.* quit, leave empty —**vaca'tion** *n.* time when schools and law courts are closed; period of rest from work *etc.*, *esp.* spent away from home; act of vacating —*vi.* take a vacation —**vaca'tionist, vaca'tioner** *n.*

vac'cinate [vak's-] *vt.* inoculate with vaccine as protection against a specific disease —**vaccina'tion** *n.* —**vac'cine** [-sēn] *n.* any substance used for inoculation against disease

vac'illate [vas'-] *vi.* fluctuate in opinion; waver; move to and fro —**vacilla'tion** *n.*

vac'uum [-yoom] *n.* place, region containing no matter and from which all or most air, gas has been removed (*pl.* **-uums, -ua**) —*v.* clean with vacuum cleaner —**vacu'ity** *n.* —**vac'uous** *a.* vacant; expressionless; unintelligent —**vacuum cleaner** apparatus for removing dust by suction —**vacuum flask** double-walled flask with vacuum between walls, for keeping contents of inner flask at temperature at which they were inserted —**vacuum tube** part of radio or television which controls flow of current

vag'abond *n.* person with no fixed home; wandering beggar or thief —*a.* like a vagabond

va'gary [*or* və-gā'-] *n.* something unusual, erratic; whim

vagi'na [-jī'-] *n.* passage from womb to exterior —**vagi'nal** *a.*

va'grant *n.* vagabond, tramp —*a.* wandering, *esp.* without purpose —**va'grancy** *n.*

vague [vāg] *a.* indefinite or uncertain; indistinct; not clearly expressed; absent-minded

vain *a.* conceited; worthless, useless; unavailing; foolish —**vain'ly** *adv.*

vain'glory *n.* boastfulness, vanity —**vainglo'rious** *a.*

val'ance *n.* short curtain round base of bed *etc.*

vale *n. Poet.* valley

valedic'tion *n.* farewell —**valedic'tory** *n.* farewell address, *esp.* at school commencement —*a.*

va'lence *n. Chem.* combining power of element or atom

val'entine *n.* (one receiving) card, gift, expressing affection, on Saint Valentine's Day, 14th Feb.

valer'ian *n.* flowering herb

val'et [*or* -ā] *n.* gentleman's personal servant

valetu'dinary *a.* sickly; infirm —**valetudina'rian** *n.* person obliged or disposed to live the life of an invalid

Valhall'a *n. Norse Myth.* place of immortality for heroes slain in battle

val'iant *a.* brave, courageous

val'id *a.* sound; capable of being justified; of binding force in law —**valid'ity** *n.* soundness; power to convince; legal force —**val'idate** *vt.* make valid

valise' [-ēz'] *n.* travelling bag

Valky'rie [-kē'-] *n.* one of the Norse war-goddesses who chose the slain and guided them to Valhalla

vall'ey *n.* low area between hills; river basin

val'o(u)r [-ər] *n.* bravery —**val'orous** *a.*

val'ue *n.* worth; utility; equivalent; importance —*pl.* principles, standards —*vt.* estimate value of; hold in respect; prize —**val'uable** *a.* precious; worthy; capable of being valued —*n.* (*usu. pl.*) valuable thing —**valua'tion** *n.* estimated worth —**val'ueless** *a.* worthless —**val'uer** *n.*

valve *n.* device to control passage of

fluid *etc.* through pipe; *Anat.* part of body allowing one-way passage of fluids; **UK** vacuum tube; any of separable parts of shell of mollusc; *Mus.* device on brass instrument for lengthening tube **—val'vular** *a.* of, like valves

vamoose' *v. sl.* depart quickly

vamp[1] *inf. n.* woman who deliberately allures men *—v.* exploit (man) as vamp

vamp[2] *n.* something patched up (*also* **revamp'**); front part of shoe upper *—vt.* patch up, rework

vamp'ire *n.* (in folklore) corpse that rises from dead to drink blood of the living **—vampire bat** one that sucks blood of animals

van[1] *n.* covered vehicle, *esp.* for goods

van[2] *n. short for* VANGUARD

vana'dium *n.* metallic element used in manufacture of hard steel

van'dal *n.* one who wantonly and deliberately damages or destroys **—van'dalism** *n.* **—van'dalize** *vt.*

vane *n.* weathercock; blade of propeller; fin on bomb *etc.*; sight on quadrant

van'guard *n.* leading, foremost group, position *etc.*

vanill'a *n.* tropical climbing orchid; its seed(pod); essence of this for flavouring

van'ish *vi.* disappear; fade away

van'ity *n.* excessive pride or conceit; ostentation

van'quish *vt.* subdue in battle; conquer, overcome **—van'quishable** *a.* **—van'quisher** *n.*

van'tage [vahn'-] *n.* advantage

vap'id *a.* flat, dull, insipid **—vapid'ity** *n.*

va'po(u)r [-ər] *n.* gaseous form of a substance more familiar as liquid or solid; steam, mist; invisible moisture in air **—va'porize** *v.* convert into, pass off in, vapour **—va'porizer** *n.* **—va'porous** *a.*

va'riable *see* VARY

var'icose [va'ri-] *a.* of vein, swollen, twisted

va'riegate *vt.* diversify by patches of different colours **—va'riegated** *a.* streaked, spotted, dappled **—variega'tion** *n.*

vari'ety *n.* state of being varied or various; diversity; varied assortment; sort or kind

vario'rum *a./n.* (edition) with notes by various commentators

va'rious *a.* manifold, diverse, of several kinds

var'let *n.* formerly, menial servant, rascal

var'nish *n.* resinous solution put on a surface to make it hard and shiny *—vt.* apply varnish to

va'ry *v.* (cause to) change, diversify, differ, deviate (**va'ried, va'rying**) **—variabil'ity** *n.* **—va'riable** *a.* changeable; unsteady or fickle *—n.* something subject to variation **—va'riance** *n.* state of discord, discrepancy **—va'riant** *a.* different *—n.* difference in form; alternative form or reading **—varia'tion** *n.* alteration; extent to which thing varies; modification **—va'ried** *a.* diverse; modified; variegated

vas *n.* vessel, tube carrying bodily fluid (*pl.* **va'sa**)

vas'cular *a.* of, with vessels for conveying sap, blood *etc.*

vase [vahz] *n.* vessel, jar as ornament or for holding flowers

vasec'tomy *n.* contraceptive measure of surgical removal of part of vas bearing sperm from testicle

Vas'eline [-ēn] *n.* **R** jellylike petroleum product

vass'al *n.* holder of land by feudal tenure; dependant **—vass'alage** *n.*

vast [-ah-] *a.* very large **—vast'ly** *adv.* **—vast'ness** *n.*

vat *n.* large tub, tank

Vat'ican *n.* Pope's palace; papal authority

vau'deville [vō'də-vil] *n.* theatrical entertainment with songs, juggling acts, dance *etc.*

vault[1] *n.* arched roof; arched apartment; cellar; burial chamber; place for storing valuables *—vt.* build with arched roof

vault[2] *v.* spring, jump over with the hands resting on something *—n.* such jump

vaunt *v./n.* boast

VC Vice Chairman; Vice Chancellor; Victoria Cross; Viet Cong

VCR video cassette recorder

VD venereal disease

VDU visual display unit

veal *n.* calf flesh as food

vec'tor *n.* quantity (*eg* force) having both magnitude and direction; disease-carrying organism, *esp.* insect; compass direction, course

veer *vi.* change direction; change one's mind

ve'gan *n.* strict vegetarian, who does not eat animal products

veg'etable [vej'-] *n.* plant, *esp.* edible one; *inf.* person who has lost use of mental faculties; *inf.* dull person —*a.* of, from, concerned with plants —**vegetable marrow** plant with long, green-striped fruit, eaten as vegetable

vegeta'rian *n.* one who does not eat meat —*a.* —**vegeta'rianism** *n.*

veg'etate [vej'-] *vi.* (of plants) grow, develop; (of person) live dull, unproductive life —**vegeta'tion** *n.* plants collectively; plants growing in a place; process of plant growth —**veg'etative** *a.*

ve'hement [vē'im-] *a.* marked by intensity of feeling; vigorous; forcible —**ve'hemence** *n.* —**ve'hemently** *adv.*

ve'hicle [vē'ikl] *n.* means of conveying; means of expression; medium —**vehic'ular** [vi-hik'-] *a.*

veil [vāl] *n.* light material to cover face or head; mask, cover —*vt.* cover with, as with, veil —**veiled** *a.* disguised —**take the veil** become a nun

vein [vān] *n.* tube in body taking blood to heart; rib of leaf or insect's wing; fissure in rock filled with ore; streak; distinctive trait, strain *etc.*; mood —*vt.* mark with streaks —**ve'nous** *a.* of veins

veld, veldt [velt] *n.* elevated grassland in S Afr.

vell'um *n.* parchment of calf skin used for manuscripts or bindings; paper resembling this

veloc'ity [-os'-] *n.* rate of motion in given direction, *esp.* of inanimate things; speed

ve'lodrome *n.* area with banked track for cycle racing

velour(s)' [-loor'] *n.* fabric with velvety finish

ve'lum *n. Zool.* membranous covering or organ; soft palate (*pl.* **ve'la**)

vel'vet *n.* silk or cotton fabric with thick, short pile —**velveteen'** *n.* cotton fabric resembling velvet —**vel'vety** *a.* of, like velvet; soft and smooth

ve'nal *a.* guilty of taking, prepared to take, bribes; corrupt —**venal'ity** *n.*

vend *vt.* sell —**vend'or** *n.* —**vending machine** one that automatically dispenses goods when money is inserted

vendett'a *n.* bitter, prolonged feud

veneer' *n.* thin layer of fine wood; superficial appearance —*vt.* cover with veneer

ven'erable *a.* worthy of reverence —**ven'erate** *vt.* look up to, respect, revere —**venera'tion** *n.*

vene'real *a.* (of disease) transmitted by sexual intercourse; infected with venereal disease; of, relating to genitals or sexual intercourse

vene'tian blind window blind made of thin horizontal slats arranged to turn so as to admit or exclude light

ven'geance *n.* revenge; retribution for wrong done —**venge'ful** *a.* —**venge'fully** *adv.*

ve'nial *a.* pardonable

ven'ison *n.* flesh of deer as food

ven'om *n.* poison; spite —**ven'omous** *a.* poisonous

ve'nous *see* VEIN

vent[1] *n.* small hole or outlet —*vt.* give outlet to; utter; pour forth

vent[2] *n.* vertical slit in garment *esp.* at back of jacket

vent'ilate *vt.* supply with fresh air; bring into discussion —**ventila'tion** *n.* —**vent'ilator** *n.*

ven'tral *a.* abdominal

ven'tricle *n.* cavity, hollow in body, *esp.* in heart or brain —**ventric'ular** *a.*

ventril'oquist *n.* one who can so speak that the sounds seem to come from some other person or place —**ventril'oquism** *n.*

ven'ture *vt.* expose to hazard; risk —*vi.* dare; have courage to do something or go somewhere —*n.* risky undertaking; speculative commercial undertaking —**ven'turesome** *a.*

ven'ue *n. Law* district in which case is tried; meeting place; location

Ve'nus *n.* Roman goddess of love; planet between earth and Mercury —**Venus's flytrap** insect-eating plant

vera'cious *a.* truthful; true —**verac'ity** [-as'-] *n.*

veran'da(h) *n.* open or partly enclosed porch on outside of house

verb *n.* part of speech used to express action or being —**verb'al** *a.* of, by, or relating to words spoken rather than written; of, like a verb —**verb'alize** *v.* put into words, speak —**verb'ally** *adv.* —**verba'tim** *adv./a.* word for word, literal

verbe'na *n.* genus of fragrant, beautiful plants; their characteristic scent

verb'iage *n.* excess of words —**verbose'** *a.* wordy, long-winded —**verbos'ity** *n.*

verd'ant *a.* green and fresh —**ver'dure** *n.* greenery; freshness —**ver'durous** *a.*

ver'dict *n.* decision of a jury; opinion reached after examination of facts

ver'digris *n.* green film on copper

verd'ure *see* VERDANT

verge *n.* edge; brink ; grass border along a road —*vi.* come close to; be on the border of

ver'ger *n.* caretaker and attendant in church; bearer of wand of office

ver'ify [ve'ri-] *vt.* prove, confirm truth of; test accuracy of (**-ified, -ifying**) —**ver'ifiable** *a.* —**verifica'tion** *n.*

ver'ily [ve'ri-] *obs. adv.* truly; in truth

verisimil'itude *n.* appearance of truth; likelihood

ver'itable [ve'ri-] *a.* actual, true, genuine —**ver'itably** *adv.*

ver'ity [ve'ri-] *n.* truth; reality; true assertion

vermicell'i [-sel'-] *n.* pasta in fine strands, used in soups; tiny chocolate strands used to coat cakes *etc.*

verm'icide *n.* substance to destroy worms —**verm'iform** *a.* shaped like a worm (*eg* **vermiform appendix**)

vermil'ion *a./n.* (of) bright red colour or pigment

ver'min *pl.n.* injurious animals, parasites *etc.* —**ver'minous** *a.*

ver'mouth [-məth] *n.* wine flavoured with aromatic herbs *etc.*

vernac'ular *n.* commonly spoken language or dialect of particular country or place —*a.* of vernacular; native

vern'al *a.* of spring

vern'ier *n.* sliding scale for obtaining fractional parts of subdivision of graduated scale

veron'ica *n.* genus of plants including speedwell

verru'ca [-rōō'-] *n.* wart, *esp.* on foot

ver'satile *a.* capable of or adapted to many different uses, skills *etc.*; liable to change —**versatil'ity** *n.*

verse *n.* stanza or short subdivision of poem or the Bible; poetry; line of poetry —**ver'sify** *v.* turn into verse (**-ified, -ifying**) —**versifica'tion** *n.* —**versed in** skilled

ver'sion *n.* description from certain point of view; translation; adaptation

ver'so *n.* back of sheet of printed paper, left-hand page

ver'sus *prep.* against

vert'ebra *n.* single section of backbone (*pl.* **-brae** [-brē]) —**vert'ebral** *a.* of the spine —**vert'ebrate** *n.* animal with backbone —*a.*

vert'ex *n.* summit (*pl.* **vert'ices** [-sēz])

vert'ical *a.* at right angles to the horizon; upright; overhead

vert'igo *n.* giddiness (*pl.* **-goes, vertig'ines** [-tij'i-nēz]) —**vertig'inous** [-ij'-] *a.* dizzy

ver'vain *n.* plant of the genus *Verbena*

verve *n.* enthusiasm; spirit; energy, vigour

ver'y [ve'ri] *a.* exact, ideal; same; complete; actual —*adv.* extremely, to great extent

ves'icle *n.* small blister, bubble, or cavity —**vesic'ular** *a.*

ves'pers *pl.n.* evening church service; evensong

vess'el *n.* any object used as a container, *esp.* for liquids; ship, large boat; tubular structure conveying liquids (*eg* blood) in body

vest *n.* sleeveless garment worn under jacket or coat; **UK** undershirt —*vt.* place; bestow; confer; clothe —**vest'ment** *n.* robe or official garment —**vested interest** strong personal interest in particular state of affairs —**vest-pocket** *a.* small enough to fit into vest pocket

ves'tal *a.* pure, chaste

vest'ibule *n.* entrance hall, lobby

vest'ige [-ij] *n.* small trace, amount —**vestig'ial** *a.*

vest'ry *n.* room in church for keeping vestments, holding meetings *etc.*; *Anglican and Episcopalian Churches* committee of church members chosen to manage temporal affairs of church

vet[1] *n. short for* VETERINARIAN

vet[2] *short for* VETERAN

vet. veteran; veterinary

vetch *n.* plant of bean family

vet'eran *n.* person who has served in military forces; one who has served a long time —*a.* long-serving

vet'erinary *a.* of, concerning the health of animals —*n.* veterinarian —**veterina'rian** *n.* one qualified to treat animal ailments

ve'to *n.* power of rejecting piece of legislation, or preventing it from coming into effect; any prohibition (*pl.* **-toes**) —*vt.* enforce veto against; forbid with authority

vex *vt.* annoy; distress —**vexa'tion** *n.* cause of irritation; state of distress —**vexa'tious** *a.* —**vexed** *a.* cross; annoyed; much discussed

vg very good

VHF very high frequency

VI Vancouver Island

vi'a *adv.* by way of

vi'able *a.* practicable; able to live and grow independently —**viabil'ity** *n.*

vi'aduct *n.* bridge over valley for a road or railway

vi'al *n. same as* PHIAL

vi'ands *pl.n.* food

vibes *pl.n. inf. short for* VIBRATIONS, VIBRAPHONE

vi'braphone *n.* musical instrument like xylophone, but with electronic resonators, that produces a gentle vibrato

vibrate' *v.* (cause to) move to and fro rapidly and continuously; give off (light or sound) by vibration —*vi.* oscillate; quiver —**vi'brant** *a.* throbbing; vibrating; appearing vigorous, lively —**vibra'tion** *n.* a vibrating —*pl. inf.* instinctive feelings about a place, person *etc.* —**vibra'to** [-ah'tō] *n.* vibrating effect in music (*pl.* **-os**) —**vibra'tor** *n.* —**vi'bratory** *a.*

vibur'num *n.* subtropical shrub with white flowers and berrylike fruits

vic'ar *n.* clergyman in charge of parish —**vic'arage** *n.* vicar's house —**vica'rial** *a.* of vicar

vica'rious *a.* obtained, enjoyed or undergone through sympathetic experience of another's experiences; suffered, done *etc.* as substitute for another —**vica'riously** *adv.* —**vica'riousness** *n.*

vice[1] *n.* evil or immoral habit or practice; criminal immorality; fault, imperfection

vice[2] *n.* appliance with screw jaw for holding things while working on them

vice- (*comb. form*) in place of, second to, as in *vice-chairman, viceroy etc.* These are not given here where meaning may be inferred from simple word

vice'roy [vīs'-] *n.* ruler acting for king in province or dependency (**vicereine'** [-rān'] *n. fem.*) —**vicere'gal** *a.* of viceroy —**viceroy'alty** *n.*

vi'ce ver'sa [-si-] *Lat.* conversely, the other way round

vicin'ity *n.* neighbourhood

vi'cious [vish'əs] *a.* wicked, cruel; ferocious, dangerous; leading to vice —**vi'ciously** *adv.*

viciss'itude *n.* change of fortune —*pl.* ups and downs of fortune —**vicissitu'dinous** *a.*

vic'tim *n.* person or thing killed, injured *etc.* as result of another's deed, or accident, circumstances *etc.*; person cheated; sacrifice —**victimiza'tion** *n.* —**vic'timize** *vt.* punish unfairly; make victim of

vic'tor *n.* conqueror; winner —**victo'rious** *a.* winning; triumphant —**vic'tory** *n.* winning of battle *etc.*

vict'ual [vit'l] *n.* (*usu. in pl.*) food —*v.* supply with or obtain food (**-ll-**) —**vict'ualler** *n.*

vicu'na *n.* S Amer. animal like llama; fine, light cloth made from its wool

vi'de *Lat.* see —**vide infra** see below —**vide supra** see above

vide'licet [-li-set] *Lat.* namely

vid'eo *a.* relating to or used in transmission or production of television image —*n.* apparatus for recording television programmes —**video cassette** cassette containing video tape —**video cassette recorder** tape recorder for vision and sound signals, used for recording and playing back TV programmes and movies on cassette (*also* **video**) —**video game** any of various games played on video screen using electronic control —**video nasty** movie, *usu.* made for video, that is explicitly horrific and pornographic —**video tape** magnetic tape on which to record television programme —**video tape recorder** tape recorder for vision signals using open spools for TV broadcast —**vid'eotext** *n.* means of providing written or graphical representation of computerized information on TV screen

vie [vī] *vi.* (*with* with *or* for) contend, compete against or for someone, something (**vied, vy'ing**)

view [vyōō] *n.* survey by eyes or mind; range of vision; picture; scene; opinion; purpose —*vt.* look at; survey; consider —**view'er** *n.* one who views; one who watches television; optical device to assist viewing of photographic slides —**view'finder** *n.* device on camera enabling user to see what will be included in photograph —**view'point** *n.* way of regarding a subject; position commanding view of landscape

view'data *n.* service in which consumer is linked to a computer by telephone and can select information required

vig'il [vij'-] *n.* a keeping awake, watch; eve of feast day —**vig'ilance** *n.* —**vig'ilant** *a.* watchful, alert

vigilan'te [vij-] *n.* one (*esp.* as member of group) who unofficially takes it upon himself to enforce law

vignette' [vin-yet'] *n.* short literary essay, sketch; photograph or portrait with the background shaded off

vig'o(u)r [-ər] *n.* force, strength; energy, activity —**vig'orous** *a.* strong; energetic; flourishing —**vig'orously** *adv.*

Vi'king *n.* medieval Scandinavian seafarer, raider, settler

vile *a.* very wicked, shameful; disgusting; despicable —**vile'ly** *adv.* —**vile'ness** *n.* —**vilifica'tion** *n.* —**vil'ify** *vt.* speak ill of; slander (**-ified, -ifying**)

vill'a *n.* large, luxurious, country house; detached or semidetached suburban house

vill'age *n.* small group of houses in country area —**vill'ager** *n.*

vill'ain [-ən] *n.* wicked person; *inf.* mischievous person —**vill'ainous** *a.* wicked; vile —**vill'ainy** *n.*

vim *n. inf.* force, energy

vinaigrette' *n.* small bottle of smelling salts; type of salad dressing

vin'dicate *vt.* clear of charges; justify; establish the truth or merit of —**vindica'tion** *n.* —**vin'dicator** *n.* —**vin'dicatory** *a.*

vindic'tive *a.* revengeful; inspired by resentment

vine *n.* climbing plant bearing grapes —**vine'yard** [vin'-] *n.* plantation of vines —**vin'tage** *n.* gathering of the grapes; the yield; wine of particular year; time of origin —*a.* best and most typical —**vint'ner** *n.* dealer in wine

vin'egar *n.* acid liquid obtained from wine and other alcoholic liquors —**vin'egary** *a.* like vinegar; sour; bad-tempered

vi'nyl *n.* plastic material with variety of domestic and industrial uses

vi'ol *n.* early stringed instrument preceding violin

vio'la[1] *n. see* VIOLIN

vi'ola[2] *n.* single-coloured variety of pansy

vi'olate *vt.* break (law, agreement *etc.*), infringe; rape; outrage, desecrate —**vi'olable** *a.* —**viola'tion** *n.* —**vi'olator** *n.*

vi'olent *a.* marked by, due to, extreme force, passion or fierceness; of great force; intense —**vi'olence** *n.* —**vi'olently** *adv.*

vi'olet *n.* plant with small bluish-purple or white flowers; the flower; bluish-purple colour —*a.* of this colour

violin' *n.* small four-stringed musical instrument —**vio'la** *n.* large violin with lower range —**violin'ist** *n.* —**violoncel'lo** *n. see* CELLO

VIP very important person

vi'per *n.* venomous snake

virag'o [-rahg'-] *n.* abusive woman (*pl.* **-go(e)s**)

vir'gin *n.* one who has not had sexual intercourse —*a.* without experience of sexual intercourse; unsullied, fresh; (of land) untilled —**vir'ginal** *a.* of, like virgin —*n.* type of spinet —**virgin'ity** *n.*

Virgin'ia creep'er climbing plant that turns red in autumn

Vir'go *n.* (the virgin) 6th sign of the zodiac, operative c. Aug. 22-Sept. 21

vir'ile [vi'rīl] *a.* (of male) capable of copulation or procreation; strong, forceful —**viril'ity** *n.*

virol'ogy *see* VIRUS

vir'tual *a.* so in effect, though not in appearance or name —**vir'tually** *adv.* practically, almost

vir'tue *n.* moral goodness; good quality; merit; inherent power —**vir'tuous** *a.* morally good; chaste —**vir'tuously** *adv.*

virtuo'so [-zō] *n.* one with special skill, *esp.* in a fine art (*pl.* **-sos, -si** [-sē])

—**virtuos'ity** *n.* great technical skill, *esp.* in a fine art as music

vir'ulent *a.* very infectious, poisonous *etc.*; malicious

vi'rus *n.* various submicroscopic organisms, some causing disease —**virol'ogy** *n.* study of viruses

Vis. Viscount

vi'sa [vē'zə] *n.* endorsement on passport permitting the bearer to travel into country of issuing government —**vi'saed** [-zəd] *a.*

vis'age [viz'ij] *n.* face

vis-à-vis' [vēz-ah-vē'] *Fr.* in relation to, regarding; opposite to

visc'era [vis'-] *pl.n.* large internal organs of body, *esp.* of abdomen —**vis'ceral** *a.*

visc'id [vis'-] *a.* sticky, of a consistency like treacle

vis'cose *n.* (substance used to produce) synthetic fabric

vis'count [vī'-] *n.* Brit. nobleman ranking below earl and above baron (**vis'countess** *fem.*)

vis'cous *a.* thick and sticky —**viscos'ity** *n.*

vis'ible [viz'-] *a.* that can be seen —**visibil'ity** *n.* degree of clarity of atmosphere, *esp.* for navigation —**vis'ibly** *adv.*

vis'ion [vizh'ən] *n.* sight; insight; dream; phantom; imagination —**vis'ionary** *a.* marked by vision; impractical —*n.* mystic; impractical person

vis'it [viz'-] *v.* go, come and see, stay temporarily with (someone); *inf.* chat —*n.* stay; call at person's home *etc.*; official call; *inf.* chat —**visita'tion** *n.* formal visit or inspection; affliction or plague —**vis'itor** *n.*

vi'sor, vi'zor [-z-] *n.* front part of helmet made to move up and down before the face; eyeshade, *esp.* on car; peak on cap

vis'ta *n.* view, *esp.* distant view

vis'ual [viz'-] *a.* of sight; visible —**visualiza'tion** *n.* —**vis'ualize** *vt.* form mental image of

vi'tal *a.* necessary to, affecting life; lively, animated; essential; highly important —**vi'tals** *pl.n.* vital organs of body —**vital'ity** *n.* life, vigour —**vi'talize** *vt.* give life to; lend vigour to —**vi'tally** *adv.*

vit'amin *n.* any of group of substances occurring in foodstuffs and essential to health

vi'tiate [vish'-] *vt.* spoil; deprive of efficacy; invalidate —**vitia'tion** *n.*

vit'reous *a.* of glass; glassy —**vitrifica'tion** *n.* —**vit'rify** *v.* convert into glass, or glassy substance (**-ified, -ifying**)

vit'riol *n.* sulphuric acid; caustic speech —**vitriol'ic** *a.*

vitu'perate [vi-tyōō'-] *vt.* abuse in words, revile —**vitupera'tion** *n.* —**vitu'perative** *a.*

viva'cious *a.* lively, gay, sprightly —**vivac'ity** [-as'-] *n.*

vi'va vo'ce [-chi] *Lat. adv.* by word of mouth —*n.* oral examination (*oft.* **vi'va**)

viv'id *a.* bright, intense; clear; lively, animated; graphic —**viv'idly** *adv.* —**viv'idness** *n.*

viv'ify *vt.* animate, inspire (**-ified, -ifying**)

vivip'arous *a.* bringing forth young alive

vivisec'tion *n.* dissection of, or operating on, living animals —**vivisec'tionist** *n.*

vix'en *n.* female fox; spiteful woman —**vix'enish** *a.*

viz. *short for* VIDELICET

vizier' *n.* high official in some Muslim countries

vi'zor *see* VISOR

vocab'ulary *n.* list of words, usu. in alphabetical order; stock of words used in particular language *etc.*

vo'cal *a.* of, with, or giving out voice; outspoken, articulate —*n.* piece of popular music that is sung —**vo'calist** *n.* singer —**vo'calize** *vt.* utter with voice —**vo'cally** *adv.*

vocal'ic *a.* of vowel(s)

voca'tion *n.* (urge, inclination, predisposition to) particular career, profession *etc.* —**voca'tional** *a.*

voc'ative *n.* in some languages, case of nouns used in addressing a person

vocif'erate *v.* exclaim, cry out —**vocifera'tion** *n.* —**vocif'erous** *a.* shouting, noisy

vod'ka *n.* Russian spirit distilled from grain, potatoes *etc.*

vogue [vōg] *n.* fashion, style; popularity

voice *n.* sound given out by person in speaking, singing *etc.*; quality of the sound; expressed opinion; (right to) share in discussion; verbal forms proper to relation of subject and action —*vt.* give utterance to, express —**voice'less** *a.*

void *a.* empty; destitute; not legally binding —*n.* empty space —*vt.* make ineffectual or invalid; empty out

voile *n.* light semitransparent fabric

vol. volume

vol'atile *a.* evaporating quickly; lively; fickle, changeable —**volatil'ity** *n.* —**volatiliza'tion** *n.* —**volat'ilize** *v.* (cause to) evaporate

volca'no *n.* hole in earth's crust through which lava, ashes, smoke *etc.* are discharged; mountain so formed (*pl.* **-no(e)s**) —**volcan'ic** *a.*

vole *n.* small rodent

voli'tion [-ish'-] *n.* act, power of willing; exercise of the will —**voli'tional, voli'tionary** *a.*

voll'ey *n.* simultaneous discharge of weapons or missiles; rush of oaths, questions *etc.*; *Sports* kick, stroke *etc.* at moving ball before it touches ground —*v.* discharge; utter; fly, strike *etc.* in volley —**voll'eyball** *n.* team game where large ball is hit by hand over high net

volt [-ō-] *n.* unit of electric potential —**volt'age** *n.* electric potential difference expressed in volts —**volt'meter** *n.*

volte'-face' [-fahs'] *Fr. n.* complete reversal of opinion or direction

vol'uble *a.* talking easily, readily and at length —**volubil'ity** *n.* —**vol'ubly** *adv.*

vol'ume *n.* space occupied; bulk, mass; amount; power, fullness of voice or sound; control on radio *etc.* for adjusting this; book; part of book bound in one cover —**volumet'ric** *a.* pert. to measurement by volume —**volu'minous** *a.* bulky, copious

vol'untary *a.* having, done by free will; done without payment; supported by freewill contributions; spontaneous —*n.* organ solo in church service —**vol'untarily** *adv.* —**volunteer'** *n.* one who offers service, joins force *etc.* of his own free will —*v.* offer oneself or one's services

volup'tuous *a.* of, contributing to pleasures of the senses —**volup'tuary** *n.* one given to luxury and sensual pleasures

vol'ute [*or* -lo͞ot'] *n.* spiral or twisting turn, form or object

vom'it *v.* eject (contents of stomach) through mouth —*n.* matter vomited

voo'doo *n.* practice of black magic, *esp.* in W Indies, witchcraft —*vt.* affect by voodoo

vora'cious *a.* greedy, ravenous —**vora'ciously** *adv.* —**vora'city** [-as'-] *n.*

vor'tex *n.* whirlpool; whirling motion (*pl.* **vor'tices** [-ti-sēz])

vo'tary *n.* one vowed to service or pursuit (**vo'taress** *fem.*) —**vo'tive** *a.* given, consecrated by vow

vote *n.* formal expression of choice; individual pronouncement; right to give it, in question or election; result of voting; that which is given or allowed by vote —*v.* express, declare opinion, choice, preference *etc.* by vote; authorize, enact *etc.* by vote —**vo'ter** *n.*

vouch *vi.* (*usu. with* for) guarantee, make oneself responsible for —**vouch'er** *n.* document proving correctness of item in accounts, or to establish facts; ticket as substitute for cash —**vouchsafe'** *vt.* condescend to grant or do

vow *n.* solemn promise, *esp.* religious one —*vt.* promise, threaten by vow

vow'el *n.* any speech sound pronounced without stoppage or friction of the breath; letter standing for such sound, as *a, e, i, o, u*

vox pop interviews with public on radio or TV programme

voy'age *n.* journey, *esp.* long one, by sea or air —*vi.* make voyage —**voy'ager** *n.* —**voyageur'** [vwah-yah-zher'] *n.* guide, trapper in N regions

voyeur' *n.* one obtaining sexual pleasure by watching sexual activities of others

vs. versus

VSOP very superior old pale

VTR video tape recorder

vul'canize *vt.* treat (rubber) with sulphur at high temperature to increase its durability —**vul'canite** *n.* rubber so hardened —**vulcaniza'tion** *n.*

vul'gar *a.* offending against good taste; coarse; common —**vulga'rian** *n.* vulgar (rich) person —**vul'garism** *n.* coarse, obscene word, phrase —**vulgar'ity** *n.* —**vulgariza'tion** *n.* —**vul'garize** *vt.*

make vulgar or too common —**vul'garly** *adv.*

Vul'gate *n.* fourth century Latin version of the Bible

vul'nerable *a.* capable of being physically or emotionally wounded or hurt; exposed, open to attack, persuasion *etc.* —**vulnerabil'ity** *n.*

vul'pine *a.* of foxes; foxy

vul'ture *n.* large bird which feeds on carrion

vul'va *n.* external genitals of human female

v.v. vice versa

vy'ing *pr.p. of* VIE

W

W *Chem.* tungsten; watt; Wednesday; west(ern)

w. week; weight; width

wad [wod] *n.* small pad of fibrous material; thick roll of banknotes; *sl.* large sum of money —*vt.* line, pad, stuff *etc.* with wad (**-dd-**) —**wadd'ing** *n.* stuffing

wad'dle [wod'l] *vi.* walk like duck —*n.* this gait

wade *vi.* walk through something that hampers movement, *esp.* water; proceed with difficulty —**wa'der** *n.* person or bird that wades —*pl.* angler's high waterproof boots

wad'y, wad'i [wod'i] *n.* in the East, watercourse which is dry, except in wet season

wa'fer *n.* thin, crisp biscuit; thin slice of anything; thin disc of unleavened bread used in the Eucharist

waf'fle[1] [wof'l] *n.* kind of pancake with deep indentations on both sides from **waffle iron** in which cooked

waf'fle[2] [wof'l] **UK** *vi. inf.* speak, write in vague wordy manner —*n. inf.* vague speech *etc.*; nonsense

waft [-ah-] *vt.* convey smoothly through air or water —*n.* breath of wind; odour, whiff

wag *v.* (cause to) move rapidly from side to side (**-gg-**) —*n.* instance of wagging; *inf.* humorous, witty person —**wagg'ish** *a.*

wage *n.* payment for work done (*oft. in pl.*) —*vt.* carry on

wa'ger *n./vt.* bet

wag'gle *vt.* wag —**wag'gly** *a.*

wag(g)'on *n.* four-wheeled vehicle for heavy loads; child's four-wheeled cart; police truck for transporting prisoners; *see* STATION WAGON —**wag(g)'oner** *n.*

waif *n.* homeless person, *esp.* child

wail *v.* cry out, lament —*n.* mournful cry

wain *n. Poet.* wagon

wains'cot *n.* wooden lining of walls of room —*vt.* line thus (**-tt-**)

waist *n.* part of body between hips and ribs; various narrow central parts —**waist'coat** *n.* **UK** vest —**waist'line** *n.* line, size of waist (of person, garment)

wait *v.* stay in one place, remain inactive in expectation (of something); be prepared (for something); delay —*vi.* serve in restaurant *etc.* —*n.* act or period of waiting —*pl.* street musicians, carol singers —**wait'er** *n.* attendant on guests at hotel, restaurant *etc.* (**wait'ress** *fem.*); one who waits

waive *vt.* forgo; not to insist on —**wai'ver** *n.* (written statement of) this act

wake[1] *v.* rouse from sleep; stir up (**woke, wo'ken, wa'king**) —*n.* vigil; watch beside corpse —**wa'ken** *v.* wake —**wake'ful** *a.*

wake[2] *n.* track or path left by anything that has passed, as track of turbulent water behind ship

walk [wawk] *v.* (cause, assist to) move, travel on foot at ordinary pace —*vt.* cross, pass through by walking; escort, conduct by walking —*n.* act, instance of walking; path or other place or route for walking; manner of walking; occupation, career —**walk'er** *n.* —**walkie-talkie** *n.* portable radio set containing both transmission and receiver units —**walking papers** *sl.* notice of dismissal —**walking stick** stick, cane carried while walking —**walk'out** *n.* strike; act of leaving as a protest —**walk'over** *n.* unopposed or easy victory —**walk-up** *n.* apartment block having no elevator

Walk'man R small portable cassette player with light headphones, personal stereo

wall [wawl] *n.* structure of brick, stone *etc.* serving as fence, side of building *etc.*; surface of one; anything resembling this —*vt.* enclose with wall; block up with wall —**wall'flower** *n.* garden flower, often growing on walls; at dance, woman who remains seated for lack of partner

—**wall'paper** *n.* paper, usu. patterned, to cover interior walls

wall'aby [wol'-] *n.* Aust. marsupial similar to and smaller than kangaroo

wall'et [wol'-] *n.* small folding case, *esp.* for paper money, documents *etc.*, billfold

wall'eyed [wawl'-] *a.* squinting; having eyes with pale irises

wall'op [wol'-] *inf. vt.* beat soundly; strike hard —*n.* stroke or blow —**wal'loper** *n. inf.* one who wallops —**wal'loping** *inf. n.* thrashing —*a./adv.* very, great(ly)

wall'ow [wol'ō] *vi.* roll (in liquid or mud); revel (in) —*n.*

wal'nut [wawl'-] *n.* large nut with crinkled shell splitting easily into two halves; the tree; its wood

wal'rus [wawl'-] *n.* large sea mammal with long tusks

waltz [wawls] *n.* ballroom dance; music for it —*v.*

wam'pum [wom'-] *n.* beads made of shells, formerly used by N Amer. Indians as money and for ornament; *inf.* money or wealth

wan [won] *a.* pale, sickly complexioned, pallid

wand [wond] *n.* stick, usu. straight and slender, *esp.* as carried by magician *etc.*

wand'er [won'-] *v.* roam, ramble —*vi.* go astray, deviate —*n.* —**wand'erer** *n.* —**wand'erlust** *n.* irrepressible urge to wander or travel

wane *vi./n.* decline; (of moon) decrease in size

wan'gle [-ng'gl] *inf. vt.* manipulate, manage in skilful way —*n.* intrigue, trickery, something obtained by craft

want [wont] *v.* desire; lack —*n.* desire; need; deficiency —**want'ed** *a.* being sought, *esp.* by the police —**wan'ting** *a.* lacking; below standard

want'on [won'-] *a.* dissolute; without motive, thoughtless; unrestrained —*n.* wanton person

wap'iti [wop'-] *n.* large N Amer. deer

war [wawr] *n.* fighting between nations; state of hostility; conflict, contest —*vi.* make war (**-rr-**) —**war'like** *a.* of, for war; fond of war —**warr'ior** [wo'ri-] *n.* fighter —**war cry** cry used by attacking troops in war; distinctive word, phrase used by political party *etc.* —**war'fare** *n.* hostilities —**war'head** *n.* part of missile *etc.* containing explosives —**war'monger** *n.* one fostering, encouraging war —**war'ship** *n.* vessel armed, armoured for naval warfare

war'ble *vi.* sing with trills —**war'bler** *n.* person or bird that warbles; any of various kinds of small songbirds

ward [-aw-] *n.* division of city, hospital *etc.*; minor under care of guardian; guardianship; bar in lock, groove in key that prevents incorrectly cut key opening lock —**ward'er** *n.* jailer (**ward'ress** *fem.*) —**ward'ship** *n.* office of guardian; state of being under guardian —**ward'room** *n.* senior officers' mess on warship —**ward off** avert, repel

ward'en [-aw-] *n.* person, officer in charge of building, institution, college *etc.* —**ward'enship** *n.*

ward'robe *n.* closet or piece of furniture for hanging clothes in; person's supply of clothes; costumes of theatrical company

ware *n.* goods; articles collectively —*pl.* goods for sale; commodities; merchandise —**ware'house** *n.* storehouse for goods prior to distribution and sale

war'lock [-aw'-] *n.* wizard, sorcerer

warm [-aw-] *a.* moderately hot; serving to maintain heat; affectionate; ardent; earnest; hearty; (of colour) having yellow or red for a basis —*v.* make, become warm —**warm'ly** *adv.* —**warmth** *n.* mild heat; cordiality; vehemence, anger

warn [-aw-] *vt.* put on guard; caution, admonish; give advance information to; notify authoritatively —**warn'ing** *n.* hint of harm *etc.*; admonition; advance notice of

warp [-aw-] *v.* (cause to) twist (out of shape); pervert or be perverted —*n.* state, condition of being warped; lengthwise threads on loom

warr'ant [wo'rənt] *n.* authority; document giving authority —*vt.* guarantee; authorize, justify —**warrantee'** *n.* person given warranty —**warr'antor** *n.* person, company giving warranty —**war'ranty** *n.* guarantee of quality of goods; security —**warrant officer** in the army, a noncommissioned officer ranking next above a sergeant

warr'en [wo'rən] *n.* (burrows inhabited by) colony of rabbits

warr'ior *n. see* WAR

wart [-aw-] *n.* small hard growth on skin —**wart hog** kind of Afr. wild pig

wa'ry *a.* watchful, cautious, alert —**wa'rily** *adv.*

was *pt.* first and third person sing. of BE

wash [wosh] *v.* clean (oneself, clothes *etc.*) *esp.* with water, soap *etc.* —*vi.* be washable; *inf.* be able to be proved true —*vt.* move, be moved by water; flow, sweep over, against —*n.* act of washing; clothes washed at one time; sweep of water, *esp.* set up by moving ship; thin coat of colour —**wash'able** *a.* capable of being washed without damage *etc.* —**wash'er** *n.* one who, that which, washes; ring put under a nut —**wash'ing** *n.* clothes to be washed —**wash'y** *a.* dilute; watery; insipid —**wash'basin** *n.* sink for washing hands and face —**wash'cloth** *n.* small piece of cloth for washing face and hands —**wash'out** *n.* *inf.* complete failure —**wash'room** *n.* (room with washbasin and) toilet —**wash'tub** *n.* tub for washing clothes in —**washed-up** *a.* *inf.* no longer successful, useful *etc.*; exhausted

Wasp, WASP [wosp] *n.* *oft. derogatory* White Anglo-Saxon Protestant

wasp [wosp] *n.* striped stinging insect resembling bee —**wasp'ish** *a.* irritable, snappish —**wasp waist** very small waist

waste [wāst] *vt.* expend uselessly, use extravagantly; fail to take advantage of; lay desolate —*vi.* dwindle; pine away —*n.* act of wasting; what is wasted; desert —*a.* worthless, useless; desert; wasted —**wast'age** *n.* loss by use or decay; reduction in numbers, *esp.* of workforce —**waste'ful** *a.* extravagant —**waste'fully** *adv.* —**waste'lot** *n.* piece of waste ground in city —**wast'rel** *n.* wasteful person, idler

watap' *n.* thread made from roots by N Amer. Indians

watch [woch] *vt.* observe closely; guard —*vi.* wait expectantly (for); be on watch —*n.* portable timepiece for wrist, pocket *etc.*; state of being on the lookout; guard; spell of duty —**watch'ful** *a.* —**watch'fully** *adv.* —**watch'maker** *n.* one skilled in making and repairing watches —**watch'man** *n.* man guarding building *etc.*, *esp.* at night —**watch'word** *n.* password; rallying cry

wat'er [wawt'-] *n.* transparent, colourless, odourless, tasteless liquid, substance of rain, river *etc.*; body of water; river; lake; sea; tear; urine —*vt.* put water on or into; irrigate or provide with water —*vi.* salivate; (of eyes) fill with tears; take in or obtain water —**wat'ery** *a.* —**wat'erbuck** *n.* Afr. antelope —**water buffalo** oxlike Asian animal —**water closet** sanitary convenience flushed by water —**wat'ercolour** *n.* pigment mixed with water; painting in this —**wat'ercourse** *n.* stream —**wat'ercress** *n.* plant growing in clear ponds and streams —**wat'erfall** *n.* perpendicular descent of waters of river —**water lily** plant that floats on surface of fresh water —**wat'erlogged** *a.* saturated, filled with water —**wat'ermark** *n.* faint translucent design stamped on substance of sheet of paper —**wat'erproof** *a.* not letting water through —*v.* make waterproof —*n.* waterproof garment —**wat'ershed** *n.* line separating two river systems; divide —**water-skiing** *n.* sport of riding over water on ski towed by speedboat —**water sport** any of various sports, as swimming, windsurfing, that take place in or on water —**wat'ertight** *a.* so fitted as to prevent water entering or escaping; with no loopholes or weak points

watt [wot] *n.* unit of electric power —**watt'age** *n.* electric power expressed in watts

wat'tle [wot'-] *n.* frame of woven branches *etc.* as fence; fleshy pendent lobe of neck of certain birds, *eg* turkey

wave *v.* move to and fro, as hand in greeting or farewell; signal by waving; give, take shape of waves (as hair *etc.*) —*n.* ridge and trough on water *etc.*; act, gesture of waving; vibration, as in radio waves, of electric and magnetic forces alternating in direction; prolonged spell of something; upsurge; wavelike shapes in the hair *etc.* —**wa'vy** *a.* —**wave'length** *n.* distance between same points of two successive sound waves

wa'ver *vi.* hesitate, be irresolute; be, become unsteady —**wa'verer** *n.*

wa'vey *n.* snow goose or other wild goose (*also* **wawa**)

wax[1] *n.* yellow, soft, pliable material made by bees; this or similar substance used for sealing, making candles *etc.*; waxy secretion of ear —*vt.* put wax on —**wax'y** *a.* like wax —**wax bean** yellow string bean —**wax'wing** *n.* small songbird —**wax'work** *n.* lifelike figure, *esp.* of famous person, reproduced in wax

wax[2] *vi.* grow, increase

way *n.* manner; method, means; track; direction; path; passage; course; route; progress; state or condition —**way'farer** *n.* traveller, *esp.* on foot —**waylay'** *vt.* lie in wait for and accost, attack (**-laid', -lay'ing**) —**way'side** *n.* side or edge of a road —*a.* —**way'ward** *a.* capricious, perverse, wilful —**way'wardly** *adv.* —**way'wardness** *n.*

WC water closet

we *pron.* first person plural pronoun

weak *a.* lacking strength; feeble; fragile; defenceless; easily influenced; faint —**weak'en** *v.* —**weak'ling** *n.* feeble creature —**weak'ly** *a.* weak; sickly —*adv.* —**weak'ness** *n.*

weal *n.* streak left on flesh by blow of stick or whip

wealth [welth] *n.* riches; abundance —**wealth'iness** *n.* —**wealth'y** *a.*

wean *vt.* accustom to food other than mother's milk; win over, coax away from

weap'on [wep'n] *n.* implement to fight with; anything used to get the better of an opponent

wear [wār] *vt.* have on the body; show; produce (hole *etc.*) by rubbing *etc.*; harass or weaken; *inf.* allow, tolerate —*vi.* last; become impaired by use; (of time) pass slowly (**wore, worn, wear'ing**) —*n.* act of wearing; things to wear; damage caused by use; ability to resist effects of constant use —**wear'er** *n.*

wear'y [wēr'i] *a.* tired, exhausted, jaded; tiring; tedious —*v.* make, become weary (**wear'ied, wear'ying**) —**wear'ily** *adv.* —**wear'iness** *n.* —**wear'isome** *a.* causing weariness

weas'el [wēz'-] *n.* small carnivorous mammal with long body and short legs; *inf.* sly or treacherous person —**weasel out** go back on commitment —**weasel words** *inf.* intentionally evasive or misleading speech

weath'er [weTH'-] *n.* day-to-day meteorological conditions, *esp.* temperature, cloudiness *etc.* of a place —*a.* towards the wind —*vt.* affect by weather; endure; resist; come safely through; sail to windward of —**weath'erboard** *n.* timber boards used as external cladding of house —**weath'ercock** *n.* revolving vane to show which way wind blows

weave *vt.* form into texture or fabric by interlacing, *esp.* on loom; fashion, construct; make one's way, *esp.* with side to side motion (**weaved** *pt.*) —*vi.* practise weaving (**wove, wo'ven, weav'ing**) —**weav'er** *n.*

web *n.* woven fabric; net spun by spider; membrane between toes of waterfowl, frogs *etc.* —**webb'ing** *n.* strong fabric woven in strips

we'ber [vā'-] *n.* SI unit of magnetic flux

wed *vt.* marry; unite closely (**-dd-**) —**wed'ding** *n.* act of marrying, nuptial ceremony —**wed'lock** *n.* marriage

wedge *n.* piece of wood, metal *etc.*, thick at one end, tapering to a thin edge —*vt.* fasten, split with wedge; stick by compression or crowding

Wedg'wood R kind of pottery with ornamental reliefs

Wednes'day [wenz'-] *n.* fourth day of the week

wee *a.* small; little

weed *n.* plant growing where undesired; *inf.* tobacco; *inf.* marijuana; *inf.* thin, sickly person, animal —*vt.* clear of weeds —**weed'y** *a.* full of weeds; *inf.* thin, weakly —**weed out** remove, eliminate what is unwanted

weeds *pl.n.* *obs.* (widow's) mourning clothes

week *n.* period of seven days, *esp.* one beginning on Sunday and ending on Saturday; hours, days of work in seven-day period —**week'ly** *a./adv.* happening, done, published *etc.* once a week —*n.* —**week'day** *n.* any day of week except Sunday and *usu.* Saturday —**weekend'** *n.* Saturday and Sunday, *esp.* considered as rest period

weep *v.* shed tears (for); grieve (**wept, weep'ing**) —**weep'y** *a.* —**weeping willow** willow with drooping branches

wee'vil *n.* small beetle harmful to grain *etc.*

weft *n.* cross threads in weaving, woof

weigh [wā] *vt.* find weight of; consider; raise (anchor) —*vi.* have weight; be burdensome —**weight** *n.* measure of the heaviness of an object; quality of heaviness; heavy mass; object of known mass for weighing; unit of measurement of weight; importance, influence *—vt.* add weight to **—weight'ily** *adv.* **—weight'y** *a.* heavy; onerous; important; momentous **—weigh'bridge** *n.* machine for weighing vehicles *etc.* by means of metal plate set into road

weir [wēr] *n.* river dam

weird [wērd] *a.* unearthly, uncanny; strange, bizarre

wel'come *a.* received gladly; freely permitted *—n.* kindly greeting *—vt.* greet with pleasure; receive gladly (**-comed, -coming**)

weld *vt.* unite metal by softening with heat; unite closely *—n.* welded joint **—weld'er** *n.* tradesman who welds; machine used in welding

wel'fare *n.* wellbeing **—welfare state** system in which the government takes responsibility for the social, economic *etc.* security of its citizens

well[1] *adv.* in good manner or degree; suitably; intimately; fully; favourably, kindly; to a considerable degree *—a.* in good health; suitable (**better** *comp.*, **best** *sup.*) *—interj.* exclamation of surprise, interrogation *etc.* **—well'be'ing** *n.* state of being well, happy, or prosperous **—well-disposed** *a.* inclined to be friendly, kindly (towards) **—well-mannered** *a.* having good manners **—well-off** *a.* fairly rich **—well-read** *a.* having read much **—well-spoken** *a.* speaking fluently, graciously, aptly

well[2] *n.* hole sunk into the earth to reach water, gas, oil *etc.*; spring; any shaft like a well *—vi.* spring, gush

well'ingtons *pl.n.* high waterproof boots

Welsh *a.* of Wales *—n.* language, people of Wales **—Welsh rabbit, rarebit** savoury dish of melted cheese on toast

welsh, welch *vi.* fail to pay debt or fulfil obligation **—welsh'er, welch'er** *n.*

welt *n.* raised, strengthened seam; weal *—vt.* provide with welt; thrash

welt'er *vi.* roll or tumble *—n.* turmoil, disorder

wel'terweight *n. Boxing* weight between light and middle; boxer of this weight

wen *n.* cyst, *esp.* on scalp

wench *n. obs. now oft. facetious* young woman

wend *v.* go, travel

wen'digo *n. see* SPLAKE

went *pt. of* GO

wept *pt./pp. of* WEEP

were imperfect indicative, plural and subjunctive sing. and pl. of BE

were'wolf [wēr'-] *n.* (in folklore) human being turned into wolf

west *n.* part of sky where sun sets; part of country *etc.* lying to this side; occident *—a.* that is toward or in this region *—adv.* to the west **—west'erly** *a.* **—west'ward** *a./adv.* **—west'wards** *adv.* towards the west **—west'ern** *a.* of, in the west *—n.* movie, story *etc.* about cowboys or frontiersmen in western U.S. **—western larch** N Amer. larch having oval cones; its wood **—go west** *inf.* disappear; die; be lost

wet *a.* having water or other liquid on a surface or being soaked in it; rainy; not yet dry (paint, ink *etc.*); permitting sale of alcoholic beverages (**wett'er** *comp.*, **wett'est** *sup.*) *—vt.* make wet (**wett'ed, wett'ing**) *—n.* moisture, rain; person advocating sale of alcoholic beverages **—wet blanket** *inf.* one depressing spirits of others **—wet'land** *n.* area of swamp or marsh **—wet nurse** woman suckling another's child **—wet suit** close-fitting rubber suit worn by divers *etc.*

weth'er [weTH'-] *n.* castrated ram

whack *vt.* strike with sharp resounding blow *—n.* such blow; *inf.* share; *inf.* attempt **—whack'ing** *a. inf.* big, enormous

whale *n.* large fish-shaped sea mammal **—wha'ler** *n.* man, ship employed in hunting whales **—whale'bone** *n.* horny elastic substance from projections of upper jaw of certain whales **—a whale of a** *inf.* very large, fine, example of something

wharf [-awrf] *n.* platform at harbour, on river *etc.* for loading and unloading ships **—wharf'age** *n.* accommodation or dues at wharf

what [wot] *pron.* which thing; that which; request for statement to be repeated *—a.* which; as much as; how great, surprising *etc.* *—interj.* exclamation of surprise, anger *etc.* **—whatev'er**

pron. anything which; of what kind it may be —**what'not** *n. inf.* person, thing whose name is unknown, forgotten *etc.;* small stand with shelves

wheat *n.* cereal plant with thick four-sided seed spikes of which bread is chiefly made —**wheat'en** *a.* —**wheat'ear** *n.* small songbird —**wheat germ** embryo of wheat kernel

whee'dle *v.* coax, cajole

wheel *n.* circular frame or disc (with spokes) revolving on axle; anything like a wheel in shape or function; act of turning; steering wheel; *inf.* bicycle; *inf.* influential person, as in **big wheel** —*pl. inf.* automobile —*v.* (cause to) turn as if on axis; (cause to) move on or as if on wheels; (cause to) change course, *esp.* in opposite direction —**wheel'barrow** *n.* barrow with one wheel —**wheel'base** *n.* distance between front and rear hubs of vehicle —**wheel'chair** *n.* chair mounted on large wheels, used by people who cannot walk —**wheel'house** *n.* deckhouse for steersman

wheeze *vi.* breathe with difficulty and whistling noise —*n.* this sound —**wheez'y** *a.*

whelk *n.* sea snail *esp.* edible variety

whelp *n.* (*oft. jocular, disparaging*) pup, cub —*v.* produce whelps

when *adv.* at what time —*conj.* at the time that; although; since —*pron.* at which (time) —**whenev'er** *adv./conj.* at whatever time

whence *adv./conj. obs.* from what place or source; how

where *adv./conj.* at what place; at or to the place in which —**where'abouts** *adv./conj.* in what, which place —*n.* present position —**whereas'** *conj.* considering that; while, on the contrary —**whereby'** *conj.* by which —**where'fore** *adv. obs.* why —*conj.* consequently —**whereupon'** *conj.* at which point —**wherev'er** *adv.* at whatever place —**where'withal** *n.* necessary funds, resources *etc.*

wherr'y *n.* barge; light rowing boat

whet *vt.* sharpen; stimulate (**-tt-**) —**whet'stone** *n.* stone for sharpening tools

wheth'er [weTH'-] *conj.* introduces the first of two alternatives, of which the second may be expressed or implied

whey [wā] *n.* watery part of milk left after separation of curd in cheese making

which *a.* used in requests for a selection from alternatives —*pron.* which person or thing; the thing "who" —**whichev'er** *pron.*

whiff *n.* brief smell or suggestion of; puff of air —*v.* smell

Whig *n.* member of British political party that preceded the Liberal Party

while *conj.* in the time that; in spite of the fact that, although; whereas —*vt.* pass (time, usu. idly) —*n.* period of time —**whilst** *conj.* while

whim *n.* sudden, passing fancy —**whim'sical** *a.* fanciful; full of whims —**whimsical'ity** *n.* —**whim'sy** *n.* whim; caprice —*a.*

whim'per *vi.* cry or whine softly; complain in this way —*n.* such cry or complaint

whin *n.* gorse

whine *n.* high-pitched plaintive cry; peevish complaint —*vi.* utter this

whinge *inf. vi.* whine, complain —*n.*

whinn'y *vi.* neigh softly (**whinn'ied, whinn'ying**) —*n.*

whip *vt.* strike with whip; thrash; beat (cream, eggs) to a froth; lash; *inf.* pull, remove, insert *etc.* quickly; *inf.* defeat —*vi.* dart (**-pp-**) —*n.* lash attached to handle for urging or punishing; one who enforces attendance of political party; call made on members of legislature to attend for important votes; elastic quality permitting bending in mast, fishing rod *etc.*; whipped dessert —**whiplash injury** injury to neck as result of sudden jerking of unsupported head —**whipping boy** scapegoat

whipp'et *n.* racing dog like small greyhound

whir *v.* (cause to) fly, spin *etc.* with buzzing or whizzing sound (**-rr-**) —*n.* this sound

whirl *v.* swing rapidly round; move rapidly in a circular course; drive at high speed —*n.* whirling movement; confusion, bustle, giddiness —**whirl'igig** *n.* spinning toy; merry-go-round —**whirl'pool** *n.* circular current, eddy —**whirl'wind** *n.* wind whirling round while moving forwards —*a.*

whisk *v.* brush, sweep, beat lightly;

move, remove, quickly; beat to a froth —*n.* light brush; egg-beating implement

whisk'er *n.* any of the long stiff hairs at side of mouth of cat or other animal; any of hairs on a man's face —**by a whisker** *inf.* only just

whisk'(e)y *n.* spirit distilled from fermented cereals

whisp'er *v.* speak in soft, hushed tones, without vibration of vocal cords; rustle —*n.* such speech; trace or suspicion; rustle

whist *n.* card game

whis'tle [-sl] *vi.* produce shrill sound by forcing breath through rounded, nearly closed lips; make such a sound —*vt.* utter, summon *etc.* by whistle —*n.* such sound; any similar sound; instrument to make it —**whis'tler** *n.* —**whistle-blower** *n. inf.* person who informs on or puts stop to something

whit *n.* jot, particle (*usu. in* **not a whit**)

white *a.* of the colour of snow; pale; light in colour; having a light-coloured skin —*n.* colour of snow; white pigment; white part; clear fluid round yolk of egg; (**W-**) white person —**whi'ten** *v.* —**white'ness** *n.* —**whi'tish** *a.* —**white ant** termite —**white-collar** *a.* denoting nonmanual salaried workers —**white elephant** useless, unwanted, gift or possession —**white flag** white banner or cloth used as signal of surrender or truce —**white hope** one expected to bring honour or glory to his group, team *etc.* —**white lie** minor, unimportant lie —**white paper** government report on matter recently investigated —**white slave** woman, child forced or enticed away for purposes of prostitution —**white'wash** *n.* substance for whitening walls *etc.* —*vt.* apply this; cover up, gloss over, suppress

whith'er [wiTH'-] *adv. obs.* to what place; to which

whi'ting *n.* edible sea fish

whit'low [-lō] *n.* abscess on finger, *esp.* round nail

Whit'sun [wit'sən] *n.* week following **Whit Sunday**, seventh Sunday after Easter

whit'tle *vt.* cut, carve with knife; pare away —**whittle down** reduce gradually, wear (away)

whiz(z) *n.* loud hissing sound; *inf.* person skilful at something —*v.* move with such sound, or make it; *inf.* move quickly (**-zz-**)

WHO World Health Organization

who [hōō] *pron.* relative and interrogative pronoun, always referring to persons —**whodun'it** *n. inf.* detective story —**whoev'er** *pron.* who, any one or every one that

whole [hōl] *a.* complete; containing all elements or parts; entire; not defective or imperfect; healthy —*n.* complete thing or system —**who'lly** *adv.* —**whole-heart'ed** *a.* sincere; enthusiastic —**whole note** musical note, now the longest in common use —**whole'sale** *n.* sale of goods by large quantities to retailers —*a.* dealing by wholesale; extensive —**whole'saler** *n.* —**whole'some** *a.* producing good effect, physically or morally —**whole-wheat** *a.* made from entire wheat kernels —**on the whole** taking everything into consideration; in general

whom [hōōm] *pron.* objective case of WHO

whoop [wōōp] *n.* shout or cry expressing excitement *etc.*

whoo'pee *n. inf.* gay, riotous time —**make whoopee** participate in wild noisy party; go on spree

whooping cough [hōōp'-] *n.* infectious disease of mucous membrane lining air passages, marked by convulsive coughing with loud whoop or indrawing of breath

whopp'er *inf. n.* anything unusually large; monstrous lie —**whopp'ing** *a.*

whore [h-] *n.* prostitute

whorl *n.* ring of leaves or petals; turn of spiral; anything forming part of circular pattern, *eg* lines of human fingerprint

whose [hōōz] *pron.* possessive case of WHO and WHICH

why *adv.* for what cause or reason

wick *n.* strip of thread feeding flame of lamp or candle with oil, grease *etc.*

wick'ed *a.* evil, sinful; very bad; mischievous —**wick'edly** *adv.* —**wick'edness** *n.*

wick'er(work) *n.* woven cane *etc.*, basketwork

wick'et *n.* small gate; *Cricket* set of three stumps and bails; cricket pitch

wick'iup [-up] *n.* shelter made of brush-wood, mats *etc.* used by nomadic Indians

wide *a.* having a great extent from side to side, broad; having considerable distance between; spacious; liberal; vast; far from the mark; opened fully —*adv.* to the full extent; far from the intended target —**wi'den** *v.* —**wide'ly** *adv.* —**width, wide'ness** *n.* breadth —**wide'spread** *a.* extending over a wide area

wid'ow [-ō] *n.* woman whose husband is dead and who has not married again —*vt.* make a widow of —**wid'ower** *n.* man whose wife is dead and who has not married again —**wid'owhood** *n.*

wield *vt.* hold and use; brandish; manage

wie'ner [wē'nər] *n.* smoked sausage; frankfurter

Wiener schnitzel [vē'nər] thin slice of veal, crumbed and fried

wife *n.* a man's partner in marriage, married woman (*pl.* **wives**) —**wife'ly** *a.*

wig *n.* artificial hair for the head —**wigged** *a.*

wig'gle *v.* (cause to) move jerkily from side to side —*n.* —**wig'gly** *a.*

wight [wīt] *n. obs.* person

wig'wam *n.* N Amer. Indian's hut or tent

wild [wīld] *a.* not tamed or domesticated; not cultivated; savage; stormy; uncontrolled; random; excited; rash; frantic; *inf.* (of party *etc.*) rowdy, exciting —**wild'ly** *adv.* —**wild'ness** *n.* —**wild'-cat** *n.* any of various undomesticated European and Amer. feline animals; *inf.* wild, savage person; exploratory oil well; unsound commercial enterprise; unscheduled locomotive, *esp.* running without cars, or trucks —*a.* unsound, irresponsible; sudden, unofficial, unauthorized —**wild-goose chase** futile pursuit —**wild'life** *n.* wild animals and plants collectively

wil'debeest [-di-bēst] *n.* gnu

wil'derness *n.* desert, waste place; state of desolation or confusion

wild'fire *n.* raging, uncontrollable fire; anything spreading, moving fast

wile *n.* trick —**wi'ly** *a.* crafty, sly

wil'ful *a. see* WILLFUL

will *v. aux.* forms moods and tenses indicating intention or conditional result (**would** *pt.*) —*vi.* have a wish —*vt.* wish; intend; leave as legacy —*n.* faculty of deciding what one will do; purpose; volition; determination; wish; directions written for disposal of property after death —**will'ing** *a.* ready; given cheerfully —**will'ingly** *adv.* —**will'ingness** *n.* —**will'power** *n.* ability to control oneself, one's actions, impulses

will'ful *a.* obstinate, self-willed; intentional —**will'fully** *adv.* —**will'fulness** *n.*

will-o'-the-wisp *n.* brief pale flame or phosphorescence sometimes seen over marshes; elusive person or hope

will'ow [-ō] *n.* tree (*eg* **weeping willow**) with long thin flexible branches; its wood —**will'owy** *a.* lithe, slender, supple —**will'owherb** *n.* tall plant with mauve flowers

willy-nilly *adv./a.* (occurring) whether desired or not

wilt *v.* (cause to) become limp, drooping or lose strength *etc.*

wimp *n. inf.* feeble, ineffective person

wim'ple *n.* garment worn by nun, around face

win *vi.* be successful, victorious —*vt.* get by labour or effort; reach; allure; be successful in; gain the support, consent *etc.* of (**won, winn'ing**) —*n.* victory, *esp.* in games —**winn'er** *n.* —**winn'ing** *a.* charming —**winn'ings** *pl.n.* sum won in game, betting *etc.*

wince *vi.* flinch, draw back, as from pain *etc.* —*n.* this act

winch *n.* machine for hoisting or hauling using cable wound round drum —*vt.* move (something) by using a winch

wind[1] [wind] *n.* air in motion; breath; flatulence; idle talk; hint or suggestion; scent borne by air —*vt.* render short of breath, *esp.* by blow *etc.*; get the scent of —**wind'ward** *n.* side against which wind is blowing —**wind'y** *a.* exposed to wind; flatulent; *sl.* nervous, scared; *inf.* talking too much —**wind'fall** *n.* unexpected good luck ; fallen fruit —**wind instrument** musical instrument played by blowing or air pressure —**wind'mill** *n.* wind-driven apparatus with fanlike sails for raising water, crushing grain *etc.* —**wind'pipe** *n.* passage from throat to lungs —**wind'screen** *n.* **UK** windshield —**wind'shield** *n.* protective sheet of glass *etc.* in front of driver or pilot —**wind'sock** *n.* cone of material flown on mast at airfield to indicate wind direction —**wind'surfing** *n.* sport of sailing standing up on sailboard holding special boom to control sail

wind[2] [wīnd] *vi.* twine; meander —*vt.* twist round, coil; wrap; make ready for working by tightening spring (**wound** [wownd], **wind'ing**) —*n.* act of winding; single turn of something wound; a turn, curve —**wind-up** *n.* act of concluding; end

wind'lass *n.* winch, *esp.* simple one worked by a crank

win'dow [-ō] *n.* hole in wall (with glass) to admit light, air *etc.*; anything similar in appearance or function; area for display of goods behind glass of shop front —**window-dressing** *n.* arrangement of goods in a shop window; deceptive display

wine *n.* fermented juice of grape *etc.* —**wine'press** *n.* apparatus for extracting juice from grape —**wi'nery** *n.* place where wine is made

wing *n.* feathered limb a bird uses in flying; one of organs of flight of insect or some animals; main lifting surface of aircraft; lateral extension; side portion of building projecting from main central portion; one of sides of a stage; flank corps of army on either side; **UK** fender of automobile; *Sport* (player on) either side of pitch; faction *esp.* of political party —*pl.* insignia worn by qualified aircraft pilot; sides of stage —*vi.* fly; move, go very fast —*vt.* disable, wound slightly —**winged** *a.* having wings

wink *v.* close and open (an eye) rapidly, *esp.* to indicate friendliness or as signal; twinkle —*n.* act of winking

win'kle *n.* shellfish, periwinkle

winn'ow [-ō] *vt.* blow free of chaff; sift, examine

win'some *a.* charming, winning

win'ter *n.* the coldest season —*vi.* pass, spend the winter —**win'try** *a.* of, like winter; cold —**win'terize** *vt.* prepare (house, automobile *etc.*) to withstand winter weather —**win'terkill** *v.* kill (crops or other plants) by exposure to frost *etc.* or (of plants) to die by this means —**winter sports** sports held in open air on snow or ice

wipe *vt.* rub so as to clean —*n.* wiping —**wi'per** *n.* one that wipes; automatic wiping apparatus (*esp.* **windshield wiper**) —**wipe out** erase; annihilate; *sl.* kill

wire *n.* metal drawn into thin, flexible strand; something made of wire, *eg* fence; telegram; finishing line on racetrack —*vt.* provide, fasten with wire; send by telegraph —**wi'ring** *n.* system of wires —**wi'ry** *a.* like wire; lean and tough —**wire-haired** *a.* (of various breeds of dog) with short stiff hair —**wire'puller** *n.* person who uses private influence for his own ends —**wire service** agency supplying news *etc.* to newspapers, radio and television stations *etc.* —**pull wires** exert influence behind scenes

wire'less *n. esp. Brit. old-fashioned term for* radio, radio set —*a.*

wise[1] [wīz] *a.* having intelligence and knowledge; sensible; *sl.* cocksure or insolent —**wis'dom** *n.* (accumulated) knowledge, learning; erudition —**wise'ly** *adv.* —**wise'acre** *n.* one who wishes to seem wise —**wisdom tooth** third molar usually cut about 20th year —**wise up** *sl.* (cause to) become aware or informed (of)

wise[2] [wīz] *n. obs.* manner

wise'crack *n. inf.* flippant, (would-be) clever remark

wish *vi.* have a desire —*vt.* desire —*n.* desire; thing desired —**wish'ful** *a.* desirous; too optimistic —**wish'bone** *n.* V-shaped bone above breastbone of fowl

wisp *n.* light, delicate streak, as of smoke; twisted handful, usu. of straw *etc.*; stray lock of hair —**wisp'y** *a.*

wiste'ria *n.* climbing shrub with usu. mauve flowers

wist'ful *a.* longing, yearning; sadly pensive —**wist'fully** *adv.*

wit *n.* ingenuity in connecting amusingly incongruous ideas; person gifted with this power; sense; intellect; understanding; ingenuity; humour —**witt'icism** *n.* witty remark —**witt'ily** *adv.* —**witt'ingly** *adv.* on purpose; knowingly —**wit'less** *a.* foolish —**witt'y** *a.*

witch[1] *n.* person, usu. female, believed to practise, practising, or professing to practise (black) magic, sorcery; ugly, wicked woman; fascinating woman —**witch'ery** *n.* —**witch'craft** *n.* —**witch doctor** in certain societies, man appearing to cure or cause injury, disease by magic

witch[2] *see* WYCH-

with *prep.* in company or possession of; against; in relation to; through; by means of —**withal'** [-awl'] *adv.* also, likewise —**within'** *prep./adv.* in, inside —**without'** *prep.* lacking; *obs.* outside

withdraw' *v.* draw back or out (**-drew', -drawn', -draw'ing**) —**withdraw'al** *n.* —**withdrawn'** *a.* reserved, unsociable

with'er *v.* (cause to) wilt, dry up, decline —**with'ering** *a.* (of glance *etc.*) scornful

with'ers *pl.n.* ridge between a horse's shoulder blades

withhold' *vt.* restrain; keep back; refrain from giving (**-held', -hold'ing**) —**withhold'er** *n.*

withstand' *vt.* oppose, resist, *esp.* successfully (**-stood', -stand'ing**)

with'y [-THi] *n.* willow tree; (*also* **withe**) its twig

wit'ness *n.* one who sees something; testimony; one who gives testimony —*vi.* give testimony —*vt.* see; attest; see and sign as having seen

wiz'ard *n.* sorcerer, magician; conjurer —**wiz'ardry** *n.*

wiz'ened *a.* shrivelled, wrinkled

woad *n.* blue dye from plant

wob'ble *vi.* move unsteadily; sway —*n.* an unsteady movement —**wob'bly** *a.*

woe *n.* grief —**woe'begone** *a.* looking sorrowful —**woe'ful** *a.* sorrowful; pitiful; wretched —**woe'fully** *adv.*

wold [wōld] *n.* open downs, moorland

wolf [woolf] *n.* wild predatory doglike animal of northern countries; *inf.* man who habitually tries to seduce women (*pl.* **wolves**) —*vt.* eat ravenously —**wolf whistle** whistle by man expressing admiration for a woman —**cry wolf** raise false alarm

wolf'ram [-oo-] *n.* tungsten

wol'verine [wool'və-rēn] *n.* carnivorous mammal inhabiting Arctic regions

wom'an [woom'-] *n.* adult human female; women collectively (*pl.* **wom'en** [wim'-]) —**wom'anhood** *n.* —**wom'anish** *a.* effeminate —**wom'anize** *vi. inf.* (of man) indulge in many casual affairs with women —**wom'ankind** *n.* —**wom'anly** *a.* of, proper to woman —**Women's Liberation** movement for removal of attitudes, practices that preserve social, economic *etc.* inequalities between women and men (*also* **women's lib**)

womb [wo͞om] *n.* female organ of conception and gestation, uterus

wom'bat *n.* Aust. burrowing marsupial with heavy body, short legs and dense fur

won [wun] *pt./pp. of* WIN

won'der [wun'-] *n.* emotion excited by amazing or unusual thing; marvel, miracle —*vi.* be curious about; feel amazement —**won'derful** *a.* remarkable; very fine —**won'derfully** *adv.* —**won'derment** *n.* surprise —**won'drous** *a.* inspiring wonder; strange —**won'drously** *adv.*

wont [-ō-] *n.* custom —*a.* accustomed —**wont'ed** *a.* habitual, established

woo *vt.* court, seek to marry —**woo'er** *n.* suitor

wood *n.* substance of trees, timber; firewood; tract of land with growing trees —**wood'ed** *a.* having (many) trees —**wood'en** *a.* made of wood; obstinate; without expression —**wood'sy** *a. inf.* of, reminiscent of, or connected with woods —**wood'y** *a.* —**wood'bine** *n.* honeysuckle —**wood'chuck** *n.* groundhog —**wood'cock** *n.* game bird —**wood'craft** *n.* ability and experience in living in woods or forest; skill in carving wood; skill in caring for trees —**wood'cut** *n.* engraving on wood; impression from this —**wood'land** *n.* woods, forest —**wood'louse** *n.* small grey land crustacean with seven pairs of legs —**wood'pecker** *n.* bird which searches tree trunks for insects —**wood'wind** *a./n.* (of) wind instruments of orchestra, *orig.* made of wood —**wood'worm** *n.* insect larva that bores into wood

woof [-o͞o-] *n.* the threads that cross the warp in weaving

woof'er *n.* loudspeaker for reproducing low-frequency sounds

wool *n.* soft hair of sheep, goat *etc.*; yarn spun from this —**wooll'en** *a.* —**wooll'y** *a.* of wool; vague, muddled —*n.* knitted woollen garment —**wool'gathering** *a./n.* daydreaming —**wool'sack** *n.* Lord Chancellor's seat in British House of Lords

wop *n. sl. offens.* S European immigrant, *esp.* Italian

word [wurd] *n.* unit of speech or writing regarded by users of a language as the smallest separate meaningful unit; term; message; brief remark; information; promise; command —*vt.* express in words, *esp.* in particular way —**word'ily** *adv.* —**word'ing** *n.* choice and arrangement of words —**word'y** *a.* using more words than necessary, verbose —**word processor** keyboard, microprocessor and VDU for electronic organization and storage of written text

wore *pt.*, **worn** *pp. of* WEAR

work [wurk] *n.* labour; employment; occupation; task; toil; something made or accomplished; production of art or science; book; needlework —*pl.* factory; total of person's deeds, writings *etc.*; *inf.* everything, full or extreme treatment; mechanism of clock *etc.* —*vt.* cause to operate; make, shape; solve (mathematical problem) —*vi.* apply effort; labour; operate; be engaged in trade, profession *etc.*; turn out successfully; ferment —**work'able** *a.* —**work'er** *n.* —**workahol'ic** *n.* person addicted to work —**work'day** *n.* day on which work is done; that part of day allocated to work —**work'house** *n. Hist.* institution offering food, lodgings for unpaid menial work —**working class** social class consisting of wage earners, *esp.* manual —**working-class** *a.* —**work'man** *n.* manual worker —**work'manship** *n.* skill of workman; way thing is finished; style —**work'shop** *n.* place where things are made —**work'week** *n.* number of hours or days in week allocated to work —**work to rule** adhere strictly to all working regulations to reduce rate of work as form of protest

world [wurld] *n.* the universe; the planet earth; sphere of existence; mankind, people generally; society —**world'ly** *a.* earthly; mundane; absorbed in the pursuit of material gain, advantage; carnal —**world war** war involving many countries

worm [wurm] *n.* small limbless creeping snakelike creature; anything resembling worm in shape or movement; gear wheel with teeth forming part of screw threads; *inf.* weak, despised person —*pl.* (disorder caused by) infestation of worms, *esp.* in intestines —*vi.* crawl —*vt.* work (oneself) in insidiously; extract (secret) craftily; rid of worms —**worm-eaten** *a.* full of holes gnawed by worms; old, antiquated —**worm'y** *a.*

worm'wood [wurm'-] *n.* bitter herb; bitterness

worn *pp. of* WEAR

worr'y [wu'ri] *vi.* be (unduly) concerned —*vt.* trouble, pester, harass; (of dog) seize, shake with teeth (**worr'ied, wor'rying**) —*n.* (cause of) anxiety, concern —**worr'ier** *n.* —**worri'ment** *n. inf.* anxiety or trouble that causes it

worse [wurs] *a./adv. comp. of* BAD *or* BADLY —*n.* —**worst** *a./adv. sup. of* BAD *or* BADLY —*n.* —**wors'en** *v.* make, grow worse; impair; deteriorate

wor'ship [wur'-] *vt.* show religious devotion to; adore; love and admire (**-pp-**) —*n.* act of worshipping; title used to address mayor, magistrate *etc.* —**wor'shipful** *a.* —**wor'shipper** *n.*

wors'ted [woos'tid] *n.* woollen yarn —*a.* made of woollen yarn; spun from wool

wort [wurt] *n. obs.* plant, herb; infusion of malt before fermentation

worth [wurth] *a.* having or deserving to have value specified; meriting —*n.* excellence; merit, value; virtue; usefulness; price; quantity to be had for a given sum —**wor'thy** [-THi] *a.* virtuous; meriting —*n.* one of eminent worth; celebrity —**wor'thily** *adv.* —**wor'thiness** *n.* —**worth'less** *a.* useless —**worthwhile'** *a.* worth the time, effort *etc.* involved

would [wood] *v. aux.* expressing wish, intention, probability; *pt. of* WILL —**would-be** *a.* wishing, pretending to be

wound[1] [wo͞ond] *n.* injury, hurt from cut, stab *etc.* —*vt.* inflict wound on, injure; pain

wound[2] [wownd] *pt./pp. of* WIND[2]

wove *pt.*, **wo'ven** *pp. of* WEAVE

wow *interj.* of astonishment —*n. inf.* object of astonishment, admiration *etc.*; variation, distortion in pitch in record player *etc.* —*vt. sl.* arouse great enthusiasm in

wpm words per minute

wrack [rak] *n.* seaweed

wraith *n.* apparition of a person seen shortly before or after death; spectre

wran'gle [-ng'gl] *vi.* quarrel (noisily);

dispute; herd cattle —*n.* noisy quarrel; dispute —**wran'gler** *n.* cowboy

wrap *v.* cover, *esp.* by putting something round; put round (**-pp-**) —**wrap, wrap'per** *n.* loose garment; covering —**wrap'ping** *n.* material used to wrap

wrasse [ras] *n.* type of sea fish

wrath [roth] *n.* anger —**wrath'ful** *a.* —**wrath'fully** *adv.*

wreak *vt.* inflict (vengeance); cause

wreath [rēth] *n.* something twisted into ring form, *esp.* band of flowers *etc.* as memorial or tribute on grave *etc.* —**wreathe** [rēTH] *vt.* form into wreath; surround; wind round

wreck *n.* destruction of ship; wrecked ship; ruin; something ruined —*vt.* cause the wreck of —**wreck'age** *n.* —**wreck'er** *n.* person or thing that destroys, ruins; one whose job is to demolish houses; motor vehicle equipped for towing away wrecked or disabled automobiles *etc.*

wren *n.* kind of small songbird, as **house wren** or **winter wren**

wrench *vt.* twist; distort; seize forcibly; sprain —*n.* violent twist; tool for twisting or screwing; spanner; sudden pain caused *esp.* by parting

wrest *vt.* take by force; twist violently

wres'tle [-sl] *vi.* fight (*esp.* as sport) by grappling and trying to throw down; strive (with); struggle —*n.* —**wrest'ler** *n.* —**wrest'ling** *n.*

wretch *n.* despicable person; miserable creature —**wretch'ed** *a.* miserable, unhappy; worthless —**wretch'edly** *adv.* —**wretch'edness** *n.*

wrig'gle *v.* move with twisting action, as worm; squirm —*n.* this action

wright [rīt] *n. obs.* workman, maker, builder

wring *vt.* twist; extort; pain; squeeze out (**wrung, wring'ing**)

wrin'kle [-ng'kl] *n.* slight ridge or furrow on surface; crease in the skin; fold; pucker; *inf.* (useful) trick, hint —*v.* make, become wrinkled, pucker

wrist *n.* joint between hand and arm —**wrist'let** *n.* band worn on wrist

writ *n.* written command from law court or other authority

write *vi.* mark paper *etc.* with the symbols which are used to represent words or sounds; compose; send a letter —*vt.* set down in words; compose; communicate in writing (**wrote, writt'en, wri't-ing**) —**wri'ter** *n.* one who writes; author —**write-off** *n. inf.* something damaged beyond repair —**write-up** *n.* written (published) account of something

writhe [rīTH] *v.* twist, squirm in or as in pain *etc.* —*vi.* be acutely embarrassed *etc.* (**writhed** *pt.*, **writhed,** *Poet.* **writh'en** *pp.*, **wri'thing** *pr.p.*)

wrong *a.* not right or good; not suitable; wicked; incorrect; mistaken; not functioning properly —*n.* that which is wrong; harm; evil —*vt.* do wrong to; think badly of without justification —**wrong'doer** *n.* one who acts immorally or illegally —**wrong'ful** *a.* —**wrong'fully** *adv.* —**wrong'ly** *adv.*

wrote *pt. of* WRITE

wrought [rawt] *pt./pp. of* WORK —*a.* (of metals) shaped by hammering or beating —**wrought iron** pure form of iron used *esp.* in decorative railings *etc.*

wrung *pt./pp. of* WRING

wry *a.* turned to one side, contorted, askew; sardonic, dryly humorous —**wry'neck** *n.* type of woodpecker

wt. weight

WWI World War One

WWII World War Two

wych- (*comb. form*) (of tree) with pliant branches, as **wych-elm**

X Christ; Christian; Cross; Roman numeral, 10; mark indicating something wrong, a choice, a kiss, signature *etc.* —*n.* unknown, mysterious person, factor

x *Maths.* unknown quantity

Xe *Chem.* xenon

xen'on *n.* colourless, odourless gas occurring in very small quantities in air

xenopho'bia *n.* dislike, hatred, fear, of strangers or aliens

xerog'raphy *n.* photocopying process —**Xe'rox** R xerographic copying process, machine

X'mas [eks'məs] *n. short for* CHRISTMAS

x-rays *pl.n.* radiation of very short wavelengths, capable of penetrating solid bodies, and printing on photographic plate shadow picture of objects not permeable by rays —**x-ray** *v.* photograph by x-rays

xy'lophone *n.* musical instrument of wooden bars which sound when struck

Y

yacht [yot] *n.* vessel propelled by sail or power, used for racing, pleasure *etc.* —**yachts'man** *n.*

yahoo' *n.* crude, coarse person

Yah'weh [yah'wā] *n.* God

yak *n.* shaggy-haired, long-horned ox of Central Asia

yam *n.* large edible tuber, sweet potato

yank *v.* jerk, tug; pull quickly —*n.* quick tug

Yank, Yank'ee *a./n. sl.* American

yap *vi.* bark (as small dog); talk idly; gossip (**-pp-**) —*n.* bark; *sl.* jabber; *sl.* mouth

yard[1] *n.* unit of length, .915 metre; spar slung across ship's mast to extend sails —**yard'stick** *n.* formula or standard of measurement or comparison

yard[2] *n.* piece of enclosed ground, oft. attached to or adjoining building and used for some specific purpose, as garden, storage, holding livestock *etc.*; winter pasture of deer, moose *etc.*

yarn *n.* spun thread; tale —*vi.* tell a tale

yarr'ow *n.* plant with flat white flower clusters

yash'mak *n.* face veil worn by Muslim women

yaw *vi.* of aircraft *etc.*, turn about vertical axis; deviate temporarily from course

yawl *n.* two-masted sailing vessel

yawn *vi.* open mouth wide, *esp.* in sleepiness; gape —*n.* a yawning

yaws *pl.n.* contagious tropical skin disease

yd. yard

YDT Yukon Daylight Time

ye [yē] *pron. obs.* you

yea [yā] *interj. obs.* yes

year *n.* time taken by one revolution of earth round sun, about 365¼ days; twelve months —**year'ling** *n.* animal one year old —**year'ly** *adv.* every year, once a year —*a.* happening *etc.* once a year

yearn [yern] *vi.* feel longing, desire; be filled with pity, tenderness —**yearn'ing** *n.*

yeast *n.* substance used as fermenting agent, *esp.* in raising bread —**yeast'y** *a.* of, like yeast; frothy, fermenting —**yeast cake** yeast compressed with starch into small cake for baking or brewing

yell *v.* cry out in loud shrill tone; *inf.* call —*n.* loud shrill cry; *inf.* call; rhythmic cry used in cheering in unison

yell'ow [-ō] *a.* of the colour of lemons, gold *etc.*; *inf.* cowardly —*n.* this colour —**yellow fever** acute infectious disease of (sub)tropical climates —**yell'owhammer** *n.* type of Amer. woodpecker; small European bunting —**yell'owjacket** *n.* any of several social wasps

yelp *vi./n.* (produce) quick, shrill cry

yen[1] *n.* Japanese monetary unit

yen[2] *n. inf.* longing, craving

yeo'man [yō'-] *n. Hist.* farmer cultivating his own land; assistant, subordinate

yes *interj.* affirms or consents, gives an affirmative answer —**yes man** weak person willing to agree to anything

yes'terday *n.* day before today; recent time —*adv.*

yet *adv.* now, still, besides, hitherto; nevertheless —*conj.* but, at the same time, nevertheless

yet'i *n. see* ABOMINABLE SNOWMAN

yew *n.* evergreen tree with dark leaves; its wood

Yidd'ish *a./n.* (of, in) dialect of mixed German and Hebrew used by many Jews in Europe

yield *vt.* give or return as food; produce; provide; concede; give up, surrender —*vi.* produce; submit; comply; surrender, give way —*n.* amount produced, return, profit, result

YMCA Young Men's Christian Association

yo'del, yo'dle *vi.* warble in falsetto tone (**-ll-**) —*n.* falsetto warbling as practised by Swiss mountaineers

yo'ga *n.* Hindu philosophical system

aiming at spiritual, mental and physical wellbeing by means of certain physical and mental exercises —**yo'gi** *n.* one who practises yoga

yog(h)'urt [yog'ət] *n.* thick, custard-like preparation of curdled milk

yoke *n.* wooden bar put across the necks of two animals to hold them together and to which plough *etc.* may be attached; various objects like a yoke in shape or use; fitted part of garment, *esp.* round neck, shoulders; bond or tie; domination —*vt.* put a yoke on, couple, unite

yo'kel *n.* disparaging term for (old-fashioned) country dweller

yolk [yōk] *n.* yellow central part of egg; oily secretion of skin of sheep

yon *a. obs. or dial.* that or those over there —**yon'der** *a.* yon —*adv.* over there, in that direction

yore *n. Poet.* the distant past

York'shire pudding savoury baked batter eaten with roast beef

you [yo͞o] *pron.* referring to person(s) addressed, or to unspecified person(s)

young [yung] *a.* not far advanced in growth, life or existence; not yet old; immature; junior; recently formed; vigorous —*n.* offspring —**young'ster** *n.* child

your [yawr] *a.* belonging to you —**yours** *pron.* —**yourself'** *pron.* (*pl.* **yourselves'**)

youth [-o͞o-] *n.* state or time of being young; state before adult age; young man; young people —**youth'ful** *a.*

yowl *v./n.* (produce) mournful cry

yo'-yo *n.* toy consisting of a spool attached to a string, by which it can be spun out and reeled in while attached to the finger (*pl.* **-s**)

YST Yukon Standard Time

Y.T. Yukon Territory

yucc'a *n.* tropical plant with stiff lance-like leaves

Yule *n.* the Christmas festival or season

Yup'pie *n.* young urban professional —*a.*

YWCA Young Women's Christian Association

Z

za'ny *a.* comical, funny in unusual way

zap *vt. sl.* attack, kill or destroy; *Computers* clear from screen, erase —*vi.* change television channels rapidly by remote control (**-pp-**)

zeal [zēl] *n.* fervour; keenness, enthusiasm —**zeal'ot** [zel'-] *n.* fanatic; enthusiast —**zeal'ous** *a.* ardent; enthusiastic; earnest —**zeal'ously** *adv.*

zeb'ra *n.* striped Afr. animal like a horse

ze'bu *n.* humped Indian ox or cow

Zen *n.* Japanese school teaching contemplation, meditation

zen'ith *n.* point of the heavens directly above an observer; point opposite nadir; summit, peak; climax —**zen'ithal** *a.*

zeph'yr [zef'ər] *n.* soft, gentle breeze

zepp'elin *n.* large, cylindrical, rigid airship

ze'ro *n.* nothing; figure 0; point on graduated instrument from which positive and negative quantities are reckoned; the lowest point (*pl.* **-ro(e)s**)

zest *n.* enjoyment; excitement, interest, flavour; peel of orange or lemon

zig'zag *n.* line or course characterized by sharp turns in alternating directions —*vi.* move along in zigzag course (**-zagged** *pt./pp.*, **-zagging** *pr.p.*)

zinc *n.* bluish-white metallic element with wide variety of uses, *esp.* in alloys as brass *etc.*

zinn'ia *n.* plant with daisylike, brightly coloured flowers

Zi'on *n.* hill on which Jerusalem stands; Judaism; Christian Church; heaven —**Zi'onism** *n.* movement to found, support Jewish homeland in Palestine —**Zi'onist** *n./a.*

zip *n.* short whizzing sound; energy, vigour —*v.* move with zip

zipp'er *n.* device for fastening with two rows of flexible metal or nylon teeth, interlocked and opened by a sliding clip (*also* **slide fastener**) —*vt.* fasten with zipper

zir'con *n.* mineral used as gemstone and in industry

zith'er *n.* flat stringed instrument

zlot'y *n.* Polish coin

Zn *Chem.* zinc

zo'diac *n.* imaginary belt of the heavens along which the sun, moon, and chief planets appear to move, divided crosswise into twelve equal areas, called **signs of the zodiac**, each named after a constellation —**zodi'acal** *a.*

zom'bi(e) *n.* person appearing lifeless, apathetic *etc.*; corpse supposedly brought to life by supernatural spirit

zone *n.* region with particular characteristics or use; any of the five belts into which tropics and arctic and antarctic circles divide the earth —**zo'nal** *a.*

zoo *n.* place where wild animals are kept, studied, bred and exhibited (*in full* **zoological gardens**)

zoogeog'raphy [zō-ə-] *n.* science of geographical distribution of animals

zoog'raphy [zō-og'-] *n.* descriptive zoology —**zoog'rapher, zoog'raphist** *n.* —**zoograph'ic(al)** *a.*

zo'olite *n.* fossil animal —**zoolit'ic** *a.*

zool'ogy [zō-ol'- *or* zōō-ol'-] *n.* scientific study of animals; characteristics of particular animals or of fauna of particular area —**zoolog'ical** *a.* —**zool'ogist** *n.*

zoom *v.* (cause to) make loud buzzing, humming sound; (cause to) go fast or rise, increase sharply —*vi.* (of camera) use lens of adjustable focal length to make subject appear to move closer or further away —**zoom lens** lens used in this way

zo'ophyte *n.* plantlike animal, *eg* sponge —**zoophyt'ic** *a.*

zucchi'ni [zōō-kē'ni] *n.* type of small vegetable marrow

Zu'lu [zōō'-] *n.* member, language of native S Afr. tribe

zy'gote *n.* fertilized egg cell

zymot'ic [zī-] *a.* of, or caused by fermentation; of, caused by infection

PUNCTUATION MARKS AND OTHER SYMBOLS

Symbol	Meaning
,	comma
;	semicolon
:	colon
.	period
—	dash
!	exclamation mark
?	interrogation or doubt
-	hyphen; as in *knick-knack*
’	apostrophe; as in *Peter's pence*
( )	parentheses
[ ]	brackets
}	brace, to enclose two or more lines
´	acute accent; as in *blasé*
`	grave accent } as in *tête-à-tête*
^	circumflex } as in *tête-à-tête*
~	tilde, used over *n* in certain Spanish words to denote the sound of *ny*; as in *señor*
¸	cedilla, to denote that *c* is pronounced soft; as in *façade*
“ ”	quotation marks
‘ ’	quotation marks, when used within a quotation; as in *“He said, ‘I will go at once’ and jumped into the car.”*
¯	macron, to mark length of sound; as in *cōbra*
˘	breve, marking a short sound; as in *lĭnen*
¨	diaeresis: as in *daïs*
¨	in German, used to denote modification of the vowel sound; as in *Köln* (Cologne)
‸	caret, marking a word or letter to be inserted in the line
* *	* .. .. .. — or - - - - ellipsis to indicate a break in a narrative, or an omission
⁂	or ⁂ asterism, used to call attention to a particular passage
. . .	. . or - - - - leaders, to direct the eye to a certain point
¶	paragraph
*	star, asterisk; (1) a reference mark; (2) used in philology to denote forms assumed to have existed though not recorded
†	dagger, obelisk; (1) a reference mark; (2) obsolete or dead
‡	double dagger, a reference mark
^{2}	superior figure, used (1) as a reference mark; (2) to indicate the number of a verse or line; as in *St. Mark* 4^{16}
^{a}	superior letter
§	section mark
‖	parallel mark
☛	index, hand, fist
#	number; space
”	ditto
&	ampersand, and
&c	et cetera
@	at
℔	per
%	per cent, per hundred
©	copyright
®	registered; registered trademark
♂	male
♀	female

PUNCTUATION AND THE USE OF CAPITAL LETTERS

apostrophe The sign ('), used to indicate possession. In the singular -'s is used (eg *day's end*); in the plural the apostrophe is added to the end of the word (eg *the neighbours' dog*). Plurals that do not end in -s also take -'s (eg *sheep's eyes*). Except for a few traditional exceptions (like *Jesus', Keats'*) proper names ending in -s take -'s at the end (eg *Thomas's, the Jones's*).

brackets These serve to isolate part of a sentence which could be omitted and still leave an intelligible statement. Punctuation of the rest of the sentence should run as if the bracketed portion were not there, eg *That house over there (with the blue door) is ours.* Square brackets are used where the writer inserts his own information into a quotation, eg *I knew Pitt [the Younger] as a boy.*

capital letters These are used at the beginning of a sentence or quoted speech, and for proper names and titles of people and organizations, eg *Mr Robertson, Dr Smith, Canadian Pacific.* They are not used when speaking of a general topic like *the pay of miners, the manufacture of cosmetics.* If an initial *the* is included in a title it has a capital, eg *We went to see The Tempest.*

colons and semicolons The function of these is to provide more of a break than a comma, and less than a period. The colon is used to make an abrupt break between two related statements, eg *Take it or leave it: the choice is yours.* It is also used to introduce a list, quotation, or summary and may be followed by a dash if the following matter begins on a separate line. Semicolons can be used instead of conjunctions to link two sentences or parts of them, eg *Two of the lights were working; two were out.*

commas 1. These make divisions or slight pauses in sentences, eg *She stormed out, slamming the door behind her.*
2. Commas are used to divide units in a series of nouns, adjectives, or phrases, eg *The cupboard was full of pots, pans, and crockery.* In such a series the last comma (ie before 'and' or 'or') is optional. It is not usual to place a comma between the last of a series of adjectives and the noun, eg *It was a long, hot, humid day.*
3. Commas also serve to mark off a word or phrase in a sentence which can stand grammatically complete on its own, as can dashes and brackets. Commas give the lightest degree of separation, dashes produce a jerky effect, and brackets cut off part of a sentence most firmly, eg *He hurried home, taking a short cut, but still arrived too late. It's a long time – over two years – since last we met. They both went to Athens (unaware of each other's plans) and stayed in the same hotel.*
4. When two phrases are linked by a conjunction a comma is used if there is a contrast, eg *She was dark, but her brother was fair.*
5. When addressing a person commas are used before and after the person's name or title, eg *Well, Mrs Smith, how are you today?*

exclamation marks These should only be used after genuine exclamations and not after ordinary statements.

hyphens Compound words, like *lay-by* or *manor house,* or words with a prefix, like *unpick,* may or may not contain a hyphen. It is generally used when the compound is new and dropped as it becomes familiar. When a compound adjective comes before a noun it should be hyphenated to stress that the constituent parts are not to be used independently, eg *He has a half-Italian wife.*

inverted commas (quotation marks, quotes) 1. These are used for direct quotation, not for indirect speech. It is usual to have a comma before and after a quotation if the sentence is resumed, eg *He said, "Follow me", and set off down the street.*
2. Single quotation marks can be used to indicate a title or quotation within a speech, eg *"I loved 'War and Peace'," she said, "but it took so long to read."*

periods (full stops) Normally these appear only at the end of a complete sentence containing a main verb, except in reported speech and where a passage takes the form of an argument, eg *You may think you can get away with it. Not a chance.* Periods are also used after abbreviations and initial letters standing for the whole word (as in *fig.*, *a.m.*, *R.C.*) but they are often omitted after abbreviations which include the first and last letters of a word (*Dr*, *Mr*, *ft*) and in much-used titles like *CTV*, *USA*. As usage is currently in a state of flux the above should be taken only as a guide to common practice.

question marks These are used at the end of direct questions, but not after reported ones.

forms of address Letters to men can be addressed as follows: *Mr. Bates, Mr. T. Bates,* or *Mr. Thomas Bates.* If the courtesy title *Esq.* is used the surname must be preceded by a first name or initials, and any letters must be put after the *Esq.* eg *Thomas Bates Esq., M.A.* Young boys can be addressed as *Master.* The plural form *Messrs.* is only used with names of business firms which contain a personal name, eg *Messrs. Jackson and Sons.*

Unmarried women and young girls can be addressed as *Miss.* Married women are often identified by their husband's first name or initial, eg *Mrs. R(obert) Henderson,* but it is increasingly common for them to appear as in *Mrs. M(ary) Henderson,* which is also the usual form for a widow. It is possible to use *Ms.* instead of *Miss* or *Mrs.*

Professional titles are used instead of *Mr.* etc., as in *Dr. H. Stevens, The Rev. Simon Clifford.* First names are always used with the titles *Sir* and *Dame,* as in *Sir John Gielgud, Dame Margot Fonteyn.*

Orders, decorations, degrees, qualifications, and letters denoting professions appear in that order. Degrees start with the lowest, but orders start with the highest, eg *Joseph Halliday Esq., O.B.E., D.S.O., M.A., F.S.A., M.D.* Orders and decorations are usually included in addresses, but qualifications etc. are only used where appropriate, as when writing to a person in his official capacity.

A list of some ceremonious forms of address follows at the end of this article.

postal addresses In Canada the recommended form of postal address has the addressee's name first, followed by the street address on the second line, the town or city and the province on the third line, followed with the postal code, eg

Miss Joan Bannerman
6 Overton Drive
Toronto, Ontario
M5A 3G4

address of a letter The writer's address should appear in the top right-hand corner with the date underneath. The name and address of the intended recipient should come below the date, on the left-hand side of the page.

beginnings and endings These depend on the degree of formality required. The most commonly used forms are as follows:

very formal	
Sir,	I am, Sir, *or*
Gentlemen,	I remain, Sir,
Madam,	Your obedient
Mesdames,	servant,
formal	
Dear Sir(s),	Yours faithfully,
Dear Madam,	
Mesdames,	Yours truly,
when correspondent is known	
Dear Mr.	Yours sincerely,
(Mrs. etc.) —	Yours truly,
between friends	
Dear —	Yours ever,
My dear —	Yours affectionately,

postscript This abbreviates to PS (not P.S.). An additional postscript is labelled PPS.

CEREMONIOUS FORMS OF ADDRESS

The Queen *Address* The Queen's Most Excellent Majesty *Begin* Madam *or* May it please Your Majesty *Refer to as* Your Majesty *End* I have the honour to remain, Your Majesty's faithful subject,

Prince *Address* His Royal Highness Prince (Christian name) *Or, if a duke* His Royal Highness the Duke of — *Begin* Sir *Refer to as* Your Royal Highness *End* I have the honour to remain, Your Royal Highness's most dutiful subject,

Princess *Address* Her Royal Highness the Princess (Christian name) *Or, if a duchess* Her Royal Highness the Duchess of — *Begin* Madam *Refer to as* Your Royal Highness *End* I have the honour to remain, Your Royal Highness's dutiful and obedient subject,

Member of Parliament *Address* according to rank, with the addition of M.P. *Begin etc.* according to rank.

Ambassador, British *Address* His Excellency (rank), H.B.M.'s Ambassador and Plenipotentiary *Begin* Sir, My Lord etc. (according to rank) *Refer to as* Your Excellency *End* I am, etc. (according to rank), Your obedient servant,

Consul-General *Address* (name) Esq., H.B.M.'s Consul-General, Consul, Vice-Consul etc. *Begin* Sir *End* I am, Sir, Your obedient servant,

SIGNS OF THE ZODIAC

Aries, the Ram	21 March—19 April
Taurus, the Bull	20 April—20 May
Gemini, the Twins	21 May—21 June
Cancer, the Crab	22 June—22 July
Leo, the Lion	23 July—22 August
Virgo, the Virgin	23 August—22 September
Libra, the Balance	23 September—21 October
Scorpio, the Scorpion	22 October—21 November
Sagittarius, the Archer	22 November—21 December
Capricorn, the Goat	22 December—19 January
Aquarius, the Water Bearer	20 January—18 February
Pisces, the Fish	19 February—20 March

ROMAN NUMERALS

I	= 1	XX	= 20
II	= 2	XXX	= 30
III	= 3	XL	= 40
IV or IIII	= 4	L	= 50
V	= 5	LX	= 60
VI	= 6	LXX	= 70
VII	= 7	LXXX	= 80
VIII	= 8	XC	= 90
IX	= 9	C	= 100
X	= 10	CC	= 200
XI	= 11	CCC	= 300
XII	= 12	CCCC or CD	= 400
XIII	= 13	D	= 500
XIV	= 14	DC	= 600
XV	= 15	DCC	= 700
XVI	= 16	DCCC	= 800
XVII	= 17	CM	= 900
XVIII	= 18	M	= 1000
XIX	= 19	MM	= 2000

PLURALS OF NOUNS

Plurals are formed by adding -s except in the following cases.

1. When a word ends in -ch, -s, -sh, -ss, or -x the plural is formed by adding -es (eg *benches, gases, dishes, crosses, taxes*).
2. When a word ends in -y preceded by a consonant the plural form is -ies (eg *parties, bodies, policies*). When a word ends in -y preceded by a vowel the plural is formed by adding -s (eg *trays, joys, keys*).
3. When a word ends in -o the more common plural ending is -oes (eg *cargoes, potatoes, heroes, goes*). In many less familiar words or when the final -o is preceded by a vowel the plural ending is -os (eg *avocados, armadillos, studios, cameos*).
4. When a word ends in -f the plural is formed either by adding -s (eg *beliefs, cuffs, whiffs*) or by changing the -f to -v and adding -es (eg *wives, thieves, loaves*). Some words may take both forms (eg *scarf, hoof, wharf*).
5. When a word ends in -ex or -ix the more formal plural ending is -ices. In more general contexts -es is used (eg *appendices, appendixes; indices, indexes*).
6. When a word from Latin ends in -is the plural form is -es (eg *crises, analyses*).

With compound words (like *court-martial*) it is usually the most important part which is pluralized (eg *courts-martial, lord-justices, mothers-in-law*).

In certain cases the plural form of a word is the same as the singular (eg *deer, sheep, grouse*) and in some words both forms end in -s (eg *measles, corps, mews*).

There are two main types of plural which take either singular or plural verbs:

a. words like *media* and *data*. These are in common use as singular nouns although, strictly, this is incorrect.
b. words ending in -ics. Generally, these are treated as plural when the word relates to an individual person or thing (eg *his mathematics are poor; the hall's acoustics are good*) and as singular when it is regarded more strictly as a science (eg *mathematics is an important subject*).

GROUP NAMES AND COLLECTIVE NOUNS

barren of mules
bevy of quails
bevy of roes
brace or lease of bucks
brood or covey of grouse
brood of hens or chickens
building or clamour of rooks
bunch, company or knob of wigeon (in the water)
bunch, knob or spring of teal
cast of hawks
cete of badgers
charm of goldfinches
chattering of choughs
clowder of cats
colony of gulls (breeding)
covert of coots
covey of partridges
cowardice of curs
desert of lapwings
dopping of sheldrakes
down or husk of hares
drove or herd of cattle (kine)
exaltation of larks
fall of woodcocks
field or string of racehorses
flight of wigeon (in the air)
flight or dule of doves
flight of swallows
flight of dunlins
flight, rush, bunch or knob of pochards
flock or flight of pigeons
flock of sheep
flock of swifts
flock or gaggle of geese
flock, congregation, flight or volery of birds
gaggle of geese (on the ground)
gang of elk
haras (stud) of horses
herd of antelopes
herd of buffaloes
herd, sedge or siege of cranes
herd of curlews
herd of deer
herd of giraffes
herd or tribe of goats
herd or pod of seals
herd or bevy of swans
herd of ponies
herd of swine
hill of ruffs
host of sparrows
kindle of kittens
labour of moles
leap of leopards
litter of cubs
litter of pups or pigs
litter of whelps
murmuration of starlings
muster of peacocks
nest of rabbits
nye or nide of pheasants
pace or herd of asses
pack of grouse
pack, mute or cry of hounds
pack, rout or herd of wolves
paddling of ducks
plump, sord or sute of wildfowl
pod of whiting

pride or troup of lions
rag of colts
richesse of martens
run of poultry
school or run of whales
school or gam of porpoises
sedge or siege of bitterns
sedge or siege of herons
shoal or glean of herrings
shoal, draught, haul, run or catch of fish
shrewdness of apes
skein of geese (in flight)
skulk of foxes
sleuth of bears
sord or sute of mallards
sounder of boars
sounder or dryft of swine
stand or wing of plovers
stud of mares
swarm of insects
swarm or grist of bees, or flies
swarm or cloud of gnats
tok of capercailzies
team of ducks (in flight)
troop of kangaroos
troop of monkeys
walk or wisp of snipe
watch of nightingales
yoke, drove, team or herd of oxen

NAMES AND SYMBOLS OF METRIC UNITS

Quantity	*Name of Unit*	*Value*	*Symbol*
LENGTH	metre	base unit	m
	centimetre	0.01 m	cm
	millimetre	0.001 m	mm
	micrometre	0.000 001 m	µm (or um)
	kilometre	1 000 m	km
	international nautical mile (for navigation)	1 852 m	n mile
MASS (weight)	kilogram	base unit	kg
	milligram	0.000 001 kg	mg
	gram	0.001 kg	g
	tonne	1 000 kg	t
TIME	second	base unit	s
	minute	60 s	min
	hour	60 min	h
	day	24 h	d
AREA	square metre	SI unit	m^2
	square millimetre	0.000 001 m^2	mm^2
	square centimetre	0.000 1 m^2	cm^2
	hectare	10 000 m^2	ha
	square kilometre	1 000 000 m^2	km^2
VOLUME	cubic metre	SI unit	m^3
	cubic centimetre	0.000 001 m^3	cm^3
VOLUME (for fluids)	litre	0.001 m^3	l
	millilitre	0.001 l	ml
	kilolitre	1 000 l (1 m^3)	kl
VELOCITY	metre per second	SI unit	m/s
	kilometre per hour	0.27 m/s	km/h
	knot	1 n mile/h or 0.514 m/s	kn
FORCE	newton	SI unit	N
	kilonewton	1 000 N	kN
	meganewton	1 000 000 N	MN
ENERGY	joule	SI unit	J
	kilojoule	1 000 J	kJ
	megajoule	1 000 000 J	MJ

NAMES AND SYMBOLS OF METRIC UNITS

Quantity	*Name of Unit*	*Value*	*Symbol*
POWER	watt	SI unit	W
	kilowatt	1 000 W	kW
	megawatt	1 000 000 W	MW
DENSITY	kilogram per cubic metre	SI unit	kg/m^3
	tonne per cubic metre	1 000 kg/m^3	t/m^3
	gram per cubic metre	0.001 kg/m^3	g/m^3
DENSITY (for fluids)	kilogram per litre	1 000 kg/m^3	kg/l
PRESSURE	pascal	SI unit (N/m^2)	Pa
	kilopascal	1 000 Pa	kPa
	megapascal	1 000 000 Pa	MPa
PRESSURE (for meteorology)	millibar	100 Pa	mb
ELECTRIC CURRENT	ampere	base unit	A
	milliampere	0.001 A	mA
POTENTIAL DIFFERENCE	volt	SI unit	V
	microvolt	0.000 001 V	µV
	millivolt	0.001 V	mV
	kilovolt	1 000 V	kV
	megavolt	1 000 000 V	MV
ELECTRICAL RESISTANCE	ohm	SI unit	Ω
	microhm	0.000 001 Ω	µΩ
	megohm	1 000 000 Ω	MΩ
FREQUENCY	hertz	SI unit	Hz
	kilohertz	1 000 Hz	kHz
	megahertz	1 000 000 Hz	MHz
	gigahertz	1 000 000 000 Hz	GHz
TEMPERATURE	kelvin	SI unit	K
	degree Celsius	K-273.15	°C

METRIC/IMPERIAL CONVERSION FACTORS

Imperial to Metric Units		*Metric to Imperial Units*	
LENGTH			
1 in	= 25.4 mm	1 cm	= 0.394 in
1 ft	= 30.5 cm	1 m	= 3.28 ft
1 yd	= 0.914 m	1 m	= 1.09 yd
1 mile	= 1.61 km	1 km	= 0.621 mile
MASS			
1 oz	= 28.35 g	1 g	= 0.0353 oz
1 lb	= 454 g	1 kg	= 2.20 lb
1 ton	= 1.02 tonne	1 tonne	= 0.984 ton
AREA			
1 in^2	= 6.45 cm^2	1 cm^2	= 0.155 in^2
1 ft^2	= 929 cm^2	1 m^2	= 10.8 ft^2
1 yd^2	= 0.836 m^2	1 m^2	= 1.20 yd^2
1 ac	= 0.405 ha	1 ha	= 2.47 ac
1 sq mile	= 259 ha	1 km^2	= 247 ac
VOLUME			
1 in^3	= 16.4 cm^3	1 cm^3	= 0.0610 in^3
1 ft^3	= 0.0283 m^3	1 m^3	= 35.3 ft^3
1 yd^3	= 0.765 m^3	1 m^3	= 1.31 yd^3
1 bushel	= 0.364 m^3	1 m^3	= 27.5 bushels
VOLUME (fluids)			
1 fl oz	= 28.4 ml	1 ml	= 0.0352 fl oz
1 pint	= 568 ml	1 litre	= 1.76 pint
1 gallon	= 4.55 litre	1 m^3	= 220 gallons
FORCE			
1 lbf (pound-force)	= 4.45 N	1N (newton)	= 0.225 lbf
PRESSURE			
1 psi (lb/sq in)	= 6.89 kPa	1 kPa (kilo-pascal)	= 0.145 psi
VELOCITY			
1 mph	= 1.61 km/h	1 km/h	= 0.621 mph
TEMPERATURE			
°C	$= \frac{5}{9}$ (°F − 32)	°F	$= \frac{9 \times °C}{5} + 32$
ENERGY			
1 Btu (British thermal unit)	= 1.06 kJ	1 kJ (kilo-joule)	= 0.948 Btu
POWER			
1 hp	= 0.746 kW	1 kW	= 1.34 hp
FUEL CONSUMPTION			
mpg	$= \frac{282}{\text{litres/100 km}}$	litres/100 km	$= \frac{282}{\text{mpg}}$

TEMPERATURE CONVERSION TABLE

CELSIUS TO FAHRENHEIT

Conversion formulae:

See METRIC/IMPERIAL CONVERSION FACTORS

°C	°F	°C	°F	°C	°F
50	122	20	68	−10	14
49	120.2	19	66.2	−11	12.2
48	118.4	18	64.4	−12	10.4
47	116.6	17	62.6	−13	8.6
46	114.8	16	60.8	−14	6.8
45	113	15	59	−15	5
44	111.2	14	57.2	−16	3.2
43	109.4	13	55.4	−17	1.4
42	107.6	12	53.6	−18	−0.4
41	105.8	11	51.8	−19	−2.2
40	104	10	50	−20	−4
39	102.2	9	48.2	−21	−5.8
38	100.4	8	46.4	−22	−7.6
37	98.6	7	44.6	−23	−9.4
36	96.8	6	42.8	−24	−11.2
35	95	5	41	−25	−13
34	93.2	4	39.2	−26	−14.8
33	91.4	3	37.4	−27	−16.6
32	89.6	2	35.6	−28	−18.4
31	87.8	1	33.8	−29	−20.2
30	86	0	32	−30	−22
29	84.2	−1	30.2	−31	−23.8
28	82.4	−2	28.4	−32	−25.6
27	80.6	−3	26.6	−33	−27.4
26	78.8	−4	24.8	−34	−29.2
25	77	−5	23	−35	−31
24	75.2	−6	21.2	−36	−32.8
23	73.4	−7	19.4	−37	−34.6
22	71.6	−8	17.6	−38	−36.4
21	69.8	−9	15.8	−39	−38.2

MATHEMATICAL SYMBOLS

$+$	1. plus, addition sign 2. positive
$-$	1. minus, subtraction sign 2. negative
$\times$	multiplied by
$\div$	divided by; also indicated by oblique stroke (8/2) or horizontal line $\frac{8}{2}$
$=$	equals; is equal to
$\neq$	is not equal to
$\equiv$	is identical with; is congruent to
$\sim$	difference between; is equivalent to
$\simeq$, $\approx$	is approximately equal to
$>$	is greater than
$<$	is less than
$\ngtr$	is not greater than
$\nless$	is not less than
$\leqslant$	less than or equal to
$\geqslant$	greater than or equal to
$\cong$	is isomorphic to
$:$	is to; ratio sign
$::$	as: used between ratios
∞	infinity
$\propto$	varies as, proportional to
$\therefore$	therefore
$\because$	since, because
$\angle$	angle
$\llcorner$	right angle
$\perp$	is perpendicular to

MATHEMATICAL SYMBOLS

$\parallel$	is parallel to
$\bigcirc$	circle; circumference
$\frown$	arc of a circle
$\triangle$	triangle
$\square$	square
▭	rectangle
▱	parallelogram
$\surd$	radical sign (ie square root sign)
$\sum$	sum
$\int$	integral
$\cup$	union
$\cap$	intersection
$\in$	is a member of; is an element of; belongs to
$\subseteq$	is contained as subclass within
$\supseteq$	contains as subclass
$\{\ \}$	set braces
$\varnothing$	the empty set
$\mid\ \mid$	absolute value of; modulus of
$\lhd$	is a normal subgroup of
μ	mean (population)
σ	standard deviation (population)
$\bar{x}$	mean (sample)
s	standard deviation (sample)
π	ratio of circumference of any circle to its diameter
e	base of natural logarithms
$^\circ$	degrees of arc or temperature
$'$	minutes of arc or time; feet
$''$	seconds of arc or time; inches

CHEMICAL SYMBOLS

Each element is placed in alphabetical order of its symbol and is followed by its atomic number.

Ac actinium, 89
Ag silver, 47
Al aluminum, 13
Am americium, 95
Ar argon, 18
As arsenic, 33
At astatine, 85
Au gold, 79
B boron, 5
Ba barium, 56
Be beryllium, 4
Bi bismuth, 83
Bk berkelium, 97
Br bromine, 35
C carbon, 6
Ca calcium, 20
Cd cadmium, 48
Ce cerium, 58
Cf californium, 98
Cl chlorine, 17
Cm curium, 96
Co cobalt, 27
Cr chromium, 24
Cs caesium, 55
Cu copper, 29
Dy dysprosium, 66
Er erbium, 68
Es einsteinium, 99
Eu europium, 63
F fluorine, 9
Fe iron, 26
Fm fermium, 100
Fr francium, 87
Ga gallium, 31
Gd gadolinium, 64
Ge germanium, 32
H hydrogen, 1
Ha hahnium, 105
He helium, 2
Hf hafnium, 72
Hg mercury, 80
Ho holmium, 67
I iodine, 53
In indium, 49
Ir iridium, 77
K potassium, 19
Kr krypton, 36
La lanthanum, 57
Li lithium, 3
Lr lawrencium, 103
Lu lutetium, 71
Md mendelevium, 101
Mg magnesium, 12
Mn manganese, 25
Mo molybdenum, 42
N nitrogen, 7
Na sodium, 11
Nb niobium, 41
Nd neodymium, 60
Ne neon, 10
Ni nickel, 28
No nobelium, 102
Np neptunium, 93
O oxygen, 8
Os osmium, 76
P phosphorus, 15
Pa protactinium, 91
Pb lead, 82
Pd palladium, 45
Pm promethium, 61
Po polonium, 84
Pr praseodymium, 59
Pt platinum, 78
Pu plutonium, 94
Ra radium, 88
Rb rubidium, 37
Re rhenium, 75
Rf rutherfordium, 104
Rh rhodium, 45
Rn radon, 86
Ru ruthenium, 44
S sulphur, 16
Sb antimony, 51
Sc scandium, 21
Se selenium, 34
Si silicon, 14
Sm samarium, 62
Sn tin, 50
Sr strontium, 38
Ta tantalum, 73
Tb terbium, 65
Tc technetium, 43
Te tellurium, 52
Th thorium, 90
Ti titanium, 22
Tl thallium, 81
Tm thulium, 69
U uranium, 92
V vanadium, 23
W tungsten, 74
Xe xenon, 54
Y yttrium, 39
Yb ytterbium, 70
Zn zinc, 30
Zr zirconium, 40

Canada

Confederation: July 1, 1867
Capital: Ottawa
Area of land: 9 203 054 km^2
Population: 24 343 181

Newfoundland

Entered Confed.: March 31, 1949
Capital: St John's
Area of land: 371 635 km^2
Pop.: 567 681 (2.3% of Canada)

Prince Edward Island

Entered Confed.: July 1, 1873
Capital: Charlottetown
Area of land: 5 660 km^2
Pop.: 122 506 (0.5% of Canada)

Nova Scotia

Entered Confed.: July 1, 1867
Capital: Halifax
Area of land: 52 841 km^2
Pop.: 847 442 (3.5% of Canada)

New Brunswick

Entered Confed.: July 1, 1867
Capital: Fredericton
Area of land: 71 569 km^2
Pop.: 696 403 (2.9% of Canada)

Quebec

Entered Confed.: July 1, 1867
Capital: Quebec
Area of land: 1 357 655 km^2
Pop.: 6 438 403 (26.4% of Canada)

Ontario

Entered Confed.: July 1, 1867
Capital: Toronto
Area of land: 916 734 km^2
Pop.: 8 625 107 (35.4% of Canada)

Manitoba

Entered Confed.: July 15, 1870
Capital: Winnipeg
Area of land: 547 704 km^2
Pop.: 1 026 241 (4.2% of Canada)

Saskatchewan

Entered Confed.: Sept. 1, 1905
Capital: Regina
Area of land: 570 113 km^2
Pop.: 968 313 (4.0% of Canada)

Alberta

Entered Confed.: Sept. 1, 1905
Capital: Edmonton
Area of land: 638 233 km^2
Pop.: 2 237 724 (9.2% of Canada)

British Columbia

Entered Confed.: July 20, 1871
Capital: Victoria
Area of land: 892 677 km^2
Pop.: 2 744 467 (11.3% of Canada)

Yukon Territory

Entered Confed.: July 13, 1898
Capital: Whitehorse
Area of land: 531 844 km^2
Pop.: 23 153 (0.1% of Canada)

Northwest Territories

Entered Confed.: July 15, 1870
Capital: Yellowknife
Area of land: 3 246 389 km^2
Pop.: 45 741 (0.2% of Canada)

DISTANCES BY AIR

The flight distances shown in the following tables are quoted in kilometres via the shortest normal airline routing from airport to airport. For cities with more than one airport a mean distance is given.

Distances from Toronto

Amsterdam	5989	Lisbon	5727
Athens	8098	London	5727
Auckland	13894	Los Angeles	3494
Baghdad	9741	Madrid	6038
Bangkok	13637	Melbourne	16108
Berlin	6472	Mexico City	3268
Bermuda	1803	Miami	1996
Bombay	13119	Milan	6659
Buenos Aires	8968	Montreal	518
Cairo	9209	Moscow	7487
Calcutta	12400	Nairobi	12188
Calgary	2687	Nassau	2083
Cape Town	13123	New York	589
Caracas	3880	Oslo	5941
Chicago	692	Ottawa	395
Cologne	6633	Paris	6005
Colombo	14023	Peking	10594
Copenhagen	6247	Prague	6682
Dakar	7029	Regina	2656
Darwin	15471	Rio de Janeiro	8275
Delhi	11624	Rome	7084
Edmonton	2687	St John's	1103
Frankfurt	6348	San Francisco	4630
Freeport	1908	Santiago	10513
Geneva	6392	Shanghai	12380
Glasgow	5281	Shannon	5104
Halifax	1286	Singapore	15005
Hong Kong	12537	Stockholm	6327
Honolulu	7487	Sydney	15875
Istanbul	8195	Tokyo	10352
Jakarta	15794	Tripoli	7744
Johannesburg	13347	Vancouver	3344
Karachi	11656	Vienna	6923
Kingston	2866	Warsaw	6923
Lima	6197	Winnipeg	1502

Distances from Vancouver

Amsterdam	7696	Los Angeles	1739
Bangkok	11817	Madrid	8420
Buenos Aires	11302	Mexico	3945
Cairo	10835	New York	3912
Honolulu	4363	Paris	7921
Istanbul	9177	Peking	8517
Johannesburg	16454	Rome	9000
London	7599	Tokyo	7551

Distances from Winnipeg

Amsterdam	6505	Honolulu	6134
Auckland	12928	Kingston	3993
Bangkok	12735	Miami	3059
Berlin	6891	Port of Spain	5458
Bermuda	3301	Rio de Janeiro	9676
Colombo	13701	Singapore	13975
Geneva	7036	Sydney	14313
Hong Kong	11399	Warsaw	7261

Distances from Montreal

Athens	7599	Honolulu	7905
Bangkok	13411	Istanbul	7712
Berlin	6005	Kingston	3075
Bermuda	1658	Los Angeles	3977
Calcutta	12236	Miami	2270
Colombo	13621	Moscow	7068
Geneva	5893	Rio de Janeiro	8195
Hong Kong	12429	Singapore	14812

Distances from Halifax

Amsterdam	4927	Moscow	6649
Berlin	5458	Nairobi	10932
Buenos Aires	8839	New York	950
Cairo	8066	Paris	4894
Johannesburg	12139	Peking	10610
Kingston	3204	Rome	5941
London	4653	Shannon	4009
Mexico City	4315	Tokyo	10787

WORLD STANDARD TIMES

At noon, GMT, 1300 BST

For each degree of longitude, time differs by 4 minutes; west of Greenwich is earlier, east of Greenwich later, than GMT.

Place	*Time*	*Place*	*Time*
Adelaide	2130	Malta	1300
Algiers	1300	Melbourne	2200
Amsterdam	1300	Mexico City	0600
Athens	1400	Montevideo	0830
Auckland	2400	Montreal	0700
Beirut	1400	Moscow	1500
Belgrade	1300	Nairobi	1500
Berlin	1300	New York	0700
Bern	1300	Ottawa	0700
Bombay	1730	Panama	0700
Brisbane	2200	Paris	1300
Brussels	1300	Peking	2000
Bucharest	1400	Perth, Australia	2000
Budapest	1300	Prague	1300
Buenos Aires	0800	Quebec	0700
Cairo	1400	Regina	0600
Calgary	0500	Rio de Janeiro	0900
Cape Town	1400	Rome	1300
Chicago	0600	St John's, Nfld.	0830
Colombo	1730	San Francisco	0400
Edmonton	0500	Santiago	0800
Halifax	0800	Singapore	1930
Hamilton	0700	Sofia	1400
Hong Kong	2000	Stockholm	1300
Istanbul	1400	Sydney	2200
Jerusalem	1400	Tehran	1530
Karachi	1700	Tokyo	2100
Lagos	1300	Toronto	0700
Leningrad	1500	Vancouver	0400
Lima	0700	Warsaw	1300
Lisbon	1200	Whitehorse	0400
Madras	1730	Winnipeg	0600
Madrid	1300	Yellowknife	0500

SELECTED MOUNTAIN HEIGHTS

	Metres
Everest, China-Nepal	8848
K2 (Godwin Austen), Kashmir-Sinkiang	8611
Kangchenjunga, India-Nepal	8598
Makalu, China-Nepal	8481
Dhaulagiri, Nepal	8167
Nanga Parbat, Kashmir	8126
Annapurna, Nepal	8091
Xixabangma, Tibet	8012
Distaghil Sar, Kashmir	7989
Nanda Devi, India	7816
Rakaposhi, Kashmir	7788
Namcha Barwa, Tibet	7756
Kamet, China-India	7756
Gurla Mandhata, Tibet	7728
Muztag (Ulugh Muztagh), Sinkiang-Tibet	7723
Kongur (Kungur), China	7719
Tirich Mir, Pakistan	7690
Gongga Shan (Minya Konka), China	7556
Muztagata, China	7546
Pik Kommunizma, USSR	7495
Pik Pobedy, USSR-China	7439
Aconcagua, Argentina	6960
Ojos del Salado, Argentina-Chile	6880
Bonete, Argentina	6872
Huascarán, Peru	6768
Sajama, Bolivia	6542
Illampu, Bolivia	6485
Chimborazo, Ecuador	6310
McKinley, USA	6190

	Metres
Logan, Canada	6050
Cotopaxi, Ecuador	5896
Kilimanjaro, Tanzania	5895
Bolivar, Colombia	5775
Citlaltépetl, Mexico	5699
Damavand, Iran	5670
Elbrus, USSR	5642
St Elias, USA	5489
Popocatépetl, Mexico	5452
Kirinyaga, Kenya	5200
Ararat, Turkey	5165
Vinson Massif, Antarctica	5140
Stanley, Uganda-Zaïre	5110
Jaya (Carstensz), New Guinea	5030
Mont Blanc, France-Italy	4807
Fairweather, Canada	4663
Monte Rosa, Italy-Switzerland	4634
Matterhorn (Cervino), Italy-Switzerland	4477
Whitney, USA	4418
Elbert, USA	4398
Rainier, USA	4392
Mauna Kea, Hawaii, USA	4205
Kinabalu, Sabah, Malaysia	4094
Waddington, Canada	4042
Robson, Canada	3954
Erebus, Antarctica	3794
Fuji, Japan	3776
Cook, New Zealand	3764
Columbia, Canada	3747

RIVER LENGTHS

	km
Nile, Africa	6695
Amazon, S America	6516
Yangtze, Asia	6380
Mississippi-Missouri, N America	6019
Ob-Irtysh, Asia	5570
Yenisey-Angara, Asia	5550
Huang Ho, Asia	5464
Zaïre (Congo), Africa	4667
Paraná, S America	4500
Mekong, Asia	4425
Amur, Asia	4416
Lena, Asia	4400
Mackenzie, N America	4250
Niger, Africa	4030
Missouri, N America	3969
Mississippi, N America	3779
Murray-Darling, Australia	3750
Volga, Europe	3688
Madeira, S America	3200
Yukon, N America	3185
Indus, Asia	3180
Syr Darya, Asia	3078
Salween, Asia	3060
St Lawrence, N America	3058
São Francisco, S America	2900
Rio Grande, N America	2870
Danube, Europe	2850
Brahmaputra, Asia	2840
Euphrates, Asia	2815
Pará-Tocantins, S America	2750
Zambezi, Africa	2650
Amu Darya, Asia	2620

	km
Paraguay, S America	2600
Nelson-Saskatchewan, N America	2570
Ural, Asia	2534
Kolyma, Asia	2513
Ganges, Asia	2510
Orinoco, S America	2500
Shabeelle, Africa	2490
Arkansas, N America	2348
Colorado, N America	2333
Dnieper, Europe	2285
Columbia, N America	2250
Negro, S America	2250
Irrawaddy, Asia	2150
Xi Jiang, Asia	2129
Saskatchewan, N America	1939
Peace, N America	1923
Don, Europe	1870
Orange, Africa	1860
Pechora, Europe	1809
Churchill, N America	1609
Marañón, S America	1609
Magdalena, S America	1550
Dniester, Europe	1411
Fraser, N America	1368
Rhine, Europe	1320
Ottawa, N America	1271
Athabasca, N America	1231
Elbe, Europe	1159
Gambia, Africa	1094
Yellowstone, N America	1080
Donets, Europe	1078
Vistula, Europe	1014
Loire, Europe	1012
Tagus, Europe	1006

POPULATIONS

(estimated) of selected urban agglomerations

City	Population
New York — NE New Jersey, USA	16 121 297
Mexico City, Mexico	14 750 182
Tokyo, Japan	11 676 264
Los Angeles — Long Beach, USA	11 497 568
Shanghai, China	10 820 000
Buenos Aires, Argentina	9 927 404
Calcutta, India	9 165 650
Paris, France	8 510 000
Seoul, S Korea	8 364 379
Bombay, India	8 227 332
Moscow, USSR	8 011 000
Chicago, USA	7 869 542
Beijing (Peking), China	7 570 000
São Paulo, Brazil	7 033 529
London, England	6 696 008
Jakarta, Indonesia	6 503 449
Delhi — New Delhi, India	5 713 581
Philadelphia, USA	5 547 902
San Francisco — Oakland, USA	5 179 784
Karachi, Pakistan	5 103 000
Rio de Janeiro, Brazil	5 093 232
Cairo, Egypt	5 074 016
Hong Kong	4 986 560
Bangkok (Krung Thep), Thailand	4 697 071
Detroit, USA	4 618 161
Lima, Peru	4 600 891
Tehran (Teheran), Iran	4 589 201
Leningrad, USSR	4 588 000
Tianjin (Tientsin), China	4 280 000
Madras, India	4 276 635
Boston, USA	3 448 122
Sydney, Australia	3 280 900
Santiago, Chile	3 234 066
Madrid, Spain	3 188 297
Toronto, Canada	3 067 100
Washington DC, USA	3 060 922
Berlin, W Germany	1 869 584
Berlin, E Germany	1 179 442
Dallas — Fort Worth, USA	2 974 805
Istanbul, Turkey	2 948 856
Montreal, Canada	2 862 300
Cleveland, USA	2 834 062
Rome, Italy	2 830 569
Melbourne, Australia	2 803 600
Miami — Fort Lauderdale, USA	2 643 981
Osaka, Japan	2 623 124
Singapore	2 517 000
Shenyang, China	2 411 000
St Louis, USA	2 356 460
Kiev, USSR	2 355 000
Pittsburgh, USA	2 263 894
Wuhan, China	2 146 000
Athens, Greece	2 101 103
Budapest, Hungary	2 064 026
Havana, Cuba	1 951 373
Bucharest, Romania	1 934 025
Essen — Dortmund — Duisburg, W Germany	1 792 907
Barcelona, Spain	1 754 900
Milan, Italy	1 634 638
Manila, Philippines	1 630 485
Vancouver, Canada	1 310 600
Ottawa — Hull, Canada	737 600
Edmonton, Canada	698 600
Calgary, Canada	634 500
Winnipeg, Canada	600 700
Quebec City, Canada	580 400
Hamilton, Canada	548 100
St Catharines, Canada	304 400
Halifax, Canada	280 700
Victoria, Canada	240 400
Regina, Canada	172 700
St John's, Canada	155 500
Whitehorse, Canada	15 800
Yellowknife, Canada	10 400

COUNTRIES, RELATED NOUNS, ADJECTIVES, AND CURRENCIES

Country	*Noun/Adjective*	*Currency Unit*
Afghanistan	Afghan	afghani
Albania	Albanian	lek
Algeria	Algerian	dinar
Andorra	Andorran	franc/peseta
Angola	Angolan	kwanza
Argentina	Argentine *or* Argentinian	austral
Australia	Australian	dollar
Austria	Austrian	schilling
Bahamas	Bahamian	dollar
Bahrain	Bahraini	dinar
Bangladesh	Bangladeshi	taka
Barbados	Barbadian	dollar
Belgium	Belgian	franc
Benin	Beninese	franc
Bermuda	Bermudan	dollar
Bhutan	Bhutanese	ngultrum
Bolivia	Bolivian	peso boliviano
Botswana		pula
Brazil	Brazilian	cruzeiro
Brunei		dollar
Bulgaria	Bulgarian	lev
Burkina		franc
Burma	Burmese	kyat
Burundi	Burundian	franc
Cameroon	Cameroonian	franc
Canada	Canadian	dollar
Cape Verde	Cape Verdean	escudo
Central African Republic		franc
Chad	Chadian	franc
Chile	Chilean	peso
China	Chinese	yuan
China (Taiwan)	Chinese	dollar
Colombia	Colombian	peso
Congo	Congolese	franc
Costa Rica	Costa Rican	colon
Cuba	Cuban	peso
Cyprus	Cypriot	pound
Czechoslovakia	Czech, Czechoslovak *or* Czechoslovakian	koruna
Denmark	Dane; Danish	krone
Djibouti		franc

COUNTRIES, RELATED NOUNS, ADJECTIVES, & CURRENCIES

Country	*Noun/Adjective*	*Currency Unit*
Dominica	Dominican	dollar
Dominican Republic	Dominican	peso
Ecuador	Ecuadorean	sucre
Egypt	Egyptian	pound
El Salvador	Salvadorean	colon
Equatorial Guinea		ekpwele
Ethiopia	Ethiopian	birr
Fiji	Fijian	dollar
Finland	Finn; Finnish	markka
France	Frenchman, -woman; French	franc
Gabon	Gabonese	franc
Gambia	Gambian	dalasi
Germany, East	East German	mark
Germany, West	West German	deutschmark
Ghana	Ghanaian	cedi
Greece	Greek	drachma
Grenada	Grenadian	dollar
Guatemala	Guatemalan	quetzal
Guinea	Guinean	franc
Guinea-Bissau		peso
Guyana	Guyanese	dollar
Haiti	Haitian	gourde
Honduras	Honduran	lempira
Hungary	Hungarian	forint
Iceland	Icelander; Icelandic	krona
India	Indian	rupee
Indonesia	Indonesian	rupiah
Iran	Iranian	rial
Iraq	Iraqi	dinar
Ireland, Republic of	Irishman, -woman; Irish	pound
Israel	Israeli	shekel
Italy	Italian	lira
Ivory Coast		franc
Jamaica	Jamaican	dollar
Japan	Japanese	yen
Jordan	Jordanian	dinar
Kampuchea	Kampuchean	riel
Kenya	Kenyan	shilling
Korea, North	North Korean	won
Korea, South	South Korean	won
Kuwait	Kuwaiti	dinar

COUNTRIES, RELATED NOUNS, ADJECTIVES, & CURRENCIES

Country	*Noun/Adjective*	*Currency Unit*
Laos	Laotian	kip
Lebanon	Lebanese	pound
Lesotho		rand
Liberia	Liberian	dollar
Libya	Libyan	dinar
Liechtenstein		franc
Luxembourg		franc
Madagascar	Madagascan	franc
Malawi	Malawian	kwacha
Malaysia	Malaysian	ringgit
Maldives	Maldivian	rupee
Mali	Malian	franc
Malta	Maltese	pound
Mauritania	Mauritanian	ouguiya
Mauritius	Mauritian	rupee
Mexico	Mexican	peso
Monaco	Monegasque	franc
Mongolian People's Republic	Mongolian	tugrik
Morocco	Moroccan	dirham
Mozambique	Mozambican	escudo
Nauru	Nauruan	dollar
Nepal	Nepalese	rupee
Netherlands	Dutchman, -woman, Netherlander; Dutch	guilder
New Zealand	New Zealander	dollar
Nicaragua	Nicaraguan	cordoba
Niger		franc
Nigeria	Nigerian	naira
Norway	Norwegian	krone
Oman	Omani	rial
Pakistan	Pakistani	rupee
Panama	Panamanian	balboa
Papua New Guinea	Papuan	kina
Paraguay	Paraguayan	guarani
Peru	Peruvian	inti
Philippines	Filipino *or* Philippine	peso
Poland	Pole; Polish	zloty
Portugal	Portuguese	escudo
Qatar	Qatari	riyal
Romania	Romanian	leu
Rwanda	Rwandan	franc

Country	*Noun/Adjective*	*Currency Unit*
San Marino	San Marinese *or* Sammarinese	lira
Saudi Arabia	Saudi Arabian	riyal
Senegal	Senegalese	franc
Seychelles		rupee
Sierra Leone	Sierra Leonean	leone
Singapore	Singaporean	dollar
Somalia	Somalian	shilling
South Africa	South African	rand
Spain	Spaniard; Spanish	peseta
Sri Lanka	Sri Lankan	rupee
Sudan	Sudanese	pound
Surinam	Surinamese	guilder
Swaziland	Swazi	lilangani
Sweden	Swede; Swedish	krona
Switzerland	Swiss	franc
Syria	Syrian	pound
Tanzania	Tanzanian	shilling
Thailand	Thai	baht
Togo	Togolese	franc
Tonga	Tongan	pa'anga
Trinidad and Tobago	Trinidadian, Tobagan	dollar
Tunisia	Tunisian	dinar
Turkey	Turk; Turkish	lira
Uganda	Ugandan	shilling
USSR	Russian *or* Soviet	ruble
United Arab Emirates		dirham
United Kingdom	Briton; British	pound
USA	American	dollar
Uruguay	Uruguayan	peso
Vatican City		lira
Venezuela	Venezuelan	bolivar
Vietnam	Vietnamese	dong
Western Samoa	Samoan	dollar
Yemen, People's Democratic Republic	Yemeni	dinar
Yemen, Arab Republic	Yemeni	riyal
Yugoslavia	Yugoslav *or* Yugoslavian	dinar
Zaïre	Zaïrean	zaïre
Zambia	Zambian	kwacha
Zimbabwe	Zimbabwean	dollar

GEOLOGICAL TIME CHART

Main Divisions of Geological Time

Eras	**Periods or Systems**	Epochs or Series	**Principal Physical & Biological Features**
Cainozoic	QUATERNARY	Recent 12,000*	Glaciers restricted to Antarctica and Greenland; development and spread of modern human culture.
		Pleistocene 600,000	Great glaciers covered much of Northern Hemisphere; appearance of modern man late in Pleistocene.
	TERTIARY	Pliocene 10,000,000	W North America uplifted; continued development of mammals; first possible apelike men appeared in Africa.
		Miocene 25,000,000	Renewed uplift of Alpine mountains: mammals began to acquire present-day characters; dogs, solid-hoofed horses, manlike apes appeared.
		Oligocene 35,000,0000	Many older types of mammals became extinct, mastodons, first monkeys, and apes appeared.
		Eocene 55,000,000	Alpine mountain building (Himalayas, Alps, Andes, Rockies); expansion of early mammals; primitive horses appeared.
		Paleocene 65,000,000	Great development of primitive mammals.
Mesozoic	CRETACEOUS 135,000,000		Chalk deposits laid down; dinosaurs reached maximum development & then became extinct; mammals small & very primitive.
	JURASSIC 180,000,000		Rocks of S and C Europe laid down; conifers & cycads dominant among plants; primitive birds appeared.
	TRIASSIC 230,000,000		Modern corals appeared & some insects of present-day types; great expansion of reptiles including earliest dinosaurs.

*Figures indicate approximate number of years since the beginning of each division.

GEOLOGICAL TIME CHART

Main Divisions of Geological Time			
Eras	**Periods or Systems**		**Principal Physical & Biological Features**
Paleozoic	PERMIAN 280,000,000		Trees of coal-forming forests declined; ferns abundant; conifers present; trilobites became extinct; reptiles surpassed amphibians.
	CARBONIFEROUS	UPPER CARBONIFEROUS 310,000,000	Hercynian mountain building (C Europe, E coast of North America); great coal-forming swamp forests flourished in N Hemisphere; seed-bearing ferns abundant; cockroaches & first reptiles appeared.
		LOWER CARBONIFEROUS 345,000,000	Land plants became diversified; crinoids achieved greatest development; sharks of relatively modern types appeared; land animals little known.
	DEVONIAN 405,000,000		Land plants evolved rapidly, large trees appeared; brachiopods reached maximum development; many kinds of primitive fishes; first sharks, insects, & amphibians appeared.
	SILURIAN 425,000,000		Great mountains formed in NW Europe; first small land plants appeared; shelled cephalopods abundant; trilobites began decline; first jawed fish appeared.
	ORDOVICIAN 500,000,000		Caledonian mountain building; much limestone deposited in shallow seas; many marine invertebrates, first primitive jawless fish appeared.
	CAMBRIAN 600,000,000		Shallow seas covered parts of continents; abundant record of marine life, esp. trilobites & brachiopods; other fossils rare.
Precambrian	LATE PRECAMBRIAN** 2,000,000,000		Metamorphosed sedimentary rocks and granite formed; first evidence of life, calcareous algae & invertebrates.
	EARLY PRECAMBRIAN** 4,500,000,000		Crust formed on molten earth; crystalline rocks much disturbed; history unknown.

**Regarded as separate eras.